D1325139

THE
CARAVAN
& CAMPING
GUIDE
2015

AA Lifestyle Guides

Published by AA Publishing, a trading name of AA Media Limited, whose registered office is Fanum House, Basing View, Basingstoke RG21 4EA. Registered number 06112600

47th edition November 2014
© AA Media Limited 2014

Assessments of the AA campsites are based on the experience of the AA Caravan & Camping Inspectors on the occasion(s) of their visit(s) and therefore descriptions given in this guide necessarily contain an element of subjective opinion which may not reflect or dictate a reader's own opinion on another occasion. See pages 10-11 for a clear explanation of how, based on our Inspectors' inspection experiences, campsites are graded.

AA Media Limited strives to ensure accuracy of the information in this guide at the time of printing. Nevertheless, the Publisher cannot be held responsible for any errors or omissions, or for changes in the details given in this guide, or for the consequences of any reliance on the information provided by the same. This does not affect your statutory rights. Due to the constantly evolving nature of the subject matter the information is subject to change. AA Media Limited will gratefully receive any advice from our readers of any necessary updated information.

Please contact:
Advertising Sales Department: advertisingsales@theAA.com
Editorial Department: lifestyleguides@theAA.com

Photographs in the gazetteer are provided by the establishments.

Typeset/Repro by Servis Filmsetting Ltd, Stockport
Printed and bound by Printer Trento SRL, Trento

Directory compiled by the AA Lifestyle Guides Department and managed in the Librios Information Management System.

Country and county opening pages: Nick Channer

Maps prepared by the Mapping Services Department of AA Publishing.

Maps © AA Media Limited 2014.

Contains Ordnance Survey data © Crown copyright and database right 2014.

This is based upon Crown Copyright and is reproduced with the permission of Land & Property Services under delegated authority from the Controller of Her Majesty's Stationery Office.
© Crown copyright and database rights 2014 PMLPA No. 100497

Republic of Ireland mapping based on © Ordnance Survey Ireland/ Government of Ireland Copyright Permit number MP0000314

Information on National Parks in England provided by the Countryside Agency (Natural England).

Information on National Parks in Scotland provided by Scottish Natural Heritage.

Information on National Parks in Wales provided by The Countryside Council for Wales.

A CIP catalogue for this book is available from the British Library.

ISBN: 978-0-7495-7672-1

A05210

Contents

Welcome to the
AA Caravan & Camping Guide 2015

Welcome to the 47th edition of the AA's bestselling *Caravan & Camping Guide* featuring 900 fully inspected and independently graded camping parks across England, Scotland, Wales, Northern Ireland and the Republic of Ireland

Who's in the guide?

Within these pages you'll find simple rural campsites, beautifully landscaped parks with top quality toilet facilities and excellent customer care, and self-contained Holiday Centres that offer a wide range of sport, leisure and entertainment facilities. All have touring facilities for caravanners and campers. We also include Holiday Home Parks offering holiday caravans and lodges for hire. The sites pay an annual fee for the inspection, recognition and rating.

AA Pennant classification

Campsites apply for AA recognition and they receive an unannounced visit each year by one of the AA's qualified Campsite Inspectors. Touring pitches, facilities and hospitality are fully checked and campsites are graded from 1 to 5 Pennants, or rated as a Holiday Centre or Holiday Home Park, using fixed criteria for each Pennant rating. A qualitative assessment score is also given to each campsite. Gold Pennants identify the top quality parks that score 90% and above within the 2 to 5 Pennant ratings.

AA Campsites of the Year

Following nominations by our inspectors we award an overall winner from three national finalists; five regional winners and a Holiday Centre winner – all are selected for their outstanding overall quality and high levels of customer care. Our two special awards recognise the best small campsite, and the most improved campsite.

Oakdown Country Holiday Park, Sidmouth, Devon is the worthy overall winner for 2015 – see page 14 for details.

An in-depth look

This year we highlight what it's like to camp on one of the islands located off the shores of the British Isles, and in particular what you can expect on a visit to one of the excellent campsites on Jersey and Guernsey. Whether taking your caravan, motorhome or just a tent, our camping inspector tells you how to get to, and travel around, the islands and what the AA-rated sites have to offer (see page 20).

In our second feature (see page 26) we look at staying at a Holiday Centre in north Wales and consider why it might just have the advantage over travelling abroad in search of a top quality camping experience.

The best sites for...

Our quick reference list (pages 30-31) highlights our inspectors favourite campsites for stunning views, waterside pitches, on-site fishing, great places to stay with your children, good restaurants on site, those that are eco-friendly and even where the toilets are really top-notch.

Glamping

This ever growing camping trend embraces many diverse ways of enjoying the great outdoors without foregoing home comforts, and at the same time indulging in a little bit of luxury.

In this edition of the guide we have introduced a ⛺ symbol to show that a site offers a glamping experience. This type of accommodation could be wooden pods, yurts, tipis, safari tents, bell tents, vintage caravans, Airstream caravans or shepherd's huts. For a list of AA-rated sites that offer glamping see pages 492–494.

How to use the
AA Caravan & Camping Guide

1.
2.
3.

ROBIN HOOD'S BAY   Map 19 NZ90

Places to visit

Whitby Abbey, WHITBY, YO22 4JT, 01947 603568
www.english-heritage.org.uk/daysout/properties/whitby-abbey

Scarborough Castle, SCARBOROUGH, YO11 1HY, 01723 372451
www.english-heritage.org.uk/daysout/properties/scarborough-castle

Great for kids: Scarborough Sea Life Sanctuary, SCARBOROUGH, YO12 6RP,
01723 373414 www.sealife.co.uk

4.
Grouse Hill Caravan Park
▶▶▶▶ 90%

17.
16.
15.

5.
tel: 01947 880543 & 880560 **Flask Bungalow Farm, Fylingdales YO22 4QH**
6.
email: info@grousehill.co.uk **web:** www.grousehill.co.uk
dir: From A171 (Whitby-Scarborough road), take loop road for Flask Inn (brown site sign).
7.
grid ref: NZ928002

14.

8.
A spacious family park on a south-facing slope with attractive, mostly level, terraced pitches overlooking The North Yorkshire National Park. The site has quality, solar-heated toilet blocks, a treatment plant to ensure excellent drinking water, security barriers, new play areas (including a woodland adventure play area), CCTV and WiFi. Camping pods and four new wigwams were added for the 2014 season. Please note that there are no hardstandings for tourers, only grass pitches, and this sloping site is not suitable for disabled visitors (there are no disabled facilities). This is an ideal base for walking and touring. 14 acre site. 175 touring pitches. 30 hardstandings. Caravan pitches. Motorhome pitches. Tent pitches. 1 static. 12 wooden pods.

9.
Open: Mar-Oct (rs Etr-May shop & reception restricted) **Last arrival:** 20.30hrs
Last departure: noon
10.
Pitches: ⊕ ⊕ Å ⋔
Leisure: ⚙ ✿
11.
Facilities: ➤ ⅋ ☺ ℘ ☀ ⅋ ⅃ ⅋ ⅓ ➤ WiFi ♻ ⅋
Services: ⅋ ⅋ ⅋ ⅋ ⅃ ⅋ ⅋
Within 3 miles: ⅃ ⅋ ⅋ ∪
12.
Notes: No noise after 22.30hrs. Dogs must be kept on leads.
13.
AA Pubs & Restaurants nearby: Laurel Inn, ROBIN HOOD'S BAY, YO22 4SE, 01947 880400

1. Location
Place names are listed alphabetically within each county.

2. Map reference
Each site is given a map reference for use in conjunction with the atlas section at the back of the guide. The map reference comprises the guide map page number, the National Grid location square and a two-figure map location reference.
For example: **Map 19 NZ90.**
19 refers to the page number of the map section at the back of the guide.
NZ is the National Grid lettered square (representing 100,000sq metres) in which the location will be found.
9 is the figure reading across the top or bottom of the map page.
0 is the figure reading down each side of the map page.

3. Places to visit
Suggestions of nearby places to visit for adults and children.

4. Site name and rating
▶ Campsites are listed in descending order of their Pennant Quality rating. Sites are rated from 1 to 5 Pennants and are also awarded a score ranging from 50%–100% according to how they compare with other parks within the same Pennant rating. Some sites are given a HOLIDAY CENTRE grading. For a fuller explanation see pages 10-11.
RV indicates a category of park catering only for recreational vehicles (no toilet facilities are provided at these sites).

Where the name of the site appears in italic type, the information that follows has not been confirmed by the campsite for the 2015 edition.

NEW indicates that the site is new in the guide this year.

5. Contact details

6. Directions

Brief directions from a recognisable point, such as a main road, are included in each entry. Please contact the individual site for more detailed directions or use the AA Route Planner at **theAA.com**, and enter the site's postcode.

7. Grid reference

Each entry includes a six-figure National Grid reference as many sites are in remote locations. Use the reference alongside the relevant Ordnance Survey map and in conjunction with the atlas at the back of this guide to help you find the precise location.

8. Description

Descriptions are based on information supplied by the AA inspector at the time of the last visit.

Please note: The AA Pennant classification is based on the touring pitches and the facilities only. AA inspectors do not visit or report on statics or chalets for hire under the AA Caravan & Camping quality standards scheme. However, the AA has a category of **HOLIDAY HOME PARK** and these static caravan, chalet or lodge-only parks are inspected. For sites other than those listed as **HOLIDAY HOME PARK** we only include the number of static caravan pitches in order to give an indication of the nature and size of the site.

9. Opening, arrival and departure times

Parks are not necessarily open all year and while most sites permit arrivals at any time, checking beforehand is advised (see page 12).

10. Pitches

Rates given after each appropriate symbol 🚐 (caravan), 🚍 (motorhome), 🛆 (tent) are the overnight cost for one unit. The prices can vary according to the number of people in the party, but some parks have a fixed fee per pitch regardless of the number of people. Please note that some sites charge separately for certain facilities, including showers; and some sites charge a different rate for pitches with or without electricity. Prices are supplied to us in good faith by the site operators and are as accurate as possible. They are, however, only a guide and are subject to change during the currency of this publication. 🏠 indicates that the campsite offers one or more types of glamping accommodation (see 15, below).

* If this symbol appears before the prices, it indicates that the site has not advised us of the prices for 2015; they relate to 2014.

11. Symbols and abbreviations

These are divided into Pitches, Leisure, Facilities, Services and Within 3 miles sections. A guide to abbreviations and symbols can be found on page 9 and on pages throughout the guide.

12. Notes

This includes information about additional facilities and any restrictions the site would like their visitors to be aware of. (💳) As most sites now accept credit and debit cards, we have only indicated those that don't accept cards.

13. AA pubs and restaurants

An entry may include suggestions for nearby pubs and/or restaurants recognised by the AA. Some of these establishments will have been awarded Rosettes for food excellence. To find out the distance by road between the campsite and the pub or restaurant, enter both postcodes into a Sat Nav or the AA Route Planner at **theAA.com**.

14. Photograph

Optional photograph/s supplied by the campsite.

15. Glamping

 The campsite offers one or more types of 'glamorous camping' accommodation, i.e. wooden pods, tipis, yurts, bell tents, safari tents, shepherd's huts, Airstream caravans, vintage caravans etc. Check with the site to see what type of glamping experience they offer.

16. Best of British

Bestof British A group of over 50 parks, both large and small, which focus on high quality facilities and amenities. www.bob.org.uk

17. David Bellamy Awards

Many AA recognised sites are also recipients of a David Bellamy Award for Conservation. The awards are graded Gold, Silver and Bronze. The symbols we show indicate the 2013/14 winners as this was the most up-to-date information at the time of going to press. For the 2014/15 winners please contact: British Holiday & Homes Parks Association Tel: 01452 526911 www.bellamyparks.co.uk

Facilities for disabled guests

The Equality Act 2010 provides legal rights for disabled people including access to goods, services and facilities, and means that service providers may have to consider making adjustments to their premises. For more information about the Act see: www.gov.uk/definition-of-disability-under-equality-act-2010

If a site has told us that they provide facilities for disabled visitors their entry in the guide will include the following symbol: ♿. The sites in this guide should be aware of their responsibilities under the Act. However, we recommend that you always phone in advance to ensure the site you have chosen has facilities to suit your needs.

Find your perfect coastal escape with Haven

You can't beat a touring or camping seaside holiday

- 22 parks with heated pools
- You have a choice of 6 pitch types - from basic grass to fully services hard-standing
- Shower blocks and toilet cubicles
- Bring your furry friend for just £1*
- Family friendly entertainment every night
- A choice of tasty places to eat on park

Don't forget your bucket and spade - most of our parks are by the sea

Save up to **50%*** on 2015 holidays

Burnham touring area

Haggerston indoor pool

The Orchards touring are

If you fancy a camping or touring break to the seaside with Haven then we are just a call or click away:

haventouring.com/AAGUIDE

0843 320 9680

Quote: AAGUIDE

Calls cost 10p per minute plus network extras.

Haven touring + camping

Britain's favourite seaside holiday

Symbols and abbreviations

Pitches

Caravan

Motorhome

Tent

Glamping-style accommodation

Leisure

Indoor swimming pool

Outdoor swimming pool

Tennis court

Games room

Children's playground

Kid's club

Stables & horse riding

9/18-hole Golf Course (within 3 miles)

9-hole golf course on site

Boats for hire

Cinema

Entertainment

Fishing

Mini golf

Watersports

Gym

Sports field

Spa   Spa

Separate TV room

Facilities

Bath

Shower

Electric shaver

Hairdryer

Ice pack facility

Disabled facilities

Public telephone

Shop on site or within 200yds

Mobile shop (calling at least 5 days per week)

BBQ area

Picnic area

WiFi access

Internet access

Recycling facilities

Tourist information

Dog exercise area

Services

Toilet fluid

Café or restaurant

Fast food/Takeaway

Baby care

Electric hook up

Motorvan service point

Launderette

(Other facilities column)

Licensed bar

Calor Gas

Camping Gaz

Battery charging

Other

No dogs

No credit or debit cards

Children of all ages accepted

Abbreviations

BH   Bank Holiday/s

Etr   Easter

Spring BH
Spring Bank Holiday (late May)

fr   from

hrs   hours

m   mile

mdnt   midnight

rdbt   roundabout

rs   restricted service

RV   Recreational vehicles

rating not confirmed

wk   week

wknd   weekend

The AA classification scheme

AA parks are classified on a 5-point scale according to their style and the range of facilities they offer. As the number of pennants increases, so the quality and variety of facilities is generally greater.

What can you expect at an AA-rated park?

All AA parks must meet a minimum standard: they should be clean, well maintained and welcoming. In addition they must have a local authority site licence (unless specially exempted), and satisfy local authority fire regulations.

The AA inspection

Each campsite that applies for AA recognition receives an unannounced visit each year by one of the AA's highly qualified team of inspectors. They make a thorough check of the site's touring pitches, facilities and hospitality. The sites pay an annual fee for the inspection, recognition and rating, and receive a text entry in the *AA Caravan & Camping Guide*.

AA inspectors pay when they stay overnight on a site. The criteria used by the inspectors in awarding the AA Pennant rating is shown on the opposite page.

AA Quality percentage score

AA Rated Campsites, Caravan Parks, Holiday Centres and Holiday Home Parks are awarded a percentage score alongside their pennant rating, Holiday Centre or Holiday Home Park status. This is a qualitative assessment of various factors including customer care and hospitality, toilet facilities and park landscaping. The % score runs from 50% to 100% and indicates the relative quality of parks with the same number of pennants. For example, one 3-pennant park may score 70%, while another 3-pennant park may achieve 90%.
Holiday Centres and Holiday Home Parks also receive a percentage score between 50% and 100% to differentiate between quality levels within this grading. Like the Pennant rating, the percentage is reassessed annually.

The Pennant criteria

 One Pennant parks

These parks offer a fairly simple standard of facilities including:

- No more than 30 pitches per acre
- At least 5% of the total pitches allocated to touring caravans
- An adequate drinking water supply and reasonable drainage
- Washroom with flush toilets and toilet paper provided, unless no sanitary facilities are provided in which case this should be clearly stated
- Chemical disposal arrangements, ideally with running water, unless tents only
- Adequate refuse disposal arrangements that are clearly signed
- Well-drained ground and some level pitches
- Entrance and access roads of adequate width and surface
- Location of emergency telephone clearly signed
- Emergency telephone numbers fully displayed

 Two Pennant parks

Parks in this category should meet all of the above requirements, but offer an increased level of facilities, services, customer care, security and ground maintenance. They should include the following:

- Separate washrooms, including at least two male and two female WCs and wash basins per 30 pitches
- Hot and cold water direct to each basin
- Externally lit toilet blocks
- Warden available during day, times to be indicated
- Whereabouts of shop/chemist is clearly signed
- Dish-washing facilities, covered and lit
- Basic security (i.e. lockable gate and/or CCTV)
- Reception area

 Three Pennant parks

Many parks come within this rating and the range of facilities is wide. All parks will be of a very good standard and will meet the following minimum criteria:

- Facilities, services and park grounds are clean and well

maintained, with buildings in good repair and attention paid to customer care and park security

- Evenly surfaced roads and paths
- Clean modern toilet blocks with all-night lighting and containing toilet seats in good condition, soap and hand dryers or paper towels, mirrors, shelves and hooks, shaver and hairdryer points, and lidded waste bins in female toilets
- Modern shower cubicles with sufficient hot water and attached, private changing space
- Electric hook-ups
- Some hardstanding/wheel runs/firm, level ground
- Laundry with automatic washing and drying facilities, separate from toilets
- Children's playground with safe equipment
- 24-hour public telephone on site or nearby where mobile reception is poor
- Warden availability and 24-hour contact number clearly signed

Four Pennant parks

These parks have achieved an excellent standard in all areas, including landscaping of grounds, natural screening and attractive park buildings, and customer care and park security. Toilets are smart, modern and immaculately maintained, and generally offer the following facilities:

- Spacious vanitory-style washbasins, at least two male and two female per 25 pitches
- Fully-tiled shower cubicles with doors, dry areas, shelves and hooks, at least one male and one female per 30 pitches
- Availability of washbasins in lockable cubicles, or combined toilet/washing cubicles, or a private/family room with shower/toilet/washbasin

Other requirements are:

- Baby changing facilities
- A shop on site, or within reasonable distance
- Warden available 24 hours
- Reception area open during the day, with tourist information available
- Internal roads, paths and toilet blocks lit at night
- Maximum 25 pitches per campable acre
- Toilet blocks heated October to Easter
- Approximately 50% of pitches with electric hook-ups
- Approximately 10% of pitches have hardstandings
- Late arrivals enclosure
- Security barrier and/or CCTV

Five Pennant premier parks

Premier parks are of an extremely high standard, set in attractive surroundings with superb mature landscaping.

Facilities, security and customer care are of an exceptional quality. As well as the above they will also offer:

- First-class toilet facilities including several designated self-contained cubicles, ideally with WC, washbasin and shower.
- Ideally electric hook-ups to 75% of pitches
- Approximately 20% of pitches have hardstandings
- Some fully-serviced 'super' pitches: of larger size, with water and electricity supplies connected
- A motorhome service point
- Toilet block/s should be heated
- Excellent security - coded barrier or number plate recognition and CCTV

Many Premier Parks will also provide:

- Heated swimming pool
- Well-equipped shop
- Café or restaurant and bar
- A designated walking area for dogs (if accepted)

Gold Pennants ▶▶▶▶▶

AA Gold Pennants are awarded to the very best camping parks with a Quality Score of 90% and above within the 2, 3, 4 and 5 Pennant ratings.

Holiday Centres and Holiday Home Parks

There are separate categories for Holiday Centres and Holiday Home Parks. The AA inspects these sites and awards an appropriate quality percentage score.

HOLIDAY CENTRES

In this category we distinguish parks which cater for all holiday needs including cooked meals and entertainment. They provide:

- A wide range of on-site sports, leisure and recreational facilities
- Supervision and security at a very high level
- A choice of eating outlets
- Facilities for touring caravans that equal those available to rented holiday accommodation
- A maximum density of 25 pitches per acre
- Clubhouse with entertainment
- Laundry with automatic washing machines

HOLIDAY HOME PARKS

Parks in this category are static only parks offering holiday caravans, chalets or lodges for hire and catering for all holiday needs. They provide:

- Quality holiday hire caravans and chalets or luxurious lodges
- A wide range of on-site sports, leisure and recreational facilities
- Supervision and security at a very high level
- A choice of eating outlets
- Clubhouse with entertainment

Useful information

Booking information

It is advisable to book in advance during peak holiday seasons and in school or public holidays. It is also wise to check whether or not a reservation entitles you to a particular pitch. It does not necessarily follow that an early booking will secure the best pitch; you may simply have the choice of what is available at the time you check in.

Some parks may require a deposit on booking which may be non-returnable if you have to cancel your holiday. If you do have to cancel, notify the proprietor at once because you may be held legally responsible for partial or full payment unless the pitch can be re-let. Consider taking out insurance such as AA Travel Insurance, tel: 0800 975 5819 or visit theAA.com for details to cover a lost deposit or compensation. Some parks will not accept overnight bookings unless payment for the full minimum period (e.g. two or three days) is made.

Last arrival Unless otherwise stated, parks will usually accept arrivals at any time of the day or night, but some have a special 'late arrivals' enclosure where you have to make temporary camp to avoid disturbing other people on the park. Please note that on some parks access to the toilet block is by key or pass card only, so if you know you will be late, do check what arrangements can be made.

Last departure Most parks will specify their overnight period e.g. noon to noon. If you overstay the departure time you can be charged for an extra day.

Chemical closet disposal point

You will usually find one on every park, except those catering only for tents. It must be a specially constructed unit, or a WC permanently set aside for the purpose of chemical disposal and with adjacent rinsing and soak-away facilities. However, some local authorities are concerned about the effect of chemicals on bacteria in cesspools etc, and may prohibit or restrict provision of chemical closet disposal points in their areas.

Complaints

If you have any complaints speak to the park proprietor or supervisor immediately, so that the matter can be sorted out on the spot. If this personal approach fails you may decide, if the matter is serious, to approach the local authority or tourist board. AA guide users may also write to:

The Editor, AA Caravan & Camping Guide,
AA Lifestyle Guides, 13th floor, Fanum House,
Basing View, Basingstoke, RG21 4EA

The AA may at its sole discretion investigate any complaints received from guide users for the purpose of making any necessary amendments to the guide. The AA will not in any circumstances act as representative or negotiator or undertake to obtain compensation or enter into further correspondence or deal with the matter in any other way whatsoever. The AA will not guarantee to take any specific action.

Dogs

Dogs may or may not be accepted at parks; this is entirely at the owner's or warden's discretion (assistance dogs should be accepted). Even when the park states that they accept dogs, it is still discretionary, and certain breeds may not be considered as suitable, so we strongly advise that you check when you book. Some sites have told us they do not accept dangerous breeds. (The following breeds are covered under the Dangerous Dogs Act 1991 – Pit Bull Terrier, Japanese Tosa, Dogo Argentino and Fila Brazilerio). Dogs should always be kept on a lead and under control, and letting them sleep in cars is not encouraged.

Electric hook-up

Many parks now have electric hook-ups available on some of their pitches, however if you need electric you should request it when making your booking. Generally the voltage is 240v AC, 50 cycles. Although this can vary slightly according to the location. The supply however can vary considerably from 5 amps to 16 amps although these days' 16 amps is becoming the norm, again you should check with the campsite if this is important to you. Remember if your consumption is greater than the supply the electric supply will trip out and need resetting.

Electric hook-up connections are now standardised in the UK with the blue coloured safety connectors. However it is good practice to always connect your cable to your caravan, motorhome or tent electric distribution unit before connecting to the hook-up supply.

It is also important that tents or trailer tents have a Residual Circuit Device (RCD) for safety reasons and to avoid overloading the circuit. Caravans and motorhomes have RCDs built in. You should remember that if your RCD trips out at 16 amps and the campsite supply is say 10 amps you can easily overload the supply and cause the hook-up to trip out.

It is quite easy to check what demands your appliances can place on the supply at any one time. Details are normally available in the caravan or motorhome handbooks which show the wattage of appliances fitted.

The amperage used is based on the wattage of appliance divided by the supply voltage.

The following table is a quick check of electrical consumption, depending what is switched on.

Average amperage (based on a 240v supply)

Caravan fridge (125 watts)	0.5 amps
Caravan heater set at (500 watts)	2.1 amps
Caravan heater set at (1000 watts)	4.2 amps
Caravan heater set at (2000 watts)	8.4 amps
Caravan water heater (850 watts)	3.5 amps
Kettle (domestic type) (1500 watts)	6.3 amps
Kettle (low wattage type) (750 watts)	3.1 amps
Hairdryer (2100 watts)	8.8 amps
Microwave (750 watts)	3.1 amps
Colour TV (flat-screen LED type) (30 watts)	0.13 amps
Battery charger (built-in type) (200 watts)	0.8 amps

Motorhomes

At some parks motorhomes are only accepted if they remain static throughout the stay. Also check that there are suitable level pitches at the parks where you plan to stay.

Overflow pitches

Campsites are legally entitled to use an overflow field which is not a normal part of their camping area for up to 28 days in any one year as an emergency method of coping with additional numbers at busy periods. When this 28 day rule is being invoked site owners should increase the numbers of sanitary facilities accordingly. In these circumstances the extra facilities are sometimes no more than temporary buildings.

Parking

Some park operators insist that cars are left in a parking area separate from the pitches; others will not allow more than one car for each caravan or tent.

Park restrictions

Many parks in our guide are selective about the categories of people they will accept on their parks. In the caravan and camping world there are many restrictions and some categories of visitor are banned altogether. Where a park has told us of a restriction/s this is included in notes in their entry.

On many parks in this guide, unaccompanied young people, single-sex groups, single adults, and motorcycle groups will not be accepted. The AA takes no stance in this matter, basing its Pennant classification on facilities, quality and maintenance. On the other hand, some parks cater well for teenagers and offer magnificent sporting and leisure facilities as well as discos; others have only very simple amenities. A small number of parks in our guide exclude all children in order to create an environment aimed at holiday makers in search of total peace and quiet (see page 41).

Pets

The importation of animals into the UK is subject to strict controls. Penalties for trying to avoid these controls are severe. However, the Pet Travel Scheme (PETS) allows cats, dogs, ferrets and certain other pets coming from the EU and certain other countries to enter the UK without quarantine provided the appropriate conditions are met.
For more details: www.gov.uk/take-pet-abroad/overview
PETS Helpline: 0370 241 1710

Pets resident in the British Isles (UK, Republic of Ireland, Isle of Man and Channel Islands) are not subject to any quarantine or PETS rules when travelling within the British Isles.

Seasonal touring pitches

Some park operators allocate a number of their hardstanding pitches for long-term seasonal caravans. These pitches can be reserved for the whole period the campsite is open, generally between Easter and September, and a fixed fee is charged for keeping the caravan on the park for the season. These pitches are in great demand, especially in popular tourist areas, so enquire well in advance if you wish to book one.

Shops

The range of provisions in shops is usually in proportion to park's size. As far as AA Pennant requirements are concerned, a mobile shop calling several times a week, or a general store within easy walking distance of the park is acceptable.

AA Campsites of the Year

Following nominations by our inspectors we award an overall winner from three national finalists; five regional winners and a Holiday Centre winner — all are selected for their outstanding overall quality and high levels of customer care. Our two special awards recognise the best small campsite, and the most improved campsite.

OAKDOWN COUNTRY HOLIDAY PARK ▷▷▷▷ 94%
SIDMOUTH, DEVON page 176

For nearly 40 years, this popular, well-established park has been lovingly developed and continuously upgraded by the Franks family and is now one of Britain's top holiday parks. The touring area is divided up into 'groves' or 'drives', each separated by a lovely array of trees or shrubs, which afford plenty of privacy to many of the pitches. Careful consideration of privacy and pitch density is one of the park's strengths and sets it apart from most other sites. The main toilet and shower block, built inside of an old wartime radar building, can only be described as 'stunning', housing very modern and spotlessly clean facilities, including excellent family rooms and bathrooms. In addition to the touring area, there is a beautifully landscaped and imaginatively laid out holiday home area which offers top quality caravans and lodges for purchase or hire. The park also has a well-stocked shop and a really good café, which also doubles as a reception for the popular 9-hole par 3 golf course. Oakdown, situated on the Jurassic Coast just a few miles from Sidmouth, is the perfect holiday base, with spacious pitches, very comfortable facilities and a warm welcome from the Franks family and their attentive team. A worthy winner of the Best in England and Overall Campsite of the Year Award.

SCOTLAND

WITCHES CRAIG CARAVAN & CAMPING PARK ▶▶▶▶ 90%
BLAIRLOGIE, STIRLING page 409

In an attractive setting, deep in 'Braveheart' country, this beautifully maintained park stands at the foot of the dramatic Ochil Hills, which form an impressive backdrop. Witches Craig has been tastefully developed by the Dewar family and features an immaculate facility block and mature landscaping, with terrific displays of colourful shrubs and plants, all lovingly cared for by Veda Dewar. All the touring pitches are on large hardstandings set in small areas to provide a feeling of seclusion, while tents are located in a large, well-drained field to the rear of the site, replete with cooking shelters and picnic benches. Year-on-year improvements have recently included WiFi access, a new garden area and a new security barrier, which all clearly demonstrate that the owners are keeping abreast of customer expectations. First time visitors or campers that have been visiting the site since childhood, are guaranteed a warm and friendly welcome from Veda and her staff. A regular bus to Stirling passes the entrance and many historical sites are just a short distance away. This is not a big site, with a bar and swimming pool, but certainly a very popular one, annually attracting customers to this stunning area. It is an obvious choice for an AA campsite award.

WALES

BRON DERW TOURING CARAVAN PARK ▶▶▶▶▶ 85%
LLANRWST, CONWY page 424

It is difficult to imagine that this was the location of a dairy farm until six years ago when John and Beryl Edwards decided to change their lifestyle by creating this stunningly located camping park, surrounded by mountains and within easy walking distance of historic Llanrwst. Following development of the first touring field, a separate adults-only area was later constructed with 23 fully serviced pitches, and each area has its own excellent, stone built, heated amenities block, equipped with modern, top quality fixtures and fittings. Bron Derw has been designed and beautifully landscaped to a very high standard and is now fully mature, and all the facility blocks are immaculately maintained. Superb displays of seasonal flowers along the entrance road greet guests as they arrive, and in the touring areas, the now well-established plants and shrubs surround the generous, well-spaced pitches. Recent improvements include extending one of the toilet blocks, adding three extra toilets and resurfacing the driveway from the main road to both touring fields. This Welsh winner, run by passionate and hard working owners, is the perfect base for exploring Snowdonia – Betws-y-Coed is just five miles away – and for visiting Llandudno and the north Wales coast, including the Isle of Anglesey.

AA Campsites of the Year *continued*

SOUTH WEST ENGLAND

FAUXQUETS VALLEY CAMPSITE ▶▶▶▶▶ 81%
CASTEL, GUERNSEY page 373

Set in a beautiful sheltered valley, Fauxquets offers a truly peaceful camping environment for all the family. Roland and Teresa Guille, the young owners, have worked exceptionally hard at developing the campsite and its facilities. Each year has seen a 'project' undertaken to improve something and this has resulted in the park achieving a 5 Pennant rating for 2015, a first for a Guernsey campsite. All the facilities are now up-to-date and of an excellent standard. They place great emphasis on customer care and service, and the reception area has become a real focal point for guests to meet, read a newspaper or just chill out, with a decked area, tables, chairs, a gazebo, plus free WiFi and take-away barbecue food. The campsite offers a good variety of pitches, including some that can take the largest tents and these enjoy lovely sea views. Two well-appointed log cabins are available for hire and there is also a super swimming pool as well as some cute farm animals to keep the children amused. Roland and Teresa, plus their young daughter Eva and Morley the dog, are very much part of the day-to-day running of Fauxquets, making all their guests feel very much at home. It's the first time a Channel Islands' campsite has won this prestigious award.

SOUTH EAST ENGLAND

THE ORCHARDS HOLIDAY CARAVAN PARK ▶▶▶▶▶ 93%
NEWBRIDGE, ISLE OF WIGHT page 235

One of the standout and most well known campsites on the Isle of Wight, Orchards is a much-loved park that has been painstakingly upgraded over the years and now ranks among the best parks in the country. It really does offer a complete holiday experience for both couples and families. There is a stunning facility centre that provides very spacious shower rooms, replete with toilet and washbasin, and one of the best dishwashing areas to be found, with picture windows affording lovely views over the surrounding countryside. The high-spec building has underfloor heating, water is heated by solar panels backed by a bio-mass boiler, and the latest technology in renewable energy includes timers for showers, slow-release taps, and systemiser controls to save water. Leisure facilities include excellent indoor and outdoor swimming pools, plus there is a poolside coffee shop with a garden conservatory atmosphere, a well-stocked shop, and a take-away food bar offering fish and chips and freshly made pizzas. Situated on the quieter west side of the island, in a peaceful village location amid downs and meadowland, the park is well positioned for visiting The Needles and the more remote coast around Freshwater and Yarmouth. Guests can be assured of a friendly welcome from the helpful staff.

HEART OF ENGLAND

LONGNOR WOOD HOLIDAY PARK ▷▷▷▷▷ **90%**
LONGNOR, STAFFORDSHIRE page 312

Tucked away up a long drive and enjoying a secluded and very peaceful setting in the heart of the Peak District National Park, this spacious adults-only park is a hidden gem, surrounded by meadows and beautiful rolling countryside and sheltered by woodland, where there are walks to enjoy and a variety of wildlife to observe. Visitors can expect a warm, friendly welcome from the O'Neill family and excellent, well-maintained facilities, which include spotlessly clean modern toilets, good, spacious hardstanding pitches, high levels of security, a putting green, badminton courts, a 4-acre dog walk and super walks from the park gate. John O'Neill continues to invest and improve the park, extending the reception in 2014 to include a small shop, edging and resurfacing all the hardstandings and internal roads, installing central heating in the toilet block, and adding an excellent information chalet. The park also looks a real picture in summer, festooned with colourful hanging baskets and troughs. The O'Neill's passion and enthusiasm to invest in and develop the park year-on-year, and to ensure a high standard of customer care, has resulted in the award of Gold Pennants for 2015 and they thoroughly deserve the Heart of England Campsite of the Year Award.

NORTH WEST ENGLAND

MANOR WOOD COUNTRY CARAVAN PARK ▷▷▷▷▷ **90%**
CODDINGTON, CHESHIRE page 51

Enjoying a tranquil country setting with extensive views across the Cheshire Plain to the Welsh hills, this secluded landscaped park has experienced major investment in recent years, which has lifted the overall quality at this notable holiday destination. Improvements include the superb new amenities block that provides excellent privacy options combined with first-class interior fixtures and fittings and underfloor heating. Additionally, the grounds are immaculately maintained, with a wide variety of seasonal and indigenous trees, colourful foliage and stunning floral displays that create an air of peace and tranquillity. Generous pitch density provides optimum privacy; some super pitches have hardstandings and full services, and additional facilities include a heated outdoor swimming pool, an all-weather tennis court and coarse fishing on several lakes. Avid anglers should consider booking the holiday home that overlooks the adult-only fishing lake as they can cast a line from the decked balcony. Campers here can simply relax and enjoy the many varieties of wildlife, which is encouraged on the site – there are bird tables, bat and owl boxes, and informative nature signs that detail the flora and fauna. Happy memories are sure to be made following a stay at this park.

AA Campsites of the Year *continued*

NORTH EAST ENGLAND

GOLDEN SQUARE CARAVAN & CAMPING PARK
▶▶▶▶▶ 83% HELMSLEY, NORTH YORKSHIRE page 356

This friendly, immaculately maintained park is set in a quiet rural location with panoramic views across farm, forest and moorland towards the North York Moors. Sheltered and terraced on three levels and surrounded by mature trees, it caters particularly well for families, with two excellent outdoor play areas, an indoor play area, plus crazy golf and a field for ball games. There is a spacious feel to the touring area – with beautifully mown grass and the carefully planted, mature hedges and shrubs offering shade and privacy to the individual pitches, some of which are fully serviced with larger hardstandings, a grass patio and picnic benches. The spotless, well-maintained facilities include two stone-built and fully tiled toilet and shower blocks, each with underfloor heating and a well-equipped fully served cubicle, replete with bath and shower. The reception building has now been extended to include an excellent shop, which offers a range of home-baked bread and cakes, in addition to newspapers, books and caravan accessories. Country walks and mountain bike trails start from the park gate and routes are available from reception. This award is well deserved and the owners are to be congratulated for their enthusiasm, high levels of customer care and the continuous investment in the park.

HOLIDAY CENTRE OF THE YEAR

PARK FOOT CARAVAN & CAMPING PARK
HOLIDAY CENTRE 87% POOLEY BRIDGE, CUMBRIA page 138

In a stunning location, surrounded by dramatic fells and overlooking Lake Ullswater, Park Foot Caravan & Camping Park provides the perfect base for exploring the Lake District National Park. Set on the shores of Ullswater it offers a superb and memorable holiday destination for families who wish to enjoy a range of activities while benefiting from excellent on-site facilities. Pitch density is generous and most, including tent pitches, have electric hook-ups. There are three touring areas, each with its own modern and very well-equipped amenity block; the Aikbeck camping field has direct access to the lake. The park has its own beach and launching facilities, so boating and canoeing are very popular activities, as are pony trekking, mountain biking, tennis and fishing, all of which are available on the park. The Country Club bar and restaurant is open each evening, providing a wide range of interesting meals, from breakfast to dinner, large screen TVs and regular entertainment in high season. The park also has a well-stocked shop, two excellent adventure playgrounds, a games room and a summer kids' club. There are also many areas where you can simply relax and enjoy the stunning surroundings, including direct access to Barton Fell for some wonderful Lakeland views.

ROGER ALMOND MOST IMPROVED CAMPSITE

WELLS HOLIDAY PARK ►►►► 87%
WELLS, SOMERSET page 309

Jason and Debbie Wilton and their enthusiastic team have successfully transformed this popular, adults-only park, situated within walking distance of Wells and its cathedral, from a relatively poor quality 3 Pennant park to a high quality 5 Pennant park in just three years. A new, spotlessly clean and well-appointed toilet and shower block has been built and the park has been completely re-landscaped to offer a wide variety of pitches, many of which have hardstandings; some are fully serviced and spacious enough to accommodate large RVs. All of the changes to this park have been carried out to the highest standards. A small function room, with outside patio area and tables, and a petanque pitch have been added, plus an area for private luxury lodges, and the park also boasts a beauty salon. The whole park, which is set on slight sloping land with lovely views over the nearby Mendip Hills, is always kept in tip-top condition making it a really pleasant place to stay. It is also well positioned for visiting Wookey Hole Caves and Cheddar Gorge, with Bath and Weston-Super-Mare a short drive away. Wells Holiday Park receives this award in recognition of the tremendous improvements that Jason and Debbie and all their team have achieved.

SMALL CAMPSITE OF THE YEAR

CHURCHILL FARM CAMPSITE ► 89%
BUCKFASTLEIGH, DEVON page 156

Set in the hills above Buckfast Abbey, between the villages of Buckfastleigh and Buckfast, this small, beautifully maintained campsite is part of a working farm owned by the Pedrick family. It's a real hidden gem for those who love traditional camping; the two neatly mown paddocks, separated by post and wire fencing from pedigree Charollais and Dorper sheep, offer total peace and quiet. There are 25 spacious grass pitches (eight with electric hook-up) for caravans, motorhomes and tents, and stunning panoramic views towards Dartmoor from every pitch. Both Andrew and Ann Pedrick are just as passionate about running the campsite as they are about looking after their sheep, so visitors can expect a high level of customer care and spotlessly clean unisex toilet facilities. Housed in refurbished farm buildings across the drive from the paddock, these facilities may be simple but they're freshly decorated each year, boast smartly tiled, free showers, and are always well maintained. Churchill Farm is a relaxing and peaceful base from which to explore the South Hams area and Dartmoor, and it's close to a local bus service and within walking distance of Buckfastleigh, the Abbey and the South Devon Steam Railway.

Island Camping

AA Camping Inspector, Colin Church, knows all about camping on islands around Britain. Here, he reveals just what is so appealing about choosing to stay on Jersey and Guernsey.

As a campsite inspector for the AA, I do get to see some lovely parts of the country and have the opportunity to visit great campsites set in stunning locations. As part of my patch I cover the Channel Islands which is always guaranteed to raise the odd eyebrow or two when talking to my fellow inspectors or other campers. You can see from the questioning look that they are curious as to what the islands are like regarding caravanning or camping – how easy is it to get there? What are the islands like? What are the campsites like? Is island camping different?

We have many islands around our coast and most have campsites, so island camping does offer something a little different; each island has its own unique atmosphere and there is something quite exciting when you board a ferry or maybe travel by air to reach these islands – it's a true get-away feeling.

I've been visiting the Channel Islands for several years now and have got to know them well, and more importantly what the campsites are like, so hopefully I can offer a glimpse of what you can expect. There's a unique blend of British and French influences which combine to make these islands so different – just one look at the road names and you'd think you were in France.

The Channel Islands form an archipelago in the English Channel off the Normandy coast, some 80 miles from the English mainland. They are divided into two British Crown Dependencies, the Bailiwicks (area of jurisdiction) of Guernsey and Jersey. The former includes the islands of Alderney, Herm and Sark. The islands are not part of the United Kingdom or European Union, but rather are possessions of the British Crown with independent administrations, however, their inhabitants remain British subjects.

Jersey

The largest of the Channel Islands, Jersey is approximately 46 square miles, (compared to the Isle of Wight at 146 square miles) and embraces a mix of the cosmopolitan and rural. St Helier, the island's capital has seen major investment and growth over recent years and, as well as the main ferry port, it also has a wide variety of shops, restaurants and entertainment. In recent years it has also seen the building of luxury apartments and the accompanying infrastructure of wine bars, eating places and cinemas etc. The rest of the island has retained much of its original charm with plenty of lovely beaches or coves to explore. You can even watch motor racing on the beach at St Ouen's Bay, which also happens to be brilliant for surfing.

Jersey has three campsites and now allows caravans and motor homes from mainland UK or France, subject to a permit.

Beuvelande Camp Site This AA 5 Pennant campsite is run by Alice and Danny, a young couple who have brought a fresh approach to this well-established site. It currently has three

"I love the area, which has spectacular sea views across to France"

camping areas, all very level, and can take tents, caravans or motorhomes. If you are looking for something different or are into "glamping" the site has some fully equipped luxury yurts, safari tents or more conventional euro style tents available for hire. The facilities are both modern and exceptionally clean, and Beuvelande has the added benefit of a good outdoor swimming pool and a tasteful restaurant with a good value menu plus a small bar. For young children there is a good play area and Wendy house. Very much a family campsite but also suitable for couples.

Rozel Camping Park A high quality site that has just been awarded the coveted AA Gold Pennant status. This campsite is well established and celebrates its 40th anniversary in 2015. It is run by David Germain and his family and you are guaranteed a very warm welcome and any help you need during your stay. Rozel has two well-appointed toilet and shower blocks with good family facilities and there is a choice of several camping areas, many with good privacy. I have a slightly biased view as I love the area, which has spectacular sea views across to France, but all camping areas are good. There are also some fully-equipped euro style tents available for hire. There is a lovely outdoor swimming pool plus TV lounge etc. Fresh bread and croissants can be ordered daily.

Daisy Cottage Campsite This small site in St Ouen's is certainly different and has a wow factor. The emphasis is on peace

and relaxation. You can bring your own tent, caravan or motorhome but you can also spoil yourself and stay in a luxurious Setareh yurt, SoulPad bell tent or even a shepherd's hut. Each pitch offers plenty of space, many with picnic tables and BBQs. There is a small but nicely appointed swimming pool where you can take a dip and then relax. The site has a tasteful café and small bar which has a patio with tables and chairs making it a focal point for guests to meet or chill out. What makes Daisy Cottage really different however, is its Retreat offering a wide range of therapies. This relatively new campsite is owned run by Michelle and Les, who along with their attentive team, go out of their way to ensure an enjoyable stay.

Getting to Jersey

If you intend to stay in the accommodation offered by the campsites you have a wide choice of transport and many use air travel, from all parts of the UK, and then just hire a car at the airport, which is quite cheap.

If taking your own car, caravan or motorhome you arrive by sea. By car – most travel by Condor's fast ferry from Weymouth or Poole (4 to 4½ hours). Small motorhomes and campervans – can travel on the fast ferry but you need to check with ferry operator for availability. With a caravan or by larger motorhome – go via conventional ferry also operated by Condor, from Portsmouth.

However you first need to contact your chosen campsite to arrange your booking and importantly to arrange a permit in order to bring your caravan or motorhome to Jersey – they will do the rest, it's all quite straightforward. Caravans can also be escorted from the ferry port to the campsites, you just need to contact the sites for more information on this, and more importantly, if you intend making your own way to the campsite, they will advise on the best route to the campsite (some approaches can be quite narrow and difficult especially for caravans).

Parking can be difficult in and around St Helier; Jersey has a Paycard system, so it's a good idea to purchase some cards on the ferry or at the ferry terminal in Jersey. Expect to pay around 50p per hour.

If you are a first timer to Jersey, and travel by fast ferry, make sure you go on deck to see the south coast from Corbiere lighthouse through to St Helier, it's quite spectacular as you travel close to the shoreline at fairly high speed!

Guernsey

This island tends to offer a quieter pace of life and even its capital, St Peter Port, seems very relaxed. There is a good range of shops and some really excellent restaurants on the seafront, many specialising in mouth-watering seafood. Guernsey, with its wonderful beaches, is about 30 square miles so it is very easy to see all the island even on a short break, by car or bus. Make sure you pick up a free map of the island as road signs tend to be small and infrequent. Unfortunately, caravans are not permitted on Guernsey, however motorhomes up to 6.9 metres are allowed from the UK providing you have a permit which can be arranged by the campsite.

There are three campsites on the island all offering a peaceful holiday base in which to explore Guernsey.

Fauxquets Valley Campsite Now awarded 5 AA Pennants and the winner of the South West of England Campsite of the Year for 2015, this valley site is run by Roland and Teresa, a young couple who have transformed it in the past 4 or 5 years. They are always on site to help their guests, supported by Eva, their young daughter and Morley the dog. The reception area has now become quite a focal point with its decking, tables and chairs plus gazebo and BBQ takeaway. There is also free WiFi around the reception so it's a great place to chill out with a coffee or drink.

At the other end of the site is a very inviting swimming pool, and for the children there's the animals to visit. There is a wide range of pitch sizes including some very spacious ones that can cope with the largest of tents.

La Bailloterie Camping & Leisure This is the longest established campsite on Guernsey and has recently gone through, in its own words, 'a re-invention'. This has resulted in a central stone building being completely refurbished to house superb modern toilet and shower facilities on the ground floor. On the first floor is the reception, small shop and imaginative decked area where you can meet up with your fellow campers and relax. There are also some well-appointed fully-equipped tents for hire and new for 2014 are two camping cabins each with two bedrooms plus lounge – great for when the weather is not so good or in the shoulder season. There are also BBQs in the main season and just to keep in the French mood they even have a boules pitch. The campsite is run by enthusiastic owners Richard and Caryl who will ensure that your stay is memorable.

Le Vaugrat Camp Site Set in the grounds of a beautiful 15th-century farmhouse and within walking distance of a lovely beach, this well-appointed site has been in the Laine family for

△ St Peter Port, Guernsey

many years and all family members are now involved in its running. The site is perfect for people with motorhomes, as there is a regular bus that stops right outside the entrance. There are several camping fields and the one at the top of the site has some fabulous view of the coast and is very popular with tenters. There is a pleasant TV lounge where people can meet up or charge their phones or tablets.

Getting to Guernsey

Similar to Jersey, there is a wide choice of air routes from the UK. By car – most travel by Condor's fast ferry from Weymouth or Poole (3 to 3½ hours) or you can travel on the conventional ferry.

Guernsey is a really easy place to drive around and parking is quite easy even in the main holiday period. Look out for the blue Disk Zone signs which means you have to use a parking clock to indicate your time of arrival. These parking clocks are available from garages and most retail shops and cost around £2.25.

Herm, Sark and Alderney

Herm and Sark can be reached by regular boat service from Guernsey; both are truly lovely and well worth a visit. Cars are not allowed on either island, but on Sark you can hire a bike which is really the best way to explore. Herm is a small, spectacular place with a stunning beach but you'll have to get there on foot, so be warned.

Alderney (just 3 miles by 1.5 miles) is the nearest island to the UK and just eight miles from France. You can travel to Alderney by air, or by boat via Guernsey or Jersey.

It's not all that cheap getting to the Channel Islands, but they do provide a real alternative from camping in the UK or Europe, and you can be sure of a very warm welcome wherever you stay. Being on a small scale means you'll have time to see virtually everything in just one visit; each island has stunning scenery and excellent beaches and offers visitors the prospect of a relaxing vacation – so why not give it a try?

Camping on other islands around our shores

Isle of Man

Motor caravans may enter with prior permission. Trailer caravans are not allowed on the island without a permit. Written application for permission should be made to the Secretary, Planning Committee, Department of Infrastructure, Murray House, Mount Havelock, Douglas IM1 2SF. The shipping line cannot accept caravans without this written permission.

Isles of Scilly

Caravans and motor caravans are not allowed, and campers must stay at official sites. Booking is advisable on all sites, especially during school holidays.

Inner Hebrides

Skye is accessible to caravans and motor caravans, and has official camping sites, but its sister isles of **Rhum** and **Eigg** have no car ferries, and take only backpackers. On the **Isle of Bute** only official camping is allowed. The islands of **Mull, Islay, Coll** and **Arran** have official campsites, and welcome caravans, motor caravans and tenters; offsite camping is also allowed with the usual permission. **Iona**, a backpacker's paradise, does not permit non-residents' vehicles. Wild camping is permitted on **Tiree** in accordance with the Scottish Outdoor Access Code (see www.isleoftiree.com). Prior arrangements must be made if you wish to camp with a motor vehicle, or go wild camping on **Colonsay** or **Cumbrae** (see www.colonsay.org.uk) and **Great Cumbrae** does not permit caravanning or camping, although organized groups may stay with official permission. **Jura** and **Gigha** have small, designated areas, and **Lismore** bans caravans but permits camping, although there are no official sites and few suitable places.

Orkney

There are no camping and caravanning restrictions, and plenty of beauty spots in which to pitch camp.

Shetland

There are seven official campsites on the Shetlands, but visitors can camp anywhere with prior permission. Caravans and motor caravans must stick to the main roads. Camping 'böds' offer budget accommodation in unisex dormitories for campers with their own bed rolls and sleeping bags. There is a campsite on **Fetler** (see www.fetler.org), but no camping or caravanning is permitted on **Noss** and **Fair Isle**.

Western Isles (Outer Hebrides)

There are official campsites on these islands, but wild camping is allowed within reason, and with the landowner's prior permission.

Sligachan, Cuillins, Isle of Skye ▷

Discovering a haven in north Wales

AA Campsite Inspector, Brian Jones decided to experience a family stay at a holiday centre in north Wales to find out what it offers for those wishing to stay nearer home.

Growing up on the outskirts of Dublin, I enjoyed a wonderful childhood, and each year my three brothers and I would embark on a summer family holiday, usually to our father's favourite location, Rosapenna in County Donegal. Occasionally, we would take the ferry from Newtownards to Stranrar and motor down to my aunt and uncle's house in Barrow-in-Furness. Here we enjoyed the delights of Walney Island with our cousins – picnicking on the sands, swimming in the sea or just kicking a football in the garden. Happy days!

In 1948, a forward thinking entrepreneur called Billy Butlin opened a holiday camp at Mosney, north of Dublin and many of my school friends were wildly excited about their experiences there; something my brothers and I only enjoyed as day visitors. As our parents took only around two weeks leave from their business interests each year and with my father away during the working week, weekends and the annual holidays became important times for us all to be together. Both dad and mum owned cars, a luxury in those days, and they were keen for their boys to visit places further afield than the Dublin area.

Fast forward many years

When my own family was growing up, we were fortunate to travel to many areas in Europe, only by car in the early days. Package holidays were becoming more affordable and many families were travelling to Spain, Portugal and Italy, at a time then the pound sterling had greater buying power.

My children now have their own children and also wish them to experience foreign travel, but today it seems that all-too-frequent airport delays just add to everyone's stress levels especially when there are young ones in tow. They have often wondered about taking a holiday in the UK, but the stumbling block, it seems, is our unreliable weather.

So what has changed about UK holidays since my own childhood half a century ago? For one thing, the growth and investment at holiday centres has been phenomenal; as an AA Campsite Inspector, each year I encounter improvements and innovations at sites run by the top companies. Due to our unpredictable climate, a wide range of all-weather attractions ensures holidaymakers leave their chosen park with happy memories. I decided that the only way I could understand the concept of a UK break, or 'staycation' was to stopover at one of these parks myself.

Destination north Wales

Bourne Leisure markets itself under under the Haven brand, and runs holiday home parks and holiday centres throughout the UK, usually in Areas of Outstanding Natural Beauty. My chosen destination was Hafan y Môr*

*Hafan y Môr, Pwhelli, LL53 6HJ Page 436

"Old tourers never die, they just go static"

on the beautiful Lleyn peninsula in Gwynedd, north Wales – the winner of the 2014 AA Holiday Centre of the Year award. Like many Haven parks, this one has direct access to an award-winning beach, in addition to providing many all-weather attractions and facilities. It is also within easy travelling distance of many historical sites including Abersoch, Portmerion, Caernarfon Castle and Snowdonia.

Hafan y Môr offers three distinct types of accommodation – touring and camping; holiday letting accommodation and holiday home ownership.

The touring area was re-located to a peaceful wooded area a couple of years ago and comprises 75 very spacious euro electric pitches, sub-divided by colourful, maturing shrubs and hedging that ensures optimum privacy; each pitch has water, electricity, TV connection and waste water disposal. The top notch amenities block has superb interior decor, under-floor heating and quality modern facilities, including power showers. This area also has its own dedicated and caring wardens.

The holiday letting option offers a choice of static caravans, adapted caravans, apartments and chalets; all are well sited and equipped with central heating and quality furnishings.

Holiday home ownership is proving a real strength at the Haven's parks because many families and active older visitors appreciate having their own holiday destination; retirees, especially, are enjoying many happy and affordable breaks on their own or with their children and grandchildren.

In creating and developing Hafan y Môr, Bourne Leisure was mindful of the original landscape with its many varieties of indigenous trees, shrubs and wilderness areas. Ground maintenance is particularly noteworthy on the park, with a dedicated team out in all weathers. Possibly the only distractions for anyone staying here are wildlife sightings and birdsong. Canada geese, ducks, rabbits and many wild bird species can all be spotted, and on the second morning of our stay, we were visited at breakfast time by a duck and her eight newly hatched ducklings.

Our home away from home

To carry out my research, I decided that my four grandsons, ages 7 to 13, would join me on a weekend adventure. Charlie, James, Julian and Frankie were looking forward to the experience on a weekend that promised good weather, and for once we were not to be disappointed. On arrival, shouts of glee from the back seat included "Wow", "I'm going to do that" and "look at those slides". With gentle requests for patience, I was allowed to collect the keys to our static caravan which had a delightful location beside a superb weeping willow, and was within easy walking distance of all attractions. Our holiday home was a Moselle, created exclusively for Bourne Leisure by Swift Caravans. On entering, I was amazed by the quality of the interior, with superb open-plan living areas, comprising a modern fitted kitchen, a dining section and spacious L-shaped lounge, with comfortable sofas, a gas fire and flat-screen TV. The subtle

decor schemes create a Mediterranean atmosphere and in addition to a modern shower room with toilet and washbasin, the double room, which I 'bagged', also had an en suite toilet and washbasin of similar, excellent quality. Everything is supplied – good crockery, cutlery, glassware and cooking utensils for those wishing to self cater.

There are three strategically located Spar mini-markets on the park, selling everything from fresh, frozen and convenience foods (including local specialities) to gifts, confectionary, newspapers plus a well-stocked licensed section. Fresh, daily-baked croissants and pastries are also available, and with opening hours of 8am to 10pm, seven days per week, there is no need to waste valuable leisure time travelling into town for supplies.

On-site eating options are very good in terms of quality and choice. The Mash and Barrel, a tried and tested concept found at all Haven Parks, is a stylish continental bar and brasserie that offers a selection of good value dishes suitable for all ages and tastes. From traditional 'pub grub' to grills, pasta and pizza, you can mix and match to create your own ideal meal. This bar, and other on-site bars, provides an impressive range of draught and bottles beers, and I was particularly struck by the wine choices, available either by the bottle or by the glass. At the Traditional Fish and Chips takeaway, based on the original outlet in nearby Pwhelli, high standards are assured, and a Starbucks is conveniently situated directly opposite; Burger King is also on site.

Plenty of things to do

If you just want to eat, drink and relax that's fine, but Hafan y Môr has a dedicated and energetic activities and entertainments team to oversee every conceivable pastime to suit all ages, from tiny tots to mature visitors and the less able. This skilled team is always on hand to guide and protect children, ensuring they enjoy everything to the full.

The weekly schedule of activities starts each day at 9am. Take your pick – there's mini archery, mini football, bushcraft, roller discos, high ropes, go-karting, an adventure trail, adventure golf, boat hire, an all-weather multi-sports court with football and basketball pitches plus much more; coaching is on hand for basketball, fencing and archery too.

Indoor attractions feature a well-equipped SportsDrome and gym and a real favourite – The Splash Zone, featuring pools to suit all ages, one with slides, rapids and wave creation for the serious thrill seeker. Intrepid Charlie and James visited here three times and I happily escorted the younger two, Julian and Frankie, proving that you can behave like a kid, whatever your age. Over our short break, the boys took full advantage of the sports facilities and they easily made new friends playing football.

As the sun goes down

Evening entertainment is provided each night in both The Cove and Boardwalk Showbar, again geared to different ages – tots from 6pm in the Boardwalk at the same time as bingo is available in The Cove. As the evening progresses, talent contests or professional live acts provide a varied programme of entertainment. From 10.30pm, a disco rounds off the evening's activities.

The friendly staff at this park are highly motivated so the standards of service and hospitality are impressive. In a former life I was a hotel manager and realised that in the hospitality industry, whatever luxury is provided, a business is only successful with the right team in place.

Michael in the shop, Michelle and Lauren in The Mash and Barrel, Joff on bar duty and Natalie in reception (to name but a few), all without

exception, greeted every customer with a smile, while delivering efficient and professional service. Observing the interaction between the staff and visitors, demonstrated to me that they genuinely enjoy working here; the mood was infectious and the atmosphere everywhere is a happy one.

On our last morning, the boys wanted to visit Splash Zone yet again followed by a second round of adventure golf so I welcomed the opportunity to enjoy an espresso at Starbucks. Sitting there in the late morning sunshine there was time to reflect on the weekend and previous holiday experiences. I came to the conclusion that whilst foreign travel is important to broaden the mind, you won't miss out on creating happy

childhood memories if you find the right place in the UK. Holidaying abroad sometimes has its downside, and in response companies like Bourne Leisure have created quality parks that seriously compete with options abroad. Many holidaymakers think that taking a break within these shores has the added bonus of saving on travel time, and are more than happy to discover new and truly wonderful locations, the Lleyn peninsula among them.

I will seriously consider a return visit to Hafan y Môr and when I hang up my boots and park my motorhome at the end of my campsite inspecting career, perhaps I will be mindful of that slogan at many Haven Parks – "Old tourers never die, they just go static".

▽ Hafan y Môr rock pooling

The best sites for...

THE AA THINKS THESE ARE THE BEST SITES FOR...

...WATERSIDE PITCHES

ENGLAND
South End Caravan Park,
  Barrow-in-Furness, Cumbria
Sleningford Watermill Cc Park,
  North Stainley, North Yorkshire

SCOTLAND
Inver Mill Farm Caravan Park,
  Dunkeld, Perth & Kinross
Skye C&C Club Site,
  Edinbane, Isle of Skye

WALES
Riverside Camping,
  Caernarfon, Gwynedd

NORTHERN IRELAND
Drumaheglis Marina & Caravan Park,
  Ballymoney, Co Antrim

...STUNNING VIEWS

ENGLAND
Tristram C&C Park,
  Polzeath, Cornwall
Troutbeck C&C Club Site,
  Troutbeck, Cumbria
Sykeside Camping Park,
  Patterdale, Cumbria
Galmpton Touring Park,
  Brixham, Devon
Highlands End Holiday Park,
  Bridport, Dorset
New Hall Farm Touring Park,
  Southwell, Nottinghamshire

Wimbleball Lake,
  Dulverton, Somerset
Howgill Lodge,
  Bolton Abbey, North Yorkshire
Wolds Way Caravan & Camping,
  West Knapton, North Yorkshire

CHANNEL ISLANDS
Rozel Camping Park,
  St Martin, Jersey

SCOTLAND
Oban C&C Park,
  Oban, Argyll & Bute
Linnhe Lochside Holidays,
  Corpach, Highland
Invercoe C&C Park,
  Glencoe, Highland
John O'Groats Caravan Site,
  John O'Groats, Highland

WALES
St David's Park,
  Pentraeth, Isle of Anglesey
Bron-Y-Wendon Caravan Park,
  Llanddulas, Conwy
Bodnant Caravan Park,
  Llanwrst, Conwy
Hendwr Country Park,
  Llandrillo, Denbighshire
Beach View Caravan Park,
  Abersoch, Gwynedd
Tyn-Y-Mur Touring & Camping,
  Abersoch, Gwynedd
Trawsdir Touring C&C Park,
  Barmouth, Gwynedd
Eisteddfa, Criccieth, Gwynedd
Barcdy Touring C&C Park,
  Talsarnau, Gwynedd
Fishguard Bay C&C Park,
  Fishguard, Pembrokeshire
Carreglwyd C&C Park,
  Port Einon, Swansea

...GOOD ON-SITE RESTAURANTS

ENGLAND
Stroud Hill Park,
  St Ives, Cambridgeshire
Tristram C&C Park,
  Polzeath, Cornwall
Bingham Grange T&C Park,
  Bridport, Dorset
Highlands End Holiday Park,
  Bridport, Dorset
Bay View Holiday Park,
  Bolton-Le-Sands, Lancashire
The Old Brick Kilns,
  Barney, Norfolk
Beaconsfield Farm Caravan Park,
  Shrewsbury, Shropshire

CHANNEL ISLANDS
Beuvelande Camp Site,
  St Martin, Jersey

SCOTLAND
Glen Nevis C&C Park,
  Fort William, Highland

WALES
St David's Park,
  Pentraeth, Isle of Anglesey

...TOP TOILETS

ENGLAND
Carnon Downs C&C Park,
  Truro, Cornwall
Beech Croft Farm,
  Buxton, Derbyshire
Riverside C&C Park,
  South Molton, Devon
Shamba Holidays,
  St Leonards, Dorset
Teversal C&C Club Site,
  Teversal, Nottinghamshire

Dell Touring Park,
 Bury St Edmunds, Suffolk
Moon & Sixpence,
 Woodbridge, Suffolk
Riverside Caravan Park,
 High Bentham, North Yorkshire
Wayside Holiday Park,
 Pickering, North Yorkshire
Moor Lodge Park,
 Leeds, West Yorkshire

SCOTLAND
Skye C&C Club Site,
 Edinbane, Isle of Skye
Beecraigs C&C Site,
 Linlithgow, West Lothian

...ON-SITE FISHING

ENGLAND
Fields End Water Cp, & Fishery,
 Doddington, Cambridgeshire
Back Of Beyond Touring Park,
 St Leonards, Dorset
Blackmore Vale C&C Park,
 Shaftesbury, Dorset
Woodland Waters,
 Ancaster, Lincolnshire
Lakeside Caravan Park & Fisheries,
 Downham Market, Norfolk
Northam Farm Caravan & Touring Park,
 Brean, Somerset
Thorney Lakes Caravan Park,
 Langport, Somerset
Marsh Farm Caravan Site, & Carlton Meres Country Park, Saxmundham, Suffolk
Sumners Ponds Fishery & Campsite,
 Barns Green, West Sussex

SCOTLAND
Hoddom Castle Caravan Park,
 Ecclefechan, Dumfries & Galloway
Milton of Fonab Caravan Park,
 Pitlochry, Perth & Kinross

Gart Caravan Park,
 Callander, Stirling

WALES
Afon Teifi C&C Park,
 Newcastle Emlyn, Carmarthenshire
Ynysymaengwyn Caravan Park,
 Tywyn, Gwynedd

...THE KIDS

ENGLAND
Trevornick Holiday Park,
 Holywell Bay, Cornwall
Eden Valley Holiday Park,
 Lostwithiel, Cornwall
Golden Valley C&C Park,
 Ripley, Derbyshire
Freshwater Beach Holiday Park,
 Bridport, Dorset
Sandy Balls Holiday Village,
 Fordingbridge, Hampshire
Heathland Beach Caravan Park,
 Kessingland, Suffolk
Golden Square Touring Caravan Park,
 Helmsley, North Yorkshire
Riverside Caravan Park,
 High Bentham, North Yorkshire
Goosewood Caravan Park,
 Sutton-On-The-Forest, North Yorkshire

SCOTLAND
Blair Castle Caravan Park,
 Blair Atholl, Perth & Kinross

WALES
Home Farm Caravan Park,
 Marian-Glas, Isle of Anglesey
Hendre Mynach Touring C&C Park,
 Barmouth, Gwynedd
Trawsdir Touring C&C Park,
 Barmouth, Gwynedd

...BEING ECO-FRIENDLY

ENGLAND
South Penquite Farm,
 Blisland, Cornwall
River Dart Country Park,
 Ashburton, Devon
Brook Lodge Farm C&C Park (Bristol),
 Cowslip Green, Somerset

SCOTLAND
Shieling Holidays,
 Craignure, Isle Of Mull

WALES
Caerfai Bay Caravan & Tent Park,
 St Davids, Pembrokeshire

►►►►► Premier parks

5 GOLD PENNANTS
►►►►►

ENGLAND

CAMBRIDGESHIRE
ST IVES
Stroud Hill Park

CHESHIRE
CODDINGTON
Manor Wood Country Caravan Park

WHITEGATE
Lamb Cottage Caravan Park

CORNWALL
BUDE
Wooda Farm Holiday Park

MEVAGISSEY
Seaview International Holiday Park

PADSTOW
Padstow Touring Park

ST IVES
Polmanter Touring Park

ST JUST-IN-ROSELAND
Trethem Mill Touring Park

TRURO
Carnon Downs Caravan
   & Camping Park

CUMBRIA
AMBLESIDE
Skelwith Fold Caravan Park

WINDERMERE
Park Cliffe Camping
   & Caravan Estate

DEVON
DARTMOUTH
Woodlands Grove Caravan
   & Camping Park

NEWTON ABBOT
Dornafield
Ross Park

SIDMOUTH
Oakdown Country Holiday Park

DORSET
BRIDPORT
Bingham Grange Touring
   & Camping Park
Highlands End Holiday Park

CHARMOUTH
Wood Farm Caravan
   & Camping Park

POOLE
South Lytchett Manor Caravan
   & Camping Park

WAREHAM
Wareham Forest Tourist Park

WEYMOUTH
East Fleet Farm Touring Park

HEREFORDSHIRE
PEMBRIDGE
Townsend Touring Park

ISLE OF WIGHT
NEWBRIDGE
The Orchards Holiday Caravan Park

RYDE
Whitefield Forest Touring Park

LANCASHIRE
SILVERDALE
Silverdale Caravan Park

NORFOLK
BARNEY
The Old Brick Kilns

CLIPPESBY
Clippesby Hall

NORTHUMBERLAND
BELFORD
South Meadows Caravan Park

NOTTINGHAMSHIRE
TEVERSAL
Teversal Camping & Caravanning
   Club Site

OXFORDSHIRE
HENLEY-ON-THAMES
Swiss Farm Touring & Camping

STANDLAKE
Lincoln Farm Park Oxfordshire

SHROPSHIRE
SHREWSBURY
Beaconsfield Farm Caravan Park

SOMERSET
BISHOP SUTTON
Bath Chew Valley Caravan Park

GLASTONBURY
The Old Oaks Touring Park

STAFFORDSHIRE
LONGNOR
Longnor Wood Holiday Park

SUFFOLK
WOODBRIDGE
Moon & Sixpence

YORKSHIRE, NORTH
HIGH BENTHAM
Riverside Caravan Park

SCOTLAND

ABERDEENSHIRE
HUNTLY
Huntly Castle Caravan Park

FIFE
ST ANDREWS
Cairnsmill Holiday Park
Craigtoun Meadows Holiday Park

LOTHIAN, EAST
DUNBAR
Thurston Manor Leisure Park

PERTH & KINROSS
BLAIR ATHOLL
Blair Castle Caravan Park

WALES

ANGLESEY, ISLE OF
DULAS
Tyddyn Isaf Caravan Park

MARIAN-GLAS
Home Farm Caravan Park

GWYNEDD
BARMOUTH
Trawsdir Touring Caravans & Camp-
   ing Park

TAL-Y-BONT
Islawrffordd Caravan Park

PEMBROKESHIRE
ST DAVIDS
Caerfai Bay Caravan & Tent Park

POWYS
BRECON
Pencelli Castle Caravan & Camping
   Park

WREXHAM
EYTON
Plassey Holiday Park

NORTHERN IRELAND

COUNTY ANTRIM
BUSHMILLS
Ballyness Caravan Park

5 BLACK PENNANTS
▶▶▶▶▶

ENGLAND

BERKSHIRE
HURLEY
Hurley Riverside Park

CAMBRIDGESHIRE
DODDINGTON
Fields End Water Caravan Park
  & Fishery

CORNWALL
CARLYON BAY
Carlyon Bay Caravan
  & Camping Park

CRANTOCK
Trevella Tourist Park

GOONHAVERN
Silverbow Park

HOLYWELL BAY
Trevornick Holiday Park

LANDRAKE
Dolbeare Park Caravan
  and Camping

LEEDSTOWN
Calloose Caravan & Camping Park

LOSTWITHIEL
Eden Valley Holiday Park

NEWQUAY
Hendra Holiday Park

PENTEWAN
Sun Valley Resort

REDRUTH
Globe Vale Holiday Park

REJERRAH
Newperran Holiday Park

ST AUSTELL
River Valley Holiday Park

ST IVES
Ayr Holiday Park

ST MERRYN
Atlantic Bays Holiday Park

ST MINVER
Gunvenna Caravan Park

TRURO
Cosawes Park
Truro Caravan and Camping Park

WATERGATE BAY
Watergate Bay Touring Park

CUMBRIA
APPLEBY-IN-WESTMORLAND
Wild Rose Park

BOOT
Eskdale Camping & Caravanning
  Club Site

KESWICK
Castlerigg Hall Caravan
  & Camping Park

KIRKBY LONSDALE
Woodclose Caravan Park

PENRITH
Lowther Holiday Park

TROUTBECK [NEAR KESWICK]
Troutbeck Camping and
  Caravanning Club Site

ULVERSTON
Bardsea Leisure Park

DERBYSHIRE
BIRCHOVER
Barn Farm Campsite

DEVON
BRAUNTON
Hidden Valley Park

CLYST ST MARY
Crealy Meadows Caravan and
  Camping Park

COMBE MARTIN
Newberry Valley Park

DAWLISH
Cofton Country Holidays
Lady's Mile Holiday Park

DREWSTEIGNTON
Woodland Springs Adult
  Touring Park

KINGSBRIDGE
Parkland Caravan and Camping Site

PAIGNTON
Beverley Parks Caravan
  & Camping Park

SAMPFORD PEVERELL
Minnows Touring Park

TAVISTOCK
Langstone Manor Camping &
  Caravan Park
Woodovis Park

DORSET
ALDERHOLT
Hill Cottage Farm Camping
  and Caravan Park

CHARMOUTH
Newlands Caravan & Camping Park

CHRISTCHURCH
Meadowbank Holidays

ST LEONARDS
Shamba Holidays

SWANAGE
Ulwell Cottage Caravan Park

WIMBORNE MINSTER
Merley Court
Wilksworth Farm Caravan Park

HAMPSHIRE
FORDINGBRIDGE
Sandy Balls Holiday Village

ROMSEY
Hill Farm Caravan Park

ISLE OF WIGHT
WROXALL
Appuldurcombe Gardens
  Holiday Park

KENT
ASHFORD
Broadhembury Caravan
  & Camping Park

MARDEN
Tanner Farm Touring Caravan
  & Camping Park

LANCASHIRE
THORNTON
Kneps Farm Holiday Park

LINCOLNSHIRE
WOODHALL SPA
Woodhall Country Park

NORFOLK
BELTON
Rose Farm Touring & Camping Park

Continued on next page ▷

▶▶▶▶▶ Premier parks *continued*

KING'S LYNN
King's Lynn Caravan and
  Camping Park

NORTH WALSHAM
Two Mills Touring Park

NORTHUMBERLAND
BELLINGHAM
Bellingham Camping
  & Caravanning Club Site

BERWICK-UPON-TWEED
Ord House Country Park

HALTWHISTLE
Herding Hill Farm

SHROPSHIRE
BRIDGNORTH
Stanmore Hall Touring Park

SHREWSBURY
Oxon Hall Touring Park

TELFORD
Severn Gorge Park

WHEATHILL
Wheathill Touring Park

SOMERSET
CROWCOMBE
Quantock Orchard Caravan Park

PORLOCK
Porlock Caravan Park

WELLS
Wells Holiday Park

WIVELISCOMBE
Waterrow Touring Park

SUFFOLK
LEISTON
Cakes & Ale

WILTSHIRE
LANDFORD
Greenhill Farm Caravan
  & Camping Park

WORCESTERSHIRE
HONEYBOURNE
Ranch Caravan Park

YORKSHIRE, NORTH
ALLERSTON
Vale of Pickering Caravan Park

ALNE
Alders Caravan Park

HARROGATE
Ripley Caravan Park
Rudding Holiday Park

HELMSLEY
Golden Square Touring Caravan Park

OSMOTHERLEY
Cote Ghyll Caravan & Camping Park

RIPON
Riverside Meadows Country
  Caravan Park

SCARBOROUGH
Jacobs Mount Caravan Park

SUTTON-ON-THE-FOREST
Goosewood Caravan Park

WYKEHAM
St Helens Caravan Park

CHANNEL ISLANDS

GUERNSEY
CASTEL
Fauxquets Valley Campsite

JERSEY
ST MARTIN
Beuvelande Camp Site

SCOTLAND
DUMFRIES & GALLOWAY
BRIGHOUSE BAY
Brighouse Bay Holiday Park

CREETOWN
Castle Cary Holiday Park

ECCLEFECHAN
Hoddom Castle Caravan Park

KIRKCUDBRIGHT
Seaward Caravan Park

DUNBARTONSHIRE, WEST
BALLOCH
Lomond Woods Holiday Park

HIGHLAND
CORPACH
Linnhe Lochside Holidays

MORAY
LOSSIEMOUTH
Silver Sands Leisure Park

PERTH & KINROSS
BLAIR ATHOLL
River Tilt Caravan Park

STIRLING
ABERFOYLE
Trossachs Holiday Park

WALES
CARMARTHENSHIRE
LLANDOVERY
Erwlon Caravan & Camping Park

NEWCASTLE EMLYN
Cenarth Falls Holiday Park

CONWY
LLANDDULAS

Bron-Y-Wendon Caravan Park

LLANRWST
Bron Derw Touring Caravan Park

GWYNEDD
BARMOUTH
Hendre Mynach Touring Caravan
  & Camping Park

MONMOUTHSHIRE
USK
Pont Kemys Caravan
  & Camping Park

POWYS
BUILTH WELLS
Fforest Fields Caravan
  & Camping Park

CHURCHSTOKE
Daisy Bank Caravan Park

SWANSEA
PONTARDDULAIS
River View Touring Park

NORTHERN IRELAND

COUNTY ANTRIM
BALLYMONEY
Drumaheglis Marina
  & Caravan Park

COUNTY FERMANAGH
BELCOO
Rushin House Caravan Park

After Bite

Fast relief from bites and stings.

Don't let bites and stings stop the family fun
– take After Bite away with you.

Easy-to-apply, fast-acting After Bite provides
instant relief from the effects of mosquitoes,
bees, wasps, nettles and jellyfish.

From Boots, Superdrug, Tesco, Lloydspharmacy
and good chemists everywhere.
Online at **www.afterbite.co.uk**
Contains ammonia 3.5% w/v. Always read the label.

Gold Pennant parks

ENGLAND

CAMBRIDGESHIRE

COMBERTON
▶▶▶▶ Highfield Farm
Touring Park

ST IVES
▶▶▶▶▶ Stroud Hill Park

CHESHIRE

CODDINGTON
▶▶▶▶▶ Manor Wood Country
Caravan Park

WHITEGATE
▶▶▶▶▶ Lamb Cottage
Caravan Park

CORNWALL

BUDE
▶▶▶▶▶ Wooda Farm
Holiday Park

GWITHIAN
▶▶▶▶ Gwithian Farm Campsite

MEVAGISSEY
▶▶▶▶▶ Seaview International
Holiday Park

PADSTOW
▶▶▶▶▶ Padstow Touring Park

PORTHTOWAN
▶▶▶▶ Porthtowan Tourist Park

ST IVES
▶▶▶▶▶ Polmanter Touring Park

ST JUST-IN-ROSELAND
▶▶▶▶▶ Trethem Mill
Touring Park

SUMMERCOURT
▶▶▶▶ Carvynick Country Club

TRURO
▶▶▶▶▶ Carnon Downs Caravan
& Camping Park

WADEBRIDGE
▶▶▶▶▶ St Mabyn Holiday Park

CUMBRIA

AMBLESIDE
▶▶▶▶▶ Skelwith Fold
Caravan Park

WINDERMERE
▶▶▶▶▶ Park Cliffe Camping
& Caravan Estate

DERBYSHIRE

BUXTON
▶▶▶ Clover Fields Touring
Caravan Park

DEVON

COMBE MARTIN
▶▶▶▶ Stowford Farm Meadows

DARTMOUTH
▶▶▶▶▶ Woodlands Grove
Caravan & Camping Park

NEWTON ABBOT
▶▶▶▶▶ Dornafield
▶▶▶▶▶ Ross Park

SIDMOUTH
▶▶▶▶▶ Oakdown Country
Holiday Park

SOUTH MOLTON
▶▶▶▶ Riverside Caravan &
Camping Park

WOODBURY SALTERTON
▶▶▶ Browns Farm Caravan Park

DORSET

BRIDPORT
▶▶▶▶ Bingham Grange
Touring & Camping Park
▶▶▶▶▶ Highlands End
Holiday Park

CHARMOUTH
▶▶▶ Manor Farm Holiday Centre
▶▶▶▶▶ Wood Farm Caravan
& Camping Park

CORFE CASTLE
▶▶▶▶ Corfe Castle Camping
& Caravanning Club Site

POOLE
▶▶▶▶▶ South Lytchett Manor
Caravan & Camping Park

WAREHAM
▶▶▶▶▶ Wareham Forest
Tourist Park

WEYMOUTH
▶▶▶ West Fleet Holiday Farm
▶▶▶▶▶ East Fleet Farm
Touring Park

HEREFORDSHIRE

PEMBRIDGE
▶▶▶▶▶ Townsend Touring Park

ISLE OF WIGHT

NEWBRIDGE
▶▶▶▶▶ The Orchards Holiday
Caravan Park

RYDE
▶▶▶▶▶ Whitefield Forest
Touring Park

LANCASHIRE

FAR ARNSIDE
▶▶▶▶ Hollins Farm Camping
& Caravanning

SILVERDALE
▶▶▶▶▶ Silverdale Caravan Park

NORFOLK

BARNEY
▶▶▶▶▶ The Old Brick Kilns

CLIPPESBY
▶▶▶▶▶ Clippesby Hall

NORTHUMBERLAND

BELFORD
▶▶▶▶▶ South Meadows
Caravan Park

NOTTINGHAMSHIRE

TEVERSAL
▶▶▶▶▶ Teversal Camping
& Caravanning Club Site

OXFORDSHIRE

HENLEY-ON-THAMES
▶▶▶▶▶ Swiss Farm Touring
& Camping

STANDLAKE
▶▶▶▶▶ Lincoln Farm
Park Oxfordshire

RUTLAND

GREETHAM
▶▶▶▶ Rutland Caravan
& Camping

SHROPSHIRE

SHREWSBURY
Beaconsfield Farm Caravan Park
▶▶▶▶▶

SOMERSET

BISHOP SUTTON
▷▷▷▷▷ Bath Chew Valley
Caravan Park

BREAN
▷▷▷▷ Northam Farm Caravan
& Touring Park

BRIDGETOWN
▷▷▷▷ Exe Valley Caravan Site

GLASTONBURY
▷▷▷▷▷ The Old Oaks
Touring Park

PORLOCK
▷▷▷▷ Burrowhayes Farm
Caravan & Camping Site
& Riding Stables

SHEPTON MALLET
▷▷ Greenacres Camping

STAFFORDSHIRE

LONGNOR
▷▷▷▷ Longnor Wood
Holiday Park

SUFFOLK

WOODBRIDGE
▷▷▷▷▷ Moon & Sixpence

WEST MIDLANDS

MERIDEN
▷▷▷▷ Somers Wood
Caravan Park

WILTSHIRE

SALISBURY
▷▷▷▷ Coombe Touring Park

YORKSHIRE, NORTH

HIGH BENTHAM
▷▷▷▷▷ Riverside Caravan Park

ROBIN HOOD'S BAY
▷▷▷▷ Grouse Hill Caravan Park

WHITBY
▷▷▷▷ Ladycross Plantation
Caravan Park

CHANNEL ISLANDS

JERSEY

ST MARTIN
▷▷▷▷ Rozel Camping Park

SCOTLAND

ABERDEENSHIRE

HUNTLY
▷▷▷▷▷ Huntly Castle
Caravan Park

ARGYLL & BUTE

CARRADALE
▷▷▷ Carradale Bay Caravan Park

DUMFRIES & GALLOWAY

WIGTOWN
▷▷▷ Drumroamin Farm Camping
& Touring Site

FIFE

ST ANDREWS
▷▷▷▷▷ Cairnsmill Holiday Park
▷▷▷▷▷ Craigtoun Meadows
Holiday Park

HIGHLAND

EDINBANE
▷▷▷▷ Skye Camping &
Caravanning Club Site

FORT WILLIAM
▷▷▷▷ Glen Nevis Caravan
& Camping Park

LOTHIAN, EAST

DUNBAR
▷▷▷▷▷ Thurston Manor
Leisure Park

PERTH & KINROSS

BLAIR ATHOLL
▷▷▷▷▷ Blair Castle
Caravan Park

STIRLING

BLAIRLOGIE
▷▷▷▷ Witches Craig Caravan
& Camping Park

WALES

ANGLESEY, ISLE OF

DULAS
▷▷▷▷▷ Tyddyn Isaf
Caravan Park

MARIAN-GLAS
▷▷▷▷▷ Home Farm
Caravan Park

CARMARTHENSHIRE

LLANGENNECH
▷▷▷ South Wales Caravan Park

CEREDIGION

ABERAERON
▷▷▷ Aeron Coast Caravan Park

DENBIGHSHIRE

RHUALLT
▷▷▷▷ Penisar Mynydd
Caravan Park

GWYNEDD

BARMOUTH
▷▷▷▷ Trawsdir Touring
Caravans & Camping Park

TAL-Y-BONT
▷▷▷▷▷ Islawrffordd
Caravan Park

PEMBROKESHIRE

FISHGUARD
▷▷▷ Fishguard Bay Caravan
& Camping Park

ST DAVIDS
▷▷▷▷ Caerfai Bay Caravan
& Tent Park

POWYS

BRECON
▷▷▷▷▷ Pencelli Castle Caravan
& Camping Park

SWANSEA

RHOSSILI
▷▷▷ Pitton Cross Caravan
& Camping Park

WREXHAM

EYTON
▷▷▷▷▷ Plassey Holiday Park

NORTHERN IRELAND

COUNTY ANTRIM

BUSHMILLS
▷▷▷▷▷ Ballyness Caravan Park

AA Holiday Centres

These parks cater for all holiday needs. See page 11 for further information.

ENGLAND

CORNWALL

HAYLE
St Ives Bay Holiday Park
Holywell Bay
Holywell Bay Holiday Park

LOOE
Tencreek Holiday Park

MULLION
Mullion Holiday Park

NEWQUAY
Newquay Holiday Park

PERRANPORTH
Perran Sands Holiday Park

ST MERRYN
Harlyn Sands Holiday Park
Widemouth Bay
Widemouth Bay Caravan Park

CUMBRIA

FLOOKBURGH
Lakeland Leisure Park

POOLEY BRIDGE
Park Foot Caravan & Camping Park

SILLOTH
Stanwix Park Holiday Centre

DEVON

CROYDE BAY
Ruda Holiday Park

EXMOUTH
Devon Cliffs Holiday Park

SHALDON
Coast View Holiday Park

WOOLACOMBE
Golden Coast Holiday Village
Twitchen House Holiday Village
Woolacombe Bay Holiday Village

DORSET

BRIDPORT
Freshwater Beach Holiday Park
West Bay Holiday Park

HOLTON HEATH
Sandford Holiday Park

POOLE
Rockley Park

WEYMOUTH
Littlesea Holiday Park
Seaview Holiday Park

DURHAM, COUNTY

BLACKHALL COLLIERY
Crimdon Dene

ESSEX

CLACTON-ON-SEA
Highfield Grange
Martello Beach Holiday Park

MERSEA ISLAND
Waldegraves Holiday Park

ST LAWRENCE
Waterside St Lawrence Bay

ST OSYTH
The Orchards Holiday Park
Walton On The Naze
Naze Marine

ISLE OF WIGHT

COWES
Thorness Bay Holiday Park

ST HELENS
Nodes Point Holiday Park

SHANKLIN
Lower Hyde Holiday Park

WHITECLIFF BAY
Whitecliff Bay Holiday Park

KENT

EASTCHURCH
Warden Springs Caravan Park

LANCASHIRE

BLACKPOOL
Marton Mere Holiday Village

LINCOLNSHIRE

CLEETHORPES
Thorpe Park Holiday Centre

MABLETHORPE
Golden Sands Holiday Park

SALTFLEET
Sunnydale

SKEGNESS
Southview Leisure Park

MERSEYSIDE

SOUTHPORT
Riverside Holiday Park

NORFOLK

BELTON
Wild Duck Holiday Park

BURGH CASTLE
Breydon Water

CAISTER-ON-SEA
Caister Holiday Park

GREAT YARMOUTH
Vauxhall Holiday Park

HUNSTANTON
Manor Park Holiday Village
Searles Leisure Resort

NORTHUMBERLAND

BERWICK-UPON-TWEED
Haggerston Castle

NORTH SEATON
Sandy Bay

SOMERSET

BREAN
Holiday Resort Unity
Warren Farm Holiday Centre

BRIDGWATER
Mill Farm Caravan & Camping Park

BURNHAM-ON-SEA
Burnham-On-Sea Holiday Village

SUFFOLK

KESSINGLAND
Kessingland Beach Holiday Park

SUSSEX, EAST

CAMBER
Camber Sands

SUSSEX, WEST

SELSEY
Warner Farm Touring Park

YORKSHIRE, EAST RIDING OF

SKIPSEA
Skipsea Sands
Skirlington Leisure Park

TUNSTALL
Sand Le Mere Holiday Village

WITHERNSEA
Withernsea Sands

YORKSHIRE, NORTH

FILEY
Blue Dolphin Holiday Park
Flower Of May Holiday Park
Primrose Valley Holiday Park
Reighton Sands Holiday Park

SCOTLAND

AYRSHIRE, NORTH
SALTCOATS
Sandylands

AYRSHIRE, SOUTH
AYR
Craig Tara Holiday Park

COYLTON
Sundrum Castle Holiday Park

DUMFRIES & GALLOWAY
GATEHOUSE OF FLEET
Auchenlarie Holiday Park

SOUTHERNESS
Southerness Holiday Village

HIGHLAND
DORNOCH
Grannie's Heilan Hame Holiday Park

NAIRN
Nairn Lochloy Holiday Park

PERTH & KINROSS
TUMMEL BRIDGE
Tummel Valley Holiday Park

SCOTTISH BORDERS
EYEMOUTH
Eyemouth

WALES

CEREDIGION
BORTH
Brynowen Holiday Park

CONWY
TOWYN
Ty Mawr Holiday Park

DENBIGHSHIRE
PRESTATYN
Presthaven Sands Holiday Park

GWYNEDD
PORTHMADOG
Greenacres Holiday Park

PWLLHELI
Hafan y Môr Holiday Park

PEMBROKESHIRE
TENBY
Kiln Park Holiday Centre

SWANSEA
SWANSEA
Riverside Caravan Park

CASTLE CARY HOLIDAY PARK

Creetown, Nr Newton Stewart, Wigtownshire DG8 7DQ
Telephone: 01671 820264
Fax: 01671 820670
www.castlecary-caravans.com
enquiries@castlecarypark.f9.co.uk

For that quiet relaxing holiday in the heart of romantic Galloway, Castle Cary has much to offer, and constantly adds to and improves its facilities year after year. It has views over fields, woodlands and the estuary of the River Cree.

Having your very own luxurious holiday home on Castle Cary Holiday Park is no longer a dream. It has became a reality for more and more customers who are aware of the advantages of having your own holiday home. We have a comprehensive selection of new and used caravans, and a wide range of luxury lodges for sale.

FACILITIES

- Shower and toilets; Family room
- Outdoor heated swimming pool; Games room; Shop
- Indoor heated swimming pool; Donkey park
- Snooker room; Restaurant/Inn
- Giant Draughts; Crazy Golf
- Coarse Fishing; Glamping
- Children's Play Park; C.W. Points
- Tourers, tents, motor homes all welcome
- Special 10% discount for weekly bookings

Adults only – no children parks

ENGLAND

CAMBRIDGESHIRE
DODDINGTON
Fields End Water Caravan Park
& Fishery

ST IVES
Stroud Hill Park

CHESHIRE
WETTENHALL
New Farm Caravan Park

WHITEGATE
Lamb Cottage Caravan Park

CORNWALL
CHACEWATER
Killiwerris Touring Park

ST HILARY
Wayfarers Caravan & Camping Park

CUMBRIA
CARLISLE
Green Acres Caravan Park

MEALSGATE
Larches Caravan Park

DERBYSHIRE
BUXTON
Clover Fields Touring Caravan Park

DEVON
DREWSTEIGNTON
Woodland Springs Adult Touring Park

EAST ANSTEY
Zeacombe House Caravan Park

TORQUAY
Widdicombe Farm Touring Park

DORSET
BRIDPORT
Bingham Grange Touring
& Camping Park

HURN
Fillybrook Farm Touring Park

ST LEONARDS
Back Of Beyond Touring Park

ESSEX
GREAT SALING
Golden Grove

HEREFORDSHIRE
MORETON ON LUGG
Cuckoo's Corner Campsite

LANCASHIRE
BLACKPOOL
Manor House Caravan Park

LINCOLNSHIRE
BOSTON
Long Acres Touring Park
Orchard Park

NORFOLK
NORTH WALSHAM
Two Mills Touring Park

SAHAM HILLS
Lowe Caravan Park

STANHOE
The Rickels Caravan & Camping Park

SWAFFHAM
Breckland Meadows Touring Park
Three Holes
Lode Hall Holiday Park

NORTHAMPTONSHIRE
BULWICK
New Lodge Farm Caravan
& Camping Site

NORTHUMBERLAND
SEAHOUSES
Westfield Paddock

NOTTINGHAMSHIRE
SOUTHWELL
New Hall Farm Touring Park

OXFORDSHIRE
BURFORD
Wysdom Touring Park

SHROPSHIRE
SHREWSBURY
Beaconsfield Farm Caravan Park

TELFORD
Severn Gorge Park

WHEATHILL
Wheathill Touring Park

SOMERSET
BISHOP SUTTON
Bath Chew Valley Caravan Park

BRIDGETOWN
Exe Valley Caravan Site

CHEDDAR
Cheddar Bridge Touring Park

GLASTONBURY
The Old Oaks Touring Park

SPARKFORD
Long Hazel Park

WELLINGTON
Greenacres Touring Park

WELLS
Homestead Park
Wells Holiday Park

WIVELISCOMBE
Waterrow Touring Park

STAFFORDSHIRE
LONGNOR
Longnor Wood Holiday Park

SUFFOLK
WOODBRIDGE
Moat Barn Touring Caravan Park

WEST MIDLANDS
MERIDEN
Somers Wood Caravan Park

YORKSHIRE, EAST RIDING OF
BRANDESBURTON
Blue Rose Caravan Country Park

YORKSHIRE, NORTH
HARROGATE
Shaws Trailer Park

HELMSLEY
Foxholme Caravan Park

YORK
Rawcliffe Manor Caravan Park

YORKSHIRE, WEST
LEEDS
Moor Lodge Park
St Helena's Caravan Park

SCOTLAND

ABERDEENSHIRE
MINTLAW
Aden Caravan And Camping Park

WALES

CARMARTHENSHIRE
LLANGENNECH
South Wales Caravan Park

MONMOUTHSHIRE
ABERGAVENNY
Wernddu Caravan Park

POWYS
CHURCHSTOKE
Daisy Bank Caravan Park

CRICKHOWELL
Riverside Caravan & Camping Park

LLANDRINDOD WELLS
Dalmore Camping
& Caravanning Park

WREXHAM
OVERTON
The Trotting Mare Caravan Park

AA GUIDES

WE KNOW BRITAIN

▸ THE BEST PLACES TO VISIT

▸ CLEAR TOWN PLANS AND MAPPING

▸ WRITTEN BY LOCAL EXPERTS

▸ RECOMMENDED PLACES TO EAT

▸ TRUSTED LISTINGS

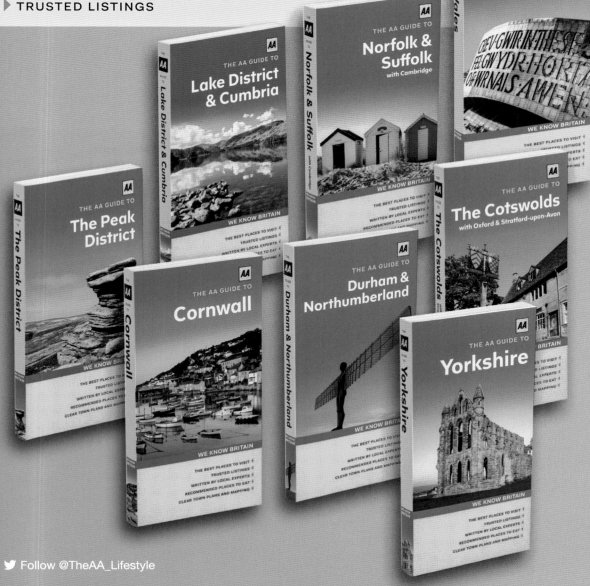

THE AA GUIDE TO
Wales
WE KNOW BRITAIN

THE AA GUIDE TO
Norfolk & Suffolk
with Cambridge
WE KNOW BRITAIN

THE AA GUIDE TO
Lake District & Cumbria
WE KNOW BRITAIN

THE AA GUIDE TO
The Cotswolds
with Oxford & Stratford-upon-Avon

The Peak District
WE KNOW BRITAIN

THE AA GUIDE TO
Cornwall
WE KNOW BRITAIN

THE AA GUIDE TO
Durham & Northumberland

THE AA GUIDE TO
Yorkshire
WE KNOW BRITAIN

Follow @TheAA_Lifestyle

England

BERKSHIRE

FINCHAMPSTEAD
Map 5 SU76

Places to visit

West Green House Gardens, HARTLEY WINTNEY, RG27 8JB, 01252 844611
www.westgreenhouse.co.uk

Museum of English Rural Life, READING, RG1 5EX, 0118 378 8660
www.merl.org.uk

Great for kids: The Look Out Discovery Centre, BRACKNELL, RG12 7QW,
01344 354400 www.bracknell-forest.gov.uk/be

California Chalet & Touring Park
►►► 80%

tel: 0118 973 3928 & 07447 475833 **Nine Mile Ride RG40 4HU**
email: enquiries@californiapark.co.uk
dir: *From A321 (S of Wokingham), right onto B3016 to Finchampstead. Follow Country
Park signs on Nine Mile Ride.* **grid ref:** *SU788651*

A simple, peaceful woodland site with secluded pitches among the trees, adjacent
to the country park. Several pitches have a prime position beside the lake with their
own fishing area. The site has large hardstandings, with more planned for 2015;
the chalet accommodation has been upgraded and the toilet block has quality
vanity units and fully tiled showers. The thinned out trees allow sunshine onto
pitches, and future investment plans are very positive for this well located park. 5.5
acre site. 44 touring pitches. 44 hardstandings. Caravan pitches. Motorhome
pitches. Tent pitches.

Open: all year **Last arrival:** flexible **Last departure:** noon
Pitches: * ⛺ £23-£27 ⛺ £23-£27 ▲ £23-£27
Facilities: ⚑⊙⚲⛤🚿♿🔌 WiFi ♲ ❶
Services: ⚡🔋 🚽T♨↯
Within 3 miles: ⚓🏇⚲◎🛒⛳♞
Notes: No ground fires, no washing of caravans. Dogs must be kept on leads.
AA Pubs & Restaurants nearby: The Broad Street Tavern, WOKINGHAM, RG40 1AU,
0118 977 3706

L'Ortolan, SHINFIELD, RG2 9BY, 0118 988 8500

HURLEY

Places to visit

Cliveden, CLIVEDEN, SL6 0JA, 01628 605069 www.nationaltrust.org.uk/cliveden

The Hell-Fire Caves, WEST WYCOMBE, HP14 3AJ, 01494 524411 (office)
www.hellfirecaves.co.uk

Great for kids: Bekonscot Model Village and Railway, BEACONSFIELD, HP9 2PL,
01494 672919 www.bekonscot.co.uk

HURLEY
Map 5 SU88

PREMIER PARK

Hurley Riverside Park
►►►►► 84%

GOLD

tel: 01628 824493 & 823501 **Park Office SL6 5NE**
email: info@hurleyriversidepark.co.uk **web:** www.hurleyriversidepark.co.uk
dir: *Signed on A4130 (Henley to Maidenhead road), just W of Hurley.*
grid ref: *SU826839*

A large Thames-side site with a good touring area close to the river. A quality
park with three beautifully appointed toilet blocks, one of which houses
excellent, fully serviced unisex facilities. Level grassy pitches are sited in small,
sectioned areas, and this is a generally peaceful setting. There are furnished
tents for hire. 15 acre site. 200 touring pitches. 36 hardstandings. Caravan
pitches. Motorhome pitches. Tent pitches. 290 statics.

Open: Mar-Oct **Last arrival:** 20.00hrs **Last departure:** noon
Pitches: * ⛺ £15-£30 ⛺ £15-£30 ▲ £13-£26 **Leisure:** ⚑❖
Facilities: ⚑⊙⚲⛤✳♿🔌📞🛒🎯🚿 WiFi ♲ ❶
Services: ⚡🔋 🚽⚑◎T↯ **Within 3 miles:** ⚓☲🏇⚲🛒🔋
Notes: No unsupervised children, no young groups, no commercial vehicles, no fires or
fire pits, quiet park policy, max 2 dogs per pitch. Dogs must be kept on leads. Fishing
in season, slipway, nature trail, riverside picnic grounds.
AA Pubs & Restaurants nearby: The Olde Bell Inn, HURLEY, SL6 5LX, 01628 825881

Hotel du Vin Henley-on-Thames, HENLEY-ON-THAMES, RG9 2BP, 01491 848400

See advert on opposite page

NEWBURY
Map 5 SU46

Places to visit

Highclere Castle & Gardens, HIGHCLERE, RG20 9RN, 01635 253210
www.highclerecastle.co.uk

Great for kids: The Living Rainforest, HAMPSTEAD NORREYS, RG18 0TN,
01635 202444 www.livingrainforest.org

Bishops Green Farm Camp Site
►►►81%

tel: 01635 268365 **Bishops Green RG20 4JP**
dir: Exit A339 (opposite New Greenham Park) towards Bishops Green & Ecchinswell. Site on left, approx 0.5m by barn. **grid ref:** SU502630

A sheltered and secluded meadowland park close to the Hampshire/Berkshire border, offering very clean and well-maintained facilities, including a toilet block with a disabled/family room. There are woodland and riverside walks to be enjoyed around the farm, and coarse fishing is also available. The site is very convenient for visiting the nearby market town of Newbury with its attractive canal in the town centre. 1.5 acre site. 30 touring pitches. 6 hardstandings. Caravan pitches. Motorhome pitches. Tent pitches.

Open: Apr-Oct **Last arrival:** 21.30hrs

Pitches: ⌂ ⌂ Å

Facilities: ⌂ ✳ ⌂

Services: ⌂ ⌂ ⌂

Within 3 miles: ↓ ⌂ ⌂

Notes: ⌂ Dogs must be kept on leads.

RISELEY
Map 5 SU76

Places to visit

Basildon Park, LOWER BASILDON, RG8 9NR, 0118 984 3040
www.nationaltrust.org.uk/basildonpark

Mapledurham House, MAPLEDURHAM, RG4 7TR, 0118 972 3350
www.mapledurham.co.uk

Great for kids: Beale Park, LOWER BASILDON, RG8 9NH, 0844 826 1761
www.bealepark.co.uk

Wellington Country Park
►►►86%

tel: 0118 932 6444 **Odiham Rd RG7 1SP**
email: info@wellington-country-park.co.uk **web:** www.wellington-country-park.co.uk
dir: M4 junct 11, A33 S towards Basingstoke. Or M3 junct 5, B3349 N towards Reading.
grid ref: SU728628

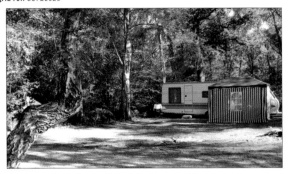

A peaceful woodland site, popular with families, set within an extensive country park, which comes complete with lakes and nature trails; these are accessible to

continued

PITCHES: ⌂ Caravans ⌂ Motorhomes Å Tents ⌂ Glamping-style accommodation **SERVICES:** ⌂ Electric hook up ⌂ Launderette ⌂ Licensed bar
⌂ Calor Gas ⌂ Camping Gaz ⌂ Toilet fluid ⌂ Café/Restaurant ⌂ Fast Food/Takeaway ⌂ Battery charging ⌂ Baby care ⌂ Motorvan service point
ABBREVIATIONS: BH/bank hols – bank holidays Etr – Easter Spring BH – Spring Bank Holiday fr – from hrs – hours m – mile mdnt – midnight
rdbt – roundabout rs – restricted service wk – week wknd – weekend x-rds – cross roads ⌂ No credit or debit cards ⌂ No dogs ⌂ Children of all ages accepted

RISELEY *continued*

campers after the country park closes. The park offers good facilities that include a refurbished laundry and a new motorhome service point. There's also a herd of Red and Fallow deer that roam the meadow area. This site is ideal for those travelling on the M4. 80 acre site. 87 touring pitches. 18 hardstandings. Caravan pitches. Motorhome pitches. Tent pitches.

Open: Mar-Nov **Last arrival:** 17.30hrs **Last departure:** noon

Pitches: 🚐 🚙 Å

Leisure: 🛝 🎵

Facilities: 🐾 ⊙ 🏳 ✳ ❤ © ⑤ 🗟 WiFi 🖥 ♻ ❶

Services: 🔌 🗑 🔋 🍴 🚌

Within 3 miles: 🎣 ◎ 🎿 🛒 ⑤ ∪

Notes: No open fires, last arrival time 16.30hrs in low season. Dogs must be kept on leads. Miniature railway, crazy golf, animal farm, access to Wellington Country Park.

AA Pubs & Restaurants nearby: The George & Dragon, SWALLOWFIELD, RG7 1TJ, 0118 988 4432

Open: Apr-Oct **Last arrival:** 20.00hrs **Last departure:** 14.00hrs

Pitches: * 🚐 £20-£25 🚙 £20-£25 Å £15-£20

Facilities: 🐾 ⊙ 🏳 ✳ © 🗟 🛒 WiFi ❶ **Services:** 🔌 🗑 🔋 🚿 Ⓣ 🚌 ⚓

Within 3 miles: 🎣 ∮ ⑤ ∪

Notes: Dogs must be kept on leads. Postbox.

AA Pubs & Restaurants nearby: The Three Horseshoes, MADINGLEY, CB23 8AB, 01954 210221

Restaurant 22, CAMBRIDGE, CB4 3AX, 01223 351880

BRISTOL

BRISTOL

See Cowslip Green (Somerset)

CAMBRIDGESHIRE

COMBERTON Map 12 TL35

Places to visit

IWM Duxford, DUXFORD, CB22 4QR, 01223 835000 www.iwm.org.uk

Chilford Hall Vineyard, LINTON, CB21 4LE, 01223 895600 www.chilfordhall.co.uk

Great for kids: Linton Zoological Gardens, LINTON, CB21 4NT, 01223 891308 www.lintonzoo.com

Highfield Farm Touring Park

 ►►►► 91%

Best of British

tel: 01223 262308 **Long Rd CB23 7DG**
email: enquiries@highfieldfarmtouringpark.co.uk
web: www.highfieldfarmtouringpark.co.uk
dir: *M11 junct 12, A603 (Sandy). 0.5m, right onto B1046 to Comberton.*
grid ref: *TL389572*

Run by a very efficient and friendly family, the park is on a well-sheltered hilltop, with spacious pitches including a cosy backpackers/cyclists' area, and separate sections for couples and families. Around the family farm there is a one and a half mile marked walk, that has stunning views. 8 acre site. 120 touring pitches. 52 hardstandings. Caravan pitches. Motorhome pitches. Tent pitches.

DODDINGTON Map 12 TL49

Places to visit

WWT Welney Wetland Centre, WELNEY, PE14 9TN, 01353 860711 www.wwt.org.uk

Flag Fen Archaeology Park, PETERBOROUGH, PE6 7QJ, 01733 313414 www.vivacity-peterborough.com/museums-and-heritage/flag-fen

PREMIER PARK

Fields End Water Caravan Park & Fishery

►►►►► 83%

tel: 01354 740199 **Benwick Rd PE15 0TY**
email: info@fieldsendfishing.co.uk
dir: *Exit A141, follow signs to Doddington. At clock tower in Doddington turn right into Benwick Rd. Site 1.5m on right after sharp bends.* **grid ref:** *TL378908*

This meticulously planned and executed park makes excellent use of its slightly elevated position in The Fens. The 33 fully serviced pitches, all with very generous hardstandings, are on smart terraces with sweeping views of the countryside. The two toilet blocks contain several combined cubicle spaces, and there are shady walks through mature deciduous woodland adjacent to two large and appealingly landscaped fishing lakes. Three high quality pine lodges are available as holiday lets. 20 acre site. 52 touring pitches. 17 hardstandings. Caravan pitches. Motorhome pitches. Tent pitches.

Open: all year **Last arrival:** 20.30hrs **Last departure:** noon

Pitches: * 🚐 £14-£19.50 🚙 £14-£19.50 Å £15-£16.50

Facilities: 🐾 ⊙ 🏳 ✳ ❤ ⑤ 🛒 WiFi ♻ ❶

Services: 🔌 🗑 🔋 Ⓣ **Within 3 miles:** 🎣 ∮ ◎ ⑤ 🗟

Notes: Adults only. Dogs must be kept on leads.

AA Pubs & Restaurants nearby: The Crown Inn, BROUGHTON, PE28 3AY, 01487 824428

The Old Bridge Hotel, HUNTINGDON, PE29 3TQ, 01480 424300

GUYHIRN · Map 12 TF40

Places to visit

Peckover House & Garden, WISBECH, PE13 1JR, 01945 583463 www.nationaltrust.org.uk/peckover

Great for kids: WWT Welney Wetland Centre, WELNEY, PE14 9TN, 01353 860711 www.wwt.org.uk

---

NEW Tall Trees Leisure Park
►►►74%

tel: 01945 450952 **Gull Rd PE13 4ER**
email: enquiries@talltreesleisurepark.co.uk
dir: A47 from Peterborough towards Wisbech. Left onto B1187 signed Guyhirn.
grid ref: TF393035

Tall Trees Leisure Park is a family-run caravan site set in 35 acres of a former commercial fruit farm. There are 59 electric pitches, each with its own water tap, set out in two perfectly level and maturely landscaped fields. There is also a separate, large rally field. Toilets are provided in well-maintained raised cabins, and the reception also houses a small shop and café. Security is given a high priority with an entrance barrier and CCTV. 35 acre site. 94 touring pitches. Caravan pitches. Motorhome pitches. Tent pitches.

Open: all year **Last arrival:** 17.00hrs **Last departure:** noon

Pitches: * 🚐 £11-£15 🚌 £11-£15 ▲ £11-£15

HEMINGFORD ABBOTS · Map 12 TL27

Quiet Waters Caravan Park
►►►79%

tel: 01480 463405 **PE28 9AJ**
email: quietwaters.park@btopenworld.com **web:** www.quietwaterscaravanpark.co.uk
dir: Follow village signs from A14 junct 25, E of Huntingdon, site in village centre.
grid ref: TL283712

This is an attractive little site on the banks of the Great Ouse that has been in the same family ownership for over 80 years. It is found in a really charming village

---

just a mile from the A14, making an ideal centre from which to tour the Cambridgeshire area. There are fishing opportunities, rowing boats for hire and many walks and cycling routes directly from the park. There are holiday statics for hire. 1 acre site. 20 touring pitches. 18 hardstandings. Caravan pitches. Motorhome pitches. Tent pitches. 40 statics.

Open: Apr-Oct **Last arrival:** 20.00hrs **Last departure:** noon

Pitches: * 🚐 £17-£21 🚌 £17-£21 ▲ £17-£21

Facilities: 🅿️☉🄿🌣🕭🕓🆆🅸🅵🄘 ❶

Services: 🔌🅓🖤🖉

Within 3 miles: 🚶‍♂️🚵🍴🛡️🐟🍺⛵

Notes: Dogs must be kept on leads.

AA Pubs & Restaurants nearby: The Cock Pub and Restaurant, HEMINGFORD GREY, PE28 9BJ, 01480 463609

The Old Bridge Hotel, HUNTINGDON, PE29 3TQ, 01480 424300

HUNTINGDON · Map 12 TL27

Places to visit

Ramsey Abbey Gatehouse, RAMSEY, PE26 1DG, 01480 301494 www.nationaltrust.org.uk

WWT Welney Wetland Centre, WELNEY, PE14 9TN, 01353 860711 www.wwt.org.uk

Great for kids: The Raptor Foundation, WOODHURST, PE28 3BT, 01487 741140 www.raptorfoundation.org.uk

---

Huntingdon Boathaven & Caravan Park
►►►80%

tel: 01480 411977 **The Avenue, Godmanchester PE29 2AF**
email: boathaven.hunts@virgin.net
dir: S of town. Exit A14 at Godmanchester junct, through Godmanchester on B1043 to site (on left by River Ouse). **grid ref:** TL249706

A small, well laid out site overlooking a boat marina and the River Ouse, set close to the A14 and within walking distance of Huntingdon town centre. The toilets are clean and well kept. A pretty area has been created for tents beside the marina, with wide views across the Ouse Valley. Weekend family activities are organised throughout the season. 2 acre site. 24 touring pitches. 18 hardstandings. Caravan pitches. Motorhome pitches. Tent pitches.

Open: all year (rs Winter open subject to weather) **Last arrival:** 21.00hrs

Pitches: * 🚐 £15-£20 🚌 £15-£20 ▲ £11-£19

Facilities: 🅿️☉🄿🌣🕭🕓🛋️🆆🅸🅵🄘 ❶

Services: 🔌🖤🖉🅣🔋

Within 3 miles: 🚶‍♂️🚵🍴🛡️🐟🍺

Notes: No cars by tents. Dogs must be kept on leads.

AA Pubs & Restaurants nearby: The Old Bridge Hotel, HUNTINGDON, PE29 3TQ, 01480 424300

King William IV, FENSTANTON, PE28 9JF, 01480 462467

HUNTINGDON *continued*

The Willows Caravan Park
►►► 79%

tel: 01480 437566 **Bromholme Ln, Brampton PE28 4NE**
email: willows@willows33.freeserve.co.uk
dir: *Exit A14/A1 signed Brampton, follow Huntingdon signs. Site on right near Brampton Mill pub.* **grid ref:** *TL224708*

A small, friendly site in a pleasant setting beside the River Ouse, on the Ouse Valley Walk. Bay areas have been provided for caravans and motorhomes, and planting for screening is gradually maturing. There are launching facilities and free river fishing. 4 acre site. 50 touring pitches. 10 hardstandings. 10 seasonal pitches. Caravan pitches. Motorhome pitches. Tent pitches.

Open: all year **Last arrival:** 20.00hrs **Last departure:** noon

Pitches: 🚐 �17 ▲

Leisure: 🛝 ⚽

Facilities: 🌳 ☉ ✳ ♿ 📶 ❶

Services: 🚽 🖭 🛁

Within 3 miles: ⬇ 🎣 🗄 ✐ 🛒

Notes: 🐕 No cars by tents. 5mph one-way system, no generators, no groundsheets, ball games allowed on field only. Dogs must be kept on leads. Free book lending/exchange.

AA Pubs & Restaurants nearby: The Old Bridge Hotel, HUNTINGDON, PE29 3TQ, 01480 424300

| ST IVES | Map 12 TL37 |

Places to visit

The Farmland Museum and Denny Abbey, WATERBEACH, CB25 9PQ, 01223 860988 www.english-heritage.org.uk/daysout/properties/denny-abbey-and-the-farmland-museum

Oliver Cromwell's House, ELY, CB7 4HF, 01353 662062 www.visitely.org.uk

---

PREMIER PARK

Stroud Hill Park
►►►►► 95%

Best of British

tel: 01487 741333 **Fen Rd, Pidley PE28 3DE**
email: stroudhillpark@btconnect.com
dir: *Exit B1040 in Pidley follow signs for Lakeside Lodge Complex, into Fen Rd, site on right.* **grid ref:** *TL335787*

A superb adults-only caravan park designed to a very high specification in a secluded and sheltered spot not far from St Ives. A modern timber-framed barn houses the exceptional facilities. These include the beautifully tiled toilets with spacious cubicles, each containing a shower, washbasin and toilet. A bar and café, AA-rosette restaurant (The Barn), small licensed shop, tennis court and coarse fishing are among the attractions. There are three pay-as-you-go golf courses plus ten-pin bowling nearby. 6 acre site. 60 touring pitches. 44 hardstandings. Caravan pitches. Motorhome pitches. Tent pitches.

Open: all year **Last arrival:** 20.00hrs **Last departure:** noon

Pitches: 🚐 £25-£27 �17 £25-£27 ▲ £17

Leisure: 🎣

Facilities: 🌳 ☉ 📮 ✳ ♿ ☎ 🛒 📶 ♻ ❶

Services: 🚽 🖭 🍴 🏧 🛁 ✐ 🅃 🍽

Within 3 miles: ⬇ 🗄 🏕 ✐ ◎ ⬇ 🛒 🛒 ∪

Notes: Adults only. No large motorhomes. Dogs must be kept on leads.

AA Pubs & Restaurants nearby: The Crown Inn, BROUGHTON, PE28 3AY, 01487 824428

The Lazy Otter, STRETHAM, CB6 3LU, 01353 649780

| WISBECH | Map 12 TF40 |

Places to visit

Peckover House & Garden, WISBECH, PE13 1JR, 01945 583463 www.nationaltrust.org.uk/peckover

African Violet Centre, KING'S LYNN, PE34 4PL, 01553 828374 www.africanvioletandgardencentre.com

Great for kids: WWT Welney Wetland Centre, WELNEY, PE14 9TN, 01353 860711 www.wwt.org.uk

---

Little Ranch Leisure
►►► 85%

tel: 01945 860066 **Begdale, Elm PE14 0AZ**
web: www.littleranchleisure.co.uk
dir: *From rdbt on A47 (SW of Wisbech) take Redmoor Lane to Begdale.* **grid ref:** *TF456062*

A friendly family site set in an apple orchard, with 25 fully serviced pitches and a beautifully designed, spacious toilet block. Now enlarged, with an extra 15 lakeside pitches, the site overlooks two fishing lakes; the famous horticultural auctions at Wisbech are nearby. 10 acre site. 40 touring pitches. 40 hardstandings. Caravan pitches. Motorhome pitches. Tent pitches.

Open: all year

Pitches: 🚐 �17 ▲

Facilities: 🌳 ☉ 📮 ✳ ♿ 🛒 ♻ ❶

Services: 🚽 🖭 🏧

Within 3 miles: ✐ 🛒

Notes: 🐕 Dogs must be kept on leads.

AA Pubs & Restaurants nearby: Crown Lodge Hotel, WISBECH, PE14 8SE, 01945 773391

The Hare Arms, STOW BARDOLPH, PE34 3HT, 01366 382229

LEISURE: 🏊 Indoor swimming pool 🏊 Outdoor swimming pool 🛝 Children's playground 🪁 Kid's club 🎾 Tennis court 🎱 Games room 📺 Separate TV room ⛳ golf course 🚣 Boats for hire 🎬 Cinema 🎭 Entertainment 🎣 Fishing ◎ Mini golf 🏄 Watersports 🏋 Gym Sports field Spa ∪ Stables
FACILITIES: 🛁 Bath 🌳 Shower ☉ Electric shaver 📮 Hairdryer ✳ Ice Pack Facility ♿ Disabled facilities ☎ Public telephone 🛒 Shop on site or within 200yds 🚐 Mobile shop (calls at least 5 days a week) BBQ area 🏕 Picnic area 📶 Wi-fi 💻 Internet access ♻ Recycling ❶ Tourist info Dog exercise area

CHESHIRE

CODDINGTON
Map 15 SJ45

Places to visit

Cholmondeley Castle Gardens, CHOLMONDELEY, SY14 8AH, 01829 720383
www.cholmondeleycastle.com

Hack Green Secret Nuclear Bunker, NANTWICH, CW5 8AP, 01270 629219
www.hackgreen.co.uk

Great for kids: Dewa Roman Experience, CHESTER, CH1 1NL, 01244 343407
www.dewaromanexperience.co.uk

Chester Zoo, CHESTER, CH2 1LH, 01244 380280 www.chesterzoo.org

REGIONAL WINNER – NORTH WEST ENGLAND AA CAMPSITE OF THE YEAR 2015

PREMIER PARK

Manor Wood Country Caravan Park
▶▶▶▶▶ 90%

GOLD

tel: 01829 782990 & 07762 817827 **Manor Wood CH3 9EN**
email: info@manorwoodcaravans.co.uk
dir: From A534 at Barton, turn opposite Cock O'Barton pub signed Coddington. Left in 100yds. Site 0.5m on left. **grid ref:** SJ453553

A secluded landscaped park in a tranquil country setting with extensive views towards the Welsh Hills across the Cheshire Plain. The park offers fully serviced pitches, a heated outdoor swimming pool and all-weather tennis courts. The generous pitch density provides optimum privacy and the superb amenities block has excellent decor, under-floor heating and smart modern facilities with very good privacy options. Wildlife is encouraged and there is a fishing lake; country walks and nearby pubs are added attractions. 8 acre site. 45 touring pitches. 38 hardstandings. 30 seasonal pitches. Caravan pitches. Motorhome pitches. Tent pitches. 18 statics.

Open: all year (rs Oct-May swimming pool closed) **Last arrival:** 19.00hrs **Last departure:** 11.00hrs
Pitches: * ⊞ £13.50-£25 ⊞ £13.50-£25 Å £13.50-£25
Leisure: ⊜ ⋒ ⊰ ⊙ ⊛
Facilities: ⌂ ⊙ ⌁ ⊹ ⅄ ⊙ ⊓ ⊼ WiFi ▣ ⊕ ⊘
Services: ⊞ ⊠ ⌄
Within 3 miles: ⌁ ⌁ ⊞ ⊠
Notes: No cars by caravans. No cycles, no noise after 23.00hrs. Dogs must be kept on leads.
AA Pubs & Restaurants nearby: The Calveley Arms, HANDLEY, CH3 9DT, 01829 770619
1851 Restaurant at Peckforton Castle, PECKFORTON, CW6 9TN, 01829 260930

DELAMERE
Map 15 SJ56

Places to visit

Jodrell Bank Discovery Centre, JODRELL BANK, SK11 9DL, 01477 571766
www.jodrellbank.net

Little Moreton Hall, CONGLETON, CW12 4SD, 01260 272018
www.nationaltrust.org.uk

Great for kids: Chester Zoo, CHESTER, CH2 1LH, 01244 380280
www.chesterzoo.org

Fishpool Farm Caravan Park
▶▶▶▶ 84%

tel: 01606 883970 & 07501 506583 **Fishpool Rd CW8 2HP**
email: enquiries@fishpoolfarmcaravanpark.co.uk
dir: From A49 (Tarporley to Cuddington road) onto A54 signed Chester. At Fishpool Inn left onto B5152 (Fishpool Rd). Site on right. **grid ref:** SJ567672

Developed on a former hay field on the owner's farm, this excellent park has a shop/reception, a superb purpose-built toilet block with laundry facilities, a picnic area, and 50 spacious pitches, all with electric hook-up. There is a lakeside lodge, coarse fishing and a nature walk. 5.5 acre site. 50 touring pitches. 14 hardstandings. Caravan pitches. Motorhome pitches. Tent pitches. 1 static.

Open: 15 Feb-15 Jan **Last arrival:** 19.00hrs **Last departure:** noon
Pitches: * ⊞ fr £23 ⊞ fr £23 Å fr £22
Leisure: ⋒ ⊙ ⊛ ⊡
Facilities: ⌂ ⊙ ⌁ ⊹ ⅄ ⊡ ⊓ ⊼ WiFi ⊕ ⊘
Services: ⊞ ⊠ ⊞ ⌄
Within 3 miles: ⌁ ⌁ ⊚ ⊰ ⊡ ⊠ ◡
Notes: Dogs must be kept on leads. Dog walks, fresh eggs from own hens.
AA Pubs & Restaurants nearby: The Dysart Arms, BUNBURY, CW6 9PH, 01829 260183
Alvanley Arms Inn, TARPORLEY, CW6 9DS, 01829 760200

KNUTSFORD
Map 15 SJ77

Places to visit

The Tabley House Collection, KNUTSFORD, WA16 0HB, 01565 750151
www.tableyhouse.co.uk

Great for kids: Jodrell Bank Discovery Centre, JODRELL BANK, SK11 9DL,
01477 571766 www.jodrellbank.net

Woodlands Park
▶▶▶ 77%

tel: 01565 723429 & 01332 810818 **Wash Ln, Allostock WA16 9LG**
dir: M6 junct 18 take A50 N to Holmes Chapel for 3m, turn into Wash Ln by Boundary Water Park. Site 0.25m on left. **grid ref:** SJ743710

A very tranquil and attractive park in the heart of rural Cheshire, and set in 16 acres of mature woodland where in spring the rhododendrons look stunning. Tourers are located in three separate wooded areas that teem with wildlife and you will wake up to the sound of birdsong. This park is just five miles from Jodrell Bank. 16 acre site. 40 touring pitches. Caravan pitches. Motorhome pitches. Tent pitches. 140 statics.

continued

PITCHES: ⊞ Caravans ⊞ Motorhomes Å Tents ⋒ Glamping-style accommodation **SERVICES:** ⊞ Electric hook up ⊠ Launderette ⊞ Licensed bar ⊟ Calor Gas ⊘ Camping Gaz ⊡ Toilet fluid ⊙ Café/Restaurant ⊞ Fast Food/Takeaway ⊞ Battery charging ⊞ Baby care ⌄ Motorvan service point
ABBREVIATIONS: BH/bank hols – bank holidays Etr – Easter Spring BH – Spring Bank Holiday fr – from hrs – hours m – mile mdnt – midnight
rdbt – roundabout rs – restricted service wk – week wknd – weekend x-rds – cross roads ⊛ No credit or debit cards ⊗ No dogs ⊞ Children of all ages accepted

KNUTSFORD *continued*

Open: Mar-6 Jan **Last arrival:** 21.00hrs **Last departure:** 11.00hrs

Pitches: * ⊞ £13-£15 ⊞ £13-£15 ▲ £13-£15

Facilities: ↑⊙& **Services:** ⊞⑤ **Within 3 miles:** ↓↗⑤⑥

Notes: ⊘ No skateboards or rollerblades. Dogs must be kept on leads.

AA Pubs & Restaurants nearby: The Dog Inn, KNUTSFORD, WA16 8UP, 01625 861421

The Duke of Portland, LACH DENNIS, CW9 7SY, 01606 46264

SIDDINGTON   Map 15 SJ87

Places to visit

Capesthorne Hall, CAPESTHORNE, SK11 9JY, 01625 861221
www.capesthorne.com

Gawsworth Hall, GAWSWORTH, SK11 9RN, 01260 223456
www.gawsworthhall.com

Great for kids: Jodrell Bank Discovery Centre, JODRELL BANK, SK11 9DL,
01477 571766 www.jodrellbank.net

Capesthorne Hall
►►►► 88%

tel: 01625 861221 **Congleton Rd SK11 9JY**
email: info@capesthorne.com
dir: *Access to site from A34 between Congleton to Wilmslow. Phone for detailed directions.*
grid ref: *SJ841727*

Located within the grounds of the notable Jacobean Capesthorne Hall, this lush, all level site provides generously sized pitches, all with electricity and most with hardstandings. The Scandanavian-style amenities block has a smart, quality, modern interior and very good privacy levels. Guests also have the opportunity to visit the award-winning gardens on certain days and there are many extensive walking opportunities directly from the camping areas. 5 acre site. 50 touring pitches. 30 hardstandings. Caravan pitches. Motorhome pitches.

Open: Apr-Oct **Last arrival:** 22.00hrs **Last departure:** noon

Pitches: ⊞ ⊞

Facilities: ↑&⊙⊬⊞ ♻ ❸ **Services:** ⊞⑤ ⑩ **Within 3 miles:** ↓⊚⑤

Notes: Minimum 3 night stay on BH wknds. No motorised scooters or skateboards. Only gas BBQs permitted. Dogs must be kept on leads. Access to Capesthorne Hall & Gardens (additional cost for hall only).

AA Pubs & Restaurants nearby: The Davenport Arms, MARTON, SK11 9HF, 01260 224269

Egerton Arms, CHELFORD, SK11 9BB, 01625 861366

WETTENHALL   Map 15 SJ66

New Farm Caravan Park
►►► 86%

tel: 01270 528213 & 07970 221112 **Long Ln CW7 4DW**
email: info@newfarmcheshire.com
dir: *M6 junct 16, A500 towards Nantwich, right onto Nantwich bypass (A51). At lights turn right, follow A51 Caster & Tarporely signs. After Calveley right into Long Ln (follow site sign). Site in 2m.* **grid ref:** *SJ613608*

Diversification at New Farm led to the development of four fishing lakes and the creation of a peaceful small touring park. The proprietors provide a very welcome

touring destination within this peaceful part of Cheshire. Expect good landscaping, generous hardstanding pitches, a spotless toilet block, and good attention to detail throughout. New super pitches are planned for 2015. Please note there is no laundry. 40 acre site. 24 touring pitches. 17 hardstandings. 6 seasonal pitches. Caravan pitches. Motorhome pitches.

Open: all year **Last arrival:** 20.00hrs **Last departure:** noon

Pitches: * ⊞ £21-£26 ⊞ £21-£26

Facilities: ↑↗✳⊟⊬⊞ ❸

Services: ⊞∅⛟⎘

Within 3 miles: ↓⌖↗⑤∪

Notes: Adults only. Dogs must be kept on leads.

AA Pubs & Restaurants nearby: The Nags Head, HAUGHTON MOSS, CW6 9RN, 01829 260265

Crewe Hall, CREWE, CW1 6UZ, 01270 253333

WHITEGATE   Map 15 SJ66

Places to visit

Beeston Castle, BEESTON, CW6 9TX, 01829 260464 www.english-heritage.org.uk/daysout/properties/beeston-castle-and-woodland-park

Chester Cathedral, CHESTER, CH1 2HU, 01244 500961
www.chestercathedral.com

PREMIER PARK

Lamb Cottage Caravan Park
►►►►► 92%

tel: 01606 882302 **Dalefords Ln CW8 2BN**
email: info@lambcottage.co.uk
dir: *From A556 turn at Sandiway lights into Dalefords Ln, signed Winsford. Site 1m on right.* **grid ref:** *SJ613692*

A secluded and attractively landscaped adults-only park in a glorious location where the emphasis is on peace and relaxation. The serviced pitches are spacious with wide grass borders for sitting out and the high quality toilet block is spotlessly clean and immaculately maintained. A good central base for exploring this area, with access to nearby woodland walks and cycle trails. 6 acre site. 45 touring pitches. 45 hardstandings. 14 seasonal pitches. Caravan pitches. Motorhome pitches. 26 statics.

Open: Mar-Oct **Last arrival:** 20.00hrs **Last departure:** noon

Pitches: * ⊞ £23-£28 ⊞ £21-£26

Facilities: ↑⊙↗&⊙⊬⊞ ♻ ❸

Services: ⊞⑤ ⛟⎘

Within 3 miles: ↓↗⑤∪

Notes: Adults only. No tents (except trailer tents), no commercial vehicles. Dogs must be kept on leads.

AA Pubs & Restaurants nearby: The Fishpool Inn, DELAMARE, CW8 2HP, 01606 883277

Fox & Barrel, COTEBROOK, CW6 9DZ, 01829 760529

LEISURE: ⊜ Indoor swimming pool ⊜ Outdoor swimming pool ⋔ Children's playground ⬇ Kid's club ⊃ Tennis court ● Games room ▭ Separate TV room ↓ golf course ⊱ Boats for hire ⊟ Cinema ♫ Entertainment ⌕ Fishing ◉ Mini golf ⊱ Watersports ⋔ Gym ⊛ Sports field Spa ∪ Stables
FACILITIES: ⊟ Bath ↑ Shower ⊙ Electric shaver ⊮ Hairdryer ✳ Ice Pack Facility & Disabled facilities ⊙ Public telephone ⑤ Shop on site or within 200yds ⊠ Mobile shop (calls at least 5 days a week) ⊟ BBQ area ⊐ Picnic area ⊞ Wi-fi ▬ Internet access ♻ Recycling ❸ Tourist info ⊬ Dog exercise area

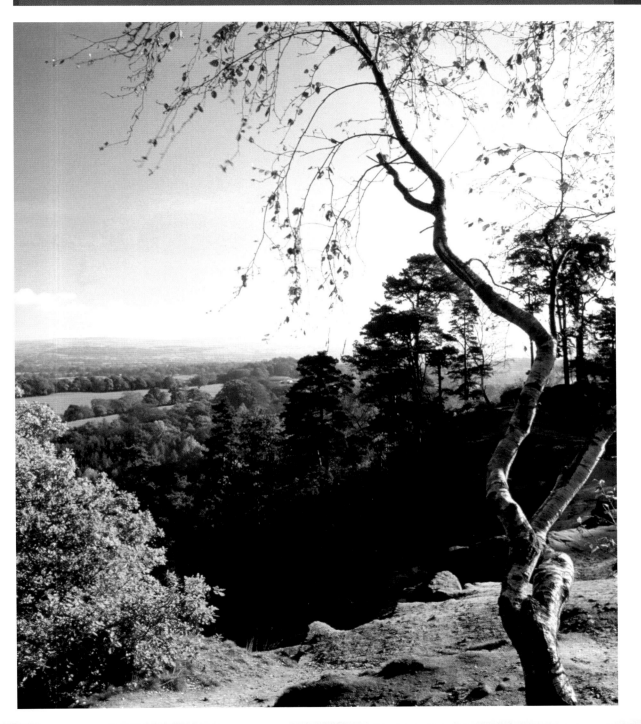

PITCHES: 🚐 Caravans 🚐 Motorhomes 🛖 Tents 🏠 Glamping-style accommodation **SERVICES:** 🔌 Electric hook up 🔘 Launderette 🍷 Licensed bar
🔋 Calor Gas 🔧 Camping Gaz T Toilet fluid 🍽️ Café/Restaurant 🏢 Fast Food/Takeaway 🔌 Battery charging 👶 Baby care ♿ Motorvan service point
ABBREVIATIONS: BH/bank hols – bank holidays Etr – Easter Spring BH – Spring Bank Holiday fr – from hrs – hours m – mile mdnt – midnight
rdbt – roundabout rs – restricted service wk – week wknd – weekend x-rds – cross roads 🚫 No credit or debit cards 🚫 No dogs 👨‍👧 Children of all ages accepted

Cornwall

It's not hard to see why thousands of tourists and holidaymakers flock to Cornwall every year. It has just about everything — wild moorland landscapes, glorious river valley scenery, picturesque villages and miles of breathtaking coastline. It has long been acknowledged as one of Britain's top holiday destinations.

Cornwall's southerly latitude and the influence of the Gulf Stream make the county the mildest and sunniest climate in Britain. It's not surprising therefore that one of its greatest and most popular pursuits is surfing. With more than 80 surfing spots, and plenty of sporting enthusiasts who make their way here to enjoy other similar coastal activities, such as wave-surfing, kite surfing and blokarting, the county is an internationally famous surfing hot spot. Blessed with wonderful surf beaches, Newquay is Cornwall's surfing capital. Nearby Watergate Bay is renowned for its glassy waves and Sennen, near Land's End, is where you might even get to surf with dolphins. Certainly the sea is strikingly blue here and the sands dazzlingly white.

A long-running TV series, filmed in a scenic location, is often a guaranteed way to boost tourism and that is certainly the case at Port Isaac on the north Cornwall coast. The village doubles as Portwenn in the drama *Doc Martin*, starring Martin Clunes as the irascible local GP. Much of Port Isaac has been used for location shooting over the years and it's quite common to bump into actors from the series at different points in the village when filming is taking place. Many films and TV series have been shot in Cornwall – including productions of Daphne du Maurier's *Jamaica Inn* and *Rebecca*, though the original version of the latter, made in 1940, was Alfred Hitchcock's first film in Hollywood and shot entirely in California.

In the book, the setting is a large house on the Cornish coast where the atmosphere is decidedly gothic. Daphne du Maurier modelled the house – which she called Manderley – and its location on the Menabilly estate, near Fowey. *Rebecca* was

published in 1938 and five years later the writer made Menabilly her home. The house is not open to the public, but it is possible to explore the setting for the story on foot, following a leafy path from the car park at Menabilly Barton Farm to Polridmouth Bay where there are two secluded and remote coves. A bird's eye view of the entire area is possible from the path to Gribben Head, though Menabilly, at the heart of the story, is hidden by trees, thus preserving the mystery of the book.

The Cornish coastline offers breathtakingly beautiful scenery. The north coast is open and exposed; the 735-ft High Cliff, between Boscastle and St Gennys, represents the highest sheer drop cliff in the county. The Lizard, at Cornwall's most southerly point, is a geological masterpiece of awesome cliffs, stacks and arches.

In recent years new or restored visitor attractions have helped to increase tourism in the region – Tim Smit has been the inspiration and driving force behind two of the county's most visited attractions. The Eden Project is famous for its giant geodesic domes housing exotic plants from different parts of the globe, while nearby the Lost Gardens of Heligan at Pentewan has impressive kitchen gardens and a wildlife hide.

Perhaps the last word on this magical corner of Britain should go to Daphne du Maurier. In her book *Vanishing Cornwall*, published in 1967, she wrote: 'A county known and loved in all its moods becomes woven into the pattern of life, something to be shared. As one who sought to know it long ago…in a quest for freedom, and later put down roots and found content, I have come a small way up the path. The beauty and the mystery beckon still.'

◁ Wreck of the RMS Mulheim at Castle Zawn

CORNWALL & ISLES OF SCILLY

ASHTON
Map 2 SW62

Places to visit

Godolphin House, GODOLPHIN CROSS, TR13 9RE, 01736 763194
www.nationaltrust.org.uk/godolphin

Poldark Mine and Heritage Complex, WENDRON, TR13 0ER, 01326 573173
www.poldark-mine.co.uk

Great for kids: The Flambards Theme Park, HELSTON, TR13 0QA, 01326 573404
www.flambards.co.uk

Boscrege Caravan & Camping Park
►►►78%

tel: 01736 762231 **TR13 9TG**
email: enquiries@caravanparkcornwall.com **web:** www.caravanparkcornwall.com
dir: A394 from Helston signed Penzance. In Ashton (Lion & Lamb pub on right) right into Higher Lane, approx 1.5m (thatched cottage on right) left at site sign. NB for recommended towing route contact the park. **grid ref:** SW595305

A quiet and bright little touring park divided into small paddocks with hedges, that offers plenty of open spaces for children to play in. This family-owned park has clean, well-painted toilet facilities and neatly trimmed grass. By an Area of Outstanding Natural Beauty at the foot of Tregonning Hill, this site makes an ideal base for touring the southern tip of Cornwall; Penzance, Land's End, St Ives and the beaches in between are all within easy reach. 14 acre site. 50 touring pitches. 10 seasonal pitches. Caravan pitches. Motorhome pitches. Tent pitches. 38 statics.

Open: Mar-Nov (rs Jan-Dec statics open) **Last arrival:** 22.00hrs **Last departure:** 11.00hrs

Pitches: * ⊞ £13.50-£20 ⊞ £13.50-£20 ▲ £13.50-£20

Leisure: ⚐ ✿

Facilities: ⬅ ☉ ⌗ ☀ ☉ 🛱 ⌁ 📶 ♻ ❶

Services: ⊟ 🖾 🛢 ⊘ ⊤ 🖳

Within 3 miles: ↨ ⅄ ⌒ ◎ ⇘ ⑤ 🖾 ↻

Notes: No fires, no noise after 23.00hrs. Dogs must be kept on leads. Microwave & freezer available, nature trail.

AA Pubs & Restaurants nearby: The Victoria Inn, PERRANUTHNOE, TR20 9NP, 01736 710309

New Yard Restaurant, HELSTON, TR12 6AF, 01326 221595

BLACKWATER
Map 2 SW74

Places to visit

Royal Cornwall Museum, TRURO, TR1 2SJ, 01872 272205
www.royalcornwallmuseum.org.uk

East Pool Mine, POOL, TR15 3NP, 01209 315027 www.nationaltrust.org.uk

Great for kids: National Maritime Museum Cornwall, FALMOUTH, TR11 3QY, 01326 313388 www.nmmc.co.uk

Chiverton Park
►►►►83%

tel: 01872 560667 & 07789 377169 **East Hill TR4 8HS**
email: chivertonpark@btopenworld.com **web:** www.chivertonpark.co.uk
dir: Exit A30 at Chiverton rdbt (Starbucks) onto unclassified road signed Blackwater (3rd exit). 1st right, site 300mtrs on right. **grid ref:** SW743468

A small, well-maintained site with some mature hedges dividing pitches, sited midway between Truro and St Agnes. Facilities include a good toilet block and a steam room, sauna and gym. All touring pitches are fully serviced. There is a games room with pool table, and the children's outside play equipment proves popular with families. 4 acre site. 12 touring pitches. 10 hardstandings. Caravan pitches. Motorhome pitches. Tent pitches. 50 statics.

Open: Mar-end Oct **Last arrival:** 19.00hrs **Last departure:** noon

Pitches: ⊞ ⊞ ▲

Leisure: ⛹ ⚐ �€ Spa

Facilities: ⬅ ☉ ⌗ ☀ ⅊ 🛱 📶 ♻ ❶

Services: 🔌 🗑 ♨

Within 3 miles: ⚓ 🎯 ✎ 🏊 🛒 🗑 ∪

Notes: No ball games. Dogs must be kept on leads. Drying lines.

AA Pubs & Restaurants nearby: Driftwood Spars, ST AGNES, TR5 0RT, 01872 552428

The Miners Arms, MITHIAN, TR5 0QF, 01872 552375

Trevarth Holiday Park
►►►► 82%

tel: 01872 560266 **TR4 8HR**

email: trevarth@btconnect.com **web:** www.trevarth.co.uk

dir: *Exit A30 at Chiverton rdbt onto B3277 signed St Agnes. At next rdbt take road signed Blackwater. Site on right in 200mtrs.* **grid ref:** *SW744468*

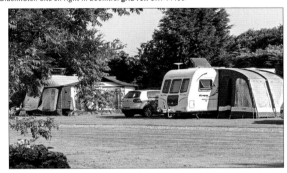

A neat and compact park with touring pitches laid out on attractive, well-screened high ground adjacent to the A30 and A39 junction. This pleasant little park is centrally located for touring, and is maintained to a very good standard. There is a large grassed area for children to play on which is away from all tents. 4 acre site. 30 touring pitches. 10 hardstandings. 6 seasonal pitches. Caravan pitches. Motorhome pitches. Tent pitches. 20 statics.

Open: Apr-Oct **Last arrival:** 21.30hrs **Last departure:** 11.30hrs

Pitches: * 🚐 £12.50-£20 🚗 £12.50-£20 ▲ £12.50-£20

Leisure: 🎱 🎣

Facilities: 🚿 ⊙ 🍽 ☼ 📶 ♻ ❗

Services: 🔌 🗑 🔋 🚰 ♨

Within 3 miles: ✎ 🏊 🗑 ∪

Notes: Dogs must be kept on leads.

AA Pubs & Restaurants nearby: Driftwood Spars, ST AGNES, TR5 0RT, 01872 552428

The Miners Arms, MITHIAN, TR5 0QF, 01872 552375

Places to visit

Lanhydrock, LANHYDROCK, PL30 5AD, 01208 265950 www.nationaltrust.org.uk

Tintagel Old Post Office, TINTAGEL, PL34 0DB, 01840 770024 www.nationaltrust.org.uk/main/w-tintageloldpostoffice

South Penquite Farm
►►► 85%

tel: 01208 850491 **South Penquite PL30 4LH**

email: thefarm@bodminmoor.co.uk

dir: *From Exeter on A30 exit at 1st sign to St Breward on right, (from Bodmin 2nd sign on left). Follow narrow road across Bodmin Moor. Ignore left & right turns until South Penquite Farm Lane on right in 2m.* **grid ref:** *SX108751*

This genuine 'back to nature' site is situated high on Bodmin Moor on a farm committed to organic agriculture. As well as camping there are facilities for adults and children to learn about conservation, organic farming and the local environment, including a fascinating and informative farm trail (pick up a leaflet); there is also a Geocaching trail. Toilet facilities are enhanced by a timber building with quality showers and a good disabled facility. The site has designated areas where fires may be lit. Organic home-reared lamb burgers and sausages are for sale, and one field contains four Mongolian yurts, available for holiday let. 4 acre site. 40 touring pitches. Motorhome pitches. Tent pitches. 4 bell tents/yurts.

Open: Apr-Oct **Last arrival:** dusk **Last departure:** 14.00hrs

Pitches: 🚐 £16 ▲ £16 🏕

Leisure: 🎱 🎣

Facilities: 🚿 ⊙ 🍽 ☼ ♿ 🚰 ♻ ❗

Services: 🗑

Within 3 miles: ⚓ ✎ 🏊 🗑 🗑 ∪

Notes: 🚫 No caravans, no pets.

AA Pubs & Restaurants nearby: St Tudy Inn, ST TUDY, PL30 3NN, 01208 850656

The Old Inn & Restaurant, ST BREWARD, PL30 4PP, 01208 850711

BODMIN
Map 2 SX06

Places to visit
Restormel Castle, RESTORMEL, PL22 0EE, 01208 872687
www.english-heritage.org.uk/daysout/properties/restormel-castle

Great for kids: Eden Project, ST AUSTELL, PL24 2SG, 01726 811911
www.edenproject.com

Mena Caravan & Camping Park
►►►► 79%

tel: 01208 831845 **PL30 5HW**
email: mena@campsitesincornwall.co.uk **web:** www.campsitesincornwall.co.uk
dir: *Exit A30 onto A389 N signed Lanivet & Wadebridge. In 0.5m 1st right & pass under A30. 1st left signed Lostwithiel & Fowey. In 0.25m right at top of hill. 0.5m then 1st right. Entrance 100yds on right.* **grid ref:** SW041626

This grassy site is about four miles from the Eden Project and midway between the north and south Cornish coasts. Set in a secluded, elevated position with high hedges for shelter, it offers plenty of peace and quiet. There is a small coarse fishing lake on site, hardstanding pitches, a shop and a café, with an alfresco decking area, where breakfasts, cream teas and takeaway food can be purchased. The site is on the Saint's Way, and nearby is the neolithic hill fort of Helman Tor, the highest point on Bodmin Moor. There is a fish and chip restaurant in Lanivet (approximately one mile) - from here there is a bus service to Bodmin. 15 acre site. 25 touring pitches. 4 hardstandings. Caravan pitches. Motorhome pitches. Tent pitches. 2 statics.

Open: all year **Last arrival:** 22.00hrs **Last departure:** noon
Pitches: * ⊞ £14-£24 ⊞ £14-£24 ▲ £14-£24
Leisure: ♨ ♜
Facilities: ⌂⊙☂⚡✳⚓⛊☐ㄲ☂✿❶
Services: ⊡⊡⚓⌀⊤⊩⚌
Within 3 miles: ↨⌀⚓☐⊡∪

AA Pubs & Restaurants nearby: The Borough Arms, DUNMERE, PL31 2RD, 01208 73118
Trehellas House Hotel & Restaurant, BODMIN, PL30 3AD, 01208 72700

BOSCASTLE
Map 2 SX09

Places to visit
Tintagel Castle, TINTAGEL, PL34 0HE, 01840 770328
www.english-heritage.org.uk/daysout/properties/tintagel-castle

Tintagel Old Post Office, TINTAGEL, PL34 0DB, 01840 770024
www.nationaltrust.org.uk/main/w-tintageloldpostoffice

Lower Pennycrocker Farm
►► 80%

tel: 01840 250613 **PL35 0BY**
email: karyn.heard@yahoo.com
dir: *Exit A39 at Marshgate onto B3263 towards Boscastle, site signed in 2m.*
grid ref: SX125927

Mature Cornish hedges provide shelter for this small, family-run site on a dairy farm. Spectacular scenery and the nearby coastal footpath are among the many attractions, along with fresh eggs, milk and home-made clotted cream for sale. The excellent toilets and showers enhance this site's facilities. Two traditional Cornish cottages are available to let. 6 acre site. 40 touring pitches. Caravan pitches. Motorhome pitches. Tent pitches. 1 wooden pod.

Open: Etr-Oct **Last arrival:** 20.30hrs **Last departure:** anytime
Pitches: ⊞ ⊞ ▲ ⋒
Facilities: ⌂⊙☂✳⚓ㄲ☂
Services: ⊡⚌↯
Within 3 miles: ↨⊟⌀☐∪

Notes: ⊛ No noise after 22.00hrs. Dogs must be kept on leads.
AA Pubs & Restaurants nearby: The Port William, TREBARWITH, PL34 0HB, 01840 770230
The Wellington Hotel, BOSCASTLE, PL35 0AQ, 01840 250202

BRYHER (ISLES OF SCILLY)
Map 2 SV81

Bryher Camp Site
►►► 81%

tel: 01720 422886 **TR23 0PR**
email: relax@bryhercampsite.co.uk
dir: *Accessed by boat from main island of St Mary's.* **grid ref:** SV880155

Set on the smallest inhabited Scilly Isle with spectacular scenery and white beaches, this tent-only site is in a sheltered valley surrounded by hedges. Pitches are located in paddocks at the northern end of the island which is only a short walk from the quay. There is a good, modern toilet block, and plenty of peace and quiet. Although located in a very quiet area, the Fraggle Rock Bar and Restaurant and a well-equipped shop are within easy reach. There is easy boat access to all the other islands. 2.25 acre site. 38 touring pitches. Tent pitches.

Open: Apr-Oct
Pitches: * ▲ fr £20.50 **Leisure:** ⚽
Facilities: ⌂⊙☂✳✿❶
Services: ⊡⚓⌀⚌
Within 3 miles: ↨↨⌀◎☐⊡∪
Notes: No cars by tents. No pets.
AA Pubs & Restaurants nearby: Hell Bay, BRYHER, TR23 0PR, 01720 422947

LEISURE: 🏊 Indoor swimming pool 🏊 Outdoor swimming pool 🎠 Children's playground 👶 Kid's club 🎾 Tennis court 🎱 Games room 📺 Separate TV room ⛳ golf course ⛵ Boats for hire 🎬 Cinema 🎵 Entertainment 🎣 Fishing ⛳ Mini golf 🏄 Watersports 🏋 Gym ⚽ Sports field Spa ∪ Stables

FACILITIES: 🛁 Bath 🚿 Shower ⊙ Electric shaver ✂ Hairdryer ✳ Ice Pack Facility ♿ Disabled facilities ☎ Public telephone 🏪 Shop on site or within 200yds 🏪 Mobile shop (calls at least 5 days a week) 🍖 BBQ area 🪑 Picnic area 📶 Wi-fi 💻 Internet access ♻ Recycling ❶ Tourist info 🐕 Dog exercise area

BUDE
Map 2 SS20

See also Kilkhampton, Bridgerule (Devon) & Holsworthy (Devon)

PREMIER PARK

Wooda Farm Holiday Park
►►►►► 91%

tel: 01288 352069 **Poughill EX23 9HJ**
email: enquiries@wooda.co.uk **web:** www.wooda.co.uk
dir: *2m E. From A39 at outskirts of Stratton follow unclassified road signed Poughill.*
grid ref: *SS229080*

An attractive park set on raised ground overlooking Bude Bay, with lovely sea views. The park is divided into paddocks by hedges and mature trees, and offers high quality facilities in extensive colourful gardens. A variety of activities is provided by way of the large sports hall and hard tennis court, and there's a super children's playground. There are holiday static caravans for hire. An interactive information screen in the reception area is for customer use. 50 acre

site. 200 touring pitches. 80 hardstandings. 5 seasonal pitches. Caravan pitches. Motorhome pitches. Tent pitches. 55 statics.

Open: Apr-Oct (rs Apr-May & mid Sep-Oct shop hours limited, bar & takeaway) **Last arrival:** 20.00hrs **Last departure:** 10.30hrs
Pitches: * 🚐 £17-£33 🚐 £12-£33 ▲ £12-£28
Leisure: 🎯🎿♒♻🎪⚫□♪
Facilities: 🚻📻☉📻🔆🔥🧑📮🧺📶♻ℹ
Services: 🔌🗑🚽🍴📮📞🍽🛒🚮🏍
Within 3 miles: 🚶🏊‍♂️📆🏌⊚🎣🚴🏇U

Notes: Restrictions on certain dog breeds, no skateboards, rollerblades or scooters. Dogs must be kept on leads. Coarse fishing, clay pigeon shooting, pets' corner, woodland walks.

AA Pubs & Restaurants nearby: Bay View Inn, WIDEMOUTH BAY, EX23 0AW, 01288 361273

See advert below

PITCHES: 🚐 Caravans 🚐 Motorhomes ▲ Tents 🏕 Glamping-style accommodation **SERVICES:** 🔌 Electric hook up 🗑 Launderette 🍻 Licensed bar 🔋 Calor Gas 🔥 Camping Gaz T Toilet fluid 🍴 Café/Restaurant 🍟 Fast Food/Takeaway 🔋 Battery charging 🍼 Baby care 🏍 Motorvan service point
ABBREVIATIONS: BH/bank hols – bank holidays Etr – Easter Spring BH – Spring Bank Holiday fr – from hrs – hours m – mile mdnt – midnight rdbt – roundabout rs – restricted service wk – week wknd – weekend x-rds – cross roads ⊗ No credit or debit cards ⊗ No dogs 👫 Children of all ages accepted

BUDE *continued*

Budemeadows Touring Park
►►►►87%

tel: 01288 361646 **Widemouth Bay EX23 0NA**
email: holiday@budemeadows.com **web:** www.budemeadows.com
dir: *3m S of Bude on A39. Follow signs after turn to Widemouth Bay. Site accessed via layby from A39.* **grid ref:** *SS215012*

This is a very well-kept site of distinction, with good quality facilities, hardstandings and eight fully serviced pitches. Budemeadows is set on a gentle sheltered slope in nine acres of naturally landscaped parkland, surrounded by mature hedges. The internal doors in the facility block have all been painted in pastel colours to resemble beach huts. The site is just one mile from Widemouth Bay, and three miles from the unspoilt resort of Bude. 9 acre site. 145 touring pitches. 34 hardstandings. 4 seasonal pitches. Caravan pitches. Motorhome pitches. Tent pitches.

Open: all year (rs Sep-late May shop, bar & pool closed, takeaway summer only) **Last arrival:** 21.00hrs **Last departure:** 11.00hrs
Pitches: * ⚐ £16-£28.50 ⛟ £16-£28.50 ▲ £12-£28.50
Leisure: ⚏ ⚑ ⚊ ▢
Facilities: ⚇ ⚑ ⊙ ⚑ ✳ ⚅ ⚕ ⚑ ⚏ ⚑ ⚀ ⚕ ❂ ❼
Services: ⚐ ⚑ ⚑ ⚑ ⚑ ⊤ ⚑ ⚑ ⚑
Within 3 miles: ⚑ ✦ ⚑ ⚑ ⚑ ⚑ ⚑ ⚑ ⚑

Notes: No noise after 23.00hrs, breatheable groundsheets only. Dogs must be kept on leads. Table tennis, giant chess, baby changing facility.

AA Pubs & Restaurants nearby: Bay View Inn, WIDEMOUTH BAY, EX23 0AW, 01288 361273

Pentire Haven Holiday Park
►►►►87%

tel: 01288 321601 **Stibb Rd, Kilkhampton EX23 9QY**
email: holidays@pentirehaven.co.uk **web:** www.pentirehaven.co.uk
dir: *A39 from Bude towards Bideford, in 3m turn left signed Sandymouth Bay.*
grid ref: *SS246111*

A very open grass site handy for many beautiful beaches, but in particular the surfing beach of Bude only four miles away. The management and enthusiastic staff continue to make a real impression on this improving park. There are excellent toilet facilities in addition to a very good children's playground and a small swimming pool, which is open during the busy season. There is a rally field and holiday static caravans are available for hire or to buy. 23 acre site. 120 touring pitches. 46 hardstandings. 40 seasonal pitches. Caravan pitches. Motorhome pitches. Tent pitches. 18 statics.

Open: all year **Last arrival:** 23.30hrs **Last departure:** 10.30hrs
Pitches: ⚐ £9.95-£20 ⛟ £9.95-£20 ▲ £9.95-£20
Leisure: ⚏ ⚊ ⚑ ⚑ ⚑ ⚑ ⚑ ⚑
Facilities: ⚇ ⚑ ✳ ⚅ ⚕ ⚑ ⚏ ❂ ❼
Services: ⚐ ⚑ ⚑ ⚑ ⚑ ⊤ ⚑ ⚑ ⚑ ⚑
Within 3 miles: ⚑ ✦ ⚑ ⚑ ⚑ ⚑ ⚑
Notes: No fires. Dogs must be kept on leads.
AA Pubs & Restaurants nearby: Bay View Inn, WIDEMOUTH BAY, EX23 0AW, 01288 361273
See advert on opposite page

Widemouth Fields Caravan & Camping Park

►►►►86%

tel: 01288 361351 & 01489 781256 **Park Farm, Poundstock EX23 0NA**
email: enquiries@widemouthbaytouring.co.uk **web:** www.widemouthbaytouring.co.uk
dir: *M5 junct 27 (signed Barnstaple). A361 to rdbt before Barnstaple. Take A39 signed Bideford & Bude. (NB do not exit A39 at Stratton). S for 3m, follow sign just past x-rds to Widemouth Bay. Into layby, entrance on left.* **grid ref:** *SS215010*

In a quiet location with far reaching views over rolling countryside, this site is only one mile from the golden beach at Widemouth Bay, and just three miles from the resort of Bude. The park has a well-stocked shop, many hardstanding pitches and a cosy bar that offers takeaway breakfasts. The toilets are of outstanding quality with a many combined fully serviced cubicles. All the buildings resemble log cabins which certainly adds to the appeal of the site. There is a courtesy shuttle bus into Bude and to the Widemouth Bay Holiday Village, where the facilities can be used by the touring campers. 15 acre site. 156 touring pitches. 156 hardstandings. 40 seasonal pitches. Caravan pitches. Motorhome pitches. Tent pitches. 5 statics.

Open: Apr-Sep **Last arrival:** 21.00hrs **Last departure:** noon
Pitches: * ➡ £14.50-£28 ➡ £14.50-£28 Å £14.50-£28

Leisure: 🅰 ☺ ❑
Facilities: ➡ 🐾 ☺ ℗ ⚒ ⚒ ⚙ ☺ 🗑 🚿 🪑 WiFi ♻ ❼
Services: 🔌 ⭕ 🛒 ⊘ T ⓘ 🍴 ➡ 🐕 ⚱
Within 3 miles: 🚴 ⚘ 日 ℗ ◎ ⚓ 🗑 🗑 ∪

Notes: Entry to site by swipecard only, deposit taken at time of check in. Bus service to beaches & into Bude (Spring BH-Aug only), access to indoor heated pool.
AA Pubs & Restaurants nearby: Bay View Inn, WIDEMOUTH BAY, EX23 0AW, 01288 361273

Willow Valley Holiday Park

►►►►82%

tel: 01288 353104 **Bush EX23 9LB**
email: willowvalley@talk21.com
dir: *On A39, 0.5m N of junct with A3072 at Stratton.* **grid ref:** *SS236078*

A small sheltered park in the Strat Valley with level grassy pitches and a stream running through it. The friendly family owners have improved all areas of this attractive park, including a smart toilet block and an excellent reception/shop. The park has direct access from the A39, and is only two miles from the sandy beaches at Bude. There are four pine lodges for holiday hire. 4 acre site. 41 touring pitches. Caravan pitches. Motorhome pitches. Tent pitches. 4 statics.

Open: Mar-end Oct **Last arrival:** 21.00hrs **Last departure:** 11.00hrs
Pitches: * ➡ £13-£18 ➡ £13-£18 Å £13-£18
Leisure: 🅰
Facilities: 🐾 ☺ ℗ ⚒ ⚙ ☺ 🗑 🚿 🪑 ♻ ❼
Services: 🔌 ⭕ 🛒 ⊘ T ⚱
Within 3 miles: 🚴 ⚘ ℗ ◎ ⚓ 🗑 🗑 ∪

Notes: ⊗ Dogs must be kept on leads.

BUDE *continued*

Upper Lynstone Caravan Park
►►►86%

tel: 01288 352017 **Lynstone EX23 0LP**
email: reception@upperlynstone.co.uk
dir: *0.75m S of Bude on coastal road to Widemouth Bay.* **grid ref:** *SS205053*

There are extensive views over Bude to be enjoyed from this quiet, sheltered family-run park, a terraced grass site suitable for all units. There's a spotlessly clean and top quality toilet block, plus a children's playground and a reception with a shop that sells basic food supplies and camping spares. Static caravans for holiday hire. A path leads directly to the coastal footpath with its stunning sea views, and the old Bude Canal is just a stroll away. 6 acre site. 65 touring pitches. Caravan pitches. Motorhome pitches. Tent pitches. 41 statics.

Open: Apr-Oct **Last arrival:** 22.00hrs **Last departure:** 10.00hrs

Pitches: * ➡ £17-£23 ⇆ £17-£23 ▲ £14.50-£21

Leisure: ⚠

Facilities: ⌐⊙⏣☀⚒⚏⊟ WiFi ♻ ⚆

Services: ⚇⌷ ⚍⊘⊤⚏

Within 3 miles: ⚓⚑⚏⚏⚗⚏⚏⚏⚏↻

Notes: No groups. Baby changing room.

AA Pubs & Restaurants nearby: Bay View Inn, WIDEMOUTH BAY, EX23 0AW, 01288 361273

| CAMELFORD | Map 2 SX18 |

Places to visit

Tintagel Castle, TINTAGEL, PL34 0HE, 01840 770328
www.english-heritage.org.uk/daysout/properties/tintagel-castle

Tintagel Old Post Office, TINTAGEL, PL34 0DB, 01840 770024
www.nationaltrust.org.uk/main/w-tintageloldpostoffice

Juliot's Well Holiday Park
►►►►85%

SILVER

tel: 01840 213302 **PL32 9RF**
email: holidays@juliotswell.com
dir: *Through Camelford, A39 at Valley Truckle turn right onto B3266, 1st left signed Lanteglos, site 300yds on right.* **grid ref:** *SX095829*

Set in the wooded grounds of an old manor house, this quiet site enjoys lovely and extensive views across the countryside. A rustic inn on site offers occasional entertainment, and there is plenty to do, both on the park and in the vicinity. The superb, fully serviced toilet facilities are very impressive. There are also self-catering pine lodges, static caravans and five cottages for hire. 33 acre site. 39 touring pitches. Caravan pitches. Motorhome pitches. Tent pitches. 82 statics.

Open: all year **Last arrival:** 20.00hrs **Last departure:** 11.00hrs

Pitches: ➡ ⇆ ▲

Leisure: ⚘ ⚠ ⚙

Facilities: ⛴⌐⏣⚒⚏⊙⚏⊟ ⚏ WiFi

Services: ⚇⌷ ⚍⊘⊤⊘⚏

Within 3 miles: ⚓⚏⚏⚏↻

Notes: Complimentary use of cots & high chairs.

AA Pubs & Restaurants nearby: The Mill House Inn, TREBARWITH, PL34 0HD, 01840 770200

The Old Inn & Restaurant, ST BREWARD, PL30 4PP, 01208 850711

Lakefield Caravan Park
►►►78%

tel: 01840 213279 **Lower Pendavey Farm PL32 9TX**
email: lakefieldcaravanpark@btconnect.com
dir: *From A39 in Camelford onto B3266, right at T-junct, site 1.5m on left.*
grid ref: *SX095853*

Set in a rural location, this friendly park is part of a specialist equestrian centre, and offers good quality services. All the facilities are immaculate and spotlessly clean. Riding lessons and hacks are always available, with a BHS qualified instructor. Newquay, Padstow and Bude are all easily accessed from this site. 5 acre site. 40 touring pitches. Caravan pitches. Motorhome pitches. Tent pitches.

Open: Etr or Apr-Sep **Last arrival:** 22.00hrs **Last departure:** 11.00hrs

Pitches: ➡ ⇆ ▲

Facilities: ⌐⊙⏣☀⚏⚆

Services: ⚇⚏ ⊘⊤⊘⚏

Within 3 miles: ⚓⚏⚏⚏↻

Notes: Dogs must be kept on leads. On-site lake.

AA Pubs & Restaurants nearby: The Old Inn & Restaurant, ST BREWARD, PL30 4PP, 01208 850711

The Port William, TREBARWITH, PL34 0HB, 01840 770230

| CARLYON BAY |

Places to visit

Charlestown Shipwreck & Heritage Centre, ST AUSTELL, PL25 3NJ, 01726 69897
www.shipwreckcharlestown.com

The Lost Gardens of Heligan, PENTEWAN, PL26 6EN, 01726 845100
www.heligan.com

Great for kids: Wheal Martyn, ST AUSTELL, PL26 8XG, 01726 850362
www.wheal-martyn.com

Eden Project, ST AUSTELL, PL24 2SG, 01726 811911 www.edenproject.com

---

LEISURE: 🏊 Indoor swimming pool 🏊 Outdoor swimming pool ⚠ Children's playground 🪁 Kid's club 🎾 Tennis court ⚐ Games room 🖵 Separate TV room ⚓ golf course ⚓ Boats for hire 🎬 Cinema 🎵 Entertainment 🎣 Fishing ◎ Mini golf ⚑ Watersports ⚐ Gym ⚏ Sports field Spa ↻ Stables **FACILITIES:** 🛁 Bath ⌐ Shower ⊙ Electric shaver ⏣ Hairdryer ☀ Ice Pack Facility ⚒ Disabled facilities ⚏ Public telephone ⚏ Shop on site or within 200yds ⚏ Mobile shop (calls at least 5 days a week) ⚍ BBQ area ⊟ Picnic area WiFi Wi-fi ⚏ Internet access ♻ Recycling ⚆ Tourist info ⚏ Dog exercise area

CARLYON BAY   Map 2 SX05

PREMIER PARK

Carlyon Bay Caravan & Camping Park
►►►►► 89%

tel: 01726 812735 **Bethesda, Cypress Av PL25 3RE**
email: holidays@carlyonbay.net **web:** www.carlyonbay.net
dir: *Exit A390 W of St Blazey, left onto A3092 for Par, right in 0.5m. On private road to Carlyon Bay.* **grid ref:** *SX052526*

An attractive, secluded site set amongst a belt of trees with background woodland. The spacious grassy park is beautifully landscaped and offers quality toilet and shower facilities and plenty of on-site attractions, including a well-equipped games room, TV room, café, an inviting swimming pool, and occasional family entertainment. It is less than half a mile from a sandy beach

and the Eden Project is only two miles away. 35 acre site. 180 touring pitches. 12 hardstandings. Caravan pitches. Motorhome pitches. Tent pitches.

Open: Etr-28 Sep (rs Etr-mid May & mid-end Sep swimming pool, takeaway & shop closed) **Last arrival:** 21.00hrs **Last departure:** 11.00hrs

Pitches: 🚐 🚐 Å

Leisure: ⚓ ⚙ 👋 ⚾ 🎣 ▢

Facilities: 🐾 ☉ 🍴 ✳ ⚙ 🕓 ⑤ 🐕 📶 ♻ ❶

Services: 🚽 ⑥ 🛢 ⊘ Ⓣ 🍽 🛒 🛆 ↯

Within 3 miles: ⬆ ⚘ ⛳ 🚴 ◎ 🏄 ⑤ ⑤ ∪

Notes: No noise after 23.00hrs. Dogs must be kept on leads. Crazy golf. Children's entertainment in Jul-Aug only.

AA Pubs & Restaurants nearby: Austell's, ST AUSTELL, PL25 3PH, 01726 813888

The Britannia Inn & Restaurant, PAR, PL24 2SL, 01726 812889

See advert below

PITCHES: 🚐 Caravans 🚐 Motorhomes Å Tents 🏕 Glamping-style accommodation **SERVICES:** 🚽 Electric hook up ⑥ Launderette 🍺 Licensed bar 🛢 Calor Gas ⊘ Camping Gaz Ⓣ Toilet fluid 🍽 Café/Restaurant 🛒 Fast Food/Takeaway 🔋 Battery charging 👶 Baby care ↯ Motorvan service point **ABBREVIATIONS:** BH/bank hols – bank holidays Etr – Easter Spring BH – Spring Bank Holiday fr – from hrs – hours m – mile mdnt – midnight rdbt – roundabout rs – restricted service wk – week wknd – weekend x-rds – cross roads 🚫 No credit or debit cards 🚫 No dogs 👫 Children of all ages accepted

CARLYON BAY *continued*

East Crinnis Camping & Caravan Park
►►►►80%

tel: 01726 813023 & 07950 614780 **Lantyan, East Crinnis PL24 2SQ**
email: eastcrinnis@btconnect.com
dir: *From A390 (Lostwithiel to St Austell) take A3082 signed Fowey at rdbt by Britannia Inn, site on left.* **grid ref:** *SX062528*

A small rural park with spacious pitches set in individual bays about one mile from the beaches at Carlyon Bay, and just two miles from the Eden Project. The friendly owners keep the site very clean and well maintained, and also offer three self-catering holiday lodges and two yurts for hire. It is a short walk to Par where restaurant food can be found. 2 acre site. 25 touring pitches. 6 hardstandings. Caravan pitches. Motorhome pitches. Tent pitches. 2 bell tents/yurts.

Open: Etr-Oct **Last arrival:** 21.00hrs **Last departure:** 11.00hrs

Pitches: 🚐 🚕 Å ⌂ **Leisure:** ⚠ ✪
Facilities: �r ⊙ ⟰ ✳ ⅋ 🔥 🛒 ⅏ 🛒 ♻ ⓲
Services: 🔋 🔲 **Within 3 miles:** ⚓ ⊱ ⊟ ⌐ ⊚ ⊱ 🔋 ⊙ ∪

Notes: Dogs must be kept on leads. Coarse fishing, wildlife & pond area with dog walk.

AA Pubs & Restaurants nearby: The Britannia Inn & Restaurant, PAR, PL24 2SL, 01726 812889

The Rashleigh Inn, POLKERRIS, PL24 2TL, 01726 813991

Austell's, ST AUSTELL, PL25 3PH, 01726 813888

CHACEWATER   Map 2 SW74

Places to visit
Royal Cornwall Museum, TRURO, TR1 2SJ, 01872 272205
www.royalcornwallmuseum.org.uk

Trelissick Garden, TRELISSICK GARDEN, TR3 6QL, 01872 862090
www.nationaltrust.org.uk/trelissick

CHACEWATER   Map 2 SW74

Killiwerris Touring Park
►►►►80%

tel: 01872 561356 & 07734 053593 **Penstraze TR4 8PF**
email: killiwerris@aol.com
dir: *Take A30 towards Penzance, at Chiverton Cross rdbt take 3rd exit signed St Agnes. At next mini rdbt take Blackwater exit, in 500yds left into Kea Downs Rd, park 1m on right.* **grid ref:** *SW753454*

A small, adults-only, family-run touring park, just five miles from Truro and four miles from the coastal village of St Agnes, making it an ideal base for exploring west Cornwall. The site has a sunny aspect yet is sheltered by mature trees giving it a very private feel. The facilities are of an exceptionally high standard and include a modern and smart amenities block. It is a peaceful spot in which to relax and get away from the crowds. 2.2 acre site. 20 touring pitches. 17 hardstandings. 3 seasonal pitches. Caravan pitches. Motorhome pitches.

Open: all year **Last arrival:** 21.00hrs **Last departure:** 11.00hrs

Pitches: * 🚐 £20-£24 🚕 £20-£24
Facilities: r ⟰ ✳ ⅋ 🔋 ♻ ⓲ **Services:** 🔋 🔲 **Within 3 miles:** ⚓ ⊟ ⌐ 🔋 ⊙ ∪

Notes: Adults only. Dogs must be kept on leads.

COVERACK   Map 2 SW71

Places to visit
Great for kids: Cornish Seal Sanctuary, GWEEK, TR12 6UG, 01326 221361
www.sealsanctuaries.com

The Flambards Theme Park, HELSTON, TR13 0QA, 01326 573404
www.flambards.co.uk

Little Trevothan Caravan & Camping Park
►►►80%

tel: 01326 280260 **Trevothan TR12 6SD**
email: sales@littletrevothan.co.uk
dir: *A3083 onto B3293 signed Coverack, approx 2m after Goonhilly ESS, right at Zoar Garage onto unclassified road. Approx 1m, 3rd left. Site 0.5m on left.* **grid ref:** *SW772179*

A secluded site, with excellent facilities, near the unspoilt fishing village of Coverack, with a large recreation area and good play equipment for children. The nearby sandy beach has lots of rock pools for children to play in, and the many walks both from the park and the village offer stunning scenery. 10.5 acre site. 70 touring pitches. 10 hardstandings. 9 seasonal pitches. Caravan pitches. Motorhome pitches. Tent pitches. 22 statics.

Open: Mar-Oct **Last arrival:** 21.00hrs **Last departure:** noon

Pitches: * 🚐 £13-£16 🚕 £13-£16 Å £13-£16
Leisure: ⚠ ✪ ✎ ⌐
Facilities: r ⊙ ⟰ ✳ ⓦ 🔋 🔥 ♻ ⓲
Services: 🔋 🔲 🗄 ⌽ Ⓣ 🔋
Within 3 miles: ⌐ ⊱ 🔋 🔲

Notes: ⓧ No noise between 22.00hrs-08.30hrs. Dogs must be kept on leads.

Who has won England Campsite of the Year?
See page 14

Prefer a child-free site?
See our list on page 41

LEISURE: 🏊 Indoor swimming pool 🏊 Outdoor swimming pool ⚠ Children's playground 👋 Kid's club 🎾 Tennis court 🎱 Games room 🖵 Separate TV room ⛳ golf course ⛵ Boats for hire 🎬 Cinema 🎵 Entertainment 🎣 Fishing ⊚ Mini golf 🏄 Watersports 🏋 Gym ✪ Sports field Spa ∪ Stables
FACILITIES: 🛁 Bath r Shower ⊙ Electric shaver ⟰ Hairdryer ✳ Ice Pack Facility ⅋ Disabled facilities 🕿 Public telephone 🔋 Shop on site or within 200yds 🔲 Mobile shop (calls at least 5 days a week) 🍖 BBQ area 🔥 Picnic area ⓦⓘⓕ Wi-fi 🖥 Internet access ♻ Recycling ⓲ Tourist info ⅏ Dog exercise area

CRANTOCK (NEAR NEWQUAY) — Map 2 SW76

Places to visit

Trerice, TRERICE, TR8 4PG, 01637 875404 www.nationaltrust.org.uk/trerice/

PREMIER PARK

Trevella Tourist Park
▶▶▶▶▶ 89%

tel: 01637 830308 **TR8 5EW**
email: holidays@trevella.co.uk **web:** www.trevella.co.uk
dir: Between Crantock & A3075. **grid ref:** SW801599

A well-established and very well-run family site, with outstanding floral displays. Set in a rural area close to Newquay, this stunning park boasts three teeming fishing lakes for the both experienced and novice angler, and a superb outdoor swimming pool and paddling area. The toilet facilities include excellent en suite wet rooms. All areas are neat and clean and the whole park looks stunning. Yurts, eurotents and safari tents are available for hire. 15 acre site. 171 touring pitches. 73 hardstandings. Caravan pitches. Motorhome pitches. Tent pitches. 142 statics. Bell tents/yurts.

Open: Etr-Oct (rs Etr-mid May & mid Sep-Oct pool closed) **Last arrival:** 21.00hrs **Last departure:** 10.00hrs

Pitches: 🚐 🚙 ▲ 🏠
Leisure: 🏊 ⛰ 🎣 ⬜ **Facilities:** 🍴 ☉ 🏧 ✳ ☕ 🚿 🔥 WiFi ♻ ❶
Services: 🔌 🗑 🛢 🧺 🚽 🍴 🔋 🍔 🚼 🛒 ↯
Within 3 miles: 🚶 ⛳ 🎣 🐎 ⑨ ⛴ 🏌 📮 🎡 U

Notes: Families & couples. Dogs must be kept on leads. Crazy golf, safari & ready tents (8 of each), charge for WiFi.

AA Pubs & Restaurants nearby: The Smugglers' Den Inn, CUBERT, TR8 5PY, 01637 830209

The Lewinnick Lodge Bar & Restaurant, NEWQUAY, TR7 1NX, 01637 878117

See advert on page 90

Treago Farm Caravan Site
▶▶▶▶ 85%

tel: 01637 830277 **TR8 5QS**
email: info@treagofarm.co.uk
dir: From A3075 (W of Newquay) turn right for Crantock. Site signed beyond village. **grid ref:** SW782601

A grass site in open farmland in a south-facing sheltered valley with a fishing lake. This friendly family park has spotless toilet facilities, which include three excellent heated family rooms, a good shop and bar with takeaway food, and it has direct access to Crantock and Polly Joke beaches, National Trust land and many natural beauty spots. 5 acre site. 90 touring pitches. Caravan pitches. Motorhome pitches. Tent pitches. 10 statics.

Open: mid May-mid Sep **Last arrival:** 22.00hrs **Last departure:** 18.00hrs

Pitches: 🚐 🚙 ▲ **Leisure:** 🎣 ⬜
Facilities: 🍴 ☉ 🏧 ✳ ☕ 🚿 🔥 🧺 ❶ **Services:** 🔌 🗑 🧺 🛢 🚽 🛒
Within 3 miles: 🚶 ⛳ 🎣 ⑨ ⛴ 🏌 📮 U

Notes: Dogs must be kept on leads.

AA Pubs & Restaurants nearby: The Smugglers' Den Inn, CUBERT, TR8 5PY, 01637 830209

The Lewinnick Lodge Bar & Restaurant, NEWQUAY, TR7 1NX, 01637 878117

CRANTOCK (NEAR NEWQUAY) *continued*

Quarryfield Holiday Park
►►►83%

tel: 01637 872792 & 830338 **TR8 5RJ**
email: quarryfield@crantockcaravans.orangehome.co.uk **web:** www.quarryfield.co.uk
dir: *From A3075 Newquay-Redruth road follow Crantock signs. Site signed.*
grid ref: *SW793608*

This park has a private path down to the dunes and golden sands of Crantock Beach, about 10 minutes away, and it is within easy reach of all that Newquay has to offer, particularly for families. The park has very modern facilities, and provides plenty of amenities including a great swimming pool. Extensive improvements have been made to the bar and the children's play area. 10 acre site. 145 touring pitches. 12 seasonal pitches. Caravan pitches. Motorhome pitches. Tent pitches. 43 statics.

Open: Etr-Oct **Last arrival:** 23.00hrs **Last departure:** 10.00hrs

Pitches: * ⊞ £14-£20 ⊞ £14-£20 ▲ £14-£20

Leisure: ⊕ ⚠ ◖

Facilities: ⬀⊙ℱ✳⚒⚖⊙⑤⬚☂ 🐾 WiFi 🖳 ♺

Services: ☎⑤ 🛢🛢⊘⑩⬚🏪⬇

Within 3 miles: ⚘⚘∺🕮ℰ◎⑤⑤ʊ

Notes: No campfires, quiet after 22.30hrs. Dogs must be kept on leads.

AA Pubs & Restaurants nearby: The Smugglers' Den Inn, CUBERT, TR8 5PY, 01637 830209

The Lewinnick Lodge Bar & Restaurant, NEWQUAY, TR7 1NX, 01637 878117

Visit the AA.com/shop for the latest AA Pub and Restaurant guides

---

Crantock Plains Touring Park
►►►81%

tel: 01637 830955 & 07837 534964 **TR8 5PH**
email: crantockp@btconnect.com
dir: *Exit Newquay on A3075, 2nd right signed to park & Crantock. Site on left in 0.75m on narrow road.* **grid ref:** *SW805589*

A small rural park with pitches on either side of a narrow lane, surrounded by mature trees for shelter. This spacious, family-run park has good modern toilet facilities and is ideal for campers who appreciate peace and quiet; it is situated approximately 1.2 miles from pretty Crantock, and Newquay is within easy reach. 6 acre site. 60 touring pitches. 20 seasonal pitches. Caravan pitches. Motorhome pitches. Tent pitches.

Open: mid Apr-end Sep **Last arrival:** 22.00hrs **Last departure:** noon

Pitches: ⊞ ⊞ ▲

Leisure: ⚠ ⚽

Facilities: ⬀⊙ℱ✳⚖⊙⑤🐾 🟡

Services: ☎⑤ ⬚

Within 3 miles: ⚘⚘∺🕮ℰ◎⚖⑤⑤ʊ

Notes: No skateboards. Dogs must be kept on leads.

AA Pubs & Restaurants nearby: The Smugglers' Den Inn, CUBERT, TR8 5PY, 01637 830209

The Lewinnick Lodge Bar & Restaurant, NEWQUAY, TR7 1NX, 01637 878117

CUBERT — Map 2 SW75

Places to visit

Trerice, TRERICE, TR8 4PG, 01637 875404 www.nationaltrust.org.uk/trerice/

Great for kids: Dairy Land Farm World, NEWQUAY, TR8 5AA, 01872 510246 www.dairylandfarmworld.com

---

Cottage Farm Touring Park
►►►81%

tel: 01637 831083 **Treworgans TR8 5HH**
email: info@cottagefarmpark.co.uk
dir: *From A392 towards Newquay, left onto A3075 towards Redruth. In 2m right signed Cubert, right again in 1.5m signed Crantock, left in 0.5m.* **grid ref:** *SW786589*

A small grassy touring park situated in the tiny hamlet of Treworgans, in sheltered open countryside close to a lovely beach at Holywell Bay. This quiet family-run park boasts very good quality facilities including a fenced playground for children, with a climbing frame, swings, slides etc. 2 acre site. 45 touring pitches. 2 hardstandings. Caravan pitches. Motorhome pitches. Tent pitches. 1 static.

Open: Apr-Sep **Last arrival:** 22.30hrs **Last departure:** noon

Pitches: * ⊞ £12-£17 ⊞ £12-£17 ▲ £12-£17

Facilities: ⬀⊙ℱ✳♺🟡

Services: ☎⑤ ⬚

Within 3 miles: ⚘⚘∺🕮ℰ◎⚖⑤⑤ʊ

Notes: No noise after 23.00hrs. Dogs must be kept on leads.

AA Pubs & Restaurants nearby: The Smugglers' Den Inn, CUBERT, TR8 5PY, 01637 830209

The Plume of Feathers, MITCHELL, TR8 5AX, 01872 510387

LEISURE: 🏊 Indoor swimming pool ⚮ Outdoor swimming pool ⚠ Children's playground 🎣 Kid's club 🎾 Tennis court ◖ Games room ⬚ Separate TV room ⚘ golf course ⚘ Boats for hire 🎬 Cinema 🎵 Entertainment ℰ Fishing ◎ Mini golf ⚖ Watersports 🏋 Gym ⚽ Sports field Spa ʊ Stables
FACILITIES: 🛁 Bath ⬀ Shower ⊙ Electric shaver ℱ Hairdryer ✳ Ice Pack Facility ⚖ Disabled facilities ⊙ Public telephone ⑤ Shop on site or within 200yds 🏪 Mobile shop (calls at least 5 days a week) 🍴 BBQ area 🏞 Picnic area WiFi Wi-fi 🖳 Internet access ♺ Recycling 🟡 Tourist info 🐾 Dog exercise area

EDGCUMBE
Map 2 SW73

Places to visit

Poldark Mine and Heritage Complex, WENDRON, TR13 0ER, 01326 573173
www.poldark-mine.co.uk

Great for kids: Cornish Seal Sanctuary, GWEEK, TR12 6UG, 01326 221361
www.sealsanctuaries.com

The Flambards Theme Park, HELSTON, TR13 0QA, 01326 573404
www.flambards.co.uk

Retanna Holiday Park
►►►81%

tel: 01326 340643 **TR13 0EJ**
email: retannaholpark@btconnect.com
dir: On A394 towards Helston, site signed on right. Site in 100mtrs. **grid ref:** SW711327

A small family-owned and run park in a rural location midway between Falmouth and Helston, and only about eight miles from Redruth. Its well-sheltered grassy pitches make this an ideal location for visiting the lovely beaches and towns nearby. For a fun day out the Flambards Experience is only a short drive away, and for sailing enthusiasts Stithians Lake is on the doorstep. 8 acre site. 24 touring pitches. Caravan pitches. Tent pitches. 23 statics.

Open: Apr-Oct **Last arrival:** 21.00hrs **Last departure:** noon
Pitches: * ♙ £16.50-£22.50 ▲ £16.50-£22.50
Leisure: ⁄Ⅾ ⬡ ⚫ ◻
Facilities: ⌐ ☉ ⚹ ⅙ ⌷ ⊓ WIFI ☐ ♺ ❼
Services: ⊞ ⊙ 🗋 ⊘ Ⓣ ≡ ➘
Within 3 miles: ⅃ ⅄ ⅁ ◎ ⅙ ⓐ ⓑ ∪

Notes: No pets, no disposable BBQs, no open fires. Free use of fridge-freezer in laundry room, free air bed inflation, free mobile phone charging.

AA Pubs & Restaurants nearby: Trengilly Wartha Inn, CONSTANTINE, TR11 5RP, 01326 340332

FALMOUTH

Places to visit

Pendennis Castle, FALMOUTH, TR11 4LP, 01326 316594
www.english-heritage.org.uk/daysout/properties/pendennis-castle

Trebah Garden, MAWNAN SMITH, TR11 5JZ, 01326 252200
www.trebah-garden.co.uk

Glendurgan, MAWNAN SMITH, TR11 5JZ, 01326 252020
www.nationaltrust.org.uk/glendurgan-garden

Great for kids: National Maritime Museum Cornwall, FALMOUTH, TR11 3QY, 01326 313388 www.nmmc.co.uk

FALMOUTH
Map 2 SW83

Tregedna Farm Touring Caravan & Tent Park
►►►80%

tel: 01326 250529 **Maenporth TR11 5HL**
email: enquiries@tregednafarmholidays.co.uk
dir: Take A39 from Truro to Falmouth. Turn right at Hill Head rdbt. Site 2.5m on right.
grid ref: SW785305

Set in the picturesque Maen Valley, this gently-sloping, south-facing park is part of a 100-acre farm. It is surrounded by beautiful wooded countryside just minutes from the beach, with spacious pitches and well-kept facilities. 12 acre site. 40 touring pitches. 6 hardstandings. Caravan pitches. Motorhome pitches. Tent pitches.

Open: Apr-Sep **Last arrival:** 22.00hrs **Last departure:** 13.00hrs
Pitches: ♙ ➿ ▲
Leisure: ⁄Ⅾ
Facilities: ⌐ ☉ ⚹ ⊙ ⌷ ⊓ ♺ ❼
Services: ⊞ ⊙ ⊘
Within 3 miles: ⅃ ⅄ ⅁ ◎ ⅙ ⓐ ⓑ

Notes: ⊛ Only 1 dog per pitch. Dogs must be kept on leads.

AA Pubs & Restaurants nearby: Trengilly Wartha Inn, CONSTANTINE, TR11 5RP, 01326 340332

Budock Vean - The Hotel on the River, MAWNAN SMITH, TR11 5LG, 01326 252100

Pennance Mill Farm Touring Park
►►►76%

tel: 01326 317431 **Maenporth TR11 5HJ**
dir: From A39 (Truro to Falmouth road) follow brown camping signs towards Maenporth Beach. At Hill Head rdbt take 2nd exit for Maenporth Beach. **grid ref:** SW792307

The safe, sandy bay at Maenporth, just half a mile away, can be accessed via a private woodland walk and cycle ride directly from this park. It is a mainly level, grassy park in a rural location sheltered by mature trees and shrubs and divided into three meadows. It has a modern toilet block. 6 acre site. 75 touring pitches. 12 hardstandings. Caravan pitches. Motorhome pitches. Tent pitches. 4 statics.

Open: Etr-Nov **Last arrival:** 22.00hrs **Last departure:** 10.00hrs
Pitches: ♙ ➿ ▲
Leisure: ⁄Ⅾ ⬡ ⚫
Facilities: ⌐ ☉ ⚹ ⊙ ⌷ ⊓ ♺ ❼
Services: ⊞ ⊙ 🗋 ⊘ ≡ ⚏ ⅄
Within 3 miles: ⅃ ⅄ ⅃ ⅁ ◎ ⅙ ⓐ ⓑ ∪

Notes: ⊛ No noise after 23.00hrs.

AA Pubs & Restaurants nearby: Trengilly Wartha Inn, CONSTANTINE, TR11 5RP, 01326 340332

Budock Vean - The Hotel on the River, MAWNAN SMITH, TR11 5LG, 01326 252100

FOWEY
Map 2 SX15

Places to visit

St Catherine's Castle, FOWEY, 0870 333 1181
www.english-heritage.org.uk/daysout/properties/st-catherines-castle

Restormel Castle, RESTORMEL, PL22 0EE, 01208 872687
www.english-heritage.org.uk/daysout/properties/restormel-castle

Great for kids: Wheal Martyn, ST AUSTELL, PL26 8XG, 01726 850362
www.wheal-martyn.com

Eden Project, ST AUSTELL, PL24 2SG, 01726 811911 www.edenproject.com

---

Penmarlam Caravan & Camping Park
►►► 83%

tel: 01726 870088 **Bodinnick PL23 1LZ**
email: info@penmarlampark.co.uk
dir: *From A390 at East Taphouse take B3359 signed Looe & Polperro. Follow signs for Bodinnick & Fowey, via ferry. Site on right at entrance to Bodinnick.* **grid ref:** *SX134526*

This continually improving, tranquil park (with access to the water) is set above the Fowey Estuary in an Area of Outstanding Natural Beauty. The pitches are level and sheltered by trees and bushes in two paddocks, while the toilets are spotlessly clean and well maintained. The shop is licensed and sells local and other Cornish produce. Online booking is now available. Good walks surrounding the site include one to the Polruan passenger ferry, and one to the Bodinnick car ferry so offering easy access to Fowey. 4 acre site. 63 touring pitches. 20 seasonal pitches. Caravan pitches. Motorhome pitches. Tent pitches.

Open: Apr-Oct **Last departure:** noon

Pitches: * 🚐 £16.50-£28 🚗 £16.50-£28 ▲ £16.50-£28
Facilities: 🅿️☉🅿️⚡☀️⚲🚻📤🚮📶🖥️♻️❶
Services: 🔌🚽🛒⛽🚾🚮
Within 3 miles: ⚓🏇🎍⚲🏊🅱️🚲⛵

Notes: Dogs must be kept on leads. Private slipway, small boat storage.

AA Pubs & Restaurants nearby: The Ship Inn, FOWEY, PL23 1AZ, 01726 832230
The Fowey Hotel, FOWEY, PL23 1HX, 01726 832551

GOONHAVERN
See also Rejerrah

Places to visit

Trerice, TRERICE, TR8 4PG, 01637 875404 www.nationaltrust.org.uk/trerice/

Blue Reef Aquarium, NEWQUAY, TR7 1DU, 01637 878134
www.bluereefaquarium.co.uk

Great for kids: Dairy Land Farm World, NEWQUAY, TR8 5AA, 01872 510246
www.dairylandfarmworld.com

Newquay Zoo, NEWQUAY, TR7 2LZ, 0844 474 2244 www.newquayzoo.org.uk

---

GOONHAVERN
Map 2 SW75

PREMIER PARK

Silverbow Park
►►►►► 84%

tel: 01872 572347 **Perranwell TR4 9NX**
email: silverbowhols@btconnect.com **web:** www.chycor.co.uk/parks/silverbow
dir: *Adjacent to A3075, 0.5m S of village.* **grid ref:** *SW782531*

This park, on the main road to Newquay, has a quiet garden atmosphere and appeals to families with young children. The superb landscaped grounds and good quality toilet facilities (with four family rooms) that are housed in an attractive chalet-style building, are maintained to a very high standard. Leisure facilities include two inviting swimming pools (outdoor and indoor), a bowling green, a nature walk around small lakes, and a summer house where children can take part in a number of nature activities. There are new, top quality eco-lodges available for hire. 14 acre site. 90 touring pitches. 2 hardstandings. 30 seasonal pitches. Caravan pitches. Motorhome pitches. Tent pitches. 15 statics. 1 wooden pod.

Open: May-end Sep **Last arrival:** 22.00hrs **Last departure:** 10.30hrs
Pitches: * 🚐 £17-£30 🚗 £17-£30 ▲ £17-£30 🏠
Leisure: 🏊🏊🎠⚽🎱
Facilities: 🛁🅿️☉🅿️⚡☀️⚲🚻📤🚮📶♻️❶
Services: 🔌🚽🛒⛽🚾⬇️
Within 3 miles: ⚓🏇🎣◎🏊🅱️🚲⛵

Notes: No cycling, no skateboards, no noise after 21.00hrs. Short mat bowls rink, conservation & information area, indoor & outdoor table tennis, all weather tennis courts.

AA Pubs & Restaurants nearby: The Smugglers' Den Inn, CUBERT, TR8 5PY, 01637 830209

The Plume of Feathers, MITCHELL, TR8 5AX, 01872 510387

See advert below

Penrose Holiday Park
►►►►86%

tel: 01872 573185 **TR4 9QF**
email: info@penroseholidaypark.com
dir: *From Exeter take A30, past Bodmin & Indian Queens. Just after Wind Farm take B3285 towards Perranporth, site on left on entering Goonhavern.* **grid ref:** *SW795534*

A quiet sheltered park set in five paddocks divided by hedges and shrubs, only a short walk from the village. Lovely floral displays enhance the park's appearance, and the grass and hedges are neatly trimmed. The four cubicle family rooms prove very popular, and there is a good laundry, a smart reception building and an internet café. Static caravans are now available for hire. 9 acre site. 110 touring pitches. 48 hardstandings. 34 seasonal pitches. Caravan pitches. Motorhome pitches. Tent pitches. 24 statics.

Open: Apr-Oct **Last arrival:** 21.30hrs **Last departure:** 10.00hrs
Pitches: * ⊞ £15-£25 ⊞ £15-£25 ▲ £15-£25
Leisure: ⚙ **Facilities:** ⚹⊙☞☀&©⊟⚟WIFI■♺❶
Services: ⚡⑤🔲⌀Ⓣ†⊙†☎⛟⚒
Within 3 miles: ⚘⚱☞◎⚶🅱⑤U

Notes: Families & couples only. Dogs must be kept on leads. Campers' kitchen. Fridge freezer, microwave & bottle warmer available.

AA Pubs & Restaurants nearby: The Smugglers' Den Inn, CUBERT, TR8 5PY, 01637 830209

The Plume of Feathers, MITCHELL, TR8 5AX, 01872 510387

Little Treamble Farm Touring Park
►►►83%

tel: 01872 573823 & 07971 070760 **Rose TR4 9PR**
email: info@treamble.co.uk
dir: *A30 onto B3285 signed Perranporth. Approx 0.5m right into Scotland Rd signed Newquay. Approx 2m to T-junct, right onto A3075 signed Newquay. 0.25m left at Rejerrah sign. Site signed 0.75m on right.* **grid ref:** *SW785560*

This site, within easy reach of Padstow, Newquay and St Ives, is set in a quiet rural location with extensive countryside views across an undulating valley. There is a small toilet block with a disabled facility and a well-stocked shop. This working farm is adjacent to a Caravan Club site. 1.5 acre site. 20 touring pitches. Caravan pitches. Motorhome pitches. Tent pitches.

Open: all year **Last departure:** noon
Pitches: ⊞ ⊞ ▲
Facilities: ⚹☞☀🅱♺❶
Services: ⚡⑤Ⓣ☎
Within 3 miles: ⚱☞◎🅱U

AA Pubs & Restaurants nearby: The Smugglers' Den Inn, CUBERT, TR8 5PY, 01637 830209

The Plume of Feathers, MITCHELL, TR8 5AX, 01872 510387

Discover a great day out at theaa.com/event-and-days-out

PITCHES: ⊞ Caravans ⊞ Motorhomes ▲ Tents 🏠 Glamping-style accommodation **SERVICES:** ⚡ Electric hook up ⑤ Launderette 🔲 Licensed bar 🔋 Calor Gas ⌀ Camping Gaz Ⓣ Toilet fluid †⊙† Café/Restaurant ☎ Fast Food/Takeaway 🔋 Battery charging ☎ Baby care ⛟ Motorvan service point
ABBREVIATIONS: BH/bank hols – bank holidays Etr – Easter Spring BH – Spring Bank Holiday fr – from hrs – hours m – mile mdnt – midnight rdbt – roundabout rs – restricted service wk – week wknd – weekend x-rds – cross roads ⊛ No credit or debit cards ⊗ No dogs ⅋ Children of all ages accepted

GORRAN
Map 2 SW94

Places to visit

Caerhays Castle Gardens, GORRAN, PL26 6LY, 01872 501310
www.caerhays.co.uk

The Lost Gardens of Heligan, PENTEWAN, PL26 6EN, 01726 845100
www.heligan.com

Great for kids: Wheal Martyn, ST AUSTELL, PL26 8XG, 01726 850362
www.wheal-martyn.com

Treveague Farm Caravan & Camping Site
►►►82%

tel: 01726 842295 **PL26 6NY**
email: treveague@btconnect.com
dir: B3273 from St Austell towards Mevagissey, pass Pentewan at top of hill, right signed Gorran. Past Heligan Gardens towards Gorran Churchtown. Follow brown tourist signs from fork in road. (NB roads to site are single lane & very narrow. It is advisable to follow guide directions & not Sat Nav). **grid ref:** SX002410

Spectacular panoramic coastal views can be enjoyed from this rural park, which is set on an organic farm and well equipped with modern facilities. A stone-faced toilet block with a Cornish slate roof is an attractive feature, as is the building that houses the smart reception, café and shop, which sells meat produced on the farm. There is an aviary with exotic birds, and also chinchillas. A footpath leads to the fishing village of Gorran Haven in one direction, and the secluded sandy Vault Beach in the other. The site is close to a bus route. 4 acre site. 46 touring pitches. Caravan pitches. Motorhome pitches. Tent pitches.

Open: Apr-Sep **Last arrival:** 21.00hrs **Last departure:** noon
Pitches: * � £9-£22 �	£9-£22 ▲ £7.50-£20
Leisure: 🄰 ✪
Facilities: 🅵⊙🄿✳ & ⓢ 🄰 🛒 📺 🖥 ♻ ❼
Services: 🔌🅾 🅣 🍴📦 ⛽
Within 3 miles: 🗡 🎣 🏊 ⓢ 🅾
Notes: Bird & animal hide with wide-screen monitors.
AA Pubs & Restaurants nearby: The Ship Inn, MEVAGISSEY, PL26 6UQ, 01726 843324
The Crown Inn, ST EWE, PL26 6EY, 01726 843322

Who has won England Campsite of the Year?
See page 14

Treveor Farm Caravan & Camping Site
►►►82%

tel: 01726 842387 **PL26 6LW**
email: info@treveorfarm.co.uk **web:** www.treveorfarm.co.uk
dir: From St Austell bypass left onto B3273 for Mevagissey. On hilltop before descent to village turn right onto unclassified road for Gorran. Right in 5m, site on right.
grid ref: SW988418

A small family-run camping park set on a working farm, with grassy pitches backing onto mature hedging. This quiet site, with good facilities, is close to beaches and offers a large coarse fishing lake. 4 acre site. 50 touring pitches. Caravan pitches. Motorhome pitches. Tent pitches.

Open: Apr-Oct **Last arrival:** 20.00hrs **Last departure:** 11.00hrs
Pitches: * � £6-£19 �	£6-£19 ▲ £6-£19
Leisure: 🄰
Facilities: 🅵⊙🄿✳ ♻ ❼
Services: 🔌🅾
Within 3 miles: 🗡 🏊 ⓢ
Notes: No hard balls, kites or frizbees. Dogs must be kept on leads.
AA Pubs & Restaurants nearby: The Ship Inn, MEVAGISSEY, PL26 6UQ, 01726 843324
The Crown Inn, ST EWE, PL26 6EY, 01726 843322

GORRAN HAVEN

Places to visit

Caerhays Castle Gardens, GORRAN, PL26 6LY, 01872 501310
www.caerhays.co.uk

The Lost Gardens of Heligan, PENTEWAN, PL26 6EN, 01726 845100
www.heligan.com

Great for kids: Wheal Martyn, ST AUSTELL, PL26 8XG, 01726 850362
www.wheal-martyn.com

| GORRAN HAVEN | Map 2 SX04 |

Trelispen Caravan & Camping Park
►►74%

tel: 01726 843501 **PL26 6NT**
email: trelispen@care4free.net
dir: *B3273 from St Austell towards Mevagissey, on hilltop at x-roads before descent into Mevagissey turn right on unclassified road to Gorran. Through village, 2nd right towards Gorran Haven, site signed on left in 250mtrs. NB it is advisable to use guide directions not Sat Nav.* **grid ref:** *SX008421*

A quiet rural site set in three paddocks, and sheltered by mature trees and hedges. The simple toilets have plenty of hot water, and there is a small laundry. Sandy beaches, pubs and shops are nearby, and Mevagissey is two miles away. There is a bus stop 100yds from the site with a regular service to Mevagissey and St Austell. 2 acre site. 40 touring pitches. Caravan pitches. Motorhome pitches. Tent pitches.

Open: Etr & Apr-Oct **Last arrival:** 22.00hrs **Last departure:** noon

Pitches: 🚐 🚈 ▲

Leisure: 🅿 **Facilities:** � ☺ ❋

Services: 🔌 🔁

Within 3 miles: ⚓ 🎣 🛒🔁

Notes: ⊘ 30-acre nature reserve.

AA Pubs & Restaurants nearby: The Ship Inn, MEVAGISSEY, PL26 6UQ, 01726 843324
The Crown Inn, ST EWE, PL26 6EY, 01726 843322

| GWITHIAN | Map 2 SW54 |

Places to visit
East Pool Mine, POOL, TR15 3NP, 01209 315027 www.nationaltrust.org.uk

Gwithian Farm Campsite
►►►►91%

tel: 01736 753127 **Gwithian Farm TR27 5BX**
email: camping@gwithianfarm.co.uk
dir: *Exit A30 at Hayle rdbt, 4th exit signed Hayle, 100mtrs. At 1st mini-rdbt right onto B3301 signed Portreath. Site 2m on left on entering village.* **grid ref:** *SW586412*

An unspoilt site located behind the sand dunes of Gwithian's golden beach, which can be reached by footpath directly from the site, making this an ideal location for surfers. The site boasts stunning floral displays, a superb toilet block with excellent facilities, including a bathroom and baby-changing unit, and first-class hardstanding pitches. Each attractive pitch has been screened by hedge planting. There is a good pub opposite. 7.5 acre site. 87 touring pitches. 32 hardstandings. Caravan pitches. Motorhome pitches. Tent pitches.

Open: 31 Mar-1 Oct **Last arrival:** 21.00hrs **Last departure:** 17.00hrs

Pitches: 🚐 £19-£30 🚈 £19-£30 ▲ £15-£26 **Leisure:** ✪

Facilities: � ☺ 🅿 ❋ 🔥 🏤 📶 ♻ ❶

Services: 🔌 🔁 🔋 ⊘ T 🍽 ⚲ **Within 3 miles:** ↯ 🏌 ◎ 🏊 🛒🔁 ♻

Notes: No ball games after 21.00hrs, no noise after 22.30hrs, debit cards (no credit cards) accepted. Dogs must be kept on leads. Surf board & wet suit hire, table tennis.

AA Pubs & Restaurants nearby: Basset Arms, PORTREATH, TR16 4NG, 01209 842077
Porthminster Beach Restaurant, ST IVES, TR26 2EB, 01736 795352

| HAYLE | Map 2 SW53 |

Places to visit
Tate St Ives, ST IVES, TR26 1TG, 01736 796226 www.tate.org.uk/stives

Barbara Hepworth Museum & Sculpture Garden, ST IVES, TR26 1AD, 01736 796226 www.tate.org.uk/stives

St Ives Bay Holiday Park
HOLIDAY CENTRE 89%

tel: 01736 752274 **73 Loggans Rd, Upton Towans TR27 5BH**
email: enquiries@stivesbay.co.uk
dir: *Exit A30 at Hayle then immediate right onto B3301 at mini-rdbts. Site entrance 0.5m on left.* **grid ref:** *SW577398*

An extremely well-maintained holiday park with a relaxed atmosphere situated adjacent to a three mile beach. The various camping fields are set in hollows amongst the sand dunes and are very tastefully laid out, with the high camping fields enjoying stunning views over St Ives Bay. The touring sections are in a number of separate locations around the extensive site. The park is specially geared for families and couples, and as well as the large indoor swimming pool there are two pubs with seasonal entertainment. 90 acre site. 240 touring pitches. Caravan pitches. Motorhome pitches. Tent pitches. 250 statics. 17 wooden pods.

Open: Etr-1 Oct **Last arrival:** 21.00hrs **Last departure:** 09.00hrs

Pitches: 🚐 🚈 ▲ 🏠 **Leisure:** 🏊 🅿 ⚲ 🎱 ▭ 🎵

Facilities: � ☺ 🅿 ❋ ♿ 🔁 🛁 🔥 📶 🖥 ♻ ❶

Services: 🔌 🔁 🍺 🔋 ⊘ T 🍽 🍔 ⚲

Within 3 miles: ↯ 🏌 ◎ 🛒🔁 ♻

Notes: ⊗ No pets. Crazy golf, video room.

AA Pubs & Restaurants nearby: The Red River Inn, GWITHIAN, TR27 5BW, 01736 753223
Porthminster Beach Restaurant, ST IVES, TR26 2EB, 01736 795352

Atlantic Coast Caravan Park
►►►87%

tel: 01736 752071 **53 Upton Towans, Gwithian TR27 5BL**
email: enquiries@atlanticcoastpark.co.uk
dir: *From A30 into Hayle, turn right at double rdbt. Site 1.5m on left.* **grid ref:** *NW580400*

Fringed by the sand dunes of St Ives Bay and close to the golden sands of Gwithian Beach, the small, friendly touring area offers fully serviced pitches. There's freshly baked bread, a takeaway and a bar next door. This park is ideally situated for visitors to enjoy the natural coastal beauty and attractions of south-west Cornwall. Recent improvements include superb new landscaping and planting, an upgraded toilet block with the addition of facilities (kettle, microwave) for campers. Static caravans for holiday hire. 4.5 acre site. 15 touring pitches. 5 seasonal pitches. Caravan pitches. Motorhome pitches. Tent pitches. 50 statics.

Open: Mar-early Jan **Last arrival:** 20.00hrs **Last departure:** 11.00hrs

Pitches: * 🚐 £21.50-£27 🚈 £21.50-£27 ▲ £21.50-£27

Facilities: � ☺ 🅿 ❋ ♿ 🔁 🛁 📶 ♻ ❶

Services: 🔌 🔁 T 🍽 ⚲ 🚰 **Within 3 miles:** ↯ 🏌 ◎ 🏊 🛒🔁 ♻

Notes: No commercial vehicles, gazebos or day tents. Dogs must be kept on leads.

AA Pubs & Restaurants nearby: The Red River Inn, GWITHIAN, TR27 5BW, 01736 753223
Porthminster Beach Restaurant, ST IVES, TR26 2EB, 01736 795352

PITCHES: 🚐 Caravans 🚈 Motorhomes ▲ Tents 🏠 Glamping-style accommodation **SERVICES:** 🔌 Electric hook up 🔁 Launderette 🍺 Licensed bar
🔋 Calor Gas ⊘ Camping Gaz T Toilet fluid 🍽 Café/Restaurant 🍔 Fast Food/Takeaway 🔋 Battery charging ⚲ Baby care 🚰 Motorvan service point
ABBREVIATIONS: BH/bank hols – bank holidays Etr – Easter Spring BH – Spring Bank Holiday fr – from hrs – hours m – mile mdnt – midnight
rdbt – roundabout rs – restricted service wk – week wknd – weekend x-rds – cross roads ⊘ No credit or debit cards ⊗ No dogs 👪 Children of all ages accepted

HAYLE *continued*

Higher Trevaskis Caravan & Camping Park

►►►84%

tel: 01209 831736 **Gwinear Rd, Connor Downs TR27 5JQ**
web: www.highertrevaskiscaravanpark.co.uk
dir: *On A30 at Hayle rdbt take exit signed Connor Downs, in 1m right signed Carnhell Green. Site 0.75m just after level crossing.* **grid ref:** *SW611381*

An attractive paddocked and terraced park in a sheltered rural position on a valley side with views towards St Ives. The terrace areas are divided by hedges. This secluded park is personally run by owners who keep it quiet and welcoming. Three unisex showers are a great hit with visitors. Fluent German is spoken. 6.5 acre site. 82 touring pitches. 3 hardstandings. Caravan pitches. Motorhome pitches. Tent pitches.

Open: mid Apr-Sep **Last arrival:** 20.00hrs **Last departure:** 10.30hrs

Pitches: * ⊞ £12-£22 ⊞ £12-£22 ▲ £12-£22

Leisure: ⚑ ✪

Facilities: ↰ ⊙ ℙ ✳ ◐ ⑤ ♻ ✪

Services: ⊡ ⑤ ⬛ ⌀ ⊤ ≞

Within 3 miles: ↧ ℘ ◎ ≋ ⑤ ⑤

Notes: ✪ Max speed 5mph, balls permitted on field only, max 2 dogs, no dangerous dogs. Dogs must be kept on leads.

AA Pubs & Restaurants nearby: The Red River Inn, GWITHIAN, TR27 5BW, 01736 753223
Porthminster Beach Restaurant, ST IVES, TR26 2EB, 01736 795352

Treglisson Touring Park

►►►81%

tel: 01736 753141 **Wheal Alfred Rd TR27 5JT**
email: treglisson@hotmail.co.uk
dir: *4th exit off rdbt on A30 at Hayle. 100mtrs, left at 1st mini-rdbt. Approx 1.5m past golf course, site sign on left.* **grid ref:** *SW581367*

A small secluded site in a peaceful wooded meadow and a former apple and pear orchard. This quiet rural site has level grass pitches and a well-planned modern toilet block, and is just two miles from the glorious beach at Hayle with its vast stretch of golden sand. 3 acre site. 26 touring pitches. 6 hardstandings. Caravan pitches. Motorhome pitches. Tent pitches.

Open: Etr-Sep **Last arrival:** 20.00hrs **Last departure:** 11.00hrs

Pitches: * ⊞ £11-£18.50 ⊞ £11-£18.50 ▲ £11-£18.50

Leisure: ⚑

Facilities: ↰ ⊙ ℙ ✳ ⬧ ☰ WiFi ♻ ✪

Services: ⊡ ⑤ ≞

Within 3 miles: ↧ ℘ ≋ ⑤ ⑤

Notes: Max 6 people per pitch. Dogs must be kept on leads.

AA Pubs & Restaurants nearby: The Red River Inn, GWITHIAN, TR27 5BW, 01736 753223
Porthminster Beach Restaurant, ST IVES, TR26 2EB, 01736 795352

Riviere Sands Holiday Park

HOLIDAY HOME PARK 86%

GOLD

tel: 01736 752132 **Riviere Towans TR27 5AX**
email: rivieresands@haven.com **web:** www.haven.com/rivieresands
dir: *A30 towards Redruth. Follow signs into Hayle, cross double mini rdbt. Turn right opposite petrol station towards Towans and beaches. Park 1m on right.*
grid ref: *SW556386*

Close to St Ives and with direct access to a safe, white-sand beach, Riviere Sands is an exciting holiday park with much to offer families. Children can enjoy the crazy golf, amusements, swimming pool complex, and the beach of course; evening entertainment for adults is extensive and lively. There are a good range of holiday caravans and apartments.

Open: Mar-Oct

Change over day: Mon, Fri, Sat

Arrival and departure times: Please contact the site

Statics: 295 Sleeps 6-8 Bedrms 2-3 Bathrms 1-2 Toilets 1-2 Microwave Freezer TV Sky/FTV Elec inc Gas inc Grass area

Children: ♦♦ Cots Highchair

Leisure: ≋ ≋ Cycle hire ♨ ⚑

LEISURE: ≋ Indoor swimming pool ≋ Outdoor swimming pool ⚑ Children's playground ♨ Kid's club ♘ Tennis court ♜ Games room ▭ Separate TV room ↧ golf course ♨ Boats for hire ☰ Cinema ♫ Entertainment ℘ Fishing ◎ Mini golf ≋ Watersports ♟ Gym ✪ Sports field ▢ Spa ♡ Stables
FACILITIES: ⬦ Bath ↰ Shower ⊙ Electric shaver ℙ Hairdryer ✳ Ice Pack Facility ⬧ Disabled facilities ◐ Public telephone ⑤ Shop on site or within 200yds ⑥ Mobile shop (calls at least 5 days a week) ☰ BBQ area ☴ Picnic area WiFi Wi-fi ▤ Internet access ♻ Recycling ✪ Tourist info ✦ Dog exercise area

See also Ashton

Places to visit

Great for kids: The Flambards Theme Park, HELSTON, TR13 0QA, 01326 573404 www.flambards.co.uk

Cornish Seal Sanctuary, GWEEK, TR12 6UG, 01326 221361 www.sealsanctuaries.com

Lower Polladras Touring Park
►►►►86%

tel: 01736 762220 **Carleen, Breage TR13 9NX**
email: lowerpolladras@btinternet.com **web:** www.lower-polladras.co.uk
dir: *From Helston take A394 then B3302 (Hayle road) at Ward Garage, 2nd left to Carleen, site 2m on right.* **grid ref:** SW617308

An attractive rural park with extensive views of surrounding fields, appealing to families who enjoy the countryside. The planted trees and shrubs are maturing, and help to divide the area into paddocks with spacious grassy pitches. The site has a dish-washing area, a games room, a dog and nature walk, two fully serviced family rooms and WiFi. 4 acre site. 39 touring pitches. 23 hardstandings. Caravan pitches. Motorhome pitches. Tent pitches. 3 statics.

Open: Apr-Jan **Last arrival:** 22.00hrs **Last departure:** noon

Pitches: ⌖ ⌖ Å

Leisure: ⌂ ⬤

Facilities: ⌖⊙⌖✳⌖⌖⌖⌖ ⌖ WiFi

Services: ⌖⌖ ⌖⌖⌖⌖⌖⌖

Within 3 miles: ⌖⌖⌖⌖⊙⌖⌖⌖⌖U

Notes: ⌖ Caravan storage area.

AA Pubs & Restaurants nearby: The Ship Inn, PORTHLEVEN, TR13 9JS, 01326 564204

Kota Restaurant with Rooms, PORTHLEVEN, TR13 9JA, 01326 562407

New Yard Restaurant, HELSTON, TR12 6AF, 01326 221595

Skyburriowe Farm
►►►80%

tel: 01326 221646 **Garras TR12 6LR**
email: bkbenney@hotmail.co.uk **web:** www.skyburriowefarm.co.uk
dir: *From Helston take A3083 to The Lizard. After Culdrose Naval Airbase continue straight on at rdbt, in 1m left at Skyburriowe Ln sign. In 0.5m right at Skyburriowe B&B/ Campsite sign. Pass bungalow to farmhouse. Site on left.* **grid ref:** SW698227

A leafy no-through road leads to this picturesque farm park in a rural location on the Lizard Peninsula. The toilet block offers excellent quality facilities, and most pitches have electric hook-ups. There are some beautiful coves and beaches nearby, and for a great day out Flambards Experience is also close by. Under the supervision of the owner, children are permitted to watch his herd of Friesian cows being milked. 4 acre site. 30 touring pitches. 4 hardstandings. Caravan pitches. Motorhome pitches. Tent pitches.

Open: Apr-Oct **Last arrival:** 22.00hrs **Last departure:** 11.00hrs

Pitches: ⌖ £14-£20 ⌖ £14-£20 Å £14-£20

Facilities: ⌖⊙✳⌖⌖⌖⌖⌖

Services: ⌖⌖

Within 3 miles: ⌖⌖⌖⌖⌖⌖⌖U

Notes: ⌖ Quiet after 23.00hrs. Dogs must be kept on leads.

AA Pubs & Restaurants nearby: The Ship Inn, PORTHLEVEN, TR13 9JS, 01326 564204

Kota Restaurant with Rooms, PORTHLEVEN, TR13 9JA, 01326 562407

New Yard Restaurant, HELSTON, TR12 6AF, 01326 221595

PITCHES: ⌖ Caravans ⌖ Motorhomes Å Tents ⌖ Glamping-style accommodation **SERVICES:** ⌖ Electric hook up ⌖ Launderette ⌖ Licensed bar ⌖ Calor Gas ⌖ Camping Gaz ⌖ Toilet fluid ⌖ Café/Restaurant ⌖ Fast Food/Takeaway ⌖ Battery charging ⌖ Baby care ⌖ Motorvan service point
ABBREVIATIONS: BH/bank hols – bank holidays Etr – Easter Spring BH – Spring Bank Holiday fr – from hrs – hours m – mile mdnt – midnight rdbt – roundabout rs – restricted service wk – week wknd – weekend x-rds – cross roads ⌖ No credit or debit cards ⌖ No dogs ⌖ Children of all ages accepted

HELSTON *continued*

Poldown Caravan Park
►►► 79%

tel: 01326 574560 **Poldown, Carleen TR13 9NN**
email: stay@poldown.co.uk
dir: *From Helston follow Penzance signs for 1m, right onto B3302 to Hayle, 2nd left to Carleen, 0.5m to site.* **grid ref:** *SW629298*

Ideally located for visiting the towns of Helston, Penzance and St Ives, this small, quiet site is set in attractive countryside. The park is sheltered by mature trees and shrubs. All the level grass pitches have electricity, and there are toilet facilities. 2 acre site. 13 touring pitches. 2 hardstandings. Caravan pitches. Motorhome pitches. Tent pitches. 7 statics. 2 bell tents/yurts.

Open: Apr-Sep **Last arrival:** 21.00hrs **Last departure:** noon

Pitches: 🚐 £16.25-£21.25 🚍 £12.50-£17.50 ▲ £12.50-£17.50 🏠

Leisure: 🅰 **Facilities:** 🏠⊙ℱ☀⚹🅮🛒🚻🐾 WIFI 🖥 ♻ 🛈

Services: 🔌🗑🛢🔱 **Within 3 miles:** 🎣🏇🛒🏌ℱ◎🛶🐟🛍🎣⛹

Notes: Debit cards accepted (no credit cards). Dogs must be kept on leads. Table tennis.

AA Pubs & Restaurants nearby: The Ship Inn, PORTHLEVEN, TR13 9JS, 01326 564204

Kota Restaurant with Rooms, PORTHLEVEN, TR13 9JA, 01326 562407

HOLYWELL BAY   Map 2 SW75

Places to visit

Trerice, TRERICE, TR8 4PG, 01637 875404 www.nationaltrust.org.uk/trerice/

Blue Reef Aquarium, NEWQUAY, TR7 1DU, 01637 878134 www.bluereefaquarium.co.uk

Great for kids: Newquay Zoo, NEWQUAY, TR7 2LZ, 0844 474 2244 www.newquayzoo.org.uk

---

Holywell Bay Holiday Park
HOLIDAY CENTRE 79%

tel: 0844 335 3756 **TR8 5PR**
email: touringandcamping@parkdeanholidays.com
dir: *Exit A30 onto A392, take A3075 signed Redruth, right in 2m signed Holywell/Cubert. Through Cubert past Trevornick to site on left.* **grid ref:** *SW773582*

Close to lovely beaches in a rural location, this level grassy park borders on National Trust land, and is only a short distance from the Cornish Coastal Path. The touring area is at the rear in a very quiet and flat area. The park provides a popular entertainment programme for the whole family (including evening entertainment), and there is an outdoor pool with a water slide and children's clubs. Newquay is just a few miles away. 16 acre site. 39 touring pitches. Caravan pitches. Motorhome pitches. Tent pitches. 156 statics.

Open: Apr-Oct (rs 3 May-22 Sep pool open) **Last arrival:** 23.00hrs
Last departure: 10.00hrs

Pitches: 🚐🚍▲ **Leisure:** 🏊🅰🛶🎮🎵

Facilities: 🏠⊙🅮🚻🏪🛒 **Services:** 🔌🗑🍴🚰🍽🛢🛒🚿

Within 3 miles: 🎣ℱ◎🛶🛍🎣⛹

Notes: Dogs must be kept on leads. Surf school & hire shop.

Trevornick Holiday Park
►►►► 84%

Best of British

tel: 01637 830531 **TR8 5PW**
email: info@trevornick.co.uk
dir: *3m from Newquay exit A3075 towards Redruth. Follow Cubert & Holywell Bay signs.* **grid ref:** *SW776586*

A large seaside holiday complex with excellent facilities and amenities. There is plenty of entertainment including a children's club and an evening cabaret, adding up to a full holiday experience for all the family. A sandy beach is just a 15-minute footpath walk away. The park has 68 ready-erected tents for hire. 20 acre site. 688 touring pitches. 53 hardstandings. 8 seasonal pitches. Caravan pitches. Motorhome pitches. Tent pitches.

Open: Etr & mid May-mid Sep **Last arrival:** 21.00hrs hrs **Last departure:** 10.00hrs

Pitches: 🚐🚍▲

Leisure: 🏊🅰🛶🎮🎵 Spa

Facilities: 🛁🏠⊙ℱ☀⚹🅮🏪🛒🚻🐾 WIFI ♻ 🛈

Services: 🔌🗑🍴🚰🛢🚰T🍽🛢🛒

Within 3 miles: 🎣🏇🛒🏌ℱ◎🛶🐟🛍🎣⛹

Notes: Families & couples only. Dogs must be kept on leads. Fishing, golf course, entertainment, fun park.

AA Pubs & Restaurants nearby: The Smugglers' Den Inn, CUBERT, TR8 5PY, 01637 830209

LEISURE: 🏊 Indoor swimming pool 🏊 Outdoor swimming pool 🅰 Children's playground 🛶 Kid's club 🎾 Tennis court 🎮 Games room 📺 Separate TV room 🏌 golf course 🚣 Boats for hire 🎬 Cinema 🎵 Entertainment ℱ Fishing ◎ Mini golf 🛶 Watersports 🏋 Gym 🏟 Sports field Spa ⛹ Stables
FACILITIES: 🛁 Bath 🏠 Shower ⊙ Electric shaver ℱ Hairdryer ☀ Ice Pack Facility 🅮 Disabled facilities 🕐 Public telephone 🛍 Shop on site or within 200yds 🏪 Mobile shop (calls at least 5 days a week) 🍴 BBQ area 🚻 Picnic area WIFI Wi-fi 🖥 Internet access ♻ Recycling 🛈 Tourist info 🐾 Dog exercise area

INDIAN QUEENS
Map 2 SW95

Places to visit
Wheal Martyn, ST AUSTELL, PL26 8XG, 01726 850362 www.wheal-martyn.com

Trerice, TRERICE, TR8 4PG, 01637 875404 www.nationaltrust.org.uk/trerice/

Gnome World Caravan & Camping Park
►►►76%

tel: 01726 860812 & 860101 **Moorland Rd TR9 6HN**
email: gnomesworld@btconnect.com
dir: Signed from slip road at A30 & A39 rdbt in village of Indian Queens - site on old A30, now unclassified road. **grid ref:** SW890599

Set in open countryside, this spacious park is set on level grassy land only half a mile from the A30 (Cornwall's main arterial route) and in a central holiday location for touring the county, and accessing the sandy beaches on the north Cornwall coast. Please note that there are no narrow lanes to negotiate. 4.5 acre site. 50 touring pitches. 25 hardstandings. Caravan pitches. Motorhome pitches. Tent pitches. 60 statics.

Open: Mar-Dec **Last arrival:** 22.00hrs **Last departure:** noon

Pitches: 🚐 🚍 ▲

Leisure: ⚲

Facilities: 🏪 ☺ ⚒ & 🚻 🐾

Services: 🔌 🗑 🛒

Within 3 miles: ⚓ ⑤ 🗑 ↻

Notes: Dogs must be kept on leads. Nature trail.

AA Pubs & Restaurants nearby: The Plume of Feathers, MITCHELL, TR8 5AX, 01872 510387

See advert below

ISLES OF SCILLY
See St Mary's and Bryher

JACOBSTOW
Map 2 SX19

Places to visit
Launceston Castle, LAUNCESTON, PL15 7DR, 01566 772365
www.english-heritage.org.uk/daysout/properties/launceston-castle

Tamar Otter & Wildlife Centre, LAUNCESTON, PL15 8GW, 01566 785646
www.tamarotters.co.uk

Great for kids: Launceston Steam Railway, LAUNCESTON, PL15 8DA, 01566 775665 www.launcestonsr.co.uk

JACOBSTOW
Map 2 SX19

Edmore Tourist Park
►►►78%

tel: 01840 230467 **Edgar Rd, Wainhouse Corner EX23 0BJ**
email: enquiries@cornwallvisited.co.uk
dir: Exit A39 at Wainhouse Corner onto Edgar Rd, site signed on right in 200yds. **grid ref:** SX184955

A quiet family-owned site in a rural location with extensive views, set close to the sandy surfing beaches of Bude, and the unspoilt sandy beach and rock pools at Crackington Haven. The friendly owners keep all facilities in a very good condition including the lovely grounds, and the site has hardstanding pitches and gravel access roads. There is an excellent children's play area. The site is handy for bus routes as it is close to the A39. 3 acre site. 28 touring pitches. 5 hardstandings. 2 seasonal pitches. Caravan pitches. Motorhome pitches. Tent pitches. 3 statics.

Open: 1 wk before Etr-Oct **Last arrival:** 21.00hrs **Last departure:** noon

Pitches: * 🚐 £16-£18 🚍 £16-£18 ▲ £16-£18 **Leisure:** ⚲

Facilities: 🏪 ☺ 🏴 ⚒ ⓒ ♻ ❶ **Services:** 🔌 🗑 🛒🔋 **Within 3 miles:** ⑤

Notes: 🚫 Dogs must be kept on leads.

AA Pubs & Restaurants nearby: Bay View Inn, WIDEMOUTH BAY, EX23 0AW, 01288 361273

PITCHES: 🚐 Caravans 🚍 Motorhomes ▲ Tents 🏠 Glamping-style accommodation **SERVICES:** 🔌 Electric hook up 🗑 Launderette 🍺 Licensed bar 🛒 Calor Gas ⊘ Camping Gaz Ⓣ Toilet fluid 🍽 Café/Restaurant 🍔 Fast Food/Takeaway 🔋 Battery charging 🍼 Baby care ⚡ Motorvan service point
ABBREVIATIONS: BH/bank hols – bank holidays Etr – Easter Spring BH – Spring Bank Holiday fr – from hrs – hours m – mile mdnt – midnight rdbt – roundabout rs – restricted service wk – week wknd – weekend x-rds – cross roads 🚫 No credit or debit cards 🚫 No dogs 👫 Children of all ages accepted

KENNACK SANDS
Map 2 SW71

Places to visit

Cornish Seal Sanctuary, GWEEK, TR12 6UG, 01326 221361
www.sealsanctuaries.com

Great for kids: The Flambards Theme Park, HELSTON, TR13 0QA, 01326 573404
www.flambards.co.uk

Chy Carne Holiday Park
►►►►87%

tel: 01326 290200 & 291161 **Kuggar, Ruan Minor TR12 7LX**
email: enquiries@camping-cornwall.com
dir: From A3083 onto B3293 after Culdrose Naval Air Station. At Goonhilly ESS right onto
unclassified road signed Kennack Sands. Left in 3m at junct. **grid ref:** SW725164

This spacious 12-acre park is in a quiet rural location and has excellent family
facilities. There are extensive sea and coastal views over the sandy beach at
Kennack Sands, less than half a mile away. Food is available from the site
takeaway, and the local hostelry is not far away in the village. 12 acre site. 30
touring pitches. 4 hardstandings. Caravan pitches. Motorhome pitches. Tent
pitches. 18 statics.

Open: Etr-Oct **Last arrival:** dusk

Pitches: 🚐 🚌 Å

Leisure: ⚠ 🎱

Facilities: 🏕 ⊙ ℗ ☀ ⅍ 🖺 🚻 ⤬ 📶

Services: 🗺 🗓 🛢 ⌁ 🗨 🍴 🔌 🔔

Within 3 miles: ⌦ ⇞ ⌿ ◉ 🛒 🛍 ↺

AA Pubs & Restaurants nearby: Cadgwith Cove Inn, CADGWITH, TR12 7JX, 01326 290513

Silver Sands Holiday Park
►►►86%

tel: 01326 290631 **Gwendreath TR12 7LZ**
email: info@silversandsholidaypark.co.uk **web:** www.silversandsholidaypark.co.uk
dir: From Helston follow signs to St Keverne. After BT Goonhilly Station turn right at x-rds
signed Kennack Sands, 1.5m, left at Gwendreath sign, site 1m. NB it is recommended
that guide directions are followed not Sat Nav. **grid ref:** SW727166

A small, family-owned park in a remote location, with individually screened pitches
providing sheltered suntraps. The owners continue to upgrade the park, improving

the landscaping, access roads and toilets; lovely floral displays greet you on arrival.
A footpath through the woods leads to the beach and the local pub. One of the
nearby beaches is the historic Mullion Cove, and for the children a short car ride
will ensure a great day out at the Flambards Experience. 9 acre site. 35 touring
pitches. Caravan pitches. Motorhome pitches. Tent pitches. 17 statics.

Open: 21 Mar-2 Nov **Last arrival:** 21.00hrs **Last departure:** 11.00hrs

Pitches: 🚐 £14.50-£23 🚌 £14.50-£23 Å £12.50-£19

Leisure: ⚠ 🎱 ▢

Facilities: 🏕 ⊙ ℗ ☀ ⊙ 🚻 ⤬ 📶 ♻ ❶

Services: 🗺 🗓 🛢 ⌁

Within 3 miles: ⌿ ⇞ 🛍 ↺

Notes: No noise after 23.00hrs. Dogs must be kept on leads.

AA Pubs & Restaurants nearby: Cadgwith Cove Inn, CADGWITH, TR12 7JX, 01326 290513

KILKHAMPTON
Map 2 SS21

Places to visit

Hartland Abbey, BIDEFORD, EX39 6DT, 01237 441234
www.hartlandabbey.com

Great for kids: The Milky Way Adventure Park, CLOVELLY, EX39 5RY,
01237 431255 www.themilkyway.co.uk

Upper Tamar Lake
►►75%

tel: 01288 321712 **Upper Tamar Lake EX23 9SB**
email: info@swlakestrust.org.uk
dir: From A39 at Kilkhampton onto B3254, left in 0.5m onto unclassified road, follow
signs approx 4m to site. **grid ref:** SS288118

A well-trimmed, slightly sloping site overlooking the lake and surrounding
countryside, with several signed walks. The site benefits from the excellent facilities
provided for the watersports centre and coarse anglers, with a rescue launch on the
lake when the flags are flying. A good family site, with Bude's beaches and surfing
waves only eight miles away. 1 acre site. 28 touring pitches. 2 hardstandings.
Caravan pitches. Motorhome pitches. Tent pitches. 3 wooden pods.

Open: Apr-Oct **Last departure:** 11.00hrs

Pitches: 🚐 🚌 Å 🛖

Leisure: ⚠

Facilities: 🏕 ℗ ☀ ⅍ 🚻 ♻ ❶

Services: ⌁ 🍴 🔔

Within 3 miles: ⌦ ⇞ ⌿ 🛍 ↺

Notes: No open fires, off-ground BBQs only, no swimming in lake. Dogs must be kept on
leads. Canoeing, sailing, windsurfing, cycle hire.

LEISURE: 🏊 Indoor swimming pool 🏊 Outdoor swimming pool ⚠ Children's playground 🧒 Kid's club 🎾 Tennis court 🎱 Games room 📺 Separate TV room
⌦ golf course ⇞ Boats for hire 🎬 Cinema 🎵 Entertainment ⌿ Fishing ◉ Mini golf 🏄 Watersports 🏋 Gym 🎯 Sports field Spa ↺ Stables
FACILITIES: 🛁 Bath 🏕 Shower ⊙ Electric shaver ℗ Hairdryer ☀ Ice Pack Facility ⅍ Disabled facilities 🕾 Public telephone 🛍 Shop on site or within 200yds
🛒 Mobile shop (calls at least 5 days a week) 🍴 BBQ area 🚻 Picnic area 📶 Wi-fi 💻 Internet access ♻ Recycling ❶ Tourist info ⤬ Dog exercise area

LANDRAKE
Map 3 SX36

Places to visit

Cotehele, CALSTOCK, PL12 6TA, 01579 351346
www.nationaltrust.org.uk/cotehele

Mount Edgcumbe House & Country Park, TORPOINT, PL10 1HZ, 01752 822236
www.mountedgcumbe.gov.uk

Great for kids: The Monkey Sanctuary, LOOE, PL13 1NZ, 0844 2721271
www.monkeysanctuary.org

PREMIER PARK

Dolbeare Park Caravan and Camping
►►►►► 85%

Best of British
GOLD

tel: 01752 851332 **St Ive Rd PL12 5AF**
email: reception@dolbeare.co.uk **web:** www.dolbeare.co.uk
dir: A38 to Landrake, 4m W of Saltash. At footbridge over A38 turn right, follow signs to site (0.75m from A38). **grid ref:** SX363616

Set in meadowland close to the A38 and the Devon/Cornwall border, this attractive touring park is run by innovative, forward-thinking owners who have adopted a very 'green' approach to running the park. The smart toilet block is very eco-friendly — electronic sensor showers, an on-demand boiler system, flow control valves on the taps, and low-energy lighting, as well as an impressive family room. The park is extremely well presented, with excellent hardstanding pitches, a good tenting field that offers spacious pitches, and good provision for children with a separate ball games paddock and nature trail. Expect high levels of customer care and cleanliness. The on-site shop sells fresh bread and local produce. One pre-erected, fully equipped Eurotent is available for hire. 9 acre site. 60 touring pitches. 54 hardstandings. 12 seasonal pitches. Caravan pitches. Motorhome pitches. Tent pitches.

Open: all year **Last arrival:** 18.00hrs **Last departure:** noon

Pitches: 🚐 🚐 ⛺

Leisure: ⚽ ⊕

Facilities: 🖐 ⊙ 🅿 ✳ ♿ ⊙ 🗑 🖰 📶 💻 ♻ ❷

Services: 🔌 🔲 🛢 ⊘ 🚽 🍴 🛒 🛠

Within 3 miles: ⬇ 🎣 🅿 🖰 🔲 ∪

Notes: No cycling, no kite flying, late arrival fee payable after 18.00hrs. Dogs must be kept on leads. Off-licence, free use of fridge & freezer.

AA Pubs & Restaurants nearby: The Crooked Inn, SALTASH, PL12 4RZ, 01752 848177

See advert below

PITCHES: 🚐 Caravans 🚐 Motorhomes ⛺ Tents 🏕 Glamping-style accommodation **SERVICES:** 🔌 Electric hook up 🅾 Launderette 🍺 Licensed bar 🛢 Calor Gas ⊘ Camping Gaz 🚽 Toilet fluid 🍴 Café/Restaurant 🍟 Fast Food/Takeaway 🔋 Battery charging 🍼 Baby care 🛠 Motorvan service point
ABBREVIATIONS: BH/bank hols – bank holidays Etr – Easter Spring BH – Spring Bank Holiday fr – from hrs – hours m – mile mdnt – midnight rdbt – roundabout rs – restricted service wk – week wknd – weekend x-rds – cross roads 🚫 No credit or debit cards 🚫 No dogs ⭐ Children of all ages accepted

LEEDSTOWN (NEAR HAYLE)
Map 2 SW63

Places to visit

East Pool Mine, POOL, TR15 3NP, 01209 315027 www.nationaltrust.org.uk

Godolphin House, GODOLPHIN CROSS, TR13 9RE, 01736 763194
www.nationaltrust.org.uk/godolphin

PREMIER PARK

Calloose Caravan & Camping Park
►►►► 83%

tel: 01736 850431 & 0800 328 7589 **TR27 5ET**
email: calloose@hotmail.com
dir: *From Hayle take B3302 to Leedstown, turn left opposite village hall before entering village. Site 0.5m on left at bottom of hill.* **grid ref:** *SW597352*

A comprehensively equipped leisure park in a remote rural setting in a small river valley. This very good park is busy and bustling, and offers bright, clean toilet facilities, an excellent games room, an inviting pool, a good children's play area, and log cabins and static caravans for holiday hire. 12.5 acre site. 109 touring pitches. 29 hardstandings. Caravan pitches. Motorhome pitches. Tent pitches. 25 statics.

Open: all year **Last arrival:** 22.00hrs **Last departure:** 11.00hrs

Pitches: ⊡ ⊡ Å

Leisure: ⚞ ⋀ ⌷ ⚟ ⊡

Facilities: ⋔ ⊙ ⨍ ☼ ⅋ ⚲ ⓢ ⓕ ⚲

Services: ⊡ ⊡ ⚟ ⅟ ⓪ ⊘ Ⓣ Ⓞ ⚟ ⚞

Within 3 miles: ⚟ ⓢ ⓢ

Notes: No noise after mdnt, no pets in statics or lodges. Crazy golf, skittle alley.

AA Pubs & Restaurants nearby: Mount Haven Hotel & Restaurant, MARAZION, TR17 0DQ, 01736 710249

LOOE

Places to visit

Antony House, TORPOINT, PL11 2QA, 01752 812191
www.nationaltrust.org.uk/antony

Mount Edgcumbe House & Country Park, TORPOINT, PL10 1HZ, 01752 822236
www.mountedgcumbe.gov.uk

Great for kids: The Monkey Sanctuary, LOOE, PL13 1NZ, 0844 2721271
www.monkeysanctuary.org

LOOE
Map 2 SX25

Tencreek Holiday Park
HOLIDAY CENTRE 81%

tel: 01503 262447 **Polperro Rd PL13 2JR**
email: reception@tencreek.co.uk **web:** www.dolphinholidays.co.uk
dir: *Take A387 1.25m from Looe. Site on left.* **grid ref:** *SX233525*

Occupying a lovely position with extensive countryside and sea views, this holiday centre is in a rural spot but close to Looe and Polperro. There is a full family entertainment programme, with indoor and outdoor swimming pools, an adventure playground and an exciting children's club. The superb amenities blocks include several private family shower rooms with WC and washbasin. 24 acre site. 254 touring pitches. 12 hardstandings. 120 seasonal pitches. Caravan pitches. Motorhome pitches. Tent pitches. 101 statics.

Open: all year **Last arrival:** 23.00hrs **Last departure:** 10.00hrs
Pitches: * ⊡ £12.50-£23.50 ⊡ £12.50-£23.50 Å £12.50-£23.50
Leisure: ⚞ ⋀ ⚟ ⌷ ⚟ ⚟ ♫
Facilities: ⋔ ⊙ ⨍ ☼ ⅋ ⓢ ⓕ ⚲ Ⓦⓘⓕⓘ ⌨ ⚟ ⓘ
Services: ⊡ ⊡ ⚟ ⅟ ⓪ ⊘ Ⓣ Ⓞ ⚟ ⚞ ⚟ ⚟
Within 3 miles: ⌷ ⚟ ⊟ ⅋ ◎ ⚟ ⓢ ⓢ ∪
Notes: Families & couples only. Dogs must be kept on leads.
AA Pubs & Restaurants nearby: Barclay House, LOOE, PL13 1LP, 01503 262929

Trelaske Hotel & Restaurant, LOOE, PL13 2JS, 01503 262159

See advert on opposite page

LEISURE: ⚞ Indoor swimming pool ⚞ Outdoor swimming pool ⋀ Children's playground ⚟ Kid's club ⚟ Tennis court ⚟ Games room ⊡ Separate TV room
⚟ golf course ⚟ Boats for hire ⊟ Cinema ♫ Entertainment ⅋ Fishing ◎ Mini golf ⚞ Watersports ⚟ Gym ⚟ Sports field ⚟ Spa ∪ Stables
FACILITIES: ⚟ Bath ⋔ Shower ⊙ Electric shaver ⨍ Hairdryer ☼ Ice Pack Facility ⅋ Disabled facilities ⓢ Public telephone ⓢ Shop on site or within 200yds
⚟ Mobile shop (calls at least 5 days a week) ⚟ BBQ area ⚟ Picnic area Ⓦⓘⓕⓘ Wi-fi ⌨ Internet access ⚟ Recycling ⓘ Tourist info ⚟ Dog exercise area

Looe Country Park Caravan & Campsite
►►►►84%

tel: 01503 240265 **Bucklawren Rd, St Martin PL13 1NZ**
email: info@looecountrypark.co.uk
dir: *From A38 (Liskeard to Saltash road) at rdbt take A374 signed Looe. Right signed Hessenford. Through Hessenford & Widegates. In No Mans Land follow Monkey Sanctuary signs, turn left to site entrance on right. NB for Sat Nav use PL13 1QS. Roads are narrow.* **grid ref:** *SX283557*

A very neat and well-kept small grassy site on high ground above Looe in a peaceful rural setting. Friendly and enthusiastic owners continue to invest in the park. The toilet facilities have upmarket fittings (note the infra-red operated taps and under floor heating). A bus stops at the bottom of the lane, but you must flag down the driver. A coastal walk runs by the site, and it is a 20-minute walk to the beach at Looe. 3.3 acre site. 31 touring pitches. 19 hardstandings. Caravan pitches. Motorhome pitches. Tent pitches. 5 statics.

Open: all year **Last arrival:** 22.00hrs **Last departure:** 11.00hrs
Pitches: * ⭷ £11-£23.50 ⭷ £11-£23.50 ⭘ £11-£23.50
Leisure: ⺍
Facilities: ⭐☉⭐✳☺⭐⭐⭐ ♻ ⭐
Services: ⭐⭐⭐⭐⭐⭐
Within 3 miles: ⭐⭐⭐◎⭐⭐⭐∪
Notes: Dogs must be kept on leads.
AA Pubs & Restaurants nearby: Barclay House, LOOE, PL13 1LP, 01503 262929
Trelaske Hotel & Restaurant, LOOE, PL13 2JS, 01503 262159

Camping Caradon Touring Park
►►►►82%

tel: 01503 272388 **Trelawne PL13 2NA**
email: enquiries@campingcaradon.co.uk
dir: *Site signed from junct of A387 & B3359, between Looe & Polperro. Take B3359 towards Pelynt & Lanreath. Site on right.* **grid ref:** *SX218539*

Set in a quiet rural location between the popular coastal resorts of Looe and Polperro, this family-run and developing eco-friendly park is just one and half miles from the beach at Talland Bay. The site caters for both families and couples. The owners take great pride in the site and offer some quality facilities and service to their campers throughout their stay; their constant aim is to provide a carefree and relaxing holiday. The local bus stops inside the park entrance. 3.5 acre site. 75 touring pitches. 23 hardstandings. Caravan pitches. Motorhome pitches. Tent pitches.

Open: all year (rs Nov-Mar by booking only) **Last arrival:** 21.00hrs **Last departure:** noon
Pitches: ⭷ ⭷ ⭘
Leisure: ⺍ ⭐
Facilities: ⭐☉⭐✳⭐⭐⭐⭐ ♻ ⭐
Services: ⭐⭐⭐⭐⭐⭐⭐⭐⭐
Within 3 miles: ⭐⭐◎⭐⭐⭐
Notes: Quiet from 23.00hrs-07.00hrs & barrier not operational. Dogs must be kept on leads. Family room with TV, undercover washing-up area, RCD lead hire, rallies welcome.
AA Pubs & Restaurants nearby: The Ship Inn, LOOE, PL13 1AD, 01503 263124
Barclay House, LOOE, PL13 1LP, 01503 262929

PITCHES: ⭷ Caravans ⭷ Motorhomes ⭘ Tents ⭐ Glamping-style accommodation **SERVICES:** ⭐ Electric hook up ⭐ Launderette ⭐ Licensed bar ⭐ Calor Gas ⭐ Camping Gaz ⭐ Toilet fluid ⭐ Café/Restaurant ⭐ Fast Food/Takeaway ⭐ Battery charging ⭐ Baby care ⭐ Motorvan service point
ABBREVIATIONS: BH/bank hols – bank holidays   Etr – Easter   Spring BH – Spring Bank Holiday   fr – from   hrs – hours   m – mile   mdnt – midnight
rdbt – roundabout   rs – restricted service   wk – week   wknd – weekend   x-rds – cross roads   ⭐ No credit or debit cards   ⭐ No dogs   ⭐ Children of all ages accepted

LOOE *continued*

Tregoad Park
▶▶▶▶ 82%

tel: 01503 262718 **St Martin PL13 1PB**
email: info@tregoadpark.co.uk
dir: *Signed with direct access from B3253, or from E on A387 follow B3253 for 1.75m towards Looe. Site on left.* **grid ref:** *SX272560*

Investment continues at this smart, terraced park with extensive sea and rural views, about a mile and a half from Looe. All pitches are level. The facilities are well maintained and spotlessly clean, and there is a swimming pool with adjacent jacuzzi and sun patio, and a licensed bar where bar meals are served in the conservatory. The site has fishing lakes stocked with carp, tench and roach. There is a bus stop at the bottom of the drive for the Plymouth and Truro routes. Static caravans, holiday cottages and two camping pods are available for holiday hire. 55 acre site. 200 touring pitches. 60 hardstandings. Caravan pitches. Motorhome pitches. Tent pitches. 7 statics. Wooden pods.

Open: all year (rs Low season bistro closed) **Last arrival:** 20.00hrs
Last departure: 11.00hrs

Pitches: 🚐 🚗 Å 🏠
Leisure: 🏊 🛝 🎱 ❑
Facilities: 🛁 🚿 ☉ 🪒 ✳ ♿ 🕐 🛒 🎍 🐕 **WiFi**
Services: 🔌 🗑 🍴 🛢 🚮 T 🍽 🛒 🏪 ⬇
Within 3 miles: 🎣 🚤 🎪 🖊 ◎ 🛥 🛒 🎯 ⛵

Notes: Dogs must be kept on leads. Crazy golf, ball sports area.
AA Pubs & Restaurants nearby: Barclay House, LOOE, PL13 1LP, 01503 262929
Trelaske Hotel & Restaurant, LOOE, PL13 2JS, 01503 262159

Trelay Farmpark
▶▶▶ 82%

tel: 01503 220900 **Pelynt PL13 2JX**
email: stay@trelay.co.uk
dir: *From A390 at East Taphouse, take B3359 S towards Looe. After Pelynt, site 0.5m on left. NB due to single track roads it is advisable to follow guide directions not Sat Nav.* **grid ref:** *SX210544*

A small site with a friendly atmosphere set in a pretty rural area with extensive views. The good-size grass pitches are on slightly-sloping ground, and the toilets are immaculately kept, as is the excellent washing-up room. Looe and Polperro are just three miles away. 6.5 acre site. 75 touring pitches. 75 hardstandings. 7 seasonal pitches. Caravan pitches. Motorhome pitches. Tent pitches. 60 statics.

Open: Dec-Oct **Last arrival:** 21.00hrs **Last departure:** 11.00hrs

Pitches: 🚐 🚗 Å
Leisure: 🛝
Facilities: 🚿 ☉ 🪒 ✳ ♿ 🕐 🛒 **WiFi** ♻ ❓
Services: 🔌 🗑 🛢 🚮 T 🏪 ⬇
Within 3 miles: 🚤 🖊 🛥 🛒 ⛵

Notes: No skateboards, ball games or kites. Dogs must be kept on leads. Fridge & freezer.
AA Pubs & Restaurants nearby: The Ship Inn, LOOE, PL13 1AD, 01503 263124
Barclay House, LOOE, PL13 1LP, 01503 262929

LOSTWITHIEL   Map 2 SX15

Places to visit
Restormel Castle, RESTORMEL, PL22 0EE, 01208 872687
www.english-heritage.org.uk/daysout/properties/restormel-castle

Lanhydrock, LANHYDROCK, PL30 5AD, 01208 265950 www.nationaltrust.org.uk

Great for kids: Eden Project, ST AUSTELL, PL24 2SG, 01726 811911
www.edenproject.com

PREMIER PARK

Eden Valley Holiday Park
▶▶▶▶▶ 82%

tel: 01208 872277 **PL30 5BU**
email: enquiries@edenvalleyholidaypark.co.uk
dir: *1.5m SW of Lostwithiel on A390 turn right at brown/white sign in 400mtrs. NB it is advisable to follow guide directions not Sat Nav.* **grid ref:** *SX083593*

A grassy park set in attractive paddocks with mature trees. A gradual upgrading of facilities continues, and both buildings and grounds are carefully maintained and contain an impressive children's play area. This park is ideally located for visiting the Eden Project, the nearby golden beaches and sailing at Fowey. There are also two self-catering lodges. 12 acre site. 56 touring pitches. 40 hardstandings. 20 seasonal pitches. Caravan pitches. Motorhome pitches. Tent pitches. 38 statics.

Open: Etr or Apr-Oct **Last arrival:** 22.00hrs **Last departure:** 11.30hrs

Pitches: 🚐 £13-£17 🚗 £13-£17 Å £13-£17
Leisure: 🛝 ⚽ 🎱
Facilities: 🚿 ☉ 🪒 ✳ ♿ 🕐 🐕 **WiFi** ♻ ❓
Services: 🔌 🗑 🛢 🚮 T 🏪 ⬇
Within 3 miles: 🎣 🚤 🖊 ◎ 🛥 🛒 🎯 ⛵

Notes: Dogs must be kept on leads. Table football, pool, table tennis, football.
AA Pubs & Restaurants nearby: The Crown Inn, LANLIVERY, PL30 5BT, 01208 872707

This symbol indicates that a site offers glamping-style accommodation

---

LEISURE: 🏊 Indoor swimming pool 🏊 Outdoor swimming pool 🛝 Children's playground 🧒 Kid's club 🎾 Tennis court 🎱 Games room ❑ Separate TV room 🏌 golf course 🚤 Boats for hire 🎬 Cinema 🎵 Entertainment 🖊 Fishing ◎ Mini golf 🏄 Watersports 💪 Gym 🏟 Sports field Spa ⛵ Stables
FACILITIES: 🛁 Bath 🚿 Shower ☉ Electric shaver 🪒 Hairdryer ✳ Ice Pack Facility ♿ Disabled facilities 🕐 Public telephone 🛒 Shop on site or within 200yds 🏪 Mobile shop (calls at least 5 days a week) 🍖 BBQ area 🎍 Picnic area **WiFi** Wi-fi 🖥 Internet access ♻ Recycling ❓ Tourist info 🐕 Dog exercise area

LUXULYAN	Map 2 SX05

Places to visit

Restormel Castle, RESTORMEL, PL22 0EE, 01208 872687
www.english-heritage.org.uk/daysout/properties/restormel-castle

Eden Project, ST AUSTELL, PL24 2SG, 01726 811911 www.edenproject.com

Great for kids: Wheal Martyn, ST AUSTELL, PL26 8XG, 01726 850362
www.wheal-martyn.com

Croft Farm Holiday Park
►►►78%

tel: 01726 850228 **PL30 5EQ**
email: enquiries@croftfarm.co.uk
dir: *Exit A30 at Bodmin onto A391 towards St Austell. In 7m left at double rdbt onto unclassified road towards Luxulyan/Eden Project, continue to rdbt at Eden, left signed Luxulyan. Site 1m on left. NB do not approach any other way as roads are very narrow.* **grid ref:** *SX044568*

A peaceful, picturesque setting at the edge of a wooded valley, and only one mile from The Eden Project. Facilities include a well-maintained toilet block, a well-equipped dishwashing area, replete with freezer and microwave, and a revamped children's play area reached via an attractive woodland trail. There is a good bus service to St Austell and Luxulyan (the bus stop is at the site's entrance) and trains run to Newquay. 10.5 acre site. 22 touring pitches. 18 hardstandings. 10 seasonal pitches. Caravan pitches. Motorhome pitches. Tent pitches. 63 statics.

Open: 21 Mar-21 Jan **Last arrival:** 18.00hrs **Last departure:** 11.00hrs

Pitches: * ⌂ £20 ⌂ £20 ⚑ £15

Leisure: ⚑ ✦

Facilities: ⚐⊙ℱ✳☉⑤⩆⚑ WiFi ♻ ❶

Services: ⚑⑤ ⚑⊘⊤⚑

Within 3 miles: ⚑⚑☰ℱ⚑⑤⑤

Notes: No skateboarding, ball games only in playing field, quiet between 23.00hrs-07.00hrs. Dogs must be kept on leads. Woodland walk, information room.

AA Pubs & Restaurants nearby: The Crown Inn, LANLIVERY, PL30 5BT, 01208 872707

Follow us on twitter
@TheAA_Lifestyle

MARAZION	Map 2 SW53

See also St Hilary

Places to visit

St Michael's Mount, MARAZION, TR17 0HT, 01736 710507
www.stmichaelsmount.co.uk

Trengwainton Garden, PENZANCE, TR20 8RZ, 01736 363148
www.nationaltrust.org.uk/trengwainton

Wheal Rodney Holiday Park
►►►82%

tel: 01736 710605 **Gwallon Ln TR17 0HL**
email: reception@whealrodney.co.uk **web:** www.whealrodney.co.uk
dir: *Exit A30 at Crowlas, signed Rospeath. Site 1.5m on right. From Marazion centre turn opposite Fire Engine Inn, site 500mtrs on left.* **grid ref:** *SW525315*

Set in a quiet rural location surrounded by farmland, with level grass pitches and well-kept facilities. Within half a mile are the beach at Marazion and the causeway or ferry to St Michael's Mount. A cycle route is within 400 yards; Penzance is only a short car or cycle ride away. 2.5 acre site. 30 touring pitches. Caravan pitches. Motorhome pitches. Tent pitches.

Open: Etr-Oct **Last arrival:** 20.00hrs **Last departure:** 11.00hrs

Pitches: * ⌂ £16-£24 ⌂ £16-£24 ⚑ £14-£20

Leisure: ⚑

Facilities: ⚐⊙ℱ✳☉⑤ WiFi ♻ ❶

Services: ⚑⑤⚑

Within 3 miles: ⚑ℱ◎⚑⑤⑤U

Notes: Quiet after 22.00hrs. Dogs must be kept on leads.

AA Pubs & Restaurants nearby: The Victoria Inn, PERRANUTHNOE, TR20 9NP, 01736 710309

Mount Haven Hotel & Restaurant, MARAZION, TR17 0DQ, 01736 710249

PITCHES: ⌂ Caravans ⌂ Motorhomes ⚑ Tents ⌂ Glamping-style accommodation **SERVICES:** ⚑ Electric hook up ⑤ Launderette ⬚ Licensed bar ⬛ Calor Gas ⊘ Camping Gaz ⊤ Toilet fluid ℡ Café/Restaurant ⬚ Fast Food/Takeaway ⚑ Battery charging ⚑ Baby care ⚑ Motorvan service point
ABBREVIATIONS: BH/bank hols – bank holidays Etr – Easter Spring BH – Spring Bank Holiday fr – from hrs – hours m – mile mdnt – midnight rdbt – roundabout rs – restricted service wk – week wknd – weekend x-rds – cross roads ⊘ No credit or debit cards ⊗ No dogs ⚑ Children of all ages accepted

MAWGAN PORTH
Map 2 SW86

Sun Haven Valley Holiday Park
►►►► 83%

tel: 01637 860373 & 0800 6346744 **TR8 4BQ**
email: sunhaven@sunhavenvalley.com
dir: Exit A30 at Highgate Hill junct for Newquay; follow signs for airport. At T-junct turn right. At beach level in Mawgan Porth take only road inland, then 0.25m. Site 0.5m beyond 'S' bend. **grid ref:** SW861669

An attractive site with level pitches on the side of a river valley; being just off the B3276 this makes an ideal base for touring the Padstow and Newquay areas. The very high quality facilities include a TV lounge and a games room in a Swedish-style chalet, and a well-kept adventure playground. Trees and hedges fringe the park, and the ground is well drained. 5 acre site. 109 touring pitches. 11 hardstandings. Caravan pitches. Motorhome pitches. Tent pitches. 38 statics.

Open: Apr-Oct **Last arrival:** 22.00hrs **Last departure:** 10.30hrs

Pitches: ⊕ ⇌ Å

Leisure: ⚑ ◀ ⬚

Facilities: ⊨ ⌢ ⊙ ℱ ⚹ ⅙ ⊘ ⑤ WiFi ▦ ♻ ❶

Services: ⊡ ⑤ ⬛ ⊘ T

Within 3 miles: ↨ ℐ ◎ ⩦ ⑤ ⑤ ↻

Notes: Families & couples only. Dogs must be kept on leads. Microwave available, pizza ovens.

AA Pubs & Restaurants nearby: The Falcon Inn, ST MAWGAN, TR8 4EP, 01637 860225
The Scarlet Hotel, MAWGAN PORTH, TR8 4DQ, 01637 861800

Trevarrian Holiday Park
►►► 80%

tel: 01637 860381 & 0845 2255910 **TR8 4AQ**
email: holiday@trevarrian.co.uk
dir: From A39 at St Columb rdbt turn right onto A3059 towards Newquay. Fork right in approx 2m for St Mawgan onto B3276. Turn right, site on left. **grid ref:** SW853661

A well-established and well-run holiday park overlooking Mawgan Porth beach. This park has a wide range of attractions including a free entertainment programme in peak season and a 10-pin bowling alley with licensed bar. It is only a short drive to Newquay and approximately 20 minutes to Padstow. 7 acre site. 185 touring pitches. 10 hardstandings. Caravan pitches. Motorhome pitches. Tent pitches.

Open: all year **Last arrival:** 22.00hrs **Last departure:** 11.00hrs

Pitches: ⊕ ⇌ Å

Leisure: ⇌ ⚑ ☺ ◀ ⬚ ♫

Facilities: ⊨ ⌢ ⊙ ℱ ⚹ ⅙ ⊘ ⑤ ⇥ WiFi ♻ ❶

Services: ⊡ ⑤ ⑪ ⬛ ⊘ T ⑪ ⬚ ⬛ ↯

Within 3 miles: ↨ ⩱ ⽬ ℐ ◎ ⑤ ⑤ ↻

Notes: No noise after mdnt. Dogs must be kept on leads. Crazy golf.

AA Pubs & Restaurants nearby: The Falcon Inn, ST MAWGAN, TR8 4EP, 01637 860225

MEVAGISSEY
Map 2 SX04

See also Gorran & Pentewan

PREMIER PARK

Seaview International Holiday Park
►►►►► 93%

tel: 01726 843425 **Boswinger PL26 6LL**
email: holidays@seaviewinternational.com **web:** www.seaviewinternational.com
dir: From St Austell take B3273 signed Mevagissey. Turn right before entering village. Follow brown tourist signs to site. NB very narrow lanes to this site; it is advisable to follow guide directions not Sat Nav. **grid ref:** SW990412

An attractive holiday park set in a beautiful environment overlooking Veryan Bay, with colourful landscaping, including attractive flowers and shrubs. It continues to offer an outstanding holiday experience, with its luxury family pitches, super toilet facilities, takeaway, shop and an alfresco eating area complete with a TV screen. The beach is just half a mile away. There is also an 'off the lead' dog walk, and a 'ring and ride' bus service to Truro, St Austell and Plymouth stops at the park gate. Static caravans are available for holiday hire. 28 acre site. 201 touring pitches. 29 hardstandings. 15 seasonal pitches. Caravan pitches. Motorhome pitches. Tent pitches. 39 statics.

Open: Mar-end Sep (rs mid Sep-end May swimming pool closed) **Last arrival:** 20.00hrs **Last departure:** 10.00hrs

Pitches: ⊕ ⇌ Å

Leisure: ⇌ ⚑ ⬔ ☺

Facilities: ⊨ ⌢ ⊙ ℱ ⚹ ⅙ ⑤ ⇥ ⇥ WiFi ▦ ♻ ❶

Services: ⊡ ⑤ ⬛ ⊘ T ⑪ ⬚ ⬛ ↯

LEISURE: ⚐ Indoor swimming pool ⚐ Outdoor swimming pool ⚑ Children's playground ⚑ Kid's club ☺ Tennis court ◀ Games room ⬚ Separate TV room ↨ golf course ⩱ Boats for hire ⽬ Cinema ♫ Entertainment ℐ Fishing ◎ Mini golf ⩦ Watersports ⑪ Gym ⬔ Sports field Spa ↻ Stables
FACILITIES: ⊨ Bath ⌢ Shower ⊙ Electric shaver ℱ Hairdryer ⚹ Ice Pack Facility ⅙ Disabled facilities ⊘ Public telephone ⑤ Shop on site or within 200yds ⑤ Mobile shop (calls at least 5 days a week) ⬛ BBQ area ⇥ Picnic area WiFi Wi-fi ▦ Internet access ♻ Recycling ❶ Tourist info ⇥ Dog exercise area

Within 3 miles: ⚓ 🎣 ◎ ⛷ 🏠 🗿

Notes: Restrictions on certain dog breeds. Dogs must be kept on leads. Crazy golf, volleyball, badminton, scuba diving, boules, tennis.

AA Pubs & Restaurants nearby: The Ship Inn, MEVAGISSEY, PL26 6UQ, 01726 843324

See advert below

MULLION
Map 2 SW61

Places to visit

Great for kids: Cornish Seal Sanctuary, GWEEK, TR12 6UG, 01326 221361 www.sealsanctuaries.com

The Flambards Theme Park, HELSTON, TR13 0QA, 01326 573404 www.flambards.co.uk

---

Mullion Holiday Park
HOLIDAY CENTRE 78%

tel: 0844 335 3756 & 01326 240428 **Ruan Minor TR12 7LJ**
email: touringandcamping@parkdeanholidays.com
dir: *A30 onto A39 through Truro towards Falmouth. A394 to Helston, A3083 for The Lizard. Site 7m on left.* **grid ref:** *SW699182*

A comprehensively-equipped leisure park geared mainly for self-catering holidays, and set close to the sandy beaches, coves and fishing villages on The Lizard peninsula. There is plenty of on-site entertainment for all ages, with indoor and outdoor swimming pools and a bar and grill. 49 acre site. 80 touring pitches. 9 hardstandings. Caravan pitches. Motorhome pitches. Tent pitches. 305 statics.

Open: Apr-Oct (rs 3 May-22 Sep outdoor pool open) **Last arrival:** 22.00hrs
Last departure: 10.00hrs

Pitches: 🚐 🚙 🛖 Å

Leisure: 🏊 🏊 ⚑ 🎣 ◎ ⚲ ⬛ 🎵

Facilities: 🐾 ⊙ 🎣 ✳ ⚃ ◐ 🛁 🚻 🚿 WiFi 🖥 ♻ ✪

Services: 🔌 🛢 🍺 🛒 🧺 ☍ 🚽 🍽 ⛲

Within 3 miles: 🛶 🎣 ◎ ⛷ 🏠 🗿 ∪

Notes: Dogs must be kept on leads. Scuba diving, football pitch, surf & cycle hire, multi-sports court.

AA Pubs & Restaurants nearby: The Halzephron Inn, GUNWALLOE, TR12 7QB, 01326 240406

Franchis Holiday Park
▶▶▶ 77%

tel: 01326 240301 **Cury Cross Lanes TR12 7AZ**
email: enquiries@franchis.co.uk **web:** www.franchis.co.uk
dir: *Exit A3083 on left 0.5m past Wheel Inn PH, between Helston & The Lizard.*
grid ref: *SW698203*

A mainly grassy site surrounded by hedges and trees, located on Goonhilly Downs and in an ideal position for exploring the Lizard Peninsula. The site is divided into two paddocks for tourers, and the pitches are a mix of level and slightly sloping. There are good facilities for families, and for a fun-filled family day out Flambards

continued

PITCHES: 🚐 Caravans 🚙 Motorhomes Å Tents ⛺ Glamping-style accommodation **SERVICES:** 🔌 Electric hook up 🛢 Launderette 🍺 Licensed bar 🛢 Calor Gas 🫗 Camping Gaz T Toilet fluid 🍽 Café/Restaurant ⛲ Fast Food/Takeaway 🔋 Battery charging 🍼 Baby care 🛠 Motorvan service point
ABBREVIATIONS: BH/bank hols – bank holidays Etr – Easter Spring BH – Spring Bank Holiday fr – from hrs – hours m – mile mdnt – midnight rdbt – roundabout rs – restricted service wk – week wknd – weekend x-rds – cross roads 🚫 No credit or debit cards 🚫 No dogs 👶 Children of all ages accepted

MULLION *continued*

Experience is less than 20 minutes' drive away in Helston. 16 acre site. 57 touring pitches. 14 seasonal pitches. Caravan pitches. Motorhome pitches. Tent pitches. 12 statics.

Franchis Holiday Park

Open: Apr-Oct **Last arrival:** 20.00hrs **Last departure:** 10.30hrs

Pitches: 🚐 🚏 ▲

Facilities: 🏪 ☉ ❋ 🛒 🚽 📶 ♻ ❶

Services: 🔲 🔊 🛢 🧹 🅣 🏬

Within 3 miles: 🎣 🦆 🏌 🛒 🛍 ∪

Notes: Dogs must be kept on leads.

AA Pubs & Restaurants nearby: The Halzephron Inn, GUNWALLOE, TR12 7QB, 01326 240406

See advert below

NEWQUAY Map 2 SW86

See also Rejerrah

Places to visit

Blue Reef Aquarium, NEWQUAY, TR7 1DU, 01637 878134
www.bluereefaquarium.co.uk

Trerice, TRERICE, TR8 4PG, 01637 875404 www.nationaltrust.org.uk/trerice/

Great for kids: Dairy Land Farm World, NEWQUAY, TR8 5AA, 01872 510246
www.dairylandfarmworld.com

Newquay Zoo, NEWQUAY, TR7 2LZ, 0844 474 2244 www.newquayzoo.org.uk

Newquay Holiday Park
HOLIDAY CENTRE 81%

tel: 0844 335 3756 **TR8 4HS**
email: touringandcamping@parkdeanholidays.com
dir: *From Bodmin on A30, under low bridge, right towards RAF St Mawgan. Take A3059 towards Newquay, site past Treloy Golf Club.* **grid ref:** *SW853626*

A well-maintained park with a wide range of indoor and outdoor activities. A children's playground and bar and grill enhance the facilities, and the club and bars offer quality entertainment. Three heated outdoor pools and a giant waterslide are very popular. 60 acre site. 53 touring pitches. 10 hardstandings. Caravan pitches. Motorhome pitches. Tent pitches. 312 statics.

Open: Apr-Oct (rs 3 May-22 Sep outdoor pool complex open) **Last arrival:** 21.00hrs
Last departure: 10.00hrs

Pitches: 🚐 🚏 ▲ **Leisure:** ⛱ ⚟ 🏓 🎱 ▢ 🎵

Facilities: 🏪 ☉ 🏌 ❋ ⛵ ⏰ 🛍 🎋 🚽 📶

Services: 🔲 🔊 🍴 🛢 🧹 🅣 🍴 🏬 ⛲ 🚿

Within 3 miles: 🎣 🦆 🏌 ◎ 🛍 🛍 ∪

Notes: Dogs must be kept on leads.

AA Pubs & Restaurants nearby: The Lewinnick Lodge Bar & Restaurant, NEWQUAY, TR7 1NX, 01637 878117

LEISURE: 🏊 Indoor swimming pool 🏊 Outdoor swimming pool ⚟ Children's playground 👦 Kid's club 🎾 Tennis court 🎱 Games room ▢ Separate TV room 🏌 golf course 🚣 Boats for hire 🎬 Cinema 🎵 Entertainment 🎣 Fishing ◎ Mini golf 🏄 Watersports 🏋 Gym 🏟 Sports field Spa ∪ Stables
FACILITIES: 🛁 Bath 🚿 Shower ☉ Electric shaver 🎀 Hairdryer ❋ Ice Pack Facility ♿ Disabled facilities 📞 Public telephone 🛍 Shop on site or within 200yds 🛒 Mobile shop (calls at least 5 days a week) 🍴 BBQ area 🌲 Picnic area 📶 Wi-fi 💻 Internet access ♻ Recycling ❶ Tourist info 🐕 Dog exercise area

Hendra Holiday Park
►►►►►84%

Best of British

tel: 01637 875778 **TR8 4NY**
email: enquiries@hendra-holidays.com **web:** www.hendra-holidays.com
dir: *A30 onto A392 signed Newquay. At Quintrell Downs over rdbt, signed Lane, site 0.5m on left.* **grid ref:** *SW833601*

A large complex with holiday statics and superb facilities including an indoor fun pool and an outdoor pool. There is a children's club for the over 6s, evening entertainment during high season, a skateboard park, fish and chip shop and a fantastic coffee shop. The 12 touring pitches are set amongst mature trees and shrubs, and some have fully serviced facilities. All amenities are open to the public. This site generates most of its own electricity from a 1.5 megawatt solar farm. The glamping pod area has 10 kitted-out pods for hire. 80 acre site. 548 touring pitches. 28 hardstandings. Caravan pitches. Motorhome pitches. Tent pitches. 307 statics. 6 wooden pods.

Open: 25 Mar-4 Nov (rs Apr-Spring BH & Sep-Oct outdoor pool closed)
Last arrival: dusk **Last departure:** 10.00hrs
Pitches: * 🚐 £12.90-£22.23 🚙 £12.90-£22.23 Å £12.90-£22.23 🏠
Leisure: 🏊 🏊 🎯 🎢 ⚽ 🎣 🎱 🎵
Facilities: 🎣 ☉ 🍴 ☼ ♿ ⓒ 🛁 🚻 🌐 💻 ♻ ❶
Services: 🔌 🔥 🍴 🛢 🚰 T ☕ 🧺 🍴 🚐 ♿
Within 3 miles: 🎿 🚴 🎡 🏌 ◎ 🛥 🏰 🏰 U

Notes: Families & couples only. Dogs must be kept on leads. Solarium, train rides, skate & scooter park.
AA Pubs & Restaurants nearby: The Lewinnick Lodge Bar & Restaurant, NEWQUAY, TR7 1NX, 01637 878117
See advert on page 89

Trencreek Holiday Park
►►►►86%

tel: 01637 874210 **Hillcrest, Higher Trencreek TR8 4NS**
email: trencreek@btconnect.com
dir: *A392 to Quintrell Downs, right towards Newquay, left at 2 mini-rdbts into Trevenson Rd to site.* **grid ref:** *SW828609*

An attractively landscaped park in the village of Trencreek, with modern toilet facilities of a very high standard. Two well-stocked fishing lakes, and evening entertainment in the licensed clubhouse, are extra draws. Located about two miles from Newquay with its beaches and surfing opportunities. 10 acre site. 194 touring pitches. 8 hardstandings. Caravan pitches. Motorhome pitches. Tent pitches. 6 statics.

Open: Spring BH-mid Sep **Last arrival:** 22.00hrs **Last departure:** noon
Pitches: 🚐 🚙 Å
Leisure: 🏊 🎢 🎣 🖵
Facilities: 🎣 ☉ 🍴 ☼ ♿ ⓒ 🛁 🚻 🌐 💻 ❶
Services: 🔌 🔥 🍴 🛢 🚰 T ☕ 🧺 🚐
Within 3 miles: 🎿 🚴 🎡 🏌 ◎ 🛥 🏰 🏰 U

Notes: 🚫 Families & couples only.
AA Pubs & Restaurants nearby: The Lewinnick Lodge Bar & Restaurant, NEWQUAY, TR7 1NX, 01637 878117

Porth Beach Tourist Park
►►►►82%

🏰 BRONZE

tel: 01637 876531 **Porth TR7 3NH**
email: info@porthbeach.co.uk **web:** www.porthbeach.co.uk
dir: *1m NE off B3276 towards Padstow.* **grid ref:** *SW834629*

This attractive, popular park offers level, grassy pitches in neat and tidy surroundings. It is a well-run site set in meadowland in a glorious location adjacent to excellent sands of Porth Beach. The site offers two fully-equipped camping pods

continued

NEWQUAY *continued*

positioned on a raised terrace. 6 acre site. 200 touring pitches. 19 hardstandings. Caravan pitches. Motorhome pitches. Tent pitches. 18 statics. 2 wooden pods.

Porth Beach Tourist Park

Open: Mar-Nov **Last arrival:** 18.00hrs **Last departure:** 10.00hrs

Pitches: 🚐 🚙 ▲ 🛖

Leisure: ⚠

Facilities: ⌂ ⊙ 🚿 ⚹ 🔅 WiFi ♻ ℹ

Services: 🔲 🔲 🔒 🛒 🚽

Within 3 miles: ⤢ 🐟 ⚽ 🎯 ◎ 🏊 🔲 🔲 ♨

Notes: Families & couples only. Dogs must be kept on leads.

AA Pubs & Restaurants nearby: The Lewinnick Lodge Bar & Restaurant, NEWQUAY, TR7 1NX, 01637 878117

See advert on page 89

Treloy Touring Park
▶▶▶▶81%

tel: 01637 872063 **TR8 4JN**
email: stay@treloy.co.uk **web:** www.treloy.co.uk
dir: On A3059 (St Columb Major-Newquay road). **grid ref:** SW858625

SILVER

An attractive site with fine countryside views, that is within easy reach of resorts and beaches. The pitches are set in four paddocks with mainly level but some slightly sloping grassy areas. Maintenance and cleanliness are very high. There is a heated swimming pool and separate paddling pool surrounded by a paved patio

---

area with tables; a new reception, shop and first aid room were added in 2014. 18 acre site. 223 touring pitches. 30 hardstandings. 15 seasonal pitches. Caravan pitches. Motorhome pitches. Tent pitches.

Open: Etr or Apr-Sep (rs Apr-mid May & Sep pool, takeaway, shop & bar closed)
Last arrival: 21.00hrs **Last departure:** 10.00hrs

Pitches: 🚐 🚙 ▲

Leisure: ⚽ ⚠ ⚽ ⊙ ● 🔲 🎵

Facilities: ⌂ ⊙ 🚿 ⚹ 🔅 ⊙ 🔲 🚻 WiFi ♻ ℹ

Services: 🔲 🔲 🍽 🔒 🛒 ⊤ 🍴 🚽 🛒 🚽

Within 3 miles: ⤢ 🐟 ⚽ 🎯 ◎ 🏊 🔲 🔲 ♨

Notes: Concessionary green fees at Treloy Golf Club.

AA Pubs & Restaurants nearby: The Lewinnick Lodge Bar & Restaurant, NEWQUAY, TR7 1NX, 01637 878117

See advert on opposite page

Trethiggey Holiday Park
▶▶▶▶81%

GOLD

tel: 01637 877672 **Quintrell Downs TR8 4QR**
email: enquiries@trethiggey.co.uk **web:** www.trethiggey.co.uk
dir: A30 onto A392 signed Newquay at Quintrell Downs rdbt, left onto A3058, pass Newquay Pearl centre. Site 0.5m on left. **grid ref:** SW846596

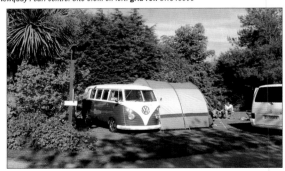

A family-owned park in a rural setting that is ideal for touring this part of Cornwall. It is pleasantly divided into paddocks with maturing trees and shrubs, and offers coarse fishing and tackle hire. This site has a car park for campers as the camping fields are set in a car-free zone for children's safety. 15 acre site. 200 touring

---

pitches. 35 hardstandings. 12 seasonal pitches. Caravan pitches. Motorhome pitches. Tent pitches. 12 statics.

Open: Mar-Dec **Last arrival:** 22.00hrs **Last departure:** 10.30hrs

Pitches: * ⊞ £11.30-£17.90 ⊞ £11.30-£17.90 Å £11.30-£17.90

Leisure: ⚙ ◖ ▢

Facilities: ➤ ⋔ ☉ ⌕ ☀ ⅋ ⚲ ⓢ 丹 ⌁ WiFi ▭ ♻ ❶

Services: ⊡ ⊟ ⊞ 🗋 ⊘ T ⦿ 🏋 ⛟ ➷ ⛛

Within 3 miles: ⅃ ⚵ 彐 ⌒ ◎ ⩥ ⑤ ⊟ ∪

Notes: No noise after mdnt. Dogs must be kept on leads. Off-licence, recreation field.

AA Pubs & Restaurants nearby: The Lewinnick Lodge Bar & Restaurant, NEWQUAY, TR7 1NX, 01637 878117

See advert on page 88

Trenance Holiday Park
►►►►78%

tel: 01637 873447 **Edgcumbe Av TR7 2JY**
email: enquiries@trenanceholidaypark.co.uk
dir: *Exit A3075 near viaduct. Site by boating lake rdbt.* **grid ref:** *SW818612*

A mainly static park popular with tenters, close to Newquay's vibrant nightlife, and serving excellent breakfasts and takeaways. Set on high ground in an urban area of town, with cheerful owners and clean facilities. The local bus stops at the site entrance. 12 acre site. 50 touring pitches. Caravan pitches. Motorhome pitches. Tent pitches. 190 statics.

Open: 21 Apr-22 Sep **Last arrival:** 22.00hrs **Last departure:** 10.00hrs

Pitches: ⊞ ⊞ Å

Leisure: ◖

Facilities: ⋔ ☉ ⌕ ☀ ⅋ ⚲ ⓢ WiFi ▭ ♻ ❶

Services: ⊡ ⊟ 🗋 ⊘ T ⦿ 🏋 ⛟ ➷

Within 3 miles: ⅃ ⚵ 彐 ⌒ ◎ ⩥ ⑤ ⊟ ∪

Notes: No pets.

AA Pubs & Restaurants nearby: The Lewinnick Lodge Bar & Restaurant, NEWQUAY, TR7 1NX, 01637 878117

PITCHES: ⊞ Caravans ⊞ Motorhomes Å Tents ⋒ Glamping-style accommodation **SERVICES:** ⊡ Electric hook up ⊟ Launderette 🍺 Licensed bar 🗋 Color Gas ⊘ Camping Gaz T Toilet fluid ⦿ Café/Restaurant 🏋 Fast Food/Takeaway ⛟ Battery charging ➷ Baby care ⛛ Motorvan service point
ABBREVIATIONS: BH/bank hols – bank holidays Etr – Easter Spring BH – Spring Bank Holiday fr – from hrs – hours m – mile mdnt – midnight
rdbt – roundabout rs – restricted service wk – week wknd – weekend x-rds – cross roads 🚫 No credit or debit cards 🚫 No dogs ⅊ Children of all ages accepted

NEWQUAY *continued*

Trebellan Park
►►►84%

tel: 01637 830522 **Cubert TR8 5PY**
email: enquiries@trebellan.co.uk
dir: *4m S of Newquay, turn W off A3075 at Cubert sign. Left in 0.75m onto unclassified road.* **grid ref:** *SW790571*

A terraced grassy rural park within a picturesque valley with views of Cubert Common, and adjacent to the Smuggler's Den, a 16th-century thatched inn. This park has a very inviting swimming pool and three well-stocked coarse fishing lakes. 8 acre site. 150 touring pitches. Caravan pitches. Motorhome pitches. Tent pitches. 7 statics.

Open: May-Oct **Last arrival:** 21.00hrs **Last departure:** 10.00hrs

Pitches: * � £20-£26 ⌔ £20-£26 Å £15-£19

Leisure: 🏊 ⛰ ▭

Facilities: 🚿 ☺ 🪒 ✳ ♿ 🕓 🛒 📶 🖥

Services: 🔌 🛢 🛒

Within 3 miles: 🎣 ⚡ ◎ ≋ 🐴 🛍 ♿ ↻

Notes: Families & couples only. Dogs must be kept on leads.

AA Pubs & Restaurants nearby: The Smugglers' Den Inn, CUBERT, TR8 5PY, 01637 830209

The Lewinnick Lodge Bar & Restaurant, NEWQUAY, TR7 1NX, 01637 878117

Riverside Holiday Park
►►►80%

tel: 01637 873617 **Gwills Ln TR8 4PE**
email: info@riversideholidaypark.co.uk **web:** www.riversideholidaypark.co.uk
dir: *A30 onto A392 signed Newquay. At Quintrell Downs cross rdbt signed Lane. 2nd left in 0.5m onto unclassified road signed Gwills. Site in 400yds.* **grid ref:** *SW829592*

A sheltered valley beside a river in a quiet location is the idyllic setting for this lightly wooded park that caters for families and couples only; the site is well placed for exploring Newquay and Padstow. There is a lovely swimming pool. The site is close to the wide variety of attractions offered by this major resort. Self-catering lodges, cabins and static vans are for hire. 11 acre site. 65 touring pitches. Caravan pitches. Motorhome pitches. Tent pitches. 65 statics.

Open: Mar-Oct **Last arrival:** 22.00hrs **Last departure:** 10.00hrs

Pitches: ⌔ £15-£20 ⌔ £15-£20 Å £15-£20

Leisure: 🏊 ⛰ 🔫 ▭ **Facilities:** 🚿 ☺ 🪒 ✳ ♿ 🕓 🛒 📶 ♻ ❶

Services: 🔌 🛢 🛒 🛢 🔧 📦 🚽 🛒 🪣

Within 3 miles: 🎣 ⛵ 🎬 ⚡ ◎ ≋ 🐴 🛍 ♿ ↻

Notes: Families & couples only. Dogs must be kept on leads.

AA Pubs & Restaurants nearby: The Lewinnick Lodge Bar & Restaurant, NEWQUAY, TR7 1NX, 01637 878117

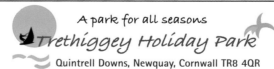
LEISURE: 🏊 Indoor swimming pool 🏊 Outdoor swimming pool ⛰ Children's playground 🔫 Kid's club 🎾 Tennis court 🔫 Games room ▭ Separate TV room 🎣 golf course ⛵ Boats for hire 🎬 Cinema 🎵 Entertainment ⚡ Fishing ◎ Mini golf ≋ Watersports 🐴 Gym ❂ Sports field Spa ↻ Stables
FACILITIES: 🛁 Bath 🚿 Shower ☺ Electric shaver 🪒 Hairdryer ✳ Ice Pack Facility ♿ Disabled facilities 🕓 Public telephone 🛒 Shop on site or within 200yds 🏪 Mobile shop (calls at least 5 days a week) 🍖 BBQ area 🪑 Picnic area 📶 Wi-fi 🖥 Internet access ♻ Recycling ❶ Tourist info 🐕 Dog exercise area

PADSTOW

Map 2 SW97

See also Rumford

Places to visit

Prideaux Place, PADSTOW, PL28 8RP, 01841 532411 www.prideauxplace.co.uk

Great for kids: Devon's Crealy Great Adventure Park, CLYST ST MARY, EX5 1DR, 01395 233200 www.crealy.co.uk

PREMIER PARK

Padstow Touring Park

►►►►► 96%

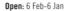

GOLD

tel: 01841 532061 **PL28 8LE**
email: bookings@padstowtouringpark.co.uk
dir: *1m S of Padstow, on E side of A389 Padstow to Wadebridge road.*
grid ref: SW913738

Improvements continue at this top quality park set in open countryside above the quaint fishing town of Padstow, which can be approached via a footpath directly from the park. This site is divided into paddocks by maturing bushes and hedges that create a peaceful and relaxing holiday atmosphere. The main facility block, extended and upgraded for 2014, has been designed and decorated to a very high standard, plus there is an improved children's play area, a well-stocked shop and an excellent café with a decked terrace offering country views. 13.5 acre site. 150 touring pitches. 39 hardstandings. Caravan pitches. Motorhome pitches. Tent pitches. 12 statics.

Open: all year **Last arrival:** 21.00hrs **Last departure:** 11.00hrs

Pitches: * ⊞ £17–£30.50 ⊞ £12–£30.50 ▲ £12–£30.50

Leisure: ⚐

Facilities: ⬡⊙☞✳⬣⬢⬣☴⊞ WIFI ▣ ♻ ❶

Services: ▣⬡ ⬢⬢⊤⬢⬢⬢

Within 3 miles: ⬥⬢⬢⬢⬢⬢⬢⬢

Notes: No groups, no noise after 22.00hrs. Dogs must be kept on leads. Coffee shop.

AA Pubs & Restaurants nearby: The Seafood Restaurant, PADSTOW, PL28 8BY, 01841 532700

Paul Ainsworth at No. 6, PADSTOW, PL28 8AP, 01841 532093

Padstow Holiday Park

HOLIDAY HOME PARK 78%

BRONZE

tel: 01841 532289 **Cliffdowne PL28 8LB**
email: alex@padstowholidaypark.co.uk
dir: *Exit A39 onto either A389 or B3274 to Padstow. Site signed 1.5m before Padstow.*
grid ref: SW009073

In an Area of Outstanding Natural Beauty and within a mile of the historic fishing village of Padstow, which can be reached via a footpath, this static-only park with 12 well-equipped units for hire aims to provide comfortable relaxing accommodation in a quiet and peaceful atmosphere. With no clubhouse or pool on site, it is ideal for families and couples who want a quiet base that is convenient for all the attractions Cornwall has to offer.

Open: 6 Feb-6 Jan

Statics: 12 Sleeps 4 Bedrms 2 Bathrms 1 (inc en suite) Toilets 2 Microwave Freezer TV Sky/FTV DVD Modem/Wi-fi Elec inc Gas inc Grass area Garden/patio furniture Low season £200–£220 High season £520–£690

Children: ⬤⬤ Cots Highchair Child gate

Leisure: ⚐

Within 3 miles: ⬢⬢⬢

PENTEWAN

Map 2 SX04

Places to visit

The Lost Gardens of Heligan, PENTEWAN, PL26 6EN, 01726 845100 www.heligan.com

Charlestown Shipwreck & Heritage Centre, ST AUSTELL, PL25 3NJ, 01726 69897 www.shipwreckcharlestown.com

Great for kids: Eden Project, ST AUSTELL, PL24 2SG, 01726 811911 www.edenproject.com

PREMIER PARK

Sun Valley Resort

►►►►► 85%

tel: 01726 843266 & 844393 **Pentewan Rd PL26 6DJ**
email: hello@sunvalleyresort.co.uk **web:** www.sunvalleyresort.co.uk
dir: *From St Austell take B3273 towards Mevagissey. Site 2m on right.*
grid ref: SX005486

In a picturesque wooded valley, this neat park has new, experienced owners and the high standards have been maintained, with excellent improvements to the bar, restaurant and pool areas. The extensive amenities include tennis courts, indoor swimming pool, takeaway, licensed clubhouse and restaurant. The sea is just a mile away, and can be accessed via a footpath and cycle path along the river bank. Bicycles can be hired on site. A public bus stops at the site entrance. 20 acre site. 29 touring pitches. 13 hardstandings. Caravan pitches. Motorhome pitches. Tent pitches. 75 statics.

Open: all year (rs Winter pool, restaurant & touring field) **Last arrival:** 22.00hrs
Last departure: 10.30hrs

Pitches: 🚐 🚑 🏕 **Leisure:** 🏊 ⚠ ⚽ 🎱 🎵

Facilities: 🐾 ⊙ 🅿 ❋ ♿ 🕤 🛉 🚻 🛒 WIFI 🗑 🚻 ℹ

Services: 🔌 🗑 🍺 🛢 🗑 🍽 ⛽ 🔋 ↯ **Within 3 miles:** 🚶 🎣 🗓 🗑 🛒 🗑 ⛳

Notes: No motorised scooters, skateboards or bikes at night, certain pet restrictions apply - please contact the site for details. Dogs must be kept on leads. Pets' corner, outdoor & indoor play areas.

AA Pubs & Restaurants nearby: The Crown Inn, ST EWE, PL26 6EY, 01726 843322

See advert below

Heligan Woods

▶▶▶ 85%

tel: 01726 842714 & 844414 **PL26 6BT**
email: info@pentewan.co.uk
dir: From A390 take B3273 for Mevagissey at x-roads signed 'No caravans beyond this point'. Right onto unclassified road towards Gorran, site 0.75m on left.
grid ref: SW998470

A pleasant peaceful park adjacent to the Lost Gardens of Heligan, with views over St Austell Bay and well-maintained facilities. Guests can also use the extensive amenities at the sister park, Pentewan Sands, and there's a footpath with direct access to Heligan Gardens. 12 acre site. 89 touring pitches. 24 hardstandings. 3 seasonal pitches. Caravan pitches. Motorhome pitches. Tent pitches. 17 statics.

Open: 16 Jan–26 Nov (rs 9-11am & 5-6pm reception open) **Last arrival:** 22.00hrs
Last departure: 10.30hrs

Pitches: 🚐 🚑 🏕

Leisure: ⚠

Facilities: 🛁 🐾 ⊙ 🅿 🕤 🛉 🚻

Services: 🔌 🗑 🍺 🗑 🔋 ↯

Within 3 miles: 🚶 🎣 🗓 🗑 🛒 🗑 ⛳

AA Pubs & Restaurants nearby: Austell's, ST AUSTELL, PL25 3PH, 01726 813888

PITCHES: 🚐 Caravans 🚑 Motorhomes 🏕 Tents ⛺ Glamping-style accommodation **SERVICES:** 🔌 Electric hook up 🗑 Launderette 🍺 Licensed bar 🛢 Calor Gas ⊘ Camping Gaz 🅣 Toilet fluid 🍽 Café/Restaurant 🍟 Fast Food/Takeaway 🔋 Battery charging 👶 Baby care ↯ Motorvan service point
ABBREVIATIONS: BH/bank hols – bank holidays Etr – Easter Spring BH – Spring Bank Holiday fr – from hrs – hours m – mile mdnt – midnight rdbt – roundabout rs – restricted service wk – week wknd – weekend x-rds – cross roads 🚫 No credit or debit cards 🚫 No dogs 👫 Children of all ages accepted

PENTEWAN *continued*

Little Winnick Touring Park
► ► ►85%

tel: 01726 843687 **PL26 6DL**
email: mail@littlewinnick.co.uk **web:** www.littlewinnick.co.uk
dir: *A390 to St Austell, then B3273 towards Mevagissey, site in 3m on left.*
grid ref: SX007482

A small, well maintained rural site within walking distance of Pentewan and its beautiful beach. It has neat level pitches, including some hardstanding pitches, an excellent children's play area, and quality toilet and facility blocks. It borders the River Winnick and also the Pentewan cycle trail from St Austell to Pentewan, and The Lost Gardens of Heligan and Mevagissey are nearby. There is a bus stop outside the park to Mevagissey and Gorran Haven or St Austell (Asda), Charlestown and Fowey. 14 acre site. 90 touring pitches. 28 hardstandings. 2 seasonal pitches. Caravan pitches. Motorhome pitches. Tent pitches.

Open: Etr-end Oct **Last arrival:** 21.00hrs **Last departure:** noon

Pitches: * ⚏ £8-£25 ⚎ £8-£25 ▲ £6-£25

Leisure: ⚠ 🐾 **Facilities:** 🐾⊙🖤☀🏪🎋🏕🛜🖥♻🛈

Services: 🔌🖨🚰♨ **Within 3 miles:** 🚲🛶🎡🎣🏊🏪🛒

Notes: No noise 22.00hrs-07.00hrs. Dogs must be kept on leads.

AA Pubs & Restaurants nearby: The Ship Inn, MEVAGISSEY, PL26 6UQ, 01726 843324
The Crown Inn, ST EWE, PL26 6EY, 01726 843322

PENZANCE   Map 2 SW43

See also Rosudgeon

Places to visit

Trengwainton Garden, PENZANCE, TR20 8RZ, 01736 363148
www.nationaltrust.org.uk/trengwainton

St Michael's Mount, MARAZION, TR17 0HT, 01736 710507
www.stmichaelsmount.co.uk

Bone Valley Caravan & Camping Park
► ► ►78%

tel: 01736 360313 **Heamoor TR20 8UJ**
email: wardmandie@yahoo.co.uk
dir: *Exit A30 at Heamoor/Madron rdbt. 4th on right into Josephs Ln. 800yds left into Bone Valley. Entrance 200yds on left.* **grid ref:** SW472316

A compact grassy park on the outskirts of Penzance with well-maintained facilities. It is divided into paddocks by mature hedges, and a small stream runs alongside. 1 acre site. 17 touring pitches. 8 hardstandings. Caravan pitches. Motorhome pitches. Tent pitches. 3 statics.

Open: all year **Last arrival:** 22.00hrs **Last departure:** 10.00hrs

Pitches: ⚏ ⚎ ▲

Leisure: 🖵

Facilities: 🛁🐾⊙🖤☀🛜🏪🎋🛜🖥♻

Services: 🔌🖨🚰🁔

Within 3 miles: 🚲🎡🏪🛒🐴

Notes: No noise after mdnt. Dogs must be kept on leads. Campers' lounge, kitchen & laundry room.

AA Pubs & Restaurants nearby: Dolphin Tavern, PENZANCE, TR18 4BD, 01736 364106
Harris's Restaurant, PENZANCE, TR18 2LZ, 01736 364408

LEISURE: 🏊 Indoor swimming pool 🏊 Outdoor swimming pool ⚠ Children's playground 👶 Kid's club 🎾 Tennis court 🎱 Games room 🖵 Separate TV room ⛳ golf course 🚣 Boats for hire 🎬 Cinema 🎵 Entertainment 🎣 Fishing ⛳ Mini golf 🏄 Watersports 🏋 Gym ⚽ Sports field Spa 🐴 Stables
FACILITIES: 🛁 Bath 🚿 Shower ⊙ Electric shaver 🖤 Hairdryer ☀ Ice Pack Facility ♿ Disabled facilities 📞 Public telephone 🏪 Shop on site or within 200yds 🚐 Mobile shop (calls at least 5 days a week) 🍖 BBQ area 🎋 Picnic area 🛜 Wi-fi 🖥 Internet access ♻ Recycling 🛈 Tourist info 🐕 Dog exercise area

PERRANPORTH | Map 2 SW75

See also Rejerrah

Places to visit

Royal Cornwall Museum, TRURO, TR1 2SJ, 01872 272205
www.royalcornwallmuseum.org.uk

Trerice, TRERICE, TR8 4PG, 01637 875404 www.nationaltrust.org.uk/trerice/

Great for kids: Blue Reef Aquarium, NEWQUAY, TR7 1DU, 01637 878134
www.bluereefaquarium.co.uk

Perran Sands Holiday Park
HOLIDAY CENTRE 88%

GOLD

tel: 0871 231 0871 **TR6 0AQ**
email: perransands@haven.com **web:** www.haven.com/perransands
dir: A30 onto B3285 towards Perranporth. Site on right before descent on hill into
Perranporth. **grid ref:** SW767554

Situated amid 500 acres of protected dune grassland, and with a footpath through
to the surf and three miles of golden sandy beach, this lively park is set in a large
village-style complex. It offers a complete range of on-site facilities and
entertainment for all the family, which makes it an extremely popular park. There
are two top-of-the-range facility blocks. 550 acre site. 363 touring pitches. 28
hardstandings. Caravan pitches. Motorhome pitches. Tent pitches. 600 statics.

Open: mid Mar-end Oct (rs mid Mar-May & Sep-Oct some facilities may be reduced) **Last arrival:** 22.00hrs **Last departure:** 10.00hrs

Pitches: ⚌ ⚌ Å
Leisure: 🏊 🏊 🎨 🖐 ⚽ 🎵
Facilities: 🚿 🍴 🎱 ✗ ♿ 🕐 $ WiFi ♻ ℹ
Services: 🔌 🛢 🍴 🎁 🧴 🍴 🛒
Within 3 miles: ⚓ 🎣 🎯 🏊 🏆 🛢 U

Notes: No commercial vehicles, no bookings by persons under 21yrs unless a family
booking, max 2 dogs per booking, certain dog breeds banned. Dogs must be kept on
leads.

AA Pubs & Restaurants nearby: Driftwood Spars, ST AGNES, TR5 0RT, 01872 552428

See advert below

PITCHES: ⚌ Caravans ⚌ Motorhomes Å Tents 🏠 Glamping-style accommodation **SERVICES:** 🔌 Electric hook up 🛢 Launderette 🍴 Licensed bar
🛢 Calor Gas ⊘ Camping Gaz 🚽 Toilet fluid 🍴 Café/Restaurant 🍟 Fast Food/Takeaway 🔋 Battery charging 🍼 Baby care ⚓ Motorvan service point
ABBREVIATIONS: BH/bank hols – bank holidays Etr – Easter Spring BH – Spring Bank Holiday fr – from hrs – hours m – mile mdnt – midnight
rdbt – roundabout rs – restricted service wk – week wknd – weekend x-rds – cross roads 🚫 No credit or debit cards 🚫 No dogs 👫 Children of all ages accepted

PERRANPORTH *continued*

Tollgate Farm Caravan & Camping Park

►►►►82%

tel: 01872 572130 **Budnick Hill TR6 0AD**
email: enquiries@tollgatefarm.co.uk   **web:** www.tollgatefarm.co.uk
dir: *Exit A30 onto B3285 to Perranporth. Site on right 1.5m after Goonhavern.*
grid ref: *SW768547*

A quiet site in a rural location with spectacular coastal views. Pitches are divided into four paddocks sheltered and screened by mature hedges. Children will like the play equipment and pets' corner, while adults can enjoy the food at the Farm Kitchen, which is open daily. The three miles of sand at Perran Bay are just a walk away through the sand dunes, or by car it is a three-quarter mile drive. There are now five camping pods for hire. 10 acre site. 102 touring pitches. 10 hardstandings. 12 seasonal pitches. Caravan pitches. Motorhome pitches. Tent pitches. 5 wooden pods.

Open: Etr-Sep **Last arrival:** 20.00hrs **Last departure:** 11.00hrs

Pitches: ⊞ ⊟ Å ⋒

Leisure: ⚠ ✿

Facilities: ⌿ ⊙ ⊓ ⚲ ✳ ⅋ ⊙ ⑤ ⊟ ⊩ ㎺ ♺ ❶

Services: ⊟ ⑤ 🔒 ⊘ Ⓣ 🞄 ⚒ ⍓

Within 3 miles: ⅃ ⅄ ⊟ ℘ ⊚ ⌂ ⑤ ⑤ ∪

Notes: No large groups. Dogs must be kept on leads.

AA Pubs & Restaurants nearby: Driftwood Spars, ST AGNES, TR5 0RT, 01872 552428

See advert below

LEISURE: 🏊 Indoor swimming pool   🏊 Outdoor swimming pool   ⚠ Children's playground   🧒 Kid's club   🎾 Tennis court   🎱 Games room   📺 Separate TV room   ⛳ golf course   🚣 Boats for hire   🎬 Cinema   🎵 Entertainment   🎣 Fishing   ⛳ Mini golf   🏄 Watersports   🏋 Gym   ⚽ Sports field   Spa   ∪ Stables
FACILITIES: 🛁 Bath   🚿 Shower   ⊙ Electric shaver   ⚲ Hairdryer   ✳ Ice Pack Facility   ♿ Disabled facilities   ☎ Public telephone   ⑤ Shop on site or within 200yds   ⑤ Mobile shop (calls at least 5 days a week)   🍖 BBQ area   🪑 Picnic area   📶 Wi-fi   💻 Internet access   ♺ Recycling   ❶ Tourist info   🐕 Dog exercise area

Higher Golla Touring & Caravan Park

►►► 82%

tel: 01872 573963 & 07800 558407 **Penhallow TR4 9LZ**
email: trevor.knibb@gmail.com **web:** www.highergollatouringpark.co.uk
dir: *A30 onto B3284 towards Perranporth (straight on at junct with A3075). Approx 2m. Site signed on right.* **grid ref:** *SW756514*

This peacefully located park is just two miles from Perranporth and its stunning beach, and extensive country views can be enjoyed from all pitches. It has high quality and immaculate toilet facilities, and every pitch has electricity and a water tap. 3 acre site. 30 touring pitches. 2 hardstandings. 4 seasonal pitches. Caravan pitches. Motorhome pitches. Tent pitches. 2 statics.

Open: Etr-end Sep (rs Spring BH wk & peak season shop open) **Last arrival:** 20.00hrs **Last departure:** 10.30hrs

Pitches: ⊞ £14-£21 ⊞ £14-£21 ▲ £10-£15

Facilities: ⬤⊙☞✳☖🚻⛬🛜♻❶
Services: ⬤◙🍺Ⓣ⬇
Within 3 miles: ⬇✐◎♨🛒🛍⛳
Notes: No kite flying, quiet between 21.00hrs-08.00hrs. Dogs must be kept on leads.
AA Pubs & Restaurants nearby: Driftwood Spars, ST AGNES, TR5 0RT, 01872 552428

Perranporth Camping & Touring Park

►►► 71%

tel: 01872 572174 **Budnick Rd TR6 0DB**
dir: *0.5m E off B3285.* **grid ref:** *SW768542*

A pleasant site, great for families and just a five-minute, easy walk to Perranporth's beautiful beach and less than 10 minutes to the shops and restaurants in the town centre. There is a clubhouse/bar and heated swimming pool for the sole use of

continued

PITCHES: ⊞ Caravans ⊞ Motorhomes ▲ Tents ⛺ Glamping-style accommodation **SERVICES:** ⬤ Electric hook up ◙ Launderette 🍺 Licensed bar 🛢 Calor Gas ⊘ Camping Gaz Ⓣ Toilet fluid 🍽 Café/Restaurant 🍟 Fast Food/Takeaway 🔋 Battery charging 👶 Baby care ⬇ Motorvan service point
ABBREVIATIONS: BH/bank hols – bank holidays Etr – Easter Spring BH – Spring Bank Holiday fr – from hrs – hours m – mile mdnt – midnight rdbt – roundabout rs – restricted service wk – week wknd – weekend x-rds – cross roads 🚫 No credit or debit cards 🚫 No dogs 👪 Children of all ages accepted

PERRANPORTH *continued*

those staying on the site. There is also a takeaway food outlet and small shop. Nine static caravans are available for holiday hire. 6 acre site. 120 touring pitches. 4 hardstandings. Caravan pitches. Motorhome pitches. Tent pitches. 9 statics.

Perranporth Camping & Touring Park

Open: Spring BH-Sep (rs Etr & end Sep shop, swimming pool & club facilities closed) **Last arrival:** 23.00hrs **Last departure:** noon

Pitches: * ⚌ £19.50-£24 ⛺ £19.50-£24 ▲ £19.50-£24

Leisure: ⚐ ⋀ ⚓ ☐

Facilities: ⚋ ⚑ ☉ ℱ ✳ ⚒ ⑤ ⋒ ⊁ ❼

Services: ⚑ ⑤ ⛨ ⛁ ⊘ Ⓣ ⚎

Within 3 miles: ⚲ ⚶ ℱ ◎ ⚴ ⑤ ⑤ ∪

Notes: No noise after 23.00hrs. Dogs must be kept on leads.

AA Pubs & Restaurants nearby: Driftwood Spars, ST AGNES, TR5 0RT, 01872 552428

See advert on page 97

Great Kellow Farm Caravan & Camping Site
►►78%

tel: 01503 272387 **Lansallos PL13 2QL**
email: kellow.farm@virgin.net
dir: *From Looe to Pelynt. In Pelynt left at church follow Lansallos sign. Left at x-rds, 0.75m. At staggered x-rds left, follow site signs. NB access is via single track lanes. It is advisable to follow guide directions not Sat Nav.* **grid ref:** *SX201522*

Set on a high level grassy paddock with extensive views of Polperro Bay, this attractive site is on a working dairy and beef farm, and close to National Trust

properties and gardens. It is situated in a very peaceful location close to the fishing village of Polperro. 3 acre site. 30 touring pitches. 25 seasonal pitches. Caravan pitches. Motorhome pitches. Tent pitches. 10 statics.

Open: Mar-3 Jan **Last arrival:** 22.00hrs **Last departure:** noon

Pitches: ⚌ ⛺ ▲

Facilities: ⚑ ☉ ✳ ⊁ ❤ ❼

Services: ⚑

Within 3 miles: ⚶ ℱ ⑤

Notes: ⊛ No noise after 23.00hrs. Dogs must be kept on leads.

AA Pubs & Restaurants nearby: Talland Bay Hotel, TALLAND BAY, PL13 2JB, 01503 272667

Barclay House, LOOE, PL13 1LP, 01503 262929

Polruan Holidays - Camping & Caravanning
►►►88%

GOLD

tel: 01726 870263 **Polruan-by-Fowey PL23 1QH**
email: polholiday@aol.com
dir: *A38 to Dobwalls, left onto A390 to East Taphouse. Left onto B3359. Right in 4.5m signed Polruan.* **grid ref:** *SX133509*

A very rural and quiet site in a lovely elevated position above the village, with good views of the sea. The River Fowey passenger ferry is close by, and the site has a good shop, and barbecues to borrow. The bus for Polperro and Looe stops outside the gate, and the foot ferry to Fowey, which runs until 11pm, is only a 10-minute walk away. 3 acre site. 47 touring pitches. 7 hardstandings. Caravan pitches. Motorhome pitches. Tent pitches. 10 statics.

Open: Etr-Oct **Last arrival:** 21.00hrs **Last departure:** 11.00hrs

Pitches: ⚌ ⛺ ▲

Leisure: ⋀

Facilities: ⚑ ☉ ℱ ✳ ⊙ ⑤ ⋒ WiFi ⬜ ❤ ❼

Services: ⚑ ⑤ ⛁ ⊘ Ⓣ ⚎ ⚐

Within 3 miles: ⚶ ℱ ⚴ ⑤ ⑤ ∪

Notes: No skateboards, rollerskates, bikes, water pistols or water bombs. Dogs must be kept on leads.

AA Pubs & Restaurants nearby: The Ship Inn, FOWEY, PL23 1AZ, 01726 832230

The Fowey Hotel, FOWEY, PL23 1HX, 01726 832551

POLZEATH
Map 2 SW97

South Winds Caravan & Camping Park
►►►87%

tel: 01208 863267 & 862215 Polzeath Rd PL27 6QU
email: info@southwindscamping.co.uk web: www.polzeathcamping.co.uk
dir: Exit B3314 onto unclassified road signed Polzeath, site on right just past turn to New Polzeath. grid ref: SW948790

A peaceful site with beautiful sea and panoramic rural views, within walking distance of a golf complex, and just three quarters of a mile from beach and village. There's an impressive reception building, replete with tourist information, TV, settees and a range of camping spares. 16 acre site. 165 touring pitches. Caravan pitches. Motorhome pitches. Tent pitches.

Open: May-mid Sep Last arrival: 21.00hrs Last departure: 10.30hrs

Pitches: * 🚐 £16-£30 🚌 £16-£30 ▲ £8.50-£30

Facilities: 🅟⊙🅿☀⅋Ⓛ🄳🔌 📶 ♻ ❼

Services: 🔌🄻 🔋⌀Ⓣ🔋⅄

Within 3 miles: ⅃⅂🗓🎣◎≋🄻🄻∪

Notes: Families & couples only, no disposable BBQs, no noise 23.00hrs-07.00hrs. Dogs must be kept on leads. Restaurant & farm shop adjacent, Stepper Field open mid Jul-Aug.

AA Pubs & Restaurants nearby: Restaurant Nathan Outlaw, ROCK, PL27 6LA, 01208 862737

See advert below

PITCHES: 🚐 Caravans 🚌 Motorhomes ▲ Tents 🏕 Glamping-style accommodation SERVICES: 🔌 Electric hook up 🄻 Launderette 🍺 Licensed bar 🔋 Calor Gas ⌀ Camping Gaz Ⓣ Toilet fluid 🍽 Café/Restaurant 🍔 Fast Food/Takeaway 🔋 Battery charging 🍼 Baby care ⅄ Motorvan service point
ABBREVIATIONS: BH/bank hols – bank holidays Etr – Easter Spring BH – Spring Bank Holiday fr – from hrs – hours m – mile mdnt – midnight rdbt – roundabout rs – restricted service wk – week wknd – weekend x-rds – cross roads No credit or debit cards No dogs Children of all ages accepted

POLRUAN *continued*

Tristram Caravan & Camping Park
►►►87%

tel: 01208 862215 **PL27 6TP**
email: info@tristramcampsite.co.uk **web:** www.polzeathcamping.co.uk
dir: *From B3314 onto unclassified road signed Polzeath. Through village, up hill, site 2nd right.* **grid ref:** SW936790

An ideal family site, positioned on a gently sloping cliff with grassy pitches and glorious sea views, which are best enjoyed from the terraced premier pitches, or over lunch or dinner at the Café India adjacent to the reception overlooking the beach. There is direct, gated access to the beach, where surfing is very popular, and the park has a holiday bungalow for rent. The local amenities of the village are only a few hundred yards away. 10 acre site. 100 touring pitches. Caravan pitches. Motorhome pitches. Tent pitches.

Open: Mar-Nov (rs mid Sep reseeding the site) **Last arrival:** 21.00hrs
Last departure: 10.00hrs

Pitches: * 🚐 £28-£65 🚍 £28-£65 ▲ £22-£65

Facilities: 🍴☉🅿☀🔥🕒🅂 📶 ♻ 🛈

Services: 🔌🔲 🔋🚰Ⓣ🍽🧺

Within 3 miles: ⬇🐴🎢🅿◎🏊🐟🅂🛶U

Notes: No ball games, no disposable BBQs, no noise between 23.00hrs-07.00hrs. Dogs must be kept on leads. Surf equipment hire.

AA Pubs & Restaurants nearby: Restaurant Nathan Outlaw, ROCK, PL27 6LA, 01208 862737

See advert on page 99

Porthtowan Tourist Park
►►►►94%

tel: 01209 890256 **Mile Hill TR4 8TY**
email: admin@porthtowantouristpark.co.uk **web:** www.porthtowantouristpark.co.uk
dir: *Exit A30 at junct signed Redruth/Porthtowan. Take 3rd exit at rdbt. 2m, right at T-junct. Site on left at top of hill.* **grid ref:** SW693473

A neat, level grassy site on high ground above Porthtowan, with plenty of shelter from mature trees and shrubs. The superb toilet facilities considerably enhance the appeal of this peaceful rural park, which is almost midway between the small seaside resorts of Portreath and Porthtowan, with their beaches and surfing. There is a purpose-built games/meeting room with a good library where tourist information leaflets are available. 5 acre site. 80 touring pitches. 11 hardstandings. 8 seasonal pitches. Caravan pitches. Motorhome pitches. Tent pitches.

Open: Apr-Sep **Last arrival:** 21.30hrs **Last departure:** 11.00hrs
Pitches: * 🚐 £11-£19 🚍 £11-£19 ▲ £11-£19
Leisure: ⋀ ♻ ⚽
Facilities: 🍴☉🅿☀🔥🕒🅂🔲🛒 📶 ♻ 🛈
Services: 🔌🔲 🔋🚰Ⓣ🧺
Within 3 miles: ⬇🅿🏊🅂🛶U
Notes: No bikes or skateboards in Jul & Aug. Dogs must be kept on leads.

AA Pubs & Restaurants nearby: Driftwood Spars, ST AGNES, TR5 0RT, 01872 552428
See advert on page 91

LEISURE: 🏊 Indoor swimming pool 🏊 Outdoor swimming pool ⋀ Children's playground 👋 Kid's club ♟ Tennis court ⚽ Games room ▭ Separate TV room
⛳ golf course ⛵ Boats for hire 🎬 Cinema 🎵 Entertainment 🎣 Fishing ◎ Mini golf 🏄 Watersports 🏋 Gym ◉ Sports field Spa U Stables
FACILITIES: 🛁 Bath 🍴 Shower ☉ Electric shaver 🅿 Hairdryer ☀ Ice Pack Facility 🔥 Disabled facilities 🕒 Public telephone 🅂 Shop on site or within 200yds
🛒 Mobile shop (calls at least 5 days a week) 🔲 BBQ area 🔲 Picnic area 📶 Wi-fi 🖥 Internet access ♻ Recycling 🛈 Tourist info 🐕 Dog exercise area

Wheal Rose Caravan & Camping Park

►►►►73%

tel: 01209 891496 **Wheal Rose TR16 5DD**
email: whealrose@aol.com **web:** www.whealrosecaravanpark.co.uk
dir: *Exit A30 at Scorrier sign, follow signs to Wheal Rose. Site 0.5m on left on the Wheal Rose to Porthtowan road.* **grid ref:** *SW717449*

A quiet, peaceful park in a secluded valley setting, which is well placed for visiting both the lovely countryside and the surfing beaches of Porthtowan (two miles away). The friendly owner works hard to keep this park in immaculate condition, with a bright toilet block and well-trimmed pitches. There is a swimming pool and a games room. 6 acre site. 50 touring pitches. 6 hardstandings. Caravan pitches. Motorhome pitches. Tent pitches. 3 statics.

Open: Mar-Dec **Last arrival:** 21.00hrs **Last departure:** 11.00hrs

Pitches: * ⊞ £12-£18 ⊞ £12-£18 ▲ £12-£18

Leisure: 🏊 ⚙ 🎮 🎣

Facilities: 📻 ☉ 🅿 ✳ ☕ ⚲ 📻 🛒 ♻ ❶

Services: 🔌 🔄 🔋 🚽 🛒

Within 3 miles: 🎿 🏇 🚴 🛶 ☕ 📻 🛒 ⛳

Notes: 5mph speed limit, minimum noise after 23.00hrs, gates locked 23.00hrs. Dogs must be kept on leads.

AA Pubs & Restaurants nearby: Basset Arms, PORTREATH, TR16 4NG, 01209 842077

PORTREATH Map 2 SW64

Places to visit

East Pool Mine, POOL, TR15 3NP, 01209 315027 www.nationaltrust.org.uk

Tehidy Holiday Park

►►►►85%

tel: 01209 216489 **Harris Mill, Illogan TR16 4JQ**
email: holiday@tehidy.co.uk **web:** www.tehidy.co.uk
dir: *Exit A30 at Redruth/Portreath junct onto A3047 to 1st rdbt. Left onto B3300. At junct straight over signed Tehidy Holiday Park. Past Cornish Arms pub, site 800yds at bottom of hill on left.* **grid ref:** *SW682432*

An attractive wooded location in a quiet rural area only two and a half miles from popular beaches. Mostly level pitches on tiered ground, and the toilet facilities are bright and modern. Holiday static caravans for hire. 4.5 acre site. 18 touring pitches. 11 hardstandings. 4 seasonal pitches. Caravan pitches. Motorhome pitches. Tent pitches. 32 statics. 2 wooden pods.

Open: all year (rs Nov-Mar part of shower block & shop closed) **Last arrival:** 20.00hrs **Last departure:** 10.00hrs

Pitches: * ⊞ £14-£23 ⊞ £14-£23 ▲ £14-£23 🏠

Leisure: ⚙ 🎮 🎣 🏓 **Facilities:** 📻 ☉ 🅿 ✳ ☕ ⚲ 📻 ♻ ❶

Services: 🔌 🔄 🚽 🛒 🚚

Within 3 miles: 🎿 ⛷ 🏇 🚴 ◎ 🛶 ☕ 📻 🛒 ⛳

Notes: No pets, no noise after 23.00hrs. Trampoline, off-licence, cooking shelter.

AA Pubs & Restaurants nearby: Basset Arms, PORTREATH, TR16 4NG, 01209 842077

See advert on page 90

PITCHES: ⊞ Caravans ⊞ Motorhomes ▲ Tents 🏠 Glamping-style accommodation **SERVICES:** 🔌 Electric hook up 🔄 Launderette 🍺 Licensed bar 🔋 Calor Gas ⚙ Camping Gaz 🚽 Toilet fluid 🍽 Café/Restaurant 🍟 Fast Food/Takeaway 🔋 Battery charging 👶 Baby care 🚐 Motorvan service point
ABBREVIATIONS: BH/bank hols – bank holidays Etr – Easter Spring BH – Spring Bank Holiday fr – from hrs – hours m – mile mdnt – midnight rdbt – roundabout rs – restricted service wk – week wknd – weekend x-rds – cross roads ⊗ No credit or debit cards ⊗ No dogs 👫 Children of all ages accepted

PORTSCATHO
Map 2 SW83

Places to visit

St Mawes Castle, ST MAWES, TR2 3AA, 01326 270526
www.english-heritage.org.uk/daysout/properties/st-mawes-castle

Trelissick Garden, TRELISSICK GARDEN, TR3 6QL, 01872 862090
www.nationaltrust.org.uk/trelissick

Trewince Farm Touring Park
►►►80%

tel: 01872 580430 **TR2 5ET**
email: info@trewincefarm.co.uk
dir: *From St Austell take A390 towards Truro. Left on B3287 to Tregony, following signs to St Mawes. At Trewithian, turn left to St Anthony. Site 0.75m past church.*
grid ref: *SW868339*

A site on a working farm with spectacular sea views from its elevated position. There are many quiet golden sandy beaches close by, and boat launching facilities and mooring can be arranged at the nearby Percuil River Boatyard. The village of Portscatho with shops and pubs and attractive harbour is approximately one mile away. 3 acre site. 25 touring pitches. Caravan pitches. Motorhome pitches. Tent pitches.

Open: May-Sep **Last arrival:** 23.00hrs **Last departure:** 11.00hrs

Pitches: * ⊕ fr £12 ⊞ Å

Facilities: ⏻ ☉ ℱ ☀ ☴ ⤞ ♻ ❶

Services: ⊞ ⊡ ≛

Within 3 miles: ⅄ ℐ ⩣ ⑤

Notes: ⊛ Dogs must be kept on leads.

AA Pubs & Restaurants nearby: The New Inn, VERYAN, TR2 5QA, 01872 501362
The Victory Inn, ST MAWES, TR2 5DQ, 01326 270324

REDRUTH

Places to visit

East Pool Mine, POOL, TR15 3NP, 01209 315027 www.nationaltrust.org.uk

Pendennis Castle, FALMOUTH, TR11 4LP, 01326 316594
www.english-heritage.org.uk/daysout/properties/pendennis-castle

Great for kids: National Maritime Museum Cornwall, FALMOUTH, TR11 3QY,
01326 313388 www.nmmc.co.uk

REDRUTH
Map 2 SW64

PREMIER PARK

Globe Vale Holiday Park
►►►►►87%

tel: 01209 891183 **Radnor TR16 4BH**
email: info@globevale.co.uk **web:** www.globevale.co.uk
dir: *A30 take Redruth/Porthtowan exit then Portreath/North Country exit from rdbt, right at x-rds into Radnor Rd, left after 0.5m, site on left after 0.5m.*
grid ref: *SW708447*

A family owned and run park set in a quiet rural location yet close to some stunning beaches and coastline. The park's touring area has a number of full facility hardstanding pitches, a high quality toilet block, a comfortable lounge bar serving bar meals, and holiday static caravans. 13 acre site. 138 touring pitches. 25 hardstandings. Caravan pitches. Motorhome pitches. Tent pitches. 10 statics.

Open: all year **Last arrival:** 20.00hrs **Last departure:** 10.00hrs

Pitches: ⊕ ⊞ Å

Leisure: ⩜ ⚲

Facilities: ⏻ ☀ ⅏ ⤞ WiFi ♻ ❶

Services: ⊞ ⊡ ⅌ ⬛ 📶 ⌁ T ⑩ ≛ ⅏

Within 3 miles: ⅃ ⊞ ⩣ ⑤ ⊡

Notes: Dogs must be kept on leads. Shower block heated in winter.

AA Pubs & Restaurants nearby: Basset Arms, PORTREATH, TR16 4NG, 01209 842077

See advert on page 90

LEISURE: 🏊 Indoor swimming pool 🏊 Outdoor swimming pool ⩜ Children's playground 👣 Kid's club 🎾 Tennis court 🎱 Games room 📺 Separate TV room
🏌 golf course ⛵ Boats for hire 🎦 Cinema 🎵 Entertainment 🎣 Fishing ⊙ Mini golf 🏄 Watersports 🏋 Gym 🏟 Sports field Spa ♨ Stables
FACILITIES: 🛁 Bath 🚿 Shower ☉ Electric shaver ✂ Hairdryer ☀ Ice Pack Facility ♿ Disabled facilities ☎ Public telephone 🏪 Shop on site or within 200yds
🏪 Mobile shop (calls at least 5 days a week) 🍖 BBQ area 🌲 Picnic area WiFi Wi-fi 💻 Internet access ♻ Recycling ❶ Tourist info ⤞ Dog exercise area

Lanyon Holiday Park
► ► ► ► 81%

tel: 01209 313474 **Loscombe Ln, Four Lanes TR16 6LP**
email: info@lanyonholidaypark.co.uk **web:** www.lanyonholidaypark.co.uk
dir: *Signed 0.5m off B2397 on Helston side of Four Lanes village.* **grid ref:** *SW684387*

Small, friendly rural park in an elevated position with fine views to distant St Ives Bay. This family owned and run park continues to be upgraded in all areas, and is close to a cycling trail. There is a well-stocked bar and a very inviting swimming pool. Stithians Reservoir for fishing, sailing and windsurfing is two miles away. Two holiday cottages are available. 14 acre site. 25 touring pitches. Caravan pitches. Motorhome pitches. Tent pitches. 49 statics.

Open: Mar-Oct **Last arrival:** 21.00hrs **Last departure:** noon
Pitches: * 🚐 £13-£25 🚍 £13-£25 ▲ £13-£25
Leisure: 🏊 🅰 🏐 🎣 🎵
Facilities: 🛒 🐾 ⊙ 🅿 ✳ 🚿 📞 🕙 📶 🖥 ♻ 🛈
Services: 🔌 🔲 🍴 🍽 🔋 🚰
Within 3 miles: 🚴 🥾 🎌 🎿 ◎ 🚣 🏧 🗄 ⛳
Notes: Families only. Dogs must be kept on leads.
AA Pubs & Restaurants nearby: Basset Arms, PORTREATH, TR16 4NG, 01209 842077

See advert on page 91

Cambrose Touring Park
► ► ► 79%

tel: 01209 890747 **Portreath Rd TR16 4HT**
email: cambrosetouringpark@gmail.com
dir: *A30 onto B3300 towards Portreath. Approx 0.75m at 1st rdbt right onto B3300. Take unclassified road on right signed Porthtowan. Site 200yds on left.* **grid ref:** *SW684453*

Situated in a rural setting surrounded by trees and shrubs, this park is divided into grassy paddocks. It is about two miles from the harbour village of Portreath. The site has an excellent swimming pool with a sun bathing area. 6 acre site. 60 touring pitches. 6 seasonal pitches. Caravan pitches. Motorhome pitches. Tent pitches.

Open: Apr-Oct **Last arrival:** 22.00hrs **Last departure:** 11.30hrs
Pitches: * 🚐 £11-£18.50 🚍 £11-£18.50 ▲ £11-£18.50
Leisure: 🏊 🅰 🏐 🎣
Facilities: 🐾 ⊙ 🅿 ✳ 🕙 🕙 🗄 🚾 📶 🖥 ♻ 🛈
Services: 🔌 🔲 🍴 🔋 🗄 🚰
Within 3 miles: 🥾 🎌 🎿 ◎ 🗄 🗄 ⛳
Notes: No noise after 23.30hrs. Dogs must be kept on leads. Mini football pitch.
AA Pubs & Restaurants nearby: Basset Arms, PORTREATH, TR16 4NG, 01209 842077

Stithians Lake Country Park
► ► ► 74%

tel: 01209 860301 **Stithians Lake, Menherion TR16 6NW**
email: stithianswatersports@swlakestrust.org.uk
dir: *From Redruth take B3297 towards Helston. Follow brown tourist signs to Stithians Lake, entrance by Golden Lion Inn.* **grid ref:** *SW705369*

This simple campsite is a two-acre field situated adjacent to the Watersports Centre, which forms part of a large activity complex beside Stithians Lake. Campers are required to use the functional toilet and shower facilities at the centre, and there is an excellent waterside café that also serves breakfasts. This is the perfect campsite for watersport enthusiasts. 2.1 acre site. 40 touring pitches. Caravan pitches. Motorhome pitches. Tent pitches.

Open: all year **Last arrival:** 17.30hrs **Last departure:** noon
Pitches: * 🚐 £14-£18 🚍 £14-£18 ▲ £14-£18
Leisure: 🅰
Facilities: 🐾 ✳ 🕙 📶 🚾 ♻ 🛈
Services: 🔌 🔲 🍴
Within 3 miles: 🥾 🎌 🎿 🎿 🗄 🗄 ⛳
Notes: No noise after mdnt, no swimming in lake. Dogs must be kept on leads.
AA Pubs & Restaurants nearby: Basset Arms, PORTREATH, TR16 4NG, 01209 842077

REJERRAH
Map 2 SW75

Places to visit

Trerice, TRERICE, TR8 4PG, 01637 875404 www.nationaltrust.org.uk/trerice/

Blue Reef Aquarium, NEWQUAY, TR7 1DU, 01637 878134
www.bluereefaquarium.co.uk

Great for kids: Newquay Zoo, NEWQUAY, TR7 2LZ, 0844 474 2244
www.newquayzoo.org.uk

PREMIER PARK

Newperran Holiday Park
►►►►► 87%

tel: 01872 572407 **TR8 5QJ**
email: holidays@newperran.co.uk **web:** www.newperran.co.uk
dir: 4m SE of Newquay & 1m S of Rejerrah on A3075. Or A30 (Redruth), exit B3275 Perranporth, at 1st T-junct right onto A3075 towards Newquay, site 300mtrs on left. **grid ref:** SW801555

A family site in a lovely rural position near several beaches and bays. This airy park offers screening to some pitches, which are set in paddocks on level ground. High season entertainment is available in the park's high quality country inn, and the café has an extensive menu. There is also a swimming pool with a separate toddlers' paddling area. 25 acre site. 357 touring pitches. 27 hardstandings. 15 seasonal pitches. Caravan pitches. Motorhome pitches. Tent pitches. 30 statics.

Open: Etr-Oct **Last arrival:** mdnt **Last departure:** 10.00hrs
Pitches: 🚐 �655 Å

Leisure: 🏊 ⚠ ⚙ 🎱 🎵
Facilities: 🛁 ☉ 🚿 ❄ ♿ 🕐 🛒 🗑 WiFi ♻ 🛈
Services: 🔌 🚽 🍽 🛒 🚰 T 🍴 ⛽ ⚒
Within 3 miles: ⛳ 🚣 🎬 🎣 ◎ 🏄 🛒 🗑 ∪

Notes: Families & couples only. Dogs must be kept on leads.
AA Pubs & Restaurants nearby: The Smugglers' Den Inn, CUBERT, TR8 5PY, 01637 830209
See advert on page 91

ROSUDGEON
Map 2 SW52

Places to visit

Trengwainton Garden, PENZANCE, TR20 8RZ, 01736 363148
www.nationaltrust.org.uk/trengwainton

Great for kids: The Flambards Theme Park, HELSTON, TR13 0QA, 01326 573404
www.flambards.co.uk

Kenneggy Cove Holiday Park
►►►► 87%

tel: 01736 763453 **Higher Kenneggy TR20 9AU**
email: enquiries@kenneggycove.co.uk **web:** www.kenneggycove.co.uk
dir: On A394 between Penzance & Helston, turn S into signed lane to site & Higher Kenneggy. **grid ref:** SW562287

Set in an Area of Outstanding Natural Beauty with spectacular sea views, this family-owned park is quiet and well kept, with a well-equipped children's play area, superb toilets, and a takeaway food facility offering home-cooked meals. A short walk along a country footpath leads to the Cornish Coastal Path, and on to the golden sandy beach at Kenneggy Cove. It's a half mile walk to the main road to pick up the local bus which goes to Penzance or Helston, with many pretty Cornish coves en route. There is a fish and chip shop and Chinese restaurant with takeaway a short drive away. 4 acre site. 45 touring pitches. Caravan pitches. Motorhome pitches. Tent pitches. 7 statics.

Open: 12 May-Sep **Last arrival:** 21.00hrs **Last departure:** 11.00hrs
Pitches: 🚐 �655 Å
Leisure: ⚠ ⚙
Facilities: 🛁 ☉ 🚿 ❄ 🗑 WiFi ♻ 🛈
Services: 🔌 🚽 🛒 🚰 T 🍴 ⚒
Within 3 miles: ⛳ 🚣 🎣 🛒 🗑 ∪

Notes: ⊘ No large groups, no noise after 22.00hrs. Dogs must be kept on leads. Fresh bakery items, breakfasts, home-made evening meals.

AA Pubs & Restaurants nearby: The Victoria Inn, PERRANUTHNOE, TR20 9NP, 01736 710309

The Ship Inn, PORTHLEVEN, TR13 9JS, 01326 564204

RUMFORD   Map 2 SW87

Places to visit

Prideaux Place, PADSTOW, PL28 8RP, 01841 532411 www.prideauxplace.co.uk

Great for kids: Devon's Crealy Great Adventure Park, CLYST ST MARY, EX5 1DR, 01395 233200 www.crealy.co.uk

Music Water Touring Park
▶▶▶81%

tel: 01841 540257 **PL27 7SJ**
dir: A39 at Winnards Perch rdbt onto B3274 signed Padstow. Left in 2m onto unclassified road signed Rumford & St Eval. Site 500mtrs on right. **grid ref:** SW906685

Set in a peaceful location yet only a short drive to the pretty fishing town of Padstow, and many sandy beaches and coves. This family owned and run park has grassy paddocks, and there is a quiet lounge bar and a separate children's games room. 8 acre site. 55 touring pitches. 2 hardstandings. Caravan pitches. Motorhome pitches. Tent pitches. 2 statics.

Open: Apr-Oct **Last arrival:** 23.00hrs **Last departure:** 10.30hrs

Pitches: * £15-£20 ⌷ £12-£20 **Å** £12-£20

Leisure: ⌷ ⌷ ⌷

Facilities: ⌷ ⊙ ⌷ ✳ ⌷ ⌷ ⌷ ⌷

Services: ⌷ ⌷ ⌷ ⌷ ⌷ ⌷

Within 3 miles: ⌷ ⌷ ⌷ ⌷ ⌷ U

Notes: ⊘ One tent per pitch, maximum 2 dogs per pitch, no pit bull terriers. Dogs must be kept on leads. Pets' corner (ponies, chickens).

AA Pubs & Restaurants nearby: The Seafood Restaurant, PADSTOW, PL28 8BY, 01841 532700

RUTHERNBRIDGE

Places to visit

Prideaux Place, PADSTOW, PL28 8RP, 01841 532411 www.prideauxplace.co.uk

Cornwall's Regimental Museum, BODMIN, PL31 1EG, 01208 72810

Great for kids: Pencarrow, BODMIN, PL30 3AG, 01208 841369 www.pencarrow.co.uk

Devon's Crealy Great Adventure Park, CLYST ST MARY, EX5 1DR, 01395 233200 www.crealy.co.uk

---

RUTHERNBRIDGE   Map 2 SX06

Ruthern Valley Holidays
▶▶▶79%   GOLD

tel: 01208 831395 **PL30 5LU**
email: camping@ruthernvalley.com
dir: A389 through Bodmin, follow St Austell signs, then Lanivet signs. At top of hill right onto unclassified road signed Ruthernbridge. Follow signs. **grid ref:** SX014665

An attractive woodland site peacefully located in a small river valley west of Bodmin Moor. This away-from-it-all park is ideal for those wanting a quiet holiday, and the informal pitches are spread in four natural areas, with plenty of sheltered space. There are also 12 lodges, heated wooden wigwams, camping pods, and static holiday vans for hire. 7.5 acre site. 26 touring pitches. 2 hardstandings. Caravan pitches. Motorhome pitches. Tent pitches. 3 statics. 3 tipis. 3 wooden pods.

Open: all year **Last arrival:** 20.30hrs **Last departure:** noon

Pitches: ⌷ ⌷ **Å** ⌷ **Leisure:** ⌷

Facilities: ⌷ ⊙ ✳ ⌷ ⌷ ⌷ ⌷ **WiFi** ⌷ ⌷

Services: ⌷ ⌷ ⌷ ⌷ ⌷ ⌷

Within 3 miles: ⌷ ⌷ ⌷ ⌷ U

Notes: ⊗ No noise 22.30hrs-07.00hrs, no fires. Farm animals.

AA Pubs & Restaurants nearby: The Borough Arms, DUNMERE, PL31 2RD, 01208 73118

Trehellas House Hotel & Restaurant, BODMIN, PL30 3AD, 01208 72700

ST AGNES   Map 2 SW75

Places to visit

Royal Cornwall Museum, TRURO, TR1 2SJ, 01872 272205 www.royalcornwallmuseum.org.uk

Trerice, TRERICE, TR8 4PG, 01637 875404 www.nationaltrust.org.uk/trerice/

Beacon Cottage Farm Touring Park
▶▶▶▶80%

tel: 01872 552347 & 07879 413862 **Beacon Dr TR5 0NU**
email: beaconcottagefarm@lineone.net
dir: From A30 at Threeburrows rdbt take B3277 to St Agnes, left into Goonvrea Rd, right into Beacon Drive, follow brown sign to site. **grid ref:** SW705502

A neat and compact site on a working farm, utilising a cottage and outhouses, an old orchard and adjoining walled paddock. The unique location on a headland looking north-east along the coast comes with stunning views towards St Ives, and the keen friendly family owners keep all areas very well maintained. 5 acre site. 70 touring pitches. 5 hardstandings. 2 seasonal pitches. Caravan pitches. Motorhome pitches. Tent pitches.

Open: Apr-Oct **Last arrival:** 20.00hrs **Last departure:** noon

Pitches: ⌷ £17-£24 ⌷ £17-£24 **Å** £17-£24 **Leisure:** ⌷ ⌷

Facilities: ⌷ ⊙ ⌷ ✳ ⌷ ⌷ ⌷ **WiFi** ⌷ ⌷ ⌷

Services: ⌷ ⌷ ⌷ ⌷ ⌷ ⌷

Within 3 miles: ⌷ ⌷ ⌷ ◎ ⌷ ⌷ ⌷ U

Notes: No large groups, no noise after 22.00hrs. Dogs must be kept on leads. Secure year-round caravan storage.

AA Pubs & Restaurants nearby: Driftwood Spars, ST AGNES, TR5 0RT, 01872 552428

PITCHES: ⌷ Caravans ⌷ Motorhomes **Å** Tents ⌷ Glamping-style accommodation **SERVICES:** ⌷ Electric hook up ⌷ Launderette ⌷ Licensed bar ⌷ Calor Gas ⌷ Camping Gaz ⌷ Toilet fluid ⌷ Café/Restaurant ⌷ Fast Food/Takeaway ⌷ Battery charging ⌷ Baby care ⌷ Motorvan service point
ABBREVIATIONS: BH/bank hols – bank holidays Etr – Easter Spring BH – Spring Bank Holiday fr – from hrs – hours m – mile mdnt – midnight rdbt – roundabout rs – restricted service wk – week wknd – weekend x-rds – cross roads ⊘ No credit or debit cards ⊗ No dogs ⌷ Children of all ages accepted

ST AGNES *continued*

Presingoll Farm Caravan & Camping Park
▶▶▶82%

tel: 01872 552333 **TR5 0PB**
email: pam@presingollfarm.co.uk **web:** www.presingollfarm.co.uk
dir: *From A30 Chiverton rdbt take B3277 towards St Agnes. Site 3m on right.*
grid ref: *SW721494*

An attractive rural park adjoining farmland, with extensive views of the coast beyond. Family owned and run, with level grass pitches, and a modernised toilet block in smart converted farm buildings. There is also a campers' room with microwave, freezer, kettle and free coffee and tea, and a children's play area. This is an ideal base for touring the Newquay and St Ives areas. 5 acre site. 90 touring pitches. 6 hardstandings. Caravan pitches. Motorhome pitches. Tent pitches.

Open: Etr & Apr-Oct **Last departure:** 10.00hrs
Pitches: * ⛺ fr £15 ⛟ fr £15 ▲ fr £15
Leisure: ⚠
Facilities: ⌂⊙⅋☀⅏🔥🐾♻🛈
Services: 🔌🔲🛒
Within 3 miles: ⅏🛍U
Notes: 🚫 No large groups. Dogs must be kept on leads.
AA Pubs & Restaurants nearby: Driftwood Spars, ST AGNES, TR5 0RT, 01872 552428

NEW Blue Hills Touring Park
▶▶▶78%

tel: 01872 552999 **Cross Combe, Trevellas TR5 0XP**
email: camping@blue-hills.co.uk
dir: *From A30 at Boxheater junct take B3285 signed Perranporth & St Agnes. In Trevellas, right, follow Cross Coombe & site signs. NB It is advisable not to use Sat Nav; do not arrive via Wheal Killy or Mithian School as roads are very narrow.* **grid ref:** *SW732521*

In an Area of Outstanding Natural Beauty, this small and tranquil campsite enjoys superb views over the Cornish countryside. Located on the rugged north Cornish coast, just a short walk away from the dog-friendly Trevellas Porth cove, the site is split into three attractive, slightly sloping areas, offering mainly level pitches and 28 with electric hook-ups. The facilities are good and include a laundry and utility room, and the reception stocks limited essentials; there are fridges and freezers for campers' use. At busy periods, a breakfast van visits the site in the mornings. Please note that from November to February the site is only open from Fridays to Mondays. 2.5 acre site. 30 touring pitches. Caravan pitches. Motorhome pitches. Tent pitches.

Open: all year (rs Nov-Feb open Fri-Mon only) **Last arrival:** 22.00hrs
Last departure: 11.00hrs
Pitches: ⛺ £12-£18 ⛟ £12-£18 ▲ £12-£18
Leisure: ⊛
Facilities: ⌂☀⅊🔥🛒WiFi♻🛈
Services: 🔌🔲🛒⅂
Within 3 miles: ⅏⅊🄷⅋⅄🛍🛍U
Notes: Dogs must be kept on leads.
AA Pubs & Restaurants nearby: Driftwood Spars, ST AGNES, TR5 0RT, 01872 552428
Rose-in-Vale Country House Hotel, ST AGNES, TR5 0QD, 01872 552202

ST ALLEN	Map 2 SW85

Places to visit

Royal Cornwall Museum, TRURO, TR1 2SJ, 01872 272205
www.royalcornwallmuseum.org.uk

Trerice, TRERICE, TR8 4PG, 01637 875404 www.nationaltrust.org.uk/trerice/

Great for kids: Dairy Land Farm World, NEWQUAY, TR8 5AA, 01872 510246
www.dairylandfarmworld.com

Tolcarne Campsite
▶▶▶82%

tel: 01872 540652 & 07881 965477 **Tolcarne Bungalow TR4 9QX**
email: dianemcd@talktalk.net
dir: *A30 towards Redruth. Approx 1m W of Carland Cross rdbt 2nd left to St Allen. 1m, 3rd left to site.* **grid ref:** *SW826513*

A rural site with fantastic countryside views from the terraced pitches. Expect level, beautifully mown pitches, and a spotlessly clean and purpose-built facilities block with bathrooms and a fully-equipped laundry room. Tenters have use of a campers' kitchen. Please note that the approach is via a narrow lane and the access to the camping field is quite steep. 1 acre site. 10 touring pitches. 5 seasonal pitches. Caravan pitches. Motorhome pitches. Tent pitches.

Open: all year **Last arrival:** 22.00hrs **Last departure:** noon
Pitches: ⛺ ⛟ ▲
Facilities: ⌂⊙☀⅊🔥⅋🛈
Services: 🔌🔲⊘🛒
Within 3 miles: ⅏⅊🛍
Notes: 🚫 No noise after 22.30hrs. Dogs must be kept on leads.
AA Pubs & Restaurants nearby: The Plume of Feathers, MITCHELL, TR8 5AX, 01872 510387

ST AUSTELL
Map 2 SX05

See also Carlyon Bay

Places to visit

Charlestown Shipwreck & Heritage Centre, ST AUSTELL, PL25 3NJ, 01726 69897
www.shipwreckcharlestown.com

Eden Project, ST AUSTELL, PL24 2SG, 01726 811911 www.edenproject.com

Great for kids: Wheal Martyn, ST AUSTELL, PL26 8XG, 01726 850362
www.wheal-martyn.com

PREMIER PARK

River Valley Holiday Park
▶▶▶▶▶ 86%

tel: 01726 73533 **London Apprentice PL26 7AP**
email: mail@rivervalleyholidaypark.co.uk **web:** www.rivervalleyholidaypark.co.uk
dir: *Take B3273 from St Austell to London Apprentice. Site signed, direct access to site from B3273.* **grid ref:** *SX010503*

A neat, well-maintained family-run park set in a pleasant river valley. The quality toilet block and attractively landscaped grounds make this a delightful base for a holiday. All pitches are hardstanding, mostly divided by low fencing and neatly trimmed hedges, and the park offers a good range of leisure facilities, including an inviting swimming pool, a games room, an internet room, and an excellent children's play area. There is direct access to river walks and an off-road cycle trail to the beach at Pentewan. The site is on the bus route to St Austell. 2 acre site. 45 touring pitches. 45 hardstandings. Caravan pitches. Motorhome pitches. Tent pitches. 40 statics.

Open: Apr-end Sep **Last arrival:** 21.00hrs **Last departure:** 11.00hrs

Pitches: * 🚐 £13-£34 🚍 £13-£34 ▲ £13-£34

Leisure: 🏊 ⚺ 🎣

Facilities: 🅿️ ⊙ ℗ ⚒ ♿ ⑤ 🚮 📶 🖥 ♻ 🔧

Services: 🔌 ⑤ 🚽

Within 3 miles: ⚓ 🎣 🗓 🛒 🐎 🎱 🎳 ↺

Notes: Dogs must be kept on leads.

AA Pubs & Restaurants nearby: Austell's, ST AUSTELL, PL25 3PH, 01726 813888

See advert below

PITCHES: 🚐 Caravans 🚍 Motorhomes ▲ Tents ⋒ Glamping-style accommodation **SERVICES:** 🔌 Electric hook up ⑤ Launderette 🍺 Licensed bar 🛢 Calor Gas ⊘ Camping Gaz Ⓣ Toilet fluid 🍽 Café/Restaurant 🍔 Fast Food/Takeaway 🔋 Battery charging 🍼 Baby care 🚐 Motorvan service point **ABBREVIATIONS:** BH/bank hols – bank holidays Etr – Easter Spring BH – Spring Bank Holiday fr – from hrs – hours m – mile mdnt – midnight rdbt – roundabout rs – restricted service wk – week wknd – weekend x-rds – cross roads ⊗ No credit or debit cards ⊗ No dogs 👫 Children of all ages accepted

ST AUSTELL *continued*

Meadow Lakes
►►►►81%

tel: 01726 882540 **Hewas Water PL26 7JG**
email: info@meadow-lakes.co.uk **web:** www.meadow-lakes.co.uk
dir: *From A390 4m SW of St Austell onto B3287, Tregony. 1m, site on left.*
grid ref: *SW966485*

Set in a quiet rural area, this extensive park is divided into paddocks with mature hedges and trees, and has its own coarse fishing lakes. This friendly, family park has enthusiastic and hands-on owners — all facilities are immaculate and spotlessly clean. The park offers organised indoor and outdoor activities for children in the summer holidays (there is a play barn for when the weather is unsuitable for using the two outdoor play areas), and at other times caters for adult breaks. There are animals in pens which children can enter. Self-catering lodges, static caravans and nine bungalows are also found at this site. The bus to Truro and St Austell stops within half a mile of the site. 56 acre site. 200 touring pitches. 11 hardstandings. 30 seasonal pitches. Caravan pitches. Motorhome pitches. Tent pitches. 35 statics. 4 wooden pods.

Open: mid Mar-end Oct **Last arrival:** 20.00hrs
Pitches: 🚐🚏⚠🏠 **Leisure:** ⚓🎢🎾🏊🕹🎱
Facilities: 🛁🚿📡☀♿🛍📱🍴🐕📶🖥♻❶
Services: 🔌🔋🛒🚽
Within 3 miles: ⚓🏇🎣♿🎢🛍🎮♻
Notes: Dogs must be kept on leads. Table tennis, tots' TV room.
AA Pubs & Restaurants nearby: Austell's, ST AUSTELL, PL25 3PH, 01726 813888
See advert on opposite page

Court Farm Holidays
►►►80%

tel: 01726 823684 & 07973 773681 **St Stephen PL26 7LE**
email: info@courtfarmcornwall.co.uk
dir: *Take A3058 towards St Austell, through St Stephen (pass Peugeot garage), right at St Stephen/Coombe Hay/Langreth/Industrial site sign. Site 400yds on right.*
grid ref: *SW953524*

Set in a peaceful rural location, this large camping field offers plenty of space, and is handy for the Eden Project and the Lost Gardens of Heligan. Coarse fishing, and star-gazing facilities at the Roseland Observatory (including astronomy lectures) are among the on-site attractions. It is a five-minute walk to a Co-op store, and also to the bus stop on the Newquay to St Austell route. 4 acre site. 50 touring pitches. 5 hardstandings. Caravan pitches. Motorhome pitches. Tent pitches.

Open: Apr-Sep **Last arrival:** by dark **Last departure:** 11.00hrs
Pitches: * 🚐 £11-£21.50 🚏 £11-£21.50 ⚠ £8-£18
Leisure: ⚠
Facilities: 📡☀♿🍴🐕📶❶
Services: 🔌🔋🛒🚽
Within 3 miles: ⚓🏇🎣🛍🎮♻
Notes: No noise after dark. Dogs must be kept on leads.
AA Pubs & Restaurants nearby: Austell's, ST AUSTELL, PL25 3PH, 01726 813888

| ST BLAZEY GATE | Map 2 SX05 |

Places to visit

Eden Project, ST AUSTELL, PL24 2SG, 01726 811911 www.edenproject.com

St Catherine's Castle, FOWEY, 0870 333 1181
www.english-heritage.org.uk/daysout/properties/st-catherines-castle

Great for kids: Wheal Martyn, ST AUSTELL, PL26 8XG, 01726 850362
www.wheal-martyn.com

Doubletrees Farm
►►►84%

tel: 01726 812266 **Luxulyan Rd PL24 2EH**
email: doubletreesfarm@gmail.com
dir: *On A390 at Blazey Gate. Turn by Leek Seed Chapel, almost opposite BP filling station. After approx 300yds turn right by public bench into site.* grid ref: *SX060540*

A popular park with terraced pitches offering superb sea and coastal views. It is close to beaches, and the Eden Project is only a 20-minute walk away. This site is very well maintained by friendly owners. There is a Chinese restaurant and a fish and chip shop; the local bus stops outside the park entrance. 1.57 acre site. 32 touring pitches. 6 hardstandings. Caravan pitches. Motorhome pitches. Tent pitches.

Open: all year **Last arrival:** 22.30hrs **Last departure:** 11.30hrs
Pitches: * 🚐 fr £15 🚏 fr £15 ⚠ fr £15
Facilities: 📡☀♿🍴🐕 **Services:** 🔌🔋🚽
Within 3 miles: ⚓🏇🎣◎🛍🎮♻
Notes: 🐾 No noise after mdnt. Dogs must be kept on leads.
AA Pubs & Restaurants nearby: Austell's, ST AUSTELL, PL25 3PH, 01726 813888

ST BURYAN
Map 2 SW42

Treverven Touring Caravan & Camping Park
►►►88%

tel: 01736 810200 & 810318 **Treverven Farm TR19 6DL**
email: info@treverventouringpark.co.uk **web:** www.treverventouringpark.co.uk
dir: A30 onto B3283 1.5m after St Buryan, left onto B3315. Site on right in 1m.
grid ref: SW410237

Situated in a quiet Area of Outstanding Natural Beauty, with panoramic sea and country views, this family-owned site is located off a traffic-free lane leading directly to the coastal path. The toilet facilities are very good, and Treverven is ideally placed for exploring west Cornwall. There is an excellent takeaway facility on site. 6 acre site. 115 touring pitches. Caravan pitches. Motorhome pitches. Tent pitches.

Open: Etr-Oct **Last departure:** noon

Pitches: 🚐 🚐 ▲

Leisure: 🛝

Facilities: 🏕️☉🏳️✳️🔥🕙🖐️🏳️🚶🖥️ ♻️ 🚻

Services: 🔌🗑️ 🔋📁ⓉΞ🏧🚻

Within 3 miles: 🗓️🚶🌳🍴🔌🖐️

Notes: No noise after 22.00hrs. Dogs must be kept on leads. Toaster & kettle available.

ST COLUMB MAJOR
Map 2 SW96

Places to visit
Prideaux Place, PADSTOW, PL28 8RP, 01841 532411 www.prideauxplace.co.uk

Cornwall's Regimental Museum, BODMIN, PL31 1EG, 01208 72810

Great for kids: Pencarrow, BODMIN, PL30 3AG, 01208 841369 www.pencarrow.co.uk

Devon's Crealy Great Adventure Park, CLYST ST MARY, EX5 1DR, 01395 233200 www.crealy.co.uk

---

Trewan Hall
►►►►80%

tel: 01637 880261 & 07900 677397 **TR9 6DB**
email: enquiries@trewan-hall.co.uk
dir: From A39 N of St Columb Major (do not enter town) turn left signed Talskiddy & St Eval. Site 1m on left. **grid ref:** SW911646

Trewan Hall lies at the centre of a Cornish estate amid 36 acres of wooded grounds. The site's extensive amenities include upgraded toilet facilities, hook-ups and good security, plus a 25-metre swimming pool, and a free, live theatre in a stone barn throughout July and August. The campsite shop stocks everything from groceries to camping equipment. The site also has fine gardens, four acres of woods for dog walking and a field available for ball games. St Columb is just a short walk away. 14.27 acre site. 200 touring pitches. Caravan pitches. Motorhome pitches. Tent pitches.

Open: 2 May-15 Sep (rs Low season shop open shorter hours) **Last arrival:** 22.00hrs **Last departure:** noon

Pitches: * 🚐 £14-£20.60 🚐 £14-£20.60 ▲ £14-£20.60

Leisure: 🏊🏸🛝⊙🎣🎵 **Facilities:** 🛁🏕️☉🏳️✳️🖐️📁🚶🖥️ 🚻 ♻️ 🚻

Services: 🔌🗑️ 🔋📁Ⓣ🚻🏧

Within 3 miles: 🚶🏌️◎🌳🔌🖐️⛳

Notes: Families & couples only, no cycling, no driving on fields from mdnt-08.00hrs, no noise after mdnt. Dogs must be kept on leads. Library, billiard room.

AA Pubs & Restaurants nearby: The Falcon Inn, ST MAWGAN, TR8 4EP, 01637 860225

PITCHES: 🚐 Caravans 🚐 Motorhomes ▲ Tents 🏠 Glamping-style accommodation **SERVICES:** 🔌 Electric hook up 🗑️ Launderette 🍺 Licensed bar
🔋 Calor Gas 🔥 Camping Gaz Ⓣ Toilet fluid 🍴 Café/Restaurant 🏧 Fast Food/Takeaway 🔋 Battery charging 👶 Baby care 🚻 Motorvan service point
ABBREVIATIONS: BH/bank hols – bank holidays Etr – Easter Spring BH – Spring Bank Holiday fr – from hrs – hours m – mile mdnt – midnight
rdbt – roundabout rs – restricted service wk – week wknd – weekend x-rds – cross roads 🚫 No credit or debit cards 🚫 No dogs 👪 Children of all ages accepted

ST COLUMB MAJOR *continued*

Southleigh Manor Naturist Park
►►►87%

tel: 01637 880938 **TR9 6HY**
email: enquiries@southleigh-manor.com
dir: *Exit A30 at junct with A39 signed Wadebridge. At Highgate Hill rdbt take A39. At Halloon rdbt take A39. At Trekenning rdbt take 4th exit signed RSPCA & Springfield Centre. Site 500mtrs on right.* **grid ref:** *SW918623*

A very well maintained, naturist park in the heart of the Cornish countryside, catering for families and couples only. Seclusion and security are very well planned, and the lovely gardens provide a calm setting. There are two lodges and static caravans for holiday hire. A bus stop at the entrance gate gives easy access to Newquay, Padstow or St Ives. 4 acre site. 50 touring pitches. Caravan pitches. Motorhome pitches. Tent pitches.

Open: Etr-Oct **Last arrival:** 20.00hrs **Last departure:** 10.30hrs

Pitches: ⌂ ⌂ Å

Leisure: ⌂ ⋀

Facilities: ⌂ ⊙ ⌂ ✳ ⊙ ⌂ ⌂ ⌂ ❶

Services: ⌂ ⌂ ⌂ ⌂ ⌂ ⊤ ⌂ ⌂

Within 3 miles: ⌂ ⌂ ⌂ ⌂ Ｕ

Notes: ⌂ Dogs to remain beside pitch/caravan except when exercising off site. Sauna, spa bath, pool table, putting green.

AA Pubs & Restaurants nearby: The Falcon Inn, ST MAWGAN, TR8 4EP, 01637 860225

ST GILES-ON-THE-HEATH

See Chapmans Well (Devon)

ST HILARY   Map 2 SW53

Places to visit
Godolphin House, GODOLPHIN CROSS, TR13 9RE, 01736 763194
www.nationaltrust.org.uk/godolphin

St Michael's Mount, MARAZION, TR17 0HT, 01736 710507
www.stmichaelsmount.co.uk

Great for kids: The Flambards Theme Park, HELSTON, TR13 0QA, 01326 573404
www.flambards.co.uk

Wayfarers Caravan & Camping Park
►►►►85%

tel: 01736 763326 **Relubbus Ln TR20 9EF**
email: elaine@wayfarerspark.co.uk
dir: *Exit A30 onto A394 towards Helston. Left at rdbt onto B3280 after 2m. Site 1.5m on left on bend.* **grid ref:** *SW558314*

Located in the centre of St Hilary, two and half miles from St Michael's Mount, this is a quiet sheltered park in a peaceful rural setting. It offers spacious, well-drained pitches and very well cared for facilities. It has a separate car park for campers which makes the camping area safer. 4.8 acre site. 32 touring pitches. 25 hardstandings. Caravan pitches. Motorhome pitches. Tent pitches. 3 statics.

Open: May-Sep **Last arrival:** 19.00hrs **Last departure:** 11.00hrs

Pitches: * ⌂ £19.50-£27 ⌂ £19.50-£27 Å £17-£24

Facilities: ⌂ ⊙ ⌂ ✳ ⌂ ⌂ ⌂ ⌂ ❶

Services: ⌂ ⌂ ⌂ ⌂ ⊤ ⌂ ⌂

Within 3 miles: ⌂ ⌂ ⌂ ◎ ⌂ ⌂ ⌂ Ｕ

Notes: Adults only. ⌂ No pets.

AA Pubs & Restaurants nearby: The Victoria Inn, PERRANUTHNOE, TR20 9NP, 01736 710309

Trevair Touring Park
►►►79%

tel: 01736 740647 **South Treveneague TR20 9BY**
email: info@trevairtouringpark.co.uk
dir: *A30 onto A394 signed Helston. 2m to rdbt, left onto B3280. Through Goldsithney. Left at brown site sign. Through 20mph zone to site, 1m on right.* **grid ref:** *SW548326*

Set in a rural location adjacent to woodland, this park is level and secluded, with grassy pitches. Marazion's beaches and the famous St Michael's Mount are just three miles away. The friendly owners live at the farmhouse on the park. 3.5 acre site. 40 touring pitches. Caravan pitches. Motorhome pitches. Tent pitches. 2 statics.

Open: Etr-Nov **Last arrival:** 22.00hrs **Last departure:** 11.00hrs

Pitches: ⌂ ⌂ Å

Facilities: ⌂ ⊙ ✳ ❸ ❶

Services: ⌂ ⌂ ⌂

Within 3 miles: ⌂ ⌂ ⌂ ⌂ Ｕ

Notes: ⌂ No noise after 23.00hrs. Dogs must be kept on leads.

AA Pubs & Restaurants nearby: The Victoria Inn, PERRANUTHNOE, TR20 9NP, 01736 710309

ST IVES

Places to visit
Barbara Hepworth Museum & Sculpture Garden, ST IVES, TR26 1AD, 01736 796226 www.tate.org.uk/stives

Tate St Ives, ST IVES, TR26 1TG, 01736 796226 www.tate.org.uk/stives

---

LEISURE: ⌂ Indoor swimming pool ⌂ Outdoor swimming pool ⋀ Children's playground ⌂ Kid's club ⌂ Tennis court ⌂ Games room ⌂ Separate TV room ⌂ golf course ⌂ Boats for hire ⊟ Cinema ⌂ Entertainment ⌂ Fishing ◎ Mini golf ⌂ Watersports ⌂ Gym ⌂ Sports field Spa Ｕ Stables
FACILITIES: ⌂ Bath ⌂ Shower ⊙ Electric shaver ⌂ Hairdryer ✳ Ice Pack Facility ⌂ Disabled facilities ⌂ Public telephone ⌂ Shop on site or within 200yds ⌂ Mobile shop (calls at least 5 days a week) ⌂ BBQ area ⌂ Picnic area ⌂ Wi-fi ⌂ Internet access ❸ Recycling ❶ Tourist info ⌂ Dog exercise area

---

ST IVES   Map 2 SW54

PREMIER PARK

Polmanter Touring Park
▶▶▶▶▶ 95%

Best of British

tel: 01736 795640 **Halsetown TR26 3LX**
email: reception@polmanter.com **web:** www.polmanter.com
dir: *Signed from B3311 at Halsetown.* **grid ref:** *SW510388*

A well-developed touring park on high ground, Polmanter is an excellent choice for family holidays and offers high quality in all areas, from the immaculate modern toilet blocks to the outdoor swimming pool and hard tennis courts. Pitches are individually marked and sited in meadows, and the park has been tastefully landscaped, which includes a field with full-facility hardstanding pitches to accommodate larger caravans and motorhomes. The fishing port and beaches of St Ives are just a mile and a half away, and there is a bus service in high season. 20 acre site. 270 touring pitches. 60 hardstandings. Caravan pitches. Motorhome pitches. Tent pitches.

Open: Spring BH-10 Sep (rs Spring BH shop, pool, bar & takeaway food closed, bus does not run) **Last arrival:** 21.00hrs **Last departure:** 10.00hrs
Pitches: 🚐 🚍 ▲   **Leisure:** ⋞ 🅰 ♨ 😊 🔍
Facilities: 🏕⊙ℱ☀♿⊙Ⓢ 🚻 WiFi 🖳 ♻ 𝒊
Services: 🔌🅖 🍴🥫⊘Ⓣ🍴🛒♨
Within 3 miles: ♪🐟🅷ℓ◎⌛🔥🎱🅖U
Notes: Family camping only, no skateboards, roller blades or heelys. Dogs must be kept on leads. Putting green.
AA Pubs & Restaurants nearby: The Tinners Arms, ZENNOR, TR26 3BY, 01736 796927
See advert on page 112

PREMIER PARK

Ayr Holiday Park
▶▶▶▶▶ 87%

GOLD

tel: 01736 795855 **TR26 1EJ**
email: recept@ayrholidaypark.co.uk **web:** www.ayrholidaypark.co.uk
dir: *From A30 follow St Ives 'large vehicles' route via B3311 through Halsetown onto B3306. Site signed towards St Ives town centre.* **grid ref:** *SW509408*

A well-established park on a cliff side overlooking St Ives Bay, with a heated toilet block that makes winter holidaying more attractive. There are stunning views from most pitches, and the town centre, harbour and beach are only half a mile away, with direct access to the coastal footpath. This makes an excellent base for surfing enthusiasts. Please note that it is advisable not to follow Sat Nav; use guide directions and avoid the town centre. 4 acre site. 40 touring pitches. 20 hardstandings. Caravan pitches. Motorhome pitches. Tent pitches.

Open: all year **Last arrival:** 22.00hrs **Last departure:** 10.00hrs
Pitches: * 🚐 £18-£37 🚍 £18-£37 ▲ £18-£37
Leisure: 🅰 🔍
Facilities: 🛁🏕⊙ℱ☀♿⊙ 🚻 🐕 WiFi 🖳 ♻ 𝒊
Services: 🔌🅖 🍴⊘Ⓣ🛒♨
Within 3 miles: ♪🐟🅷ℓ◎⌛🔥🎱🅖U
Notes: No disposable BBQs. Dogs must be kept on leads.
AA Pubs & Restaurants nearby: The Sloop Inn, ST IVES, TR26 1LP, 01736 796584
The Queens, ST IVES, TR26 1RR, 01736 796468

PITCHES: 🚐 Caravans 🚍 Motorhomes ▲ Tents 🏠 Glamping-style accommodation   **SERVICES:** 🔌 Electric hook up 🅖 Launderette 🍴 Licensed bar 🅖 Calor Gas ⊘ Camping Gaz Ⓣ Toilet fluid 🍴 Café/Restaurant 🛒 Fast Food/Takeaway ♨ Battery charging 🥫 Baby care ♨ Motorvan service point
ABBREVIATIONS: BH/bank hols – bank holidays Etr – Easter Spring BH – Spring Bank Holiday fr – from hrs – hours m – mile mdnt – midnight rdbt – roundabout rs – restricted service wk – week wknd – weekend x-rds – cross roads 🚫 No credit or debit cards 🚫 No dogs 👪 Children of all ages accepted

ST IVES *continued*

Trevalgan Touring Park
►►►► 88%

tel: 01736 791892 **Trevalgan TR26 3BJ**
email: reception@trevalgantouringpark.co.uk **web:** www.trevalgantouringpark.co.uk
dir: *From A30 follow holiday route to St Ives. B3311 through Halsetown to B3306. Left towards Land's End. Site signed 0.5m on right.* **grid ref:** *SW490402*

Serious investment by hands-on owners over the past two seasons has totally transformed this welcoming park, set in a rural area on the coastal road from St Ives to Zennor. The park is surrounded by mature hedges but there are still extensive views over the sea. There is now a new entrance (with barriers) and a smart wood-clad reception and shop (daily-baked bread and pastries are available); excellent new and upmarket toilet facilities which have family rooms and underfloor heating, and extensive landscaping across the park that has resulted in more spacious pitches which offer both privacy and shelter. A regular bus service connects the park with St Ives from late May to September. 9 acre site. 120 touring pitches. Caravan pitches. Motorhome pitches. Tent pitches.

Open: Spring BH-Sep **Last arrival:** 22.00hrs **Last departure:** 11.00hrs
Pitches: 🚐 🚍 Å
Leisure: ⚠ 🎠 🔍
Facilities: 🐾 ☺ ☎ ⚡ ✳ ♿ 🔟 🆔 🖳 ♻ ❂

Services: 🔌🗑🍺🚿🚽⚓

Within 3 miles: 🎣🛝🎯🏌🐾◎⛳🏧🛒⛵

Notes: Dogs must be kept on leads.

AA Pubs & Restaurants nearby: The Queens, ST IVES, TR26 1RR, 01736 796468

The Sloop Inn, ST IVES, TR26 1LP, 01736 796584

See advert below

Higher Penderleath Caravan & Camping Park
►►►► 81%

tel: 01736 798403 & 07840 208542 **Towednack TR26 3AF**
email: holidays@penderleath.co.uk **web:** www.penderleath.co.uk
dir: *From A30 take A3074 towards St Ives. Left at 2nd mini-rdbt, approx 3m to T-junct. Left then immediately right. Next left.* **grid ref:** *SW496375*

Set in a rugged rural location, this tranquil park has extensive views towards St Ives Bay and the north coast. Facilities are all housed in modernised granite barns, and include spotless toilets with fully serviced shower rooms, and there's a quiet licensed bar with beer garden, a food takeaway, breakfast room and bar meals. The owners are welcoming and helpful. There is a bus service to St Ives available in high season. 10 acre site. 75 touring pitches. Caravan pitches. Motorhome pitches. Tent pitches.

Open: Etr-Oct **Last arrival:** 21.30hrs **Last departure:** 10.30hrs

Pitches: 🚐🚌🏕

Leisure: ⚘🎣

Facilities: 🛡◎📮🚿🔥🐕♻🚗❓

Services: 🔌🗑🍺🍺🚿🚽🏧🍴🛒🧺

Within 3 miles: 🎣🛝🎯🏌🐾◎⛳🏧🛒⛵

Notes: No campfires, no noise after 23.00hrs, dogs must be well behaved and kept on leads.

AA Pubs & Restaurants nearby: The Watermill, ST IVES, TR27 6LQ, 01736 757912

Balnoon Camping Site
►► 88%

tel: 01736 795431 & 07751 600555 **Halsetown TR26 3JA**
email: nat@balnoon.fsnet.co.uk
dir: *From A30 take A3074, at 2nd mini-rdbt 1st left signed Tate/St Ives. In 3m turn right after The Lodge at Balnoon.* **grid ref:** *SW509382*

Small, quiet and friendly, this sheltered site offers superb views of the adjacent rolling hills. The two paddocks are surrounded by mature hedges, and the toilet facilities are kept spotlessly clean. The beaches of Carbis Bay and St Ives are about two miles away. 1 acre site. 23 touring pitches. Caravan pitches. Motorhome pitches. Tent pitches.

Open: Etr-Oct **Last arrival:** 20.00hrs **Last departure:** 11.00hrs

Pitches: * 🚐 £12-£16 🚌 🏕 **Facilities:** 🛡◎📮🚿♻

Services: 🔌🚿🚽🛒

Within 3 miles: 🎣🛝🎯🏌🐾◎⛳🏧🛒⛵

Notes: 🚫 No noise between 23.00hrs-07.30hrs. Dogs must be kept on leads. Provisions for sale (peak season).

AA Pubs & Restaurants nearby: The Watermill, ST IVES, TR27 6LQ, 01736 757912

ST JUST (NEAR LAND'S END)

Map 2 SW33

Places to visit

Geevor Tin Mine, PENDEEN, TR19 7EW, 01736 788662 www.geevor.com

Carn Euny Ancient Village, SANCREED, 0870 333 1181
www.english-heritage.org.uk/daysout/properties/carn-euny-ancient-village

Roselands Caravan and Camping Park
►►►84%

tel: 01736 788571 & 07718 745065 **Dowran TR19 7RS**
email: info@roselands.co.uk
dir: *From A30 Penzance bypass onto A3071 for St Just. 5m, left at sign after tin mine chimney, follow signs to site.* **grid ref:** *SW387305*

A small, friendly park in a sheltered rural setting, an ideal location for a quiet family holiday. The owners continue to upgrade the park, and in addition to the attractive little bar there is an indoor games room, children's playground and good toilet facilities. 4 acre site. 35 touring pitches. 5 seasonal pitches. Caravan pitches. Motorhome pitches. Tent pitches. 15 statics.

Open: Mar-Oct **Last arrival:** 21.00hrs **Last departure:** 11.00hrs

Pitches: ⛺ ⛟ Å

Leisure: 🅰 🔍 ⬜ **Facilities:** 🛁 ☉ 🧴 ❄ 🕐 🖬 🍴 ♿ 🐕 🔤 💻 ♻ 🛈
Services: 🔌 ⑤ 🔧 🛢 🍴 ⑪ 🍴 🍽 ♿ **Within 3 miles:** 🛥 ✏ 🚣 ⑥ 🛍 ↺

Notes: Dogs must be kept on leads. Dog walks on moors.

AA Pubs & Restaurants nearby: Harris's Restaurant, PENZANCE, TR18 2LZ, 01736 364408

The Navy Inn, PENZANCE, TR18 4DE, 01736 333232

See which sites have been awarded Gold Pennants
on page 36

Trevaylor Caravan & Camping Park
►►►82%

tel: 01736 787016 & 07816 992519 **Botallack TR19 7PU**
email: trevaylor@cornishcamping.co.uk **web:** www.cornishcamping.co.uk
dir: *On B3306 (St Just-St Ives road), site on right 0.75m from St Just.* **grid ref:** *SW368222*

A sheltered grassy site located off the beaten track in a peaceful location at the western tip of Cornwall; it makes an ideal base for discovering Penzance and Land's End. The dramatic coastline and the pretty villages nearby are truly unspoilt. Clean, well-maintained facilities including a good shop are offered along with a bar serving meals. The enthusiastic owners offer pitches with electric hook-ups and a shower block with heating. An open-top bus stops at the entrance to the site. 6 acre site. 50 touring pitches. 6 hardstandings. Caravan pitches. Motorhome pitches. Tent pitches. 6 statics.

Open: all year **Last arrival:** 21.00hrs **Last departure:** 11.00hrs

Pitches: ⛺ ⛟ Å

Leisure: 🅰 🔍 ⬜

Facilities: 🛁 🧴 ❄ 🖬 🔤 ♻ 🛈

Services: 🔌 ⑤ 🔧 🛢 🍴 ⑪ 🍴 🍽 ♿

Within 3 miles: 🛥 ✏ 🚣 ⑥ 🛍 ↺

Notes: Quiet after 22.00hrs. Dogs must be kept on leads.

AA Pubs & Restaurants nearby: Harris's Restaurant, PENZANCE, TR18 2LZ, 01736 364408

The Navy Inn, PENZANCE, TR18 4DE, 01736 333232

Kelynack Caravan & Camping Park

►►►80%

tel: 01736 787633 **Kelynack TR19 7RE**
email: enquiries@kelynackholidays.co.uk **web:** www.kelynackholidays.co.uk
dir: *1m S of St Just, 5m N of Land's End on B3306.* **grid ref:** *SW374301*

A small secluded park that sits alongside a stream in an unspoilt rural location. The level grass pitches are in two areas. The park is within reach of Land's End, Sennen Cove, Minack Theatre and Penzance. 3 acre site. 28 touring pitches. 3 hardstandings. Caravan pitches. Motorhome pitches. Tent pitches. 13 statics.

Open: all year **Last arrival:** 22.00hrs **Last departure:** 10.00hrs

Pitches: * ⊡ £6.50-£7.50 ⊡ £6.50-£7.50 ▲ £6.50-£7.50

Leisure: ⚙ ✎ **Facilities:** ⚙⊙⟋⚘⟐⌂⟐⟐ⅢⅡ ✿ ❶

Services: ⊡⟐⟐⟐⟐⟐⟐

Within 3 miles: ⚙⟋⟐⟐⟐⟐

Notes: Dogs must be kept on leads. Dining & cooking shelter.

AA Pubs & Restaurants nearby: Harris's Restaurant, PENZANCE, TR18 2LZ, 01736 364408

The Navy Inn, PENZANCE, TR18 4DE, 01736 333232

Secret Garden Caravan & Camping Park

►►►77%

tel: 01736 788301 **Bosavern House TR19 7RD**
email: mail@bosavern.com
dir: *Exit A3071 near St Just onto B3306 (Land's End road). Site 0.5m on left.*
grid ref: *SW370305*

A neat little site in a walled garden behind a guest house, where visitors can enjoy breakfast, and snacks in the bar in the evening. This site is in a fairly sheltered location with all grassy pitches. Please note that there is no children's playground. 1.5 acre site. 12 touring pitches. Caravan pitches. Motorhome pitches. Tent pitches.

Open: Mar-Oct **Last arrival:** 22.00hrs **Last departure:** noon

Pitches: * ⊡ fr £17 ⊡ fr £17 ▲ fr £17

Leisure: ▱ **Facilities:** ⚙⊙⟐⟐Ⅲ ⟐ ✿ ❶

Services: ⊡⟐⟐⟐⟐⟐ **Within 3 miles:** ⚙⟋⟐⟐ **Notes:** No pets.

AA Pubs & Restaurants nearby: Harris's Restaurant, PENZANCE, TR18 2LZ, 01736 364408

The Navy Inn, PENZANCE, TR18 4DE, 01736 333232

ST JUST-IN-ROSELAND Map 2 SW83

Places to visit

St Mawes Castle, ST MAWES, TR2 3AA, 01326 270526
www.english-heritage.org.uk/daysout/properties/st-mawes-castle

Trelissick Garden, TRELISSICK GARDEN, TR3 6QL, 01872 862090
www.nationaltrust.org.uk/trelissick

PREMIER PARK

Trethem Mill Touring Park

►►►►►92%

tel: 01872 580504 **TR2 5JF**
email: reception@trethem.com **web:** www.trethem.com
dir: *From Tregony on A3078 to St Mawes. 2m after Trewithian, follow signs to site.*
grid ref: *SW860365*

A quality park in all areas, with upgraded amenities including a reception, shop, laundry, and disabled/family room. This carefully-tended and sheltered park is in a lovely rural setting, with spacious pitches separated by young trees and shrubs. The very keen family who own the site are continually looking for ways to enhance its facilities. 11 acre site. 84 touring pitches. 61 hardstandings. Caravan pitches. Motorhome pitches. Tent pitches.

Open: Apr-mid Oct **Last arrival:** 20.00hrs **Last departure:** 11.00hrs

Pitches: * ⊡ £19-£27 ⊡ £19-£27 ▲ £19-£27

Leisure: ⚙ ⟐

Facilities: ⚙⊙⟋⚘⟐⟐⟐⟐Ⅲ ✿ ❶

Services: ⊡⟐⟐⟐⟐⟐⟐

Within 3 miles: ⟐⟋⟐⟐⟐

Notes: No skateboards or rollerblades. Dogs must be kept on leads. Information centre, mobile takeaway.

AA Pubs & Restaurants nearby: The Victory Inn, ST MAWES, TR2 5DQ, 01326 270324

Hotel Tresanton, ST MAWES, TR2 5DR, 01326 270055

Driftwood, PORTSCATHO, TR2 5EW, 01872 580644

PITCHES: ⊡ Caravans ⊡ Motorhomes ▲ Tents ⊙ Glamping-style accommodation **SERVICES:** ⊡ Electric hook up ⟐ Launderette ⟐ Licensed bar ⟐ Calor Gas ⟐ Camping Gaz ⟐ Toilet fluid ⟐ Café/Restaurant ⟐ Fast Food/Takeaway ⟐ Battery charging ⟐ Baby care ⟐ Motorvan service point **ABBREVIATIONS:** BH/bank hols – bank holidays Etr – Easter Spring BH – Spring Bank Holiday fr – from hrs – hours m – mile mdnt – midnight rdbt – roundabout rs – restricted service wk – week wknd – weekend x-rds – cross roads ⟐ No credit or debit cards ⟐ No dogs ⟐⟐ Children of all ages accepted

ST MARY'S (ISLES OF SCILLY)   Map 2 SV91

Places to visit

Isles of Scilly Museum, ST MARY'S, TR21 0JT, 01720 422337
www.iosmuseum.org

Garrison Campsite
►►►82%

tel: 01720 422670 **Tower Cottage, The Garrison TR21 0LS**
email: info@garrisonholidays.com
dir: 10 mins' walk from quay to site. **grid ref:** SV897104

Set on the top of an old fort with superb views, this park offers tent-only pitches in
a choice of well-sheltered paddocks, including fully-equipped ready erected tents
which are available for hire. There are modern toilet facilities (with powerful
showers), a superb children's play area and a good shop at this attractive site,
which is only 10 minutes from the town, the quay and the nearest beaches. There is
easy access to the other islands via the direct boat service from the Hugh Town
quay; the campsite owners will transport all luggage, camping equipment etc to
and from the quay. Good food is available in the many hostelries in the main town.
9.5 acre site. 120 touring pitches. Tent pitches.

Open: Etr-Oct **Last arrival:** 20.00hrs **Last departure:** 19.00hrs

Pitches: * ▲ £17.60-£22

Facilities: ⓝ☉♚☀☉⑤ℹ️WiFi♻️❼   **Services:** ⬛⭕🔋🧹🚮

Within 3 miles: ⚓➹⚑⛵⑤⑤○

Notes: No cars on site, no open fires, dogs by prior arrangement only.
Dogs must be kept on leads.

ST MERRYN (NEAR PADSTOW)   Map 2 SW87

Places to visit

Prideaux Place, PADSTOW, PL28 8RP, 01841 532411 www.prideauxplace.co.uk

Great for kids: Devon's Crealy Great Adventure Park, CLYST ST MARY, EX5 1DR,
01395 233200 www.crealy.co.uk

Harlyn Sands Holiday Park
HOLIDAY CENTRE 81%

tel: 01841 520720 & 01752 841485 **Lighthouse Rd, Trevose Head PL28 8SQ**
email: enquiries@harlynsands.co.uk
dir: Exit B3276 in St Merryn centre onto unclassified road towards Constantine Bay &
Trevose Golf Club. Through golf club, left to site. **grid ref:** SW873752

A family park for 'bucket and spade' holidays, surrounded by seven bays each with
its own sandy beach. The on-site entertainment for children and adults is extensive,
and there is an indoor swimming pool complex, excellent restaurant and takeaway,
and a quiet over-30s lounge bar. 21 acre site. 160 touring pitches. 6 hardstandings.
60 seasonal pitches. Caravan pitches. Motorhome pitches. Tent pitches. 350
statics.

Open: Etr-end Oct **Last arrival:** 22.00hrs **Last departure:** 10.00hrs

Pitches: ⬜⬜▲   **Leisure:** ♨️⚿🏐✦🎱⬜🎵

Facilities: ⓝ☉♚☀☉⑤ℹ️🛒WiFi♻️❼

Services: ⬛⭕🔋🧹🔋⛟Ⓣ🍴🚮   **Within 3 miles:** ⚓⚑⑤⑤○

Notes: Families only. Dogs must be kept on leads. Arcade, clubhouse, chip shop.

Atlantic Bays Holiday Park
►►►►►85%

tel: 01841 520855 **St Merryn PL28 8PY**
email: info@atlanticbaysholidaypark.co.uk **web:** www.atlanticbaysholidaypark.co.uk
dir: From A30 SW of Bodmin take exit signed Victoria & Roche, 1st exit at rdbt. At
Trekenning rdbt 4th exit signed A39 & Wadebridge. At Winnards Perch rdbt left B3274
signed Padstow. Left in 3m, follow signs. **grid ref:** SW890717

Atlantic Bays has a mix of hardstanding and grass pitches, a high quality toilet
and shower block and a comfortable bar and restaurant. The park is set in a
rural area yet only two miles from the coast and beautiful sandy beaches, and
within easy reach of the quaint fishing village of Padstow, and Newquay for
fantastic surfing. 27 acre site. 70 touring pitches. 50 hardstandings. Caravan
pitches. Motorhome pitches. Tent pitches. 171 statics.

Open: Mar-2 Jan **Last arrival:** 21.00hrs **Last departure:** noon

Pitches: ⬜⬜▲

Leisure: ⚿⚽✦

Facilities: ⓝ☉♚☀🍀⑤ℹ️🅿️🛒🚽WiFi🖥️♻️❼

Services: ⬛⭕🔋Ⓣ🛒⛟

Within 3 miles: ⚓➹🎯⚑◎♨️⑤⑤○

Notes: Dogs must be kept on leads.

AA Pubs & Restaurants nearby: The Seafood Restaurant, PADSTOW, PL28 8BY,
01841 532700

See advert opposite

Carnevas Holiday Park & Farm Cottages

►►►► 83%

tel: 01841 520230 & 521209 **Carnevas Farm PL28 8PN**
email: carnevascampsite@aol.com **web:** www.carnevasholidaypark.com
dir: *From St Merryn on B3276 towards Porthcothan Bay. Approx 2m turn right at site sign onto unclassified road opposite Tredrea Inn. Site 0.25m on right.* **grid ref:** *SW862728*

A family-run park on a working farm, divided into four paddocks on slightly sloping grass. The toilets are central to all areas, and there is a small licensed bar serving bar meals. An ideal base for exploring the fishing town of Padstow or the surfing beach at Newquay. 8 acre site. 195 touring pitches. Caravan pitches. Motorhome pitches. Tent pitches. 14 statics.

Open: Apr-Oct (rs Apr-Spring BH & mid Sep-Oct shop, bar & restaurant closed)
Pitches: * ⊞ £10.50-£18.50 ⊞ £10.50-£18.50 ▲ £10.50-£18.50
Leisure: ⚙ ♠
Facilities: ⊓ ⊙ ⌁ ✳ ⧖ ⊛ ⑤ WiFi ♻ ❶
Services: ⊡ ⑥ ⧉ 🔋 ⌀ T ⊙⌶ ⊨ ⌄
Within 3 miles: ↓ ✎ ⤓ ⑤ ⑥ ∪

Notes: No skateboards, no supermarket deliveries. Dogs must be kept on leads.
AA Pubs & Restaurants nearby: The Seafood Restaurant, PADSTOW, PL28 8BY, 01841 532700

See advert on page 91

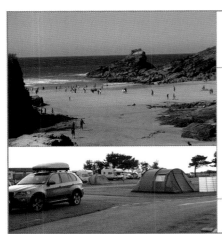
PITCHES: ⊞ Caravans ⊞ Motorhomes ▲ Tents ⋒ Glamping-style accommodation **SERVICES:** ⊡ Electric hook up ⑥ Launderette ⧉ Licensed bar ⬛ Calor Gas ⌀ Camping Gaz T Toilet fluid ⊙⌶ Café/Restaurant ⊞ Fast Food/Takeaway ⊨ Battery charging ⌁ Baby care ⌄ Motorvan service point
ABBREVIATIONS: BH/bank hols – bank holidays Etr – Easter Spring BH – Spring Bank Holiday fr – from hrs – hours m – mile mdnt – midnight rdbt – roundabout rs – restricted service wk – week wknd – weekend x-rds – cross roads ⊘ No credit or debit cards ⊗ No dogs ♦♦ Children of all ages accepted

ST MERRYN (NEAR PADSTOW) *continued*

Tregavone Touring Park
▶▶81%

tel: 01841 520148 **Tregavone Farm PL28 8JZ**
email: info@tregavone.co.uk
dir: *From A389 towards Padstow, right after Little Petherick. In 1m just beyond Padstow Holiday Park turn left onto unclassified road signed Tregavone. Site on left, approx 1m.*
grid ref: *SW898732*

Situated on a working farm with unspoilt country views, this spacious grassy park, run by friendly family owners, makes an ideal base for exploring the north Cornish coast and the seven local golden beaches with surfing areas, or for enjoying quiet country walks from the park. 3 acre site. 40 touring pitches. Caravan pitches. Motorhome pitches. Tent pitches. 1 static.

Open: Mar-Oct

Pitches: * ⊞ £10-£12 ⊞ £10-£12 ▲ £10-£12

Facilities: ♠⊙℗☀☇

Services: ❏⬚

Within 3 miles: ⬇♣☰℗◎⬗⬚⬚U

Notes: ☺

AA Pubs & Restaurants nearby: The Seafood Restaurant, PADSTOW, PL28 8BY, 01841 532700

ST MINVER	Map 2 SW97

PREMIER PARK

Gunvenna Holiday Park
▶▶▶▶▶82%

tel: 01208 862405 **PL27 6QN**
email: gunvenna.bookings@gmail.com **web:** www.gunvenna.com
dir: *From A39 N of Wadebridge take B3314 (Port Isaac road), site 4m on right.*
grid ref: *SW969782*

An attractive park with extensive rural views in a quiet country location, yet within three miles of Polzeath. This popular park is family owned and run, and provides good facilities in an ideal position for touring north Cornwall. The park has excellent hardstanding pitches, maturing landscaping and a beautiful indoor swimming pool with a glass roof. Two wooden mini glamping lodges, a holiday cottage and static caravans are for hire. The beach at Polzeath is very popular with the surfers. 10 acre site. 75 touring pitches. 24 hardstandings. 15 seasonal pitches. Caravan pitches. Motorhome pitches. Tent pitches. 44 statics. 2 wooden pods.

Open: Etr-Oct **Last arrival:** 20.30hrs **Last departure:** 11.00hrs

Pitches: ⊞⊞▲⌂

Leisure: ♨⌂◥♪

Facilities: ⬅♠⊙℗☀&⊙⑤⬚⌴☇Wifi ♻ ❼

Services: ❏⑤⬛⊘T⬚⬗⬥

Within 3 miles: ⬇♣℗⬗⬚⬚

Notes: No under 16yrs in pool unless accompanied by an adult, owners must clear up after their dogs. Dogs must be kept on leads.

AA Pubs & Restaurants nearby: The Maltsters Arms, CHAPEL AMBLE, PL27 6EU, 01208 812473

Restaurant Nathan Outlaw, ROCK, PL27 6LA, 01208 862737

See advert on opposite page

SENNEN

Places to visit
Carn Euny Ancient Village, SANCREED, 0870 333 1181
www.english-heritage.org.uk/daysout/properties/carn-euny-ancient-village

Chysauster Ancient Village, CHYSAUSTER ANCIENT VILLAGE, TR20 8XA, 07831 757934
www.english-heritage.org.uk/daysout/properties/chysauster-ancient-village

Great for kids: Geevor Tin Mine, PENDEEN, TR19 7EW, 01736 788662
www.geevor.com

SENNEN
Map 2 SW32

Trevedra Farm Caravan & Camping Site
►►►85%

tel: 01736 871818 & 871835 **TR19 7BE**
email: trevedra@btconnect.com
dir: *Take A30 towards Land's End. After junct with B3306 turn right into farm lane. NB Sat Nav directs beyond site entrance to next lane which is unsuitable for caravans.*
grid ref: *SW368276*

A working farm with dramatic sea views over to the Scilly Isles, just a mile from Land's End. This popular campsite offers well-appointed toilets, a well-stocked shop, and a cooked breakfast or evening meal from the food bar. There is direct access to the coastal footpath, and two beautiful beaches are a short walk away. 8 acre site. 100 touring pitches. Caravan pitches. Motorhome pitches. Tent pitches.

Open: Etr or Apr-Oct **Last arrival:** 19.00hrs **Last departure:** 10.30hrs

Pitches: ⌖ ⌖ Å

Facilities: ⌖⌖⌖⌖⌖⌖⌖⌖⌖ ⌖ ⌖

Services: ⌖⌖ ⌖⌖⌖⌖⌖⌖⌖⌖

Within 3 miles: ⌖⌖⌖⌖⌖

Notes: No open fires, no noise 22.00hrs-08.00hrs. Dogs must be kept on leads.

SUMMERCOURT
Map 2 SW85

Places to visit
Trerice, TRERICE, TR8 4PG, 01637 875404 www.nationaltrust.org.uk/trerice/

Blue Reef Aquarium, NEWQUAY, TR7 1DU, 01637 878134 www.bluereefaquarium.co.uk

Great for kids: Dairy Land Farm World, NEWQUAY, TR8 5AA, 01872 510246 www.dairylandfarmworld.com

Carvynick Country Club
RV ►►►► 93%

tel: 01872 510716 **TR8 5AF**
email: info@carvynick.co.uk
dir: *Accessed from A3058.* **grid ref:** *SW878564*

Set within the gardens of an attractive country estate, this spacious, dedicated American RV Park (also home to the 'Itchy Feet' retail company) provides full facility pitches on hardstandings. The extensive on-site amenities, shared by the high-quality time share village, include an indoor leisure area with swimming pool, fitness suite, badminton court and a bar and restaurant serving good food. 47 touring pitches. Caravan pitches. Motorhome pitches.

Open: all year (rs Jan-early Feb restricted leisure facilities)

Pitches: ⌖ ⌖

Leisure: ⌖⌖⌖⌖⌖ **Facilities:** ⌖⌖⌖⌖⌖ ⌖

Services: ⌖⌖⌖⌖⌖ **Within 3 miles:** ⌖⌖⌖⌖

Notes: Dogs must be exercised off site. Dogs must be kept on leads. 5-hole golf course.

AA Pubs & Restaurants nearby: The Plume of Feathers, MITCHELL, TR8 5AX, 01872 510387

PITCHES: ⌖ Caravans ⌖ Motorhomes Å Tents ⌖ Glamping-style accommodation **SERVICES:** ⌖ Electric hook up ⌖ Launderette ⌖ Licensed bar ⌖ Calor Gas ⌖ Camping Gaz ⌖ Toilet fluid ⌖ Café/Restaurant ⌖ Fast Food/Takeaway ⌖ Battery charging ⌖ Baby care ⌖ Motorvan service point
ABBREVIATIONS: BH/bank hols – bank holidays Etr – Easter Spring BH – Spring Bank Holiday fr – from hrs – hours m – mile mdnt – midnight rdbt – roundabout rs – restricted service wk – week wknd – weekend x-rds – cross roads ⌖ No credit or debit cards ⌖ No dogs ⌖ Children of all ages accepted

TINTAGEL	Map 2 SX08

See also Camelford

Places to visit

Tintagel Castle, TINTAGEL, PL34 0HE, 01840 770328 www.english-heritage.org.uk/daysout/properties/tintagel-castle

Tintagel Old Post Office, TINTAGEL, PL34 0DB, 01840 770024 www.nationaltrust.org.uk/main/w-tintageloldpostoffice

Great for kids: Tamar Otter & Wildlife Centre, LAUNCESTON, PL15 8GW, 01566 785646 www.tamarotters.co.uk

Headland Caravan & Camping Park
►►►76%

tel: 01840 770239 **Atlantic Rd PL34 0DE**
email: headland.caravan@talktalkbusiness.net **web:** www.headlandcaravanpark.co.uk
dir: *From B3263 follow brown tourist signs through village to Headland.*
grid ref: *SX056887*

A peaceful family-run site in the mystical village of Tintagel, close to the ruins of King Arthur's Castle. There are two well-terraced camping areas with sea and countryside views, immaculately clean toilet facilities, and good, colourful planting across the park. The Cornish coastal path and the spectacular scenery are just two of the attractions here, and there are safe bathing beaches nearby. There are holiday statics for hire. 5 acre site. 62 touring pitches. Caravan pitches. Motorhome pitches. Tent pitches. 28 statics.

Open: Etr-Oct **Last arrival:** 21.00hrs

Pitches: ⊞ ⊞ Å

Leisure: ⚠

Facilities: ⌐ ⊙ ℙ ✳ ⑤ WiFi ❼

Services: ⊡ ⑤ 🛢 ⊘ Ⓣ ≝ ⛟

Within 3 miles: ⊁ ℘ ≜ ⑤ ⑤ ∪

Notes: Quiet after 23.00hrs. Dogs must be kept on leads & exercised off site.
AA Pubs & Restaurants nearby: The Port William, TREBARWITH, PL34 0HB, 01840 770230

TORPOINT	Map 3 SX45

Places to visit

Antony House, TORPOINT, PL11 2QA, 01752 812191 www.nationaltrust.org.uk/antony

Mount Edgcumbe House & Country Park, TORPOINT, PL10 1HZ, 01752 822236 www.mountedgcumbe.gov.uk

Great for kids: The Monkey Sanctuary, LOOE, PL13 1NZ, 0844 2721271 www.monkeysanctuary.org

Whitsand Bay Lodge & Touring Park
►►►►81%

tel: 01752 822597 **Millbrook PL10 1JZ**
email: enquiries@whitsandbayholidays.co.uk
dir: *From Torpoint take A374, left at Anthony onto B3247 for 1.25m to T-junct. Turn left, 0.25m, right into Cliff Rd. Site 2m on left.* **grid ref:** *SX410515*

A very well-equipped park with panoramic coastal, sea and countryside views from its terraced pitches. A quality park with upmarket toilet facilities and other amenities. There is a guided historic walk around The Battery most Sundays, and a bus stop close by. 27 acre site. 49 touring pitches. 30 hardstandings. 15 seasonal pitches. Caravan pitches. Motorhome pitches. Tent pitches. 5 statics.

Open: all year (rs Sep-Mar opening hours at shop, pool & bar restricted)
Last arrival: 19.00hrs **Last departure:** 10.00hrs

Pitches: * ⊞ £15-£30 ⊞ £15-£30 Å £12.50-£30

Leisure: ⚞ ⚠ ⚓ ◣ ♫

Facilities: ⌐ ⊙ ✳ ⚅ ⑤ ☐ ⊓ WiFi ⬜ ♻ ❼

Services: ⊡ ⑤ 🍽 ⊘ ⑩ ≝ ⛟

Within 3 miles: ⚹ ⊁ ℘ ◎ ≜ ⑤ ⑤ ∪

Notes: Families & couples only. Dogs must be kept on leads. Putting green, chapel, library, heritage centre.
AA Pubs & Restaurants nearby: The Finnygook Inn, CRAFTHOLE, PL11 3BQ, 01503 230338

TRURO	

See also Portscatho

Places to visit

Royal Cornwall Museum, TRURO, TR1 2SJ, 01872 272205 www.royalcornwallmuseum.org.uk

Trelissick Garden, TRELISSICK GARDEN, TR3 6QL, 01872 862090 www.nationaltrust.org.uk/trelissick

TRURO	Map 2 SW84

PREMIER PARK

Carnon Downs Caravan & Camping Park
►►►►► 94%

GOLD

tel: 01872 862283 **Carnon Downs TR3 6JJ**
email: info@carnon-downs-caravanpark.co.uk
dir: *Take A39 from Truro towards Falmouth. Site just off main Carnon Downs rdbt, on left.* **grid ref:** *SW805406*

A beautifully mature park set in meadowland and woodland close to the village amenities of Carnon Downs. The four toilet blocks provide exceptional facilities in bright modern surroundings. An extensive landscaping programme has been carried out to give more spacious pitch sizes, and there is an exciting children's playground with modern equipment, plus a football pitch. 33 acre site. 150 touring pitches. 80 hardstandings. Caravan pitches. Motorhome pitches. Tent pitches. 2 statics.

Open: all year **Last arrival:** 22.00hrs **Last departure:** 11.00hrs

Pitches: * ➡ £22-£32 ➡ £22-£32 ▲ £19-£32

Leisure: ⚓ ▢

Facilities: ➡ ◖ ☉ ◗ ☀ & ⓒ ⌁ ▥ 🐕 ♻ ❷

Services: ➡ ⓖ ➡ ⊘ Ⓣ ➡ ⬆

Within 3 miles: ⌘ ⊱ 日 ⌀ ⊱ ⓖ ⓖ ∪

Notes: No children's bikes in Jul & Aug. Baby & child bathroom.

AA Pubs & Restaurants nearby: The Pandora Inn, MYLOR BRIDGE, TR11 5ST, 01326 372678

Tabb's, TRURO, TR1 3BZ, 01872 262110

PREMIER PARK

Cosawes Park
►►►►► 82%

GOLD

tel: 01872 863724 **Perranarworthal TR3 7QS**
email: info@cosawes.com
dir: *Exit A39 midway between Truro & Falmouth. Direct access at site sign after Perranarworthal.* **grid ref:** *SW768376*

A small touring park, close to Perranarworthal, in a peaceful wooded valley, midway between Truro and Falmouth, with a two-acre touring area. There are spotless toilet facilities (with underfloor heating) that include two smart family rooms. Its stunning location is ideal for visiting the many nearby hamlets and villages close to the Carrick Roads, a stretch of tidal water, which is a centre for sailing and other boats. 2 acre site. 59 touring pitches. 25 hardstandings. 15 seasonal pitches. Caravan pitches. Motorhome pitches. Tent pitches.

Open: all year **Last arrival:** 21.00hrs **Last departure:** 10.00hrs

Pitches: ➡ ➡ ▲

Facilities: ◖ ☉ ◗ ☀ & ⓒ ⌂ 🐕 ▥ ♻ ❷

Services: ➡ ⓖ ➡ Ⓣ ➡ ⬆

Within 3 miles: ⌘ ⊱ 日 ⌀ ◎ ⊱ ⓖ ⓖ ∪

Notes: Dogs must be kept on leads. Pizza (Thursday evenings).

AA Pubs & Restaurants nearby: The Pandora Inn, MYLOR BRIDGE, TR11 5ST, 01326 372678

PREMIER PARK

Truro Caravan and Camping Park
►►►►► 82%

tel: 01872 560274 **TR4 8QN**
email: info@trurocaravanandcampingpark.co.uk
dir: *Exit A390 at Threemilestone rdbt onto unclassified road towards Chacewater. Site signed on right in 0.5m.* **grid ref:** *SW772452*

An attractive south-facing and well-laid out park with spacious pitches, including good hardstandings, and quality modern toilets that are kept spotlessly clean. It is situated on the edge of Truro yet close to many beaches, with St Agnes just 10 minutes away by car. It is equidistant from both the rugged north coast and the calmer south coastal areas. There is a good bus service from the gate of the park to Truro. 8.5 acre site. 51 touring pitches. 26 hardstandings. Caravan pitches. Motorhome pitches. Tent pitches. 49 statics.

Open: all year **Last arrival:** 18.00hrs **Last departure:** 10.30hrs

Pitches: ➡ £20-£22 ➡ £20-£22 ▲ £20

Facilities: ➡ ◖ ☉ ◗ ☀ & ⓒ ⌁ ▥ 🖳 ♻ ❷

Services: ➡ ⓖ ➡ ⊘ Ⓣ ➡ ⬆

Within 3 miles: ⌘ 日 ⌀ ◎ ⓖ ⓖ ∪

Notes: Dogs must be kept on leads.

AA Pubs & Restaurants nearby: The Wig & Pen, TRURO, TR1 3DP, 01872 273028

Old Ale House, TRURO, TR1 2HD, 01872 271122

Summer Valley
►►► 81%

tel: 01872 277878 **Shortlanesend TR4 9DW**
email: res@summervalley.co.uk
dir: *3m NW off B3284.* **grid ref:** *SW800479*

A very attractive and secluded site in a rural setting midway between the A30 and the cathedral city of Truro. The keen owners maintain the facilities to a good standard. 3 acre site. 60 touring pitches. Caravan pitches. Motorhome pitches. Tent pitches.

Open: Apr-Oct **Last arrival:** 20.00hrs **Last departure:** 11.00hrs

Pitches: ➡ ➡ ▲

Leisure: ⚓

Facilities: ◖ ☉ ◗ ☀ ⓒ ⓖ ⌂ ▥ ♻ ❷

Services: ➡ ⓖ ➡ ⊘ Ⓣ ➡

Within 3 miles: ⌘ 日 ⌀ ◎ ⓖ ⓖ ∪

Notes: Dogs must be kept on leads. Campers' lounge.

AA Pubs & Restaurants nearby: Old Ale House, TRURO, TR1 2HD, 01872 271122

Bustophers Bar Bistro, TRURO, TR1 2PN, 01872 279029

PITCHES: ➡ Caravans ➡ Motorhomes ▲ Tents ⌂ Glamping-style accommodation **SERVICES:** ➡ Electric hook up ⓖ Launderette ➡ Licensed bar ➡ Calor Gas ⊘ Camping Gaz Ⓣ Toilet fluid ⓘ Café/Restaurant ➡ Fast Food/Takeaway ➡ Battery charging ➡ Baby care ⬆ Motorvan service point
ABBREVIATIONS: BH/bank hols – bank holidays Etr – Easter Spring BH – Spring Bank Holiday fr – from hrs – hours m – mile mdnt – midnight rdbt – roundabout rs – restricted service wk – week wknd – weekend x-rds – cross roads ⓖ No credit or debit cards ⊗ No dogs ⓫ Children of all ages accepted

WADEBRIDGE
Map 2 SW97

Places to visit
Prideaux Place, PADSTOW, PL28 8RP, 01841 532411 www.prideauxplace.co.uk

Cornwall's Regimental Museum, BODMIN, PL31 1EG, 01208 72810

Great for kids: Pencarrow, BODMIN, PL30 3AG, 01208 841369
www.pencarrow.co.uk

Devon's Crealy Great Adventure Park, CLYST ST MARY, EX5 1DR, 01395 233200
www.crealy.co.uk

St Mabyn Holiday Park
►►►► 90%

GOLD

tel: 01208 841677 **Longstone Rd, St Mabyn PL30 3BY**
email: info@stmabyn.co.uk
dir: *S of Camelford on A39, left after BP garage onto B3266 to Bodmin, 6m to Longstone, right at x-rds to St Mabyn, site approx 400mtrs on right.* **grid ref:** *SX055733*

A family-run site situated close to the picturesque market town of Wadebridge and within easy reach of Bodmin; it is centrally located for exploring both the north and south coasts of Cornwall. The park offers peace and tranquillity in a country setting and at the same time provides plenty of on-site activities including a swimming pool and children's play areas. Holiday chalets and fully-equipped holiday homes are available to rent, along with a choice of pitches. 12 acre site. 120 touring pitches. 49 hardstandings. Caravan pitches. Motorhome pitches. Tent pitches. 20 statics. 1 wooden pod.

Open: 15 Mar-Oct (rs 15 Mar-Spring BH & mid Sep-Oct swimming pool may be closed) **Last arrival:** 21.00hrs **Last departure:** 11.00hrs

Pitches: ⊞ £12-£26 ⊞ £12-£26 ▲ £10-£20 ⋒

Leisure: ⊛ ⋀ ◕ ▭

Facilities: ⋔ ⊙ ℘ ✳ ᵹ ⓒ ⓢ ⋒ ⋒ ⓦⁱⁱ ▤ ♻ ❶

Services: ⊡ ⓢ ⋒ ⊘ Ⓣ ⋈ ⋈

Within 3 miles: ↓ ℘ ⓢ ⓢ ⎍

Notes: Quiet from 23.00hrs-07.00hrs, information book given on arrival. Small animal area with goats.

AA Pubs & Restaurants nearby: The Borough Arms, DUNMERE, PL31 2RD, 01208 73118
Trehellas House Hotel & Restaurant, BODMIN, PL30 3AD, 01208 72700

Who are the AA's award-winning campsites this year?
See pages 14-19

The Laurels Holiday Park
►►►► 89%

tel: 01209 313474 **Padstow Rd, Whitecross PL27 7JQ**
email: info@thelaurelsholidaypark.co.uk
dir: *A39 onto A389 signed Padstow, follow signs. Site entrance 1st right.*
grid ref: *SW957715*

A very smart and well-equipped park with individual pitches screened by hedges and young shrubs. The enclosed dog walk is of great benefit to pet owners, and the Camel (cycle) Trail and Padstow are not far away. An excellent base if visiting the Royal Cornwall Showground. 2.2 acre site. 30 touring pitches. 2 hardstandings. Caravan pitches. Motorhome pitches. Tent pitches.

Open: Etr or Apr-Oct **Last arrival:** 20.00hrs **Last departure:** 11.00hrs

Pitches: * ⊞ £13-£25 ⊞ £13-£25 ▲ £13-£25

Leisure: ⋀

Facilities: ⋔ ⊙ ℘ ✳ ⋒ ⋒ ⓦⁱⁱ ▤ ♻ ❶

Services: ⊡ ⓢ ⋈

Within 3 miles: ↓ ⋈ ⊟ ℘ ⋈ ⓢ ⓢ ⎍

Notes: Family park. No group bookings. Dogs must be kept on leads. Wet suit dunking bath & drying area.

AA Pubs & Restaurants nearby: The Quarryman Inn, WADEBRIDGE, PL27 7JA, 01208 816444

See advert on page 91

Little Bodieve Holiday Park
►►► 84%

tel: 01208 812323 **Bodieve Rd PL27 6EG**
email: info@littlebodieve.co.uk
dir: *From A39 rdbt on Wadebridge by-pass take B3314 signed Rock & Port Isaac, site 0.25m on right.* **grid ref:** *SW995734*

Rurally located with pitches in three large grassy paddocks, this family park is close to the Camel Estuary. The licensed clubhouse provides bar meals, with an entertainment programme in high season, and there is a swimming pool with sun terrace plus a separate waterslide and splash pool. This makes a good base from which to visit the Royal Cornwall Showground. 22 acre site. 195 touring pitches. Caravan pitches. Motorhome pitches. Tent pitches. 75 statics.

Open: Apr-Oct (rs Early & late season pool, shop & clubhouse closed)
Last arrival: 21.00hrs **Last departure:** 11.00hrs

Pitches: ⊞ ⊞ ▲

Leisure: ⊛ ⋀ ◕ ♫

Facilities: ⋔ ⋔ ⊙ ℘ ✳ ᵹ ⓒ ⓢ ⋒ ⋒ ⓦⁱⁱ ▤ ♻ ❶

Services: ⊡ ⓢ ⋈ ⋒ ⊘ Ⓣ ⓞ ⋈ ⋒

Within 3 miles: ↓ ⊟ ℘ ◎ ⋈ ⓢ ⓢ ⎍

Notes: Families & couples only. Dogs must be kept on leads. Crazy golf.

AA Pubs & Restaurants nearby: The Quarryman Inn, WADEBRIDGE, PL27 7JA, 01208 816444

LEISURE: ⓈⒾ Indoor swimming pool ⓢ Outdoor swimming pool ⋀ Children's playground ⋓ Kid's club ⓈⒾ Tennis court ◕ Games room ▭ Separate TV room ↓ golf course ⋈ Boats for hire ⊟ Cinema ♫ Entertainment ℘ Fishing ◎ Mini golf ⋈ Watersports ⋓ Gym ⓈⒾ Sports field Spa ⎍ Stables
FACILITIES: ⋔ Bath ⋔ Shower ⊙ Electric shaver ℘ Hairdryer ✳ Ice Pack Facility ᵹ Disabled facilities ⓒ Public telephone ⓢ Shop on site or within 200yds ⓢ Mobile shop (calls at least 5 days a week) ⋈ BBQ area ⋒ Picnic area ⓦⁱⁱ Wi-fi ▤ Internet access ♻ Recycling ❶ Tourist info ⋈ Dog exercise area

WATERGATE BAY	Map 2 SW86

Watergate Bay Touring Park

►►►►►87%

tel: 01637 860387 **TR8 4AD**
email: email@watergatebaytouringpark.co.uk
web: www.watergatebaytouringpark.co.uk
dir: *From Bodmin on A30 follow Newquay airport signs. Continue past airport, left at T-junct, site 0.5m on right. NB for Sat Nav use TR8 4AE.* **grid ref:** *SW850653*

A well-established park above Watergate Bay, where acres of golden sand, rock pools and surf are all contribute to making this a holidaymakers' paradise. The toilet facilities are appointed to a high standard and include new, top quality family/disabled rooms; there is a well-stocked shop and café, an inviting swimming pool, and a wide range of activities including tennis. There is regular entertainment in the clubhouse and outdoor facilities are tailored for all ages.

30 acre site. 171 touring pitches. 14 hardstandings. Caravan pitches. Motorhome pitches. Tent pitches. 2 statics.

Open: Mar-Nov (rs Mar-Spring BH & Sep-Oct restricted bar, café, shop & pool)
Last arrival: 22.00hrs **Last departure:** noon

Pitches: * 🚐 £11-£22 🚌 £11-£22 ▲ £11-£22

Leisure: 🏊🚣⛰🏐🏇⚽🎱🏹🎯🎵

Facilities: 🚿📻☉🅿✳♿🛝🛒🏧 wifi 💻♻ℹ

Services: 🔌🔔🍴🛢⛽🚽🍴♨🗑♿

Within 3 miles: 🚴🎣◉⛳🏪🛒

Notes: Dogs must be kept on leads. Free mini bus to beach during main school holidays.

AA Pubs & Restaurants nearby: Fifteen Cornwall, WATERGATE BAY, TR8 4AA, 01637 861000

See advert below

WHITE CROSS
Map 2 SW96

Places to visit
Trerice, TRERICE, TR8 4PG, 01637 875404 www.nationaltrust.org.uk/trerice/

Great for kids: Dairy Land Farm World, NEWQUAY, TR8 5AA, 01872 510246 www.dairylandfarmworld.com

---

NEW Piran Meadows Resort and Spa
HOLIDAY HOME PARK 94%

tel: 01726 860415 **TR8 4LW**
email: enquiries@piranmeadows.co.uk
dir: *Telephone for directions.* **grid ref:** *SW889597*

A stunning new development that opened in early July 2014, providing excellent standards and facilities for couples and families. Generously spaced, superbly equipped lodges and static holiday homes are equipped with both practical and thoughtful extras and have unrivalled countryside views. The stylish main building with a welcoming reception is decorated and furnished with quality and comfort, and the many facilities include a modern swimming pool, special areas and attractions for children, and the excellent Serenity Spa offering a wide range of treatments. The 'Go Active' sports programme has its own instructors and the restaurant with bar has a spacious exterior area for alfresco dining.

Open: 9 Feb-9 Jan

Change over day: Mon, Fri & Sat

Arrival and departure times: Please contact the site

Statics: 104 Sleeps 6 Bedrms 2-3 Bathrms 1-2 (inc en suite) Toilets 1-2 Dishwasher Microwave Freezer TV Sky/FTV DVD Modem/Wi-fi Linen inc Towels inc Elec inc Gas inc Grass area Garden/patio furniture BBQ

Lodges: 11 Sleeps 8 Bedrms 3-4 Bathrms 2-3 (inc en suite) Toilets 2-3 Dishwasher Wash Machine T/drier Freezer TV Sky/FTV DVD Modem/Wi-fi Linen inc Towels inc Elec inc Gas inc Grass area Garden/patio furniture BBQ

Children: ♦♦ Cots Highchair **Dogs:** 1 on leads

Leisure: 🏊 Spa 🎾 ⚽ ⛹

Within 3 miles: 🏊 Spa 🎣 ⛴ 🚣

WIDEMOUTH BAY
Map 2 SS20

Widemouth Bay Caravan Park
HOLIDAY CENTRE 72%

tel: 01271 866766 **EX23 0DF**
email: bookings@jfhols.co.uk
dir: *From A39 take Widemouth Bay coastal road, turn left. Site on left.* **grid ref:** *SS199008*

A partly sloping rural site set in countryside overlooking the sea and one of Cornwall's finest beaches. There's nightly entertainment in the high season with an emphasis on children's and family club programmes. This park is located less than half a mile from the sandy beaches of Widemouth Bay. A superb base for surfing. 58 acre site. 220 touring pitches. 90 hardstandings. 4 seasonal pitches. Caravan pitches. Motorhome pitches. Tent pitches. 200 statics. 1 wooden pod.

Open: Etr-Oct (rs Etr week pools & clubhouse closed) **Last arrival:** dusk
Last departure: 10.00hrs

Pitches: * 🚐 £12-£34 🚙 £12-£34 ▲ £8-£22 🏠

Leisure: 🏊 ⛹ 🛶 🎱 🎵

Facilities: 🚿 ⊙ 🌡 ✳ ♿ 🔌 🛒 🛝 📶 🖥

Services: 🔌 🗑 🚽 🍴 🍺 🚛

Within 3 miles: 🎣 ⛴ 🎬 🎿 ◎ 🚣 🛒 🛍 ⛴

Notes: Crazy golf.

AA Pubs & Restaurants nearby: Bay View Inn, WIDEMOUTH BAY, EX23 0AW, 01288 361273

Cornish Coasts Caravan & Camping Park
►►► 80%

tel: 01288 361380 **Middle Penlean, Poundstock, Bude EX23 0EE**
email: admin@cornishcoasts.co.uk **web:** www.cornishcoasts.co.uk
dir: *5m S of Bude on A39, 0.5m S of Rebel Cinema on right.* **grid ref:** *SS202981*

Situated on the A39 midway between Padstow and the beautiful surfing beaches of Bude and Widemouth Bay, this is a quiet park with lovely terraced pitches that make the most of the stunning views over the countryside to the sea. The reception is in a 13th-century cottage, and the park is well equipped and tidy, with the well maintained and quirky toilet facilities (note the mosaic vanity units) housed in a freshly painted older-style building. 3.5 acre site. 46 touring pitches. 8 hardstandings. Caravan pitches. Motorhome pitches. Tent pitches. 4 statics.

Open: Apr-Oct **Last arrival:** 22.00hrs **Last departure:** 10.30hrs

Pitches: 🚐 £12-£16 🚙 £12-£16 ▲ £12-£16

Leisure: ⛹ **Facilities:** 🚿 ⊙ 🌡 ✳ ♿ 🛒 📶 ♻ 🛈

Services: 🔌 🗑 🛒 ⚡ 🚽 🛒

Within 3 miles: 🎣 ⛴ 🎬 🎿 ◎ 🚣 🛒 🛍 ⛴

Notes: Quiet after 22.00hrs. Dogs must be kept on leads. Post office.

AA Pubs & Restaurants nearby: Bay View Inn, WIDEMOUTH BAY, EX23 0AW, 01288 361273

LEISURE: 🏊 Indoor swimming pool 🏊 Outdoor swimming pool ⛹ Children's playground 🛶 Kid's club 🎾 Tennis court 🎱 Games room ▭ Separate TV room 🏌 golf course 🚤 Boats for hire 🎬 Cinema 🎵 Entertainment 🎣 Fishing ◎ Mini golf 🎿 Watersports 🏋 Gym ⚽ Sports field Spa ⛴ Stables
FACILITIES: 🛁 Bath 🚿 Shower ⊙ Electric shaver 🌡 Hairdryer ✳ Ice Pack Facility ♿ Disabled facilities 🕾 Public telephone 🛒 Shop on site or within 200yds 🛍 Mobile shop (calls at least 5 days a week) 🍖 BBQ area 🪧 Picnic area 📶 Wi-fi 🖥 Internet access ♻ Recycling 🛈 Tourist info 🛝 Dog exercise area

Penhalt Farm Holiday Park
▶▶▶ 75%

tel: 01288 361210 **EX23 0DG**
email: info@penhaltfarm.co.uk **web:** www.penhaltfarm.co.uk
dir: *From Bude on A39 take 2nd right to Widemouth Bay road, left at end by Widemouth Manor signed Millook onto coastal road. Site 0.75m on left.* **grid ref:** *SS194003*

Splendid views of the sea and coast can be enjoyed from all pitches on this sloping but partly level site, set in a lovely rural area on a working farm. About one mile away is one of Cornwall's finest beaches which proves popular with all the family as well as surfers. 8 acre site. 100 touring pitches. 12 hardstandings. Caravan pitches. Motorhome pitches. Tent pitches. 1 static.

Open: Etr-Oct

Pitches: * 🚐 £12-£23 🚍 £12-£23 ⚊ £10-£23

Leisure: ⚐ 🔍

Facilities: 🦮 ⊙ ℘ ☀ ⅋ 🕓 ⑤ 🐾

Services: 🔌 ⑤ 🔋 ⊘ 🛒

Within 3 miles: ⅃ ⚬ 目 ℘ ⟆ ⑤ ↻

Notes: No rollerblades, no noise after mdnt. Dogs must be kept on leads. Pool table, netball & football posts, air hockey & table tennis.

AA Pubs & Restaurants nearby: Bay View Inn, WIDEMOUTH BAY, EX23 0AW, 01288 361273

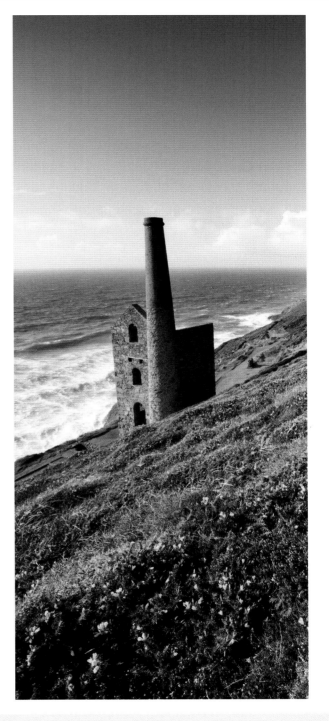

Cumbria

Cumbria means the Lake District really – a rumpled, rugged landscape that is hard to beat for sheer natural beauty and grandeur. It is almost certainly England's best known and most scenic national park, famous for Lake Windermere, the country's largest lake, and Derwentwater, described as the 'Queen of the English Lakes.'

The Lake District is a region of Britain that leaves some visitors relaxed, others completely exhausted. The list of activities and places to visit is endless. The old adage 'always leave something to come back for' is certainly apt in this remote corner of the country.

This region has long been inextricably associated with poets, artists and writers. Not surprisingly, it was this beautiful countryside that inspired William Wordsworth, Samuel Taylor Coleridge, Arthur Ransome and Robert Southey. Born in the Cumbrian town of Cockermouth, Wordsworth and his sister Dorothy moved to Dove Cottage in Grasmere in 1799. Their annual rent was £5. The poet later moved to Rydal Mount in Ambleside, a family home with a 4-acre garden and a charming setting on the banks of Rydal Water. Today, both Dove Cottage and Rydal Mount are among the most visited of all the Lake District attractions. Another house with strong literary links is Hill Top, the 17th-century farmhouse home of Beatrix Potter who moved here in 1905. Located near Windermere, Hill Top and its surroundings sparked Potter's imagination and she painstakingly reproduced much of what she saw and cherished in her charming book illustrations. Tom Kitten, Samuel Whiskers and Jemima Puddleduck were all created here and the outstanding success of the recent film about Potter's life has introduced her extraordinary work to new audiences.

Walkers are spoilt for choice in Cumbria and the Lake District. The 70-mile Cumbria Way follows the valley floors rather than the mountain summits, while the 190-mile Coast to Coast has just about every kind of landscape and terrain imaginable. The route, pioneered by the well-known fell walker and writer Alfred Wainwright, cuts across the Lake District, the Yorkshire Dales and the North York Moors, spanning the width of England between St Bees on the Cumbrian west coast, and Robin Hood's Bay on the North Yorkshire and Cleveland Heritage Coast. The region is also popular with cyclists and there are a great many cycle hire outlets and plenty of routes available.

As with any popular scenic region of the country, the Lake District has an abundance of attractions but there are plenty of places within its boundaries and outside them where you can experience peace, tranquillity and a true sense of solitude. The southern half of Cumbria is often overlooked in favour of the more obvious attractions of the region. The Lune Valley, for example, remains as lovely as it was when Turner came here to paint. In the 19th century, writer John Ruskin described the view from 'The Brow', a walk running behind Kirkby Lonsdale's parish church, as 'one of the loveliest scenes in England.'

The Cumbrian coast is also one of the county's secret gems. Overlooking the Solway Firth and noted in the area for its wide cobbled streets and spacious green, the town of Silloth is one of the finest examples of a Victorian seaside resort in the north of England and yet outside Cumbria few people know its name. There are other historic towns along this coastline, including Whitehaven, Workington and Maryport. The Roman defences at Ravenglass are a reminder of the occupation, as is the Cumbrian section of Hadrian's Wall where it follows the county's northern coast. Well worth a visit is the ancient and historic city of Carlisle. Once a Roman camp – its wall still runs north of the city – it was captured during the Jacobean rising of 1745. The cathedral dates back to the early 12th century.

Windermere, Lake District National Park ▷

CUMBRIA

AMBLESIDE
Map 18 NY30

Places to visit

The Armitt Museum & Library, AMBLESIDE, LA22 9BL, 015394 31212
www.armitt.com

Beatrix Potter Gallery, HAWKSHEAD, LA22 0NS, 015394 36269
www.nationaltrust.org.uk

PREMIER PARK

Skelwith Fold Caravan Park
►►►►► 90%

GOLD

tel: 015394 32277 **LA22 0HX**
email: info@skelwith.com
dir: *From Ambleside on A593 towards Coniston, left at Clappersgate onto B5286 (Hawkshead road). Site 1m on right.* **grid ref:** NY355029

In the grounds of a former mansion, this park is in a beautiful setting close to Lake Windermere. Touring areas are dotted in paddocks around the extensively wooded grounds, and the all-weather pitches are set close to the many facility buildings. The premium pitches are quite superb. There is a five-acre family recreation area, which has spectacular views of Loughrigg Fell. 130 acre site. 150 touring pitches. 130 hardstandings. 30 seasonal pitches. Caravan pitches. Motorhome pitches. 320 statics.

Open: Mar-15 Nov **Last arrival:** dusk **Last departure:** noon

Pitches: 🚐 🚌

Leisure: 🎠 ⚽ 🎯

Facilities: 🚿 ⊙ 🌡 🖐 ✻ ♿ ☎ ⓢ 🍴 ♻ 🎪 🛒 ♻

Services: 🔌 🗑 🛢 🚿 📭 🛁 ⚐

Within 3 miles: ⚑ ⚑ 🎣 ◎ 🍴 ⓢ 🍴 ♻

Notes: Dogs must be kept on leads.

AA Pubs & Restaurants nearby: Wateredge Inn, AMBLESIDE, LA22 0EP, 015394 32332

Drunken Duck Inn, AMBLESIDE, LA22 0NG, 015394 36347

The Croft Caravan & Campsite
►►►► 80%

tel: 015394 36374 **North Lonsdale Rd, Hawkshead LA22 0NX**
email: enquiries@hawkshead-croft.com
dir: *From B5285 in Hawkshead turn into site opposite main public car & coach park.* **grid ref:** SD352981

In the historic village of Hawkshead, which is now a popular destination for Beatrix Potter fans, this former working farm has a large tent and touring field, bordering a beck and the sound of running water and birdsong are welcome distractions. Most pitches are fully serviced with water, electricity, TV hook-up and waste water disposal. The smart amenities block provides family bathrooms. In an adjoining field there are stylish wood-clad lodges. 5 acre site. 75 touring pitches. 26 hardstandings. Caravan pitches. Motorhome pitches. Tent pitches. 20 statics.

Open: Mar-Jan **Last arrival:** 21.30hrs **Last departure:** noon

Pitches: 🚐 🚌 ⛺

Leisure: 🎣
Facilities: 🖐 🚿 ⊙ 🌡 ✻ ♿ ☎ 🍴 🐕 **WiFi** ♻ 🎪 ❶

Services: 🔌 🗑 ⚐

Within 3 miles: 🎣 ⓢ 🍴

Notes: No noise 23.00hrs-07.00hrs. Dogs must be kept on leads.

AA Pubs & Restaurants nearby: The Queen's Head Inn & Restaurant, HAWKSHEAD, LA22 0NS, 015394 36271

Kings Arms, HAWKSHEAD, LA22 0NZ, 015394 36372

Low Wray National Trust Campsite
►►► 79%

🏛

tel: 015394 32733 & 32039 **Low Wray LA22 0JA**
email: campsite.bookings@nationaltrust.org.uk
dir: *3m SW of Ambleside on A593 to Clappersgate, then B5286. Approx 1m left at Wray sign. Site approx 1m on left.* **grid ref:** NY372013

Picturesquely set on the wooded shores of Lake Windermere, this site is a favourite with tenters and watersport enthusiasts. The toilet facilities are housed in wooden cabins, and tents can be pitched in wooded glades with lake views or open grassland; here there are wooden camping pods and a mini-reservation of tipis and solar-heated bell tents. In partnership with Quest 4 Adventure, many outdoor activities are available for families (bookable during school holidays). Fresh bread is now baked daily on site, and opposite reception there is a rustic covered area with a pizza oven; there are also visits from the hot-food van in high season. 10 acre site. 140 touring pitches. Motorhome pitches. Tent pitches. 10 wooden pods.

Open: wk before Etr-Oct **Last arrival:** variable **Last departure:** 11.00hrs

Pitches: 🚌 ⛺ 🏛

Leisure: 🎠

Facilities: 🚿 ⊙ 🌡 ✻ ♿ 🍴 ♻ ❶

Services: 🗑 🛢 ⚐

Within 3 miles: ⚑ 🎣 ◎ 🍴 ⓢ 🍴

Notes: No cars by tents. No groups of more than 4 unless a family group with children, no noise between 23.00hrs-07.00hrs. Dogs must be kept on leads. Launching area for sailing craft, orienteering course, bike hire.

AA Pubs & Restaurants nearby: Wateredge Inn, AMBLESIDE, LA22 0EP, 015394 32332

Drunken Duck Inn, AMBLESIDE, LA22 0NG, 015394 36347

Kings Arms, HAWKSHEAD, LA22 0NZ, 015394 36372

Hawkshead Hall Farm
►►► 77%

tel: 015394 36221 **Hawkshead LA22 0NN**
email: enquiries@hawksheadhall-campsite.com
dir: *From Ambleside take A593 signed Coniston, then B5286 signed Hawkshead. Site signed on left just before Hawkshead. Or from Coniston take B5285 to T-junct. Left, then 1st right into site.* **grid ref:** SD349988

A mainly camping site a few minutes' walk from village centre in a landscape of gentle rolling hills. The pitch sizes are generous and there's a very well-equipped, purpose-built amenities block. Surrounded by unspoiled countryside, the adjoining fields are a delight for families, especially during the lambing season. 55 touring pitches. Caravan pitches. Motorhome pitches. Tent pitches.

Open: Mar-Oct **Last arrival:** 21.00hrs **Last departure:** noon

---

LEISURE: 🏊 Indoor swimming pool 🏊 Outdoor swimming pool 🎠 Children's playground 🪁 Kid's club 🎾 Tennis court 🎱 Games room 📺 Separate TV room ⛳ golf course 🚣 Boats for hire 🎬 Cinema 🎵 Entertainment 🎣 Fishing ◎ Mini golf 🏄 Watersports 🏋 Gym ⚽ Sports field Spa ♻ Stables
FACILITIES: 🖐 Bath 🚿 Shower ⊙ Electric shaver 🌡 Hairdryer ✻ Ice Pack Facility ♿ Disabled facilities ☎ Public telephone ⓢ Shop on site or within 200yds 🏪 Mobile shop (calls at least 5 days a week) 🍴 BBQ area 🍴 Picnic area **WiFi** Wi-fi 🖥 Internet access ♻ Recycling ❶ Tourist info 🐕 Dog exercise area

Pitches: 🚐 🚏 🛦

Facilities: 🌣⊙🅟✳🏧♻🛈

Services: 🔌

Within 3 miles: ⇞✎⏌🛒🛍🔄⟲

Notes: No noise 23.00hrs-07.00hrs.

AA Pubs & Restaurants nearby: The Queen's Head Inn & Restaurant, HAWKSHEAD, LA22 0NS, 015394 36271

Kings Arms, HAWKSHEAD, LA22 0NZ, 015394 36372

APPLEBY-IN-WESTMORLAND
Map 18 NY62

Places to visit

Acorn Bank Garden and Watermill, TEMPLE SOWERBY, CA10 1SP, 017683 61893 www.nationaltrust.org.uk

Great for kids: Wetheriggs Animal Rescue & Conservation Centre, PENRITH, CA10 2DH, 01768 866657 www.wetheriggsanimalrescue.co.uk

---

PREMIER PARK

Wild Rose Park
►►►►►88%

tel: 017683 51077 **Ormside CA16 6EJ**
email: reception@wildrose.co.uk
dir: *Signed on unclassified road to Great Ormside, off B6260.* **grid ref:** *NY698165*

Situated in the Eden Valley, this large leisure group-run park has been carefully landscaped and offers superb facilities maintained to an extremely high standard, including four wooden wigwams for hire. There are several individual pitches, and extensive views from most areas of the park. Traditional stone walls and the planting of lots of indigenous trees help the site to blend into the environment; wildlife is actively encouraged. New for 2014 — a stylish reception with adjacent internet café, the Cock-a-Hoop bar with slate floor and pub games (and where dogs are welcome) and a choice of adults-only and family entertainment rooms have all been added. Please note, tents are no longer accepted. 85 acre site. 226 touring pitches. 140 hardstandings. Caravan pitches. Motorhome pitches. 273 statics. 4 tipis.

Open: all year (rs Nov-Mar shop closed, restaurant restricted opening times, pool closed 6 Sep-27 May) **Last arrival:** 22.00hrs **Last departure:** noon

Pitches: 🚐 £20-£40 🚏 £20-£40 🏠

Leisure: ⇆⋀🎱⌨🎵

Facilities: 🌣⊙🅟✳🖐⏱🕙🏧🚻 WiFi 🖥♻🛈

Services: 🔌🛢🍺🔋🚽🎪🎮🍴🚼⚰

Within 3 miles: ⬇✎◎🛍🔄

Notes: No unaccompanied teenagers, no group bookings, no noise after 22.30hrs, no dangerous dogs. Dogs must be kept on leads. Pitch & putt, fishing.

AA Pubs & Restaurants nearby: Tufton Arms Hotel, APPLEBY-IN-WESTMORLAND, CA16 6XA, 017683 51593

Appleby Manor Country House Hotel, APPLEBY-IN-WESTMORLAND, CA16 6JB, 017683 51571

BARROW-IN-FURNESS
Map 18 SD26

Places to visit

The Dock Museum, BARROW-IN-FURNESS, LA14 2PW, 01229 876400 www.dockmuseum.org.uk

Furness Abbey, BARROW-IN-FURNESS, LA13 0PJ, 01229 823420 www.english-heritage.org.uk/daysout/properties/furness-abbey

Great for kids: South Lakes Wild Animal Park, DALTON-IN-FURNESS, LA15 8JR, 01229 466086 www.wildanimalpark.co.uk

---

South End Caravan Park
►►►85%

tel: 01229 472823 & 471556 **Walney Island LA14 3YQ**
email: enquiries@secp.co.uk **web:** www.walneyislandcaravanpark.co.uk
dir: *M6 junct 36, A590 to Barrow, follow signs for Walney Island. Cross bridge, turn left. Site 6m south.* **grid ref:** *SD208628*

A friendly family-owned and run park next to the sea and close to a nature reserve, on the southern end of Walney Island. It offers an extensive range of quality amenities including an adult lounge, and high standards of cleanliness and maintenance. 7 acre site. 50 touring pitches. 15 hardstandings. 34 seasonal pitches. Caravan pitches. Motorhome pitches. 250 statics.

Open: Mar-Oct (rs Mar-Etr & Oct pool closed) **Last arrival:** 22.00hrs **Last departure:** noon
Pitches: * 🚐 £16-£24 🚏 £16-£24 **Leisure:** ⇆⋀🎱🎱⌨
Facilities: 🌣⊙✳🖐⏱🏧 WiFi 🖥♻ **Services:** 🔌🛢🍺🔋🚼⚰
Within 3 miles: ⬇✎🛍🔄⟲
Notes: Dogs must be kept on leads. Bowling green, snooker table.
AA Pubs & Restaurants nearby: The Stan Laurel Inn, ULVERSTON, LA12 0AB, 01229 582814

BOOT
Map 18 NY10

Places to visit
Great for kids: Ravenglass & Eskdale Railway, RAVENGLASS, CA18 1SW, 01229 717171 www.ravenglass-railway.co.uk

PREMIER PARK

Eskdale Camping & Caravanning Club Site
►►►►►84%

tel: 019467 23253 & 0845 130 7633 **CA19 1TH**
email: eskdale.site@thefriendlyclub.co.uk
dir: Exit A595 at Gosforth or Holmrook to Eskdale Green, then signs for Boot. Site on left towards Hardknott Pass after railway, 150mtrs after Brook House Inn.
grid ref: NY179011

Stunningly located in Eskdale, a feeling of peace and tranquillity prevails at this top quality campsite, with the sounds of running water and birdsong the only distractions. Although mainly geared to campers, the facilities here are very impressive, with a smart amenities block, equipped with efficient modern facilities including an excellent fully serviced wet room-style family room with power shower. The surrounding mountains, and the mature trees and shrubs create a wonderful 'back to nature' feeling. There's a nest of camping pods under the trees, with gravel access paths and barbecues, a super backpackers' field and a self-catering camping barn. Expect great attention to detail and a high level of customer care. The park is only a quarter of a mile from Boot station on the Ravenglass/Eskdale railway (La'al Ratty). 8 acre site. 100 touring pitches. Motorhome pitches. Tent pitches. 10 wooden pods.

Open: Mar-14 Jan **Last arrival:** 20.00hrs **Last departure:** noon
Pitches: * ⌂ £20.75-£30.50 Å £20.75-£30.50 ⌂
Leisure: ⚠ ✿
Facilities: ⬧⊙ℙ✳⬧⊕⬧⧄⬧ ⬧ ⬧
Services: ⬧⬧ ⬧⬧⬧⬧⬧⬧⬧
Within 3 miles: ⬧⬧⬧⬧⬧

Notes: Site gates closed & no noise 23.00hrs-07.00hrs, no open fires. Dogs must be kept on leads. Camping barn, free drying room, hot & cold drinks station, toast & hot snacks.
AA Pubs & Restaurants nearby: Brook House Inn, BOOT, CA19 1TG, 019467 23288

BOWNESS-ON-WINDERMERE
Sites are listed under Windermere

Find out about staying at a Holiday Centre
in our feature on page 26

CARLISLE
Map 18 NY35

Places to visit
Lanercost Priory, BRAMPTON, CA8 2HQ, 01697 73030 www.english-heritage.org.uk/daysout/properties/lanercost-priory

Tullie House Museum & Art Gallery Trust, CARLISLE, CA3 8TP, 01228 618718 www.tulliehouse.co.uk

Great for kids: Carlisle Castle, CARLISLE, CA3 8UR, 01228 591992 www.english-heritage.org.uk/daysout/properties/carlisle-castle

Green Acres Caravan Park
►►►►86%

tel: 01228 675418 & 07720 343820 **High Knells, Houghton CA6 4JW**
email: info@caravanpark-cumbria.com
dir: M6 junct 44, A689 E towards Brampton for 1m. Left at Scaleby sign. Site 1m on left.
grid ref: NY416614

A small, adults-only touring park in rural surroundings close to the M6 with distant views of the fells. A convenient stopover, this pretty park is run by keen, friendly owners who maintain high standards throughout. The site has a caravan and motorhome pressure-washer area, a field and woodland dog walk and two superb unisex shower rooms which include toilet and wash basin. 3 acre site. 30 touring pitches. 30 hardstandings. 12 seasonal pitches. Caravan pitches. Motorhome pitches. Tent pitches.

Open: Apr-Oct **Last arrival:** 21.00hrs **Last departure:** noon
Pitches: ⌂ £17-£19 ⌂ £17-£19 Å £12-£17
Leisure: ✿
Facilities: ⬧⊙ℙ✳⬧⧄⬧⬧
Services: ⬧⬧
Within 3 miles: ⬧⬧
Notes: Adults only. Dogs must be kept on leads.

Dandy Dinmont Caravan & Camping Park
►►►87%

tel: 01228 674611 **Blackford CA6 4EA**
email: dandydinmont@btopenworld.com
dir: M6 junct 44, A7 N. Site 1.5m on right after Blackford sign. **grid ref:** NY399620

A sheltered, rural site, screened on two sides by hedgerows and only one mile from the M6 and Carlisle. The grass pitches are immaculately kept, and there are some larger hardstandings for motor homes. This park attracts mainly adults; please note that cycling and ball games are not allowed. Touring customers are invited to view the private award-winning garden. 4.5 acre site. 47 touring pitches. 14 hardstandings. Caravan pitches. Motorhome pitches. Tent pitches. 15 statics.

Open: Mar-Oct **Last arrival:** 21.00hrs **Last departure:** noon
Pitches: ⌂ fr £17 ⌂ fr £17 Å £15-£16
Facilities: ⬧⊙ℙ✳⬧⬧⬧⬧
Services: ⬧⬧⬧
Within 3 miles: ⬧⬧⬧⬧⬧⬧
Notes: Children's activities are restricted, Dogs must be kept on leads & exercised off site. Covered dishwashing area.

LEISURE: 🏊 Indoor swimming pool 🏊 Outdoor swimming pool ⚠ Children's playground 🪁 Kid's club 🎾 Tennis court 🎱 Games room ▭ Separate TV room ⛳ golf course ⛵ Boats for hire ▯ Cinema 🎵 Entertainment 🎣 Fishing ◎ Mini golf 🏄 Watersports 🏋 Gym 🏟 Sports field Spa ♘ Stables
FACILITIES: 🛁 Bath ⬧ Shower ⊙ Electric shaver 🪮 Hairdryer ✳ Ice Pack Facility ⬧ Disabled facilities ◷ Public telephone ⬧ Shop on site or within 200yds 🛒 Mobile shop (calls at least 5 days a week) 🍖 BBQ area 🌲 Picnic area ⬧ Wi-fi 🖥 Internet access ♺ Recycling ⬧ Tourist info 🐾 Dog exercise area

CARTMEL
Map 18 SD37

Places to visit
Holker Hall & Gardens, HOLKER, LA11 7PL, 015395 58328 www.holker.co.uk

Hill Top, NEAR SAWREY, LA22 0LF, 015394 36269
www.nationaltrust.org.uk/hilltop

Great for kids: Lakes Aquarium, LAKESIDE, LA12 8AS, 015395 30153
www.lakesaquarium.co.uk

Greaves Farm Caravan Park
►►►80%

tel: 015395 36587 & 36329 **Field Broughton LA11 6HR**
dir: M6 junct 36, A590 signed Barrow. Approx 1m before Newby Bridge, turn left at x-rds signed Cartmel/Staveley. Site 2m on left just before church. **grid ref:** SD391823

A small family-owned park close to a working farm in a peaceful rural area. Motorhomes are parked in a paddock which has spacious hardstandings, and there is a large field for tents and caravans. This simple park is carefully maintained, offers electric pitches (6amp), and there is always a sparkle to the toilet facilities. Static holiday caravans for hire. 3 acre site. 20 touring pitches. 9 hardstandings. Caravan pitches. Motorhome pitches. Tent pitches. 20 statics.

Open: Mar-Oct **Last arrival:** 21.00hrs **Last departure:** noon

Pitches: * ⊞ fr £16 ⊞ fr £16 ▲ fr £16

Facilities: ⚑⊙🅿❄🕓🗡♻𝟶

Services: 🖳🛢

Within 3 miles: ↨⅄🖉≽🖺↻

Notes: ⊛ Couples & families only, no noise after 23.00hrs, no open fires. Dogs must be kept on leads. Separate chalet for dishwashing, small freezer & fridge available.

AA Pubs & Restaurants nearby: The Cavendish Arms, CARTMEL, LA11 6QA, 015395 36240

The Masons Arms, CARTMEL, LA11 6NW, 015395 68486

Rogan & Company Restaurant, CARTMEL, LA11 6QD, 015395 35917

CROOKLANDS
Map 18 SD58

Places to visit
Levens Hall, LEVENS, LA8 0PD, 015395 60321 www.levenshall.co.uk

RSPB Leighton Moss & Morecambe Bay Nature Reserve, SILVERDALE, LA5 0SW, 01524 701601 www.rspb.org.uk/leightonmoss

Waters Edge Caravan Park
►►►►82%

tel: 015395 67708 & 67527 **LA7 7NN**
email: info@watersedgecaravanpark.co.uk
dir: M6 junct 36, A65 towards Kirkby Lonsdale, at 2nd rdbt follow signs for Crooklands/Endmoor. Site 1m on right at Crooklands garage, just beyond 40mph limit. **grid ref:** SD533838

A peaceful, well-run park close to the M6, pleasantly bordered by streams and woodland. A Lakeland-style building houses a shop and bar, and the attractive toilet block is clean and modern. This is ideal either as a stopover or for longer stays. 3 acre site. 26 touring pitches. 26 hardstandings. 8 seasonal pitches. Caravan pitches. Motorhome pitches. Tent pitches. 20 statics.

Open: Mar-14 Nov (rs Low season bar not always open on wkdays) **Last arrival:** 22.00hrs **Last departure:** noon

Pitches: * ⊞ £17.35-£24.90 ⊞ £17.35-£24.90 ▲ £15.50-£27.50

Leisure: ⚓▭

Facilities: ⚑⊙🅿❄🕓🗡🖺⧗📶🖥𝟶

Services: 🖳🗄🚽🛢🖉⊙🅣

Within 3 miles: 🖉🖺↻

Notes: No cars by tents. Dogs must be kept on leads.

AA Pubs & Restaurants nearby: The Plough Inn Lupton, LUPTON, LA6 1PJ, 015395 67700

CUMWHITTON
Map 18 NY55

Places to visit
Lanercost Priory, BRAMPTON, CA8 2HQ, 01697 73030
www.english-heritage.org.uk/daysout/properties/lanercost-priory

Cairndale Caravan Park
►►►69%

tel: 01768 896280 **CA8 9BZ**
dir: Exit A69 at Warwick Bridge on unclassified road through Great Corby to Cumwhitton, left at village sign, site 1m. **grid ref:** NY518523

Lovely grass site set in the tranquil Eden Valley with good views to distant hills. The all-weather touring pitches have electricity, and are located close to the immaculately maintained toilet facilities. Static holiday caravans for hire. 2 acre site. 5 touring pitches. 5 hardstandings. Caravan pitches. Motorhome pitches. 15 statics.

Open: Mar-Oct **Last arrival:** 22.00hrs

Pitches: ⊞ £12-£15 ⊞ £12-£15

Facilities: ⚑⊙❄♻ **Services:** 🖳🛢📦 **Within 3 miles:** ↨⅄🖉≽ **Notes:** ⊛

AA Pubs & Restaurants nearby: The String of Horses Inn, FAUGH, CA8 9EG, 01228 670297

This symbol indicates that a site offers glamping-style accommodation

FLOOKBURGH	Map 18 SD37

Places to visit

Holker Hall & Gardens, HOLKER, LA11 7PL, 015395 58328 www.holker.co.uk

Lakeland Leisure Park
HOLIDAY CENTRE 85%

GOLD

tel: 0871 231 0883 **Moor Ln LA11 7LT**
email: lakeland@haven.com **web:** www.haven.com/lakeland
dir: *On B5277 through Grange-over-Sands to Flookburgh. Left at village square, site 1m.*
grid ref: *SD372743*

A complete leisure park with full range of activities and entertainments, making this flat, grassy site ideal for families. The touring area, which includes 24 fully serviced pitches, is quietly situated away from the main amenities, but the swimming pools, all-weather bowling green and evening entertainment are just a short stroll away. There is a lake offering water sporting opportunities. 105 acre site. 185 touring pitches. 24 hardstandings. Caravan pitches. Motorhome pitches. Tent pitches. 800 statics.

Open: mid Mar-end Oct (rs mid Mar-May & Sep-Oct reduced activities, outdoor pool closed) **Last arrival:** anytime **Last departure:** 10.00hrs

Pitches: 🚐 🚙 🅰

Leisure: ♨ ⛱ ⚄ 👶 ⚽ ♫ ♪

Facilities: 🚿 ⊙ ♿ 🛒 WIFI 🖥 ♻ ❶

Services: 🔌 🗑 🍴 ♿ 🚽 🍽 🧹

Within 3 miles: ⚓ ⚙ ◎ ⛳ 🛒 🗑 ♾

Notes: No cars by caravans or tents. No commercial vehicles, no bookings by persons under 21yrs unless a family booking, max 2 dogs per booking, certain dog breeds banned. Dogs must be kept on leads.

AA Pubs & Restaurants nearby: The Cavendish Arms, CARTMEL, LA11 6QA, 015395 36240

The Masons Arms, CARTMEL, LA11 6NW, 015395 68486

Rogan & Company Restaurant, CARTMEL, LA11 6QD, 015395 35917

See advert below

LEISURE: 🏊 Indoor swimming pool ♨ Outdoor swimming pool 🎠 Children's playground 👶 Kid's club 🎾 Tennis court 🎱 Games room 📺 Separate TV room ⛳ golf course ⛵ Boats for hire 🎬 Cinema ♫ Entertainment 🎣 Fishing ◎ Mini golf 🏄 Watersports 💪 Gym ⚽ Sports field Spa ♾ Stables
FACILITIES: 🛁 Bath 🚿 Shower ⊙ Electric shaver ✂ Hairdryer ❄ Ice Pack Facility ♿ Disabled facilities ☏ Public telephone 🛒 Shop on site or within 200yds 🛒 Mobile shop (calls at least 5 days a week) 🍴 BBQ area 🍽 Picnic area WIFI Wi-fi 🖥 Internet access ♻ Recycling ❶ Tourist info 🐕 Dog exercise area

GRANGE-OVER-SANDS

Map 18 SD47

See also Cartmel

Oak Head Caravan Park
►►►80%

tel: 015395 31475 **Ayside LA11 6JA**
dir: *M6 junct 36, A590 towards Newby Bridge, 14m. From A590 bypass follow signs for Ayside.* **grid ref:** *SD389839*

Three miles from Grange-over-Sands and with direct access from A590 south of Newby Bridge, this is a pleasant terraced site with two separate areas – grass for tents and all gravel pitches for caravans and motorhomes. The site is enclosed within mature woodland and surrounded by hills; it is located in a less busy area but convenient for all the Lake District attractions. 10 acre site. 60 touring pitches. 30 hardstandings. Caravan pitches. Motorhome pitches. Tent pitches. 71 statics.

Open: Mar-Oct **Last arrival:** 20.00hrs **Last departure:** noon

Pitches: ⊕ £20 ⊕ £20 ▲ £18-£20

Leisure: ☺

Facilities: ⬤☉☝✳⛐☺

Services: ⊕☐⬤⊘⇶

Within 3 miles: ⬇⬆⬤⬆☐∪

Notes: ☺ No open fires, no noise after 23.00hrs. Dogs must be kept on leads.

AA Pubs & Restaurants nearby: The Cavendish Arms, CARTMEL, LA11 6QA, 015395 36240

The Masons Arms, CARTMEL, LA11 6NW, 015395 68486

Rogan & Company Restaurant, CARTMEL, LA11 6QD, 015395 35917

GREAT LANGDALE

Map 18 NY20

Great Langdale National Trust Campsite
►►►77%

tel: 015394 63862 & 32733 **LA22 9JU**
email: campsite.bookings@nationaltrust.org.uk
dir: *From Ambleside, A593 to Skelwith Bridge, right onto B5343, approx 5m to New Dungeon Ghyll Hotel. Site on left just before hotel.* **grid ref:** *NY286059*

Situated in a green valley, sheltered by mature trees and surrounded by stunning fell views, this site is an ideal base for campers, climbers and fell walkers. The large grass tent area has some gravel parking for cars, and there is a separate area for groups, and one for families with a children's play area. Attractive wooden cabins house the toilets, the reception and shop (selling fresh baked bread and pastries), and drying rooms, and there are wooden camping pods and two yurts for hire. Additionally, it is a gentle 10 minute walk to The Sticklebarn Tavern, the only National Trust run pub. 9 acre site. 220 touring pitches. Motorhome pitches. Tent pitches. 3 wooden pods.

Open: all year **Last departure:** 11.00hrs

Pitches: ⊕ ▲ ⛺

Leisure: ⬟

Facilities: ⬤☉✳⛐☺⑀♻

Services: ☐⬤⊘

Within 3 miles: ⬤⑀

Notes: No cars by tents. No noise between 23.00hrs-07.00hrs, no groups of 4 or more unless a family with children. Dogs must be kept on leads.

AA Pubs & Restaurants nearby: The New Dungeon Ghyll Hotel, GREAT LANGDALE, LA22 9JX, 015394 37213

The Britannia Inn, ELTERWATER, LA22 9HP, 015394 37210

Langdale Hotel & Spa, ELTERWATER, LA22 9JD, 015394 37302

HOLMROOK

Map 18 SD09

Places to visit

Great for kids: Ravenglass & Eskdale Railway, RAVENGLASS, CA18 1SW, 01229 717171 www.ravenglass-railway.co.uk

Seven Acres Caravan Park
►►►75%

tel: 01946 822777 **CA19 1YD**
email: reception@seacote.com
dir: *Site signed on A595 between Holmrook & Gosforth.* **grid ref:** *NY078014*

This sheltered park is close to quiet west Cumbrian coastal villages and beaches, and also handy for Eskdale and Wasdale. There is a good choice of pitches, some with hedged bays for privacy and some with coastal views. The park has a heated toilet block. 7 acre site. 37 touring pitches. 20 hardstandings. Caravan pitches. Motorhome pitches. Tent pitches. 16 statics.

Open: Mar-15 Jan **Last arrival:** 21.00hrs **Last departure:** 10.30hrs

Pitches: ⊕ £18-£21 ⊕ £18-£21 ▲ £10-£24

Facilities: ⬤☉☝✳⌂⑀♻⊘

Services: ⊕☐⑁

Within 3 miles: ⬇⑀◎☐∪

Notes: Dogs must be kept on leads.

AA Pubs & Restaurants nearby: Bower House Inn, ESKDALE GREEN, CA19 1TD, 019467 23244

Bridge Inn, SANTON BRIDGE, CA19 1UX, 019467 26221

Follow us on twitter
@TheAA_Lifestyle

PITCHES: ⊕ Caravans ⊕ Motorhomes ▲ Tents ⛺ Glamping-style accommodation **SERVICES:** ⊕ Electric hook up ☐ Launderette ⑁ Licensed bar ⬤ Calor Gas ⊘ Camping Gaz ⊤ Toilet fluid ⦿ Café/Restaurant ⇶ Fast Food/Takeaway ⇶ Battery charging ⬤ Baby care ⑁ Motorvan service point
ABBREVIATIONS: BH/bank hols – bank holidays Etr – Easter Spring BH – Spring Bank Holiday fr – from hrs – hours m – mile mdnt – midnight rdbt – roundabout rs – restricted service wk – week wknd – weekend x-rds – cross roads ⊗ No credit or debit cards ⊗ No dogs ♦ Children of all ages accepted

KESWICK
Map 18 NY22

Places to visit

The Pencil Museum, KESWICK, CA12 5NG, 017687 73626
www.pencilmuseum.co.uk

Honister Slate Mine, BORROWDALE, CA12 5XN, 01768 777230
www.honister-slate-mine.co.uk

Great for kids: Mirehouse, KESWICK, CA12 4QE, 017687 72287
www.mirehouse.com

PREMIER PARK

Castlerigg Hall Caravan & Camping Park
►►►►►87%

tel: 017687 74499 **Castlerigg Hall CA12 4TE**
email: info@castlerigg.co.uk **web:** www.castlerigg.co.uk
dir: 1.5m SE of Keswick on A591, turn right at sign. Site 200mtrs on right past Heights Hotel. **grid ref:** NY282227

Spectacular views over Derwent Water to the mountains beyond are among the many attractions at this lovely Lakeland park. Old farm buildings have been tastefully converted into excellent toilets with private washing cubicles and a family bathroom, reception and a well-equipped shop, and there is a kitchen/dining area for campers, and a restaurant/takeaway. There is a superb toilet block, and wooden camping pods and a further ten all-weather pitches are located in the tent field. 8 acre site. 48 touring pitches. 48 hardstandings. Caravan pitches. Motorhome pitches. Tent pitches. 30 statics. Wooden pods.

Open: mid Mar-7 Nov **Last arrival:** 21.00hrs **Last departure:** 11.30hrs

---

Pitches: � � 🏕
Leisure: 📺
Facilities: 🛁🚿⊙ℙ❄️♿⏱🅂✈WiFi
Services: 🔌🔲🛢⌀🅃🍽🛒⚒♨
Within 3 miles: ↧✝️日ℐ◎⛵🅂🅂∪
Notes: Dogs must not be left unattended & kept on leads. Campers' kitchen, sitting room.
AA Pubs & Restaurants nearby: The Kings Head, KESWICK, CA12 4TN, 017687 72393
See advert on opposite page

Burns Farm Caravan Park
►►►77%

tel: 017687 79225 & 79112 **St Johns in the Vale CA12 4RR**
email: linda@burns-farm.co.uk **web:** www.burns-farm.co.uk
dir: Exit A66 signed Castlerigg Stone Circle, Youth Centre & Burns Farm. Site on right in 0.5m. **grid ref:** NY307244

Lovely views of Blencathra and Skiddaw can be enjoyed from this secluded park, set on a working farm which extends a warm welcome to families. This is a good choice for exploring the beautiful and interesting countryside. Food can be found in the pub at Threlkeld. 2.5 acre site. 32 touring pitches. Caravan pitches. Motorhome pitches. Tent pitches.

Open: Mar-4 Nov **Last departure:** noon (peak season)
Pitches: 🚐🚉🏕
Facilities: 🚿⊙❄️♿⏱WiFi♻️
Services: 🔌🔲🛢📇
Within 3 miles: ↧✝️日ℐ◎⛵🅂🅂∪
Notes: 🚫 No noise after mdnt. Dogs must be kept on leads.
AA Pubs & Restaurants nearby: The Horse & Farrier Inn, KESWICK, CA12 4SQ, 017687 79688

KIRKBY LONSDALE
Map 18 SD67

Places to visit
Sizergh, SIZERGH, LA8 8AE, 015395 60951 www.nationaltrust.org.uk

PREMIER PARK

Woodclose Caravan Park
►►►►► 86%

tel: 015242 71597 **High Casterton LA6 2SE**
email: info@woodclosepark.com **web:** www.woodclosepark.com
dir: *On A65, 0.25m after Kirkby Lonsdale towards Skipton, park on left.*
grid ref: *SD618786*

A peaceful, well-managed park set in idyllic countryside within the beautiful Lune Valley, and centrally located for exploring the Lakes and Dales. Ideal for that 'back to nature' experience, with riverside walks, on-site woodland walks for both families and dogs, and top notch amenities blocks with fully serviced cubicles with one allocated for the 'Wigwam' pod village and camping field. The generous pitches are surrounded by mature trees and seasonal planting. Parts of the site are havens for wildlife. 9 acre site. 29 touring pitches. 28

hardstandings. Caravan pitches. Motorhome pitches. Tent pitches. 65 statics. 11 wooden pods.

Open: Mar-Oct **Last arrival:** 21.00hrs **Last departure:** noon

Pitches: 🚐 🚎 Å ⋔

Leisure: 🎣 ⚽

Facilities: 🌳 ⊙ 🅿 ✳ ⛄ ⚴ 🕐 📶 🗗 🚻 WiFi 🖥 ♻ 🛈

Services: 🔌 🔄 🛢 🌿 **Within 3 miles:** 🛶 🏌 🛒 🔄 ↻

Notes: No arrivals before 13.00hrs. Dogs must be kept on leads. Cycle hire, crock boxes for hire.

AA Pubs & Restaurants nearby: The Sun Inn, KIRKBY LONSDALE, LA6 2AU, 015242 71965
The Whoop Hall, KIRKBY LONSDALE, LA6 2GY, 015242 71284
The Pheasant Inn, KIRKBY LONSDALE, LA6 2RX, 01524 271230

New House Caravan Park
►►►► 81%

tel: 015242 71590 **LA6 2HR**
email: colinpreece9@aol.com
dir: *1m SE of Kirkby Lonsdale on A65, turn right into site entrance 300yds past Whoop Hall Inn.* **grid ref:** *SD628774*

Colourful floral displays greet new arrivals, creating an excellent first impression at this former farm, which has been carefully changed to provide well-spaced pitches, with hardstandings sheltered by surrounding mature trees and shrubs. An ideal base for exploring the Yorkshire Dales and the Lake District. 3 acre site. 50 touring pitches. 50 hardstandings. Caravan pitches. Motorhome pitches.

Open: Mar-Oct **Last arrival:** 21.00hrs

Pitches: 🚐 £18 🚎 £18

Facilities: 🌳 ⊙ 🅿 ✳ ⛄ ⚴ 🕐 🚻 WiFi 🖥 ♻ 🛈 **Services:** 🔌 🔄 🛢 🌿 🚰 ♨ 🔧

Within 3 miles: 🛶 🏌 🛒 🔄 **Notes:** 🚲 No cycling. Dogs must be kept on leads.

AA Pubs & Restaurants nearby: The Sun Inn, KIRKBY LONSDALE, LA6 2AU, 015242 71965
The Whoop Hall, KIRKBY LONSDALE, LA6 2GY, 015242 71284
The Pheasant Inn, KIRKBY LONSDALE, LA6 2RX, 01524 271230

PITCHES: 🚐 Caravans 🚎 Motorhomes Å Tents ⋔ Glamping-style accommodation **SERVICES:** 🔌 Electric hook up 🔄 Launderette 🍺 Licensed bar 🛢 Calor Gas 🌿 Camping Gaz 🚰 Toilet fluid 🍽 Café/Restaurant 🍟 Fast Food/Takeaway ♨ Battery charging 🍼 Baby care 🔧 Motorvan service point
ABBREVIATIONS: BH/bank hols – bank holidays Etr – Easter Spring BH – Spring Bank Holiday fr – from hrs – hours m – mile mdnt – midnight rdbt – roundabout rs – restricted service wk – week wknd – weekend x-rds – cross roads 🚫 No credit or debit cards 🐕 No dogs 👪 Children of all ages accepted

LONGTOWN   Map 21 NY36

See also Penton

Places to visit

Carlisle Castle, CARLISLE, CA3 8UR, 01228 591992
www.english-heritage.org.uk/daysout/properties/carlisle-castle

Tullie House Museum & Art Gallery Trust, CARLISLE, CA3 8TP, 01228 618718
www.tulliehouse.co.uk

Camelot Caravan Park
►► 75%

tel: 01228 791248 **CA6 5SZ**
dir: M6 junct 44, A7, site 5m N & 1m S of Longtown. **grid ref:** NY391666

A very pleasant level grassy site in a wooded setting near the M6, with direct
access from the A7, and simple, clean toilet facilities. The park is an ideal stopover
site. 1.5 acre site. 20 touring pitches. Caravan pitches. Motorhome pitches. Tent
pitches. 2 statics.

Open: Mar-Oct **Last arrival:** 20.00hrs **Last departure:** noon

Pitches: 🚐 🚏 Å

Facilities: 🏕☉✳🐕❶

Services: 🔌

Within 3 miles: 🖉🏪🛒 U

Notes: 🐾

MEALSGATE   Map 18 NY24

Places to visit

Jennings Brewery Tour and Shop, COCKERMOUTH, CA13 9NE, 01900 820362
www.jenningsbrewery.co.uk

Wordsworth House and Garden, COCKERMOUTH, CA13 9RX, 01900 824805
www.nationaltrust.org.uk/wordsworthhouse

Larches Caravan Park
►►►► 83%

tel: 016973 71379 & 71803 **CA7 1LQ**
dir: On A595 (Carlisle to Cockermouth road). **grid ref:** NY205415

This over 18s-only park is set in wooded rural surroundings on the fringe of the
Lake District National Park. Touring units are spread out over two sections. The
friendly family-run park offers constantly improving facilities, including a well-
stocked shop that also provides a very good range of camping and caravanning
spares. 20 acre site. 35 touring pitches. 30 hardstandings. Caravan pitches.
Motorhome pitches. Tent pitches.

Open: Mar-Oct (rs Early & late season) **Last arrival:** 21.30hrs **Last departure:** noon

Pitches: 🚐 🚏 Å **Facilities:** 🏕☉🍴✳🔥🐾🏪 🐕

Services: 🔌🛢🎯🚽 Ⓣ🌐

Within 3 miles: ↓🖉🛒 U

Notes: Adults only. 🐾

AA Pubs & Restaurants nearby: Oddfellows Arms, CALDBECK, CA7 8EA, 016974 78227

MILNTHORPE   Map 18 SD48

Places to visit

RSPB Leighton Moss & Morecambe Bay Nature Reserve, SILVERDALE, LA5 0SW,
01524 701601 www.rspb.org.uk/leightonmoss

Levens Hall, LEVENS, LA8 0PD, 015395 60321 www.levenshall.co.uk

Hall More Caravan Park
►►►► 77%

tel: 01524 781453 **Hale LA7 7BP**
email: enquiries@pureleisure-holidays.co.uk
dir: M6 junct 35, A6 towards Milnthorpe for 4m. Left at Lakeland Wildlife Oasis, follow
brown signs. **grid ref:** SD502771

Set on former meadowland and surrounded by mature trees, this constantly
improving rural park provides neat, well-spaced pitches with colourful hedged
areas enhanced by pretty seasonal flowers. The site is adjacent to a fishery where
fly fishing for trout is possible, and near a farm with stables offering pony trekking.
There are seven wooden camping pods for hire. 4 acre site. 44 touring pitches.
7 hardstandings. Caravan pitches. Motorhome pitches. Tent pitches. 60 statics.
Wooden pods.

Open: Mar-Jan **Last arrival:** 22.00hrs **Last departure:** 10.00hrs

Pitches: 🚐 🚏 Å 🏕 **Facilities:** 🏕☉🍴✳Ⓒ🐕

Services: 🔌🛢🎯🚽⬇ **Within 3 miles:** ↓🖉🏪🛒 U

AA Pubs & Restaurants nearby: The Wheatsheaf at Beetham, BEETHAM, LA7 7AL,
015395 62123

PATTERDALE   Map 18 NY31

Sykeside Camping Park
►►► 78%

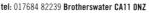

tel: 017684 82239 **Brotherswater CA11 0NZ**
email: info@sykeside.co.uk
dir: Direct access from A592 (Windermere to Ullswater road) at foot of Kirkstone Pass.
grid ref: NY403119

A camper's delight, this family-run park is sited at the foot of Kirkstone Pass, under
the 2,000ft Hartsop Dodd in a spectacular area with breathtaking views. The park
has mainly grass pitches with a few hardstandings, an area with tipis for hire, and
for those campers without a tent there is bunkhouse accommodation. There's a
small campers' kitchen and the bar serves breakfast and bar meals. There is
abundant wildlife. 10 acre site. 86 touring pitches. 25 hardstandings. Caravan
pitches. Motorhome pitches. Tent pitches. Tipis.

Open: all year **Last arrival:** 22.30hrs **Last departure:** 14.00hrs

Pitches: * 🚐 £17.50-£22.50 🚏 £17.50-£22.50 Å £13.50-£20.50 🏕

Leisure: 🎢 **Facilities:** 🏕☉🍴✳Ⓒ🏪🐾🖥❸❶

Services: 🔌🛢🎯🎾🛢Ⓣ🍽🎪🍺

Within 3 miles: 🎣🖉🚣🏪🛒

Notes: No noise after 23.00hrs. Laundry & drying room.

AA Pubs & Restaurants nearby: Queen's Head, TROUTBECK, LA23 1PW, 015394 32174
The Inn on the Lake, GLENRIDDING, CA11 0PE, 017684 82444

LEISURE: 🏊 Indoor swimming pool 🏊 Outdoor swimming pool 🎢 Children's playground 🪁 Kid's club 🎾 Tennis court 🎱 Games room ▢ Separate TV room
🏌 golf course 🚣 Boats for hire 🎦 Cinema 🎵 Entertainment 🎣 Fishing ◉ Mini golf 🏄 Watersports 🏋 Gym 🏐 Sports field Spa U Stables
FACILITIES: 🛁 Bath 🏕 Shower ☉ Electric shaver 🪒 Hairdryer ✳ Ice Pack Facility ♿ Disabled facilities Ⓒ Public telephone 🏪 Shop on site or within 200yds
🏪 Mobile shop (calls at least 5 days a week) 🍴 BBQ area 🍽 Picnic area 🌐 Wi-fi ▣ Internet access ♻ Recycling ❶ Tourist info 🐾 Dog exercise area

PENRITH
Map 18 NY53

Places to visit

Dalemain Mansion & Historic Gardens, DALEMAIN, CA11 0HB, 017684 86450
www.dalemain.com

Shap Abbey, SHAP, CA10 3NB, 0870 333 1181
www.english-heritage.org.uk/daysout/properties/shap-abbey

Great for kids: The Rheged Centre, PENRITH, CA11 0DQ, 01768 868000
www.rheged.com

PREMIER PARK

Lowther Holiday Park
►►►►►86%

tel: 01768 863631 **Eamont Bridge CA10 2JB**
email: alan@lowther-holidaypark.co.uk **web:** www.lowther-holidaypark.co.uk
dir: *3m S of Penrith on A6.* **grid ref:** *NY527265*

A secluded natural woodland site with lovely riverside walks and glorious countryside surroundings. The park is home to a rare colony of red squirrels, and trout fishing is available on the two-mile stretch of the River Lowther which runs through it. A birdwatch scheme with a coloured brochure has been introduced, inviting guests to spot some of the 30 different species that can be seen on the park. 50 acre site. 180 touring pitches. 50 hardstandings. 80 seasonal pitches. Caravan pitches. Motorhome pitches. Tent pitches. 403 statics. 2 wooden pods.

Open: mid Mar-mid Nov **Last arrival:** 22.00hrs **Last departure:** 22.00hrs

Pitches: * 🚐 £20-£33 🚎 £20-£33 ▲ £20-£33 🏕

Leisure: 🅰 🌊 🎱 🎵

Facilities: 🛒 🌳 ☉ ☂ ✳ ♿ 🚿 🐾 📶 🖥 ♻ 🅕

Services: 🔌 🔄 🍴 🧺 🚿 🚰 🛢 🍴 🔋 🍼 🚌 ⚡ ↯

Within 3 miles: ⚓ 🏇 ✏ ◎ 🚣 🛥 🛥 🛥 ∪

Notes: Families only, no commercial vehicles, no cats, rollerblades or skateboards. Dogs must be kept on leads.

AA Pubs & Restaurants nearby: The Yanwath Gate Inn, YANWATH, CA10 2LF, 01768 862386

Cross Keys Inn, PENRITH, CA11 8TP, 01768 865588

Flusco Wood
►►►►87%

tel: 017684 80020 & 07818 552931 **Flusco CA11 0JB**
email: info@fluscowood.co.uk
dir: *From Penrith to Keswick on A66 turn right signed Flusco. Approx 800mtrs, up short incline to right. Site on left.* **grid ref:** *NY345529*

Flusco Wood is set in mixed woodland with outstanding views towards Blencathra and the fells around Keswick. It combines two distinct areas, one of which has been designed specifically for touring caravans in neat glades with hardstandings, all within close proximity of the excellent log cabin-style toilet facilities. 24 acre site. 36 touring pitches. 36 hardstandings. 20 seasonal pitches. Caravan pitches. Motorhome pitches.

Open: 22 Mar-Oct **Last arrival:** 20.00hrs **Last departure:** noon

Pitches: 🚐 🚎 **Leisure:** 🅰

Facilities: 🌳 ☉ ☂ ✳ ♿ 🕐 🚿 🐾 📶 🖥 ♻ 🅕

Services: 🔌 🔄 🛢 🍴

Within 3 miles: 🏇

Notes: Quiet site, not suitable for large groups. Dogs must be kept on leads.

AA Pubs & Restaurants nearby: The Yanwath Gate Inn, YANWATH, CA10 2LF, 01768 862386

Cross Keys Inn, PENRITH, CA11 8TP, 01768 865588

PENRUDDOCK
Map 18 NY42

Beckses Caravan Park
►►►80%

tel: 01768 483224 **CA11 0RX**
dir: *M6 junct 40, A66 towards Keswick. Approx 6m, at caravan park sign turn right onto B5288. Site on right in 0.25m.* **grid ref:** *NY419278*

A small, pleasant site on sloping ground with level pitches and views of distant fells, on the edge of the National Park. This sheltered park is in a good location for touring the north lakes. 4 acre site. 25 touring pitches. 25 hardstandings. Caravan pitches. Motorhome pitches. Tent pitches. 18 statics.

Open: Etr-Oct **Last arrival:** 20.00hrs **Last departure:** 11.00hrs

Pitches: 🚐 🚎 ▲

Facilities: 🌳 ☉ ☂ 🐾 ♻

Services: 🔌 🛢 🚿 🚌

Within 3 miles: ✏ ∪

Notes: No noise after 23.00hrs. Dogs must be kept on leads.

AA Pubs & Restaurants nearby: Queen's Head, TROUTBECK, LA23 1PW, 015394 32174

PITCHES: 🚐 Caravans 🚎 Motorhomes ▲ Tents 🏕 Glamping-style accommodation **SERVICES:** 🔌 Electric hook up 🔄 Launderette 🍴 Licensed bar 🛢 Calor Gas 🚿 Camping Gaz 🅣 Toilet fluid 🍴 Café/Restaurant 🚌 Fast Food/Takeaway 🔋 Battery charging 🍼 Baby care ↯ Motorvan service point
ABBREVIATIONS: BH/bank hols – bank holidays Etr – Easter Spring BH – Spring Bank Holiday fr – from hrs – hours m – mile mdnt – midnight rdbt – roundabout rs – restricted service wk – week wknd – weekend x-rds – cross roads ⊘ No credit or debit cards ⊗ No dogs 👪 Children of all ages accepted

PENTON
Map 21 NY47

Twin Willows
►►► 76%

tel: 01228 577313 & 07850 713958 **The Beeches CA6 5QD**
email: davidson_b@btconnect.com
dir: M6 junct 44, A7 signed Longtown, right into Netherby St, 6m to Bridge Inn pub. Right then 1st left, site 300yds on right. **grid ref:** NY449771

Located close to Longtown, Twin Willows is a spacious park in a rural location on a ridge overlooking the Scottish border. All facilities, including all-weather pitches, are of a high quality. The park is suited to those who enjoy being away-from-it-all yet at the same time like to explore the area's rich history. A seasonal marquee is erected to hold regular barbecue and hog roast parties. 3 acre site. 16 touring pitches. 16 hardstandings. 10 seasonal pitches. Caravan pitches. Motorhome pitches. Tent pitches. 1 static. 1 tipi. 1 wooden pod.

Open: all year **Last arrival:** 22.00hrs **Last departure:** 10.00hrs
Pitches: * ⊕ £20-£25 ⊕ £20-£25 ▲ £15 ⊕ ⋒
Leisure: 🏊 ⚽ 🎿 ⋔ ⊙
Facilities: ↾ ⊙ ⌒ ✳ ⅋ ⊙ ⑤ ⋒ ⼌ WiFi 🖳 ♻ ❶
Services: ⊕ ⑤ ⅋ 🛢 ⟋ T ⼌ ⼌ ⺩ ⼌
Within 3 miles: ⌒ ⑤ ⑤ ∪
Notes: 🐕 Dogs must be kept on leads.

POOLEY BRIDGE
Map 18 NY42

AA HOLIDAY CENTRE OF THE YEAR 2015

Park Foot Caravan & Camping Park
HOLIDAY CENTRE 87%

tel: 017684 86309 **Howtown Rd CA10 2NA**
email: holidays@parkfootullswater.co.uk **web:** www.parkfootullswater.co.uk
dir: M6 junct 40, A66 towards Keswick, then A592 to Ullswater. Turn left for Pooley Bridge, right at church, right at x-rds signed Howtown. **grid ref:** NY469235

A lively park with good outdoor sports facilities, and boats can be launched directly onto Lake Ullswater. The attractive, mainly tenting, park has many mature trees, lovely views across the lake, and a superb amenities block in the family-only field. The Country Club bar and restaurant provides good meals, as well as discos, live music and entertainment in a glorious location. There are lodges and static

caravans for holiday hire. 40 acre site. 323 touring pitches. 32 hardstandings. Caravan pitches. Motorhome pitches. Tent pitches. 131 statics.

Open: Mar-Oct (rs Mar-Apr & mid Sep-Oct clubhouse open wknds only)
Last arrival: 22.00hrs **Last departure:** noon
Pitches: ⊕ £21-£39 ⊕ £21-£39 ▲ £14-£29
Leisure: ⋒ 🎿 🎾 ♣ ⊡ ♫
Facilities: ↾ ⊙ ⌒ ✳ ⅋ ⊙ ⑤ ⋒ ⼌ WiFi 🖳 ♻ ❶
Services: ⊕ ⑤ ⅋ 🛢 ⟋ T ⼌ ⼌ ⺩ ⼌
Within 3 miles: 🎿 ⌒ ⑤ ⑤ ∪
Notes: Families & couples only. Dogs must be kept on leads. Boat launch, pony trekking, pool table, table tennis, bike hire, kids' club in summer holidays.
AA Pubs & Restaurants nearby: The Yanwath Gate Inn, YANWATH, CA10 2LF, 01768 862386

Waterfoot Caravan Park
►►► 85%

tel: 017684 86302 **CA11 0JF**
email: enquiries@waterfootpark.co.uk **web:** www.waterfootpark.co.uk
dir: M6 junct 40, A66 for 1m, A592 for 4m, site on right before lake. (NB do not leave A592 until site entrance; Sat Nav not compatible). **grid ref:** NY462246

A quality touring park with neat, hardstanding pitches in a grassy glade within the wooded grounds of an elegant Georgian mansion. Toilet facilities are clean and well maintained, and the lounge bar with a separate family room enjoys lake views, and there is a path to Ullswater. Aira Force waterfall, Dalemain House and Gardens and Pooley Bridge are all close by. Please note that there is no access via Dacre. 22 acre site. 34 touring pitches. 30 hardstandings. Caravan pitches. Motorhome pitches. 146 statics. 2 wooden pods.

Open: Mar-14 Nov **Last arrival:** 21.30hrs **Last departure:** noon
Pitches: ⊕ ⊕ ⋒
Leisure: ⋒ ⊙ ♣ ♫
Facilities: ⼌ ↾ ⊙ ⌒ ✳ ⅋ ⊙ ⑤ ⋒ ⼌ WiFi 🖳 ♻ ❶
Services: ⊕ ⑤ ⅋ 🛢 ⟋ T ⼌ ⼌
Within 3 miles: 🎿 ⼌ ⊟ ⌒ ◎ 🎿 ⑤ ⑤ ∪
Notes: No tents. Dogs must be kept on leads.
AA Pubs & Restaurants nearby: The Yanwath Gate Inn, YANWATH, CA10 2LF, 01768 862386

LEISURE: 🏊 Indoor swimming pool 🏊 Outdoor swimming pool ⋒ Children's playground 🎿 Kid's club 🎾 Tennis court ♣ Games room ⊡ Separate TV room 🎿 golf course 🎿 Boats for hire ⊟ Cinema ♫ Entertainment ⌒ Fishing ◎ Mini golf 🎿 Watersports 🎾 Gym ⊙ Sports field Spa ∪ Stables
FACILITIES: ⼌ Bath ↾ Shower ⊙ Electric shaver ⌒ Hairdryer ✳ Ice Pack Facility ⅋ Disabled facilities ⊙ Public telephone ⑤ Shop on site or within 200yds ⑤ Mobile shop (calls at least 5 days a week) ⼌ BBQ area ⋒ Picnic area WiFi Wi-fi 🖳 Internet access ♻ Recycling ❶ Tourist info ⼌ Dog exercise area

SANTON BRIDGE | Map 18 NY10

The Old Post Office Campsite
►►► 78%

tel: 01946 726286 & 01785 822866 **CA19 1UY**
email: enquiries@theoldpostofficecampsite.co.uk
dir: *From A595 at Holmrook follow Santon Bridge signs, at T-junct left, site on right before river (NB Sat Nav may suggest a route via Wrynose & Hardknott Passes which may not be suitable for your vehicle at night or in bad weather).* **grid ref:** *NY110016*

A family-run campsite in a delightful riverside setting, beside an attractive stone bridge, that has very pretty pitches. The enthusiastic owner is steadily upgrading the park. Permits for salmon, sea and brown trout fishing are available, and there is an adjacent pub. Camping pods are available for hire. 2.2 acre site. 40 touring pitches. 5 hardstandings. Caravan pitches. Motorhome pitches. Tent pitches. 5 wooden pods.

Open: all year **Last departure:** noon

Pitches: 🚐 🚌 ▲ 🏠

Leisure: 🎣

Facilities: 🔦 ⊙ 🌂 ❋ ♿ 🗑 🛒

Services: 🔌 🖥 ⚒

Within 3 miles: 🖊 🗑 ∪

Notes: Dogs must be kept on leads.
AA Pubs & Restaurants nearby: Bridge Inn, SANTON BRIDGE, CA19 1UX, 019467 26221

Bower House Inn, ESKDALE GREEN, CA19 1TD, 019467 23244

Wasdale Head Inn, WASDALE HEAD, CA20 1EX, 019467 26229

SILLOTH | Map 18 NY15

Stanwix Park Holiday Centre
HOLIDAY CENTRE 90%

tel: 016973 32666 **Greenrow CA7 4HH**
email: enquiries@stanwix.com **web:** www.stanwix.com
dir: *1m SW on B5302. From A596 (Wigton bypass), follow signs to Silloth on B5302. In Silloth follow signs to site, approx 1m on B5300.* **grid ref:** *NY108527*

A large well-run family park within easy reach of the Lake District. Attractively laid out, with lots of amenities to ensure a lively holiday, including a 4-lane automatic, 10-pin bowling alley. Excellent touring areas with hardstandings, one in a peaceful glade well away from the main leisure complex, and there's a campers' kitchen and clean, well-maintained toilet facilities. Four camping pods are now available to hire

continued

PITCHES: 🚐 Caravans 🚌 Motorhomes ▲ Tents 🏠 Glamping-style accommodation **SERVICES:** 🔌 Electric hook up 🖥 Launderette 🍺 Licensed bar
🔥 Calor Gas ⊘ Camping Gaz Ⓣ Toilet fluid 🍽 Café/Restaurant 🍟 Fast Food/Takeaway 🔋 Battery charging 👶 Baby care ⚒ Motorvan service point
ABBREVIATIONS: BH/bank hols – bank holidays Etr – Easter Spring BH – Spring Bank Holiday fr – from hrs – hours m – mile mdnt – midnight
rdbt – roundabout rs – restricted service wk – week wknd – weekend x-rds – cross roads 🚫 No credit or debit cards ⊗ No dogs 👫 Children of all ages accepted

SILLOTH *continued*

in Skiddaw touring field. 4 acre site. 121 touring pitches. 100 hardstandings. Caravan pitches. Motorhome pitches. Tent pitches. 212 statics. 4 wooden pods.

Stanwix Park Holiday Centre

Open: all year (rs Nov-Feb (ex New Year) no entertainment, shop closed)
Last arrival: 21.00hrs **Last departure:** 11.00hrs

Pitches: * ⌭ £21.70-£27.30 ⌭ £21.70-£27.30 ▲ £21.70-£27.30 ⌂

Leisure: 🏊 🏊 🎯 ⚽ 🎱 ♫ Spa

Facilities: 🛁 🚿 ⊙ ☂ ✳ ♿ © ⑤ WiFi ♻ ❢

Services: ⬛ ⑤ ⬛ ⬛ T ⚊ ➤ ⬆

Within 3 miles: ⬍ ♪ ◎ ⑤ ⑤

Notes: Families only. Dogs must be kept on leads. Amusement arcade.

See advert on page 139

Hylton Caravan Park
►►►► 88%

tel: 016973 31707 & 32666 **Eden St CA7 4AY**
email: enquiries@stanwix.com **web:** www.stanwix.com
dir: *On entering Silloth on B5302 follow signs for site, approx 0.5m on left, at end of Eden St.* **grid ref:** NY113533

A smart, modern touring park with excellent toilet facilities including several bathrooms. This high quality park is a sister site to Stanwix Park, which is just a

mile away and offers all the amenities of a holiday centre, which are available to Hylton tourers. 18 acre site. 90 touring pitches. Caravan pitches. Motorhome pitches. Tent pitches. 213 statics.

Open: Mar-15 Nov **Last arrival:** 21.00hrs **Last departure:** 11.00hrs

Pitches: * ⌭ £19.10-£23.40 ⌭ £19.10-£23.40 ▲ £19.10-£23.40

Leisure: ⚑

Facilities: 🛁 🚿 ⊙ ☂ ♿

Services: ⬛ ⑤ ⬛ ⬆

Within 3 miles: ⬍ ♪ ◎ ⑤ ⑤

Notes: Families only. Dogs must be kept on leads. Use of facilities at Stanwix Park Holiday Centre.

TEBAY
Map 18 NY60

Tebay Services Caravan Site
►►► 77%

GOLD

tel: 01539 711322 **Orton CA10 3SB**
email: caravans@westmorland.com **web:** www.westmorland.com/caravan
dir: *Exit M6 at Westmorland Services, 1m from junct 38. Site accessed through service area from either N'bound or S'bound carriageways. Follow park signs.* **grid ref:** NY609060

An ideal stopover site adjacent to the Tebay service station on the M6, and handy for touring the Lake District. The park is screened by high grass banks, bushes and trees, and is within walking distance of the excellent farm shop and restaurant within the services complex, where caravan park customers enjoy a 10% discount. 4 acre site. 70 touring pitches. 70 hardstandings. 43 seasonal pitches. Caravan pitches. Motorhome pitches. 7 statics.

Open: Mar-Nov **Last arrival:** anytime **Last departure:** noon

Pitches: ⌭ ⌭

Facilities: 🚿 ⊙ ☂ ✳ ♿ © ⑤ ⬛ 🐕 WiFi 💻 ♻ ❢

Services: ⬛ ⑤ ⬛ ⬛ T ⚊ ⬆

Within 3 miles: ♪ ⑤ ⑤

Notes: 3 service pitches.

AA Pubs & Restaurants nearby: The Fat Lamb Country Inn, RAVENSTONEDALE, CA17 4LL, 015396 23242

The Black Swan, RAVENSTONEDALE, CA17 4NG, 015396 23204

LEISURE: 🏊 Indoor swimming pool 🏊 Outdoor swimming pool ⚑ Children's playground 🏑 Kid's club 🎾 Tennis court 🎱 Games room ⬛ Separate TV room ⬍ golf course 🚣 Boats for hire 🎬 Cinema ♫ Entertainment 🎣 Fishing ◎ Mini golf 🏄 Watersports 🏋 Gym ⚽ Sports field Spa ⚲ Stables
FACILITIES: 🛁 Bath 🚿 Shower ⊙ Electric shaver ☂ Hairdryer ✳ Ice Pack Facility ♿ Disabled facilities © Public telephone ⑤ Shop on site or within 200yds ⬛ Mobile shop (calls at least 5 days a week) ⬛ BBQ area ⬛ Picnic area WiFi Wi-fi 💻 Internet access ♻ Recycling ❢ Tourist info 🐕 Dog exercise area

TROUTBECK (NEAR KESWICK) — Map 18 NY32

PREMIER PARK

Troutbeck Camping and Caravanning Club Site
►►►►►81%

tel: 017687 79149 **Hutton Moor End CA11 0SX**
dir: *M6 junct 40, A66 towards Keswick. In 9.5m sharp left for Wallthwaite. Site 0.5m on left.* **grid ref:** *NY365271*

Beautifully situated between Penrith and Keswick, this quiet, well-managed Lakeland campsite offers two immaculate touring areas, one a sheltered paddock for caravans and motorhomes, with serviced hardstanding pitches, and a maturing lower field, which has spacious hardstanding pitches and a superb and very popular small tenting area that enjoys stunning and extensive views of the surrounding fells. The toilet block is appointed to a very high standard and includes two family cubicles, and the log cabin reception/shop stocks local and organic produce. A luxury caravan, sleeping six, is available for hire. The enthusiastic franchisees offer high levels of customer care and are constantly improving the park, which is well-placed for visited Keswick, Ullswater and the north lakes. Non-members are also very welcome. 5 acre site. 54 touring pitches. 36 hardstandings. Caravan pitches. Motorhome pitches. Tent pitches. 20 statics.

Open: 9 Mar-11 Nov & 26 Dec-2 Jan **Last arrival:** 20.00hrs **Last departure:** noon
Pitches: 🚐 🚐 ⛺
Leisure: 🄰 **Facilities:** 🌂⊙ℙ⚡🔥🕭♿ 🛁 WiFi ♻ ❶
Services: 🔌🔄 🔋⚖ T🛒♨ **Within 3 miles:** ↧🟦 ⚘
Notes: Site gates closed 23.00hrs-07.00hrs. Dogs must be kept on leads. Dog walk.

ULVERSTON — Map 18 SD27

Places to visit
The Dock Museum, BARROW-IN-FURNESS, LA14 2PW, 01229 876400 www.dockmuseum.org.uk

Furness Abbey, BARROW-IN-FURNESS, LA13 0PJ, 01229 823420 www.english-heritage.org.uk/daysout/properties/furness-abbey

Great for kids: South Lakes Wild Animal Park, DALTON-IN-FURNESS, LA15 8JR, 01229 466086 www.wildanimalpark.co.uk

ULVERSTON — Map 18 SD27

PREMIER PARK

Bardsea Leisure Park
►►►►►87%

tel: 01229 584712 & 484363 **Priory Rd LA12 9QE**
email: reception@bardsealeisure.co.uk
dir: *M6 junct 36, A590 towards Barrow. At Ulverston take A5087, site 1m on right.* **grid ref:** *SD292765*

An attractively landscaped former quarry, making a quiet and very sheltered site. Many of the generously-sized pitches offer all-weather full facilities, and a luxury toilet block provides plenty of fully serviced cubicles. Set on the southern edge of the town, it is convenient for both the coast and the Lake District and

there's an excellent caravan accessories shop on site. Please note that this site does not accept tents. 5 acre site. 83 touring pitches. 83 hardstandings. 50 seasonal pitches. Caravan pitches. Motorhome pitches. 88 statics.

Open: all year **Last arrival:** 21.00hrs **Last departure:** noon
Pitches: 🚐 £17-£24 🚐 £17-£24
Leisure: 🄰 ⚽
Facilities: 🌂⊙ℙ⚡♿🕭🛁🔥♨ WiFi 🖥
Services: 🔌🔄 🔋⚖T🛒♨⚖
Within 3 miles: ↧🟦 ⚘ 🛁🟦⚘
Notes: No noise after 22.30hrs. Dogs must be kept on leads.
AA Pubs & Restaurants nearby: Farmers Arms Hotel, ULVERSTON, LA12 7BA, 01229 584469

WASDALE HEAD — Map 18 NY10

Wasdale Head National Trust Campsite
►►►76%

tel: 015394 63862 & 32733 **CA20 1EX**
email: campsite.bookings@nationaltrust.org.uk
dir: *From A595 N towards Whitehaven turn left at Gosforth; from Whitehaven S on A595 right at Holmrook for Santon Bridge, follow signs to Wasdale Head.* **grid ref:** *NY183076*

Set in a remote and beautiful spot at Wasdale Head, under the stunning Scafell peaks at the head of the deepest lake in England. Clean, well-kept facilities are set centrally amongst open grass pitches and trees, where camping pods and tipis are also located. There are eight hardstandings for motorhomes and eight electric hook-ups for tents. The renowned Wasdale Head Inn is close by. 5 acre site. 120 touring pitches. 6 hardstandings. Motorhome pitches. Tent pitches. 2 tipis. 3 wooden pods.

Open: all year (rs Wknds Nov-Feb shop open) **Last arrival:** 20.00hrs **Last departure:** 11.00hrs
Pitches: 🚐 ⛺🏠
Facilities: 🌂⊙ℙ⚡♿🕭🛁♻
Services: 🔌🔄⚖
Within 3 miles: 🛁
Notes: No cars by tents. No groups of more than 4 unless a family with children. Dogs must be kept on leads.
AA Pubs & Restaurants nearby: Wasdale Head Inn, WASDALE HEAD, CA20 1EX, 019467 26229

Who are the AA's award-winning campsites this year? See pages 14-19

WATERMILLOCK
Map 18 NY42

The Quiet Site
►►►►88%

tel: 07768 727016 **Ullswater CA11 0LS**
email: info@thequietsite.co.uk
dir: *M6 junct 40, A592 towards Ullswater. Right at lake junct, then right at Brackenrigg Hotel. Site 1.5m on right.* **grid ref:** *NY431236*

A well-maintained site in a lovely, peaceful location, with good terraced pitches offering great fell views, very good toilet facilities including family bathrooms, and a charming 'olde-worlde' bar. Their policy of green sustainability is commendable, with solar panels and a biomass boiler delivering heat and hot water to the amenity blocks, even when the site is busy. There are wooden camping pods and a self-catering stone cottage for hire. 10 acre site. 100 touring pitches. 60 hardstandings. Caravan pitches. Motorhome pitches. Tent pitches. 23 statics. 13 wooden pods.

Open: all year (rs Low season bar closed some wkdays only) **Last arrival:** 22.00hrs
Last departure: noon

Pitches: 🚐 🚍 ▲ 🏠

Leisure: ⋀ ⚽ 🎱 ▢

Facilities: 🛁 📷 ⊙ 🗗 ✳ ⚿ 🕓 🖫 🍴 🚿 WiFi 🖳 ♻ 🛈

Services: 🖴 🖥 🍽 🛢 🖉 T 🚽 🖐

Within 3 miles: ⅂ 🎣 ⚗ 🖫 🖫 ∪

Notes: Quiet from 22.00hrs. Pool table, soft play area for toddlers, caravan storage.

AA Pubs & Restaurants nearby: Macdonald Leeming House, WATERMILLOCK, CA11 0JJ, 0844 879 9142

Rampsbeck Country House Hotel, WATERMILLOCK, CA11 0LP, 017684 86442

Cove Caravan & Camping Park
►►►►83%

tel: 017684 86549 **Ullswater CA11 0LS**
email: info@cove-park.co.uk
dir: *M6 junct 40, A592 for Ullswater. Right at lake junct, then right at Brackenrigg Inn. Site 1.5m on left.* **grid ref:** *NY431236*

A peaceful family site in an attractive and elevated position with extensive fell views and glimpses of Ullswater Lake. Extensive ground works have been carried out in order to provide spacious, mostly level pitches. Pretty, seasonal flowers are planted amid the wide variety of mature trees and shrubs. 3 acre site. 50 touring pitches. 27 hardstandings. 10 seasonal pitches. Caravan pitches. Motorhome pitches. Tent pitches. 39 statics.

Open: Mar-Oct **Last arrival:** 21.00hrs **Last departure:** noon

Pitches: * 🚐 £20-£34 🚍 £20-£34 ▲ £15-£30

Leisure: ⋀

Facilities: 📷 ⊙ 🗗 ✳ ⚿ 🖫 ♻ 🛈

Services: 🖴 🖥 🛢 🖉

Within 3 miles: ⅂ 🎣 ⚗ 🖫 🖫 ∪

Notes: No open fires, no noise after 22.30hrs. Dogs must be kept on leads.

AA Pubs & Restaurants nearby: Macdonald Leeming House, WATERMILLOCK, CA11 0JJ, 0844 879 9142

Rampsbeck Country House Hotel, WATERMILLOCK, CA11 0LP, 017684 86442

Ullswater Caravan, Camping & Marine Park
►►►►81%

tel: 017684 86666 **High Longthwaite CA11 0LR**
email: info@ullswatercaravanpark.co.uk
dir: *M6 junct 40, A592, W towards Ullswater for 5m. Right, alongside Ullswater for 2m, right at phone box. Site 0.5m on right.* **grid ref:** *NY438232*

A pleasant rural site with its own nearby boat launching and marine storage facility, making it ideal for sailors. The family-owned and run park enjoys fell and lake views, and there is a bar, a stylish new café, a splendid undercover area for campers, and a shop on site. Many of the pitches are fully serviced and there are wooden cabins with barbecues. Please note that the Marine Park is one mile from the camping area. 12 acre site. 160 touring pitches. 58 hardstandings. Caravan pitches. Motorhome pitches. Tent pitches. 55 statics. 4 wooden pods.

Open: Mar-Nov (rs Low season bar open wknds only) **Last arrival:** 21.00hrs
Last departure: noon

Pitches: * 🚐 £14.50-£27.50 🚍 £14.50-£27.50 ▲ £14.50-£27.50 🏠

Leisure: ⋀ 🎱

Facilities: 📷 ⊙ 🗗 ✳ ⚿ 🖫 🖈 WiFi 🖳 ♻

Services: 🖴 🖥 🍽 🛢 🖉 T 🚽

Within 3 miles: ⅂ 🎣 ⚗ 🖫 🖫 ∪

Notes: No open fires, no noise after 23.30hrs. Dogs must be kept on leads. Boat launching & moorings 1m.

AA Pubs & Restaurants nearby: Macdonald Leeming House, WATERMILLOCK, CA11 0JJ, 0844 879 9142

Rampsbeck Country House Hotel, WATERMILLOCK, CA11 0LP, 017684 86442

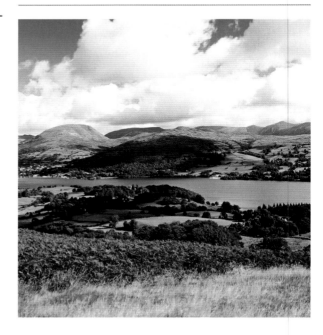

WINDERMERE
Map 18 SD49

Places to visit

Holehird Gardens, WINDERMERE, LA23 1NP, 015394 46008
www.holehirdgardens.org.uk

Blackwell The Arts & Crafts House, BOWNESS-ON-WINDERMERE, LA23 3JT, 015394 46139 www.blackwell.org.uk

Great for kids: Lake District Visitor Centre at Brockhole, WINDERMERE, LA23 1LJ, 015394 46601 www.brockhole.co.uk

---

PREMIER PARK

Park Cliffe Camping & Caravan Estate

►►►►► 90%

tel: 015395 31344 **Birks Rd, Tower Wood LA23 3PG**
email: info@parkcliffe.co.uk **web:** www.parkcliffe.co.uk
dir: *M6 junct 36, A590. Right at Newby Bridge onto A592. 3.6m right into site. NB due to difficult access from main road this is the only advised direction for approaching the site.* **grid ref:** *SD391912*

A lovely hillside park set in 25 secluded acres of fell land. The camping area is sloping and uneven in places, but well drained and sheltered; some pitches have spectacular views of Lake Windermere and the Langdales. The park offers a high level of customer care and is very well equipped for families (family bathrooms), and there is an attractive bar and brasserie restaurant serving quality food; three static holiday caravans are for hire. 25 acre site. 60 touring pitches. 60 hardstandings. 25 seasonal pitches. Caravan pitches. Motorhome pitches. Tent pitches. 56 statics. 7 wooden pods.

Open: Mar-8 Nov (rs Wknds & school hols facilities open fully) **Last arrival:** 22.00hrs **Last departure:** noon

Pitches: * ➡ £26-£31 ➡ £26-£31 ▲ £20-£25 ⋔

Leisure: ⅄ ⚲

Facilities: ⋔ ⊙ ⌿ ☼ ⅋ ⊙ ⑤ ⊓ ⊓ WiFi ♻ ❼

Services: ⊕ ⑤ ⋓ ⛽ ⌀ ⊤ ⋔ ⛟ ⛟ ⛟

Within 3 miles: ↓ ⅟ ⊟ ⌿ ◎ ⅙ ⓪ ⑤ ∪

Notes: No noise 23.00hrs-07.30hrs. Dogs must be kept on leads. Off-licence.

AA Pubs & Restaurants nearby: Eagle & Child Inn, WINDERMERE, LA8 9LP, 01539 821320

Beech Hill Hotel, WINDERMERE, LA23 3LR, 015394 42137

Hill of Oaks & Blakeholme
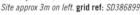
►►►► 84%

tel: 015395 31578 **LA12 8NR**
email: enquiries@hillofoaks.co.uk **web:** www.hillofoaks.co.uk
dir: *M6 junct 36, A590 towards Barrow. At rdbt signed Bowness turn right onto A592. Site approx 3m on left.* **grid ref:** *SD386899*

A secluded, heavily wooded park on the shores of Lake Windermere. Pretty lakeside picnic areas, woodland walks and a play area make this a delightful park for families, with excellent serviced pitches, a licensed shop and a heated toilet block. Watersports include sailing and canoeing, with private jetties for boat launching. 31 acre site. 43 touring pitches. 43 hardstandings. Caravan pitches. Motorhome pitches. 215 statics.

Open: Mar-14 Nov **Last departure:** noon

Pitches: ➡ ➡

Leisure: ⅄ ⚲

Facilities: ⋔ ⊙ ⌿ ☼ ⅋ ⊙ ⑤ ⊓ ⊓ WiFi ▬ ♻ ❼

Services: ⊕ ⑤ ⛽ ⊤ ⛟

Within 3 miles: ↓ ⅟ ⊟ ⌿ ◎ ⅙ ⓪ ⑤ ∪

Notes: No tents (except trailer tents), no groups. Dogs must be kept on leads.

AA Pubs & Restaurants nearby: Eagle & Child Inn, WINDERMERE, LA8 9LP, 01539 821320

Beech Hill Hotel, WINDERMERE, LA23 3LR, 015394 42137

Who has won England Campsite of the Year? See page 14

PITCHES: ➡ Caravans ➡ Motorhomes ▲ Tents ⋔ Glamping-style accommodation **SERVICES:** ⊕ Electric hook up ⑤ Launderette ⋓ Licensed bar ⛽ Calor Gas ⌀ Camping Gaz ⊤ Toilet fluid ⊙ Café/Restaurant ⛟ Fast Food/Takeaway ⛟ Battery charging ⛟ Baby care ⛟ Motorvan service point
ABBREVIATIONS: BH/bank hols – bank holidays Etr – Easter Spring BH – Spring Bank Holiday fr – from hrs – hours m – mile mdnt – midnight rdbt – roundabout rs – restricted service wk – week wknd – weekend x-rds – cross roads ⊘ No credit or debit cards ⊗ No dogs ♦ Children of all ages accepted

DERBYSHIRE

ASHBOURNE
Map 10 SK14

Places to visit

Kedleston Hall, KEDLESTON HALL, DE22 5JH, 01332 842191
www.nationaltrust.org.uk

Carsington Fields Caravan Park
►►► 80%

tel: 01335 372872 **Millfields Ln, Nr Carsington Water DE6 3JS**
email: bookings@carsingtoncaravaning.co.uk
dir: From Belper towards Ashbourne on A517, right approx 0.25m past Hulland Ward into Dog Ln. 0.75m right at x-rds signed Carsington. Site on right approx 0.75m.
grid ref: SK251493

A very well-presented and spacious park with a good toilet block, open views and a large fenced pond that attracts plenty of wildlife. The popular tourist attraction of Carsington Water is a short stroll away, with its variety of leisure facilities including fishing, sailing, windsurfing and children's play area. The park is also a good base for walkers. 6 acre site. 58 touring pitches. 10 hardstandings. 10 seasonal pitches. Caravan pitches. Motorhome pitches. Tent pitches.

Open: Mar-Sep **Last arrival:** 21.00hrs **Last departure:** 14.00hrs

Pitches: * ⊕ £20-£25 ⊕ £20-£25 ⋀ £20-£25

Facilities: 🐾 ⊙ 𝒫 ✳ ⚐ 🚻 WiFi ♻ 𝟋

Services: ⊕ ≛

Within 3 miles: ⊁ ⌿ ⩘ 🛒 ⎈ ∪

Notes: No large groups or group bookings, no noise after 23.00hrs. Dogs must be kept on leads. Indian takeaway free delivery to site.

AA Pubs & Restaurants nearby: The Coach and Horses Inn, FENNY BENTLEY, DE6 1LB, 01335 350246

Bentley Brook Inn, FENNY BENTLEY, DE6 1LF, 01335 350278

BAKEWELL
Map 16 SK26

Places to visit

Chatsworth, CHATSWORTH, DE45 1PP, 01246 565300 www.chatsworth.org

Greenhills Holiday Park
►►► 81%

tel: 01629 813052 & 813467 **Crowhill Ln DE45 1PX**
email: info@greenhillsholidaypark.co.uk
dir: 1m NW of Bakewell on A6. Signed before Ashford-in-the-Water, onto unclassified road on right. **grid ref:** SK202693

A well-established park set in lovely countryside within the Peak District National Park. Many pitches enjoy uninterrupted views, and there is easy accessibility to all facilities. A clubhouse, shop and children's playground are popular features. 8 acre site. 172 touring pitches. 30 hardstandings. Caravan pitches. Motorhome pitches. Tent pitches. 73 statics.

Open: Feb-Nov (rs Feb-Apr & Oct-Nov bar & shop closed) **Last arrival:** 22.00hrs
Last departure: noon

Pitches: * ⊕ fr £20 ⊕ fr £20 ⋀ fr £15

Leisure: ⌂ ⚽ 🎵
Facilities: 🐾 ⊙ 𝒫 ✳ ⚐ ⚲ 🛒 🚻 WiFi 🖥 ♻ 𝟋
Services: ⊕ 🔄 ⛽ 🛢 ⌿ ⎕ 🍽 ≛ ⩊
Within 3 miles: ⌿ ⩘ ◎ 🛒 ⎈ ∪

AA Pubs & Restaurants nearby: The Monsal Head Hotel, BAKEWELL, DE45 1NL, 01629 640250

Piedaniel's, BAKEWELL, DE45 1BX, 01629 812687

BIRCHOVER
Map 16 SK26

Places to visit

Haddon Hall, HADDON HALL, DE45 1LA, 01629 812855 www.haddonhall.co.uk

The Heights of Abraham Cable Cars, Caverns & Hilltop Park, MATLOCK BATH, DE4 3PD, 01629 582365 www.heightsofabraham.com

PREMIER PARK

Barn Farm Campsite
►►►► 80%

tel: 01629 650245 **Barn Farm DE4 2BL**
email: gilberthh@msn.com
dir: From A6 take B5056 towards Ashbourne. Follow brown signs to site.
grid ref: SK238621

An interesting park on a former dairy farm with the many and varied facilities housed in high quality conversions of old farm buildings. The three large and well-maintained touring fields offer sweeping views across the Peak National Park. There is an excellent choice of privacy cubicles, including shower and washbasin cubicles, a new, fully serviced family room, and even a shower and sauna. New hardstandings were created for 2014, and there are five stylish, self-catering camping barns for hire. 15 acre site. 62 touring pitches. 13 hardstandings. Caravan pitches. Motorhome pitches. Tent pitches.

Open: Apr-Oct **Last arrival:** 21.00hrs **Last departure:** 11.00hrs

Pitches: * ⊕ £22 ⊕ £22 ⋀ £10-£15

Leisure: ⌂ ⚽ 🎱 ⎕
Facilities: 🐾 ⊙ 𝒫 ✳ ⚲ 🛒 🚻 🖥 ♻ 𝟋
Services: ⊕ 🔄 🛢 ⌿ ⎕
Within 3 miles: ⌖ ⌿ ◎ 🛒 ⩘ 🛒 ⎈ ∪

Notes: No music after 22.30hrs, minimum noise 22.30hrs-07.00hrs. Dogs must be kept on leads. Vending machines.

AA Pubs & Restaurants nearby: The Druid Inn, BIRCHOVER, DE4 2BL, 01629 653836

The Peacock at Rowsley, ROWSLEY, DE4 2EB, 01629 733518

LEISURE: 🏊 Indoor swimming pool 🏊 Outdoor swimming pool ⌂ Children's playground 👶 Kid's club 🎾 Tennis court 🎱 Games room ⎕ Separate TV room ⌖ golf course ⛵ Boats for hire 🎬 Cinema 🎵 Entertainment ⌿ Fishing ◎ Mini golf ⩘ Watersports 💪 Gym ⚽ Sports field Spa ∪ Stables
FACILITIES: 🛁 Bath 🐾 Shower ⊙ Electric shaver 𝒫 Hairdryer ✳ Ice Pack Facility ⚲ Disabled facilities ⚐ Public telephone 🛒 Shop on site or within 200yds 🛒 Mobile shop (calls at least 5 days a week) 🍖 BBQ area 🪑 Picnic area WiFi Wi-fi 🖥 Internet access ♻ Recycling 𝟋 Tourist info 🚻 Dog exercise area

BUXTON
Map 16 SK07

Places to visit

Poole's Cavern (Buxton Country Park), BUXTON, SK17 9DH, 01298 26978
www.poolescavern.co.uk

Great for kids: Go Ape Buxton, BUXTON, SK17 9DH, 0845 643 9215
www.goape.co.uk/buxton

Lime Tree Park
►►►►86%

tel: 01298 22988 **Dukes Dr SK17 9RP**
email: info@limetreeparkbuxton.com
dir: *1m S of Buxton, between A515 & A6.* **grid ref:** *SK070725*

A most attractive and well-designed site, set on the side of a narrow valley in an elevated location, with separate, neatly landscaped areas for statics, tents, touring caravans and motorhomes. There's good attention to detail throughout including the clean toilets and showers, and WiFi is free of charge. Its backdrop of a magnificent old railway viaduct and views over Buxton and the surrounding hills, make this a sought-after destination. There are eight static caravans, a pine lodge and two apartments available for holiday lets. 10.5 acre site. 106 touring pitches. 22 hardstandings. Caravan pitches. Motorhome pitches. Tent pitches. 43 statics.

Open: Mar-Oct **Last arrival:** 18.00hrs **Last departure:** noon

Pitches: ⌖ £25-£31 ⌖ £25-£31 ⅄ £25-£31

Leisure: ⌂ ⚲ ⊡

Facilities: ⌖⊙⌖☀⅄⌚⌅⌖⌖⌗⌗ ⌂ ⊛

Services: ⌖⌖ ⌖⌖⌖⌖⌖

Within 3 miles: ⌖⊙⌖⌖⌖⌖

Notes: No noise after 22.00hrs, no fires. Dogs must be kept on leads.

AA Pubs & Restaurants nearby: The Queen Anne Inn, GREAT HUCKLOW, SK17 8RF, 01298 871246

Beech Croft Farm
►►►►83%

tel: 01298 85330 **Beech Croft, Blackwell in the Peak SK17 9TQ**
email: mail@beechcroftfarm.co.uk **web:** www.beechcroftfarm.co.uk
dir: *Exit A6 midway between Buxton & Bakewell. Site signed.* **grid ref:** *SK122720*

A small terraced farm site with lovely Peak District views. There's a fine stone-built toilet block with ultra-modern fittings, under-floor heating and additional unisex

facilities, fully-serviced hardstanding pitches, gravel roads, a campers' shelter, and a super tarmac pathway leading from the camping field to the toilet block. This makes an ideal site for those touring or walking in the Peak District. 3 acre site. 30 touring pitches. 30 hardstandings. Caravan pitches. Motorhome pitches. Tent pitches.

Open: all year (rs Nov-Feb not open for tents) **Last arrival:** 21.30hrs **Last departure:** noon

Pitches: * ⌖ £20-£22.50 ⌖ £20-£22.50 ⅄ £14-£16

Leisure: ⌂ ⊛

Facilities: ⌖⊙☀⅄⌅⌗⌗ ⌂ ⊛

Services: ⌖⌖ ⌖⌖⌖

Notes: No noise after 22.00hrs. Dogs must be kept on leads. Breakfast & jacket potato van (high season).

AA Pubs & Restaurants nearby: The Queen Anne Inn, GREAT HUCKLOW, SK17 8RF, 01298 871246

Clover Fields Touring Caravan Park
►►►91%

tel: 01298 78731 **1 Heath View, Harpur Hill SK17 9PU**
email: cloverfields@tiscali.co.uk
dir: *A515, B5053, then immediately right. Site 0.5m on left.* **grid ref:** *SK075704*

A developing and spacious adults-only park, just over a mile from the attractions of Buxton, with very good facilities, including an upmarket, timber chalet-style toilet block. All pitches are fully serviced and have individual barbecues, and are set out on terraces, each with extensive views over the countryside. Swathes of natural meadow grasses and flowers cloak the terraces and surrounding fields. A café will be opened for the 2015 season. 12 acre site. 25 touring pitches. 25 hardstandings. Caravan pitches. Motorhome pitches. Tent pitches.

Open: all year **Last arrival:** 20.00hrs **Last departure:** 18.00hrs

Pitches: ⌖ ⌖ ⅄

Facilities: ⌖⊙☀⅄⌚⌗ ⌂ ⊛

Services: ⌖⌖ ⌖⌖⌖

Within 3 miles: ⌖⌖⌖⌖⌖

Notes: Adults only. No commercial vehicles. Dogs must be kept on leads. Small fishing pond, boules area.

AA Pubs & Restaurants nearby: The Queen Anne Inn, GREAT HUCKLOW, SK17 8RF, 01298 871246

PITCHES: ⌖ Caravans ⌖ Motorhomes ⅄ Tents ⌂ Glamping-style accommodation **SERVICES:** ⌖ Electric hook up ⌖ Launderette ⌖ Licensed bar ⌖ Calor Gas ⌖ Camping Gaz ⌖ Toilet fluid ⌖ Café/Restaurant ⌖ Fast Food/Takeaway ⌖ Battery charging ⌖ Baby care ⌖ Motorvan service point
ABBREVIATIONS: BH/bank hols – bank holidays Etr – Easter Spring BH – Spring Bank Holiday fr – from hrs – hours m – mile mdnt – midnight rdbt – roundabout rs – restricted service wk – week wknd – weekend x-rds – cross roads ⌖ No credit or debit cards ⌖ No dogs ⌖ Children of all ages accepted

HOPE
Map 16 SK18

Places to visit
Peveril Castle, CASTLETON, S33 8WQ, 01433 620613
www.english-heritage.org.uk/daysout/properties/peveril-castle

Speedwell Cavern, CASTLETON, S33 8WA, 01433 620512
www.speedwellcavern.co.uk

Pindale Farm Outdoor Centre
►►►77%

tel: 01433 620111 **Pindale Rd S33 6RN**
email: pindalefarm@btconnect.com
dir: *From A6187 in Hope follow Pindale sign between church & Woodroffe Arms. Site 1m on left.* **grid ref:** *SK163825*

Set around a 13th-century farmhouse and a former lead mine pump house (now converted to a self-contained bunkhouse for up to 60 people), this simple, off-the-beaten-track site is an ideal base for walking, climbing, caving and various outdoor pursuits. Around the farm are several deeply wooded areas available for tents, and old stone buildings that have been converted to house modern toilet facilities. 4 acre site. 60 touring pitches. Tent pitches.

Open: Mar-Oct
Pitches: * ▲ fr £15
Facilities: 🌧 ☺ ✲ 🐕 WiFi
Services: 🖭 🗑
Within 3 miles: 🛒 ∪

Notes: No anti-social behaviour, noise must be kept to minimum after 21.00hrs, no fires. Dogs must be kept on leads. Charge for WiFi.

AA Pubs & Restaurants nearby: Cheshire Cheese Inn, HOPE, S33 6ZF, 01433 620381

Ye Olde Nags Head, CASTLETON, S33 8WH, 01433 620248

The Peaks Hotel, CASTLETON, S33 8WJ, 01433 620247

MATLOCK

Places to visit
Peak District Mining Museum, MATLOCK BATH, DE4 3NR, 01629 583834
www.peakmines.co.uk

Haddon Hall, HADDON HALL, DE45 1LA, 01629 812855 www.haddonhall.co.uk

Great for kids: The Heights of Abraham Cable Cars, Caverns & Hilltop Park, MATLOCK BATH, DE4 3PD, 01629 582365 www.heightsofabraham.com

MATLOCK
Map 16 SK35

Lickpenny Caravan Site
►►►►87%

tel: 01629 583040 **Lickpenny Ln, Tansley DE4 5GF**
email: enquiries@lickpennycaravanpark.co.uk
dir: *From Matlock take A615 towards Alfreton for 3m. Site signed to left, into Lickpenny Ln, right into site near end of road.* **grid ref:** *SK339597*

A picturesque site in the grounds of an old plant nursery with areas broken up and screened by a variety of shrubs, and with spectacular views, which are best enjoyed from the upper terraced areas. Pitches, several fully serviced, are spacious, well screened and well marked, and facilities are kept to a very good standard. The bistro/coffee shop is popular with visitors. 16 acre site. 80 touring pitches. 80 hardstandings. 20 seasonal pitches. Caravan pitches. Motorhome pitches.

Open: all year **Last arrival:** 20.00hrs **Last departure:** noon
Pitches: * 🚐 £15-£29 🚗 £15-£29
Leisure: 🛝
Facilities: 🌧 ☺ 🅿 🚿 ☎ 🗑 🛒 🐕 WiFi 💻 ♻ ℹ
Services: 🖭 🗑 🚽 T 🛒 ↯
Within 3 miles: ⚓ ✈ ℐ ◎ 🛒 🗑 ∪

Notes: No noise after 23.00hrs, 1 car per pitch, late departure until 18.00hrs (charge applies). Dogs must be kept on leads. Child bath available.

AA Pubs & Restaurants nearby: The Red Lion, MATLOCK, DE4 3BT, 01629 584888

Stones Restaurant, MATLOCK, DE4 3LT, 01629 56061

NEWHAVEN
Map 16 SK16

Places to visit
Middleton Top Engine House, MIDDLETON, DE4 4LS, 01629 823204
www.derbyshire.gov.uk/countryside

Peak District Mining Museum, MATLOCK BATH, DE4 3NR, 01629 583834
www.peakmines.co.uk

Newhaven Caravan & Camping Park
►►►►82%

tel: 01298 84300 **SK17 0DT**
email: newhavencaravanpark@btconnect.com
dir: *Between Ashbourne & Buxton at A515 & A5012 junct.* **grid ref:** *SK167602*

Pleasantly situated within the Peak District National Park, this park has mature trees screening the three touring areas. Very good toilet facilities cater for touring vans and a large tent field, and there's a restaurant adjacent to the site. 30 acre site. 125 touring pitches. 60 hardstandings. 40 seasonal pitches. Caravan pitches. Motorhome pitches. Tent pitches. 73 statics.

Open: Mar-Oct **Last arrival:** 20.00hrs **Last departure:** noon
Pitches: * 🚐 £15.25-£19.75 🚗 £15.25-£19.75 ▲ £11.50-£16
Leisure: 🛝 🎱   **Facilities:** 🌧 ☺ 🅿 🚿 🗑 🛒 🐕 ♻ ℹ
Services: 🖭 🗑 🚽 🚿 T 🛒   **Within 3 miles:** ℐ ✈ 🛒 🗑 ∪

Notes: No noise after 23.00hrs. Dogs must be kept on leads.

AA Pubs & Restaurants nearby: Red Lion Inn, BIRCHOVER, DE4 2BN, 01629 650363

The Druid Inn, BIRCHOVER, DE4 2BL, 01629 653836

LEISURE: 🏊 Indoor swimming pool 🏊 Outdoor swimming pool 🛝 Children's playground 👦 Kid's club 🎾 Tennis court 🎱 Games room 📺 Separate TV room 🏌 golf course ⛵ Boats for hire 🎬 Cinema 🎵 Entertainment 🎣 Fishing ◎ Mini golf 🏄 Watersports 💪 Gym 🏟 Sports field Spa ∪ Stables
FACILITIES: 🛁 Bath 🌧 Shower ☺ Electric shaver 🅿 Hairdryer ✳ Ice Pack Facility 🐕 Disabled facilities ☎ Public telephone 🛒 Shop on site or within 200yds 🗑 Mobile shop (calls at least 5 days a week) 🍖 BBQ area 🏕 Picnic area WiFi Wi-fi 💻 Internet access ♻ Recycling ℹ Tourist info 🐕 Dog exercise area

RIPLEY
Map 16 SK35

Places to visit

Midland Railway Butterley, RIPLEY, DE5 3QZ, 01773 747674
www.midlandrailwaycentre.co.uk

Denby Pottery Visitor Centre, DENBY, DE5 8NX, 01773 740799
www.denbyvisitorcentre.co.uk

Golden Valley Caravan & Camping Park
►►►►84%

tel: 01773 513881 & 746786 **Coach Rd DE55 4ES**
email: enquiries@goldenvalleycaravanpark.co.uk
web: www.goldenvalleycaravanpark.co.uk
dir: *M1 junct 26, A610 to Codnor. Right at lights. Right into Alfreton Rd. In 1m left into Coach Rd, park on left. NB it is advised that Sat Nav is ignored for last few miles & guide directions are followed.* **grid ref:** *SK408513*

This superbly landscaped park is set within 30 acres of woodland in the Amber Valley. The fully serviced pitches are set out in informal groups in clearings amongst the trees. The park has a cosy bar and bistro with outside patio, a fully stocked fishing lake, an innovative and well-equipped play area, an on-site jacuzzi and fully equipped fitness suite. There is also a wildlife pond and a nature trail. 30 acre site. 45 touring pitches. 45 hardstandings. 12 seasonal pitches. Caravan pitches. Motorhome pitches. Tent pitches. 1 static.

Open: all year (rs Wknds only in low season bar & café open, children's activities)
Last arrival: 21.00hrs **Last departure:** noon

Pitches: ⊟ £22-£30 ⊟ £22-£30 ⋀ £15-£30

Leisure: ⍓ ⌂ ◖ ⊡

Facilities: ⊷ ⋔ ⊙ ⑂ ⋇ ⓺ ⑤ ☴ ⊶ WiFi ⊒ ♻ ❶

Services: ⊡ ⊡ ⊡ ∅ ⓣ ⑩ ⌸ ⛴ ↓

Within 3 miles: ⌕ ≵ ⊟ ⌇ ⑤ ⑤ ∪

Notes: No vehicles on grass, no open fires or disposable BBQs, no noise after 22.30hrs. Dogs must be kept on leads. Zip slide, donkey rides, tractor train, water walking balls, log flume ride.

AA Pubs & Restaurants nearby: Santo's Higham Farm Hotel, HIGHAM, DE55 6EH, 01773 833812

ROSLISTON
Map 10 SK21

Places to visit

Ashby-de-la-Zouch Castle, ASHBY-DE-LA-ZOUCH, LE65 1BR, 01530 413343
www.english-heritage.org.uk/daysout/properties/ashby-de-la-zouch-castle

Great for kids: Conkers, MOIRA, DE12 6GA, 01283 216633
www.visitconkers.com

Beehive Woodland Lakes
►►►►81%

tel: 01283 763981 **DE12 8HZ**
email: info@beehivefarm-woodlandlakes.co.uk
dir: *From A444 in Castle Gresley into Mount Pleasant Rd, follow Rosliston signs for 3.5m through Linton to T-junct. Left signed Beehive Farms.* **grid ref:** *SK249161*

A small, informal and rapidly developing caravan area secluded from an extensive woodland park in the heart of the National Forest National Park. Toilet facilities include four family rooms. Young children will enjoy the on-site animal farm and playground, whilst anglers can pass many a happy hour fishing at the park's three lakes; bikes can be hired. There is an adults-only area and more camping pods were added for 2014. The Honey Pot tearoom provides snacks and is open most days. 2.5 acre site. 46 touring pitches. 46 hardstandings. Caravan pitches. Motorhome pitches. Tent pitches. Wooden pods.

Open: all year **Last arrival:** 20.00hrs **Last departure:** noon

Pitches: ⊟ ⊟ ⋀ ⋔

Leisure: ⌂

Facilities: ⋔ ⊙ ⑂ ⋇ ⓺ ⑤ ☴ WiFi ❶

Services: ⊡ ⊡ ⊡ ⌸

Within 3 miles: ⌕ ⊟ ⌇ ⑤ ⑤

Notes: Last arrival time 18.00hrs low season. Dogs must be kept on leads. Takeaway food delivered to site.

AA Pubs & Restaurants nearby: The Waterfront, BARTON-UNDER-NEEDWOOD, DE13 8DZ, 01283 711500

PITCHES: ⊟ Caravans ⊟ Motorhomes ⋀ Tents ⋔ Glamping-style accommodation **SERVICES:** ⊡ Electric hook up ⑤ Launderette ⊡ Licensed bar ⬛ Calor Gas ∅ Camping Gaz ⓣ Toilet fluid ⑩ Café/Restaurant ⌸ Fast Food/Takeaway ⛴ Battery charging ♥ Baby care ↓ Motorvan service point **ABBREVIATIONS:** BH/bank hols – bank holidays Etr – Easter Spring BH – Spring Bank Holiday fr – from hrs – hours m – mile mdnt – midnight rdbt – roundabout rs – restricted service wk – week wknd – weekend x-rds – cross roads ⊘ No credit or debit cards ⊗ No dogs ⍟ Children of all ages accepted

ROWSLEY
Map 16 SK26

Places to visit

Temple Mine, MATLOCK BATH, DE4 3NR, 01629 583834 www.peakmines.co.uk

Great for kids: The Heights of Abraham Cable Cars, Caverns & Hilltop Park, MATLOCK BATH, DE4 3PD, 01629 582365 www.heightsofabraham.com

Grouse & Claret
►►► 74%

tel: 01629 733233 **Station Rd DE4 2EB**
email: grouseandclaret.matlock@marstons.co.uk
dir: M1 junct 29. Site on A6, 5m from Matlock & 3m from Bakewell. **grid ref:** SK258660

A well-designed, purpose-built park at the rear of an eating house on the A6 between Bakewell and Chatsworth, and adjacent to the New Peak Shopping Village. The park comprises a level grassy area running down to the river, and all pitches have hardstandings and electric hook-ups. Please note there is no TV signal here. 2.5 acre site. 28 touring pitches. 28 hardstandings. Caravan pitches. Motorhome pitches.

Open: all year **Last arrival:** 22.00hrs **Last departure:** 11.00hrs

Pitches: * ⚐ £20 ⚐ £20

Leisure: ⚑

Facilities: ♠ ⊙ ⌂ WiFi

Services: ⚐ ⚐ ⊙ ⊞ ✓

Within 3 miles: ↧ ⌒ Ⓢ ↻

Notes: Dogs must be kept on leads.

AA Pubs & Restaurants nearby: The Grouse & Claret, ROWSLEY, DE4 2EB, 01629 733233

The Peacock at Rowsley, ROWSLEY, DE4 2EB, 01629 733518

SHARDLOW
Map 11 SK43

Places to visit

Melbourne Hall & Gardens, MELBOURNE, DE73 8EN, 01332 862502 www.melbournehall.com

Shardlow Marina Caravan Park
►►► 71%

tel: 01332 792832 **London Rd DE72 2GL**
email: admin@shardlowmarina.co.uk
dir: M1 junct 24a, A50 signed Derby. Exit junct 1 at rdbt signed Shardlow. Site 1m on right. **grid ref:** SK444303

A large marina site with restaurant facilities, situated on the Trent and Merseyside Canal. Pitches are on grass surrounded by mature trees, and for the keen angler, the site offers fishing within the marina. The attractive grass touring area overlooks the marina. 25 acre site. 35 touring pitches. 26 hardstandings. 10 seasonal pitches. Caravan pitches. Motorhome pitches. Tent pitches. 73 statics.

Open: Mar-Jan **Last arrival:** 17.00hrs **Last departure:** noon

Pitches: * ⚐ £13.50-£17.50 ⚐ £13.50-£17.50 ▲ £13.50-£21.50

Facilities: ♠ ⊙ ✳ ⅙ Ⓢ ⌁ ❼

Services: ⚐ ⚐ ⊞ ⌾ ⊘ Ⓣ ⊙ ⌸

Within 3 miles: ↧ ✦ ⊟ ⌒ Ⓢ Ⓢ ↻

Notes: Max 2 dogs per unit, dogs must be kept on leads, not be left unattended or tied up outside, office closed between 13.00hrs-14.00hrs.

AA Pubs & Restaurants nearby: The Old Crown Inn, SHARDLOW, DE72 2HL, 01332 792392

The Priest House Hotel, CASTLE DONINGTON, DE74 2RR, 0845 072 7502

LEISURE: 🏊 Indoor swimming pool 🏊 Outdoor swimming pool ⚑ Children's playground 🎣 Kid's club 🎾 Tennis court 🎱 Games room ⬚ Separate TV room ⛳ golf course 🚣 Boats for hire 🎬 Cinema 🎵 Entertainment 🎣 Fishing ⛳ Mini golf 🏄 Watersports 🏋 Gym ⚽ Sports field Spa ↻ Stables
FACILITIES: 🛁 Bath 🚿 Shower ⊙ Electric shaver ✂ Hairdryer ✳ Ice Pack Facility ⅙ Disabled facilities ☎ Public telephone Ⓢ Shop on site or within 200yds 🏪 Mobile shop (calls at least 5 days a week) 🍖 BBQ area ⌂ Picnic area WiFi Wi-fi 🖥 Internet access ♻ Recycling ❼ Tourist info ⌁ Dog exercise area

Devon

With magnificent coastlines, two historic cities and the world-famous Dartmoor National Park, Devon sums up all that is best about the British landscape. For centuries it has been a fashionable and much loved holiday destination – especially south Devon's glorious English Riviera.

When the crime writer Agatha Christie was born in Torquay on Devon's glorious south coast, the town was a popular seaside resort. It was 1890, the start of Queen Victoria's last decade as monarch, and Torquay was a fashionable destination for all sorts of people; those looking for a permanent home by the sea as well as holidaymakers in search of long hours of sunshine and a mild climate. In many ways, Torquay remains much the same today and its impressive setting still evokes a sense of its Victorian heyday. A local steam train attraction adds to the atmosphere; you can travel from Paignton to Dartmouth, alighting on the way at the small station at Churston, just as Hercule Poirot does in Christie's 1930s detective novel *The ABC Murders*. The Queen of Crime herself used this station when she had a summer home nearby. The house, Greenway, overlooks a glorious sweep of the River Dart and is now managed as a popular visitor attraction by the National Trust.

Close to the English Riviera lies Dartmoor, one of the south-west's most spectacular landscapes. The contrast between the traditional attractions of the coast and this expanse of bleak, brooding moorland could not be greater. The National Park, which contains Dartmoor, covers 365 square miles and includes many fascinating geological features – isolated granite tors and two summits exceeding 2,000 feet among them. Dartmoor's waterfalls, including the tumbling Whitelady Waterfall at Lydford Gorge, can be seen in full spate even in the depths of winter. Everywhere you venture on Dartmoor, there are stone circles, burial chambers and mysterious clues to the distant past. The place oozes antiquity. Sir Arthur Conan Doyle set his classic Sherlock Holmes story *The Hound of the Baskervilles* on Dartmoor, and Agatha Christie stayed at a local hotel for two weeks at the height of the First World War in order to finish writing her first detective novel *The Mysterious Affair at Styles*, first published in 1920.

Not surprisingly, Dartmoor equates with walking and the opportunities are enormous. For something really adventurous, try the Two Moors Way. This long-distance route begins at Ivybridge and crosses the National Park to enter neighbouring Exmoor, which straddles the Devon/Somerset border. At Lynton and Lynmouth the trail connects with the South West Coast Path, which takes walkers on a breathtaking journey to explore north Devon's gloriously rugged coastline, renowned for its extraordinary collection of peaks and outcrops. Cycling in the two National Parks is also extremely popular and there is a good choice of off-road routes taking you to the heart of Dartmoor and Exmoor.

Devon's towns and cities offer a pleasing but stimulating alternative to the rigours of the countryside. There are scores of small market towns in the region – for example there is Tavistock with its popular farmers' market, one of many in the county. Plymouth lies in Devon's south-west corner and is a striking city and naval port. Much of its transformation over the years is a reminder of the devastation it suffered, together with Exeter, during the Second World War. The city places particular emphasis, of course, on the Spanish Armada and the voyage of the Pilgrim Fathers to America.

On the theme of sailing, Devon is synonymous with this most invigorating of boating activities. Salcombe, on the county's south coast, is a sailing playground. Situated on a tree-fringed estuary beneath lush rolling hills, the town thrives on boats – it hosts the week-long Salcombe Regatta in August. It's even suitable for swimming, with several sandy beaches and sheltered bays.

◁ Dartmoor National Park

DEVON

ASHBURTON
Map 3 SX77

Places to visit

Compton Castle, COMPTON, TQ3 1TA, 01803 842382
www.nationaltrust.org.uk/comptoncastle

Tuckers Maltings, NEWTON ABBOT, TQ12 4AA, 01626 334734
www.tuckersmaltings.com

Great for kids: Prickly Ball Farm and Hedgehog Hospital, NEWTON ABBOT, TQ12 6BZ, 01626 362319 www.pricklyballfarm.com

---

River Dart Country Park
▶▶▶▶ 85%

tel: 01364 652511 **Holne Park TQ13 7NP**
email: info@riverdart.co.uk
dir: *M5 junct 31, A38 towards Plymouth. In Ashburton at Peartree junct follow brown site signs. Site 1m on left. NB Peartree junct is 2nd exit at Ashburton - do not exit at Linhay junct as narrow roads are unsuitable for caravans.* **grid ref:** *SX734700*

Set in 90 acres of magnificent parkland that was once part of a Victorian estate, with many specimen and exotic trees, this peaceful, hidden-away touring park occupies several camping areas, all served with good quality toilet facilities. In spring the park is a blaze of colour from the many azaleas and rhododendrons. There are numerous outdoor activities for all ages including abseiling, caving and canoeing, plus high quality, well-maintained facilities. The open moorland of Dartmoor is only a few minutes away. 90 acre site. 170 touring pitches. 23 hardstandings. Caravan pitches. Motorhome pitches. Tent pitches.

Open: Apr-Sep (rs Low season café bar restricted opening hours) **Last arrival:** 21.00hrs **Last departure:** 11.00hrs

Pitches: * ⊞ £14-£31.50 ⊞ £14-£31.50 Å £14-£31.50

Leisure: ⚘ ♨ ⚲

Facilities: ➽ ⌁ ☉ ☞ ⚹ ⅋ ⊙ ⑤ ⤴ ⛢ ⅏ WiFi ♻ ❂

Services: ⊞ ⑤ ⊕⊞ ⬛ ⊘ T ⅋◌⅋ ⬛ ⬆ ↯

Within 3 miles: ↯ ⌁ ⑤ ⑤ ∪

Notes: Dogs must be kept on leads. Adventure playground.

AA Pubs & Restaurants nearby: Agaric, ASHBURTON, TQ13 7QD, 01364 654478

Parkers Farm Holiday Park
▶▶▶▶ 84%

tel: 01364 654869 **Higher Mead Farm TQ13 7LJ**
email: parkersfarm@btconnect.com
dir: *From Exeter on A38, 2nd left after Plymouth (29m) sign, signed Woodland & Denbury. From Plymouth on A38 take A383 Newton Abbot exit, turn right across bridge, rejoin A38, then as above.* **grid ref:** *SX779713*

A well-developed site terraced into rising ground with stunning views across rolling countryside to the Dartmoor tors. Part of a working farm, this park offers excellent fully serviced hardstanding pitches, which make the most of the fine views; it is beautifully maintained and has good quality toilet facilities, a popular games room and a bar/restaurant that serves excellent meals. Large family rooms with two shower cubicles, a large sink and a toilet are especially appreciated by families with small children. There are regular farm walks when all the family can meet and feed the various animals. 25 acre site. 100 touring pitches. 20 hardstandings. Caravan pitches. Motorhome pitches. Tent pitches. 18 statics.

Open: Etr-end Oct (rs Out of season bar & restaurant open wknds only)
Last arrival: 22.00hrs **Last departure:** 10.00hrs

Pitches: * ⊞ £12-£25 ⊞ £12-£25 Å £10-£20

Leisure: ⚘ ♨ ⚲ ☐ ⅏

Facilities: ⌁ ☉ ⚹ ⅋ ⊙ ⑤ ⤴ ⛢ WiFi ♻ ❂

Services: ⊞ ⑤ ⊕⊞ ⬛ ⊘ T ⅋◌⅋ ⬛ ⬆ ↯

Within 3 miles: ⌁ ⑤ ⑤

Notes: Dogs must be kept on leads. Large field for dog walking.

AA Pubs & Restaurants nearby: The Rising Sun, ASHBURTON, TQ13 7JT, 01364 652544
Agaric, ASHBURTON, TQ13 7QD, 01364 654478

AXMINSTER
Map 4 SY29

Places to visit

Branscombe - The Old Bakery, Manor Mill and Forge, BRANSCOMBE, EX12 3DB, 01752 346585 www.nationaltrust.org.uk

Allhallows Museum, HONITON, EX14 1PG, 01404 44966
www.honitonmuseum.co.uk

Great for kids: Pecorama Pleasure Gardens, BEER, EX12 3NA, 01297 21542 www.pecorama.info

---

Andrewshayes Holiday Park
▶▶▶▶ 86%

tel: 01404 831225 **Dalwood EX13 7DY**
email: info@andrewshayes.co.uk **web:** www.andrewshayes.co.uk
dir: *3m from Axminster (towards Honiton) on A35, right at Taunton Cross signed Dalwood & Stockland. Site 150mtrs on right.* **grid ref:** *ST248088*

An attractive family park within easy reach of Lyme Regis, Seaton, Branscombe and Sidmouth in an ideal touring location. This popular park offers modern toilet facilities, an outdoor swimming pool, a quiet, cosy bar and restaurant, and good, new play facilities for children. 12 acre site. 150 touring pitches. 105 hardstandings. 100 seasonal pitches. Caravan pitches. Motorhome pitches. Tent pitches. 80 statics.

Open: Jul-Aug & wknds (rs Off-peak shop, bar hours, takeaway limited)
Last arrival: 22.00hrs **Last departure:** 11.00hrs

Pitches: * ⊞ £15-£32 ⊞ £15-£32 Å £15-£32

LEISURE: 🏊 Indoor swimming pool 🏊 Outdoor swimming pool ⚘ Children's playground 👶 Kid's club 🎾 Tennis court 🎱 Games room 📺 Separate TV room ⛳ golf course 🚣 Boats for hire 🎬 Cinema ♪ Entertainment 🎣 Fishing ⛳ Mini golf 🏄 Watersports 💪 Gym ⚽ Sports field Spa ∪ Stables

FACILITIES: 🛁 Bath 🚿 Shower ☉ Electric shaver ☂ Hairdryer ❄ Ice Pack Facility ♿ Disabled facilities ☎ Public telephone 🛒 Shop on site or within 200yds 🏪 Mobile shop (calls at least 5 days a week) 🍖 BBQ area ⛱ Picnic area WiFi Wi-fi 💻 Internet access ♻ Recycling ❂ Tourist info ⌁ Dog exercise area

Leisure: 🏖 🅿 🌀 🎣 💻

Facilities: 📶 ☉ 🅿 ✳ ⚹ ♿ 🕐 ⓢ 🚻 📶 ♻ ❶

Services: 🔌 ⓢ 🍽 🔧 🗑 ⊘ 🧳 🛒 🚽

Within 3 miles: 📎 ⓢ ⓢ

Notes: Children under 12 must be supervised by an adult in pool. Dogs must be kept on leads.

AA Pubs & Restaurants nearby: The Old Inn, KILMINGTON, EX13 7RB, 01297 32096

BERRYNARBOR
Map 3 SS54

Places to visit
Arlington Court, ARLINGTON, EX31 4LP, 01271 850296
www.nationaltrust.org.uk/arlington-court

Exmoor Zoological Park, BLACKMOOR GATE, EX31 4SG, 01598 763352
www.exmoorzoo.co.uk

Great for kids: Combe Martin Wildlife Park & Dinosaur Park, COMBE MARTIN, EX34 0NG, 01271 882486 www.wildlifedinosaurpark.co.uk

---

Mill Park Touring Site

►►►85%

tel: 01271 882647 **Mill Ln EX34 9SH**
email: millparkdevon@btconnect.com
dir: M5 junct 27, A361 towards Barnstaple. Right onto A399 towards Combe Martin. At Sawmills Inn take turn opposite Berrynarbor sign. **grid ref:** SS559471

This family-owned and run park is set in an attractive wooded valley with a stream running into a lake where coarse fishing is available. There is a quiet bar/restaurant with a family room, and the park has two wooden lakeside cocoons, three wooden 'glampods', and a four-bedroom apartment to let. The park is two miles from Combe Martin and Ilfracombe and just a stroll across the road from the small harbour at Watermouth. 23 acre site. 178 touring pitches. 20 hardstandings. Caravan pitches. Motorhome pitches. Tent pitches. 5 wooden pods.

Open: Mar-30 Oct (rs Low season on-site facilities closed) **Last arrival:** 22.00hrs **Last departure:** 10.00hrs

Pitches: * 🚐 £10-£23 🚍 £10-£23 ▲ £9.50-£23 🏕

Leisure: 🅿 🎣

Facilities: 📶 ☉ 🅿 ✳ ⚹ ♿ ⓢ 🚻 📶 💻 ♻ ❶

Services: 🔌 ⓢ 🍽 🔧 🗑 ⊘ T 🍴 🛒

Within 3 miles: ⚓ 🚤 🎯 📎 ◎ 🏌 ⓢ ⓢ ∪

Notes: Beauty therapy room.

AA Pubs & Restaurants nearby: Sandy Cove Hotel, ILFRACOMBE, EX34 9SR, 01271 882243

11 The Quay, ILFRACOMBE, EX34 9EQ, 01271 868090

BICKINGTON (NEAR ASHBURTON)
Map 3 SX87

Places to visit
Bradley Manor, NEWTON ABBOT, TQ12 6BN, 01803 843235
www.nationaltrust.org.uk/devoncornwall

Lemonford Caravan Park
►►►►82%

tel: 01626 821242 **TQ12 6JR**
email: info@lemonford.co.uk **web:** www.lemonford.co.uk
dir: From Exeter on A38 take A382, 3rd exit at rdbt, follow Bickington signs.
grid ref: SX793723

Small, secluded and well-maintained park with a good mixture of attractively laid out pitches. The friendly owners pay a great deal of attention to detail, and the toilets in particular are kept spotlessly clean. This good touring base is only one mile from Dartmoor and 10 miles from the seaside at Torbay. The bus to Exeter, Plymouth and Torbay stops outside the park. 7 acre site. 82 touring pitches. 55 hardstandings. Caravan pitches. Motorhome pitches. Tent pitches. 44 statics.

Open: all year **Last arrival:** 22.00hrs **Last departure:** 11.00hrs

Pitches: 🚐 🚍 ▲ **Leisure:** 🅿

Facilities: 🚿 📶 ☉ 🅿 ✳ ⚹ ♿ ⓢ 🚻 📶 ♻ ❶

Services: 🔌 ⓢ 🗑 ⊘ T 🧳 🛒 🚽 ⚓ **Within 3 miles:** 🎯 🎯 ⓢ ⓢ ∪

Notes: No noise after 23.00hrs. Dogs must be kept on leads. Clothes drying area.

AA Pubs & Restaurants nearby: The Wild Goose Inn, NEWTON ABBOT, TQ12 4RA, 01626 872241

See advert on page 154

PITCHES: 🚐 Caravans 🚍 Motorhomes ▲ Tents 🏕 Glamping-style accommodation **SERVICES:** 🔌 Electric hook up ⓢ Launderette 🍽 Licensed bar 🔋 Calor Gas ⊘ Camping Gaz T Toilet fluid 🍴 Café/Restaurant 🛒 Fast Food/Takeaway 🧳 Battery charging 🍼 Baby care 🚽 Motorvan service point **ABBREVIATIONS:** BH/bank hols — bank holidays Etr — Easter Spring BH — Spring Bank Holiday fr — from hrs — hours m — mile mdnt — midnight rdbt — roundabout rs — restricted service wk — week wknd — weekend x-rds — cross roads 🚫 No credit or debit cards 🚫 No dogs 👫 Children of all ages accepted

BRAUNTON

Map 3 SS43

Places to visit

Marwood Hill Gardens, BARNSTAPLE, EX31 4EB, 01271 342528
swww.marwoodhillgarden.co.uk

Great for kids: Combe Martin Wildlife Park & Dinosaur Park, COMBE MARTIN,
EX34 0NG, 01271 882486 www.wildlifedinosaurpark.co.uk

PREMIER PARK

Hidden Valley Park

►►►►► 86%

Best of British

tel: 01271 813837 **West Down EX34 8NU**
dir: Direct access from A361, 8m from Barnstaple & 2m from Mullacott Cross.
grid ref: SS499408

A delightful, well-appointed family site set in a wooded valley, with superb
facilities and a café. The park is set in a very rural, natural location not far from
the beautiful coastline around Ilfracombe. The woodland is home to nesting
buzzards and woodpeckers, and otters have taken up residence by the lake. WiFi
is available. There are three fully equipped timber cabins for hire, and the
Lakeside Restaurant and Bar serves good home-cooked meals. 32 acre site. 100
touring pitches. 50 hardstandings. 15 seasonal pitches. Caravan pitches.
Motorhome pitches. Tent pitches. 3 statics.

Open: all year **Last arrival:** 21.00hrs **Last departure:** 10.30hrs

Pitches: * 🚐 fr £10 🚗 fr £10 ▲ fr £10

Leisure: 🅰

Facilities: 🛁 🚿 ⊙ ℘ ☀ ⚙ 🖫 🚰 ⚑ WiFi 🖳 ♻ 🄋

Services: 🚱 🔄 🛢 🖉 🇹 🍴 ✇

Within 3 miles: ⬇ 🏇 ℘ ◎ ⚓ 🛒 🔄 🌀 ∪

AA Pubs & Restaurants nearby: The Williams Arms, BRAUNTON, EX33 2DE,
01271 812360

Lobb Fields Caravan & Camping Park

►►► 81%

tel: 01271 812090 **Saunton Rd EX33 1HG**
email: info@lobbfields.com **web:** www.lobbfields.com
dir: At x-rds in Braunton take B3231 towards Croyde. Site signed on right.
grid ref: SS475378

A bright, tree-lined park with gently-sloping grass pitches divided into two open
areas, plus a camping field in August. Braunton is an easy walk away, and a bus
service from the entrance makes the golden beaches of Saunton and Croyde, or the
market town of Barnstaple, easily accessible. 14 acre site. 180 touring pitches. 11
hardstandings. Caravan pitches. Motorhome pitches. Tent pitches.

Open: 27 Mar-1 Nov **Last arrival:** 22.00hrs **Last departure:** 10.30hrs

Pitches: 🚐 £11-£30 🚗 £11-£30 ▲ £10-£30

Leisure: 🅰 **Facilities:** 🚿 ⊙ ℘ ☀ ⚙ ⓒ 🚰 WiFi 🖳 ♻ 🄋

Services: 🚱 🔄 🛢 🖉 🍴 🛒 ✇

Within 3 miles: ⬇ ℘ ⚓ 🛒 🔄 ∪

Notes: No under 18s unless accompanied by an adult. Dogs must be kept on leads.
Surfing, boards & wet suits for hire, wet suit washing areas.

AA Pubs & Restaurants nearby: The Williams Arms, BRAUNTON, EX33 2DE,
01271 812360

LEISURE: 🏊 Indoor swimming pool 🏊 Outdoor swimming pool 🅰 Children's playground 🧒 Kid's club 🎾 Tennis court 🎱 Games room 📺 Separate TV room
⛳ golf course 🚣 Boats for hire 🎬 Cinema 🎵 Entertainment ℘ Fishing ◎ Mini golf 🏄 Watersports 🏋 Gym ⚽ Sports field Spa ∪ Stables
FACILITIES: 🛁 Bath 🚿 Shower ⊙ Electric shaver ℘ Hairdryer ☀ Ice Pack Facility ⚙ Disabled facilities ⓒ Public telephone 🛒 Shop on site or within 200yds
🖫 Mobile shop (calls at least 5 days a week) 🍴 BBQ area 🚰 Picnic area WiFi Wi-fi 🖳 Internet access ♻ Recycling 🄋 Tourist info 🚩 Dog exercise area

BRIDESTOWE
Map 3 SX58

Places to visit

Lydford Castle and Saxon Town, LYDFORD, EX20 4BH, 0870 333 1181
www.english-heritage.org.uk/daysout/properties/lydford-castle-and-saxon-town

Museum of Dartmoor Life, OKEHAMPTON, EX20 1HQ, 01837 52295
www.museumofdartmoorlife.org.uk

Bridestowe Caravan Park
►►►75%

tel: 01837 861261 **EX20 4ER**
email: ali.young53@btinternet.com
dir: Exit A30 at A386 & Sourton Cross junct, follow B3278 signed Bridestowe, left in 3m. In village centre, left onto unclassified road for 0.5m. **grid ref:** SX519893

A small, well-established park in a rural setting close to Dartmoor National Park. This mainly static park has a small, peaceful touring space, and there are many activities to enjoy in the area including fishing and riding. Part of the National Cycle Route 27 (the Devon coast to coast) passes close to this park. 1 acre site. 13 touring pitches. 3 hardstandings. Caravan pitches. Motorhome pitches. Tent pitches. 40 statics.

Open: Mar-Dec **Last arrival:** 22.30hrs **Last departure:** noon

Pitches: * ⚏ £13-£18 ⛟ £13-£18 ▲ £10-£15

Leisure: ⚠ 🎣

Facilities: 🌳⊙✳️⑤♻️🅹

Services: 🔌⑤🔋⌀Ⓣ🔋

Within 3 miles: ⑤⑤

Notes: 🐕 Dogs must be kept on leads.

AA Pubs & Restaurants nearby: The Highwayman Inn, SOURTON, EX20 4HN, 01837 861243

Lewtrenchard Manor, LEWDOWN, EX20 4PN, 01566 783222

Interested in camping on an island? Take a look at page 20

BRIDGERULE
Map 2 SS20

Hedleywood Caravan & Camping Park
►►►82%

tel: 01288 381404 **EX22 7ED**
email: alan@hedleywood.co.uk **web:** www.hedleywood.co.uk
dir: From Exeter, A30 to Launceston, B3254 towards Bude. Left into Tackbear Rd signed Marhamchurch & Widemouth (at Devon/Cornwall border). Site on right.
grid ref: SS262013

Set in a very rural location about four miles from Bude, this relaxed family-owned site has a peaceful, easy-going atmosphere. Pitches are in separate paddocks, some with extensive views, and this wooded park is quite sheltered in the lower areas. The restaurant/club house is a popular place to relax. 16.5 acre site. 120 touring pitches. 30 hardstandings. 27 seasonal pitches. Caravan pitches. Motorhome pitches. Tent pitches. 16 statics.

Open: all year (rs Except main hols shop, bar & restaurant may be closed)
Last arrival: anytime **Last departure:** anytime

Pitches: * ⚏ £13.50-£23 ⛟ £13.50-£23 ▲ £13.50-£23

Leisure: ⚠🎣⊡

Facilities: 🌳⊙🄿✳️♿⓵⑤🄰🚾💻♻️🅹

Services: 🔌⑤🍺🔋⌀Ⓣ🍽🔋🛒🚮⚡

Within 3 miles: ⚓🎣⑤⑤∪

Notes: Dogs must be kept on leads. Dog kennels, dog walk & nature trail, caravan storage.

AA Pubs & Restaurants nearby: The Bickford Arms, HOLSWORTHY, EX22 7XY, 01409 221318

Bay View Inn, WIDEMOUTH BAY, EX23 0AW, 01288 361273

BRIXHAM — Map 3 SX95

Places to visit

Greenway, CHURSTON FERRERS, TQ5 0ES, 01803 842382
www.nationaltrust.org.uk/devoncornwall

Great for kids: Paignton Zoo Environmental Park, PAIGNTON, TQ4 7EU,
0844 474 2222 www.paigntonzoo.org.uk

Galmpton Touring Park
►►►►80%

tel: 01803 842066 **Greenway Rd TQ5 0EP**
email: enquiries@galmptontouringpark.co.uk
dir: *A380 or A385 to Paignton, A3022 towards Brixham. Turn right into Manor Vale Rd, follow Galmpton sign. Left into Greenway Rd to site on right.* **grid ref:** *SX885558*

A stunningly located site, set on high ground overlooking the River Dart and with outstanding views of the creek and anchorage. The park looks smart, and pitches are set on level terraces; the toilet facilities has been upgraded to provide good quality amenities. 10 acre site. 120 touring pitches. 46 hardstandings. Caravan pitches. Motorhome pitches. Tent pitches.

Open: 21 Mar-Oct **Last arrival:** 20.00hrs (late arrival times require prior notice) **Last departure:** 10.00hrs

Pitches: * ⬛ £14.50-£27.50 ⬛ £14.50-£27.50 Å £14.50-£23.50

Leisure: ⚠

Facilities: ⬛ ☺ ⬛ ✳ ⬛ ⬛ ⬛ ⬛ WiFi ⬛ ♻ 🄸

Services: ⬛ ⬛ ⬛ ⬛ Ⓣ ⬛ ⬛

Within 3 miles: ⬛ ⬛ ⬛ ⬛ ◎ ⬛ ⬛ ⬛

Notes: Families & couples only. Dogs must be kept on leads. Bathroom for under 5s (charges apply).

BROADWOODWIDGER — Map 3 SX48

Places to visit

Lydford Gorge, LYDFORD, EX20 4BH, 01822 820320
www.nationaltrust.org.uk/lydford-gorge

Launceston Steam Railway, LAUNCESTON, PL15 8DA, 01566 775665
www.launcestonsr.co.uk

Great for kids: Tamar Otter & Wildlife Centre, LAUNCESTON, PL15 8GW,
01566 785646 www.tamarotters.co.uk

Roadford Lake
►►►80%

tel: 01409 211507 **Lower Goodacre PL16 0JL**
email: info@swlakestrust.org.uk
dir: *Exit A30 between Okehampton & Launceston at Roadford Lake signs, cross dam wall, site 0.25m on right.* **grid ref:** *SX421900*

Located right at the edge of Devon's largest inland water, this popular rural park is well screened by mature trees and shrubs. There is an excellent watersports school for sailing, windsurfing, rowing and kayaking, with hire and day launch facilities. This is an ideal location for brown trout fly fishing. 3 acre site. 50 touring pitches. 6 hardstandings. Caravan pitches. Motorhome pitches. Tent pitches.

Open: all year **Late arrivals:** available if pre-booked. **Last departure:** 11.00hrs

Pitches: ⬛ ⬛ Å

Facilities: ⬛ ☺ ⬛ ✳ ⬛ ⬛ ♻ 🄸

Services: ⬛ ⬛ ⬛

Within 3 miles: ⬛ ⬛ ⬛ ⬛

Notes: Off-ground BBQs only, no open fires, Dogs must be kept on leads. Climbing wall, archery, high ropes, watersports.

AA Pubs & Restaurants nearby: Arundell Arms, LIFTON, PL16 0AA, 01566 784666

BUCKFASTLEIGH — Map 3 SX76

Places to visit

Buckfast Abbey, BUCKFASTLEIGH, TQ11 0EE, 01364 645500
www.buckfast.org.uk

Great for kids: Buckfast Butterfly Farm & Dartmoor Otter Sanctuary, BUCK-FASTLEIGH, TQ11 0DZ, 01364 642916 www.ottersandbutterflies.co.uk

AA BEST SMALL CAMPSITE OF THE YEAR 2015

Churchill Farm Campsite
►89%

tel: 01364 642844 & 07977 113175 **TQ11 0EZ**
email: apedrick@btinternet.com
dir: *From A38 Dart Bridge exit for Buckfastleigh & Totnes towards Buckfast Abbey. Pass Abbey entrance, up hill, left at x-rds to site opposite Holy Trinity Church.*
grid ref: *SX743664*

A working family farm in a relaxed and peaceful setting, with keen, friendly owners. Set on the hills above Buckfast Abbey, this attractive park is maintained to a good standard. The spacious pitches in the neatly trimmed paddock enjoy extensive country views towards Dartmoor, and the clean, simple toilet facilities include smart showers. This is a hidden gem for those who love traditional camping. Close to a local bus service and within walking distance of Buckfastleigh, the Abbey and the South Devon Steam Railway. 3 acre site. 25 touring pitches. Caravan pitches. Motorhome pitches. Tent pitches.

Open: May-Sep **Last arrival:** 22.00hrs

Pitches: * ⬛ fr £12 ⬛ fr £12 Å fr £12

Facilities: ⬛ ☺ ✳ ⬛ ♻ 🄸

Services: ⬛ ⬛

Within 3 miles: ⬛

Notes: No ball games. Dogs must be kept on leads. Within a Site of Special Scientific Interest (SSSI).

AA Pubs & Restaurants nearby: Agaric, ASHBURTON, TQ13 7QD, 01364 654478

LEISURE: 🏊 Indoor swimming pool 🏊 Outdoor swimming pool ⚠ Children's playground ♦ Kid's club ♦ Tennis court ♦ Games room ▭ Separate TV room ♦ golf course ♦ Boats for hire ▤ Cinema ♫ Entertainment ♦ Fishing ◎ Mini golf ♦ Watersports ♦ Gym ♦ Sports field ♦ Stables
FACILITIES: ♦ Bath ♦ Shower ☺ Electric shaver ♦ Hairdryer ✳ Ice Pack Facility ♦ Disabled facilities ♦ Public telephone ⬛ Shop on site or within 200yds ♦ Mobile shop (calls at least 5 days a week) ♦ BBQ area ♦ Picnic area WiFi Wi-fi ▤ Internet access ♻ Recycling 🄸 Tourist info ♦ Dog exercise area

Beara Farm Caravan & Camping Site
► 84%

tel: 01364 642234 **Colston Rd TQ11 0LW**
dir: *From Exeter take Buckfastleigh exit at Dart Bridge, follow South Devon Steam Railway & Butterfly Farm signs. 200mtrs past entrance to South Devon Steam Railway 1st left into Old Totnes Rd, 0.5m right at red brick cottages signed Beara Farm. Approx 1m to site.*
grid ref: *SX751645*

A very good farm park, with clean unisex facilities, run by very keen and friendly owners. A well-trimmed camping field offers peace and quiet. Close to the River Dart and the Dart Valley Steam Railway line, within easy reach of the sea and moors. Please note that the approach to the site is narrow, with passing places, and care needs to be taken. 3.63 acre site. 30 touring pitches. 1 hardstanding. Caravan pitches. Motorhome pitches. Tent pitches.

Open: all year **Last arrival:** 21.00hrs **Last departure:** anytime

Pitches: * ⊟ fr £11 ⊟ fr £11 ▲ fr £11

Facilities: ⚑☉⚬⛨⚑⚑♻❶

Services: ⛟

Within 3 miles: ⚲ ⓢ

Notes: ⊗ No noise after 22.30hrs. Dogs must be kept on leads. Access to River Dart.

AA Pubs & Restaurants nearby: Agaric, ASHBURTON, TQ13 7QD, 01364 654478

Pooh Cottage Holiday Park
►►► 82%

tel: 01395 442354 & 07875 685595 **Bear Ln EX9 7AQ**
email: bookings@poohcottage.co.uk
dir: *M5 junct 30, A376 towards Exmouth. Left onto B3179 towards Woodbury & Budleigh Salterton. Left into Knowle onto B3178. Through village, at brow of hill take sharp left into Bear Lane. Site 200yds.* **grid ref:** *SY053831*

A rural park with wide views of the sea and surrounding peaceful countryside. Expect a friendly welcome to this attractive site, with its lovely play area, and easy access to plenty of walks, as well as the Buzzard Cycle Way. On site cycle hire, and there's a bus stop within walking distance. 8 acre site. 16 touring pitches. 45 seasonal pitches. Caravan pitches. Motorhome pitches. Tent pitches. 3 statics.

Open: 15 Mar-Oct **Last arrival:** 21.00hrs **Last departure:** 11.30hrs

Pitches: * ⊟ £14-£20 ⊟ £14-£20 ▲ £14-£20

Leisure: ⚑

Facilities: ⚑☉⚬⛨⚑⚑WiFi♻❶

Services: ⚡⛟🍺⚙T

Within 3 miles: ⚲⚵⊟⚲◎⛉ⓢⓢU

Notes: No gazebos, no open fires, 5mph speed limit. Dogs must be kept on leads.

AA Pubs & Restaurants nearby: Blue Ball Inn, SIDMOUTH, EX10 9QL, 01395 514062
The Salty Monk, SIDMOUTH, EX10 9QP, 01395 513174

Chapmanswell Caravan Park
►►► 84%

tel: 01409 211382 **St Giles-on-the-Heath PL15 9SG**
email: george@chapmanswellcaravanpark.co.uk
dir: *A338 from Launceston towards Holsworthy, 6m. Site on left at Chapmans Well.*
grid ref: *SX354931*

Set on the borders of Devon and Cornwall in peaceful countryside, this park is just waiting to be discovered. It enjoys extensive views towards Dartmoor from level pitches, and is within easy driving distance of Launceston (7 miles) and the golden beaches at Bude (14 miles). 10 acre site. 50 touring pitches. 35 hardstandings. 32 seasonal pitches. Caravan pitches. Motorhome pitches. Tent pitches. 50 statics.

Open: all year **Last arrival:** anytime by prior arrangement
Last departure: anytime by prior arrangement

Pitches: ⊟ ⊟ ▲

Leisure: ⚑ ♫

Facilities: ⚑☉⚬⛨🛁ⓢWiFi♻❶

Services: ⚡⛟🍺🔋⚙T🍴⛟🚽♿

Within 3 miles: ⚲⚵⚲⛉ⓢⓢU

Notes: Dogs must be kept on leads.

AA Pubs & Restaurants nearby: The Bickford Arms, HOLSWORTHY, EX22 7XY, 01409 221318

Looking for a golf course near your campsite?
Visit theaa.com/golf-course

Prefer a child-free site?
See our list on page 41

CHUDLEIGH
Map 3 SX87

Places to visit

Canonteign Falls, CHUDLEIGH, EX6 7NT, 01647 252434
www.canonteignfalls.co.uk

Exeter's Underground Passages, EXETER, EX1 1GA, 01392 665887
www.exeter.gov.uk/passages

Great for kids: Prickly Ball Farm and Hedgehog Hospital, NEWTON ABBOT, TQ12 6BZ, 01626 362319 www.pricklyballfarm.com

Holmans Wood Holiday Park
▶▶▶85%

tel: 01626 853785 **Harcombe Cross TQ13 0DZ**
email: enquiries@holmanswood.co.uk
dir: M5 junct 31, A38. After racecourse at top of Haldon Hill left at BP petrol station signed Chudleigh, site entrance on left of slip road. **grid ref:** SX881812

A delightful small park set back from the A38 in a secluded wooded area, handy for touring Dartmoor National Park, and the lanes and beaches of south Devon. The facilities are bright and clean, and the grounds are attractively landscaped. 12 acre site. 73 touring pitches. 71 hardstandings. Caravan pitches. Motorhome pitches. Tent pitches. 34 statics.

Open: mid Mar-end Oct **Last arrival:** 22.00hrs **Last departure:** 11.00hrs
Pitches: * 🚐 £19-£25 🚕 £19-£25 ▲ £12-£16 **Leisure:** 🄰
Facilities: 🏧⊙🅿☀️🅰🔌🛒📶💻🛈
Services: 🔌🔲🔩🗑 **Within 3 miles:** 🔌🛒🅄
Notes: No cycling or skateboards, pets only allowed at the management's discretion. Dogs must be kept on leads.
AA Pubs & Restaurants nearby: Cridford Inn, TRUSHAM, TQ13 0NR, 01626 853694

Find out about the AA's Pennant rating scheme on pages 10-11

CLYST ST MARY
Map 3 SX99

Places to visit

Exeter Cathedral, EXETER, EX1 1HS, 01392 285983 www.exeter-cathedral.org.uk

Exeter's Underground Passages, EXETER, EX1 1GA, 01392 665887
www.exeter.gov.uk/passages

Great for kids: The World of Country Life, EXMOUTH, EX8 5BU, 01395 274533
www.worldofcountrylife.co.uk

PREMIER PARK

Crealy Meadows Caravan and Camping Park
▶▶▶▶▶84%

tel: 01395 234888 **Sidmouth Rd EX5 1DR**
email: stay@crealymeadows.co.uk
dir: M5 junct 30, A3052 signed Exmouth. At rdbt take A3052 signed Seaton. Follow brown Crealy Great Adventure Park signs. Turn right. **grid ref:** SY001906

A quality park with excellent toilet facilities, spacious, fully serviced pitches and good security, adjacent to the popular Crealy Adventure Park, with free or discounted entry available for all campers. The park is within a short drive of Exeter and the seaside attractions at Sidmouth. Free WiFi is available and free kennels can be used on request. Pre-erected luxury safari tents are for hire, and also in the Camelot Village there are medieval pavillion tents for a real glamping holiday. For children there is a unique 'own pony' experience. 14.65 acre site. 120 touring pitches. 21 hardstandings. Caravan pitches. Motorhome pitches. Tent pitches. 18 bell tents/yurts.

Open: Mar-Oct **Last arrival:** 20.00hrs **Last departure:** 10.00hrs
Pitches: * 🚐 fr £10 🚕 fr £10 ▲ fr £10 🏠
Leisure: 🄰👶🎵
Facilities: 🛁🏧🅿☀️🅰🔌🅂🛒🅰📶💻♻️🛈
Services: 🔌🔲🔩🔨🗑🍽🏪
Within 3 miles: 🔌🅿🛒🔲
Notes: Dogs must be kept on leads.
AA Pubs & Restaurants nearby: The Black Horse Inn, SOWTON, EX5 2AN, 01392 366649

Bridge Inn, TOPSHAM, EX3 0QQ, 01392 873862

LEISURE: 🏊 Indoor swimming pool 🏊 Outdoor swimming pool 🄰 Children's playground 👶 Kid's club 🎾 Tennis court 🎱 Games room ▢ Separate TV room ⛳ golf course ⛵ Boats for hire 🎬 Cinema 🎵 Entertainment 🎣 Fishing ◎ Mini golf 🏄 Watersports 🏋 Gym ⚽ Sports field Spa 🅄 Stables
FACILITIES: 🛁 Bath 🚿 Shower ⊙ Electric shaver 🅿 Hairdryer ☀️ Ice Pack Facility ♿ Disabled facilities 📞 Public telephone 🅂 Shop on site or within 200yds 🏪 Mobile shop (calls at least 5 days a week) 🍖 BBQ area 🅰 Picnic area 📶 Wi-fi 💻 Internet access ♻️ Recycling 🛈 Tourist info 🐕 Dog exercise area

COMBE MARTIN
Map 3 SS54

See also Berrynarbor

Places to visit

Arlington Court, ARLINGTON, EX31 4LP, 01271 850296
www.nationaltrust.org.uk/arlington-court

Great for kids: Combe Martin Wildlife Park & Dinosaur Park, COMBE MARTIN, EX34 0NG, 01271 882486 www.wildlifedinosaurpark.co.uk

PREMIER PARK

Newberry Valley Park
►►►►► 85%

GOLD

tel: 01271 882334 **Woodlands EX34 0AT**
email: relax@newberryvalleypark.co.uk
dir: *M5 junct 27, A361 towards Barnstaple. Right at North Aller rdbt onto A399, through Combe Martin to sea. Left into site.* **grid ref:** *SS576473*

A family owned and run touring park on the edge of Combe Martin, with all its amenities just a five-minute walk away. The park is set in a wooded valley with its own coarse fishing lake and has a stunning toilet block with underfloor heating and excellent unisex privacy cubicles. The safe beaches of Newberry and Combe Martin are reached by a short footpath opposite the park entrance, where the South West Coastal Path is located. 20 acre site. 110 touring pitches. 25 hardstandings. 20 seasonal pitches. Caravan pitches. Motorhome pitches. Tent pitches.

Open: 15 Mar-Oct (rs Low season office hours limited) **Last arrival:** 20.45hrs (last arrival time dusk in winter) **Last departure:** 11.00hrs

Pitches: * ⬛ £16-£38 ⬛ £16-£38 ▲ £16-£38

Leisure: ⛰

Facilities: 🚰🔥☉🅿☀️🚿🔒🛁🐾⋔ WiFi ♻ ❼

Services: 🔌🛆 🎛 🔋⬆

Within 3 miles: ⬇🔗🏊🛝🍴🛒U

Notes: No camp fires. Dogs must be kept on leads. Veg prep area, fridge & microwave available.

AA Pubs & Restaurants nearby: 11 The Quay, ILFRACOMBE, EX34 9EQ, 01271 868090

The Fox & Goose, PARRACOMBE, EX31 4PE, 01598 763239

Stowford Farm Meadows
►►►► 90%

GOLD

tel: 01271 882476 **Berry Down EX34 0PW**
email: enquiries@stowford.co.uk
dir: *M5 junct 27, A361 to Barnstaple. Take A39 from town centre towards Lynton, in 1m left onto B3230. Right at garage at Lynton Cross onto A3123, site 1.5m on right.* **grid ref:** *SS560427*

Very gently sloping, grassy, sheltered and south-facing site approached down a wide, well-kept driveway. This family friendly site is set in 500 acres of rolling countryside, and offers many quality amenities including a large swimming pool and horse riding. A woodland walk is an added attraction, as is the 'petorama' with its stock of friendly animals. 100 acre site. 700 touring pitches. 115 hardstandings. Caravan pitches. Motorhome pitches. Tent pitches.

Open: all year (rs Winter at certain times bars closed & catering not available) **Last arrival:** 20.00hrs **Last departure:** 10.00hrs

Pitches: * ⬛ £10.45-£24.50 ⬛ £11.45-£25.50 ▲ £10.45-£24.50

Leisure: 🏊⛰☺🏊❓🎵♪

Facilities: 🚰🔥☉🅿☀️🚿🔒🛁🐾⋔ WiFi ♻ ❼

Services: 🔌🛆 🎛🔋⬛⬆⬇ 🎛🍴🔋⬛⬆⬇

Within 3 miles: ⬇🔗◎🛝🛒U

Notes: Dogs must be kept on leads. Caravan accessory shop, storage, workshop & sales.

AA Pubs & Restaurants nearby: 11 The Quay, ILFRACOMBE, EX34 9EQ, 01271 868090

The Fox & Goose, PARRACOMBE, EX31 4PE, 01598 763239

CROYDE
Map 3 SS43

Places to visit

Marwood Hill Gardens, BARNSTAPLE, EX31 4EB, 01271 342528
www.marwoodhillgarden.co.uk

Great for kids: Watermouth Castle & Family Theme Park, ILFRACOMBE, EX34 9SL, 01271 863879 www.watermouthcastle.com

Bay View Farm Caravan & Camping Park
►►►► 78%

tel: 01271 890501 **EX33 1PN**
dir: *M5 junct 27, A361, through Barnstaple to Braunton, left onto B3231. Site at entrance to Croyde.* **grid ref:** *SS443388*

A very busy and popular park close to surfing beaches and rock pools, with a public footpath leading directly to the sea. Set in a stunning location with views out over the Atlantic to Lundy Island, it is just a short stroll from Croyde. Facilities are clean and well maintained; a family bathroom is available. There is a fish and chip shop on site. Please note that no dogs are allowed. 10 acre site. 70 touring pitches. 38 hardstandings. 10 seasonal pitches. Caravan pitches. Motorhome pitches. Tent pitches. 3 statics.

Open: Mar-Oct **Last arrival:** 21.30hrs **Last departure:** 11.00hrs

Pitches: ⬛ ⬛ ▲

Leisure: ⛰

Facilities: 🚰🔥☉🅿☀️🚿🔒🛁 WiFi ♻ ❼

Services: 🔌🛆 🔋⬛⬇🍴⬛⬆

Within 3 miles: ⬇🛏🔗◎🛝🛒U

Notes: 🚫 No noise after mdnt.

AA Pubs & Restaurants nearby: The Williams Arms, BRAUNTON, EX33 2DE, 01271 812360

The Rock Inn, GEORGEHAM, EX33 1JW, 01271 890322

11 The Quay, ILFRACOMBE, EX34 9EQ, 01271 868090

PITCHES: ⬛ Caravans ⬛ Motorhomes ▲ Tents ⛰ Glamping-style accommodation **SERVICES:** 🔌 Electric hook up 🛆 Launderette 🍸 Licensed bar 🔋 Calor Gas 🛢 Camping Gaz 🎛 Toilet fluid 🍴 Café/Restaurant ⬛ Fast Food/Takeaway 🔋 Battery charging 🚼 Baby care ⬆ Motorvan service point **ABBREVIATIONS:** BH/bank hols – bank holidays Etr – Easter Spring BH – Spring Bank Holiday fr – from hrs – hours m – mile mdnt – midnight rdbt – roundabout rs – restricted service wk – week wknd – weekend x-rds – cross roads 🚫 No credit or debit cards 🚫 No dogs 👪 Children of all ages accepted

CROYDE BAY
Map 3 SS43

Ruda Holiday Park
HOLIDAY CENTRE 87%

GOLD

tel: 0844 335 3756 **EX33 1NY**
email: touringandcamping@parkdeanholidays.com
dir: M5 junct 27, A361 to Braunton. Left at main lights, follow Croyde signs.
grid ref: SS438397

A spacious, well-managed park with its own glorious award-winning sandy beach, a surfer's paradise. Set in well-landscaped grounds, it offers a full leisure programme plus daytime and evening entertainment for all the family. The Cascades Tropical Adventure Pool and the entertainment lounge are very popular features. A summer activity programme is available to suit all age groups. The local bus stops outside the park. 220 acre site. 312 touring pitches. Caravan pitches. Motorhome pitches. Tent pitches. 312 statics.

Open: mid Mar-Oct **Last arrival:** 21.00hrs **Last departure:** 10.00hrs

Pitches: 🚐 🚐 ▲

Leisure: 🏊 ⚙ ⚓ ⚽ 🎱 📺 🎵

Facilities: 🛁 🚿 ☺ 🧴 ❄ 🚹 🅿 🛒 ₩ⅈⅎⅈ

Services: 🔌 📷 🏪 🍴 🛒 🚽 🚛

Within 3 miles: 🎣 🏊 🛒 ♺

Notes: No pets.

AA Pubs & Restaurants nearby: The Williams Arms, BRAUNTON, EX33 2DE, 01271 812360

The Rock Inn, GEORGEHAM, EX33 1JW, 01271 890322

11 The Quay, ILFRACOMBE, EX34 9EQ, 01271 868090

CULLOMPTON

See Kentisbeare

DARTMOUTH

Places to visit

Dartmouth Castle, DARTMOUTH, TQ6 0JN, 01803 833588
www.english-heritage.org.uk/daysout/properties/dartmouth-castle

DARTMOUTH
Map 3 SX85

PREMIER PARK

Woodlands Grove Caravan & Camping Park
▶▶▶▶▶ 90%

Best of British

tel: 01803 712598 **Blackawton TQ9 7DQ**
email: holiday@woodlandsgrove.com **web:** www.woodlands-caravanpark.com
dir: From Dartmouth take A3122, 4m. Or from A38 take A385 to Totnes. Then A381 towards Salcombe, after Halwell take A3122 towards Dartmouth, site signed (brown tourist signs). **grid ref:** SX813522

A quality caravan and tent park with smart toilet facilities (including excellent family rooms), spacious pitches, including decent hardstandings, and good attention to detail throughout, all set in an extensive woodland environment with a terraced grass camping area. Free entry to the adjoining Woodlands Theme Park makes an excellent package holiday for families, but also good for adults travelling without children who are perhaps seeking a low season break. Please check with the site regarding their minimum stay policy. There is a bus stop at the entrance. 16 acre site. 350 touring pitches. 129 hardstandings. Caravan pitches. Motorhome pitches. Tent pitches.

Open: 28 Mar-2 Nov **Last arrival:** 22.00hrs **Last departure:** 11.00hrs

Pitches: * 🚐 £13.50-£23 🚐 £13.50-£23 ▲ £13.50-£23

Leisure: ⚙ 🎱 📺 🎵

Facilities: 🛁 🚿 ☺ 🧴 ❄ 🚹 🅿 🛒 🐕 ₩ⅈⅎⅈ 💻 ♺ ⓘ

Services: 🔌 📷 🛒 🚽 🍴 🚛 🏪

Within 3 miles: 🚣 ◎ 🛒

LEISURE: 🏊 Indoor swimming pool 🏊 Outdoor swimming pool ⚙ Children's playground 🖐 Kid's club 🎾 Tennis court 🎱 Games room 📺 Separate TV room 🏌 golf course ⚓ Boats for hire 🎬 Cinema 🎵 Entertainment 🎣 Fishing ◎ Mini golf 🏄 Watersports 🏋 Gym 🏅 Sports field ♨ Spa ⛲ Stables
FACILITIES: 🛁 Bath 🚿 Shower ☺ Electric shaver 💇 Hairdryer ❄ Ice Pack Facility 🚹 Disabled facilities 🕐 Public telephone 🅿 Shop on site or within 200yds 🛒 Mobile shop (calls at least 5 days a week) 🍴 BBQ area 🌲 Picnic area ₩ⅈⅎⅈ Wi-fi 💻 Internet access ♺ Recycling ⓘ Tourist info 🐕 Dog exercise area

Notes: No open fires, fire pits or chimeneas, quiet 22.30hrs-08.00hrs. Dogs must be kept on leads. Falconry centre, woodland walk, mini golf, zoo, farm, dog kennels.

AA Pubs & Restaurants nearby: The George Inn, BLACKAWTON, TQ9 7BG, 01803 712342

The Normandy Arms, BLACKAWTON, TQ9 7BN, 01803 712884

The Seahorse, DARTMOUTH, TQ6 9BH, 01803 835147

Little Cotton Caravan Park
►►►►85%

tel: 01803 832558 **Little Cotton TQ6 0LB**
email: enquiries@littlecotton.co.uk
dir: Exit A38 at Buckfastleigh, A384 to Totnes, A381 to Halwell, take A3122 (Dartmouth Rd), site on right at entrance to town. **grid ref:** SX858508

A very good grassy touring park set on high ground above Dartmouth, with quality facilities, and park-and-ride to the town from the gate. The immaculate toilet blocks are heated and superbly maintained. Spacious hardstandings are available. The friendly owners offer high levels of customer care and are happy to offer advice on touring in this pretty area. Excellent base for visiting Totnes, Slapton Sands and Kingsbridge. 7.5 acre site. 95 touring pitches. 42 hardstandings. Caravan pitches. Motorhome pitches. Tent pitches.

Open: 15 Mar-Oct **Last arrival:** 19.00hrs **Last departure:** 11.00hrs

Pitches: * ➡ £14-£23 ➡ £14-£23 ▲ £14-£23

Facilities: 🛠️⊙🅿️✳️♿🕒🚮🚻📶♻️🔧

Services: 🔌🅾️ 🧴🚮🚽🅃🧺

Within 3 miles: ↕️🚴🏼🕒🎣◎🛶🛒🅾️

Notes: No noise after 22.30hrs, no footballs. Dogs must be kept on leads.

AA Pubs & Restaurants nearby: The Seahorse, DARTMOUTH, TQ6 9BH, 01803 835147

Royal Castle Hotel, DARTMOUTH, TQ6 9PS, 01803 833033

DAWLISH
Places to visit

Powderham Castle, POWDERHAM, EX6 8JQ, 01626 890243
www.powderham.co.uk

PREMIER PARK

Cofton Country Holidays
►►►►►86%

tel: 01626 890111 & 0800 085 8649 **Starcross EX6 8RP**
email: info@coftonholidays.co.uk **web:** www.coftonholidays.co.uk
dir: On A379 (Exeter to Dawlish road), 3m from Dawlish. **grid ref:** SX967801

This park is set in a rural location surrounded by spacious open grassland, with plenty of well-kept flowerbeds throughout. Most pitches overlook either the swimming pool complex or the coarse fishing lakes and woodlands. A purpose-built toilet block offers smart modern facilities and the on-site pub serves drinks, meals and snacks for all the family, and a mini-market caters for most shopping needs. 45 acre site. 450 touring pitches. 30 hardstandings. 110 seasonal pitches. Caravan pitches. Motorhome pitches. Tent pitches. 76 statics.

Open: all year **Last arrival:** 20.00hrs **Last departure:** 11.00hrs

Pitches: * ➡ £14.50-£33 ➡ £14.50-£33 ▲ £14.50-£33

Leisure: 🏊🎣🏌️🎡◎⚽🎵

Facilities: 🛠️🛠️⊙🅿️✳️♿🕒🚮🚻📶♻️🔧

Services: 🔌🅾️ 🍺🧴🚮🚽🅃🍴🧺🛒🛒🛗 **Within 3 miles:** ↕️🚴🕒🎣◎🛶🛒🅾️

Notes: Dogs must be kept on leads. Soft play area, sauna & steam room, bowling.

AA Pubs & Restaurants nearby: The Elizabethan Inn, LUTON (NEAR CHUDLEIGH), TQ13 0BL, 01626 775425

The Anchor Inn, COCKWOOD, EX6 8RA, 01626 890203

See advert on page 162

PITCHES: ➡ Caravans ➡ Motorhomes ▲ Tents ⌂ Glamping-style accommodation **SERVICES:** 🔌 Electric hook up 🅾️ Launderette 🍺 Licensed bar
🧴 Calor Gas ⊘ Camping Gaz 🅃 Toilet fluid 🍴 Café/Restaurant 🍟 Fast Food/Takeaway 🔋 Battery charging 🚮 Baby care 🛗 Motorvan service point
ABBREVIATIONS: BH/bank hols – bank holidays Etr – Easter Spring BH – Spring Bank Holiday fr – from hrs – hours m – mile mdnt – midnight
rdbt – roundabout rs – restricted service wk – week wknd – weekend x-rds – cross roads 🚫 No credit or debit cards 🚫 No dogs 🚼 Children of all ages accepted

DAWLISH *continued*

Lady's Mile Holiday Park

►►►►► 82%

tel: 01626 863411 **EX7 0LX**
email: info@ladysmile.co.uk
dir: *1m N of Dawlish on A379.* **grid ref:** *SX968784*

A family owned and run touring park with a wide variety of pitches, including some that are fully serviced. There are plenty of activities for everyone, including two swimming pools with waterslides, a children's splash pool, a well-equipped gym, a sauna in the main season, a large adventure playground, and a bar with entertainment in high season. Facilities are kept very clean, and the surrounding beaches are easily accessed. Holiday homes and two, high quality glamping pods are also available. 18 acre site. 570 touring pitches. 67 hardstandings.

150 seasonal pitches. Caravan pitches. Motorhome pitches. Tent pitches. 100 statics. 2 wooden pods.

Open: all year (rs Facilities open 23 Mar-Oct) **Last arrival:** 20.00hrs
Last departure: 11.00hrs

Pitches: * 🚐 £15-£36.50 🚲 £15-£36.50 ▲ £15-£29.50 🏠

Leisure: 🏊 🏊 🎾 ⚴ 👶 ☺ 🎱 🎵 Spa

Facilities: 🛁 🚿 ☺ 🚻 ♿ 🎫 🛒 🅿 🐎 WiFi ♻ ℹ

Services: 🚽 🗑 🍴 🔌 🚰 Ⓣ 🍴 🛒 🛍

Within 3 miles: ↓ ⛳ 🎣 🏌 ◎ 🚣 🛍 🛍 ♨

Notes: No noise after mdnt. Dogs must be kept on leads. Bowling alley.

AA Pubs & Restaurants nearby: The Elizabethan Inn, LUTON (NEAR CHUDLEIGH), TQ13 0BL, 01626 775425

The Anchor Inn, COCKWOOD, EX6 8RA, 01626 890203

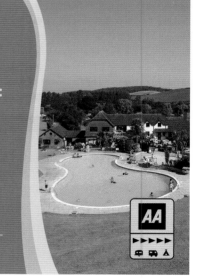

Leadstone Camping
►►►82%

tel: 01626 864411 **Warren Rd EX7 0NG**
email: info@leadstonecamping.co.uk **web:** www.leadstonecamping.co.uk
dir: M5 junct 30, A379 to Dawlish. Before village turn left on brow of hill, signed Dawlish Warren. Site 0.5m on right. **grid ref:** SX974782

A traditional, mainly level, grassy camping park approximately a half-mile walk from the sands and dunes at Dawlish Warren - a nature reserve and Blue Flag beach. This mainly tented park has been run by the same friendly family for many years, and is an ideal base for touring south Devon. A regular bus service from outside the gate takes in a wide area. The smart, well-equipped timber cabin toilet facility includes some privacy cubicles. There is a pub a short walk away. 8 acre site. 137 touring pitches. 14 seasonal pitches. Caravan pitches. Motorhome pitches. Tent pitches.

Open: 22 May-6 Sep **Last arrival:** 22.00hrs **Last departure:** noon
Pitches: * ⊞ £19-£26 ⊞ £15-£22 ▲ £15-£22
Leisure: ⚒
Facilities: ⬚⊙℘✻☖⑤ℿ ♻ ❼
Services: ⬛⑤ ⬛⌀➴↯
Within 3 miles: ↧℘◎⑤⑥

Notes: No noise after 23.00hrs. Portable/disposable BBQs permitted. Dogs must be kept on leads.
AA Pubs & Restaurants nearby: The Elizabethan Inn, LUTON (NEAR CHUDLEIGH), TQ13 0BL, 01626 775425
The Anchor Inn, COCKWOOD, EX6 8RA, 01626 890203

DREWSTEIGNTON   Map 3 SX79

Places to visit
Castle Drogo, DREWSTEIGNTON, EX6 6PB, 01647 433306
www.nationaltrust.org.uk/castle-drogo

Finch Foundry, STICKLEPATH, EX20 2NW, 01837 840046
www.nationaltrust.org.uk

PREMIER PARK

Woodland Springs Adult Touring Park
►►►►►81%

tel: 01647 231695 **Venton EX6 6PG**
email: enquiries@woodlandsprings.co.uk
dir: Exit A30 at Whiddon Down junct onto A382 towards Moretonhampstead. Site 1.5m on left. **grid ref:** SX695912

An attractive park in a rural area within Dartmoor National Park. This site is surrounded by woodland and farmland, and is very peaceful. The toilet block offers superb facilities, including some for disabled visitors. Please note that children are not accepted. 4 acre site. 81 touring pitches. 48 hardstandings. 19 seasonal pitches. Caravan pitches. Motorhome pitches. Tent pitches.

Open: all year **Last arrival:** 20.00hrs **Last departure:** 11.00hrs
Pitches: * ⊞ £20-£26 ⊞ £20-£26 ▲ £17-£23
Facilities: ⬚⊙℘✻☖⑤ℿ ☆ ⛶ ♻ ❼
Services: ⬛⑤ ⬛⌀↴➴↯
Within 3 miles: ℘⑤

Notes: Adults only. No fires, no noise 23.00hrs-08.00hrs. Dogs must be kept on leads. Day kennels, freezer, coffee vending machine.
AA Pubs & Restaurants nearby: The Old Inn, DREWSTEIGNTON, EX6 6QR, 01647 281276
Sandy Park Inn, CHAGFORD, TQ13 8JW, 01647 433267

EAST ALLINGTON
Map 3 SX74

Places to visit

Kingsbridge Cookworthy Museum, KINGSBRIDGE, TQ7 1AW, 01548 853235
www.kingsbridgemuseum.org.uk

Great for kids: Woodlands Family Theme Park, DARTMOUTH, TQ9 7DQ,
01803 712598 www.woodlandspark.com

Mounts Farm Touring Park
►►►76%

tel: 01548 521591 **The Mounts TQ9 7QJ**
email: mounts.farm@lineone.net
dir: A381 from Totnes towards Kingsbridge (NB ignore signs for East Allington). At
'Mounts', site 0.5m on left. **grid ref:** SX757488

A neat, grassy park divided into four paddocks by mature natural hedges. Three of
the paddocks are for the tourers and campers, and the fourth is a children's play
area. The laundry, toilets and well-stocked little shop are in converted farm
buildings. There's an on-site snack bar and Calor Gaz retailer. 7 acre site. 50
touring pitches. 10 seasonal pitches. Caravan pitches. Motorhome pitches. Tent
pitches.

Open: Mar-Nov **Last arrival:** 22.00hrs **Last departure:** 16.00hrs

Pitches: 🚐 🚃 Å

Leisure: ⚑ ✿

Facilities: ♍ ☉ ℱ ✳ ⑤ ♻ ❶

Services: 🔌 🔄 🚽 ⊘ Ⓣ 🚿

Within 3 miles: ⟁ �︙ ℘ ⤳ ⑤ ⑥ ∪

Notes: Dogs must be kept on leads. Camping accessories shop on site.

AA Pubs & Restaurants nearby: The Fortescue Arms, EAST ALLINGTON, TQ9 7RA,
01548 521215

EAST ANSTEY
Map 3 SS82

Places to visit

Quince Honey Farm, SOUTH MOLTON, EX36 3AZ, 01769 572401
www.quincehoneyfarm.com

Tiverton Museum of Mid Devon Life, TIVERTON, EX16 6PJ, 01884 256295
www.tivertonmuseum.org.uk

Zeacombe House Caravan Park
►►►►86%

tel: 01398 341279 **Blackerton Cross EX16 9JU**
email: enquiries@zeacombeadultretreat.co.uk
dir: M5 junct 27, A361 signed Barnstaple, right at next rdbt onto A396 signed Dulverton
& Minehead. In 5m at Exeter Inn left, 1.5m, at Black Cat junct left onto B3227 towards
South Molton, site 7m on left. **grid ref:** SS860240

Set on the southern fringes of Exmoor National Park, this sheltered, adult-only,
'garden' park is nicely landscaped in a tranquil location and enjoys panoramic

views towards Exmoor. There is a choice of grass or hardstanding pitches and a
unique restaurant-style meal service allows you to eat a home-cooked evening meal
in the comfort of your own unit. 5 acre site. 50 touring pitches. 12 hardstandings.
Caravan pitches. Motorhome pitches. Tent pitches.

Open: 7 Mar-Oct **Last arrival:** 21.00hrs **Last departure:** noon

Pitches: * 🚐 £15-£21 🚃 £15-£21 Å £15-£21

Facilities: ♍ ☉ ℱ ✳ ♿ ⑤ 🚽 ❶

Services: 🔌 🔄 🚽 ⊘ Ⓣ 🚿 🛒 ⬇

Within 3 miles: ℘ ⑤ ⑥ ∪

Notes: Adults only. No awning ground sheets. Dogs must be kept on leads.
Caravan store & stay system.

AA Pubs & Restaurants nearby: The Masons Arms, KNOWSTONE, EX36 4RY,
01398 341231

Woods Bar & Dining Room, DULVERTON, TA22 9BU, 01398 324007

EAST WORLINGTON
Map 3 SS71

Yeatheridge Farm Caravan Park
►►►►82%

tel: 01884 860330 **EX17 4TN**
email: yeatheridge@talk21.com
dir: M5 junct 27, A361, at 1st rdbt at Tiverton take B3137 for 9m towards Witheridge. Fork
left 1m past Nomansland onto B3042. Site on left in 3.5m. (NB do not enter East
Worlington). **grid ref:** SS768110

A well-kept park in a remote woodland setting on the edge of the Tamar Valley. It is
peacefully located at the end of a private, half-mile, tree-lined drive; it offers
superb on-site facilities and high levels of customer care from the hands-on
owners. The toilets are immaculate and well maintained, plus there is an indoor
swimming pool, sauna and a good information and games room, all in a friendly
atmosphere. 12 acre site. 103 touring pitches. 8 hardstandings. Caravan pitches.
Motorhome pitches. Tent pitches. 19 statics.

Open: 15 Mar-end Sep **Last arrival:** 22.00hrs **Last departure:** 10.00hrs

Pitches: * 🚐 £9-£18.50 🚃 £9-£18.50 Å £9-£18.50

Leisure: 🏊 ⚑ ✿ ⚲

Facilities: 🛁 ♍ ☉ ℱ ✳ ♿ ⊙ ⑤ 🚽 WiFi ♻ ❶

Services: 🔌 🔄 🍴 🚽 ⊘ Ⓣ ⊚ 🚿 🛒 ⬇ ⬇

Within 3 miles: ℘ ⑤ ⑥ ∪

Notes: Dogs must be kept on leads. Fishing, pool table.

AA Pubs & Restaurants nearby: The Grove Inn, KINGS NYMPTON, EX37 9ST,
01769 580406

EXETER

See Kennford

See Kennford

LEISURE: 🏊 Indoor swimming pool 🏊 Outdoor swimming pool ⚑ Children's playground 👶 Kid's club 🎾 Tennis court 🎱 Games room 📺 Separate TV room
⛳ golf course 🚣 Boats for hire 🎬 Cinema 🎵 Entertainment 🎣 Fishing 🏌 Mini golf 🏄 Watersports 🏋 Gym ✿ Sports field Spa ∪ Stables
FACILITIES: 🛁 Bath ♍ Shower ☉ Electric shaver ℱ Hairdryer ✳ Ice Pack Facility ♿ Disabled facilities ⊙ Public telephone ⑤ Shop on site or within 200yds
🛒 Mobile shop (calls at least 5 days a week) 🍴 BBQ area 🌲 Picnic area WiFi Wi-fi ⬛ Internet access ♻ Recycling ❶ Tourist info 🚿 Dog exercise area

EXMOUTH
Map 3 SY08

See also Woodbury Salterton

Places to visit

A la Ronde, EXMOUTH, EX8 5BD, 01395 265514
www.nationaltrust.org.uk/alaronde

Bicton Park Botanical Gardens, BICTON, EX9 7BJ, 01395 568465
www.bictongardens.co.uk

Great for kids: The World of Country Life, EXMOUTH, EX8 5BU, 01395 274533
www.worldofcountrylife.co.uk

Devon Cliffs Holiday Park
HOLIDAY CENTRE 91%

GOLD

tel: 0871 231 0870 **Sandy Bay EX8 5BT**
email: devoncliffs@haven.com **web:** www.haven.com/devoncliffs
dir: *M5 junct 30, A376 towards Exmouth, follow brown signs to Sandy Bay.*
grid ref: *SY036807*

A large and exciting holiday park on a hillside setting close to Exmouth, with spectacular views across Sandy Bay. This all-action park offers a superb

entertainment programme for all ages throughout the day, with very modern sports and leisure facilities available for everyone. An internet café is just one of the quality amenities, and though some visitors may enjoy relaxing and watching others play, the temptation to join in is overwhelming. South Beach Café, which overlooks the sea, is well worth a visit. Please note that this park does not accept tents. 163 acre site. 43 touring pitches. 43 hardstandings. Caravan pitches. Motorhome pitches. 1800 statics.

Open: mid Mar-end Oct (rs mid Mar-May & Sep-Oct some facilities may be reduced) **Last arrival:** anytime **Last departure:** 10.00hrs

Pitches: 🚐 🚐 **Leisure:** 🏊 🏊 🎯 🛝 🛶 🎵 Spa
Facilities: 🚿 🕯 ⊙ 🔌 ♿ 🕐 🗑 🍴 WiFi 🖥 ♻
Services: 🔌 🗑 🍴 🛡 🍴 🎂
Within 3 miles: ⬇ 🏇 ⊙ ⛳ 🚣 🎣 U

Notes: No commercial vehicles, no bookings by persons under 21yrs unless a family booking, max 2 dogs per booking, certain dog breeds banned, no dogs on beach May-Sep. Dogs must be kept on leads. Crazy golf, fencing, archery, bungee trampoline, aqua jets.

AA Pubs & Restaurants nearby: The Globe Inn, LYMPSTONE, EX8 5EY, 01395 263166

Les Saveurs, EXMOUTH, EX8 1NT, 01395 269459

See advert below

PITCHES: 🚐 Caravans 🚐 Motorhomes ⬥ Tents ⛺ Glamping-style accommodation **SERVICES:** 🔌 Electric hook up 🗑 Launderette 🍴 Licensed bar 🔋 Calor Gas 🔥 Camping Gaz 🅃 Toilet fluid 🍴 Café/Restaurant 🍔 Fast Food/Takeaway ⚡ Battery charging 👶 Baby care 🚐 Motorvan service point
ABBREVIATIONS: BH/bank hols – bank holidays Etr – Easter Spring BH – Spring Bank Holiday fr – from hrs – hours m – mile mdnt – midnight rdbt – roundabout rs – restricted service wk – week wknd – weekend x-rds – cross roads 🚫 No credit or debit cards 🚫 No dogs 👪 Children of all ages accepted

HOLSWORTHY — Map 3 SS30

Places to visit

Dartington Crystal, GREAT TORRINGTON, EX38 7AN, 01805 626242
www.dartington.co.uk

RHS Garden Rosemoor, GREAT TORRINGTON, EX38 8PH, 0845 265 8072
www.rhs.org.uk/rosemoor

Great for kids: The Milky Way Adventure Park, CLOVELLY, EX39 5RY,
01237 431255 www.themilkyway.co.uk

Headon Farm Caravan Site
►►►80%

tel: 01409 254477 **Headon Farm, Hollacombe EX22 6NN**
email: reader@headonfarm.co.uk
dir: *From Holsworthy A388 signed Launceston. 0.5m, at hill brow left into Staddon Rd.
1m, (follow site signs) right signed Ashwater. 0.5m, left at hill brow. Site 25yds.*
grid ref: SS367023

Set on a working farm in a quiet rural location. All pitches have extensive views of
the Devon countryside, yet the park is only two and a half miles from the market
town of Holsworthy, and within easy reach of roads to the coast and beaches of
north Cornwall. 2 acre site. 19 touring pitches. 11 hardstandings. Caravan pitches.
Motorhome pitches. Tent pitches.

Open: all year **Last arrival:** 19.00hrs **Last departure:** noon

Pitches: * 🚐 £15-£17 🚌 £15-£17 ▲

Leisure: ⁄Ⅲ ♣

Facilities: 🏳⊙✳☴🛏♻ ❶

Services: 🖳 🛒

Within 3 miles: ⚓ 🖊 ⑤ 🔵 ∪

Notes: Breathable groundsheets only. Dogs must be kept on leads. Caravan & motorhome
storage (outside & undercover).

AA Pubs & Restaurants nearby: The Bickford Arms, HOLSWORTHY, EX22 7XY,
01409 221318

Tamarstone Farm
►►77%

tel: 01288 381734 **Bude Rd, Pancrasweek EX22 7JT**
email: camping@tamarstone.co.uk
dir: *A30 to Launceston, B3254 towards Bude, approx 14m. Right onto A3072 towards
Holsworthy, approx 1.5m, site on left.* **grid ref:** SS286056

Four acres of river-bordered meadow and woodland providing a wildlife haven for
those who enjoy peace and seclusion. The wide, sandy beaches of Bude are just five
miles away, and free coarse fishing is provided on site for visitors. 1 acre site. 16
touring pitches. Caravan pitches. Motorhome pitches. Tent pitches. 1 static.

Open: Etr-end Oct **Last arrival:** 22.00hrs **Last departure:** noon

Pitches: * 🚐 £10-£13 🚌 £10-£13 ▲ £10-£13

Leisure: 🎣

Facilities: 🏳⊙✳☴🛏♻ ❶

Services: 🖳

Within 3 miles: ⚓ 🖊 ⑤

Notes: 🐕 No noise after mdnt, pitch must be kept clean & tidy. Dogs must be kept on
leads. BT hot spot.

AA Pubs & Restaurants nearby: The Bickford Arms, HOLSWORTHY, EX22 7XY,
01409 221318

Noteworthy Farm Caravan and Campsite
►►76%

tel: 01409 253731 & 07811 000071 **Noteworthy, Bude Rd EX22 7JB**
email: enquiries@noteworthy-devon.co.uk
dir: *On A3072 between Holsworthy & Bude. 3m from Holsworthy on right.*
grid ref: SS303052

This campsite is owned by a friendly young couple with their own children. There are
good views from the quiet rural location, and simple toilet facilities. The local bus
stops outside the gate on request. 5 acre site. 5 touring pitches. 3 hardstandings.
Caravan pitches. Motorhome pitches. Tent pitches. 3 statics.

Open: all year **Last departure:** 11.00hrs

Pitches: * 🚐 £10-£15 🚌 £10-£15 ▲ £10-£15

Leisure: ⁄Ⅲ

Facilities: 🏳⊙✳☉🛏♻

Services: 🖳 🛒

Within 3 miles: ⚓ 🖊 ⛷ ⑤ 🔵 ∪

Notes: 🐕 No open fires, no noise after 22.30hrs. Dogs must be kept on leads. Dog
grooming available.

AA Pubs & Restaurants nearby: The Bickford Arms, HOLSWORTHY, EX22 7XY,
01409 221318

ILFRACOMBE — Map 3 SS54

See also Berrynarbor

Places to visit

Arlington Court, ARLINGTON, EX31 4LP, 01271 850296
www.nationaltrust.org.uk/arlington-court

Exmoor Zoological Park, BLACKMOOR GATE, EX31 4SG, 01598 763352
www.exmoorzoo.co.uk

Great for kids: Watermouth Castle & Family Theme Park, ILFRACOMBE,
EX34 9SL, 01271 863879 www.watermouthcastle.com

Hele Valley Holiday Park
►►►►87%

tel: 01271 862460 **Hele Bay EX34 9RD**
email: holidays@helevalley.co.uk
dir: *M5 junct 27, A361, through Barnstaple & Braunton to Ilfracombe. Take A399 towards
Combe Martin. Follow brown Hele Valley signs. In 400mtrs sharp right to T-junct. Park on
left.* **grid ref:** SS533472

A deceptively spacious park set in a picturesque valley with glorious tree-lined hilly
views from most pitches. High quality toilet facilities are provided, and the park is
within walking distance of a lovely beach and on a regular bus route. Camping
pods are available to hire. The harbour and other attractions of Ilfracombe are just
a mile away. 17 acre site. 55 touring pitches. 18 hardstandings. Caravan pitches.
Motorhome pitches. Tent pitches. 80 statics. 3 wooden pods.

LEISURE: 🏊 Indoor swimming pool 🏊 Outdoor swimming pool ⁄Ⅲ Children's playground 🎣 Kid's club ⚹ Tennis court 🎱 Games room ▭ Separate TV room
⚓ golf course ⛵ Boats for hire ▤ Cinema ♫ Entertainment 🖊 Fishing ◎ Mini golf ⛷ Watersports 🏋 Gym ⊕ Sports field Spa ∪ Stables
FACILITIES: 🛁 Bath 🏳 Shower ⊙ Electric shaver 🖊 Hairdryer ✳ Ice Pack Facility ♿ Disabled facilities 🕾 Public telephone ⑤ Shop on site or within 200yds
📷 Mobile shop (calls at least 5 days a week) 🍴 BBQ area 🌲 Picnic area 📶 Wi-fi 🖥 Internet access ♻ Recycling ❶ Tourist info 🛏 Dog exercise area

Open: Etr-Oct **Last arrival:** 21.00hrs **Last departure:** 11.00hrs

Pitches: ⛟ ⛺ Å ⛺

Leisure: ⚘ Spa

Facilities: 🏸☺🄲❄&🛠🚻 WiFi 🖥 ♻ 🄸

Services: 🔌🄻 🛢⌀🅣🧺⇊

Within 3 miles: ⤋⚘🕀🕐🅿◎⛵🅑🅢🅕∪

Notes: Groups, motorhomes & tourers by arrangement only. Dogs must be kept on leads. Nature trail, postal collection.

AA Pubs & Restaurants nearby: 11 The Quay, ILFRACOMBE, EX34 9EQ, 01271 868090

KENNFORD — Map 3 SX98

Places to visit

St Nicholas Priory, EXETER, EX4 3BL, 01392 665858 www.exeter.gov.uk/priory

Quay House Visitor Centre, EXETER, EX2 4AN, 01392 271611 www.exeter.gov.uk/quayhouse

Great for kids: Devon's Crealy Great Adventure Park, CLYST ST MARY, EX5 1DR, 01395 233200 www.crealy.co.uk

Kennford International Caravan Park
►►►► 80%

tel: 01392 833046 **EX6 7YN**
email: ian@kennfordinternational.com
dir: At end of M5 take A38, site signed at Kennford slip road. **grid ref:** SX912857

Screened from the A38 by trees and shrubs, this park offers many pitches divided by hedging for privacy. A high quality toilet block complements the park's facilities. A good, centrally-located base for touring the coast and countryside of Devon, and Exeter is easily accessible via buses that stop nearby. 15 acre site. 22 touring pitches. 4 hardstandings. Caravan pitches. Motorhome pitches. Tent pitches. 65 statics.

Open: all year **Last arrival:** 21.00hrs (winter arrival times vary)
Last departure: 11.00hrs

Pitches: ⛟ ⛺ Å

Leisure: ⚘ ✎

Facilities: 🛠🏸☺&🛠 WiFi ♻ 🄸

Services: 🔌🄻 🍴🛢🅣🧺⬆⇊

Within 3 miles: ⤋⚘🕀🕐🅿🅑🅢🅕∪

Notes: Dogs must be kept on leads.

AA Pubs & Restaurants nearby: Bridge Inn, TOPSHAM, EX3 0QQ, 01392 873862

KENTISBEARE

Places to visit

Killerton House & Garden, KILLERTON, EX5 3LE, 01392 881345 www.nationaltrust.org.uk

Allhallows Museum, HONITON, EX14 1PG, 01404 44966 www.honitonmuseum.co.uk

Great for kids: Diggerland, CULLOMPTON, EX15 2PE, 0871 227 7007 www.diggerland.com

---

KENTISBEARE — Map 3 ST00

Forest Glade Holiday Park
►►►► 80%

tel: 01404 841381 **EX15 2DT**
email: enquiries@forest-glade.co.uk **web:** www.forest-glade.co.uk
dir: Tent traffic: from A373 turn left past Keepers Cottage Inn (2.5m E of M5 junct 28). NB due to narrow roads, touring caravans & larger motorhomes must approach from Honiton direction. Please phone for access details. **grid ref:** ST101073

A quiet, attractive park in a forest clearing with well-kept gardens and beech hedge screening. One of the main attractions is the site's immediate proximity to the forest which offers magnificent hillside walks with surprising views over the valleys. Camping pods are available for hire. Please note that because the roads are narrow around the site, it is best to phone the site for suitable route details. 16 acre site. 80 touring pitches. 40 hardstandings. 28 seasonal pitches. Caravan pitches. Motorhome pitches. Tent pitches. 57 statics. 2 wooden pods.

Open: mid Mar-end Oct (rs Low season limited shop hours) **Last arrival:** 21.00hrs
Last departure: noon

Pitches: ⛟ £14.50-£22.50 ⛺ £14.50-£22.50 Å £14.50-£22.50 ⛺

Leisure: 🏊⚘♨☺✎

Facilities: 🏸☺🄲❄&🄲🅑🚻🛠 WiFi ♻ 🄸

Services: 🔌🄻 🛢⌀🅣🧺⬆⇊

Within 3 miles: 🅿🅕∪

Notes: Families & couples only. Dogs must be kept on leads. Adventure & soft play area, wildlife information room, paddling pool.

AA Pubs & Restaurants nearby: The Blacksmiths Arms, PLYMTREE, EX15 2JU, 01884 277474

PITCHES: ⛟ Caravans ⛺ Motorhomes Å Tents ⛺ Glamping-style accommodation **SERVICES:** 🔌 Electric hook up 🄻 Launderette 🍴 Licensed bar 🛢 Calor Gas ⌀ Camping Gaz 🅣 Toilet fluid 🍽 Café/Restaurant 🍟 Fast Food/Takeaway 🧺 Battery charging ⬆ Baby care ⇊ Motorvan service point **ABBREVIATIONS:** BH/bank hols — bank holidays Etr — Easter Spring BH — Spring Bank Holiday fr — from hrs — hours m — mile mdnt — midnight rdbt — roundabout rs — restricted service wk — week wknd — weekend x-rds — cross roads ❷ No credit or debit cards ❌ No dogs 👪 Children of all ages accepted

KINGSBRIDGE
Map 3 SX74

Places to visit
Kingsbridge Cookworthy Museum, KINGSBRIDGE, TQ7 1AW, 01548 853235 www.kingsbridgemuseum.org.uk

Overbeck's, SALCOMBE, TQ8 8LW, 01548 842893 www.nationaltrust.org.uk

PREMIER PARK

Parkland Caravan and Camping Site
►►►►►78%

tel: 01548 852723 & 07968 222008 **Sorley Green Cross TQ7 4AF**
email: enquiries@parklandsite.co.uk
dir: A384 to Totnes, A381 towards Kingsbridge. 12m, at Stumpy Post Cross rdbt turn right, 1m. Site 200yds on left after Sorley Green Cross. **grid ref:** SX728462

Expect a high level of customer care at this family-run park set in the glorious South Hams countryside; it has panoramic views over Salcombe and the rolling countryside towards Dartmoor. The immaculately maintained grounds offer generous grass pitches, hardstandings and super pitches. The seasonal on-site shop sells local produce and pre-ordered hampers; the toilet facilities feature quality, fully serviced cubicles, family washrooms, a bathroom and a fully fitted disabled suite. Babysitting is available by arrangement. A bus stops close to the site entrance, which is handy for exploring the local towns and villages. 3 acre site. 50 touring pitches. 30 hardstandings. 15 seasonal pitches. Caravan pitches. Motorhome pitches. Tent pitches.

Open: all year **Last arrival:** 22.00hrs **Last departure:** 11.30hrs
Pitches: ⊞ £10-£28 ⊞ £10-£28 ▲ £10-£28
Leisure: ⚑ ✎
Facilities: ⊯⋔⊙℘✳⅊⚅⌂⛶▦⬛♻❶
Services: ⬛⬛⬛⬛⬛⬛⬛⬛
Within 3 miles: ⬛⬛⬛⬛⬛⬛⬛⬛⬛

Notes: ⊗ No camp fires, no noise after 23.00hrs, children must be accompanied by an adult when using facilities. Fridge freezers available, storage facility.

AA Pubs & Restaurants nearby: The Fortescue Arms, EAST ALLINGTON, TQ9 7RA, 01548 521215

The Crabshell Inn, KINGSBRIDGE, TQ7 1JZ, 01548 852345

Island Lodge Caravan & Camping Site
►►►►78%

tel: 01548 852956 & 07968 222007 **Stumpy Post Cross TQ7 4BL**
email: enquiries@islandlodgesite.co.uk
dir: Take A381 from Totnes towards Kingsbridge. In 12m, at rdbt (Stumpy Post Cross) right, 300mtrs left into lane, site signed. 200mtrs on left. **grid ref:** SX738470

A small, peaceful and well-established park, with extensive views over the South Hams, which has been run by the same family for many years. The toilet facilities are of good quality; food orders can delivered by arrangement. A scenic two-mile walk will take you to Kingsbridge, or the Kingsbridge bus stops close to the site.

There are several dog-friendly beaches nearby. 2 acre site. 30 touring pitches. 2 hardstandings. 15 seasonal pitches. Caravan pitches. Motorhome pitches. Tent pitches.

Open: all year **Last arrival:** 20.30hrs **Last departure:** noon
Pitches: ⊞ ⊞ ▲
Leisure: ⚑
Facilities: ⋔⊙℘✳⅊⚅⌂▦⬛♻❶
Services: ⬛⬛⬛⬛⬛⬛⬛⬛
Within 3 miles: ⬛⬛⬛⬛⬛⬛⬛⬛⬛

Notes: ⊗ No generators. Play area open 09.00hrs-21.00hrs. Dogs must be kept on leads. Restrictions on certain dog breeds .Secure caravan storage yard, boat park.

AA Pubs & Restaurants nearby: The Fortescue Arms, EAST ALLINGTON, TQ9 7RA, 01548 521215

The Crabshell Inn, KINGSBRIDGE, TQ7 1JZ, 01548 852345

LYNTON
Map 3 SS74

See also Oare (Somerset)

Places to visit
Arlington Court, ARLINGTON, EX31 4LP, 01271 850296 www.nationaltrust.org.uk/arlington-court

Great for kids: Exmoor Zoological Park, BLACKMOOR GATE, EX31 4SG, 01598 763352 www.exmoorzoo.co.uk

Channel View Caravan and Camping Park
►►►►71%

GOLD

tel: 01598 753349 **Manor Farm EX35 6LD**
email: relax@channel-view.co.uk **grid ref:** SS724482
dir: A39 E for 0.5m on left past Barbrook. **grid ref:** SS724482

On the top of the cliffs overlooking the Bristol Channel, this is a well-maintained park on the edge of Exmoor, and close to both Lynton and Lynmouth. Pitches can be selected from either those in a hidden hedged area or those with panoramic views over the coast. 6 acre site. 76 touring pitches. 15 hardstandings. Caravan pitches. Motorhome pitches. Tent pitches. 31 statics.

Open: 15 Mar-15 Nov **Last arrival:** 22.00hrs **Last departure:** noon
Pitches: * ⊞ £13-£21 ⊞ £13-£21 ▲ £13-£21
Leisure: ⚑
Facilities: ⊯⋔⊙℘✳⚅⛶⌂♜▦♻❶
Services: ⬛⬛⬛⬛⬛⬛⬛
Within 3 miles: ⬛℘◎⬛⬛⬛⬛

Notes: Groups by prior arrangement only. Dogs must be kept on leads. Parent & baby room.

AA Pubs & Restaurants nearby: Rising Sun Hotel, LYNMOUTH, EX35 6EG, 01598 753223

Rockford Inn, BRENDON, EX35 6PT, 01598 741214

LEISURE: 🏊 Indoor swimming pool 🏊 Outdoor swimming pool ⚑ Children's playground 🧒 Kid's club 🎾 Tennis court ✎ Games room 📺 Separate TV room ⛳ golf course 🚤 Boats for hire 🎭 Cinema 🎵 Entertainment ℘ Fishing ◎ Mini golf 🏄 Watersports 💪 Gym ⚽ Sports field Spa ⛎ Stables
FACILITIES: 🛁 Bath ⋔ Shower ⊙ Electric shaver ℘ Hairdryer ✳ Ice Pack Facility ⚅ Disabled facilities ⌚ Public telephone 🏪 Shop on site or within 200yds 🚚 Mobile shop (calls at least 5 days a week) 🍖 BBQ area 🪑 Picnic area ▦ Wi-fi ⬛ Internet access ♻ Recycling ❶ Tourist info 🐕 Dog exercise area

Sunny Lyn Holiday Park

▶▶▶76%

tel: 01598 753384 **Lynbridge EX35 6NS**
email: info@caravandevon.co.uk **web:** www.caravandevon.co.uk
dir: *M5 junct 27, A361 to South Molton. Right onto A399 to Blackmoor Gate, right onto A39, left onto B3234 towards Lynmouth. Site 1m on right.* **grid ref:** *SS719486*

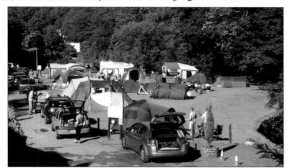

Set in a sheltered riverside location in a wooded combe within a mile of the sea, in Exmoor National Park. This family-run park offers good facilities including an excellent café. 4.5 acre site. 9 touring pitches. 5 hardstandings. Caravan pitches. Motorhome pitches. Tent pitches. 7 statics.

Open: Mar-Oct **Last arrival:** 20.00hrs **Last departure:** 11.00hrs

Pitches: * 🚐 £16-£17.50 🚐 £16-£17.50 ▲ £15-£16

Facilities: 🅿️☉🅿️⚹♿🕙💲🅆🄸🄵 🖥 ♻ ❶

Services: 🔌🅕 🔋⊘🍽🔋🛒

Within 3 miles: ⚓🗓🅿️⚓◎🗼🅕🅕↺

Notes: No cars by tents. No wood fires, quiet after 22.30hrs. Dogs must be kept on leads.
AA Pubs & Restaurants nearby: Rising Sun Hotel, LYNMOUTH, EX35 6EG, 01598 753223
Rockford Inn, BRENDON, EX35 6PT, 01598 741214

Pennymoor Camping & Caravan Park

▶▶▶82%

tel: 01548 830542 **PL21 0SB**
email: enquiries@pennymoor-camping.co.uk **web:** www.pennymoor-camping.co.uk
dir: *Exit A38 at Wrangaton Cross. Left & then right at x-rds. After by-passing Ermington, turn left onto A379. Turn left at Harraton Cross. Site on left.* **grid ref:** *SX685516*

A well-established rural park on part level, part gently sloping grass with good views over distant Dartmoor and the countryside in between. The park has been owned and run by the same family since 1935, and is very carefully tended, with clean, well-maintained toilets and a relaxing atmosphere. 12.5 acre site. 119 touring pitches. 3 hardstandings. Caravan pitches. Motorhome pitches. Tent pitches. 76 statics.

Open: 15 Mar-15 Nov (rs 15 Mar-mid May only one toilet & shower block open)
Last arrival: 20.00hrs **Last departure:** 11.00hrs

Pitches: * 🚐 £14-£20 🚐 £14-£20 ▲ £14-£20

Leisure: ⚑

Facilities: 🅿️☉🅿️⚹♿🅕➡🅆🄸🄵 ♻ ❶

Services: 🔌🅕 🔋⊘🅃🛒↯

Within 3 miles: ⚓🅕

Notes: No skateboards or scooters, no noise after 22.00hrs. Dogs must be kept on leads. Emergency phone.
AA Pubs & Restaurants nearby: California Country Inn, MODBURY, PL21 0SG, 01548 821449
Rose & Crown, YEALMPTON, PL8 2EB, 01752 880223

MORTEHOE
Map 3 SS44

See also Woolacombe

Places to visit

Marwood Hill Gardens, BARNSTAPLE, EX31 4EB, 01271 342528 www.marwoodhillgarden.co.uk

Great for kids: Watermouth Castle & Family Theme Park, ILFRACOMBE, EX34 9SL, 01271 863879 www.watermouthcastle.com

North Morte Farm Caravan & Camping Park
►►►►85%

tel: 01271 870381 **North Morte Rd EX34 7EG**
email: info@northmortefarm.co.uk **web:** www.northmortefarm.co.uk
dir: From B3343 into Mortehoe, right at post office. Site 500yds on left.
grid ref: SS462455

Set in spectacular coastal countryside close to National Trust land and 500 yards from Rockham Beach. This attractive park is very well run and maintained by friendly family owners, and the quaint village of Mortehoe with its cafés, shops and pubs, is just a five-minute walk away. 22 acre site. 180 touring pitches. 25 hardstandings. 13 seasonal pitches. Caravan pitches. Motorhome pitches. Tent pitches. 73 statics.

Open: Apr-Oct **Last arrival:** 22.00hrs **Last departure:** noon
Pitches: 🚐 🚙 Å
Leisure: ⚑
Facilities: ⚑⊙☞✳&⊙⑤🛒📶 ♻ ❶
Services: 🔌⑤🛢⊘Ⓣ🛒🚽♨
Within 3 miles: ⚓ℐ◎⑤⑤∪
Notes: No large groups. Dogs must be kept on leads.
AA Pubs & Restaurants nearby: Watersmeet Hotel, WOOLACOMBE, EX34 7EB, 01271 870333

11 The Quay, ILFRACOMBE, EX34 9EQ, 01271 868090

Warcombe Farm Caravan & Camping Park
►►►►85%

tel: 01271 870690 **Station Rd EX34 7EJ**
email: info@warcombefarm.co.uk **web:** www.warcombefarm.co.uk
dir: On B3343 towards Woolacombe turn right towards Mortehoe. Site less than 1m on right. **grid ref:** SS478445

Extensive views over the Bristol Channel can be enjoyed from the open areas of this attractive park, while other pitches are sheltered in paddocks with maturing trees. The site has 14 excellent super pitches with hardstandings. The superb sandy, Blue Flag beach at Woolacombe Bay is only a mile and a half away, and there is a fishing lake with direct access from some pitches. The local bus stops outside the park entrance. 35 acre site. 250 touring pitches. 82 hardstandings. 12 seasonal pitches. Caravan pitches. Motorhome pitches. Tent pitches.

Open: 15 Mar-Oct **Last arrival:** 21.00hrs **Last departure:** 11.00hrs
Pitches: * 🚐 £15-£33 🚙 £15-£33 Å £12.50-£28
Leisure: ⚑❄
Facilities: ⚑⊙☞✳&⑤🛒📶 ♻ ❶
Services: 🔌⑤🛢⊘Ⓣ🛒♨
Within 3 miles: ⚓♨⧓ℐ◎≋⑤⑤∪
Notes: No noise after 22.30hrs. Dogs must be kept on leads.
AA Pubs & Restaurants nearby: Watersmeet Hotel, WOOLACOMBE, EX34 7EB, 01271 870333

11 The Quay, ILFRACOMBE, EX34 9EQ, 01271 868090

NEWTON ABBOT

See also Bickington

Places to visit

Tuckers Maltings, NEWTON ABBOT, TQ12 4AA, 01626 334734 www.tuckersmaltings.com

Bradley Manor, NEWTON ABBOT, TQ12 6BN, 01803 843235 www.nationaltrust.org.uk/devoncornwall

Great for kids: Prickly Ball Farm and Hedgehog Hospital, NEWTON ABBOT, TQ12 6BZ, 01626 362319 www.pricklyballfarm.com

---

LEISURE: 🏊 Indoor swimming pool 🏊 Outdoor swimming pool ⚑ Children's playground 🧒 Kid's club 🎾 Tennis court 🎱 Games room 📺 Separate TV room ⛳ golf course ⛵ Boats for hire 🎦 Cinema 🎵 Entertainment 🎣 Fishing ◎ Mini golf 🏄 Watersports 🏋 Gym ❄ Sports field ∪ Stables
FACILITIES: 🛁 Bath ⚑ Shower ⊙ Electric shaver ☞ Hairdryer ✳ Ice Pack Facility & Disabled facilities ⊙ Public telephone ⑤ Shop on site or within 200yds 🏪 Mobile shop (calls at least 5 days a week) 🍖 BBQ area 🎋 Picnic area 📶 Wi-fi 💻 Internet access ♻ Recycling ❶ Tourist info 🛒 Dog exercise area

PREMIER PARK

Ross Park
▶▶▶▶▶ 96%

tel: 01803 812983 **Park Hill Farm, Ipplepen TQ12 5TT**
email: enquiries@rossparkcaravanpark.co.uk **web:** www.rossparkcaravanpark.co.uk
dir: *N of Ipplepen on A381 follow brown site signs & sign for Woodland opposite Texaco garage.* **grid ref:** *SX845671*

A top-class park in every way, with large secluded pitches, high quality toilet facilities (which include excellent family rooms) and colourful flower displays throughout - note the wonderful floral walk to the toilets. The beautiful tropical conservatory also offers a breathtaking show of colour. There's a conservation walk through glorious wild flower meadows, replete with nature trail, a dog shower/grooming area, and six fully serviced pitches. This very rural park enjoys superb views of Dartmoor, and good quality meals to suit all tastes and pockets are served in the restaurant. Expect high levels of customer care — this park gets better each year. Home-grown produce and honey are sold in the shop. A bus, which stops close to the entrance, runs to Totnes and Newton Abbot. 32 acre site. 110 touring pitches. 110 hardstandings. Caravan pitches. Motorhome pitches. Tent pitches.

Open: Mar-2 Jan (rs Nov-Jan & 1st 3 wks in Mar restaurant/bar closed (ex Xmas/New Year)) **Last arrival:** 21.00hrs **Last departure:** 11.00hrs
Pitches: * ▤ £15.50-£28.60 ▤ £15.50-£28.60 ▲ £14.50-£28.60
Leisure: ⚙ 🌊 ⚲ ▭
Facilities: ⟟ ☉ ℰ ✳ ⚙ ⚲ ⓢ 🎣 🖊 📶 ♻ ❂
Services: 🔌 🗑 🍺 🔋 ⊘ Ⓣ 🍽 📸 🚮 ⬇
Within 3 miles: ⚓ 🎋 ✐ 🏪 ⚲ ♻

Notes: Bikes, skateboards & scooters permitted only on leisure field. Snooker, table tennis, badminton.

AA Pubs & Restaurants nearby: The Church House Inn, MARLDON, TQ3 1SL, 01803 558279

The Union Inn, DENBURY, TQ12 6DQ, 01803 812595

PREMIER PARK

Dornafield
▶▶▶▶▶ 94%

tel: 01803 812732 **Dornafield Farm, Two Mile Oak TQ12 6DD**
email: enquiries@dornafield.com **web:** www.dornafield.com
dir: *From Newton Abbot take A381 signed Totnes for 2m. At Two Mile Oak Inn right, left at x-rds in 0.5m. Site on right.* **grid ref:** *SX838683*

An immaculately kept park in a tranquil wooded valley between Dartmoor and Torbay, divided into three areas. At the heart of the 30-acre site is Dornafield, a 14th-century farmhouse, adapted for campers' use but still retaining much charm. The friendly family owners are always available for help or to give advice. The site has superb facilities in two ultra modern toilet blocks. On-site there is the Quarry Café which provides takeaway fish and chips or jacket potatoes daily. This is a quiet and peaceful location convenient for Torbay, Dartmoor and the charming coastal villages of the South Hams. A bus service to Totnes or Newton Abbot runs nearby. 30 acre site. 135 touring pitches. 119 hardstandings. 13 seasonal pitches. Caravan pitches. Motorhome pitches. Tent pitches.

Open: 13 Mar-3 Jan **Last arrival:** 22.00hrs **Last departure:** 11.00hrs
Pitches: * ▤ £16-£32 ▤ £16-£32 ▲ £14.80-£26
Leisure: ⚙ 🌊 ⚲
Facilities: ⟟ ☉ ℰ ✳ ⚙ ⚲ ⓢ 🎣 🖊 📶 ♻ ❂
Services: 🔌 🗑 🔋 ⊘ Ⓣ 🚮 🚽 ⬇
Within 3 miles: ⚓ 🎋 ✐ 🏪 ♻

Notes: No commercial vehicles with signs. Dogs must be kept on leads. All year caravan storage.

AA Pubs & Restaurants nearby: The Church House Inn, MARLDON, TQ3 1SL, 01803 558279

The Union Inn, DENBURY, TQ12 6DQ, 01803 812595

NEWTON ABBOT *continued*

Twelve Oaks Farm Caravan Park
►►► 79%

tel: 01626 335015 **Teigngrace TQ12 6QT**
email: info@twelveoaksfarm.co.uk web: www.twelveoaksfarm.co.uk
dir: *A38 from Exeter left signed Teigngrace (only), 0.25m before Drumbridges rdbt. 1.5m, through village, site on left. Or from Plymouth pass Drumbridges rdbt, take slip road for Chudleigh Knighton. Right over bridge, rejoin A38 towards Plymouth. Left for Teigngrace (only), then as above.* **grid ref:** *SX852737*

An attractive small park on a working farm close to Dartmoor National Park, and bordered by the River Teign. The tidy pitches are located amongst trees and shrubs, and the modern facilities are very well maintained. There are two well-stocked fishing lakes and children will enjoy visiting all the farm animals. Close by is Stover Country Park and also the popular Templar Way walking route. 2 acre site. 50 touring pitches. 25 hardstandings. 15 seasonal pitches. Caravan pitches. Motorhome pitches. Tent pitches.

Open: all year **Last arrival:** 21.00hrs **Last departure:** 10.30hrs
Pitches: * ⊞ £10-£17.50 ⊞ £10-£17.50 ▲ £10-£17.50
Leisure: ⇌ ⋀
Facilities: ⋔ ⊙ ℱ ✳ ⅁ ◍ ⑤ ⊨ WiFi ♳ ❼
Services: ⊟⑤ ⬛ T ⊍
Within 3 miles: ↨ 目 ℱ ◎ ≋ ⑤ ⑤ ∪
Notes: No noise after 23.00hrs. Dogs must be kept on leads.
AA Pubs & Restaurants nearby: The Elizabethan Inn, LUTON (NEAR CHUDLEIGH), TQ13 0BL, 01626 775425
The Union Inn, DENBURY, TQ12 6DQ, 01803 812595

See which sites have been awarded Gold Pennants
on page 36

See which sites have been awarded Gold Pennants on page 36

PAIGNTON
Map 3 SX86

Places to visit
Dartmouth Steam Railway & River Boat Company, PAIGNTON, TQ4 6AF, 01803 555872 www.dartmouthrailriver.co.uk

Kents Cavern, TORQUAY, TQ1 2JF, 01803 215136 www.kents-cavern.co.uk

Great for kids: Paignton Zoo Environmental Park, PAIGNTON, TQ4 7EU, 0844 474 2222 www.paigntonzoo.org.uk

PREMIER PARK

Beverley Parks Caravan & Camping Park
►►►►► 86%

tel: 01803 661979 **Goodrington Rd TQ4 7JE**
email: info@beverley-holidays.co.uk web: www.beverley-holidays.co.uk
dir: *On A380, A3022, 2m S of Paignton left into Goodrington Rd. Beverley Park on right.* **grid ref:** *SX886582*

A high quality family-run park with extensive views of the bay and plenty of on-site amenities. The park boasts indoor and outdoor heated swimming pools, plus good bars and restaurants. The toilet facilities are modern and very clean and include excellent fully serviced family rooms. The park complex is attractively laid out with the touring areas divided into nicely screened areas. 12 acre site. 172 touring pitches. 49 hardstandings. Caravan pitches. Motorhome pitches. Tent pitches.

Open: all year **Last arrival:** 21.00hrs **Last departure:** 10.00hrs
Pitches: ⊞ ⊞ ▲
Leisure: ⇌ ⇌ ⵷ ⋀ ⌕ ⚓ ♬ Spa
Facilities: ⊨ ⋔ ⊙ ℱ ✳ ⅁ ◍ ⑤ ⊨ WiFi ▦ ♳ ❼
Services: ⊟⑤ ⬛⬛ ⌀ T ◍ ⬛ ⊍ ⊍
Within 3 miles: ↨ ⵷ 目 ℱ ◎ ≋ ⑤ ⑤ ∪
Notes: No pets. Table tennis, sauna, crazy golf, letter box trail.
AA Pubs & Restaurants nearby: The Church House Inn, MARLDON, TQ3 1SL, 01803 558279
The Cary Arms, TORQUAY, TQ1 3LX, 01803 327110
The Elephant Restaurant and Brasserie, TORQUAY, TQ1 2BH, 01803 200044

LEISURE: ⛱ Indoor swimming pool ⇌ Outdoor swimming pool ⋀ Children's playground ⵷ Kid's club ⚲ Tennis court ⚓ Games room ⬚ Separate TV room ⛳ golf course ⵷ Boats for hire ▤ Cinema ♬ Entertainment ℱ Fishing ◎ Mini golf ≋ Watersports ⵷ Gym ⚘ Sports field Spa ∪ Stables
FACILITIES: ⊨ Bath ⋔ Shower ⊙ Electric shaver ℱ Hairdryer ✳ Ice Pack Facility ⅁ Disabled facilities ◍ Public telephone ⑤ Shop on site or within 200yds ⑤ Mobile shop (calls at least 5 days a week) ⬛ BBQ area ⊨ Picnic area WiFi Wi-fi ▦ Internet access ♳ Recycling ❼ Tourist info ⊨ Dog exercise area

Whitehill Country Park
►►►► 80%

GOLD

tel: 01803 782338 **Stoke Rd TQ4 7PF**
email: info@whitehill-park.co.uk **web:** www.whitehill-park.co.uk
dir: *A385 through Totnes towards Paignton. Turn right by Parkers Arms into Stoke Rd towards Stoke Gabriel. Site on left after approx 1.5m.* **grid ref:** *SX857588*

A family-owned and run park set in rolling countryside, with many scenic beaches just a short drive away. This extensive country park covers 40 acres with woodland walks, plenty of flora and fauna and an excellent outdoor swimming pool, a café, plus a bar/restaurant with summer entertainment. It offers ideal facilities, including luxury lodges and camping pods, for an excellent holiday. 40 acre site. 260 touring pitches. Caravan pitches. Motorhome pitches. Tent pitches. 60 statics. 5 wooden pods.

Open: Etr-Sep **Last arrival:** 21.00hrs **Last departure:** 10.00hrs

Pitches: 🚐 🚍 ⛺ 🏠

Leisure: 🏊 🎡 🎣 🖥

Facilities: 🕯 📮 ✳ ♿ 🕑 🔥 WiFi 🖥 ♻ ⓘ

Services: 🔌 🔲 🍺 🔋 🐕 🍽 🚮 🚐 ♿

Within 3 miles: ⚓ 🎣 🎯 🛒 🏌 ◎ 🍽 🛍 🛒 U

Notes: Dogs must be kept on leads. Walking & cycling trails, letter box trail, craft room, table tennis.

AA Pubs & Restaurants nearby: The Church House Inn, MARLDON, TQ3 1SL, 01803 558279

The Cary Arms, TORQUAY, TQ1 3LX, 01803 327110

The Elephant Restaurant and Brasserie, TORQUAY, TQ1 2BH, 01803 200044

PLYMOUTH

Places to visit
Plymouth City Museum & Art Gallery, PLYMOUTH, PL4 8AJ, 01752 304774
www.plymouthmuseum.gov.uk

The Elizabethan House, PLYMOUTH, PL1 2NA, 01752 304774
www.plymouth.gov.uk/museums

Great for kids: National Marine Aquarium, PLYMOUTH, PL4 0LF, 01752 275200
www.national-aquarium.co.uk

PLYMOUTH Map 3 SX45

Riverside Caravan Park
►►►► 84%

tel: 01752 344122 **Leigham Manor Dr PL6 8LL**
email: office@riversidecaravanpark.com **web:** www.riversidecaravanpark.com
dir: *A38 follow signs at Marsh Mills rdbt, take 3rd exit, then left. 400yds turn right (keep River Plym on right) to site.* **grid ref:** *SX515575*

A well-groomed site on the outskirts of Plymouth on the banks of the River Plym, in a surprisingly peaceful location surrounded by woodland. The toilet facilities are appointed to a very good standard, and include private cubicles, plus there's a good games room and bar/restaurant serving food. This park is an ideal stopover for the ferries to France and Spain, and makes an excellent base for touring Dartmoor and the coast. The local bus stop is just a ten-minute walk from the site. 11 acre site. 259 touring pitches. Caravan pitches. Motorhome pitches. Tent pitches. 22 statics.

Open: all year (rs Oct-Etr bar, restaurant, takeaway & pool closed) **Last arrival:** 22.00hrs **Last departure:** 10.00hrs

Pitches: * 🚐 £15.50-£23.50 🚍 £18.50-£26.50 ⛺ £11.50-£21.50

Leisure: 🏊 🎡 🎣 🖥

Facilities: 🕯 ☺ 📮 ✳ ♿ 🕑 🔥 ♻ ⓘ

Services: 🔌 🔲 🍺 🔋 🐕 🍽 🔋 🚮 ♿

Within 3 miles: ⚓ 🎣 🎯 🛒 🏌 ◎ 🍽 🛍 🛒 U

Notes: Dogs must be kept on leads.

AA Pubs & Restaurants nearby: Artillery Tower Restaurant, PLYMOUTH, PL1 3QR, 01752 257610

Tanners Restaurant, PLYMOUTH, PL1 2AE, 01752 252001

PITCHES: 🚐 Caravans 🚍 Motorhomes ⛺ Tents 🏠 Glamping-style accommodation **SERVICES:** 🔌 Electric hook up 🔲 Launderette 🍺 Licensed bar 🔋 Calor Gas 🔋 Camping Gaz 🔲 Toilet fluid 🍽 Café/Restaurant 🚮 Fast Food/Takeaway 🔋 Battery charging 🐕 Baby care ♿ Motorvan service point
ABBREVIATIONS: BH/bank hols – bank holidays Etr – Easter Spring BH – Spring Bank Holiday fr – from hrs – hours m – mile mdnt – midnight rdbt – roundabout rs – restricted service wk – week wknd – weekend x-rds – cross roads 🚫 No credit or debit cards 🚫 No dogs 👪 Children of all ages accepted

Karrageen Caravan & Camping Park

►►►►78%

tel: 01548 561230 **Bolberry, Malborough TQ7 3EN**
email: phil@karrageen.co.uk
dir: At Malborough on A381, sharp right through village, in 0.6m right again, 0.9m, site on right. **grid ref:** SX686395

A small friendly, family-run park with secluded hidden dells for tents and terraced grass pitches giving extensive sea and country views. There is a well-stocked shop and an excellent toilet block that has two cubicled units — one suitable for families and for less able visitors. This park is just one mile from the beach and pretty hamlet of Hope Cove and is a really peaceful park from which to explore the South Hams coast. 7.5 acre site. 70 touring pitches. Caravan pitches. Motorhome pitches. Tent pitches. 25 statics.

Open: Etr-Sep **Last arrival:** 21.00hrs **Last departure:** 11.30hrs

Pitches: * ⊡ £15-£25 ⊡ £15-£25 ▲ £10-£30

Facilities: ⬤☉☂✳⬤⬤⬤⬤⬤⬤

Services: ⬤⬤⬤⬤⬤⬤⬤⬤

Within 3 miles: ⬤⬤⬤⬤⬤⬤

Notes: ⬤ Dogs must be kept on leads.

AA Pubs & Restaurants nearby: The Victoria Inn, SALCOMBE, TQ8 8BU, 01548 842604

Soar Mill Cove Hotel, SALCOMBE, TQ7 3DS, 01548 561566

Higher Rew Caravan & Camping Park

►►►80%

tel: 01548 842681 **Higher Rew, Malborough TQ7 3BW**
email: enquiries@higherrew.co.uk
dir: A381 to Malborough. Right at Townsend Cross, follow signs to Soar for 1m. Left at Rew Cross. **grid ref:** SX714383

A long-established park in a remote location within sight of the sea. The spacious, open touring field has some tiered pitches in the sloping grass, and there are lovely countryside or sea views from every pitch. The friendly family owners are continually improving the facilities. 5 acre site. 90 touring pitches. Caravan pitches. Motorhome pitches. Tent pitches.

Open: Etr-Oct **Last arrival:** 22.00hrs **Last departure:** noon

Pitches: * ⊡ £15-£21 ⊡ £15-£21 ▲ £14-£20

Leisure: ⬤⬤

Facilities: ⬤☉☂✳⬤⬤⬤⬤⬤

Services: ⬤⬤⬤⬤⬤⬤

Within 3 miles: ⬤⬤⬤⬤⬤

Notes: ⬤ Minimum noise after 23.00hrs. Dogs must be kept on leads. Play barn.

AA Pubs & Restaurants nearby: The Victoria Inn, SALCOMBE, TQ8 8BU, 01548 842604

Soar Mill Cove Hotel, SALCOMBE, TQ7 3DS, 01548 561566

Bolberry House Farm Caravan & Camping Park

►►►79%

tel: 01548 561251 **Bolberry TQ7 3DY**
email: enquiries@bolberryparks.co.uk
dir: At Malborough on A381 turn right signed Hope Cove & Bolberry. Take left fork after village signed Soar & Bolberry. Right in 0.6m. Site signed in 0.5m. **grid ref:** SX687395

A very popular park in a peaceful setting on a coastal farm with sea views, fine cliff walks and nearby beaches. Customers are assured of a warm welcome and the nicely tucked-away portaloo facilities are smart and beautifully maintained. Ten hardstandings are available. A mobile fish and chip van calls weekly in high season. There's a super dog-walking area. 6 acre site. 70 touring pitches. Caravan pitches. Motorhome pitches. Tent pitches. 10 statics.

Open: Etr-Oct **Last arrival:** 20.00hrs **Last departure:** 11.30hrs

Pitches: ⬤⬤▲

Leisure: ⬤

Facilities: ⬤☉☂✳⬤⬤⬤⬤⬤⬤⬤

Services: ⬤⬤⬤

Within 3 miles: ⬤⬤⬤⬤⬤⬤⬤⬤⬤⬤

Notes: ⬤

AA Pubs & Restaurants nearby: The Victoria Inn, SALCOMBE, TQ8 8BU, 01548 842604

Soar Mill Cove Hotel, SALCOMBE, TQ7 3DS, 01548 561566

Alston Camping and Caravan Site

►►69%

tel: 01548 561260 & 0780 803 0921 **Malborough, Kingsbridge TQ7 3BJ**
email: info@alstoncampsite.co.uk
dir: 1.5m W of town off A381 towards Malborough. **grid ref:** SX716406

An established farm site in a rural location adjacent to the Kingsbridge/Salcombe estuary. The site is well sheltered and screened, and approached down a long, well-surfaced narrow farm lane with passing places. The toilet facilities are basic. 16 acre site. 90 touring pitches. Caravan pitches. Motorhome pitches. Tent pitches. 58 statics.

Open: 15 Mar-Oct

Pitches: ⬤⬤▲

Leisure: ⬤

Facilities: ⬤☉☂✳⬤⬤⬤⬤⬤⬤

Services: ⬤⬤⬤⬤⬤⬤

Within 3 miles: ⬤⬤⬤⬤⬤⬤⬤

Notes: Dogs must be kept on leads.

AA Pubs & Restaurants nearby: The Victoria Inn, SALCOMBE, TQ8 8BU, 01548 842604

Soar Mill Cove Hotel, SALCOMBE, TQ7 3DS, 01548 561566

SAMPFORD PEVERELL
Map 3 ST01

Places to visit

Tiverton Castle, TIVERTON, EX16 6RP, 01884 253200 www.tivertoncastle.com

Tiverton Museum of Mid Devon Life, TIVERTON, EX16 6PJ, 01884 256295 www.tivertonmuseum.org.uk

Great for kids: Diggerland, CULLOMPTON, EX15 2PE, 0871 227 7007 www.diggerland.com

PREMIER PARK

Minnows Touring Park
►►►►►81%

tel: 01884 821770 **Holbrook Ln EX16 7EN**
email: admin@minnowstouringpark.co.uk
dir: *M5 junct 27, A361 signed Tiverton & Barnstaple. In 600yds take 1st slip road, right over bridge, site ahead.* **grid ref:** SS042148

A small, well-sheltered park, peacefully located amidst fields and mature trees. The toilet facilities are of a high quality in keeping with the rest of the park, and there is a good laundry. The park has direct gated access to the canal towpath; a brisk 20-minute walk leads to a choice of pubs and a farm shop, and the bus stop is 15 minutes away. All pitches are hardstanding with some large enough for American RVs; fully serviced pitches are also available. The park has WiFi. 5.5 acre site. 59 touring pitches. 59 hardstandings. Caravan pitches. Motorhome pitches. Tent pitches. 1 static.

Open: 2 Mar-2 Nov **Last arrival:** 20.00hrs **Last departure:** noon
Pitches: 🚐 🚃 ▲
Leisure: �Ⓐ
Facilities: 🏕️☉ℱ☀️🔥🅒🔥🗑️🎏📶 ♲ ❶
Services: 🔌🌀 🔋⊘Ⓣ🔋⊥
Within 3 miles: ⌿ℓ🚣🚲

Notes: No cycling, no groundsheets on grass. Dogs must be kept on leads. RVs welcome, caravan storage.

AA Pubs & Restaurants nearby: The Butterleigh Inn, BUTTERLEIGH, EX15 1PN, 01884 855433

SHALDON
Map 3 SX97

Places to visit

'Bygones', TORQUAY, TQ1 4PR, 01803 326108 www.bygones.co.uk

Great for kids: Babbacombe Model Village, TORQUAY, TQ1 3LA, 01803 315315 www.model-village.co.uk

Coast View Holiday Park
HOLIDAY CENTRE 77%

tel: 01626 818350 **Torquay Rd TQ14 0BG**
email: holidays@coastview.co.uk
dir: *M5 junct 31, A38 then A380 towards Torquay. A381 towards Teignmouth. Right in 4m at lights, over Shaldon Bridge. 0.75m, up hill, site on right.* **grid ref:** SX935716

This park has stunning sea views from its spacious pitches. The family-run park has a full entertainment programme every night for all the family, plus outdoor and indoor activities for children; this site will certainly appeal to lively families. 30 acre site. 38 touring pitches. 6 hardstandings. 21 seasonal pitches. Caravan pitches. Motorhome pitches. Tent pitches. 27 statics.

Open: mid Mar-end Oct **Last arrival:** 20.00hrs **Last departure:** 10.00hrs
Pitches: 🚐 🚃 ▲
Leisure: 🏊⚑🎣🎵
Facilities: 🏕️☉ℱ☀️🅒🗑️🔥🎏📶 🖥️ ♲ ❶
Services: 🔌🌀 🍽️🔋🍴🔋⊥
Within 3 miles: ⌿🚣♿🎣ℓ◎🚣🚲

Notes: No noise after 23.00hrs. Dogs must be kept on leads.

AA Pubs & Restaurants nearby: ODE dining, SHALDON, TQ14 0DE, 01626 873977

PITCHES: 🚐 Caravans 🚃 Motorhomes ▲ Tents 🏕️ Glamping-style accommodation **SERVICES:** 🔌 Electric hook up 🌀 Launderette 🍺 Licensed bar 🔋 Calor Gas ⊘ Camping Gaz Ⓣ Toilet fluid 🍽️ Café/Restaurant 🍴 Fast Food/Takeaway 🔋 Battery charging 🍼 Baby care ⊥ Motorvan service point
ABBREVIATIONS: BH/bank hols – bank holidays Etr – Easter Spring BH – Spring Bank Holiday fr – from hrs – hours m – mile mdnt – midnight rdbt – roundabout rs – restricted service wk – week wknd – weekend x-rds – cross roads 🚫 No credit or debit cards 🚫 No dogs 👫 Children of all ages accepted

SIDMOUTH

Map 3 SY18

Places to visit

Branscombe - The Old Bakery, Manor Mill and Forge, BRANSCOMBE, EX12 3DB, 01752 346585 www.nationaltrust.org.uk

Otterton Mill, OTTERTON, EX9 7HG, 01395 568521 www.ottertonmill.com

Great for kids: Pecorama Pleasure Gardens, BEER, EX12 3NA, 01297 21542 www.pecorama.info

---

ENGLAND & OVERALL WINNER OF THE AA CAMPSITE OF THE YEAR 2015

PREMIER PARK

Oakdown Country Holiday Park

▶▶▶▶▶ 94%

tel: 01297 680387 **Gatedown Ln, Weston EX10 0PT**
email: enquiries@oakdown.co.uk **web:** www.oakdown.co.uk
dir: Exit A3052, 2.5m E of junct with A375. **grid ref:** SY167902

A quality, friendly, well-maintained park with good landscaping and plenty of maturing trees that make it well screened from the A3052. Pitches are grouped in groves surrounded by shrubs, with a 50-pitch development replete with an upmarket toilet block. The park has excellent facilities including a 9-hole par 3 golf course and a good shop and café. The park's conservation areas, with their natural flora and fauna, offer attractive walks, and there is a hide by the Victorian reed bed for both casual and dedicated bird watchers. A delightful park in every respect. 16 acre site. 150 touring pitches. 90 hardstandings. 35 seasonal pitches. Caravan pitches. Motorhome pitches. Tent pitches. 15 statics.

Open: Apr-Oct **Last arrival:** 22.00hrs **Last departure:** 10.30hrs

Pitches: * ⊞ £16.70-£30.25 ⊞ £16.70-£30.25 ▲ £16.70-£24.20

Leisure: 🅰 🎯 ▢ ♪

Facilities: 🚿 🅝 ⊙ ℱ ✳ ♿ 🕔 ⓢ 🗷 📶 🖥 ♻ ❶

Services: 🔧 ⓢ 🛢 🖊 Ⓣ 🍽 ♨ 🚮 ⛽

Within 3 miles: ⌓ ⛵ 🎬 ℱ ◉ ♨ ⛳ ⓢ U

Notes: No bikes, skateboards or kite flying. Dogs must be kept on leads. Microwave available. Field trail to donkey sanctuary.

AA Pubs & Restaurants nearby: Blue Ball Inn, SIDMOUTH, EX10 9QL, 01395 514062

The Salty Monk, SIDMOUTH, EX10 9QP, 01395 513174

Dukes, SIDMOUTH, EX10 8AR, 01395 513320

See advert below

LEISURE: 🏊 Indoor swimming pool 🏊 Outdoor swimming pool 🅰 Children's playground 🧒 Kid's club ♞ Tennis court 🎱 Games room ▢ Separate TV room ⛳ golf course ⛵ Boats for hire 🎬 Cinema 🎵 Entertainment ℱ Fishing ◉ Mini golf ⛱ Watersports 💪 Gym ⚽ Sports field Spa U Stables

FACILITIES: 🛁 Bath 🅝 Shower ⊙ Electric shaver ℱ Hairdryer ✳ Ice Pack Facility ♿ Disabled facilities 🕔 Public telephone ⓢ Shop on site or within 200yds 🏪 Mobile shop (calls at least 5 days a week) 🍖 BBQ area 🏕 Picnic area 📶 Wi-fi 🖥 Internet access ♻ Recycling ❶ Tourist info 🐕 Dog exercise area

Kings Down Tail Caravan & Camping Park
►►►►80%

tel: 01297 680313 & 07796 618668 **Salcombe Regis EX10 0PD**
email: info@kingsdowntail.co.uk **web:** www.kingsdowntail.co.uk
dir: *M5, junct 30. A3052 towards Sidmouth. Continue through Sidford, up the hill for 2m then turn left just before Branscombe Cross.* **grid ref:** *SY173907*

This well managed family run park (now under new ownership) is well located near Sidmouth. There are new facilities for the 2015 season, including well-appointed family rooms. There is also a new play area for children including a pirate ship and den. The park is perfect for visiting south-east Devon, including Sidmouth, Beer, and Lyme Regis in Dorset. 5 acre site. 80 touring pitches. 68 hardstandings. 20 seasonal pitches. Caravan pitches. Motorhome pitches. Tent pitches.

Open: 15 Mar-15 Nov **Last departure:** 11.00hrs
Pitches: 🚐 £18-£20 🚙 £18-£20 ▲ £18-£20
Leisure: 🎡 🔍
Facilities: 🏪 ⊙ 🍴 ✳ 🚿 💲 ✈ 📶 🖥 ♻ 🛈
Services: 🔌 🖲 🛢 🗑 🅣 🍴 🚐
Within 3 miles: ⚘ 🎯 🍴 ◎ 👟 🛍 ♻
Notes: Dogs must be kept on leads.
AA Pubs & Restaurants nearby: Blue Ball Inn, SIDMOUTH, EX10 9QL, 01395 514062
The Salty Monk, SIDMOUTH, EX10 9QP, 01395 513174
Dukes, SIDMOUTH, EX10 8AR, 01395 513320
See advert below

PITCHES: 🚐 Caravans 🚙 Motorhomes ▲ Tents 🏠 Glamping-style accommodation **SERVICES:** 🔌 Electric hook up 🖲 Launderette 🍺 Licensed bar 🛢 Calor Gas 🗑 Camping Gaz 🅣 Toilet fluid 🍴 Café/Restaurant 🍟 Fast Food/Takeaway 🔋 Battery charging 🍼 Baby care 🚐 Motorvan service point
ABBREVIATIONS: BH/bank hols – bank holidays Etr – Easter Spring BH – Spring Bank Holiday fr – from hrs – hours m – mile mdnt – midnight
rdbt – roundabout rs – restricted service wk – week wknd – weekend x-rds – cross roads ⊘ No credit or debit cards ⊗ No dogs 👫 Children of all ages accepted

SIDMOUTH *continued*

Salcombe Regis Caravan & Camping Park
►►►►79%

tel: 01395 514303 **Salcombe Regis EX10 0JH**
email: contact@salcombe-regis.co.uk
dir: *Exit A3052 1m E of junct with A375. From opposite direction turn left past Donkey Sanctuary.* **grid ref:** *SY153892*

Set in quiet countryside with glorious views, this spacious park has well-maintained facilities, and a good mix of grass and hardstanding pitches. A footpath runs from the park to the coastal path and the beach. There is a self-catering holiday cottage and static caravans for hire. This is a perfect location for visiting Sidmouth, Lyme Regis and the coastal area of south-east Devon. 16 acre site. 100 touring pitches. 40 hardstandings. 26 seasonal pitches. Caravan pitches. Motorhome pitches. Tent pitches. 10 statics.

Open: Etr-end Oct **Last arrival:** 20.15hrs **Last departure:** 10.30hrs

Pitches: * 🚐 £12.75-£23.65 🚎 £12.75-£23.65 ▲ £12.75-£23.65

Leisure: ⚫

Facilities: 🚿📷⊙☂✳🕐🔃☰📶♻🔆

Services: 🔌📷🔒🖊🚽🚮⬇

Within 3 miles: ♨⚓🚴📷◎🏊🏧🛍⛵

Notes: Quiet at 22.00hrs, no noise from 23.00hrs. Dogs must be kept on leads. Putting green.

AA Pubs & Restaurants nearby: Blue Ball Inn, SIDMOUTH, EX10 9QL, 01395 514062

The Salty Monk, SIDMOUTH, EX10 9QP, 01395 513174

Dukes, SIDMOUTH, EX10 8AR, 01395 513320

SOURTON CROSS   Map 3 SX59

Places to visit

Lydford Gorge, LYDFORD, EX20 4BH, 01822 820320
www.nationaltrust.org.uk/lydford-gorge

Okehampton Castle, OKEHAMPTON, EX20 1JB, 01837 52844
www.english-heritage.org.uk/daysout/properties/okehampton-castle

---

Bundu Camping & Caravan Park
►►►80%

tel: 01837 861747 & 861611 **EX20 4HT**
email: bundu@btconnect.com
dir: *From A30, W of Okehampton towards Launceston, left onto A386 signed Tavistock. 1st left & left again.* **grid ref:** *SX546916*

The welcoming, friendly owners set the tone for this well-maintained site, ideally positioned on the border of the Dartmoor National Park. Along with fine views, well-maintained toilet facilities and level grassy pitches, the Granite Way cycle track from Lydford to Okehampton that runs along the old railway line (part of the Devon Coast to Coast cycle trail) passes the edge of the park. There is a bus stop and cycle hire a few minutes' walk away. Dogs are accepted. 4.5 acre site. 38 touring pitches. 16 hardstandings. Caravan pitches. Motorhome pitches. Tent pitches.

Open: all year **Last arrival:** 22.30hrs **Last departure:** noon

Pitches: * 🚐 £13-£18 🚎 £13-£18 ▲ £8-£12

Facilities: 📷⊙☂✳🕐🏧☰📶♻🔆

Services: 🔌📷🔒🖊🚽🚮

Within 3 miles: ♨⚓🚴📷🏧

Notes: Dogs must be kept on leads.

AA Pubs & Restaurants nearby: The Highwayman Inn, SOURTON, EX20 4HN, 01837 861243

SOUTH MOLTON   Map 3 SS72

Places to visit

Quince Honey Farm, SOUTH MOLTON, EX36 3AZ, 01769 572401
www.quincehoneyfarm.com

Cobbaton Combat Collection, CHITTLEHAMPTON, EX37 9RZ, 01769 540740
www.cobbatoncombat.co.uk

Great for kids: Exmoor Zoological Park, BLACKMOOR GATE, EX31 4SG, 01598 763352 www.exmoorzoo.co.uk

---

Riverside Caravan & Camping Park
►►►►90%

tel: 01769 579269 **Marsh Ln, North Molton Rd EX36 3HQ**
email: relax@exmoorriverside.co.uk **web:** www.exmoorriverside.co.uk
dir: *M5 junct 27, A361 towards Barnstaple. Site signed 1m before South Molton on right.* **grid ref:** *SS723274*

A family-run park, set alongside the River Mole, where supervised children can play, and fishing is available. This is an ideal base for exploring Exmoor, as well as north Devon's golden beaches. There's on-site entertainment during the school holidays and on Bank Holidays. The site has an award for the excellence of the toilets. The local bus stops at park entrance. 70 acre site. 54 touring pitches. 54 hardstandings. Caravan pitches. Motorhome pitches. Tent pitches. 3 statics.

Open: all year **Last arrival:** 22.00hrs **Last departure:** 11.00hrs

Pitches: 🚐 £18-£30 🚎 £18-£30 ▲ £10-£28

Leisure: ⚫🎣🎵

Facilities: 📷⊙☂✳🕐🏧☰📶💻♻🔆

Services: 🔌📷🍴🔒🖊🚽🍽🚮🛒⬇

Within 3 miles: ♨🚴📷🏊🏧🛍⛵

Notes: Dogs must be kept on leads.

STARCROSS

See Dawlish

STOKE GABRIEL
Map 3 SX85

Places to visit

Berry Pomeroy Castle, TOTNES, TQ9 6NJ, 01803 866618
www.english-heritage.org.uk/daysout/properties/berry-pomeroy-castle

Totnes Museum, TOTNES, TQ9 5RU, 01803 863821
www.devonmuseums.net/totnes

Great for kids: Paignton Zoo Environmental Park, PAIGNTON, TQ4 7EU, 0844 474 2222 www.paigntonzoo.org.uk

Higher Well Farm Holiday Park
►►►84%

tel: 01803 782289 **Waddeton Rd TQ9 6RN**
email: higherwell@talk21.com
dir: *From Exeter A380 to Torbay, turn right onto A385 for Totnes, in 0.5m left for Stoke Gabriel, follow signs.* **grid ref:** *SX857577*

Set on a quiet farm yet only four miles from Paignton, this rural holiday park is on the outskirts of the picturesque village of Stoke Gabriel. A toilet block, with some en suite facilities, is an excellent amenity, and tourers are housed in an open field with very good views. 10 acre site. 80 touring pitches. 3 hardstandings. Caravan pitches. Motorhome pitches. Tent pitches. 19 statics.

Open: 28 Mar-1 Nov **Last arrival:** 22.00hrs **Last departure:** 10.00hrs

Pitches: 🚐 £12.50-£20 🚐 £12.50-£20 ▲ £12.50-£20

Facilities: 🅿️⊙🄿✳️🔥🟢🚿🔋♻️❶

Services: 🔌🔲🔒🧺🚽🚿⚡

Within 3 miles: 🔥🔒🚿🔲

Notes: No commercial vehicles, pets must not be left unattended in caravans, motorhomes or tents. Dogs must be kept on leads.

AA Pubs & Restaurants nearby: The Durant Arms, TOTNES, TQ9 7UP, 01803 732240

Steam Packet Inn, TOTNES, TQ9 5EW, 01803 863880

The White Hart Bar & Restaurant, TOTNES, TQ9 6EL, 01803 847111

Broadleigh Farm Park
►►►80%

tel: 01803 782110 **Coombe House Ln, Aish TQ9 6PU**
email: enquiries@broadleighfarm.co.uk
dir: *From Exeter on A38 then A380 towards Torbay. Right onto A385 for Totnes. In 0.5m right at Whitehill Country Park. Site approx 0.75m on left.* **grid ref:** *SX851587*

Set in a very rural location on a working farm bordering Paignton and Stoke Gabriel. The large sloping field with a timber-clad toilet block in the centre is sheltered and peaceful, surrounded by rolling countryside but handy for the beaches. There is also an excellent rally field with good toilets and showers. 7 acre site. 80 touring pitches. Caravan pitches. Motorhome pitches. Tent pitches.

Open: Mar-Oct **Last arrival:** 21.00hrs **Last departure:** 11.30hrs

Pitches: * 🚐 £12-£20.50 🚐 £12-£20.50 ▲ £12-£20.50

Facilities: 🅿️⊙🄿✳️🔥🚿⚡♻️❶

Services: 🔌🔲 📠🚿

Within 3 miles: 🔥🔒🚿♻️🔲🔲

Notes: Dogs must be kept on leads. Fish & chip van every Sat in high season.

AA Pubs & Restaurants nearby: Rumour, TOTNES, TQ9 5RY, 01803 864682

Royal Seven Stars Hotel, TOTNES, TQ9 5DD, 01803 862125

TAVISTOCK
Map 3 SX47

Places to visit

Morwellham Quay, MORWELLHAM, PL19 8JL, 01822 832766
www.morwellham-quay.co.uk

PREMIER PARK

Woodovis Park
►►►►►87%

tel: 01822 832968 **Gulworthy PL19 8NY**
email: info@woodovis.com
dir: *A390 from Tavistock signed Callington & Gunnislake. At hill top right at rdbt signed Lamerton & Chipshop. Site 1m on left.* **grid ref:** *SX431745*

A well-kept park in a remote woodland setting on the edge of the Tamar Valley. A peacefully located park at the end of a private, half-mile, tree-lined drive, it offers superb on-site facilities and high levels of customer care from hands-on owners. The toilets are immaculate and well maintained, plus there is an indoor swimming pool, sauna and a good information/games room, all creating a friendly atmosphere. 14.5 acre site. 50 touring pitches. 33 hardstandings. 8 seasonal pitches. Caravan pitches. Motorhome pitches. Tent pitches. 35 statics. 4 wooden pods.

Open: 22 Mar-1 Nov **Last arrival:** 20.00hrs **Last departure:** 11.00hrs

Pitches: * 🚐 £18-£40 🚐 £18-£40 ▲ £18-£40 🏠

Leisure: 🏊🎢🟢🔍

Facilities: 🚿🅿️⊙🄿✳️🔥🚿🔋📶🖥️♻️❶

Services: 🔌🔲🔒🧺🚽🚿🔌⚡

Within 3 miles: 🔥🔒🚿♻️🔲🔲↻

Notes: No open fires. Dogs must be kept on leads. Archery, water-walking, physiotherm infra-red therapy cabin, petanque court, outdoor table tennis, hog roast takeaway, story teller in school holidays.

AA Pubs & Restaurants nearby: The Cornish Arms, TAVISTOCK, PL19 8AN, 01822 612145

Who has won England Campsite of the Year?
See page 14

PITCHES: 🚐 Caravans 🚐 Motorhomes ▲ Tents 🏠 Glamping-style accommodation **SERVICES:** 🔌 Electric hook up 🔲 Launderette 🍺 Licensed bar 🔥 Calor Gas 🔥 Camping Gaz 🔲 Toilet fluid 🍽️ Café/Restaurant 📠 Fast Food/Takeaway 🔋 Battery charging 🚿 Baby care ⚡ Motorvan service point
ABBREVIATIONS: BH/bank hols – bank holidays Etr – Easter Spring BH – Spring Bank Holiday fr – from hrs – hours m – mile mdnt – midnight rdbt – roundabout rs – restricted service wk – week wknd – weekend x-rds – cross roads 🚫 No credit or debit cards 🚫 No dogs 👫 Children of all ages accepted

TAVISTOCK *continued*

Langstone Manor Camping & Caravan Park
►►►►► 80%

tel: 01822 613371 **Moortown PL19 9JZ**
email: jane@langstone-manor.co.uk **web:** www.langstone-manor.co.uk
dir: *Take B3357 from Tavistock to Princetown. Approx 1.5m turn right at x-rds, follow signs. Over bridge, cattle grid, up hill, left at sign, left again to park.*
grid ref: *SX524738*

A secluded and very peaceful site set in the well-maintained grounds of a manor house in Dartmoor National Park. Many attractive mature trees provide screening within the park, yet the west-facing terraced pitches on the main park enjoy the superb summer sunsets. There are excellent toilet facilities, a popular lounge bar with an excellent menu of reasonably priced evening meals. Plenty of activities and places of interest can be found within the surrounding moorland. Dogs are accepted. 6.5 acre site. 40 touring pitches. 10 hardstandings. 4 seasonal pitches. Caravan pitches. Motorhome pitches. Tent pitches. 25 statics. 7 wooden pods.

Open: 15 Mar-15 Nov (rs 15 Mar-15 Nov bar & restaurant closed weekdays (excl BH & school hols)) **Last arrival:** 21.00hrs **Last departure:** 11.00hrs
Pitches: 🚐 🚲 Å 🏠
Leisure: 🅰 🔍
Facilities: 🛁 🖙 ⊙ 🅿 ✳ ♿ 🕒 🚻 📶 ♻ 🛈
Services: 🔌 🗑 ⛽ ⊘ Ⓣ 🍴 🛒 💷 🖕
Within 3 miles: 🎣 🔦 ◎ ⛵ 🛒 🔺 ∪

Notes: Dogs must be kept on leads. Baguettes, croissants etc available.
AA Pubs & Restaurants nearby: The Cornish Arms, TAVISTOCK, PL19 8AN, 01822 612145

Harford Bridge Holiday Park
►►►► 80%

tel: 01822 810349 & 07773 251457 **Peter Tavy PL19 9LS**
email: stay@harfordbridge.co.uk **web:** www.harfordbridge.co.uk
dir: *2m N of Tavistock, off A386 Okehampton Rd, take Peter Tavy turn, entrance 200yds on right.* **grid ref:** *SX504767*

This beautiful spacious park is set beside the River Tavy in the Dartmoor National Park. Pitches are located beside the river and around the copses, and the park is very well equipped for holidaymakers. An adventure playground and games room keep children entertained, and there is fly-fishing and a free tennis court. A lovely, authentic shepherd's hut complete with fridge and woodburner is available to let. 16 acre site. 125 touring pitches. 5 hardstandings. 5 seasonal pitches. Caravan pitches. Motorhome pitches. Tent pitches. 80 statics.

Open: all year (rs 15 Nov-14 Mar statics only) **Last arrival:** 21.00hrs **Last departure:** noon
Pitches: * 🚐 £15.40-£23.40 🚲 £15.40-£23.40 Å £15.40-£23.40 🏠
Leisure: 🅰 🏊 ⊙ 🔍 🖵
Facilities: 🖙 ⊙ 🅿 ✳ ♿ 🕒 🗑 🚻 🔺 📶 🖥 ♻ 🛈
Services: 🔌 🗑 ⛽ ⊘ Ⓣ 🛒 🖕
Within 3 miles: 🎣 🎣 🔦 ⛵ 🛒 🔺 ∪

Notes: Expedition groups & rallies welcome by prior arrangement. Dogs must be kept on leads. Baguettes, croissants, snacks, sweets, cold drinks, ices & grocery basics available.
AA Pubs & Restaurants nearby: Peter Tavy Inn, TAVISTOCK, PL19 9NN, 01822 810348

TEDBURN ST MARY
Map 3 SX89

Places to visit

Finch Foundry, STICKLEPATH, EX20 2NW, 01837 840046
www.nationaltrust.org.uk

Castle Drogo, DREWSTEIGNTON, EX6 6PB, 01647 433306
www.nationaltrust.org.uk/castle-drogo

Springfield Holiday Park
►►►► 82%

tel: 01647 24242 **EX6 6EW**
email: enquiries@springfieldholidaypark.co.uk
dir: *M5 junct 31, A30 towards Okehampton, exit at junct, signed to Cheriton Bishop. Follow brown tourist signs to site. NB for Sat Nav use EX6 6JN.* **grid ref:** *SX788935*

Set in a quiet rural location with countryside views, this park continues to be upgraded to a smart standard. It has the advantage of being close to Dartmoor National Park, with village pubs and stores less than a mile away. There is a very inviting heated outdoor swimming pool. 9 acre site. 48 touring pitches. 38 hardstandings. 25 seasonal pitches. Caravan pitches. Motorhome pitches. Tent pitches. 49 statics.

Open: 15 Mar-15 Nov **Last arrival:** 22.00hrs **Last departure:** noon

Pitches: 🚐 £15-£20 🚛 £15-£25 ▲ £10-£20

Leisure: 🏊 🎱 🎣

Facilities: 🚿 ☉ ❄ 🛒 🚼 WiFi 💻 ♻ ⓘ

Services: 🔌 🧺 🪪 🛢 ⌀ ↯

Within 3 miles: ↕ 🖉 🛒 🛒

Notes: Dogs must be kept on leads.

AA Pubs & Restaurants nearby: The Old Inn, DREWSTEIGNTON, EX6 6QR, 01647 281276

TIVERTON

See East Worlington

TORQUAY
Map 3 SX96

See also Newton Abbot

Places to visit

Torre Abbey, TORQUAY, TQ2 5JE, 01803 293593 www.torre-abbey.org.uk

'Bygones', TORQUAY, TQ1 4PR, 01803 326108 www.bygones.co.uk

Great for kids: Living Coasts, TORQUAY, TQ1 2BG, 01803 202470
www.livingcoasts.org.uk

Widdicombe Farm Touring Park
►►►► 85%

tel: 01803 558325 **Marldon TQ3 1ST**
email: info@widdicombefarm.co.uk **web:** www.widdicombefarm.co.uk
dir: *On A380, midway between Torquay & Paignton ring road.* **grid ref:** *SX876643*

A friendly family-run park on a working farm with good quality facilities, extensive views and easy access as there are no narrow roads. The level pitches are terraced to take advantage of the views towards the coast and Dartmoor. This is the only adult touring park within Torquay, and is also handy for Paignton and Brixham. There's a bus service from the park to the local shopping centre and Torquay's harbour. It has a small shop, a restaurant and a bar with entertainment from Easter to the end of September. Club WiFi is available throughout the park and The Nippy Chippy van calls regularly. 8 acre site. 180 touring pitches. 180 hardstandings. 20 seasonal pitches. Caravan pitches. Motorhome pitches. Tent pitches. 3 statics.

Open: mid Mar-end Oct **Last arrival:** 20.00hrs **Last departure:** 11.00hrs

Pitches: 🚐 🚛 ▲

Leisure: 🎵

Facilities: 🚿 ☉ 🅿 ❄ ♿ 🛒 🚼 WiFi ♻ ⓘ

Services: 🔌 🧺 🍴 🪪 ⌀ 🅣 🍽 🔋 🍔 ↯

Within 3 miles: ↕ ✈ 🚲 🖉 ◎ 🛶 🛒 🛒

Notes: Adults only. No groups. Most dog breeds accepted. Dogs must be kept on leads.

AA Pubs & Restaurants nearby: The Church House Inn, MARLDON, TQ3 1SL, 01803 558279

The Cary Arms, TORQUAY, TQ1 3LX, 01803 327110

The Elephant Restaurant and Brasserie, TORQUAY, TQ1 2BH, 01803 200044

PITCHES: 🚐 Caravans 🚛 Motorhomes ▲ Tents 🏠 Glamping-style accommodation **SERVICES:** 🔌 Electric hook up 🧺 Launderette 🍷 Licensed bar
🪪 Calor Gas ⌀ Camping Gaz 🅣 Toilet fluid 🍴 Café/Restaurant 🍔 Fast Food/Takeaway 🔋 Battery charging 🚼 Baby care ↯ Motorvan service point
ABBREVIATIONS: BH/bank hols – bank holidays Etr – Easter Spring BH – Spring Bank Holiday fr – from hrs – hours m – mile mdnt – midnight
rdbt – roundabout rs – restricted service wk – week wknd – weekend x-rds – cross roads 🚫 No credit or debit cards 🚫 No dogs 👫 Children of all ages accepted

WOODBURY SALTERTON
Map 3 SY08

Places to visit

The World of Country Life, EXMOUTH, EX8 5BU, 01395 274533
www.worldofcountrylife.co.uk

A la Ronde, EXMOUTH, EX8 5BD, 01395 265514
www.nationaltrust.org.uk/alaronde

Great for kids: Devon's Crealy Great Adventure Park, CLYST ST MARY, EX5 1DR,
01395 233200 www.crealy.co.uk

Browns Farm Caravan Park
► ► ► 90%

tel: 01395 232895 **Browns Farm EX5 1PS**
dir: *M5 junct 30, A3052. In 3.7m right at White Horse Inn signed Woodbury Salterton, left at fork. At t-junct right into Village Rd. Park on left.* **grid ref:** *SY016885*

A small farm park adjoining a 14th-century thatched farmhouse, and located in a quiet village. Pitches back onto hedgerows, and the friendly owners keep the excellent facilities very clean. The tourist information and games room, with table tennis, chess etc, is housed in a purpose-built building. The park is just a mile from the historic heathland of Woodbury Common with its superb views. The local bus to Exeter and Exmouth stops at site entrance. 2.5 acre site. 29 touring pitches. 24 hardstandings. Caravan pitches. Motorhome pitches. Tent pitches.

Open: all year **Last departure:** 11.00hrs
Pitches: * 🚐 £12-£15 🚌 £12-£16 ▲ £13-£15
Leisure: 🎱 ⬜
Facilities: 🚿 ☉ 🅿 ✳ ⛧ 🕐 🖊
Services: 🔌 🔋 🛢 🗑 🚐
Within 3 miles: ♨ 🖊 🏪 ∪

Notes: 🚫 No ground sheets in awnings, no music. Dogs must be kept on leads. Hardstandings for winter period, caravan storage.

AA Pubs & Restaurants nearby: The Digger's Rest, WOODBURY SALTERTON, EX5 1PQ, 01395 232375

The Golden Lion Inn, TIPTON ST JOHN, EX10 0AA, 01404 812881

Find out about staying at a Holiday Centre in our feature on page 26

WOOLACOMBE
Map 3 SS44

See also Mortehoe

Twitchen House Holiday Village
HOLIDAY CENTRE 85%

tel: 0844 7700 365 **Mortehoe Station Rd, Mortehoe EX34 7ES**
email: goodtimes@woolacombe.com **web:** www.woolacombe.co.uk
dir: *M5 junct 27, A361 to Ilfracombe. From Mullacott Cross rdbt take B3343 (Woolacombe road) to Turnpike Cross junct. Take right fork, site 1.5m on left.* **grid ref:** *SS465447*

A very attractive, seaside park with excellent leisure facilities, all-weather activities and entertainment; visitors can use the amenities at all three of the group's holiday parks and a bus service connects them all with the beach. Continuing investment has resulted in a show room, indoor soft play area, a 2D and 3D cinema, and craft centre. The touring area features many fully serviced pitches and 80 that are available for tents; they have either sea views or a woodland countryside outlook. 45 acre site. 334 touring pitches. 110 hardstandings. Caravan pitches. Motorhome pitches. Tent pitches. 253 statics.

Open: Mar-Nov (rs Mar-mid May & mid Sep-Nov outdoor pool closed) **Last arrival:** mdnt
Last departure: 10.00hrs
Pitches: 🚐 🚌 ▲
Leisure: 🏊 🏖 🎢 ⬇ 🎱 ⬜ 🎵
Facilities: 🚿 ☉ 🅿 ✳ ⛧ 🕐 🛢 🍴 🍽 📶 🖥 ♻
Services: 🔌 🔋 🔧 🗑 📞 🍴 🚐 🛒 🚽
Within 3 miles: ♨ 🚣 🍴 🖊 ◎ ⛳ 🏪 ∪

Notes: Dogs must be kept on leads. Table tennis, sauna, swimming & surfing lessons, climbing wall, bungee trampoline.

AA Pubs & Restaurants nearby: Watersmeet Hotel, WOOLACOMBE, EX34 7EB, 01271 870333

See advert opposite & inside front cover

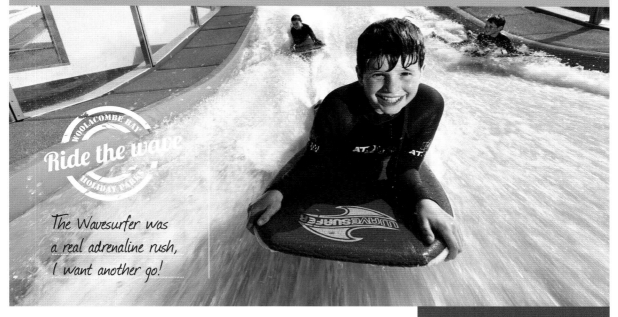

Escape to North Devon

Right next to Woolacombe's three miles of golden sandy beach

Ride the wave

The Wavesurfer was a real adrenaline rush, I want another go!

What we've got to offer...

- Sea view touring & super pitches
- 400 all weather pitches
- 16 amp electric hookups
- Modern amenity blocks

- Level pitches with easy access
- 4 award winning Holiday Parks
- Outstanding leisure facilities
- Activities for all ages

Pitches from just

£6 per night

Call **0844 7700 365**
or visit **woolacombe.com/aac**

WOOLACOMBE BAY
HOLIDAY PARKS

We're here

WOOLACOMBE *continued*

Woolacombe Bay Holiday Village
HOLIDAY CENTRE 84%

tel: 0844 7700 365 **Sandy Ln EX34 7AH**
email: goodtimes@woolacombe.com **web:** www.woolacombe.co.uk
dir: *M5 junct 27, A361 to Ilfracombe. At Mullacott rdbt take 1st exit to Woolacombe.*
Follow Mortehoe signs. **grid ref:** *SS465442*

There's a well-developed touring section at this seaside holiday complex that offers a full entertainment and leisure programme. There are super pitches with TV aerial, water, drainage, electricity and a night light. The park has excellent amenities including a steam room and sauna, and an outdoor sports area with a circular Ocean Bar. For a small charge, a bus takes holidaymakers to the other Woolacombe Bay holiday centres where they can take part in any of the many activities offered, and there is also a bus to the beach. The sports complex features a surfing simulator, high ropes course and a climbing wall. 8.5 acre site. 171 touring pitches. Motorhome pitches. Tent pitches. 237 statics.

Open: May-Sep (rs Etr) **Last arrival:** mdnt **Last departure:** 10.00hrs

Pitches: ⊡ Å

Leisure: ≋ ⚌ ⵏ ⋀ ⤋ ⚲ ⊕ ⚡ ♫ Spa ⚘

Facilities: ↿ ⊙ ⌘ ✳ ⅏ ⓢ ⓢ 冊 ⌷ ▆ ♻

Services: ⊕⊡ ⊞⊘⊤⏚⍓ ⚒

Within 3 miles: ⅃ ⚐ ⺙ ⌀ ◎ ⚘ ⓢ ⓢ ∪

Notes: 21ft motorhome maximum, site not ideal for guests with mobility problems due to hills & stairs. Dogs must be kept on leads. Crazy golf, bungee trampoline.

AA Pubs & Restaurants nearby: Watersmeet Hotel, WOOLACOMBE, EX34 7EB, 01271 870333

See advert on page 183 & inside front cover

Golden Coast Holiday Village
HOLIDAY CENTRE 80%

tel: 0844 7700 365 **Station Rd EX34 7HW**
email: goodtimes@woolacombe.com **web:** www.woolacombe.co.uk
dir: *M5 junct 27, A361 to Ilfracombe. At Mullacott rdbt 1st exit to Woolacombe.*
grid ref: *SS482436*

A seaside holiday village, set beside a three mile sandy beach, that offers excellent leisure facilities together with the amenities available at the other Woolacombe Bay holiday parks. There is a neat touring area with a unisex toilet block that has under-floor heating and individual cubicles - all maintained to a high standard; the super pitches have water, drainage, electricity, TV aerial and night light. The sports complex features ten-pin bowling, high ropes course, climbing wall, surfing simulator and adventure golf and much more; there are over 40 free activities available to try. 10 acre site. 93 touring pitches. 87 hardstandings. Caravan pitches. Motorhome pitches. Tent pitches. 324 statics.

Open: Feb-Nov (rs mid Sep-May outdoor pool closed) **Last arrival:** mdnt
Last departure: 10.00hrs

Pitches: ⊕ ⊡ Å

Leisure: ≋ ⚌ ⋀ ⤋ ⚲ ⊕ ⚡ ▢ ♫

Facilities: ↿ ⊙ ⌘ ✳ ⅏ ⓢ ⓢ 冊 ⌷ ᵂᴵᶠᴵ ▆ ♻

Services: ⊕⊡ ⊞⊘⊤⍓ ⚒ ⚒ ⌄

Within 3 miles: ⅃ ⚐ ⺙ ⌀ ◎ ⚘ ⓢ ⓢ ∪

Notes: No pets on touring pitches. Sauna, solarium, fishing, snooker, cinema, bungee trampoline, swimming & surfing lessons.

AA Pubs & Restaurants nearby: Watersmeet Hotel, WOOLACOMBE, EX34 7EB, 01271 870333

See advert on page 183 & inside front cover

Easewell Farm Holiday Village
▶▶▶84%

tel: 0844 7700 365 **Mortehoe Station Rd, Mortehoe EX34 7EH**
email: goodtimes@woolacombe.com **web:** www.woolacombe.co.uk
dir: *M5 junct 27, A361 to Ilfracombe. At Mullacott rdbt 1st exit to Woolacombe. Follow Mortehoe signs.* **grid ref:** *SS465455*

A peaceful cliff-top park with superb views that offers full facility pitches for caravans and motorhomes. The shower rooms have under-floor heating and individual cubicles, plus there's a sauna, steam room, launderette, washing up area and chemical disposal facilities. The sports complex has a surfing simulator, high ropes course and climbing wall; the 40 activities available include indoor bowling, snooker and a 9-hole golf course. All the facilities at the three other nearby holiday centres within this group are open to everyone. 17 acre site. 318 touring pitches. 186 hardstandings. Caravan pitches. Motorhome pitches. Tent pitches. 1 static.

Open: Mar-Nov (rs Etr) **Last arrival:** 22.00hrs **Last departure:** 10.00hrs

Pitches: ⊞ ⊞ Å

Leisure: ☞ ⋔ ⬇ ◕ ♫

Facilities: ⋔ ☉ ☞ ✳ ♿ ⓢ 🗑 ☶ 🛒 ♻

Services: ⊞ ⓢ ⅊ ∅ T ⑪ 🔋 🚬

Within 3 miles: ⚓ ⅊ 🎣 ◎ ⬇ ⓢ ⓢ ∪

Notes: Dogs must be kept on leads.

AA Pubs & Restaurants nearby: Watersmeet Hotel, WOOLACOMBE, EX34 7EB, 01271 870333

See advert on page 183 & inside front cover

Europa Park
▶▶▶77%

tel: 01271 871425 **Beach Rd EX34 7AN**
email: europaparkwoolacombe@yahoo.co.uk **web:** www.europapark.co.uk
dir: *M5 junct 27, A361 through Barnstaple to Mullacott Cross. Left onto B3343 signed Woolacombe. Site on right at Spa shop/garage.* **grid ref:** *SS475435*

A very lively family-run site handy for the beach at Woolacombe, and catering well for surfers but maybe not suitable for a quieter type of stay (please make sure the site is suitable for you before making your booking). Set in a stunning location high above the bay, it provides a wide range of accommodation including surf cabins, surf pods, a yurt and generous touring pitches. Visitors can enjoy the indoor pool and sauna, games room, restaurant/café/bar and clubhouse. 16 acre site. 200 touring pitches. 20 hardstandings. Caravan pitches. Motorhome pitches. Tent pitches. 22 statics. 1 yurt.

Open: all year **Last arrival:** 23.00hrs **Last departure:** 10.00hrs

Pitches: ⊞ ⊞ Å ⋔

Leisure: ☞ ⋔ ♦ ▭

Facilities: ⋔ ☉ ✳ ⓢ ⓢ

Services: ⊞ ⓢ ⅊ ∅ T ⑪ 🔋 🚬 ⅄

Within 3 miles: ⚓ ⅊ ◎ ⬇ ⓢ ⓢ ∪

Notes: Beer deck, off licence, pub, big-screen TV.

AA Pubs & Restaurants nearby: Watersmeet Hotel, WOOLACOMBE, EX34 7EB, 01271 870333

11 The Quay, ILFRACOMBE, EX34 9EQ, 01271 868090

The Williams Arms, BRAUNTON, EX33 2DE, 01271 812360

Dorset

Dorset means rugged varied coastlines and high chalk downlands with more than a hint of Thomas Hardy, its most famous son. Squeezed in among the cliffs and set amid some of Britain's most beautiful scenery is a chain of picturesque villages and seaside towns.

Along the coast you'll find the Lulworth Ranges, which run from Kimmeridge Bay in the east to Lulworth Cove in the west. Walking is the most obvious and rewarding recreational activity here, but the British Army firing ranges mean that access to this glorious landscape is restricted. This is Britain's Jurassic Coast, a UNESCO World Heritage Site and Area of Outstanding Natural Beauty, noted for its layers of shale and numerous fossils embedded in the rock. Among the best-known natural landmarks on this stretch of the Dorset coast is Durdle Door, a rocky arch that has been shaped and sculpted to perfection by the elements. The whole area has the unmistakable stamp of prehistory. The landscape and coastal views may be spectacular but the up-and-down nature of the walking here is often physically demanding.

This designated coastline stretches from Swanage and the Isle of Purbeck to east Devon, offering miles of breathtaking scenery. Beyond the seaside town of Weymouth is Chesil Beach, a long shingle reef running for 10 miles between Portland and Abbotsbury. The beach is covered by a vast wall of shingle left by centuries of dramatic weather-induced activity along the Devon and Dorset coast. Beyond Bridport and West Bay, where the hugely successful TV series *Broadchurch* is filmed, lies quaint Lyme Regis, with its sturdy breakwater, known as The Cobb. It's the sort of place where Georgian houses and pretty cottages jostle with historic pubs and independently run shops. With its blend of architectural styles and old world charm, Lyme Regis looks very much like a film set. Perhaps that is why film producers chose this setting as a location for the making of *The French Lieutenant's Woman* in 1981. Jeremy Irons and Meryl Streep starred in the film, based on the novel by John Fowles.

Away from Dorset's magical coastline lies a landscape with a very different character and atmosphere, but one that is no less appealing. Here, winding, hedge-lined country lanes lead beneath lush, green hilltops to snug, sleepy villages hidden from view and the wider world. The main roads lead to the country towns of Sherborne, Blandford Forum, Wareham and Shaftesbury and in September these routes fill with even more traffic as the county prepares to host the annual Dorset Steam Fair. This famous event draws many visitors who come to admire the various vintage and classic vehicles on display. The same month is also set aside for the two-day County Show, an eagerly anticipated annual fixture.

Inland there are further links with literature. Dorset is justifiably proud of the achievements of Thomas Hardy, and much of the county is immortalized in his writing. He was born at Higher Bockhampton, near Dorchester, and this quaint old cob-and-thatch cottage was where the writer lived until he was 34. As a child, Hardy spent much of his time here reading and writing poems about the countryside. The cottage contains the desk where he wrote *Far from the Madding Crowd*. In later years Hardy lived at Max Gate on the edge of Dorchester and here he was visited by many distinguished writers of the day, including Rudyard Kipling and Virginia Woolf. Even the Prince of Wales called on him one day in 1923. Both homes are now in the care of the National Trust.

One of Thomas Hardy's great friends was T. E. (Thomas Edward) Lawrence, better known as Lawrence of Arabia, who lived nearby in a modest cottage known as Clouds Hill. The cottage, also managed by the National Trust, was Lawrence's secluded retreat from the world, where he could read and play music.

◁ Durdle Door

DORSET

ALDERHOLT
Map 5 SU11

Places to visit

Breamore House & Countryside Museum, BREAMORE, SP6 2DF, 01725 512468
www.breamorehouse.com

Great for kids: Rockbourne Roman Villa, ROCKBOURNE, SP6 3PG, 01725 518541
www.hants.gov.uk/rockbourne-roman-villa

PREMIER PARK

Hill Cottage Farm Camping and Caravan Park
►►►►►80%

tel: 01425 650513 & 07714 648690 **Sandleheath Rd SP6 3EG**
email: hillcottagefarmcaravansite@supanet.com
dir: *Take B3078 W of Fordingbridge. Exit at Alderholt, site 0.25m on left after railway bridge.* **grid ref:** *SU119133*

Set within extensive grounds, this rural and beautifully landscaped park is under new ownership and offers fully serviced pitches set in individual hardstanding bays with mature dividing hedges that give adequate pitch privacy. The modern toilet block is kept immaculately clean, and there's a good range of leisure facilities. In high season there is an area available for tents. Rallies are very welcome. A function room with skittle alley is available, and there is a fully-equipped shepherd's hut for hire. 40 acre site. 95 touring pitches. 35 hardstandings. Caravan pitches. Motorhome pitches. Tent pitches.

Open: Mar-Oct **Last arrival:** 20.00hrs **Last departure:** 11.00hrs

Pitches: * 🚐 £18-£27 🚌 £18-£27 ▲ £14-£31 🏠

Leisure: 🎢 🔍

Facilities: 🛁⊙📮✳👶🕐🏪🛒🚻🚾 💻 ♻ ❶

Services: 🚐🗑 🛢🧺🛗

Within 3 miles: 🏌🎣 🛶🛒🗑 ⛹

Notes: No noise after 22.30hrs. Dogs must be kept on leads.

AA Pubs & Restaurants nearby: The Augustus John, FORDINGBRIDGE, SP6 1DG, 01425 652098

This symbol indicates that a site offers glamping-style accommodation

BERE REGIS
Map 4 SY89

Places to visit

Kingston Lacy, WIMBORNE, BH21 4EA, 01202 883402 (Mon-Fri)
www.nationaltrust.org.uk/kingston-lacy

Priest's House Museum and Garden, WIMBORNE, BH21 1HR, 01202 882533
www.priest-house.co.uk

Great for kids: Monkey World-Ape Rescue Centre, WOOL, BH20 6HH,
01929 462537 www.monkeyworld.org

Rowlands Wait Touring Park
►►►86%

tel: 01929 472727 **Rye Hill BH20 7LP**
email: enquiries@rowlandswait.co.uk **web:** www.rowlandswait.co.uk
dir: *From A35 or A31 to Bere Regis, follow Bovington Tank Museum signs. 0.75m, at top of Rye Hill turn right. 200yds to site.* **grid ref:** *SY842933*

This park lies in a really attractive setting overlooking Bere Regis and the Dorset countryside, and is set amongst undulating areas of trees and shrubs. It is located within a few miles of The Tank Museum (Bovingdon Camp) with its mock battles, and is also very convenient for visiting the Dorchester, Poole and Swanage areas. The toilet facilities include two family rooms. The park now has four new fully-equipped safari tents (Glampotel canvas cottages) for hire complete with their own shower, toilet and washbasin, as well as a wood-burning stove. 8 acre site. 71 touring pitches. 2 hardstandings. 23 seasonal pitches. Caravan pitches. Motorhome pitches. Tent pitches.

Open: mid Mar-Oct (winter by arrangement) (rs Nov-Feb own facilities required)
Last arrival: 21.00hrs **Last departure:** noon

Pitches: * 🚐 £17-£22.50 🚌 £17-£22.50 ▲ £15-£19 🏠

Leisure: 🎢 🔍

Facilities: 🛁⊙📮✳👶🏪🚻🚾 💻 ♻ ❶

Services: 🚐🗑 🛢🧺🖳🛒🛗

Within 3 miles: 🏌🎣 ◎🛒🗑 ⛹

Notes: No open fires. Dogs must be kept on leads.

AA Pubs & Restaurants nearby: Botany Bay Inne, WINTERBORNE ZELSTON, DT11 9ET, 01929 459227

BLANDFORD FORUM   Map 4 ST80

Places to visit

Kingston Lacy, WIMBORNE, BH21 4EA, 01202 883402 (Mon-Fri)
www.nationaltrust.org.uk/kingston-lacy

Old Wardour Castle, TISBURY, SP3 6RR, 01747 870487
www.english-heritage.org.uk/daysout/properties/old-wardour-castle

Great for kids: Monkey World-Ape Rescue Centre, WOOL, BH20 6HH,
01929 462537 www.monkeyworld.org

The Inside Park
► ► ► ► 81%

tel: 01258 453719 **Down House Estate DT11 9AD**
email: mail@theinsidepark.co.uk
dir: *From Blandford Forum follow Winterborne Stickland signs. Site in 1.5m.*
grid ref: *ST869046*

An attractive, well-sheltered and quiet park, half a mile along a country lane in a
wooded valley. The spacious pitches are divided by mature trees and shrubs, and
the amenities are housed in an 18th-century coach house and stables. There are
some lovely woodland walks within the park, an excellent fenced play area for
children and a dog-free area. This makes the perfect base for those visiting the
Blandford Steam Fair in August. 12 acre site. 125 touring pitches. Caravan pitches.
Motorhome pitches. Tent pitches.

Open: Etr-Oct **Last arrival:** 22.00hrs **Last departure:** noon

Pitches: * 🚐 £17.50-£25.45 🚚 £17.50-£25.45 ⛺ £17.50-£25.45

Leisure: 🅰 🔍

Facilities: 🏠☉🅿✳&🕒ⓢ🚻 WiFi ♻ 🄋

Services: 🔌🅖🛢🖉Ⓣ🔋

Within 3 miles: ↨🏌🅗🅖∪

Notes: Dogs must be kept on leads. Kennels (charges apply).

AA Pubs & Restaurants nearby: The Anvil Inn, BLANDFORD FORUM, DT11 8UQ,
01258 453431

BRIDPORT

Places to visit

Dorset County Museum, DORCHESTER, DT1 1XA, 01305 262735
www.dorsetcountymuseum.org

Great for kids: Abbotsbury Swannery, ABBOTSBURY, DT3 4JG, 01305 871858
www.abbotsbury-tourism.co.uk

BRIDPORT   Map 4 SY49

Freshwater Beach Holiday Park
HOLIDAY CENTRE 91%

tel: 01308 897317 **Burton Bradstock DT6 4PT**
email: office@freshwaterbeach.co.uk **web:** www.freshwaterbeach.co.uk
dir: *Take B3157 from Bridport towards Burton Bradstock. Site 1.5m from Crown rdbt on
right.* **grid ref:** *SY493892*

A family holiday centre sheltered by a sand bank and enjoying its own private
beach. The park offers a wide variety of leisure and entertainment programmes for
all the family, plus the Jurassic Fun Centre with indoor pool, gym, 6-lane bowling
alley, restaurant and bar is excellent. The park is well placed at one end of the
Weymouth/Bridport coast with spectacular views of Chesil Beach. There are three
immaculate toilet blocks with excellent private rooms. 40 acre site. 500 touring
pitches. 25 hardstandings. Caravan pitches. Motorhome pitches. Tent pitches. 250
statics.

Open: mid Mar-mid Nov **Last arrival:** 22.00hrs **Last departure:** 10.00hrs

Pitches: * 🚐 £16-£44 🚚 £16-£44 ⛺ £16-£44

Leisure: 🏊🏖✝🅰👋☉🔍🎵 Spa **Facilities:** 🏠☉🅿✳&🕒ⓢ🚻 WiFi 🖥 🄋

Services: 🔌🅖🍺🛢🖉Ⓣ🍴🔋🚲 **Within 3 miles:** ↨🍴🅗🏌◎🅖🅖

Notes: Families & couples only. Dogs must be kept on leads. Large TV, kids' club in high
season & BHs.

AA Pubs & Restaurants nearby: The Shave Cross Inn, BRIDPORT, DT6 6HW, 01308 868358

Riverside Restaurant, BRIDPORT, DT6 4EZ, 01308 422011

The Anchor Inn, CHIDEOCK, DT6 6JU, 01297 489215

See advert on page 190

PITCHES: 🚐 Caravans 🚚 Motorhomes ⛺ Tents 🏕 Glamping-style accommodation **SERVICES:** 🔌 Electric hook up 🅖 Launderette 🍺 Licensed bar
🛢 Calor Gas 🖉 Camping Gaz Ⓣ Toilet fluid 🍴 Café/Restaurant 🍟 Fast Food/Takeaway 🔋 Battery charging 🍼 Baby care 🚲 Motorvan service point
ABBREVIATIONS: BH/bank hols – bank holidays Etr – Easter Spring BH – Spring Bank Holiday fr – from hrs – hours m – mile mdnt – midnight
rdbt – roundabout rs – restricted service wk – week wknd – weekend x-rds – cross roads 🚫 No credit or debit cards 🚫 No dogs 👪 Children of all ages accepted

BRIDPORT *continued*

West Bay Holiday Park
HOLIDAY CENTRE 84%

tel: 0844 335 3756 **West Bay DT6 4HB**
email: touringandcamping@parkdeanholidays.com
dir: *From A35 (Dorchester road), W towards Bridport, take 1st exit at 1st rdbt, 2nd exit at 2nd rdbt into West Bay, site on right.* **grid ref:** *SY461906*

Overlooking the pretty little harbour at West Bay, and close to the shingle beach, this park offers a full entertainment programme for all ages. There are children's clubs and an indoor pool with flume for all the family, and plenty of evening fun with shows and cabaret etc. The large adventure playground is very popular. The terraced touring section, with its own reception and warden, offers excellent sea views and has hardstandings and super pitches. 6 acre site. 116 touring pitches. 18 hardstandings. Caravan pitches. Motorhome pitches. Tent pitches. 298 statics.

Open: mid Mar-Oct **Last arrival:** 23.00hrs **Last departure:** 10.00hrs

Pitches: 🚐 �281 ▲

Leisure: 🏊 🄰 ⛵ 🔍

Facilities: 🛁 🚿 ☉ 🍴 ⚡ ✕ ⚐ ⏰ 🏪 🎴 📶

Services: 🚙 🗄 🍴 🛢 🧺 🚰 [T] 🍽 🛒 🏪 ♿

Within 3 miles: ⚒ ⛳ 🎣 ◎ 🏪 ⚓ ♻ ∪

Notes: No skateboards.

AA Pubs & Restaurants nearby: Riverside Restaurant, BRIDPORT, DT6 4EZ, 01308 422011

Highlands End Holiday Park
►►►►► 91%

tel: 01308 422139 & 426947 **Eype DT6 6AR**
email: holidays@wdlh.co.uk **web:** www.wdlh.co.uk
dir: *1m W of Bridport on A35, follow signs for Eype. Site signed.* **grid ref:** *SY454913*

A well-screened site with magnificent cliff-top views over the Channel and the Dorset coast, adjacent to National Trust land and overlooking Lyme Bay. The pitches are mostly sheltered by hedging and well spaced on hardstandings. The excellent facilities include a tasteful bar and restaurant, indoor pool, leisure centre and The Cowshed, a very good coffee shop. There is a mixture of statics and tourers, but the tourers enjoy the best cliff-top positions. 9 acre site. 195

---

touring pitches. 45 hardstandings. Caravan pitches. Motorhome pitches. Tent pitches. 160 statics.

Open: 21 Mar-1 Nov **Last arrival:** 22.00hrs **Last departure:** 11.00hrs

Pitches: * 🚐 £16-£36 �281 £16-£36 ▲ £13.75-£26

Leisure: 🏊 ⛵ 🄰 🔍 🎯 🔍 🎵

Facilities: 🚿 ☉ 🍴 ✕ ⚐ ⏰ 🏪 🎴 🎴 📶 ♻ 🛈

Services: 🚙 🗄 🍴 🛢 🧺 [T] 🍽 🛒 🏪 🚰 ♿ **Within 3 miles:** ⚒ 🎣 🏪 🏪

Notes: Dogs must be kept on leads. Steam room, sauna, pitch & putt.

AA Pubs & Restaurants nearby: The Shave Cross Inn, BRIDPORT, DT6 6HW, 01308 868358

Riverside Restaurant, BRIDPORT, DT6 4EZ, 01308 422011

The Anchor Inn, CHIDEOCK, DT6 6JU, 01297 489215

See advert on page 191

Bingham Grange Touring & Camping Park
►►►►► 90%

tel: 01308 488234 **Melplash DT6 3TT**
email: enquiries@binghamgrange.co.uk
dir: *From A35 at Bridport take A3066 N towards Beaminster. Site on left in 3m.* **grid ref:** *SY478963*

Set in a quiet rural location but only five miles from the Jurassic Coast, this adults-only park enjoys views over the west Dorset countryside. The mostly level pitches are attractively set amongst shrub beds and ornamental trees. There is an excellent restaurant with lounge bar and takeaway, and all facilities are of a high quality. This is a very dog-friendly site. 20 acre site. 150 touring pitches. 85 hardstandings. 50 seasonal pitches. Caravan pitches. Motorhome pitches. Tent pitches.

Open: 16 Mar-end Oct (approx) (rs Wed (all year), Tue (mid-low season) restaurant & bar closed)

Pitches: * 🚐 £19.50-£28 �281 £18.50-£28 ▲ £16-£27

Facilities: 🚿 ☉ 🍴 ✕ ⚐ ⏰ 🏪 📶 ♻ 🛈

Services: 🚙 🗄 🍴 🛢 🧺 [T] 🍽 ♿ **Within 3 miles:** ⚒ 🎣 🎣 🏪 🏪 ∪

Notes: Adults only. No under 18s may stay or visit, no noise after 23.00hrs. Dogs must be kept on leads. Woodland walks.

AA Pubs & Restaurants nearby: The Shave Cross Inn, BRIDPORT, DT6 6HW, 01308 868358

LEISURE: 🏊 Indoor swimming pool 🏊 Outdoor swimming pool 🄰 Children's playground ⛵ Kid's club 🎾 Tennis court 🔍 Games room ▭ Separate TV room ⛳ golf course ⛵ Boats for hire ▤ Cinema 🎵 Entertainment 🎣 Fishing ◎ Mini golf ⛵ Watersports 🏌 Gym 🎯 Sports field ∪ Stables
FACILITIES: 🛁 Bath 🚿 Shower ☉ Electric shaver 🍴 Hairdryer ✕ Ice Pack Facility ⚐ Disabled facilities ⏰ Public telephone 🏪 Shop on site or within 200yds 🎴 Mobile shop (calls at least 5 days a week) 🎴 BBQ area 🏪 Picnic area 📶 Wi-fi 🖥 Internet access ♻ Recycling 🛈 Tourist info 🎴 Dog exercise area

Graston Copse Holiday Park
►►►87%

tel: 01308 426912 & 422139 **Annings Ln, Burton Bradstock DT6 4QP**
email: enquiries@wdlh.co.uk
dir: *From Dorchester take A35 to Bridport. In Bridport follow 'Westbound through traffic' sign at mini rdbt. At next rdbt left onto B3157 to Burton Bradstock.* **grid ref:** *SY491893*

This small, peaceful site is located near the village of Burton Bradstock making it a perfect base for visiting the stunning cliffs and beaches along the Jurassic coastline. The facilities are modern and spotlessly clean. Please note, care is needed if driving through Burton Bradstock to the site. 9 acre site. 26 touring pitches. Caravan pitches. Motorhome pitches. Tent pitches. 90 statics. 2 wooden pods.

Open: 17 Apr-7 Sep **Last arrival:** 22.00hrs **Last departure:** 11.00hrs

Pitches: * ⊟ £15-£25 ⊟ £15-£25 ▲ £12.50-£23 ⋔

Facilities: ⋔ ⊙ ℙ ✳ ⋔ ⊞ WiFi ♻ ❶

Services: ⊟ Ⓢⓘⓝ

Within 3 miles: ⅃ ⅄ ☰ ℘ ⊚ ⇆ ⑤ ⓢ ∪

Notes: Dogs must be kept on leads.

AA Pubs & Restaurants nearby: Riverside Restaurant, BRIDPORT, DT6 4EZ, 01308 422011

The Crown Inn, PUNCKNOWLE, DT2 9BN, 01308 897711

| CERNE ABBAS | Map 4 ST60 |

Places to visit

Athelhampton House & Gardens, ATHELHAMPTON, DT2 7LG, 01305 848363 www.athelhampton.co.uk

Hardy's Cottage, DORCHESTER, DT2 8QJ, 01305 262366 www.nationaltrust.org.uk

Great for kids: Maiden Castle, DORCHESTER, DT2 9PP, 0870 333 1181 www.english-heritage.org.uk/daysout/properties/maiden-castle

Lyons Gate Caravan and Camping Park
►►►►79%

tel: 01300 345260 **Lyons Gate DT2 7AZ**
email: info@lyons-gate.co.uk
dir: *Direct access from A352, 3m N of Cerne Abbas, site signed.* **grid ref:** *ST660062*

A peaceful park with pitches set out around the four attractive coarse fishing lakes. It is surrounded by mature woodland, with many footpaths and bridleways. Other easily accessible attractions include the Cerne Giant carved into the hills, the old market town of Dorchester, and the superb sandy beach at Weymouth. Holiday homes are available for sale. 10 acre site. 90 touring pitches. 24 hardstandings. Caravan pitches. Motorhome pitches. Tent pitches. 14 statics.

Open: all year **Last arrival:** 20.00hrs **Last departure:** 11.30hrs

Pitches: ⊟ ⊟ ▲ **Leisure:** ⚑ ● ▭

Facilities: ⋔ ⊙ ℙ ✳ ⅃ ⓢ ⊟ ⋔ WiFi ❶

Services: ⊟ Ⓢⓝ **Within 3 miles:** ⅃ ℘ ⓢ ∪

Notes: Dogs must be kept on leads.

AA Pubs & Restaurants nearby: The New Inn, CERNE ABBAS, DT2 7JF, 01300 341274

The Poachers Inn, PIDDLETRENTHIDE, DT2 7QX, 01300 348358

Giants Head Caravan & Camping Park
►►►78%

tel: 01300 341242 **Giants Head Farm, Old Sherborne Rd DT2 7TR**
email: holidays@giantshead.co.uk
dir: *From Dorchester into town avoiding by-pass, at Top O'Town rdbt take A352 (Sherborne road), in 500yds right fork at BP (Loder's) garage, site signed.* **grid ref:** *ST675029*

A pleasant, though rather simple, park set in Dorset downland near the Cerne Giant (the famous landmark figure cut into the chalk) with stunning views and a smart toilet block. This is a good stopover site especially for tenters and backpackers on The Ridgeway National Trail. Holiday chalets are available to let. 4 acre site. 50 touring pitches. Caravan pitches. Motorhome pitches. Tent pitches.

Open: Etr-Oct (rs Etr shop & bar closed) **Last arrival:** anytime **Last departure:** 13.00hrs

Pitches: ⊟ £12-£20 ⊟ £12-£20 ▲ £12-£20

Facilities: ⋔ ⊙ ℙ ✳ ⋔ ⊞ ♻ ❶

Services: ⊟ Ⓢ ▮ ⊘ ⇞ **Within 3 miles:** ℘ ⓢ ⓝ

Notes: Dogs must be kept on leads.

AA Pubs & Restaurants nearby: The Greyhound Inn, SYDLING ST NICHOLAS, DT2 9PD, 01300 341303

| CHARMOUTH | Map 4 SY39 |

Places to visit

Forde Abbey, THORNCOMBE, TA20 4LU, 01460 221290 www.fordeabbey.co.uk

Great for kids: Abbotsbury Swannery, ABBOTSBURY, DT3 4JG, 01305 871858 www.abbotsbury-tourism.co.uk

PREMIER PARK

Wood Farm Caravan & Camping Park
►►►►► 92%

Best of British

tel: 01297 560697 **Axminster Rd DT6 6BT**
email: holidays@woodfarm.co.uk **web:** www.woodfarm.co.uk
dir: *Accessed directly from A35 rdbt, on Axminster side of Charmouth.*
grid ref: *SY356940*

This top quality park, the perfect place to relax, is set amongst mature native trees with the various levels of the site falling away into a beautiful valley below. The park offers excellent facilities including family rooms and fully serviced

PITCHES: ⊟ Caravans ⊟ Motorhomes ▲ Tents ⋔ Glamping-style accommodation **SERVICES:** ⊟ Electric hook up Ⓢ Launderette ⓝ Licensed bar ▮ Calor Gas ⊘ Camping Gaz Ⓣ Toilet fluid ⓘ Café/Restaurant ⊞ Fast Food/Takeaway ⇞ Battery charging ⇖ Baby care ⚐ Motorvan service point **ABBREVIATIONS:** BH/bank hols – bank holidays Etr – Easter Spring BH – Spring Bank Holiday fr – from hrs – hours m – mile mdnt – midnight rdbt – roundabout rs – restricted service wk – week wknd – weekend x-rds – cross roads ⊗ No credit or debit cards ⊗ No dogs ✦ Children of all ages accepted

CHARMOUTH *continued*

pitches. Everything throughout the park is spotless. At the bottom end of the park there is an indoor swimming pool and leisure complex, plus the licensed, conservatory-style Offshore Café. There's a very good children's play room in addition to tennis courts and a well-stocked, coarse-fishing lake. The park is well positioned on the Heritage Coast near Lyme Regis. Static holiday homes are also available for hire. 13 acre site. 175 touring pitches. 175 hardstandings. 20 seasonal pitches. Caravan pitches. Motorhome pitches. Tent pitches. 92 statics.

Wood Farm Caravan & Camping Park

Open: Etr-Oct **Last arrival:** 19.00hrs **Last departure:** noon

Pitches: * 🚐 £15.50-£28 🚙 £15.50-£28 ▲ £12.50-£26

Leisure: 🏊⚲♨♦⚄ **Facilities:** 🛁📷⦿📠✳🕭🕙🛍🐕📶🖥♻ℹ

Services: 🔌🗑🛢🧴🚽🍴🛒🔽 **Within 3 miles:** ↓✦⌑♦⦿♨🛍🛢⛎

Notes: No bikes, skateboards, scooters or roller skates. Dogs must be kept on leads.

AA Pubs & Restaurants nearby: The Mariners, LYME REGIS, DT7 3HS, 01297 442753

See advert on opposite page

PREMIER PARK

Newlands Caravan & Camping Park
▶▶▶▶▶81%

tel: 01297 560259 **DT6 6RB**

email: enq@newlandsholidays.co.uk **web:** www.newlandsholidays.co.uk

dir: *4m W of Bridport on A35.* **grid ref:** SY374935

A very smart site with excellent touring facilities, set on gently sloping ground in hilly countryside near the sea. The park offers a full cabaret and entertainment programme for all ages, and boasts an indoor swimming pool and an outdoor pool with water slide. Lodges, apartments and motel rooms are available, plus there are four new camping pods for hire. 23 acre site. 240 touring pitches. 52 hardstandings. 40 seasonal pitches. Caravan pitches. Motorhome pitches. Tent pitches. 86 statics. 4 wooden pods.

Open: 10 Mar-4 Nov **Last arrival:** 21.00hrs **Last departure:** 10.00hrs

Pitches: * 🚐 £14-£40 🚙 £14-£40 ▲ £14-£40 🏠

Leisure: 🏊⚲♨♦⚄🎵

Facilities: 📷⦿📠✳🕭🕙🛍🐕📶🖥♻ℹ

Services: 🔌🗑🛢🧴🚽🍴🛒🔽

Within 3 miles: ↓✦⌑♦⦿♨🛍🛢⛎

Notes: Dogs must be kept on leads. Kids' club during school holidays.

AA Pubs & Restaurants nearby: The Mariners, LYME REGIS, DT7 3HS, 01297 442753

See advert on opposite page

Manor Farm Holiday Centre
▶▶▶ 90%

tel: 01297 560226 **Manor Farm Holiday Centre DT6 6QL**

email: enquiries@manorfarmholidaycentre.co.uk

dir: *From E: A35 into Charmouth, site 0.75m on right.* **grid ref:** SY368937

Set just a short walk from the safe sand and shingle beach at Charmouth, this popular family park offers a good range of facilities. There is an indoor/outdoor swimming pool plus café, a fully-equipped gym and sauna. Children enjoy the activity area and the park also offers a lively programme in the extensive bar and entertainment complex. In addition there are 16 luxury cottages available to let. 30 acre site. 400 touring pitches. 80 hardstandings. 100 seasonal pitches. Caravan pitches. Motorhome pitches. Tent pitches. 29 statics.

Open: all year (rs Open all year round statics only) **Last arrival:** 20.00hrs **Last departure:** 10.00hrs

Pitches: * 🚐 £14-£34 🚙 £14-£34 ▲ £14-£34

Leisure: 🏊⚲🏌♨♦🎵 Spa

Facilities: 📷⦿📠✳🕭🕙🛍🐕📶♻ℹ

Services: 🔌🗑🛢🧴🚽🍴🛒🔽

Within 3 miles: ↓✦⌑♦⦿♨🛍🛢⛎

Notes: No skateboards. Dogs must be kept on leads.

AA Pubs & Restaurants nearby: The Mariners, LYME REGIS, DT7 3HS, 01297 442753

LEISURE: 🏊 Indoor swimming pool 🏊 Outdoor swimming pool 🎢 Children's playground 👶 Kid's club ♨ Tennis court ♦ Games room ⚄ Separate TV room ↓ golf course ⚓ Boats for hire 🎬 Cinema 🎵 Entertainment ♦ Fishing ⦿ Mini golf ♨ Watersports 🏌 Gym ✦ Sports field Spa ⛎ Stables
FACILITIES: 🛁 Bath 📷 Shower ⦿ Electric shaver 📠 Hairdryer ✳ Ice Pack Facility 🕭 Disabled facilities 🕙 Public telephone 🛍 Shop on site or within 200yds 🗑 Mobile shop (calls at least 5 days a week) 🍴 BBQ area 🔽 Picnic area 📶 Wi-fi 🖥 Internet access ♻ Recycling ℹ Tourist info 🐕 Dog exercise area

CHIDEOCK
Map 4 SY49

Places to visit
Mapperton, BEAMINSTER, DT8 3NR, 01308 862645 www.mapperton.com

---

Golden Cap Holiday Park
▶▶▶▶85%

tel: 01308 422139 & 426947 **Seatown DT6 6JX**
email: holidays@wdlh.co.uk
dir: On A35, in Chideock follow Seatown signs, site signed. **grid ref:** SY422919

A grassy site, overlooking the sea and beach and surrounded by National Trust parkland. This uniquely placed park slopes down to the sea, although pitches are generally level. A slight dip hides the view of the beach from the back of the park, but this area benefits from having trees, scrub and meadows, unlike the barer areas closer to the sea which do have a spectacular outlook. This makes an ideal base for touring Dorset and Devon. Lake fishing is possible (a licence can be obtained locally). 11 acre site. 108 touring pitches. 24 hardstandings. Caravan pitches. Motorhome pitches. Tent pitches. 234 statics. 3 wooden pods.

Open: 21 Mar-2 Nov **Last arrival:** 22.00hrs **Last departure:** 11.00hrs

Pitches: * 🚐 £16-£45 🚗 £16-£45 ▲ £16-£32 🛖

Leisure: 🎠

Facilities: 🚿⊙☂✳&🕐🖐🍴🎪WiFi♻🅸

Services: 🚱🗑🛢🧺T🍴🛒🛒

Within 3 miles: 🛶🎣🅢🗑

Notes: Dogs must be kept on leads.

AA Pubs & Restaurants nearby: Riverside Restaurant, BRIDPORT, DT6 4EZ, 01308 422011

CHRISTCHURCH

Places to visit
Red House Museum & Gardens, CHRISTCHURCH, BH23 1BU, 01202 482860 www3.hants.gov.uk/redhouse

Great for kids: Oceanarium, BOURNEMOUTH, BH2 5AA, 01202 311993 www.oceanarium.co.uk

---

CHRISTCHURCH
Map 5 SZ19

PREMIER PARK

Meadowbank Holidays
▶▶▶▶▶85%

SILVER

tel: 01202 483597 **Stour Way BH23 2PQ**
email: enquiries@meadowbank-holidays.co.uk
web: www.meadowbank-holidays.co.uk
dir: A31 onto A338 towards Bournemouth. 5m, left towards Christchurch on B3073. Right at 1st rdbt into St Catherine's Way, becomes River Way. 3rd right into Stour Way to site. **grid ref:** SZ136946

A very smart park on the banks of the River Stour, with a colourful display of hanging baskets and flower-filled tubs placed around the superb reception area. The facility block is excellent. Visitors can choose between the different pitch sizes, including luxury, fully serviced ones. There is also an excellent play area, a good shop on site and coarse fishing. Statics are available for hire. 2 acre site. 41 touring pitches. 22 hardstandings. Caravan pitches. Motorhome pitches. 180 statics.

Open: Mar-Oct **Last arrival:** 21.00hrs **Last departure:** noon

Pitches: 🚐 🚗

Leisure: 🎠 🔍

Facilities: 🛁🚿⊙☂&🕐🖐🍴WiFi🖥♻🅸

Services: 🚱🗑🛢🧺T🛒🛒

Within 3 miles: 🛶🎿🎱🎣◎🏊🅢🗑U

Notes: ⊗ No pets.

AA Pubs & Restaurants nearby: The Ship In Distress, CHRISTCHURCH, BH23 3NA, 01202 485123

Splinters Restaurant, CHRISTCHURCH, BH23 1BW, 01202 483454

LEISURE: 🏊 Indoor swimming pool 🏖 Outdoor swimming pool 🎠 Children's playground 🪁 Kid's club 🎾 Tennis court 🔍 Games room ▭ Separate TV room 🏌 golf course 🚣 Boats for hire 🎬 Cinema 🎵 Entertainment 🎣 Fishing ◎ Mini golf 🏄 Watersports 🏋 Gym 🏅 Sports field Spa U Stables
FACILITIES: 🛁 Bath 🚿 Shower ⊙ Electric shaver 🖐 Hairdryer ✳ Ice Pack Facility & Disabled facilities 🕐 Public telephone 🅢 Shop on site or within 200yds 🅰 Mobile shop (calls at least 5 days a week) 🍴 BBQ area 🍴 Picnic area WiFi Wi-fi 🖥 Internet access ♻ Recycling 🅸 Tourist info 🐾 Dog exercise area

CORFE CASTLE
Map 4 SY98

Places to visit
Great for kids: Swanage Railway, SWANAGE, BH19 1HB, 01929 425800
www.swanagerailway.co.uk

Corfe Castle Camping & Caravanning Club Site
▶▶▶▶ 90%

tel: 01929 480280 & 0845 130 7633 **Bucknowle BH20 5PQ**
dir: *A351 from Wareham towards Swanage. In 4m right at foot of Corfe Castle signed Church Knowle. 0.75m right to site on left at top of lane.* **grid ref:** *SY953818*

This lovely campsite, where non-members are also very welcome, is set in woodland near the famous Corfe Castle at the foot of the Purbeck Hills. It has a stone reception building, on-site shop and modern toilet and shower facilities, which are spotless. Although the site is sloping, pitches are level and include spacious hardstandings. The site is perfect for visiting the many attractions of the Purbeck area, including the award-winning beaches at Studland and Swanage, and the seaside towns of Poole, Bournemouth and Weymouth. There is also a station at Corfe for the Swanage Steam Railway. The site is pet friendly. 6 acre site. 80 touring pitches. 33 hardstandings. Caravan pitches. Motorhome pitches. Tent pitches.

Open: Mar-Oct **Last arrival:** 20.00hrs (later arrivals by prior arrangement only)
Last departure: noon

Pitches: 🚐 � 🛆 **Leisure:** 🅰
Facilities: 🎣⊙🎥✳🔥🛢♻️ⓘ **Services:** 🔌🗑 🛢⊘🅣🛗⛟
Within 3 miles: ⬇️🐟🎯🎣◎🔥🛢🛍️U

Notes: Site gates closed 23.00hrs-07.00hrs. Dogs must be kept on leads.
AA Pubs & Restaurants nearby: The New Inn, CHURCH KNOWLE, BH20 5NQ, 01929 480357

Woodyhyde Camp Site
▶▶▶ 80%

tel: 01929 480274 **Valley Rd BH20 5HT**
email: camp@woodyhyde.co.uk **web:** www.woodyhyde.co.uk
dir: *From Corfe Castle towards Swanage on A351, site approx 1m on right.*
grid ref: *SY974804*

A large grassy campsite in a sheltered location for tents and motorhomes only, divided into three paddocks - one is dog free. There is a well-stocked shop on site, a modern toilet and shower block, and a regular bus service that stops near the site entrance. Electric hook-ups and some hardstandings are available. This site offers

traditional camping in a great location between Corfe Castle and Swanage. 13 acre site. 150 touring pitches. 25 hardstandings. Motorhome pitches. Tent pitches.

Open: Mar-Oct **Pitches:** * 🚐 £8-£25 🛆 £8-£25
Facilities: 🎣⊙🎥✳🔥🛢♻️ⓘ **Services:** 🔌🛢⊘🅣🛗⛟
Within 3 miles: ⬇️🐟🎯🎣◎🔥🛢🛍️U

Notes: No noise after 23.00hrs, no open fires. Dogs must be kept on leads.
AA Pubs & Restaurants nearby: The New Inn, CHURCH KNOWLE, BH20 5NQ, 01929 480357

DORCHESTER
See Cerne Abbas

DRIMPTON
Map 4 ST40

Places to visit
Forde Abbey, THORNCOMBE, TA20 4LU, 01460 221290 www.fordeabbey.co.uk

Mapperton, BEAMINSTER, DT8 3NR, 01308 862645 www.mapperton.com

Oathill Farm Touring and Camping Site
▶▶▶▶ 83%

tel: 01460 30234 **Oathill TA18 8PZ**
email: oathillfarm@btconnect.com **web:** www.oathillfarmleisure.co.uk
dir: *From Crewkerne take B3165. Site on left just after Clapton.* **grid ref:** *ST404055*

This small peaceful park borders Somerset and Devon, with the Jurassic Coast at Lyme Regis, Charmouth and Bridport only a short drive away. The modern facilities are spotless and there are hardstandings and fully serviced pitches available. Lucy's Tea Room serves breakfast and meals. The well-stocked, landscaped fishing ponds prove a hit with anglers. Three luxury lodges are available for hire. 10 acre site. 13 touring pitches. 13 hardstandings. 3 seasonal pitches. Caravan pitches. Motorhome pitches. Tent pitches. 3 statics.

Open: all year **Last arrival:** 20.00hrs **Last departure:** noon
Pitches: 🚐 � 🛆
Leisure: ✪ **Facilities:** 🎣⊙🎥✳🔥🛢🅙🎢WiFi🖥️♻️ⓘ
Services: 🔌🗑 🛢⊘🅣🍴🛗⛟ **Within 3 miles:** ⬇️🎣🛢🛍️U

Notes: No washing lines, no quad bikes, no noise after 23.00hrs. Separate recreational areas.
AA Pubs & Restaurants nearby: The George Inn, CREWKERNE, TA18 7LP, 01460 73650

PITCHES: 🚐 Caravans 🚐 Motorhomes 🛆 Tents 🏕 Glamping-style accommodation **SERVICES:** 🔌 Electric hook up 🗑 Launderette 🍺 Licensed bar
🛢 Calor Gas ⊘ Camping Gaz 🅣 Toilet fluid 🍴 Café/Restaurant 🛗 Fast Food/Takeaway 🔋 Battery charging 🍼 Baby care ⛟ Motorvan service point
ABBREVIATIONS: BH/bank hols – bank holidays Etr – Easter Spring BH – Spring Bank Holiday fr – from hrs – hours m – mile mdnt – midnight
rdbt – roundabout rs – restricted service wk – week wknd – weekend x-rds – cross roads 🚫 No credit or debit cards 🚫 No dogs 👪 Children of all ages accepted

FERNDOWN
Map 5 SU00

Places to visit

Kingston Lacy, WIMBORNE, BH21 4EA, 01202 883402 (Mon-Fri)
www.nationaltrust.org.uk/kingston-lacy

Great for kids: Oceanarium, BOURNEMOUTH, BH2 5AA, 01202 311993
www.oceanarium.co.uk

St Leonards Farm Caravan & Camping Park
▶▶▶82%

tel: 01202 872637 **Ringwood Rd, West Moors BH22 0AQ**
email: enquiries_stleonards@yahoo.co.uk **web:** www.stleonardsfarm.biz
dir: *From Ringwood on A31 (dual carriageway) towards Ferndown, exit left into slip road at site sign. From Wimborne Minster on A31 at rdbt (junct of A31 & A347) follow signs for Ringwood (A31)(pass Texaco garage on left) to next rdbt. 3rd exit (ie double back towards Ferndown) exit at slip road for site.* **grid ref:** SU093014

A private road accessed from the A31 leads to this well-screened park divided into paddocks that have spacious pitches; the site has an excellent secure children's play area, and is well located for visiting nearby Bournemouth and the New Forest National Park. 12 acre site. 151 touring pitches. 30 seasonal pitches. Caravan pitches. Motorhome pitches. Tent pitches. 6 statics.

Open: Apr-Sep **Last departure:** 14.00hrs

Pitches: 🚐 🚃 ▲

Leisure: 🎢

Facilities: 🌳⊙☂☀♿🛒♻️ℹ️

Services: 🔌🖥️🔧💧🚿📆

Within 3 miles: ⛳🛒🛒

Notes: No large groups, no noise after 23.00hrs, no disposable BBQs, no gazebos, no dogs during Jul-Aug. Dogs must be kept on leads.

AA Pubs & Restaurants nearby: Les Bouviers Restaurant with Rooms, WIMBORNE MINSTER, BH21 3BD, 01202 889555

HOLTON HEATH
Map 4 SY99

Places to visit

Great for kids: Farmer Palmer's Farm Park, ORGANFORD, BH16 6EU, 01202 622022 www.farmerpalmers.co.uk

Sandford Holiday Park
HOLIDAY CENTRE 86%

tel: 0844 335 3756 & 01202 631600 **Organford Rd BH16 6JZ**
email: touringandcamping@parkdeanholidays.com
dir: *A35 from Poole towards Dorchester, at lights onto A351 towards Wareham. Right at Holton Heath. Site 100yds on left.* **grid ref:** SY939916

With touring pitches set individually in 20 acres surrounded by woodland, this park offers a full range of leisure activities and entertainment for the whole family. The touring area, situated at the far end of the park, is neat and well maintained, and there are children's clubs in the daytime and entertainment nightly. A reception area with lounge, bar, café and restaurant creates an excellent and attractive entrance, with a covered area outside with tables and chairs and well-landscaped gardens. Static holiday homes are available for hire or purchase. 64 acre site. 353 touring pitches. 20 hardstandings. 78 seasonal pitches. Caravan pitches. Motorhome pitches. Tent pitches. 344 statics.

Open: Mar-Oct (rs Mar-3 May & 22 Sep-Oct outdoor pool closed) **Last arrival:** 20.00hrs **Last departure:** 10.00hrs

Pitches: 🚐 🚃 ▲

Leisure: 🏊🏊🎢🖐️♟️🎾🎵

Facilities: 🛁🌳⊙☂☀♿🛒🍴📶🖥️♻️ℹ️

Services: 🔌🖥️🔧💧🚿🔧🍴📆🛒⛽

Within 3 miles: ⛳🚴⛳🛒◎🛒🛒🐴

Notes: No noise after 23.00hrs, no motorised scooters or carts, max 2 dogs per pitch. Dogs must be kept on leads. Bowling, crazy golf, bike hire.

AA Pubs & Restaurants nearby: The New Inn, CHURCH KNOWLE, BH20 5NQ, 01929 480357

HURN

Places to visit

Red House Museum & Gardens, CHRISTCHURCH, BH23 1BU, 01202 482860
www3.hants.gov.uk/redhouse

Oceanarium, BOURNEMOUTH, BH2 5AA, 01202 311993 www.oceanarium.co.uk

Great for kids: Moors Valley Country Park and Forest, RINGWOOD, BH24 2ET, 01425 470721 www.moors-valley.co.uk

HURN
Map 5 SZ19

Fillybrook Farm Touring Park
▶▶85%

tel: 01202 478266 **Matchams Ln BH23 6AW**
email: enquiries@fillybrookfarm.co.uk
dir: *M27 junct 1, A31 to Ringwood, then Poole, left immediately after Texaco Garage signed Verwood & B3081, left into Hurn Ln signed Matchams. Site on right in 4m.*
grid ref: *SZ128997*

A small adults-only park well located on the edge of Hurn Forest, with Bournemouth, Christchurch, Poole and the New Forest within easy reach. Fillybrook provides a pleasant, peaceful camping environment, and the facilities are both modern and very clean. A dry-ski slope, with an adjoining restaurant and small bar, is a short walk from the site. There is also a separate rally field. 1 acre site. 18 touring pitches. Caravan pitches. Motorhome pitches. Tent pitches.

Open: Etr-Oct **Last arrival:** 20.00hrs **Last departure:** 11.00hrs

Pitches: ⬚ ⬚ ⚊

Facilities: ⬚ ⊙ ⬚ ※ ⬚ ✿ ⬚

Services: ⬚ ⬚ ⬚

Within 3 miles: ⬚ ⬚ ⬚ ⬚ ⬚

Notes: Adults only. ⬚ No large groups, no commercial vehicles, no campfires. Dogs must be kept on leads.

AA Pubs & Restaurants nearby: The Three Tuns, BRANSGORE, BH23 8JH, 01425 672232

LYME REGIS
Map 4 SY39

See also Charmouth

Places to visit
Pecorama Pleasure Gardens, BEER, EX12 3NA, 01297 21542 www.pecorama.info

Shrubbery Touring Park
▶▶▶▶87%

tel: 01297 442227 **Rousdon DT7 3XW**
email: info@shrubberypark.co.uk **web:** www.shrubberypark.co.uk
dir: *3m W of Lyme Regis on A3052 (coast road).* **grid ref:** *SY300914*

Mature trees enclose this peaceful park, which has distant views of the lovely countryside. The modern facilities are well kept, the hardstanding pitches are

spacious, and there is plenty of space for children to play in the grounds. Well located for visiting Lyme Regis, Sidmouth and Seaton, the park is right on the Jurassic Coast bus route, which is popular with visitors to this area. 10 acre site. 120 touring pitches. 28 hardstandings. Caravan pitches. Motorhome pitches. Tent pitches.

Open: Apr-1 Nov **Last arrival:** 21.00hrs **Last departure:** 11.00hrs

Pitches: * ⬚ £12-£17.50 ⬚ £12-£17.50 ⚊ £12-£17.50

Leisure: ⬚

Facilities: ⬚ ⊙ ⬚ ※ ⬚ ⬚ ✿ ⬚ ⬚

Services: ⬚ ⬚ ⬚ ⬚ ⬚

Within 3 miles: ⬚ ⬚ ⬚ ⬚ ⬚ ⬚ ⬚ ⬚ ⬚

Notes: No groups (except rallies), no motor scooters, roller skates or skateboards. Dogs must be kept on leads. Crazy golf.

AA Pubs & Restaurants nearby: The Mariners, LYME REGIS, DT7 3HS, 01297 442753

Hook Farm Caravan & Camping Park
▶▶▶85%

tel: 01297 442801 **Gore Ln, Uplyme DT7 3UU**
email: information@hookfarm-uplyme.co.uk
dir: *A35 onto B3165 towards Lyme Regis & Uplyme at Hunters Lodge pub. In 2m right into Gore Ln, site 400yds on right.* **grid ref:** *SY323930*

Set in a peaceful and very rural location, this popular farm site enjoys lovely views of Lym Valley and is just a mile from the seaside at Lyme Regis. There are modern toilet facilities and good on-site amenities. Most pitches are level due to excellent terracing – a great site for tents but is also suited to motorhomes and caravans. Please note, it is advised that if arriving in a motorhome or if towing a caravan that Sat Nav is not used; there are many narrow roads that only have few passing places. 5.5 acre site. 100 touring pitches. 4 hardstandings. Caravan pitches. Motorhome pitches. Tent pitches. 17 statics.

Open: Mar-Oct **Last arrival:** 20.00hrs **Last departure:** 11.00hrs

Pitches: * ⬚ £12-£28 ⬚ £12-£28 ⚊ £10-£30

Leisure: ⬚

Facilities: ⬚ ⊙ ⬚ ※ ⬚ ⬚ ⬚ ⬚ WiFi ✿ ⬚

Services: ⬚ ⬚ ⬚ ⬚ ⬚ ⬚

Within 3 miles: ⬚ ⬚ ⬚ ⬚ ⬚ ⬚ ⬚ ⬚ ⬚

Notes: ⬚ No groups of 5 adults or more, no dangerous dog breeds. Dogs must be kept on leads. Bicycle storage.

AA Pubs & Restaurants nearby: The Mariners, LYME REGIS, DT7 3HS, 01297 442753

Find out about the AA's Pennant rating scheme on pages 10-11

PITCHES: ⬚ Caravans ⬚ Motorhomes ⚊ Tents ⬚ Glamping-style accommodation **SERVICES:** ⬚ Electric hook up ⬚ Launderette ⬚ Licensed bar ⬚ Calor Gas ⬚ Camping Gaz ⬚ Toilet fluid ⬚ Café/Restaurant ⬚ Fast Food/Takeaway ⬚ Battery charging ⬚ Baby care ⬚ Motorvan service point
ABBREVIATIONS: BH/bank hols – bank holidays Etr – Easter Spring BH – Spring Bank Holiday fr – from hrs – hours m – mile mdnt – midnight rdbt – roundabout rs – restricted service wk – week wknd – weekend x-rds – cross roads ⬚ No credit or debit cards ⬚ No dogs ⬚ Children of all ages accepted

Huntick Farm Caravan Park
►►►79%

tel: 01202 622222 **Huntick Rd BH16 6BB**
email: huntickcaravans@btconnect.com
dir: *Site between Lytchett Minster & Lytchett Matravers. From A31 take A350 towards Poole. Follow Lytchett Minster signs, then Lytchett Matravers signs. Into Huntick Rd by Rose & Crown pub.* **grid ref:** *SY955947*

A really attractive little park situated in rural surroundings edged by woodland, a mile from the village amenities of Lytchett Matravers. This neat grassy park is divided into three, peaceful paddocks, yet it is close to the attractions that both Poole and Bournemouth have to offer. A new toilet and shower block is planned. 4 acre site. 30 touring pitches. Caravan pitches. Motorhome pitches. Tent pitches.

Open: Apr-Oct **Last arrival:** 21.00hrs **Last departure:** noon
Pitches: * 🚐 £21-£32 🚍 £21-£32 ▲ £15-£22.50
Leisure: 🅰 ✪
Facilities: 🅵 ☉ ✳ 🐾 WiFi ♻ 🛈
Services: 🔌 🛒
Within 3 miles: 🛒 ▾ ↻
Notes: No ball games on site. Dogs must be kept on leads.
AA Pubs & Restaurants nearby: Botany Bay Inne, WINTERBORNE ZELSTON, DT11 9ET, 01929 459227

Pear Tree Holiday Park
►►►►85%

tel: 01202 622434 **Organford Rd, Holton Heath BH16 6LA**
email: enquiries@peartreepark.co.uk
dir: *From Poole take A35 towards Dorchester, onto A351 towards Wareham, at 1st lights turn right, site 300yds on left.* **grid ref:** *SY938915*

A quiet, sheltered country park with many colourful flowerbeds, and toilet facilities that offer quality and comfort. The touring area is divided into terraces with mature hedges for screening, with a separate level tenting area on the edge of woodland. The friendly atmosphere at this attractive park helps to ensure a relaxing holiday. A bridle path leads into Wareham Forest. 9 acre site. 154 touring pitches. 82 hardstandings. Caravan pitches. Motorhome pitches. Tent pitches. 40 statics.

Open: Mar-Oct **Last arrival:** 19.00hrs **Last departure:** 11.00hrs
Pitches: 🚐 🚍 ▲
Leisure: 🅰
Facilities: 🅵 ☉ 🅿 ✳ ♿ ☏ 🛒 🐾 WiFi ♻ 🛈
Services: 🔌 🛒 🛢 ✎ 🚽 🛒
Within 3 miles: ◎
Notes: No noise after 22.30hrs. Dogs must be kept on leads.
AA Pubs & Restaurants nearby: Botany Bay Inne, WINTERBORNE ZELSTON, DT11 9ET, 01929 459227

Sandyholme Holiday Park
►►►81%

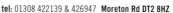

tel: 01308 422139 & 426947 **Moreton Rd DT2 8HZ**
email: holidays@wdlh.co.uk
dir: *From A352 (Wareham to Dorchester road) turn right towards Owermoigne for 1m. Site on left.* **grid ref:** *SY768863*

A pleasant quiet site surrounded by trees and within easy reach of the coast at Lulworth Cove, and handy for several seaside resorts, including Weymouth, Portland, Purbeck and Swanage. The facilities are good, including a children's play area, small football pitch, a shop and tourist information. 6 acre site. 46 touring pitches. 20 seasonal pitches. Caravan pitches. Motorhome pitches. Tent pitches. 52 statics.

Open: 21 Mar-2 Nov (rs Etr) **Last arrival:** 22.00hrs **Last departure:** 11.00hrs
Pitches: * 🚐 £14-£23 🚍 £14-£23 ▲ £12-£17.50
Leisure: 🅰 ✪ ✪ 🔍
Facilities: 🅵 🅿 ✳ ♿ ☏ 🛒 🐾 WiFi ♻ 🛈
Services: 🔌 🛒 🛢 ✎ 🚽 🛒 ⚘
Within 3 miles: 🎣 🛒 🛒
Notes: Dogs must be kept on leads. Table tennis, wildlife lake.
AA Pubs & Restaurants nearby: The Smugglers Inn, OSMINGTON MILLS, DT3 6HF, 01305 833125

Lulworth Cove Inn, WEST LULWORTH, BH20 5RQ, 01929 400333

POOLE
Map 4 SZ09

See also Organford & Wimborne Minster

Places to visit

Brownsea Island, BROWNSEA ISLAND, BH13 7EE, 01202 707744
www.nationaltrust.org.uk/brownsea

Poole Museum, POOLE, BH15 1BW, 01202 262600
www.boroughofpoole.com/museums

Great for kids: Oceanarium, BOURNEMOUTH, BH2 5AA, 01202 311993
www.oceanarium.co.uk

Rockley Park
HOLIDAY CENTRE 88%

GOLD

tel: 0871 231 0880 **Hamworthy BH15 4LZ**
email: rockleypark@haven.com **web:** www.haven.com/rockleypark
dir: *M27 junct 1, A31 to Poole centre, then follow signs to site.* **grid ref:** *SY982909*

A complete holiday experience, including a wide range of day and night entertainment, and plenty of sports and leisure activities, notably watersports.

There is also mooring and launching from the park. The touring area has 60 fully serviced pitches and an excellent toilet and shower block. A great base for all the family that's set in a good location for exploring Poole and Bournemouth. 105 holiday homes are available for hire. 90 acre site. 60 touring pitches. 60 hardstandings. Caravan pitches. Motorhome pitches. Tent pitches. 1077 statics.

Open: mid Mar-end Oct (rs mid Mar-May & Sep-Oct some facilities may be reduced)
Last departure: 10.00hrs

Pitches: 🚐 🚐 🛖

Leisure: 🏊 ⛱ /🛝 👋 👟 ♨ 🎵 Spa

Facilities: 🏪 ⊙ 🍴 ⚡ 🔥 ♿ 🛁 🚿 WiFi ♻ ✱

Services: 🔌 🗄 🚻 T 🍴 🍻

Within 3 miles: ⛳ 🎯 🐎 ◎ 👟 🗄 🗄

Notes: No commercial vehicles, no bookings by persons under 21yrs unless a family booking, max 2 dogs per booking, certain dog breeds banned. Dogs must be kept on leads. Sailing school.

AA Pubs & Restaurants nearby: The Rising Sun, POOLE, BH15 1NZ, 01202 771246
See advert below

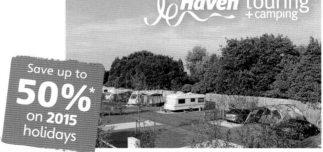
PITCHES: 🚐 Caravans 🚐 Motorhomes 🛖 Tents 🏠 Glamping-style accommodation SERVICES: 🔌 Electric hook up 🗄 Launderette 🍸 Licensed bar
🔥 Calor Gas ⊘ Camping Gaz T Toilet fluid 🍴 Café/Restaurant 🍟 Fast Food/Takeaway 🔋 Battery charging 🍼 Baby care 🚗 Motorvan service point
ABBREVIATIONS: BH/bank hols – bank holidays Etr – Easter Spring BH – Spring Bank Holiday fr – from hrs – hours m – mile mdnt – midnight
rdbt – roundabout rs – restricted service wk – week wknd – weekend x-rds – cross roads ⊘ No credit or debit cards ⊗ No dogs 👪 Children of all ages accepted

POOLE *continued*

South Lytchett Manor Caravan & Camping Park
▶▶▶▶▶ 94%

Best of British

tel: 01202 622577 **Dorchester Rd, Lytchett Minster BH16 6JB**
email: info@southlytchettmanor.co.uk **web:** www.southlytchettmanor.co.uk
dir: *Exit A35 onto B3067, 1m E of Lytchett Minster, 600yds on right after village.*
grid ref: *SY954926*

Situated in the grounds of a historic manor house, the park has modern facilities that are spotless and well maintained. A warm and friendly welcome awaits at this lovely park which is well located for visiting Poole and Bournemouth; the Jurassic X53 bus route (Exeter to Poole) has a stop just outside the park. This site continues to improve each year. 22 acre site. 150 touring pitches. 85 hardstandings. Caravan pitches. Motorhome pitches. Tent pitches.

Open: Mar-2 Jan **Last arrival:** 21.00hrs **Last departure:** 11.00hrs
Pitches: 🚐 🚐 ▲
Leisure: 🛝 😊 🎱 🖵
Facilities: 🌡️ ☉ 🌢 🔆 ♿ 🖬 🎡 🚽 📶 🖵 ♻️ ℹ️
Services: 🔌 🛢️ 🔒 ⚕️ 🚻 ♨️ ♿
Within 3 miles: ♨️ 🎬 🎣 🛒 🖵 🛢️ ♈

Notes: No camp fires or Chinese lanterns. Dogs must be kept on leads. TV hook-up on all pitches, free WiFi.
AA Pubs & Restaurants nearby: The Rising Sun, POOLE, BH15 1NZ, 01202 771246
The Cock & Bottle, EAST MORDEN, BH20 7DL, 01929 459238

Beacon Hill Touring Park
▶▶▶ 77%

tel: 01202 631631 **Blandford Road North BH16 6AB**
email: bookings@beaconhilltouringpark.co.uk
dir: *On A350, 0.25m N of junct with A35, 3m NW of Poole.* **grid ref:** *SY977945*

Set in an attractive, wooded area with conservation very much in mind. There are two large ponds for coarse fishing within the grounds, and the terraced pitches, with fine views, are informally sited so that visitors can choose their favourite spot. The outdoor swimming pool and tennis court are popular during the summer period. 30 acre site. 170 touring pitches. 10 hardstandings. Caravan pitches. Motorhome pitches. Tent pitches.

Open: Etr-end Oct (rs Low & mid season some services closed/restricted opening)
Last arrival: 23.00hrs **Last departure:** 11.00hrs
Pitches: 🚐 £10.50-£25.50 🚐 £8.50-£23.50 ▲ £8.50-£25.50
Leisure: 🏊 🛝 🎱 🎾 🖵
Facilities: 🌡️ ☉ 🌢 🔆 ♿ 🖬 🎡 🚽 📶 ♻️ ℹ️
Services: 🔌 🛢️ 🔒 ⚕️ 🚽 📞 ♨️ 🛒 ♿
Within 3 miles: ♨️ 🎬 🎣 🖵 🎣 ◎ 🛒 🛢️ ♈

Notes: Groups of young people not accepted during high season.
AA Pubs & Restaurants nearby: The Rising Sun, POOLE, BH15 1NZ, 01202 771246

Places to visit
Tutankhamun Exhibition, DORCHESTER, DT1 1UW, 01305 269571
www.tutankhamun-exhibition.co.uk

Maiden Castle, DORCHESTER, DT2 9PP, 0870 333 1181
www.english-heritage.org.uk/daysout/properties/maiden-castle

Great for kids: Teddy Bear Museum, DORCHESTER, DT1 1JU, 01305 266040
www.teddybearmuseum.co.uk

Portesham Dairy Farm Campsite
▶▶▶▶ 80%

tel: 01305 871297 **Weymouth DT3 4HG**
email: info@porteshamdairyfarm.co.uk
dir: *From Dorchester take A35 towards Bridport. In 5m left at Winterbourne Abbas, follow Portesham signs. Through village, left at Kings Arms pub, site 350yds on right.*
grid ref: *SY602854*

Located at the edge of the picturesque village of Portesham close to the Dorset coast. This family-run, level park is part of a small working farm in a quiet rural location. Fully serviced and seasonal pitches are available. Near the site entrance is a pub where meals are served, and it has a garden for children to play in. 8 acre site. 90 touring pitches. 61 hardstandings. 60 seasonal pitches. Caravan pitches. Motorhome pitches. Tent pitches.

Open: Apr-Sep **Last arrival:** 18.30hrs **Last departure:** 11.00hrs
Pitches: * 🚐 £12-£28 🚐 £12-£28 ▲ £12-£28
Leisure: 🛝 **Facilities:** 🌡️ ☉ 🌢 🔆 🚽 📶 ℹ️
Services: 🔌 🛢️ 🔒 **Within 3 miles:** 🎣 🛢️

Notes: No commercial vehicles, no groups, no camp fires, minimal noise after 22.00hrs. Dogs must be kept on leads. Caravan storage.

PUNCKNOWLE
Map 4 SY58

Places to visit

Dinosaur Museum, DORCHESTER, DT1 1EW, 01305 269880
www.thedinosaurmuseum.com

Hardy's Cottage, DORCHESTER, DT2 8QJ, 01305 262366
www.nationaltrust.org.uk

Great for kids: Abbotsbury Swannery, ABBOTSBURY, DT3 4JG, 01305 871858
www.abbotsbury-tourism.co.uk

Home Farm Caravan and Campsite
►►87%

tel: 01308 897258 **Home Farm, Rectory Ln DT2 9BW**
dir: *From Dorchester towards Bridport on A35, left at start of dual carriageway, at hill bottom right to Litton Cheney. Through village, 2nd left to Puncknowle (Hazel Ln). Left at T-junct, left at phone box. Site 150mtrs on right. Caravan route: approach via A35 Bridport, then Swyre on B3157, continue to Swyre Lane & Rectory Lane.*
grid ref: SY535887

This quiet site, hidden away on the edge of a little hamlet, has good facilities and is an excellent place to camp. It offers sweeping views of the Dorset countryside from most pitches, and is just five miles from Abbotsbury, and one and a half miles from the South West Coast Path. A really good base from which to tour this attractive area. 6.5 acre site. 47 touring pitches. 14 seasonal pitches. Caravan pitches. Motorhome pitches. Tent pitches.

Open: Apr-Oct **Last arrival:** 21.00hrs (late arrival time by prior arrangement)
Last departure: noon

Pitches: ♣ ♣ Å

Facilities: ♠ ⊙ ℰ ☀ ⊙ ♃ ♻ ❶

Services: ♠ ⬛ ⬛ ⬛ ⬛

Within 3 miles: ℰ ⑤

Notes: ⊗ No cats, no wood-burning fires, skateboards, rollerblades, motorised toys or loud music. Dogs must be kept on leads. Calor gas exchange.

AA Pubs & Restaurants nearby: The Crown Inn, PUNCKNOWLE, DT2 9BN, 01308 897711
The Manor Hotel, WEST BEXINGTON, DT2 9DF, 01308 897660

ST LEONARDS

Places to visit

Rockbourne Roman Villa, ROCKBOURNE, SP6 3PG, 01725 518541
www.hants.gov.uk/rockbourne-roman-villa

Red House Museum & Gardens, CHRISTCHURCH, BH23 1BU, 01202 482860
www3.hants.gov.uk/redhouse

Great for kids: Moors Valley Country Park and Forest, RINGWOOD, BH24 2ET,
01425 470721 www.moors-valley.co.uk

ST LEONARDS
Map 5 SU10

PREMIER PARK

Shamba Holidays
►►►►► 85%

Best of British   GOLD

tel: 01202 873302 **230 Ringwood Rd BH24 2SB**
email: enquiries@shambaholidays.co.uk **web:** www.shambaholidays.co.uk
dir: *From Poole on A31, pass Woodman Pub on left, straight on at rdbt (keep in left lane), immediately left into East Moors Ln. Site 1m on right.* **grid ref:** SU105029

This top quality park has excellent modern facilities particularly suited to families, and you can be certain of a warm welcome from the friendly staff. There is a really good indoor/outdoor heated pool, plus a tasteful bar supplying a good range of meals. The park is well located for visiting the south coast, which is just a short drive away, and also for the New Forest National Park. 7 acre site. 150 touring pitches. 40 seasonal pitches. Caravan pitches. Motorhome pitches. Tent pitches.

Open: Mar-Oct (rs Low/mid season some facilities open only at wknds)
Last arrival: 20.00hrs (late arrivals by prior arrangement only)
Last departure: 11.00hrs

Pitches: ♣ ♣ Å   **Leisure:** ♠ ♠ ⋀ ⊛ ♦

Facilities: ♠ ♠ ⊙ ℰ ☀ ⅗ ⊙ ⑤ ⋈ WiFi ♻ ❶

Services: ♠ ⬛ ⬛ ⬛ ⬛ ⊤ ⎯ ⬛ ⬛ ⬛   **Within 3 miles:** ⅃ ℰ ⑤ ⬛ U

Notes: No large groups or commercial vehicles, no noise after 23.00hrs. Dogs must be kept on leads. Phone card top-up facility.

AA Pubs & Restaurants nearby: The Kings Arms, FERNDOWN, BH22 9AA,
01202 577490

See advert on page 204

PITCHES: ♣ Caravans ♣ Motorhomes Å Tents ⋒ Glamping-style accommodation **SERVICES:** ♠ Electric hook up ⑤ Launderette ♈ Licensed bar
♠ Calor Gas ⊘ Camping Gaz ⊤ Toilet fluid ⑩ Café/Restaurant ⬛ Fast Food/Takeaway ⬛ Battery charging ⬛ Baby care ⬛ Motorvan service point
ABBREVIATIONS: BH/bank hols – bank holidays Etr – Easter Spring BH – Spring Bank Holiday fr – from hrs – hours m – mile mdnt – midnight
rdbt – roundabout rs – restricted service wk – week wknd – weekend x-rds – cross roads ⊛ No credit or debit cards ⊗ No dogs ⬛ Children of all ages accepted

ST LEONARDS *continued*

Back of Beyond Touring Park
▶▶▶▶85%

tel: 01202 876968 **234 Ringwood Rd BH24 2SB**
email: info@backofbeyondtouringpark.co.uk
dir: *From E: on A31 over Little Chef rdbt, pass St Leonard's Hotel, at next rdbt U-turn into lane immediately left. Site at end of lane. From W: on A31 pass Texaco garage & Woodman Inn, immediately left to site.* **grid ref:** SU103034

Set well off the beaten track in natural woodland surroundings, with its own river and fishing lake, yet close to many attractions, this tranquil park is run by keen, friendly owners, and the quality facilities are for adults only. There is a 9-hole pitch and putt course, boules and many woodland walks; the park is a haven for wildlife. 30 acre site. 80 touring pitches. 40 seasonal pitches. Caravan pitches. Motorhome pitches. Tent pitches.

Open: Mar-Oct **Last arrival:** 18.00hrs **Last departure:** 11.00hrs

Pitches: * ♣ £25-£29 ♠ £25-£29 ▲ £20-£29

Facilities: ♟⊙♉⚹⚒️🖼️🚻🔌Ⓦ♻⊘ **Services:** ♣⊡🛢⊘Ⓣ⚒⬇

Within 3 miles: ⚓♥♪⚓◎♨🖼️🔵∪

Notes: Adults only. No commercial vehicles. Visiting food vans.

AA Pubs & Restaurants nearby: The Kings Arms, FERNDOWN, BH22 9AA, 01202 577490

Forest Edge Touring Park
▶▶▶79%

tel: 01590 648331 **229 Ringwood Rd BH24 2SD**
email: holidays@shorefield.co.uk **web:** www.shorefield.co.uk
dir: *From E: on A31 over 1st rdbt (Little Chef), pass St Leonards Hotel, left at next rdbt into Boundary Ln, site 100yds on left. From W: on A31 pass Texaco garage & Woodman Inn, right at rdbt into Boundary Ln.* **grid ref:** SU104024

A tree-lined park set in grassland with plenty of excellent amenities for all the family, including an outdoor heated swimming pool, a toddlers' pool and an adventure playground. Visitors are invited to use the superb leisure club plus all amenities and entertainment at the sister site of Oakdene Forest Park, which is less than a mile away. Holiday homes are available for hire. 9 acre site. 72 touring pitches. 29 seasonal pitches. Caravan pitches. Motorhome pitches. Tent pitches. 30 statics.

Open: Feb-3 Jan (rs School & summer hols pool open) **Last arrival:** 21.00hrs
Last departure: 10.00hrs

Pitches: * ♣ £13-£44 ♠ £13-£44 ▲ £11-£33

Leisure: ⚡🅰🔍 **Facilities:** ♟⊙♉⚹Ⓒ🖼️♻⊘

Services: ♣⊡🛢⊘Ⓣ **Within 3 miles:** ⚓♪◎🖼️🔵∪

Notes: Families & couples only, rallies welcome, 1 car & 1 dog per pitch, no gazebos, no noise after 22.00hrs. Dogs must be kept on leads.

AA Pubs & Restaurants nearby: The Kings Arms, FERNDOWN, BH22 9AA, 01202 577490

See advert on page 215

SHAFTESBURY	Map 4 ST82

Places to visit

Shaftesbury Abbey Museum & Garden, SHAFTESBURY, SP7 8JR, 01747 852910
www.shaftesburyabbey.org.uk

Blackmore Vale Caravan & Camping Park
▶▶▶▶84%

tel: 01747 851523 & 01225 290924 **Sherborne Causeway SP7 9PX**
email: info@dche.co.uk
dir: *From Shaftesbury's Ivy Cross rdbt take A30 signed Sherborne. Site 2m on right.* **grid ref:** ST835233

This small park set in open countryside just outside Shaftesbury (famous for the steep, cobbled street known as Gold Hill) now offers a wide range of camping opportunities, including touring pitches with some large hardstandings; a luxury lodge area (four are available for hire); an expanding glamping area which includes stargazer pods; a shepherd's hut; an Airstream caravan; yurts; bell tents and vintage caravans. The facilities are modern and very clean. There is also a fully equipped gym that's available for all customers. 3 acre site. 16 touring pitches. 3 hardstandings. Caravan pitches. Motorhome pitches. Tent pitches. 8 bell tents/yurts. 3 wooden pods.

Open: all year **Last arrival:** 21.00hrs

Pitches: ♣ £15-£25 ♠ £15-£25 ▲ £10-£26 🍽🏠

Leisure: 🏋 **Facilities:** ♟⊙♉⚹ⒸⒼ🖼️🚻🔌♻⊘

Services: ♣⊡🛢⊘Ⓣ⚒🏪 **Within 3 miles:** ♪🖼️🔵

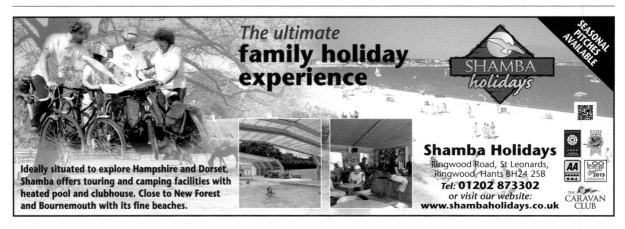

LEISURE: 🏊 Indoor swimming pool 🏊 Outdoor swimming pool 🅰 Children's playground 🎯 Kid's club 🎾 Tennis court 🎱 Games room 📺 Separate TV room ⛳ golf course 🚣 Boats for hire 🎬 Cinema 🎵 Entertainment 🎣 Fishing ◎ Mini golf 🏄 Watersports 🏋 Gym 🏟 Sports field Spa ∪ Stables
FACILITIES: 🛁 Bath 🚿 Shower ⊙ Electric shaver 🔱 Hairdryer ⚹ Ice Pack Facility ♿ Disabled facilities ☎ Public telephone 🏪 Shop on site or within 200yds 🏪 Mobile shop (calls at least 5 days a week) 🍖 BBQ area 🪑 Picnic area Ⓦ Wi-fi 💻 Internet access ♻ Recycling ⊘ Tourist info 🐕 Dog exercise area

Notes: No noise after 23.00hrs. Dogs must be kept on leads. Caravan sales & accessories.

AA Pubs & Restaurants nearby: The Kings Arms Inn, GILLINGHAM, SP8 5NB, 01747 838325

The Coppleridge Inn, MOTCOMBE, SP7 9HW, 01747 851980

SIXPENNY HANDLEY   Map 4 ST91

Places to visit

Larmer Tree Gardens, TOLLARD ROYAL, SP5 5PT, 01725 516971
www.larmertreegardens.co.uk

Shaftesbury Abbey Museum & Garden, SHAFTESBURY, SP7 8JR, 01747 852910
www.shaftesburyabbey.org.uk

Great for kids: Moors Valley Country Park and Forest, RINGWOOD, BH24 2ET, 01425 470721 www.moors-valley.co.uk

Church Farm Caravan & Camping Park
▶▶▶▶85%

tel: 01725 552563 & 07766 677525 **The Bungalow, Church Farm, High St SP5 5ND**
email: churchfarmcandcpark@yahoo.co.uk **web:** www.churchfarmcandcpark.co.uk
dir: *1m S of Handley Hill rdbt. Exit for Sixpenny Handley, right by school, site 300yds by church.* **grid ref:** *ST994173*

A spacious park located within the Cranborne Chase Area of Outstanding Natural Beauty; the site is split into several camping areas including one for adults only. There is a first-class facility block with good private facilities and an excellent café/restaurant. The pretty village of Sixpenny Handley with all its amenities is just 200 yards away, and the site is well positioned for visiting the New Forest National Park, Bournemouth, Poole and Stonehenge. 10 acre site. 35 touring pitches. 4 hardstandings. 5 seasonal pitches. Caravan pitches. Motorhome pitches. Tent pitches. 2 statics.

Open: all year (rs Nov-Mar 10 vans max) **Last arrival:** 21.00hrs **Last departure:** 11.00hrs

Pitches: ⌕ £18-£20 ⌕ £18-£20 ▲ £18-£20

Leisure: ⚠ **Facilities:** ⌕☉⚬☀⚬⌕⌕ ⌕ 🄆 ⌕ ♻ ❶

Services: ⌕⌕ ⌕⌕⌕⌕⌕⌕⌕⌕⌕ **Within 3 miles:** ⌕⌕

Notes: Quiet after 23.00hrs. Dogs must be kept on leads. Use of fridge/freezer & microwave.

AA Pubs & Restaurants nearby: The Museum Inn, FARNHAM, DT11 8DE, 01725 516261

The Drovers Inn, GUSSAGE ALL SAINTS, BH21 5ET, 01258 840084

SWANAGE   Map 5 SZ07

Places to visit

Corfe Castle, CORFE CASTLE, BH20 5EZ, 01929 481294
www.nationaltrust.org.uk

Brownsea Island, BROWNSEA ISLAND, BH13 7EE, 01202 707744
www.nationaltrust.org.uk/brownsea

Great for kids: Swanage Railway, SWANAGE, BH19 1HB, 01929 425800
www.swanagerailway.co.uk

PREMIER PARK

Ulwell Cottage Caravan Park
▶▶▶▶▶81%

tel: 01929 422823 **Ulwell Cottage, Ulwell BH19 3DG**
email: enq@ulwellcottagepark.co.uk **web:** www.ulwellcottagepark.co.uk
dir: *From Swanage N for 2m on unclassified road towards Studland.*
grid ref: *SZ019809*

Sitting under the Purbeck Hills and surrounded by scenic walks, this park is only two miles from the beach. This is a family-run park that caters well for families and couples, and offers a toilet and shower block complete with good family rooms, all appointed to a high standard. There are fully serviced pitches, a good indoor swimming pool and the village inn offers a good range of meals. 13 acre site. 77 touring pitches. 23 hardstandings. Caravan pitches. Motorhome pitches. Tent pitches. 140 statics.

Open: Mar-7 Jan (rs Mar-Spring BH & mid Sep-early Jan takeaway closed, shop open variable hrs) **Last arrival:** 22.00hrs **Last departure:** 11.00hrs

Pitches: ⌕ ⌕ ▲

Leisure: ⚲ ⚠ ✪

Facilities: ⌕☉⌕☀⚬⌕⌕ 🄆 ♻ ❶

Services: ⌕⌕ ⌕⌕⌕⌕⌕⌕

Within 3 miles: ⌕⌕⌕⌕⌕◎⌕⌕⌕U

Notes: No bonfires or fireworks. Dogs must be kept on leads.

AA Pubs & Restaurants nearby: The Bankes Arms Hotel, STUDLAND, BH19 3AU, 01929 450225

The Square and Compass, WORTH MATRAVERS, BH19 3LF, 01929 439229

SWANAGE *continued*

Herston Caravan & Camping Park
►►►79%

tel: 01929 422932 **Washpond Ln BH19 3DJ**
email: office@herstonleisure.co.uk
dir: *From Wareham on A351 towards Swanage. Washpond Ln on left just after 'Welcome to Swanage' sign.* **grid ref:** *SZ018785*

Set in a rural area, with extensive views of the Purbecks, this tree-lined park has fully serviced pitches plus large camping areas. Herston Halt, a stop for the famous Swanage Steam Railway between the town centre and Corfe Castle, is within walking distance. There are also six yurts available for hire. 10 acre site. 100 touring pitches. 71 hardstandings. Caravan pitches. Motorhome pitches. Tent pitches. 5 statics. 6 bell tents/yurts.

Open: all year

Pitches: ⊕ ⇔ Å ⋒

Leisure: ⚑

Facilities: ⌂ ☉ ⅌ ✳ ⅊ 🖽 ⊟ 🖿 🛱 WiFi ♻ ❻

Services: ⊕ ⑤ ⬚ ⬗ T 🍴 ⊞ ♨ ⊎

Within 3 miles: ⌇ ╪ 目 ⅌ ◎ ≼ ⑤ ⑤ ∪

Notes: No noise after 23.00hrs. Dogs must be kept on leads.

AA Pubs & Restaurants nearby: The Bankes Arms Hotel, STUDLAND, BH19 3AU, 01929 450225

The Square and Compass, WORTH MATRAVERS, BH19 3LF, 01929 439229

Acton Field Camping Site
►►77%

tel: 01929 424184 & 439424 **Acton Field, Langton Matravers BH19 3HS**
email: enquiries@actonfieldcampsite.co.uk **web:** www.actonfieldcampsite.co.uk
dir: *From A351 right after Corfe Castle onto B3069 to Langton Matravers, 2nd right after village (bridleway) sign.* **grid ref:** *SY991785*

The informal campsite, bordered by farmland on the outskirts of Langton Matravers, with good toilet facilities. There are superb views of the Purbeck Hills and towards the Isle of Wight, and a footpath leads to the coastal path. The site occupies what was once a stone quarry so rock pegs may be required. 7 acre site. 80 touring pitches. Caravan pitches. Motorhome pitches. Tent pitches.

Open: mid Jul-early Sep (rs Apr-Oct open for organised groups) **Last arrival:** 22.00hrs
Last departure: noon

Pitches: ⊕ ⇔ Å

Facilities: ⌂ ☉ ✳ ⅊ ♻ **Services:** ⊞

Within 3 miles: ⌇ ╪ ⅌ ◎ ≼ ⑤ ⑤ ∪

Notes: ⊘ No open fires, no noise after 23.00hrs. Dogs must be kept on leads.

AA Pubs & Restaurants nearby: The Bankes Arms Hotel, STUDLAND, BH19 3AU, 01929 450225

The Square and Compass, WORTH MATRAVERS, BH19 3LF, 01929 439229

THREE LEGGED CROSS   **Map 5 SU00**

Places to visit
Moors Valley Country Park and Forest, RINGWOOD, BH24 2ET, 01425 470721
www.moors-valley.co.uk

Woolsbridge Manor Farm Caravan Park
►►►►82%

GOLD

tel: 01202 826369 **BH21 6RA**
email: woolsbridge@btconnect.com **web:** www.woolsbridgemanorcaravanpark.co.uk
dir: *From Ringwood take A31 towards Ferndown. Approx 1m, follow signs for Three Legged Cross & Horton. Site 2m on right.* **grid ref:** *SU099052*

A small farm site with spacious pitches on a level field. This quiet site is an excellent central base for touring the New Forest National Park, Salisbury and the

LEISURE: 🏊 Indoor swimming pool 🏊 Outdoor swimming pool ⚑ Children's playground 🧒 Kid's club 🎾 Tennis court ⚫ Games room ▭ Separate TV room ⅃ golf course ⛵ Boats for hire 🎬 Cinema 🎵 Entertainment ⌁ Fishing ◎ Mini golf ≼ Watersports ⅋ Gym ⊕ Sports field Spa ∪ Stables
FACILITIES: 🛁 Bath 🚿 Shower ☉ Electric shaver ⅌ Hairdryer ✳ Ice Pack Facility ♿ Disabled facilities ☎ Public telephone ⑤ Shop on site or within 200yds 🏪 Mobile shop (calls at least 5 days a week) ▦ BBQ area 🛱 Picnic area WiFi Wi-fi 💻 Internet access ♻ Recycling ❻ Tourist info 🛱 Dog exercise area

south coast, and is close to Moors Valley Country Park for outdoor family activities. Facilities are good and very clean and there are excellent family rooms available. 6.75 acre site. 60 touring pitches. Caravan pitches. Motorhome pitches. Tent pitches.

Open: Mar-Oct **Last arrival:** 20.00hrs **Last departure:** 10.30hrs

Pitches: * ⊞ £17.50-£24.50 ⊞ £17.50-£24.50 ▲ £17.50-£24.50

Leisure: ⚲

Facilities: ⬥⊙☏✳⚴⑤☴⌁☸𝟘

Services: ⊡⑤⬛⊘Ⓣ⬛

Within 3 miles: ⚲⚲⑤⑤Ⓤ

Notes: Dogs must be kept on leads.

AA Pubs & Restaurants nearby: The Star Inn, RINGWOOD, BH24 1AW, 01425 473105

See advert below

WAREHAM　　　　　　　　　　　　　　　　　**Map 4 SY98**

Places to visit

Brownsea Island, BROWNSEA ISLAND, BH13 7EE, 01202 707744
www.nationaltrust.org.uk/brownsea

PREMIER PARK

Wareham Forest Tourist Park
▶ ▶ ▶ ▶ ▶ 94%

tel: 01929 551393 **North Trigon BH20 7NZ**
email: holiday@warehamforest.co.uk
dir: *From A35 between Bere Regis & Lytchett Minster follow Wareham sign into Sugar Hill. Site on left.* **grid ref:** SY894912

A woodland park within the tranquil Wareham Forest, with its many walks and proximity to Poole, Dorchester and the Purbeck coast. Two luxury blocks, with combined washbasin and toilets for total privacy, are maintained to a high standard of cleanliness. A heated outdoor swimming pool, off licence, shop and games room add to the pleasure of a stay on this top quality park. 55 acre site. 200 touring pitches. 70 hardstandings. 70 seasonal pitches. Caravan pitches. Motorhome pitches. Tent pitches.

Open: all year (rs Off-peak season limited services) **Last arrival:** 21.00hrs
Last departure: 11.00hrs

Pitches: ⊞ ⊞ ▲

Leisure: ⚲ ⚲ ⚲

Facilities: ⬥⊙☏✳⚴⑤⑤☴⌁WiFi ☸𝟘

Services: ⊡⑤⬛⊘Ⓣ⬛⬆

Within 3 miles: ⚲⚲⊟⚲⑤⑤Ⓤ

Notes: Families & couples only, no group bookings. Dogs must be kept on leads.

AA Pubs & Restaurants nearby: The New Inn, CHURCH KNOWLE, BH20 5NQ, 01929 480357

PITCHES: ⊞ Caravans ⊞ Motorhomes ▲ Tents ⋒ Glamping-style accommodation **SERVICES:** ⊡ Electric hook up ⑤ Launderette ⬛ Licensed bar ⬛ Calor Gas ⊘ Camping Gaz Ⓣ Toilet fluid ⑂ Café/Restaurant ⬛ Fast Food/Takeaway ⬛ Battery charging ⬛ Baby care ⬆ Motorvan service point
ABBREVIATIONS: BH/bank hols – bank holidays　Etr – Easter　Spring BH – Spring Bank Holiday　fr – from　hrs – hours　m – mile　mdnt – midnight
rdbt – roundabout　rs – restricted service　wk – week　wknd – weekend　x-rds – cross roads　⊗ No credit or debit cards　⊗ No dogs　⬥⬥ Children of all ages accepted

WAREHAM *continued*

Birchwood Tourist Park
►►►►80%

tel: 01929 554763 **Bere Rd, Coldharbour BH20 7PA**
email: birchwoodtouristpark@hotmail.com **web:** www.birchwoodtouristpark.co.uk
dir: *From Poole (A351) or Dorchester (A352) on N side of railway line at Wareham, follow Bere Regis signs (unclassified). 2nd park after 2.25m.* **grid ref:** *SY896905*

Set in 50 acres of parkland located within Wareham Forest, this site offers direct access into ideal areas for walking, mountain biking, and horse and pony riding. This is a spacious open park with plenty of room for young people to play games including football. The modern facilities are in two central locations and are very clean. There is a good security barrier system. 25 acre site. 175 touring pitches. 25 hardstandings. Caravan pitches. Motorhome pitches. Tent pitches.

Open: 13 Dec-23 Nov (rs 31 Oct-1 Mar shop/reception open for 2-3 hrs daily)
Last arrival: 21.00hrs **Last departure:** 11.30hrs

Pitches: 🚐 🚃 Å
Leisure: 🎢 ⚽ 🔍
Facilities: 🏕 ⊙ 🌡 ⚙ 🕐 🚿 🖈 📶 ♻ ❶
Services: 🖭 📶 💧 ⊘ 🚽 ♨ 🛒
Within 3 miles: ⚓ 🎣 📎 🛍

Notes: No groups on BH, no generators or camp fires. Dogs must be kept on leads. Pitch & putt, paddling pool.

AA Pubs & Restaurants nearby: The New Inn, CHURCH KNOWLE, BH20 5NQ, 01929 480357

See advert below

LEISURE: 🏊 Indoor swimming pool 🏊 Outdoor swimming pool 🎢 Children's playground 👶 Kid's club 🎾 Tennis court 🎯 Games room 📺 Separate TV room ⛳ golf course 🚣 Boats for hire 🎬 Cinema 🎵 Entertainment 🎣 Fishing ⊙ Mini golf 🏄 Watersports 🏋 Gym ⚽ Sports field Spa ♨ Stables
FACILITIES: 🛁 Bath 🚿 Shower ⊙ Electric shaver 💈 Hairdryer ❄ Ice Pack Facility ♿ Disabled facilities 🕐 Public telephone 🛍 Shop on site or within 200yds 🛒 Mobile shop (calls at least 5 days a week) 🍖 BBQ area 🪑 Picnic area 📶 Wi-fi 💻 Internet access ♻ Recycling ❶ Tourist info 🐕 Dog exercise area

Lookout Holiday Park
►►►►80%

tel: 01929 552546 **Stoborough BH20 5AZ**
email: enquiries@caravan-sites.co.uk **web:** www.thelookoutholidaypark.co.uk
dir: *Take A351 through Wareham, cross River Frome, through Stoborough, site signed on left.* **grid ref:** *SY927858*

Divided into two paddocks and set well back from the Swanage road, this touring park is separated from the static part of the operation (32 static holiday homes are for hire). There are very good facilities including a refurbished toilet block and five camping pods, while a superb children's playground and plenty of other attractions make this an ideal centre for families. The site is very convenient for visiting Corfe and Swanage. 15 acre site. 150 touring pitches. 99 hardstandings. Caravan pitches. Motorhome pitches. Tent pitches. 89 statics. 2 wooden pods.

Open: Mar-Dec (rs no tourers before 22 Mar) **Last arrival:** 22.00hrs **Last departure:** noon
Pitches: 🚐 🚐 ▲ 🏠
Leisure: /🏊 🎣
Facilities: 🚿 ⊙ 🍽 ☀ 🚿 🕙 📷 WiFi ♻ 🔧
Services: 🔌 🗑 🧺 🧴 T 🔋 🍔
Within 3 miles: 🚣 ♨ ⛳ 🏇 📷 🗑 🎬 U
Notes: No pets.
AA Pubs & Restaurants nearby: The New Inn, CHURCH KNOWLE, BH20 5NQ, 01929 480357
See advert below

PITCHES: 🚐 Caravans 🚐 Motorhomes ▲ Tents 🏠 Glamping-style accommodation **SERVICES:** 🔌 Electric hook up 🗑 Launderette 🍷 Licensed bar 🔥 Calor Gas 🔥 Camping Gaz T Toilet fluid 🍽 Café/Restaurant 🍔 Fast Food/Takeaway 🔋 Battery charging 🚼 Baby care ⛟ Motorvan service point **ABBREVIATIONS:** BH/bank hols – bank holidays Etr – Easter Spring BH – Spring Bank Holiday fr – from hrs – hours m – mile mdnt – midnight rdbt – roundabout rs – restricted service wk – week wknd – weekend x-rds – cross roads 🚫 No credit or debit cards 🚫 No dogs ♿ Children of all ages accepted

WAREHAM *continued*

Norden Farm Touring Caravan and Camping Site
►►►►80%

tel: 01929 480098 **Norden Farm, Corfe Castle BH20 5DS**
email: campsite@nordenfarm.com
dir: *On A351 from Wareham towards Swanage, 3.5m to site on right.* **grid ref:** *SY950828*

This delightful farm site offers traditional camping but with excellent toilet and shower facilities. It is a very dog-friendly site and is ideally suited for those who enjoy country pursuits. Its location is very close to Corfe Castle so it's very convenient for visiting the Isle of Purbeck and Swanage (maybe by using the park and ride at Norden railway station and taking the train). There is a holiday cottage for hire plus an AA rated bed & breakfast operation, with a restaurant that's open to all. 10 acre site. 140 touring pitches. variable seasonal pitches. Caravan pitches. Motorhome pitches. Tent pitches.

Open: Mar-Oct **Last arrival:** 22.00hrs **Last departure:** 11.00hrs

Pitches: * 🚐 £14-£20.50 🚈 £14-£20.50 ▲ £14-£20.50

Leisure: ⚤

Facilities: 🌂⊙📁☀🕭🕔🛋🛄🚻🌐♻🛈

Services: 🔌🗑🔋🏠🚽🍽🚚⚒

Within 3 miles: 🎣🏊🎡🚴🛍🗑

Notes: Strict speed limit of 10mph on site, no noise after 23.00hrs. Dogs must be kept on leads. Hot shower washroom for dogs.

AA Pubs & Restaurants nearby: The New Inn, CHURCH KNOWLE, BH20 5NQ, 01929 480357

East Creech Farm Campsite
►►►82%

tel: 01929 480519 & 481312 **East Creech Farm, East Creech BH20 5AP**
email: east.creech@virgin.net
dir: *From Wareham on A351 S towards Swanage. On bypass at 3rd rdbt take Furzebrook/ Blue Pool Rd exit, approx 2m site on right.* **grid ref:** *SY928827*

This grassy park set in a peaceful location beneath the Purbeck Hills, with extensive views towards Poole and Brownsea Island. The park boasts a woodland play area, bright, clean toilet facilities and a farm shop selling milk, eggs and bread. There are also four coarse fishing lakes teeming with fish. The park is close to Norden Station on the Swanage to Norden steam railway line, and is well located for visiting Corfe Castle, Swanage and the Purbeck coast. 4 acre site. 80 touring pitches. Caravan pitches. Motorhome pitches. Tent pitches.

Open: Apr-Oct **Last arrival:** 20.00hrs **Last departure:** noon

Pitches: * 🚐 £12-£15.50 🚈 £12-£15.50 ▲ £12-£15.50

Leisure: ⚤

Facilities: 🌂⊙📁☀♻🛈

Services: 🔌🗑

Within 3 miles: 🎣🏊🎡🚴🛍🗑

Notes: No camp fires, no loud noise. Dogs must be kept on leads.

AA Pubs & Restaurants nearby: The New Inn, CHURCH KNOWLE, BH20 5NQ, 01929 480357

Ridge Farm Camping & Caravan Park
►►►78%

tel: 01929 556444 **Barnhill Rd, Ridge BH20 5BG**
email: info@ridgefarm.co.uk
dir: *From Wareham take B3075 towards Corfe Castle, cross river, into Stoborough, left to Ridge. Follow site signs for 1.5m.* **grid ref:** *SY939868*

A quiet rural park, adjacent to a working farm and surrounded by trees and bushes. This away-from-it-all park is ideally located for touring this part of Dorset, and especially for birdwatchers, or those who enjoy walking and cycling. This site is perfect for visiting the Arne Nature Reserve, the Blue Pool and Corfe Castle. 3.47 acre site. 60 touring pitches. 2 hardstandings. Caravan pitches. Motorhome pitches. Tent pitches.

Open: Etr-Sep **Last arrival:** 21.00hrs **Last departure:** noon

Pitches: 🚐 🚈 ▲

Facilities: 🌂⊙📁☀🕔🛍♻🛈

Services: 🔌🗑🔋🏠🚽🚚

Within 3 miles: 🎣🏊🎡🚴🛍🗑🐴

Notes: 🐾 No dogs Jul-Aug. Dogs must be kept on leads.

AA Pubs & Restaurants nearby: The New Inn, CHURCH KNOWLE, BH20 5NQ, 01929 480357

LEISURE: 🏊 Indoor swimming pool 🏊 Outdoor swimming pool ⚤ Children's playground 🪁 Kid's club 🎾 Tennis court 🎱 Games room 📺 Separate TV room 🏌 golf course ⛵ Boats for hire 🎬 Cinema 🎵 Entertainment 🎣 Fishing ⛳ Mini golf 🏄 Watersports 🏋 Gym 🏟 Sports field Spa ♆ Stables
FACILITIES: 🛁 Bath 🚿 Shower ⊙ Electric shaver 📁 Hairdryer ☀ Ice Pack Facility 🛋 Disabled facilities 🕔 Public telephone 🛍 Shop on site or within 200yds 🛒 Mobile shop (calls at least 5 days a week) 🍖 BBQ area 🏕 Picnic area 🌐 Wi-fi 📶 Internet access ♻ Recycling 🛈 Tourist info 🐾 Dog exercise area

WEYMOUTH

Map 4 SY67

Littlesea Holiday Park
HOLIDAY CENTRE 86%

tel: 0871 231 0879 **Lynch Ln DT4 9DT**
email: littlesea@haven.com **web:** www.haven.com/littlesea
dir: *A35 onto A354 signed Weymouth. Right at 1st rdbt, 3rd exit at 2nd rdbt towards Chickerell. Left into Lynch Lane after lights. Site at far end of road.* **grid ref:** *SY654783*

Open: end Mar-end Oct (rs end Mar-May & Sep-Oct facilities may be reduced)
Last arrival: mdnt **Last departure:** 10.00hrs

Pitches: ⛺ 🚐 ⛺

Leisure: 🏊 🏊 🎱 ✋ 🎯 🎪 ⚽ 🎵

Facilities: 🐕 ⊙ 📷 ✳ ⛱ 🕐 🛁 🛒 🚾 ♻ ⓘ

Services: 🔌 🔋 🍴 🔋 🚿 Ⓣ 🍴 🍺

Within 3 miles: 🚶 🎣 🛒 📷 ◎ 🛒 🏦 🚌 ⛵

Notes: No commercial vehicles, no bookings by persons under 21yrs unless a family booking, no boats, max 2 dogs per booking, certain dog breeds banned.

AA Pubs & Restaurants nearby: The Old Ship Inn, WEYMOUTH, DT3 5QQ, 01305 812522

See advert below

Just three miles from Weymouth with its lovely beaches and many attractions, Littlesea has a cheerful family atmosphere and fantastic facilities. Indoor and outdoor entertainment and activities are on offer for all the family, and the toilet facilities on the touring park are of a good quality. The touring section of this holiday complex is at the far end of the site adjacent to the South West Coast Path in a perfect location. 100 acre site. 120 touring pitches. Caravan pitches. Motorhome pitches. Tent pitches. 720 statics.

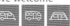

WEYMOUTH *continued*

Seaview Holiday Park
HOLIDAY CENTRE 83%

tel: 0871 231 0877 **Preston DT3 6DZ**
email: seaview@haven.com **web:** www.haven.com/seaview
dir: *A354 to Weymouth, follow signs for Preston/Wareham onto A353. Site 3m on right just after Weymouth Bay Holiday Park.* **grid ref:** SY707830

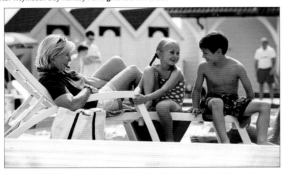

A fun-packed holiday centre for all the family, with plenty of activities and entertainment during the day and evening. Terraced pitches are provided for caravans, and there is a separate field for tents. The park is close to Weymouth and other coastal attractions. There's a smart toilet and shower block, plus fully serviced hardstanding pitches. Holiday homes available for hire. 20 acre site. 87 touring pitches. 35 hardstandings. Caravan pitches. Motorhome pitches. Tent pitches. 259 statics.

Open: mid Mar-end Oct (rs mid Mar-May & Sep-Oct facilities may be reduced)
Last arrival: mdnt **Last departure:** 10.00hrs
Pitches: 🚐 🚃 🛆   **Leisure:** 🏊 🏊 🛝 🛝 🎾 🎱 🎵
Facilities: 🛁 📷 ☉ 🕳 🚹 🕙 🛐 🔺 WIFI ♻ ❶
Services: 🚐 🛢 🍴 🛢 🏠 🍴 🚽
Within 3 miles: ⚓ 🎣 🎳 🏌 ⑥ 🏊 🛒 🛐 🛒 ⛳

Notes: No commercial vehicles, no bookings by persons under 21yrs unless a family booking, max 2 dogs per booking, certain dog breeds banned. Dogs must be kept on leads.
AA Pubs & Restaurants nearby: The Old Ship Inn, WEYMOUTH, DT3 5QQ, 01305 812522

The Smugglers Inn, OSMINGTON MILLS, DT3 6HF, 01305 833125

See advert on opposite page

East Fleet Farm Touring Park
►►►►► 90%

tel: 01305 785768 **Chickerell DT3 4DW**
email: enquiries@eastfleet.co.uk
dir: *On B3157 (Weymouth to Bridport road), 3m from Weymouth.* **grid ref:** SY640797

Set on a working organic farm overlooking Fleet Lagoon and Chesil Beach, with direct access to the coastal path, this park offers a wide range of amenities and quality toilet facilities, with family rooms, housed in a Scandinavian log cabin facility block. The friendly owners, over 25 years at the park, are welcoming and helpful, and their family bar serving meals and takeaway food is open from Easter and has glorious views from the patio area. There is also a good accessory shop. 21 acre site. 400 touring pitches. 90 hardstandings. 40 seasonal pitches. Caravan pitches. Motorhome pitches. Tent pitches.

Open: 16 Mar-Oct **Last arrival:** 22.00hrs **Last departure:** 10.30hrs
Pitches: * 🚐 £16-£26 🚃 £16-£26 🛆 £16-£26
Leisure: 🛝 🎱 🔍
Facilities: 🛁 📷 ☉ 🕳 🚹 🕙 🛐 🔺 WIFI 🖥 ♻ ❶
Services: 🚐 🛢 🍴 🛢 🛢 🍴 🍴 🛒 🚽
Within 3 miles: ⚓ 🎣 🎳 🏌 ⑥ 🏊 🛒 🛐 ⛳

Notes: Dogs must be kept on leads.
AA Pubs & Restaurants nearby: The Old Ship Inn, WEYMOUTH, DT3 5QQ, 01305 812522

Bagwell Farm Touring Park
►►►► 85%

tel: 01305 782575 **Knights in the Bottom, Chickerell DT3 4EA**
email: aa@bagwellfarm.co.uk
dir: *From A354 follow signs for Weymouth town centre, then B3157 to Chickerell & Abbotsbury, 1m past Chickerell left into site 500yds after Victoria Inn.* **grid ref:** SY627816

This well located park is set in a small valley with access to the South West Coast Path and is very convenient for visiting Weymouth and Portland. It has excellent facilities including a good shop, pets' corner, children's play area plus the Red Barn bar and restaurant. A good range of hardstandings are available, including some fully serviced pitches. 14 acre site. 320 touring pitches. 25 hardstandings. 70 seasonal pitches. Caravan pitches. Motorhome pitches. Tent pitches.

Open: all year (rs Winter bar closed) **Last arrival:** 21.00hrs **Last departure:** 11.00hrs
Pitches: * 🚐 £16.50-£30.50 🚃 £16.50-£30.50 🛆 £13-£28
Leisure: 🛝
Facilities: 🛁 📷 ☉ 🕳 🚹 🕙 🛐 🔺 WIFI ♻ ❶
Services: 🚐 🛢 🍴 🛢 🛢 🍴 🍴 🛒 🚽
Within 3 miles: 🛐 🛐 ⛳

Notes: Families & couples only, no noise after 23.00hrs. Dogs must be kept on leads. Wet suit shower, campers' shelter.
AA Pubs & Restaurants nearby: The Old Ship Inn, WEYMOUTH, DT3 5QQ, 01305 812522

West Fleet Holiday Farm

►►► 90%

tel: 01305 782218 **Fleet DT3 4EF**
email: aa@westfleetholidays.co.uk
dir: *From Weymouth take B3157 towards Abbotsbury for 3m. Past Chickerell turn left at mini-rdbt to Fleet, site 1m on right.* **grid ref:** SY625811

A spacious farm site with both level and sloping pitches divided into paddocks and screened by hedges. This site has good views of the Dorset countryside, and is a relaxing place for a family holiday, particularly suited to tents and small motorhomes or campervans. There is a spacious clubhouse with bar, restaurant and entertainment area. WiFi is also available. 12 acre site. 250 touring pitches. Caravan pitches. Motorhome pitches. Tent pitches.

Open: Etr-Sep (rs May-Sep clubhouse & pool only during high season)
Last arrival: 21.00hrs **Last departure:** 11.00hrs

Pitches: * 🚐 £16-£27 🚐 £13-£27 ⛺ £13-£27

Leisure: 🏊 🄰 🎾 🎵 **Facilities:** 🚿 📵 ⊙ 🎣 ✳ ♿ 🖵 📶 ♻ ❶

Services: 🔌 🔘 🍺 🛢 🔥 ⌷ 🍴 🛒 ↯

Within 3 miles: 🚶 🖢 ∪

Notes: Non-family groups by arrangement only. Dogs must be kept on leads & are restricted to certain areas.

AA Pubs & Restaurants nearby: The Old Ship Inn, WEYMOUTH, DT3 5QQ, 01305 812522

Pebble Bank Caravan Park

►►► 86%

tel: 01305 774844 **Camp Rd, Wyke Regis DT4 9HF**
email: info@pebblebank.co.uk
dir: *From Weymouth take Portland road. At last rdbt turn right, then 1st left to Army Tent Camp. Site opposite.* **grid ref:** SY659775

This site, although only one and a half miles from Weymouth, is in a peaceful location overlooking Chesil Beach and the Fleet, and is an excellent place to stay. There is a friendly little bar, which offers even better views. The toilet and shower block is very modern and spotlessly clean. 4 acre site. 40 touring pitches. Caravan pitches. Motorhome pitches. Tent pitches. 80 statics.

Open: Etr-mid Oct (rs High season & wknds only bar open) **Last arrival:** 18.00hrs
Last departure: 11.00hrs

Pitches: * 🚐 £15.50-£28.50 🚐 £15.50-£28.50 ⛺ £10-£26

Leisure: 🄰 **Facilities:** 🚿 📵 ⊙ 🎣 ✳ ♿ 📶 ❶

Services: 🔌 🔘 🍺 🛢 ⌷ 🔋

Within 3 miles: 🚶 🖢 🎯 🎣 ⊚ 🛶 🖢 🍴 🔘 ∪

Notes: Dogs must be kept on leads.

AA Pubs & Restaurants nearby: The Old Ship Inn, WEYMOUTH, DT3 5QQ, 01305 812522

Sea Barn Farm

►►► 82%

tel: 01305 782218 **Fleet DT3 4ED**
email: aa@seabarnfarm.co.uk
dir: *From Weymouth take B3157 towards Abbotsbury for 3m. Past Chickerell turn left at mini-rdbt towards Fleet. Site 1m on left.* **grid ref:** SY625807

This site is set high on the Dorset coast and has spectacular views over Chesil Beach, The Fleet and Lyme Bay, and it is also on the South West Coast Path. Optional use of the clubhouse and swimming pool at West Fleet Holiday Farm is available. Pitches are sheltered by hedging, and there is an excellent toilet facility block, and plenty of space for games. Suitable mainly for tents and small motorhomes or campervans. 12 acre site. 250 touring pitches. Motorhome pitches. Tent pitches. 1 static.

Open: 15 Mar-Oct (rs Mar-Jun & Sep-Oct use of facilities at West Fleet)
Last arrival: 21.00hrs **Last departure:** 11.00hrs

Pitches: * 🚐 £12-£26 ⛺ £12-£26

Leisure: 🄰

Facilities: 🚿 📵 ⊙ 🎣 ✳ ♿ 🖵 🔥 📶 ♻ ❶

Services: 🔌 🔘 🛢 ⌷ ⌷

Within 3 miles: 🚶 🖢 ∪

Notes: Non-family groups by prior arrangement only. Dogs must be kept on leads. Use of West Fleet facilities including outdoor pool & motorhome service point.

AA Pubs & Restaurants nearby: The Old Ship Inn, WEYMOUTH, DT3 5QQ, 01305 812522

PITCHES: 🚐 Caravans 🚐 Motorhomes ⛺ Tents 🏠 Glamping-style accommodation   **SERVICES:** 🔌 Electric hook up 🔘 Launderette 🍺 Licensed bar
🛢 Calor Gas 🔥 Camping Gaz ⌷ Toilet fluid 🍴 Café/Restaurant 🛒 Fast Food/Takeaway 🔋 Battery charging 👶 Baby care ↯ Motorvan service point
ABBREVIATIONS: BH/bank hols – bank holidays Etr – Easter Spring BH – Spring Bank Holiday fr – from hrs – hours m – mile mdnt – midnight
rdbt – roundabout rs – restricted service wk – week wknd – weekend x-rds – cross roads 🚫 No credit or debit cards 🚫 No dogs 👪 Children of all ages accepted

WEYMOUTH *continued*

Rosewall Camping
►►►81%

tel: 01305 832248 **East Farm Dairy, Osmington Mills DT3 6HA**
email: holidays@weymouthcamping.com
dir: *Take A353 towards Weymouth. At Osmington Mills sign (opposite garage) turn left, 0.25m, site on 1st right.* **grid ref:** SY736820

This well positioned, sloping tent site is close to the coast and the South West Coast Path and has great views of Weymouth Bay. There are good toilet and shower blocks at the top and bottom of the site, and also a good shop. This site is a spacious place to camp and very suitable for families. 13 acre site. 225 touring pitches. Motorhome pitches. Tent pitches.

Open: Etr-Oct (rs Apr-May & Oct shop opening times vary) **Last arrival:** 22.00hrs
Last departure: 10.00hrs

Pitches: ⇔ ▲

Leisure: ⌂

Facilities: ┌ ☺ ✳ ⅗ ⑤ ♻ ❼

Services: ▤ ⬛ ⌀ ⛟

Within 3 miles: ⊟ ℘ ≶ ⑤ ⑤ ↻

Notes: Families & couples only, no noise after 23.00hrs. Dogs must be kept on leads. Riding stables & coarse fishing.

AA Pubs & Restaurants nearby: The Old Ship Inn, WEYMOUTH, DT3 5QQ, 01305 812522
The Smugglers Inn, OSMINGTON MILLS, DT3 6HF, 01305 833125

Weymouth Bay Holiday Park
HOLIDAY HOME PARK 91%

tel: 01305 832271 **Preston DT3 6BQ**
email: weymouthbay@haven.com **web:** www.haven.com/weymouthbay
dir: *From A35 towards Dorchester take A354 signed Weymouth. Follow towards Preston signs onto A353. At Chalbury rdbt 1st left into Preston Rd. Park on right.*
grid ref: SY705830

This well-located holiday park, just a short drive away from Weymouth beach, offers the complete holiday experience for the whole family. It has excellent indoor and outdoor pools complete with a 'Lazy River' attraction. There is an excellent choice of eating outlets as well as a full entertainment programme for all. The holiday homes are well appointed throughout. The park is conveniently placed for visiting Portland Bill, Lulworth Cove and Chesil Beach.

Open: Mar-Oct

Change over day: Mon, Fri, Sat

Arrival and departure times: Please contact the site

Statics: 83 Sleeps 6-8 Bedrms 2-3 Bathrms 1-2 Toilets 1-2 Microwave Freezer TV Sky/FTV Elec inc Gas inc Grass area

Children: ♦♦ Cots Highchair **Dogs:** 2 on leads No dangerous dogs

Leisure: ≋ ≋ ⤜ ⌂

PREMIER PARK

Wilksworth Farm Caravan Park
►►►►►87%

tel: 01202 885467 **Cranborne Rd BH21 4HW**
email: info@wilksworthfarmcaravanpark.co.uk
dir: *1m N of Wimborne on B3078.* **grid ref:** SU004018

A popular and attractive park peacefully set in the grounds of a listed house in the heart of rural Dorset. This spacious site has much to offer visitors, including an excellent heated swimming pool, takeaway and café, a bar and restaurant plus a games room and an excellent new Tiny Town play area for young children. The modern toilet facilities contain en suite rooms and good family rooms. 11 acre site. 85 touring pitches. 20 hardstandings. Caravan pitches. Motorhome pitches. Tent pitches. 77 statics.

Open: Apr-Oct (rs Oct no shop) **Last arrival:** 20.00hrs **Last departure:** 11.00hrs

Pitches: ＊ ⇔ £16-£32 ⇔ £16-£32 ▲ £16-£32

Leisure: ≋ ⌂ ⊕ ⚽

Facilities: ⤙ ┌ ☺ ℘ ✳ ⅗ ⓒ ⑤ ⊓ ♙ 📶 ▯ ♻ ❼

Services: ▣ ▤ ⬛ ⌀ Ⓣ ⊙ ⛟ ⤴ ⬇

Within 3 miles: ⌁ ⊟ ℘ ⑤ ⑤

Notes: No cars by tents. Max 2 dogs per pitch, no noise 23.00hrs-07.00 hrs. Dogs must be kept on leads. Paddling pool, volley ball, mini football pitch.

AA Pubs & Restaurants nearby: Les Bouviers Restaurant with Rooms, WIMBORNE MINSTER, BH21 3BD, 01202 889555

Botany Bay Inne, WINTERBORNE ZELSTON, DT11 9ET, 01929 459227

LEISURE: ≋ Indoor swimming pool ≋ Outdoor swimming pool ⌂ Children's playground ⤜ Kid's club ⊕ Tennis court ♙ Games room ▭ Separate TV room ⌁ golf course ⤜ Boats for hire ⊟ Cinema ♪ Entertainment ℘ Fishing ◎ Mini golf ≋ Watersports ♙ Gym ⊕ Sports field Spa ↻ Stables
FACILITIES: ⤙ Bath ┌ Shower ☺ Electric shaver ℘ Hairdryer ✳ Ice Pack Facility ⅗ Disabled facilities ⓒ Public telephone ⑤ Shop on site or within 200yds ⓢ Mobile shop (calls at least 5 days a week) ♙ BBQ area ⊓ Picnic area 📶 Wi-fi ▯ Internet access ♻ Recycling ❼ Tourist info ♙ Dog exercise area

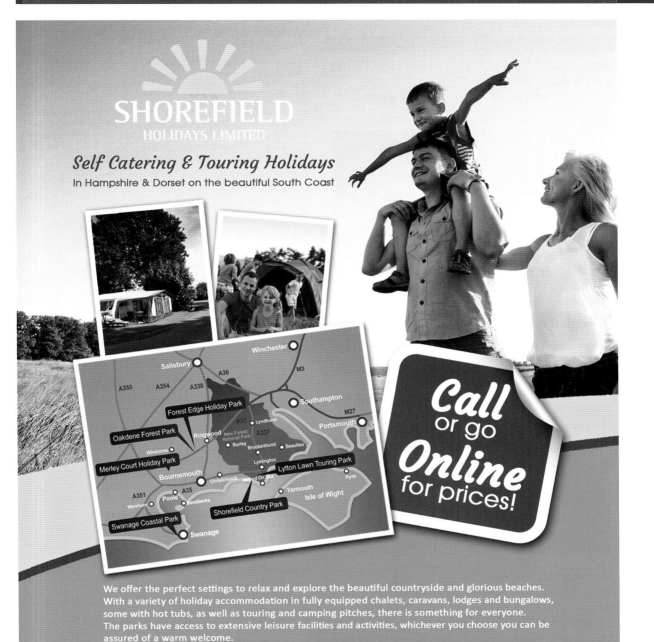

WIMBORNE MINSTER *continued*

Merley Court
►►►►►86%

tel: 01590 648331 **Merley BH21 3AA**
email: holidays@shorefield.co.uk **web:** www.shorefield.co.uk
dir: *Site signed on A31, Wimborne by-pass & Poole junct rdbt.* **grid ref:** *SZ008984*

A superb site in a quiet rural position on the edge of Wimborne, with woodland on two sides and good access roads. The park is well landscaped and offers generous individual pitches in sheltered grassland. There are plenty of amenities for all the family, including a heated outdoor pool, tennis court and adventure playground plus a tastefully appointed bar and restaurant. This park tends to get busy in summer, so advance booking is advised. Three Eurotents are available for hire. 20 acre site. 160 touring pitches. 50 hardstandings. Caravan pitches. Motorhome pitches. Tent pitches. 6 statics. 2 bell tents/yurts.

Open: 6 Feb-2 Jan (rs Low season pool closed & bar, shop open limited hrs)
Last arrival: 21.00hrs **Last departure:** 10.00hrs

Pitches: * ⊞ £13-£44 ⊞ £13-£44 ▲ £13-£40 ⋒

Leisure: ⚄ ⋀ ⚲ ⊙ ❀ **Facilities:** ➤ ⋔ ⊙ ☞ ✳ ⅊ ⓒ ⑤ ⊞ ☵ ▤ ♻ ❶

Services: ⊡ ⑤ ⬟ ⬛ ⬙ ⊘ Ⓣ ⅋ ☷ ⛟ ⛏

Within 3 miles: ⌇ ⧓ ⊟ ⅊ ◎ ⑤ ⑤ ∪

Notes: Families & couples only, no noise after 22.00hrs, rallies welcome. Dogs must be kept on leads. Use of facilities at Oakdene Forest Park (7m).

AA Pubs & Restaurants nearby: Botany Bay Inne, WINTERBORNE ZELSTON, DT11 9ET, 01929 459227

See advert on page 215

Springfield Touring Park
►►►84%

tel: 01202 881719 **Candys Ln, Corfe Mullen BH21 3EF**
email: john.clark18@btconnect.com
dir: *From Wimborne on Wimborne by-pass (A31) at W end turn left after Caravan Sales, follow brown sign.* **grid ref:** *SY987989*

A small touring park with extensive views over the Stour Valley and a quiet and friendly atmosphere. It is well positioned for visiting Poole, Bournemouth or the really lovely town of Wimborne. The park is maintained immaculately, has a well-stocked shop, and is a great place to stay. 3.5 acre site. 45 touring pitches. 30 hardstandings. Caravan pitches. Motorhome pitches. Tent pitches.

Open: Apr-14 Oct **Last arrival:** 21.00hrs **Last departure:** 11.00hrs

Pitches: ⊞ £22-£24 ⊞ £22-£24 ▲ £18-£22

Leisure: ⋀

Facilities: ➤ ⊙ ☞ ✳ ⅊ ⓒ ⑤ ♻ ❶

Services: ⊡ ⑤ ⬟ ☷

Within 3 miles: ⌇ ⧓ ⊟ ⅊ ⑤ ⑤ ∪

Notes: ⊘ No skateboards. Dogs must be kept on leads.

AA Pubs & Restaurants nearby: Les Bouviers Restaurant with Rooms, WIMBORNE MINSTER, BH21 3BD, 01202 889555

Botany Bay Inne, WINTERBORNE ZELSTON, DT11 9ET, 01929 459227

Charris Camping & Caravan Park
►►►81%

tel: 01202 885970 **Candy's Ln, Corfe Mullen BH21 3EF**
email: bookings@charris.co.uk
dir: *From E, exit Wimborne bypass (A31) W end. 300yds after Caravan Sales, follow brown sign. From W on A31, over A350 rdbt, take next turn after B3074, follow brown signs.* **grid ref:** *SY992988*

A sheltered park of grassland lined with trees on the edge of the Stour Valley. Customers can be assured of a warm welcome at this well located park, now under new ownership. Poole and the south coast resorts are only a short drive away. Facilities are very clean, some hardstandings are available, and social get-togethers are held for customers including barbecues which are very popular. 3.5 acre site. 45 touring pitches. 12 hardstandings. 10 seasonal pitches. Caravan pitches. Motorhome pitches. Tent pitches.

Open: all year **Last arrival:** 21.00hrs (earliest possible arrival 11.00hrs by prior arrangement) **Last departure:** 11.00hrs

Pitches: * ⊞ £17.25-£19.25 ⊞ £17.25-£19.25 ▲ £13.50-£15.50

Facilities: ➤ ⊙ ☞ ✳ ⑤ Ⓦ ♻ ❶

Services: ⊡ ⑤ ⬟ ⬙ Ⓣ ☷ **Within 3 miles:** ⌇ ⅊ ⑤ ⑤ ∪

Notes: No noise after 23:00hrs. Dogs must be kept on leads.

AA Pubs & Restaurants nearby: Les Bouviers Restaurant with Rooms, WIMBORNE MINSTER, BH21 3BD, 01202 889555

Botany Bay Inne, WINTERBORNE ZELSTON, DT11 9ET, 01929 459227

LEISURE: ⌂ Indoor swimming pool ⚲ Outdoor swimming pool ⋀ Children's playground ⚲ Kid's club ⚲ Tennis court ❀ Games room ⬚ Separate TV room ⌇ golf course ⧓ Boats for hire ⊟ Cinema ♫ Entertainment ⅊ Fishing ◎ Mini golf ⚱ Watersports ⚐ Gym ⊕ Sports field Spa ∪ Stables
FACILITIES: ⬟ Bath ⋔ Shower ⊙ Electric shaver ☞ Hairdryer ✳ Ice Pack Facility ⓒ Disabled facilities Ⓒ Public telephone ⑤ Shop on site or within 200yds ⑤ Mobile shop (calls at least 5 days a week) ☷ BBQ area ⅋ Picnic area Ⓦ Wi-fi ▤ Internet access ♻ Recycling ❶ Tourist info ⛏ Dog exercise area

WOOL
Map 4 SY88

Places to visit

The Tank Museum, BOVINGTON CAMP, BH20 6JG, 01929 405096
www.tankmuseum.org

Clouds Hill, BOVINGTON CAMP, BH20 7NQ, 01929 405616
www.nationaltrust.org.uk

Great for kids: Monkey World-Ape Rescue Centre, WOOL, BH20 6HH,
01929 462537 www.monkeyworld.org

Whitemead Caravan Park
►►►► 84%

tel: 01929 462241 **East Burton Rd BH20 6HG**
email: whitemeadcp@aol.com **web:** www.whitemeadcaravanpark.co.uk
dir: *Signed from A352 at level crossing on Wareham side of Wool.* **grid ref:** *SY841869*

A well laid-out site in the valley of the River Frome, close to the village of Wool, and
surrounded by woodland. A shop and games room enhance the facilities here, and
the spotless, modern toilets are heated, providing an excellent amenity. Only a short
walk away are the shops and pubs, plus the main bus route and mainline station to
Poole, Bournemouth and Weymouth. 5 acre site. 95 touring pitches. 20 seasonal
pitches. Caravan pitches. Motorhome pitches. Tent pitches.

Open: mid Mar-Oct **Last arrival:** 22.00hrs **Last departure:** noon
Pitches: * 🚐 £16-£23.50 🚍 £16-£23.50 ▲ £13-£20.50
Leisure: ⚫🔍
Facilities: ⚫☉♟☀⚫⚫🚽WiFi ♻ ⚫
Services: ⚫⚫⚫⚫�🚽
Within 3 miles: ⚫♟⚫⚫U
Notes: Dogs must be kept on leads.
AA Pubs & Restaurants nearby: The New Inn, CHURCH KNOWLE, BH20 5NQ,
01929 480357

COUNTY DURHAM

BARNARD CASTLE
Map 19 NZ01

Places to visit

Barnard Castle, BARNARD CASTLE, DL12 8PR, 01833 638212
www.english-heritage.org.uk/daysout/properties/barnard-castle

The Bowes Museum, BARNARD CASTLE, DL12 8NP, 01833 690606
www.thebowesmuseum.org.uk

Great for kids: Raby Castle, STAINDROP, DL2 3AH, 01833 660202
www.rabycastle.com

Pecknell Farm Caravan Park
►►► 79%

tel: 01833 638357 **Lartington DL12 9DF**
dir: *1.5m from Barnard Castle. From A66 take B6277. Site on right 1.5m from junct with
A67.* **grid ref:** *NZ028178*

A small well laid out site on a working farm in beautiful rural meadowland, with
spacious marked pitches on level ground. There are many walking opportunities
that start directly from this friendly site. 1.5 acre site. 20 touring pitches. 5
hardstandings. Caravan pitches. Motorhome pitches.

Open: Apr-Oct **Last arrival:** 20.00hrs **Last departure:** noon
Pitches: 🚐 £13-£19 🚍 £13-£19
Facilities: ⚫☉♟⚫⚫⚫
Services: ⚫🚽
Within 3 miles: ⚫♟⚫⚫⚫U
Notes: ⚫ No noise after 22.30hrs, maximum 2 dogs. Dogs must be kept on leads.
AA Pubs & Restaurants nearby: The Fox and Hounds, COTHERSTONE, DL12 9PF,
01833 650241

The Morritt Arms Hotel, BARNARD CASTLE, DL12 9SE, 01833 627232

The Rose & Crown, ROMALDKIRK, DL12 9EB, 01833 650213

Prefer a child-free site?
See our list on page 41

PITCHES: 🚐 Caravans 🚍 Motorhomes ▲ Tents ⚫ Glamping-style accommodation **SERVICES:** ⚫ Electric hook up ⚫ Launderette ⚫ Licensed bar
⚫ Calor Gas ⚫ Camping Gaz ⚫ Toilet fluid ⚫ Café/Restaurant ⚫ Fast Food/Takeaway ⚫ Battery charging ⚫ Baby care ⚫ Motorvan service point
ABBREVIATIONS: BH/bank hols – bank holidays Etr – Easter Spring BH – Spring Bank Holiday fr – from hrs – hours m – mile mdnt – midnight
rdbt – roundabout rs – restricted service wk – week wknd – weekend x-rds – cross roads ⚫ No credit or debit cards ⚫ No dogs ⚫ Children of all ages accepted

BEAMISH — Map 19 NZ25

Places to visit

Beamish Museum, BEAMISH, DH9 0RG, 0191 370 4000 www.beamish.org.uk

Great for kids: Diggerland, LANGLEY PARK, DH7 9TT, 0871 227 7007 www.diggerland.com

Bobby Shafto Caravan Park
►►►81%

tel: 0191 370 1776 **Cranberry Plantation DH9 0RY**
dir: *From A693 signed Beamish to sign for Beamish Museum. Take approach road, turn right immediately before museum, left at pub to site 1m on right.* **grid ref:** *NZ232545*

A tranquil rural park surrounded by trees, with very clean and well organised facilities. The suntrap touring area has plenty of attractive hanging baskets, and there is a clubhouse with bar, TV and pool. The hardstandings and the 28 fully serviced pitches enhance the amenities. 9 acre site. 83 touring pitches. 47 hardstandings. Caravan pitches. Motorhome pitches. Tent pitches. 54 statics.

Open: Mar-Oct **Last arrival:** 23.00hrs **Last departure:** 11.00hrs

Pitches: * ➡ £22-£31 ➡ £22-£31 ▲ £22-£31 **Leisure:** ⚠☺⚡●▢♫

Facilities: ⬈☉☂✳⚓⚑⛶⚷ WiFi 🖥 ♻ ❂

Services: ⚡🗑 ⚒⚙🖥⛟⚒⛏

Within 3 miles: ⚒⚓☷⚑⛶⚷U

Notes: Dogs must be kept on leads.

AA Pubs & Restaurants nearby: The Stables Pub and Restaurant, STANLEY, DH9 0YB, 01207 288750

BLACKHALL COLLIERY — Map 19 NZ43

Places to visit

Hartlepool's Maritime Experience, HARTLEPOOL, TS24 0XZ, 01429 860077 www.hartlepoolsmaritimeexperience.com

Crimdon Dene
HOLIDAY CENTRE 80%

GOLD

tel: 0871 664 9737 **Coast Rd TS27 4BN**
email: crimdon.dene@park-resorts.com
dir: *From A19 just S of Peterlee, take B1281 signed Blackhall. Through Castle Eden, left in 0.5m signed Blackhall. Approx 3m right at T-junct onto A1086 towards Crimdon. Site in 1m signed on left, by Seagull pub.* **grid ref:** *NZ477378*

A large, popular coastal holiday park, handily placed for access to Teeside, Durham and Newcastle. The park contains a full range of holiday centre facilities for both children and their parents. Touring facilities are appointed to a very good standard. 44 touring pitches. 44 hardstandings. 12 seasonal pitches. Caravan pitches. Motorhome pitches. 586 statics.

Open: Apr-Oct **Last arrival:** 23.00hrs **Last departure:** 10.00hrs

Pitches: ➡ ➡ **Leisure:** ⚑⚠⛶●♫

Facilities: ⬈☉☂⚷⛶ WiFi ♻ ❂

Services: ⚡🗑 ⚒⛟⛏ **Within 3 miles:** ⚒☷⚑⛶⚷U

Notes: No cars by caravans. No quad bikes. Dogs must be kept on leads.

ESSEX

CLACTON-ON-SEA — Map 7 TM11

Places to visit

Harwich Redoubt Fort, HARWICH, CO12 3TE, 01255 503429 www.harwich-society.com

The Beth Chatto Gardens, COLCHESTER, CO7 7DB, 01206 822007

www.bethchatto.co.uk

Great for kids: Colchester Zoo, COLCHESTER, CO3 0SL, 01206 331292 www.colchesterzoo.org

Highfield Grange
HOLIDAY CENTRE 78%

SILVER

tel: 0871 664 9746 **London Rd CO16 9QY**
email: highfield.grange@park-resorts.com
dir: *A12 to Colchester, A120 (Harwich), A133 to Clacton-on-Sea. Site on B1441 clearly signed on left.* **grid ref:** *TM173175*

The modern leisure facilities at this attractively planned park make it an ideal base for a lively family holiday. The swimming complex with both indoor and outdoor pools and a huge water shoot is especially popular. There are fully serviced touring pitches, each with its own hardstanding, located at the heart of the park. The nearby resorts of Walton on the Naze, Frinton and Clacton all offer excellent beaches and a wide range of popular seaside attractions. 30 acre site. 43 touring pitches. 43 hardstandings. Caravan pitches. Motorhome pitches. 509 statics.

Open: Apr-Oct **Last arrival:** mdnt **Last departure:** 10.00hrs

Pitches: ➡ ➡

Leisure: ⚓⚑⚠⚡⛶☺●♫

Facilities: ⬈☉☂⚷☮⛶ WiFi 🖥

Services: ⚡🗑 ⚒⚙⛏

Within 3 miles: ⚒☷⚑⛶◉⚷⛶⚷U

Notes: No fold-in campers or trailer tents.

AA Pubs & Restaurants nearby: The Rose & Crown Hotel, COLCHESTER, CO1 2TZ, 01206 866677

The Whalebone, FINGRINGHOE, CO5 7BG, 01206 729307

Find out about staying at a Holiday Centre in our feature on page 26

LEISURE: 🏊 Indoor swimming pool 🏊 Outdoor swimming pool ⚠ Children's playground 🚣 Kid's club ⚑ Tennis court ● Games room ▢ Separate TV room ⛳ golf course ⛵ Boats for hire ⛶ Cinema ♫ Entertainment ⚓ Fishing ◉ Mini golf ⛴ Watersports 💪 Gym ⚽ Sports field Spa U Stables
FACILITIES: 🛁 Bath ⬈ Shower ☉ Electric shaver ☂ Hairdryer ✳ Ice Pack Facility ⚷ Disabled facilities ☏ Public telephone ⛶ Shop on site or within 200yds 🏪 Mobile shop (calls at least 5 days a week) 🍖 BBQ area ⛶ Picnic area WiFi Wi-fi 🖥 Internet access ♻ Recycling ❂ Tourist info ⛏ Dog exercise area

Martello Beach Holiday Park
HOLIDAY CENTRE 77%

BRONZE

tel: 0871 664 9782 & 01442 830100 **Belsize Av, Jaywick CO15 2LF**
email: martello.beach@park-resorts.com
dir: *Phone for detailed directions.* **grid ref:** *TM136128*

Direct access to a seven-mile long Blue Flag beach is an undoubted attraction at this holiday park. The touring area is next to the leisure complex, where an indoor and outdoor swimming pool, shops, cafés and bars and evening entertainment are all provided. 40 acre site. 100 touring pitches. Caravan pitches. Motorhome pitches. Tent pitches. 294 statics.

Open: Apr-Oct **Last arrival:** 21.30hrs **Last departure:** 10.00hrs

Pitches: 🚐 🚛 Å

Leisure: 🎣 🏊 ⚓ 🎯 ⊙ 🎱 🎵

Facilities: 🛁 ⊙ 🍴 ✳ 🕹 🕐 💲 📶 🖥

Services: 🔌 🗑 🍴 🚿 🍴 ♨

Within 3 miles: 🚴 🎣 🏊 💲 🗑 ∪

Notes: 🚫 Watersports.

AA Pubs & Restaurants nearby: The Rose & Crown Hotel, COLCHESTER, CO1 2TZ, 01206 866677

The Whalebone, FINGRINGHOE, CO5 7BG, 01206 729307

GREAT SALING
Map 12 TL72

Places to visit

Paycocke's, COGGESHALL, CO6 1NS, 01376 561305
www.nationaltrust.org.uk/paycockes

Golden Grove
▶ 78%

tel: 07917 592310 **Piccotts Ln CM7 5DW**
email: louise@salinggrove.com
dir: *M11 junct 8A, A120 (Colchester). S of Dunmow take B1256 towards Braintree. In 8m left signed Great Saling. Enter village, right into Piccotts Lane.* **grid ref:** *TL704252*

This site has just nine pitches and enjoys a peaceful and secluded location behind a large country house, screened by a high line of trees and with a wide expanse of meadow to the front. The all-electric pitches are set out on a wide swathe of gravel and a timber chalet houses a single unisex cubicle with washbasins and toilet, a small lounge and library. The whole setting is very rural and abounds with wildlife. 6 acre site. 9 touring pitches. 9 hardstandings. Caravan pitches. Motorhome pitches. Tent pitches.

Open: all year **Last arrival:** 18.00hrs **Last departure:** noon

Pitches: * 🚐 £12 🚛 £12 Å £10

Facilities: 🍴 🎯 🎱 ♨ ⓘ

Services: 🔌 T 🚿

Within 3 miles: 💲

Notes: Adults only. 🚫 No noise after 22.00hrs. Dogs must be kept on leads.

MERSEA ISLAND
Map 7 TM01

Places to visit

Layer Marney Tower, LAYER MARNEY, CO5 9US, 01206 330784
www.layermarneytower.co.uk

Waldegraves Holiday Park
HOLIDAY CENTRE 80%

GOLD

tel: 01206 382898 **CO5 8SE**
email: holidays@waldegraves.co.uk **web:** www.waldegraves.co.uk
dir: *A12 junct 26, B1025 to Mersea Island across The Strood. Left to East Mersea, 2nd right, follow tourist signs to site.* **grid ref:** *TM033133*

A spacious and pleasant site located between farmland and its own private beach on the Blackwater Estuary. The facilities include two freshwater fishing lakes, a heated swimming pool, café, club, amusements and golf; there is generally good provision for families. Holiday static caravans are available for hire. 25 acre site. 60 touring pitches. 30 seasonal pitches. Caravan pitches. Motorhome pitches. Tent pitches. 250 statics.

Open: Mar-Nov (rs Mar-Jun & Sep-Nov (excl BH & school half terms) pool, shop & clubhouse reduced opening hrs; pool open May-Sep weather permitting)
Last arrival: 22.00hrs **Last departure:** 13.00hrs

Pitches: 🚐 £18-£30 🚛 £18-£30 Å £18-£30 **Leisure:** 🎣 ⚓ 🎯 ⊙ 🎱 🎵

Facilities: 🛁 ⊙ 🍴 ✳ 🕹 🕐 💲 🍴 🎯 📶 ♨ ⓘ

Services: 🔌 🗑 🍴 🛢 🚿 T 🍴 🚿 ♨ 🚼 ⚡ **Within 3 miles:** 🚴 🎣 ⊙ 🏊 💲 🗑

Notes: No groups of under 21s. Dogs must be kept on leads. Boating, slipway, pitch & putt, driving range, crazy golf, family games room, family entertainment.

AA Pubs & Restaurants nearby: The Peldon Rose, PELDON, CO5 7QJ, 01206 735248

MERSEA ISLAND *continued*

Fen Farm Caravan Site
►►►►80%

GOLD

tel: 01206 383275 **Moore Ln, East Mersea CO5 8FE**
email: havefun@fenfarm.co.uk
dir: B1025 from Colchester to Mersea Island, left signed East Mersea. 1st right after Dog & Pheasant pub into Moore Lane. NB road is tidal, please check tide times.
grid ref: TM059143

The first tents were pitched at Fen Farm in 1923 and over the years the farm gave way entirely to becoming a caravan park. Enjoying an enviable location beside the Blackwater Estuary, it has unique atmosphere with a mixture of meadow, woodland and marine shore, and varied wildlife to match each environment. There are two excellent solar-heated toilet blocks, which include three family rooms and privacy cubicles, with the newest block constructed in the local style of black clapboard and a red tile roof. There is a woodland dog walk and two well-equipped play areas, while crabbing in the beach pools is also a popular pastime. 65 touring pitches. 3 hardstandings. 65 seasonal pitches. Caravan pitches. Motorhome pitches. Tent pitches. 90 statics.

Open: Mar-Oct
Pitches: ⌂ ⌂ Å
Leisure: ⌂ ⊙
Facilities: ⌂ ⌂ ✳ ⌂ ⊙ ⌂ ⌂ ⌂ ♻ ⊙
Services: ⌂ ⌂ ⌂ ⌂ ⊤ ⌂
Within 3 miles: ⌂ ◎ ⌂ ⌂
Notes: No open fires, no noise after 23.00hrs. Dogs must be kept on leads.
AA Pubs & Restaurants nearby: The Peldon Rose, PELDON, CO5 7QJ, 01206 735248

Seaview Holiday Park
►►►79%

tel: 01206 382534 **Seaview Av, West Mersea CO5 8DA**
email: seaviewholidaypark@googlemail.com
dir: From A12 (Colchester) onto B1025 (Mersea Island), cross causeway, left towards East Mersea, 1st right, follow signs. **grid ref:** TM025125

With sweeping views across the Blackwater estuary, this interesting, well-established park has its own private beach, complete with boat slipway and attractive beach cabins, a modern shop, café and a stylish clubhouse which offers evening meals and drinks in a quiet family atmosphere. The touring area is well maintained and has 40 fully serviced pitches. 30 acre site. 106 touring pitches. 40 hardstandings. 30 seasonal pitches. Caravan pitches. Motorhome pitches. 240 statics.

Open: Apr-Oct **Last arrival:** 18.00hrs (phone site if late arrival expected)
Last departure: noon
Pitches: ⌂ ⌂
Facilities: ⌂ ⌂ ⊙ ⌂ ⌂ ⊙
Services: ⌂ ⌂ ⌂ ⌂ ⌂ ⌂
Within 3 miles: ⌂ ⌂ ⌂ ⌂ ⌂ ∪
Notes: No noise after mdnt, no boats or jet skis. Dogs must be kept on leads. Private beach.
AA Pubs & Restaurants nearby: The Peldon Rose, PELDON, CO5 7QJ, 01206 735248

Riverside Village Holiday Park
►►►79%

tel: 01702 258297 **Creeksea Ferry Rd, Wallasea Island, Canewdon SS4 2EY**
email: riversidevillage@tiscali.co.uk
dir: M25 junct 29, A127 towards Southend-on-Sea. Take B1013 towards Rochford. Follow signs for Wallasea Island & Baltic Wharf. **grid ref:** TQ929951

Situated next to a nature reserve beside the River Crouch, this holiday park is surrounded by wetlands but only eight miles from Southend. A modern toilet block, with disabled facilities, is provided for tourers and there's a handsome reception area. The park has several fishing lakes for site guests (permits available at reception). Several restaurants and pubs are within a short distance. 25 acre site. 60 touring pitches. Caravan pitches. Motorhome pitches. Tent pitches. 159 statics.

Open: Mar-Oct
Pitches: * ⌂ fr £24 ⌂ fr £24 Å fr £16
Leisure: ⌂
Facilities: ⌂ ⊙ ⌂ ✳ ⌂ ⊙ ⌂ ⌂ ⌂ ♻ ⊙
Services: ⌂ ⌂ ⌂ ⌂ ⊤
Within 3 miles: ⌂ ⌂ ⌂ ⌂ ∪
Notes: No dogs in tents. Dogs must be kept on leads. Mobile newspaper vendor Sun & BHs.

Waterside St Lawrence Bay
HOLIDAY CENTRE 79%

SILVER

tel: 0871 664 9794 **Main Rd CM0 7LY**
email: waterside@park-resorts.com
dir: A12 towards Chelmsford, A414 signed Maldon. Follow B1010 & signs to Latchingdon, then signs for Mayland/Steeple/St Lawrence. Left towards St Lawrence. Site on right.
grid ref: TL953056

Waterside occupies a scenic location overlooking the Blackwater Estuary. In addition to the range of on-site leisure facilities there are opportunities for beautiful coastal walks and visits to the attractions of Southend. Tents are welcome on this expansive site, which has some touring pitches with electricity and good toilet facilities. The park has its own boat storage and slipway onto the Blackwater. 72 touring pitches. Caravan pitches. Motorhome pitches. Tent pitches. 271 statics.

Open: Apr-Oct (rs Wknds) **Last arrival:** 22.00hrs **Last departure:** 10.00hrs
Pitches: ⌂ ⌂ Å
Leisure: ⌂ ⌂ ⌂ ⌂ ⌂
Facilities: ⌂ ⌂ ⊙ ⌂ ⊙ ⌂ ⌂ ⌂ ⌂
Services: ⌂ ⌂ ⌂ ⌂ ⌂
Within 3 miles: ⌂ ⌂ ⌂ ⌂
Notes: Sauna, spa pool.
AA Pubs & Restaurants nearby: Ye Olde White Harte Hotel, BURNHAM-ON-CROUCH, CM0 8AS, 01621 782106

The Ferry Boat Inn, NORTH FAMBRIDGE, CM3 6LR, 01621 740208

LEISURE: ⌂ Indoor swimming pool ⌂ Outdoor swimming pool ⌂ Children's playground ⌂ Kid's club ⌂ Tennis court ⌂ Games room ⌂ Separate TV room ⌂ golf course ⌂ Boats for hire ⌂ Cinema ⌂ Entertainment ⌂ Fishing ◎ Mini golf ⌂ Watersports ⌂ Gym ⊙ Sports field Spa ∪ Stables
FACILITIES: ⌂ Bath ⌂ Shower ⊙ Electric shaver ⌂ Hairdryer ✳ Ice Pack Facility ⌂ Disabled facilities ⊙ Public telephone ⌂ Shop on site or within 200yds ⌂ Mobile shop (calls at least 5 days a week) ⌂ BBQ area ⌂ Picnic area ⌂ Wi-fi ⌂ Internet access ♻ Recycling ⊙ Tourist info ⌂ Dog exercise area

ST OSYTH

Map 7 TM11

Places to visit

Colchester, St Botolph's Priory, COLCHESTER
www.english-heritage.org.uk/daysout/properties/colchester-st-botolphs-priory

Colchester Castle Museum, COLCHESTER, CO1 1TJ, 01206 282939
www.colchestermuseums.org.uk

Great for kids: Colchester Zoo, COLCHESTER, CO3 0SL, 01206 331292
www.colchesterzoo.org

The Orchards Holiday Park
HOLIDAY CENTRE 79%

tel: 0871 231 0861 **CO16 8LJ**
email: theorchards@haven.com **web:** www.haven.com/theorchards
dir: *From Clacton-on-Sea take B1027 towards Colchester. Left after petrol station, straight on at x-rds in St Osyth. Follow signs to Point Clear. Park in 3m.*
grid ref: *TM125155*

The Orchards offers good touring facilities with a quality toilet block which includes a laundry, play area and two very spacious family rooms. The touring pitches are generously sized. There's also direct access to all the leisure, entertainment and dining outlets available on this large popular holiday park on the Essex coast. 140 acre site. 63 touring pitches. Caravan pitches. Tent pitches. 1000 statics.

Open: end Mar-end Oct (rs end Mar-May & Sep-end Oct some facilities may be reduced) **Last arrival:** anytime **Last departure:** 10.00hrs

Pitches: 🚐 ⛺

Leisure: 🏊 🏊 ⚙ 🎵 🎿

Facilities: 🌂 ☉ 🍳 ♿ 🕐 💲 📶 🖥 ♻ ❶

Services: 🔌 🗄 🍴 🛍 🍽 🛒

Within 3 miles: 🎣 🐾 ◎ 🚣 🛍 🗄 ⛳ ↺

Notes: No cars by tents. No commercial vehicles, no bookings by persons under 21yrs unless a family booking, max 2 dogs per booking, certain dog breeds banned.

AA Pubs & Restaurants nearby: The Rose & Crown Hotel, COLCHESTER, CO1 2TZ, 01206 866677

The Whalebone, FINGRINGHOE, CO5 7BG, 01206 729307

See advert below

PITCHES: 🚐 Caravans 🚙 Motorhomes ⛺ Tents 🏠 Glamping-style accommodation **SERVICES:** 🔌 Electric hook up 🗄 Launderette 🍷 Licensed bar 🛍 Calor Gas ⛽ Camping Gaz Ⓣ Toilet fluid 🍽 Café/Restaurant 🍴 Fast Food/Takeaway 🔋 Battery charging 👶 Baby care 🚐 Motorvan service point
ABBREVIATIONS: BH/bank hols – bank holidays Etr – Easter Spring BH – Spring Bank Holiday fr – from hrs – hours m – mile mdnt – midnight rdbt – roundabout rs – restricted service wk – week wknd – weekend x-rds – cross roads 🚫 No credit or debit cards 🚫 No dogs 👫 Children of all ages accepted

WALTON ON THE NAZE
Map 7 TM22

Naze Marine
HOLIDAY CENTRE 73%

tel: 0871 664 9755 **Hall Ln CO14 8HL**
email: naze.marine@park-resorts.com
dir: *A12 to Colchester. Then A120 (Harwich road), then A133 to Weeley. Take B1033 to Walton on the Naze seafront. Site on left.* **grid ref:** *TM255226*

With its modern indoor swimming pool, show bar, bar/restaurant and amusements, this park offers a variety of on-site attractions. The park is within easy access of the beaches and attractions of Walton on the Naze, Frinton and Clacton, and the more historic places of interest inland. Please note that this site does not cater for tents. 46 acre site. 41 touring pitches. Caravan pitches. Motorhome pitches. 540 statics.

Open: Apr-Oct **Last arrival:** anytime **Last departure:** 10.00hrs

Pitches: ⊕ ⊕

Leisure: ≋ ⋀ ⋓ ♫

Facilities: ⋔ ⊙ ⅇ ⅅ ⑤ ⇧ ⇧ 🖵

Services: ⊕ ⑤ ⋢ ⦿ ⊜

Within 3 miles: ⅃ ⅇ ⅍ ⑤ ⑤

Notes: Dogs must be kept on leads. Nature walk, natural meadowland.

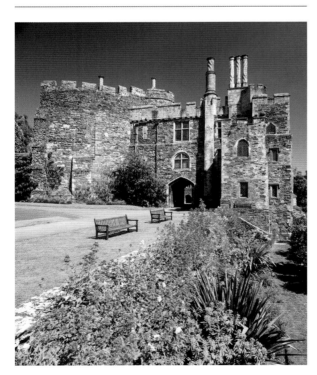

GLOUCESTERSHIRE

BERKELEY
Map 4 ST69

Places to visit
Dr Jenner's House, BERKELEY, GL13 9BN, 01453 810631
www.jennermuseum.com

WWT Slimbridge Wetland Centre, SLIMBRIDGE, GL2 7BT, 01453 891900
www.wwt.org.uk/slimbridge

Great for kids: Berkeley Castle & Butterfly House, BERKELEY, GL13 9BQ, 01453 810303 www.berkeley-castle.com

Hogsdown Farm Caravan & Camping Park
▶▶▶ 79%

tel: 01453 810224 **Hogsdown Farm, Lower Wick GL11 6DD**
web: www.hogsdownfarm.co.uk
dir: *M5 junct 14 (Falfield), A38 towards Gloucester. Through Stone & Woodford. After Newport turn right signed Lower Wick.* **grid ref:** *ST710974*

A pleasant site with good toilet facilities, located between Bristol and Gloucester. It is well positioned for visiting Berkeley Castle and the Cotswolds, and makes an excellent overnight stop when travelling to or from the West Country. 5 acre site. 45 touring pitches. 12 hardstandings. Caravan pitches. Motorhome pitches. Tent pitches.

Open: all year **Last arrival:** 21.00hrs **Last departure:** 16.00hrs

Pitches: ⊕ ⊕ ⋀

Leisure: ⋀

Facilities: ⋔ ⊙ ✳ ♻ ❼

Services: ⊕ ⑤ ⬛ ⋢

Within 3 miles: ⅃ ⅇ ⑤ ⑤ ∪

Notes: No skateboards or bicycles. Dogs must be kept on leads.

AA Pubs & Restaurants nearby: The Malt House, BERKELEY, GL13 9BA, 01453 511177
The Anchor Inn, OLDBURY-ON-SEVERN, BS35 1QA, 01454 413331

LEISURE: ≋ Indoor swimming pool ≋ Outdoor swimming pool ⋀ Children's playground ⋓ Kid's club ⊛ Tennis court ⦿ Games room ▯ Separate TV room
⅃ golf course ⛵ Boats for hire ▤ Cinema ♫ Entertainment ℘ Fishing ◎ Mini golf ⋧ Watersports ⋇ Gym ⊕ Sports field Spa ∪ Stables
FACILITIES: ⬿ Bath ⋔ Shower ⊙ Electric shaver ℘ Hairdryer ✳ Ice Pack Facility ⅇ Disabled facilities ⓒ Public telephone ⑤ Shop on site or within 200yds
⑤ Mobile shop (calls at least 5 days a week) ⛭ BBQ area ⇧ Picnic area ⇧ Wi-fi 🖵 Internet access ♻ Recycling ❼ Tourist info ⇥ Dog exercise area

CHELTENHAM — Map 10 SO92

Places to visit

Holst Birthplace Museum, CHELTENHAM, GL52 2AY, 01242 524846
www.holstmuseum.org.uk

Sudeley Castle, Gardens & Exhibitions, WINCHCOMBE, GL54 5JD, 01242 609485
www.sudeleycastle.co.uk

Great for kids: Gloucester City Museum & Art Gallery, GLOUCESTER, GL1 1HP,
01452 396131 www.gloucester.gov.uk/citymuseum

Briarfields Motel & Touring Park
►►►► 86%

tel: 01242 235324 **Gloucester Rd GL51 0SX**
email: briarfields@hotmail.co.uk
dir: M5 junct 11, A40 towards Cheltenham. At rdbt left onto B4063, site 200mtrs on left.
grid ref: SO909218

A well-designed level park, with a motel, where the facilities are modern and very clean. The park is well-positioned between Cheltenham and Gloucester, with easy access to the Cotswolds. And, being close to the M5, it makes a perfect overnight stopping point. 5 acre site. 72 touring pitches. 72 hardstandings. Caravan pitches. Motorhome pitches. Tent pitches.

Open: all year **Last arrival:** 21.00hrs **Last departure:** noon
Pitches: * ⚐ £16-£19 ⚐ £16-£19 ▲ £12-£15
Facilities: various
Services: various
Within 3 miles: various
Notes: No noise after 22.00hrs. Dogs must be kept on leads.
AA Pubs & Restaurants nearby: The Gloucester Old Spot, CHELTENHAM, GL51 9SY, 01242 680321
The Royal Oak Inn, CHELTENHAM, GL52 3DL, 01242 522344

CIRENCESTER — Map 5 SP00

Places to visit

Corinium Museum, CIRENCESTER, GL7 2BX, 01285 655611
www.coriniummuseum.org

Mayfield Touring Park
►►►► 81%

tel: 01285 831301 **Cheltenham Rd GL7 7BH**
email: mayfield-park@cirencester.fsbusiness.co.uk
dir: In Cirencester at rdbt junct of A429 & A417, take A417 signed Cheltenham & A435. Right onto A435, follow brown camping signs to site on left. **grid ref:** SP020055

A gently sloping park on the edge of the Cotswolds, with level pitches and a warm welcome. Popular with couples and families, it offers a good licensed shop selling a wide selection of home-cooked takeaway food. This lovely park makes an ideal base for exploring the Cotswolds and its many attractions, and for walking the nearby Monarch's Way and the Cotswold Way long-distance paths. 12 acre site. 72 touring pitches. 31 hardstandings. 10 seasonal pitches. Caravan pitches. Motorhome pitches. Tent pitches. 33 statics.

Open: all year **Last arrival:** 20.00hrs **Last departure:** noon
Pitches: * ⚐ £16-£24 ⚐ £16-£24 ▲ £13-£21
Facilities: various
Services: various
Within 3 miles: various
Notes: No cycles or skateboards. Dogs only by prior arrangement. Dogs must be kept on leads.
AA Pubs & Restaurants nearby: The Crown of Crucis, CIRENCESTER, GL7 5RS, 01285 851806
Hare & Hounds, CHEDWORTH, GL54 4NN, 01285 720288

GLOUCESTER — Map 10 SO81

Places to visit

Gloucester Folk Museum, GLOUCESTER, GL1 2PG, 01452 396868
www.gloucester.gov.uk/folkmuseum

Nature in Art, GLOUCESTER, GL2 9PA, 01452 731422 www.nature-in-art.org.uk

Great for kids: The Gloucester Waterways Museum, GLOUCESTER, GL1 2EH,
01452 318200 www.canalrivertrust.org.uk/gloucester-waterways-museum

Red Lion Caravan & Camping Park
►►► 76%

tel: 01452 731810 & 01299 400787 **Wainlode Hill, Norton GL2 9LW**
dir: Exit A38 at Norton, follow road to river. **grid ref:** SO849258

An attractive meadowland park, adjacent to a traditional pub, with the River Severn just across a country lane. There is a private lake for freshwater fishing. This makes an ideal touring base. 24 acre site. 60 touring pitches. 10 hardstandings. 60 seasonal pitches. Caravan pitches. Motorhome pitches. Tent pitches. 85 statics.

Open: all year **Last arrival:** 22.00hrs **Last departure:** 11.00hrs
Pitches: ⚐ ⚐ ▲
Leisure: various
Facilities: various
Services: various
Within 3 miles: various
Notes: various
AA Pubs & Restaurants nearby: Queens Head, GLOUCESTER, GL2 9EJ, 01452 301882
The Queens Arms, ASHLEWORTH, GL19 4HT, 01452 700395

PITCHES: Caravans Motorhomes Tents Glamping-style accommodation **SERVICES:** Electric hook up Launderette Licensed bar Calor Gas Camping Gaz Toilet fluid Café/Restaurant Fast Food/Takeaway Battery charging Baby care Motorvan service point **ABBREVIATIONS:** BH/bank hols – bank holidays Etr – Easter Spring BH – Spring Bank Holiday fr – from hrs – hours m – mile mdnt – midnight rdbt – roundabout rs – restricted service wk – week wknd – weekend x-rds – cross roads No credit or debit cards No dogs Children of all ages accepted

NEWENT
Map 10 SO72

Places to visit

Odda's Chapel, DEERHURST, 0870 333 1181
www.english-heritage.org.uk/daysout/properties/oddas-chapel

Westbury Court Garden, WESTBURY-ON-SEVERN, GL14 1PD, 01452 760461
www.nationaltrust.org.uk

Great for kids: International Centre for Birds of Prey, NEWENT, GL18 1JJ,
01531 820286 www.icbp.org

Pelerine Caravan and Camping
►►►83%

tel: 01531 822761 & 07909 914262 **Ford House Rd GL18 1LQ**
email: pelerine@hotmail.com
dir: *1m from Newent.* **grid ref:** *SO645183*

A pleasant, French-themed site divided into separate areas (Rue de Pelerine and
Avenue des Families), plus one for adults-only; there are some hardstandings and
electric hook-ups in each area. Facilities are very good, especially for families. It is
close to several vineyards, and well positioned in the north of the Forest of Dean
with Tewkesbury, Cheltenham and Ross-on-Wye within easy reach. 5 acre site. 35
touring pitches. 2 hardstandings. Caravan pitches. Motorhome pitches. Tent
pitches.

Open: Mar-Nov **Last arrival:** 22.00hrs **Last departure:** 16.00hrs

Pitches: 🚐 fr £20 🚳 fr £20 ▲ fr £20

Facilities: 🏟⊙☝✳️🚿🛜 ♻️ ❶

Services: 🚘📶 ➿

Within 3 miles: ♨️🖿🖋🛒🏪♻️∪

Notes: 🐕 Dogs must be kept on leads. Woodburners, chimneas, burning pits available.

AA Pubs & Restaurants nearby: The Yew Tree, CLIFFORD'S MESNE, GL18 1JS,
01531 820719

Three Choirs Vineyards, NEWENT, GL18 1LS, 01531 890223

SLIMBRIDGE
Map 4 SO70

Places to visit

Berkeley Castle & Butterfly House, BERKELEY, GL13 9BQ, 01453 810303
www.berkeley-castle.com

Great for kids: WWT Slimbridge Wetland Centre, SLIMBRIDGE, GL2 7BT,
01453 891900 www.wwt.org.uk/slimbridge

Tudor Caravan & Camping
►►►►88%

tel: 01453 890483 **Shepherds Patch GL2 7BP**
email: aa@tudorcaravanpark.co.uk **web:** www.tudorcaravanpark.com
dir: *M5 juncts 13 & 14 follow WWT Wetlands Wildlife Centre-Slimbridge signs. Site at rear
of Tudor Arms pub.* **grid ref:** *SO728040*

This park benefits from one of the best locations in the county, situated right
alongside the Sharpness to Gloucester canal and just a short walk from the famous
Wildfowl & Wetlands Trust at Slimbridge. The site has two areas, one for adults
only, and a more open area with a facility block. There are both grass and gravel
pitches complete with electric hook-ups. Being next to the canal, there are excellent
walks plus the National Cycle Network route 41 can be accessed from the site.
There is a pub and restaurant adjacent to the site. 8 acre site. 75 touring pitches.
48 hardstandings. 4 seasonal pitches. Caravan pitches. Motorhome pitches. Tent
pitches.

Open: all year **Last arrival:** 20.00hrs **Last departure:** 11.00hrs

Pitches: * 🚐 £13-£23 🚳 £13-£23 ▲ £8-£23

Facilities: 🏟⊙✳️🚿🛒🏪➿🛜 ♻️ ❶

Services: 🚘📶 🍴🛢🏪⊘🅣🍽➿⟳

Within 3 miles: ✳️🖋🛒🏪∪

Notes: Debit cards accepted (no credit cards). Dogs must be kept on leads.

AA Pubs & Restaurants nearby: The Old Passage Inn, ARLINGHAM, GL2 7JR,
01452 740547

STONEHOUSE
Map 4 SO80

Places to visit
Painswick Rococo Garden, PAINSWICK, GL6 6TH, 01452 813204
www.rococogarden.org.uk

WWT Slimbridge Wetland Centre, SLIMBRIDGE, GL2 7BT, 01453 891900
www.wwt.org.uk/slimbridge

Apple Tree Park Caravan and Camping Site
►►►► 88%

tel: 01452 742362 & 07708 221457 **A38, Claypits GL10 3AL**
email: appletreepark@hotmail.co.uk
dir: *M5 junct 13, A38. Take 1st exit at rdbt. Site 0.7m on left, 400mtrs beyond filling station.* **grid ref:** *SO766063*

This is a family-owned park conveniently located on the A38, not far from the M5. A peaceful site with glorious views of the Cotswolds, it offers modern and spotlessly clean toilet facilities with under-floor heating. The park is well located for visiting Slimbridge Wildfowl & Wetlands Trust and makes an excellent stopover for M5 travellers. There is a bus stop directly outside the park which is handy for those with motorhomes who wish to visit nearby Gloucester and Cheltenham. 6.5 acre site. 65 touring pitches. 14 hardstandings. 10 seasonal pitches. Caravan pitches. Motorhome pitches. Tent pitches.

Open: Feb-Nov **Last arrival:** 21.00hrs **Last departure:** noon

Pitches: 🚐 🚙 ⛺ **Leisure:** ⚽

Facilities: 🛱⊙ℙ✳👍🔥📶🖥♻️ℹ️ **Services:** 🔌🔒⊘ T ↯

Within 3 miles: 🚶 ℘ 🚲 📷

Notes: Minimum noise after 22.30hrs. Dogs must be kept on leads.

AA Pubs & Restaurants nearby: The Old Passage Inn, ARLINGHAM, GL2 7JR, 01452 740547

GREATER MANCHESTER

LITTLEBOROUGH
Map 16 SD91

Hollingworth Lake Caravan Park
►►► 70%

tel: 01706 378661 & 373919 **Round House Farm, Rakewood Rd, Rakewood OL15 0AT**
dir: *From Littleborough or Milnrow (M62 junct 21), follow Hollingworth Lake Country Park signs to Fishermans Inn/The Wine Press. Take 'No Through Road' to Rakewood, then 2nd right.* **grid ref:** *SD943146*

A popular park adjacent to Hollingworth Lake, at the foot of the Pennines, within easy reach of many local attractions. Backpackers walking the Pennine Way are welcome at this family-run park, and there are also large rally fields. 5 acre site. 50 touring pitches. 25 hardstandings. Caravan pitches. Motorhome pitches. Tent pitches. 53 statics.

Open: all year **Last arrival:** 20.00hrs **Last departure:** noon

Pitches: 🚐 £14-£18 🚙 £14-£20 ⛺ £14-£18

Facilities: 🛱⊙✳👍🔥ℹ️ **Services:** 🔌🔒⊘ T 🔋↯

Within 3 miles: 🚶 ℘ 🚲 📷🔋⛳ **Notes:** 🚯🚳 Family groups only. Pony trekking.

AA Pubs & Restaurants nearby: The White House, LITTLEBOROUGH, OL15 0LG, 01706 378456

HAMPSHIRE

BRANSGORE
Map 5 SZ19

Places to visit
Sammy Miller Motorcycle Museum, NEW MILTON, BH25 5SZ, 01425 620777 www.sammymiller.co.uk

Red House Museum & Gardens, CHRISTCHURCH, BH23 1BU, 01202 482860 www3.hants.gov.uk/redhouse

Great for kids: Moors Valley Country Park and Forest, RINGWOOD, BH24 2ET, 01425 470721 www.moors-valley.co.uk

Harrow Wood Farm Caravan Park
►►► 86%

tel: 01425 672487 **Harrow Wood Farm, Poplar Ln BH23 8JE**
email: harrowwood@caravan-sites.co.uk **web:** www.caravan-sites.co.uk
dir: *From Ringwood take B3347 towards Christchurch. At Sopley, left for Bransgore, to T-junct. Turn right. Straight on at x-rds. Left in 400yds (just after garage) into Poplar Lane.* **grid ref:** *SZ194978*

A well laid-out, well-drained and spacious site in a pleasant rural position adjoining woodland and fields. Free on-site coarse fishing is available at this peaceful park. Well located for visiting Christchurch, the New Forest National Park and the south coast. 6 acre site. 60 touring pitches. 60 hardstandings. Caravan pitches. Motorhome pitches. Tent pitches. 14 bell tents/yurts.

Open: Mar-6 Jan **Last arrival:** 22.00hrs **Last departure:** noon

Pitches: 🚐 🚙 ⛺ 🏕

Facilities: 🛱⊙ℙ✳👍🕓📶ℹ️

Services: 🔌🔒 🔒🔋↯

Within 3 miles: ℘ 📷

Notes: 🚳 No open fires.

AA Pubs & Restaurants nearby: The Three Tuns, BRANSGORE, BH23 8JH, 01425 672232

PITCHES: 🚐 Caravans 🚙 Motorhomes ⛺ Tents 🏕 Glamping-style accommodation **SERVICES:** 🔌 Electric hook up 🔒 Launderette 🍺 Licensed bar 🔋 Calor Gas ⊘ Camping Gaz T Toilet fluid 🍽 Café/Restaurant 🍔 Fast Food/Takeaway 🔋 Battery charging 🚼 Baby care ↯ Motorvan service point **ABBREVIATIONS:** BH/bank hols – bank holidays Etr – Easter Spring BH – Spring Bank Holiday fr – from hrs – hours m – mile mdnt – midnight rdbt – roundabout rs – restricted service wk – week wknd – weekend x-rds – cross roads 🚯 No credit or debit cards 🚳 No dogs 👶 Children of all ages accepted

FORDINGBRIDGE
Map 5 SU11

Places to visit

Rockbourne Roman Villa, ROCKBOURNE, SP6 3PG, 01725 518541
www.hants.gov.uk/rockbourne-roman-villa

Breamore House & Countryside Museum, BREAMORE, SP6 2DF, 01725 512468
www.breamorehouse.com

Great for kids: Moors Valley Country Park and Forest, RINGWOOD, BH24 2ET,
01425 470721 www.moors-valley.co.uk

PREMIER PARK

Sandy Balls Holiday Village
►►►►►88%

Best of British

GOLD

tel: 0844 693 1336 **Sandy Balls Estate Ltd, Godshill SP6 2JZ**
email: post@sandyballs.co.uk
dir: *M27 junct 1, B3078, B3079, 8m to Godshill. Site 0.25m after cattle grid.*
grid ref: *SU167148*

A large, mostly wooded New Forest holiday complex with good provision of
touring facilities on terraced, well laid-out fields. Pitches are fully serviced with
shingle bases, and groups can be sited beside the river and away from the main
site. There are excellent sporting, leisure and entertainment facilities for the
whole family including a jacuzzi, sauna, beauty therapy, horse riding and
children's activities. There's also a bistro, information centre and ready-erected
tents, lodges and eight camping pods (added in 2014) for hire. 120 acre site.
225 touring pitches. 225 hardstandings. Caravan pitches. Motorhome pitches.
Tent pitches. 37 statics. Wooden pods.

Open: all year (rs Nov-Feb pitches reduced, no activities) **Last arrival:** 21.00hrs
Last departure: 11.00hrs

Pitches: ⌂ ⌂ Å ⌂

Leisure: ≋ ≋ ⅄ ⅍ ☺ ♞ ♫ Spa

Facilities: ⌂ ⌂ ☺ ⌂ ☀ ⌂ ⌂ ⌂ ⌂ ⌂ ⌂ WiFi ⌂ ⌂

Services: ⌂ ⌂ ⌂ ⌂ ⌂ ⌂ ⌂ ⌂ ⌂ ⌂ ⌂

Within 3 miles: ⌂ ⌂ ⌂ ⌂ ⌂

Notes: Groups only by arrangement, no gazebos, no noise after 23.00hrs. Dogs must
be kept on leads.

AA Pubs & Restaurants nearby: The Augustus John, FORDINGBRIDGE, SP6 1DG,
01425 652098

HAMBLE-LE-RICE
Map 5 SU40

Riverside Holidays
►►►►82%

tel: 023 8045 3220 **Satchell Lane SO31 4HR**
email: enquiries@riversideholidays.co.uk **web:** www.riversideholidays.co.uk
dir: *M27 junct 8, follow signs to Hamble on B3397. Left into Satchell Lane, site in 1m.*
grid ref: *SU481081*

A small, peaceful park next to the marina, and close to the pretty village of Hamble.
The park is neatly kept, and there are two toilet and shower blocks, with the central
facilities block having excellent private rooms. A pub and restaurant are very close
by and there are good river walks alongside the Hamble. Lodges and static
caravans are available for hire. 6 acre site. 60 touring pitches. Caravan pitches.
Motorhome pitches. Tent pitches. 45 statics.

Open: Mar-Oct **Last arrival:** 22.00hrs **Last departure:** 11.00hrs

Pitches: ⌂ ⌂ Å

Facilities: ⌂ ⌂ ☺ ⌂ ☀ ⌂ ⌂ ⌂

Services: ⌂ ⌂ ⌂ ⌂

Within 3 miles: ⌂ ⌂ ⌂ ⌂ ⌂ ⌂ ⌂

Notes: Dogs must be kept on leads. Bike hire, baby-changing facilities.

AA Pubs & Restaurants nearby: The Bugle, HAMBLE-LE-RICE, SO31 4HA, 023 8045 3000

See advert on opposite page

LEISURE: ≋ Indoor swimming pool ≋ Outdoor swimming pool ⅍ Children's playground ⅄ Kid's club ☺ Tennis court ♞ Games room ⌂ Separate TV room
⌂ golf course ⌂ Boats for hire ⌂ Cinema ♫ Entertainment ⌂ Fishing ◎ Mini golf ≋ Watersports ⅄ Gym ☺ Sports field Spa ⌂ Stables
FACILITIES: ⌂ Bath ⌂ Shower ☺ Electric shaver ⌂ Hairdryer ☀ Ice Pack Facility ⌂ Disabled facilities ⌂ Public telephone ⌂ Shop on site or within 200yds
⌂ Mobile shop (calls at least 5 days a week) ⌂ BBQ area ⌂ Picnic area WiFi Wi-fi ⌂ Internet access ⌂ Recycling ⌂ Tourist info ⌂ Dog exercise area

LINWOOD
Map 5 SU10

Places to visit

The New Forest Centre, LYNDHURST, SO43 7NY, 023 8028 3444
www.newforestcentre.org.uk

Furzey Gardens, MINSTEAD, SO43 7GL, 023 8081 2464 www.furzey-gardens.org

Great for kids: Paultons Park, OWER, SO51 6AL, 023 8081 4442
www.paultonspark.co.uk

Red Shoot Camping Park
▶▶▶85%

tel: 01425 473789 **BH24 3QT**
email: enquiries@redshoot-campingpark.com
dir: *A31 onto A338 towards Fordingbridge & Salisbury. Right at brown signs for caravan park towards Linwood on unclassified roads, site signed.* **grid ref:** *SU187094*

Located behind the Red Shoot Inn in one of the most attractive parts of the New Forest, this park is in an ideal spot for nature lovers and walkers. It is personally supervised by friendly owners, and offers many amenities including a children's play area. There are modern and spotless facilities plus a smart reception and shop. 3.5 acre site. 130 touring pitches. Caravan pitches. Motorhome pitches. Tent pitches.

Open: Mar-Oct **Last arrival:** 19.00hrs **Last departure:** 13.00hrs

Pitches: * 🚐 £17-£28 🚍 £17-£28 ▲ £17-£28

Leisure: 🅰

Facilities: 🖊️☺️🎣✳️♿🕒🅂♻️

Services: 🔌🅘🍴🛒🚿🅣🍽️🔋

Within 3 miles: 🎣⛵🅿️🅂🅅↻

Notes: Quiet after 22.30hrs. Dogs must be kept on leads.

AA Pubs & Restaurants nearby: The Alice Lisle, ROCKFORD, BH24 3NA, 01425 474700

MILFORD ON SEA
Map 5 SZ29

Places to visit

Sammy Miller Motorcycle Museum, NEW MILTON, BH25 5SZ, 01425 620777
www.sammymiller.co.uk

Exbury Gardens & Railway, EXBURY, SO45 1AZ, 023 8089 1203 www.exbury.co.uk

Great for kids: Beaulieu, BEAULIEU, SO42 7ZN, 01590 612345
www.beaulieu.co.uk

Lytton Lawn Touring Park
▶▶▶▶86%

tel: 01590 648331 **Lymore Ln SO41 0TX**
email: holidays@shorefield.co.uk
dir: *From Lymington A337 to Christchurch for 2.5m to Everton. Left onto B3058 to Milford on Sea. 0.25m, left into Lymore Lane.* **grid ref:** *SZ293937*

A pleasant well-run park with good facilities, located near the coast. The park is peaceful and quiet, but the facilities of a sister park 2.5 miles away are available to campers, including a swimming pool, tennis courts, bistro and bar/carvery, and large club with family entertainment. Fully serviced pitches provide good screening, and standard pitches are on gently-sloping grass. 8 acre site. 136 touring pitches. 53 hardstandings. Caravan pitches. Motorhome pitches. Tent pitches.

Open: 6 Feb-2 Jan (rs Low season shop/reception limited hrs, no grass pitches)
Last arrival: 21.00hrs **Last departure:** 10.00hrs

Pitches: * 🚐 £18-£44 🚍 £18-£44 ▲ £13-£40

Leisure: 🅰♻️🔍

Facilities: 🖊️☺️🎣✳️♿🕒🅂🐕WiFi♻️ℹ️

Services: 🔌🅘🛒🚿🅣↯

Within 3 miles: ⚓🎣◎⛵🅿️🅂🅅↻

Notes: Families & couples only, no noise after 22.00hrs, rallies welcome. Dogs must be kept on leads.

AA Pubs & Restaurants nearby: Mayflower Inn, LYMINGTON, SO41 3QD, 01590 672160

See advert on page 215

PITCHES: 🚐 Caravans 🚍 Motorhomes ▲ Tents 🏕 Glamping-style accommodation **SERVICES:** 🔌 Electric hook up 🅘 Launderette 🍴 Licensed bar 🛒 Calor Gas 🅖 Camping Gaz 🅣 Toilet fluid 🍽️ Café/Restaurant 🍟 Fast Food/Takeaway 🔋 Battery charging 🛒 Baby care ↯ Motorvan service point **ABBREVIATIONS:** BH/bank hols – bank holidays Etr – Easter Spring BH – Spring Bank Holiday fr – from hrs – hours m – mile mdnt – midnight rdbt – roundabout rs – restricted service wk – week wknd – weekend x-rds – cross roads ⊗ No credit or debit cards ⊗ No dogs 🚸 Children of all ages accepted

RINGWOOD

See St Leonards (Dorset)

ROMSEY
Map 5 SU32

Places to visit

The Sir Harold Hillier Gardens, AMPFIELD, SO51 0QA, 01794 369318
www.hilliergardens.org.uk

Mottisfont, MOTTISFONT, SO51 0LP, 01794 340757
www.nationaltrust.org.uk/mottisfont

Great for kids: Longdown Activity Farm, ASHURST, SO40 7EH, 023 8029 2837
www.longdownfarm.co.uk

PREMIER PARK

Hill Farm Caravan Park
►►►►► 85%

tel: 01794 340402 **Branches Ln, Sherfield English SO51 6FH**
email: gjb@hillfarmpark.com
dir: Signed from A27 (Salisbury to Romsey road) in Sherfield English. 4m NW of
Romsey & M27 junct 2. **grid ref:** SU287238

A small, well-sheltered park peacefully located amidst mature trees and
meadows. The two toilet blocks offer smart unisex showers as well as a fully en
suite family/disabled room and plenty of privacy in the washrooms. The Garden
Room, a good café/restaurant, with an outside patio, serves a wide range of
snacks and meals. This attractive park is well placed for visiting Salisbury and
the New Forest National Park, and the south coast is only a short drive away,
making it an appealing holiday location. There is a separate caravan sales and
full repair centre - South Coast Caravans. 10.5 acre site. 100 touring pitches. 60
hardstandings. Caravan pitches. Motorhome pitches. Tent pitches. 6 statics.

Open: Mar-Oct **Last arrival:** 20.00hrs **Last departure:** noon

Pitches: ⊕ ⇔ Å

Leisure: ⚠ ✪

Facilities: ⌐ ⊙ ⨍ ✳ ⅋ ₼ ₷ ⅋ ⊼ ⊼ Wifi ⊒ ♻ 𝟢

Services: ⊕ ◙ 🛢 ⌀ T ⊙ 📥 ⟱

Within 3 miles: ↓ ⊟ ⌀ ◎ ₷ ⅁ ∪

Notes: Minimum noise at all times & no noise after 23.00hrs, one unit per pitch,
site unsuitable for teenagers. 9-hole pitch & putt.

AA Pubs & Restaurants nearby: The Cromwell Arms, ROMSEY, SO51 8HG,
01794 519515

The Three Tuns, ROMSEY, SO51 8HL, 01794 512639

Green Pastures Farm Camping & Touring Park
►►► 84%

tel: 023 8081 4444 **Ower SO51 6AJ**
email: enquiries@greenpasturesfarm.com
dir: M27 junct 2. Follow Salisbury signs for 0.5m, then brown tourist signs for Green
Pastures. Also signed from A36 & A3090 at Ower. **grid ref:** SU321158

This pleasant site offers a variety of easily accessed pitches, including those with
electric hook-up. There is a code access security barrier to the site. Green Pastures
is well located for visiting Paultons Theme Park, Southampton and the New Forest
National Park, and being close to the M27 it is convenient for overnight stops. There
are kennels where dogs can be left while you visit the theme park or go shopping. 6
acre site. 53 touring pitches. 6 hardstandings. Caravan pitches. Motorhome
pitches. Tent pitches.

Open: 13 Mar-Oct **Last arrival:** 20.30hrs **Last departure:** 11.00hrs

Pitches: * ⊕ £19-£24 ⇔ £19-£24 Å £14-£31

Facilities: ⌐ ✳ ⅋ ₷ ♻ 𝟢

Services: ⊕ ◙ 🛢 ⌀ T 📥 ⟱

Within 3 miles: ↓ ⌀ ₷ ⅁

Notes: No water games, off-ground BBQs only. Dogs must be kept on leads.

AA Pubs & Restaurants nearby: Sir John Barleycorn, CADNAM, SO40 2NP, 023 8081 2236

WARSASH
Map 5 SU40

Places to visit

Explosion Museum of Naval Firepower, GOSPORT, PO12 4LE, 023 9250 5600
www.explosion.org.uk

Portchester Castle, PORTCHESTER, PO16 9QW, 023 9237 8291
www.english-heritage.org.uk/daysout/properties/portchester-castle

Great for kids: Blue Reef Aquarium, PORTSMOUTH, PO5 3PB, 023 9287 5222
www.bluereefaquarium.co.uk

Dibles Park
►►►► 84%

tel: 01489 575232 **Dibles Rd SO31 9SA**
email: dibles.park@btconnect.com
dir: M27 junct 9, at rdbt 5th exit (Parkgate A27), 3rd rdbt 1st exit, 4th rdbt 2nd exit. Site
500yds on left. Or M27 junct 8, at rdbt 1st exit (Parkgate), next rdbt 3rd exit (Brook Ln),
4th rdbt 2nd exit. Site 500yds on left. **grid ref:** SU505060

A small peaceful touring park adjacent to a private residential park. The facilities
are excellent and spotlessly clean. A warm welcome awaits visitors to this well-
managed park, which is very convenient for the Hamble, the Solent and the cross-
channel ferries. Excellent information on walks that start from the site is available.
0.75 acre site. 14 touring pitches. 14 hardstandings. Caravan pitches. Motorhome
pitches. Tent pitches. 46 statics.

Open: all year **Last arrival:** 20.30hrs **Last departure:** 11.00hrs

Pitches: ⊕ ⇔ Å

Facilities: ⌐ ⊙ ⨍ ✳ ◐ ♻ 𝟢   **Services:** ⊕ ◙ 🛢 ⟱

Within 3 miles: ⅊ ⌀ ₷ ⅁ ∪   **Notes:** Dogs must be kept on leads.

AA Pubs & Restaurants nearby: The Jolly Farmer Country Inn, WARSASH, SO31 9JH,
01489 572500

LEISURE: 🏊 Indoor swimming pool 🏊 Outdoor swimming pool ⚠ Children's playground 🛝 Kid's club 🎾 Tennis court ⚫ Games room ⬜ Separate TV room
⅃ golf course ⚓ Boats for hire 🎬 Cinema 🎵 Entertainment ⌀ Fishing ◎ Mini golf ⚓ Watersports 🏋 Gym ✪ Sports field Spa ∪ Stables
FACILITIES: 🛁 Bath ⌐ Shower ⊙ Electric shaver ⨍ Hairdryer ✳ Ice Pack Facility ⅋ Disabled facilities ◐ Public telephone ₷ Shop on site or within 200yds
⅁ Mobile shop (calls at least 5 days a week) ₼ BBQ area ⊼ Picnic area Wifi Wi-fi ⊒ Internet access ♻ Recycling 𝟢 Tourist info ⊼ Dog exercise area

HEREFORDSHIRE

EARDISLAND
Map 9 SO45

Places to visit

Berrington Hall, ASHTON, HR6 0DW, 01568 615721
www.nationaltrust.org.uk/berringtonhall

Hergest Croft Gardens, KINGTON, HR5 3EG, 01544 230160 www.hergest.co.uk

Great for kids: Croft Castle & Parkland, CROFT, HR6 9PW, 01568 780246
www.nationaltrust.org.uk/main/w-croftcastle

Arrow Bank Holiday Park
►►►► 86%

tel: 01544 388312 **Nun House Farm HR6 9BG**
email: info@arrowbank.co.uk
dir: From Leominster A44 towards Rhayader. Right to Eardisland, follow signs.
grid ref: SO419588

This peaceful park is set in the beautiful 'Black and White' village of Eardisland with its free exhibitions, tea rooms and heritage centre. The park is well positioned for visiting the many local attractions, as well as those further afield such as Ludlow Castle, Ross-on-Wye and Shrewsbury; the Welsh border is just down the road. The modern toilet facilities are spotlessly clean and there are 36 fully-serviced pitches. 65 acre site. 38 touring pitches. 38 hardstandings. 16 seasonal pitches. Caravan pitches. Motorhome pitches. Tent pitches. 60 statics. 4 bell tents/yurts.

Open: Mar-Nov **Last arrival:** 21.00hrs **Last departure:** 11.30hrs
Pitches: * ⚏ £18-£22 ⚌ £18-£22 Å £18-£22 ⌂
Facilities: ⚡☉⚘♿☾⊞ ⛟ WiFi ❶
Services: ⚕⚒ ⚔⚗T⚓
Within 3 miles: ⚘⚒⚒
Notes: No ball games, skateboards or cycles. Dogs must be kept on leads.
AA Pubs & Restaurants nearby: New Inn, PEMBRIDGE, HR6 9DZ, 01544 388427
The Stagg Inn and Restaurant, KINGTON, HR5 3RL, 01544 230221

HEREFORD

Places to visit

Cider Museum, HEREFORD, HR4 0LW, 01432 354207 www.cidermuseum.co.uk

Great for kids: Goodrich Castle, GOODRICH, HR9 6HY, 01600 890538
www.english-heritage.org.uk/daysout/properties/goodrich-castle

HEREFORD
Map 10 SO53

Ridge Hill Caravan and Campsite
► 69%

tel: 01432 351293 **HR2 8AG**
email: ridgehill@fsmail.net
dir: From Hereford on A49, take B4399 signed Rotherwas. At 1st rdbt follow Dinedor & Little Dewchurch signs, in 1m signed Ridge Hill & Twyford turn right. Right at phone box, 200yds, site on right. **grid ref:** SO509355

A simple, basic site set high on Ridge Hill a few miles south of Hereford. This peaceful site offers outstanding views over the countryside. It does not have toilets or showers, and therefore own facilities are essential, although toilet tents can be supplied on request at certain times of the year. (NB please do not rely on Sat Nav directions to this site - guidebook directions should be used for caravans and motorhomes). 1.3 acre site. 5 touring pitches. Caravan pitches. Motorhome pitches. Tent pitches.

Open: Mar-Oct **Last departure:** noon
Pitches: ⚏ ⚌ Å
Facilities: ♻ ❶
Within 3 miles: ⚓⊟⚘⚒⚒
Notes: ⊘ Dogs must be kept on leads.
AA Pubs & Restaurants nearby: Castle House, HEREFORD, HR1 2NW, 01432 356321

MORETON ON LUGG
Map 10 SO54

Places to visit

The Weir Gardens, SWAINSHILL, HR4 7QF, 01981 590509
www.nationaltrust.org.uk

Cuckoo's Corner Campsite
►►► 86%

tel: 01432 760234 **Cuckoo's Corner HR4 8AH**
email: cuckooscorner@gmail.com
dir: Direct access from A49. From Hereford 2nd left after Moreton on Lugg sign. From Leominster 1st right (non gated road) after brown sign. Right just before island.
grid ref: SO501456

This small adults-only site is well positioned just north of Hereford, with easy access to the city. The site has two areas and offers hardstandings and also some electric pitches. It is an ideal spot for an overnight stop or for longer stay in order to visit the attractions of the area. Two new unisex rooms with shower, washbasin and toilet were added for the 2014 season. There's a bus stop just outside the site and a full timetable is available from the reception office. 3 acre site. 19 touring pitches. 15 hardstandings. Caravan pitches. Motorhome pitches. Tent pitches.

Open: all year **Last arrival:** 21.00hrs **Last departure:** 13.00hrs
Pitches: ⚏ £15 ⚌ £15 Å £15
Facilities: ⚡☉☀⛟ WiFi ▬ ♻ ❶
Services: ⚕⚒⚑ **Within 3 miles:** ⚓⚘⚒
Notes: Adults only. ⊘ No large groups, no noise after 22.30hrs. Dogs must be kept on leads. DVD library, books & magazines.
AA Pubs & Restaurants nearby: The Bell, TILLINGTON, HR4 8LE, 01432 760395
The Wellington, WELLINGTON, HR4 8AT, 01432 830367

PITCHES: ⚏ Caravans ⚌ Motorhomes Å Tents ⌂ Glamping-style accommodation **SERVICES:** ⚕ Electric hook up ⚒ Launderette ⚑ Licensed bar ⚔ Calor Gas ⚘ Camping Gaz T Toilet fluid ⚙ Café/Restaurant ⚑ Fast Food/Takeaway ⚓ Battery charging ⚗ Baby care ⚖ Motorvan service point **ABBREVIATIONS:** BH/bank hols – bank holidays Etr – Easter Spring BH – Spring Bank Holiday fr – from hrs – hours m – mile mdnt – midnight rdbt – roundabout rs – restricted service wk – week wknd – weekend x-rds – cross roads ⊘ No credit or debit cards ⊗ No dogs ♦♦ Children of all ages accepted

PEMBRIDGE
Map 9 SO35

PREMIER PARK

Townsend Touring Park
▶▶▶▶▶ 90%

tel: 01544 388527 **Townsend Farm HR6 9HB**
email: info@townsend-farm.co.uk
dir: A44 through Pembridge. Site 40mtrs from 30mph on E side of village.
grid ref: SO395583

This outstanding park is spaciously located on the edge of one of Herefordshire's most beautiful Black and White villages. The park offers excellent facilities, and all hardstanding pitches are fully serviced, and it has its own award-winning farm shop and butchery. Coarse fishing is possible on the site's lake. It also makes an excellent base from which to explore the area, including Ludlow Castle and Ironbridge. There are camping pods available for hire. 12 acre site. 60 touring pitches. 23 hardstandings. 14 seasonal pitches. Caravan pitches. Motorhome pitches. Tent pitches. 4 wooden pods.

Open: Mar-mid Jan **Last arrival:** 22.00hrs **Last departure:** 11.00hrs

Pitches: * ⊞ £18-£26 ⊞ £19-£26 ⛺ £18-£26 🏠

Leisure: 🛝 ✦

Facilities: 🛁 ⋔ ☉ 🗡 ⅃ ☏ ⑤ ⋏ ♻ ✦

Services: ⊡ ⑤ 🛒 ⌄

Within 3 miles: ⑤ ⑤ ∪

Notes: Bike trails.

AA Pubs & Restaurants nearby: New Inn, PEMBRIDGE, HR6 9DZ, 01544 388427
The Stagg Inn and Restaurant, KINGTON, HR5 3RL, 01544 230221

SYMONDS YAT (WEST)

Places to visit

The Nelson Museum & Local History Centre, MONMOUTH, NP25 3XA, 01600 710630

Great for kids: Goodrich Castle, GOODRICH, HR9 6HY, 01600 890538
www.english-heritage.org.uk/daysout/properties/goodrich-castle

SYMONDS YAT (WEST)
Map 10 SO51

Doward Park Camp Site
▶▶▶ 85%

tel: 01600 890438 **Great Doward HR9 6BP**
email: enquiries@dowardpark.co.uk
dir: A40 from Monmouth towards Ross-on-Wye. In 2m left signed Crockers Ash, Ganarew & The Doward. Cross over A40, 1st left at T-junct, in 0.5m 1st right signed The Doward. Follow park signs up hill. NB it is advised that Sat Nav is not used for end of journey.
grid ref: SO539167

This delightful little park is set in peaceful woodlands on the hillside above the Wye Valley. It is ideal for campers and motorhomes but not caravans due to the narrow, twisting approach roads. A warm welcome awaits and the facilities are kept spotless. The Bluebell Wood children's play area is a great place for imaginative games. 1.5 acre site. 28 touring pitches. 6 seasonal pitches. Motorhome pitches. Tent pitches.

Open: Mar-Oct **Last arrival:** 20.00hrs **Last departure:** 11.30hrs

Pitches: ⊞ ⛺

Leisure: 🛝

Facilities: ⋔ ☉ 🗡 ✳ ☏ ⑤ 🛜 ✦

Services: ⊡ ⑤ 🛒 ⌀ ⌄

Within 3 miles: ⅃ ✦ ✎ ◎ ⚓ ⑤ ⑤

Notes: No fires, quiet after 22.00hrs. Dogs must be kept on leads.

AA Pubs & Restaurants nearby: The Mill Race, WALFORD, HR9 5QS, 01989 562891

HERTFORDSHIRE

HODDESDON
Map 6 TL30

Lee Valley Caravan Park Dobbs Weir
▶▶▶ 77%

tel: 0845 677 0609 **Charlton Meadows, Essex Rd EN11 0AS**
email: dobbsweircampsite@leevalleypark.org.uk
dir: From A10 follow Hoddesdon signs, at 2nd rdbt left signed Dobbs Weir. At next rdbt take 3rd exit. 1m to site on right. **grid ref:** TL382080

This site provides much needed extra camping facilities close to London. Situated on level ground beside the River Lee, the smallest of the three London Authority parks has a modernised toilet block with good facilities, a large timber chalet housing the reception and shop, and an extremely innovative motorhome service point. On-site fishing is available. 11 acre site. 158 touring pitches. 15 hardstandings. Caravan pitches. Motorhome pitches. Tent pitches. 24 statics. 3 bell tents/yurts.

Open: Mar-Jan **Last arrival:** 21.00hrs **Last departure:** noon

Pitches: * ⊞ £13.50-£22 ⊞ £13.50-£22 ⛺ £13.50-£22 🏠

Leisure: 🛝

Facilities: ⋔ ☉ ✳ ☏ ⑤ ⅃ ⋏ 🛜 ♻ ✦

Services: ⊡ ⑤ 🛒 ⌀ Ⓣ ⌄

Within 3 miles: ✦ ✎ ⚓ ⑤ ⑤

Notes: No commercial vehicles. Dogs must be kept on leads. Cycle hire.

AA Pubs & Restaurants nearby: The Fox and Hounds, HUNSDON, SG12 8NH, 01279 843999

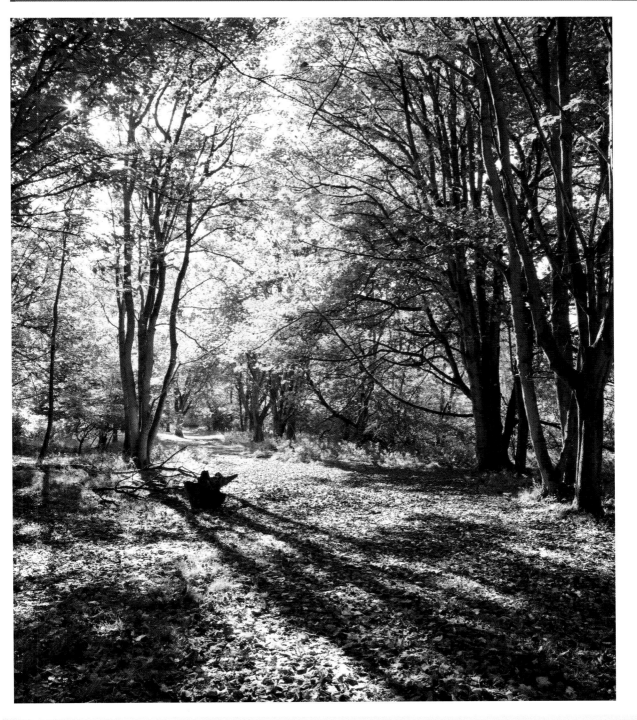

PITCHES: 🚐 Caravans 🚌 Motorhomes ▲ Tents ⛺ Glamping-style accommodation **SERVICES:** 🔌 Electric hook up ⑤ Launderette 🍸 Licensed bar
🛢 Calor Gas ⊘ Camping Gaz Ⓣ Toilet fluid 🍽 Café/Restaurant 🏬 Fast Food/Takeaway 🔋 Battery charging 🍼 Baby care ⚓ Motorvan service point
ABBREVIATIONS: BH/bank hols – bank holidays Etr – Easter Spring BH – Spring Bank Holiday fr – from hrs – hours m – mile mdnt – midnight
rdbt – roundabout rs – restricted service wk – week wknd – weekend x-rds – cross roads ⓩ No credit or debit cards ⊗ No dogs 👨‍👦 Children of all ages accepted

Isle of Wight

There is a timeless quality to the Isle of Wight. For many it embodies the spirit and atmosphere of English seaside holidays over the years, and being an island, it has a unique and highly distinctive identity. Small and intimate — it's just 23 miles by 13 miles — it's a great place to get away-from-it-all, and with its mild climate, long hours of sunshine and colourful architecture, it has something of a continental flavour.

The Isle of Wight is probably most famous for the world's premier sailing regatta. Cowes Week, which takes place at the height of summer, is a key annual fixture in the country's sporting calendar, with the regatta drawing more than 1,000 boats and around 100,000 spectators. It is a hugely colourful event attracting Olympic veterans, weekend sailors and top names from the worlds of sport and the media. Various spectator boats offer good views of the action, but for something less hectic and more sedate, take to the island's 65-mile Coast Path, which offers a continual, unfolding backdrop of magnificent coastal scenery and natural beauty. The sea is seen at numerous points along the route and during Cowes Week, you get constant views of the energetic sailing activity. The regatta is held in the first week of August.

The Isle of Wight Coast Path is a good way to explore the island's varied coastline at any time of the year. Even in the depths of winter, the weather conditions are often favourable for walking. Much of the trail in the southern half of the island represents a relatively undemanding walk over majestic chalk downs. Beyond Freshwater Bay the coast is largely uninhabited with a palpable air of isolation. It is on this stretch that walkers can appreciate how the elements have shaped and weathered the island over many centuries. Away from the coast an intricate network of paths offers the chance to discover a rich assortment of charming villages, hidden valleys and country houses. In all, the Isle of Wight has more than 500 miles of public rights of way and over half the island is acknowledged as an Area of Outstanding Natural Beauty. There is an annual walking festival in May and a weekend walking festival in October. Cycling is also extremely popular here, with the Round the Island Cycle Route attracting many enthusiasts. The route runs for 49 miles and there are starting points at Yarmouth, Cowes and Ryde.

Away from walking and cycling, the Isle of Wight offers numerous attractions and activities. You could plan a week's itinerary on the island and not set foot on the beach. The island's history is a fascinating and crucial aspect of its story. It was long considered as a convenient stepping stone for the French in their plan to invade the mainland, and various fortifications — including Fort Victoria and Yarmouth Castle — reflect its key strategic role in the defence of our coastline. Carisbrooke Castle at Newport — the island's capital — is where Charles I was held before his execution in 1649.

The Isle of Wight has been a fashionable destination for the rich and famous over the years, and members of royalty made their home here. Queen Victoria and Prince Albert boosted tourism hugely when they chose the island as the setting for their summer home, Osborne House, which is now open to the public. Elsewhere, there are echoes of the Isle of Wight's fascinating literary links. Charles Dickens is said to have written six chapters of *David Copperfield* in the village of Bonchurch, near Ventnor, and the Victorian Poet Laureate Alfred Lord Tennyson lived at Faringford House, near Freshwater Bay. He claimed that the air on the coast here was worth 'sixpence a pint.'

Coastal path near Sandown ▷

ISLE OF WIGHT

BEMBRIDGE

See Whitecliff Bay

BRIGHSTONE

Map 5 SZ48

Places to visit

Mottistone Gardens, MOTTISTONE, PO30 4ED, 01983 741302
www.nationaltrust.org.uk/isleofwight

Grange Farm
▶▶▶▶ 79%

tel: 01983 740296 **Grange Chine PO30 4DA**
email: grangefarmholidays@gmail.com
dir: *From Freshwater Bay take A3055 towards Ventnor, 5m (pass Isle of Wight Pearl). Site approx 0.5m on right.* grid ref: SZ421820

This family-run site is set in a stunning location on the south-west coast of the island in Brighstone Bay. The facilities are very good. For children there is an imaginative play area and a wide range of animals to see including llamas and water buffalo. This site is ideally located for those who like walking and cycling. There are static homes and camping pods for hire. 8 acre site. 60 touring pitches. 8 hardstandings. Caravan pitches. Motorhome pitches. Tent pitches. 12 statics. 8 wooden pods.

Open: Mar-Oct **Last arrival:** noon **Last departure:** noon

Pitches: ⊞ ⊞ ▲ ⋒

Leisure: ⋒

Facilities: ⋔ ⊙ ⋔ ✳ ⊙ ⑤ ⋒ ⋔ WiFi ♻ ✱

Services: ⊕ ⑤ ⋔ ⊘ T ⋔ ⋓

Within 3 miles: ⋔ ⋨ ⑤ ⑤

Notes: No fires. Dogs must be kept on leads. Bakery.

AA Pubs & Restaurants nearby: The Crown Inn, SHORWELL, PO30 3JZ, 01983 740293

COWES

Map 5 SZ49

Places to visit

Osborne House, OSBORNE HOUSE, PO32 6JX, 01983 200022
www.english-heritage.org.uk/daysout/properties/osborne

Colemans Farm Park, PORCHFIELD, PO30 4LX, 01983 522831
www.colemansfarmpark.co.uk

Great for kids: Robin Hill Country Park, ARRETON, PO30 2NU, 01983 527352
www.robin-hill.com

Thorness Bay Holiday Park
HOLIDAY CENTRE 84%

tel: 01983 523109 **Thorness PO31 8NJ**
email: holidaysales.thornessbay@park-resorts.com web: www.park-resorts.com
dir: *On A3054 towards Yarmouth, 1st right after BMW garage, signed Thorness Bay.*
grid ref: SZ448928

Splendid views of The Solent can be enjoyed from this rural park located just outside Cowes. A footpath leads directly to the coast, while on site there is an all-weather sports court, entertainment clubs for children, cabaret shows, and a bar for all the family. There are 23 serviced pitches, with TV boosters, in the separate touring area. 130 holiday homes are for hire. 148 acre site. 124 touring pitches. 21 hardstandings. 8 seasonal pitches. Caravan pitches. Motorhome pitches. Tent pitches. 560 statics.

Open: Apr-1 Nov **Last arrival:** anytime **Last departure:** 10.00hrs

Pitches: ⊞ ⊞ ▲ **Leisure:** ≋ ⋒ ⋔ ❀ ⊙ ♪

Facilities: ⋔ ⋔ ⊙ ⋔ ⋔ ⊙ ⑤ ⋔ WiFi ▤ ♻ ✱

Services: ⊕ ⑤ ⋔ ⋔ ⊘ ⋔ ⊙ ⋔ **Within 3 miles:** ⋔ ⋨ ⑤ ⑤

Notes: Dogs must be kept on leads. Water slide.

AA Pubs & Restaurants nearby: The Fountain Inn, COWES, PO31 7AW, 01983 292397
Duke of York Inn, COWES, PO31 7BT, 01983 295171
The Folly, WHIPPINGHAM, PO32 6NB, 01983 297171

See advert below

LEISURE: ≋ Indoor swimming pool ≋ Outdoor swimming pool ⋀ Children's playground ⋓ Kid's club ⋐ Tennis court ⋔ Games room ⊡ Separate TV room ⋔ golf course ⋔ Boats for hire ⊟ Cinema ♪ Entertainment ⋔ Fishing ◎ Mini golf ⋐ Watersports ⋔ Gym ⋔ Sports field Spa ⋓ Stables
FACILITIES: ⋔ Bath ⋔ Shower ⊙ Electric shaver ⋔ Hairdryer ✳ Ice Pack Facility ⋔ Disabled facilities ⋔ Public telephone ⑤ Shop on site or within 200yds ⑤ Mobile shop (calls at least 5 days a week) ⋔ BBQ area ⋔ Picnic area WiFi Wi-fi ▤ Internet access ♻ Recycling ✱ Tourist info ⋔ Dog exercise area

FRESHWATER
Map 5 SZ38

Places to visit
Yarmouth Castle, YARMOUTH, PO41 0PB, 01983 760678
www.english-heritage.org.uk/daysout/properties/yarmouth-castle

Dimbola Lodge Museum, FRESHWATER, PO40 9QE, 01983 756814
www.dimbola.co.uk

Great for kids: The Needles Park, ALUM BAY, PO39 0JD, 0871 720 0022
www.theneedles.co.uk

Heathfield Farm Camping
▶▶▶▶ 87%

tel: 01983 407822 **Heathfield Rd PO40 9SH**
email: web@heathfieldcamping.co.uk **web:** www.heathfieldcamping.co.uk
dir: *2m W from Yarmouth ferry port on A3054, left to Heathfield Rd, entrance 200yds on right.* **grid ref:** *SZ335879*

A very good quality park with friendly and welcoming staff. There are lovely views across the Solent to Hurst Castle. The toilet facilities, the amenities, which include an excellent backpackers' area, and the very well maintained grounds, make this park amongst the best on the island. 10 acre site. 60 touring pitches. Caravan pitches. Motorhome pitches. Tent pitches.

Open: May-Sep **Last arrival:** 20.00hrs **Last departure:** 11.00hrs

Pitches: * 🚐 £13.50-£21.50 🚍 £13.50-£21.50 ▲ £6-£8

Leisure: 🌣

Facilities: 🔦⊙ℙ⚙☀️🔥🕔🚿🏕️ WiFi ❖ 🕄

Services: 🔌🖬 🥄⚊

Within 3 miles: ↧↟⌁◎🐾🏧🛒🔄∪

Notes: Families camping only. Dogs must be kept on leads.

AA Pubs & Restaurants nearby: The Red Lion, FRESHWATER, PO40 9BP, 01983 754925

NEWBRIDGE
Map 5 SZ48

Places to visit
Newtown Old Town Hall, NEWTOWN, PO30 4PA, 01983 531785
www.nationaltrust.org.uk/isleofwight

Great for kids: Yarmouth Castle, YARMOUTH, PO41 0PB, 01983 760678
www.english-heritage.org.uk/daysout/properties/yarmouth-castle

REGIONAL WINNER – SOUTH EAST ENGLAND
AA CAMPSITE OF THE YEAR 2015

PREMIER PARK

The Orchards Holiday Caravan Park
▶▶▶▶▶ 93%

Best of British

tel: 01983 531331 & 531350 **Main Rd PO41 0TS**
email: info@orchards-holiday-park.co.uk **web:** www.orchards-holiday-park.co.uk
dir: *A3054 from Yarmouth, right in 3m at Horse & Groom Inn. Follow signs to Newbridge. Entrance opposite post office. Or from Newport, 6m, via B3401.* **grid ref:** *SZ411881*

A really excellent, well-managed park set in a peaceful village location amid downs and meadowland, with glorious downland views. The pitches are terraced and offer a good provision of hardstandings, including those that are water serviced. There is a high quality facility centre offering excellent, spacious showers and family rooms, plus there is access for less able visitors to all site facilities and disabled toilets. The park has indoor and outdoor swimming pools, a takeaway and licensed shop. Static homes are available for hire and 'ferry plus stay' packages are on offer. 15 acre site. 160 touring pitches. 52 hardstandings. Caravan pitches. Motorhome pitches. Tent pitches. 65 statics.

Open: 28 Mar-3 Nov (rs late May-early Sep outdoor pool open) **Last arrival:** 23.00hrs **Last departure:** 11.00hrs

Pitches: * 🚐 £18.75-£34.50 🚍 £18.75-£34.50 ▲ £18.75-£34.50

Leisure: 🏊🏊♨🎱

Facilities: 🛁🔦⊙ℙ☀️🕔🚿🏕️🔥 WiFi 🕄

Services: 🔌🖬 🔋Ⓣ🍽️🚼👶⚊

Within 3 miles: ↧🏧🛒

Notes: No cycling, no noise after mdnt. Dogs must be kept on leads. Table tennis room, poolside coffee shop.

AA Pubs & Restaurants nearby: The New Inn, SHALFLEET, PO30 4NS, 01983 531314

RYDE

Map 5 SZ59

Places to visit

Nunwell House & Gardens, BRADING, PO36 0JQ, 01983 407240

Bembridge Windmill, BEMBRIDGE, PO35 5SQ, 01983 873945
www.nationaltrust.org.uk/isleofwight

Great for kids: Robin Hill Country Park, ARRETON, PO30 2NU, 01983 527352
www.robin-hill.com

PREMIER PARK

Whitefield Forest Touring Park

► ► ► ► ► 94%

tel: 01983 617069 **Brading Rd PO33 1QL**
email: pat&louise@whitefieldforest.co.uk
dir: *From Ryde follow A3055 towards Brading, after Tesco rdbt site 0.5m on left.*
grid ref: *SZ604893*

This park is beautifully laid out in the Whitefield Forest, and offers a wide variety of pitches, including some that are fully serviced; it is conveniently located on a bus route. It offers excellent modern facilities which are kept spotlessly clean. The park takes great care to retain the natural beauty of the forest, and is a haven for wildlife; red squirrels can be spotted throughout the park, including along the nature walk. 23 acre site. 90 touring pitches. 38 hardstandings. Caravan pitches. Motorhome pitches. Tent pitches.

Open: 28 Mar-6 Oct **Last arrival:** 21.00hrs **Last departure:** 11.00hrs

Pitches: 🚐 🚍 ▲

Leisure: 🅰

Facilities: 🍴 ⊙ 🎨 ❄ 🚹 🛒 🛜 ♻ ❶

Services: 🔌 🛢 🚽 🧺 🅣 🛒 ↯

Within 3 miles: ↓ ⛵ 🎡 ℓ 🛒 🛒 🛒

Notes: Dogs must be kept on leads.

AA Pubs & Restaurants nearby: The Boathouse, SEAVIEW, PO34 5AW, 01983 810616
The Seaview Hotel & Restaurant, SEAVIEW, PO34 5EX, 01983 612711

ST HELENS

Places to visit

Nunwell House & Gardens, BRADING, PO36 0JQ, 01983 407240

Bembridge Windmill, BEMBRIDGE, PO35 5SQ, 01983 873945
www.nationaltrust.org.uk/isleofwight

Great for kids: Lilliput Antique Doll & Toy Museum, BRADING, PO36 0DJ, 01983 407231 www.lilliputmuseum.co.uk

ST HELENS

Map 5 SZ68

Nodes Point Holiday Park

HOLIDAY CENTRE 88%

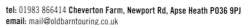

tel: 01983 872401 **Nodes Rd PO33 1YA**
email: gm.nodespoint@park-resorts.com
dir: *From Ryde take B3330 signed Seaview & Puckpool. At junct for Puckpool bear right. 1m past Road Side Inn in Nettlestone, site on left.* **grid ref:** *SZ636897*

A well-equipped holiday centre on an elevated position overlooking Bembridge Bay with direct access to the beach. The touring area is mostly sloping with some terraces. Activities are organised for youngsters, and there is entertainment for the whole family. Buses pass the main entrance road. The touring area has very well appointed, ready-erected tents for hire. Holiday homes are also available for hire or purchase. 16 acre site. 150 touring pitches. 4 hardstandings. 4 seasonal pitches. Caravan pitches. Motorhome pitches. Tent pitches. 195 statics.

Open: Apr-Oct **Last arrival:** 21.00hrs **Last departure:** 10.00hrs

Pitches: 🚐 🚍 ▲

Leisure: 🏊 🅰 🛝 🎾 🎵

Facilities: 🛁 🍴 ⊙ 🎨 ❄ 🚹 🛒 🛒 🛒 🅟 🅷 🛜 🖥

Services: 🔌 🛢 🚽 🧺 🅣 🛒

Within 3 miles: ↓ ⛵ 🎡 ℓ ◎ 🛒 🛒 🛒 ∪

AA Pubs & Restaurants nearby: The Crab & Lobster Inn, BEMBRIDGE, PO35 5TR, 01983 872244

SANDOWN

Map 5 SZ58

Places to visit

Nunwell House & Gardens, BRADING, PO36 0JQ, 01983 407240

Bembridge Windmill, BEMBRIDGE, PO35 5SQ, 01983 873945
www.nationaltrust.org.uk/isleofwight

Great for kids: Dinosaur Isle, SANDOWN, PO36 8QA, 01983 404344
www.dinosaurisle.com

Old Barn Touring Park

► ► ► ► 79%

tel: 01983 866414 **Cheverton Farm, Newport Rd, Apse Heath PO36 9PJ**
email: mail@oldbarntouring.co.uk
dir: *On A3056 from Newport, site on left after Apse Heath rdbt.* **grid ref:** *SZ571833*

A terraced site with several secluded camping areas that are divided by hedges. This site is well positioned for visiting the eastern side of the island, and customers can be sure of a warm welcome from the friendly staff. Rallies are very welcome, plus there are three fully equipped tents for hire. 5 acre site. 60 touring pitches. 9 hardstandings. 6 seasonal pitches. Caravan pitches. Motorhome pitches. Tent pitches.

Open: May-Sep **Last arrival:** 21.00hrs **Last departure:** noon

Pitches: * 🚐 £18-£25 🚗 £18-£25 ⛺ £18-£25

Leisure: 🎱 ⚲ ▭

Facilities: �📶 ⊙ ☂ ✳ ⚅ 🛒 📶 🖥 ♻ ❶

Services: 🔌 🔲 ⛽ ⌀ T 🔋 ↯

Within 3 miles: ↯ ⚓ ₽ ◎ ≋ ⊞ ⊟ ∪

Notes: Dogs must be kept on leads.

AA Pubs & Restaurants nearby: The Crab & Lobster Inn, BEMBRIDGE, PO35 5TR, 01983 872244

Queenbower Dairy Caravan Park
► 78%

tel: 01983 403840 **Alverstone Rd, Queenbower PO36 0NZ**
email: queenbowerdairy@btconnect.com
dir: *3m N of Sandown from A3056 right into Alverstone Rd, site 1m on left.*
grid ref: *SZ567846*

A small site with basic amenities that will appeal to campers keen to escape the crowds and the busy larger sites. The enthusiastic owners keep the facilities very clean. 2.5 acre site. 20 touring pitches. Caravan pitches. Motorhome pitches. Tent pitches.

Open: May-Oct

Pitches: * 🚐 £7-£11 🚗 £7-£11 ⛺ £7-£11

Facilities: ✳ ⚅ ❶

Services: 🔌 🔋

Within 3 miles: ↯ ⚓ ₽ ◎ ≋ ⊞ ⊟

Notes: 🚫 Dogs must be kept on leads & exercised off site.

AA Pubs & Restaurants nearby: The Crab & Lobster Inn, BEMBRIDGE, PO35 5TR, 01983 872244

Lower Hyde Holiday Park
HOLIDAY CENTRE 86%
GOLD

tel: 01983 866131 **Landguard Rd PO37 7LL**
email: holidaysales.lowerhyde@park-resorts.com **web:** www.park-resorts.com
dir: *From Fishbourne ferry terminal follow A3055 to Shanklin. Site signed just past lake.*
grid ref: *SZ575819*

A popular holiday park on the outskirts of Shanklin, close to the sandy beaches. There is an outdoor swimming pool and plenty of organised activities for youngsters of all ages. In the evening there is a choice of family entertainment. The touring facilities are located in a quiet area away from the main complex, with good views over the downs. Holiday homes are available for hire or purchase. 65 acre site. 151 touring pitches. 25 hardstandings. Caravan pitches. Motorhome pitches. Tent pitches.

Open: Mar-end Oct **Last arrival:** 17.00hrs **Last departure:** noon

Pitches: 🚐 🚗 ⛺

Leisure: 🏊 🏊 🎱 🎿 ♾ ☺ ⚲ 🎵

Facilities: ⬅ �📶 ✳ ⚅ ⊙ ⊡ ☂ 🔥 🛒 📶 ♻ ❶

Services: 🔌 🔲 🍴 ⛽ ⌀ ⊙ ⧦ 🔋 ⬛ ♻

Within 3 miles: ↯ ⚓ ⊟ ₽ ◎ ≋ ⊞ ⊟ ∪

Notes: Dogs must be kept on leads.

AA Pubs & Restaurants nearby: The Bonchurch Inn, BONCHURCH, PO38 1NU, 01983 852611

The Taverners, GODSHILL, PO38 3HZ, 01983 840707

See advert below

PITCHES: 🚐 Caravans 🚗 Motorhomes ⛺ Tents 🏕 Glamping-style accommodation **SERVICES:** 🔌 Electric hook up 🔲 Launderette 🍴 Licensed bar
⛽ Calor Gas ⌀ Camping Gaz T Toilet fluid 🍴 Café/Restaurant ⬛ Fast Food/Takeaway 🔋 Battery charging ⬅ Baby care ↯ Motorvan service point
ABBREVIATIONS: BH/bank hols – bank holidays Etr – Easter Spring BH – Spring Bank Holiday fr – from hrs – hours m – mile mdnt – midnight
rdbt – roundabout rs – restricted service wk – week wknd – weekend x-rds – cross roads 🚫 No credit or debit cards 🚫 No dogs 👪 Children of all ages accepted

SHANKLIN *continued*

Ninham Country Holidays
►►►►86%

tel: 01983 864243 **Ninham PO37 7PL**
email: office@ninham-holidays.co.uk **web:** www.ninham-holidays.co.uk
dir: *Signed from A3056 Newport to Sandown road.* **grid ref:** SZ573825

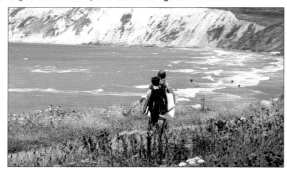

Enjoying a lofty rural location with fine country views, this delightful, spacious park occupies two separate, well-maintained areas in a country park setting near the sea and beach. It has an excellent toilet and shower block in The Orchards that has a good layout of pitches; there is also a good outdoor pool, a games room and an excellent children's play area. Willow Bank is a separate camping area that provides more basic, but adequate, facilities. There are also static holiday homes for hire. 12 acre site. 150 touring pitches. Caravan pitches. Motorhome pitches. Tent pitches. 6 statics.

Open: Early Spring BH-Sep **Last arrival:** 20.00hrs **Last departure:** 10.00hrs
Pitches: * 🚐 £18-£24.75 🚍 £18-£24.75 ▲ £15.25-£21.75
Leisure: 🏊 /ᴧ 😊 🎱 ▭
Facilities: 🟢 ☉ ☀ ⚲ ⛊ 📶 ♻ ❶
Services: 🔌 🔋 🛢 ⊘ 🍴 🛒 ⚒
Within 3 miles: ⚡ ≛ ⌁ ⌀ ◎ ⚲ 🏪 🛍 U

Notes: Swimming pool & coarse fishing rules apply, late night arrival area available. Dogs must be kept on leads.

AA Pubs & Restaurants nearby: The Bonchurch Inn, BONCHURCH, PO38 1NU, 01983 852611

The Taverners, GODSHILL, PO38 3HZ, 01983 840707

Landguard Camping
►►►80%

tel: 01983 863100 **Manor Rd PO37 7PJ**
email: holidaysales.landguard@park-resorts.com
dir: *A3056 towards Sandown. After Morrisons on left, turn right into Whitecross Ln. Follow brown signs to site.* **grid ref:** SZ580825

Owned by Park Resorts, this peaceful and secluded park offers good touring facilities. Customers here also have the benefit of using the swimming pool and entertainment facilities at Lower Hyde Holiday Park nearby. Please note, this park will only open for six weeks in the main summer period. Please check with Park Resorts - Lower Hyde Holiday Park for further details. 142 touring pitches. 6 hardstandings. Caravan pitches. Motorhome pitches. Tent pitches.

Open: Mar-end Oct **Last arrival:** 17.00hrs **Last departure:** noon
Pitches: 🚐 🚍 ▲
Leisure: 🏊 🏊 /ᴧ 🎣 🎱 🎵
Facilities: 🟢 ☉ ☀ ⚲ ⛊ 🍴 📶 ♻ ❶
Services: 🔌 🔋 🛢 🛢 ⊘ 🍴 🛒 ⚒
Within 3 miles: ⚡ ≛ 🗓 ⌀ ◎ ⚲ 🏪 🛍 U

Notes: Dogs must be kept on leads.

AA Pubs & Restaurants nearby: The Bonchurch Inn, BONCHURCH, PO38 1NU, 01983 852611

The Taverners, GODSHILL, PO38 3HZ, 01983 840707

TOTLAND BAY	Map 5 SZ38

Places to visit

Dimbola Lodge Museum, FRESHWATER, PO40 9QE, 01983 756814
www.dimbola.co.uk

Mottistone Gardens, MOTTISTONE, PO30 4ED, 01983 741302
www.nationaltrust.org.uk/isleofwight

Great for kids: Yarmouth Castle, YARMOUTH, PO41 0PB, 01983 760678
www.english-heritage.org.uk/daysout/properties/yarmouth-castle

---

Stoats Farm Caravan & Camping
►►►76%

tel: 01983 755258 & 753416 **PO39 0HE**
email: david@stoats-farm.co.uk
dir: *0.75m S of Totland. NB For caravans & motorhomes approach via Moons Hill advised (do not approach via Weston Ln which is narrow).* **grid ref:** SZ324865

A friendly, personally run site in a quiet country setting close to Alum Bay, Tennyson Down and The Needles. It has good laundry and shower facilities, and the shop, although small, is well stocked. Popular with families, walkers and cyclists, it makes the perfect base for campers wishing to explore this part of the island. 10 acre site. 100 touring pitches. Caravan pitches. Motorhome pitches. Tent pitches.

Open: Apr-Oct
Pitches: 🚐 🚍 ▲
Facilities: 🟢 ☉ 🎣 ☀ ⚲ ⛊ 🛍 ⚲ ❶
Services: 🔌 🔋 ⚒
Within 3 miles: ⚡ ≛ ⌀ ◎ ⚲ 🛍 U

Notes: No loud noise after 23.00hrs, no camp fires. Dogs must be kept on leads. Campers' fridge available.

AA Pubs & Restaurants nearby: The Red Lion, FRESHWATER, PO40 9BP, 01983 754925

LEISURE: 🏊 Indoor swimming pool 🏊 Outdoor swimming pool /ᴧ Children's playground 🎣 Kid's club 🎾 Tennis court 🎱 Games room ▭ Separate TV room ⚡ golf course ≛ Boats for hire 🎦 Cinema 🎵 Entertainment ⌀ Fishing ◎ Mini golf ⚲ Watersports 🏋 Gym 😊 Sports field Spa U Stables
FACILITIES: 🛁 Bath 🟢 Shower ☉ Electric shaver 🎣 Hairdryer ☀ Ice Pack Facility ⚲ Disabled facilities ⛊ Public telephone 🛍 Shop on site or within 200yds 🏪 Mobile shop (calls at least 5 days a week) 🍴 BBQ area 🎋 Picnic area 📶 Wi-fi 🖥 Internet access ♻ Recycling ❶ Tourist info ⚒ Dog exercise area

WHITECLIFF BAY   Map 5 SZ68

Places to visit

Bembridge Windmill, BEMBRIDGE, PO35 5SQ, 01983 873945
www.nationaltrust.org.uk/isleofwight

Nunwell House & Gardens, BRADING, PO36 0JQ, 01983 407240

Great for kids: Lilliput Antique Doll & Toy Museum, BRADING, PO36 0DJ,
01983 407231 www.lilliputmuseum.co.uk

Whitecliff Bay Holiday Park
HOLIDAY CENTRE 86%

tel: 01983 872671 **Hillway Rd, Bembridge PO35 5PL**
email: holiday.sales@away-resorts.com
dir: *1m S of Bembridge, signed from B3395 in village.* **grid ref:** *SZ637862*

This is a large seaside complex on two sites, with camping on one and self-catering
chalets and statics on the other. There is an indoor pool with flume and spa pool,
and an outdoor pool with a kiddies' pool, a family entertainment club, and plenty of
traditional on-site activities including crazy golf and table tennis, plus an indoor
soft play area, a restaurant and a choice of bars. Activities include a My Active
programme for all the family in partnership with Fit4Life. There is access to a
secluded beach from the park. The glamping area offers fully-equipped Cottage
Tents (with heating, TV and a hot tub); equipped, canvas tents; and three vintage
caravans for hire. 49 acre site. 400 touring pitches. 50 hardstandings. 400
seasonal pitches. Caravan pitches. Motorhome pitches. Tent pitches. 227 statics.
12 bell tents/yurts.

Open: all year (rs Off peak facilities restricted) **Last arrival:** flexible
Last departure: 10.00hrs

Pitches: * ⛺ £5-£30 🚐 £5-£30 ▲ £4-£25 🏠

Leisure: 🏊 🏊 🎢 🎣 🎯 🎱 ▢ 🎵

Facilities: 🎣 ☉ 🅿 ✳ ♿ 🕐 💲 🚿 🚽 WiFi 🖥 ♻ 🛈

Services: 🔌 🗄 🍽 🛢 🗑 🚰 🍴 🍴 🏧 🚼 🔧

Within 3 miles: 🎿 ⛵ 🚶 🏌 ◎ 🏊 🎣 🏰 🗄 ⛳

Notes: Adults & families only. Dogs must be kept on leads. Sauna, hot tubs, sports TV
lounge, outdoor cinema.

AA Pubs & Restaurants nearby: The Crab & Lobster Inn, BEMBRIDGE, PO35 5TR,
01983 872244

WOOTTON BRIDGE   Map 5 SZ59

Places to visit

Osborne House, OSBORNE HOUSE, PO32 6JX, 01983 200022
www.english-heritage.org.uk/daysout/properties/osborne

Carisbrooke Castle, CARISBROOKE, PO30 1XY, 01983 522107
www.english-heritage.org.uk/daysout/properties/carisbrooke-castle

Great for kids: Robin Hill Country Park, ARRETON, PO30 2NU, 01983 527352
www.robin-hill.com

Kite Hill Farm Caravan & Camping Park
▶▶▶87%

tel: 01983 883261 **Firestone Copse Rd PO33 4LE**
email: welcome@kitehillfarm.co.uk **web:** www.kitehillfarm.co.uk
dir: *Signed from A3054 at Wootton Bridge, between Ryde & Newport.* **grid ref:** *SZ549906*

The park, on a gently sloping field, is tucked away behind the owners' farm, just a
short walk from the village and attractive river estuary. The facilities are excellent
and very clean, and even include a defibrulator at reception. This park provides a
pleasant relaxing atmosphere for a stay on the island. Rallies are welcome. 12.5
acre site. 50 touring pitches. Caravan pitches. Motorhome pitches. Tent pitches.

Open: all year **Last arrival:** anytime **Last departure:** noon

Pitches: ⛺ £14-£17.50 🚐 £14-£17.50 ▲ £14-£17.50

Leisure: 🎢

Facilities: 🎣 ☉ ✳ ♿ 🕐 🚽 🛈

Services: 🔌 🗄 🚰 🏧

Within 3 miles: 🎿 ⛵ 🚶 🏌 ◎ 🏊 🎣 🏰 🗄 ⛳

Notes: Owners must clean up after their pets. Dogs must be kept on leads.

AA Pubs & Restaurants nearby: The Folly, WHIPPINGHAM, PO32 6NB, 01983 297171

The Fountain Inn, COWES, PO31 7AW, 01983 292397

Duke of York Inn, COWES, PO31 7BT, 01983 295171

PITCHES: ⛺ Caravans 🚐 Motorhomes ▲ Tents 🏠 Glamping-style accommodation **SERVICES:** 🔌 Electric hook up 🗄 Launderette 🍽 Licensed bar
🛢 Calor Gas 🗑 Camping Gaz 🚽 Toilet fluid 🍴 Café/Restaurant 🏧 Fast Food/Takeaway 🔋 Battery charging 🚼 Baby care 🔧 Motorvan service point
ABBREVIATIONS: BH/bank hols – bank holidays Etr – Easter Spring BH – Spring Bank Holiday fr – from hrs – hours m – mile mdnt – midnight
rdbt – roundabout rs – restricted service wk – week wknd – weekend x-rds – cross roads 🚫 No credit or debit cards 🚫 No dogs 👪 Children of all ages accepted

WROXALL
Map 5 SZ57

Places to visit

Appuldurcombe House, WROXALL, PO38 3EW, 01983 852484
www.english-heritage.org.uk/daysout/properties/appuldurcombe-house

Great for kids: Blackgang Chine Fantasy Park, BLACKGANG, PO38 2HN, 01983 730330 www.blackgangchine.com

PREMIER PARK

Appuldurcombe Gardens Holiday Park
►►►►► 87%

GOLD

tel: 01983 852597 **Appuldurcombe Rd PO38 3EP**
email: info@appuldurcombegardens.co.uk
dir: *From Newport take A3020 towards Shanklin & Ventnor. Through Rookley & Godshill. Right at Whiteley Bank rdbt towards Wroxall village, then follow brown signs.*
grid ref: SZ546804

This well-appointed park is set in a unique setting fairly close to the town of Ventnor. It has modern and smart facilities including a spotless toilet and shower block, and a very tasteful lounge bar and function room. There is an excellent, screened outdoor pool and paddling pool plus café and shop. The site is close to cycle routes and is only 150 yards from the bus stop, making it perfect for those with a motorhome or those not wanting to use their car. Static caravans and apartments are also available for hire. 14 acre site. 130 touring pitches. 40 hardstandings. Caravan pitches. Motorhome pitches. Tent pitches. 40 statics.

Open: Mar-Nov **Last arrival:** 21.00hrs **Last departure:** 11.00hrs

Pitches: 🚐 🚏 🛖

Leisure: ⛱ ⛺ 🎣

Facilities: 🚻 📷 ⊙ 🎯 ✳ 🖰 🖹 🎋 WIFI ♻ ❶

Services: 🔌 🗑 🗠 ⌗ T 🍽 🧺 🛒 ↯

Within 3 miles: 🎣 🛶 ☷ 🏌 ⊚ 🚴 🖹 🗒 ∪

Notes: No skateboards. Dogs must be kept on leads. Entertainment in high season.

AA Pubs & Restaurants nearby: The Pond Café, VENTNOR, PO38 1RG, 01983 855666

YARMOUTH

See Newbridge

KENT

ASHFORD
Map 7 TR04

Places to visit

Kent & East Sussex Railway, TENTERDEN, TN30 6HE, 01580 765155
www.kesr.org.uk

Great for kids: Port Lympne Wild Animal Park, LYMPNE, CT21 4LR, 0844 842 4647 www.aspinallfoundation.org/portlympne

PREMIER PARK

Broadhembury Caravan & Camping Park
►►►►► 87%

Best of British

tel: 01233 620859 **Steeds Ln, Kingsnorth TN26 1NQ**
email: holidaypark@broadhembury.co.uk **web:** www.broadhembury.co.uk
dir: *M20 junct 10, A2070 towards Brenzett. Straight on at 1st rdbt. Left at 2nd rdbt (avoid fork left). Straight on at next rdbt. Left at 2nd x-rds in village.*
grid ref: TR009387

A well-run and well-maintained small family park surrounded by open pasture; it is neatly landscaped with pitches sheltered by mature hedges. There is a well-equipped campers' kitchen adjacent to the spotless toilet facilities and children will love the play areas, games room and football pitch. The adults-only area, close to the excellent reception building, includes popular fully serviced hardstanding pitches; this area has its own first-class, solar heated toilet block. 10 acre site. 110 touring pitches. 20 hardstandings. Caravan pitches. Motorhome pitches. Tent pitches. 25 statics.

Open: all year **Last arrival:** 22.00hrs **Last departure:** noon

Pitches: * 🚐 £19-£30 🚏 £19-£30 🛖 £19-£53

Leisure: ⛺ ⚽ 🎣 🖵

Facilities: 🚻 📷 ⊙ 🎯 ✳ 🖰 🕓 🖹 🎋 WIFI 🖥 ♻ ❶

Services: 🔌 🗑 🛢 ⌗ T 🛒 ↯

Within 3 miles: 🎣 ☷ 🏌 ⊚ 🖹 🗒 ∪

Notes: No noise after 22.00hrs. Dogs must be kept on leads.

LEISURE: 🏊 Indoor swimming pool 🏊 Outdoor swimming pool 🎠 Children's playground 👶 Kid's club 🎾 Tennis court 🎱 Games room 🖵 Separate TV room 🏌 golf course 🚣 Boats for hire 🎬 Cinema 🎵 Entertainment 🎣 Fishing ⊚ Mini golf 🏄 Watersports 🏋 Gym 🎯 Sports field Spa ∪ Stables

FACILITIES: 🛁 Bath 🚿 Shower ⊙ Electric shaver 🖰 Hairdryer ✳ Ice Pack Facility 🖰 Disabled facilities 🕓 Public telephone 🖹 Shop on site or within 200yds 🏪 Mobile shop (calls at least 5 days a week) 🍖 BBQ area 🎋 Picnic area WIFI Wi-fi 🖥 Internet access ♻ Recycling ❶ Tourist info 🐕 Dog exercise area

BIRCHINGTON
Map 7 TR36

Places to visit

Reculver Towers & Roman Fort, RECULVER, CT6 6SU, 01227 740676
www.english-heritage.org.uk/daysout/properties/reculver-towers-and-roman-fort

Ramsgate Maritime Museum, RAMSGATE, CT11 8LS, 01843 570622
www.ramsgatemaritimemuseum.org

Great for kids: Richborough Roman Fort & Amphitheatre, RICHBOROUGH,
CT13 9JW, 01304 612013 www.english-heritage.org.uk/daysout/properties/
richborough-roman-fort-and-amphitheatre

Two Chimneys Caravan Park
►►►83%

tel: 01843 841068 & 843157 **Shottendane Rd CT7 0HD**
email: info@twochimneys.co.uk **web:** www.twochimneys.co.uk
dir: From A28 to Birchington Sq right into Park Lane (B2048). Left at Manston Rd
(B2050), 1st left. **grid ref:** TR320684

An impressive entrance leads into this busy, family-run site, which boasts two
swimming pools, a fully-licensed clubhouse, crazy golf, an amusement arcade and
a café/bistro. Other attractions include a tennis court and children's play area. The
immaculately clean toilet facilities fully meet the needs of visitors at this popular
family park. 60 acre site. 250 touring pitches. 5 hardstandings. 20 seasonal
pitches. Caravan pitches. Motorhome pitches. Tent pitches. 200 statics.

Open: all year (rs Off peak shop, bar, pool & diner restricted) **Last arrival:** 22.00hrs
Last departure: 11.00hrs

Pitches: * ♣ £15.50-£32 ♣ £15.50-£32 Å £15.50-£29

Leisure: ♨ ⚄ ♫

Facilities: ♠ ☉ ☞ ✻ ⚷ ⚟ ⑤ 🏧 WiFi ♺ ❶

Services: ♦ ⑤ ⛽ ⌀ Ⓣ ⑩ 🍴 ♨ ⌂ ⚱

Within 3 miles: ↳ ⚓ 日 ⚲ ◎ ⟲ 🏧 🏪 U

Notes: ⊗ No gazebos, no noise between 23.00hrs-07.00hrs, no bikes after dusk.

AA Pubs & Restaurants nearby: The Ambrette, MARGATE, CT9 1QE, 01843 231504

EASTCHURCH
Map 7 TQ97

Warden Springs Caravan Park
HOLIDAY CENTRE 74%

tel: 01795 880216 **Warden Point ME12 4HF**
email: warden.springs@pdk-resorts.com
dir: M2 junct 5 (Sheerness/Sittingbourne), A249 for 8m, right onto B2231 to Eastchurch.
In Eastchurch left after church, follow park signs. **grid ref:** TR019722

Panoramic views from the scenic cliff-top setting can be enjoyed at their best from
the touring area of this holiday park. All of the many and varied leisure activities
provided by the park are included in the pitch tariff, ie the heated outdoor
swimming pool, adventure playground, family entertainment and a good choice of
food outlets. 66 touring pitches. Caravan pitches. Motorhome pitches. Tent pitches.
198 statics.

Open: Apr-Oct (rs BH & peak wks) **Last arrival:** 22.00hrs **Last departure:** noon

Pitches: ♣ ♣ Å **Leisure:** ♨ ⚄ ♨ ♫

Facilities: ♠ ☉ ☞ ⚷ ⚟ 🏧 ♫ WiFi ♨

Services: ♦ ⑤ ⛽ 🍴 ♨ **Within 3 miles:** ⚲ 🏧 🏪 U

Notes: No cars by caravans or tents.

AA Pubs & Restaurants nearby: The Ferry House Inn, LEYSDOWN-ON-SEA, ME12 4BQ,
01795 510214

FOLKESTONE
Map 7 TR23

Places to visit

Dymchurch Martello Tower, DYMCHURCH, CT16 1HU, 01304 211067
www.english-heritage.org.uk/daysout/properties/dymchurch-martello-tower

Dover Castle & Secret Wartime Tunnels, DOVER, CT16 1HU, 01304 211067
www.english-heritage.org.uk/daysout/properties/dover-castle

Great for kids: Port Lympne Wild Animal Park, LYMPNE, CT21 4LR,
0844 842 4647 www.aspinallfoundation.org/portlympne

Little Switzerland Camping & Caravan Site
►►75%

tel: 01303 252168 **Wear Bay Rd CT19 6PS**
email: btony328@aol.com
dir: M20 junct 13, A259 (Folkestone Harbour). At 2nd rdbt follow brown Country Park sign
(A260). Right at next rdbt (Country Park). 8th left into Swiss Way, site signed.
grid ref: TR248380

Set on a narrow plateau below the White Cliffs and above The Warren, this unique
site offers sheltered, traditional camping in secluded dells and enjoys fine views
across the English Channel to the French coast — probably best enjoyed from the
grassy alfresco area at the popular café. The toilet facilities are basic and
unsuitable for disabled visitors. 3 acre site. 32 touring pitches. Caravan pitches.
Motorhome pitches. Tent pitches. 13 statics.

Open: Mar-Oct **Last arrival:** mdnt **Last departure:** noon

Pitches: ♣ ♣ Å **Facilities:** ♠ ☉ ✻ ⚟ 🏧 WiFi ♨ ❶

Services: ♦ ⑤ ⛽ ⌀ ⑩ ♨ ⌂ ⚱

Within 3 miles: ↳ ⚓ 日 ⚲ ◎ ⟲ 🏧 🏪 U

Notes: ◎ No open fires. Dogs must be kept on leads.

AA Pubs & Restaurants nearby: Rocksalt Rooms, FOLKESTONE, CT19 6NN, 01303 212070

PITCHES: ♣ Caravans ♣ Motorhomes Å Tents ⋒ Glamping-style accommodation **SERVICES:** ♦ Electric hook up ⑤ Launderette ⛽ Licensed bar
♠ Calor Gas ⌀ Camping Gaz Ⓣ Toilet fluid 🍴 Café/Restaurant ♨ Fast Food/Takeaway ♨ Battery charging ♨ Baby care ⚱ Motorvan service point
ABBREVIATIONS: BH/bank hols – bank holidays Etr – Easter Spring BH – Spring Bank Holiday fr – from hrs – hours m – mile mdnt – midnight
rdbt – roundabout rs – restricted service wk – week wknd – weekend x-rds – cross roads ⊛ No credit or debit cards ⊗ No dogs ♟ Children of all ages accepted

LEYSDOWN-ON-SEA
Map 7 TR07

Priory Hill
►►► 71%

tel: 01795 510267 **Wing Rd ME12 4QT**
email: touringpark@prioryhill.co.uk
dir: *M2 junct 5, A249 signed Sheerness, then B2231 to Leysdown, follow brown tourist signs.* **grid ref:** *TR038704*

A small well-maintained touring area on an established family-run holiday park close to the sea, with views of the north Kent coast. Amenities include a clubhouse and a swimming pool. The pitch price includes membership of the clubhouse with live entertainment, and use of the indoor swimming pool. 1.5 acre site. 37 touring pitches. Caravan pitches. Motorhome pitches. Tent pitches.

Open: Mar-Oct (rs Low season shorter opening times for pool & club)
Last arrival: 20.00hrs **Last departure:** noon

Pitches: * ⊞ £18-£30 ⇌ £16-£30 Å £16-£30

Leisure: ≋ ⊙ ◗ ⊡

Facilities: ⋔ ⊙ ℱ ※ ⓑ ⑤ ⋔ 📶 ✪

Services: ⊡ ⑤ ⬛ ◉ ⊞

Within 3 miles: ⌒ ◎ ⑤ ⑤

Notes: Dogs must be kept on leads.

AA Pubs & Restaurants nearby: The Ferry House Inn, LEYSDOWN-ON-SEA, ME12 4BQ, 01795 510214

MARDEN
Map 6 TQ74

Places to visit
Finchcocks Musical Museum, GOUDHURST, TN17 1HH, 01580 211702 www.finchcocks.co.uk

Scotney Castle, LAMBERHURST, TN3 8JN, 01892 893868 www.nationaltrust.org.uk/scotneycastle

PREMIER PARK

Tanner Farm Touring Caravan & Camping Park
►►►►► 89%

Best of British
GOLD

tel: 01622 832399 & 831214 **Tanner Farm, Goudhurst Rd TN12 9ND**
email: enquiries@tannerfarmpark.co.uk
dir: *From A21 or A229 onto B2079. Midway between Marden & Goudhurst.* **grid ref:** *TQ732415*

At the heart of a 150-acre Wealden farm, this extensive, long-established touring park is peacefully tucked away down a quiet farm drive deep in unspoilt Kent countryside, yet close to Sissinghurst Castle and within easy reach of London (Marden station is three miles away). Perfect for families, as it has farm animals, two excellent play areas and a recreation/wet weather room (with TV); it offers quality toilet blocks with privacy cubicles, a good shop, spacious hardstandings (12 fully serviced), and high levels of security and customer care. 15 acre site. 130 touring pitches. 34 hardstandings. 11 seasonal pitches. Caravan pitches. Motorhome pitches. Tent pitches.

Open: 14 Feb-mid Nov **Last arrival:** 20.00hrs **Last departure:** noon

Pitches: ⊞ ⇌ Å

Leisure: ⚠ ⊙ ◗

Facilities: ⋔ ⋔ ⊙ ℱ ※ ⓑ ⑤ ⋔ 📶 ♻ ✪

Services: ⊡ ⑤ 🔒 ◍ ⊞ ⬗

Within 3 miles: ⌒ ⑤ ⑤

Notes: No groups, 1 car per pitch, no commercial vehicles. Dogs must be kept on leads.

AA Pubs & Restaurants nearby: The Bull Inn, LINTON, ME17 4AW, 01622 743612

The Star & Eagle, GOUDHURST, TN17 1AL, 01580 211512

Green Cross Inn, GOUDHURST, TN17 1HA, 01580 211200

ROCHESTER
Map 6 TQ76

Places to visit
Guildhall Museum, ROCHESTER, ME1 1PY, 01634 332900 www.guildhallmuseumrochester.co.uk

Upnor Castle, UPNOR, ME2 4XG, 01634 718742 www.english-heritage.org.uk/daysout/properties/upnor-castle

Great for kids: Diggerland, STROOD, ME2 2NU, 0871 227 7007 www.diggerland.com

Allhallows Holiday Park
HOLIDAY HOME PARK 82%

GOLD

tel: 01634 270385 **Allhallows-on-Sea ME3 9QD**
email: allhallows@haven.com **web:** www.haven.com/allhallows
dir: *M25 junct 2, A2 signed Rochester, A289 signed Gillingham. A228 signed Grain. Follow site signs.* **grid ref:** *TQ841784*

Located in a peaceful country park setting close to Rochester, Allhallows is a static-only holiday park offering a wide range of sporting and leisure activities for all the family, including swimming pools, tennis courts, coarse fishing, a 9-hole golf course and fencing. Children will love the kids' club and play area, while there is a restaurant and bar with evening entertainment for adults.

Open: Mar-Oct

Change over day: Mon, Fri, Sat

Arrival and departure times: Please contact the site

Statics: 93 Sleeps 6-8 Bedrms 2-3 Bathrms 1-2 Toilets 1-2 Dishwasher Microwave Freezer TV Sky/FTV Elec inc Gas inc Grass area

Children: ⓘ Cots inc Highchair **Dogs:** 2 on leads No dangerous dogs

Leisure: ≋ ≋ ◡ ◡ ⌒ Cycle hire ⚒ ⚠

ST NICHOLAS AT WADE

Places to visit
Reculver Towers & Roman Fort, RECULVER, CT6 6SU, 01227 740676 www.english-heritage.org.uk/daysout/properties/reculver-towers-and-roman-fort

Great for kids: Richborough Roman Fort & Amphitheatre, RICHBOROUGH, CT13 9JW, 01304 612013 www.english-heritage.org.uk/daysout/properties/richborough-roman-fort-and-amphitheatre

---

LEISURE: ≋ Indoor swimming pool ≋ Outdoor swimming pool ⚠ Children's playground ⚒ Kid's club ◡ Tennis court ◖ Games room ⊡ Separate TV room ↓ golf course ⚓ Boats for hire ⊟ Cinema ♫ Entertainment ⌒ Fishing ◎ Mini golf ≋ Watersports ⚐ Gym ⊙ Sports field Spa ◡ Stables
FACILITIES: ⋔ Bath ⋔ Shower ⊙ Electric shaver ℱ Hairdryer ※ Ice Pack Facility ⓑ Disabled facilities ◔ Public telephone ⑤ Shop on site or within 200yds ⓕ Mobile shop (calls at least 5 days a week) ⬛ BBQ area ⊟ Picnic area 📶 Wi-fi ⬛ Internet access ♻ Recycling ✪ Tourist info ⋔ Dog exercise area

ST NICHOLAS AT WADE
Map 7 TR26

St Nicholas Camping Site
►►78%

tel: 01843 847245 **Court Rd CT7 0NH**
web: www.stnicholascampingsite.co.uk
dir: Signed from A299 & A28, site at W end of village near church. **grid ref:** TR254672

A gently-sloping field with mature hedging, on the edge of the village close to the shop. This pretty site offers good facilities, including a family/disabled room, and is conveniently located close to primary routes and the north Kent coast. 3 acre site. 75 touring pitches. 6 seasonal pitches. Caravan pitches. Motorhome pitches. Tent pitches.

Open: Etr-Oct **Last arrival:** 22.00hrs **Last departure:** 14.00hrs

Pitches: * ⛺ £20-£21.50 🚐 £19-£21 ▲ £17-£20

Leisure: 🅰 **Facilities:** 🅿⊙🄿✳🅑🏍🅘

Services: 🔋🅐🅐🅣 **Within 3 miles:** 🄿🅢U

Notes: ⊘ No music after 22.30hrs. Dogs must be kept on leads. Baby changing area.

WHITSTABLE
Map 7 TR16

Places to visit

Canterbury Westgate Towers Museum, CANTERBURY, CT1 2BZ, 07768 535766
www.canterburywestgatetowers.com

The Canterbury Tales, CANTERBURY, CT1 2TG, 01227 479227
www.canterburytales.org.uk

Great for kids: Druidstone Park, CANTERBURY, CT2 9JR, 01227 765168
www.druidstone.net

Homing Park
►►►►84%

tel: 01227 771777 **Church Ln, Seasalter CT5 4BU**
email: info@homingpark.co.uk
dir: Exit A299 for Whitstable & Canterbury, left at brown camping-caravan sign into Church Ln. Site entrance has 2 large flag poles. **grid ref:** TR095645

A small touring park close to Seasalter Beach and Whitstable, which is famous for its oysters. All pitches are generously sized and fully serviced, and most are separated by hedging and shrubs. A clubhouse and swimming pool are available on site with a small cost for the use of the swimming pool. 12.6 acre site. 43 touring pitches. Caravan pitches. Motorhome pitches. Tent pitches. 195 statics. 3 wooden pods.

Open: Etr-Oct **Last arrival:** 20.00hrs **Last departure:** 11.00hrs

Pitches: * ⛺ £19.50-£27 🚐 £19.50-£27 ▲ £19.50-£27 🏠

Leisure: 🏊🅰🎱 **Facilities:** 🅿⊙🄿✳🅑WiFi🅐🅘

Services: 🔋🅓🅑🅐🅐🅣🍴 **Within 3 miles:** 🄳🄷🄿🅢🅢🅢U

Notes: No commercial vehicles, no tents greater than 8 berth or 5mtrs, no unaccompanied minors, no cycles or scooters. Dogs must be kept on leads.

AA Pubs & Restaurants nearby: The Sportsman, WHITSTABLE, CT5 4BP, 01227 273370

WROTHAM HEATH
Map 6 TQ65

Places to visit

Ightham Mote, IGHTHAM, TN15 0NT, 01732 810378 www.nationaltrust.org.uk

St Leonard's Tower, WEST MALLING, ME19 6PE, 01732 870872
www.english-heritage.org.uk/daysout/properties/st-leonards-tower

Great for kids: Kent Life, MAIDSTONE, ME14 3AU, 01622 763936
ww.kentlife.org.uk

Gate House Wood Touring Park
►►►80%

tel: 01732 843062 **Ford Ln TN15 7SD**
email: contact@gatehousewoodtouringpark.com
web: www.gatehousewoodtouringpark.com
dir: M26 junct 2a, A20 S towards Maidstone, through lights at Wrotham Heath. 1st left signed Trottiscliffe, left at next junct into Ford Ln. Site 100yds on left. **grid ref:** TQ635585

A well-sheltered and mature site in a former quarry surrounded by tall deciduous trees and gorse banks. The well-designed facilities include a reception, shop and smart toilets, and there is good entrance security and high levels of customer care. The colourful flower beds and hanging baskets are impressive and give a positive first impression. Conveniently placed for the M20 and M25 and a fast rail link to central London. 3.5 acre site. 55 touring pitches. Caravan pitches. Motorhome pitches. Tent pitches.

Open: Mar-Oct **Last arrival:** 21.00hrs **Last departure:** noon

Pitches: ⛺🚐▲ **Leisure:** 🅰

Facilities: 🅿⊙🄿✳🅑🄰🅑WiFi🅐🅘

Services: 🔋🅓🅐🅐🅣🄳 **Within 3 miles:** 🄳🅢🄿🅢🅢U

Notes: ⊘ ⊗ No commercial vehicles, no noise after 23.00hrs.

AA Pubs & Restaurants nearby: The Bull, WROTHAM, TN15 7RF, 01732 789800

PITCHES: 🚐 Caravans 🚐 Motorhomes ▲ Tents 🏠 Glamping-style accommodation **SERVICES:** 🔋 Electric hook up 🅓 Launderette 🅑 Licensed bar
🅐 Calor Gas ⌀ Camping Gaz 🅣 Toilet fluid 🍴 Café/Restaurant 🍟 Fast Food/Takeaway 🔋 Battery charging 🍼 Baby care ⚡ Motorvan service point
ABBREVIATIONS: BH/bank hols – bank holidays Etr – Easter Spring BH – Spring Bank Holiday fr – from hrs – hours m – mile mdnt – midnight
rdbt – roundabout rs – restricted service wk – week wknd – weekend x-rds – cross roads ⊘ No credit or debit cards ⊗ No dogs 👪 Children of all ages accepted

LANCASHIRE

See also sites under Greater Manchester & Merseyside

BLACKPOOL
Map 18 SD33

See also Lytham St Annes & Thornton

Places to visit

Blackpool Zoo, BLACKPOOL, FY3 8PP, 01253 830830 www.blackpoolzoo.org.uk

Marton Mere Holiday Village
HOLIDAY CENTRE 87%

tel: 0871 231 0881 **Mythop Rd FY4 4XN**
email: martonmere@haven.com **web:** www.haven.com/martonmere
dir: *M55 junct 4, A583 towards Blackpool. Right at Clifton Arms lights into Mythop Rd. Site 150yds on left.* **grid ref:** *SD347349*

A very attractive holiday centre in an unusual setting on the edge of the mere, with plenty of birdlife to be spotted. A stylish Mediterranean seaside themed Boathouse Restaurant was added to the park ready for the 2014 season. The on-site entertainment is tailored for all ages, and includes a superb show bar. There's a regular bus service into Blackpool for those who want to explore further afield. The separate touring area is well equipped with hardstandings and electric pitches, and there are good quality facilities, including a superb amenities block. 30 acre site. 82 touring pitches. 82 hardstandings. Caravan pitches. Motorhome pitches. 700 statics.

Open: mid Mar-end Oct (rs Mar-end May & Sep-Oct reduced facilities, splash zone closed) **Last arrival:** 22.00hrs **Last departure:** 10.00hrs

Pitches: 🚐 🚏
Leisure: 🏊 ⌂ 🎣 🎵
Facilities: 🛁 🚿 ☉ 🍴 ✳ ✿ 🔒 🐕 🛒 💻 ♻ ❶
Services: 🔌 🖪 🍴 🛒 🖊 🍽 ⛲
Within 3 miles: ⚓ 🚴 🎱 🎣 ◎ ⚓ 🛒 🛒 ♻

Notes: No commercial vehicles, no bookings by persons under 21yrs unless a family booking, max 2 dogs per booking, certain dog breeds banned. Dogs must be kept on leads.
See advert below

LEISURE: 🏊 Indoor swimming pool 🏊 Outdoor swimming pool ⌂ Children's playground 🎣 Kid's club 🎾 Tennis court 🎱 Games room ▭ Separate TV room ⛳ golf course 🚣 Boats for hire 🎬 Cinema 🎵 Entertainment 🎣 Fishing ◎ Mini golf 🏄 Watersports 🏋 Gym 🏟 Sports field Spa ⛲ Stables
FACILITIES: 🛁 Bath 🚿 Shower ☉ Electric shaver 🎣 Hairdryer ✳ Ice Pack Facility ♿ Disabled facilities 📞 Public telephone 🛒 Shop on site or within 200yds 🏪 Mobile shop (calls at least 5 days a week) 🍴 BBQ area 🍴 Picnic area 📶 Wi-fi 💻 Internet access ♻ Recycling ❶ Tourist info 🐕 Dog exercise area

Manor House Caravan Park

►►►►81%

tel: 01253 764723 **Kitty Ln, Marton Moss FY4 5EG**

email: info@manorhousecaravanpark.co.uk

dir: *At rdbt at end of M55 junct 4, take A5230 signed Sq Gate. At next rdbt take 3rd exit (Blackpool/Sq Gate/A5230). In 0.5m left at lights into Midgeland Rd. 500yds, straight on at x-rds. 250yds, right into Kitty Ln. 250yds site on right (NB it is advised not to follow Sat Nav).* **grid ref:** SD336318

A sympathetically converted former small holding close to both Lytham St Annes and Blackpool, this peacefully located adults-only park is surrounded by high neat hedges and generous sized hardstanding pitches ensure optimum privacy. A warm welcome is assured by the resident owners and although there is no shop or launderette, both services are within a 10-minute drive. There are caravan pitches and motorhome pitches. Please note that tents are not accepted. 1 acre site. 10 touring pitches. 10 hardstandings. Caravan pitches. Motorhome pitches.

Open: all year **Last arrival:** 20.00hrs **Last departure:** 11.30hrs

Pitches: 🚐 🚃 **Facilities:** 🎄♻️🅰️

Services: 🔌 🛠️ **Within 3 miles:** ⛳🏕️⛳🎣◎⚓🏧🛒🎬🔄

Notes: Adults only. 🚫 No ball games or loud music. Pets accepted by prior arrangement only. Dogs must be kept on leads.

BOLTON-LE-SANDS   Map 18 SD46

Places to visit

Lancaster Maritime Museum, LANCASTER, LA1 1RB, 01524 382264
www.lancashire.gov.uk/museums

Lancaster City Museum, LANCASTER, LA1 1HT, 01524 64637
www.lancashire.gov.uk/museums

Great for kids: Lancaster Castle, LANCASTER, LA1 1YJ, 01524 64998
www.lancastercastle.com

Bay View Holiday Park

►►►►86%

tel: 01524 701508 **LA5 9TN**

email: info@holgatesleisureparks.co.uk **web:** www.holgates.co.uk

dir: *M6 junct 25, A6 through Carnforth to Bolton-le-Sands. Site on right.* **grid ref:** SD478683

A high quality, family-oriented seaside destination with fully serviced all-weather pitches, many of which have views of Morecambe Bay and the Cumbrian hills. A

stylish bar/restaurant is just one of the park's amenities, and there is a wide range of activities and attractions on offer within a few miles. This makes a good choice for a family holiday by the sea. 10 acre site. 100 touring pitches. 50 hardstandings. 127 seasonal pitches. Caravan pitches. Motorhome pitches. Tent pitches. 100 statics. 2 wooden pods.

Open: all year **Last arrival:** 20.00hrs **Last departure:** noon

Pitches: * 🚐 £21-£26 🚃 £21-£26 ⛺ £16-£21 🏕️

Leisure: 🏊♻️🎣🖥️

Facilities: 🎄☀️❄️♿🅱️🕐🅰️🛁🖥️ ♻️ 🅰️

Services: 🔌🛒🍺🔋⚡🎯🍴🍟🚰🚂

Within 3 miles: ⛳🏕️⛳🎣🏧🎬

Notes: No noise after 23.00hrs. Dogs must be kept on leads.

AA Pubs & Restaurants nearby: The Longlands Inn and Restaurant, CARNFORTH, LA6 1JH, 01524 781256

Hest Bank Inn, HEST BANK, LA2 6DN, 01524 824339

See advert advert on page 251

Sandside Caravan & Camping Park

►►►84%

tel: 01524 822311 **The Shore LA5 8JS**

email: sandside@btconnect.com

dir: *M6 junct 35, A6 through Carnforth. Right after Far Pavillion in Bolton-le-Sands, over level crossing to site.* **grid ref:** SD472681

A well-kept family park located in a pleasant spot overlooking Morecambe Bay, with distant views of the Lake District. The site is next to a West Coast railway line with a level crossing. The shop and reception certainly are assets at this welcoming park. Booking is advisable at peak periods. 9 acre site. 70 touring pitches. 70 hardstandings. Caravan pitches. Motorhome pitches. Tent pitches. 33 statics.

Open: Mar-Oct **Last arrival:** 19.00hrs **Last departure:** 13.00hrs

Pitches: 🚐 🚃 ⛺

Facilities: 🎄☀️🅿️🅰️ **Services:** 🔌🖥️

Within 3 miles: ⛳🏕️⛳🎣🏧🎬🔄

Notes: No noise after mdnt. Dogs must be kept on leads. LPG (gas) available.

AA Pubs & Restaurants nearby: The Longlands Inn and Restaurant, CARNFORTH, LA6 1JH, 01524 781256

Hest Bank Inn, HEST BANK, LA2 6DN, 01524 824339

Red Bank Farm

►►►80%

tel: 01524 823196 **LA5 8JR**

email: mark.archer@hotmail.co.uk

dir: *From Morecambe take A5015 towards Carnforth. After Hest Bank left into Pastures Ln (follow brown site sign). Over rail bridge, right (follow site sign). At T-junct left into The Shore to site at end.* **grid ref:** SD472681

A gently sloping grassy field with mature hedges, close to the sea shore and a RSPB reserve. This farm site has smart toilet facilities, a superb view across Morecambe Bay to the distant Lake District hills, and is popular with tenters. Archers Café serves a good range of cooked food, including home-reared marsh lamb dishes. 3 acre site. 60 touring pitches. Motorhome pitches. Tent pitches.

Open: Mar-Oct

continued

PITCHES: 🚐 Caravans 🚃 Motorhomes ⛺ Tents 🏕️ Glamping-style accommodation **SERVICES:** 🔌 Electric hook up 🖥️ Launderette 🍺 Licensed bar 🅱️ Calor Gas 🔥 Camping Gaz ⊤ Toilet fluid 🍴 Café/Restaurant 🍟 Fast Food/Takeaway 🔋 Battery charging 👶 Baby care 🔄 Motorvan service point **ABBREVIATIONS:** BH/bank hols – bank holidays Etr – Easter Spring BH – Spring Bank Holiday fr – from hrs – hours m – mile mdnt – midnight rdbt – roundabout rs – restricted service wk – week wknd – weekend x-rds – cross roads 🚫 No credit or debit cards 🚫 No dogs 👫 Children of all ages accepted

BOLTON-LE-SANDS *continued*

Pitches: * ⊞ fr £12 ▲ fr £12

Facilities: ♠ ⊙ ☞ ✳ ♻ ❼

Services: ⊡ ⓢ

Within 3 miles: ↓ ≱ ⊟ ℰ ◎ ≋ ⓢ ⓢ

Notes: No noise after 22.30hrs. Dogs must be kept on leads. Pets' corner.

AA Pubs & Restaurants nearby: The Longlands Inn and Restaurant, CARNFORTH, LA6 1JH, 01524 781256

Hest Bank Inn, HEST BANK, LA2 6DN, 01524 824339

CAPERNWRAY   Map 18 SD57

Places to visit

Leighton Hall, CARNFORTH, LA5 9ST, 01524 734474 www.leightonhall.co.uk

RSPB Leighton Moss & Morecambe Bay Nature Reserve, SILVERDALE, LA5 0SW, 01524 701601 www.rspb.org.uk/leightonmoss

Old Hall Caravan Park
▶▶▶▶ 88%

tel: 01524 733276 **LA6 1AD**

email: info@oldhallcaravanpark.co.uk

dir: *M6 junct 35 follow signs to Over Kellet, left onto B6254, left at village green signed Capernwray. Site 1.5m on right.* **grid ref:** *SD533716*

A lovely secluded park set in a clearing amongst trees at the end of a half-mile long drive. This peaceful park is home to a wide variety of wildlife, and there are marked walks in the woods. A pathway over a meandering brook through woodland separates the reception from the touring area. The facilities are well maintained by friendly owners, and booking is advisable. 3 acre site. 38 touring pitches. 38 hardstandings. 30 seasonal pitches. Caravan pitches. Motorhome pitches. 240 statics.

Open: Mar-Oct **Last departure:** noon

Pitches: * ⊞ fr £20 ⊞ fr £20

Leisure: ⚠

Facilities: ♠ ⊙ ☞ ♿ ⓢ ♒ 🎾 WiFi 🖥 ♻ ❼

Services: ⊡ ⓢ 🔒 ⊘ ≋

Within 3 miles: ≱ ℰ ≋ ⓢ ⓢ ∪

Notes: No skateboards, rollerblades or roller boots. Dogs must be kept on leads.

AA Pubs & Restaurants nearby: The Highwayman, BURROW, LA6 2RJ, 01524 273338

The Lunesdale Arms, TUNSTALL, LA6 2QN, 015242 74203

COCKERHAM

Places to visit

Lancaster Maritime Museum, LANCASTER, LA1 1RB, 01524 382264 www.lancashire.gov.uk/museums

Lancaster City Museum, LANCASTER, LA1 1HT, 01524 64637 www.lancashire.gov.uk/museums

Great for kids: Blackpool Zoo, BLACKPOOL, FY3 8PP, 01253 830830 www.blackpoolzoo.org.uk

COCKERHAM   Map 18 SD45

Moss Wood Caravan Park
▶▶▶▶ 83%

GOLD

tel: 01524 791041 **Crimbles Ln LA2 0ES**

email: info@mosswood.co.uk

dir: *M6 junct 33, A6, approx 4m to site. From Cockerham take W A588. Left into Crimbles Lane to site.* **grid ref:** *SD456497*

A tree-lined grassy park with sheltered, level pitches, located on peaceful Cockerham Moss. The modern toilet block is attractively clad in stained wood, and the facilities include cubicled washing facilities and a launderette. 25 acre site. 25 touring pitches. 25 hardstandings. Caravan pitches. Motorhome pitches. Tent pitches. 143 statics.

Open: Mar-Oct **Last arrival:** 20.00hrs **Last departure:** 16.00hrs

Pitches: ⊞ ⊞ ▲

Leisure: ⚽

Facilities: ♠ ⊙ ☞ ♿ ⓢ ⓢ 🎾 ♒

Services: ⊡ ⓢ 🔒 ⊘ Ⓣ

Within 3 miles: ↓ ℰ ⓢ ∪

Notes: Dogs must be kept on leads. Woodland walks.

AA Pubs & Restaurants nearby: The Bay Horse Inn, FORTON, LA2 0HR, 01524 791204

CROSTON   Map 15 SD41

Places to visit

Harris Museum & Art Gallery, PRESTON, PR1 2PP, 01772 258248 www.harrismuseum.org.uk

Rufford Old Hall, RUFFORD, L40 1SG, 01704 821254 www.nationaltrust.org.uk/ruffordoldhall

Royal Umpire Caravan Park
▶▶▶ 84%

tel: 01772 600257 **Southport Rd PR26 9JB**

email: info@royalumpire.co.uk

dir: *From N: M6 junct 28 (from S: M6 junct 27), onto B5209, right onto B5250.* **grid ref:** *SD504190*

A large park with tree- or hedge-lined bays for touring caravans and motorhomes, plus a large camping field in open countryside. There are many areas for children's activities and a several pubs and restaurants within walking distance. Four camping pods are available for hire. 60 acre site. 195 touring pitches. 180 hardstandings. Caravan pitches. Motorhome pitches. Tent pitches. 4 wooden pods.

Open: all year **Last arrival:** 20.00hrs **Last departure:** 16.00hrs

Pitches: * ⊞ £17-£35 ⊞ £17-£35 ▲ £15-£26 ⌂

Leisure: ⚠ ⚽

Facilities: ♠ ⊙ ☞ ✳ ♿ ⓢ 🎾 WiFi ♻ ❼

Services: ⊡ ⓢ 🔒 ⊘ ≋

Within 3 miles: ↓ ≱ ℰ ≋ ⓢ ⓢ ∪

Notes: Dogs must be kept on leads.

AA Pubs & Restaurants nearby: Farmers Arms, HESKIN GREEN, PR7 5NP, 01257 451276

LEISURE: 🏊 Indoor swimming pool 🏊 Outdoor swimming pool ⚠ Children's playground 👶 Kid's club 🎾 Tennis court 🎱 Games room 📺 Separate TV room ⛳ golf course 🚤 Boats for hire 🎦 Cinema 🎵 Entertainment 🎣 Fishing ◎ Mini golf 🏄 Watersports 🏋 Gym ⚽ Sports field Spa ∪ Stables
FACILITIES: 🛁 Bath 🚿 Shower ⊙ Electric shaver 💈 Hairdryer ✳ Ice Pack Facility ♿ Disabled facilities ☎ Public telephone 🏪 Shop on site or within 200yds 🛒 Mobile shop (calls at least 5 days a week) 🍖 BBQ area 🎍 Picnic area WiFi Wi-fi 🖥 Internet access ♻ Recycling ❼ Tourist info 🐕 Dog exercise area

FAR ARNSIDE
Map 18 SD47

Places to visit

Rufford Old Hall, RUFFORD, L40 1SG, 01704 821254
www.nationaltrust.org.uk/ruffordoldhall

RSPB Leighton Moss & Morecambe Bay Nature Reserve, SILVERDALE, LA5 0SW,
01524 701601 www.rspb.org.uk/leightonmoss

Hollins Farm Camping & Caravanning
▶▶▶▶ 90%

tel: 01524 701508 **LA5 0SL**
email: reception@holgates.co.uk **web:** www.holgates.co.uk
dir: M6 junct 35, A601(Carnforth). Left in 1m at rdbt to Carnforth. Right in 1m at lights
signed Silverdale. Left in 1m into Sands Ln, signed Silverdale. 2.4m over auto-crossing,
0.3m to T-junct. Right, follow signs to site, in approx 3m take 2nd left after passing
Holgates. **grid ref:** SD450764

Hollins Farm is a long established park that continues to be upgraded by the
owners. There are 50 fully serviced hardstanding pitches for tourers and 25 fully
serviced tent pitches; the excellent amenities block provides very good facilities and
privacy options. It has a traditional family camping feel and offers high standard
facilities; most pitches offer views towards Morecambe Bay. The leisure and
recreation facilities of the nearby, much larger, sister park (Silverdale Holiday Park)
can be accessed by guests here. 30 acre site. 12 touring pitches. 12 hardstandings.
38 seasonal pitches. Caravan pitches. Motorhome pitches. Tent pitches.

Open: 14 Mar-7 Nov **Last arrival:** 20.00hrs **Last departure:** noon
Pitches: * 🚐 £30 🚐 £30 ⛺ £28
Facilities: 🍴 ☉ ☀ 🛈
Services: 🔌 🔲 🛢 ⊘
Within 3 miles: ↓ ❊ ◎ 🖥 🔲
Notes: No unaccompanied children. Dogs must be kept on leads.
See advert on page 251

FLEETWOOD

Places to visit

Blackpool Zoo, BLACKPOOL, FY3 8PP, 01253 830830 www.blackpoolzoo.org.uk

---

FLEETWOOD
Map 18 SD34

Cala Gran Holiday Park
HOLIDAY HOME PARK 84%

tel: 01253 872555 **Fleetwood Rd FY7 8JY**
email: calagran@haven.com **web:** www.haven.com/calagran
dir: M55 junct 3, A585 signed Fleetwood. At 4th rdbt (Nautical College on left) take 3rd
exit. Park 250yds on left. **grid ref:** SD330451

Cala Gran is a lively holiday park close to Blackpool with a range of quality holiday
caravans and apartments. The park is all about fun, and the entertainment
includes live music, comedy shows and resident DJs, while for children there are
swimming pools and SplashZone.

Open: Mar-Oct
Change over day: Mon, Fri, Sat   **Arrival and departure times:** Please contact the site
Statics: 226 Sleeps 6-8 Bedrms 2-3 Bathrms 1-2 Toilets 1-2 Microwave Freezer TV Sky/
FTV Elec inc Gas inc Grass area
Children: 🛉 Cots Highchair **Dogs:** 2 on leads No dangerous dogs
Leisure: 🚲 Cycle hire 🖐 /�️

GARSTANG
Map 18 SD44

Places to visit

Lancaster Maritime Museum, LANCASTER, LA1 1RB, 01524 382264
www.lancashire.gov.uk/museums

Lancaster City Museum, LANCASTER, LA1 1HT, 01524 64637
www.lancashire.gov.uk/museums

Great for kids: Lancaster Castle, LANCASTER, LA1 1YJ, 01524 64998
www.lancastercastle.com

Claylands Caravan Park
▶▶▶▶ 85%

tel: 01524 791242 **Cabus PR3 1AJ**
email: alan@claylands.com
dir: From M6 junct 33, A6 towards Garstang, approx 6m, past Thorpy's chipshop, left into
Weavers Lane. **grid ref:** SD496485

Colourful seasonal floral displays create an excellent first impression. A well-
maintained site with lovely river and woodland walks and good views over the River
Wyre towards the village of Scorton. This friendly park is set in delightful
countryside where guests can enjoy fishing, and the atmosphere is very relaxed. The
quality facilities and amenities are of a high standard, and everything is
immaculately maintained. 14 acre site. 30 touring pitches. 30 hardstandings.
Caravan pitches. Motorhome pitches. Tent pitches. 68 statics.

Open: Mar-Jan **Last arrival:** 23.00hrs **Last departure:** noon
Pitches: * 🚐 £20-£26 🚐 £20-£26 ⛺ £17-£23
Leisure: /�️ 🎵 **Facilities:** 🍴 ☉ ☀ ♿ 🛈 🖥 🎣 ⛲ 🚻 [Wifi] ♻ 🛈
Services: 🔌 🔲 🍴 ⊘ [T] 🍽 🛒 🚰
Within 3 miles: ↓ ❧ ✎ 🖥 🔲 ⛳
Notes: No roller blades or skateboards. Dogs must be kept on leads.
AA Pubs & Restaurants nearby: Owd Nell's Tavern, BILSBORROW, PR3 0RS,
01995 640010

PITCHES: 🚐 Caravans 🚐 Motorhomes ⛺ Tents 🏕 Glamping-style accommodation **SERVICES:** 🔌 Electric hook up 🔲 Launderette 🍴 Licensed bar
🛢 Calor Gas ⊘ Camping Gaz [T] Toilet fluid 🍽 Café/Restaurant 🛒 Fast Food/Takeaway 🔋 Battery charging 🚼 Baby care ⚒ Motorvan service point
ABBREVIATIONS: BH/bank hols – bank holidays Etr – Easter Spring BH – Spring Bank Holiday fr – from hrs – hours m – mile mdnt – midnight
rdbt – roundabout rs – restricted service wk – week wknd – weekend x-rds – cross roads 🚫 No credit or debit cards 🚫 No dogs 🛉 Children of all ages accepted

GARSTANG *continued*

Bridge House Marina & Caravan Park
►►►78%

tel: 01995 603207 **Nateby Crossing Ln, Nateby PR3 0JJ**
email: edwin@bridgehousemarina.co.uk
dir: *Exit A6 at pub & Knott End sign, immediately right into Nateby Crossing Ln, over canal bridge to site on left.* **grid ref:** *SD483457*

A well-maintained site in attractive countryside by the Lancaster Canal, with good views towards the Trough of Bowland. The boatyard atmosphere is interesting, and there is a good children's playground. 4 acre site. 50 touring pitches. 50 hardstandings. Caravan pitches. Motorhome pitches. 40 statics.

Open: Feb-Jan **Last arrival:** 22.00hrs **Last departure:** 13.00hrs

Pitches: * ⚎ £21.75-£23.50 ⚎ £21.75-£23.50

Leisure: 🅰 **Facilities:** 🏕⊙🄿⚹&🕒🖳WiFi 🄿

Services: 🄿🖥🔧⊘🅣🖷 **Within 3 miles:** 🚶🎣🖺

Notes: Dogs must be kept on leads.

AA Pubs & Restaurants nearby: Owd Nell's Tavern, BILSBORROW, PR3 0RS, 01995 640010

New Parkside Farm Caravan Park
►►►82%

tel: 015247 70723 **Denny Beck, Caton Rd LA2 9HH**
email: enquiries@newparksidefarm.co.uk
dir: *M6 junct 34, A683 towards Caton/Kirkby Lonsdale. Site 1m on right.*
grid ref: *SD507633*

A peaceful, friendly, grassy park on a working farm convenient for exploring the historic City of Lancaster and the delights of the Lune Valley. 4 acre site. 40 touring pitches. 40 hardstandings. Caravan pitches. Motorhome pitches. Tent pitches. 16 statics.

Open: Mar-Oct **Last arrival:** 20.00hrs **Last departure:** 16.00hrs

Pitches: * ⚎ £15-£17 ⚎ £15-£17 ⚑ £12-£14

Facilities: 🏕⊙🄿&🗘🄿

Services: 🄿🔒 **Within 3 miles:** 🚶🖺

Notes: 🚫 No football. Dogs must be kept on leads.

AA Pubs & Restaurants nearby: The Sun Hotel and Bar, LANCASTER, LA1 1ET, 01524 66006

The White Cross, LANCASTER, LA1 4XT, 01524 33999

The Stork Inn, LANCASTER, LA2 0AN, 01524 751234

Little Orchard Caravan Park
►►►80%

tel: 01253 836658 **Shorrocks Barn, Back Ln, Kirkham PR4 3HN**
email: info@littleorchardcaravanpark.com
dir: *M55 junct 3, A585 signed Fleetwood. Left in 0.5m opposite Ashiana Tandoori restaurant into Greenhalgh Ln in 0.75m, right at T-junct, site entrance 1st left.*
grid ref: *SD399355*

Set in a quiet rural location in an orchard, this attractive park welcomes mature visitors. The toilet facilities are to a very high standard. Two excellent fisheries are within easy walking distance. The site advises that bookings should be made by phone only, not on-line. 7 acre site. 45 touring pitches. 45 hardstandings. 20 seasonal pitches. Caravan pitches. Motorhome pitches. Tent pitches.

Open: 14 Feb-1 Jan **Last arrival:** 20.00hrs **Last departure:** noon

Pitches: ⚎ £20-£26 ⚎ £20-£26 ⚑ £15-£20

Facilities: 🏕⊙🄿&🗘⛱🄿 **Services:** 🄿🖥 **Within 3 miles:** 🖺🛁

Notes: 🚫 No cars by tents. No ball games or skateboards, no noise after 23.00hrs, children must be supervised when in toilet blocks, no dangerous dog breeds. Dogs must be kept on leads.

AA Pubs & Restaurants nearby: The Ship at Elswick, ELSWICK, PR4 3ZB, 01995 672777

Eastham Hall Caravan Park
►►►81%

tel: 01253 737907 **Saltcotes Rd FY8 4LS**
email: info@easthamhall.co.uk **web:** www.easthamhall.co.uk
dir: *M55 junct 3. Straight over 3 rdbts onto B5259. Through Wrea Green & Moss Side, site 1m after level crossing.* **grid ref:** *SD379291*

A large family-run park in a tranquil rural setting, surrounded by trees and mature shrubs. The pitch density is very good and some are fully serviced, plus the amenities blocks were refurbished for the 2014 season. 15 acre site. 160 touring pitches. 99 hardstandings. 133 seasonal pitches. Caravan pitches. Motorhome pitches. 150 statics.

Open: Mar-Nov (rs Nov only hardstanding pitches available) **Last arrival:** 21.00hrs
Last departure: noon

Pitches: 🚐 🚌

Leisure: ⚐ ⊙

Facilities: 🌡⊙🏳✳🔥⚲🆔🛒🌀❶

Services: 🔌🔲🔋🚿🅃

Within 3 miles: 🚴‍♂️🛶🦌⛳◎♨🐾💰🔲∪

Notes: No tents. Breathable groundsheets in awnings only. Dogs must be kept on leads. Football field, night touring pitches available.

AA Pubs & Restaurants nearby: Greens Bistro, LYTHAM ST ANNES, FY8 1SX, 01253 789990

See advert below

MORECAMBE	Map 18 SD46

Places to visit
Leighton Hall, CARNFORTH, LA5 9ST, 01524 734474
www.leightonhall.co.uk

Lancaster City Museum, LANCASTER, LA1 1HT, 01524 64637
www.lancashire.gov.uk/museums

Venture Caravan Park
►►►81%

tel: 01524 412986 **Langridge Way, Westgate LA4 4TQ**
email: mark@venturecaravanpark.co.uk
dir: M6 junct 34, A683, follow Morecambe signs. At rdbt 3rd exit, into Westgate. 1st right after fire station (site signed). **grid ref:** SD436633

A large family park close to the town centre, with good modern facilities, including a small indoor heated pool, a licensed clubhouse and a family room with children's entertainment. The site has many statics, some of which are for holiday hire. 17.5 acre site. 56 touring pitches. 40 hardstandings. Caravan pitches. Motorhome pitches. Tent pitches. 304 statics.

Open: all year (rs Winter one toilet block open) **Last arrival:** 22.00hrs
Last departure: noon

Pitches: * 🚐 £17-£24 🚌 £17-£24 ▲ £17-£24

Leisure: ⚐⚐⊙🔍

Facilities: ⬅🌡⊙🏳✳🔥⚲🆔🌀❶

Services: 🔌🔲🚱🔋🅃🔋♨🛗↯

Within 3 miles: 🚴‍♂️🏇🦌💰🔲

Notes: Dogs must be kept on leads. Amusement arcade, off licence, seasonal entertainment.

AA Pubs & Restaurants nearby: Hest Bank Inn, HEST BANK, LA2 6DN, 01524 824339

Places to visit

Rufford Old Hall, RUFFORD, L40 1SG, 01704 821254
www.nationaltrust.org.uk/ruffordoldhall

WWT Martin Mere Wetland Centre, MARTIN MERE, L40 0TA, 01704 895181
ww.wwt.org.uk/martinmere

Shaw Hall Holiday Park
►►►►82%

tel: 01704 840298 **Smithy Ln, Scarisbrick L40 8HJ**
email: shawhall@btconnect.com
dir: *Take A570 from Ormskirk towards Southport. At Pinfold School, right into Smithy Lane.* **grid ref:** *SD397119*

Ideally located between Southport and historic Ormskirk, this constantly improving holiday destination stands on open countryside and has the benefit of a waterside area, with boating holidays, in addition to well-equipped static homes and lodges. All touring pitches are fully serviced with water, waste water disposal, electric hook-up and TV connection, and future plans include a boating marina and a new serviced camping field. A well-stocked shop, stylish bar and entertainment room are additional benefits. 75 acre site. 37 touring pitches. 37 hardstandings. Caravan pitches. Motorhome pitches. Tent pitches. 247 statics.

Open: all year **Last arrival:** 22.00hrs **Last departure:** 10.30hrs

Pitches: 🚐 🚍 Å

Leisure: 🄰 ⊙ 🎵 **Facilities:** 🖈 ⊙ ✳ 🕭 🕓 🗑 🛱 🛒 📶 ♻ ❶

Services: 🔌 🗑 🍴 🛢 🍴 🚮 **Within 3 miles:** ↨ ⌖ ◎ 🗐 🗐

Notes: No noise after mdnt. Dogs must be kept on leads. Putting green, bowling green.

AA Pubs & Restaurants nearby: The Eagle & Child, PARBOLD, L40 3SG, 01257 462297

Abbey Farm Caravan Park
►►►►81%

tel: 01695 572686 **Dark Ln L40 5TX**
email: abbeyfarm@yahoo.com
dir: *M6 junct 27, A5209 to Burscough. 4m, left onto B5240, immediately right into Hobcross Lane. Site 1.5m on right.* **grid ref:** *SD434098*

Delightful hanging baskets and flower beds brighten this garden-like rural park which is sheltered by hedging and mature trees. Modern, very clean facilities include a family bathroom, and there are suitable pitches, close to the toilet facilities, for disabled visitors. A superb recreation field caters for children of all ages, and there is an indoor games room, large library, fishing lake and dog walk. Tents have their own area with a BBQ and picnic tables. 6 acre site. 56 touring pitches. 18 hardstandings. 46 seasonal pitches. Caravan pitches. Motorhome pitches. Tent pitches. 39 statics.

Open: Mar-Oct **Last arrival:** 21.00hrs **Last departure:** noon

Pitches: * 🚐 £16.10-£22.20 🚍 £19.70-£22.20 Å £16.10-£24.80

Leisure: 🄰 ⊙ 🔍 **Facilities:** 🖈 ⊙ 🄿 ✳ 🕭 🕓 🗑 🛱 🛒 📶 ♻ ❶

Services: 🔌 🗑 🛢 🗑 Ⓣ **Within 3 miles:** ↨ ⌖ 🗐 🗐 ∪

Notes: No camp fires, no noise after 23.00hrs. Dogs must be kept on leads. Off-licence, farm walk.

AA Pubs & Restaurants nearby: The Eagle & Child, PARBOLD, L40 3SG, 01257 462297

Places to visit

Leighton Hall, CARNFORTH, LA5 9ST, 01524 734474 www.leightonhall.co.uk

Great for kids: RSPB Leighton Moss & Morecambe Bay Nature Reserve, SILVERDALE, LA5 0SW, 01524 701601 www.rspb.org.uk/leightonmoss

PREMIER PARK

Silverdale Caravan Park
►►►►►95%

tel: 01524 701508 **Middlebarrow Plain, Cove Rd LA5 0SH**
email: caravan@holgates.co.uk **web:** www.holgates.co.uk
dir: *M6 junct 35. 5m NW of Carnforth. From Carnforth centre take unclassified Silverdale road & follow tourist signs after Warton.* **grid ref:** *SD455762*

A superb family holiday destination set in extensive wooded countryside overlooking the sea. All areas of the park are maintained in excellent condition with mature trees, shrubs and pretty, seasonal flowers creating a peaceful and relaxing atmosphere. The pitch density is generous and the spotlessly clean amenities blocks are conveniently located. An indoor swimming pool, smart bar/bistro and well-stocked shop are just a few of the additional amenities on offer. 100 acre site. 80 touring pitches. 80 hardstandings. 2 seasonal pitches. Caravan pitches. Motorhome pitches. Tent pitches. 339 statics. 3 wooden pods.

Open: all year **Last arrival:** 20.00hrs **Last departure:** noon

Pitches: * 🚐 £33.50 🚍 £33.50 Å £33.50 🏠

Leisure: 🏊 🎯 🄰 ⊙ 🔍

LEISURE: 🏊 Indoor swimming pool 🏖 Outdoor swimming pool 🄰 Children's playground 🪁 Kid's club ⚷ Tennis court 🔍 Games room ⬜ Separate TV room
↨ golf course 🚣 Boats for hire 🎬 Cinema 🎵 Entertainment 🎣 Fishing ◎ Mini golf 🏄 Watersports 🎯 Gym 🏟 Sports field   Spa ∪ Stables
FACILITIES: 🛁 Bath 🖈 Shower ⊙ Electric shaver 🄿 Hairdryer ✳ Ice Pack Facility 🕭 Disabled facilities 🕓 Public telephone 🗑 Shop on site or within 200yds
🗐 Mobile shop (calls at least 5 days a week) 🛱 BBQ area 🛒 Picnic area 📶 Wi-fi 🖥 Internet access ♻ Recycling ❶ Tourist info 🛒 Dog exercise area

Facilities: ⬛⬛⬛⬛⬛⬛⬛⬛⬛⬛ ⬛ ⬛

Services: ⬛⬛ ⬛⬛⬛⬛⬛⬛⬛⬛⬛ **Within 3 miles:** ⬛⬛⬛⬛⬛⬛

Notes: No unaccompanied children. Dogs must be kept on leads. Sauna, spa pool, steam room, mini-golf.

AA Pubs & Restaurants nearby: The Longlands Inn and Restaurant, CARNFORTH, LA6 1JH, 01524 781256

The Wheatsheaf at Beetham, BEETHAM, LA7 7AL, 015395 62123

See advert below

THORNTON
Map 18 SD34

Places to visit

Blackpool Zoo, BLACKPOOL, FY3 8PP, 01253 830830 www.blackpoolzoo.org.uk

---

PREMIER PARK

Kneps Farm Holiday Park
▶▶▶▶▶ 82%

tel: 01253 823632 **River Rd, Stanah FY5 5LR**
email: enquiries@knepsfarm.co.uk
dir: *Exit A585 at rdbt onto B5412 to Little Thornton. Right at mini-rdbt after school into Stanah Rd, over 2nd mini-rdbt, leading to River Rd.* **grid ref:** *SD353429*

A quality park, quietly located, adjacent to the River Wyre and the Wyre Estuary Country Park, handily placed for the attractions of Blackpool and the Fylde

coast. This family-run park offers an excellent toilet block with immaculate facilities, and a mixture of hard and grass pitches (no tents), plus there are camping pods for hire. 10 acre site. 40 touring pitches. 40 hardstandings. 5 seasonal pitches. Caravan pitches. Motorhome pitches. 40 statics. 6 wooden pods.

Open: Mar-mid Nov (rs Mar & early Nov shop closed) **Last arrival:** 20.00hrs
Last departure: noon

Pitches: * ⬛ £20-£24.50 ⬛ £20-£24.50 ⬛

Leisure: ⬛

Facilities: ⬛⬛⬛⬛⬛⬛⬛⬛⬛⬛ ⬛ ⬛

Services: ⬛⬛ ⬛⬛⬛⬛⬛

Within 3 miles: ⬛⬛⬛⬛⬛⬛⬛

Notes: No commercial vehicles, max 2 dogs (chargeable) per unit. Dogs must be kept on leads.

AA Pubs & Restaurants nearby: Twelve Restaurant and Lounge Bar, THORNTON, FY5 4JZ, 01253 821212

PITCHES: ⬛ Caravans ⬛ Motorhomes ⬛ Tents ⬛ Glamping-style accommodation **SERVICES:** ⬛ Electric hook up ⬛ Launderette ⬛ Licensed bar ⬛ Calor Gas ⬛ Camping Gaz ⬛ Toilet fluid ⬛ Café/Restaurant ⬛ Fast Food/Takeaway ⬛ Battery charging ⬛ Baby care ⬛ Motorvan service point
ABBREVIATIONS: BH/bank hols – bank holidays Etr – Easter Spring BH – Spring Bank Holiday fr – from hrs – hours m – mile mdnt – midnight rdbt – roundabout rs – restricted service wk – week wknd – weekend x-rds – cross roads ⬛ No credit or debit cards ⬛ No dogs ⬛ Children of all ages accepted

LEICESTERSHIRE

See also Wolvey (Warwickshire)

CASTLE DONINGTON — Map 11 SK42

Places to visit

Calke Abbey, CALKE, DE73 7LE, 01332 863822 www.nationaltrust.org.uk

Ashby-de-la-Zouch Castle, ASHBY-DE-LA-ZOUCH, LE65 1BR, 01530 413343 www.english-heritage.org.uk/daysout/properties/ashby-de-la-zouch-castle

Great for kids: Snibston Discovery Museum, COALVILLE, LE67 3LN, 01530 278444 www.snibston.com

Donington Park Farmhouse

►►► 75%

tel: 01332 862409 **Melbourne Rd, Isley Walton DE74 2RN**
email: info@parkfarmhouse.co.uk
dir: *M1 junct 24, pass airport to Isley Walton, right towards Melbourne. Site 0.5m on right.* **grid ref:** *SK414254*

A secluded touring site, at the rear of a hotel beside Donington Park motor racing circuit, which is very popular on race days so booking is essential. Please note that both daytime and night flights from nearby East Midlands Airport may cause disturbance. 7 acre site. 60 touring pitches. 18 hardstandings. Caravan pitches. Motorhome pitches. Tent pitches.

Open: Jan-23 Dec (rs Winter hardstanding only) **Last arrival:** 21.00hrs
Last departure: noon

Pitches: * 🚐 £16-£28 🚙 £16-£28 ▲ £13-£23

Leisure: �

Facilities: 🏠 ☉ ⚒ ⚹ 📶 🖥 ♻ ❶

Services: 🔌 🗄 🍽 🛢 🍴 ⚒

Within 3 miles: ⚓ 🚴 ⛴ 🛒 🎬 ↻

Notes: Dogs must be kept on leads. Bread & milk sold, hotel on site for bar & dining.

Looking for a golf course near your campsite?
Visit theaa.com/golf-course

Visit the AA.com/shop for the latest AA Pub and Restaurant guides

LINCOLNSHIRE

ANCASTER — Map 11 SK94

Places to visit

Belton House Park & Gardens, BELTON, NG32 2LS, 01476 566116 www.nationaltrust.org.uk

Woodland Waters

►►► 85%

tel: 01400 230888 **Willoughby Rd NG32 3RT**
email: info@woodlandwaters.co.uk
dir: *On A153 W of junct with B6403.* **grid ref:** *SK979435*

Peacefully set around five impressive fishing lakes, with a few log cabins in a separate area, this is a pleasant open park. The access road is through mature woodland, and there is an excellent heated toilet block, and a pub/club house with restaurant. 72 acre site. 128 touring pitches. 5 hardstandings. Caravan pitches. Motorhome pitches. Tent pitches.

Open: all year **Last arrival:** 20.00hrs **Last departure:** noon

Pitches: 🚐 £16.50-£20 🚙 £16.50-£20 ▲ £16.50-£20

Leisure: ⚙ 🎣

Facilities: 🏠 ☉ ⚒ ⚹ 📶 ❶

Services: 🔌 🗄 🍽 🛢 🍴 🛒 ⚒

Within 3 miles: ⚓ 🚴 🛒 ↻

Notes: No noise after 23.00hrs. Dogs must be kept on leads.

AA Pubs & Restaurants nearby: The Bustard Inn & Restaurant, SLEAFORD, NG34 8QG, 01529 488250

The Brownlow Arms, HOUGH-ON-THE-HILL, NG32 2AZ, 01400 250234

BOSTON — Map 12 TF34

Places to visit

Battle of Britain Memorial Flight Visitor Centre, CONINGSBY, LN4 4SY, 01522 782040 www.lincolnshire.gov.uk/bbmf

Tattershall Castle, TATTERSHALL, LN4 4LR, 01526 342543 www.nationaltrust.org.uk

Long Acres Touring Park

►►►► 87%

Best of British
GOLD

tel: 01205 871555 **Station Rd, Old Leake PE22 9RF**
email: enquiries@longacres-caravanpark.co.uk
dir: *From A16 take B1184 at Sibsey (by church); approx 1m at T-junct turn left. 1.5m, after level crossing take next right into Station Rd. Park entrance approx 0.5m on left.* **grid ref:** *TF384531*

A small rural adults-only park in an attractive setting within easy reach of Boston, Spalding and Skegness. The park has a smart toilet block, which is very clean and has an appealing interior, with modern, upmarket fittings. Excellent shelter is provided by the high, mature boundary hedging. A holiday cottage is available to let. 2 acre site. 40 touring pitches. 40 hardstandings. Caravan pitches. Motorhome pitches. Tent pitches.

Open: Mar-8 Jan Last arrival: 20.00hrs Last departure: 11.00hrs

Pitches: * 🚐 £18-£22 🚍 £18-£22 ▲ £18-£22

Facilities: 🅿️⊙🄿❄️&🔥 WiFi ♻️ ❶

Services: 🔌🛁⇩ Within 3 miles: ⌀🛒

Notes: Adults only. Dogs must be kept on leads.

Orchard Park
▶▶▶▶ 85%

tel: 01205 290328 Frampton Ln, Hubbert's Bridge PE20 3QU
email: info@orchardpark.co.uk web: www.orchardpark.co.uk
dir: On B1192 between A52 (Boston to Grantham road) & A1121 (Boston to Sleaford road). grid ref: TF274432

Ideally located for exploring the unique fenlands, this rapidly improving park has two lakes - one for fishing and the other set aside for conservation. The very attractive restaurant and bar prove popular with visitors, and Sandy's Café offers a delivery service to those fishing at the lake. 51 acre site. 87 touring pitches. 15 hardstandings. Caravan pitches. Motorhome pitches. Tent pitches. 164 statics.

Open: all year (rs Dec-Feb bar, shop & café closed) Last arrival: 22.30hrs
Last departure: 16.00hrs

Pitches: * 🚐 £18 🚍 £18 ▲ £9-£18

Leisure: 🔄🎣🎵 Facilities: 🛁🅿️⊙🄿❄️&🕒🔥 WiFi 🖥️ ♻️ ❶
Services: 🔌🛁🍽️⇩🄣🛒🍴⇩⚑ Within 3 miles: ⌀🅿️◎🛒🛒∪

Notes: Adults only. 🚫 No washing lines. Dogs must be kept on leads.

Pilgrims Way Caravan & Camping Park
▶▶▶▶ 81%

tel: 01205 366646 & 07973 941955 Church Green Rd, Fishtoft PE21 0QY
email: holidays@pilgrimswaycaravanandcamping.co.uk
dir: E from Boston on A52. In 1m, after junct with A16, at Ball House pub turn right. Follow tourist signs to site. grid ref: TF358434

A beautifully maintained and peaceful park within easy walking distance of the town centre that has many attractions. All pitches, named after birds species, are screened by well trimmed hedges to create optimum privacy; a lush tent field is also available. Regular barbecue evenings with entertainment are held during the warmer months. 2.5 acre site. 22 touring pitches. 15 hardstandings. Caravan pitches. Motorhome pitches. Tent pitches.

Open: all year Last arrival: 22.00hrs Last departure: noon

Pitches: * 🚐 fr £15 🚍 fr £15 ▲ fr £7

Leisure: 🎱🎵

Facilities: 🅿️⊙🄿❄️&🔥 WiFi 🖥️ ♻️ ❶

Services: 🔌🛁🛒🍴⚑

Within 3 miles: ⌀🎣🛒🅿️◎🛒🛒∪

Notes: 🚫 Dogs must be kept on leads. Tea house & sun terrace, day dog kennels.

Follow us on twitter
@TheAA_Lifestyle

PITCHES: 🚐 Caravans 🚍 Motorhomes ▲ Tents 🎪 Glamping-style accommodation **SERVICES:** 🔌 Electric hook up 🄣 Launderette 🍷 Licensed bar 🔋 Calor Gas 🔥 Camping Gaz 🅣 Toilet fluid 🍴 Café/Restaurant 🍟 Fast Food/Takeaway 🛒 Battery charging 🚼 Baby care ⛟ Motorvan service point
ABBREVIATIONS: BH/bank hols — bank holidays Etr — Easter Spring BH — Spring Bank Holiday fr — from hrs — hours m — mile mdnt — midnight rdbt — roundabout rs — restricted service wk — week wknd — weekend x-rds — cross roads 🚫 No credit or debit cards ⊗ No dogs ❖ Children of all ages accepted

CLEETHORPES
Map 17 TA30

Thorpe Park Holiday Centre
HOLIDAY CENTRE 83%

tel: 0871 231 0885 **DN35 0PW**
email: thorpepark@haven.com web: www.haven.com/thorpepark
dir: *From A180 at Cleethorpes take unclassified road signed Humberstone & Holiday Park.*
grid ref: *TA321035*

A large static site, adjacent to the beach, with touring facilities, including fully serviced pitches and pitches with hardstandings. This holiday centre offers excellent recreational and leisure activities including an indoor pool with bar, bowling greens, crazy golf, 9-hole golf course, lake coarse fishing, tennis courts and a games area. Parts of the site overlook the sea. 300 acre site. 141 touring pitches. 81 hardstandings. Caravan pitches. Motorhome pitches. Tent pitches. 1357 statics.

Open: mid Mar-end Oct (rs mid Mar-May & Sep-Oct some facilities may be reduced) **Last arrival:** anytime **Last departure:** 10.00hrs

Pitches: ▭ ▭ Å

Leisure: 🏊 🏊 Ⓜ 🎿 ⚲ ♫ ♪ **Facilities:** 🚿 ⊙ 📷 ♿ Ⓒ 🛁 🚻 📶 🖥 ♻ ❶

Services: 🔌 🔲 🍴 💧 🛒 🍽 🛒 📦

Within 3 miles: ♿ 🏋 ♿ 🌊 🍽 🛒 🛒 🐴

Notes: No commercial vehicles, no bookings by persons under 21yrs unless a family booking, max 2 dogs per booking, certain dog breeds banned. Dogs must be kept on leads.

AA Pubs & Restaurants nearby: The Ship Inn, BARNOLDBY LE BECK, DN37 0BG, 01472 822308

See advert on page 253

GREAT CARLTON
Map 17 TF48

Places to visit
Cadwell Park, LOUTH, LN11 9SE, 01507 343248 www.cadwellpark.co.uk

West End Farm
►►►86%

tel: 01507 450949 & 07766 278740 **Salters Way LN11 8BF**
email: westendfarm1@btconnect.com
dir: *From A157 follow Great Carlton signs at Gayton Top. Follow brown sign for West End Farm in 0.5m, right into site.* grid ref: *TF418842*

A neat and well-maintained four-acre touring park situated on the edge of the Lincolnshire Wolds. Surrounded by mature trees and bushes and well away from the busy main roads, yet connected by walking and cycling paths, it offers enjoyable peace and quiet close to the popular holiday resort of Mablethorpe. The site has good, clean facilities throughout and there's a passionate approach to everything 'green', with a reed bed sewage system, wild areas, bird and bat boxes and wildlife identification charts. 4 acre site. 35 touring pitches. 4 seasonal pitches. Caravan pitches. Motorhome pitches. Tent pitches.

Open: 28 Mar-2 Oct **Last arrival:** 20.30hrs **Last departure:** 14.00hrs

Pitches: * ▭ £17 ▭ £17 Å £17

Leisure: Ⓜ **Facilities:** 🚿 📷 ♿ ☀ 🚻 🖥 ❶

Services: 🔌 🔲 📦 **Within 3 miles:** ♿ 🏋 ♿ 🛒 🐴 🐴 🐴

Notes: No fires, quiet after 22.30hrs. Dogs must be kept on leads. Fridge available.

AA Pubs & Restaurants nearby: Kings Head Inn, THEDDLETHORPE ALL SAINTS, LN12 1PB, 01507 339798

LANGWORTH
Map 17 TF07

Places to visit
The Collection: Art & Archaeology in Lincolnshire, LINCOLN, LN2 1LP, 01522 550990 www.thecollectionmuseum.com

Lincoln Castle, LINCOLN, LN1 3AA, 01522 782040 www.lincolnshire.gov.uk/lincolncastle

NEW Barlings Country Holiday Park
►►►77%

tel: 01522 753200 **Barlings Ln LN3 5DF**
email: sean@barlingscountrypark.co.uk
dir: *From Lincoln take A158 towards Horncastle. In Langham right into Barlings Ln signed Barlings & Reepham.* grid ref: *TF065762*

Set in rural Lincolnshire and only a short car journey from Lincoln, this idyllic 26-acre site offers both seasonal and touring pitches positioned around four lakes. With wildlife in abundance, the park is well landscaped, with beautifully mown grass and trimmed shrubs, a new wooden reception chalet, spotlessly clean, older-style toilet facilities, and fishing from purpose-built jetties on two of the lakes. 26 acre site. 84 touring pitches. Caravan pitches. Motorhome pitches. Tent pitches. 27 statics.

Open: all year **Last arrival:** 18.00hrs **Last departure:** noon

Pitches: * ▭ £16-£19.50 ▭ £16-£19.50 Å £14-£16

AA Pubs & Restaurants nearby: The Victoria, LINCOLN, LN1 3BJ, 01522 541000

Wig & Mitre, LINCOLN, LN2 1LU, 01522 535190

LEISURE: 🏊 Indoor swimming pool 🏊 Outdoor swimming pool Ⓜ Children's playground 🎿 Kid's club ⚲ Tennis court ♦ Games room ▭ Separate TV room
🏌 golf course 🚤 Boats for hire 🎬 Cinema ♫ Entertainment 🎣 Fishing ⊙ Mini golf 🎿 Watersports 🏋 Gym ♦ Sports field ♿ Stables
FACILITIES: 🛁 Bath 🚿 Shower ⊙ Electric shaver 📷 Hairdryer ☀ Ice Pack Facility ♿ Disabled facilities ☎ Public telephone 🛒 Shop on site or within 200yds
🏪 Mobile shop (calls at least 5 days a week) 🍖 BBQ area 🍽 Picnic area 📶 Wi-fi 🖥 Internet access ♻ Recycling ❶ Tourist info 🐴 Dog exercise area

MABLETHORPE

Map 17 TF58

Places to visit

Great for kids: Skegness Natureland Seal Sanctuary, SKEGNESS, PE25 1DB, 01754 764345 www.skegnessnatureland.co.uk

Golden Sands Holiday Park

HOLIDAY CENTRE 84%

tel: 0871 231 0884 **Quebec Rd LN12 1QJ**
email: goldensands@haven.com **web:** www.haven.com/goldensands
dir: *From centre of Mablethorpe turn left into Quebec Rd (seafront road). Site on left.*
grid ref: *TF501861*

A large, well-equipped seaside holiday park with many all-weather attractions and a good choice of entertainment and eating options. The large touring area is serviced by two amenities blocks and is close to the mini market and laundry.

23 acre site. 222 touring pitches. 20 hardstandings. Caravan pitches. Motorhome pitches. Tent pitches. 1500 statics.

Open: mid Mar-end Oct **Last arrival:** anytime **Last departure:** 10.00hrs

Pitches: 🚐 🚎 ⚊

Leisure: ♨ ♨ ⚏ ⚐ ♦ ♫

Facilities: 🛁 🚻 ⊙ ☕ ❄ ♿ 🕐 S WiFi

Services: 🔌 🗑 🍽 🛢 ⊘ T 🍴 ⚒ 🛠

Within 3 miles: ↨ ⊟ ⚲ ◎ 🛍 🛍

Notes: No commercial vehicles, no bookings by persons under 21yrs unless a family booking, max 2 dogs per booking, certain dog breeds banned. Dogs must be kept on leads. Mini bowling alley, snooker & pool, indoor fun palace.

AA Pubs & Restaurants nearby: Red Lion Inn, PARTNEY, PE23 4PG, 01790 752271

See advert below

PITCHES: 🚐 Caravans 🚎 Motorhomes ⚊ Tents ⛺ Glamping-style accommodation **SERVICES:** 🔌 Electric hook up 🗑 Launderette 🍸 Licensed bar 🛢 Calor Gas ⊘ Camping Gaz T Toilet fluid 🍴 Café/Restaurant ⚒ Fast Food/Takeaway 🔋 Battery charging 🍼 Baby care 🛠 Motorvan service point **ABBREVIATIONS:** BH/bank hols – bank holidays Etr – Easter Spring BH – Spring Bank Holiday fr – from hrs – hours m – mile mdnt – midnight rdbt – roundabout rs – restricted service wk – week wknd – weekend x-rds – cross roads 🚫 No credit or debit cards 🚫 No dogs ♦ Children of all ages accepted

MABLETHORPE *continued*

Kirkstead Holiday Park
►►►80%

tel: 01507 441483 **North Rd, Trusthorpe LN12 2QD**
email: mark@kirkstead.co.uk
dir: *From Mablethorpe town centre take A52 S towards Sutton-on-Sea. 1m, sharp right by phone box into North Rd. Site signed in 300yds.* **grid ref:** *TF509835*

A well-established family-run park catering for all age groups, just a few minutes' walk from Trusthorpe and the sandy beaches of Mablethorpe. The main touring area, which is serviced by good quality toilet facilities, has 37 fully serviced pitches on what was once the football pitch, and here toilets have been installed. The site is particularly well maintained. 12 acre site. 60 touring pitches. 3 hardstandings. 30 seasonal pitches. Caravan pitches. Motorhome pitches. Tent pitches. 70 statics.

Open: Mar-Nov **Last arrival:** 22.00hrs **Last departure:** 15.00hrs

Pitches: * ⛟ £14-£28 ⛟ £14-£28 ▲ £10-£22

Leisure: 🅰🌀🎯🎱🎵 **Facilities:** 🚿⊙🔍✳🔥🕐🛒🔥🐕 WiFi 🖥 ♻ 🚻

Services: 🔋🔷🍽🏪⛽🚮 **Within 3 miles:** ⚓🎣🛒⊙🔷🛒🐎

Notes: No dogs in tents. Dogs must be kept on leads.

AA Pubs & Restaurants nearby: Kings Head Inn, THEDDLETHORPE ALL SAINTS, LN12 1PB, 01507 339798

MARSTON
Map 11 SK84

Places to visit

Belton House Park & Gardens, BELTON, NG32 2LS, 01476 566116
www.nationaltrust.org.uk

Newark Air Museum, NEWARK-ON-TRENT, NG24 2NY, 01636 707170
www.newarkairmuseum.org

Wagtail Country Park
►►►►87%

GOLD

tel: 01400 251955 & 07814 481088 (bookings) **Cliff Ln NG32 2HU**
email: info@wagtailcountrypark.co.uk
dir: *From A1 exit at petrol station signed Barkston & Marston, right signed Barkston into Green Ln, follow park signs.* **grid ref:** *SK897412*

The park, on a gently sloping field, is tucked away behind the owners' farm, just a short walk from the village and attractive river estuary. The facilities are excellent and very clean, and even include a defibrulator in reception. This park provides a relaxing atmosphere for a pleasant stay on the island. Rallies are welcome. 20 acre site. 76 touring pitches. 76 hardstandings. 10 seasonal pitches. Caravan pitches. Motorhome pitches.

Open: all year **Last arrival:** 17.00hrs **Last departure:** 11.00hrs

Pitches: ⛟ ⛟

Facilities: 🚿🔍⊙🔥🐕♻ **Services:** 🔋🔷🔒 T

Within 3 miles: ⚓🛒🔷

Notes: No noise after 23.00hrs. Dogs must be kept on leads. Fishing bait, milk & ice creams available.

AA Pubs & Restaurants nearby: The Brownlow Arms, HOUGH-ON-THE-HILL, NG32 2AZ, 01400 250234

OLD LEAKE
Map 17 TF45

Places to visit

Lincolnshire Aviation Heritage Centre, EAST KIRKBY, PE23 4DE, 01790 763207
www.lincsaviation.co.uk

Battle of Britain Memorial Flight Visitor Centre, CONINGSBY, LN4 4SY, 01522 782040 www.lincolnshire.gov.uk/bbmf

---

Old Leake Leisure Park
►►►75%

tel: 01205 870121 **Shaw Ln PE22 9LQ**
email: oldleakeleisure@yahoo.co.uk
dir: *From Boston take A52 towards Skegness. In Old Leake right at x-rds into Shaw Lane, follow brown camping sign. At left bend turn right.* **grid ref:** *TF415498*

A pleasant, well-maintained small touring park set down a rural lane just off the A52, surrounded by the tranquillity of the Fenlands. It makes a peaceful base for exploring Boston and the Lincolnshire coast, and there are two holiday statics for hire. 2.5 acre site. 30 touring pitches. Caravan pitches. Motorhome pitches. Tent pitches.

Open: Mar-Oct **Last arrival:** 22.00hrs **Last departure:** noon

Pitches: * ⛟ £18 ⛟ £18 ▲ £18

Leisure: ♻

Facilities: 🚿🔍✳🛒 WiFi ♻ 🚻

Services: 🔋

Within 3 miles: 🎣🔷🛒

Notes: ⊘ No noise after 22.00hrs. Dogs must be kept on leads.

SALTFLEET
Map 17 TF49

Sunnydale
HOLIDAY CENTRE 83%

GOLD

tel: 0871 664 9776 **Sea Ln LN11 7RP**
email: sunnydale@park-resorts.com
dir: *From A16 towards Louth take B1200 through Manby & Saltfleetby. Left into Saltfleet. Sea Lane on right. Site in approx 400mtrs.* **grid ref:** *TF455941*

Set in a peaceful and tranquil location in the village of Saltfleet between the seaside resorts of Cleethorpes and Mablethorpe. This park offers modern leisure facilities including an indoor pool, the tavern bar with entertainment, amusements and a coarse fishing pond. There is also direct access to the huge expanse of Saltfleet Beach. The touring facilities are incorporated into the leisure complex, and are modern and well cared for. 38 touring pitches. Caravan pitches. Motorhome pitches. 260 statics.

Open: Mar-Oct (rs BH & peak wks) **Last arrival:** noon **Last departure:** 10.00hrs

Pitches: ⛟ ⛟

Leisure: 🏊🅰🎯🎵

Facilities: 🚿🛒🕐🔥 WiFi 🖥

Services: 🔋🔷🍽🏪

Within 3 miles: 🔷⊙🛒🔷🐎

AA Pubs & Restaurants nearby: Kings Head Inn, THEDDLETHORPE ALL SAINTS, LN12 1PB, 01507 339798

LEISURE: 🏊 Indoor swimming pool 🏊 Outdoor swimming pool 🅰 Children's playground 🪁 Kid's club 🎾 Tennis court 🎱 Games room ▢ Separate TV room
🏌 Golf course ⛵ Boats for hire 🎬 Cinema 🎵 Entertainment 🎣 Fishing ◎ Mini golf 🌊 Watersports 💪 Gym 🏐 Sports field Spa ∪ Stables
FACILITIES: 🛁 Bath 🚿 Shower ⊙ Electric shaver 🔍 Hairdryer ✳ Ice Pack Facility 🛒 Disabled facilities 🕐 Public telephone 🛒 Shop on site or within 200yds
🏪 Mobile shop (calls at least 5 days a week) 🍽 BBQ area 🔥 Picnic area WiFi Wi-fi 🖥 Internet access ♻ Recycling 🛈 Tourist info 🐕 Dog exercise area

SKEGNESS — Map 17 TF56

Places to visit

Skegness Natureland Seal Sanctuary, SKEGNESS, PE25 1DB, 01754 764345
www.skegnessnatureland.co.uk

The Village-Church Farm Museum, SKEGNESS, PE25 2HF, 01754 766658
www.churchfarmvillage.org.uk

Southview Leisure Park
HOLIDAY CENTRE 83%

tel: 01754 896001 **Burgh Rd PE25 2LA**
email: southview@park-resorts.com
dir: *A158 towards Skegness. Park on left.* **grid ref:** *TF541645*

A well-presented holiday and leisure park close to the resort of Skegness. The leisure and entertainment facilities are modern and well maintained, and are just a short walk from the touring area with its neat pitches and clean and tidy amenity block. The staff are friendly and efficient. 98 touring pitches. Caravan pitches. Motorhome pitches.

Open: Apr-Oct **Last arrival:** noon **Last departure:** 10.00hrs

Pitches: 🚐 🚎

Leisure: 🏊 ❄ 🎮 🛝 ⚽ 🎯 🎵

Facilities: 🚿 📶 ♿ 🕐 🏧 📶 💻 ♻ ⊘

Services: 🔌 🗑 🍴 T 🍽 🛒

Within 3 miles: ⛳ 🚶 🐾 🎣 🏪 🛒

NEW Eastview Caravan Park
►►►►80%

tel: 01754 875324 & 07710 336145 **Trunch Ln, Chapel St Leonards PE24 5UA**
email: enquiries@eastviewcaravans.co.uk
dir: *A52 from Skegness to Chapel St Leonards. Turn left into Trunch Ln. 2nd caravan park on left.* **grid ref:** *TF555778*

Set in 15 acres and only a short walk from one of Lincolnshire's finest beaches, Eastview Caravan Park is neat and tidy and a good all-round campsite. It has beautifully mown grass, well-trimmed shrubbery and spotlessly clean and modern toilet facilities. The children's playground has now been extended and a shop has opened. It is well placed for exploring both the coast and the countryside, especially the beautiful Lincolnshire Wolds. 15 acre site. 53 touring pitches. 56 hardstandings. 112 seasonal pitches. Caravan pitches. Motorhome pitches. Tent pitches.

Open: Mar-Oct **Last arrival:** 20.00hrs **Last departure:** 10.30hrs (late departure up to 17.00hrs available for fee)
Pitches: * 🚐 £17-£23.50 🚎 £17-£23.50 ▲ £15.50-£17.50
Leisure: 🎮 **Facilities:** 🚿 ⊙ ❄ ♿ 🏧 📶 💻 ⊘
Services: 🔌 🗑 🛒 **Within 3 miles:** ⛳ 🚶 🐾 🎣 🏪 🛒 ∪

Notes: No motorised scooters, BB guns or kites. Maximum 2 dogs, BBQs at least 1ft off ground, quiet after 22.30hrs. Dogs must be kept on leads.

TATTERSHALL — Map 17 TF25

Places to visit

Tattershall Castle, TATTERSHALL, LN4 4LR, 01526 342543
www.nationaltrust.org.uk

Tattershall Lakes Country Park
►►►►83%

tel: 01526 348800 **Sleaford Rd LN4 4LR**
email: tattershall.holidays@away-resorts.com
dir: *A153 to Tattershall.* **grid ref:** *TF234587*

Set amongst woodlands, lakes and parkland on the edge of Tattershall in the heart of the Lincolnshire Fens, this mature country park has been created from old gravel pits and the flat, well-drained and maintained touring area offers plenty of space for campers. There's a lot to entertain the youngsters as well as the grown-ups, with good fishing on excellent lakes, an 18-hole golf course, water-ski and jet ski lakes and an indoor heated pool with spa facilities. There is a separate adults-only field. 365 acre site. 186 touring pitches. 20 hardstandings. 25 seasonal pitches. Caravan pitches. Motorhome pitches. Tent pitches. 500 statics. 3 bell tents/yurts.

Open: end Mar-end Oct (rs Off peak restricted services) **Last arrival:** 19.00hrs **Last departure:** 10.00hrs

Pitches: 🚐 🚎 ▲ 🏕

Leisure: 🏊 ❄ 🎮 🛝 ⚽ 🎯 🎣 🎵 Spa

Facilities: 🚿 ⊙ 📶 ♿ 🏧 🏧 🍴 📶 💻 ♻ ⊘

Services: 🔌 🗑 🍴 🔋 🍽 🛒 🚐

Within 3 miles: ⛳ 🚶 🐾 🎣 🏪 🛒

Notes: No excessive noise after mdnt. Dogs must be kept on leads.

AA Pubs & Restaurants nearby: The Lea Gate Inn, CONINGSBY, LN4 4RS, 01526 342370

WADDINGHAM
Map 17 SK99

Brandy Wharf Leisure Park
▶▶▶75%

tel: 01673 818010 **Brandy Wharf DN21 4RT**
email: brandywharflp@freenetname.co.uk **web:** www.brandywharfleisurepark.co.uk
dir: *From A15 onto B1205 through Waddingham. Site in 3m.* **grid ref:** *TF014968*

A delightful site in a very rural area on the banks of the River Ancholme, where fishing is available. The toilet block has unisex rooms with combined facilities as well as a more conventional ladies and gents with washbasins and toilets. All the grassy pitches have electricity, and there's a play and picnic area. This site will appeal to bikers, groups, music lovers, and also cider aficionados as there is a renowned cider hostelry next door. Advance booking is necessary for weekend pitches. 5 acre site. 50 touring pitches. Caravan pitches. Motorhome pitches. Tent pitches.

Open: all year (rs Nov-Etr no tents) **Last arrival:** dusk **Last departure:** 17.00hrs

Pitches: ⌖ ⌖ Å

Leisure: ⌂

Facilities: ⌖ ☉ ☀ ⌖ ⌖ ⌖ ⌖ ♻ ⓘ

Services: ⌖ ⌖ ⌖ ⌖ ⌖ ⌖ ⌖

Within 3 miles: ⌖ ⌖ ⌖ ⌖ ⌖ ↻

Notes: No disposable BBQs on grass, no music after 01.00hrs. Boat mooring & slipway, canoe hire, pedalos, pets' corner.

AA Pubs & Restaurants nearby: The George, KIRTON IN LINDSEY, DN21 4LX, 01652 640600

WOODHALL SPA

Places to visit

Tattershall Castle, TATTERSHALL, LN4 4LR, 01526 342543
www.nationaltrust.org.uk

Battle of Britain Memorial Flight Visitor Centre, CONINGSBY, LN4 4SY,
01522 782040 www.lincolnshire.gov.uk/bbmf

LEISURE: 🏊 Indoor swimming pool 🏊 Outdoor swimming pool ⌂ Children's playground 👶 Kid's club 🎾 Tennis court 🎱 Games room 🖵 Separate TV room ⛳ golf course ⛵ Boats for hire 🎬 Cinema 🎵 Entertainment 🎣 Fishing ◎ Mini golf 🏄 Watersports 🏋 Gym ⊕ Sports field Spa ↻ Stables
FACILITIES: 🛁 Bath 🚿 Shower ☉ Electric shaver 💈 Hairdryer ❄ Ice Pack Facility ♿ Disabled facilities ☏ Public telephone 🏪 Shop on site or within 200yds 🛒 Mobile shop (calls at least 5 days a week) 🍖 BBQ area 🌲 Picnic area 📶 Wi-fi 💻 Internet access ♻ Recycling ⓘ Tourist info 🐕 Dog exercise area

PREMIER PARK

Woodhall Country Park
►►►►►88%

tel: 01526 353710 **Stixwold Rd LN10 6UJ**
email: info@woodhallcountrypark.co.uk **web:** www.woodhallcountrypark.co.uk
dir: *In Woodhall Spa at rdbt in High St take Stixwold Rd. 1m, site on right, just before Village Limits pub.* **grid ref:** *TF189643*

A peaceful and attractive touring park situated just a short walk from Woodhall Spa. The owners transformed part of the woodland area into a countryside retreat for campers who wish to escape from a hectic lifestyle. Well organised and well laid out, the park offers fishing lakes, three log cabin amenity blocks, fully serviced pitches and high levels of customer care. There's a strong ethos towards sustainability and a bio-mass boiler provides all heating and hot water supplies to the three superb amenities blocks, plus there are bird hides around the park. Camping pods are now available on the site. 80 acre site. 115 touring pitches. 88 hardstandings. Caravan pitches. Motorhome pitches. Tent pitches. 12 wooden pods.

Open: Mar-Nov **Last arrival:** 20.00hrs **Last departure:** noon
Pitches: * 🚐 £18-£24 🚐 £18-£24 ▲ £15-£22 🏠
Leisure: ⚽ **Facilities:** ➡️⊙ᚷ⚹⚿🛁🚿🚻⛽🛒♻️❓
Services: 🔌🅓 🛢️⚿⎕ **Within 3 miles:** ↨🎣🛒📮🅤
Notes: No cars by tents. No fires, Chinese lanterns or fireworks, no noise between 23.00hrs-07.00hrs, BBQs must be off ground. Dogs must be kept on leads.
AA Pubs & Restaurants nearby: Village Limits Country Pub, Restaurant & Motel, WOODHALL SPA, LN10 6UJ, 01526 353312
See advert on opposite page

NEW Petwood Caravan Park
►►►►84%

tel: 01526 354799 **Off Stixwould Rd LN10 6QH**
email: info@petwoodcaravanpark.co.uk
dir: *From Lincoln take A15 towards Sleaford. Left onto B1188 signed Woodhall Spa. Approx 7.5m at Metheringham left onto B1189 (signed Billinghay). 3.7m left onto B1191 (Woodhall Spa). Approx 6m at rdbt in Woodhall Spa, 1st exit into Stixwould Rd. In 0.3m left into Jubilee Park, follow site signs.* **grid ref:** *TF191633*

Covering seven immaculate acres of beautifully manicured grounds, Petwood Caravan Park is a hidden gem of a touring park located behind a much larger static park in the heart of Woodhall Spa. There are 98 pitches, all with electric hook ups; 18 have spacious hardstandings for caravans and motorhomes. There is a modern reception and shop, and two excellent heated toilet blocks, each containing a spotless family room. Dogs are welcome at no extra charge. 7 acre site. 98 touring pitches. Caravan pitches. Motorhome pitches. Tent pitches.

Open: 21 Mar-2 Nov **Last arrival:** 21.00hrs **Last departure:** noon
Pitches: * 🚐 £16-£24 🚐 £16-£24 ▲ £16-£24
AA Pubs & Restaurants nearby: Village Limits Country Pub, Restaurant & Motel, WOODHALL SPA, LN10 6UJ, 01526 353312

LONDON

Places to visit
Waltham Abbey Gatehouse, Bridge & Entrance to Cloisters, WALTHAM ABBEY, 01992 702200 www.english-heritage.org.uk/daysout/properties/waltham-abbey-gatehouse-and-bridge

Lee Valley Campsite
►►►►83%

tel: 020 8529 5689 **Sewardstone Rd, Chingford E4 7RA**
email: sewardstonecampsite@leevalleypark.org.uk
web: www.visitleevalley.org.uk/wheretostay
dir: *M25 junct 26, A112. Site signed.* **grid ref:** *TQ381970*

Overlooking King George's Reservoir and close to Epping Forest, this popular and very peaceful park features very good modern facilities and excellent hardstanding pitches including nine that are able to accommodate larger motorhomes. This impressive park is maintained to a high standard and there are camping pods in a

continued

PITCHES: 🚐 Caravans 🚐 Motorhomes ▲ Tents 🏠 Glamping-style accommodation **SERVICES:** 🔌 Electric hook up 🅓 Launderette 🍺 Licensed bar
🛢️ Calor Gas ⌀ Camping Gaz ⎕ Toilet fluid 🍽️ Café/Restaurant 🍔 Fast Food/Takeaway 🔋 Battery charging 👶 Baby care 🔧 Motorvan service point
ABBREVIATIONS: BH/bank hols – bank holidays Etr – Easter Spring BH – Spring Bank Holiday fr – from hrs – hours m – mile mdnt – midnight
rdbt – roundabout rs – restricted service wk – week wknd – weekend x-rds – cross roads 🚫 No credit or debit cards 🚫 No dogs 👶 Children of all ages accepted

LONDON E4, CHINGFORD *continued*

separate shady glade for hire, and timber cabins. A bus calls at the site hourly to take passengers to the nearest tube station, and Enfield is easily accessible. 12 acre site. 81 touring pitches. 65 hardstandings. Caravan pitches. Motorhome pitches. Tent pitches. 46 statics. 17 wooden pods.

Lee Valley Campsite

Open: Mar-Jan **Last arrival:** 21.00hrs **Last departure:** noon
Pitches: * 🚐 £14-£22 🚍 £14-£22 ▲ £14-£22 🏚
Leisure: 🅰 **Facilities:** 📷☉🅿☀️♿⏰🖊✂♻🛈
Services: 🔌🗑🛒✏️🇹🚜♻ **Within 3 miles:** ↧🎠🚠♨️🗑🗑⛎
Notes: Under 18s must be accompanied by an adult, no commercial vehicles. Dogs must be kept on leads.
See advert below

N9 EDMONTON **Map 6 TQ39**

Lee Valley Camping & Caravan Park
▶▶▶▶83%

tel: 020 8803 6900 **Meridian Way N9 0AR**
email: edmontoncampsite@leevalleypark.org.uk
dir: *M25 junct 25, A10 S, 1st left onto A1055, approx 5m to Leisure Complex. From A406 (North Circular), N on A1010, left after 0.25m, right into Pickets Lock Ln.*
grid ref: *TQ360945*

A pleasant, open site within easy reach of London yet peacefully located close to two large reservoirs. There are excellent gravel access roads to the camping field, good signage and lighting, and smartly refurbished toilets. The site has the advantage of being adjacent to a restaurant and bar, and a multi-screen cinema. There are also camping pods and timber cabins for hire. A convenient bus stop provides a direct service to central London. 7 acre site. 100 touring pitches. 54 hardstandings. Caravan pitches. Motorhome pitches. Tent pitches. 12 wooden pods.

Open: all year **Last arrival:** 20.00hrs **Last departure:** noon
Pitches: * 🚐 £14-£22 🚍 £14-£22 ▲ £14-£22 🏚
Leisure: 🅰🎣
Facilities: 📷☉🅿☀️♿⏰🗑🖊📶♻🛈
Services: 🔌🗑🛒🇹🍴🚜⛎
Within 3 miles: ↧🗑
Notes: Under 18s must be accompanied by an adult. Dogs must be kept on leads.

MERSEYSIDE

SOUTHPORT
Map 15 SD31

Places to visit

The British Lawnmower Museum, SOUTHPORT, PR8 5AJ, 01704 501336
www.lawnmowerworld.com

Great for kids: Dunes Splash World, SOUTHPORT, PR8 1RX, 01704 537160
www.splashworldsouthport.com

Riverside Holiday Park
HOLIDAY CENTRE 86%

tel: 01704 228886 **Southport New Rd PR9 8DF**
email: reception@harrisonleisureuk.com
dir: M6 junct 27, A5209 towards Parbold/Burscough, right onto A59. Left onto A565 at lights in Tarleton. Continue to dual carriageway. At rdbt straight across, site 1m on left. **grid ref:** SD405192

A family friendly park north of Southport, with many indoor attractions, including a swimming pool, sauna, steam room and jacuzzi. The generously sized pitches are located on carefully landscaped grounds and served by two well-equipped, modern amenities blocks. Free WiFi is provided in an attractive café, and cycle hire is also available. 80 acre site. 260 touring pitches. 130 hardstandings. Caravan pitches. Motorhome pitches. Tent pitches. 355 statics.

Open: 14 Feb-Jan **Last arrival:** 17.00hrs **Last departure:** 11.00hrs

Pitches: 🚐 🚌 ▲

Leisure: 🏊 ⚄ 🎣 🎵 **Facilities:** 🗼 🏐 🅿 ⚅ 🛁 🐕 🖥 🛒 ❓

Services: 🔌 🗑 🍽 🍺 💧 🚽 🍴 **Within 3 miles:** 🛶 🎿 🐟 🔒 ❓

Notes: One car per pitch. Dogs must be kept on leads.

AA Pubs & Restaurants nearby: Warehouse Kitchen & Bar, SOUTHPORT, PR8 1QN, 01704 544662

Bistrot Vérité, SOUTHPORT, PR8 4AR, 01704 564199

Vincent Hotel, SOUTHPORT, PR8 1JR, 01704 883800

Hurlston Hall Country Caravan Park
►►►►80%

tel: 01704 840400 & 842829 **Southport Rd L40 8HB**
email: enquiries@hurlstonhallcaravanpark.co.uk
dir: On A570, 3m from Ormskirk towards Southport. **grid ref:** SD398107

A peaceful tree-lined touring park next to a static site in attractive countryside about 10 minutes' drive from Southport. The park is maturing well, with growing trees and a coarse fishing lake, and the excellent on-site facilities include golf, a bistro, a well-equipped health centre, a bowling green and model boat lake. Please note that neither tents nor dogs are accepted at this site. 5 acre site. 60 touring pitches. Caravan pitches. Motorhome pitches. 68 statics.

Open: Etr-Oct **Last arrival:** 20.30hrs (18.30hrs at wknds & BHs.)
Last departure: 17.00hrs

Pitches: * 🚐 fr £25 🚌 fr £25

Leisure: 🏊 ⛳ ⚄ Spa 🎵 **Facilities:** 🗼 ⊙ 🅿 ⚅ 🔔 🛒 ♻

Services: 🔌 🗑 🍽 🍺 🍴 **Within 3 miles:** 🛶 🔒 **Notes:** 🚫

AA Pubs & Restaurants nearby: Warehouse Kitchen & Bar, SOUTHPORT, PR8 1QN, 01704 544662

Willowbank Holiday Home & Touring Park
►►►86%

tel: 01704 571566 **Coastal Rd, Ainsdale PR8 3ST**
email: info@willowbankcp.co.uk **web:** www.willowbankcp.co.uk
dir: From A565 between Formby & Ainsdale exit at Woodvale lights onto coast road, site 150mtrs on left. From N: M6 junct 31, A59 towards Preston, A565, through Southport & Ainsdale, right at Woodvale lights. **grid ref:** SD305110

Set in woodland on a nature reserve next to sand dunes, this constantly improving park is a peaceful and relaxing holiday destination with mature trees, shrubs and colourful seasonal flowers surrounding neat pitches and modern amenities blocks. 8 acre site. 87 touring pitches. 61 hardstandings. Caravan pitches. Motorhome pitches. 228 statics.

Open: 14 Feb-31 Jan **Last arrival:** 21.00hrs **Last departure:** noon

Pitches: * 🚐 £15.20-£20.25 🚌 £15.20-£20.25

Leisure: ⚄ ♺

Facilities: 🗼 ⊙ 🅿 ✱ ⚅ 🛁 🔔 🛒 📶 ♻ ❓

Services: 🔌 🗑 🍺 💧 🛠

Within 3 miles: 🛶 🎿 🎯 🏌 🐟 ◎ 🔒 ❓ 🏊

Notes: Cannot site continental door entry units, no commercial vehicles, no dangerous dog breeds. Dogs must be kept on leads. Baby changing facility, bike hire.

AA Pubs & Restaurants nearby: Warehouse Kitchen & Bar, SOUTHPORT, PR8 1QN, 01704 544662

Bistrot Vérité, SOUTHPORT, PR8 4AR, 01704 564199

Vincent Hotel, SOUTHPORT, PR8 1JR, 01704 883800

PITCHES: 🚐 Caravans 🚌 Motorhomes ▲ Tents ⛺ Glamping-style accommodation **SERVICES:** 🔌 Electric hook up 🗑 Launderette 🍺 Licensed bar 🔋 Calor Gas 🔥 Camping Gaz 🚽 Toilet fluid 🍴 Café/Restaurant 🍟 Fast Food/Takeaway 🔋 Battery charging 🍼 Baby care 🛠 Motorvan service point
ABBREVIATIONS: BH/bank hols – bank holidays Etr – Easter Spring BH – Spring Bank Holiday fr – from hrs – hours m – mile mdnt – midnight rdbt – roundabout rs – restricted service wk – week wknd – weekend x-rds – cross roads 🚫 No credit or debit cards 🚫 No dogs ♿ Children of all ages accepted

Norfolk

Think of Norfolk, and the theme of water – in particular the Norfolk Broads, a complex network of mostly navigable rivers and man-made waterways – usually springs to mind. This delightfully unspoiled region attracts thousands of visitors every year, as does the North Norfolk Coast, designated an Area of Outstanding Natural Beauty and probably the finest of its kind in Europe.

'A long way from anywhere' and 'a remote corner of England that has been able to hold on to its traditions and ancient secrets,' are two of the apt descriptions that apply to this spacious corner of the country that still seems a separate entity, as if it is strangely detached from the rest of the country.

The coastline here represents a world of lonely beaches, vast salt marshes and extensive sand dunes stretching to the far horizon. It remains essentially unchanged, a stark reminder of how this area has long been vulnerable to attack and enemy invasion.

The highly successful thriller writer Jack Higgins chose this theme as the subject of his hugely popular adventure yarn *The Eagle has Landed*, published in 1975. The book, about a wartime Nazi plot to kidnap and assassinate Winston Churchill while he is spending the weekend at a country house near the sea in this part of East Anglia, vividly conveys the strange, unsettling atmosphere of the North Norfolk Coast.

Walking is the best way to gain a flavour of that atmosphere and visit the story's memorable setting. The 93-mile Peddars Way and North Norfolk Coast Path is one of Britain's most popular national trails. Made up of two paths strung together to form one continuous route, the trail begins near Thetford on the Suffolk/Norfolk border and follows ancient tracks and sections of Roman road before reaching the coast near Hunstanton. Cycling is another popular pastime in this region and in places you can combine it with a local train ride. One option, for example, is to cycle beside the Bure Valley Railway on a 9-mile trail running from Aylsham to Wroxham, returning to the start by train. There is also the North Norfolk Coast Cycleway between King's Lynn and Cromer, among other routes.

Norfolk prides itself on its wealth of historic houses, the most famous being Sandringham, where Her Majesty the Queen and her family spend Christmas. The Grade II-listed house, which is surrounded by 20,000 acres, has been the private home of four generations of monarchs since 1862. 'Dear old Sandringham, the place I love better than anywhere in the world,' wrote King George V. The house and gardens are open to visitors. Among the other great houses in the region are Holkham Hall – the magnificent Palladian home of the Earls of Leicester – and the National Trust properties of Blickling Hall and Felbrigg Hall.

Many of Norfolk's towns have a particular charm and a strong sense of community. The quiet market towns of Fakenham and Swaffham are prime examples, and there is also Thetford, with its popular museum focusing on the iconic TV comedy series *Dad's Army*. Much of the filming for this cherished BBC production took place in the town and in nearby Thetford Forest. On the coast, you'll find a string of quaint villages and small towns. Wells-next-the-Sea is a popular destination for many visitors to Norfolk, as is Blakeney, renowned for its mudflats and medieval parish church, dedicated to the patron saint of seafarers, standing guard over the village and the estuary of the River Glaven. With its iconic pier, a key feature of coastal towns, Cromer is a classic example of a good old fashioned seaside resort where rather grand Victorian hotels look out to sea. Together with Sheringham, Cromer hosts a Crab and Lobster Festival in May.

◁ Hunstanton beach

NORFOLK

BARNEY
Map 13 TF93

Places to visit

Baconsthorpe Castle, BACONSTHORPE, NR25 6LN, 01799 322399
www.english-heritage.org.uk/daysout/properties/baconsthorpe-castle

Holkham Hall & Bygones Museum, HOLKHAM, NR23 1AB, 01328 710227
www.holkham.co.uk

Great for kids: Dinosaur Adventure Park, LENWADE, NR9 5JW, 01603 876310
www.dinosauradventure.co.uk

PREMIER PARK

The Old Brick Kilns
▶▶▶▶▶ 91%

tel: 01328 878305 **Little Barney Ln NR21 0NL**
email: enquiries@old-brick-kilns.co.uk **web:** www.old-brick-kilns.co.uk
dir: *From A148 Fakenham to Cromer road follow brown tourist signs to Barney, left into Little Barney Ln. Site at end of lane.* **grid ref:** *TG007328*

A secluded and peaceful park approached via a quiet, leafy country lane. The park is on two levels with its own boating and fishing pool and many mature trees. Excellent, well-planned toilet facilities can be found in two beautifully appointed blocks, and there is a short dog walk. Please note due to a narrow access road, no arrivals are accepted until after 1pm. There are four self-catering holiday cottages. 12.73 acre site. 65 touring pitches. 65 hardstandings. Caravan pitches. Motorhome pitches. Tent pitches.

Open: 15 Mar-15 Dec (rs Etr-Sep bar food & takeaway on selected nights only) **Last arrival:** 21.00hrs **Last departure:** 11.00hrs

Pitches: 🚐 🚗 Å

Leisure: 🎱 ♣ 🖵

Facilities: 🌠☉⚡🎇✳🕯☎Ⓢ🛒🚻📶🖥♻ⓘ

Services: 🔌🗑🍽🛢⚗️📞🍴🚮🚽

Within 3 miles: ⚓🛒🛍

Notes: No gazebos. Outdoor draughts, chess, family games, massages by appointment.

AA Pubs & Restaurants nearby: The Old Forge Seafood Restaurant, THURSFORD, NR21 0BD, 01328 878345

BELTON
Map 13 TG40

Places to visit

Burgh Castle, BURGH CASTLE, NR31 9PZ, 0870 333 1181
www.english-heritage.org.uk/daysout/properties/burgh-castle

Wild Duck Holiday Park
HOLIDAY CENTRE 74%

tel: 0871 231 0876 **Howards Common NR31 9NE**
email: wildduck@haven.com **web:** www.haven.com/wildduck
dir: *Phone for detailed directions.* **grid ref:** *TG475028*

This a large holiday complex with plenty to do for all ages both indoors and out. This level grassy site has well laid-out facilities and is set in a forest with small, cleared areas for tourers. Clubs for children and teenagers, sporting activities and evening shows all add to the fun of a stay here. 97 acre site. 119 touring pitches. Caravan pitches. Motorhome pitches. Tent pitches. 560 statics.

Open: 16 Mar-5 Nov (rs mid Mar-May & Sep-early Nov some facilities may be reduced) **Last arrival:** 21.00hrs **Last departure:** 10.00hrs

Pitches: 🚐 🚗 Å

Leisure: 🏊 🏊 🎱 ♣ 🎵 **Facilities:** 🌠☉⚡Ⓢ🛒🚻📶♻ⓘ

Services: 🔌🗑🍽🛢🍴🛒🚽 **Within 3 miles:** ⛳🚣⚓◎🛒🛍

Notes: No commercial vehicles, no bookings by persons under 21yrs unless a family booking, max 2 dogs per booking, certain dog breeds banned. Dogs must be kept on leads.

AA Pubs & Restaurants nearby: Andover House, GREAT YARMOUTH, NR30 3JB, 01493 843490

See advert opposite

PREMIER PARK

Rose Farm Touring & Camping Park
▶▶▶▶▶ 85%

tel: 01493 780896 **Stepshort NR31 9JS**
dir: *Follow signs to Belton off A143, right at lane signed Stepshort, site 1st on right.*
grid ref: *TG488033*

A former railway line is the setting for this very peaceful, beautifully presented site which enjoys rural views. It is brightened with many flower and herb beds. The toilet facilities are smart, spotlessly clean, inviting to use and include family rooms. The customer care here is truly exceptional and the quality café (open in peak season only) is very popular. 10 acre site. 145 touring pitches. 20 hardstandings. Caravan pitches. Motorhome pitches. Tent pitches.

Open: all year
Pitches: 🚐 🚐 🅰
Leisure: 🎱 ▢
Facilities: 🚿 ☉ ✳ ♿ 🗲 🛒 WiFi
Services: 🔌 🗲 ⊘ 🍴 🛒
Within 3 miles: 🎣 🛒 🅿 ⊘ 🔌 U
Notes: No dog fouling.
AA Pubs & Restaurants nearby: Andover House, GREAT YARMOUTH, NR30 3JB, 01493 843490

BURGH CASTLE Map 13 TG40

Places to visit
Burgh Castle, BURGH CASTLE, NR31 9PZ, 0870 333 1181
www.english-heritage.org.uk/daysout/properties/burgh-castle

Breydon Water
HOLIDAY CENTRE 77%

tel: 0871 664 9710 **Butt Ln NR31 9QB**
email: breydon.water@park-resorts.com
dir: *From Gt Yarmouth take A12 towards Lowestoft. Right signed Diss & Beccles onto A143. Through Bradwell, right signed Burgh Castle & Belton. At mini rdbt right into Stepshort. Site on right.* **grid ref:** *TG479042*

This large park has two village areas just a short walk apart. Yare Village offers touring facilities, family fun and superb entertainment, while Bure Village, which is a quieter base, is now static caravans only. Although the villages are separated, guests are more than welcome to use facilities at both. Yare Village has modern, well maintained toilets, and tents are welcome. The park is just a short drive from the bright lights of Great Yarmouth and the unique Norfolk Broads. 189 touring pitches. Caravan pitches. Motorhome pitches. Tent pitches. 327 statics.

Open: Apr-Oct **Last arrival:** anytime **Last departure:** 10.00hrs
Pitches: 🚐 🚐 🅰
Leisure: 🏊 ⚽ 🎱 🎵
Facilities: 🚿 🅿 ♿ 🗲 WiFi 🖥
Services: 🔌 🗲 ⊘ 🍴
Within 3 miles: 🎣 🅿 ⊘ 🔌
AA Pubs & Restaurants nearby: Andover House, GREAT YARMOUTH, NR30 3JB, 01493 843490

PITCHES: 🚐 Caravans 🚐 Motorhomes 🅰 Tents 🏠 Glamping-style accommodation **SERVICES:** 🔌 Electric hook up 🗲 Launderette 🍴 Licensed bar 🅿 Calor Gas ⊘ Camping Gaz 🅃 Toilet fluid 🍴 Café/Restaurant 🛒 Fast Food/Takeaway 🔋 Battery charging 🍼 Baby care ♿ Motorvan service point **ABBREVIATIONS:** BH/bank hols – bank holidays Etr – Easter Spring BH – Spring Bank Holiday fr – from hrs – hours m – mile mdnt – midnight rdbt – roundabout rs – restricted service wk – week wknd – weekend x-rds – cross roads ⊘ No credit or debit cards ⊗ No dogs 👨‍👦 Children of all ages accepted

CAISTER-ON-SEA — Map 13 TG51

Places to visit

Caister Roman Fort, CAISTER-ON-SEA, 0870 333 1181
www.english-heritage.org.uk/daysout/properties/caister-roman-fort

Thrigby Hall Wildlife Gardens, FILBY, NR29 3DR, 01493 369477
www.thrigbyhall.co.uk

Caister Holiday Park
HOLIDAY CENTRE 86%

tel: 0871 231 0873 **Ormesby Rd NR30 5NQ**
email: caister@haven.com **web:** www.haven.com/caister
dir: *A1064 signed Caister-on-Sea. At rdbt 2nd exit onto A149, at next rdbt 1st exit onto Caister by-pass, at 3rd rdbt 3rd exit to Caister-on-Sea. Park on left.* **grid ref:** *TG519132*

An all-action holiday park located beside the beach north of the resort of Great Yarmouth, yet close to the attractions of the Norfolk Broads. The touring area offers

46 fully serviced pitches and a modern purpose-built toilet block. Customer care is of an extremely high standard with a full time, experienced and caring warden. Please note that the park does not accept tents. 138 acre site. 46 touring pitches. Caravan pitches. Motorhome pitches. 900 statics.

Open: mid Mar-end Oct **Last arrival:** 18.00hrs **Last departure:** 10.00hrs

Pitches: 🚐 🚍

Leisure: 🏊 ⏀ 🎯 😊 🎣 🎵

Facilities: 🍴 🚿 ♿ 🕐 🛒 💈 🛜 ♻ ❓

Services: 🔌 🛒 🚽 🛢 🍴 🛒 🚏 ⚓

Within 3 miles: ⚓ ✚ 🏇 🎣 ◉ 💈 🛒

Notes: No tents, no commercial vehicles, no bookings by persons under 21yrs unless a family booking, no sleeping in awnings, max 2 dogs per booking, certain dog breeds banned. Dogs must be kept on leads.

AA Pubs & Restaurants nearby: Fishermans Return, WINTERTON-ON-SEA, NR29 4BN, 01493 393305

See advert below

LEISURE: 🏊 Indoor swimming pool 🏊 Outdoor swimming pool ⏀ Children's playground 🎣 Kid's club 🎾 Tennis court 🎱 Games room 📺 Separate TV room ⛳ golf course 🚣 Boats for hire 🎬 Cinema 🎵 Entertainment 🎣 Fishing ◉ Mini golf 🏄 Watersports 🏋 Gym ⚽ Sports field Spa ♨ Stables
FACILITIES: 🛁 Bath 🚿 Shower ⚡ Electric shaver 🔥 Hairdryer ❄ Ice Pack Facility ♿ Disabled facilities ☎ Public telephone 🛒 Shop on site or within 200yds 🏪 Mobile shop (calls at least 5 days a week) 🍖 BBQ area 🏕 Picnic area 🛜 Wi-fi 🖥 Internet access ♻ Recycling ❓ Tourist info 🐕 Dog exercise area

CLIPPESBY
Map 13 TG41

Places to visit

Fairhaven Woodland & Water Garden, SOUTH WALSHAM, NR13 6DZ, 01603 270449 www.fairhavengarden.co.uk

Great for kids: Caister Roman Fort, CAISTER-ON-SEA, 0870 333 1181 www.english-heritage.org.uk/daysout/properties/caister-roman-fort

PREMIER PARK

Clippesby Hall
▶▶▶▶▶ 93%

tel: 01493 367800 **Hall Ln NR29 3BL**
email: holidays@clippesby.com **web:** www.clippesby.com
dir: From A47 follow tourist signs for The Broads. At Acle rdbt take A1064, in 2m left onto B1152, 0.5m left opposite village sign, site 400yds on right. **grid ref:** TG423147

A lovely country house estate with secluded pitches hidden among the trees or in sheltered sunny glades. The toilet facilities, appointed to a very good standard, provide a wide choice of cubicles. Amenities include a coffee shop with both WiFi and wired internet access, a family bar and restaurant and family golf. Excellent hardstanding pitches are available as the park is open all year. There are pine lodges and cottages for holiday lets. 30 acre site. 120 touring pitches. 41 hardstandings. Caravan pitches. Motorhome pitches. Tent pitches.

Open: all year (rs Nov-Mar coffee shop, bar & restaurant closed) **Last arrival:** 17.30hrs **Last departure:** 11.00hrs

Pitches: * 🚐 £16.50-£39 🚐 £16.50-£39 ▲ £12.50-£39

Leisure: 🏊 ⚲ ♨ ☺ 🎣

Facilities: 🚿 ⌂ ⊙ 🏪 ☼ ♿ ◐ 🚽 🔥 ⛅ WiFi ▭ ♻ ❂

Services: 🔌 🔄 🍺 ▮ ⊘ 🅃 🍽 🍴 ⚡

Within 3 miles: ⌕ ⚓ ℰ ◎ ⛵ 🏌 🐟 U

Notes: No groups, no noise after 23.00hrs, no camp fires. Dogs must be kept on leads. Bicycle hire, volley ball, table tennis, cycle trail.

AA Pubs & Restaurants nearby: Fishermans Return, WINTERTON-ON-SEA, NR29 4BN, 01493 393305

The Fur & Feather Inn, WOODBASTWICK, NR13 6HQ, 01603 720003

CROMER
Map 13 TG24

Places to visit

RNLI Henry Blogg Museum, CROMER, NR27 9ET, 01263 511294 www.rnli.org/henryblogg

Felbrigg Hall, FELBRIGG, NR11 8PR, 01263 837444 www.nationaltrust.org.uk/main/w-felbrigghallgardenandpark

Forest Park
▶▶▶▶ 81%

tel: 01263 513290 **Northrepps Rd NR27 0JR**
email: info@forest-park.co.uk
dir: A140 from Norwich, left at T-junct signed Cromer, right signed Northrepps, right then immediately left, left at T-junct, site on right. **grid ref:** TG233405

Surrounded by forest, this gently sloping park offers a wide choice of pitches. Visitors have the use of a heated indoor swimming pool, and a large clubhouse with entertainment. 100 acre site. 262 touring pitches. Caravan pitches. Motorhome pitches. Tent pitches. 420 statics.

Open: 15 Mar-15 Jan **Last arrival:** 21.00hrs **Last departure:** 11.00hrs

Pitches: 🚐 🚐 ▲

Leisure: 🏊 ⚲ 🎣 **Facilities:** 🚿 ⊙ 🏪 ☼ ♿ ◐ 🚽 🔥 WiFi

Services: 🔌 🔄 🍺 ▮ ⊘ 🅃 🍽 ⛟ 🚮 **Within 3 miles:** ⌕ ⚓ 🏌 ℰ ◎ ⛵ 🏌 🐟 U

AA Pubs & Restaurants nearby: The Red Lion Food and Rooms, CROMER, NR27 9HD, 01263 514964

The White Horse Overstrand, CROMER, NR27 0AB, 01263 579237

Sea Marge Hotel, CROMER, NR27 0AB, 01263 579579

Manor Farm Caravan & Camping Site
▶▶▶▶ 81%

tel: 01263 512858 & 07760 324673 **East Runton NR27 9PR**
email: stay@manorfarmcampsite.co.uk
dir: 1m W of Cromer, exit A148 or A149 (recommended towing route) at Manor Farm sign. **grid ref:** TG198416

A well-established family-run site on a working farm enjoying panoramic sea views. There are good modern facilities across the site, including three smart toilet blocks that include two quality family rooms and privacy cubicles, two good play areas and a large expanse of grass for games - the park is very popular with families. 17 acre site. 250 touring pitches. Caravan pitches. Motorhome pitches. Tent pitches.

Open: Etr-Sep **Last arrival:** 20.30hrs **Last departure:** noon

Pitches: * 🚐 £14.50-£23 🚐 £14.50-£23 ▲ £14.50-£23

Leisure: ⚲ ✤ **Facilities:** 🚿 ⊙ ☼ ♿ 🔥 ❂ ❂

Services: 🔌 🔄 ▮ ⊘ ⛟ **Within 3 miles:** ⌕ 🏌 ℰ ◎ ⛵ 🏌 🐟

Notes: ⊘ No noise after 23.00hrs, no groups. Dogs must be kept on leads. 2 dog-free fields.

AA Pubs & Restaurants nearby: The Red Lion Food and Rooms, CROMER, NR27 9HD, 01263 514964

The White Horse Overstrand, CROMER, NR27 0AB, 01263 579237

Sea Marge Hotel, CROMER, NR27 0AB, 01263 579579

PITCHES: 🚐 Caravans 🚐 Motorhomes ▲ Tents 🏠 Glamping-style accommodation **SERVICES:** 🔌 Electric hook up 🔄 Launderette 🍺 Licensed bar ▮ Calor Gas ⊘ Camping Gaz 🅃 Toilet fluid 🍽 Café/Restaurant ⛟ Fast Food/Takeaway ⚡ Battery charging 🚼 Baby care ⚡ Motorvan service point
ABBREVIATIONS: BH/bank hols – bank holidays Etr – Easter Spring BH – Spring Bank Holiday fr – from hrs – hours m – mile mdnt – midnight rdbt – roundabout rs – restricted service wk – week wknd – weekend x-rds – cross roads 🚫 No credit or debit cards 🚫 No dogs 👪 Children of all ages accepted

DOWNHAM MARKET
Map 12 TF60

Lakeside Caravan Park & Fisheries
►►►86%

tel: 01366 387074 & 07790 272978 **Sluice Rd, Denver PE38 0DZ**
email: richesflorido@aol.com **web:** www.westhallfarmholidays.co.uk
dir: Exit A10 towards Denver, follow signs to Denver Windmill, site on right.
grid ref: TF608013

A peaceful, rapidly improving park set around five pretty fishing lakes. There are several grassy touring areas which are sheltered by mature hedging and trees, a function room for social get togethers, shop, laundry and children's play area. Electric hook-up pitches are available. Rallies are welcome. 30 acre site. 100 touring pitches. Caravan pitches. Motorhome pitches. Tent pitches. 1 static.

Open: all year (rs Oct-Mar) **Last arrival:** 21.00hrs **Last departure:** 10.30hrs

Pitches: ⊞ ⇎ Å

Leisure: ⚑

Facilities: ⬥ ☉ ☺ ⌂ ✳ ✦ ⑤ ⌦ WiFi

Services: ⬤◎ 🛢 ⊘ ⊤ ⛟

Within 3 miles: ↓ ⥥ ⽥ ⌔ ⥇ ⑤⑤

Notes: Dogs must be kept on leads. Pool table, fishing tackle & bait, caravan accessories, caravan storage.

AA Pubs & Restaurants nearby: The Hare Arms, STOW BARDOLPH, PE34 3HT, 01366 382229

> **Find out more about this area** with the *AA Guide to Norfolk & Suffolk* – see the AA.com/shop

FAKENHAM
Map 13 TF92

Places to visit
Houghton Hall, HOUGHTON, PE31 6UE, 01485 528569 www.houghtonhall.com

Great for kids: Pensthorpe Nature Reserve & Gardens, FAKENHAM, NR21 0LN, 01328 851465 www.pensthorpe.co.uk

Fakenham Fairways Campsite
►►►86%

tel: 01328 856614 **Burnham Market Rd, Sculthorpe NR21 9SA**
email: hello@fakenhamfairways.uk
dir: From Fakenham take A148 towards King's Lynn then right onto B1355 towards Burnham Market. Site on right in 400yds. **grid ref:** TF907310

Enthusiastic owners run this peaceful site that is surrounded by tranquil countryside and which is part of a 9-hole, par 3 golf complex and driving range. The toilet facilities are of good quality, and there is a golf shop and licensed bar. Please note there is no laundry. 4 acre site. 50 touring pitches. 13 hardstandings. Caravan pitches. Motorhome pitches. Tent pitches.

Open: all year **Last arrival:** 20.00hrs **Last departure:** noon

Pitches: * ⊞ £15-£19 ⇎ £15-£19 Å £12.50-£19

Leisure: ⚑ ⌁ **Facilities:** ⬥ ✳ ✦ ⌂ WiFi 🖳 ♻ ❶

Services: ⬤◎ ⊘

Within 3 miles: ↓⽥⌔⑤

Notes: No noise after 22.30hrs. Dogs must be kept on leads.

AA Pubs & Restaurants nearby: The Blue Boar Inn, GREAT RYBURGH, NR21 0DX, 01328 829212

The Wensum Lodge Hotel, FAKENHAM, NR21 9AY, 01328 862100

Caravan Club M.V.C. Site
►►►82%

tel: 01328 862388 **Fakenham Racecourse NR21 7NY**
email: caravan@fakenhamracecourse.co.uk
dir: From B1146, S of Fakenham follow brown Racecourse signs (with tent & caravan symbols) leads to site entrance. **grid ref:** TF926288

A very well laid-out site set around the racecourse, with a grandstand offering smart, newly refurbished modern toilet facilities. Tourers move to the centre of the course on race days, and enjoy free racing, and there's a wide range of sporting activities in the club house. 11.4 acre site. 120 touring pitches. 25 hardstandings. 22 seasonal pitches. Caravan pitches. Motorhome pitches. Tent pitches.

Open: all year **Last arrival:** 21.00hrs **Last departure:** noon

Pitches: ⊞ ⇎ Å

Leisure: ⌁ **Facilities:** ⬥ ☉ ⌂ ✳ ✦ ⓢ ⑤ ⌦ WiFi ♻ ❶

Services: ⬤◎ 🍴🛢 ⊘ ⊤ ◎ ⛟

Within 3 miles: ↓⽥⌔ ◎⑤⑤⟲

Notes: Max 2 dogs per unit. Dogs must be kept on leads. TV aerial hook-ups.

AA Pubs & Restaurants nearby: The Blue Boar Inn, GREAT RYBURGH, NR21 0DX, 01328 829212

The Wensum Lodge Hotel, FAKENHAM, NR21 9AY, 01328 862100

Crossways Caravan & Camping Park
►►72%

tel: 01328 878335 **Crossways, Holt Rd, Little Snoring NR21 0AX**
email: joyholland@live.co.uk
dir: From Fakenham take A148 towards Cromer. After 3m pass exit for Little Snoring. Site on A148 on left behind post office. **grid ref:** TF961321

Set on the edge of the peaceful hamlet of Little Snoring, this level site enjoys views across the fields towards the north Norfolk coast some seven miles away. Visitors can use the health suite for a small charge, and there is a shop on site, and a good village pub. 2 acre site. 26 touring pitches. 10 hardstandings. 14 seasonal pitches. Caravan pitches. Motorhome pitches. Tent pitches. 1 static.

Open: all year **Last arrival:** 22.00hrs **Last departure:** noon

Pitches: ⊕ ⊕ Å

Leisure: ✪

Facilities: ♦ ☉ ✳ ◐ ⑤ ☶ ➴ ▬ ♺ ❂

Services: ♨⑤ ☖ ◿ T

Within 3 miles: ⌿ ⻌ ♪ ◎ ⑤⑤ ∪

Notes: Dogs must be kept on leads.

AA Pubs & Restaurants nearby: The Blue Boar Inn, GREAT RYBURGH, NR21 0DX, 01328 829212

The Wensum Lodge Hotel, FAKENHAM, NR21 9AY, 01328 862100

GREAT YARMOUTH	**Map 13 TG50**

Places to visit

Yesterday's World Great Yarmouth, GREAT YARMOUTH, NR30 2EN, 01493 331148 www.yesterdaysworld.co.uk

Great for kids: Time and Tide Museum of Great Yarmouth Life, GREAT YARMOUTH, NR30 3BX, 01493 743930 www.museums.norfolk.gov.uk

---

Vauxhall Holiday Park
HOLIDAY CENTRE 89%

tel: 01493 857231 **4 Acle New Rd NR30 1TB**
email: info@vauxhallholidays.co.uk **web:** www.vauxhall-holiday-park.co.uk
dir: On A47 approaching Great Yarmouth. **grid ref:** TG520083

A very large holiday complex with plenty of entertainment and access to beach, river, estuary, lake and the A47. The touring pitches are laid out in four separate areas, each with its own amenity block, and all arranged around the main entertainment. 40 acre site. 220 touring pitches. Caravan pitches. Motorhome pitches. Tent pitches. 421 statics.

Open: Etr, mid May-Sep & Oct half term **Last arrival:** 21.00hrs **Last departure:** 10.00hrs

Pitches: ⊕ ⊕ Å

Leisure: ⪿ ⪿ ☗ ⚲ ▲ ⬇ ⚽ ✪ ◕ ☐ ♫

Facilities: ♦ ☉ ✳ ⟐ ◐ ⑤ WiFi ♺

Services: ♨⑤ ☖ ⎅ ◿ T ⎮⚬⎮ ⚏ ⇞

Within 3 miles: ⌿ ⻌ ♪ ◎ ⍆ ⑤⑤ ∪

Notes: No pets. Children's pool, sauna, solarium.

AA Pubs & Restaurants nearby: Andover House, GREAT YARMOUTH, NR30 3JB, 01493 843490

See advert on page 270

The Grange Touring Park
►►►►80%

tel: 01493 730306 & 730023 **Yarmouth Rd, Ormesby St Margaret NR29 3QG**
email: info@grangetouring.co.uk
dir: From A149, 3m N of Great Yarmouth. Site at junct of A149 & B1159, signed. **grid ref:** TG510142

A mature, ever improving park with plenty of trees, located just one mile from the sea, within easy reach of both coastal attractions and the Norfolk Broads. The level pitches have electric hook-ups and include 13 hardstanding pitches, and there are clean, modern toilets including three spacious family rooms. All pitches have WiFi. 3.5 acre site. 70 touring pitches. 7 hardstandings. Caravan pitches. Motorhome pitches. Tent pitches.

Open: Etr-Oct **Last arrival:** 21.00hrs **Last departure:** 14.00hrs

Pitches: * ⊕ £13-£25 ⊕ £13-£25 Å £12-£14

Leisure: ▲

Facilities: ♦ ☉ ☞ ✳ ⟐ WiFi ▬ ❂

Services: ♨⑤ ☖ ⎅ ◿ ⇞ ⇞

Within 3 miles: ⌿ ♪ ◎ ⑤⑤ ∪

Notes: No football, no open fires. Dogs must be kept on leads.

AA Pubs & Restaurants nearby: Andover House, GREAT YARMOUTH, NR30 3JB, 01493 843490

GREAT YARMOUTH *continued*

Seashore Holiday Park
HOLIDAY HOME PARK 87%

tel: 01493 851131 **North Denes NR30 4HG**
email: seashore@haven.com **web:** www.haven.com/seashore
dir: *A149 from Great Yarmouth to Caister. Right at 2nd lights signed seafront & racecourse. Continue to sea, turn left. Park on left.* **grid ref:** *TG653103*

Bordered by sand dunes and with direct access to a sandy beach, Seashore Holiday Park is located in Great Yarmouth yet is close enough for day trips to the peaceful Norfolk Broads. Facilities include excellent water activities and bike hire for children and lively evening entertainment for adults. There is a good range of holiday caravans and apartments.

Open: Mar-Oct

Change over day: Mon, Fri, Sat

Arrival and departure times: Please contact the site

Statics: 285 Sleeps 6-8 Bedrms 2-3 Bathrms 1-2 Toilets 1-2 Microwave Freezer TV Sky/FTV Elec inc Gas inc

Children: 🚹 Cots Highchair **Dogs:** 2 on leads No dangerous dogs

Leisure: 🚲 Cycle hire 👋 🛝

Hopton Holiday Park
HOLIDAY HOME PARK 91%

tel: 01502 730214 **NR31 9BW**
email: hopton@haven.com **web:** www.haven.com/hopton
dir: *Site signed from A12 between Great Yarmouth & Lowestoft.* **grid ref:** *TG531002*

Located between Lowestoft and Great Yarmouth, close to beaches and the town attractions, this lively holiday park offers excellent sport activities, including golf on the 9-hole course and tennis coaching, plus popular evening entertainment in the form of shows, music and dancing. There is a good range of holiday caravans and apartments.

Open: Mar-Oct

Change over day: Mon, Fri, Sat

Arrival and departure times: Please contact the site

Statics: 216 Sleeps 6-8 Bedrms 2-3 Bathrms 1-2 Toilets 1-2 Microwave Freezer TV Sky/FTV Elec inc Gas inc Grass area

Children: 🚹 Cots Highchair **Dogs:** 2 on leads No dangerous dogs

Leisure: 🚲 🚲 🚣 Cycle hire 👋 🛝

HUNSTANTON
Map 12 TF64

Places to visit

Lynn Museum, KING'S LYNN, PE30 1NL, 01553 775001
www.museums.norfolk.gov.uk

Norfolk Lavender, HEACHAM, PE31 7JE, 01485 570384
www.norfolk-lavender.co.uk

Great for kids: Hunstanton Sea Life Sanctuary, HUNSTANTON, PE36 5BH, 01485 533576 www.sealife.co.uk

---

Searles Leisure Resort
HOLIDAY CENTRE 90%

tel: 01485 534211 **South Beach Rd PE36 5BB**
email: bookings@searles.co.uk
dir: A149 from King's Lynn to Hunstanton. At rdbt follow signs for South Beach. Straight on at 2nd rdbt. Site on left. **grid ref:** TF671400

A large seaside holiday complex with well managed facilities, adjacent to sea and beach. The tourers have their own areas, including two excellent toilet blocks, and pitches are individually marked by small maturing shrubs for privacy. The bars and entertainment, restaurant, bistro and takeaway, heated indoor and outdoor pools, golf, fishing and bowling green make this park popular throughout the year. 50 acre site. 255 touring pitches. 91 hardstandings. Caravan pitches. Motorhome pitches. Tent pitches. 158 statics.

Open: all year (rs Dec-Mar excl Feb half term limited facilities & use of indoor pool & country park only)

Pitches: 🚐 🚋 ▲

Leisure: 🏊 ⛱ 🎾 🏸 🚶 ⚽ 🎣 ♪

Facilities: 🐕 ✳ ♿ 🖲 🔥 🚻 📶 🛒 ♻ ✪

Services: 🔌 🗑 🍴 🛢 ⏚ 🚽 🍴 🔋 🚼 ↯

Within 3 miles: ⛳ 📍 🏄 🎣 🍴 ∪

Notes: Dogs must be kept on leads.

AA Pubs & Restaurants nearby: The King William IV Country Inn & Restaurant, HUNSTANTON, PE36 5LU, 01485 571765

The Neptune Restaurant with Rooms, HUNSTANTON, PE36 6HZ, 01485 532122

Marco Pierre White The Lifeboat Inn, THORNHAM, PE36 6LT, 01485 512236

Manor Park Holiday Village
HOLIDAY CENTRE 80%

tel: 01485 532300 **Manor Rd PE36 5AZ**
email: manor.park@park-resorts.com
dir: Take A149 (King's Lynn Rd) to Hunstanton, left onto B1161 (Oasis Way). **grid ref:** TF671399

Situated just a few yards from the beach on the outskirts of the lively resort of Hunstanton, Manor Farm offers a range of leisure activities, including two heated outdoor swimming pools, children's playground, children's club, amusement arcade, restaurant, bar and cabaret. There are 64 electric, all-grass pitches set out in the heart of the park and adjacent to the leisure complex. Expect high standards of customer care. 64 touring pitches. 10 seasonal pitches. Caravan pitches. Motorhome pitches. 650 statics.

Open: Apr-Oct **Last arrival:** noon **Last departure:** 10.00hrs

Pitches: 🚐 🚋

Leisure: 🏊 ⛱ 🚶 🔫 ⛱ 🎣 ♪

Facilities: 🐕 ♿ 🖲 🔥 🚻 📶 🛒 ♻ ✪

Services: 🔌 🗑 🍴 🛢 🍴 ↯

Within 3 miles: ⛳ 📍 🏄 🎣 🍴 ∪

Notes: Dogs must be kept on leads. Bicycle hire.

AA Pubs & Restaurants nearby: The King William IV Country Inn & Restaurant, HUNSTANTON, PE36 5LU, 01485 571765

The Neptune Restaurant with Rooms, HUNSTANTON, PE36 6HZ, 01485 532122

KING'S LYNN
Map 12 TF62

See also Stanhoe

Places to visit

Bircham Windmill, GREAT BIRCHAM, PE31 6SJ, 01485 578393
www.birchamwindmill.co.uk

African Violet Centre, KING'S LYNN, PE34 4PL, 01553 828374
www.africanvioletandgardencentre.com

Great for kids: Castle Rising Castle, CASTLE RISING, PE31 6AH, 01553 631330
www.english-heritage.org.uk/daysout/properties/castle-rising-castle

---

PREMIER PARK

King's Lynn Caravan and Camping Park
►►►►► 84%

tel: 01553 840004 **New Rd, North Runcton PE33 0RA**
email: klcc@btconnect.com
dir: From King's Lynn take A47 signed Swaffham & Norwich, in 1.5m turn right signed North Runcton. Site 100yds on left. **grid ref:** TF645160

Set in approximately 10 acres of parkland, this developing camping park is situated on the edge of North Runcton, just a few miles south of the historic town of King's Lynn. The three very extensive touring fields are equipped with 150 electric hook-ups and one field is reserved for rallies. There is an eco-friendly toilet block which is powered by solar panels and an air-sourced heat pump which also recycles rainwater - this in itself proves a source of great interest. A second toilet block was refurbished ready for the 2014 season. High quality camping pods and four new pine lodges are for hire. 9 acre site. 150 touring pitches. 2 hardstandings. 54 seasonal pitches. Caravan pitches. Motorhome pitches. Tent pitches. 8 wooden pods.

Open: all year **Last arrival:** flexible **Last departure:** flexible

Pitches: 🚐 £17-£20 🚋 £17-£20 ▲ £12-£19 🏠

Facilities: 🐕 🖲 🔥 ✳ ♿ 🖲 🚻 📶 ♻ ✪

Services: 🔌 🗑 🛢 ⏚ 🍴 🔋 ↯

Within 3 miles: ⛳ 🎯 📍 🏄 🎣 🍴 ∪

Notes: No skateboards or fires. Dogs must be kept on leads.

AA Pubs & Restaurants nearby: The Stuart House Hotel, Bar & Restaurant, KING'S LYNN, PE30 5QX, 01553 772169

Bank House Hotel, KING'S LYNN, PE30 1RD, 01553 660492

PITCHES: 🚐 Caravans 🚋 Motorhomes ▲ Tents 🏠 Glamping-style accommodation **SERVICES:** 🔌 Electric hook up 🗑 Launderette 🍴 Licensed bar 🛢 Calor Gas ⏚ Camping Gaz T Toilet fluid 🍴 Café/Restaurant 🔋 Fast Food/Takeaway 🔋 Battery charging 🚼 Baby care ↯ Motorvan service point
ABBREVIATIONS: BH/bank hols – bank holidays Etr – Easter Spring BH – Spring Bank Holiday fr – from hrs – hours m – mile mdnt – midnight rdbt – roundabout rs – restricted service wk – week wknd – weekend x-rds – cross roads Ⓐ No credit or debit cards Ⓧ No dogs ♦♦ Children of all ages accepted

NORTH WALSHAM
Map 13 TG23

Places to visit

Blickling Estate, BLICKLING, NR11 6NF, 01263 738030
www.nationaltrust.org.uk/blickling

Wolterton Park, ERPINGHAM, NR11 7LY, 01263 584175
www.manningtongardens.co.uk

PREMIER PARK

Two Mills Touring Park
►►►►► 85%

Best of British

tel: 01692 405829 **Yarmouth Rd NR28 9NA**
email: enquiries@twomills.co.uk
dir: 1m S of North Walsham on Old Yarmouth road past police station & hospital on left. **grid ref:** TG291286

An intimate, beautifully presented park set in superb countryside in a peaceful, rural spot, which is also convenient for touring. The 'Top Acre' section is maturing and features fully serviced pitches, offering panoramic views over the site, an immaculate toilet block and good planting, plus the layout of pitches and facilities is excellent. The very friendly and helpful owners keep the park in immaculate condition. Please note this park is for adults only. 7 acre site. 81 touring pitches. 81 hardstandings. Caravan pitches. Motorhome pitches. Tent pitches.

Open: Mar-3 Jan **Last arrival:** 20.30hrs **Last departure:** noon
Pitches: * ➡ £17.45-£25 ⇔ £17.45-£25 ▲ £17.45-£25
Leisure: ☐
Facilities: ➡ ☉ ℙ ☼ & ☺ ⑤ ㅈ ㅐ WiFi 🖥 ♻ 𝒊
Services: ➡⑤ 🔒 ⌀ T ☎ ⌄
Within 3 miles: ℙ ⑤ ⑤
Notes: Adults only. Max 2 dogs per pitch. Dogs must be kept on leads. Library.

AA Pubs & Restaurants nearby: The Butchers Arms, EAST RUSTON, NR12 9JG, 01692 650237

Beechwood Hotel, NORTH WALSHAM, NR28 0HD, 01692 403231

SAHAM HILLS
Map 13 TF90

Lowe Caravan Park
►►► 85%

tel: 01953 881051 **Ashdale, 134 Hills Rd IP25 7EZ**
dir: From B1108 (High St) in Watton follow Saham Hills sign, pass Richmond Park Golf Club on left. 2nd right into Ploughboy Ln, at T-junct right into Hills Rd. 1st drive on right. **grid ref:** TF903034

A small, well-established adults-only touring park run by experienced and caring owners. Twenty five pitches occupy a level field behind the owners' house and there are clean, well-maintained toilets and exceptional levels of customer care and security. The site occupies a tranquil location deep in the Norfolk countryside, yet it is well-placed for visiting Norwich and the north Norfolk coast. 4 acre site. 31 touring pitches. Caravan pitches. Motorhome pitches. Tent pitches.

Open: all year ex Xmas & New Year **Last arrival:** 21.30hrs **Last departure:** 15.00hrs
Pitches: * ➡ £14.50-£15 ⇔ £14.50-£15 ▲ £14.50-£15
Facilities: ➡ ℙ ㅈ 𝒊
Services: ➡ 🔒
Within 3 miles: ⅃ ℙ ⑤
Notes: Adults only. 🐕 Dogs must be kept on leads.

SCRATBY
Map 13 TG51

Places to visit

Time and Tide Museum of Great Yarmouth Life, GREAT YARMOUTH, NR30 3BX, 01493 743930 www.museums.norfolk.gov.uk

Great for kids: Caister Roman Fort, CAISTER-ON-SEA, 0870 333 1181 www.english-heritage.org.uk/daysout/properties/caister-roman-fort

Scratby Hall Caravan Park
►►► 86%

tel: 01493 730283 **NR29 3SR**
email: scratbyhall@aol.com **web:** www.scratbyhall.co.uk
dir: 5m N of Great Yarmouth. Exit A149 onto B1159, site signed. **grid ref:** TG501155

A neatly-maintained site with a popular children's play area, well-equipped shop and outdoor swimming pool with sun terrace. The toilets are kept very clean. The beach and the Norfolk Broads are close by. 5 acre site. 85 touring pitches. Caravan pitches. Motorhome pitches. Tent pitches.

Open: Etr-end Sep (rs Etr-mid Jul & Sep pool closed) **Last arrival:** 21.00hrs **Last departure:** noon
Pitches: * ➡ £10-£31 ⇔ £10-£31 ▲ £10-£31
Leisure: ⚲ ⋀
Facilities: ➡ ☉ ℙ ☼ & ☺ ⑤ WiFi ♻ 𝒊
Services: ➡⑤ 🔒 ⌀ T ☎
Within 3 miles: ⅃ ⅃ ℙ ⑤ ⑤ U
Notes: No commercial vehicles. Dogs must be kept on leads. Food preparation room.

AA Pubs & Restaurants nearby: Fishermans Return, WINTERTON-ON-SEA, NR29 4BN, 01493 393305

Places to visit

Norfolk Lavender, HEACHAM, PE31 7JE, 01485 570384
www.norfolk-lavender.co.uk

Walsingham Abbey Grounds & Shirehall Museum, LITTLE WALSINGHAM,
NR22 6BP, 01328 820510 www.walsinghamabbey.com

The Rickels Caravan & Camping Park
►►►84%

tel: 01485 518671 **Bircham Rd PE31 8PU**
dir: *A148 from King's Lynn to Hillington. B1153 to Great Bircham. B1155 to x-rds, straight over, site on left.* **grid ref:** *TF794355*

Set in three acres of grassland, with sweeping country views and a pleasant, relaxing atmosphere fostered by being for adults only. The meticulously maintained grounds and facilities are part of the attraction, and the slightly sloping land has some level areas and sheltering for tents. A field is available to hire for rallies. 3 acre site. 30 touring pitches. Caravan pitches. Motorhome pitches. Tent pitches.

Open: all year **Last arrival:** 21.00hrs **Last departure:** 11.00hrs

Pitches: * ☎ £11-£16 ☎ £11-£16 **Å** £11-£14

Leisure: ▢

Facilities: ♚⊙⋇⊹⚡♻❶

Services: ☎⑤ 🔋⊘🖿

Within 3 miles: ⚓⑤

Notes: Adults only. 🚫 No groundsheets. Dogs must be kept on leads.

AA Pubs & Restaurants nearby: The Lord Nelson, BURNHAM THORPE, PE31 8HN, 01328 738241

The Hoste, BURNHAM MARKET, PE31 8HD, 01328 738777

Places to visit

Gressenhall Farm and Workhouse, GRESSENHALL, NR20 4DR, 01362 860563
www.museums.norfolk.gov.uk

Breckland Meadows Touring Park
►►►►80%

tel: 01760 721246 **Lynn Rd PE37 7PT**
email: info@brecklandmeadows.co.uk
dir: *1m W of Swaffham on old A47.* **grid ref:** *TF809094*

An immaculate, well-landscaped little park on the edge of Swaffham. For 2014, the toilet block was extended and completely refurbished and is now a very impressive facility, replete with quality fixtures and fittings, spacious cubicles, including a family/disabled room, a large, well-equipped laundry, and a high tech, and very efficient, hot water system. There are hardstandings, with electricity, and the plentiful planting makes attractive screening. 3 acre site. 45 touring pitches. 35 hardstandings. 5 seasonal pitches. Caravan pitches. Motorhome pitches. Tent pitches.

Open: all year **Last arrival:** 21.00hrs **Last departure:** noon

Pitches: * ☎ £13.50-£14.50 ☎ £13.50-£14.50 **Å** £8-£11.50

Facilities: ♚⊙⋇⊹⑤🗄♨🚻Wifi 🖥♻❶

Services: ☎⑤ 🔋⊘Ⓣ🖿 Within 3 miles: ⚓🎣⚓⑤⑤U

Notes: Adults only. Dogs must be kept on leads. Newspaper deliveries.

Places to visit

Creake Abbey, NORTH CREAKE, NR21 9LF, 0870 333 1181
www.english-heritage.org.uk/daysout/properties/creake-abbey

The Garden Caravan Site
►►►77%

tel: 01485 578220 & 578178 **Barmer Hall Farm PE31 8SR**
email: nigel@gardencaravansite.co.uk
dir: *Signed from B1454 at Barmer between A148 & Docking, 1m W of Syderstone.*
grid ref: *TF812337*

In the tranquil setting of a former walled garden beside a large farmhouse, with mature trees and shrubs, a secluded site surrounded by woodland. The site is run mainly on trust, with a daily notice indicating which pitches are available, and an honesty box for basic foods. An ideal site for the discerning camper, and well placed for touring north Norfolk. 3.5 acre site. 30 touring pitches. Caravan pitches. Motorhome pitches. Tent pitches.

Open: Mar-Nov **Last arrival:** 21.00hrs **Last departure:** noon

Pitches: * ☎ £19-£22 ☎ £19-£22 **Å** **Facilities:** ♚⊙🗄⋇⊹⑤🚻❶

Services: ☎ 🔋🖿⚓ Within 3 miles: ⑤

Notes: 🚫 Max 2 dogs per pitch. Dogs must be kept on leads. Cold drinks, ice creams & eggs available.

AA Pubs & Restaurants nearby: The Lord Nelson, BURNHAM THORPE, PE31 8HN, 01328 738241

The Hoste, BURNHAM MARKET, PE31 8HD, 01328 738777

PITCHES: ☎ Caravans ☎ Motorhomes **Å** Tents ⌂ Glamping-style accommodation **SERVICES:** ☎ Electric hook up ⑤ Launderette ▯ Licensed bar 🔋 Calor Gas ⊘ Camping Gaz Ⓣ Toilet fluid ▯🍴 Café/Restaurant ▦ Fast Food/Takeaway 🖿 Battery charging ⚓ Baby care ⚓ Motorvan service point **ABBREVIATIONS:** BH/bank hols – bank holidays Etr – Easter Spring BH – Spring Bank Holiday fr – from hrs – hours m – mile mdnt – midnight rdbt – roundabout rs – restricted service wk – week wknd – weekend x-rds – cross roads 🚫 No credit or debit cards 🚫 No dogs ⚓ Children of all ages accepted

THREE HOLES
Map 12 TF50

Places to visit

African Violet Centre, KING'S LYNN, PE34 4PL, 01553 828374
www.africanvioletandgardencentre.com

Oxburgh Hall, OXBOROUGH, PE33 9PS, 01366 328258
www.nationaltrust.org.uk/oxburgh-hall

Lode Hall Holiday Park
►►► 77%

tel: 01354 638133 **Lode Hall, Silt Rd PE14 9JW**
email: dick@lode-hall.co.uk
dir: *From Wisbech take A1101 towards Downham Market. At Outwell continue on A1101 signed Littleport. Site signed from Three Holes. Right onto B1094 to site.*
grid ref: TF529989

Peace and tranquilly is assured at this deeply rural park in the grounds of Lode Hall. The toilet facilities are located in an imaginative restoration of a former cricket pavilion and include combined toilet/wash basin cubicles and unisex showers. Please note that this is an adults-only site. 5 acre site. 20 touring pitches. 8 hardstandings. Caravan pitches. Motorhome pitches. Tent pitches.

Open: Apr-Oct
Pitches: ⇌ ⇌ ▲
Facilities: ⬅⊙🅟✳❤🛒 WiFi
Services: ⬅🔄 🏕
Within 3 miles: 🎣🏪U
Notes: Adults only. 🐕

AA Pubs & Restaurants nearby: The Hare Arms, STOW BARDOLPH, PE34 3HT, 01366 382229

WORTWELL
Map 13 TM28

Places to visit

Bressingham Steam Museum & Gardens, BRESSINGHAM, IP22 2AB, 01379 686900 www.bressingham.co.uk

---

Little Lakeland Caravan Park
►►►► 83%

tel: 01986 788646 **IP20 0EL**
email: information@littlelakeland.co.uk
dir: *From W: exit A143 at sign for Wortwell. In village turn right 300yds past garage. From E: on A143, left onto B1062, then right. After 800yds turn left.* **grid ref:** TM279849

A well-kept and pretty site built round a fishing lake, and accessed by a lake-lined drive. The individual pitches are sited in hedged enclosures for complete privacy, and the purpose-built toilet facilities are excellent. 4.5 acre site. 38 touring pitches.

---

6 hardstandings. 17 seasonal pitches. Caravan pitches. Motorhome pitches. Tent pitches. 21 statics.

Open: 15 Mar-Oct **Last arrival:** 22.00hrs **Last departure:** noon
Pitches: * ⇌ £15.50-£21.50 ⇌ £15.50-£21.50 ▲ £15.50-£21.50
Leisure: ⚠
Facilities: ⬅⊙🅟✳❤🛒 WiFi ♻ ❶
Services: ⬅🔄 🏕🛒⊘T🏕
Within 3 miles: 🎣🏪
Notes: 🐕 No noise after 22.30hrs. Dogs must be kept on leads. Library.

AA Pubs & Restaurants nearby: The Dove Restaurant with Rooms, ALBURGH, IP20 0EP, 01986 788315

Fox & Goose Inn, FRESSINGFIELD, IP21 5PB, 01379 586247

NORTHAMPTONSHIRE

BULWICK
Map 11 SP99

Places to visit

Lyveden New Bield, LYVEDEN NEW BIELD, PE8 5AT, 01832 205358
www.nationaltrust.org.uk

NEW New Lodge Farm Caravan & Camping Site
►►►► 80%

tel: 01780 450493 **New Lodge Farm NN17 3DU**
email: shop@newlodgefarm.com
dir: *On A43 between Corby (5m) & Stamford (10m) turn right at Laxton & Harringworth junct. Site signed.* **grid ref:** SP959951

Simon and Sarah Singlehurst have worked hard in creating this beautiful adults-only site on their working farm in rural Northamptonshire. The result is impressive - 52 large, fully serviced and level pitches (27 with hardstandings), all with views over the farm and rolling countryside. The heated toilet and amenity block is located in a beautifully restored stone barn, as is the site reception. The farm boasts an award-winning farm shop that sells home-reared meats, bread, cakes and locally grown fruit and vegetables. Attached to the shop is a cosy café with a patio area overlooking the site; here breakfasts, lunches and afternoon teas are served. The site is situated in the heart of Rockingham Forest, making it a good base for visiting Stamford, Oundle and Uppingham. 4 acre site. 72 touring pitches. 25 hardstandings. Caravan pitches. Motorhome pitches. Tent pitches.

Open: 3 Apr-Oct **Last arrival:** 20.00hrs **Last departure:** noon
Pitches: * ⇌ £21.50-£25 ⇌ £21.50-£25 ▲ £15
Facilities: ⬅⊙🅟✳❤🛒 WiFi 🖥 ♻ ❶
Services: ⬅🔄 🏕⊘T🏕🚲
Within 3 miles: 🎣🏪U
Notes: Adults only. No noise after 23.00hrs. Dogs must be kept on leads.
AA Pubs & Restaurants nearby: The Queen's Head, BULWICK, NN17 3DY, 01780 450272

LEISURE: 🏊 Indoor swimming pool 🏊 Outdoor swimming pool ⚠ Children's playground 🎣 Kid's club 🎾 Tennis court 🎱 Games room 📺 Separate TV room ⛳ golf course 🚣 Boats for hire 🎬 Cinema 🎵 Entertainment 🎣 Fishing ◉ Mini golf 🏄 Watersports 🏋 Gym 🏟 Sports field Spa U Stables
FACILITIES: 🛁 Bath 🚿 Shower ⊙ Electric shaver 🅟 Hairdryer ✳ Ice Pack Facility ❤ Disabled facilities 📞 Public telephone 🛒 Shop on site or within 200yds 🏪 Mobile shop (calls at least 5 days a week) 🍖 BBQ area 🎪 Picnic area WiFi Wi-fi 🖥 Internet access ♻ Recycling ❶ Tourist info 🐕 Dog exercise area

NORTHUMBERLAND

BAMBURGH	Map 21 NU13

Places to visit

Chillingham Wild Cattle Park, CHILLINGHAM, NE66 5NP, 01668 215250
www.chillinghamwildcattle.com

Great for kids: Bamburgh Castle, BAMBURGH, NE69 7DF, 01668 214515
www.bamburghcastle.com

Waren Caravan & Camping Park
►►►►83%

tel: 01668 214366 & 07730 129619 **Waren Mill NE70 7EE**
email: waren@meadowhead.co.uk
dir: *2m E of town. From A1 onto B1342 signed Bamburgh. Take unclassified road past Waren Mill, signed Budle.* **grid ref:** *NU155343*

An attractive seaside site with footpath access to the beach, surrounded by a slightly sloping grassy embankment giving shelter to caravans. The park offers excellent facilities, including smartened up toilet/shower blocks, which have several family bathrooms, new fully serviced pitches, and the on-site restaurant serves a good breakfast. There are also wooden 'wigwams' to rent. 4 acre site. 150 touring pitches. 24 hardstandings. Caravan pitches. Motorhome pitches. Tent pitches. 300 statics. 8 wooden pods.

Open: Apr-Oct **Last arrival:** 20.00hrs **Last departure:** noon

Pitches: ⌂ ⌂ ▲ ⌂

Leisure: ⌂ ⌂ ⌂

Facilities: ⌂ ⌂ ⌂ ⌂ ⌂ ⌂ ⌂ ⌂ ⌂ ⌂ ⌂ ⌂ ⌂ ⌂ ⌂ ⌂

Services: ⌂ ⌂ ⌂ ⌂ ⌂ ⌂ ⌂ ⌂ ⌂ ⌂

Within 3 miles: ⌂ ⌂ ⌂ ⌂ ⌂

Notes: Dogs must be kept on leads. 100 acres of private heathland.
AA Pubs & Restaurants nearby: The Olde Ship Inn, SEAHOUSES, NE68 7RD,
01665 720200
Blue Bell Hotel, BELFORD, NE70 7NE, 01668 213543
Waren House Hotel, BAMBURGH, NE70 7EE, 01668 214581

Glororum Caravan Park
►►►►81%

tel: 01670 860256 **Glororum Farm NE69 7AW**
email: enquiries@northumbrianleisure.co.uk
dir: *Exit A1 at junct with B1341 (Purdy's Lodge). In 3.5m left onto unclassified road. Site 300yds on left.* **grid ref:** *NU166334*

A pleasantly situated site in an open countryside setting with good views of Bamburgh Castle. A popular holiday destination where tourers have their own separate area – 42 excellent, well-spaced, fully serviced pitches have a lush grass area in addition to the hardstanding. This field also has an excellent purpose-built amenities block with a smartly clad interior and modern, efficient fittings. 6 acre site. 43 touring pitches. 43 hardstandings. 30 seasonal pitches. Caravan pitches. Motorhome pitches. 170 statics.

Open: Mar-end Nov **Last arrival:** 18.00hrs **Last departure:** noon

Pitches: ⌂ ⌂

Leisure: ⌂ ⌂

Facilities: ⌂ ⌂ ⌂ ⌂ ⌂ ⌂ ⌂ ⌂ ⌂ ⌂ ⌂ ⌂

Services: ⌂ ⌂ ⌂ ⌂

Within 3 miles: ⌂ ⌂ ⌂ ⌂ ⌂ ⌂

Notes: No commercial vehicles, no noise after 23.00hrs. Dogs must be kept on leads.
AA Pubs & Restaurants nearby: The Olde Ship Inn, SEAHOUSES, NE68 7RD,
01665 720200
The Bamburgh Castle Inn, SEAHOUSES, NE68 7SQ, 01665 720283
Blue Bell Hotel, BELFORD, NE70 7NE, 01668 213543

BELFORD	Map 21 NU13

Places to visit

Bamburgh Castle, BAMBURGH, NE69 7DF, 01668 214515
www.bamburghcastle.com

Lindisfarne Castle, HOLY ISLAND [LINDISFARNE], TD15 2SH, 01289 389244
www.nationaltrust.org.uk

PREMIER PARK

South Meadows Caravan Park
►►►►►90%

tel: 01668 213326 **South Rd NE70 7DP**
email: info@southmeadows.co.uk
dir: *From A1 between Alnwick & Berwick-upon-Tweed take B6349 towards Belford, at right bend site signed, turn left, site on right.* **grid ref:** *NU115331*

South Meadows has become a top quality touring and holiday park. Set in open countryside, it is extremely spacious and no expense has been spared in its landscaping and redevelopment. Tree planting on a grand scale has been carried out, grassy areas are expertly mown and all pitches are fully serviced. The solar heated amenity block is ultra modern, with quality fittings and smart family rooms; everywhere is spotlessly clean and fresh. There's an adventure playground complete with a zip-wire and even dogs have two walking areas, one in a bluebell wood. 50 acre site. 120 touring pitches. 71 hardstandings. 67 seasonal pitches. Caravan pitches. Motorhome pitches. Tent pitches. 55 statics.

Open: all year **Last departure:** 16.00hrs

Pitches: ⌂ ⌂ ▲

Leisure: ⌂ ⌂

Facilities: ⌂ ⌂ ⌂ ⌂ ⌂ ⌂ ⌂ ⌂ ⌂ ⌂ ⌂

Services: ⌂ ⌂ ⌂ ⌂ ⌂ ⌂ ⌂

Within 3 miles: ⌂ ⌂ ⌂

Notes: Minimum noise after 23.00hrs, under 12s must be supervised in toilet blocks. Dogs must be kept on leads.
AA Pubs & Restaurants nearby: Blue Bell Hotel, BELFORD, NE70 7NE, 01668 213543

PITCHES: ⌂ Caravans ⌂ Motorhomes ▲ Tents ⌂ Glamping-style accommodation **SERVICES:** ⌂ Electric hook up ⌂ Launderette ⌂ Licensed bar
⌂ Calor Gas ⌂ Camping Gaz ⌂ Toilet fluid ⌂ Café/Restaurant ⌂ Fast Food/Takeaway ⌂ Battery charging ⌂ Baby care ⌂ Motorvan service point
ABBREVIATIONS: BH/bank hols – bank holidays Etr – Easter Spring BH – Spring Bank Holiday fr – from hrs – hours m – mile mdnt – midnight
rdbt – roundabout rs – restricted service wk – week wknd – weekend x-rds – cross roads ⌂ No credit or debit cards ⌂ No dogs ⌂ Children of all ages accepted

BELLINGHAM
Map 21 NY88

Places to visit
Wallington, CAMBO, NE61 4AR, 01670 773600
www.nationaltrust.org.uk/wallington

PREMIER PARK

Bellingham Camping & Caravanning Club Site
▶▶▶▶▶83%

tel: 01434 220175 & 0845 130 7633 **Brown Rigg NE48 2JY**
dir: *From A69 take A6079 N to Chollerford & B6320 to Bellingham. Pass Forestry Commission land, site 0.5m S of Bellingham.* **grid ref:** *NY835826*

A beautiful and peaceful campsite set in the glorious Northumberland National Park. Exceptionally well managed, it has improved significantly in 2014 under the management of the passionate new owners, who offer high levels of customer care, maintenance and cleanliness. The excellent toilet facilities are spotlessly clean. Improvements include the installation of new family washrooms, a recreation room, a campers' kitchen and a drying room. There are four camping pods for hire. This is a perfect base for exploring an undiscovered part of England, and it is handily placed for visiting the beautiful Northumberland coast. 5 acre site. 64 touring pitches. 42 hardstandings. Caravan pitches. Motorhome pitches. Tent pitches. 4 wooden pods.

Open: 15 Mar-3 Nov **Last arrival:** 20.00hrs **Last departure:** noon

Pitches: 🚐 🚏 Å 🛖

Leisure: /🛝

Facilities: 🌳 ⊙ �📺 ✳ 🔥 🕒 🛎 🚻 📶 🖥 ♻ ❶

Services: 🚰 🗑 🔒 🧼 🚰 🛒 🛄

Within 3 miles: 🚶 🎣 🛒 🗑

Notes: Site gates closed & quiet time 23.00hrs-07.00hrs. Dogs must be kept on leads.

AA Pubs & Restaurants nearby: The Pheasant Inn, FALSTONE, NE48 1DD, 01434 240382

BERWICK-UPON-TWEED

Places to visit
Berwick-upon-Tweed Barracks, BERWICK-UPON-TWEED, TD15 1DF, 01289 304493 www.english-heritage.org.uk/daysout/properties/berwick-upon-tweed-barracks-and-main-guard

Paxton House, Gallery & Country Park, BERWICK-UPON-TWEED, TD15 1SZ, 01289 386291 www.paxtonhouse.com

Great for kids: Norham Castle, NORHAM, TD15 2JY, 01289 382329 www.english-heritage.org.uk/daysout/properties/norham-castle

BERWICK-UPON-TWEED
Map 21 NT95

Haggerston Castle
HOLIDAY CENTRE 80%

tel: 0871 231 0865 & 01289 381333 **Beal TD15 2PA**
email: haggerstoncastle@haven.com **web:** www.haven.com/haggerstoncastle
dir: *On A1, 7m S of Berwick-upon-Tweed, site signed.* **grid ref:** *NU041435*

A large holiday centre with a very well equipped touring park, offering comprehensive holiday activities. The entertainment complex contains amusements for the whole family, and there are several bars, an adventure playground, boating on the lake, a children's club, a 9-hole golf course, tennis courts, and various eating outlets. Please note that this site does not accept tents. 100 acre site. 132 touring pitches. 132 hardstandings. Caravan pitches. Motorhome pitches. 1200 statics.

Open: mid Mar-end Oct (rs mid Mar-May & Sep-Oct some facilities may be reduced) **Last arrival:** anytime **Last departure:** 10.00hrs

Pitches: 🚐 🚏

Leisure: 🏊 /🛝 👋 🎾 🎵 ♪

Facilities: 🌳 ⊙ ✳ 🔥 🛎 🚻 📶 🖥 ♻ ❶

Services: 🚰 🗑 🍴 🔒 🍽 🛒

Within 3 miles: 🚶 🚣 ◎ 🛒 🗑 ⛓

Notes: No commercial vehicles, no bookings by persons under 21yrs unless a family booking, max 2 dogs per booking, certain dog breeds banned. Dogs must be kept on leads.

AA Pubs & Restaurants nearby: Blue Bell Hotel, BELFORD, NE70 7NE, 01668 213543

See advert on opposite page

LEISURE: 🏊 Indoor swimming pool 🏊 Outdoor swimming pool /🛝 Children's playground 👋 Kid's club 🎾 Tennis court 🎱 Games room ⬜ Separate TV room 🏌 golf course 🚣 Boats for hire 🎬 Cinema 🎵 Entertainment 🎣 Fishing ◎ Mini golf 🏄 Watersports 🏋 Gym 🏟 Sports field Spa ⛓ Stables
FACILITIES: 🛁 Bath 🚿 Shower ⊙ Electric shaver 🔥 Hairdryer ✳ Ice Pack Facility ⚿ Disabled facilities 🕒 Public telephone 🛒 Shop on site or within 200yds 🛒 Mobile shop (calls at least 5 days a week) 🍴 BBQ area 🎪 Picnic area 📶 Wi-fi 🖥 Internet access ♻ Recycling ❶ Tourist info 🐕 Dog exercise area

Ord House Country Park
►►►►► 85%

Best of British

GOLD

tel: 01289 305288 **East Ord TD15 2NS**
email: enquiries@ordhouse.co.uk
dir: At rdbt junct of A1 (Berwick bypass) & A698 take exit signed East Ord, follow brown camping signs. **grid ref:** NT982515

A very well-run park set in the pleasant grounds of an 18th-century country house. Touring pitches are marked and well spaced – some are fully serviced. The very modern toilet facilities include family bath and shower suites, and first-class disabled rooms. There is an exceptional outdoor leisure shop that stocks a good range of camping and caravanning spares, as well as clothing and equipment, and an attractive licensed club selling bar meals. The provision for children is excellent, with a fantastic adventure playground, miniature golf, a football field and a new soft play area in the clubhouse. 42 acre site. 79 touring pitches. 46 hardstandings. 30 seasonal pitches. Caravan pitches. Motorhome pitches. Tent pitches. 255 statics. 10 wooden pods.

Open: all year **Last arrival:** 23.00hrs **Last departure:** noon
Pitches: * 🚐 £17.50-£28 🚐 £17.50-£28 ▲ £17.50-£28 🏠
Leisure: 🎱 🎡
Facilities: 🚾 🅿️ ⊙ 🍳 ⚒ ♿ 📷 🗄️ 🎯 📶 ♻️ 🐾 🔧
Services: 🔌 🗄️ 🍺 🧺 🛢️ 🚰 🛒 🍴 ⛽ 🛒 🚽
Within 3 miles: ⛷️ 🎣 ⛳ 🛒 ◎ 🛒

Notes: No noise after mdnt. Dogs must be kept on leads. Crazy golf, table tennis.
AA Pubs & Restaurants nearby: The Wheatsheaf at Swinton, SWINTON, TD11 3JJ, 01890 860257

Old Mill Caravan Site
►► 80%

tel: 01289 381279 & 07971 411625 **West Kyloe Farm, Fenwick TD15 2PG**
email: teresasmalley@westkyloe.demon.co.uk
dir: A1 onto B6353, 9m S of Berwick-upon-Tweed. Road signed to Lowick/Fenwick. Site 1.5m signed on left. **grid ref:** NU055401

Small, secluded site accessed through a farm complex, and overlooking a mill pond complete with resident ducks. Some pitches are in a walled garden, and the amenity block is simple but well kept. Delightful walks can be enjoyed on the 600-acre farm. A holiday cottage is also available. 2.5 acre site. 12 touring pitches. Caravan pitches. Motorhome pitches. Tent pitches.

Open: Apr-Oct **Last arrival:** 19.00hrs **Last departure:** 11.00hrs
Pitches: 🚐 🚐 ▲
Facilities: 🅿️ ⊙ ♿ 📷 ♻️ 🎯 🔧
Services: 🔌 🚽
Within 3 miles: 🛒

Notes: 🚫 No gazebos or open fires. Dogs must be kept on leads. Wet room.
AA Pubs & Restaurants nearby: Blue Bell Hotel, BELFORD, NE70 7NE, 01668 213543

This symbol indicates that a site offers glamping-style accommodation

BERWICK-UPON-TWEED *continued*

Berwick Holiday Park
HOLIDAY HOME PARK 84%

tel: 01289 307113 **Magdalene Fields TD15 1NE**
email: berwick@haven.com **web:** www.haven.com/berwick
dir: *From A1 follow Berwick-upon-Tweed signs. At Morrisons/McDonalds rdbt take 2nd exit. At mini rdbt straight on, into North Rd (pass Shell garage on left). At next mini rdbt 1st exit into Northumberland Ave. Park at end.* **grid ref:** NT998535

This all-happening, static-only holiday park has direct access to a beach on the edge of Berwick, and offers exciting family activities and entertainment including the FunWorks Amusement Centre and a multisports court.

Open: Mar-Oct

Change over day: Mon, Fri, Sat

Arrival and departure times: Please contact the site

Statics: 204 Sleeps 6-8 Bedrms 2-3 Bathrms 1-2 Toilets 1-2 Microwave Freezer TV Sky/FTV Elec inc Gas inc Grass area

Children: 🚼 Cots Highchair **Dogs:** 2 on leads No dangerous dogs

Leisure: 🏊 🏊 Cycle hire 🎣 🛝

HALTWHISTLE   Map 21 NY76

Places to visit

Corbridge Roman Site and Museum, CORBRIDGE, NE45 5NT, 01434 632349 www.english-heritage.org.uk/daysout/properties/corbridge-roman-town-hadrians-wall

Chesters Roman Fort, WALWICK, NE46 4EP, 01434 681379 www.english-heritage.org.uk/daysout/properties/chesters-roman-fort-and-museum-hadrians-wall

---

PREMIER PARK

NEW Herding Hill Farm
►►►►►86%

tel: 01434 320175 **Shield Hill NE49 9NW**
email: bookings@herdinghillfarm.co.uk
dir: *From W: exit A69 at Greenhead onto B6318 towards Chollerford. Follow brown campsite signs. From E: exit A69 at Corbridge onto A68 N, left onto B6318 towards Greenhead. Approx 12m, follow campsite signs.* **grid ref:** NY712649

In an idyllic moorland location above Haltwhistle, close to Hadrian's Wall, this beautifully developed working farm site is geared to families and offers a mix of accommodation – excellent tent pitches, quality hardstandings, a bunkhouse sleeping 28, a 6-berth lodge, and a community of tipis and wooden wigwams. The upmarket amenity block is really ultra-modern – the internal red and grey partitioning really sets off the very high standard of fixtures and fittings, and the underfloor heating is very welcoming. A drying room, barbecues and firebaskets, a playground and petting farm, an excellent shop and café, and activities such as star-gazing, geo-caching, and walking along Hadrian's Wall complete the

package. This is a top-class site developed over the last few years by the hands-on owners. 4.86 acre site. 44 touring pitches. 11 hardstandings. Caravan pitches. Motorhome pitches. Tent pitches. 4 tipis. 8 wooden pods.

Open: Feb-3 Jan **Last arrival:** 21.00hrs **Last departure:** 11.00hrs

Pitches: 🚐 £20-£24 🚍 £20-£24 ▲ £20-£24 🏕

Leisure: 🛝

Facilities: 🛁 🚿 ⊙ 🌡 ☀ 🔌 🖅 🛒 🎪 📶 ♻ ❼

Services: 🚐 🗑 🛒 🚿 Ⓣ 🛒 ↯

Notes: No noise after 23.00hrs. Dogs must be kept on leads. Unisex sauna.

HEXHAM   Map 21 NY96

Places to visit

Vindolanda (Chesterholm), BARDON MILL, NE47 7JN, 01434 344277 www.vindolanda.com

Temple of Mithras (Hadrian's Wall), CARRAWBROUGH, 0870 333 1181 www.english-heritage.org.uk/daysout/properties/temple-of-mithras-carrawburgh-hadrians-wall

Great for kids: Housesteads Roman Fort, HOUSESTEADS, NE47 6NN, 01434 344363 www.english-heritage.org.uk/daysout/properties/housesteads-roman-fort-hadrians-wall

---

Hexham Racecourse Caravan Site
►►►70%

tel: 01434 606847 & 606881 **Hexham Racecourse NE46 2JP**
email: hexrace.caravan@btconnect.com
dir: *From Hexham take B6305 signed Allendale/Alston. Left in 3m signed to racecourse. Site 1.5m on right.* **grid ref:** NY919623

A part-level and part-sloping grassy site situated on a racecourse overlooking Hexhamshire Moors. The facilities, although clean, are of an older but functional type. 4 acre site. 50 touring pitches. Caravan pitches. Motorhome pitches. Tent pitches.

Open: May-Sep **Last arrival:** 20.00hrs **Last departure:** noon

Pitches: * 🚐 £14-£17 🚍 £14-£17 ▲ fr £10

Leisure: 🛝 🎱

Facilities: 🚿 ⊙ 🌡 ☀ Ⓝ 🛒 🎪 ❼

Services: 🚐 🗑 🛒 🚿 🛒

Within 3 miles: 🚴 🎣 🍴 🏌 ◎ 🛒 🏴

Notes: No noise after 23.00hrs. Dogs must be kept on leads.

AA Pubs & Restaurants nearby: Miners Arms Inn, HEXHAM, NE46 4PW, 01434 603909 Dipton Mill Inn, HEXHAM, NE46 1YA, 01434 606577 Rat Inn, HEXHAM, NE46 4LN, 01434 602814

NORTH SEATON
Map 21 NZ28

Places to visit

Woodhorn, ASHINGTON, NE63 9YF, 01670 624455 www.experiencewoodhorn.com

Morpeth Chantry Bagpipe Museum, MORPETH, NE61 1PD, 01670 624455
www.experiencewoodhorn.com/morpeth-bagpipe-museum

Sandy Bay
HOLIDAY CENTRE 75%

GOLD

tel: 0871 664 9764 **NE63 9YD**
email: sandy.bay@park-resorts.com
dir: *From A1 at Seaton Burn take A19 signed Tyne Tunnel. Then A189 signed Ashington, approx 8m, at rdbt right onto B1334 towards Newbiggin-by-the-Sea. Site on right.*
grid ref: *NZ302858*

A beach-side holiday park on the outskirts of the small village of North Seaton, within easy reach of Newcastle. The site is handily placed for exploring the magnificent coastline and countryside of Northumberland, but for those who do not wish to travel, it offers the full range of holiday centre attractions, both for parents and their children. 48 touring pitches. Caravan pitches. Motorhome pitches. 396 statics.

Open: Apr-Oct **Last arrival:** anytime **Last departure:** noon

Pitches: ⊕ ⇔

Leisure: 🏊 ⚲ 🖐 🎵

Facilities: 🕯 🏵 🕒 🅂 WiFi 🖥

Services: ⊕ 🖭 🍽 🍴 📷

Within 3 miles: 🖉 🅂 🖭

Notes: Koi carp lake.

SEAHOUSES
Map 21 NU23

Places to visit

Bamburgh Castle, BAMBURGH, NE69 7DF, 01668 214515
www.bamburghcastle.com

Lindisfarne Castle, HOLY ISLAND [LINDISFARNE], TD15 2SH, 01289 389244
www.nationaltrust.org.uk

NEW Westfield Paddock
►70%

tel: 01665 478988 & 721380 **Westfield Farmhouse NE68 7UR**
email: info@westfieldpaddock.co.uk
dir: *From A1 (15m N of Alnwick) take B1341 to Bamburgh. Right to Seahouses on B1340. In 2m right to Elford. Site 1.5m at x-rds.* **grid ref:** *NU203318*

A peaceful, adults-only site set in a lush grassy paddock beside the owners' house. Popular with self-sufficient motorhome and caravan owners (no tents allowed),

each of the 10 pitches has its own water and electricity. It does not have toilets and showers, and therefore own facilities are essential. Fresh eggs can be bought from the owners.

Open: Mar-2 Jan **Last arrival:** 21.00hrs **Last departure:** 11.00hrs

Pitches: * ⊕ £12-£18 ⇔ £12-£18

Facilities: ❄ 🖐 WiFi 🖥 ♻ 🛈

Services: ⊕ 🖭 📷

Within 3 miles: 🖉 🖉 ◎ 🛶 🅂 🖭 ∪

Notes: Adults only. Dogs must be kept on leads.

AA Pubs & Restaurants nearby: The Bamburgh Castle Inn, SEAHOUSES, NE68 7SQ,
01665 720283

WOOLER
Map 21 NT92

Places to visit

Chillingham Castle, CHILLINGHAM, NE66 5NJ, 01668 215359
www.chillingham-castle.com

Great for kids: Chillingham Wild Cattle Park, CHILLINGHAM, NE66 5NP,
01668 215250 www.chillinghamwildcattle.com

Riverside Leisure Park
►►►78%

tel: 01668 281447 **South Rd NE71 6NJ**
email: reception@riverside-wooler.co.uk
dir: *From S: A1 to Morpeth, A697 signed Wooler & Coldstream. In Wooler, park on left. From N: From Berwick-upon-Tweed on A1, 1st right signed Wooler (B6525). Through Wooler on A697. Park on right.* **grid ref:** *NT993279*

This is the sister park to Thurston Manor Leisure Park at Dunbar in East Lothian. It is set in the heart of stunning Northumberland countryside on the edge of Wooler Water. Very much family orientated, the park offers excellent leisure facilities including swimming pools, a bar and a restaurant, weekend entertainment and riverside and woodland walks. Fly fishing for rainbow trout is possible at the site's own lake. 90 acre site. 50 touring pitches. 50 hardstandings. 35 seasonal pitches. Caravan pitches. Motorhome pitches. Tent pitches. 350 statics. 4 wooden pods.

Open: all year (rs Nov-Mar swimming pool closed) **Last departure:** noon

Pitches: ⊕ ⇔ ▲ ∩

Leisure: 🏊 ⚲ 🖐 😊 ◕ 🎵 Spa

Facilities: 🕯 ⊙ 🏵 ❄ ⚷ 🕒 🅂 🖐 WiFi ♻ 🛈

Services: ⊕ 🖭 🍽 🛢 ⊘ 🖭 🍴 🍼 🚻

Within 3 miles: 🖉 🖉 🅂 🖭 ∪

Notes: No noise after 22.00hrs. Dogs must be kept on leads.

AA Pubs & Restaurants nearby: The Red Lion Inn, MILFIELD, NE71 6JD, 01668 216224

NOTTINGHAMSHIRE

CHURCH LANEHAM — Map 17 SK87

Places to visit

Newark Air Museum, NEWARK-ON-TRENT, NG24 2NY, 01636 707170
www.newarkairmuseum.org

Trentfield Farm
►►► 81%

tel: 01777 228651 **DN22 0NJ**
email: post@trentfield.co.uk
dir: A1 onto A57 towards Lincoln for 6m. Left signed Laneham, 1.5m, through Laneham & Church Laneham (pass Ferryboat pub on left). Site 300yds on right. **grid ref:** SK815774

A delightfully rural and level grass park tucked away on the banks of the River Trent. The park has its own river frontage with free coarse fishing available to park residents. The cosy local pub, which serves food, is under the same ownership. 34 acre site. 45 touring pitches. 20 seasonal pitches. Caravan pitches. Motorhome pitches. Tent pitches.

Open: Etr-Nov **Last arrival:** 20.00hrs **Last departure:** noon
Pitches: * ⊕ fr £18 ⊕ fr £18 ▲ fr £10
Facilities: ⬠⊙⧄✳⬥⬠☐⬠⬧ WiFi ♻ ❷
Services: ⊕⬠⬠⬠ **Within 3 miles:** ⬠⬠⬠⬠⬠
Notes: Dogs must be kept on leads. 24-hour mini shop.

MANSFIELD — Map 16 SK56

Places to visit

Sherwood Forest Country Park & Visitor Centre, EDWINSTOWE, NG21 9HN, 01623 823202 www.nottinghamshire.gov.uk/sherwoodforestcp

Tall Trees Touring Park
►►► 86%

tel: 01623 626503 & 07770 661957 **Old Mill Ln, Forest Town NG19 0JP**
email: info@talltreestouringpark.co.uk **web:** www.talltreestouringpark.co.uk
dir: A60 from Mansfield towards Worksop. After 1m turn right at lights into Old Mill Lane. Site approx 0.5m on left. **grid ref:** SK551626

A very pleasant park situated just on the outskirts of Mansfield and within easy walking distance of shops and restaurants. It is surrounded on three sides by trees

and shrubs, and securely set at the back of the residential park. This site has a modern amenities block, a fishing lake to the rear of the site and an extra grassed area to give more space for caravans and tents. 10 acre site. 37 touring pitches. 10 hardstandings. Caravan pitches. Motorhome pitches. Tent pitches.

Open: all year **Last arrival:** anytime **Last departure:** anytime
Pitches: * ⊕ £12.50-£17.50 ⊕ £12.50-£17.50 ▲ £12.50-£17.50
Leisure: ⬠ ❂
Facilities: ⬠⊙⧄⬥⬠☐⬠⬧♻❷
Services: ⊕⬠
Within 3 miles: ⬠⬠⬠⬠⬠
Notes: No noise after mdnt. Dogs must be kept on leads.
AA Pubs & Restaurants nearby: Forest Lodge, EDWINSTOWE, NG21 9QA, 01623 824443
Fox & Hounds, BLIDWORTH, NG21 0NW, 01623 792383

NEWARK

See Southwell

RADCLIFFE ON TRENT — Map 11 SK63

Places to visit

Nottingham Castle Museum & Art Gallery, NOTTINGHAM, NG1 6EL, 0115 876 1400 www.nottinghamcity.gov.uk/Castle

Wollaton Hall, Gardens & Deer Park, NOTTINGHAM, NG8 2AE, 0115 915 3900 www.nottingham.gov.uk/wollatonhall

Thornton's Holt Camping Park
►►► 79%

tel: 0115 933 2125 & 933 4204 **Stragglethorpe Rd, Stragglethorpe NG12 2JZ**
email: camping@thorntons-holt.co.uk
dir: Take A52, 3m E of Nottingham. Turn S at lights towards Cropwell Bishop. Site 0.5m on left. Or A46 SE of Nottingham. N at lights. Site 2.5m on right. **grid ref:** SK638377

A well-run family site in former meadowland, with pitches located among young trees and bushes for a rural atmosphere and outlook. The toilets are housed in converted farm buildings, and an indoor swimming pool is a popular attraction. 13 acre site. 155 touring pitches. 35 hardstandings. 20 seasonal pitches. Caravan pitches. Motorhome pitches. Tent pitches.

Open: Apr-6 Nov **Last arrival:** 20.00hrs **Last departure:** noon
Pitches: ⊕ ⊕ ▲
Leisure: ⬠ ⬠
Facilities: ⬠⊙⧄✳⬥⬠☐⬧♻❷
Services: ⊕⬠⬠⬠☐⬠⬠
Within 3 miles: ⬠⬠⬠⬠⬠⬠⬠⬠
Notes: Noise curfew at 22.00hrs. Dogs must be kept on leads.
AA Pubs & Restaurants nearby: Ye Olde Trip to Jerusalem, NOTTINGHAM, NG1 6AD, 0115 947 3171

Fellows Morton & Clayton, NOTTINGHAM, NG1 7EH, 0115 950 6795

World Service, NOTTINGHAM, NG1 6AF, 0115 847 5587

SOUTHWELL   Map 17 SK65

Places to visit

The Workhouse, SOUTHWELL, NG25 0PT, 01636 817260
www.nationaltrust.org.uk/theworkhouse

New Hall Farm Touring Park
▶▶▶ 78%

tel: 01623 883041 **New Hall Farm, New Hall Ln NG22 8BS**
email: enquiries@newhallfarm.co.uk
dir: From A614 at White Post Modern Farm Centre, turn E signed Southwell. Immediately after Edingley turn S into New Hall Ln to site. **grid ref:** SK660550

A park on a working stock farm with the elevated pitching area enjoying outstanding panoramic views. It is within a short drive of medieval Newark and Sherwood Forest. A log cabin viewing gantry offers a place to relax and take in the spectacular scenery. 2.5 acre site. 25 touring pitches. 10 hardstandings. 7 seasonal pitches. Caravan pitches. Motorhome pitches. Tent pitches.

Open: Mar-Oct **Last arrival:** 21.00hrs **Last departure:** 13.00hrs
Pitches: * ⊞ £15-£20 ⊞ £15-£20 ▲ £12-£18
Facilities: 🌲☉☀🎄🦮♻️𝒊
Services: 🔌⊡🛒
Within 3 miles: ⬇️🎣🛍️⊡↺
Notes: Adults only. 🐕 Dogs must be kept on leads.
AA Pubs & Restaurants nearby: Tom Browns Brasserie, GUNTHORPE, NG14 7FB, 0115 966 3642

TEVERSAL   Map 16 SK46

Places to visit

Hardwick Hall, HARDWICK HALL, S44 5QJ, 01246 850430
www.nationaltrust.org.uk/hardwick

PREMIER PARK

Teversal Camping & Caravanning Club Site
▷▷▷▷▷ 90%

tel: 01623 551838 **Silverhill Ln NG17 3JJ**
dir: M1 junct 28, A38 towards Mansfield. Left at lights onto B6027. At top of hill straight over at lights & left at Tesco Express. Right onto B6014, left at Carnarvon Arms, site on left. **grid ref:** SK472615

A top notch park with excellent purpose-built facilities and innovative, hands-on owners. Each pitch is spacious, the excellent toilet facilities are state-of-the-art, and there are views of, and access to, the countryside and nearby Silverhill Community Woods. Both the attention to detail and the all-round quality are truly exceptional – guests can even hire a car for a day and there is a special area for washing dogs and bikes. The site has an on-site shop. Buses for Sutton

Ashfield and Chesterfield stop just a five-minute walk from the site. A six-berth holiday caravan, a luxury ready-erected safari tent and a log cabin are available for hire. Good food pub can be found only a few minutes' walk from the site. 6 acre site. 126 touring pitches. 92 hardstandings. Caravan pitches. Motorhome pitches. Tent pitches. 1 static. 1 bell tent/yurt. 1 wooden pod.

Open: all year **Last arrival:** 20.00hrs **Last departure:** noon
Pitches: ⊞ ⊞ ▲ ⋒
Leisure: ⚘ ✪
Facilities: 🌲☉℉☀🦮♿🛍️🐕🎄WiFi♻️𝒊
Services: 🔌⊡🛢️⊘⊡↯
Within 3 miles: ⬇️🎣🛍️↺
Notes: Site gates closed 23.00hrs-07.00hrs. Dogs must be kept on leads.
AA Pubs & Restaurants nearby: The Shoulder at Hardstoft, HARDSTOFT, S45 8AF, 01246 850276

TUXFORD   Map 17 SK77

Places to visit

Museum of Lincolnshire Life, LINCOLN, LN1 3LY, 01522 782040
www.lincolnshire.gov.uk/museumoflincolnshirelife

Great for kids: Lincoln Castle, LINCOLN, LN1 3AA, 01522 782040
www.lincolnshire.gov.uk/lincolncastle

Orchard Park Touring Caravan & Camping Park
▶▶▶ 83%

tel: 01777 870228 **Marnham Rd NG22 0PY**
email: info@orchardcaravanpark.co.uk
dir: Exit A1 at Tuxford, follow brown camping signs for 0.5m, right into Marnham Rd. Site 0.75m on right. **grid ref:** SK754708

A rural site set in an old fruit orchard with spacious pitches arranged in small groups separated by shrubs; many of the pitches are served with water and electricity. A network of grass pathways and picnic clearings have been created in a woodland area, and there's a superb adventure playground. 7 acre site. 60 touring pitches. 30 hardstandings. 20 seasonal pitches. Caravan pitches. Motorhome pitches. Tent pitches.

Open: mid Mar-Oct **Last arrival:** mdnt **Last departure:** 18.00hrs
Pitches: ⊞ ⊞ ▲
Leisure: ⚘
Facilities: 🌲☉℉☀🦮♿🛍️🐕🎄WiFi🖥️♻️𝒊
Services: 🔌⊡🛢️⊘⊡🛒
Within 3 miles: 🎣🛍️↺
Notes: Dogs must be kept on leads.
AA Pubs & Restaurants nearby: The Mussel & Crab, TUXFORD, NG22 0PJ, 01777 870491

PITCHES: ⊞ Caravans ⊞ Motorhomes ▲ Tents ⋒ Glamping-style accommodation **SERVICES:** 🔌 Electric hook up ⊡ Launderette 🍷 Licensed bar 🛢️ Calor Gas ⊘ Camping Gaz ⊡ Toilet fluid 🍽️ Café/Restaurant 🍟 Fast Food/Takeaway 🔋 Battery charging 🍼 Baby care ↯ Motorvan service point
ABBREVIATIONS: BH/bank hols – bank holidays Etr – Easter Spring BH – Spring Bank Holiday fr – from hrs – hours m – mile mdnt – midnight rdbt – roundabout rs – restricted service wk – week wknd – weekend x-rds – cross roads 🚫 No credit or debit cards 🚫 No dogs 👫 Children of all ages accepted

OXFORDSHIRE

BANBURY

Map 11 SP44

Places to visit

Banbury Museum, BANBURY, OX16 2PQ, 01295 753752
www.cherwell.gov.uk/banburymuseum

Great for kids: Deddington Castle, DEDDINGTON, OX15 0TE, 0870 333 1181
www.english-heritage.org.uk/daysout/properties/deddington-castle

Bo Peep Farm Caravan Park
► ► ► ► 85%

tel: 01295 810605 **Bo Peep Farm, Aynho Rd, Adderbury OX17 3NP**
email: warden@bo-peep.co.uk
dir: 1m E of Adderbury & A4260, on B4100 (Aynho road). **grid ref:** SP481348

A delightful park with good views and a spacious feel. Four well laid out camping areas including two with hardstandings and a separate tent field are all planted with maturing shrubs and trees. The two facility blocks are built in attractive Cotswold stone. There is a bay where you can clean your caravan or motorhome, and the 'Dovecote Barn' is available for weddings/corporate events and offers on-site food at selected times. There are four miles of on-site walks through woods and on the river bank. The site is well placed for visiting Banbury and the Cotswolds. 13 acre site. 104 touring pitches. 27 seasonal pitches. Caravan pitches. Motorhome pitches. Tent pitches.

Open: Mar-Oct **Last arrival:** 20.00hrs **Last departure:** noon

Pitches: ⊕ ⇔ Å

Facilities: ⬧ ⊙ ☞ ✳ ⟊ ⓒ ⑤ ⏢ ⚲ 🆆🅸🅵🅸 🖥 ♻ 🛈

Services: ⊖ ⑤ ∅ 🅣 ☷ ⏚

Within 3 miles: ⬇ ⚲ ☞ ⑤

AA Pubs & Restaurants nearby: Ye Olde Reindeer Inn, BANBURY, OX16 5NA, 01295 270972

The Wykham Arms, BANBURY, OX15 5RX, 01295 788808

Saye and Sele Arms, BROUGHTON, OX15 5ED, 01295 263348

Find out more about this area with the *AA Guide to The Cotswolds* – see the AA.com/shop

Prefer a child-free site? See our list on page 41

Barnstones Caravan & Camping Site
► ► ► ► 83%

tel: 01295 750289 **Great Bourton OX17 1QU**
dir: Take A423 from Banbury signed Southam. In 3m turn right signed Gt Bourton & Cropredy, site 100yds on right. **grid ref:** SP455454

A popular, neatly laid-out site with plenty of hardstandings, some fully serviced pitches, a smart up-to-date toilet block, and excellent rally facilities. Well run by a very personable owner, this is an excellent value park. The site is well positioned for stopovers or for visiting nearby Banbury. 3 acre site. 49 touring pitches. 44 hardstandings. Caravan pitches. Motorhome pitches. Tent pitches.

Open: all year

Pitches: ⊕ £13-£15 ⇔ £13-£15 Å £8-£13

Leisure: Ⓐ ⚽

Facilities: ⬧ ⊙ ✳ ⟊ ⓒ ⑤ ⏢ ⚲ ♻ 🛈

Services: ⊖ ⑤ 🛢 ∅ ☷ ☷ ⏚

Within 3 miles: ⬇ ☰ 🗓 ☞ ◎ ☷ ⑤ ⑤ U

Notes: 🐾 Dogs must be kept on leads.

AA Pubs & Restaurants nearby: Ye Olde Reindeer Inn, BANBURY, OX16 5NA, 01295 270972

The Wykham Arms, BANBURY, OX15 5RX, 01295 788808

Saye and Sele Arms, BROUGHTON, OX15 5ED, 01295 263348

NEW Drayton Leisure Camping
► ► ► 76%

tel: 01295 730242 **Warwick Road (B4100) OX17 1HJ**
email: info@draytonleisure.co.uk
dir: From N: M40 junct 12 at Gaydon, B4100 to Banbury. From S: M40 junct 11 at Banbury, take B4100 towards Warmington. **grid ref:** SP434426

In a beautiful countryside setting, just two miles from the centre of Banbury and ideal for both families and couples, Drayton Leisure Park makes a convenient base for exploring the northern Cotswolds. Well maintained and level, this family-owned campsite offers many activities including golf (and golf lessons), football and a 1.5-acre fishing lake, plus a popular café and bar, and a function room that offers live music nights. There is a play area for the younger children and a games room with pool, darts and table tennis. 1.5 acre site. 75 touring pitches. 5 hardstandings. Caravan pitches. Motorhome pitches. Tent pitches.

Open: 10 Feb-Oct **Last arrival:** 19.00hrs **Last departure:** noon

Pitches: ⊕ £12-£16 ⇔ £12-£16 Å £12-£16

Leisure: Ⓐ ⬥ 🎣 🎵 ⬇

Facilities: ⬧ ⊙ ☞ ✳ ⟊ ⓒ ⑤ ⏢ ⚲ 🆆🅸🅵🅸 ♻ 🛈

Services: ⊖ ⑤ 🅣 ◎ ☷ ⏚

Within 3 miles: ⬇ ☞ ⑤ ⑤ U

Notes: Children to be supervised on & around golf range & course. Dogs must be kept on leads.

AA Pubs & Restaurants nearby: Best Western Plus Wroxton House Hotel, BANBURY, OX15 6QB, 01295 730777

Ye Olde Reindeer Inn, BANBURY, OX16 5NA, 01295 270972

LEISURE: ⬤ Indoor swimming pool ⬤ Outdoor swimming pool Ⓐ Children's playground ⬥ Kid's club ⬤ Tennis court ⬤ Games room ⬜ Separate TV room
⬇ golf course ☰ Boats for hire 🖽 Cinema 🎵 Entertainment 🎣 Fishing ◎ Mini golf ⬤ Watersports ⬥ Gym ⬤ Sports field Spa U Stables
FACILITIES: ⬥ Bath ⬧ Shower ⊙ Electric shaver ☞ Hairdryer ✳ Ice Pack Facility ⟊ Disabled facilities ⓒ Public telephone ⑤ Shop on site or within 200yds
⬤ Mobile shop (calls at least 5 days a week) ☷ BBQ area ⏢ Picnic area 🆆🅸🅵🅸 Wi-fi 🖥 Internet access ♻ Recycling 🛈 Tourist info ⚲ Dog exercise area

Places to visit

Rousham House, ROUSHAM, OX25 4QX, 01869 347110 www.rousham.org

Museum of the History of Science, OXFORD, OX1 3AZ, 01865 277280 www.mhs.ox.ac.uk

Great for kids: Oxford University Museum of Natural History, OXFORD, OX1 3PW, 01865 272950 www.oum.ox.ac.uk

Greenhill Leisure Park
►►►►87%

tel: 01869 351600 **Greenhill Farm, Station Rd OX5 3BQ**
email: info@greenhill-leisure-park.co.uk **web:** www.greenhill-leisure-park.co.uk
dir: M40 junct 9, A34 S for 3m. Take B4027 to Bletchingdon. Site 0.5m after village on left. **grid ref:** SP488178

An all-year round park, with spacious pitches, set in open countryside near the village of Bletchingdon and well placed for visiting Oxford or the Cotswolds. Fishing is available in the park's two well-stocked lakes and nearby river. This a family-friendly park and is certainly in keeping with the owner's 'where fun meets the countryside' philosophy. The facilities are very good and include a new reception and shop, with plans to add a café-bar for 2015. 7 acre site. 92 touring pitches. 44 hardstandings. 20 seasonal pitches. Caravan pitches. Motorhome pitches. Tent pitches.

Open: all year (rs Oct-Mar no dogs, games room closed) **Last arrival:** 21.00hrs (20.00hrs winter) **Last departure:** noon

Pitches: ⊞ £18-£23 ⊞ £18-£23 ▲ £15-£20

Leisure: ⚠ ❧

Facilities: ⬚⊙☂⁎⚲⑤☶⾒✉♻⚙

Services: ⚡⑤⊞⚑⬛⊘⊤⚑

Within 3 miles: ⚓⌀⑤

Notes: No camp fires or firepits. Dogs must be kept on leads.

AA Pubs & Restaurants nearby: Kings Arms Hotel, WOODSTOCK, OX20 1SU, 01993 813636

The Feathers Hotel, WOODSTOCK, OX20 1SX, 01993 812291

Diamond Farm Caravan & Camping Park
►►►►83%

tel: 01869 350909 **Islip Rd OX5 3DR**
email: warden@diamondpark.co.uk
dir: M40 junct 9, A34 S for 3m, B4027 to Bletchingdon. Site 1m on left.
grid ref: SP513170

A well-run, quiet rural site in good level surroundings, and ideal for touring the Cotswolds, situated seven miles north of Oxford in the heart of the Thames Valley. This popular park has excellent facilities, and offers a heated outdoor swimming pool, a games room for children and a small bar. 3 acre site. 37 touring pitches. 20 hardstandings. Caravan pitches. Motorhome pitches. Tent pitches.

Open: Mar-Oct (rs Mar-Apr & Sep-Oct bar & swimming pool closed) **Last arrival:** dusk
Last departure: 11.00hrs

Pitches: ⊞ ⊞ ▲

Leisure: ⚲ ⚠ ❧

Facilities: ⬚⬈⊙☂⁎⑤☶✉♻⚙

Services: ⚡⑤⚑⬛⊘⊤⚑⾒

Within 3 miles: ⚓⌀⑤

Notes: ⊗ No gazebos or campfires, no groups occupying more than 3 pitches, no noise after 22.30hrs. Dogs must be kept on leads.

AA Pubs & Restaurants nearby: Kings Arms Hotel, WOODSTOCK, OX20 1SU, 01993 813636

The Feathers Hotel, WOODSTOCK, OX20 1SX, 01993 812291

Places to visit

Minster Lovell Hall & Dovecote, MINSTER LOVELL, OX29 0RR, 0870 333 1181 www.english-heritage.org.uk/daysout/properties/minster-lovell-hall-and-dovecote

Wysdom Touring Park
►►85%

tel: 01993 823207 **Cheltenham Rd OX18 4PL**
email: geoffhayes@fsmail.net
dir: Phone for detailed directions. **grid ref:** SP248117

Owned by Burford School, this small adults' only park is very much a hidden gem being just a five-minute walk from Burford, one of prettiest towns in the Cotswolds. The pitches have good privacy; all have electricity and there are many hardstandings for caravans and motorhome. The unisex toilet facilities are very clean. This makes a good base from which to explore the Cotswolds. 25 touring pitches. Caravan pitches. Motorhome pitches.

Open: all year **Last arrival:** 21.00hrs **Last departure:** noon

Pitches: ⊞ £13-£16 ⊞ £13-£16

Facilities: ⊙

Within 3 miles: ⚓⑤⑤

Notes: Adults only. Dogs must be kept on leads.

AA Pubs & Restaurants nearby: The Lamb Inn, BURFORD, OX18 4LR, 01993 823155

The Highway Inn, BURFORD, OX18 4RG, 01993 823661

The Angel at Burford, BURFORD, OX18 4SN, 01993 822714

PITCHES: ⊞ Caravans ⊞ Motorhomes ▲ Tents ⋒ Glamping-style accommodation **SERVICES:** ⚡ Electric hook up ⑤ Launderette ⚑ Licensed bar ⬛ Calor Gas ⊘ Camping Gaz ⊤ Toilet fluid ⎯ Café/Restaurant ⾒ Fast Food/Takeaway ⚑ Battery charging ⚑ Baby care ⾒ Motorvan service point
ABBREVIATIONS: BH/bank hols – bank holidays Etr – Easter Spring BH – Spring Bank Holiday fr – from hrs – hours m – mile mdnt – midnight
rdbt – roundabout rs – restricted service wk – week wknd – weekend x-rds – cross roads ⊛ No credit or debit cards ⊗ No dogs ⋔ Children of all ages accepted

CHARLBURY
Map 11 SP31

Places to visit

Blenheim Palace, WOODSTOCK, OX20 1PP, 0800 849 6500
www.blenheimpalace.com

Minster Lovell Hall & Dovecote, MINSTER LOVELL, OX29 0RR, 0870 333 1181
www.english-heritage.org.uk/daysout/properties/minster-lovell-hall-and-dovecote

Great for kids: Cogges Witney, WITNEY, OX28 3LA, 01993 772602
www.cogges.org.uk

Cotswold View Touring Park

▶▶▶▶ 84%

tel: 01608 810314 **Enstone Rd OX7 3JH**
email: bookings@gfwiddows.co.uk
dir: *From A44 in Enstone take B4022 towards Charlbury. Follow site signs. Site 1m from Charlbury.* **grid ref:** *SP365210*

A good Cotswold site, well screened and with attractive views across the countryside. The toilet facilities include fully-equipped family rooms and bathrooms, and there are spacious, sheltered pitches, some with hardstandings. Breakfasts and takeaway food are available from the shop. The site has camping pods for hire. This is the perfect location for exploring the Cotswolds and anyone heading for the Charlbury Music Festival. 10 acre site. 125 touring pitches. Caravan pitches. Motorhome pitches. Tent pitches. Wooden pods.

Open: Etr or Apr-Oct **Last arrival:** 21.00hrs **Last departure:** noon
Pitches: 🚐 🚏 Å 🏠
Leisure: /A 🏊 🎣
Facilities: 🛁 🚿 ⊙ 🗲 ✳ 🚿 🕒 💲 🛒 🚽
Services: 🚐 💲 🛒 🖊 T 🛒 ⊥
Within 3 miles: 🗲 💲 🛒
Notes: Off licence, skittle alley, chess, boules.
AA Pubs & Restaurants nearby: The Bull Inn, CHARLBURY, OX7 3RR, 01608 810689
The Crown Inn, CHURCH ENSTONE, OX7 4NN, 01608 677262

HENLEY-ON-THAMES

Places to visit

Greys Court, HENLEY-ON-THAMES, RG9 4PG, 01491 628529
www.nationaltrust.org.uk

River & Rowing Museum, HENLEY-ON-THAMES, RG9 1BF, 01491 415600
www.rrm.co.uk

Great for kids: The LEGOLAND Windsor Resort, WINDSOR, SL4 4AY, 0871 222 2001 www.legoland.co.uk

LEISURE: 🏊 Indoor swimming pool 🏊 Outdoor swimming pool /A Children's playground 👶 Kid's club 🎾 Tennis court 🎯 Games room 📺 Separate TV room ⛳ golf course ⛵ Boats for hire 🎬 Cinema 🎵 Entertainment 🎣 Fishing ◎ Mini golf 🏄 Watersports 🏋 Gym ⚽ Sports field Spa ♨ Stables
FACILITIES: 🛁 Bath 🚿 Shower ⊙ Electric shaver 🗲 Hairdryer ✳ Ice Pack Facility ♿ Disabled facilities 📞 Public telephone 💲 Shop on site or within 200yds 🏪 Mobile shop (calls at least 5 days a week) 🍖 BBQ area 🏕 Picnic area 📶 Wi-fi 🌐 Internet access ♻ Recycling ℹ Tourist info 🐕 Dog exercise area

HENLEY-ON-THAMES
Map 5 SU78

PREMIER PARK

Swiss Farm Touring & Camping

►►►►► 90%

Best of British

tel: 01491 573419 **Marlow Rd RG9 2HY**
email: enquiries@swissfarmcamping.co.uk **web:** www.swissfarmcamping.co.uk
dir: *From Henley-on-Thames take A4155, towards Marlow. 1st left after rugby club.*
grid ref: *SU759837*

This park enjoys an excellent location within easy walking distance of the town and is perfect for those visiting the Henley Regatta (but booking is essential at that time). Pitches are spacious and well appointed, and include some that are fully serviced. There is a tasteful bar plus a nice outdoor swimming pool. Luxury lodge for hire. 6 acre site. 140 touring pitches. 100 hardstandings. Caravan pitches. Motorhome pitches. Tent pitches. 6 statics.

Open: Mar-Oct (rs Mar-May & Oct pool closed) **Last arrival:** 21.00hrs
Last departure: noon

Pitches: 🚐 £21.50-£29 🚐 £21.50-£29 🔺 £18.50-£25.50

Leisure: 🏊 🎿 **Facilities:** 📶◉♇✕🅰♿⦵🗑🚿🌮 ♻ 🔧

Services: 🔌🗑🔋🚿🚽🍽️⛽ **Within 3 miles:** 🚶🎣♿🎿🗑🔄

Notes: No groups, no dogs during high season. Dogs must be kept on leads.

AA Pubs & Restaurants nearby: The Little Angel, HENLEY-ON-THAMES, RG9 2LS, 01491 411008

Crooked Billet, STOKE ROW, RG9 5PU, 01491 681048

The Five Horseshoes, HENLEY-ON-THAMES, RG9 6EX, 01491 641282

See advert on opposite page

STANDLAKE
Map 5 SP30

Places to visit

Buscot Park, BUSCOT, SN7 8BU, 01367 240786 www.buscotpark.com

Harcourt Arboretum, OXFORD, OX44 9PX, 01865 343501
www.botanic-garden.ox.ac.uk

Great for kids: Cotswold Wildlife Park and Gardens, BURFORD, OX18 4JP, 01993 823006 www.cotswoldwildlifepark.co.uk

PREMIER PARK

Lincoln Farm Park Oxfordshire

►►►►► 96%

Best of British

tel: 01865 300239 **High St OX29 7RH**
email: info@lincolnfarmpark.co.uk **web:** www.lincolnfarmpark.co.uk
dir: *Exit A415 between Abingdon & Witney, 5m SE of Witney. Follow brown campsite sign in Standlake.* **grid ref:** *SP395028*

This attractively landscaped family-run park, located in a quiet village near the River Thames, offers a truly excellent camping or caravanning experience. There are top class facilities throughout the park. It has excellent leisure facilities in the Standlake Leisure Centre complete with two pools plus gym, sauna etc. This is the perfect base for visiting the many attractions in Oxfordshire and the Cotswolds. A warm welcome is assured from the friendly staff. 9 acre site. 90 touring pitches. 75 hardstandings. Caravan pitches. Motorhome pitches. Tent pitches.

Open: Feb-Nov **Last arrival:** 20.00hrs **Last departure:** noon

Pitches: 🚐 🚐 🔺

Leisure: 🏊 🎿 ♿ 🎣 Spa

Facilities: 🚿📶◉♇✕♿⦵🗑🚿🐾📶 ♻ 🔧

Services: 🔌🗑🔋🚿🚽🍽️⛽

Within 3 miles: 🚶🎣♿🎿🗑🔄

Notes: No gazebos, no noise after 23.00hrs. Dogs must be kept on leads. Putting green, outdoor chess.

AA Pubs & Restaurants nearby: Bear & Ragged Staff, CUMNOR, OX2 9QH, 01865 862329

The Vine Inn, CUMNOR, OX2 9QN, 01865 862567

PITCHES: 🚐 Caravans 🚐 Motorhomes 🔺 Tents 🏠 Glamping-style accommodation **SERVICES:** 🔌 Electric hook up 🗑 Launderette 🍺 Licensed bar
🔋 Calor Gas ⊘ Camping Gaz 🚽 Toilet fluid 🍽️ Café/Restaurant 🍔 Fast Food/Takeaway 🔋 Battery charging 🚼 Baby care ⛽ Motorvan service point
ABBREVIATIONS: BH/bank hols – bank holidays Etr – Easter Spring BH – Spring Bank Holiday fr – from hrs – hours m – mile mdnt – midnight
rdbt – roundabout rs – restricted service wk – week wknd – weekend x-rds – cross roads 🚫 No credit or debit cards 🚫 No dogs 👶 Children of all ages accepted

RUTLAND

GREETHAM — Map 11 SK91

Places to visit

Rutland County Museum & Visitor Centre, OAKHAM, LE15 6HW, 01572 758440
www.rutland.gov.uk/museum

Great for kids: Oakham Castle, OAKHAM, LE15 6HW, 01572 758440
www.rutland.gov.uk/castle

Rutland Caravan & Camping
▶▶▶▶ 91%

tel: 01572 813520 **Park Ln LE15 7FN**
email: info@rutlandcaravanandcamping.co.uk
dir: *From A1 onto B668 towards Greetham. Before Greetham turn right at x-rds, left to site.* **grid ref:** *SK925148*

This pretty caravan park, built to a high specification and surrounded by well-planted banks, continues to improve due to the enthusiasm and vision of its owner. A swimming pool and luxury lodges are under construction at the time of our inspection, plus there are plans to add family washrooms and fully serviced pitches. From the spacious reception and the innovative play area to the toilet block, everything is of a very high standard. The spacious grassy site is close to the Viking Way and other footpath networks, and well sited for visiting Rutland Water and the many picturesque villages in the area. 5 acre site. 130 touring pitches. 65 hardstandings. Caravan pitches. Motorhome pitches. Tent pitches.

Open: all year **Last arrival:** 20.00hrs
Pitches: * ➤ £16.30-£24.90 ➤ £16.30-£24.90 ▲ £16.30-£24.90
Leisure: 🏊 ⁄𝕀 🎣
Facilities: 🅵 ⊙ 🅿 ✳ ⅃ 🖫 🎪 WiFi ♻ ❶
Services: 🅿 🖥 🛢 ⌀ 🆃 ⅃
Within 3 miles: ⅃ 🚤 🖉 ◎ 🏊 🛍 ∪
Notes: No noise after 23.00hrs. Dogs must be kept on leads. Dog shower.
AA Pubs & Restaurants nearby: The Wheatsheaf, GREETHAM, LE15 7NP, 01572 812325
The Olive Branch, CLIPSHAM, LE15 7SH, 01780 410355

OAKHAM — Map 11 SK80

Places to visit

Oakham Castle, OAKHAM, LE15 6HW, 01572 758440 www.rutland.gov.uk/castle

Rutland County Museum & Visitor Centre, OAKHAM, LE15 6HW, 01572 758440
www.rutland.gov.uk/museum

Ranksborough Hall Caravan and Camping
▶▶▶ 77%

tel: 01572 722984 & 07794 949568 **Ranksborough Hall Estates, Langham LE15 7JR**
email: sales@ranksboroughhall.com
dir: *Take A606 from Oakham towards Melton Mowbray, through Langham, left at Ranksborough Hall sign.* **grid ref:** *SK838110*

This small, intimate, tranquil touring park is situated in the grounds of Ranksborough Hall. It occupies a level, secluded and mature tree fringed area with

clean, well-maintained toilets, and a high priority is given to security. Several attractive and historic market towns are a short drive away through rolling and unspoilt countryside, plus there are opportunities for walking, sailing and cycling at nearby Rutland Water. 1.5 acre site. 33 touring pitches. 33 hardstandings. 10 seasonal pitches. Caravan pitches. Motorhome pitches. Tent pitches.

Open: all year **Last arrival:** 18.00hrs **Last departure:** anytime
Pitches: ➤ ➤ ▲
Facilities: 🅵 ⊙ 🅿 ♿ ⌀ 🎪 ❶
Services: 🅿 🛢
Within 3 miles: ⅃ 🖉 🏊 🛍 ∪
Notes: 🐕 Quiet time after 23.00hrs, BBQs must be off the ground. Dogs must be kept on leads.
AA Pubs & Restaurants nearby: The Grainstore Brewery, OAKHAM, LE15 6RE, 01572 770065
The Fox & Hounds, KNOSSINGTON, LE15 8LY, 01664 452129

WING — Map 11 SK80

Places to visit

Lyddington Bede House, LYDDINGTON, LE15 9LZ, 01572 822438
www.english-heritage.org.uk/daysout/properties/lyddington-bede-house

Great for kids: Oakham Castle, OAKHAM, LE15 6HW, 01572 758440
www.rutland.gov.uk/castle

Wing Lakes Caravan & Camping
▶▶▶ 71%

tel: 01572 737283 & 737090 **Wing Hall LE15 8RY**
email: winghall1891@aol.com
dir: *From A1 take A47 towards Leicester, 14m, follow Morcott signs. In Morcott follow Wing signs. 2.5m, follow site signs.* **grid ref:** *SK892031*

A deeply tranquil and rural park set in the grounds of an old manor house. The four grassy fields with attractive borders of mixed, mature deciduous trees have exceptional views across the Rutland countryside and are within one mile of Rutland Water. There's a good farm shop which specialises in locally sourced produce, a licensed café, and there are high quality showers and a fully-equipped laundry. Children and tents are very welcome in what is a safe environment where there is space to roam. 11 acre site. 250 touring pitches. 4 hardstandings. Caravan pitches. Motorhome pitches. Tent pitches.

Open: all year (rs Nov-Feb large motorhomes advised not to arrive if weather very wet) **Last arrival:** 21.00hrs **Last departure:** noon
Pitches: * ➤ £10-£25 ➤ £10-£25 ▲ fr £16
Facilities: 🅵 🅿 ✳ 🛍 🎪 WiFi ♻ ❶
Services: 🅿 🍽 🛢 ⌀
Within 3 miles: ⅃ 🚤 🖉 🏊 🛍 ∪
Notes: Dogs must be kept on leads. Coarse fishing.
AA Pubs & Restaurants nearby: Kings Arms, WING, LE15 8SE, 01572 737634

LEISURE: 🏊 Indoor swimming pool 🏊 Outdoor swimming pool ⅃𝕀 Children's playground 🪁 Kid's club 🎾 Tennis court 🎱 Games room 📺 Separate TV room ⅃ golf course 🚤 Boats for hire 🎬 Cinema 🎵 Entertainment 🖉 Fishing ◎ Mini golf 🏊 Watersports 🏋 Gym 🎯 Sports field Spa ∪ Stables
FACILITIES: 🛁 Bath 🅵 Shower ⊙ Electric shaver 🅿 Hairdryer ✳ Ice Pack Facility ♿ Disabled facilities ◐ Public telephone 🛍 Shop on site or within 200yds 🛒 Mobile shop (calls at least 5 days a week) 🍽 BBQ area 🎪 Picnic area WiFi Wi-fi 🖥 Internet access ♻ Recycling ❶ Tourist info 🎪 Dog exercise area

SHROPSHIRE

BRIDGNORTH   Map 10 SO79

Places to visit

Benthall Hall, BENTHALL, TF12 5RX, 01952 882159
www.nationaltrust.org.uk/main/w-benthallhall

Great for kids: Dudmaston Estate, QUATT, WV15 6QN, 01746 780866
www.nationaltrust.org.uk/dudmaston-estate

PREMIER PARK

Stanmore Hall Touring Park
▶▶▶▶▶ 88%

tel: 01746 761761 **Stourbridge Rd WV15 6DT**
email: stanmore@morris-leisure
dir: *2m E of Bridgnorth on A458.* **grid ref:** *SO742923*

An excellent park in peaceful surroundings offering outstanding facilities. The pitches, many fully serviced (with Freeview TV), are arranged around the lake close to Stanmore Hall. Arboretum standard trees include some magnificent Californian Redwoods and an oak tree that is nearly 700 years old. The site is handy for visiting Ironbridge, the Severn Valley Railway and the attractive market town of Bridgnorth. 12.5 acre site. 129 touring pitches. 68 hardstandings. Caravan pitches. Motorhome pitches. Tent pitches.

Open: all year **Last arrival:** 20.00hrs **Last departure:** noon
Pitches: * 🚐 £22.50-£31.30 🚐 £22.50-£31.30 ▲ £22.50-£31.30
Leisure: ⚙ 🎱
Facilities: 🌂☉🅿✳&⊙ⓢ🎏🚑 WiFi 🄳
Services: 🔌🗑 🛢🅃📶⚡
Within 3 miles: ↓🎣🎯🏇ⓢ🏊∪
Notes: Max 2 dogs per pitch. Dogs must be kept on leads.
AA Pubs & Restaurants nearby: Halfway House Inn, BRIDGNORTH, WV16 5LS, 01746 762670

CRAVEN ARMS   Map 9 SO48

Places to visit

Stokesay Castle, STOKESAY, SY7 9AH, 01588 672544
www.english-heritage.org.uk/daysout/properties/stokesay-castle

Great for kids: Ludlow Castle, LUDLOW, SY8 1AY, 01584 873355
www.ludlowcastle.com

Wayside Camping and Caravan Park
▶▶▶ 80%

tel: 01588 660218 **Aston on Clun SY7 8EF**
email: waysidecamping@hotmail.com
dir: *From Craven Arms on A49, W onto B4368 (Clun road) towards Clun Valley. Site approx 2m on right just before Aston-on-Clun.* **grid ref:** *SO399816*

A peaceful park with lovely views, close to excellent local walks and many places of interest. The modern toilet facilities provide a good level of comfort, and there are several electric hook-ups. You are assured of a warm welcome by the helpful owner. Out of season price reductions are available. Many places of interest are within easy reach including Stokesay Castle, Offa's Dyke and Ludlow. 2.5 acre site. 20 touring pitches. 10 hardstandings. Caravan pitches. Motorhome pitches. Tent pitches. 1 static.

Open: Apr-Oct
Pitches: 🚐 £15-£18 🚐 £15-£18 ▲ £15-£18
Facilities: 🌂☉🅿✳&ⓢ🎏🎱🄳
Services: 🔌🅃📶⚡
Within 3 miles: ↓☉ⓢ🏊
Notes: 🚫 Adults only on BHs, only 1 dog per unit. Dogs must be kept on leads. Seasonal organic vegetables on sale.
AA Pubs & Restaurants nearby: The Sun Inn, CRAVEN ARMS, SY7 9DF, 01584 861239
The Crown Country Inn, MUNSLOW, SY7 9ET, 01584 841205

ELLESMERE

See Lyneal

HUGHLEY   Map 10 SO59

Places to visit

Wenlock Priory, MUCH WENLOCK, TF13 6HS, 01952 727466
www.english-heritage.org.uk/daysout/properties/wenlock-priory

Shipton Hall, MUCH WENLOCK, TF13 6JZ, 01746 785225 www.hha.org.uk

Great for kids: Hoo Farm Animal Kingdom, TELFORD, TF6 6DJ, 01952 677917
www.hoofarm.com

Mill Farm Holiday Park
▶▶▶ 80%

GOLD

tel: 01746 785208 **SY5 6NT**
email: myrtleroberts@hotmail.com
dir: *From Much Wenlock take B4371 towards Church Stretton. Right onto unclassified road signed Hughley.* **grid ref:** *SO564979*

Peacefully located within woodland, a stream runs through the park and the only sounds to be heard are running water and birdsong. Touring pitches are terraced and the lush screened camping area ensures peace and relaxation. The older style amenities blocks are spotlessly clean and regular social events are held in the former farm outbuildings. 20 acre site. 60 touring pitches. 6 hardstandings. 10 seasonal pitches. Caravan pitches. Motorhome pitches. Tent pitches. 90 statics.

Open: all year **Last arrival:** 18.00hrs **Last departure:** noon
Pitches: 🚐 🚐 ▲
Leisure: 🎱
Facilities: 🌂☉🅿✳🎏🚑 WiFi 🎱 🄳
Services: 🔌🗑 🛢🅃📶⚡
Within 3 miles: 🏇🏊∪
Notes: Site more suitable for adults. Dogs must be kept on leads. Fishing, horse riding.
AA Pubs & Restaurants nearby: The George & Dragon, MUCH WENLOCK, TF13 6AA, 01952 727312
The Royal Oak, CARDINGTON, SY6 7JZ, 01694 771266

LYNEAL (NEAR ELLESMERE)　　　Map 15 SJ43

Places to visit

Old Oswestry Hill Fort, OSWESTRY, 0870 333 1181
www.english-heritage.org.uk/daysout/properties/old-oswestry-hill-fort

Great for kids: Hawkstone Historic Park & Follies, WESTON-UNDER-REDCASTLE, SY4 5UY, 01948 841700 www.hawkstoneparkfollies.co.uk

Fernwood Caravan Park
►►►►84%

tel: 01948 710221 **SY12 0QF**
email: enquiries@fernwoodpark.co.uk
dir: *From A495 in Welshampton take B5063, over canal bridge, turn right as signed.*
grid ref: *SJ445346*

A peaceful park set in wooded countryside, with a screened, tree-lined touring area and coarse fishing lake. The approach is past colourful flowerbeds, and the static area which is tastefully arranged around an attractive children's playing area. There is a small child-free touring area for those wanting complete relaxation, and the park has 40 acres of woodland where there are many walks to enjoy. 26 acre site. 60 touring pitches. 8 hardstandings. 30 seasonal pitches. Caravan pitches. Motorhome pitches. 165 statics.

Open: Mar-Nov (rs Mar & Nov shop closed) **Last arrival:** 21.00hrs
Last departure: 17.00hrs

Pitches: * 🚐 £23-£27 🚐 £23-£27

Leisure: 🎢

Facilities: 🌢⊙🖤✳🌢🕒🖫🛲♻🅕

Services: 🔌🖫🛢🚽🖤

Within 3 miles: ⚓🎣🖫🖫

Notes: No noise after 23.00hrs. Dogs must be kept on leads.

MINSTERLEY　　　Map 15 SJ30

Places to visit

Powis Castle & Garden, WELSHPOOL, SY21 8RF, 01938 551929
www.nationaltrust.org.uk

Great for kids: Shrewsbury Castle and Shropshire Regimental Museum, SHREWSBURY, SY1 2AT, 01743 358516
www.shropshireregimentalmuseum.co.uk

The Old School Caravan Park
►►►86%

tel: 01588 650410 **Shelve SY5 0JQ**
email: t.ward425@btinternet.com
dir: *6.5m SW of Minsterley on A488, site on left 2m after village sign for Hope.*
grid ref: *SO322977*

Situated in the Shropshire Hills, an Area of Outstanding Natural Beauty, with many excellent walks starting directly from the site, and many cycle trails close by.

Although a small site of just 1.5 acres it is well equipped. It is a really beautiful park, often described as 'a gem', that has excellent facilities and offers all the requirements for a relaxing countryside holiday. The friendly owners, Terry and Jan, are always on hand to help out with anything. Nearby Snailbreach Mine offers guided tours on certain days. Please note that there is no laundry at this park. 1.5 acre site. 22 touring pitches. 10 hardstandings. 6 seasonal pitches. Caravan pitches. Motorhome pitches. Tent pitches.

Open: Mar-Jan **Last arrival:** 21.00hrs **Last departure:** 11.00hrs

Pitches: * 🚐 £14-£18 🚐 £14-£18 ▲ £14-£18

Facilities: 🌢⊙✳🕒🛲♻🅕

Services: 🔌

Within 3 miles: 🎣🖫U

Notes: 🐾 No ball games or cycle riding. Dogs must be kept on leads.

AA Pubs & Restaurants nearby: The Sun Inn, MARTON, SY21 8JP, 01938 561211
The Lowfield Inn, MARTON, SY21 8JX, 01743 891313

SHREWSBURY　　　Map 15 SJ41

Places to visit

Attingham Park, ATCHAM, SY4 4TP, 01743 708123
www.nationaltrust.org.uk/attinghampark

Great for kids: Wroxeter Roman City, WROXETER, SY5 6PH, 01743 761330
www.english-heritage.org.uk/daysout/properties/wroxeter-roman-city

PREMIER PARK

Beaconsfield Farm Caravan Park
►►►►►90%

tel: 01939 210370 & 210399 **Battlefield SY4 4AA**
email: mail@beaconsfieldholidaypark.co.uk **web:** www.beaconsfieldholidaypark.co.uk
dir: *At Hadnall, 1.5m NE of Shrewsbury. Follow sign for Astley from A49.*
grid ref: *SJ522189*

A purpose-built family-run park on farmland in open countryside. This pleasant park offers quality in every area, including superior toilets, heated indoor swimming pool, luxury lodges for hire and attractive landscaping. Fly and coarse fishing are available from the park's own lake and The Bothy restaurant is excellent. Car hire is available directly from the site, and there's a steam room, plus free WiFi. 12 luxury lodges are available for hire or sale. Only adults over 21 years are accepted. 16 acre site. 60 touring pitches. 50 hardstandings. 10 seasonal pitches. Caravan pitches. Motorhome pitches. 35 statics.

Open: all year **Last arrival:** 19.00hrs **Last departure:** 11.00hrs

Pitches: 🚐 🚎

Leisure: 🏊

Facilities: 🌲⊙🄿✳🕏🕘🖛🛏️WiFi🖥️♻️❼

Services: 🔌🔟🔒🍴🔄

Within 3 miles: 🔱🎿🎣◎🔟🔟

Notes: Adults only. Dogs must be kept on leads. Cycle hire.

AA Pubs & Restaurants nearby: The Armoury, SHREWSBURY, SY1 1HH, 01743 340525

The Mytton & Mermaid Hotel, SHREWSBURY, SY5 6QG, 01743 761220

Albright Hussey Manor Hotel & Restaurant, SHREWSBURY, SY4 3AF, 01939 290571

Oxon Hall Touring Park
►►►►►88%

Best of British

tel: 01743 340868 **Welshpool Rd SY3 5FB**
email: oxon@morris-leisure.co.uk
dir: *Exit A5 (ring road) at junct with A458. Site shares entrance with Oxon Park & Ride.* **grid ref:** *SJ455138*

A delightful park with quality facilities and a choice of grass and fully serviced pitches. A warm welcome is assured from the friendly staff. The adults-only section proves very popular, and there is an inviting patio area next to reception and the shop, overlooking a small lake. This site is ideally located for visiting Shrewsbury and the surrounding countryside, and the site also benefits from the Oxon Park & Ride, a short walk through the park. 15 acre site. 105 touring pitches. 72 hardstandings. Caravan pitches. Motorhome pitches. Tent pitches. 60 statics.

Open: all year **Last arrival:** 20.00hrs **Last departure:** noon

Pitches: 🚐 🚎 🏕️

Leisure: 🅿️ **Facilities:** 🌲⊙🄿✳🕏🕘🖛🛏️WiFi🖥️♻️❼

Services: 🔌🔟🔒🍴🔟🔄

Within 3 miles: 🔱🎿🎣🔟🔟🏌️

Notes: Max 2 dogs per pitch. Dogs must be kept on leads.

AA Pubs & Restaurants nearby: The Armoury, SHREWSBURY, SY1 1HH, 01743 340525

The Mytton & Mermaid Hotel, SHREWSBURY, SY5 6QG, 01743 761220

Albright Hussey Manor Hotel & Restaurant, SHREWSBURY, SY4 3AF, 01939 290571

TELFORD
Map 10 SJ60

Places to visit

Lilleshall Abbey, LILLESHALL, TF10 9HW, 0121 625 6820
www.english-heritage.org.uk/daysout/properties/lilleshall-abbey

Ironbridge Gorge Museums, IRONBRIDGE, TF8 7DQ, 01952 433424
www.ironbridge.org.uk

Severn Gorge Park
►►►►►81%

tel: 01952 684789 **Bridgnorth Rd, Tweedale TF7 4JB**
email: info@severngorgepark.co.uk
dir: *Signed off A442, 1m S of Telford.* **grid ref:** *SJ705051*

A very pleasant wooded site in the heart of Telford, that is well screened and well maintained. The sanitary facilities are fresh and immaculate, and landscaping of the grounds is carefully managed. Although the touring section is small, this is a really delightful park to stay on, and it is also well positioned for visiting nearby Ironbridge and its museums. The Telford bus stops at the end of the drive. 6 acre site. 12 touring pitches. 12 hardstandings. Caravan pitches. Motorhome pitches. 120 statics.

Open: all year **Last arrival:** 20.00hrs **Last departure:** noon

Pitches: ✱ 🚐 £18.75 🚎 £18.75

Facilities: 🌲⊙🄿✳🕏🖛❼ **Services:** 🔌🔟🔒🍴🔟🔄

Within 3 miles: 🔱🎿🎣◎🔟🔟🏌️

Notes: Adults only. Well behaved dogs only. Dogs must be kept on leads.

See which sites have been awarded Gold Pennants on page 36

WEM
Map 15 SJ52

Places to visit
Hawkstone Historic Park & Follies, WESTON-UNDER-REDCASTLE, SY4 5UY, 01948 841700 www.hawkstoneparkfollies.co.uk

Attingham Park, ATCHAM, SY4 4TP, 01743 708123 www.nationaltrust.org.uk/attinghampark

Great for kids: Shrewsbury Castle and Shropshire Regimental Museum, SHREWSBURY, SY1 2AT, 01743 358516 www.shropshireregimentalmuseum.co.uk

Lower Lacon Caravan Park
►►►79%

tel: 01939 232376 **SY4 5RP**
email: info@llcp.co.uk **web:** www.llcp.co.uk
dir: A49 onto B5065. Site 3m on right. **grid ref:** SJ534304

A large, spacious park with lively club facilities and an entertainments' barn, set safely away from the main road. The park is particularly suited to families, with an outdoor swimming pool and farm animals. 57 acre site. 270 touring pitches. 30 hardstandings. 100 seasonal pitches. Caravan pitches. Motorhome pitches. Tent pitches. 50 statics. 2 wooden pods.

Open: all year (rs Winter entertainment barn & café closed) **Last arrival:** anytime **Last departure:** 16.00hrs

Pitches: 🚐 🚙 ⛺ 🛖

Leisure: 🏊 🎡 🎣 📺

Facilities: 🛁 🚿 ⊙ 🧴 ❄ ♿ 🕐 💲 🎯 📶 ♻ ❂

Services: 🔌 📶 🍴 🛢 ⊘ 🚰 🍽 🚮 🏪

Within 3 miles: ⌢ 🏌 ◎ 💲 🏪

Notes: No skateboards, no commercial vehicles, no sign-written vehicles. Dogs must be kept on leads. Crazy golf.

WENTNOR

Places to visit
Montgomery Castle, MONTGOMERY, 01443 336000 www.cadw.wales.gov.uk

Great for kids: The Shropshire Hills Discovery Centre, CRAVEN ARMS, SY7 9RS, 01588 676000 www.shropshirehillsdiscoverycentre.co.uk

WENTNOR
Map 15 SO39

The Green Caravan Park
►►►81%

tel: 01588 650605 **SY9 5EF**
email: lin@greencaravanpark.co.uk
dir: 1m NE of Bishop's Castle on A489. Right at brown tourist sign. **grid ref:** SO380932

A pleasant site in a peaceful setting convenient for visiting Ludlow or Shrewsbury. Very family orientated, with good facilities. The grassy pitches are mainly level, and some hardstandings are available. 15 acre site. 140 touring pitches. 5 hardstandings. 20 seasonal pitches. Caravan pitches. Motorhome pitches. Tent pitches. 20 statics.

Open: Etr-Oct **Last arrival:** 21.00hrs **Last departure:** noon (late departure available for a fee)

Pitches: * 🚐 £15-£18 🚙 £15-£18 ⛺ £15-£18

Leisure: 🎡 **Facilities:** 🚿 ⊙ 🧴 ❄ 💲 🍽 🎯 ♻ ❂

Services: 🔌 📶 🍴 🛢 ⊘ 🚰 🍽 🚮 **Within 3 miles:** ⌢ 💲

Notes: No open fires, quiet from 22.00hrs-08.00 hrs. Dogs must be kept on leads.

AA Pubs & Restaurants nearby: The Crown Inn, WENTNOR, SY9 5EE, 01588 650613

WHEATHILL
Map 10 SO68

Places to visit
Ludlow Castle, LUDLOW, SY8 1AY, 01584 873355 www.ludlowcastle.com

PREMIER PARK

Wheathill Touring Park
►►►►►81%

tel: 01584 823456 **WV16 6QT**
email: info@wheathillpark.co.uk
dir: On B4364 between Ludlow & Bridgnorth. (NB Sat Nav may give directions to exit B4364, this should be ignored. Site entrance well signed from B4364). **grid ref:** SO603805

Ideally located in open countryside between the historic towns of Bridgnorth and Ludlow, this development, provides spacious, fully serviced pitches, most with stunning views and a top-notch amenities block with quality fittings and good privacy options. The park is also situated adjacent to the Three Horseshoes pub serving a good range of ales and food. Please note that the on-site shop only sells caravan and camping spares but there's a licensed village shop within a 10-minute drive. 4 acre site. 25 touring pitches. 25 hardstandings. 5 seasonal pitches. Caravan pitches. Motorhome pitches.

Open: Mar-1 Jan **Last arrival:** 20.00hrs **Last departure:** noon

Pitches: 🚐 🚙

Facilities: 🚿 ⊙ 🧴 ♿ 🎯 📶 🖥 ❂ **Services:** 🔌 📶 🛢 ⊘ 🚰 🚮 ⏏

Within 3 miles: ⌢ 💲 ◎ ♻

Notes: Adults only. Dogs must be kept on leads.

AA Pubs & Restaurants nearby: Fighting Cocks, STOTTESDON, DY14 8TZ, 01746 718270

The Crown Inn, CLEOBURY MORTIMER, DY14 0NB, 01299 270372

LEISURE: 🏊 Indoor swimming pool 🏊 Outdoor swimming pool 🎡 Children's playground 🧒 Kid's club 🎾 Tennis court 🎱 Games room ⬜ Separate TV room ⛳ golf course 🚣 Boats for hire 🎬 Cinema 🎵 Entertainment 🎣 Fishing ◎ Mini golf 🏄 Watersports 🏋 Gym ⚽ Sports field Spa ♻ Stables
FACILITIES: 🛁 Bath 🚿 Shower ⊙ Electric shaver 🧴 Hairdryer ❄ Ice Pack Facility ♿ Disabled facilities 🕐 Public telephone 💲 Shop on site or within 200yds 🏪 Mobile shop (calls at least 5 days a week) 🍴 BBQ area 🚮 Picnic area 📶 Wi-fi 🖥 Internet access ♻ Recycling ❂ Tourist info 🎯 Dog exercise area

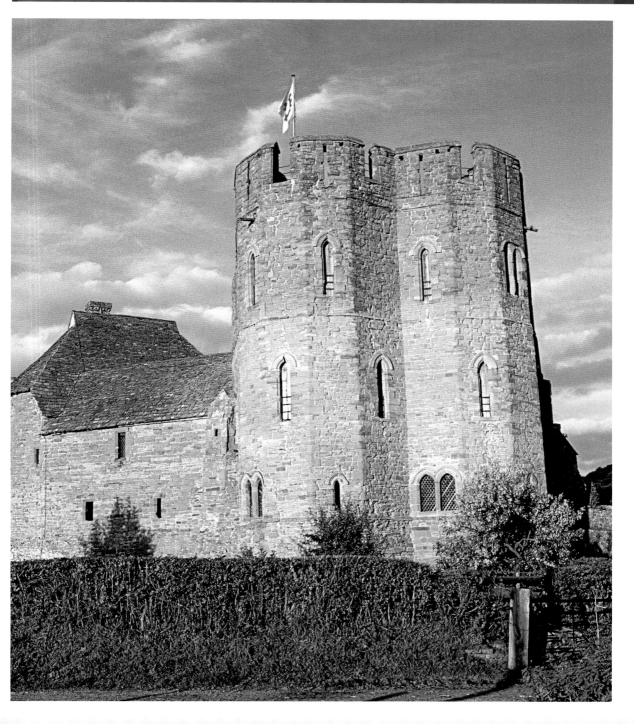

PITCHES: 🚐 Caravans 🚍 Motorhomes 🛆 Tents 🏕 Glamping-style accommodation **SERVICES:** 🔌 Electric hook up 🔳 Launderette 🍸 Licensed bar
🔒 Calor Gas 🔥 Camping Gaz 🅣 Toilet fluid 🍽 Café/Restaurant 🍟 Fast Food/Takeaway 🔋 Battery charging 🚼 Baby care 🔧 Motorvan service point
ABBREVIATIONS: BH/bank hols – bank holidays Etr – Easter Spring BH – Spring Bank Holiday fr – from hrs – hours m – mile mdnt – midnight
rdbt – roundabout rs – restricted service wk – week wknd – weekend x-rds – cross roads 💳 No credit or debit cards 🚫 No dogs 👫 Children of all ages accepted

Somerset

Somerset means 'summer pastures' — appropriate given that so much of this county remains rural and unspoiled. Ever popular areas to visit are the limestone and red sandstone Mendips Hills rising to over 1,000 feet, and by complete contrast, to the south and southwest, the flat landscape of the Somerset Levels.

At the heart of Somerset lies the city of Wells, one of the smallest in the country and surely one of the finest. The jewel in the city's crown is its splendid cathedral, with a magnificent Gothic interior; adorned with sculptures, the West Front is a masterpiece of medieval craftsmanship. Nearby are Vicar's Close, a delightful street of 14th-century houses, and the Bishop's Palace, which is 13th century and moated.

Radiating from Wells are numerous paths and tracks, offering walkers the chance to escape the noise and bustle of the city and discover Somerset's rural delights. Deep within the county are the Mendip Hills, 25 miles long by 5 miles wide, that have a distinctive character and identity.

One of Somerset's more adventurous routes, and a long-term favourite with walkers, is the West Mendip Way, running for 50 miles between the coast and the town of Frome. The starting point at Uphill is spectacular – a ruined hilltop church overlooking the coast near the classic seaside resort of Weston-Super-Mare. The town's famous pier replaces a previous structure destroyed by fire in 2008. Weston and Minehead, which lie on the edge of Exmoor National Park, are two traditional, much-loved holiday destinations on this stretch of coastline.

From Uphill, the West Mendip Way makes for Cheddar Caves and Gorge where stunning geological formations attract countless visitors who are left with a lasting impression of unique natural beauty. For almost a mile the gorge's limestone cliffs rise vertically above the road, in places giving Cheddar a somewhat sinister and oppressive air. Beyond Cheddar the trail heads for Wells. The choice of walks in Somerset is impressive, as is the range of cycle routes.

Descend to the Somerset Levels, an evocative lowland landscape that was the setting for the Battle of Sedgemoor in 1685. In the depths of winter this is a desolate place and famously prone to extensive flooding. There is also a palpable sense of the distant past among these fields and scattered communities. It is claimed that Alfred the Great retreated here after his defeat by the Danes.

One of Somerset's most famous features is the ancient, enigmatic Glastonbury Tor. Steeped in early Christian and Arthurian legend, the Isle of Avalon is one of a number of 'islands' rising above the Somerset Levels. This was once the site of the largest and richest monastery in medieval England and it is claimed that in this setting, Joseph of Arimathea founded the first Christian church in the country. Today, near this spot, modern-day pilgrims come for worship of a very different kind – every summer Glastonbury's legendary festival attracts big names from the world of music and large crowds who brave the elements to support them.

Away from the flat country are the Quantocks, once the haunt of poets. Samuel Taylor Coleridge wrote *The Ancient Mariner* while living in the area and William Wordsworth and his sister Dorothy visited on occasion and often accompanied their friend Coleridge on his country rambles among these hills. The Quantocks are noted for their gentle slopes, heather-covered moorland expanses and red deer. From the summit, the Bristol Channel is visible where it meets the Severn Estuary. So much of this hilly landscape has a timeless quality about it and large areas have hardly changed since Coleridge and William and Dorothy Wordsworth explored it on foot around the end of the 18th century.

◁ Cheddar Gorge

SOMERSET

BISHOP SUTTON
Map 4 ST55

PREMIER PARK

Bath Chew Valley Caravan Park
▶▶▶▶▶ 93%

Best of British

GOLD

tel: 01275 332127 **Ham Ln BS39 5TZ**
email: enquiries@bathchewvalley.co.uk
dir: *From A4 towards Bath take A39 towards Weston-Super-Mare. Right onto A368. 6m, right opposite The Red Lion into Ham Lane, site 250mtrs on left.*
grid ref: *ST586598*

This peaceful adults-only park can be described as 'a park in a garden', with caravan pitches set amidst lawns, shrubs and trees. There are excellent private facilities – rooms with showers, wash basins and toilets – all are spotlessly clean and well maintained and there's a good woodland walk on the park. This site is well situated for visiting Bath, Bristol, Wells, Cheddar and Wookey Hole, and for walking in the Mendip Hills. Chew Valley Lake, noted for its top quality fishing, is close by. 4.5 acre site. 45 touring pitches. 4 seasonal pitches. Caravan pitches. Motorhome pitches. Tent pitches.

Open: all year **Last arrival:** 19.00hrs **Last departure:** 11.00hrs

Pitches: 🚐 🚍 ⚊

Facilities: 📶 ⊙ 🐾 ✳ ⅃ ⌾ ⓢ 🎇 🛒 WiFi 🖥 ♻ 🅘

Services: 🚽 🔛 🛢 ⌀ 🇹 ⊙ 🚰 ⚐

Within 3 miles: ⚘ 🖉 ⓢ

Notes: Adults only. No cars by caravans or tents. Dogs must be kept on leads. Lending library.

AA Pubs & Restaurants nearby: The Carpenters Arms, STANTON WICK, BS39 4BX, 01761 490202

The Bear and Swan, CHEW MAGNA, BS40 8SL, 01275 331100

The Pony and Trap, CHEW MAGNA, BS40 8TQ, 01275 332627

BREAN

Places to visit

King John's Hunting Lodge, AXBRIDGE, BS26 2AP, 01934 732012
www.kingjohnshuntinglodge.co.uk

Weston-Super-Mare Museum, WESTON-SUPER-MARE, BS23 1PR, 01934 621028
www.weston-super-maretowncouncil.gov.uk

Great for kids: The Helicopter Museum, WESTON-SUPER-MARE, BS24 8PP, 01934 635227 www.helicoptermuseum.co.uk

BREAN
Map 4 ST25

Warren Farm Holiday Centre
HOLIDAY CENTRE 92%

tel: 01278 751227 **Brean Sands TA8 2RP**
email: enquiries@warren-farm.co.uk **web:** www.warren-farm.co.uk
dir: *M5 junct 22 , B3140 through Burnham-on-Sea to Berrow & Brean. Site 1.5m past Brean Leisure Park.* **grid ref:** *ST297564*

A large family-run holiday park just a short walk from the beach and divided up into several fields each with its own designated facilities. Pitches are spacious and level (some hardstandings available), and there are good panoramic views of the Mendip Hills and Brean Down. The park has its own Beachcomber Inn with bar, restaurant and entertainment area. The site is perfect for families and has a playbarn. Lake fishing is available on site and there is also a fishing tackle and bait shop. 100 acre site. 575 touring pitches. 70 hardstandings. Caravan pitches. Motorhome pitches. Tent pitches. 400 statics.

Open: Apr-Oct **Last arrival:** 20.00hrs **Last departure:** noon

Pitches: * 🚐 £8.50-£18.50 🚍 £8.50-£18.50 ⚊ £8.50-£18.50

Leisure: 🛝 ☺ 🎱 ⬜ ♫

Facilities: 🛁 📶 ⊙ 🐾 ✳ ⅃ ⌾ ⓢ 🎇 🛒 WiFi 🖥 🅘

Services: 🚽 🔛 🛢 ⌀ 🇹 ⊙ 🚰 🛒 ⚐

Within 3 miles: ⚘ 🖉 ⊙ ⚓ ⓢ ⓤ

Notes: No commercial vehicles.

See advert on opposite page

Holiday Resort Unity
HOLIDAY CENTRE 91%

tel: 01278 751235 **Coast Rd, Brean Sands TA8 2RB**
email: admin@hru.co.uk
dir: *M5 junct 22, B3140 through Burnham-on-Sea, through Berrow to Brean. Site on left just before Brean Leisure Park.* **grid ref:** *ST294539*

This is an excellent, family-run holiday park offering very good touring facilities plus a wide range of family oriented activities, including bowling, RJ's entertainment club plus good eating outlets etc. Brean Leisure Park and a swimming pool complex are available directly from the touring park at a discounted entry price. Ready erected, fully-equipped safari tents are also available for hire. 200 acre site. 453 touring pitches. 158 hardstandings. 168 seasonal pitches. Caravan pitches. Motorhome pitches. Tent pitches. 650 statics. 3 wooden pods.

Open: Feb-Nov **Last arrival:** 21.00hrs **Last departure:** 10.00hrs (late departures available for a fee)

Pitches: 🚐 £10-£35 🚙 £10-£35 ⛺ £10-£30 🏕

Leisure: 🏊‍♀️🏊🎯♿🎣🎱♪🎵

Facilities: 🐾🔥☕♿⚡🕐🛁🚻📶🖥♻🅿

Services: 🔌🗑🚮🔒🧺🚽🍴🍺🛒

Within 3 miles: 🛶🎠♿🎯🐾🅿⛳

Notes: Family parties of 3 or more must be over 21 (young persons' policy applies). Dogs must be kept on leads. Fishing lake, indoor play centre.

AA Pubs & Restaurants nearby: Crossways Inn, WEST HUNTSPILL, TA9 3RA, 01278 783756

PITCHES: 🚐 Caravans 🚙 Motorhomes ⛺ Tents 🏕 Glamping-style accommodation **SERVICES:** 🔌 Electric hook up 🗑 Launderette 🍺 Licensed bar 🔥 Calor Gas ⊘ Camping Gaz 🚽 Toilet fluid 🍴 Café/Restaurant 🍟 Fast Food/Takeaway ⚡ Battery charging 🚮 Baby care 🚐 Motorvan service point
ABBREVIATIONS: BH/bank hols – bank holidays Etr – Easter Spring BH – Spring Bank Holiday fr – from hrs – hours m – mile mdnt – midnight
rdbt – roundabout rs – restricted service wk – week wknd – weekend x-rds – cross roads 🚫 No credit or debit cards 🚫 No dogs 👫 Children of all ages accepted

BREAN *continued*

Northam Farm Caravan & Touring Park

►►►► 91%

tel: 01278 751244 **TA8 2SE**
email: stay@northamfarm.co.uk **web:** www.northamfarm.co.uk
dir: *M5 junct 22, B3140 to Burnham-on-Sea & Brean. Park on right 0.5m past Brean Leisure Park.* **grid ref:** ST299556

An attractive site that's just a short walk from the sea and a long sandy beach. This quality park also has lots of children's play areas, and also owns the Seagull Inn about 600 yards away, which includes a restaurant and entertainment. There is a top quality fishing lake on site, which is very popular and has been featured on TV. The facilities on this park are excellent. A DVD of the site is available on request, free of charge. 30 acre site. 350 touring pitches. 260 hardstandings. Caravan pitches. Motorhome pitches. Tent pitches.

Open: Mar-Oct (rs Mar-Oct shop, café, takeaway open limited hours)
Last arrival: 20.00hrs **Last departure:** 10.30hrs

Pitches: * ⊕ £13-£27.50 ⊕ £13-£27.50 ▲ £11.75-£21

Leisure: ⋀ ⊗

Facilities: ⊷ ⋔ ⊙ ⨍ ☀ ὁ Ⓢ ⓢ ⋤ ⋈ WiFi ♻ ❶

Services: ⊡ ⓢ ⬛ ⬚ T ⑽ ⬆ ⬛ ⬇

Within 3 miles: ⌁ ⋔ ⊚ Ⓢ ⑨ ∪

Notes: Families & couples only, no motorcycles or commercial vehicles. Dogs must be kept on leads. Fishing lake.

See advert on opposite page

| BRIDGETOWN | Map 3 SS93 |

Places to visit

Dunster Castle, DUNSTER, TA24 6SL, 01643 821314
www.nationaltrust.org.uk/dunstercastle

Cleeve Abbey, WASHFORD, TA23 0PS, 01984 640377
www.english-heritage.org.uk/daysout/properties/cleeve-abbey

Exe Valley Caravan Site

►►►► 91%

tel: 01643 851432 **Mill House TA22 9JR**
email: info@exevalleycamping.co.uk **web:** www.exevalleycamping.co.uk
dir: *Take A396 (Tiverton to Minehead road). Turn W in centre of Bridgetown, site 40yds on right.* **grid ref:** SS923333

Set in the Exmoor National Park, this adults-only park occupies an enchanting, peaceful spot in a wooded valley alongside the River Exe. There is free fly-fishing, an abundance of wildlife and excellent walks leading directly from the park. The site has good, spotlessly clean facilities. The inn opposite serves meals at lunchtime and in the evening. 4 acre site. 48 touring pitches. 10 hardstandings. Caravan pitches. Motorhome pitches. Tent pitches.

Open: 13 Mar-19 Oct **Last arrival:** 22.00hrs **Last departure:** 11.00hrs

Pitches: * ⊕ £12-£18 ⊕ £12-£18 ▲ £12-£21

Facilities: ⋔ ⊙ ⨍ ☀ ὁ Ⓢ ⓢ ⋤ ⋈ WiFi ♻ ❶

Services: ⊡ ⓢ ⬛ ⬚ T ⬆ ⬇

Within 3 miles: ⌁ ⋔ ⊚ Ⓢ ∪

Notes: Adults only. ⊛ 17th-century mill, cycle hire, TV sockets & cables.

AA Pubs & Restaurants nearby: The Rest and Be Thankful Inn, WHEDDON CROSS, TA24 7DR, 01643 841222

---

www.northamfarm.co.uk

One of Somerset's most sought after parks for Tourers, Motorhomes & Tents and *just 5 minutes stroll* from the beach and the South West's BEST entertainment…

Treat yourself!

Northam Farm Touring Park, South Road, Brean, Nr Burnham-on-Sea, Somerset TA8 2SE
For Reservations, Brochure & DVD
Phone 01278 751244 or email stay@northamfarm.co.uk

BRIDGWATER   Map 4 ST23

Mill Farm Caravan & Camping Park
HOLIDAY CENTRE 84%

tel: 01278 732286 **Fiddington TA5 1JQ**
web: www.millfarm.biz
dir: *From Bridgwater take A39 W, left at Cannington rdbt, 2m, right just beyond Apple Inn towards Fiddington. Follow camping signs.* **grid ref:** *ST219410*

A large holiday park with plenty to interest all the family, including indoor and outdoor pools, a boating lake, a gym and horse riding. There is also a clubhouse with bar, and a full entertainment programme in the main season. Although lively and busy in the main season, the park also offers a much quieter environment at other times; out of season some activities and entertainment may not be available.

6 acre site. 275 touring pitches. 40 seasonal pitches. Caravan pitches. Motorhome pitches. Tent pitches.

Open: Mar-1 Dec **Last arrival:** 23.00hrs **Last departure:** 10.00hrs
Pitches: * ⛺ £11.50-£20.50 ⛺ £11.50-£20.50 ▲ £11.50-£20.50
Leisure: 🏊 ⛱ ⚜ 🎠 🎱 🏹 ▢ 🎵
Facilities: 🛁 🚿 ☉ 🧴 ❄ 🚻 🕐 ⑤ 🎌 🚻 📶 ♻ ❶
Services: 🔌 ⑤ 🍴 🎒 📮 ⊤ 🍴 🛒
Within 3 miles: ⚓ 🎣 ◎ ⑤ ⛵ ♨

Notes: No noise after 23.00hrs. Dogs must be kept on leads. Canoeing, pool table, trampolines, pony rides, fitness classes, saunas.

AA Pubs & Restaurants nearby: The Hood Arms, KILVE, TA5 1EA, 01278 741210

See advert below

LEISURE: 🏊 Indoor swimming pool   ⛱ Outdoor swimming pool   🛝 Children's playground   👶 Kid's club   🎾 Tennis court   🎱 Games room   ▢ Separate TV room   ⛳ golf course   ⛵ Boats for hire   🎬 Cinema   🎵 Entertainment   🎣 Fishing   ◎ Mini golf   ⛵ Watersports   🏋 Gym   ✪ Sports field   Spa   ♨ Stables
FACILITIES: 🛁 Bath   🚿 Shower   ☉ Electric shaver   🧴 Hairdryer   ❄ Ice Pack Facility   🚻 Disabled facilities   🕐 Public telephone   ⑤ Shop on site or within 200yds   🏪 Mobile shop (calls at least 5 days a week)   🍴 BBQ area   🌳 Picnic area   📶 Wi-fi   💻 Internet access   ♻ Recycling   ❶ Tourist info   🐕 Dog exercise area

BURNHAM-ON-SEA
Map 4 ST34

Places to visit

The Helicopter Museum, WESTON-SUPER-MARE, BS24 8PP, 01934 635227
www.helicoptermuseum.co.uk

King John's Hunting Lodge, AXBRIDGE, BS26 2AP, 01934 732012
www.kingjohnshuntinglodge.co.uk

Burnham-on-Sea Holiday Village
HOLIDAY CENTRE 87%

GOLD

tel: 0871 231 0868 **Marine Dr TA8 1LA**
email: burnhamonsea@haven.com **web:** www.haven.com/burnhamonsea
dir: *M5 junct 22, A38 towards Highbridge. Over mini rdbt, right onto B3139 to Burnham.
After Total Garage left into Marine Drive. Park 400yds on left.* **grid ref:** *ST305485*

A large, family-orientated holiday village complex with a separate touring park
containing 43 super pitches. There is a wide range of activities, including excellent
indoor and outdoor pools, plus bars, restaurants and entertainment for all the
family. The coarse fishing lake is very popular, and the seafront at Burnham is only
half a mile away. A wide range of well laid out holiday homes are available for hire.
94 acre site. 75 touring pitches. 44 hardstandings. Caravan pitches. Motorhome
pitches. Tent pitches. 700 statics.

Open: mid Mar-end Oct (rs mid Mar-May & Sep-Oct facilities may be reduced)
Last arrival: anytime **Last departure:** 10.00hrs

Pitches: 🚐 🚌 Å
Leisure: 🏊 🏊 🎠 🎣 ⚽ 🎵
Facilities: 🐕 🍴 ✳ ♿ 🕐 💲 WiFi
Services: 🔌 🛒 🍴 🛎 🍽 🔋 🎂
Within 3 miles: 🚴 🎢 🏌 ◎ 🎣 🔋 🏊 ⛳

Notes: 🚫 No pets, no commercial vehicles, no bookings by persons under 21yrs unless a
family booking.
AA Pubs & Restaurants nearby: Crossways Inn, WEST HUNTSPILL, TA9 3RA,
01278 783756
See advert below

PITCHES: 🚐 Caravans 🚌 Motorhomes Å Tents 🏕 Glamping-style accommodation **SERVICES:** 🔌 Electric hook up 🗳 Launderette 🍷 Licensed bar
🪨 Calor Gas ⊘ Camping Gaz T Toilet fluid 🍴 Café/Restaurant 🍟 Fast Food/Takeaway 🔋 Battery charging 🍼 Baby care ⚲ Motorvan service point
ABBREVIATIONS: BH/bank hols – bank holidays Etr – Easter Spring BH – Spring Bank Holiday fr – from hrs – hours m – mile mdnt – midnight
rdbt – roundabout rs – restricted service wk – week wknd – weekend x-rds – cross roads 🚫 No credit or debit cards 🚫 No dogs 👫 Children of all ages accepted

CHEDDAR · Map 4 ST45

Places to visit

Glastonbury Abbey, GLASTONBURY, BA6 9EL, 01458 832267
www.glastonburyabbey.com

The Helicopter Museum, WESTON-SUPER-MARE, BS24 8PP, 01934 635227
www.helicoptermuseum.co.uk

Great for kids: Wookey Hole Caves & Papermill, WOOKEY HOLE, BA5 1BB,
01749 672243 www.wookey.co.uk

Cheddar Bridge Touring Park
►►►►88%

tel: 01934 743048 **Draycott Rd BS27 3RJ**
email: enquiries@cheddarbridge.co.uk
dir: M5 junct 22 (Burnham-on-Sea), A38 towards Cheddar & Bristol, approx 5m. Right onto A371 at Cross, follow Cheddar signs. Through Cheddar village towards Wells, site on right just before Caravan Club site. **grid ref:** ST459529

A peaceful adults-only park on the edge of the village of Cheddar, with the added attraction of the River Yeo that flows through the grounds. The site is handy for exploring Cheddar Gorge, Wookey Hole, Wells and Bath. The toilet and shower facilities are very good. There are three camping pods, a gypsy wagon, statics and two apartments for hire. 4 acre site. 45 touring pitches. 10 hardstandings. Caravan pitches. Motorhome pitches. Tent pitches. 4 statics. 3 wooden pods.

Open: Mar-Oct **Last arrival:** 22.00hrs **Last departure:** 11.00hrs

Pitches: ♥♣ Å ⋒

Facilities: ⚡☉ℙ⚜🔥✣ⓒⓢ⌒

Services: ⚑∅⌁

Within 3 miles: ⌁ℙ◎⚒ⓢⓈ∪

Notes: Adults only. Quiet from 23.00hrs-08.00hrs.

AA Pubs & Restaurants nearby: Wookey Hole Inn, WOOKEY HOLE, BA5 1BP, 01749 676677

Cheddar Woods Holiday Park
HOLIDAY HOME PARK 95%

tel: 01934 742610 **Axbridge Rd BS27 3DB**
email: enquiries@cheddarwoods.co.uk
dir: From M5 junct 22 follow signs to Cheddar Gorge & Caves (8m). Site midway between Cheddar & Axbridge on A371. **grid ref:** ST448547

Situated in the beatiful Mendip Hills, Cheddar Woods is the perfect place to relax and unwind. This state-of-the-art park is an ideal location for family holidays. Both large and smaller lodges are available for hire, all offering top quality accommodation. There are excellent leisure facilities including a gym, spa and swimming pool plus a 'Go Active' programme. In addition, there is a very tasteful bar and quality restaurant. The park is just outside the village of Cheddar with its famous Gorge and is well positioned for visiting Wells, Weston-Super-Mare and many other attractions of the area. It should be noted this a lodge-only park.

Open: all year (rs Xmas & New Year)

Change over day: Mon, Fri, Sun

Arrival and departure times: Please contact the site

Lodges: 79 Sleeps 8

Bedrms 4 Bathrms 2 (inc en suite) Toilets 2 Dishwasher Wash Machine T/drier Freezer TV Sky/FTV DVD Modem/WiFi Linen inc Towels inc Elec inc Gas inc Grass area Garden/patio furniture Low season £355-£745 High season £909-£1745 Weekly price £600

Children: ♦♦ Cots (cot linen charged) Highchair **Dogs:** 2 on leads

Leisure: ☜ Spa ⌣ ♉ ⋔ ⋀

Within 3 miles: ☜ Spa ∪ ℙ

COWSLIP GREEN · Map 4 ST46

Places to visit

Clevedon Court, CLEVEDON, BS21 6QU, 01275 872257
www.nationaltrust.org.uk/clevedon-court

Bristol Museum & Art Gallery, BRISTOL, BS8 1RL, 0117 922 3571
www.bristol.gov.uk/museums

Great for kids: HorseWorld, BRISTOL, BS14 0QL, 01275 540173
www.horseworld.org.uk

Brook Lodge Farm Camping & Caravan Park (Bristol)
►►►84%

tel: 01934 862311 **BS40 5RB**
email: info@brooklodgefarm.com
dir: M5 junct 22, A38 to Churchill. Site 4m on right opposite Holiday Inn. Or M5 junct 18, follow Bristol Airport signs. From A38 towards Bridgwater (airport on left). Site 3m on left at bottom of hill. **grid ref:** ST486620

A naturally sheltered country touring park sitting in a valley of the Mendip Hills, surrounded by trees and a historic walled garden. A friendly welcome is always assured by the family owners who are particularly keen on preserving the site's environment and have won a green tourism award. This park is particularly well placed for visiting the Bristol Balloon Festival, held in August, plus the many country walks in the area. 3.5 acre site. 29 touring pitches. 3 hardstandings. Caravan pitches. Motorhome pitches. Tent pitches.

Open: Mar-Oct **Last arrival:** 21.30hrs **Last departure:** noon

Pitches: ♥♣ Å

Leisure: ⋀

Facilities: ⚡☉ℙ✣ⓒⓢ⌁📶🖥♻🛈

Services: ⚑ⓢ🛡∅⌁

Within 3 miles: ⌁ℙⓢ∪

Notes: Dogs by prior arrangement only. Dogs must be kept on leads. Cycle hire, walking maps available, fire pits.

AA Pubs & Restaurants nearby: The Langford Inn, LOWER LANGFORD, BS40 5BL, 01934 863059

CREWKERNE

See Drimpton (Dorset)

CROWCOMBE

Map 3 ST13

Places to visit

Cleeve Abbey, WASHFORD, TA23 0PS, 01984 640377
www.english-heritage.org.uk/daysout/properties/cleeve-abbey

Great for kids: Dunster Castle, DUNSTER, TA24 6SL, 01643 821314
www.nationaltrust.org.uk/dunstercastle

PREMIER PARK

Quantock Orchard Caravan Park
►►►►►80%

tel: 01984 618618 **Flaxpool TA4 4AW**
email: member@flaxpool.freeserve.co.uk **web:** www.quantock-orchard.co.uk
dir: *Take A358 from Taunton, signed Minehead & Williton. In 8m turn left just past Flaxpool Garage. Park immediately on left.* **grid ref:** ST138357

This small family-run park is set at the foot of the beautiful Quantock Hills and makes an ideal base for touring Somerset, Exmoor and north Devon. It is also close to the West Somerset Railway. It has excellent facilities and there is a lovely heated outdoor swimming pool, plus gym and fitness centre; bike hire is also available. There are static homes for hire. 3.5 acre site. 60 touring pitches. 30 hardstandings. Caravan pitches. Motorhome pitches. Tent pitches. 15 statics.

Open: all year (rs 10 Sep-20 May swimming pool closed) **Last arrival:** 22.00hrs
Last departure: noon

Pitches: * ⚏ £15-£28 ⛌ £15-£28 ▲ £15-£28

Leisure: ⚤ ᛉ ⋀ ⬤ ☐ Spa

Facilities: ⬥ ⎰ ☉ ⏣ ✳ ⅋ ⓢ 🔥 ⌂ 📶 🖥 ♻ ✪

Services: ⚡ 🔄 🛢 ⊘ T 🔋 ⚓

Within 3 miles: ⅃ ⌒ 🛍 🔄 ∪

Notes: Dogs must be kept on leads. Off licence.

AA Pubs & Restaurants nearby: The White Horse, STOGUMBER, TA4 3TA, 01984 656277

The Blue Ball Inn, TRISCOMBE, TA4 3HE, 01984 618242

The Rising Sun Inn, WEST BAGBOROUGH, TA4 3EF, 01823 432575

DULVERTON

Map 3 SS92

See also East Anstey (Devon)

Places to visit

Knightshayes, KNIGHTSHAYES, EX16 7RQ, 01884 254665
www.nationaltrust.org.uk/knightshayes

Great for kids: Tiverton Castle, TIVERTON, EX16 6RP, 01884 253200
www.tivertoncastle.com

Wimbleball Lake
►►►80%

tel: 01398 371460 & 371257 **Brompton Regis TA22 9NU**
email: wimbleball@swlakestrust.org.uk
dir: *From A396 (Tiverton to Minehead road) take B3222 signed Dulverton Services, follow signs to Wimbleball Lake. Ignore 1st entry (fishing) & take 2nd entry for tea room & camping. NB care needed due to narrow roads.* **grid ref:** SS960300

A grassy site overlooking Wimbleball Lake, set high up on Exmoor National Park. The camping area is adjacent to the visitor centre and café, which also includes the camping toilets and showers. The camping field, with 14 electric hook-ups and two hardstandings, is in a quiet and peaceful setting with good views of the lake, which is nationally renowned for its trout fishing; boats can be hired with advance notice. 1.25 acre site. 30 touring pitches. 2 hardstandings. Caravan pitches. Motorhome pitches. Tent pitches. 2 wooden pods.

Open: Mar-Oct **Last departure:** 11.00hrs

Pitches: * ⚏ £18-£22 ⛌ £18-£22 ▲ £14-£18 ⋔

Leisure: ⋀ ⚽

Facilities: ⎰ ☉ ⏣ ✳ ⅋ ⓢ 🔥 ⌂ 🖥 ♻ ✪

Services: ⚡ 🔄 🍽

Within 3 miles: ⅃ ⌒ 🛍 🔄 ∪

Notes: No open fires, off-ground BBQs only, no swimming in lake, no dogs in lake. Dogs must be kept on leads. Watersports & activity centre, bird watching, cycling, lakeside walks & bushcraft.

AA Pubs & Restaurants nearby: The Masons Arms, KNOWSTONE, EX36 4RY, 01398 341231

Follow us on facebook
www.facebook.com/TheAAUK

EMBOROUGH
Map 4 ST65

Places to visit
Glastonbury Abbey, GLASTONBURY, BA6 9EL, 01458 832267

www.glastonburyabbey.com

King John's Hunting Lodge, AXBRIDGE, BS26 2AP, 01934 732012
www.kingjohnshuntinglodge.co.uk

Great for kids: East Somerset Railway, CRANMORE, BA4 4QP, 01749 880417
www.eastsomersetrailway.com

Old Down Touring Park
►►► 83%

tel: 01761 232355 **Old Down House BA3 4SA**
email: jsmallparkhomes@aol.com
dir: A37 from Farrington Gurney through Ston Easton. In 2m left onto B3139 to Radstock.
Site opposite Old Down Inn. **grid ref:** ST628513

A small family-run site set in open parkland, surrounded by well-established trees.
The excellent toilet facilities are well maintained as is every other aspect of the
park. Children are welcome. 4 acre site. 30 touring pitches. 15 hardstandings. 6
seasonal pitches. Caravan pitches. Motorhome pitches. Tent pitches.

Open: all year **Last arrival:** 20.00hrs **Last departure:** noon
Pitches: 🚐 🚐 ▲
Facilities: 🌡⊙📺⋇⑤🎋♻❶
Services: 🔌🔋⊘Ⓣ🔦
Within 3 miles: ⅃🎱⛱⑤🔘U
Notes: Dogs must be kept on leads.
AA Pubs & Restaurants nearby: The Oakhill Inn, OAKHILL, BA3 5HU, 01749 840442
The Holcombe Inn, HOLCOMBE, BA3 5EB, 01761 232478

EXFORD

Places to visit
Dunster Castle, DUNSTER, TA24 6SL, 01643 821314
www.nationaltrust.org.uk/dunstercastle

West Somerset Railway, MINEHEAD, TA24 5BG, 01643 704996
www.west-somerset-railway.co.uk

Great for kids: Exmoor Zoological Park, BLACKMOOR GATE, EX31 4SG,
01598 763352 www.exmoorzoo.co.uk

EXFORD
Map 3 SS83

Westermill Farm
►► 86%

GOLD

tel: 01643 831238 **TA24 7NJ**
email: aa@westermill.com
dir: From Exford on Porlock road. Left in 0.25m, left to Westermill, sign on tree. Fork left.
grid ref: SS825398

An idyllic site for peace and quiet, in a sheltered valley in the heart of Exmoor,
which has won awards for conservation. Highly recommended for traditional
camping. There are four waymarked walks over the 500-acre working farm and self-
catering accommodation is also available. Please note that the site should only be
approached from Exford (other approaches are difficult). 6 acre site. 60 touring
pitches. Motorhome pitches. Tent pitches.

Open: all year (rs Nov-May larger toilet block & shop closed)
Pitches: 🚐 ▲ fr £15.50
Facilities: 🌡⊙📺⋇⑤🎋🔦WiFi♻❶
Services: 🔌🔋⊘ **Within 3 miles:** ⛱⑤🔘
Notes: 🐾 No noise after 23.00hrs, well behaved dogs accepted. Dogs must be kept on
leads. Shallow river for fishing & bathing.
AA Pubs & Restaurants nearby: Crown Hotel, EXFORD, TA24 7PP, 01643 831554

FROME
Map 4 ST74

Places to visit
Stourhead, STOURHEAD, BA12 6QD, 01747 841152
www.nationaltrust.org.uk/stourhead

Nunney Castle, NUNNEY, 0870 333 1181
www.english-heritage.org.uk/daysout/properties/nunney-castle

Great for kids: Longleat Safari & Adventure Park, LONGLEAT, BA12 7NW,
01985 844400 www.longleat.co.uk

Seven Acres Caravan & Camping Site
►►► 85%

tel: 01373 464222 **Seven Acres, West Woodlands BA11 5EQ**
dir: A361 Frome bypass, onto B3092 at rdbt, 0.75m to site. **grid ref:** ST777444

A level meadowland site beside the shallow River Frome, with a bridge across to an
adjacent field, and plenty of scope for families. The facilities are spotless. Set on
the edge of the Longleat Estate with its stately home, wildlife safari park, and many
other attractions. 3 acre site. 16 touring pitches. 16 hardstandings. Caravan
pitches. Motorhome pitches. Tent pitches.

Open: Mar-Oct
Pitches: * 🚐 £17 🚐 £17 ▲ fr £12
Leisure: 🛝 **Facilities:** 🌡⊙📺⋇🎋♻
Services: 🔌 **Within 3 miles:** ⅃🎱⛱⑤🔘U
Notes: 🐾 Dogs must be kept on leads.
AA Pubs & Restaurants nearby: The George at Nunney, NUNNEY, BA11 4LW,
01373 836458

Vobster Inn, LOWER VOBSTER, BA3 5RJ, 01373 812920

LEISURE: 🏊 Indoor swimming pool 🏊 Outdoor swimming pool 🛝 Children's playground 🧒 Kid's club 🎾 Tennis court 🎱 Games room 📺 Separate TV room
⛳ golf course ⛵ Boats for hire 🎬 Cinema 🎵 Entertainment 🎣 Fishing ◉ Mini golf 🏄 Watersports 🏋 Gym 🏟 Sports field Spa U Stables
FACILITIES: 🛁 Bath 🚿 Shower ⊙ Electric shaver 📺 Hairdryer ⋇ Ice Pack Facility ♿ Disabled facilities 🕾 Public telephone ⑤ Shop on site or within 200yds
🏪 Mobile shop (calls at least 5 days a week) 🍖 BBQ area 🎋 Picnic area WiFi Wi-fi 🖥 Internet access ♻ Recycling ❶ Tourist info 🐾 Dog exercise area

GLASTONBURY

Map 4 ST53

Places to visit

Lytes Cary Manor, KINGSDON, TA11 7HU, 01458 224471
www.nationaltrust.org.uk/lytes-cary-manor

Fleet Air Arm Museum, YEOVILTON, BA22 8HT, 01935 840565
www.fleetairarm.com

Great for kids: Haynes International Motor Museum, SPARKFORD, BA22 7LH, 01963 440804 www.haynesmotormuseum.com

PREMIER PARK

The Old Oaks Touring Park

►►►►► 97%

tel: 01458 831437 **Wick Farm, Wick BA6 8JS**
email: info@theoldoaks.co.uk
dir: *M5 junct 23, A39 to Glastonbury. After Street take A39 towards Wells. At 3rd rdbt follow Wick & Brindham signs. Site 1.5m on right. NB it is advisable to not use Sat Nav for last part of journey.* **grid ref:** *ST521394*

An exceptional adults-only park offering larger than average landscaped pitches, impeccably maintained grounds and wonderful views. The perfect 'get away from it all' spot where you can enjoy walking, cycling, fishing and touring or simply relaxing amid the abundant wildlife. The top class facilities include a well-stocked shop selling locally-sourced produce and home-baked cakes, a smart new shower block, WiFi, free walking and cycling maps, a half-acre fishing lake, a daily mini bus service to nearby towns and even a hot doggy shower! Camping cabins are available for hire. 10 acre site. 98 touring pitches. 98 hardstandings. Caravan pitches. Motorhome pitches. Tent pitches. 6 wooden pods.

Open: mid Feb-mid Nov (rs Feb-Mar & Oct-Nov reduced shop & reception hours) **Last arrival:** 20.00hrs **Last departure:** noon

Pitches: ⛺ £17-£34 ⛺ £17-£34 ▲ £15-£25 ⋒

Facilities: 🚿 🏠 ⊙ 🅿 ✳ & ⏰ 🔥 🛒 WiFi 💻 ♻ ❼

Services: 🔌 🔲 🛢 ⊘ T 🍼 🏪 🚾

Within 3 miles: ᵖ 🏪 🔲

Notes: Adults only. No groups, no noise after 22.30hrs. Dogs must be kept on leads. Off-licence, local produce boxes, caravan cleaning, dog owners' information pack, dog sitting, subsidised minibus.

AA Pubs & Restaurants nearby: Ring O'Bells, ASHCOTT, TA7 9PZ, 01458 210232

Isle of Avalon Touring Caravan Park

►►►► 84%

tel: 01458 833618 **Godney Rd BA6 9AF**
email: candicehatwell@hotmail.co.uk
dir: *M5 junct 23, A39 to outskirts of Glastonbury, 2nd exit signed Wells at B&Q rdbt, straight over next rdbt, 1st exit at 3rd rdbt (B3151), site 200yds on right.* **grid ref:** *ST494397*

A popular site, on the south side of this historic town, and within easy walking distance of the centre. It is a level park, with a separate tent field, that offers a

quiet environment. It makes an ideal spot from which to explore the many local attractions that include Glastonbury Tor, Wells, Wookey Hole and Clarks Village. Approved caravan storage is available. 8 acre site. 120 touring pitches. 70 hardstandings. Caravan pitches. Motorhome pitches. Tent pitches. 2 wooden pods.

Open: all year **Last arrival:** 21.00hrs **Last departure:** 11.00hrs

Pitches: ⛺ ⛺ ▲ ⋒

Facilities: 🚿 ⊙ 🅿 ✳ & 🔲 🔥 🛒 WiFi 💻 ♻ ❼

Services: 🔌 🔲 🛢 ⊘ T 🍼 🏪 🚾

Within 3 miles: ᶜ ᵖ 🏪 🔲 ⊙

Notes: Cycle hire.

AA Pubs & Restaurants nearby: Ring O'Bells, ASHCOTT, TA7 9PZ, 01458 210232

LANGPORT

Map 4 ST42

Places to visit

Montacute House, MONTACUTE, TA15 6XP, 01935 823289
www.nationaltrust.org.uk

Lytes Cary Manor, KINGSDON, TA11 7HU, 01458 224471
www.nationaltrust.org.uk/lytes-cary-manor

Great for kids: Fleet Air Arm Museum, YEOVILTON, BA22 8HT, 01935 840565
www.fleetairarm.com

Thorney Lakes Caravan Park

►►► 85%

tel: 01458 250811 **Thorney Lakes, Muchelney TA10 0DW**
email: info@thorneylakes.co.uk
dir: *From A303 at Podimore rdbt take A372 to Langport. At Huish Episcopi Church turn left for Muchelney. In 100yds left (signed Muchelney & Crewkerne). Site 300yds after John Leach Pottery.* **grid ref:** *ST430237*

A small, peaceful site set in a cider apple orchard in the heart of the Somerset Levels. There are excellent coarse fishing lakes just a short stroll away from the campsite, and the good walks in the area include the Parrett Trail which is just 100 metres from the site. Excellent family facilities are available. 6 acre site. 36 touring pitches. Caravan pitches. Motorhome pitches. Tent pitches.

Open: Etr-Oct

Pitches: ⛺ £14-£21 ⛺ £14-£21 ▲ £14-£21

Facilities: 🚿 ⊙ ✳ 🔥 WiFi ♻ ❼

Services: 🔌

Within 3 miles: ↡ ᵖ 🔲

Notes: 🚫

AA Pubs & Restaurants nearby: Rose & Crown (Eli's), HUISH EPISCOPI, TA10 9QT, 01458 250494

The Devonshire Arms, LONG SUTTON, TA10 9LP, 01458 241271

The Halfway House, PITNEY, TA10 9AB, 01458 252513

PITCHES: ⛺ Caravans ⛺ Motorhomes ▲ Tents ⋒ Glamping-style accommodation **SERVICES:** 🔌 Electric hook up 🔲 Launderette 🍺 Licensed bar 🛢 Calor Gas ⊘ Camping Gaz T Toilet fluid 🍽 Café/Restaurant 🏪 Fast Food/Takeaway 🔋 Battery charging 🍼 Baby care 🚾 Motorvan service point
ABBREVIATIONS: BH/bank hols – bank holidays Etr – Easter Spring BH – Spring Bank Holiday fr – from hrs – hours m – mile mdnt – midnight rdbt – roundabout rs – restricted service wk – week wknd – weekend x-rds – cross roads 🚫 No credit or debit cards 🚫 No dogs 👫 Children of all ages accepted

MARTOCK
Map 4 ST41

Places to visit

Montacute House, MONTACUTE, TA15 6XP, 01935 823289
www.nationaltrust.org.uk

Great for kids: Fleet Air Arm Museum, YEOVILTON, BA22 8HT, 01935 840565
www.fleetairarm.com

Southfork Caravan Park
►►►► 82%

tel: 01935 825661 **Parrett Works TA12 6AE**
email: southforkcaravans@btconnect.com web: www.southforkcaravans.co.uk
dir: *8m NW of Yeovil, 2m off A303. From E, take exit after Cartgate rdbt. From W, 1st exit off rdbt signed South Petherton, follow camping signs.* grid ref: *ST448188*

A neat, level mainly grass park in a quiet rural area, just outside the pretty village of Martock. Some excellent spacious hardstandings are available. The facilities are always spotless and the whole site is well cared for by the friendly owners, who will ensure your stay is a happy one, a fact borne out by the many repeat customers. The park is unique in that it also has a fully-approved caravan repair and servicing centre with accessory shop. There are also static caravans available for hire. 2 acre site. 27 touring pitches. 2 hardstandings. Caravan pitches. Motorhome pitches. Tent pitches. 3 statics.

Open: all year **Last arrival:** 22.30hrs **Last departure:** noon

Pitches: ⊞ ⊞ Å

Leisure: ⅗

Facilities: ⊠⊙⌧⌖⊛⊙⑤⌁⌂⊙⌀

Services: ⊞⊙⌂⊘Ⓣ⌀

Within 3 miles: ⌀⌀⑤

Notes: Dogs must be kept on leads.

AA Pubs & Restaurants nearby: The Nag's Head Inn, MARTOCK, TA12 6NF, 01935 823432
Ilchester Arms, ILCHESTER, BA22 8LN, 01935 840220

MINEHEAD
Map 3 SS94

Places to visit

West Somerset Railway, MINEHEAD, TA24 5BG, 01643 704996
www.west-somerset-railway.co.uk

Dunster Castle, DUNSTER, TA24 6SL, 01643 821314
www.nationaltrust.org.uk/dunstercastle

Great for kids: Tropiquaria Animal and Adventure Park, WASHFORD, TA23 0QB, 01984 640688 www.tropiquaria.co.uk

Minehead & Exmoor Caravan & Camping Park
►►► 78%

tel: 01643 703074 **Porlock Rd TA24 8SW**
email: enquiries@mineheadandexmoorcamping.co.uk
dir: *1m W of Minehead town centre, take A39 towards Porlock. Site on right.* grid ref: *SS950457*

A small terraced park, on the edge of Exmoor, spread over five small paddocks and screened by the mature trees that surround it. The level pitches provide a comfortable space for each unit on this family-run park. The site is very conveniently placed for visiting Minehead and the Exmoor National Park. 3 acre site. 50 touring pitches. 9 hardstandings. 10 seasonal pitches. Caravan pitches. Motorhome pitches. Tent pitches.

Open: Mar-Oct (rs Nov-Feb open certain weeks only (phone to check))
Last arrival: 21.00hrs **Last departure:** noon

Pitches: * ⊞ £14-£20 ⊞ £14-£20 Å £14-£20

Leisure: ⅗

Facilities: ⊠⊙⌧⌖⊛⊙⑤⌂⊙⌀

Services: ⊞⌂⊘⌀

Within 3 miles: ⌀⊞⌀◎⌀⑤⑤

Notes: ⊘ No open fires or loud music. Dogs must be kept on leads. Tumble dryer.

AA Pubs & Restaurants nearby: The Luttrell Arms, DUNSTER, TA24 6SG, 01643 821555
The Stags Head Inn, DUNSTER, TA24 6SN, 01643 821229

OARE
Map 3 SS74

Places to visit

The Lyn & Exmoor Museum, LYNTON, EX35 6AF, 01598 753398
www.lyntonmuseum.org.uk

Great for kids: Exmoor Zoological Park, BLACKMOOR GATE, EX31 4SG, 01598 763352 www.exmoorzoo.co.uk

Cloud Farm
►►► 77%

tel: 01598 741278 **EX35 6NU**
email: stay@cloudfarmcamping.co.uk
dir: *M5 junct 24, A39 towards Minehead & Porlock then Lynton. Left in 6.5m, follow signs to Oare, right, site signed.* grid ref: *SS794467*

A traditional campsite set in a stunning location in Exmoor's Doone Valley. This quiet, sheltered campsite is arranged over four riverside fields with fairly basic but modern toilet and shower facilities. It offers a good shop and a café serving food all

LEISURE: 🏊 Indoor swimming pool 🏊 Outdoor swimming pool ⅗ Children's playground 🧒 Kid's club 🎾 Tennis court 🎱 Games room 📺 Separate TV room
⛳ golf course 🚣 Boats for hire 🎬 Cinema 🎵 Entertainment 🎣 Fishing ◎ Mini golf 🏄 Watersports 🏋 Gym 🏟 Sports field Spa ♻ Stables
FACILITIES: 🛁 Bath 🚿 Shower ⊙ Electric shaver 🎀 Hairdryer ❄ Ice Pack Facility ♿ Disabled facilities 📞 Public telephone 🏪 Shop on site or within 200yds
🏬 Mobile shop (calls at least 5 days a week) 🍖 BBQ area 🏕 Picnic area 📶 Wi-fi 💻 Internet access ♻ Recycling ⓘ Tourist info 🐕 Dog exercise area

day, including breakfasts; there is a walled Tea Garden for alfresco eating. There are also several self-catering cottages for hire. Food is served all day at the pub that's only a 10-minute walk away. 110 acre site. 70 touring pitches. 6 hardstandings. Caravan pitches. Motorhome pitches. Tent pitches.

Open: all year **Last arrival:** anytime **Last departure:** anytime

Pitches: * ⊂⊃ £16 ⊂⊃ £16 ▲ £16

Facilities: ⬩⊙⌐✳⬩⬩⬩⬩⬩⬩ WiFi ▦ ♻ ❸

Services: ⬩⬩ ⬩⬩⬩T⬩⬩⬩⬩

Within 3 miles: ⬩⬩⬩⬩↻

Notes: No noise after mdnt.

AA Pubs & Restaurants nearby: Rockford Inn, BRENDON, EX35 6PT, 01598 741214

PORLOCK
Map 3 SS84

Places to visit

West Somerset Railway, MINEHEAD, TA24 5BG, 01643 704996
www.west-somerset-railway.co.uk

Dunster Castle, DUNSTER, TA24 6SL, 01643 821314
www.nationaltrust.org.uk/dunstercastle

Great for kids: Tropiquaria Animal and Adventure Park, WASHFORD, TA23 0QB, 01984 640688 www.tropiquaria.co.uk

---

PREMIER PARK

Porlock Caravan Park
▶▶▶▶▶ 85%

GOLD

tel: 01643 862269 **TA24 8ND**
email: info@porlockcaravanpark.co.uk **web:** www.porlockcaravanpark.co.uk
dir: Through village fork right signed Porlock Weir, site on right. **grid ref:** SS882469

A sheltered touring park attractively laid out in the centre of lovely countryside on the edge of Porlock. The famous Porlock Hill, a few hundred yards from the site, leads to some spectacular areas of Exmoor and stunning views. The toilet facilities are superb, and there's a popular kitchen area with microwave and freezer. Seven holiday statics are available for hire. 3 acre site. 40 touring pitches. 14 hardstandings. Caravan pitches. Motorhome pitches. Tent pitches. 55 statics.

Open: 15 Mar-Oct **Last arrival:** 20.00hrs **Last departure:** 11.00hrs

Pitches: ⊂⊃ ⊂⊃ ▲

Facilities: ⬩⊙⌐✳⬩⬩⬩⬩⬩ WiFi ♻ ❸

Services: ⬩⬩ ⬩⬩⬩⬩⬩

Within 3 miles: ⬩⬩⬩⬩⬩↻

Notes: No fires, rollerblades or scooters. Dogs must be kept on leads.

AA Pubs & Restaurants nearby: The Ship Inn, PORLOCK, TA24 8QD, 01643 862507

The Bottom Ship, PORLOCK, TA24 8PB, 01643 863288

Burrowhayes Farm Caravan & Camping Site & Riding Stables
▶▶▶▶ 90%

tel: 01643 862463 **West Luccombe TA24 8HT**
email: info@burrowhayes.co.uk **web:** www.burrowhayes.co.uk
dir: A39 from Minehead towards Porlock for 5m. Left at Red Post to Horner & West Luccombe, site 0.25m on right, immediately before humpback bridge. **grid ref:** SS897460

A delightful site on the edge of Exmoor that slopes gently down to Horner Water. The farm buildings have been converted into riding stables from where escorted rides onto the moors can be taken; the excellent toilet facilities are housed in timber-clad buildings. Hardstandings are available, some of which are fully serviced, and there is a popular, well-stocked shop on site. There are many countryside walks that can be accessed directly from the site. 20 static holiday homes are for hire. 8 acre site. 120 touring pitches. 10 hardstandings. Caravan pitches. Motorhome pitches. Tent pitches. 20 statics.

Open: 15 Mar-Oct (rs Before Etr caravan hire & riding not available)
Last arrival: 22.00hrs **Last departure:** noon

Pitches: * ⊂⊃ £16-£22.50 ⊂⊃ £16-£22.50 ▲ £13-£20

Facilities: ⬩⊙⌐✳⬩⬩⬩⬩ WiFi ♻ ❸

Services: ⬩⬩ ⬩⬩⬩T⬩⬩⬩

Within 3 miles: ⬩⬩⊚⬩⬩↻

Notes: Dogs must be kept on leads.

AA Pubs & Restaurants nearby: The Ship Inn, PORLOCK, TA24 8QD, 01643 862507

The Bottom Ship, PORLOCK, TA24 8PB, 01643 863288

PITCHES: ⊂⊃ Caravans ⊂⊃ Motorhomes ▲ Tents ⋒ Glamping-style accommodation **SERVICES:** ⬩ Electric hook up ⬩ Launderette ⬩ Licensed bar ⬩ Calor Gas ⬩ Camping Gaz T Toilet fluid ⬩ Café/Restaurant ⬩ Fast Food/Takeaway ⬩ Battery charging ⬩ Baby care ⬩ Motorvan service point
ABBREVIATIONS: BH/bank hols – bank holidays Etr – Easter Spring BH – Spring Bank Holiday fr – from hrs – hours m – mile mdnt – midnight rdbt – roundabout rs – restricted service wk – week wknd – weekend x-rds – cross roads ⬩ No credit or debit cards ⬩ No dogs ⬩ Children of all ages accepted

Places to visit

Glastonbury Abbey, GLASTONBURY, BA6 9EL, 01458 832267
www.glastonburyabbey.com

The Helicopter Museum, WESTON-SUPER-MARE, BS24 8PP, 01934 635227
www.helicoptermuseum.co.uk

Great for kids: Wookey Hole Caves & Papermill, WOOKEY HOLE, BA5 1BB,
01749 672243 www.wookey.co.uk

Cheddar Mendip Heights Camping & Caravanning Club Site

▶▶▶▶88%

tel: 01749 870241 & 0845 130 7633　**Townsend BA5 3BP**
email: cheddar.site@thecampingandcaravanningclub.co.uk
dir: *From A39 take B3135 to Cheddar. Left in 4.5m. Site 200yds on right, signed.*
grid ref: ST522519

A gently sloping site set high on the Mendip Hills and surrounded by trees. This excellent campsite offers really good facilities, including top notch family rooms and private cubicles which are spotlessly maintained. Fresh bread is baked daily and available from the well-stocked shop. The site is well positioned for visiting local attractions such as Cheddar, Wookey Hole, Wells and Glastonbury, and is popular with walkers. Self-catering caravans are now available for hire. 4.5 acre site. 90 touring pitches. 37 hardstandings. Caravan pitches. Motorhome pitches. Tent pitches. 2 statics.

Open: 15 Mar-5 Nov **Last arrival:** 20.00hrs **Last departure:** noon
Pitches: * ⌗ £19.25-£27.45 ⌗ £19.25-£27.45 ▲ £10.70-£26.45
Leisure: ⋀
Facilities: ♠⊙☞✳♿⊙⑤🍴 ⬛ ♻ ❶
Services: ❷⑤🔋⟋Ⓣ🢒⚒
Within 3 miles: ⚓⑤♻
Notes: Site gates closed 23.00hrs-07.00hrs. Dogs must be kept on leads.
AA Pubs & Restaurants nearby: Wookey Hole Inn, WOOKEY HOLE, BA5 1BP, 01749 676677
The Burcott Inn, WOOKEY, BA5 1NJ, 01749 673874

Places to visit

East Somerset Railway, CRANMORE, BA4 4QP, 01749 880417
www.eastsomersetrailway.com

The Bishop's Palace, WELLS, BA5 2PD, 01749 988111 www.bishopspalace.org.uk

Great for kids: Wookey Hole Caves & Papermill, WOOKEY HOLE, BA5 1BB,
01749 672243 www.wookey.co.uk

Greenacres Camping

▶▶ 96%

tel: 01749 890497 **Barrow Ln, North Wootton BA4 4HL**
email: stay@greenacres-camping.co.uk
dir: *Approx halfway between Glastonbury & Shepton Mallet on A361 turn at Steanbow Farm signed North Wootton. Or from A39 between Upper Coxley & Wells turn at Brownes Garden Centre into Woodford Ln. Follow North Wootton & site signs.* **grid ref:** ST553417

An immaculately maintained site peacefully set within sight of Glastonbury Tor. It is mainly family orientated and there is plenty of space for children to play games in a very safe environment; many thoughtful extra facilities provided such as play houses and a children's entertainment team in the high season. There is even a 'glow worm safari' at certain times of the year. Facilities are exceptionally clean and bike hire is available. 4.5 acre site. 40 touring pitches. Motorhome pitches. Tent pitches.

Open: Apr-Sep **Last arrival:** 21.00hrs **Last departure:** 11.00hrs
Pitches: * ⌗ fr £18 ▲ fr £18
Leisure: ⋀ ❀
Facilities: ♠⊙☞✳⑤♿🍴 ⬛ ♻ ❶
Services: ❷❶⟋🢒
Within 3 miles: ⚓🢒⚒❀♻⑤♻U
Notes: ⊗ No caravans or large motorhomes. Cycle hire, fire pits, camp fires, free use of fridges & freezers, book library.
The George Inn, CROSCOMBE, BA5 3QH, 01749 342306

Places to visit

Lytes Cary Manor, KINGSDON, TA11 7HU, 01458 224471
www.nationaltrust.org.uk/lytes-cary-manor

Haynes International Motor Museum, SPARKFORD, BA22 7LH, 01963 440804
www.haynesmotormuseum.com

Long Hazel Park

▶▶▶▶84%

tel: 01963 440002 **High St BA22 7JH**
email: longhazelpark@hotmail.com
dir: *Exit A303 at Hazlegrove rdbt, follow signs for Sparkford. Site 400yds on left.*
grid ref: ST602262

A very neat, adults-only park next to the village inn in the high street. This attractive park is run by friendly owners to a very good standard. Many of the spacious pitches have hardstandings. There are also luxury lodges on site for hire or purchase. The site is close to the Haynes Motor Museum and the Yeovilton Air Museum. 3.5 acre site. 50 touring pitches. 30 hardstandings. 21 seasonal pitches. Caravan pitches. Motorhome pitches. Tent pitches. 2 statics.

Open: all year **Last arrival:** 21.00hrs **Last departure:** 11.00hrs
Pitches: * ⌗ fr £18 ⌗ fr £18 ▲ fr £18
Facilities: ♠⊙☞✳♿⊙🍴 ⬛ ♻ ❶

LEISURE: 🏊 Indoor swimming pool 🏊 Outdoor swimming pool ⋀ Children's playground 🪁 Kid's club ⚲ Tennis court 🎱 Games room ▭ Separate TV room ⛳ golf course ⛵ Boats for hire ▤ Cinema 🎵 Entertainment 🎣 Fishing ◉ Mini golf 🏄 Watersports 🏋 Gym ⚽ Sports field Spa U Stables
FACILITIES: 🛁 Bath ♠ Shower ⊙ Electric shaver ☞ Hairdryer ✳ Ice Pack Facility ♿ Disabled facilities ⓒ Public telephone ⑤ Shop on site or within 200yds 🢒 Mobile shop (calls at least 5 days a week) 🍴 BBQ area 🢒 Picnic area ⬛ Wi-fi 🖥 Internet access ♻ Recycling ❶ Tourist info 🐕 Dog exercise area

Services: 🔌🔲🔋⊘Ⓣ🔋⛟

Within 3 miles: ⌕🎣🛒

Notes: Adults only. ⊗ No open fires or firepits, no noise after 22.00hrs. Dogs must be kept on leads & exercised off site. Picnic tables available, camping spares.

AA Pubs & Restaurants nearby: The Walnut Tree, WEST CAMEL, BA22 7QW, 01935 851292

The Queens Arms, CORTON DENHAM, DT9 4LR, 01963 220317

TAUNTON	**Map 4 ST22**

Places to visit

Hestercombe Gardens, TAUNTON, TA2 8LG, 01823 413923 www.hestercombe.com

Barrington Court, BARRINGTON, TA19 0NQ, 01460 241938 www.nationaltrust.org.uk

---

Cornish Farm Touring Park
►►►► 84%

tel: 01823 327746 **Shoreditch TA3 7BS**

email: info@cornishfarm.com **web:** www.cornishfarm.com

dir: *M5 junct 25 towards Taunton. Left at lights. 3rd left into Ilminster Rd (follow Corfe signs). Right at rdbt, left at next rdbt. Right at T-junct, left into Killams Dr, 2nd left into Killams Ave. Over motorway bridge. Site on left, take 2nd entrance.* **grid ref:** *ST235217*

This smart park provides really top quality facilities throughout. Although only two miles from Taunton, it is set in open countryside and is a very convenient base for visiting the many attractions of the area such as Clarks Village, Glastonbury and Cheddar Gorge. Also makes an excellent base for watching county cricket at the nearby Somerset County Ground. 3.5 acre site. 50 touring pitches. 25 hardstandings. Caravan pitches. Motorhome pitches. Tent pitches.

Open: all year **Last arrival:** anytime **Last departure:** 11.30hrs

Pitches: * 🚐 £15-£19 🚍 £15-£19 🅰 £15-£19

Facilities: 🏕️☉🅿️♿🚿📶💻🏋️

Services: 🔌🔲🔋Ⓣ⛟

Within 3 miles: ⌕🎯🎣◎🛒🛢️🎣

Notes: Dogs must be kept on leads.

AA Pubs & Restaurants nearby: The Hatch Inn, TAUNTON, TA3 6SG, 01823 480245

The Willow Tree Restaurant, TAUNTON, TA1 4AR, 01823 352835

Ashe Farm Camping & Caravan Site
►►► 83%

tel: 01823 443764 & 07891 989482 **Thornfalcon TA3 5NW**

email: info@ashefarm.co.uk **web:** www.ashefarm.co.uk

dir: *M5 junct 25, A358 E for 2.5m. Right at Nags Head pub. Site 0.25m on right.*

grid ref: *ST279229*

A well-screened site surrounded by mature trees and shrubs, with two large touring fields. A modern facilities block includes toilets and showers plus a separate laundry room. Not far from the bustling market town of Taunton, and handy for both south and north coasts. Also makes a good stopover for people travelling on the nearby M5. 7 acre site. 30 touring pitches. 11 hardstandings. Caravan pitches. Motorhome pitches. Tent pitches. 3 statics. 10 tipis. 10 bell tents/yurts.

Open: Apr-Oct **Last arrival:** 22.00hrs **Last departure:** noon

Pitches: 🚐🚍🅰🏕️

Leisure: ⚺♨

Facilities: 🏕️☉🅿️♿♿🏋️🎣🏋️🏋️

Services: 🔌🔲

Within 3 miles: ⌕🎯🎣◎🛒🛢️🎣

Notes: ⊗ No camp fires, no noise after 22.00hrs. Dogs must be kept on leads. Baby changing facilities.

AA Pubs & Restaurants nearby: The Hatch Inn, TAUNTON, TA3 6SG, 01823 480245

The Willow Tree Restaurant, TAUNTON, TA1 4AR, 01823 352835

Find out about the AA's Pennant rating scheme
on pages 10-11

PITCHES: 🚐 Caravans 🚍 Motorhomes 🅰 Tents 🏕️ Glamping-style accommodation **SERVICES:** 🔌 Electric hook up 🔲 Launderette 🍺 Licensed bar 🔋 Calor Gas ⊘ Camping Gaz Ⓣ Toilet fluid 🍽️ Café/Restaurant 🍔 Fast Food/Takeaway 🔋 Battery charging 🛒 Baby care ⛟ Motorvan service point

ABBREVIATIONS: BH/bank hols – bank holidays Etr – Easter Spring BH – Spring Bank Holiday fr – from hrs – hours m – mile mdnt – midnight rdbt – roundabout rs – restricted service wk – week wknd – weekend x-rds – cross roads ⊗ No credit or debit cards ⊗ No dogs 🚸 Children of all ages accepted

WATCHET
Map 3 ST04

Places to visit

West Somerset Railway, MINEHEAD, TA24 5BG, 01643 704996
www.west-somerset-railway.co.uk

Dunster Castle, DUNSTER, TA24 6SL, 01643 821314
www.nationaltrust.org.uk/dunstercastle

Great for kids: Tropiquaria Animal and Adventure Park, WASHFORD, TA23 0QB, 01984 640688 www.tropiquaria.co.uk

---

Home Farm Holiday Centre
►►►►81%

tel: 01984 632487 **St Audries Bay TA4 4DP**
email: dib@homefarmholidaycentre.co.uk
dir: A39 for 17m to West Quantoxhead, B3191 after garage in village (signed Doniford), 1st right in 0.25m. **grid ref:** ST106432

In a hidden valley beneath the Quantock Hills, this park overlooks its own private beach. The atmosphere is friendly and quiet, and there are lovely sea views from the level pitches. Flowerbeds, woodland walks and the Koi carp pond all enhance this very attractive site, along with a lovely indoor swimming pool, an excellent children's play area, and a beer garden. 45 acre site. 40 touring pitches. 35 hardstandings. Caravan pitches. Motorhome pitches. Tent pitches. 230 statics.

Open: all year (rs Nov-1 Mar no camping, shop & bar closed) **Last arrival:** dusk **Last departure:** noon

Pitches: ⊞ £12-£27.50 ⊞ £12-£27.50 ▲ £12-£27.50

Leisure: ⊞ ⚶   **Facilities:** ⎎ ⊙ ⌂ ✳ ⚲ ⚲ ⑤ ⌁ 📶 ♻ 🛈

Services: ⚲ ⑤ ⌁ 🛢 ⌁ ⊤   **Within 3 miles:** ⌁ ⑤ ⊡

Notes: No cars by caravans or tents. No noise after 23.00hrs. Dogs must be kept on leads.

AA Pubs & Restaurants nearby: The Hood Arms, KILVE, TA5 1EA, 01278 741210

Doniford Bay Holiday Park
HOLIDAY HOME PARK 89%

GOLD

tel: 01984 632423 **TA23 0TJ**
email: donifordbay@haven.com **web:** www.haven.com/donifordbay
dir: M5 junct 23, A38 towards Bridgwater, A39 towards Minehead. 15m, at West Quantoxhead, right after St Audries garage. Park 1m on right. **grid ref:** ST093432

This well-appointed holiday park, situated adjacent to a shingle and sand beach, offers a wide range of activities for the whole family. The holiday homes are spacious and well-appointed and there is plenty to keep children (of all ages) interested, including great indoor and outdoor pools, a multi-sports centre, slides and archery. The park has good eating outlets including a nice café/restaurant. Being close to the Exmoor National Park, it offers visitors the chance to seek out some of the best scenery in the county.

Open: Mar-Oct

Change over day: Mon, Fri, Sat

Arrival and departure times: Please contact the site

Statics: 143 Sleeps 6-8 Bedrms 2-3 Bathrms 1-2 Toilets 1-2 Microwave Freezer TV Sky/FTV Elec inc Gas inc Grass area

Children: ⚭ Cots Highchair **Dogs:** 2 on leads No dangerous dogs

Leisure: ⊞ ⚶ Cycle hire ⚱ ⚶

WELLINGTON
Map 3 ST12

Places to visit

Hestercombe Gardens, TAUNTON, TA2 8LG, 01823 413923
www.hestercombe.com

Great for kids: Diggerland, CULLOMPTON, EX15 2PE, 0871 227 7007
www.diggerland.com

Greenacres Touring Park
►►►►85%

tel: 01823 652844 **Haywards Ln, Chelston TA21 9PH**
email: enquiries@wellington.co.uk
dir: M5 junct 26, right at rdbt signed Wellington, approx 1.5m. At Chelston rdbt, take 1st left, signed A38 West Buckland Rd. In 500mtrs follow sign for site. **grid ref:** ST156001

This attractively landscaped adults-only park is situated close to the Somerset/Devon border in a peaceful setting with great views of the Blackdown and Quantock Hills. It is in a very convenient location for overnight stays, being just one and half miles from the M5. This park is also well positioned for visiting both the north and south coasts, and it is also close to a local bus route. It has excellent facilities, which are spotlessly clean and well maintained. 2.5 acre site. 40 touring pitches. 30 hardstandings. Caravan pitches. Motorhome pitches.

Open: Apr-end Sep **Last arrival:** 19.00hrs **Last departure:** 11.00hrs

Pitches: * ⊞ £17-£18 ⊞ £17-£18

Facilities: ⎎ ⊙ ⌂ ⚲ ⚶ ♻ 🛈

Services: ⚲

Within 3 miles: ⌁ ⊞ ⌁ ⑤ ⊡ ⚶

Notes: Adults only. ⚶ No RVs. Dogs must be kept on leads.

AA Pubs & Restaurants nearby: The Globe, MILVERTON, TA4 1JX, 01823 400534

Gamlins Farm Caravan Park
►►►81%

tel: 01823 672859 & 07814 742462 **Gamlins Farm House, Greenham TA21 0LZ**
email: gamlinsfarmcaravanpark@hotmail.co.uk
dir: M5 junct 26, A38 towards Tiverton & Exeter. 5m, right for Greenham, site 1m on right. **grid ref:** ST083195

This peaceful site (only two minutes from the A38) is set in a secluded valley with excellent views of the Quantock Hills; it is well placed for visiting both Devon and Somerset. The facilities are very good and spotlessly clean, and free coarse fishing is available. Static holiday homes for hire. 4 acre site. 30 touring pitches. 6 hardstandings. Caravan pitches. Motorhome pitches. Tent pitches. 4 statics.

Open: Mar-Oct

Pitches: * ⊞ £12-£19 ⊞ £12-£19 ▲ £10-£15

Leisure: ⚲

Facilities: ⎎ ⊙ ⌂ ✳ ⚲ ⌁ 📶 ▦ ♻ 🛈

Services: ⚲ ⑤ 🛢 ⌁

Within 3 miles: ⌁ ⌁ ⑤ ⊡ ⚶

Notes: ⚶ Dogs not to be left on site without owners, no loud noise after 22.00hrs. Dogs must be kept on leads.

LEISURE: ⊞ Indoor swimming pool ⚶ Outdoor swimming pool ⚶ Children's playground ⚱ Kid's club ⚶ Tennis court ⚲ Games room ▢ Separate TV room ⌁ golf course ⚶ Boats for hire ⊟ Cinema ♬ Entertainment ⌁ Fishing ◎ Mini golf ⚶ Watersports ⚶ Gym ⚶ Sports field Spa ⚶ Stables **FACILITIES:** ⚭ Bath ⎎ Shower ⊙ Electric shaver ⌂ Hairdryer ✳ Ice Pack Facility ⚲ Disabled facilities ⑤ Public telephone ⑤ Shop on site or within 200yds ⌁ Mobile shop (calls at least 5 days a week) ⌁ BBQ area ⌁ Picnic area 📶 Wi-fi ▦ Internet access ♻ Recycling 🛈 Tourist info ⌁ Dog exercise area

WELLS
Map 4 ST54

Places to visit
Glastonbury Abbey, GLASTONBURY, BA6 9EL, 01458 832267
www.glastonburyabbey.com

The Bishop's Palace, WELLS, BA5 2PD, 01749 988111 www.bishopspalace.org.uk

ROGER ALMOND AWARD FOR THE MOST IMPROVED CAMPSITE OF THE YEAR 2015

PREMIER PARK

Wells Holiday Park
▶▶▶▶▶ 87%

tel: 01749 676869 **Haybridge BA5 1AJ**
email: jason@wellsholidaypark.co.uk
dir: A38 then follow signs for Axbridge, Cheddar & Wells. **grid ref:** ST531459

This well established, adults-only holiday park has first-class toilet facilities and many hardstandings, all with electricity. A restful park set in countryside on the outskirts of Wells, it is within easy walking distance of the city, with its spectacular cathedral and Bishop's Palace. Cheddar Gorge and Caves, Bath, Bristol, Weston-Super-Mare, Wookey Hole and Glastonbury are all within easy driving distance. The site has a function room and patio as well as a beauty salon. Holiday cottages are available for hire. 7.5 acre site. 72 touring pitches. 54 hardstandings. 20 seasonal pitches. Caravan pitches. Motorhome pitches. Tent pitches. 12 statics. 20 bell tents/yurts.

Open: all year **Last arrival:** 20.00hrs **Last departure:** noon

Pitches: ⌐ ⌐ ▲ ⌂

Facilities: ⌐⊙⌐✳⌐⌐⌐⌐⌐⌐⌐⌐⌐ 🛆 ⊙

Services: ⌐⌐ ⌐⌐⌐⌐⌐⌐⌐

Within 3 miles: ⌐⌐⌐⌐⊙⌐⌐⌐⌐

Notes: Adults only. Dogs must be kept on leads. Pètanque.

AA Pubs & Restaurants nearby: The City Arms, WELLS, BA5 2AG, 01749 673916

The Fountain Inn, WELLS, BA5 2UU, 01749 672317

Goodfellows, WELLS, BA5 2RR, 01749 673866

The Old Spot, WELLS, BA5 2SE, 01749 689099

Homestead Park
▶▶ 84%

tel: 01749 673022 **Wookey Hole BA5 1BW**
email: homesteadpark@onetel.com
dir: 0.5m NW off A371 (Wells to Cheddar road). NB weight limit on bridge into touring area now 1 tonne. **grid ref:** ST532474

This attractive, small site for tents only is set on a wooded hillside and meadowland with access to the river and nearby Wookey Hole. This park is for adults only and the statics are residential caravans. 2 acre site. 30 touring pitches. Tent pitches. 28 statics.

Open: Etr-Sep **Last arrival:** 20.00hrs **Last departure:** noon

Pitches: ▲

Facilities: ⌐⊙⌐✳ ⊙

Services: ⌐⌐⌐ **Within 3 miles:** ⌐⌐⌐⌐⌐⌐⌐⌐

Notes: Adults only. ⌐ Dogs must be kept on leads.

AA Pubs & Restaurants nearby: The City Arms, WELLS, BA5 2AG, 01749 673916

The Fountain Inn, WELLS, BA5 2UU, 01749 672317

Goodfellows, WELLS, BA5 2RR, 01749 673866

The Old Spot, WELLS, BA5 2SE, 01749 689099

WESTON-SUPER-MARE
Map 4 ST36

Places to visit
Weston-Super-Mare Museum, WESTON-SUPER-MARE, BS23 1PR, 01934 621028 www.weston-super-maretowncouncil.gov.uk

Great for kids: The Helicopter Museum, WESTON-SUPER-MARE, BS24 8PP, 01934 635227 www.helicoptermuseum.co.uk

Country View Holiday Park
▶▶▶▶ 85%

tel: 01934 627595 **Sand Rd, Sand Bay BS22 9UJ**
email: info@cvhp.co.uk **web:** www.cvhp.co.uk
dir: M5 junct 21, A370 towards Weston-Super-Mare. Immediately into left lane, follow Kewstoke & Sand Bay signs. Straight over 3 rdbts onto Lower Norton Ln. At Sand Bay right into Sand Rd, site on right. **grid ref:** ST335647

A pleasant open site in a rural area a few hundred yards from Sandy Bay and the beach. The park is also well placed for energetic walks along the coast at either end of the beach and is only a short drive away from Weston-Super-Mare. There is a touring section for tents, caravans and motorhomes with a toilet and shower block. There are 14 hardstanding pitches plus grass pitches all with electricity. The facilities are excellent and well maintained, including a nice outdoor swimming pool and small tasteful bar. 20 acre site. 190 touring pitches. 150 hardstandings. 90 seasonal pitches. Caravan pitches. Motorhome pitches. Tent pitches. 65 statics.

Open: Mar-Jan **Last arrival:** 20.00hrs **Last departure:** noon

Pitches: * ⌐ £15-£28 ⌐ £15-£28 ▲ £15-£28

Leisure: ⌐⌐⌐⌐⌐ **Facilities:** ⌐⊙⌐✳⌐⌐⌐⌐⌐⌐ 🛆 ⊙

Services: ⌐⌐⌐⌐ **Within 3 miles:** ⌐⌐⌐⌐⊙⌐⌐⌐⌐

Notes: Dogs must be kept on leads.

AA Pubs & Restaurants nearby: The Cove, WESTON-SUPER-MARE, BS23 2BX, 01934 418217

PITCHES: ⌐ Caravans ⌐ Motorhomes ▲ Tents ⌂ Glamping-style accommodation **SERVICES:** ⌐ Electric hook up ⌐ Launderette ⌐ Licensed bar ⌐ Calor Gas ⌐ Camping Gaz ⌐ Toilet fluid ⌐ Café/Restaurant ⌐ Fast Food/Takeaway ⌐ Battery charging ⌐ Baby care ⌐ Motorvan service point
ABBREVIATIONS: BH/bank hols – bank holidays Etr – Easter Spring BH – Spring Bank Holiday fr – from hrs – hours m – mile mdnt – midnight rdbt – roundabout rs – restricted service wk – week wknd – weekend x-rds – cross roads ⌐ No credit or debit cards ⌐ No dogs ⌐ Children of all ages accepted

WESTON-SUPER-MARE *continued*

West End Farm Caravan & Camping Park
►►►82%

tel: 01934 822529 **Locking BS24 8RH**
email: robin@westendfarm.org
dir: *M5 junct 21 onto A370. Follow International Helicopter Museum signs. Right at rdbt, follow signs to site.* **grid ref:** ST354600

A spacious and well laid out park bordered by hedges, with good landscaping, and well-kept facilities. Fully serviced pitches are available. It is handily located next to a helicopter museum, and offers good access to Weston-Super-Mare and the Mendips. 10 acre site. 75 touring pitches. 10 hardstandings. 30 seasonal pitches. Caravan pitches. Motorhome pitches. Tent pitches. 11 statics.

Open: all year **Last arrival:** 21.00hrs **Last departure:** noon
Pitches: * 🚐 £18.50-£23 🚉 £18.50-£23 ▲ £15-£18.50
Leisure: ♻ **Facilities:** 🏕⊙♿🛒🛗🖕♻🛈
Services: 🔌🖥🔒🖉⬇ **Within 3 miles:** 🚶🏊🎭🎣◎🏊🛍🛍U
Notes: No noise after 22.00hrs. Dogs must be kept on leads.
AA Pubs & Restaurants nearby: The Cove, WESTON-SUPER-MARE, BS23 2BX, 01934 418217

WINSFORD   Map 3 SS93

Places to visit
Dunster Castle, DUNSTER, TA24 6SL, 01643 821314
www.nationaltrust.org.uk/dunstercastle

Cleeve Abbey, WASHFORD, TA23 0PS, 01984 640377
www.english-heritage.org.uk/daysout/properties/cleeve-abbey

Great for kids: Tropiquaria Animal and Adventure Park, WASHFORD, TA23 0QB, 01984 640688 www.tropiquaria.co.uk

Halse Farm Caravan & Camping Park
►►►►80%

GOLD

tel: 01643 851259 **TA24 7JL**
email: info@halsefarm.co.uk **web:** www.halsefarm.co.uk
dir: *Signed from A396 at Bridgetown. In Winsford turn left, bear left past pub. 1m up hill, entrance on left immediately after cattle grid.* **grid ref:** SS894344

A peaceful little site on Exmoor overlooking a wooded valley with glorious views. This moorland site is quite remote, but it provides good modern toilet facilities which are kept immaculately clean. This is a good base for exploring the Exmoor National Park, and Minehead, Porlock and Lynton are only a short drive away. 3 acre site. 44 touring pitches. Caravan pitches. Motorhome pitches. Tent pitches.

Open: 20 Mar-Oct **Last arrival:** 22.00hrs **Last departure:** noon
Pitches: * 🚐 £17-£19 🚉 £17-£19 ▲
Leisure: ⚫
Facilities: 🏕⊙♿🛒🖕♿🖥🛒WiFi♻🛈
Services: 🔌🖥🔒🖉
Within 3 miles: 🎣🛍U
Notes: Dogs must be kept on leads.
AA Pubs & Restaurants nearby: Crown Hotel, EXFORD, TA24 7PP, 01643 831554
Royal Oak Inn, WINSFORD, TA24 7JE, 01643 851455

WIVELISCOMBE   Map 3 ST02

Places to visit
Cleeve Abbey, WASHFORD, TA23 0PS, 01984 640377
www.english-heritage.org.uk/daysout/properties/cleeve-abbey

Hestercombe Gardens, TAUNTON, TA2 8LG, 01823 413923 www.hestercombe.com

PREMIER PARK

Waterrow Touring Park
►►►►►88%

Best of British

tel: 01984 623464 **TA4 2AZ**
email: info@waterrowpark.co.uk **web:** www.waterrowpark.co.uk
dir: *M5 junct 25, A358 (signed Minehead) bypassing Taunton, B3227 through Wiveliscombe. Site in 3m at Waterrow, 0.25m past Rock Inn.* **grid ref:** ST053251

Under pro-active new ownership, this really delightful park for adults has spotless facilities and plenty of spacious hardstandings. The River Tone runs along a valley beneath the park, accessed by steps to a nature area created by the owners, where fly-fishing is permitted. Watercolour painting workshops and other activities are available, and the local pub is a short walk away. There is also a bus stop just outside of the site. 6 acre site. 45 touring pitches. 38 hardstandings. Caravan pitches. Motorhome pitches. Tent pitches.

Open: all year **Last arrival:** 19.00hrs **Last departure:** 11.30hrs
Pitches: 🚐🚉▲
Facilities: 🏕⊙♿🛒🖕♿🖥🛒🖕WiFi♻🛈

LEISURE: 🏊 Indoor swimming pool   🏊 Outdoor swimming pool   🎠 Children's playground   🎣 Kid's club   🎾 Tennis court   🎱 Games room   📺 Separate TV room
⛳ golf course   ⛵ Boats for hire   🎬 Cinema   🎭 Entertainment   🎣 Fishing   ◎ Mini golf   🏄 Watersports   💪 Gym   🏟 Sports field   Spa   U Stables
FACILITIES: 🛁 Bath   🚿 Shower   ⊙ Electric shaver   🖕 Hairdryer   ❄ Ice Pack Facility   ♿ Disabled facilities   ☎ Public telephone   🛍 Shop on site or within 200yds
🛒 Mobile shop (calls at least 5 days a week)   🍖 BBQ area   🌲 Picnic area   WiFi Wi-fi   💻 Internet access   ♻ Recycling   🛈 Tourist info   🖕 Dog exercise area

Services: 🔌🅾️🔋T🔋♿

Within 3 miles: ✏️🛒🅾️

Notes: Adults only. No gazebos, max 2 dogs per unit. Dogs must be kept on leads. Caravan storage.

AA Pubs & Restaurants nearby: The Rock Inn, WATERROW, TA4 2AX, 01984 623293

The Three Horseshoes, LANGLEY MARSH, TA4 2UL, 01984 623763

YEOVIL Map 4 ST51

Places to visit

Montacute House, MONTACUTE, TA15 6XP, 01935 823289
www.nationaltrust.org.uk

Lytes Cary Manor, KINGSDON, TA11 7HU, 01458 224471
www.nationaltrust.org.uk/lytes-cary-manor

Great for kids: Fleet Air Arm Museum, YEOVILTON, BA22 8HT, 01935 840565
www.fleetairarm.com

Halfway Caravan & Camping Park
▶▶82%

tel: 01935 840342 **Trees Cottage, Halfway, Ilchester Rd BA22 8RE**
email: halfwaycaravanpark@earthlink.net
dir: *On A37 between Ilchester & Yeovil.* **grid ref:** *ST530195*

An attractive little park near the Somerset and Dorset border, and next to the Halfway House pub and restaurant, which also has excellent AA-graded accommodation. It overlooks a fishing lake and is surrounded by attractive countryside. Dogs are welcome here. 2 acre site. 20 touring pitches. 10 hardstandings. Caravan pitches. Motorhome pitches. Tent pitches.

Open: Apr-Oct **Last arrival:** 19.00hrs; 21.00hrs on Fri; earliest check-in noon (please contact park) **Last departure:** noon

Pitches: 🚐 £10-£12.50 🚙 £10-£12.50 ▲ £7-£15

Facilities: 🚻🪠❓

Services: 🔌🍽️

Within 3 miles: ⚓🏕️✏️🛒🅾️

Notes: 🐕 Dogs must be kept on leads.

AA Pubs & Restaurants nearby: The Masons Arms, YEOVIL, BA22 8TX, 01935 862591

The Helyar Arms, EAST COKER, BA22 9JR, 01935 862332

STAFFORDSHIRE

CHEADLE Map 10 SK04

Places to visit

Churnet Valley Railway, CHEDDLETON, ST13 7EE, 01538 750755
www.churnetvalleyrailway.co.uk

The Potteries Museum & Art Gallery, STOKE-ON-TRENT, ST1 3DW, 01782 232323
www.stoke.gov.uk/museum

Great for kids: Alton Towers Resort, ALTON, ST10 4DB, 0871 222 3330
www.altontowers.com

Etruria Industrial Museum, STOKE-ON-TRENT, ST4 7AF, 01782 233144
www.stokemuseums.org.uk

Quarry Walk Park
▶▶▶73%

tel: 01538 723412 **Coppice Ln, Croxden Common, Freehay ST10 1RQ**
email: quarry@quarrywalkpark.co.uk
dir: *From A522 (Uttoxeter to Cheadle road) in Mobberley follow Freehay sign. In 1m at rdbt, 3rd exit signed Great Gate. 1.25m to site on right.* **grid ref:** *SK045405*

A pleasant park (for tents only), close to Alton Towers, that was developed in an old quarry; it has well-screened pitches, each with water and electricity, and surrounded by mature trees and shrubs which enhance the peaceful ambience of the park. There are seven glades of varying sizes used exclusively for tents, one with ten electric hook-ups. There are timber lodges for hire, each with its own hot tub. Please note caravans and motorhomes are not accepted. 46 acre site. 40 touring pitches. 1 wooden pod.

Open: all year **Last arrival:** 18.00hrs **Last departure:** 11.00hrs

Pitches: ▲🛖

Leisure: 🎣

Facilities: 🪠☺️🅿️❄️♿🚿🛁📶🖥️♻️❓

Services: 🔌🅾️🔋🖊️

Within 3 miles: 🏕️✏️🎣🛒🅾️⛳

Notes: No cars by tents. No noise after 23.00hrs. Dogs must be kept on leads.

AA Pubs & Restaurants nearby: The Queens At Freehay, CHEADLE, ST10 1RF, 01538 722383

PITCHES: 🚐 Caravans 🚙 Motorhomes ▲ Tents 🛖 Glamping-style accommodation **SERVICES:** 🔌 Electric hook up 🅾️ Launderette 🍽️ Licensed bar
🔋 Calor Gas 🅖 Camping Gaz T Toilet fluid 🍽️ Café/Restaurant 🍟 Fast Food/Takeaway 🔋 Battery charging 🍼 Baby care ♿ Motorvan service point
ABBREVIATIONS: BH/bank hols – bank holidays Etr – Easter Spring BH – Spring Bank Holiday fr – from hrs – hours m – mile mdnt – midnight
rdbt – roundabout rs – restricted service wk – week wknd – weekend x-rds – cross roads 🚫 No credit or debit cards 🚫 No dogs 👪 Children of all ages accepted

LONGNOR

Map 16 SK06

Places to visit

Poole's Cavern (Buxton Country Park), BUXTON, SK17 9DH, 01298 26978
www.poolescavern.co.uk

Haddon Hall, HADDON HALL, DE45 1LA, 01629 812855 www.haddonhall.co.uk

REGIONAL WINNER – HEART OF ENGLAND
AA CAMPSITE OF THE YEAR 2015

PREMIER PARK

Longnor Wood Holiday Park

▶▶▶▶▶ 90%

tel: 01298 83648 & 07866 016567 **Newtown SK17 0NG**
email: info@longnorwood.co.uk
dir: *From A53 follow Longnor sign. Site signed from village, 1.25m.* **grid ref:** *SK072640*

Enjoying a secluded and very peaceful setting in the heart of the Peak District National Park, this spacious adults-only park is a hidden gem, surrounded by beautiful rolling countryside and sheltered by woodland where there is a variety of wildlife to observe. Expect a warm welcome from the O'Neill family and excellent, well-maintained facilities, including spotlessly clean modern toilets (central heating was installed for 2014), good hardstanding pitches, high levels of security, a putting green, badminton courts, a 4-acre dog walk and super walks from the park gate. The reception was extended in 2014 to include a small shop. 10.5 acre site. 47 touring pitches. 47 hardstandings. 13 seasonal pitches. Caravan pitches. Motorhome pitches. Tent pitches.

Open: Mar-10 Jan **Last arrival:** 19.00hrs **Last departure:** noon

Pitches: 🚐 £23-£29 🚎 £23-£29 ▲ £10-£23

Facilities: 🚿⊙☊✳🕐⑤🎄🐾 Wifi 🖥 ♻ ❶

Services: 🔌⑤🔒⊘①🍴⚒

Within 3 miles: ⚓⑤↻

Notes: Adults only. No fires, no noise after 23.00hrs. Dogs must be kept on leads.

AA Pubs & Restaurants nearby: The Queen Anne Inn, GREAT HUCKLOW, SK17 8RF, 01298 871246

The George, ALSTONEFIELD, DE6 2FX, 01335 310205

LEISURE: 🏊 Indoor swimming pool 🏊 Outdoor swimming pool 🅰 Children's playground 🖐 Kid's club 🎾 Tennis court 🎱 Games room 📺 Separate TV room
🏌 golf course ⛵ Boats for hire 🎦 Cinema 🎵 Entertainment ✒ Fishing ◎ Mini golf 🏄 Watersports 🏋 Gym ⚽ Sports field Spa ♻ Stables
FACILITIES: 🛁 Bath 🚿 Shower ⊙ Electric shaver 🎀 Hairdryer ✳ Ice Pack Facility ♿ Disabled facilities 🕐 Public telephone ⑤ Shop on site or within 200yds
🏪 Mobile shop (calls at least 5 days a week) 🍴 BBQ area 🎄 Picnic area Wifi Wi-fi 🖥 Internet access ♻ Recycling ❶ Tourist info 🐾 Dog exercise area

PITCHES: 🚐 Caravans 🚌 Motorhomes ⛺ Tents ⛺ Glamping-style accommodation **SERVICES:** ⚡ Electric hook up 🔲 Launderette 🍸 Licensed bar
🔋 Calor Gas ⊘ Camping Gaz Ⓣ Toilet fluid 🍽 Café/Restaurant 🍔 Fast Food/Takeaway ⚡ Battery charging 🍼 Baby care ⚙ Motorvan service point
ABBREVIATIONS: BH/bank hols – bank holidays Etr – Easter Spring BH – Spring Bank Holiday fr – from hrs – hours m – mile mdnt – midnight
rdbt – roundabout rs – restricted service wk – week wknd – weekend x-rds – cross roads 🚫 No credit or debit cards 🚫 No dogs 👫 Children of all ages accepted

Suffolk

Suffolk is Constable country, where the county's crumbling, time-ravaged coastline spreads itself under wide skies to convey a wonderful sense of remoteness and solitude. Highly evocative and atmospheric, this is where rivers wind lazily to the sea and notorious 18th-century smugglers hid from the excise men.

It was the artist John Constable who was responsible for raising the region's profile in the 18th century. Constable immortalised these expansive flatlands in his paintings and today the marketing brochures and websites usually refer to the area as Constable Country. Situated on the River Stour at Flatford, Constable's mill is now a major tourist attraction in the area but a close look at the surroundings confirms rural Suffolk is little changed since the family lived here. Constable himself maintained that the Suffolk countryside 'made me a painter and I am grateful.'

Facing the European mainland and with easy access by the various rivers, the county's open, often bleak, landscape made Suffolk vulnerable in early times to attack from waves of invaders. In the Middle Ages, however, it prospered under the wool merchants: it was their wealth that built the great churches which dominate the countryside.

Walking is one of Suffolk's most popular recreational activities. It may be flat but the county has much to discover on foot – not least the isolated Heritage Coast, which can be accessed via the Suffolk Coast Path. Running along the edge of the shore, between Felixstowe and Lowestoft, the trail is a fascinating blend of ecology and military history. Near its southerly start, the path passes close to one of the National Trust's most unusual acquisitions – Orford Ness. Acquired by the Trust in 1993, and officially opened in 1995, this spectacular stretch of coastline had previously been closed to the public since 1915 when the Royal Flying Corps chose Orford Ness as the setting for military research. These days, it is a Site of Special Scientific Interest, recognised in particular for its rare shingle habitats. Visitors to Orford Ness cross the River Ore by National Trust ferry from Orford Quay.

Beyond Orford, the Suffolk Coast Path parts company with the North Sea, albeit briefly, to visit Aldeburgh. Nearby are Snape Maltings, renowned internationally as the home of the Aldeburgh Festival that takes place in June. Benjamin Britten lived at Snape and wrote *Peter Grimes* here. The Suffolk coast is where both the sea and the natural landscape have influenced generations of writers, artists and musicians. An annual literary festival is staged at Aldeburgh on the first weekend in March.

Back on the Suffolk coast, the trail makes for Southwold, with its distinctive, white-walled lighthouse standing sentinel above the town and its colourful beach huts and attractive pier that feature on many a promotional brochure. The final section of the walk is one of the most spectacular, with low, sandy cliffs, several shallow Suffolk broads and the occasional church tower peeping through the trees. Much of Suffolk's coastal heathland is protected as a designated Area of Outstanding Natural Beauty and shelters several rare creatures including the adder, the heath butterfly and the nightjar.

In addition to walking, there is a good choice of cycling routes. There is the Heart of Suffolk Cycle Route, which extends for 78 miles, while the National Byway, a 4,000-mile cycle route around Britain takes in part of Suffolk and is a very enjoyable way to explore the county.

For something less demanding, visit some of Suffolk's best-known towns. Bury St Edmunds, Sudbury and Ipswich feature prominently on the tourist trail, while Lavenham, Kersey and Debenham are a reminder of the county's important role in the wool industry and the vast wealth it yielded the wool merchants. In these charming old towns look out for streets of handsome, period buildings and picturesque, timber-framed houses.

◁ Aldeburgh Beach

SUFFOLK

BUCKLESHAM
Map 13 TM24

Places to visit

Ipswich Museum, IPSWICH, IP1 3QH, 01473 433550
www.cimuseums.org.uk/venues/ipswich-museum.html

Christchurch Mansion, IPSWICH, IP4 2BE, 01473 433554
www.cimuseums.org.uk/venues/christchurch-mansion.html

Westwood Caravan Park
►►►►89%

tel: 01473 659637 & 07436 813545 **Old Felixstowe Rd IP10 0BN**
email: info@westwoodcaravanpark.co.uk **web:** www.westwoodcaravanpark.co.uk
dir: *A14 towards Felixstowe, after junct 58 take 1st exit signed to Kirton. 1.5m to
Bucklesham. Site on right.* **grid ref:** *TM253411*

This constantly improving park is in the heart of rural Suffolk in an idyllic, peaceful
setting. All buildings are of traditional Suffolk style, and the toilet facilities, are of
outstanding quality. The planting and landscaping is exceptional, and
hardstanding pitches are generous in size. There is also a spacious room for
disabled visitors, plenty of space for children to play and a barbecue area with
seating and a fire pit. 4.5 acre site. 100 touring pitches. 70 hardstandings. 65
seasonal pitches. Caravan pitches. Motorhome pitches. Tent pitches.

Open: Mar-15 Jan **Last arrival:** 22.00hrs **Last departure:** 18.00hrs

Pitches: * ⊞ £18-£25 ⊞ £18-£25 ▲ £18-£20

Leisure: ⋀ ✎

Facilities: ⋔ ☉ ✻ ♿ ⑤ ⚲ ⋈ 🆆🅸🅵🅸 ♻ ❂

Services: ⊟⑤ 🔋 ⊘ Ⓣ ☷ ⎌

Within 3 miles: ♟ ◢ ⩶ ⑤⑤

Notes: Dogs must be kept on leads.

AA Pubs & Restaurants nearby: Milsoms Kesgrave Hall, IPSWICH, IP5 2PU, 01473 333741

Mariners, IPSWICH, IP4 1AX, 01473 289748

Salthouse Harbour Hotel, IPSWICH, IP4 1AX, 01473 226789

BUNGAY
Map 13 TM38

Places to visit

Norfolk & Suffolk Aviation Museum, FLIXTON, NR35 1NZ, 01986 896644
www.aviationmuseum.net

Outney Meadow Caravan Park
►►►73%

tel: 01986 892338 **Outney Meadow NR35 1HG**
email: c.r.hancy@ukgateway.net **web:** www.outneymeadow.co.uk
dir: *At Bungay, site signed from rdbt junction of A143 & A144.* **grid ref:** *TM333905*

Three pleasant grassy areas beside the River Waveney, with screened pitches. The
central toilet block offers good modern facilities, especially in the ladies, and is
open at all times. The views from the site across the wide flood plain could be
straight out of a Constable painting. Canoeing and boating, coarse fishing and
cycling are all available here. 6 acre site. 65 touring pitches. 8 hardstandings. 8
seasonal pitches. Caravan pitches. Motorhome pitches. Tent pitches. 20 statics.

Open: Mar-Oct **Last arrival:** 21.00hrs **Last departure:** 16.00hrs

Pitches: ⊞ ⊞ ▲

Facilities: ⋔ ☉ ℱ ✻ ⑤ ⚲ ♻ ❂

Services: ⊟⑤ 🔋 ⊘ Ⓣ ☷

Within 3 miles: ♟ ⩶ ◢ ⩶ ⑤⑤

Notes: Dogs must be kept on leads. Boat, canoe & cycle hire.

BURY ST EDMUNDS
Map 13 TL86

Places to visit

Moyse's Hall Museum, BURY ST EDMUNDS, IP33 1DX, 01284 757160
www.moyseshall.org

Ickworth House, Park & Gardens, HORRINGER, IP29 5QE, 01284 735270
www.nationaltrust.org.uk/ickworth

Great for kids: National Horseracing Museum and Tours, NEWMARKET, CB8 8JH, 01638 667333 www.nhrm.co.uk

Dell Touring Park
►►►► 85%

tel: 01359 270121 **Beyton Rd, Thurston IP31 3RB**
email: info@thedellcaravanpark.co.uk
dir: A14 junct 46 follow Thurston signs & brown camping signs to site. From A143 in Great Barton at x-rds follow Thurston & brown camping signs. **grid ref:** TL928640

A small site with enthusiastic owners that has been developed to a high specification. Set in a quiet spot with lots of mature trees, the quality purpose-built toilet facilities include family rooms, dishwashing and laundry. This is an ideal base for exploring this picturesque area. 6 acre site. 50 touring pitches. 12 hardstandings. Caravan pitches. Motorhome pitches. Tent pitches.

Open: Mar-Oct **Last arrival:** 20.00hrs **Last departure:** noon
Pitches: * ➡ £13-£20 ➡ £13-£20 ▲ £13-£20
Facilities: ➡ ♣ ⊙ ℙ ☀ & ➡ ⅧⅢ ♻ ❼
Services: �R ⊡ ▤ ⬚
Within 3 miles: ℐ ⓢ
Notes: No footballs, no noise after 23.00hrs. Dogs must be kept on leads.
AA Pubs & Restaurants nearby: The Old Cannon Brewery, BURY ST EDMUNDS, IP33 1JR, 01284 768769

Maison Bleue, BURY ST EDMUNDS, IP33 1RG, 01284 760623

The Leaping Hare Restaurant & Country Store, BURY ST EDMUNDS, IP31 2DW, 01359 250287

DUNWICH
Map 13 TM47

Places to visit

RSPB Nature Reserve Minsmere, WESTLETON, IP17 3BY, 01728 648281
www.rspb.org.uk/minsmere

Haw Wood Farm Caravan Park
►► 75%

tel: 01986 784248 **Hinton IP17 3QT**
email: bookings@hawwoodfarm.co.uk
dir: Exit A12, 1.5m N of Darsham level crossing at Darsham Pantry. Site 0.5m on right. **grid ref:** TM421717

An unpretentious family-orientated park set in two large fields surrounded by low hedges. The toilets are clean and functional, and there is plenty of space for children to play. There are big plans and investment scheduled for 2015 that will include a smart new service building, housing the toilets (including family rooms), a coffee shop and laundry, plus the site will have a new children's play area, and a communal BBQ. 15 acre site. 60 touring pitches. Caravan pitches. Motorhome pitches. Tent pitches. 55 statics.

Open: Mar-14 Jan **Last arrival:** 21.00hrs **Last departure:** noon
Pitches: * ➡ £16-£19 ➡ £16-£19 ▲ £8-£19
Leisure: ⋀
Facilities: ➡ ♣ ⊙ ☀ ⓢ ➡ ✈ ❼
Services: ⊠ ⊡ ▤ ∅ ⊤ ⍥ ⬚
Within 3 miles: ℐ ℙ ⓢ ⓢ ∪
Notes: Dogs must be kept on leads.
AA Pubs & Restaurants nearby: The Westleton Crown, WESTLETON, IP17 3AD, 01728 648777

The Ship at Dunwich, DUNWICH, IP17 3DT, 01728 648219

The Queen's Head, HALESWORTH, IP19 9HT, 01986 784214

FELIXSTOWE
Map 13 TM33

Places to visit

Ipswich Museum, IPSWICH, IP1 3QH, 01473 433550
www.cimuseums.org.uk/venues/ipswich-museum.html

Christchurch Mansion, IPSWICH, IP4 2BE, 01473 433554
www.cimuseums.org.uk/venues/christchurch-mansion.html

Peewit Caravan Park
►►► 78%

GOLD

tel: 01394 284511 **Walton Av IP11 2HB**
email: peewitpark@aol.com
dir: Signed from A14 in Felixstowe, 100mtrs past Dock Gate 1, 1st on left. **grid ref:** TM290338

A grass touring area fringed by trees, with well-maintained grounds and a colourful floral display. This handy urban site is not overlooked by houses, and the toilet and shower facilities are clean and well cared for. A function room contains a TV and library. The beach is a few minutes away by car. 13 acre site. 45 touring pitches. 4 hardstandings. Caravan pitches. Motorhome pitches. Tent pitches. 200 statics.

Open: Apr (or Etr if earlier)-Oct **Last arrival:** 21.00hrs **Last departure:** 11.00hrs (late departures possible by prior arrangement)
Pitches: ➡ £17-£29 ➡ £17-£29 ▲ £14-£30
Leisure: ⋀
Facilities: ♣ ⊙ ℙ ☀ & ⊙ ➡ ⅧⅢ ♻ ❼
Services: ⊠ ⊡ ▤ ⬚
Within 3 miles: ℐ ⌘ ☷ ℙ ◎ ≚ ⓢ ⓢ
Notes: 5mph speed restriction, only foam footballs permitted. Dogs must be kept on leads. Boules area, bowling green, adventure trail.

PITCHES: ➡ Caravans ➡ Motorhomes ▲ Tents ♠ Glamping-style accommodation **SERVICES:** ⊠ Electric hook up ⊡ Launderette ⍮ Licensed bar ▤ Calor Gas ∅ Camping Gaz ⊤ Toilet fluid ⍥ Café/Restaurant ⬚ Fast Food/Takeaway ⬚ Battery charging ➡ Baby care ⍘ Motorvan service point **ABBREVIATIONS:** BH/bank hols — bank holidays Etr — Easter Spring BH — Spring Bank Holiday fr — from hrs — hours m — mile mdnt — midnight rdbt — roundabout rs — restricted service wk — week wknd — weekend x-rds — cross roads ⊘ No credit or debit cards ⊗ No dogs ♦ Children of all ages accepted

HOLLESLEY
Map 13 TM34

Places to visit

Woodbridge Tide Mill, WOODBRIDGE, IP12 1BY, 01394 382815
www.woodbridgetidemill.org.uk

Sutton Hoo, WOODBRIDGE, IP12 3DJ, 01394 389700
www.nationaltrust.org.uk/suttonhoo

Great for kids: Orford Castle, ORFORD, IP12 2ND, 01394 450472
www.english-heritage.org.uk/daysout/properties/orford-castle

Run Cottage Touring Park
►►►►82%

tel: 01394 411309 **Alderton Rd IP12 3RQ**
email: info@run-cottage.co.uk **web:** www.runcottage.co.uk
dir: *From A12 (Ipswich-Saxmundham) onto A1152 at Melton. 1.5m, right at rdbt onto B1083. 0.75m, left to Hollesley. In Hollesley right into The Street, through village, down hill, over bridge, site 100yds on left.* **grid ref:** *TM350440*

Located in the peaceful village of Hollesley on the Suffolk coast, this landscaped park is set behind the owners' house; for the 2014 season the site was improved and extended. The generously-sized pitches are serviced by a well-appointed and immaculately maintained toilet block which includes two fully serviced cubicles. A newly landscaped field offers 22 extra pitches, each with an electric hook-up and TV point, and seven hardstanding pitches. This site is handy for the National Trust's Sutton Hoo, and also by travelling a little further north, the coastal centre and beach at Dunwich Heath, and the RSPB bird reserve at Minsmere. 4.25 acre site. 45 touring pitches. 14 hardstandings. 6 seasonal pitches. Caravan pitches. Motorhome pitches. Tent pitches.

Open: all year **Last arrival:** 20.00hrs **Last departure:** 11.00hrs

Pitches: * ▦ £18-£20 ⟷ £18-£20 ▲ £16-£18

Facilities: ➍ ↰ ⊙ 𝒫 ✳ ⚲ ↰ ✿ ❼

Services: ⊟ ☲

Within 3 miles: ⌖ 𝒫 ⋛ ⓢ ∪

Notes: No groundsheets, ball games or cycles. Satellite TV point on some pitches.

AA Pubs & Restaurants nearby: The Crown at Woodbridge, WOODBRIDGE, IP12 1AD, 01394 384242

Seckford Hall Hotel, WOODBRIDGE, IP13 6NU, 01394 385678

IPSWICH

See Bucklesham

KESSINGLAND
Map 13 TM58

Places to visit

East Anglia Transport Museum, LOWESTOFT, NR33 8BL, 01502 518459
www.eatm.org.uk

Maritime Museum, LOWESTOFT, NR32 1XG, 01502 567833
www.lowestoftmaritimemuseum.org.uk

Great for kids: Africa Alive!, LOWESTOFT, NR33 7TF, 01502 740291
www.africa-alive.co.uk

Kessingland Beach Holiday Park
HOLIDAY CENTRE 75%

tel: 01502 740636 **Beach Rd NR33 7RW**
email: holidaysales.kessinglandbeach@park-resorts.com **web:** www.park-resorts.com
dir: *From Lowestoft take A12 S. At Kessingland take 3rd exit at rdbt towards beach. Through village. At beach follow road to right. In 400yds fork left for park.*
grid ref: *TM535852*

A large holiday centre with direct access onto the beach, and a variety of leisure facilities. The touring area is tucked away from the statics, and served by a clean and functional toilet block. A fish and chip shop and the Boat House Restaurant are popular features. 69 acre site. 90 touring pitches. Caravan pitches. Motorhome pitches. Tent pitches. 95 statics.

Open: Apr-Oct **Last departure:** 10.00hrs

Pitches: ▦ ⟷ ▲

Leisure: ⌘ ⋛ ⋀ ↯ ◉ ⚲ ☐ ♪ **Facilities:** ↰ ⊙ 𝒫 ✳ ⚲ ⓢ ⓢ 𝅘 ▦ 🖥 ✿ ❼

Services: ⊟ ⓢ 🍴 ⍾ ↲

Within 3 miles: ⌖ ✦ 目 𝒫 ◎ ⋛ ⓢ ⓢ ∪

Notes: No loud noise after 23.00hrs, no fires. Dogs must be kept on leads.

Heathland Beach Caravan Park
►►►►89%

tel: 01502 740337 **London Rd NR33 7PJ**
email: heathlandbeach@btinternet.com
dir: *1m N of Kessingland exit A12 onto B1437.* **grid ref:** *TM533877*

A well-run and maintained park offering superb toilet facilities. The park is set in meadowland, with level grass pitches, and mature trees and bushes. There is direct access to the sea and beach, and good provisions for families on site with a heated swimming pool and three play areas. There is a well-stocked fishing lake, and sea fishing is also possible. 5 acre site. 63 touring pitches. Caravan pitches. Motorhome pitches. Tent pitches. 200 statics.

Open: Apr-Oct **Last arrival:** 21.00hrs **Last departure:** 11.00hrs

Pitches: * ▦ £20-£33 ⟷ £20-£33 ▲ £12-£33

Leisure: ⋛ ⋀ ◡ ◉ **Facilities:** ↰ ⊙ 𝒫 ✳ ⚲ ⓢ 𝅘 ↰ ▦ 🖥 ✿ ❼

Services: ⊟ ⓢ 🍴 🗎 ⌀ Ⓣ 🍴 ⍾ ↲

Within 3 miles: ⌖ ✦ 目 𝒫 ◎ ⋛ ⓢ ⓢ ∪

Notes: Only 1 dog per unit. Dogs must be kept on leads.

LEISURE: ⌘ Indoor swimming pool ⋛ Outdoor swimming pool ⋀ Children's playground ↯ Kid's club ⊸ Tennis court ◉ Games room ☐ Separate TV room ⌖ golf course ✦ Boats for hire 目 Cinema ♪ Entertainment 𝒫 Fishing ◎ Mini golf ⋛ Watersports ⚲ Gym ◉ Sports field Spa ∪ Stables
FACILITIES: ➍ Bath ↰ Shower ⊙ Electric shaver 𝒫 Hairdryer ✳ Ice Pack Facility ⚲ Disabled facilities ⓢ Public telephone ⓢ Shop on site or within 200yds ⓢ Mobile shop (calls at least 5 days a week) 🍴 BBQ area 𝅘 Picnic area ▦ Wi-fi 🖥 Internet access ✿ Recycling ❼ Tourist info ↰ Dog exercise area

LEISTON
Map 13 TM46

Cakes & Ale
▶▶▶▶▶87%

tel: 01728 831655 **Abbey Ln, Theberton IP16 4TE**
email: reception@cakesandale.co.uk **web:** www.cakesandale.co.uk
dir: *From Saxmundham E on B1119. 3m follow minor road over level crossing, turn right, in 0.5m straight on at x-rds, entrance 0.5m on left.* **grid ref:** *TM432637*

A large, well spread out and beautifully maintained site on a former World War Two airfield that has many trees and bushes. The spacious touring area includes plenty of hardstandings and 55 super pitches, and there is a good bar. In 2014 a new, high-quality, solar-powered toilet block was built, containing four fully serviced family rooms, seven cubicled toilet and washbasin rooms, dishwashing facilities, laundry, a contemporary decor and underfloor heating. 45 acre site. 55 touring pitches. 55 hardstandings. Caravan pitches. Motorhome pitches. Tent pitches. 200 statics.

Open: Apr-Oct (rs Low season club, shop & reception limited hours)
Last arrival: 19.00hrs **Last departure:** 13.00hrs
Pitches: * ⊞ £24-£30 ⊞ £24-£30 ▲ £24-£30
Leisure: ⋀ ⌇ ☺ **Facilities:** ⬅ ⬤ ⊙ ⌇ ✳ ⬤ ⑤ ⌁ WiFi ⬛ ♻ ➊
Services: ⬤ ⑤ ⑪ ⬤ ⊘ ⊤ ⬆ **Within 3 miles:** ⌇ ⬤ ⊟ ⌇ ⬤ ⑤ ∪
Notes: No group bookings, no noise between 21.00hrs-08.00hrs. Dogs must be kept on leads. Practice range and practice net, volleyball court, boules, football nets.
AA Pubs & Restaurants nearby: The Parrot and Punchbowl Inn & Restaurant, ALDRINGHAM, IP16 4PY, 01728 830221
Regatta Restaurant, ALDEBURGH, IP15 5AN, 01728 452011
See advert on page 320

LOWESTOFT
See Kessingland

SAXMUNDHAM
Map 13 TM36

Places to visit
Long Shop Museum, LEISTON, IP16 4ES, 01728 832189
www.longshopmuseum.co.uk

Leiston Abbey, LEISTON, IP16 4TD, 01728 831354
www.english-heritage.org.uk/daysout/properties/leiston-abbey

Great for kids: RSPB Nature Reserve Minsmere, WESTLETON, IP17 3BY, 01728 648281 www.rspb.org.uk/minsmere

Carlton Meres Country Park
▶▶▶▶85%

tel: 01728 603344 **Rendham Rd, Carlton IP17 2QP**
email: enquiries@carlton-meres.co.uk
dir: *From A12, W of Saxmundham, take B1119 towards Framlingham (site signed).* **grid ref:** *TM372637*

With two large fishing lakes, a modern fitness suite, a beauty salon, sauna and steam rooms, tennis court, a bar, and a heated outdoor swimming pool, Carlton Meres offers a wealth of leisure facilities, and all for the exclusive use for those staying on the site (holiday statics and lodges for hire). There is a modern heated toilet block and excellent security. This site is well-placed for all the Suffolk coast attractions. 52 acre site. 96 touring pitches. 56 hardstandings. 25 seasonal pitches. Caravan pitches. Motorhome pitches. Tent pitches.

Open: Etr-Oct **Last arrival:** 17.00hrs **Last departure:** 10.00hrs
Pitches: * ⊞ £15-£35 ⊞ £15-£70 ▲ £16-£24
Leisure: ⬤ ⌇ ⋀ ☺ ⬤ ⌁ Spa
Facilities: ⬤ ✳ ⑤ ⬅ WiFi ⬛ ♻ ➊
Services: ⬤ ⑤ ⑪ ⬤ ⊙ ♻
Within 3 miles: ⌇ ⬤ ⊟ ⌇ ⬤ ⑤ ⑤ ∪
Notes: Dogs must be kept on leads.
AA Pubs & Restaurants nearby: Sibton White Horse Inn, SIBTON, IP17 2JJ, 01728 660337
Regatta Restaurant, ALDEBURGH, IP15 5AN, 01728 452011

LEISTON *continued*

Marsh Farm Caravan Site
►►82%

tel: 01728 602168 **Sternfield IP17 1HW**
dir: *A12 onto A1094 (Aldeburgh road), at Snape x-rds left signed Sternfield, follow signs to site.* **grid ref:** *TM385608*

A very pretty site overlooking reed-fringed lakes which offer excellent coarse fishing. The facilities are very well maintained, and the park truly is a peaceful haven. 30 acre site. 45 touring pitches. Caravan pitches. Motorhome pitches. Tent pitches.

Open: all year **Last arrival:** 21.00hrs **Last departure:** 17.00hrs

Pitches: 🚐 🚙 Å

Facilities: 🏕 ☼ 🖳 🚿 🌡 ♻ ❶

Services: 🔌 🚽

Within 3 miles: 🎣 🏇 🖳 🖳 ↺

Notes: 🐕 Campers must report to reception on arrival, site closed when freezing temperatures are forecast. Dogs must be kept on leads.

AA Pubs & Restaurants nearby: The Parrot and Punchbowl Inn & Restaurant, ALDRINGHAM, IP16 4PY, 01728 830221

Regatta Restaurant, ALDEBURGH, IP15 5AN, 01728 452011

NEW Sycamore Park
►►►77%

tel: 01728 635830 **Rearoff Pump Cottages, Main Rd IP16 4RA**
email: enquiries@sycamorepark.co.uk
dir: *From A12 at Yoxford take B1122 towards Theberton.* **grid ref:** *TM435660*

Sycamore Park opened in the spring of 2014 and is a very peaceful site in the village of Theberton, within easy reach of Southwold and Aldeburgh, and only three miles from RSPB Minsmere. There are 20 electric hook-ups on grass pitches set out in a compact field surrounded by mature trees. The small, but high quality and very stylish, toilet block contains combined cubicled facilities and has underfloor heating. 3 acre site. 60 touring pitches. Caravan pitches. Motorhome pitches. Tent pitches.

Open: 3 Mar-1 Feb **Pitches:** * 🚐 fr £20 🚙 fr £20 Å fr £20 **Notes:** 🐕

WOODBRIDGE
Map 13 TM24

Places to visit

Sutton Hoo, WOODBRIDGE, IP12 3DJ, 01394 389700
www.nationaltrust.org.uk/suttonhoo

Orford Castle, ORFORD, IP12 2ND, 01394 450472
www.english-heritage.org.uk/daysout/properties/orford-castle

Great for kids: Easton Farm Park, EASTON, IP13 0EQ, 01728 746475
www.eastonfarmpark.co.uk

PREMIER PARK

Moon & Sixpence
▶▶▶▶▶ 92%

tel: 01473 736650 **Newbourn Rd, Waldringfield IP12 4PP**
email: info@moonandsixpence.eu **web:** www.moonandsixpence.eu
dir: *From A12 rdbt, E of Ipswich, follow brown caravan & Moon & Sixpence signs
(Waldringfield). 1.5m, left at x-rds, follow signs.* **grid ref:** *TM263454*

A well-planned site, with tourers occupying a sheltered valley position around an attractive boating lake with a sandy beach. Toilet facilities are housed in a smart Norwegian-style cabin, and there is a laundry and dish-washing area. Leisure facilities include two tennis courts, a bowling green, fishing, boating and a games room; there's also a lake, woodland trails, a cycle trail and 9-hole golf. The park has an adult-only area, and a strict 'no groups and no noise after 9pm' policy. 5 acre site. 50 touring pitches. 10 hardstandings. Caravan pitches. Motorhome pitches. 225 statics.

continued

PITCHES: 🚐 Caravans 🚐 Motorhomes ⛺ Tents 🏕 Glamping-style accommodation **SERVICES:** 🔌 Electric hook up ⬜ Launderette 🍺 Licensed bar
🔲 Calor Gas ⌀ Camping Gaz 🅃 Toilet fluid 🍴 Café/Restaurant 🍟 Fast Food/Takeaway 🔋 Battery charging 🍼 Baby care ⚒ Motorvan service point
ABBREVIATIONS: BH/bank hols – bank holidays Etr – Easter Spring BH – Spring Bank Holiday fr – from hrs – hours m – mile mdnt – midnight
rdbt – roundabout rs – restricted service wk – week wknd – weekend x-rds – cross roads 🚫 No credit or debit cards 🚫 No dogs 👫 Children of all ages accepted

WOODBRIDGE *continued*

Moon & Sixpence

Open: Apr-Oct (rs Low season club, shop, reception open limited hours)
Last arrival: 20.00hrs **Last departure:** noon

Pitches: 🚐 £22-£35 🚃 £22-£35

Leisure: ⚠ 🏊 🎮 🎣 ♪

Facilities: 🚿 🏪 ⊙ 🅿 ✳ 🛠 🚿 WiFi 🖥 ♻ 🛈

Services: 🚐 🗑 🚮 💧 🍴 🚽 ♿

Within 3 miles: ↓ 🎏 🚴 🏊 🛒 🗑

Notes: No group bookings or commercial vehicles, quiet 21.00hrs-08.00hrs, no tents. Dogs must be kept on leads. 10-acre sports area, 100 acre woods.

AA Pubs & Restaurants nearby: The Crown at Woodbridge, WOODBRIDGE, IP12 1AD, 01394 384242

Seckford Hall Hotel, WOODBRIDGE, IP13 6NU, 01394 385678

See on page 323

Moat Barn Touring Caravan Park
►►► 85%

tel: 01473 737520 **Dallinghoo Rd, Bredfield IP13 6BD**
dir: *Exit A12 at Bredfield, 1st right at village pump. Through village, 1m site on left.*
grid ref: TM269530

An attractive small park set in idyllic Suffolk countryside, perfectly located for touring the heritage coastline and for visiting the National Trust's Sutton Hoo. The modern toilet block is well equipped and maintained. There are 10 tent pitches and the park is located on the popular Hull to Harwich cycle route. Cycle hire is available, but there are no facilities for children. 2 acre site. 34 touring pitches. 10 seasonal pitches. Caravan pitches. Motorhome pitches. Tent pitches.

Open: Mar-15 Jan **Last arrival:** 22.00hrs **Last departure:** noon

Pitches: * 🚐 fr £19 🚃 fr £19 ⛺ fr £19

Facilities: 🏪 ⊙ 🅿 ✳ WiFi ♻ 🛈

Services: 🚐 🚽 ♿

Within 3 miles: ↓ 🎏 🚴 ◎ 🏊 🛒 🗑 ♻

Notes: Adults only. 🚫 No ball games, breathable groundsheets only. Dogs must be kept on leads.

AA Pubs & Restaurants nearby: The Crown at Woodbridge, WOODBRIDGE, IP12 1AD, 01394 384242

Seckford Hall Hotel, WOODBRIDGE, IP13 6NU, 01394 385678

LEISURE: 🏊 Indoor swimming pool 🏊 Outdoor swimming pool ⚠ Children's playground 🧒 Kid's club 🎾 Tennis court 🎱 Games room 🖥 Separate TV room ⛳ golf course 🚣 Boats for hire 🎬 Cinema ♪ Entertainment 🎣 Fishing ◎ Mini golf 🏄 Watersports 💪 Gym 🎯 Sports field Spa ♘ Stables
FACILITIES: 🚿 Bath 🏪 Shower ⊙ Electric shaver 🅿 Hairdryer ✳ Ice Pack Facility ♿ Disabled facilities 📞 Public telephone 🛒 Shop on site or within 200yds 🏪 Mobile shop (calls at least 5 days a week) 🍴 BBQ area 🎋 Picnic area WiFi Wi-fi 🖥 Internet access ♻ Recycling 🛈 Tourist info 🐕 Dog exercise area

PITCHES: 🚐 Caravans 🚎 Motorhomes ⛺ Tents ⛺ Glamping-style accommodation **SERVICES:** ⚡ Electric hook up 🔘 Launderette 🍷 Licensed bar
🪣 Calor Gas ⊘ Camping Gaz 🇹 Toilet fluid 🍽 Café/Restaurant 🍟 Fast Food/Takeaway 🔋 Battery charging 🍼 Baby care ⚡ Motorvan service point
ABBREVIATIONS: BH/bank hols – bank holidays Etr – Easter Spring BH – Spring Bank Holiday fr – from hrs – hours m – mile mdnt – midnight
rdbt – roundabout rs – restricted service wk – week wknd – weekend x-rds – cross roads 🚫 No credit or debit cards 🚫 No dogs 👫 Children of all ages accepted

Sussex

East and West Sussex are adjoining counties packed with interest. This is a land of stately homes and castles, miles of breezy chalk cliffs overlooking the English Channel, pretty rivers, picturesque villages and links to our glorious past. Since 2011 it has been the home of Britain's newest national park – the South Downs

Mention Sussex to many people and images of the South Downs immediately spring to mind – 'vast, smooth, shaven, serene,' as the writer Virginia Woolf described them. She and her husband lived at Monk's House in the village of Rodmell, near Lewes, and today, her modest home is managed by the National Trust and open to the public.

Close by, on the downs, is Charleston Farmhouse where Woolf's sister, the artist Vanessa Bell, lived a bohemian life as part of the renowned Bloomsbury group, whose members were mainly notable writers, artists and thinkers. Rudyard Kipling resided at Bateman's, near Burwash, and described the house as 'a good and peaceable place,' after moving there in 1902. 'We have loved it ever since our first sight of it,' he wrote later. Bateman's is also in the care of the National Trust, as is Uppark House at South Harting, near Petersfield. The writer H. G. Wells stayed at Uppark as a boy while his mother was employed there as housekeeper. Away to the east, inland from Hastings, lies Great Dixter, an ancient house in a magical garden. This was the home of the pioneering gardening writer Christopher Lloyd and today both Great Dixter and its garden are open to visitors.

There are a great many historic landmarks within Sussex, but probably the most famous is the battlefield where William, Duke of Normandy defeated Harold and his Saxon army to become William the Conqueror of England. By visiting Battle, near Hastings, you can, with a little imagination, picture the bloody events that led to his defeat. Before the Battle of Hastings, William vowed that if God gave him victory that day, he would build an abbey on the site of the battle at Senlac Field. This he did, with the high altar set up on the spot where Harold died. The abbey was enlarged and improved over the years and today is maintained by English Heritage.

In terms of walking in Sussex, this county is spoilt for choice. Studying the map reveals a multitude of routes – many of them to be found within the boundaries of the South Downs National Park – and an assortment of scenic long-distance trails leading towards distant horizons; all of them offer a perfect way to get to the heart of 'Sussex by the sea,' as it has long been known. The Monarch's Way, one of the region's most popular trails, broadly follows Charles II's escape route in 1651, while the most famous of them, the South Downs Way, follows hill paths and cliff-top tracks all the way from Winchester to Eastbourne. As well as a good range of walks, Sussex offers exhilarating cycle rides through the High Weald, along the South Downs Way and via coastal routes between Worthing and Rye. There is also the Forest Way through East Grinstead to Groombridge. If you enjoy cycling with the salty tang of the sea for company, try the ride between Chichester and West Wittering. You can vary the return journey by taking the Itchenor ferry to Bosham.

Sussex is renowned for its many pretty towns, of course. There is Arundel, littered with period buildings and dominated by the castle, the family home of the Duke of Norfolk, that dates back nearly 1,000 years. Midhurst, Lewes, Rye and Uckfield also have their charms, while the cities of Chichester and Brighton offer countless museums and fascinating landmarks. Brighton's best-known and grandest feature is surely the Royal Pavilion, created as the seaside palace of the Prince Regent (later George IV). The town's genteel Regency terraces and graceful crescents reflect his influence on Brighton. Often referred to as 'London by the sea,' the city has long enjoyed a colourful reputation and has been used as a location in many high profile and highly successful films, including *Brighton Rock* and *Quadrophenia*.

West Wittering Beach ▷

EAST SUSSEX

BATTLE
Map 7 TQ71

Places to visit

1066 Battle of Hastings Abbey & Battlefield, BATTLE, TN33 0AD, 01424 773792 www.english-heritage.org.uk/daysout/properties/1066-battle-of-hastings-abbey-and-battlefield

Yesterday's World - Battle, BATTLE, TN33 0AQ, 01424 777226 www.yesterdaysworld.co.uk

Great for kids: The Observatory Science Centre, HERSTMONCEUX, BN27 1RN, 01323 832731 www.the-observatory.org

---

Brakes Coppice Park
▶▶▶80%

tel: 01424 830322 **Forewood Ln TN33 9AB**
email: brakesco@btinternet.com
dir: From Battle on A2100 towards Hastings. After 2m turn right for Crowhurst. Site 1m on left. **grid ref:** TQ765134

A secluded farm site in a sunny meadow deep in woodland with a small stream and a coarse fishing lake. The toilet block has quality fittings and there's a good fully-serviced family/disabled room. Hardstanding pitches are neatly laid out on a terrace, and tents are pitched on grass edged by woodland. The hands-on owners, who added a small shop in 2014, offer high levels of customer care and this tucked-away gem proves a peaceful base for exploring Battle and the south coast. 3 acre site. 60 touring pitches. 10 hardstandings. Caravan pitches. Motorhome pitches. Tent pitches. 1 static.

Open: Mar-Oct **Last arrival:** 21.00hrs **Last departure:** noon
Pitches: * 🚐 £15-£21 🚍 £15-£21 ▲ £15-£21
Leisure: ⏢
Facilities: 🎣☺🏳✳🔥🕚🖐🛒🚷🚻 WiFi 💻 ♻ 🛈
Services: 🔌🗑 🛢🧹🚽🛒
Within 3 miles: 🎣🐾🛍🎠
Notes: No fires, footballs or kite flying. Dogs must be kept on leads.
AA Pubs & Restaurants nearby: Ash Tree Inn, ASHBURNHAM PLACE, TN33 9NX, 01424 892104
The Wild Mushroom Restaurant, WESTFIELD, TN35 4SB, 01424 751137

Senlac Wood
▶▶▶73%

tel: 01424 773969 **Catsfield Rd, Catsfield TN33 9LN**
email: senlacwood@xlninternet.co.uk
dir: A271 from Battle onto B2204 signed Bexhill. Site on left. **grid ref:** TQ722153

A woodland site with many secluded hardstanding bays and two peaceful grassy glades for tents. The functional toilet facilities are clean but there are plans to add a new toilet block in the tent area. The site is ideal for anyone looking for seclusion and shade and it is well placed for visiting nearby Battle and the south coast

---

beaches. 20 acre site. 35 touring pitches. 16 hardstandings. Caravan pitches. Motorhome pitches. Tent pitches.

Open: Mar-Oct **Last arrival:** 22.00hrs **Last departure:** noon
Pitches: 🚐 🚍 ▲
Leisure: ⏢ ⚲
Facilities: 🎣☺🏳✳🕚🖐🛒 WiFi 🛈
Services: 🔌🚽🛒
Within 3 miles: 🎣🐾🎠
Notes: No camp fires, no noise after 23.00hrs. Dogs must be kept on leads. Caravan storage.
AA Pubs & Restaurants nearby: Ash Tree Inn, ASHBURNHAM PLACE, TN33 9NX, 01424 892104
The Wild Mushroom Restaurant, WESTFIELD, TN35 4SB, 01424 751137

BEXHILL
Map 6 TQ70

Places to visit

Pevensey Castle, PEVENSEY, BN24 5LE, 01323 762604 www.english-heritage.org.uk/daysout/properties/pevensey-castle

1066 Battle of Hastings Abbey & Battlefield, BATTLE, TN33 0AD, 01424 773792 www.english-heritage.org.uk/daysout/properties/1066-battle-of-hastings-abbey-and-battlefield

Great for kids: The Observatory Science Centre, HERSTMONCEUX, BN27 1RN, 01323 832731 www.the-observatory.org

---

Cobbs Hill Farm Caravan & Camping Park
▶▶▶81%

tel: 01424 213460 & 07708 958910 **Watermill Ln TN39 5JA**
email: cobbshillfarmuk@hotmail.com
dir: Exit A269 into Watermill Ln, park 1m on left. NB it is advisable not to follow Sat Nav. **grid ref:** TQ736102

A well-established farm site tucked away in pleasant rolling countryside close to Bexhill and a short drive from Battle, the South Downs and good beaches. Neat, well-maintained camping paddocks, one with eight hardstanding pitches, are sheltered by mature trees and hedging; the toilet block is clean and freshly painted. Children will love the menagerie of farm animals. 17 acre site. 55 touring pitches. 8 hardstandings. 20 seasonal pitches. Caravan pitches. Motorhome pitches. Tent pitches. 15 statics.

Open: Apr-Oct **Last arrival:** 20.00hrs **Last departure:** noon
Pitches: * 🚐 £14-£16 🚍 £14-£16 ▲ £15-£17
Leisure: ⏢ ⚙
Facilities: 🎣☺🏳✳🔥🛍🛒♻🛈
Services: 🔌🗑 🛢🧹🚽🛒⛽
Within 3 miles: 🎣🐾🚣🛍🗑
Notes: No camp fires. Dogs must be kept on leads.
AA Pubs & Restaurants nearby: Ash Tree Inn, ASHBURNHAM PLACE, TN33 9NX, 01424 892104

LEISURE: 🏊 Indoor swimming pool 🏊 Outdoor swimming pool ⏢ Children's playground 🪁 Kid's club 🎾 Tennis court 🎱 Games room 📺 Separate TV room 🏌 golf course ⛵ Boats for hire 🎦 Cinema 🎵 Entertainment 🎣 Fishing 🏌 Mini golf 🚣 Watersports 🏋 Gym 🏟 Sports field Spa ♀ Stables
FACILITIES: 🛁 Bath 🚿 Shower ⊙ Electric shaver 🏳 Hairdryer ✳ Ice Pack Facility ♿ Disabled facilities ☎ Public telephone 🛍 Shop on site or within 200yds 🛒 Mobile shop (calls at least 5 days a week) 🍖 BBQ area 🏕 Picnic area WiFi Wi-fi 💻 Internet access ♻ Recycling 🛈 Tourist info 🐾 Dog exercise area

CAMBER
Map 7 TQ91

Places to visit

Rye Castle Museum, RYE, TN31 7JY, 01797 226728 www.ryemuseum.co.uk

Lamb House, RYE, TN31 7ES, 01580 762334
www.nationaltrust.org.uk/main/w-lambhouse

Camber Sands
HOLIDAY CENTRE 70%

tel: 0871 664 9719 & 01797 222000 **New Lydd Rd TN31 7RT**
email: camber.sands@park-resorts.com
dir: M20 junct 10 (Ashford International Station), A2070 signed Brenzett. Follow Hastings & Rye signs on A259. 1m before Rye, left signed Camber. Site in 3m. **grid ref:** TQ972184

Located opposite Camber's vast sandy beach, this large holiday centre offers a good range of leisure and entertainment facilities. The touring area is positioned close to the reception and entrance, and is served by a clean and functional toilet block. 110 acre site. 55 touring pitches. 6 hardstandings. Caravan pitches. Motorhome pitches. Tent pitches. 921 statics.

Open: Mar-Nov **Last arrival:** anytime **Last departure:** 10.00hrs

Pitches: ⌂ ⌂ Å

Leisure: 🏊 ⛰ 🛝 💆 🎱 🎵 Spa

Facilities: 🏠⊙⭐⑤📦⭳WiFi 🖥🔄 🅰

Services: 🔌⑤ 🍴🍽🍞

Within 3 miles: 🚶🎣◎🚣⑤⑤

Notes: Quiet from 23.00hrs-07.00hrs. Dogs must be kept on leads.

AA Pubs & Restaurants nearby: Mermaid Inn, RYE, TN31 7EY, 01797 223065

The Ypres Castle Inn, RYE, TN31 7HH, 01797 223248

The George in Rye, RYE, TN31 7JT, 01797 222114

FURNER'S GREEN
Map 6 TQ42

Places to visit

Sheffield Park and Garden, SHEFFIELD PARK, TN22 3QX, 01825 790231
www.nationaltrust.org.uk/sheffieldpark

Nymans, HANDCROSS, RH17 6EB, 01444 405250
www.nationaltrust.org.uk/nymans

Great for kids: Bluebell Railway, SHEFFIELD PARK STATION, TN22 3QL, 01825 720800 www.bluebell-railway.co.uk

Heaven Farm
►►81%

tel: 01825 790226 **TN22 3RG**
email: heavenfarmleisure@btinternet.com
dir: On A275 between Lewes & East Grinstead, 1m N of Sheffield Park Garden. **grid ref:** TQ403264

A delightful, small, rural site on a popular farm complex incorporating a farm museum, craft shop, tea room and nature trail. The good, clean toilet facilities are housed in well-converted outbuildings and chickens and ducks roam freely around the site. Ashdown Forest, the Bluebell Railway and Sheffield Park Garden are nearby. 1.5 acre site. 25 touring pitches. 2 hardstandings. Caravan pitches. Motorhome pitches. Tent pitches. 3 statics.

Open: all year (rs Nov-Mar) **Last arrival:** 21.00hrs **Last departure:** noon

Pitches: * ⌂ £20-£22.50 ⌂ £20-£22.50 Å fr £20

Facilities: 🏠⊙⭐⑤📦🅰🅰🅰

Services: 🔌Ⓣ🍽🔋⭳

Within 3 miles: 🚶🎣⑤◡

Notes: ⊗ Dogs must be kept on leads. Fishing.

AA Pubs & Restaurants nearby: The Coach and Horses, DANEHILL, RH17 7JF, 01825 740369

The Griffin Inn, FLETCHING, TN22 3SS, 01825 722890

HASTINGS
Map 7 TQ80

Places to visit

Old Town Hall Museum of Local History, HASTINGS & ST LEONARDS, TN34 3EW, 01424 451052 www.hmag.org.uk

Shipwreck Museum, HASTINGS & ST LEONARDS, TN34 3DW, 01424 437452
www.shipwreckmuseum.co.uk

Great for kids: Blue Reef Aquarium, HASTINGS & ST LEONARDS, TN34 3DW, 01424 718776 www.bluereefaquarium.co.uk

Smugglers Adventure, HASTINGS & ST LEONARDS, TN34 3HY, 01424 422964
www.discoverhastings.co.uk

Combe Haven Holiday Park
HOLIDAY HOME PARK 87%

tel: 01424 427891 **Harley Shute Rd, St Leonards-on-Sea TN38 8BZ**
email: combehaven@haven.com **web:** www.haven.com/combehaven
dir: A21 towards Hastings. In Hastings take A259 towards Bexhill. Park signed on right. **grid ref:** TQ779091

Close to a beach and the resort attractions of Hastings, this newly upgraded holiday park has been designed with families in mind. Activities include a pirates' adventure playground, heated swimming pools and a wealth of sports and outdoor activities.

Open: Mar-Oct

Change over day: Mon, Fri, Sat

Arrival and departure times: Please contact the site

Statics: 296 Sleeps 6-8 Bedrms 2-3 Bathrms 1-2 Toilets 1-2 Microwave Freezer TV Sky/FTV Elec inc Gas inc Grass area

Children: 🚸 Cots Highchair **Dogs:** 2 on leads No dangerous dogs

Leisure: 🏊 🏊 Cycle hire 🛝 ⛰

PEVENSEY BAY — Map 6 TQ60

Places to visit

"How We Lived Then" Museum of Shops & Social History, EASTBOURNE, BN21 4NS, 01323 737143 www.how-we-lived-then.co.uk

Alfriston Clergy House, ALFRISTON, BN26 5TL, 01323 871961 www.nationaltrust.org.uk/alfriston/

Great for kids: The Observatory Science Centre, HERSTMONCEUX, BN27 1RN, 01323 832731 www.the-observatory.org

Bay View Park
►►►85%

tel: 01323 768688 **Old Martello Rd BN24 6DX**
email: holidays@bay-view.co.uk
dir: *Signed from A259 W of Pevensey Bay. On seaward side of A259 take private road towards beach.* **grid ref:** *TQ648028*

A pleasant well-run site just yards from the beach, in an area east of Eastbourne town centre known as 'The Crumbles'. The level grassy site is very well maintained and the toilet facilities feature fully-serviced cubicles. The seasonal tent field has marked pitches and toilet facilities with toilet and washbasins, and washbasins and shower cubicles. There is a 9-hole par 4 golf course and clubhouse. 6 acre site. 94 touring pitches. 14 hardstandings. 15 seasonal pitches. Caravan pitches. Motorhome pitches. Tent pitches. 14 statics.

Open: Mar-Oct **Last arrival:** 20.00hrs **Last departure:** noon

Pitches: 🚐 🚉 ▲

Leisure: ⚠

Facilities: 🚿⊙🅿✳🚻🏪wifi ♻ ❼

Services: 🔌🖅🔋⊘Ⓣⓘ⌖↯

Within 3 miles: ♨🚴♪⌔◎🛶🏪🚺

Notes: Families & couples only, no commercial vehicles. Dogs must be kept on leads.

AA Pubs & Restaurants nearby: The Farm @ Friday Street, LANGNEY, BN23 8AP, 01323 766049

▶ Discover a great day out at theaa.com/event-and-days-out

▶ Who are the AA's award-winning campsites this year? See pages 14-19

WEST SUSSEX

ARUNDEL — Map 6 TQ00

Places to visit

Arundel Castle, ARUNDEL, BN18 9AB, 01903 882173 www.arundelcastle.org

Harbour Park, LITTLEHAMPTON, BN17 5LL, 01903 721200 www.harbourpark.com

Great for kids: Look & Sea! Visitor Centre, LITTLEHAMPTON, BN17 5AW, 01903 718984 www.lookandsea.co.uk

Ship & Anchor Marina
►►79%

GOLD

tel: 01243 551262 **Station Rd, Ford BN18 0BJ**
email: enquiries@shipandanchormarina.co.uk
dir: *From A27 at Arundel take road S signed Ford. Site 2m on left after level crossing.*
grid ref: *TQ002040*

Neatly maintained by the enthusiastic, hard working owner, this small, well located site has dated but spotlessly clean toilet facilities, a secluded tent area, and enjoys a pleasant position beside the Ship & Anchor pub and the tidal River Arun. There are good walks from the site to Arundel and the coast. 12 acre site. 120 touring pitches. 11 hardstandings. Caravan pitches. Motorhome pitches. Tent pitches.

Open: Mar-Oct **Last arrival:** 21.00hrs **Last departure:** noon

Pitches: * 🚐 £15-£21 🚉 £15-£21 ▲ £15-£21

Leisure: ⚠

Facilities: 🛁🚿⊙🅿✳🚻🏪🚺❼

Services: 🔌🖅🔋⊘Ⓣⓘ⌖↯

Within 3 miles: ♨🚴🎣🛶🚺◎🏪

Notes: 🐾 No music audible to others. Dogs must be kept on leads. River fishing from site.

AA Pubs & Restaurants nearby: The Town House, ARUNDEL, BN18 9AJ, 01903 883847

The George at Burpham, BURPHAM, BN18 9RR, 01903 883131

BARNS GREEN — Map 6 TQ12

Places to visit

Parham House & Gardens, PULBOROUGH, RH20 4HS, 01903 742021 www.parhaminsussex.co.uk

Great for kids: Bignor Roman Villa & Museum, BIGNOR, RH20 1PH, 01798 869259 www.bignorromanvilla.co.uk

Sumners Ponds Fishery & Campsite
►►►►87%

GOLD

tel: 01403 732539 **Chapel Rd RH13 0PR**
email: bookings@sumnersponds.co.uk
dir: *From A272 at Coolham x-rds, N towards Barns Green. In 1.5m take 1st left at small x-rds. 1m, over level crossing. Site on left just after right bend.* **grid ref:** *TQ125268*

Diversification towards high quality camping continues at this working farm set in attractive surroundings on the edge of the quiet village of Barns Green, with a new

LEISURE: 🏊 Indoor swimming pool 🏊 Outdoor swimming pool ⚠ Children's playground 👶 Kid's club 🎾 Tennis court 🎱 Games room 📺 Separate TV room ⛳ golf course 🚣 Boats for hire 🎬 Cinema 🎵 Entertainment 🎣 Fishing ◎ Mini golf 🏄 Watersports 🏋 Gym ⚽ Sports field Spa ♻ Stables
FACILITIES: 🛁 Bath 🚿 Shower ⊙ Electric shaver 🅿 Hairdryer ✳ Ice Pack Facility 🚻 Disabled facilities 📞 Public telephone 🏪 Shop on site or within 200yds 🏪 Mobile shop (calls at least 5 days a week) 🍖 BBQ area 🌲 Picnic area wifi Wi-fi 💻 Internet access ♻ Recycling ❼ Tourist info 🐾 Dog exercise area

reception in 2014 and plans to develop the lakeside café. There are three touring areas; one continues to develop and includes camping pods and extra hardstandings, and another, which has a stunning modern toilet block, has excellent pitches (and pods) on the banks of one of the well-stocked fishing lakes. There are many cycle paths on site and a woodland walk has direct access to miles of footpaths. The Café by the Lake serves meals from breakfast onwards. Horsham and Brighton are within easy reach. 40 acre site. 86 touring pitches. 45 hardstandings. Caravan pitches. Motorhome pitches. Tent pitches. 4 wooden pods.

Open: all year **Last arrival:** 20.00hrs **Last departure:** noon

Pitches: * ⊞ £24.50-£31.50 ⊞ £24.50-£31.50 ▲ £24.50-£31.50 🏠

Leisure: ⚟

Facilities: ⬈⊙🗠✳⚅🖲🎇🗭ᵂᴵᶠᴵ ♻ ❷

Services: 🔌🗇 🔋⊘Ⓣ🍽🛒↯

Within 3 miles: ⬇🎣🔥🎣🎲🎯∪

Notes: Only one car per pitch.

AA Pubs & Restaurants nearby: The White Horse, MAPLEHURST, RH13 6LL, 01403 891208

Limeburners Arms Camp Site
►►74%

tel: 01403 782311 **Lordings Rd, Newbridge RH14 9JA**
email: chippy.sawyer@virgin.net **web:** www.thelimeburners.com
dir: *From A29 take A272 towards Petworth for 1m, left onto B2133. Site 300yds on left.* **grid ref:** TQ072255

A secluded site in rural West Sussex, at the rear of the Limeburners Arms public house, and surrounded by fields. It makes a pleasant base for touring the South Downs and the Arun Valley. The toilets are basic but very clean. 2.75 acre site. 40 touring pitches. Caravan pitches. Motorhome pitches. Tent pitches.

Open: Apr-Oct **Last arrival:** 22.00hrs **Last departure:** 14.00hrs

---

Pitches: * ⊞ £18-£22 ⊞ £18-£22 ▲ £18-£22

Leisure: ⚟

Facilities: ⬈⊙✳Ⓒ

Services: 🔌🗎🍽🛒↯

Within 3 miles: ⬇🎲∪

Notes: Dogs must be kept on leads.

AA Pubs & Restaurants nearby: The White Horse, MAPLEHURST, RH13 6LL, 01403 891208

Ellscott Park
►►►82%

tel: 01243 512003 **Sidlesham Ln, Birdham PO20 7QL**
email: camping@ellscottpark.co.uk
dir: *From Chichester take A286 for approx 4m, left at Butterfly Farm sign, site 500yds right.* **grid ref:** SU829995

A well-kept park set in sheltered meadowland behind the owners' nursery and van storage area. The park attracts a peace-loving clientele, has spotless, well maintained toilet facilities, and is handy for the beach, Chichester, Goodwood House, the racing at Goodwood and walking on the South Downs. Home-grown produce is for sale. 2.5 acre site. 50 touring pitches. 25 seasonal pitches. Caravan pitches. Motorhome pitches. Tent pitches.

Open: Apr-3rd wk in Oct **Last arrival:** daylight **Last departure:** variable

Pitches: ⊞ ⊞ ▲

Leisure: ⚟ 🎯

Facilities: ⬈⊙✳⚅🎇🗭♻❷

Services: 🔌🗇 ⊘Ⓣ🛒

Within 3 miles: ⬇🥅🎣🎲🎯∪

Notes: 🐾 Dogs must be kept on leads.

AA Pubs & Restaurants nearby: The Crab & Lobster, SIDLESHAM, PO20 7NB, 01243 641233

DIAL POST
Map 6 TQ11

Places to visit

Parham House & Gardens, PULBOROUGH, RH20 4HS, 01903 742021
www.parhaminsussex.co.uk

RSPB Pulborough Brooks Nature Reserve, PULBOROUGH, RH20 2EL,
01798 875851 www.rspb.org.uk/pulboroughbrooks

Honeybridge Park
►►►► 85%

tel: 01403 710923 **Honeybridge Ln RH13 8NX**
email: enquiries@honeybridgepark.co.uk
dir: *10m S of Horsham, just off A24 at Dial Post. Behind Old Barn Nursery.*
grid ref: *TQ152183*

An attractive and very popular park on gently-sloping ground surrounded by hedgerows and mature trees. A comprehensive amenities building houses upmarket toilet facilities including luxury family and disabled rooms, as well as a laundry, shop and off-licence. There are plenty of hardstandings and electric hook-ups, a games room, and an excellent children's play area. 15 acre site. 130 touring pitches. 70 hardstandings. 20 seasonal pitches. Caravan pitches. Motorhome pitches. Tent pitches. 50 statics.

Open: all year **Last arrival:** 19.00hrs **Last departure:** noon

Pitches: ⚌ ⛆ ▲

Leisure: ⚙ ⚲ ▭

Facilities: ⛭ ⛏ ⊙ ⌂ ✳ ⛾ ⑤ ⋈ ⌷ ⎚ 𝗪𝗶𝗙𝗶 ▬ ❶

Services: ⚋ ⑤ ⛟ ⬧ ⦸ Ⓣ ⑩ ⛴

Within 3 miles: ⦸ ⛱ ⑤ ⛒ ∪

Notes: No open fires. Dogs must be kept on leads. Fridges available.

AA Pubs & Restaurants nearby: The Countryman Inn, SHIPLEY, RH13 8PZ, 01403 741383

The Crown Inn, DIAL POST, RH13 8NH, 01403 710902

The Queens Head, WEST CHILTINGTON, RH20 2JN, 01798 812244

HENFIELD
Map 6 TQ21

Places to visit

Bolney Wine Estate, BOLNEY, RH17 5NB, 01444 881575
www.bolneywineestate.com

Blacklands Farm Caravan & Camping
►► 72%

tel: 01273 493528 & 07773 792577 **Wheatsheaf Rd BN5 9AT**
email: info@blacklandsfarm.co.uk
dir: *A23, B2118, B2116 towards Henfield. Site approx 4m on right.* **grid ref:** *TQ231180*

Tucked away off the B2116, east of Henfield, and well placed for visiting Brighton and exploring the South Downs National Park, this simple, grassy site has great

potential, and the owners plan positive improvements that will not spoil the traditional feel of the campsite. There are spacious pitches down by fishing lakes and the basic portaloos are clean and tidy and have been smartly clad in wood, but future plans include building a new toilet block. 5 acre site. 75 touring pitches. Caravan pitches. Motorhome pitches. Tent pitches.

Open: Mar-Jan **Last arrival:** 20.00hrs **Last departure:** anytime

Pitches: ⚌ ⛆ ▲

Leisure: ⚙ ⚲

Facilities: ⛏ ⊙ ⌂ ✳ ⑤ ⋈ ⌷ ❸ ❶

Services: ⚋

Within 3 miles: ⌿ ⦸ ⑤ ⛒ ∪

Notes: No commercial vehicles. Dogs must be kept on leads. Coffee machine.

AA Pubs & Restaurants nearby: The Fountain Inn, ASHURST, BN44 3AP, 01403 710219

Royal Oak, POYNINGS, BN45 7AQ, 01273 857389

HORSHAM

See Barns Green & Dial Post

PAGHAM
Map 6 SZ89

Places to visit

Chichester Cathedral, CHICHESTER, PO19 1PX, 01243 782595
www.chichestercathedral.org.uk

Pallant House Gallery, CHICHESTER, PO19 1TJ, 01243 774557
www.pallant.org.uk

Church Farm Holiday Park
HOLIDAY HOME PARK 90%

tel: 01243 262635 **Church Ln PO21 4NR**
email: churchfarm@haven.com **web:** www.haven.com/churchfarm
dir: *At rdbt on A27 (S of Chichester) take B2145 signed Hunston & Selsey. At mini rdbt take 1st left signed North Mundham, Pagham & Bognor Regis. Site in approx 3m.*
grid ref: *SZ885974*

Close to Portsmouth, Chichester and south coast beaches, this relaxing and fun-packed holiday park is located close to Pagham Harbour Nature Reserve. On-site activities include golf on the 9-hole course, tennis coaching, shopping, kids' play areas and evening entertainment. There are a range of holiday caravans and apartments.

Open: Mar-Oct

Change over day: Mon, Fri, Sat

Arrival and departure times: Please contact the site

Statics: 189 Sleeps 6-8 Bedrms 2-3 Bathrms 1-2 Toilets 1-2 Microwave Freezer TV Sky/FTV Elec inc Gas inc Grass area

Children: ⛹ Cots Highchair **Dogs:** 2 on leads No dangerous dogs

Leisure: ⛱ ⛲ ⛵ Cycle hire ⛹ ⚙

SELSEY
Map 5 SZ89

Places to visit

Chichester Cathedral, CHICHESTER, PO19 1PX, 01243 782595
www.chichestercathedral.org.uk

Pallant House Gallery, CHICHESTER, PO19 1TJ, 01243 774557
www.pallant.org.uk

Warner Farm Touring Park
HOLIDAY CENTRE 82%

tel: 01243 604499 **Warner Ln, Selsey PO20 9EL**
email: touring@bunnleisure.co.uk **web:** www.warnerfarm.co.uk
dir: *From B2145 in Selsey turn right into School Lane & follow signs.* **grid ref:** *SZ845939*

A well-screened touring site that adjoins the three static parks under the same ownership. A courtesy bus runs around the complex to entertainment areas and

supermarkets. The park backs onto open grassland, and the leisure facilities with bar, amusements and bowling alley, and swimming pool/sauna complex are also accessible to tourers. 10 acre site. 250 touring pitches. 60 hardstandings. 25 seasonal pitches. Caravan pitches. Motorhome pitches. Tent pitches.

Open: Mar-Jan **Last arrival:** 17.30hrs **Last departure:** 10.00hrs

Pitches: 🚐 🚙 🛖

Leisure: 🏊 🎣 🎾 ⛳ 🎱 👣 🏴 🎮 ⚽ 🎵

Facilities: 🐕 ☉ ☂ ✳ ♿ 🕒 🚿 🚻 🛁 WiFi 🖥 ♻ ❶

Services: 🔌 🔄 🍽 🛢 🕳 T 🍴 🏪 ⚡

Within 3 miles: 🎣 🚣 🏌 ◎ ⛴ 🏧 🛒 🎯 ∪

Notes: Dogs must be kept on leads.

AA Pubs & Restaurants nearby: The Crab & Lobster, SIDLESHAM, PO20 7NB, 01243 641233

See advert below

PITCHES: 🚐 Caravans 🚙 Motorhomes 🛖 Tents 🏕 Glamping-style accommodation **SERVICES:** 🔌 Electric hook up 🔄 Launderette 🍽 Licensed bar 🛢 Calor Gas 🕳 Camping Gaz T Toilet fluid 🍴 Café/Restaurant 🏪 Fast Food/Takeaway ⚡ Battery charging 🍼 Baby care ⚒ Motorvan service point
ABBREVIATIONS: BH/bank hols – bank holidays Etr – Easter Spring BH – Spring Bank Holiday fr – from hrs – hours m – mile mdnt – midnight rdbt – roundabout rs – restricted service wk – week wknd – weekend x-rds – cross roads ⊗ No credit or debit cards ⊗ No dogs 👪 Children of all ages accepted

TYNE & WEAR

SOUTH SHIELDS   Map 21 NZ36

Places to visit

Arbeia Roman Fort & Museum, SOUTH SHIELDS, NE33 2BB, 0191 456 1369
www.twmuseums.org.uk/arbeia

Souter Lighthouse & The Leas, WHITBURN, SR6 7NH, 0191 529 3161
www.nationaltrust.org.uk/souterlighthouseandtheleas

Great for kids: Blue Reef Aquarium, TYNEMOUTH, NE30 4JF, 0191 258 1031
www.bluereefaquarium.co.uk

Lizard Lane Caravan & Camping Site
►►►80%

tel: 0191 454 4982 **Lizard Ln NE34 7AB**
email: info@littlehavenhotel.com
dir: *2m S of town centre on A183 (Sunderland road).* **grid ref:** *NZ399648*

This site is located in an elevated position with good sea views. All touring pitches
are fully serviced and the modern smart amenities block is equipped with superb
fixtures and fittings. A shop is also provided. Please note that tents are not
accepted. 2 acre site. 47 touring pitches. Caravan pitches. Motorhome pitches. 70
statics.

Open: Feb-28 Jan **Last arrival:** anytime **Last departure:** 11.00hrs

Pitches: ⬜ ⬜

Facilities: ⬤☉☉♟✲⬤⬤⬤⬤⬤

Services: ⬤⬤⬤

Within 3 miles: ⬤⬤⬤⬤⬤⬤⬤⬤

Notes: Dogs must be kept on leads. 9-hole putting green.

WARWICKSHIRE

ASTON CANTLOW   Map 10 SP16

Places to visit

Mary Arden's Farm, WILMCOTE, CV37 9UN, 01789 201844
www.shakespeare.org.uk

Coughton Court, COUGHTON, B49 5JA, 01789 400777
www.nationaltrust.org.uk/coughtoncourt

Great for kids: Stratford Butterfly Farm, STRATFORD-UPON-AVON, CV37 7LS,
01789 299288 www.butterflyfarm.co.uk

Island Meadow Caravan Park
►►►80%

GOLD

tel: 01789 488273 **The Mill House B95 6JP**
email: holiday@islandmeadowcaravanpark.co.uk
dir: *From A46 or A3400 follow signs for Aston Cantlow. Site signed 0.25m W off Mill Lane.*
grid ref: *SP137596*

A peacefully located site bordered by the River Alne on one side and its mill stream
on the other. Surrounded by mature trees, pitch density is generous and the well-
stocked shop also sells wines, beers and spirits. 7 acre site. 24 touring pitches. 14
hardstandings. Caravan pitches. Motorhome pitches. Tent pitches. 56 statics.

Open: Mar-Oct **Last arrival:** 21.00hrs **Last departure:** noon

Pitches: * ⬜ £23 ⬜ £23 ▲ £15-£23

Facilities: ⬤☉☉♟✲⬤⬤⬤⬤

Services: ⬤⬤⬤⬤⬤

Within 3 miles: ⬤⬤⬤⬤

Notes: Dogs must be kept on leads.

AA Pubs & Restaurants nearby: The Blue Boar Inn, TEMPLE GRAFTON, B49 6NR,
01789 750010

HARBURY   Map 11 SP35

Places to visit

Warwick Castle, WARWICK, CV34 4QU, 0871 265 2000 www.warwick-castle.com

Farnborough Hall, FARNBOROUGH, OX17 1DU, 01295 690002
www.nationaltrust.org.uk

Great for kids: Heritage Motor Centre, GAYDON, CV35 0BJ, 01926 641188
www.heritage-motor-centre.co.uk

Harbury Fields
►►►►87%

tel: 01926 612457 **Harbury Fields Farm CV33 9JN**
email: rdavis@harburyfields.co.uk
dir: *M40 junct 12, B4451 (signed Kineton/Gaydon). 0.75m, right signed Lightborne. 4m,
right at rdbt onto B4455 (signed Harbury). 3rd right by petrol station, site in 700yds by
two cottages.* **grid ref:** *SP352604*

This developing park is in a peaceful farm setting with lovely countryside views. All
pitches have hardstandings with electric and the facilities are spotless. It is well
positioned for visiting Warwick and Leamington Spa as well as the exhibition
centres at NEC Birmingham and Stoneleigh Park. Stratford is just 10 miles away,
and Upton House (NT) and Compton Valley Art Gallery are nearby. 3 acre site. 59
touring pitches. 59 hardstandings. Caravan pitches. Motorhome pitches.

Open: Feb-19 Dec **Last arrival:** 20.00hrs **Last departure:** noon

Pitches: ⬜ £16-£23 ⬜ £16-£23

Facilities: ⬤☉☉⬤⬤⬤⬤⬤

Services: ⬤⬤⬤

Within 3 miles: ⬤⬤⬤

Notes: No traffic noise mdnt-07.30hrs.

AA Pubs & Restaurants nearby: Mallory Court Hotel, ROYAL LEAMINGTON SPA, CV33 9QB,
01926 330214

The Brasserie at Mallory Court, ROYAL LEAMINGTON SPA, CV33 9QB, 01926 453939

LEISURE: 🏊 Indoor swimming pool 🏊 Outdoor swimming pool 🎢 Children's playground 🧒 Kid's club 🎾 Tennis court 🎱 Games room 📺 Separate TV room
🏌 golf course ⛵ Boats for hire 🎦 Cinema 🎵 Entertainment 🎣 Fishing ⛳ Mini golf 🏄 Watersports 🏋 Gym 🏟 Sports field Spa ♘ Stables
FACILITIES: 🛁 Bath 🚿 Shower ☉ Electric shaver 📠 Hairdryer ✳ Ice Pack Facility ♿ Disabled facilities ☎ Public telephone 🏪 Shop on site or within 200yds
🏪 Mobile shop (calls at least 5 days a week) 🍖 BBQ area 🌲 Picnic area 📶 Wi-fi 💻 Internet access ♻ Recycling 🛈 Tourist info 🐕 Dog exercise area

KINGSBURY
Map 10 SP29

Places to visit

Drayton Manor Theme Park, TAMWORTH, B78 3TW, 0844 4721950
www.draytonmanor.co.uk

Tamworth Castle, TAMWORTH, B79 7NA, 01827 709633
www.tamworthcastle.co.uk

Great for kids: Ash End House Children's Farm, MIDDLETON, B78 2BL,
0121 329 3240 www.childrensfarm.co.uk

Tame View Caravan Site
▶ 70%

tel: 01827 873853 **Cliff B78 2DR**
dir: *400yds off A51 (Tamworth-Kingsbury road), 1m N of Kingsbury. Into Cliff Hall Ln (opposite pub) to site.* **grid ref:** *SP209979*

A secluded spot overlooking the Tame Valley and river, sheltered by high hedges. Sanitary facilities are minimal but clean on this small park. The site is popular with many return visitors who like a peaceful, basic site. 5 acre site. 5 touring pitches. Caravan pitches. Motorhome pitches. Tent pitches.

Open: all year **Last arrival:** 23.00hrs **Last departure:** 23.00hrs

Pitches: ⊕ ⊕ ▲

Facilities: ✳️ ⑤ 🎏 🛒 ♻️   **Services:** 📥

Within 3 miles: ↓ ⚊ ⛱️ 🏌️ ◎ 🛒 ⑤ ⑤ U

Notes: 🐾 No noise after mdnt. Dogs must be kept on leads. Fishing.

WOLVEY
Map 11 SP48

Places to visit

Arbury Hall, NUNEATON, CV10 7PT, 024 7638 2804 www.arburyestate.co.uk

Lunt Roman Fort, COVENTRY, CV8 3AJ, 024 7678 6142 www.luntromanfort.org

Great for kids: Coventry Transport Museum, COVENTRY, CV1 1JD, 024 7623 4270 www.transport-museum.com

Wolvey Villa Farm Caravan & Camping Park
▶▶▶ 79%

tel: 01455 220493 **LE10 3HF**
dir: *M6 junct 2, B4065 follow Wolvey signs. Or M69 junct 1 & follow Wolvey signs.* **grid ref:** *SP428869*

A level grass site surrounded by trees and shrubs, on the border of Warwickshire and Leicestershire. This quiet country site has its own popular fishing lake, and is convenient for visiting Coventry and Leicester. 7 acre site. 110 touring pitches. 24 hardstandings. Caravan pitches. Motorhome pitches. Tent pitches.

Open: all year **Last arrival:** 22.00hrs **Last departure:** noon

Pitches: ⊕ £14-£17 ⊕ £14-£17 ▲ £14-£17

Leisure: ✪ 🔍   **Facilities:** 🦮 ⊙ 🏵️ ✳️ 🕹️ ⑤ 🎏 🛒 ❗

Services: ⊕ ⑤ 🔋 🌀 🚰 📥

Within 3 miles: ↓ ⚊ 🏌️ ⑤ ⑤ U

Notes: 🐾 No twin axle vehicles. Dogs must be kept on leads. Putting green, off licence.

AA Pubs & Restaurants nearby: The Bell Inn, MONKS KIRBY, CV23 0QY, 01788 832352
The Pheasant, WITHYBROOK, CV7 9LT, 01455 220480

WEST MIDLANDS

MERIDEN
Map 10 SP28

Places to visit

Blakesley Hall, BIRMINGHAM, B25 8RN, 0121 348 8120
www.bmag.org.uk/blakesley-hall

Packwood House, PACKWOOD HOUSE, B94 6AT, 01564 782024
www.nationaltrust.org.uk/main/w-packwoodhouse

Somers Wood Caravan Park
▶▶▶▶ 92%

Best of British

tel: 01676 522978 **Somers Rd CV7 7PL**
email: enquiries@somerswood.co.uk
dir: *M42 junct 6, A45 signed Coventry. Keep left, do not take flyover. Right onto A452 signed Meriden & Leamington. At next rdbt left onto B4102 Hampton Lane. Site in 0.5m on left.* **grid ref:** *SP225824*

A peaceful adults-only park set in the heart of England with spotless facilities. The park is well positioned for visiting the National Exhibition Centre (NEC), the NEC Arena and National Indoor Arena (NIA), and Birmingham is only 12 miles away. The park also makes an ideal touring base for Warwick, Coventry and Stratford-upon-Avon just 22 miles away. Please note that tents are not accepted. 4 acre site. 48 touring pitches. 48 hardstandings. Caravan pitches. Motorhome pitches.

Open: all year **Last arrival:** variable **Last departure:** variable

Pitches: ✳️ ⊕ £19-£25 ⊕ £19-£25

Facilities: 🦮 ⊙ 🏵️ ✳️ 🕹️ ⓛ 🚽 📶 ♻️ ❗   **Services:** ⊕ ⑤ 🔋 🚽 📥 🛒

Within 3 miles: ↓ 🏌️ ⑤ ⑤ U

Notes: Adults only. No noise 22.30hrs-08.00hrs. Dogs must be kept on leads.

AA Pubs & Restaurants nearby: The White Lion Inn, HAMPTON IN ARDEN, B92 0AA, 01675 442833

PITCHES: ⊕ Caravans ⊕ Motorhomes ▲ Tents 🏠 Glamping-style accommodation **SERVICES:** ⊕ Electric hook up ⑤ Launderette 🍺 Licensed bar
🔋 Color Gas 🌀 Camping Gaz ⊤ Toilet fluid 🍽️ Café/Restaurant 🍟 Fast Food/Takeaway 📥 Battery charging 🚰 Baby care 🚐 Motorvan service point
ABBREVIATIONS: BH/bank hols – bank holidays Etr – Easter Spring BH – Spring Bank Holiday fr – from hrs – hours m – mile mdnt – midnight
rdbt – roundabout rs – restricted service wk – week wknd – weekend x-rds – cross roads 🚫 No credit or debit cards 🐾 No dogs 👨‍👩‍👧 Children of all ages accepted

WILTSHIRE

AMESBURY
Map 5 SU14

Places to visit

Stonehenge, STONEHENGE, SP4 7DE, 0870 333 1181
www.english-heritage.org.uk/daysout/properties/stonehenge

Heale Gardens, MIDDLE WOODFORD, SP4 6NT, 01722 782504
www.healegarden.co.uk

Great for kids: Wilton House, WILTON [NEAR SALISBURY], SP2 0BJ,
01722 746714 www.wiltonhouse.com

Stonehenge Touring Park
►►►83%

tel: 01980 620304 **Orcheston SP3 4SH**
email: stay@stonehengetouringpark.com
dir: *From A360 towards Devizes turn right, follow lane, site at bottom of village on right.* **grid ref:** *SU061456*

A quiet site adjacent to the small village of Orcheston near the centre of Salisbury Plain and four miles from Stonehenge. There's an excellent on-site shop and some hardstandings are available. 2 acre site. 30 touring pitches. 13 hardstandings. Caravan pitches. Motorhome pitches. Tent pitches.

Open: all year **Last arrival:** 19.00hrs **Last departure:** 11.00hrs

Pitches: * 🚐 £10-£16 🚗 £10-£16 ▲ £10-£27

Leisure: ⚠

Facilities: 🅵⊙🅿✳🆂🆆🆒🅸

Services: 🅿🅾🔒🕖🅃🖿🖾

Within 3 miles: 🅂🅂🅄

Notes: No noise after 23.00hrs. Dogs must be kept on leads.

AA Pubs & Restaurants nearby: The Boot Inn, BERWICK ST JAMES, SP3 4TN, 01722 790243

Interested in camping on an island? Take a look at page 20

BERWICK ST JAMES
Map 5 SU03

Places to visit

Stonehenge, STONEHENGE, SP4 7DE, 0870 333 1181
www.english-heritage.org.uk/daysout/properties/stonehenge

Heale Gardens, MIDDLE WOODFORD, SP4 6NT, 01722 782504
www.healegarden.co.uk

Stonehenge Campsite & Glamping Pods
►►►80%

tel: 07786 734732 **SP3 4TQ**
email: stay@stonehengecampsite.co.uk
dir: *From Stonehenge Visitor Centre take A303 W, 2m. Through Winterbourne Stoke. Left onto B3083 towards Berwick St James. Site on left in 0.5m.* **grid ref:** *SU077405*

This small, award-winning site is split into three areas and has good modern toilets, and the addition of laundry facilities for the 2014 season. The lower area has hardstandings for caravans and motorhomes, as well as two luxury glamping pods. The middle field is for tents, both for families and individuals, whilst the top area is for larger groups who can perhaps enjoy some of their holiday time sitting around open fires or fire pits. The site is close to Stonehenge and Longleat; there are plenty of excellent walks from the campsite and two good pubs nearby. 4 acre site. 35 touring pitches. 10 hardstandings. Caravan pitches. Motorhome pitches. Tent pitches. 2 wooden pods.

Open: all year **Last arrival:** 21.00hrs **Last departure:** noon

Pitches: * 🚐 £20-£30 🚗 £15-£30 ▲ £15-£25 🏠

Facilities: 🅵⊙🅿✳🅖🆐🆆🅸🆆🅸🅸

Services: 🅿🅾🅃🖿🖾

Within 3 miles: 🅂🅂🅄

Notes: No noise after 23.00hrs. Dogs must be kept on leads. Fire pit & mobile fire pits.

CALNE
Map 4 ST97

Places to visit

Avebury Manor & Garden, AVEBURY, SN8 1RF, 01672 539250
www.english-heritage.org.uk/daysout/properties/avebury

Bowood House & Gardens, CALNE, SN11 0LZ, 01249 812102 www.bowood.org

Great for kids: Alexander Keiller Museum, AVEBURY, SN8 1RF, 01672 539250
www.nationaltrust.org.uk

Blackland Lakes Holiday & Leisure Centre
►►►79%

tel: 01249 810943 **Stockley Ln SN11 0NQ**
email: enquiries@blacklandlakes.co.uk
dir: *From Calne take A4 E for 1.5m, right at camp sign. Site 1m on left.* **grid ref:** *ST973687*

A rural site surrounded by the North and West Downs. The park is divided into several paddocks separated by hedges, trees and fences, and there are two well-stocked carp fisheries for the angling enthusiast. There are some excellent walks close by, and the interesting market town of Devizes is just a few miles away. 15 acre site. 180 touring pitches. 16 hardstandings. 25 seasonal pitches. Caravan pitches. Motorhome pitches. Tent pitches.

Open: all year (rs 30 Oct-1 Mar pre-paid bookings only) **Last arrival:** 22.00hrs **Last departure:** noon

Pitches: ⌑ ⌑ Å **Leisure:** ⚘

Facilities: ⌑⊙☀&⑤⊓⊓♻❂ **Services:** ⌑⑤ 🔋⌀⊤🔌⊔

Within 3 miles: ⌑⌑⑤⑤∪

Notes: No noise after 22.30hrs, no loud music, no groups of under 25s. Dogs must be kept on leads. Wildfowl sanctuary, cycle trail.

AA Pubs & Restaurants nearby: The White Horse, CALNE, SN11 8RG, 01249 813118

The Lansdowne, CALNE, SN11 0EH, 01249 812488

The George Inn, LACOCK, SN15 2LH, 01249 730263

LACOCK
Map 4 ST96

Places to visit

Lacock Abbey, Fox Talbot Museum & Village, LACOCK, SN15 2LG, 01249 730459 www.nationaltrust.org.uk/lacock

Corsham Court, CORSHAM, SN13 0BZ, 01249 701610 www.corsham-court.co.uk

Piccadilly Caravan Park
►►►► 83%

tel: 01249 730260 **Folly Lane West SN15 2LP**
email: info@piccadillylacock.co.uk **web:** www.piccadillylacock.co.uk
dir: 4m S of Chippenham just past Lacock. Exit A350 signed Gastard. Site 300yds on left. **grid ref:** ST913683

A peaceful, pleasant site, well established and beautifully laid-out, close to the village of Lacock and Lacock Abbey. Both the facilities and the grounds are immaculately maintained; there is very good screening. A section of the park has been developed to provide spacious pitches especially for tents, complete with its own toilet and shower block. 2.5 acre site. 41 touring pitches. 12 hardstandings. Caravan pitches. Motorhome pitches. Tent pitches.

Open: Etr & Apr-Oct **Last arrival:** 21.00hrs **Last departure:** noon

Pitches: ⌑ £19-£21 ⌑ £19-£21 Å £19-£21

Leisure: ⚘❂ **Facilities:** ⌑⊙⌽☀①⊓WiFi❂❂

Services: ⌑⑤ 🔋⌀🔌

Within 3 miles: ⌑⊟⌑⑤⑤∪

Notes: 🐾 Dogs must be kept on leads.

AA Pubs & Restaurants nearby: The George Inn, LACOCK, SN15 2LH, 01249 730263

LANDFORD
Map 5 SU21

Places to visit

Furzey Gardens, MINSTEAD, SO43 7GL, 023 8081 2464 www.furzey-gardens.org

Mottisfont, MOTTISFONT, SO51 0LP, 01794 340757 www.nationaltrust.org.uk/mottisfont

Great for kids: Paultons Park, OWER, SO51 6AL, 023 8081 4442 www.paultonspark.co.uk

---

PREMIER PARK

Greenhill Farm Caravan & Camping Park
►►►► 79%

tel: 01794 324117 **Greenhill Farm, New Rd SP5 2AZ**
email: info@greenhillholidays.co.uk
dir: M27 junct 2, A36 towards Salisbury, approx 3m after Hampshire/Wiltshire border, (pass Shoe Inn pub on right, BP garage on left) take next left into New Rd, signed Nomansland, 0.75m on left. **grid ref:** SU266183

A tranquil, well-landscaped park hidden away in unspoilt countryside on the edge of the New Forest National Park. Pitches overlooking the fishing lake include hardstandings and are for adults only. The other section of the park is for families and includes a play area and games room. There are excellent new toilet and shower blocks in both the family area and adults' only area. This site is also well placed for visiting Paultons Family Theme Park at Ower. 13 acre site. 160 touring pitches. 45 hardstandings. Caravan pitches. Motorhome pitches. Tent pitches.

Open: all year **Last arrival:** 21.30hrs **Last departure:** 11.00hrs

Pitches: * ⌑ £17.50-£27.50 ⌑ £17.50-£27.50 Å £13.50-£27.50

Leisure: ⚘❂❦

Facilities: ⌑⌑⊙⌽☀&①⑤♻❂❂

Services: ⌑⑤🍴🔋⌀⊤🔌⊔

Within 3 miles: ⌑⌑⑤⑤∪

Notes: No noise after 23.00hrs. Dogs must be kept on leads. Disposable BBQs.

> **Visit the AA.com/shop for the latest AA Pub and Restaurant guides**

SALISBURY

Map 5 SU12

See also Amesbury

Places to visit

The Salisbury Museum, SALISBURY, SP1 2EN, 01722 332151
www.salisburymuseum.org.com

Salisbury Cathedral, SALISBURY, SP1 2EJ, 01722 555120
www.salisburycathedral.org.uk

Great for kids: Wilton House, WILTON [NEAR SALISBURY], SP2 0BJ,
01722 746714 www.wiltonhouse.com

Coombe Touring Park

▶ ▶ ▶ ▶ 90%

tel: 01722 328451 **Race Plain, Netherhampton SP2 8PN**
email: enquiries@coombecaravanpark.co.uk **web:** www.coombecaravanpark.co.uk
dir: A36 onto A3094, 2m SW, site adjacent to Salisbury racecourse. **grid ref:** SU099282

A very neat and attractive site adjacent to the racecourse with views over the
downs. The park is well landscaped with shrubs and maturing trees, and the very
colourful beds are stocked from the owner's greenhouse. This is a lovely quiet and
peaceful park to stay on with an excellent toilet and shower block; a marquee is
erected in the main season for campers' use which proves very popular. There are
four static homes available for hire. 3 acre site. 50 touring pitches. 6
hardstandings. Caravan pitches. Motorhome pitches. Tent pitches. 4 statics.

Open: 3 Jan-20 Dec (rs Oct-May shop closed) **Last arrival:** 21.00hrs **Last departure:** noon

Pitches: 🚐 🚌 Å

Leisure: 🄰

Facilities: 🖍 ⊙ 𝌆 ✳ ⅙ 🖫 ❶

Services: 🔌 🖫 ⌀ 🛒

Within 3 miles: ⌄ 🖫 🖫 ∪

Notes: 🚫 No disposable BBQs or fires, no mini motorbikes, no noise between 23.00hrs-
07.00hrs. Dogs must be kept on leads. Children's bathroom.

AA Pubs & Restaurants nearby: The Wig and Quill, SALISBURY, SP1 2PH, 01722 335665

Alderbury Caravan & Camping Park

▶ ▶ ▶ 80%

tel: 01722 710125 **Southampton Rd, Whaddon SP5 3HB**
email: alderbury@aol.com
dir: Follow Whaddon signs from A36, 3m from Salisbury. Site opposite The Three Crowns
pub. **grid ref:** SU197259

A pleasant, attractive park set in the village of Whaddon not far from Salisbury. The
small site is well maintained by friendly owners, and is ideally positioned near the
A36 for overnight stops to and from the Southampton ferry terminals. 2 acre site.
39 touring pitches. 12 hardstandings. Caravan pitches. Motorhome pitches. Tent
pitches. 1 static.

Open: all year **Last arrival:** 21.00hrs **Last departure:** 12.30hrs

Pitches: * 🚐 £9.50-£15 🚌 £9.50-£15 Å £9.50-£15

Facilities: 🖍 ⊙ ✳ ⅙ 🛜 ❶

Services: 🔌 🖫 🔒 ⌀ 🛒

Within 3 miles: ⌄ 𝌆 🖫 🖫 ∪

Notes: No open fires. Dogs must be kept on leads. Microwave & electric kettle available.

AA Pubs & Restaurants nearby: Salisbury Seafood & Steakhouse, SALISBURY, SP1 3TE,
01722 417411

The Cloisters, SALISBURY, SP1 2DH, 01722 338102

TROWBRIDGE

Map 4 ST85

Places to visit

Great Chalfield Manor and Garden, BRADFORD-ON-AVON, SN12 8NH,
01225 782239 www.nationaltrust.org.uk

The Courts Garden, HOLT, BA14 6RR, 01225 782875 www.nationaltrust.org.uk

Great for kids: Longleat Safari & Adventure Park, LONGLEAT, BA12 7NW,
01985 844400 www.longleat.co.uk

Stowford Manor Farm

▶ ▶ 75%

tel: 01225 752253 **Stowford, Wingfield BA14 9LH**
email: stowford1@supanet.com
dir: From Trowbridge take A366 W towards Radstock. Site on left in 3m.
grid ref: ST810577

A very simple farm site set on the banks of the River Frome behind the farm
courtyard. The owners are friendly and relaxed and the park enjoys a similarly
comfortable ambience, with cream teas available at the farmhouse. Farleigh &
District Swimming Club, one of the few remaining river swimming clubs, is just half
a mile from the site. 1.5 acre site. 15 touring pitches. Caravan pitches. Motorhome
pitches. Tent pitches.

Open: Etr-Oct **Last departure:** noon

Pitches: * 🚐 £16-£19 🚌 £16-£19 Å £16-£19

Facilities: 🖍 ⊙ ✳ 🐾 🛜 ♺

Services: 🔌 🍴 🛒

Within 3 miles: ⌄ 𝌆 🖫 🖫 ♨ 🖫 🖫 ∪

Notes: No open fires (fire bowls available). Dogs must be kept on leads. Fishing, boating.

AA Pubs & Restaurants nearby: George Inn, NORTON ST PHILIP, BA2 7LH, 01373 834224

LEISURE: 🏊 Indoor swimming pool 🏊 Outdoor swimming pool 🄰 Children's playground 🪁 Kid's club 🎾 Tennis court 🎱 Games room 📺 Separate TV room
⛳ golf course ⛵ Boats for hire 🎬 Cinema 🎵 Entertainment 🎣 Fishing 🏌 Mini golf 🚣 Watersports 🏋 Gym 🏟 Sports field Spa ∪ Stables
FACILITIES: 🛁 Bath 🚿 Shower ⊙ Electric shaver 𝌆 Hairdryer ✳ Ice Pack Facility ⅙ Disabled facilities 🖫 Public telephone 🖫 Shop on site or within 200yds
🖫 Mobile shop (calls at least 5 days a week) 🍴 BBQ area 🎪 Picnic area 🛜 Wi-fi 💻 Internet access ♺ Recycling ❶ Tourist info 🐾 Dog exercise area

WESTBURY   Map 4 ST85

Places to visit

Great Chalfield Manor and Garden, BRADFORD-ON-AVON, SN12 8NH, 01225 782239 www.nationaltrust.org.uk

The Courts Garden, HOLT, BA14 6RR, 01225 782875 www.nationaltrust.org.uk

Brokerswood Country Park
▶▶▶▶84%

GOLD

tel: 01373 822238 **Brokerswood BA13 4EH**
email: info@brokerswoodcountrypark.co.uk **web:** www.brokerswoodcountrypark.co.uk
dir: M4 junct 17, S on A350. Right at Yarnbrook to Rising Sun pub at North Bradley, left at rdbt. Left on bend approaching Southwick, 2.5m, site on right. **grid ref:** ST836523

A popular site on the edge of an 80-acre woodland park with nature trails, fishing lakes and a good range of activities including archery, tree climbing and kayaking. The adventure playground offers plenty of fun for all ages, and there is a miniature railway, an indoor play centre and a café. There are high quality toilet facilities and fully-equipped, ready-erected tents are available for hire. 5 acre site. 69 touring pitches. 21 hardstandings. Caravan pitches. Motorhome pitches. Tent pitches.

Open: Apr-4 Nov **Last arrival:** 21.30hrs **Last departure:** 11.00hrs

Pitches: * ➡ £16-£32 ➡ £16-£32 ▲ £16-£32

Leisure: ⚞

Facilities: ➡ ▮ ✾ ☉ ⋔ ✳ & 🛢 ㇆ ⇌ ❖ ⊘

Services: ⊡ ⊡ ⋔ 🛢 ⊘ T ᴑ ➡ ⇌ ⇘

Within 3 miles: ⊘ ⓢ

Notes: Families only. Dogs must be kept on leads.

AA Pubs & Restaurants nearby: The Full Moon at Rudge, RUDGE, BA11 2QF, 01373 830936

The Bell Inn, GREAT CHEVERELL, SN10 5TH, 01380 813277

WORCESTERSHIRE

HONEYBOURNE   Map 10 SP14

Places to visit

Kiftsgate Court Garden, MICKLETON, GL55 6LN, 01386 438777 www.kiftsgate.co.uk

Hidcote Manor Garden, MICKLETON, GL55 6LR, 01386 438333 www.nationaltrust.org.uk/hidcote

Great for kids: Anne Hathaway's Cottage, SHOTTERY, CV37 9HH, 01789 201844 www.shakespeare.org.uk

PREMIER PARK

Ranch Caravan Park
▶▶▶▶▶83%

GOLD

tel: 01386 830744 **Station Rd WR11 7PR**
email: enquiries@ranch.co.uk **web:** www.ranch.co.uk
dir: From village x-rds towards Bidford, site 400mtrs on left. **grid ref:** SP113444

An attractive and well-run park set amidst farmland in the Vale of Evesham and landscaped with trees and bushes. Tourers have their own excellent facilities in two locations, and the use of an outdoor heated swimming pool in peak season. There is also a licensed club serving meals. Please note that this site does not accept tents. 12 acre site. 120 touring pitches. 46 hardstandings. 20 seasonal pitches. Caravan pitches. Motorhome pitches. 218 statics.

Open: Mar-Nov (rs Mar-May & Sep-Nov swimming pool closed, shorter club hours) **Last arrival:** 20.00hrs **Last departure:** noon

Pitches: * ➡ £24-£28 ➡ £24-£28

Leisure: ≋ ⅄ ⚞ ⚘ ⚲ ▢ ♫

Facilities: ▮ ☉ ⋔ ✳ & ⓢ 🛢 ㇆ ▬ ❖ ⊘

Services: ⊡ ⊡ ⋔ 🛢 ⊘ T ᴑ ➡ 🚮 ⇘

Within 3 miles: ⚲ ⊘ ⓢ ⊡ ∪

Notes: No unaccompanied minors. Dogs must be kept on leads.

AA Pubs & Restaurants nearby: The Fleece Inn, BRETFORTON, WR11 7JE, 01386 831173

The Ebrington Arms, EBRINGTON, GL55 6NH, 01386 593223

PITCHES: ➡ Caravans ➡ Motorhomes ▲ Tents ⋔ Glamping-style accommodation **SERVICES:** ⊡ Electric hook up ⊡ Launderette ⋔ Licensed bar
🛢 Calor Gas ⊘ Camping Gaz T Toilet fluid ᴑ Café/Restaurant 🚮 Fast Food/Takeaway ➡ Battery charging ⇌ Baby care ⇘ Motorvan service point
ABBREVIATIONS: BH/bank hols – bank holidays Etr – Easter Spring BH – Spring Bank Holiday fr – from hrs – hours m – mile mdnt – midnight
rdbt – roundabout rs – restricted service wk – week wknd – weekend x-rds – cross roads ⊘ No credit or debit cards ⊗ No dogs ⅋ Children of all ages accepted

WORCESTER
Map 10 SO85

Places to visit

City Museum & Art Gallery, WORCESTER, WR1 1DT, 01905 25371
www.museumsworcestershire.org.uk

The Greyfriars, WORCESTER, WR1 2LZ, 01905 23571 www.nationaltrust.org.uk

Great for kids: West Midland Safari & Leisure Park, BEWDLEY, DY12 1LF,
01299 402114 www.wmsp.co.uk

Peachley Leisure Touring Park
▶▶▶87%

SILVER

tel: 01905 641309 & 07764 540803 **Peachley Ln, Lower Broadheath WR2 6QX**
email: peachleyleisure@live.co.uk
dir: *M5 junct 7, A44 (Worcester ring road) towards Leominster. Exit at sign for Elgar's
Birthplace Museum. Pass museum, at x-rds turn right. In 0.75m at T-junct turn left. Park
signed on right.* **grid ref:** *SO807576*

The park is set in its own area in the grounds of Peachley Farm and has all
hardstanding and fully serviced pitches. There are two fishing lakes, a really
excellent quad bike course and, new for 2014, outdoor giant draughts, chess and
jenga. The park proves to be a peaceful haven, and is an excellent base from which
to explore the area, which includes The Elgar Birthplace Museum, Worcester
Racecourse and the Worcester Victorian Christmas Fayre (in late November); it is
also convenient for Malvern's Three Counties Showground. 8 acre site. 82 touring
pitches. 82 hardstandings. Caravan pitches. Motorhome pitches. Tent pitches.

Open: all year **Last arrival:** 21.30hrs **Last departure:** noon

Pitches: * 🚐 £16-£18 🚎 £16-£18 ▲

Leisure: ⚽

Facilities: 🏕⊙✳&🕿 WiFi 🖥 ♻

Services: 🚐🖭 🗑🍴

Within 3 miles: ⚓🗄📎⚓🛍🛍U

Notes: No skateboards, no riding of motorbikes or scooters. Dogs must be kept on leads.

AA Pubs & Restaurants nearby: The Talbot, KNIGHTWICK, WR6 5PH, 01886 821235

The Bear & Ragged Staff, BRANSFORD, WR6 5JH, 01886 833399

PITCHES: 🚐 Caravans 🚐 Motorhomes ⛺ Tents 🏠 Glamping-style accommodation SERVICES: 🔌 Electric hook up 🔄 Launderette 🍸 Licensed bar
🛢 Calor Gas 🍃 Camping Gaz ⊤ Toilet fluid 🍽 Café/Restaurant 🍔 Fast Food/Takeaway 🔋 Battery charging 🍼 Baby care ⚡ Motorvan service point
ABBREVIATIONS: BH/bank hols – bank holidays Etr – Easter Spring BH – Spring Bank Holiday fr – from hrs – hours m – mile mdnt – midnight
rdbt – roundabout rs – restricted service wk – week wknd – weekend x-rds – cross roads 🚫 No credit or debit cards 🚫 No dogs 👫 Children of all ages accepted

Yorkshire

There is nowhere in the British Isles quite like Yorkshire. With such scenic and cultural diversity, it is almost a country within a country. For sheer scale, size and grandeur, there is nowhere to beat it. Much of it in the spectacular Pennines, Yorkshire is a land of glorious moors, gentle dales, ruined abbeys and picturesque market towns.

'My Yorkshire, a land of pure air, rocky streams and hidden waterfalls,' was how the celebrated vet Alf Wight described his adopted home. Wight was born in Sunderland but moved to the North Yorkshire market town of Thirsk soon after the outbreak of the Second World War. He fell in love with the place and in later years his affection for the beauty, spirit and character of this great county translated to the printed page when Wight, writing under the name of James Herriot, wrote eight best-selling volumes of memoirs about the life of a Yorkshire vet, which spawned two films and a long-running TV series. Today, thousands of visitors from near and far travel to the landscape he loved so dearly to see it all for themselves. His veterinary practice, and original home, in Thirsk is open to the public.

Not surprisingly, walking features prominently on the list of things to do in Yorkshire. There are countless footpaths and bridleways to explore and miles of long-distance trails across vast open moorland and through tranquil meandering valleys. The 81-mile Dales Way is a perfect way to discover the magnificent scenery of Wharfedale, Ribblesdale and Dentdale, while the Calderdale Way offers a fascinating insight into the Pennine heartland of industrial West Yorkshire. Most famous of all the region's longer routes is surely the Pennine Way, which opened 50 years ago in April 1965. Its inception was the most important achievement in the history of the Ramblers' Association, marking Britain's first national long-distance footpath.

The Pennine Way was the brainchild of Tom Stephenson, one-time secretary of the Association but his vision for a trail for everyone was a long time in the planning. Landowners regularly thwarted his attempts to make the landscape accessible to walkers and there were countless prosecutions for trespassing 'I could never understand how anyone could own a mountain,' Stephenson wrote. 'Surely it was there for everybody.'

One of the more surprising features to be found on the route of the Pennine Way is the ruined house known as Top Withins. This is thought to be the inspiration for *Wuthering Heights*, the Earnshaw home in Emily Brontë's stirring novel of the same name. The Brontë sisters knew the area well, and their home, now the Brontë Parsonage Museum, lies just a few miles from the ruins in the village of Haworth. The parsonage draws thousands of visitors every year; its atmospheric setting amid bleak moorland and gritstone houses vividly captures the spirit of this uniquely talented trio of writers.

An easier, more comfortable way of exploring much of Yorkshire's scenic landscape is by train. A ride on the famous Settle to Carlisle railway represents one of the region's most memorable train journeys. For a while during the late 1980s the future of this line was in serious doubt, when it seemed British Rail might close it because of soaring maintenance costs. Thanks to Michael Portillo, a noted railway enthusiast who was Secretary of State for Transport at the time, the line was saved. Essentially, the Settle to Carlisle railway is a lifeline for commuters and the people of the more remote communities of the western Dales, but it is also an extremely popular tourist attraction. Carriages are regularly filled with summer visitors in search of stunning scenery and they are not disappointed. Elsewhere in Yorkshire, a very different train recalls a very different age. In the National Railway Museum at York you'll find countless locomotives, including a replica of Stephenson's Rocket and the much-loved *Flying Scotsman*.

EAST RIDING OF YORKSHIRE

BRANDESBURTON
Map 17 TA14

Places to visit
Beverley Guildhall, BEVERLEY, HU17 9AU, 01482 392783
www.eastriding.gov.uk/museums

Burton Constable Hall, SPROATLEY, HU11 4LN, 01964 562400
www.burtonconstable.com

Blue Rose Caravan Country Park
▶▶▶▶ 85%

SILVER

tel: 01964 543366 & 07504 026899 **Star Carr Ln YO25 8RU**
email: info@bluerosepark.com
dir: From A165 at rdbt into New Rd signed Brandesburton (becomes Star Carr Ln). Approx 1m, site on left. **grid ref:** TA110464

A neat and well maintained adult-only site well placed for visiting Hornsea and the Yorkshire coastline. The park is within walking distance of Brandesburton and offers an idyllic stopover for caravanners wanting a peaceful break in the countryside. 12 acre site. 58 touring pitches. 58 hardstandings. 44 seasonal pitches. Caravan pitches. Motorhome pitches. 36 statics.

Open: all year **Last arrival:** 20.00hrs **Last departure:** noon

Pitches: * 🚐 £15-£22 🚐 £15-£22

Facilities: 🃏⊙🕭🕭🖈🌿🛁🖥 ♻ 🛈

Services: 🔌🗑 🍴🛢⊘ T

Within 3 miles: 👟🚲🎣◎🛶🎮🏪 U

Notes: Adults only. Dogs must be kept on leads.

Dacre Lakeside Park
▶▶▶ 85%

tel: 0800 180 4556 & 01964 543704 **YO25 8RT**
email: dacrepark@btconnect.com
dir: From A165 (bypass) midway between Beverley & Hornsea, follow Brandesburton & brown site sign. **grid ref:** TA118468

A large lake popular with watersports enthusiasts is the focal point of this grassy site, which offers predominantly seasonal pitches - only four touring pitches are available. The clubhouse offers indoor activities; there's a fish and chip shop, a pub and a Chinese takeaway in the village, which is within walking distance. The six-acre lake is used for windsurfing, sailing, kayaking, canoeing and fishing. Camping pods are available for hire. 8 acre site. 120 touring pitches. 110 seasonal pitches. Caravan pitches. Motorhome pitches. Tent pitches. 110 statics. 9 wooden pods.

Open: Mar-Oct **Last arrival:** 21.00hrs **Last departure:** noon

Pitches: 🚐🚐 Å 🏠

Leisure: 🏊⊙🎱🎵

Facilities: 🃏⊙🌿❄🕭🖈🛁 WiFi 🖥

Services: 🔌🗑🍴⊘T🖤

Within 3 miles: 👟🚲🎣🛶🎮🏪 U

Notes: No noise 23.00hrs-08.00hrs, no craft with engines permitted on lake.

BRIDLINGTON
Map 17 TA16

See also Rudston

Places to visit
Sewerby Hall & Gardens, BRIDLINGTON, YO15 1EA, 01262 673769
www.eastriding.gov.uk/sewerby

RSPB Nature Reserve, BEMPTON, YO15 1JD, 01262 422212
www.rspb.org.uk/bemptoncliffs

Great for kids: Burton Agnes Hall, BURTON AGNES, YO25 4ND, 01262 490324
www.burtonagnes.com

Fir Tree Caravan Park
▶▶▶▶ 81%

tel: 01262 676442 **Jewison Ln, Sewerby YO16 6YG**
email: info@flowerofmay.com
dir: 1.5m from centre of Bridlington. Left onto B1255 at Marton Corner. Site 600yds on left. **grid ref:** TA195702

Fir Tree Park, a large, mainly static park, has a well laid out touring area (seasonal pitches only) with its own facilities, including a new toilet block which opened in 2014. It has an excellent swimming pool complex and the adjacent bar-cum-conservatory serves meals. There is also a family bar, games room and outdoor children's play area. 22 acre site. 45 touring pitches. 45 hardstandings. 45 seasonal pitches. Caravan pitches. Motorhome pitches. 400 statics.

Open: Mar-Oct (rs Early & late season bar & entertainment restrictions) **Last arrival:** dusk **Last departure:** noon

Pitches: 🚐🚐

Leisure: 🏊 🏠 🎱 🎵

Facilities: 🃏⊙❄🕭🕭🖈🛁 WiFi ♻ 🛈

Services: 🔌🗑🍴🛢🍴⊙🖤

Within 3 miles: 👟🚲🎣🛶🎮🏪 U

Notes: No noise after mdnt. Dogs accepted by prior arrangement only & must be kept on leads.

AA Pubs & Restaurants nearby: The Seabirds Inn, FLAMBOROUGH, YO15 1PD, 01262 850242

See advert on page 349

KINGSTON UPON HULL

See Sproatley

RUDSTON

Places to visit
Sewerby Hall & Gardens, BRIDLINGTON, YO15 1EA, 01262 673769
www.eastriding.gov.uk/sewerby

LEISURE: 🏊 Indoor swimming pool 🏊 Outdoor swimming pool 🏠 Children's playground 🙌 Kid's club 🎾 Tennis court 🎱 Games room 📺 Separate TV room
👟 golf course 🚣 Boats for hire 🎬 Cinema 🎵 Entertainment 🎣 Fishing ◎ Mini golf 🛶 Watersports 🏋 Gym ⊙ Sports field Spa U Stables
FACILITIES: 🛁 Bath 🃏 Shower ⊙ Electric shaver 🌿 Hairdryer ❄ Ice Pack Facility 🕭 Disabled facilities 🕭 Public telephone 🛒 Shop on site or within 200yds
🛍 Mobile shop (calls at least 5 days a week) 🍴 BBQ area 🌿 Picnic area WiFi Wi-fi 🖥 Internet access ♻ Recycling 🛈 Tourist info 🖈 Dog exercise area

RUDSTON
Map 17 TA06

Thorpe Hall Caravan & Camping Site
►►►►80%

tel: 01262 420393 & 420574 **Thorpe Hall YO25 4JE**
email: caravansite@thorpehall.co.uk **web:** www.thorpehall.co.uk
dir: From Bridlington take B1253 W for 5m. **grid ref:** TA108677

A delightful, peaceful small park within the walled gardens of Thorpe Hall yet within a few miles of the bustling seaside resort of Bridlington. The site offers a games field, its own coarse fishery, pitch and putt, and a games and TV lounge. There are numerous walks locally. 4.5 acre site. 92 touring pitches. Caravan pitches. Motorhome pitches. Tent pitches.

Open: Mar-Oct **Last arrival:** 22.00hrs **Last departure:** noon

Pitches: * 🚐 £13-£24 🚌 £13-£24 ⛺ £10-£21

Leisure: 🄰 😊 🎣 ▢ **Facilities:** 🚿 🐾 ⊙ ℗ ⚒ ♿ 🕙 🛉 🛒 ⽑ 📶 ♻ 🅕

Services: 🔌 🔲 🍴 🛢 Ⓣ 🔋 **Within 3 miles:** 🐎 🛝 🔲 ⛳

Notes: No ball games (field provided), no noise 23.00hrs-08.00hrs, well behaved dogs only. Dogs must be kept on leads. 4.5 acre golf practice area.

AA Pubs & Restaurants nearby: The Seabirds Inn, FLAMBOROUGH, YO15 1PD, 01262 850242

SKIPSEA
Map 17 TA15

Places to visit
Hornsea Museum, HORNSEA, HU18 1AB, 01964 533443
www.hornseamuseum.com

Sewerby Hall & Gardens, BRIDLINGTON, YO15 1EA, 01262 673769
www.eastriding.gov.uk/sewerby

Skirlington Leisure Park
HOLIDAY CENTRE 88%

tel: 01262 468213 & 468466 **YO25 8SY**
email: info@skirlington.com
dir: From M62 towards Beverley then Hornsea. Between Skipsea & Hornsea on B1242.
grid ref: TA188528

A large, well-run seaside park set close to the beach in partly-sloping meadowland with young trees and shrubs. The site has five toilet blocks, a supermarket and an amusement arcade, plus occasional entertainment in the clubhouse. The wide range of family amenities includes an indoor heated swimming pool complex with sauna, steam room and gym. A 10-pin bowling alley and indoor soft play area for children are added attractions. 140 acre site. 280 touring pitches. 15 hardstandings. 180 seasonal pitches. Caravan pitches. Motorhome pitches. 450 statics.

Open: Mar-Oct (rs Out of school hols & BHs some facilities & diner only open Fri-Sun) **Last arrival:** 20.00hrs **Last departure:** 11.00hrs

Pitches: * 🚐 £11-£26 🚌 £11-£26

Leisure: 🏊 ⚽ 🄰 😊 🎵

Facilities: 🚿 🐾 ⊙ ℗ ♿ 🕙 🛒 ⽑ 📶 🖥 ♻ 🅕

Services: 🔌 🔲 🍴 🛢 🛢 🍴 🔋 🍟

Within 3 miles: 🛝 ⧴ 🔲 ◎ 🔋 🔲 ⛳

Notes: No noise after 22.00hrs. Dogs must be kept on leads. Putting green, fishing lake, Sunday market, arcade, indoor softplay, mini bowling alley.

PITCHES: 🚐 Caravans 🚌 Motorhomes ⛺ Tents 🏕 Glamping-style accommodation **SERVICES:** 🔌 Electric hook up 🔲 Launderette 🍴 Licensed bar 🛢 Calor Gas 🛢 Camping Gaz Ⓣ Toilet fluid 🍴 Café/Restaurant 🍟 Fast Food/Takeaway 🔋 Battery charging 🍼 Baby care 🔧 Motorvan service point
ABBREVIATIONS: BH/bank hols – bank holidays Etr – Easter Spring BH – Spring Bank Holiday fr – from hrs – hours m – mile mdnt – midnight
rdbt – roundabout rs – restricted service wk – week wknd – weekend x-rds – cross roads 🚫 No credit or debit cards ⊗ No dogs 👫 Children of all ages accepted

SKIPSEA *continued*

Skipsea Sands
HOLIDAY CENTRE 83%

tel: 01262 468210 **Mill Ln YO25 8TZ**
email: skipsea.sands@park-resorts.com **web:** www.park-resorts.co.uk
dir: *From A165 (Bridlington to Kingston upon Hull road) 8m S of Bridlington take B1242 to Skipsea. Follow Skipsea Sands signed to left just after sharp left bend.*
grid ref: TA176563

A busy and popular holiday park just a stone's throw from the beach, and offering an excellent range of leisure and entertainment facilities for families and couples. There's a good, well maintained touring area with clean toilets and neat grass pitches. A dedicated team ensure that standards are high across the park. 91 touring pitches. Caravan pitches. Motorhome pitches. Tent pitches.

Open: Apr-Oct **Last arrival:** noon **Last departure:** 10.00hrs

Pitches: 🚐 🚑 🅰

See advert on page 343

SPROATLEY Map 17 TA13

Places to visit

Burton Constable Hall, SPROATLEY, HU11 4LN, 01964 562400
www.burtonconstable.com

Streetlife Museum, KINGSTON UPON HULL, HU1 1PS, 01482 613902
www.hullcc.gov.uk

Great for kids: The Deep, KINGSTON UPON HULL, HU1 4DP, 01482 381000
www.thedeep.co.uk

Burton Constable Holiday Park & Arboretum
►►►► 88%

tel: 01964 562508 **Old Lodges HU11 4LJ**
email: info@burtonconstable.co.uk **web:** www.burtonconstable.co.uk
dir: *A165 onto B1238 to Sproatley. Follow signs to site.* **grid ref:** TA186357

Within the extensive estate of Constable Burton Hall, this large and secluded holiday destination provides a wide range of attractions including fishing and

boating on the two 10-acre lakes, a snooker room, and a licensed bar with a designated family room. The grounds are immaculately maintained and generous pitch density offers good privacy. 90 acre site. 140 touring pitches. 20 hardstandings. 14 seasonal pitches. Caravan pitches. Motorhome pitches. Tent pitches. 360 statics. 2 wooden pods.

Open: Mar-mid Feb (rs Mar-Nov tourers & tents) **Last arrival:** 22.00hrs
Last departure: noon

Pitches: * 🚐 £17.50-£20.50 🚑 £17.50-£20.50 🅰 £15.50-£25.50 🏠

Leisure: 🅰 🏊 ⚽ 🎵

Facilities: 🏕 ⊙ 🅿 ⚿ ⊙ 🕿 🅂 📛 📶 🖥 ♻ ❼

Services: 🔌 🔁 🍴 🍺 ⊘ 🅃 🛒 🛗

Within 3 miles: 🎣 🎿 🅂 🅂 ∪

Notes: No skateboards or rollerblades. Dogs must be kept on leads. Snooker, table tennis.

TUNSTALL Map 17 TA33

Places to visit

Burton Constable Hall, SPROATLEY, HU11 4LN, 01964 562400
www.burtonconstable.com

Sand le Mere Holiday Village
HOLIDAY CENTRE 82%

tel: 01964 670403 **Southfield Ln HU12 0JF**
email: info@sand-le-mere.co.uk **web:** www.sand-le-mere.co.uk
dir: *From Hull A1033 signed Withernsea, B1362 (Hull Rd) signed Hedon. In Hedon continue on B3162 towards Withernsea. Turn left signed Roos. In Roos take B1242. Turn left at brown sign for site. In Tunstall right at T-junct, right into Seaside Ln to site.*
grid ref: TA305318

Ideally located between Withernsea and Bridlington, this impressive development provides first-class indoor leisure facilities with swimming pool, entertainment and a kiddies' soft ball area. The touring pitches are level and surrounded by maturing trees and shrubs. 135 acre site. 72 touring pitches. 51 hardstandings. Caravan pitches. Motorhome pitches. Tent pitches.

LEISURE: 🏊 Indoor swimming pool 🏊 Outdoor swimming pool 🅰 Children's playground 🅰 Kid's club 🎾 Tennis court 🎱 Games room 📺 Separate TV room 🏌 golf course ⛵ Boats for hire 🎬 Cinema 🎵 Entertainment 🎣 Fishing ◉ Mini golf 🏄 Watersports 🏋 Gym 🏟 Sports field Spa ∪ Stables
FACILITIES: 🛁 Bath 🚿 Shower ⊙ Electric shaver 🅿 Hairdryer ✳ Ice Pack Facility 🦽 Disabled facilities 🕿 Public telephone 🅂 Shop on site or within 200yds 🅂 Mobile shop (calls at least 5 days a week) 🍖 BBQ area 🄰 Picnic area 📶 Wi-fi 🖥 Internet access ♻ Recycling ❼ Tourist info 🅰 Dog exercise area

Open: Mar-Nov **Last arrival:** 23.00hrs **Last departure:** 11.00hrs

Pitches: 🚐 🚍 Å

Leisure: 🏊 ⛳ 🐴 🎯 ❤ 🎱 ♨ 🎵 Spa

Facilities: ℝ 🎮 ☀ ⚭ ⊙ 🛇 WiFi 🖥 ♻ 🄋

Services: 🔌 🛢 🍺 🔒 🛅 🍴 🚮 🧺 🔱

Within 3 miles: ↯ 🖉 ◎ 🛅 🖭

Notes: No noise after 23.00hrs, speed limits around site, no camp fires. Dogs must be kept on leads.

See advert below

WITHERNSEA   Map 17 TA32

Places to visit

Burton Constable Hall, SPROATLEY, HU11 4LN, 01964 562400
www.burtonconstable.com

Withernsea Sands
HOLIDAY CENTRE 80%   SILVER

tel: 0871 664 9803 **Waxholme Rd HU19 2BS**
email: withernsea.sands@park-resorts.com
dir: *M62 junct 38, A63 through Hull. At end of dual carriageway, right onto A1033, follow Withernsea signs. Through village, left at mini-rdbt onto B1242. 1st right at lighthouse. Site 0.5m on left.* **grid ref:** *TA335289*

Touring is very much at the heart of this holiday park's operation, with 100 all-electric pitches and additional space for tents. The owners, Park Resorts, continue to upgrade the facilities and attractions, and the leisure complex with its futuristic design is especially impressive. 115 touring pitches. Caravan pitches. Motorhome pitches. Tent pitches. 400 statics.

Open: Apr-Oct (rs BH & peak wknds sports available) **Last arrival:** 22.00hrs **Last departure:** noon

Pitches: 🚐 🚍 Å

Leisure: 🏊 🐴 🎯 ❤ 🎱 🎵

Facilities: 🔱 ℝ ⊙ 🎮 ☀ ⚭ ⊙ 🛅 🍴 🛒 WiFi 🖥 ♻

Services: 🔌 🛢 🍺 🔒 🛅 ⏣ 🅣 🍴 🚮

Within 3 miles: ↯ 🖉 🛅 🖭 ∪

Notes: No noise between 23.00hrs-07.00hrs. Dogs must be kept on leads. Extension leads & utilities available from reception.

PITCHES: 🚐 Caravans 🚍 Motorhomes Å Tents 🏠 Glamping-style accommodation   **SERVICES:** 🔌 Electric hook up 🛢 Launderette 🍺 Licensed bar 🔒 Calor Gas ⊘ Camping Gaz 🅣 Toilet fluid 🍴 Café/Restaurant 🚮 Fast Food/Takeaway ⏣ Battery charging 🧺 Baby care 🔱 Motorvan service point

ABBREVIATIONS: BH/bank hols – bank holidays   Etr – Easter   Spring BH – Spring Bank Holiday   fr – from   hrs – hours   m – mile   mdnt – midnight
rdbt – roundabout   rs – restricted service   wk – week   wknd – weekend   x-rds – cross roads   ⊜ No credit or debit cards   ⊗ No dogs   👫 Children of all ages accepted

NORTH YORKSHIRE

ACASTER MALBIS
Map 16 SE54

Places to visit
National Railway Museum, YORK, YO26 4XJ, 01904 621261 www.nrm.org.uk

York Minster, YORK, YO1 7HH, 01904 557200 www.yorkminster.org

Great for kids: Jorvik Viking Centre, YORK, YO1 9WT, 01904 615505
www.jorvik-viking-centre.com

Moor End Farm
►►74%

tel: 01904 706727 & 07860 405872 **YO23 2UQ**
email: moorendfarm@acaster99.fsnet.co.uk **web:** www.moor-end-farm.co.uk
dir: *Follow signs to Acaster Malbis from junct of A64 & A1237 at Copmanthorpe.*
grid ref: *SE589457*

A very pleasant farm site with modernised facilities including a heated family/disabled shower room. A river boat pickup to York is 150 yards from the site entrance, and the village inn and restaurant are a short stroll away. A very convenient site for visiting York Racecourse. 1 acre site. 12 touring pitches. Caravan pitches. Motorhome pitches. Tent pitches. 7 statics.

Open: Etr or Apr-Oct **Last arrival:** 22.00hrs **Last departure:** noon

Pitches: * 🚐 £15-£22 🚐 £15-£22 ▲ £15-£25

Leisure: ⚠

Facilities: 🍴⊙📺❄❓❤

Services: 🔌🗑🍴

Within 3 miles: ⚓⚓📅🛒🛒

Notes: 🐕 Dogs must be kept on leads. Fridge, freezer & microwave available.

AA Pubs & Restaurants nearby: Ye Old Sun Inn, COLTON, LS24 8EP, 01904 744261

ALLERSTON
Map 19 SE88

Places to visit
Scarborough Castle, SCARBOROUGH, YO11 1HY, 01723 372451
www.english-heritage.org.uk/daysout/properties/scarborough-castle

Pickering Castle, PICKERING, YO18 7AX, 01751 474989
www.english-heritage.org.uk/daysout/properties/pickering-castle

Great for kids: Flamingo Land Theme Park & Zoo, KIRBY MISPERTON, YO17 6UX, 01653 668287 www.flamingoland.co.uk

PREMIER PARK

Vale of Pickering Caravan Park
►►►►►86%

tel: 01723 859280 **Carr House Farm YO18 7PQ**
email: tony@valeofpickering.co.uk **web:** www.valeofpickering.co.uk
dir: *On B1415, 1.75m from A170 Pickering to Scarborough road.* **grid ref:** *SE879808*

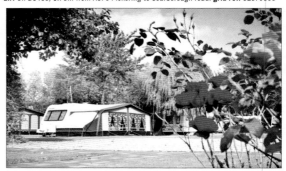

A well-maintained, spacious family park with excellent facilities including a well-stocked shop and immaculate toilet facilities, and an interesting woodland walk. Younger children will enjoy the attractive play area, while the large ball sports area will attract older ones. The park is set in open countryside bounded by hedges, has manicured grassland and stunning seasonal floral displays, and is handy for the North Yorkshire Moors and the attractions of Scarborough. 13 acre site. 120 touring pitches. 100 hardstandings. Caravan pitches. Motorhome pitches. Tent pitches.

Open: 5 Mar-3 Jan (rs Mar) **Last arrival:** 21.00hrs **Last departure:** 11.30hrs

Pitches: * 🚐 £16-£27 🚐 £16-£27 ▲ £13-£27

Leisure: ⚠⚽

Facilities: 🛁🍴⊙📺❄⚓🕐🛒🛒🐕♻ℹ

Services: 🔌🗑🍴⚓💧🚽🍴♿

Within 3 miles: ⚓🎣◎🛒🛒U

Notes: No open fires or Chinese lanterns, no noise after 23.00hrs. Microwave available.

AA Pubs & Restaurants nearby: The New Inn, THORNTON LE DALE, YO18 7LF, 01751 474226

The Coachman Inn, SNAINTON, YO13 9PL, 01723 859231

LEISURE: 🏊 Indoor swimming pool 🏊 Outdoor swimming pool ⚠ Children's playground 👶 Kid's club 🎾 Tennis court 🎱 Games room 📺 Separate TV room ⛳ golf course 🚣 Boats for hire 🎬 Cinema 🎵 Entertainment 🎣 Fishing ◎ Mini golf 🏄 Watersports 🏋 Gym 🏟 Sports field Spa U Stables
FACILITIES: 🛁 Bath 🍴 Shower ⊙ Electric shaver 📺 Hairdryer ❄ Ice Pack Facility ♿ Disabled facilities 🕐 Public telephone 🛒 Shop on site or within 200yds 🛒 Mobile shop (calls at least 5 days a week) 🍴 BBQ area 🍴 Picnic area 📶 Wi-fi 💻 Internet access ♻ Recycling ℹ Tourist info 🐕 Dog exercise area

ALNE
Map 19 SE46

Places to visit

Beningbrough Hall, Gallery & Gardens, BENINGBROUGH, YO30 1DD, 01904 472027 www.nationaltrust.org.uk/beningbrough

Sutton Park, SUTTON-ON-THE-FOREST, YO61 1DP, 01347 810249 www.statelyhome.co.uk

Great for kids: National Railway Museum, YORK, YO26 4XJ, 01904 621261 www.nrm.org.uk

PREMIER PARK

Alders Caravan Park
►►►► 80%

tel: 01347 838722 **Home Farm YO61 1RY**
email: enquiries@homefarmalne.co.uk
dir: *From A19 exit at Alne sign, in 1.5m left at T-junct, 0.5m site on left in village centre.* **grid ref:** *SE497654*

A tastefully developed park on a working farm with screened pitches laid out in horseshoe-shaped areas. This well-designed park offers excellent toilet facilities including a bathroom and fully-serviced washing and toilet cubicles. A woodland area and a water meadow are pleasant places to walk. 12 acre site. 87 touring pitches. 6 hardstandings. 71 seasonal pitches. Caravan pitches. Motorhome pitches. Tent pitches. 2 wooden pods.

Open: Mar-Oct **Last arrival:** 21.00hrs **Last departure:** 14.00hrs
Pitches: * 🚐 £19.50-£21.50 🚍 fr £19.50 🅰 fr £19.50 🏠
Facilities: 🔌🅿️☉🌡☀️♿🕐🔒🍽🐾♻️🐕‍🦺
Services: 🔌🅾 🛒🔋⚡ **Within 3 miles:** ↨🏌🛒🎣
Notes: Max 2 dogs per pitch. Dogs must be kept on leads. Summer house, farm produce for sale.
AA Pubs & Restaurants nearby: The Black Bull Inn, BOROUGHBRIDGE, YO51 9AR, 01423 322413
The Dining Room Restaurant, BOROUGHBRIDGE, YO51 9AR, 01423 326426

BISHOP MONKTON
Map 19 SE36

Places to visit

Newby Hall & Gardens, RIPON, HG4 5AE, 01423 322583 www.newbyhall.com

Fountains Abbey & Studley Royal, RIPON, HG4 3DY, 01765 608888 www.nationaltrust.org.uk/fountains-abbey

Great for kids: Lightwater Valley Theme Park, NORTH STAINLEY, HG4 3HT, 0871 720 0011 www.lightwatervalley.co.uk

Church Farm Caravan Park
►►► 75%

tel: 01765 676578 & 07861 770164 **Knaresborough Rd HG3 3QQ**
email: churchfarmcaravan@btinternet.com
dir: *From A61 at x-rds follow Bishop Monkton signs. 1.25m to village. At x-rds right into Knaresborough Rd, site approx 500mtrs on right.* **grid ref:** *SE328660*

A very pleasant rural site on a working farm, on the edge of the attractive village of Bishop Monkton with its well-stocked shop and pubs. Whilst very much a place to

relax, there are many attractions close by, including Fountains Abbey, Newby Hall, Ripon and Harrogate. 4 acre site. 45 touring pitches. 3 hardstandings. Caravan pitches. Motorhome pitches. Tent pitches. 3 statics.

Open: Mar-Oct **Last arrival:** 22.30hrs **Last departure:** 15.30hrs
Pitches: 🚐 🚍 🅰
Facilities: 🔌☉🌡♿🕐♻️🐕‍🦺
Services: 🔌🛒⚡
Within 3 miles: ↨🏌🛒🎣⛳
Notes: 🚫 No ball games. Dogs must be kept on leads.
AA Pubs & Restaurants nearby: The Black Bull Inn, BOROUGHBRIDGE, YO51 9AR, 01423 322413
The Dining Room Restaurant, BOROUGHBRIDGE, YO51 9AR, 01423 326426

BOLTON ABBEY
Map 19 SE05

Places to visit

National Park Centre, GRASSINGTON, BD23 5LB, 01756 751690 www.yorkshiredales.org.uk

Parcevall Hall Gardens, GRASSINGTON, BD23 6DE, 01756 720311 www.parcevallhallgardens.co.uk

Great for kids: Stump Cross Caverns, PATELEY BRIDGE, HG3 5JL, 01756 752780 www.stumpcrosscaverns.co.uk

Howgill Lodge
►►►► 78%

GOLD

tel: 01756 720655 **Barden BD23 6DJ**
email: info@howgill-lodge.co.uk
dir: *From Bolton Abbey take B6160 signed Burnsall. In 3m at Barden Tower right signed Appletreewick. 1.5m at phone box right into lane to site.* **grid ref:** *SE064592*

A beautifully-maintained and secluded site offering panoramic views of Wharfedale. The spacious hardstanding pitches are mainly terraced, and there is a separate tenting area with numerous picnic tables. There are three toilet facilities spread throughout the site, with the main block (including private, cubicled wash facilities) appointed to a high standard. There is also a well-stocked shop. 4 acre site. 40 touring pitches. 20 hardstandings. Caravan pitches. Motorhome pitches. Tent pitches.

Open: mid Mar-Oct **Last arrival:** 20.00hrs **Last departure:** noon
Pitches: 🚐 🚍 🅰
Leisure: ⚽
Facilities: 🔌☉🌡☀️🕐🔒🐾♻️🐕‍🦺
Services: 🔌🅾 🛒⚡🍽🔋
Within 3 miles: 🏌🛒🎣
Notes: Dogs must be kept on leads.
AA Pubs & Restaurants nearby: The Devonshire Brasserie & Bar, BOLTON ABBEY, BD23 6AJ, 01756 710710
The Fleece, ADDINGHAM, LS29 0LY, 01943 830491
The Craven Arms, APPLETREEWICK, BD23 6DA, 01756 720270

PITCHES: 🚐 Caravans 🚍 Motorhomes 🅰 Tents 🏠 Glamping-style accommodation **SERVICES:** 🔌 Electric hook up 🅾 Launderette 🍽 Licensed bar 🔋 Calor Gas ⚗ Camping Gaz 🅣 Toilet fluid 🍽 Café/Restaurant 🍟 Fast Food/Takeaway 🔋 Battery charging 🍼 Baby care ⚡ Motorvan service point **ABBREVIATIONS:** BH/bank hols – bank holidays Etr – Easter Spring BH – Spring Bank Holiday fr – from hrs – hours m – mile mdnt – midnight rdbt – roundabout rs – restricted service wk – week wknd – weekend x-rds – cross roads 🚫 No credit or debit cards 🚫 No dogs 👫 Children of all ages accepted

CHOP GATE
Map 19 SE59

NEW Lordstones Country Park
[U]

tel: 01642 778482 **Carlton Bank TS9 7JH**
email: info@lordstones.com
dir: *Please phone for directions.* **grid ref:** *NZ524030*

Situated in the North York Moors National Park with glorious views, Lordstones is a privately owned country park that has been developed into a distinctive visitor venue, with serious investment into providing a café-restaurant, a quality farm shop selling local produce, and small camping-cum-glamping park. The pitches, some with electricity, are enclosed by woodland, and the site also offerstwo fully-equipped bell tents, two bothy tents, and five luxury camping pods, each with a wood-burning stove, kitchenette, toilet and outside decking with barbecue and seating. In addition, there is a new, purpose-built amenity building housing showers and toilet facilities. 150 acre site. 21 touring pitches. Tent pitches. 4 bell tents/yurts. 5 wooden pods.

Open: all year **Last arrival:** 17.00hrs

Pitches: * ▲ £17-£24 🏠

CONSTABLE BURTON
Map 19 SE19

Places to visit

Middleham Castle, MIDDLEHAM, DL8 4RJ, 01969 623899
www.english-heritage.org.uk/daysout/properties/middleham-castle

Great for kids: Bedale Museum, BEDALE, DL8 1AA, 01677 427516
www.bedalemuseum.org.uk

Constable Burton Hall Caravan Park
▶▶▶▶81%

tel: 01677 450428 **DL8 5LJ**
email: caravanpark@constableburton.com
dir: *From Leyburn on A684 towards Bedale, approx 3m site on left.* **grid ref:** *SE158907*

A pretty site in the former deer park of the adjoining Constable Burton Hall, screened from the road by the park walls and surrounded by mature trees in a quiet rural location. The laundry is housed in a converted 18th-century deer barn and there is a pub and restaurant opposite; seasonal pitches are available. Please note that this site does not accept tents. 10 acre site. 120 touring pitches. Caravan pitches. Motorhome pitches.

Open: Apr-Oct **Last arrival:** 20.00hrs **Last departure:** noon

Pitches: * ⊞ £20-£25 ⊞ £20-£25

Facilities: 🏕️☉☞❄️🔥♿📶♻️🎯

Services: 🔌🔲💼🍴

Within 3 miles: ⛳🛒

Notes: No commercial vehicles, no games. Dogs must be kept on leads.
AA Pubs & Restaurants nearby: Sandpiper Inn, LEYBURN, DL8 5AT, 01969 622206
The White Swan, MIDDLEHAM, DL8 4PE, 01969 622093
The Wensleydale Heifer, WEST WITTON, DL8 4LS, 01969 622322

FILEY
Map 17 TA18

Flower of May Holiday Park
HOLIDAY CENTRE 90%

tel: 01723 584311 **Lebberston Cliff YO11 3NU**
email: info@flowerofmay.com **web:** www.flowerofmay.com
dir: *Take A165 from Scarborough towards Filey. Site signed.* **grid ref:** *TA085835*

A well-run, high quality family holiday park with top class facilities. This large landscaped park offers a full range of recreational activities, with plenty to occupy everyone. Grass and hard pitches are available, all on level ground, and arranged in avenues screened by shrubs. Enjoy the 'Scarborough Fair' museum, with its collection of restored fairground attractions, including rides, organs and vintage cars. 13 acre site. 300 touring pitches. 250 hardstandings. 100 seasonal pitches. Caravan pitches. Motorhome pitches. Tent pitches. 193 statics. 4 wooden pods.

Open: Etr-Oct (rs Early & late season restricted opening in café, shop & bars)
Last arrival: dusk **Last departure:** noon

Pitches: * ⊞ £22-£28 ⊞ £22-£28 ▲ £22-£28 🏠

Leisure: 🏊🎢👶🎣📺🎵🎶 **Facilities:** 🏕️☉❄️♿🔥🛒🍴📶♻️🎯

Services: 🔌🔲🍴💼🔥📺🍴💼🏪 **Within 3 miles:** ⛳🎣🏇🎿◎⛵🛒💈

Notes: No noise after mdnt, 1 dog per pitch by arrangement only. Dogs must be kept on leads. Squash, bowling, basketball court, skate park.

See advert on opposite page

LEISURE: 🏊 Indoor swimming pool 🏊 Outdoor swimming pool ⛰️ Children's playground 👶 Kid's club 🎾 Tennis court 🎱 Games room 📺 Separate TV room ⛳ golf course ⛵ Boats for hire 🎬 Cinema 🎵 Entertainment 🎣 Fishing ◎ Mini golf 🏄 Watersports 🏋️ Gym 🏟️ Sports field ♘ Stables
FACILITIES: 🛁 Bath 🚿 Shower ☉ Electric shaver 🔷 Hairdryer ❄️ Ice Pack Facility ♿ Disabled facilities 📞 Public telephone 🏪 Shop on site or within 200yds 🏬 Mobile shop (calls at least 5 days a week) 🔥 BBQ area 🪑 Picnic area 📶 Wi-fi 💻 Internet access ♻️ Recycling 🎯 Tourist info 🐕 Dog exercise area

FILEY *continued*

Blue Dolphin Holiday Park
HOLIDAY CENTRE 81%

tel: 0871 231 0893 **Gristhorpe Bay YO14 9PU**
email: bluedolphin@haven.com web: www.haven.com/bluedolphin
dir: *On A165, 2m N of Filey.* grid ref: *TA095829*

There are great cliff-top views to be enjoyed from this fun-filled holiday centre with an extensive and separate touring area. The emphasis is on non-stop entertainment, with organised sports and clubs, all-weather leisure facilities, heated swimming pools (with multi-slide), and plenty of well-planned amusements. Pitches are mainly on level or gently-sloping grass plus there are some fully serviced hardstandings. The beach is just two miles away. 85 acre site. 280 touring pitches. 42 hardstandings. 20 seasonal pitches. Caravan pitches. Motorhome pitches. Tent pitches. 850 statics.

Open: mid Mar-end Oct (rs mid Mar-May & Sep-Oct some facilities may be reduced & outdoor pool closed) **Last arrival:** mdnt **Last departure:** 10.00hrs
Pitches: 🚐 🚌 Å
Leisure: 🏊 🏊 ⚙ 👶 ☺ ♫
Facilities: 🚿 ☉ ♿ ⏰ ⑤ WiFi ♻ ❸
Services: 🚐 ⑤ 🍴 🛢 🧴 Ⓣ 🍴 ♨ ⬆
Within 3 miles: ⌱ ✒ ◎ ⑤ ⑤

Notes: No commercial vehicles, no bookings by persons under 21yrs unless a family booking, max 2 dogs per booking, certain dog breeds banned. Dogs must be kept on leads.

See advert on opposite page

Primrose Valley Holiday Park
HOLIDAY CENTRE 81%

tel: 0871 231 0892 **YO14 9RF**
email: primrosevalley@haven.com web: www.haven.com/primrosevalley
dir: *Signed from A165 (Scarboroug to Bridlington road), 3m S of Filey.* grid ref: *TA123778*

A large all-action holiday centre with a wide range of sports and leisure activities to suit everyone from morning until late in the evening. The touring area is completely separate from the main park with its own high quality amenity block. All touring pitches are fully serviced hardstandings with grassed awning strips. The touring area has its own reception and designated warden. 160 acre site. 50 touring pitches. 50 hardstandings. Caravan pitches. Motorhome pitches. 1514 statics.

Open: mid Mar-end Oct **Last arrival:** anytime **Last departure:** 10.00hrs
Pitches: 🚐 🚌
Leisure: 🏊 🏊 ⚙ 👶 ☺ ⚔ ♫
Facilities: 🚿 ✒ ♿ ⏰ ⑤ 🏠 WiFi 🖥 ♻ ❸
Services: 🚐 ⑤ 🍴 🛢 🧴 🍴 ⬆
Within 3 miles: ⌱ ✢ ✒ ◎ ⑤ ⑤

Notes: No commercial vehicles, no bookings by persons under 21yrs unless a family booking, max 2 dogs per booking, certain dog breeds banned. Dogs must be kept on leads.

See advert on opposite page

PITCHES: 🚐 Caravans 🚙 Motorhomes ⛺ Tents 🏕 Glamping-style accommodation   **SERVICES:** 🔌 Electric hook up 🧺 Launderette 🍸 Licensed bar 🛍 Calor Gas ⛽ Camping Gaz 🚽 Toilet fluid 🍽 Café/Restaurant 🍔 Fast Food/Takeaway 🔋 Battery charging 🛒 Baby care 🚐 Motorvan service point   **ABBREVIATIONS:** BH/bank hols – bank holidays Etr – Easter Spring BH – Spring Bank Holiday fr – from hrs – hours m – mile mdnt – midnight rdbt – roundabout rs – restricted service wk – week wknd – weekend x-rds – cross roads 🚫 No credit or debit cards 🚫 No dogs 👪 Children of all ages accepted

FILEY *continued*

Reighton Sands Holiday Park
HOLIDAY CENTRE 79%

tel: 0871 231 0894 **Reighton Gap YO14 9SH**
email: reightonsands@haven.com **web:** www.haven.com/reightonsands
dir: *On A165, 5m S of Filey at Reighton Gap, signed.* **grid ref:** TA142769

A large, lively holiday centre with a wide range of entertainment and all-weather leisure facilities (including an indoor play area), located just a 10-minute walk from a long sandy beach. There are good all-weather pitches and a large tenting field. The site is particularly geared towards families with young children. 229 acre site. 218 touring pitches. 68 hardstandings. 5 seasonal pitches. Caravan pitches. Motorhome pitches. Tent pitches. 800 statics.

Open: mid Mar-end Oct (rs mid Mar-May & Sep-Oct some facilities may be reduced) **Last arrival:** 22.00hrs **Last departure:** 10.00hrs

Pitches: 🚐 🚙 ▲

Leisure: 🏊 ⛱ 🛝 🎱 🎣 🎵 ⛳

Facilities: 🚿 ⊙ 🧴 ♿ 🕐 🏪 🍴 📶 🖥 ♻ ❼

Services: 🔌 🛒 🚿 T 🍴 🛒 ♿

Within 3 miles: ↕ 🚣 ✏ ◎ 🛒 🛒 ∪

Notes: No commercial vehicles, no bookings by persons under 21yrs unless a family booking, max 2 dogs per booking, certain dog breeds banned. Dogs must be kept on leads.

See advert on page 351

Lebberston Touring Park
►►►► 87%

tel: 01723 585723 **Filey Rd YO11 3PE**
email: info@lebberstontouring.co.uk **web:** www.lebberstontouring.co.uk
dir: *From A165 (Filey to Scarborough road) follow brown site signs.* **grid ref:** TA077824

A peaceful family park in a gently-sloping rural area, where the quality facilities are maintained to a high standard of cleanliness. The keen owners are friendly and helpful, and create a relaxing atmosphere. A natural area offers views of the surrounding countryside through the shrubbery. Please note that this park does not accept tents. 7.5 acre site. 125 touring pitches. 25 hardstandings. 80 seasonal pitches. Caravan pitches. Motorhome pitches.

Open: Mar-Oct **Last arrival:** 20.00hrs **Last departure:** 11.00hrs

Pitches: * 🚐 £15.50-£27 🚙 £15.50-£27

Leisure: ⚽

Facilities: 🚿 🛁 ⊙ 🧴 ☀ ♿ 🏪 🛒 📶 ♻ ❼

Services: 🔌 🛒 🚿 ∅ T **Within 3 miles:** ↕ 🚣 ✏ ◎ 🛒 🛒 ∪

Notes: No noise after 22.00hrs. Dogs must be kept on leads.

Crows Nest Caravan Park
►►►► 83%

tel: 01723 582206 **Gristhorpe YO14 9PS**
email: enquires@crowsnestcaravanpark.com **web:** www.crowsnestcaravanpark.com
dir: *5m S of Scarborough & 2m N of Filey. On seaward side of A165, signed from rdbt, near petrol station.* **grid ref:** TA094826

A beautifully situated park on the coast between Scarborough and Filey, with excellent panoramic views. This large and mainly static park offers lively

LEISURE: 🏊 Indoor swimming pool 🏊 Outdoor swimming pool 🛝 Children's playground 🧒 Kid's club 🎾 Tennis court 🎱 Games room 📺 Separate TV room 🏌 golf course ⛵ Boats for hire 🎬 Cinema 🎵 Entertainment 🎣 Fishing ◎ Mini golf 🏄 Watersports 🏋 Gym ⚽ Sports field Spa ∪ Stables
FACILITIES: 🛁 Bath 🚿 Shower ⊙ Electric shaver 🧴 Hairdryer ☀ Ice Pack Facility ♿ Disabled facilities ☎ Public telephone 🏪 Shop on site or within 200yds 🛒 Mobile shop (calls at least 5 days a week) 🍴 BBQ area 🍽 Picnic area 📶 Wi-fi 🖥 Internet access ♻ Recycling ❼ Tourist info 🐕 Dog exercise area

entertainment, and two bars. A small touring area is close to the attractions, and the main touring and camping section is at the top of the park overlooking the sea; this area is equipped with some excellent fully serviced pitches and a superb amenities block. 20 acre site. 49 touring pitches. 49 hardstandings. Caravan pitches. Motorhome pitches. Tent pitches. 220 statics.

Open: Mar-Oct **Last departure:** noon

Pitches: 🚐 � 🏕

Leisure: 🏊 ⛰ ⊕ 🏑 🎵

Facilities: 🔦 ⊙ 🗝 ❄ ⛷ © 🛢 ✚ WiFi 🖥 ♻ ❶

Services: 🔌 🔄 🍴 🛢 ⊘ T 🛒 ➡ 🔧

Within 3 miles: ⅃ 🖊 ◎ 🎿 🛢 🛢 ∪

Notes: Dogs must be kept on leads.

See advert below

Orchard Farm Holiday Village
▶▶▶▶81%

tel: 01723 891582 **Stonegate, Hunmanby YO14 0PU**
email: info@orchardfarmholidayvillage.co.uk **web:** www.orchardfarmholidayvillage.co.uk
dir: *A165 from Scarborough towards Bridlington. Turn right signed Hunmanby, site on right just after rail bridge.* **grid ref:** *TA105779*

Pitches are arranged around a large coarse fishing lake at this grassy park. The enthusiastic owners are friendly, and offer a wide range of amenities including an indoor heated swimming pool and a licensed bar. 14 acre site. 91 touring pitches. 34 hardstandings. Caravan pitches. Motorhome pitches. Tent pitches. 46 statics.

Open: Mar-Oct (rs Off peak some facilities restricted) **Last arrival:** 23.00hrs
Last departure: 11.00hrs

Pitches: * 🚐 £14-£22 🚌 £14-£22 🏕 £14-£22

Leisure: 🏊 ⛰ 🏑 ▭

Facilities: 🔦 ⊙ 🗝 ❄ ⛷ © 🛢 🛒 🔧

Services: 🔌 🔄 🍴 T 🛒

Within 3 miles: ⅃ 🖊 ◎ 🎿 🛢 🛢

Notes: Dogs must be kept on leads. Miniature railway.

PITCHES: 🚐 Caravans 🚌 Motorhomes 🏕 Tents ⛺ Glamping-style accommodation **SERVICES:** 🔌 Electric hook up 🔄 Launderette 🍴 Licensed bar 🛢 Calor Gas ⊘ Camping Gaz T Toilet fluid 🍴 Café/Restaurant 🍔 Fast Food/Takeaway 🔋 Battery charging ➡ Baby care 🔧 Motorvan service point
ABBREVIATIONS: BH/bank hols – bank holidays Etr – Easter Spring BH – Spring Bank Holiday fr – from hrs – hours m – mile mdnt – midnight
rdbt – roundabout rs – restricted service wk – week wknd – weekend x-rds – cross roads 🚫 No credit or debit cards 🚫 No dogs 👫 Children of all ages accepted

FILEY *continued*

Centenary Way Camping & Caravan Park
►►►82%

tel: 01723 516415 & 512313 **Muston Grange YO14 0HU**
dir: *From A165 onto A1039 signed Filey. 1st right to site.* **grid ref:** *TA115798*

A well set-out family-owned park, with footpath access to nearby beach. Close to the seaside resort of Filey, and caravan pitches enjoy views over open countryside. 3 acre site. 75 touring pitches. 25 hardstandings. Caravan pitches. Motorhome pitches. Tent pitches.

Open: Mar-Oct **Last arrival:** 21.00hrs **Last departure:** noon

Pitches: * ⛺ £13-£24 ⛺ £13-£24 ▲ £6-£24

Leisure: ⚏

Facilities: ⬡☉✳⬡⬡⬡⬡⬡

Services: ⬡⬡⬡⬡

Within 3 miles: ⬡⬡⬡⬡⬡⬡

Notes: ⬡ No group bookings in peak period, no 9-12 berth tents, no gazebos. Dogs must be kept on leads.

Filey Brigg Touring Caravan & Country Park
►►►77%

tel: 01723 513852 **North Cliff YO14 9ET**
email: fileybrigg@scarborough.gov.uk
dir: *A165 from Scarborough to Filey. Left onto A1039, at rdbt into Church Cliff Dr, to site.* **grid ref:** *TA115812*

A municipal park overlooking Filey Brigg with splendid views along the coast, and set in a country park. The beach is just a short walk away, as is the resort of Filey. There is a good quality amenity block, and 50 all-weather pitches are available. An excellent children's adventure playground is adjacent to the touring areas. 9 acre site. 158 touring pitches. 82 hardstandings. Caravan pitches. Motorhome pitches. Tent pitches.

Open: end Feb-2 Jan **Last arrival:** 18.00hrs **Last departure:** noon

Pitches: ⛺ ⛺ ▲

Leisure: ⚏ ⬡

Facilities: ⬡☉✳⬡⬡⬡⬡⬡⬡

Services: ⬡⬡ T ⬡⬡

Within 3 miles: ⬡⬡⬡⬡⬡⬡U

Notes: Dogs must be kept on leads.

HARROGATE   **Map 19 SE35**

PREMIER PARK

Rudding Holiday Park
►►►►►83%

tel: 01423 870439 **Follifoot HG3 1JH**
email: holiday-park@ruddingpark.com **web:** www.ruddingholidaypark.co.uk
dir: *From A1 take A59 to A658 signed Bradford. 4.5m, right & follow signs.* **grid ref:** *SE333531*

A spacious park set in beautiful 200 acres of mature parkland and walled gardens of Rudding Park. The setting has been tastefully enhanced with terraced pitches and dry-stone walls. A separate area houses super pitches where all services are supplied including a picnic table and TV connection, and there are excellent toilets. An 18-hole golf course, a 6-hole short course, driving range, golf academy, heated outdoor swimming pool, the Deer House Family Pub, and a children's play area complete the amenities. 50 acre site. 141 touring pitches. 20 hardstandings. 50 seasonal pitches. Caravan pitches. Motorhome pitches. Tent pitches. 57 statics.

Open: Mar-Jan (rs Nov-Jan shop & Deer House Pub - limited opening, summer open times only for outdoor swimming pool) **Last arrival:** 23.00hrs
Last departure: 11.00hrs

Pitches: * ⛺ £17-£42 ⛺ £17-£42 ▲ £17-£35.50

Leisure: ⬡ ⚏ ⬡ ⬡ ⬡ Spa

Facilities: ⬡⬡☉⬡✳⬡⬡⬡⬡ WiFi ⬡ ⬡

Services: ⬡⬡⬡⬡⬡⬡ T ⬡⬡⬡⬡⬡

Within 3 miles: ⬡⬡⬡⬡⬡U

Notes: Under 18s must be accompanied by an adult.

AA Pubs & Restaurants nearby: Rudding Park Hotel, Spa & Golf, HARROGATE, HG3 1JH, 01423 871350

Ripley Caravan Park
►►►►►79%

GOLD

tel: 01423 770050 **Knaresborough Rd, Ripley HG3 3AU**
email: ripleycaravanpark@talk21.com
dir: *3m N of Harrogate on A61. Right at rdbt onto B6165 signed Knaresborough. Site 300yds left.* **grid ref:** SE289610

A well-run rural site in attractive meadowland which has been landscaped with mature tree plantings. The resident owners lovingly maintain the facilities, and there is a heated swimming pool and sauna, a TV and games room, and a covered nursery playroom for small children. There is a bus every 15 minutes which gives easy access to Ripon and Leeds, and a cycleway/walkway leads from the site directly to Harrogate, a distance of four miles. 24 acre site. 110 touring pitches. 60 hardstandings. 35 seasonal pitches. Caravan pitches. Motorhome pitches. Tent pitches. 75 statics.

Open: Etr-Oct **Last arrival:** 21.00hrs **Last departure:** noon
Pitches: * 🚐 £17-£22 🚍 £17-£22 ▲ £17-£23.50
Leisure: 🏊 ⋀ 🎯 ⚽
Facilities: 🏗️⊙🍴❄🔥🔌🛒🎣 ⟳ ❶
Services: 🔌🔵 🍺⊘🚽🛒⛟
Within 3 miles: ↓🚲🗓️🐾 ◎🔵🔵∪
Notes: Family camping only, no open fires, off-ground BBQs only, no skateboards or rollerblades. Dogs must be kept on leads. Football, volleyball.

AA Pubs & Restaurants nearby: van Zeller, HARROGATE, HG1 2TQ, 01423 508762
The General Tarleton Inn, KNARESBOROUGH, HG5 0PZ, 01423 340284

High Moor Farm Park
►►►►83%

tel: 01423 563637 & 564955 **Skipton Rd HG3 2LT**
email: highmoorfarmpark@btconnect.com **web:** www.highmoorfarmpark.co.uk
dir: *4m W of Harrogate on A59 towards Skipton.* **grid ref:** SE242560

An excellent site with very good facilities, set beside a small wood and surrounded by thorn hedges. The numerous touring pitches are located in meadowland fields, each area with its own toilet block. A large heated indoor swimming pool, games room, 9-hole golf course, full-sized crown bowling green, and a bar serving meals and snacks are all popular. Please note that this park does not accept tents. 15 acre site. 320 touring pitches. 51 hardstandings. 57 seasonal pitches. Caravan pitches. Motorhome pitches. 158 statics.

Open: Etr or Apr-Oct **Last arrival:** 23.30hrs **Last departure:** 15.00hrs
Pitches: 🚐 fr £24 🚍 fr £24
Leisure: 🏊 ⋀ 🎯 ⚽ **Facilities:** 🚿🏗️⊙🍴❄🔌🔥🛒🎣🔥 ⟳ ❶
Services: 🔌🔵 🍺🍴⊘🚽🍴🛒⛟ **Within 3 miles:** ↓🗓️🐾 🔵🔵∪
Notes: Dogs must be kept on leads. Coarse fishing.

AA Pubs & Restaurants nearby: van Zeller, HARROGATE, HG1 2TQ, 01423 508762
The General Tarleton Inn, KNARESBOROUGH, HG5 0PZ, 01423 340284

NEW Harrogate Caravan Park
►►►83%

tel: 01423 546145 **Great Yorkshire Showground HG2 8NZ**
email: info@harrogatecaravanpark.co.uk
dir: *A1(M) junct 47, A59 to Harrogate. A658, then A661. At Sainsbury's supermarket lights turn left into Railway Rd.* **grid ref:** SE329542

Located on the perimeter of the Yorkshire Showground and owned by the Yorkshire Agricultural Society, this very peaceful park offers easy main road access and is popular at weekends and during the days of the shows. Investment on the park is good and ongoing, with a new, high standard amenity block, extensive tree planting and the addition of smart, gravelled hardstanding pitches. This is a good base for visiting Harrogate and the Yorkshire Dales. 3.56 acre site. 66 touring pitches. 43 hardstandings. Caravan pitches. Motorhome pitches. Tent pitches.

Open: Mar-Nov **Last arrival:** 21.00hrs **Last departure:** 11.00hrs
Pitches: 🚐 £18-£23 🚍 £18-£23 ▲ £18-£23
Leisure: ⚽ **Facilities:** 🏗️⊙🔌🔥🔥 🖥️ ⟳ ❶
Services: 🔌🔵 🛒⛟ **Within 3 miles:** ↓🚲🗓️🐾 ◎🔵🔵∪
Notes: Dogs must be kept on leads. Shop & café adjacent to site.

AA Pubs & Restaurants nearby: Hotel du Vin Harrogate, HARROGATE, HG1 1LB, 0844 7364257
Studley Hotel, HARROGATE, HG1 2SE, 01423 560425
The Fat Badger, HARROGATE, HG2 0NF, 01823 505681

Shaws Trailer Park
►►69%

tel: 01423 884432 **Knaresborough Rd HG2 7NE**
dir: *On A59 1m from town centre. 0.5m SW of Starbeck railway crossing.* **grid ref:** SE325557

A long-established site just a mile from the centre of Harrogate. The all-weather pitches are arranged around a carefully kept grass area, and the toilets are basic but functional and clean. The entrance is on the bus route to Harrogate. 11 acre site. 60 touring pitches. 24 hardstandings. Caravan pitches. Motorhome pitches. Tent pitches. 146 statics.

Open: all year **Last arrival:** 20.00hrs **Last departure:** 14.00hrs
Pitches: * 🚐 £18-£20 🚍 £18-£20 ▲ £10-£16
Facilities: 🚿🏗️⊙🔌 ❶
Services: 🔌🔵 🍺
Within 3 miles: ↓🚲🗓️🐾 🔵🔵
Notes: Adults only. Ⓧ Dogs must be kept on leads.

AA Pubs & Restaurants nearby: van Zeller, HARROGATE, HG1 2TQ, 01423 508762
The General Tarleton Inn, KNARESBOROUGH, HG5 0PZ, 01423 340284

HAWES
Map 18 SD88

Places to visit

Dales Countryside Museum & National Park Centre, HAWES, DL8 3NT,
01969 666210 www.dalescountrysidemuseum.org.uk

Bainbridge Ings Caravan & Camping Site
►►► 80%

tel: 01969 667354 **DL8 3NU**
email: janet@bainbridge-ings.co.uk
dir: *From Bainbridge towards Hawes on A684, left at Gayle sign, site 300yds on left.*
grid ref: SD879895

A quiet, well-organised site in open countryside close to Hawes in the heart of
Upper Wensleydale, popular with ramblers. Pitches are sited around the perimeter
of several fields, each bounded by traditional stone walls. 5 acre site. 70 touring
pitches. 8 hardstandings. Caravan pitches. Motorhome pitches. Tent pitches. 15
statics.

Open: Apr-Sep **Last arrival:** 20.00hrs **Last departure:** noon

Pitches: * ⊞ £18.50 ⊟ £18.50 ▲ £15.50

Facilities: ⌐⊙☞✳ WIFI ♻ ❶

Services: ⊡⊠ ❚⊘≒↻

Within 3 miles: ⌑⑂⊠

Notes: ⊘ No noise after 23.00hrs. Dogs must be kept on leads.

AA Pubs & Restaurants nearby: The Moorcock Inn, HAWES, LA10 5PU, 01969 667488

HELMSLEY

Places to visit

Duncombe Park, HELMSLEY, YO62 5EB, 01439 778625 www.duncombepark.com

Helmsley Castle, HELMSLEY, YO62 5AB, 01439 770442
www.english-heritage.org.uk/daysout/properties/helmsley-castle

Great for kids: Flamingo Land Theme Park & Zoo, KIRBY MISPERTON, YO17 6UX,
01653 668287 www.flamingoland.co.uk

HELMSLEY
Map 19 SE68

REGIONAL WINNER – NORTH EAST ENGLAND AA CAMPSITE OF THE YEAR 2015

PREMIER PARK

Golden Square Caravan & Camping Park
►►►►► 83%

GOLD

tel: 01439 788269 **Oswaldkirk YO62 5YQ**
email: reception@goldensquarecaravanpark.com
web: www.goldensquarecaravanpark.com
dir: *From York take B1363 to Oswaldkirk. Left onto B1257, 2nd left onto unclassified
road signed Ampleforth, site 0.5m on right. Or A19 from Thirsk towards York. Left,
follow 'Caravan Route avoiding Sutton Bank' signs, through Ampleforth to site in 1m.*
grid ref: SE604797

An excellent, popular and spacious site with very good facilities. This friendly,
immaculately maintained park is set in a quiet rural situation with lovely views
over the North York Moors. Terraced on three levels and surrounded by mature
trees, it caters particularly for families, with excellent play areas and space for
ball games. Country walks and mountain bike trails start here and an attractive
holiday home area is also available. 12 acre site. 129 touring pitches. 10
hardstandings. 50 seasonal pitches. Caravan pitches. Motorhome pitches. Tent
pitches. 10 statics.

Open: Mar-Oct **Last arrival:** 21.00hrs **Last departure:** noon

Pitches: * ⊞ £17-£22 ⊟ £17-£22 ▲ £15-£20

Leisure: ⚑☺🔍

Facilities: ⊯⌐⊙☞✳⚒🕓⑂⊟禾🕂WIFI🖥♻❶

Services: ⊡⊠ ❚⊘Ⓣ≒↻

Within 3 miles: ⚴⑂⌑◎⊠⊠U

Notes: No skateboards or fires. Dogs must be kept on leads. Microwave available.

AA Pubs & Restaurants nearby: The Star Inn, HAROME, YO62 5JE, 01439 770397
Feversham Arms Hotel & Verbena Spa, HELMSLEY, YO62 5AG, 01439 770766

LEISURE: 🏊 Indoor swimming pool 🏊 Outdoor swimming pool ⚑ Children's playground 🏐 Kid's club 🎾 Tennis court 🔍 Games room ⬜ Separate TV room
⛳ golf course 🚣 Boats for hire ☰ Cinema 🎵 Entertainment 🎣 Fishing ◎ Mini golf 🏄 Watersports 🏋 Gym ☺ Sports field Spa U Stables
FACILITIES: 🛁 Bath ⌐ Shower ⊙ Electric shaver ☞ Hairdryer ✳ Ice Pack Facility ⚒ Disabled facilities 🕓 Public telephone ⑂ Shop on site or within 200yds
⊠ Mobile shop (calls at least 5 days a week) 禾 BBQ area 禾 Picnic area WIFI Wi-fi 🖥 Internet access ♻ Recycling ❶ Tourist info 🕂 Dog exercise area

Foxholme Caravan Park

▶▶▶ 75%

tel: 01439 771904 & 772336 **Harome YO62 5JG**
dir: *A170 from Helmsley towards Scarborough, right signed Harome, left at church, through village, follow signs.* **grid ref:** *SE658828*

A quiet park set in secluded wooded countryside, with well-shaded pitches in individual clearings divided by mature trees. The facilities are well maintained, and the site is ideal as a touring base or a place to relax. Please note that caravans are prohibited on the A170 at Sutton Bank between Thirsk and Helmsley. 6 acre site. 60 touring pitches. 30 seasonal pitches. Caravan pitches. Motorhome pitches. Tent pitches.

Open: Etr-Oct **Last arrival:** 23.00hrs **Last departure:** noon

Pitches: 🚐 £20-£22 🚛 £20-£22 🛆 £20-£22

Facilities: 🚾📍⊙🅿❅🛁🐕🏕❶ **Services:** 🔌🗑🛢🗑Ⓣ🔋↯

Within 3 miles: 🎣🛝🛒U **Notes:** Adults only. 🚫

AA Pubs & Restaurants nearby: The Star Inn, HAROME, YO62 5JE, 01439 770397
Feversham Arms Hotel & Verbena Spa, HELMSLEY, YO62 5AG, 01439 770766

Places to visit

Lancaster Maritime Museum, LANCASTER, LA1 1RB, 01524 382264
www.lancashire.gov.uk/museums

Great for kids: Yorkshire Dales Falconry & Wildlife Conservation Centre, SETTLE, LA2 8AS, 01729 822832 www.falconryandwildlife.co.uk

PREMIER PARK

Riverside Caravan Park

▶▶▶▶▶ 90%

GOLD

tel: 015242 61272 **LA2 7FJ**
email: info@riversidecaravanpark.co.uk
dir: *M6 junct 34, A683 then Exit B6480, signed from High Bentham town centre.* **grid ref:** *SD665688*

A well-managed riverside park developed to a high standard, with level grass pitches set in avenues separated by trees, and there are excellent facilities for children, who are made to feel as important as the adults. It has an excellent, modern amenity block, including a family bathroom, a well-stocked shop, laundry and information room. The superb games room and adventure playground are hugely popular, and the market town of High Bentham is close by. Please note that this site does not accept tents. Bentham Golf Club (within one mile) is also under same ownership with facilities available for Riverside customers. 12 acre site. 61 touring pitches. 27 hardstandings. 50 seasonal pitches. Caravan pitches. Motorhome pitches. 206 statics.

Open: Mar-2 Jan **Last arrival:** 20.00hrs **Last departure:** noon

Pitches: * 🚐 £20.95-£26.75 🚛 £20.95-£26.75

Leisure: ⚠🎣 **Facilities:** 📍⊙🅿❅🛁🗑🏕📶🖥♻❶

Services: 🔌🗑🛢🗑Ⓣ🔋↯ **Within 3 miles:** 🎣🛝🛒U

Notes: Dogs must be kept on leads. Permits for private fishing (chargeable), discounted green fees at Bentham Golf Club.

AA Pubs & Restaurants nearby: The Traddock, AUSTWICK, LA2 8BY, 01524 251224

Lowther Hill Caravan Park

▶ 81%

tel: 015242 61657 & 07985 478750 **LA2 7AN**
dir: *A65 at Clapham onto B6480 signed Bentham. 3m to site on right. Or from M6 junct 34, A643 to Kirkby Lonsdale. In 6m turn right onto B6480 to Bentham. 9m, site on left between High Bentham & Clapham.* **grid ref:** *SD696695*

A simple site with stunning panoramic views from every pitch. Peace reigns on this little park, though the tourist villages of Ingleton, Clapham and Settle are not far away. All pitches have electricity, and there is a heated toilet/washroom and dishwashing facilities. 1 acre site. 9 touring pitches. 4 hardstandings. 4 seasonal pitches. Caravan pitches. Motorhome pitches. Tent pitches.

Open: Mar-Nov **Last arrival:** 21.00hrs **Last departure:** 14.00hrs

Pitches: * 🚐 £16.50 🚛 £16.50 🛆 fr £10

Facilities: 📍🛁🏕♻ **Services:** 🔌 **Within 3 miles:** 🎣🛝🛒

Notes: 🚫 Payment on arrival. Dogs must be kept on leads.

AA Pubs & Restaurants nearby: The Traddock, AUSTWICK, LA2 8BY, 01524 251224

Places to visit

Nunnington Hall, NUNNINGTON, YO62 5UY, 01439 748283
www.nationaltrust.org.uk

Rievaulx Abbey, RIEVAULX, 01439 798228
www.english-heritage.org.uk/daysout/properties/rievaulx-abbey

Great for kids: Pickering Castle, PICKERING, YO18 7AX, 01751 474989
www.english-heritage.org.uk/daysout/properties/pickering-castle

Hutton-le-Hole Caravan Park

▶▶▶▶ 81%

tel: 01751 417261 **Westfield Lodge YO62 6UG**
email: rwstrickland@farmersweekly.net
dir: *From A170 at Keldholme follow Hutton-le-Hole signs. Approx 2m, over cattle grid, left in 500yds into Park Drive, site signed.* **grid ref:** *SE705895*

A small, high quality park on a working farm in the North York Moors National Park. The purpose-built toilet block offers en suite family rooms, and there is a choice of hardstanding or grass pitches within a well-tended area surrounded by hedges and shrubs. The village facilities are a 10-minute walk away. Please note that caravans are prohibited from the A170 at Sutton Bank between Thirsk and Helmsley. 5 acre site. 42 touring pitches. 36 hardstandings. Caravan pitches. Motorhome pitches. Tent pitches.

Open: Etr-Oct **Last arrival:** 21.00hrs **Last departure:** noon

Pitches: 🚐 £17-£20 🚛 £17-£20 🛆 £14.50-£17.50

Facilities: 📍⊙🅿❅🛁🗑🏕📶♻❶ **Services:** 🔌🛢Ⓣ🔋

Within 3 miles: 🎣◎🛒U **Notes:** Boot, bike & dog washing area, farm walks.

AA Pubs & Restaurants nearby: Blacksmiths Arms, LASTINGHAM, YO62 6TN, 01751 417247
The Moors Inn, APPLETON-LE-MOORS, YO62 6TF, 01751 417435

PITCHES: 🚐 Caravans 🚛 Motorhomes 🛆 Tents 🏕 Glamping-style accommodation **SERVICES:** 🔌 Electric hook up 🗑 Launderette 🍺 Licensed bar
🛢 Calor Gas 🔧 Camping Gaz Ⓣ Toilet fluid 🍴 Café/Restaurant 🍔 Fast Food/Takeaway 🔋 Battery charging 🍼 Baby care ↯ Motorvan service point
ABBREVIATIONS: BH/bank hols – bank holidays Etr – Easter Spring BH – Spring Bank Holiday fr – from hrs – hours m – mile mdnt – midnight
rdbt – roundabout rs – restricted service wk – week wknd – weekend x-rds – cross roads 🚫 No credit or debit cards 🚫 No dogs 👫 Children of all ages accepted

KNARESBOROUGH — Map 19 SE35

Places to visit

RHS Garden Harlow Carr, HARROGATE, HG3 1QB, 0845 265 8070
www.rhs.org.uk/harlowcarr

Aldborough Roman Site, ALDBOROUGH, YO51 9ES, 01423 322768
www.english-heritage.org.uk/daysout/properties/aldborough-roman-site

Kingfisher Caravan Park
►►►78%

tel: 01423 869411 **Low Moor Ln, Farnham HG5 9JB**
email: enquiries@kingfisher-caravanpark.co.uk
dir: *From Knaresborough take A6055. Left in 1m towards Farnham, left in village signed Scotton. Site 1m on left.* **grid ref:** *SE343603*

A large grassy site with open spaces set in a wooded area in rural countryside. Whilst Harrogate, Fountains Abbey and York are within easy reach, anglers will want to take advantage of on-site coarse and fly fishing lakes. The park has a separate flat tenting field with electric hook-ups available. 14 acre site. 35 touring pitches. Caravan pitches. Motorhome pitches. Tent pitches. 80 statics.

Open: Mar-Oct **Last arrival:** 21.00hrs **Last departure:** 16.00hrs

Pitches: * ⏣ fr £16 ⏣ fr £16 ▲ fr £18

Leisure: ⏢

Facilities: 🌡️☉ℙ☼🚹🕒🛍️🍴🚻🐕➍

Services: 🔌🔄🛢️🧺

Within 3 miles: ⬇️🐎🎣🏪🛍️🍴♻️

Notes: ❌ No football. Pets must be kept under strict adult control.

AA Pubs & Restaurants nearby: The General Tarleton Inn, KNARESBOROUGH, HG5 0PZ, 01423 340284

MARKINGTON — Map 19 SE26

Places to visit

Fountains Abbey & Studley Royal, RIPON, HG4 3DY, 01765 608888
www.nationaltrust.org.uk/fountains-abbey

Newby Hall & Gardens, RIPON, HG4 5AE, 01423 322583 www.newbyhall.com

Great for kids: Brimham Rocks, BRIMHAM, HG3 4DW, 01423 780688
www.nationaltrust.org.uk

Yorkshire Hussar Inn Holiday Caravan Park
►►►82%

tel: 01765 677327 & 677715 **High St HG3 3NR**
email: yorkshirehussar@yahoo.co.uk
dir: *From A61 between Harrogate & Ripon at Wormald Green follow Markington signs, 1m, left past Post Office into High Street. Site signed on left behind The Yorkshire Hussar Inn.* **grid ref:** *SE288650*

A pleasant, terraced site behind the village inn with well-kept grass that offers spacious pitches (hardstanding and electric hook-up pitches are available) and a few holiday statics for hire. Although the Yorkshire Hussar Inn does not provide food, there is a pub that does and is within walking distance. 5 acre site. 20 touring pitches. 6 hardstandings. 12 seasonal pitches. Caravan pitches. Motorhome pitches. Tent pitches. 73 statics.

Open: Etr-Oct **Last arrival:** 19.00hrs **Last departure:** noon

Pitches: ⏣ ⏣ ▲

Leisure: ⏢

Facilities: 🌡️☉☼🕒🚹🐕📶🖥️♻️➍

Services: 🔌🔄🛢️🛍️🚰

Within 3 miles: 🎣🏪🛍️♻️U

Notes: ❌ Dogs must be kept on leads. Paddling pool.

MASHAM — Map 19 SE28

Places to visit

Theakston Brewery & Visitor Centre, MASHAM, HG4 4YD, 01765 680000
www.theakstons.co.uk

Norton Conyers, RIPON, HG4 5EQ, 01765 640333
www.weddingsatnortonconyers.co.uk

Great for kids: Lightwater Valley Theme Park, NORTH STANLEY, HG4 3HT, 0871 720 0011 www.lightwatervalley.co.uk

Old Station Holiday Park
►►►►75%

tel: 01765 689569 **Old Station Yard, Low Burton HG4 4DF**
email: oldstation@tiscali.co.uk
dir: *From S: A1(M) junct 50, B6267, left in 8m; From N: A1(M) junct 51, A684 to Bedale, then B6268, 4m to site.* **grid ref:** *SE232812*

An interesting site on a former station. The enthusiastic and caring family owners have maintained the railway theme in creating a park with high quality facilities. The small town of Masham with its Theakston and Black Sheep breweries are within easy walking distance of the park. The reception/café in a carefully restored wagon shed provides a range of meals using local produce. 3.75 acre site. 50 touring pitches. 16 seasonal pitches. Caravan pitches. Motorhome pitches. Tent pitches.

Open: Mar-Nov (rs Mar-Nov café closed wkdays) **Last arrival:** 20.00hrs
Last departure: noon

Pitches: ⏣ ⏣ ▲

Facilities: 🌡️☉ℙ☼🕒🛍️🍴🚻📶🖥️♻️➍

Services: 🔌🔄🛢️🅣🍴🚰♿🚮

Within 3 miles: ⬇️🎣🏪🛍️U

Notes: No fast cycling around site, no campfires. Dogs must be kept on leads.

AA Pubs & Restaurants nearby: The Black Sheep Brewery, MASHAM, HG4 4EN, 01765 680101

Vennell's, MASHAM, HG4 4DX, 01765 689000

LEISURE: 🏊 Indoor swimming pool 🏊 Outdoor swimming pool ⏢ Children's playground 🧒 Kid's club 🎾 Tennis court 🎱 Games room 📺 Separate TV room ⛳ golf course ⛵ Boats for hire 🎬 Cinema 🎵 Entertainment 🎣 Fishing ⛳ Mini golf 🏄 Watersports 🏋️ Gym ⚽ Sports field Spa U Stables
FACILITIES: 🛁 Bath 🚿 Shower ☉ Electric shaver ℙ Hairdryer ☼ Ice Pack Facility 🕒 Disabled facilities 📞 Public telephone 🛍️ Shop on site or within 200yds 🏪 Mobile shop (calls at least 5 days a week) 🍴 BBQ area 🚻 Picnic area 📶 Wi-fi 🖥️ Internet access ♻️ Recycling ➍ Tourist info 🐕 Dog exercise area

NABURN
Map 16 SE54

Places to visit

Clifford's Tower, YORK, YO1 9SA, 01904 646940
www.english-heritage.org.uk/daysout/properties/cliffords-tower-york

Fairfax House, YORK, YO1 9RN, 01904 655543 www.fairfaxhouse.co.uk

Great for kids: Jorvik Viking Centre, YORK, YO1 9WT, 01904 615505
www.jorvik-viking-centre.com

Naburn Lock Caravan Park
►►►►85%

tel: 01904 728697 **YO19 4RU**
email: petercatherine@naburnlock.co.uk
dir: From A64 (McArthur Glen designer outlet) take A19 N, turn left signed Naburn on
B1222, site on right 0.5m past village. **grid ref:** SE596446

A family park where the enthusiastic owners are steadily improving its quality. The
mainly grass pitches are arranged in small groups separated by mature hedges.
The park is close to the River Ouse, and the river towpath provides excellent walking
and cycling opportunities. The river bus to nearby York leaves from a jetty beside
the park. 7 acre site. 100 touring pitches. 22 hardstandings. Caravan pitches.
Motorhome pitches. Tent pitches.

Open: Mar-6 Nov **Last arrival:** 20.00hrs **Last departure:** 12.30hrs

Pitches: 🚐 🚐 ⛺

Facilities: 🌣⊙🏳☀🔥ⓢ🚽🔥 Wifi ♻ ❶

Services: 🔌🗑🛢⊘Ⓣ🔋♻

Within 3 miles: 🚲⚲ⓢ🗑U

Notes: Adults only section, quiet 23.00hrs-07.00hrs. Debit cards accepted (no credit
cards). Dogs must be kept on leads. River fishing.

AA Pubs & Restaurants nearby: Lamb & Lion Inn, YORK, YO1 7EH, 01904 612078

Blue Bell, YORK, YO1 9TF, 01904 654904

Lysander Arms, YORK, YO30 5TZ, 01904 640845

Find out more about this area
with the *AA Guide to Yorkshire*
– see the AA.com/shop

NORTHALLERTON
Map 19 SE39

Places to visit

Mount Grace Priory, OSMOTHERLEY, DL6 3JG, 01609 883494
www.english-heritage.org.uk/daysout/properties/mount-grace-priory

Theakston Brewery & Visitor Centre, MASHAM, HG4 4YD, 01765 680000
www.theakstons.co.uk

Great for kids: Falconry UK - Birds of Prey Centre, THIRSK, YO7 4EU,
01845 587522 www.falconrycentre.co.uk

Otterington Park
►►►►81%

tel: 01609 780656 **Station Farm, South Otterington DL7 9JB**
email: info@otteringtonpark.com **web:** www.otteringtonpark.com
dir: From A168 midway between Northallerton & Thirsk onto unclassified road signed
South Otterington. Site on right just before South Otterington. **grid ref:** SE378882

A high quality park on a working farm with open vistas across the Vale of York. It
enjoys a peaceful location with a lovely nature walk and on-site fishing, which is
very popular. Young children will enjoy the play area. Toilet facilities are very good.
The attractions of Northallerton and Thirsk are a few minutes' drive away. 6 acre
site. 62 touring pitches. 62 hardstandings. Caravan pitches. Motorhome pitches. 3
wooden pods.

Open: Mar-Oct **Last arrival:** 21.00hrs **Last departure:** 13.00hrs

Pitches: * 🚐 £19-£26 🚐 £19-£26 🏠

Leisure: ⚠☺

Facilities: 🔌🌣⊙🏳☀🔥ⓢ🚽🔥 Wifi ♻ ❶

Services: 🔌🗑🛢Ⓣ🔋

Within 3 miles: 🚲🅗⚲◎ⓢ🗑

Notes: Dogs must be kept on leads.

AA Pubs & Restaurants nearby: Solberge Hall, NORTHALLERTON, DL7 9ER, 01609 779191

PITCHES: 🚐 Caravans 🚐 Motorhomes ⛺ Tents 🏠 Glamping-style accommodation **SERVICES:** 🔌 Electric hook up 🗑 Launderette 🍺 Licensed bar
🛢 Calor Gas ⊘ Camping Gaz Ⓣ Toilet fluid 🍽 Café/Restaurant 🏪 Fast Food/Takeaway 🔋 Battery charging 🍼 Baby care 🚽 Motorvan service point
ABBREVIATIONS: BH/bank hols – bank holidays Etr – Easter Spring BH – Spring Bank Holiday fr – from hrs – hours m – mile mdnt – midnight
rdbt – roundabout rs – restricted service wk – week wknd – weekend x-rds – cross roads ㊙ No credit or debit cards ⊗ No dogs 👫 Children of all ages accepted

NORTH STAINLEY
Map 19 SE27

Places to visit

Norton Conyers, RIPON, HG4 5EQ, 01765 640333
www.weddingsatnortonconyers.co.uk

Theakston Brewery & Visitor Centre, MASHAM, HG4 4YD, 01765 680000
www.theakstons.co.uk

Great for kids: Lightwater Valley Theme Park, NORTH STAINLEY, HG4 3HT,
0871 720 0011 www.lightwatervalley.co.uk

Sleningford Watermill Caravan Camping Park
►►►►80%

GOLD

tel: 01765 635201 **HG4 3HQ**
email: sleningfordwatermill@gmail.com **web:** www.sleningfordwatermill.co.uk
dir: *From S: A1(M) junct 50, A61 to Ripon. A6108 through North Stainley towards West Tanfield. Site on right. From N: A1(M) junct 51, A648 to Bedale. B6268, A6108 through West Tanfield. Site on left.* **grid ref:** *SE280783*

The old watermill and the River Ure make an attractive setting for this touring park which is laid out in two areas. Pitches are placed in meadowland and close to mature woodland, and the park has two enthusiastic managers. This is a popular place with canoeists and seasonal fly fishing is possible. 14 acre site. 140 touring pitches. 8 hardstandings. 48 seasonal pitches. Caravan pitches. Motorhome pitches. Tent pitches.

Open: Etr & Apr-Oct **Last arrival:** 21.00hrs **Last departure:** 12.30hrs

Pitches: 🚐 🚛 Å

Leisure: ✪

Facilities: 🏕⊙ℱ✻⚿⑤🅰🏕♻𝒊

Services: 🚱⑤🛢∅🖴

Within 3 miles: ↨ℐ⑤⑤

Notes: No noise after 23.00hrs. Dogs must be kept on leads. Newspapers can be ordered.

AA Pubs & Restaurants nearby: The Bruce Arms, WEST TANFIELD, HG4 5JJ, 01677 470325

The Black Sheep Brewery, MASHAM, HG4 4EN, 01765 680101

Vennell's, MASHAM, HG4 4DX, 01765 689000

OSMOTHERLEY
Map 19 SE49

Places to visit

Mount Grace Priory, OSMOTHERLEY, DL6 3JG, 01609 883494
www.english-heritage.org.uk/daysout/properties/mount-grace-priory

Gisborough Priory, GUISBOROUGH, TS14 6HG, 01287 633801
www.english-heritage.org.uk/daysout/properties/gisborough-priory

Great for kids: Falconry UK - Birds of Prey Centre, THIRSK, YO7 4EU,
01845 587522 www.falconrycentre.co.uk

PREMIER PARK

Cote Ghyll Caravan & Camping Park
►►►►►86%

tel: 01609 883425 **DL6 3AH**
email: hills@coteghyll.com
dir: *Exit A19 dual carriageway at A684 (Northallerton junct). Follow signs to Osmotherley. Left in village centre. Site entrance 0.5m on right.* **grid ref:** *SE459979*

A quiet, peaceful site in a pleasant valley on the edge of moorland, close to the village. The park is divided into terraces bordered by woodland, and the extra well-appointed amenity block is a welcome addition to this attractive park. Mature trees, shrubs and an abundance of seasonal floral displays create a relaxing and peaceful atmosphere and the whole park is immaculately maintained. There are pubs and shops nearby and holiday statics for hire. 7 acre site. 77 touring pitches. 22 hardstandings. Caravan pitches. Motorhome pitches. Tent pitches. 18 statics.

Open: Mar-Oct **Last arrival:** 21.00hrs **Last departure:** noon

Pitches: 🚐 🚛 Å

Leisure: 🅰

Facilities: 🛁🏕⊙ℱ✻⚿⑤🅰🔋🆆🖥♻𝒊

Services: 🚱⑤🛢∅🗓🍽⛟🚮⛟

Within 3 miles: ↨ℐ⑤⑤↻

Notes: Quiet after 22.00hrs, no camp fires. Dogs must be kept on leads.

AA Pubs & Restaurants nearby: The Golden Lion, OSMOTHERLEY, DL6 3AA,
01609 883526

PICKERING

Places to visit

Pickering Castle, PICKERING, YO18 7AX, 01751 474989
www.english-heritage.org.uk/daysout/properties/pickering-castle

North Yorkshire Moors Railway, PICKERING, YO18 7AJ, 01751 472508
www.nymr.co.uk

Great for kids: Flamingo Land Theme Park & Zoo, KIRBY MISPERTON, YO17 6UX,
01653 668287 www.flamingoland.co.uk

LEISURE: 🏊 Indoor swimming pool 🏊 Outdoor swimming pool 🅰 Children's playground 🏑 Kid's club 🎾 Tennis court 🎱 Games room ▭ Separate TV room ⛳ golf course ⛵ Boats for hire 🎦 Cinema 🎵 Entertainment ⌒ Fishing ◎ Mini golf 🏄 Watersports 🏋 Gym ⚽ Sports field Spa ⛄ Stables
FACILITIES: 🛁 Bath 🚿 Shower ⊙ Electric shaver ℱ Hairdryer ✻ Ice Pack Facility ⚿ Disabled facilities ⓒ Public telephone ⑤ Shop on site or within 200yds 🏪 Mobile shop (calls at least 5 days a week) 🍖 BBQ area 🏕 Picnic area 🆆 Wi-fi 🖥 Internet access ♻ Recycling 𝒊 Tourist info 🐕 Dog exercise area

PICKERING
Map 19 SE78

Wayside Holiday Park
►►►► 78%

tel: 01751 472608 & 07940 938517 **Wrelton YO18 8PG**
email: wrelton@waysideholidaypark.co.uk
dir: *2.5m W of Pickering exit A170, follow signs at Wrelton.* **grid ref:** *SE764859*

Located in the village of Wrelton, this well-maintained seasonal touring and holiday home park is divided into small paddocks by mature hedging. The amenity block has smart, modern facilities. The village pub and restaurant are within a few minutes' walk of the park. Please note that this site has seasonal pitches only – caravans, motorhomes and tents are not accepted. 10 acre site. 40 seasonal pitches. 113 statics.

Open: Apr-Oct
Facilities: 🐕⊙🅿♿🕐🚻🛈 **Services:** 🔌🅾
Within 3 miles: 🛴🎠♿🅿🎣🛍🅾⛴ **Notes:** 🐕 Dogs must be kept on leads.
AA Pubs & Restaurants nearby: Fox & Hounds Country Inn, PICKERING, YO62 6SQ, 01751 431577
The White Swan Inn, PICKERING, YO18 7AA, 01751 472288
The Fox & Rabbit Inn, PICKERING, YO18 7NQ, 01751 460213

RICHMOND
Map 19 NZ10

Places to visit

Green Howards Museum, RICHMOND, DL10 4QN, 01748 826561
www.greenhowards.org.uk

Kiplin Hall, RICHMOND, DL10 6AT, 01748 818178 www.kiplinhall.co.uk

Great for kids: Richmond Castle, RICHMOND, DL10 4QW, 01748 822493
www.english-heritage.org.uk/daysout/properties/richmond-castle

Brompton Caravan Park
►►►► 80%

tel: 01748 824629 **Brompton-on-Swale DL10 7EZ**
email: brompton.caravanpark@btconnect.com **web:** www.bromptoncaravanpark.co.uk
dir: *Exit A1 signed Catterick. B6271 to Brompton-on-Swale, site 1m on left.*
grid ref: *NZ199002*

An attractive and well-managed family park where pitches have an open outlook across the River Swale. There is a good children's playground, an excellent family recreation room, a takeaway food service, and fishing is available on the river. Three

river view camping pods and holiday apartments can also be hired. 14 acre site. 177 touring pitches. 15 hardstandings. Caravan pitches. Motorhome pitches. Tent pitches. 22 statics. 3 wooden pods.

Open: mid Mar-Oct **Last arrival:** 21.00hrs **Last departure:** noon
Pitches: 🚐 £19-£23 🚐 £19-£23 ⚠ £8-£19 🏠
Leisure: 🎱 🎣
Facilities: 🐕⊙🅿♿🕐🚻🛈🎯🛍♻🛈
Services: 🔌🅾 🛢⚙🚽♨⛟
Within 3 miles: 🛴🎠🅿🛍🅾⛴
Notes: No group bookings, no motor, electric cars or scooters, no gazebos, no open fires or wood burners, no electricity for tents, quiet from mdnt. Dogs must be kept on leads.

RIPON
Map 19 SE37

See also North Stainley

Places to visit

Fountains Abbey & Studley Royal, RIPON, HG4 3DY, 01765 608888
www.nationaltrust.org.uk/fountains-abbey

Norton Conyers, RIPON, HG4 5EQ, 01765 640333
www.weddingsatnortonconyers.co.uk

Great for kids: Falconry UK - Birds of Prey Centre, THIRSK, YO7 4EU, 01845 587522 www.falconrycentre.co.uk

PREMIER PARK

Riverside Meadows Country Caravan Park
►►►►► 76%

tel: 01765 602964 **Ure Bank Top HG4 1JD**
email: info@flowerofmay.com **web:** www.flowerofmay.co.uk
dir: *On A61 at N end of bridge from Ripon, W along river (do not cross river). Site 400yds, signed.* **grid ref:** *SE317726*

This pleasant, well-maintained site stands on high ground overlooking the River Ure, one mile from the town centre. The site has an excellent club with family room and quiet lounge. There is no access to the river from the site. 28 acre site. 80 touring pitches. 40 hardstandings. 40 seasonal pitches. Caravan pitches. Motorhome pitches. Tent pitches. 269 statics.

Open: Etr-Oct (rs Low-mid season bar open wknds only) **Last arrival:** dusk **Last departure:** noon
Pitches: * 🚐 £22-£28 🚐 £22-£28 ⚠ £22-£28
Leisure: 🎱 🎣 ▭ 🎵
Facilities: 🐕⊙🅿♿🕐🚻🛈🎯🛍 WiFi ♻🛈
Services: 🔌🅾 🍽🛢⚙🚽🔋
Within 3 miles: 🛴🎿🎠🅿🛶🛍🅾⛴
Notes: No noise after mdnt, dogs accepted by prior arrangement only. Dogs must be kept on leads.
AA Pubs & Restaurants nearby: The George at Wath, RIPON, HG4 5EN, 01765 641324
The Royal Oak, RIPON, HG4 1PB, 01765 602284
See advert on page 349

PITCHES: 🚐 Caravans 🚐 Motorhomes ⚠ Tents 🏠 Glamping-style accommodation **SERVICES:** 🔌 Electric hook up 🅾 Launderette 🍽 Licensed bar 🛢 Calor Gas ⚙ Camping Gaz 🚽 Toilet fluid 🍽 Café/Restaurant ⛟ Fast Food/Takeaway 🔋 Battery charging ♨ Baby care ⛟ Motorvan service point **ABBREVIATIONS: BH**/bank hols – bank holidays **Etr** – Easter **Spring BH** – Spring Bank Holiday **fr** – from **hrs** – hours **m** – mile **mdnt** – midnight **rdbt** – roundabout **rs** – restricted service **wk** – week **wknd** – weekend **x-rds** – cross roads 🚫 No credit or debit cards 🚫 No dogs ❗ Children of all ages accepted

ROBIN HOOD'S BAY
Map 19 NZ90

See also Whitby

Places to visit

Whitby Abbey, WHITBY, YO22 4JT, 01947 603568
www.english-heritage.org.uk/daysout/properties/whitby-abbey

Scarborough Castle, SCARBOROUGH, YO11 1HY, 01723 372451
www.english-heritage.org.uk/daysout/properties/scarborough-castle

Great for kids: Scarborough Sea Life Sanctuary, SCARBOROUGH, YO12 6RP,
01723 373414 www.sealife.co.uk

Grouse Hill Caravan Park
►►►► 90%

tel: 01947 880543 & 880560 **Flask Bungalow Farm, Fylingdales YO22 4QH**
email: info@grousehill.co.uk **web:** www.grousehill.co.uk
dir: *From A171 (Whitby-Scarborough road), take loop road for Flask Inn (brown site sign).*
grid ref: *NZ928002*

A spacious family park on a south-facing slope with attractive, mostly level,
terraced pitches overlooking The North Yorkshire National Park. The site has quality,
solar-heated toilet blocks, a treatment plant to ensure excellent drinking water,
security barriers, new play areas (including a woodland adventure play area), CCTV
and WiFi. Camping pods and four new wigwams were added for the 2014 season.
Please note that there are no hardstandings for tourers, only grass pitches, and this
sloping site is not suitable for disabled visitors (there are no disabled facilities).
This is an ideal base for walking and touring. 14 acre site. 175 touring pitches. 30
hardstandings. Caravan pitches. Motorhome pitches. Tent pitches. 1 static. 12
wooden pods.

Open: Mar-Oct (rs Etr-May shop & reception restricted) **Last arrival:** 20.30hrs
Last departure: noon

Pitches: 🚐 🚎 ▲ ⛺

Leisure: ⋀ ✪

Facilities: 🛁 📷 ⊙ 🖉 ✳ ♿ 🕓 ⑤ 🎯 📶 ♻ 🛈

Services: ⊕ ⑤ 🛢 ⌁ ⊤ ⛟ ⇩

Within 3 miles: ↧ 🍴 ⑤ 🛢 ∪

Notes: No noise after 22.30hrs. Dogs must be kept on leads.

AA Pubs & Restaurants nearby: Laurel Inn, ROBIN HOOD'S BAY, YO22 4SE, 01947 880400

The Magpie Café, WHITBY, YO21 3PU, 01947 602058

See advert below

LEISURE: 🏊 Indoor swimming pool 🏊 Outdoor swimming pool ⋀ Children's playground 👷 Kid's club 🎾 Tennis court 🎱 Games room 📺 Separate TV room
⛳ golf course ⛵ Boats for hire 🎬 Cinema 🎵 Entertainment 🎣 Fishing ◎ Mini golf 🏄 Watersports 🏋 Gym ✪ Sports field Spa ∪ Stables
FACILITIES: 🛁 Bath 📷 Shower ⊙ Electric shaver 🖉 Hairdryer ✳ Ice Pack Facility ♿ Disabled facilities 🕓 Public telephone ⑤ Shop on site or within 200yds
🛒 Mobile shop (calls at least 5 days a week) 🍴 BBQ area 🏕 Picnic area 📶 Wi-fi 🌐 Internet access ♻ Recycling 🛈 Tourist info 🐕 Dog exercise area

Middlewood Farm Holiday Park
▶▶▶▶ 86%

tel: 01947 880414 **Middlewood Ln, Fylingthorpe YO22 4UF**
email: info@middlewoodfarm.com **web:** www.middlewoodfarm.com
dir: *From A171 towards Robin Hood's Bay, into Fylingthorpe. Site signed from A171.*
grid ref: *NZ945045*

A peaceful, friendly family park enjoying panoramic views of Robin Hood's Bay in a picturesque fishing village. The park has two toilet blocks with private facilities. The village pub is a five-minute walk away, and the beach can be reached via a path leading directly from the site, which is also accessible for wheelchair users. Four 5-berth camping pods are available for hire. 7 acre site. 100 touring pitches. 21 hardstandings. Caravan pitches. Motorhome pitches. Tent pitches. 30 statics. 4 wooden pods.

Open: 7 Feb-7 Jan (rs Nov-Feb no tents) **Last arrival:** 20.00hrs **Last departure:** 11.00hrs
Pitches: 🚐 🚏 ⛺ ⋒
Leisure: ⚑
Facilities: ⇟ ⋔ ☉ ℱ ⚒ ⛾ 🆘 🎡 WiFi ♻ ❼
Services: 🔌 ⬚ 🔋 ⊘ ⛽ ♨ 🛒 ↴
Within 3 miles: ↡ ⇞ ⌾ 🛍 ⬚ ∪

Notes: No radios or noise after 23.00hrs. Dangerous dog breeds are not accepted. Dogs must be kept on leads.
AA Pubs & Restaurants nearby: Laurel Inn, ROBIN HOOD'S BAY, YO22 4SE, 01947 880400
The Magpie Café, WHITBY, YO21 3PU, 01947 602058
See advert below

PITCHES: 🚐 Caravans 🚏 Motorhomes ⛺ Tents ⋒ Glamping-style accommodation **SERVICES:** 🔌 Electric hook up ⬚ Launderette 🍺 Licensed bar 🔋 Calor Gas ⊘ Camping Gaz Ⓣ Toilet fluid 🍽 Café/Restaurant 🍟 Fast Food/Takeaway ♨ Battery charging 🍼 Baby care ↴ Motorvan service point
ABBREVIATIONS: BH/bank hols – bank holidays Etr – Easter Spring BH – Spring Bank Holiday fr – from hrs – hours m – mile mdnt – midnight
rdbt – roundabout rs – restricted service wk – week wknd – weekend x-rds – cross roads ⊗ No credit or debit cards ⊗ No dogs ⫯ Children of all ages accepted

ROSEDALE ABBEY
Map 19 SE79

Places to visit

Pickering Castle, PICKERING, YO18 7AX, 01751 474989
www.english-heritage.org.uk/daysout/properties/pickering-castle

North Yorkshire Moors Railway, PICKERING, YO18 7AJ, 01751 472508
www.nymr.co.uk

Great for kids: Flamingo Land Theme Park & Zoo, KIRBY MISPERTON, YO17 6UX, 01653 668287 www.flamingoland.co.uk

Rosedale Caravan & Camping Park
►►►►81%

tel: 01751 417272 **YO18 8SA**
email: info@flowerofmay.com
dir: *From Pickering take A170 towards Sinnington for 2.25m. At Wrelton right onto unclassified road signed Cropton & Rosedale, 7m. Site on left in village.*
grid ref: *SE725958*

Set in a sheltered valley in the centre of the North Yorkshire Moors National Park, and divided into separate areas for tents, tourers and statics. A very popular park, with well-tended grounds, and close to the pretty village of Rosedale Abbey. Two toilet blocks offer private, combined facilities. There are six camping pods situated by the river. 10 acre site. 100 touring pitches. 20 seasonal pitches. Caravan pitches. Motorhome pitches. Tent pitches. 35 statics. 6 wooden pods.

Open: Mar-Oct **Last arrival:** dusk **Last departure:** noon

Pitches: * 🚐 £22-£28 🚏 £22-£28 ▲ £22-£28 🛖

Leisure: 🄰

Facilities: 🏠⊙❄🛇🕔🛁🚽🍴❔

Services: 🔌🔲🛒🖉🚽🛎

Within 3 miles: 🏌️🎣🍴🛒🛎🕯

Notes: No noise after mdnt. Dogs accepted by prior arrangement only & must be kept on leads.

AA Pubs & Restaurants nearby: Blacksmiths Arms, LASTINGHAM, YO62 6TN, 01751 417247

The New Inn, CROPTON, YO18 8HH, 01751 417330

See advert on page 349

SCARBOROUGH

See also Filey & Wykeham

Places to visit

Scarborough Castle, SCARBOROUGH, YO11 1HY, 01723 372451 www.english-heritage.org.uk/daysout/properties/scarborough-castle

Great for kids: Scarborough Sea Life Sanctuary, SCARBOROUGH, YO12 6RP, 01723 373414 www.sealife.co.uk

SCARBOROUGH
Map 17 TA08

PREMIER PARK

Jacobs Mount Caravan Park
►►►►►81%

tel: 01723 361178 **Jacobs Mount, Stepney Rd YO12 5NL**
email: jacobsmount@yahoo.co.uk **web:** www.jacobsmount.com
dir: *Direct access from A170.* **grid ref:** *TA021868*

An elevated family-run park surrounded by woodland and open countryside, yet only two miles from the beach. Touring pitches are terraced gravel stands with individual services. The Jacobs Tavern serves a wide range of appetising meals and snacks, and there is a separate well-equipped games room for teenagers. 18 acre site. 156 touring pitches. 131 hardstandings. Caravan pitches. Motorhome pitches. Tent pitches. 60 statics.

Open: Mar-Nov (rs Mar-May & Oct-Nov limited hours at shop & bar)
Last arrival: 22.00hrs **Last departure:** noon

Pitches: * 🚐 £12.50-£23.50 🚏 £12.50-£23.50 ▲ £12.50-£23.50

Leisure: 🄰🎣🔲🎵 **Facilities:** 🛁🏠⊙🅿❄🛇🕔🛁🚽📶🖥❔

Services: 🔌🔲🍴🛒🖉🚽🍽🛎🏺🚽🕯

Within 3 miles: 🏌️🎣🍴🛒🎣◎🛶🛒🛎🕯

Notes: Dogs must be kept on leads. Food preparation area.

Cayton Village Caravan Park
►►►►83%

tel: 01723 583171 **Mill Ln, Cayton Bay YO11 3NN**
email: info@caytontouring.co.uk
dir: *From Scarborough A64, B1261 signed Filey. In Cayton 2nd left after pedestrian crossing into Mill Ln. Site 150yds on left. Or from A165 from Scarborough towards Filey right at Cayton Bay rdbt into Mill Ln. Site 0.5m right. NB it is advisable to follow guide directions not Sat Nav.* **grid ref:** *TA063838*

A long established, quietly located holiday destination close to all the major coastal attractions. The immaculately maintained grounds provide excellent pitch density and many areas are hedge-screened to create privacy. The newest touring field, The Laurels, is equipped with fully serviced hardstanding pitches that include TV hook-up and free WiFi. 30 acre site. 310 touring pitches. 239 hardstandings. 180 seasonal pitches. Caravan pitches. Motorhome pitches. Tent pitches.

Open: Mar-2 Nov **Last arrival:** 18.00hrs **Last departure:** noon (late arrival/departure available if pre-booked & charges may apply)

LEISURE: 🏊 Indoor swimming pool 🏊 Outdoor swimming pool 🄰 Children's playground 🧒 Kid's club 🎾 Tennis court 🎱 Games room 📺 Separate TV room 🏌️ golf course 🚣 Boats for hire 🎬 Cinema 🎭 Entertainment 🎣 Fishing ◎ Mini golf 🏄 Watersports 💪 Gym 🏟 Sports field 🧖 Spa 🕯 Stables
FACILITIES: 🛁 Bath 🚿 Shower ⊙ Electric shaver 🅿 Hairdryer ❄ Ice Pack Facility 🛇 Disabled facilities 🕔 Public telephone 🛒 Shop on site or within 200yds 🛵 Mobile shop (calls at least 5 days a week) 🍖 BBQ area 🌲 Picnic area 📶 Wi-fi 🖥 Internet access ♻ Recycling ❔ Tourist info 🐾 Dog exercise area

Pitches: * ⛺ £13-£35 🚐 £15-£35 ⛺ £13-£28

Leisure: /Λ ✪ Facilities: ⛽☉🅿✳🔥⑤🚿🚻📶 ♻ ❶

Services: 🔌⑤ 🔥📶T🔋

Within 3 miles: ⬇❄️🅗🅙🅟◎⛳⑤⑤

Notes: No noise after 23.00hrs, children must be supervised, no campfires, . Dogs must be kept on leads.

AA Pubs & Restaurants nearby: Lanterna Ristorante, SCARBOROUGH, YO11 1HQ, 01723 363616

Scalby Close Park
▶▶▶▶ 79%

tel: 01723 365908 **Burniston Rd YO13 ODA**
email: info@scalbyclosepark.co.uk
dir: *2m N of Scarborough on A615 (coast road), 1m from junct with A171.*
grid ref: *TA020925*

An attractive, well-landscaped park that is run by enthusiastic owners. The site has a shower block, laundry, fully serviced pitches and a motorhome service point. Just two miles from Scarborough, this makes an ideal base from which to explore both the coast and lovely countryside. 3 acre site. 42 touring pitches. 42 hardstandings. Caravan pitches. Motorhome pitches. 5 statics.

Open: Mar-Oct **Last arrival:** 22.00hrs **Last departure:** noon

Pitches: * ⛺ £17-£29 🚐 £17-£29

Facilities: ⛽☉🅿✳🚿⑤📶 🖥 Services: 🔌⑤ ⊘T🔋⬆

Within 3 miles: ⬇❄️🅗🅙🅟⑤⑤U

Notes: 🐕 Dogs must be kept on leads.

AA Pubs & Restaurants nearby: The Anvil Inn, SAWDON, YO13 9DY, 01723 859896

Lanterna Ristorante, SCARBOROUGH, YO11 1HQ, 01723 363616

Arosa Caravan & Camping Park
▶▶▶ 82%

tel: 01723 862166 & 07858 694077 **Ratten Row, Seamer YO12 4QB**
email: info@arosacamping.co.uk
dir: *A64 towards Scarborough onto B1261. On entering village 1st left at rdbt signed Seamer. From Pickering on A171 right at Seamer rdbt. Last right in village.*
grid ref: *TA014830*

A mature park in a secluded location, but with easy access to coastal attractions. Touring areas are hedge-screened to provide privacy, the toilet facilities have been recently spruced up, and a well-stocked bar serving food is also available. Barbecues and hog roasts are a feature during the warmer months. 9 acre site. 118 touring pitches. 25 hardstandings. 40 seasonal pitches. Caravan pitches. Motorhome pitches. Tent pitches. 8 statics.

Open: Mar-4 Jan **Last arrival:** 21.00hrs **Last departure:** by arrangement

Pitches: ⛺ 🚐 ⛺

Leisure: /Λ🎣🎵 Facilities: ⛽🅿✳⑤📶🖥 ❶

Services: 🔌⑤ 🍴🔥⊘T🍽🔋🏧

Within 3 miles: ⬇🅟⑤⑤U

Notes: No noise after 23.00hrs, no generators, no powered bikes or scooters. Dogs must be kept on leads.

AA Pubs & Restaurants nearby: Downe Arms Country Inn, SCARBOROUGH, YO13 9QB, 01723 862471

Killerby Old Hall
▶▶▶ 80%

SILVER

tel: 01723 583799 **Killerby YO11 3TW**
email: killerbyhall@btconnect.com
dir: *Direct access via B1261 at Killerby, near Cayton.* **grid ref:** *TA063829*

A small secluded park, well sheltered by mature trees and shrubs, located at the rear of the old hall. Use of the small indoor swimming pool is shared by visitors to the hall's holiday accommodation. There is a children's play area. 2 acre site. 20 touring pitches. 20 hardstandings. Caravan pitches. Motorhome pitches.

Open: 14 Feb-4 Jan **Last arrival:** 20.00hrs **Last departure:** noon

Pitches: ⛺ 🚐

Leisure: 🏊/Λ✪🎣

Facilities: ⛽☉🅿🔥🚻📶 ♻ ❶

Services: 🔌⑤

Within 3 miles: ⬇🅟◎⛳⑤⑤U

Notes: Dogs must be kept on leads.

AA Pubs & Restaurants nearby: The Anvil Inn, SAWDON, YO13 9DY, 01723 859896
Lanterna Ristorante, SCARBOROUGH, YO11 1HQ, 01723 363616

SCOTCH CORNER
Map 19 NZ20

Places to visit
Green Howards Museum, RICHMOND, DL10 4QN, 01748 826561
www.greenhowards.org.uk

Easby Abbey, EASBY, 0870 333 1181
www.english-heritage.org.uk/daysout/properties/easby-abbey

Scotch Corner Caravan Park
▶▶▶ 75%

tel: 01748 822530 & 07977 647722 **DL10 6NS**
email: marshallleisure@aol.com
dir: *From Scotch Corner junct of A1 & A66 take A6108 towards Richmond. 250mtrs, cross central reservation, return 200mtrs to site entrance.* **grid ref:** *NZ210054*

A well-maintained site with good facilities, ideally situated as a stopover, and an equally good location for touring. The Vintage Hotel, which serves food, can be accessed from the rear of the site. 7 acre site. 96 touring pitches. 4 hardstandings. Caravan pitches. Motorhome pitches. Tent pitches. 1 static.

Open: Etr or Apr-Oct **Last arrival:** 22.30hrs **Last departure:** noon

Pitches: ⛺ 🚐 ⛺

Facilities: ⛽☉🅿✳⑤🚿🔥♻❶

Services: 🔌⑤ 🍴🔥⊘T🍽🔋⬆

Within 3 miles: ⬇🅗🅟⑤⑤U

Notes: Dogs must be kept on leads. Recreation area for children, soft ball.

AA Pubs & Restaurants nearby: The Shoulder of Mutton Inn, KIRBY HILL, DL11 7JH, 01748 822772

PITCHES: ⛺ Caravans 🚐 Motorhomes ⛺ Tents 🏕 Glamping-style accommodation **SERVICES:** 🔌 Electric hook up ⑤ Launderette 🍴 Licensed bar 🔥 Calor Gas ⊘ Camping Gaz T Toilet fluid 🍽 Café/Restaurant 🏧 Fast Food/Takeaway 🔋 Battery charging 🍼 Baby care ⬆ Motorvan service point
ABBREVIATIONS: BH/bank hols – bank holidays Etr – Easter Spring BH – Spring Bank Holiday fr – from hrs – hours m – mile mdnt – midnight rdbt – roundabout rs – restricted service wk – week wknd – weekend x-rds – cross roads ◎ No credit or debit cards ⊗ No dogs 🧒 Children of all ages accepted

SELBY
Map 16 SE63

Places to visit

The Yorkshire Waterways Museum, GOOLE, DN14 5TB, 01405 768730
www.waterwaysmuseum.org.uk

NEW The Ranch Caravan Park
►►►► 82%

tel: 01757 638984 **Cliffe Common YO8 6PA**
email: contact@theranchcaravanpark.co.uk
dir: *Exit A63 at Cliffe signed Skipwith. Site 1m N on left.* **grid ref:** *SE664337*

A compact, sheltered park set in seven acres in a peaceful area of Cliffe Common. The enthusiastic and welcoming family owners are investing in the park by planting flowers and shrubs and relocating the reception closer to the electronic gate; they have also refurbished the on-site bar. Pitches are well spaced and, like the amenity block, they are immaculately maintained. 7 acre site. 44 touring pitches. Caravan pitches. Motorhome pitches. Tent pitches.

Open: all year **Last arrival:** 21.00hrs **Last departure:** 13.00hrs
Pitches: * ⊞ £17-£25 ⊞ £17-£25 ⚠ £12.50-£38 **Notes:** ⊗

SHERIFF HUTTON
Map 19 SE66

Places to visit

Kirkham Priory, KIRKHAM, YO60 7JS, 01653 618768
www.english-heritage.org.uk/daysout/properties/kirkham-priory

Sutton Park, SUTTON-ON-THE-FOREST, YO61 1DP, 01347 810249
www.statelyhome.co.uk

Great for kids: Castle Howard, MALTON, YO60 7DA, 01653 648333
www.castlehoward.co.uk

York Meadows Caravan Park
►►►► 80%

tel: 01439 788269 & 788236 **York Rd YO60 6QP**
email: reception@yorkmeadowscaravanpark.com
web: www.yorkmeadowscaravanpark.com
dir: *From York take A64 towards Scarborough. Left signed Flaxton & Sheriff Hutton. At West Lilling left signed Strensall. Site opposite junct.* **grid ref:** *SE644653*

Peacefully located in open countryside and surrounded by mature trees, shrubs and wildlife areas, this park provides all level pitches and a modern, well-equipped amenities block. Outdoor games such as draughts and snakes and ladders are available. 12 acre site. 45 touring pitches. 45 hardstandings. 10 seasonal pitches. Caravan pitches. Motorhome pitches. Tent pitches. 15 statics.

Open: Mar-Oct **Last arrival:** 21.00hrs **Last departure:** noon
Pitches: ⊞ ⊞ ⚠
Leisure: 🅐 🅖 **Facilities:** ⊯ ☏ ℘ ⚙ ⚐ ⛟ ⬡ 🈁 ♻ ✇
Services: ⊞ ⬚ 🖤 ⊘ ⬆ **Within 3 miles:** ⚿ 🄷 ℘ ⬚ ⬚
Notes: No noise after 23.00hrs. Dogs must be kept on leads.
AA Pubs & Restaurants nearby: The Blackwell Ox Inn, SUTTON-ON-THE-FOREST, YO61 1DT, 01347 810328

The Rose & Crown, SUTTON-ON-THE-FOREST, YO61 1DP, 01347 811333

SLINGSBY
Map 19 SE67

Places to visit

Nunnington Hall, NUNNINGTON, YO62 5UY, 01439 748283
www.nationaltrust.org.uk

Castle Howard, MALTON, YO60 7DA, 01653 648333 www.castlehoward.co.uk

Robin Hood Caravan & Camping Park
►►►► 82%

tel: 01653 628391 **Green Dyke Ln YO62 4AP**
email: info@robinhoodcaravanpark.co.uk **web:** www.robinhoodcaravanpark.co.uk
dir: *Access from B1257 (Malton to Helmsley road).* **grid ref:** *SE701748*

A pleasant, well-maintained, grassy park in a good location for touring North Yorkshire. Situated on the edge of the village of Slingsby, the park has hardstandings and electricity for every pitch, and a centrally heated toilet block. There is a treasure trail and play area for children. 2 acre site. 32 touring pitches. 22 hardstandings. Caravan pitches. Motorhome pitches. Tent pitches. 35 statics.

Open: Mar-Oct **Last arrival:** 18.00hrs **Last departure:** noon
Pitches: ⊞ ⊞ ⚠
Leisure: 🅐 **Facilities:** ☏ ⚙ ℘ ⚙ ⚐ ⬡ 🆂 🈁 🔌 💻 ♻ ✇
Services: ⊞ ⬚ 🖤 ⊘ 🆃 ⬆ **Within 3 miles:** ℘ ⬚ ⬡
Notes: No noise after 23.00hrs. Dogs must be kept on leads. Caravan hire, off-licence.
AA Pubs & Restaurants nearby: The Worsley Arms Hotel, HOVINGHAM, YO62 4LA, 01653 628234

The Malt Shovel, HOVINGHAM, YO62 4LF, 01653 628264

The Royal Oak Inn, NUNNINGTON, YO62 5US, 01439 748271

See advert on opposite page

LEISURE: 🏊 Indoor swimming pool 🏊 Outdoor swimming pool 🅐 Children's playground 👶 Kid's club 🎾 Tennis court 🎱 Games room 📺 Separate TV room
⛳ golf course ⛵ Boats for hire 🎬 Cinema 🎵 Entertainment ℘ Fishing ◎ Mini golf 🏄 Watersports 🏋 Gym 🅢 Sports field Spa ♘ Stables
FACILITIES: 🛁 Bath 🚿 Shower ⊙ Electric shaver ℘ Hairdryer ✳ Ice Pack Facility ♿ Disabled facilities 📞 Public telephone 🆂 Shop on site or within 200yds
🏪 Mobile shop (calls at least 5 days a week) 🍖 BBQ area 🌲 Picnic area 🈁 Wi-fi 💻 Internet access ♻ Recycling ✇ Tourist info 🐕 Dog exercise area

SNAINTON
Map 17 SE98

Places to visit

Scarborough Castle, SCARBOROUGH, YO11 1HY, 01723 372451
www.english-heritage.org.uk/daysout/properties/scarborough-castle

Pickering Castle, PICKERING, YO18 7AX, 01751 474989
www.english-heritage.org.uk/daysout/properties/pickering-castle

Great for kids: Scarborough Sea Life Sanctuary, SCARBOROUGH, YO12 6RP, 01723 373414 www.sealife.co.uk

Jasmine Caravan Park
►►►► 88%

tel: 01723 859240 **Cross Ln YO13 9BE**
email: enquiries@jasminepark.co.uk **web:** www.jasminepark.co.uk
dir: Turn S from A170 in Snainton, then follow signs. **grid ref:** SE928813

A peaceful and beautifully-presented park on the edge of a pretty village, and sheltered by high hedges. The toilet block with individual wash cubicles is maintained to a very high standard, and there is a licensed shop. This picturesque park lies midway between Pickering and Scarborough on the southern edge of the North Yorkshire Moors. Please note there is no motorhome service point but super

pitches for motorhomes are available. 5 acre site. 68 touring pitches. 68 hardstandings. 42 seasonal pitches. Caravan pitches. Motorhome pitches. Tent pitches. 16 statics.

Open: Mar-Oct **Last arrival:** 20.00hrs **Last departure:** noon
Pitches: ⊞ ⊞ ⚊
Leisure: ⚊ ⚊
Facilities: ⚊ ⚊ ⚊ ⚊ ⚊ ⚊ ⚊ ⚊ ⚊ ⚊ ⚊ ⚊ ⚊ ⚊ ⚊ ⚊
Services: ⚊ ⚊ ⚊ ⚊ ⚊ ⚊
Within 3 miles: ⚊ ⚊ ⚊ ⚊ ⚊ ⚊
Notes: No noise after 23.00hrs. Dogs must be kept on leads. Baby changing unit.
AA Pubs & Restaurants nearby: The Anvil Inn, SAWDON, YO13 9DY, 01723 859896
The New Inn, THORNTON LE DALE, YO18 7LF, 01751 474226

STAINFORTH
Map 18 SD86

Places to visit

Malham National Park Centre, MALHAM, BD23 4DA, 01729 833200
www.yorkshiredales.org.uk

Great for kids: Yorkshire Dales Falconry & Wildlife Conservation Centre, SETTLE, LA2 8AS, 01729 822832 www.falconryandwildlife.co.uk

Knight Stainforth Hall Caravan & Campsite
►►►► 82%

tel: 01729 822200 **BD24 0DP**
email: info@knightstainforth.co.uk
dir: From W: A65 onto B6480 towards Settle, left before swimming pool signed Little Stainforth. From E: through Settle on B6480, over bridge, 1st right. **grid ref:** SD816672

Located near Settle and the River Ribble in the Yorkshire Dales National Park, this well-maintained family site is sheltered by mature woodland. It is an ideal base for walking or touring in the beautiful surrounding areas. The toilet block has been refurbished to high standard and 5000 trees were planted in the lower part of the

continued

PITCHES: ⊞ Caravans ⊞ Motorhomes ⚊ Tents ⚊ Glamping-style accommodation **SERVICES:** ⚊ Electric hook up ⚊ Launderette ⚊ Licensed bar ⚊ Calor Gas ⚊ Camping Gaz ⚊ Toilet fluid ⚊ Café/Restaurant ⚊ Fast Food/Takeaway ⚊ Battery charging ⚊ Baby care ⚊ Motorvan service point
ABBREVIATIONS: BH/bank hols – bank holidays Etr – Easter Spring BH – Spring Bank Holiday fr – from hrs – hours m – mile mdnt – midnight
rdbt – roundabout rs – restricted service wk – week wknd – weekend x-rds – cross roads ⚊ No credit or debit cards ⚊ No dogs ⚊ Children of all ages accepted

STAINFORTH *continued*

site in 2014. 6 acre site. 100 touring pitches. 30 hardstandings. Caravan pitches. Motorhome pitches. Tent pitches. 60 statics.

Open: Mar-Oct **Last arrival:** 22.00hrs **Last departure:** noon

Pitches: * ⊞ £16-£22 ⊞ £16-£22 ▲ £16-£22

Leisure: ⚑ ⊕ ✎ ▢

Facilities: ⋔ ⊙ ℱ ✳ & ⓒ ⑤ ☴ ⋌ �📶 🖥 ♻ ❶

Services: ⊟ ⑤ ⬛ ⊘ Ⓣ ☴ ⬇

Within 3 miles: ↨ ℐ ⑤ ⑤ ∪

Notes: No groups of unaccompanied minors. Dogs must be kept on leads. Fishing.

AA Pubs & Restaurants nearby: Black Horse Hotel, GIGGLESWICK, BD24 0BE, 01729 822506

The Traddock, AUSTWICK, LA2 8BY, 01524 251224

STILLINGFLEET   Map 16 SE54

Places to visit

Merchant Adventurers' Hall, YORK, YO1 9XD, 01904 654818 www.theyorkcompany.co.uk

Mansion House, YORK, YO1 9QN, 01904 613161 www.mansionhouseyork.com

Great for kids: National Railway Museum, YORK, YO26 4XJ, 01904 621261 www.nrm.org.uk

---

Home Farm Caravan & Camping
▶▶ 72%

tel: 01904 728263 **Moreby YO19 6HN**
email: home_farm@hotmail.co.uk
dir: *6m from York on B1222, 1.5m N of Stillingfleet.* **grid ref:** *SE595427*

A traditional meadowland site on a working farm bordered by parkland on one side and the River Ouse on another. Facilities are in converted farm buildings, and the family owners extend a friendly welcome to tourers. An excellent site for relaxing and unwinding, yet only a short distance from the attractions of York. There are four log cabins for holiday hire. 5 acre site. 25 touring pitches. Caravan pitches. Motorhome pitches. Tent pitches.

Open: Feb-Dec **Last arrival:** 22.00hrs

Pitches: ⊞ ⊞ ▲

Facilities: ⋔ ⊙ ℱ ✳ ⓒ ⋌ ♻ ❶

Services: ⊟ ⬛ ⊘ Ⓣ ☴

Within 3 miles: ℐ ∪

Notes: ⊚ Dogs must be kept on leads. Family washroom.

SUTTON-ON-THE-FOREST

Places to visit

Sutton Park, SUTTON-ON-THE-FOREST, YO61 1DP, 01347 810249 www.statelyhome.co.uk

Treasurer's House, YORK, YO1 7JL, 01904 624247 www.nationaltrust.org.uk

Great for kids: Jorvik Viking Centre, YORK, YO1 9WT, 01904 615505 www.jorvik-viking-centre.com

---

SUTTON-ON-THE-FOREST   Map 19 SE56

PREMIER PARK

Goosewood Caravan Park
▶▶▶▶▶ 83%

tel: 01347 810829 **YO61 1ET**
email: enquiries@goosewood.co.uk
dir: *From A1237 take B1363. In 5m turn right. Right again in 0.5m, site on right.*
grid ref: *SE595636*

A relaxing and immaculately maintained park with its own lake and seasonal fishing. It is set in attractive woodland just six miles north of York. Mature shrubs and stunning seasonal floral displays at the entrance create an excellent first impression and the well-located toilet facilities are kept spotlessly clean. The generous patio pitches, providing optimum privacy, are randomly spaced throughout the site, and in addition to an excellent outdoor children's play area, there are also an indoor swimming pool, clubhouse, games room and bar/bistro. There are holiday homes for hire. 20 acre site. 100 touring pitches. 75 hardstandings. 50 seasonal pitches. Caravan pitches. Motorhome pitches. 35 statics.

Open: Mar-2 Jan (rs Low season shop, bar & pool reduced hours) **Last arrival:** dusk **Last departure:** noon

Pitches: * ⊞ £22-£28 ⊞ £22-£28

Leisure: ⊜ ⚑ ✎

Facilities: ⋔ ⊙ ℱ ✳ & ⓒ ⑤ ☴ ⋌ 📶 ♻ ❶

Services: ⊟ ⑤ ▮ ⬛ Ⓣ ⊙ ☴ ⬇

Within 3 miles: ↨ ⊟ ℐ ⑤ ⑤

Notes: No noise after mdnt. Dogs accepted by prior arrangement only & must be kept on leads.

AA Pubs & Restaurants nearby: The Blackwell Ox Inn, SUTTON-ON-THE-FOREST, YO61 1DT, 01347 810328

The Rose & Crown, SUTTON-ON-THE-FOREST, YO61 1DP, 01347 811333

THIRSK   Map 19 SE48

Places to visit

Monk Park Farm Visitor Centre, THIRSK, YO7 2AG, 01845 597730 www.monkparkfarm.co.uk

Byland Abbey, COXWOLD, YO61 4BD, 01347 868614 www.english-heritage.org.uk/daysout/properties/byland-abbey

Great for kids: Falconry UK - Birds of Prey Centre, THIRSK, YO7 4EU, 01845 587522 www.falconrycentre.co.uk

---

Hillside Caravan Park
▶▶▶▶ 86%

GOLD

tel: 01845 537349 & 07711 643652 **Canvas Farm, Moor Rd, Knayton YO7 4BR**
email: info@hillsidecaravanpark.co.uk
dir: *From Thirsk take A19 N exit at Knayton sign. In 0.25m right (cross bridge over A19), through village. Site on left in approx 1.5m.* **grid ref:** *SE447889*

A high quality, spacious park with first-class facilities, set in open countryside. It is an excellent base for walkers and for those wishing to explore the Thirsk area.

LEISURE: ⊜ Indoor swimming pool   ⊜ Outdoor swimming pool   ⚑ Children's playground   ⛟ Kid's club   ⓢ Tennis court   ✎ Games room   ▢ Separate TV room   ↨ golf course   ⊱ Boats for hire   ⊟ Cinema   ♫ Entertainment   ℐ Fishing   ◎ Mini golf   ⊰ Watersports   ⛾ Gym   ⊕ Sports field   ∪ Stables
FACILITIES: ⊾ Bath   ⋔ Shower   ⊙ Electric shaver   ℱ Hairdryer   ✳ Ice Pack Facility   & Disabled facilities   ⓒ Public telephone   ⑤ Shop on site or within 200yds   ⑤ Mobile shop (calls at least 5 days a week)   ☴ BBQ area   ⋌ Picnic area   📶 Wi-fi   🖥 Internet access   ♻ Recycling   ❶ Tourist info   ⋌ Dog exercise area

Please note that the park does not accept tents. 9 acre site. 50 touring pitches. 50 hardstandings. Caravan pitches. Motorhome pitches.

Open: 4 Feb-4 Jan **Last arrival:** 21.00hrs **Last departure:** noon

Pitches: * ⊞ £20-£32 ⊞ £20-£32

Leisure: 🏊 ⊕

Facilities: 🚿⊙🅿♿🔥🛒 WiFi ♻ ❶

Services: 🔌⊟ 🪫🔋

Within 3 miles: ⬇🖉⊟↻

Notes: ⊛ Dogs must be kept on leads.

AA Pubs & Restaurants nearby: The Black Swan at Oldstead, OLDSTEAD, YO61 4BL, 01347 868387

Thirkleby Hall Caravan Park
▶▶▶75%

tel: 01845 501360 & 07799 641815 **Thirkleby YO7 3AR**
email: greenwood.parks@virgin.net **web:** www.greenwoodparks.com
dir: 3m S of Thirsk on A19. Turn left through arched gatehouse into site.
grid ref: SE472794

A long-established site in the grounds of the old hall, with statics in wooded areas around a fishing lake and tourers based on slightly sloping grassy pitches. There is a quality amenities block and laundry. This well-screened park has superb views of the Hambledon Hills. 53 acre site. 50 touring pitches. 3 hardstandings. 20 seasonal pitches. Caravan pitches. Motorhome pitches. Tent pitches. 185 statics.

Open: Mar-Oct **Last arrival:** 17.30hrs **Last departure:** 14.30hrs

Pitches: ⊞ ⊞ ⋏

Leisure: 🏊 ⊕

Facilities: 🚿⊙🅿✳♿🔥🛒♻

Services: 🔌⊟🍴🪫🔋

Within 3 miles: ⬇🎿🖉⊟⊟

Notes: ⊛ No noise after 23.00hrs. Dogs must be kept on leads.

AA Pubs & Restaurants nearby: The Black Swan at Oldstead, OLDSTEAD, YO61 4BL, 01347 868387

TOLLERTON Map 19 SE56

Places to visit

Beningbrough Hall, Gallery & Gardens, BENINGBROUGH, YO30 1DD, 01904 472027 www.nationaltrust.org.uk/beningbrough

Sutton Park, SUTTON-ON-THE-FOREST, YO61 1DP, 01347 810249 www.statelyhome.co.uk

Great for kids: Jorvik Viking Centre, YORK, YO1 9WT, 01904 615505 www.jorvik-viking-centre.com

Tollerton Holiday Park
▶▶▶▶78%

tel: 01347 838313 **Station Rd YO61 1RD**
email: greenwood.parks@virgin.net **web:** www.greenwoodparks.com
dir: From York take A19 towards Thirsk. At Cross Lanes left towards Tollerton. 1m to Chinese restaurant just before rail bridge. Site entrance through restaurant car park.
grid ref: SE513643

Set in open countryside within a few minutes' walk of Tollerton and just a short drive from the Park & Ride for York, this is a small park. There's an amenities block of real quality, which includes a family bathroom and laundry. There is little disturbance from the East Coast mainline which passes near to the park. 5 acre site. 50 touring pitches. 17 hardstandings. 25 seasonal pitches. Caravan pitches. Motorhome pitches. Tent pitches. 75 statics.

Open: Mar-Oct **Last arrival:** 20.00hrs **Last departure:** 15.00hrs

Pitches: ⊞ ⊞ ⋏

Leisure: 🏊 ⊕

Facilities: ➡🚿⊙🅿✳♿◐🔥🛒♻❶

Services: 🔌⊟🪫🍴🔋⊞

Within 3 miles: ⬇🖉⊟⊟

Notes: ⊛ No groups. Dogs must be kept on leads. Small fishing lake.

AA Pubs & Restaurants nearby: The Blackwell Ox Inn, SUTTON-ON-THE-FOREST, YO61 1DT, 01347 810328

The Rose & Crown, SUTTON-ON-THE-FOREST, YO61 1DP, 01347 811333

TOWTHORPE
Map 19 SE65

Places to visit

Barley Hall, YORK, YO1 8AR, 01904 615505 www.barleyhall.co.uk

York Castle Museum, YORK, YO1 9RY, 01904 687687
www.yorkcastlemuseum.org.uk

Great for kids: Jorvik Viking Centre, YORK, YO1 9WT, 01904 615505
www.jorvik-viking-centre.com

York Touring Caravan Site
▶▶▶▶ 79%

tel: 01904 499275 **Greystones Farm, Towthorpe Moor Ln YO32 9ST**
email: info@yorkcaravansite.co.uk
dir: *From A64 follow Strensall & Haxby signs, site 1.5m on left.* **grid ref:** *SE648584*

This purpose-built golf complex and caravan park is situated just over five miles from York. There is a 9-hole golf course, crazy golf, driving range and golf shop with a coffee bar/café. The generously sized, level pitches are set within well-manicured grassland with a backdrop of trees and shrubs. 6 acre site. 44 touring pitches. 12 hardstandings. Caravan pitches. Motorhome pitches. Tent pitches.

Open: 8 Feb-3 Jan **Last arrival:** 21.00hrs **Last departure:** noon

Pitches: * ⊕ £18-£23 ⊕ £18-£23 ▲ £16-£20

Leisure: ۞ ♪

Facilities: ♦ ⊙ ℱ ✳ ⅙ ♿ ㅈ ♨ 🆆 ♻ ❼

Services: ⊕ 🗑 🔋 🍴 ⅃

Within 3 miles: ⅃ ✐ ◎ ⑤ ⑤

Notes: No noise after 23.00hrs, no commercial vehicles. Dogs must be kept on leads.

AA Pubs & Restaurants nearby: The Blackwell Ox Inn, SUTTON-ON-THE-FOREST, YO61 1DT, 01347 810328

The Rose & Crown, SUTTON-ON-THE-FOREST, YO61 1DP, 01347 811333

WEST KNAPTON
Map 19 SE87

Places to visit

Pickering Castle, PICKERING, YO18 7AX, 01751 474989
www.english-heritage.org.uk/daysout/properties/pickering-castle

North Yorkshire Moors Railway, PICKERING, YO18 7AJ, 01751 472508
www.nymr.co.uk

Great for kids: Eden Camp Modern History Theme Museum, MALTON, YO17 6RT, 01653 697777 www.edencamp.co.uk

Wolds Way Caravan and Camping
▶▶▶▶ 80%

tel: 01944 728463 & 728180 **West Farm YO17 8JE**
dir: *Signed between Rillington & West Heslerton on A64 (Malton to Scarborough road). Site 1.5m.* **grid ref:** *SE896743*

A park on a working farm in a peaceful, high position on the Yorkshire Wolds, with magnificent views over the Vale of Pickering. This is an excellent walking area, with the Wolds Way passing the entrance to the park. A pleasant one and a half mile path leads to a lavender farm, with its first-class coffee shop. 7.5 acre site. 70 touring pitches. 5 hardstandings. Caravan pitches. Motorhome pitches. Tent pitches.

Open: Mar-Oct **Last arrival:** 22.30hrs **Last departure:** 19.00hrs

Pitches: ⊕ ⊕ ▲

Leisure: ⋀

Facilities: ♦ ⋔ ⊙ ✳ ⅙ ⑤ ㅈ ♨ 🆆 ♻ ❼

Services: ⊕ 🗑 🔋 ⏏ ⅃

Within 3 miles: ✐ ⑤

Notes: Free use of microwave, toaster & TV. Drinks machine, fridge & freezer.

AA Pubs & Restaurants nearby: The New Inn, THORNTON LE DALE, YO18 7LF, 01751 474226

WHITBY
Map 19 NZ81

See also Robin Hood's Bay

Places to visit

Whitby Abbey, WHITBY, YO22 4JT, 01947 603568
www.english-heritage.org.uk/daysout/properties/whitby-abbey

North Yorkshire Moors Railway, PICKERING, YO18 7AJ, 01751 472508
www.nymr.co.uk

Ladycross Plantation Caravan Park
▶▶▶▶ 91%

tel: 01947 895502 **Egton YO21 1UA**
email: enquiries@ladycrossplantation.co.uk **web:** www.ladycrossplantation.co.uk
dir: *From A171 (Whitby to Teesside road) onto unclassified road (site signed).* **grid ref:** *NZ821080*

A unique forest setting creates an away-from-it-all feeling at this peaceful touring park set in 30 acres of woodland and under enthusiastic ownership. Pitches are sited in small groups in clearings around two smartly appointed amenity blocks, which offer excellent facilities - underfloor heating, no-touch infra-red showers, cubicles, kitchen prep areas and laundry facilities. The site is well placed for visiting Whitby and exploring the North York Moors. Children will enjoy exploring the woodland and nature walk. Oak Lodges are available for hire or sale. 30 acre site.

130 touring pitches. 33 hardstandings. 60 seasonal pitches. Caravan pitches. Motorhome pitches. Tent pitches. 2 wooden pods.

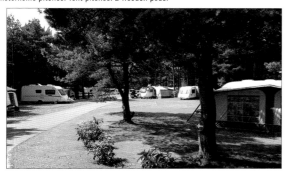

Open: Mar-Nov **Last arrival:** 20.00hrs **Last departure:** noon

Pitches: 🚐 🚐 ▲ 🏠

Facilities: 📻 ⊙ 𝒫 ☀ ⅄ © ⑤ 🖪 🚽 WiFi ♻ ❼

Services: 🔌 ⑤ 🔋 ⊘ T 📇 ✓

Within 3 miles: ⅃ 🚴 ℒ ◎ ⅍ ⑤

Notes: Dogs must be kept on leads.

AA Pubs & Restaurants nearby: The Wheatsheaf Inn, EGTON, YO21 1TZ, 01947 895271

Horseshoe Hotel, EGTON BRIDGE, YO21 1XE, 01947 895245

The Magpie Café, WHITBY, YO21 3PU, 01947 602058

WYKEHAM Map 17 SE98

Places to visit

Scarborough Castle, SCARBOROUGH, YO11 1HY, 01723 372451 www.english-heritage.org.uk/daysout/properties/scarborough-castle

Pickering Castle, PICKERING, YO18 7AX, 01751 474989 www.english-heritage.org.uk/daysout/properties/pickering-castle

Great for kids: Scarborough Sea Life Sanctuary, SCARBOROUGH, YO12 6RP, 01723 373414 www.sealife.co.uk

PREMIER PARK

St Helens Caravan Park
►►►►► 84%   🏠

tel: 01723 862771 **YO13 9QD**
email: caravans@wykeham.co.uk
dir: On A170 in village, 150yds on left beyond Downe Arms Hotel towards Scarborough. **grid ref:** SE967836

Set on the edge of the North York Moors National Park, this delightfully landscaped park is immaculately maintained and thoughtfully laid out; the stunning floral displays around the park are impressive. There are top quality facilities and a high level of customer care. The site is divided into terraces with tree-screening that creates smaller areas including an adults' zone. There are camping pods for hire (two have electricity). A cycle route leads through the

surrounding Wykeham Estate and there is a short pathway to the adjoining Downe Arms Country Inn. 25 acre site. 250 touring pitches. 40 hardstandings. Caravan pitches. Motorhome pitches. Tent pitches. 10 wooden pods.

Open: 15 Feb-15 Jan (rs Nov-Jan shop/laundry closed) **Last arrival:** 22.00hrs **Last departure:** 17.00hrs

Pitches: * 🚐 £17-£26 🚐 £17-£26 ▲ £11-£21 🏠

Leisure: 🅰

Facilities: 🚽 📻 ⊙ 𝒫 ☀ ⅄ © ⑤ 🚽 🐕 🖪 WiFi ♻ ❼

Services: 🔌 ⑤ 🔋 ⊘ T 📇 🍴 ⊟ 🏢 ✓

Within 3 miles: ⅃ 🚴 ℒ ◎ ⅍ ⑤ ⑤ U

Notes: No noise after 22.00hrs. Dogs must be kept on leads. Family & adult-only super pitches, caravan storage.

AA Pubs & Restaurants nearby: Downe Arms Country Inn, SCARBOROUGH, YO13 9QB, 01723 862471

The New Inn, THORNTON LE DALE, YO18 7LF, 01751 474226

YORK Map 16 SE65

See also Sheriff Hutton

Places to visit

York Minster, YORK, YO1 7HH, 01904 557200 www.yorkminster.org

National Railway Museum, YORK, YO26 4XJ, 01904 621261 www.nrm.org.uk

Great for kids: Jorvik Viking Centre, YORK, YO1 9WT, 01904 615505 www.jorvik-viking-centre.com

Yorvick DIG, YORK, YO1 8NN, 01904 615505 www.digyork.com

Rawcliffe Manor Caravan Park
►►►► 79%

tel: 01904 640845 **Manor Ln, Shipton Rd YO30 5TZ**
email: christine@lysanderarms.co.uk
dir: From rdbt junct of A1237 & A19, take A19 signed York, Clifton, Rawcliffe. 1st left into Manor Ln, follow brown camping signs. **grid ref:** SE583550

A lovely little adults-only site tucked away behind the Lysander Arms and located only minutes from the centre of York. Each of the 13 generous-sized pitches is fully serviced with an individual chemical disposal point, and the central toilet block is very airy, modern and spotlessly clean. The grounds have been imaginatively landscaped. The pub offers good food and the York Park & Ride facility is a 10-minute walk away. 4.5 acre site. 13 touring pitches. Caravan pitches. Motorhome pitches.

Open: all year **Last arrival:** 18.00hrs **Last departure:** 11.00hrs

Pitches: 🚐 🚐

Notes: Adults only.

AA Pubs & Restaurants nearby: Lysander Arms, YORK, YO30 5TZ, 01904 640845

Lamb & Lion Inn, YORK, YO1 7EH, 01904 612078

PITCHES: 🚐 Caravans 🚐 Motorhomes ▲ Tents 🏠 Glamping-style accommodation **SERVICES:** 🔌 Electric hook up ⑤ Launderette 🍸 Licensed bar 🔋 Calor Gas ⊘ Camping Gaz T Toilet fluid 🍴 Café/Restaurant 🏢 Fast Food/Takeaway 📇 Battery charging ⊟ Baby care ✓ Motorvan service point **ABBREVIATIONS:** BH/bank hols – bank holidays Etr – Easter Spring BH – Spring Bank Holiday fr – from hrs – hours m – mile mdnt – midnight rdbt – roundabout rs – restricted service wk – week wknd – weekend x-rds – cross roads ◎ No credit or debit cards ⊗ No dogs ♟ Children of all ages accepted

SOUTH YORKSHIRE

HATFIELD
Map 16 SE60

Places to visit

Doncaster Museum & Art Gallery, DONCASTER, DN1 2AE, 01302 734293
www.doncaster.gov.uk/museums

NEW Hatfield Outdoor Activity Centre
►►73%

tel: 01302 841572 **Old Thorne Rd DN7 6EQ**
email: hatfield@dclt.co.uk
dir: *M180 junct 1, A18 towards Doncaster. Right to site.* **grid ref:** *SE670100*

Reached via a sweeping driveway, both the Activity Centre and campsite border a beautiful lake, the latter being set amongst mature trees with well-maintained grass pitches and a central toilet block. At the well-organised Activity Centre, campers can enjoy kayaking, sailing and windsurfing, learn to build a raft, or tackle the climbing wall. Buses for Doncaster stop at the entrance. Please note, there is no laundry. 11 acre site. 49 touring pitches. 1 hardstanding. Caravan pitches. Motorhome pitches. Tent pitches.

Open: Mar-Oct **Last arrival:** 16.30hrs **Last departure:** 11.00hrs
Pitches: * ⊞ fr £13.50 ⊞ fr £13.50 Å £8.50-£13.50
Leisure: Ⓐ **Facilities:** ⚑⊙&⚒Ⓕ**ⓘ**
Services: ⊞ **Within 3 miles:** ⚓⚒⚓⚒⑤⑤
Notes: No caravans or motorhomes Sun night-Thu night. Dogs must be kept on leads.

WORSBROUGH
Map 16 SE30

Places to visit

Monk Bretton Priory, BARNSLEY, S71 5QD, 0870 333 1181
www.english-heritage.org.uk/dayout/properties/monk-bretton-priory

Millennium Gallery, SHEFFIELD, S1 2PP, 0114 278 2600
www.museums-sheffield.org.uk

Great for kids: Magna Science Adventure Centre, ROTHERHAM, S60 1DX, 01709 720002 www.visitmagna.co.uk

Greensprings Touring Park
►►79%

tel: 01226 288298 **Rockley Abbey Farm, Rockley Ln S75 3DS**
dir: *M1 junct 36, A61 to Barnsley. Left after 0.25m signed Pilley. Site 1m at bottom of hill.* **grid ref:** *SE330020*

A secluded and attractive farm site set amidst woods and farmland, with access to the river and several good local walks. There are two touring areas, one gently sloping. Although not far from the M1, there is almost no traffic noise, and this site is convenient for exploring the area's industrial heritage, as well as the Peak District. 4 acre site. 65 touring pitches. 30 hardstandings. 22 seasonal pitches. Caravan pitches. Motorhome pitches. Tent pitches.

Open: Apr-30 Oct **Last arrival:** 21.00hrs **Last departure:** noon
Pitches: ⊞ ⊞ Å

Leisure: ⊕
Facilities: ⚑⊙✳⚒Ⓕ**ⓘ**
Services: ⊞ ▮
Within 3 miles: ⚓⚒⚓⚒◎⑤⑤U
Notes: ⊕ Dogs must be kept on leads.

WEST YORKSHIRE

BARDSEY
Map 16 SE34

Places to visit

Bramham Park, BRAMHAM, LS23 6ND, 01937 846000 www.bramhampark.co.uk

Thackray Medical Museum, LEEDS, LS9 7LN, 0113 244 4343
www.thackraymedicalmuseum.co.uk

Great for kids: Leeds Industrial Museum at Armley Mills, LEEDS, LS12 2QF, 0113 263 7861 www.leeds.gov.uk/armleymills

Glenfield Caravan Park
►►►►80%

tel: 01937 574657 & 0776 1710862 **120 Blackmoor Ln LS17 9DZ**
email: glenfieldcp@aol.com **web:** www.glenfieldcaravanpark.co.uk
dir: *3m from A1 junct 45. From A58 at Bardsey into Church Ln, past church, up hill. 0.5m, site on right.* **grid ref:** *SE351421*

A quiet family-owned rural site in a well-screened, tree-lined meadow. The site has an excellent toilet block complete with family room. A convenient touring base for Leeds and the surrounding area. Discounted golf and food are both available at the local golf club. 4 acre site. 30 touring pitches. 30 hardstandings. 10 seasonal pitches. Caravan pitches. Motorhome pitches. Tent pitches. 1 static.

Open: all year **Last arrival:** 21.00hrs **Last departure:** noon
Pitches: ⊞ fr £17 ⊞ fr £17 Å fr £17
Facilities: ⚑⊙Ⓕ✳&Ⓒ⚒Ⓕ**ⓦⓘⓕ**▯♻**ⓘ**
Services: ⊞⑤▮⊘🚐🛒
Within 3 miles: ⚓⚒⚓⚒◎⑤⑤U
Notes: Children must be supervised. Dogs must be kept on leads.
AA Pubs & Restaurants nearby: The Windmill Inn, LINTON, LS22 4HT, 01937 582209

LEEDS   Map 19 SE23

Places to visit

Leeds Art Gallery, LEEDS, LS1 3AA, 0113 247 8256 www.leeds.gov.uk/artgallery

Temple Newsam Estate, LEEDS, LS15 0AE, 0113 336 7460 (House)
www.leeds.gov.uk/templenewsamhouse

Moor Lodge Park
▶▶▶▶ 83%

tel: 01937 572424 **Blackmoor Ln, Bardsey LS17 9DZ**
email: moorlodgecp@aol.com **web:** www.moorlodgecaravanpark.co.uk
dir: *From A1(M) take A659 (S of Wetherby) signed Otley. Left onto A58 towards Leeds for 5m. Right after New Inn pub (Ling Lane), right at x-rds, 1m. Site on right.*
grid ref: *SE352423*

A warm welcome is assured at this well-kept site set in a peaceful and beautiful setting, close to Harewood House and only 25 minutes' drive from York and the Dales; the centre of Leeds is just 15 minutes away. The touring area is for adults only. Please note, this site does not accept tents. 7 acre site. 12 touring pitches. Caravan pitches. Motorhome pitches. 60 statics.

Open: all year **Last arrival:** 20.00hrs **Last departure:** noon
Pitches: * 🚐 £16.50-£20 🚐 £16.50-£20
Facilities: 🌣⊙🗲✻☉🌣🗮🚾♻❶   **Services:** 🖳🖺🔋🖉🔌
Within 3 miles: ⌯🖉◎🖺∪
Notes: Adults only. No large groups. Dogs must be kept on leads.

St Helena's Caravan Park
▶▶▶ 81%

tel: 0113 284 1142 **Otley Old Rd, Horsforth LS18 5HZ**
email: info@st-helenas.co.uk
dir: *From A658 follow signs for Leeds/Bradford Airport. Then follow site signs.*
grid ref: *SE240421*

A well-maintained parkland setting surrounded by woodland yet within easy reach of Leeds with its excellent shopping and cultural opportunities, Ilkley, and the attractive Wharfedale town of Otley. Some visitors may just want to relax in this adults-only park's spacious and pleasant surroundings. 25 acre site. 60 touring pitches. 31 hardstandings. Caravan pitches. Motorhome pitches. Tent pitches. 40 statics.

Open: Apr-Oct **Last arrival:** 19.30hrs **Last departure:** 14.00hrs
Pitches: 🚐 🚐 🛆
Facilities: 🚽🌣⊙🗲✻⅏☉🗮🚻♻❶
Services: 🖳🖺🇹   **Within 3 miles:** ⌯🖉🖺🖺∪   **Notes:** Adults only.

CHANNEL ISLANDS
GUERNSEY

CASTEL   Map 24

Places to visit

Sausmarez Manor, ST MARTIN, GY4 6SG, 01481 235571
www.sausmarezmanor.co.uk

Fort Grey Shipwreck Museum, ROCQUAINE BAY, GY7 9BY, 01481 265036
www.museums.gov.gg

REGIONAL WINNER – SOUTH WEST ENGLAND
AA CAMPSITE OF THE YEAR 2015

PREMIER PARK

Fauxquets Valley Campsite
▶▶▶▶▶ 81%

tel: 01481 255460 & 07781 413333 **GY5 7QL**
email: info@fauxquets.co.uk
dir: *From pier, take 2nd exit off rdbt. At top of hill left into Queens Rd. 2m. Right into Candie Rd. Site opposite sign for German Occupation Museum.*

A beautiful, quiet farm site in a hidden valley close to the sea. The friendly and helpful owners, who understand campers' needs, offer good quality facilities and amenities, including spacious pitches and an outdoor swimming pool. There's a nature trail and sports areas, plus BBQ food is available near the reception. There are pigs, sheep and chickens for the children to visit. Fully equipped tents and two lodges are available for hire. Motorhomes up to 6.9 metres are allowed on Guernsey - contact the site for details and a permit. 3 acre site. 120 touring pitches. Motorhome pitches. Tent pitches.

Open: May-1 Sep
Pitches: 🚐 🛆
Leisure: 🏊♨⚽🎣□
Facilities: 🌣⊙🗲✻⅏☉🗮🚻🚾♻❶
Services: 🖳🖺🔋🖉🇹🍴🔌🛒🚼
Within 3 miles: ⌯🏊♨🖉◎⛵🖺🖺∪
Notes: Dogs must be kept on leads. Birdwatching.
AA Pubs & Restaurants nearby: Fleur du Jardin, CASTEL, GY5 7JT, 01481 257996

Cobo Bay Hotel, CASTEL, GY5 7HB, 01481 257102

ST SAMPSON
Map 24

Places to visit

Sausmarez Manor, ST MARTIN, GY4 6SG, 01481 235571
www.sausmarezmanor.co.uk

Castle Cornet, ST PETER PORT, GY1 1AU, 01481 721657 www.museums.gov.gg

Le Vaugrat Camp Site
►►►87%

tel: 01481 257468 **Route de Vaugrat GY2 4TA**
email: enquiries@vaugratcampsite.com **web:** www.vaugratcampsite.com
dir: *From main coast road on NW of island, site signed at Port Grat Bay into Route de Vaugrat, near Peninsula Hotel.*

Overlooking the sea and set within the grounds of a lovely 17th-century house, this level grassy park is backed by woodland, and is close to the lovely sandy beaches of Port Grat and Grand Havre. It is run by a welcoming family who pride themselves on creating magnificent floral displays. The facilities here are excellent and there are 18 electric hook ups. Motorhomes up to 6.9 metres are allowed on Guernsey - contact the site for details and permit. A 'round the island' bus stops very close to the site. 6 acre site. 150 touring pitches. Motorhome pitches. Tent pitches.

Open: May-mid Sep
Pitches: ⊕ Å
Leisure: ▢ **Facilities:** ⋒⊙ℙ☀⅋Ⓢ⑤冊 WIFI ✿ ❶
Services: ⊕⑤ ⬛⊘🛒 **Within 3 miles:** ⅃⽥⌽◎⇟⑤⑤Ս
Notes: No pets.
AA Pubs & Restaurants nearby: The Admiral de Saumarez, ST PETER PORT, GY1 2JP, 01481 721431
The Old Government House Hotel & Spa, ST PETER PORT, GY1 2NU, 01481 724921
The Absolute End, ST PETER PORT, GY1 2BG, 01481 723822
Mora Restaurant & Grill, ST PETER PORT, GY1 2LE, 01481 715053

VALE

Places to visit

Guernsey Museum & Art Gallery, ST PETER PORT, GY1 1UG, 01481 726518
www.museums.gov.gg

Great for kids: Castle Cornet, ST PETER PORT, GY1 1AU, 01481 721657
www.museums.gov.gg

VALE
Map 24

La Bailloterie Camping & Leisure
►►►88%

tel: 01481 243636 & 07781 103420 **Bailloterie Ln GY3 5HA**
email: info@campinginguernsey.com
dir: *3m N of St Peter Port take Vale road to Crossways, right into Rue du Braye. Site 1st left at sign.*

A pretty rural site with one large touring field and a few small, well-screened paddocks. This delightful site has been in the same family ownership for over 30 years and offers good facilities in converted outbuildings. There are also fully-equipped tents for hire. Motorhomes up to 6.9 metres are allowed on Guernsey - contact the site for detailed instructions. 10 acre site. 100 touring pitches. Motorhome pitches. Tent pitches.

Open: 15 May-15 Sep **Last arrival:** 23.00hrs
Pitches: ⊕ Å
Leisure: ▲ ⊛
Facilities: ⋒⊙ℙ☀⅋Ⓢ冊⚙ WIFI ❶
Services: ⊕⑤ ⬛⊘⑩🛒⬛🛒
Within 3 miles: ⅃⽥⅃⌽◎⇟⑤⑤Ս
Notes: Dogs by prior arrangement only & must be kept on leads. Volleyball net, boules pitch.
AA Pubs & Restaurants nearby: The Admiral de Saumarez, ST PETER PORT, GY1 2JP, 01481 721431
The Old Government House Hotel & Spa, ST PETER PORT, GY1 2NU, 01481 724921
The Absolute End, ST PETER PORT, GY1 2BG, 01481 723822
Mora Restaurant & Grill, ST PETER PORT, GY1 2LE, 01481 715053

JERSEY

ST MARTIN
Map 24

Places to visit

Mont Orgueil Castle, GOREY, JE3 6ET, 01534 853292 www.jerseyheritage.org

Maritime Museum & Occupation Tapestry Gallery, ST HELIER, JE2 3ND, 01534 811043 www.jerseyheritage.org

Great for kids: Elizabeth Castle, ST HELIER, JE2 3WU, 01534 723971
www.jerseyheritage.org

PREMIER PARK

Beuvelande Camp Site
►►►►►85%

tel: 01534 853575 **Beuvelande JE3 6EZ**
email: info@campingjersey.com
dir: *Take A6 from St Helier to St Martin & follow signs to site before St Martins Church.*

A well-established site with excellent toilet facilities, accessed via narrow lanes in peaceful countryside close to St Martin. An attractive bar and restaurant is the focal point of the park, especially in the evenings, and there is a small swimming pool and playground. Motorhomes and towed caravans will be met at the ferry and escorted to the site if requested when booking. Two yurts, three emperor tents, two bell tents and one safari tent are for hire. 6 acre site. 150

LEISURE: 🏊 Indoor swimming pool 🏊 Outdoor swimming pool ▲ Children's playground 🧒 Kid's club ☺ Tennis court 🎱 Games room ▢ Separate TV room ⅃ golf course ⛵ Boats for hire ⽥ Cinema ♫ Entertainment 🎣 Fishing ◎ Mini golf 🏊 Watersports 🏋 Gym ✪ Sports field Spa Ս Stables
FACILITIES: 🛁 Bath ⋒ Shower ⊙ Electric shaver ℙ Hairdryer ☀ Ice Pack Facility ⅋ Disabled facilities ℂ Public telephone ⑤ Shop on site or within 200yds ⑤ Mobile shop (calls at least 5 days a week) 🍖 BBQ area 🌳 Picnic area WIFI Wi-fi 🖥 Internet access ✿ Recycling ❶ Tourist info 🐕 Dog exercise area

touring pitches. Caravan pitches. Motorhome pitches. Tent pitches. 75 statics. 2 bell tents/yurts.

Open: Apr-Sep (rs Apr-May & Sep pool & restaurant closed, shop hours limited)

Pitches: 🚐 🚏 ▲ 🏠

Leisure: ⚓ 🎪 🎱 🎵 🎶

Facilities: 🝰 ☉ ✳ ♿ 🕙 💲 🛒 📶 💻 🅾

Services: 🔌 🗄 🗄 🎒 🚰 🚽 🍽 🔋 🛠

Within 3 miles: 🎣 ⛳ 🏊 💲 🗄 ⛳

Notes: Dogs must be kept on leads.

AA Pubs & Restaurants nearby: Royal Hotel, ST MARTIN, JE3 6UG, 01534 856289

Rozel Camping Park
▶ ▶ ▶ ▶ 90%

tel: 01534 855200 **Summerville Farm JE3 6AX**
email: enquiries@rozelcamping.com
dir: *Take A6 from St Helier through Five Oaks to St Martins Church, turn right onto A38 towards Rozel, site on right.*

Customers can be sure of a warm welcome at this delightful family-run park. Set in the north east of the island, it offers large spacious pitches, many with electric, for tents, caravans and motorhomes. The lovely Rozel Bay is just a short distance away and spectacular views of the French coast can be seen from one of the four fields on the park. The site also offers excellent facilities including a swimming pool. Motorhomes and caravans will be met at the ferry and escorted to the park if requested when booking. Fully equipped, ready-erected tents available for hire. 4 acre site. 100 touring pitches. Caravan pitches. Motorhome pitches. Tent pitches. 20 statics.

Open: May-mid Sep **Last departure:** noon

Pitches: 🚐 🚏 ▲

Leisure: ⚓ 🎪 🎯 🎱 🖵

Facilities: 🝰 ☉ 🅿 ✳ ♿ 🕙 💲 📶 💻 🅾

Services: 🔌 🗄 🎒 🚰 🚽 🔋 🛠

Within 3 miles: 🎣 ⛳ 🏊 ◎ 🏊 💲 🗄 ⛳

Notes: Dogs must be kept on leads. Mini golf.

AA Pubs & Restaurants nearby: Royal Hotel, ST MARTIN, JE3 6UG, 01534 856289

ST OUEN

Places to visit

Creux Baillot Cottage, ST OUEN, JE3 2FE, 01534 482191 www.judithqueree.com

The Channel Islands Military Museum, ST OUEN, JE3 2FN, 01534 483205

Great for kids: The Living Legend, ST PETER, JE3 7ET, 01534 485496 www.jerseyslivinglegend.co.je

ST OUEN
Map 24

NEW Daisy Cottage Campsite
▶ ▶ ▶ ▶ 85%

tel: 01534 481700 **Route de Vinchelez JE3 2DB**
email: hello@daisycottagecampsite.com
dir: *Phone for detailed directions.*

This quiet family site is the only campsite on the west side of the island. The choice of accommodation includes luxury, fully-equipped yurts, bell tents and even a shepherd's hut; or you can bring your own tent, caravan or motorhome. The campsite also has a unique Retreat offering a wide range of therapies as well as an on-site chiropractor. There is also a small, well-appointed swimming pool, and a small café and tasteful bar in keeping with the quiet and peaceful environment. The campsite is also very close to Greve de Lecq with its delightful beach. Caravan pitches. Motorhome pitches. Tent pitches. 12 bell tents/yurts.

Open: all year

Pitches: * 🚐 £20-£30 🚏 £20-£30 ▲ £20-£25 🏠

Leisure: ⚓ 🎪 Spa **Facilities:** 🝰 ✳ ♿ 💲 📶 💻 🅾

Services: 🔌 🗄 🍽 🔋 🚰 **Within 3 miles:** 🖫 ⛳ 🏊 💲 🗄

Notes: No noise after 22.00hrs.

AA Pubs & Restaurants nearby: St Mary's Country Inn, ST MARY, JE3 3DS, 01534 482897

Mark Jordan at the Beach, ST PETER, JE3 7YD, 01534 780180

ISLE OF MAN

KIRK MICHAEL
Map 24 SC39

Places to visit

Peel Castle, PEEL, IM5 1TB, 01624 648000 www.manxnationalheritage.im

House of Manannan, PEEL, IM5 1TA, 01624 648000 www.manxnationalheritage.im

Great for kids: Curraghs Wildlife Park, BALLAUGH, IM7 5EA, 01624 897323 www.gov.im/wildlife

Glen Wyllin Campsite
▶ ▶ ▶ 72%

tel: 01624 878231 & 878836 **IM6 1AL**
email: michaelcommissioners@manx.net
dir: *From Douglas take A1 to Ballacraine, right at lights onto A3 to Kirk Michael. Left onto A4 signed Peel. Site 100yds on right.* **grid ref:** SC302901

Set in a beautiful wooded glen with bridges over a pretty stream dividing the camping areas. A gently-sloping tarmac road gives direct access to a good beach. Hire tents are available. 9 acre site. 90 touring pitches. Caravan pitches. Motorhome pitches. Tent pitches. 18 statics.

Open: mid Apr-mid Sep **Last departure:** noon

Pitches: 🚐 🚏 ▲

Leisure: 🎪 🖵 **Facilities:** 🝰 ☉ 🅿 ✳ ♿ 🕙 💲 🛒 📶 ♻

Services: 🔌 🗄 🍽 🔋 🚰 **Within 3 miles:** ⛳ 💲 🗄 ⛳

Notes: No excess noise after mdnt, dogs must be kept on leads & under control.

AA Pubs & Restaurants nearby: The Creek Inn, PEEL, IM5 1AT, 01624 842216

PITCHES: 🚐 Caravans 🚏 Motorhomes ▲ Tents 🏠 Glamping-style accommodation **SERVICES:** 🔌 Electric hook up 🗄 Launderette 🍷 Licensed bar 🎒 Calor Gas 🖉 Camping Gaz 🔲 Toilet fluid 🍽 Café/Restaurant 🍔 Fast Food/Takeaway 🔋 Battery charging 🚼 Baby care 🛠 Motorvan service point **ABBREVIATIONS:** BH/bank hols – bank holidays Etr – Easter Spring BH – Spring Bank Holiday fr – from hrs – hours m – mile mdnt – midnight rdbt – roundabout rs – restricted service wk – week wknd – weekend x-rds – cross roads ⊘ No credit or debit cards ⊗ No dogs ♀♂ Children of all ages accepted

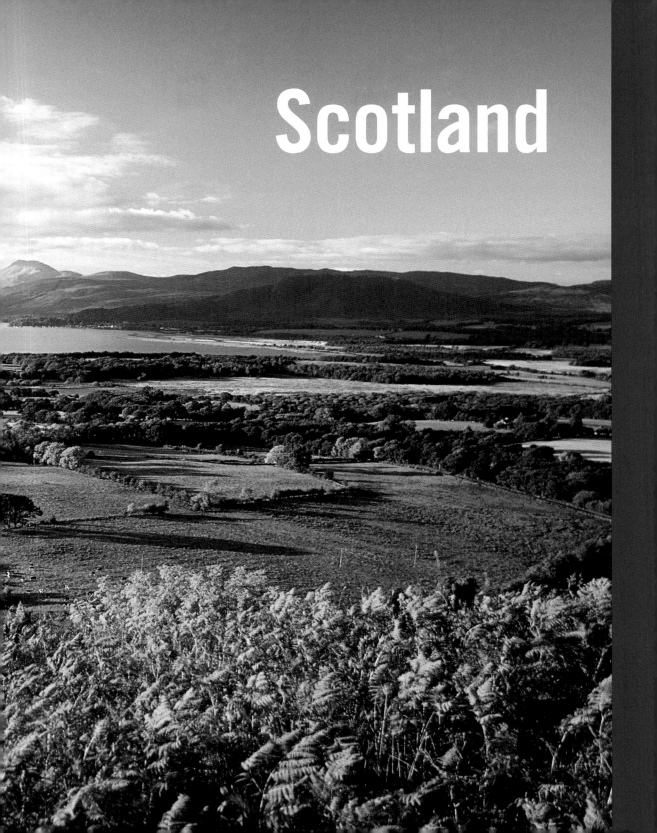

Scotland

Scotland

With its remarkable, timeless beauty, jagged coastline and long and eventful history, Scotland is a country with something very special to offer. Around half the size of England, but with barely one fifth of its population and nearly 800 islands, the statistics alone are enough make you want to pack a suitcase and head north without hesitation.

The Scottish Borders region acts as a perfect introduction and is an obvious place to begin a tour of the country. The novelist and poet Sir Walter Scott was so moved by its remoteness and grandeur that he wrote: 'To my eye, these grey hills and all this wild border country have beauties peculiar to themselves. I like the very nakedness of the land; it has something bold and stern and solitary about it. If I did not see the heather at least once a year I think I should die.' Abbotsford, Scott's turreted mansion on the banks of the River Tweed near Melrose, was re-opened to the public in the summer of 2013 following a £12 million programme of major improvements.

Consisting of 1,800 square miles of dense forest, rolling green hills and the broad sweeps of heather that lifted Scott's spirits, this region is characterised by some of the country's most majestic landscapes. Adjacent to this region is Dumfries & Galloway, where, at Gretna Green on the border with England, eloping couples have tied the knot since Lord Hardwicke's Marriage Act came into force in 1754; it still can boast around 1,500 weddings a year. Travel north and you discover mile upon mile of open moorland and swathes of seemingly endless forest that stretch to the Ayrshire coast. At a crucial time in the country's history, it is fascinating to reflect on another momentous event in the story of Scotland when, following the signing of the Declaration of Arbroath in 1320, it became independent and was ruled by Robert the Bruce. Dumfries & Galloway is littered with the relics of his battles.

Not far from Dumfries is the cottage where Robert Burns, the Bard of Scotland, was born in 1759. This tiny white-washed dwelling, constructed of thatch and clay, was built by the poet's father two years earlier. In a 2009 poll, TV viewers voted Burns the 'Greatest ever Scot' and his song *Is there for Honest Poverty*

opened the new Scottish Parliament in 1999. The cottage at Alloway is one of Scotland's most popular tourist attractions with a new museum allowing the poet's collection of precious manuscripts, correspondence and artefacts to be housed in one building.

Scotland's two greatest cities, Glasgow and Edinburgh, include innumerable historic sites, popular landmarks and innovative visitor attractions. Edinburgh is home to the annual, internationally famous Military Tattoo; Glasgow, once the second city of the British Empire and yet synonymous with the dreadful slums and the grime of industry, has, in places, been transformed beyond recognition. The city hosted the Great Exhibitions of 1888 and 1901, was designated European City of Culture in 1990 and in 2014 became the setting for the highly successful Commonwealth Games.

To the north of Glasgow and Edinburgh lies a sublime landscape of tranquil lochs, fishing rivers, wooded glens and the fine cities of Perth and Dundee. There is also the superb scenery of The Trossachs, Loch Lomond and Stirling, which, with its handsome castle perched on a rocky crag, is Scotland's heritage capital. Sooner or later the might and majesty of the Cairngorms and the Grampians beckon, drawing you into a breathtakingly beautiful landscape of mountains and remote, rugged terrain. Scotland's isolated far north is further from many parts of England than a good many European destinations. Cape Wrath is Britain's most northerly outpost.

For many visitors, the Western Highlands is the place to go, evoking a truly unique and breathtaking sense of adventure. The list of island names seems endless – Skye, Mull, Iona, Jura, Islay – each with their own individual character and identity, and the reward of everlasting and treasured memories.

Loch Lomond and the Trossachs National Park ▷

ABERDEENSHIRE

ABOYNE
Map 23 NO59

Places to visit

Alford Valley Railway, ALFORD, AB33 8AD, 019755 63942
www.alfordvalleyrailway.org.uk

Crathes Castle Garden & Estate, CRATHES, AB31 5QJ, 0844 4932166
www.nts.org.uk/Property/Crathes-Castle-Garden-and-Estate

Great for kids: Craigievar Castle, ALFORD, AB33 8JF, 0844 493 2174
www.nts.org.uk/Property/Craigievar-Castle

Aboyne Loch Caravan Park
►►►76%

GOLD

tel: 01339 886244 & 882589 **AB34 5BR**
email: heatherreid24@yahoo.co.uk
dir: On A93, 1m E of Aboyne. **grid ref:** NO538998

Located on the outskirts of Aboyne on a small outcrop which is almost surrounded by Loch Aboyne, this is a mature site within scenic Royal Deeside. The facilities are well maintained, and pitches are set amongst mature trees with most having views over the loch. Boat hire and fishing (coarse and pike) are available and there is a regular bus service from the site entrance. 6 acre site. 20 touring pitches. 25 hardstandings. Caravan pitches. Motorhome pitches. Tent pitches. 100 statics.

Open: 31 Mar-Oct **Last arrival:** 20.00hrs **Last departure:** 11.00hrs

Pitches: * ⚌ £22-£25 ⇌ £22-£25 Å £15-£25

Leisure: ⚍ ◥

Facilities: ⌕ ⊙ ⧨ ✳ ⅋ ◔ ⌁ 📶 ♻ ❶

Services: ⬒ ⬓ ⬛ ⬮ ⊤ ⬙

Within 3 miles: ⬆ ⚶ ◢ ◎ ⬌ ⑤ ⑤ ∪

Notes: ◉ Dogs must be kept on leads.

AA Pubs & Restaurants nearby: The Milton Brasserie, CRATHES, AB31 5QH, 01330 844566

ALFORD

Places to visit

Alford Valley Railway, ALFORD, AB33 8AD, 019755 63942
www.alfordvalleyrailway.org.uk

Craigievar Castle, ALFORD, AB33 8JF, 0844 493 2174
www.nts.org.uk/Property/Craigievar-Castle

ALFORD
Map 23 NJ51

Haughton House Holiday Park
►►►76%

tel: 01975 562107 **Montgarrie Rd AB33 8NA**
email: enquiries@haughtonhouse.co.uk
dir: In Alford follow Haughton Country House signs. **grid ref:** NJ577168

Located on the outskirts of Alford this site is set within a large country park with good countryside views. Now under the same ownership as Huntly Castle Caravan Park (Huntly), this park receives the same attention to detail to ensure facilities are of a high standard; the existing facilities are clean and well maintained. The pitches are set amongst mature trees and the tenting area is within the old walled garden. There is plenty to do on site and within the country park which has various activities for children, including a narrow gauge railway that runs to the Grampian Transport Museum in nearby Alford. 22 acre site. 71 touring pitches. 71 hardstandings. 20 seasonal pitches. Caravan pitches. Motorhome pitches. Tent pitches. 70 statics.

Open: 25 Mar-27 Oct **Last arrival:** 21.00hrs **Last departure:** noon

Pitches: ⚌ ⇌ Å

Leisure: ⚍ **Facilities:** ⌕ ⊙ ⧨ ✳ ⅋ ◔ ⌁ ⍾ ♻ ❶

Services: ⬒ ⬓ ⬛ ⊤ ⬚ ⬙ **Within 3 miles:** ⬆ ◢ ◎ ⑤ ⑤

Notes: No noise after 22.30hrs. Dogs must be kept on leads. Putting green, fishing permits.

BANFF
Map 23 NJ66

Places to visit

Banff Museum, BANFF, AB45 1AE, 01261 812941

Duff House, BANFF, AB45 3SX, 01261 818181 www.historic-scotland.gov.uk

---

Banff Links Caravan Park
►►►►80%

tel: 01261 812228 **Inverboyndie AB45 2JJ**
email: banfflinkscaravanpark@btconnect.com
dir: From W: A98 onto B9038 signed Whitehills. 2nd right signed Inverboyndie. 4th left to site. From E (Banff): A98, right at brown 'Banff Links Beach' sign. **grid ref:** NJ668644

A delightful small park set beside the award-winning sandy beach at Banff Links with magnificent views over the Moray Coast. Set at sea level, there is direct access to the beach and also a large grass esplanade and play area for children. A pleasant walk on good level paths by the sea will take you to either Banff or the small village of Whitehill, which has a leisure boat harbour. It is ideally located to explore this lovely coastline. The family owners at the park are keen that their visitors will have an enjoyable stay. Two static caravans are for hire. 5.78 acre site. 55 touring pitches. 10 hardstandings. 10 seasonal pitches. Caravan pitches. Motorhome pitches. Tent pitches. 38 statics.

Open: Apr-Oct

Pitches: * ⚌ £19-£22 ⇌ £19-£22 Å £11-£30

Leisure: ⚍ **Facilities:** ⌕ ⧨ ⅋ ⑤ ⍾ 📶 ♻ ❶

Services: ⬒ ⬓ ⬛ ⊤ ⬚ ⬙

Within 3 miles: ⬆ ◢ ◎ ⬌ ⑤ ⑤ ∪

Notes: Dogs must be kept on leads.

LEISURE: 🏊 Indoor swimming pool 🏊 Outdoor swimming pool ⚍ Children's playground Kid's club Tennis court Games room Separate TV room golf course Boats for hire Cinema Entertainment Fishing Mini golf Watersports Gym Sports field Spa Stables
FACILITIES: Bath Shower Electric shaver Hairdryer Ice Pack Facility Disabled facilities Public telephone Shop on site or within 200yds Mobile shop (calls at least 5 days a week) BBQ area Picnic area Wi-fi Internet access Recycling Tourist info Dog exercise area

HUNTLY
Map 23 NJ53

Places to visit

Leith Hall, Garden & Estate, RHYNIE, AB54 4NQ, 01464 831 216
www.nts.org.uk/Property/Leith-Hall-Garden-and-Estate

Glenfiddich Distillery, DUFFTOWN, AB55 4DH, 01340 820373
www.glenfiddich.com

PREMIER PARK

Huntly Castle Caravan Park
►►►►► 90%

tel: 01466 794999 **The Meadow AB54 4UJ**
email: enquiries@huntlycastle.co.uk
dir: From Aberdeen on A96 to Huntly. 0.75m after rdbt (on outskirts of Huntly) right towards town centre, left into Riverside Drive. **grid ref:** NJ525405

A quality parkland site within striking distance of the Speyside Malt Whisky Trail, the beautiful Moray coast and the Cairngorm Mountains. The park provides exceptional toilet facilities, and there are some fully serviced pitches. The indoor activity centre provides a wide range of games; the attractive town of Huntly is only a five-minute walk away, with its ruined castle plus a wide variety of restaurants and shops. 15 acre site. 90 touring pitches. 51 hardstandings. 10 seasonal pitches. Caravan pitches. Motorhome pitches. Tent pitches. 40 statics.

Open: Apr-Oct (rs Wknds & school hols indoor activity centre open)
Last arrival: 20.00hrs **Last departure:** noon

Pitches: ⊞ ⊟ Å

Leisure: ⚠

Facilities: ⬤⊙ℙ⚹⬤ rⓉ WIFI ♻ ✿

Services: ⬤⬤ ⬛Ⓣ⬛ ↯

Within 3 miles: ⬤⬤⬤⬤

Notes: Dogs must be kept on leads. Snooker table.

KINTORE

Places to visit

Pitmedden Garden, PITMEDDEN, AB41 7PD, 0844 493 2177
www.nts.org.uk/Property/Pitmedden-Garden

Tolquhon Castle, PITMEDDEN, AB41 7LP, 01651 851286
www.historic-scotland.gov.uk

Great for kids: Castle Fraser, KEMNAY, AB51 7LD, 0844 493 2164
www.nts.org.uk/Property/Castle-Fraser-Garden-and-Estate

KINTORE
Map 23 NJ71

Hillhead Caravan Park
►►►► 77%

tel: 01467 632809 & 0870 413 0870 **AB51 0YX**
email: enquiries@hillheadcaravan.co.uk
dir: 1m from village & A96 (Aberdeen-Inverness road). From A96 follow signs to site on B994, then unclassified road. **grid ref:** NJ777163

An attractive, nicely landscaped site, located on the outskirts of Kintore in the valley of the River Dee with excellent access to forest walks and within easy reach of the many attractions in rural Aberdeenshire. The toilet facilities are of a high standard. There are good play facilities for smaller children plus a small café with TV and internet access. 1.5 acre site. 29 touring pitches. 14 hardstandings. Caravan pitches. Motorhome pitches. Tent pitches.

Open: all year **Last arrival:** 21.00hrs **Last departure:** 13.00hrs

Pitches: ⊞ ⊟ Å

Leisure: ⚠ **Facilities:** ⬤⊙ℙ⚹⬤⬤⬤ rⓈ WIFI

Services: ⬤⬤ ⬤Ⓣ⬤⬤

Within 3 miles: ⬤⬤⬤⬤

Notes: Caravan storage, accessories shop.

AA Pubs & Restaurants nearby: The Cock & Bull Bar & Restaurant, BALMEDIE, AB23 8XY, 01358 743249

Old Blackfriars, ABERDEEN, AB11 5BB, 01224 581922

The Adelphi Kitchen, ABERDEEN, AB11 5BL, 01224 211414

The Silver Darling, ABERDEEN, AB11 5DQ, 01224 576229

MACDUFF
Map 23 NJ76

Places to visit

Duff House, BANFF, AB45 3SX, 01261 818181 www.historic-scotland.gov.uk

Banff Museum, BANFF, AB45 1AE, 01261 812941

Wester Bonnyton Farm Site
►► 68%

tel: 01261 832470 **Gamrie AB45 3EP**
email: westerbonnyton@fsmail.net
dir: From A98 (1m S of Macduff) take B9031 signed Rosehearty. Site 1.25m on right. **grid ref:** NJ741638

A spacious farm site, with level touring pitches, overlooking the Moray Firth. The small, picturesque fishing villages of Gardenstown and Crovie and the larger town of Macduff, which has a marine aquarium, are all within easy reach. All the touring pitches have good views of the coastline. Families with children are welcome, and there is a play area and play barn. 8 acre site. 8 touring pitches. 5 hardstandings. Caravan pitches. Motorhome pitches. Tent pitches. 65 statics.

Open: Mar-Oct

Pitches: ⊞ ⊟ Å

Leisure: ⚠ ✦ **Facilities:** ⬤⊙ℙ⬤⬤ rⓈ WIFI ♻ ✿

Services: ⬤⬤ ⬤⬤

Within 3 miles: ⬤⬤⬤⬤⬤⬤

Notes: Dogs must be kept on leads.

PITCHES: ⊞ Caravans ⊟ Motorhomes Å Tents 🏠 Glamping-style accommodation **SERVICES:** ⬤ Electric hook up ⓈLaunderette 🍺Licensed bar ⬛ Calor Gas ⊘ Camping Gaz Ⓣ Toilet fluid 🍽 Café/Restaurant ⬛ Fast Food/Takeaway ⬛ Battery charging ⬛ Baby care ↯ Motorvan service point
ABBREVIATIONS: BH/bank hols – bank holidays Etr – Easter Spring BH – Spring Bank Holiday fr – from hrs – hours m – mile mdnt – midnight rdbt – roundabout rs – restricted service wk – week wknd – weekend x-rds – cross roads 🚫 No credit or debit cards 🚫 No dogs ⬤ Children of all ages accepted

MINTLAW — Map 23 NJ94

Places to visit

Aberdeenshire Farming Museum, MINTLAW, AB42 5FQ, 01771 624590
www.aberdeenshire.gov.uk/museums

Deer Abbey, OLD DEER, 01667 460232 www.historic-scotland.gov.uk

Aden Caravan and Camping Park
►►► 82%

tel: 01771 623460 **Aden Country Park AB42 5FQ**
email: info@adencaravanandcamping.co.uk
dir: *From Mintlaw take A950 signed New Pitsligo & Aden Country Park. Park on left.*
grid ref: *NJ981479*

Situated in the heart of Buchan in Aberdeenshire and within Aden Country Park, this is a small tranquil site offering excellent facilities. It is ideally located for visiting the many tourist attractions in this beautiful north-east coastal area, not least of which is the 230-acre country park itself. The site is only a short drive from the busy fishing towns of Fraserburgh and Peterhead, and as it is only an hour from Aberdeen's city centre; this is an ideal spot for a short stay or a longer holiday. The country park plays host to numerous events throughout the year, including pipe band championships, horse events and various ranger-run activities. 11.1 acre site. 66 touring pitches. 31 hardstandings. 10 seasonal pitches. Caravan pitches. Motorhome pitches. Tent pitches. 17 statics.

Open: Apr-Oct **Last arrival:** 20.00hrs **Last departure:** 14.00hrs

Pitches: 🚐 🚎 Å
Leisure: ⚑
Facilities: 🏕️ ☉ 🅿️ 🕯️ 🛁 🚻 🐕 WiFi ♻ ❶
Services: 🔌 🗑️ 🛒 T ⚡
Within 3 miles: ⚙ 🏌️ 💲

Notes: Adults only. Dogs must be kept on leads.

NORTH WATER BRIDGE — Map 23 NO66

Places to visit

Edzell Castle and Garden, EDZELL, DD9 7UE, 01356 648631
www.historic-scotland.gov.uk

Pictavia Visitor Centre, BRECHIN, DD9 6RL, 01356 626241 www.pictavia.org.uk

Dovecot Caravan Park
►►► 77%

tel: 01674 840630 **AB30 1QL**
email: adele@dovecotcaravanpark.co.uk
dir: *Take A90, 5m S of Laurencekirk. At Edzell Woods sign turn left. Site 500yds on left.*
grid ref: *NO648663*

A level grassy site in a country area close to the A90, with mature trees screening one side and the River North Esk on the other. The immaculate toilet facilities make this a handy overnight stop in a good touring area. 6 acre site. 25 touring pitches. 8 hardstandings. 8 seasonal pitches. Caravan pitches. Motorhome pitches. Tent pitches. 44 statics.

Open: Apr-Oct **Last arrival:** 20.00hrs **Last departure:** noon

Pitches: * 🚐 £15.50-£17.50 🚎 £15.50-£17.50 Å £12.50-£14.50
Leisure: ⚑ 🎮
Facilities: 🏕️ ☉ 🅿️ 🕯️ 🛁 🕐 🐕 WiFi ♻ ❶
Services: 🔌 🛒 T ⚡

Notes: Dogs must be kept on leads.

PETERHEAD — Map 23 NK14

Places to visit

Arbuthnot Museum, PETERHEAD, AB42 1QD, 01771 622807
www.aberdeenshire.gov.uk/museums

Aberdeenshire Farming Museum, MINTLAW, AB42 5FQ, 01771 624590
www.aberdeenshire.gov.uk/museums

Lido Caravan Park
►►► 74%

tel: 01779 478950 & 473358 **South Rd AB42 2YP**
email: admin@peterheadprojects.co.uk
dir: *From A90 (Aberdeen to Peterhead) at Invernetty rdbt take A982.* grid ref: *NK123452*

This small site is located on The Lido with direct access to a small sandy beach with a nice play area and sand dunes. Each of the all-electric pitches has a view over Peterhead's busy harbour and there is always some boating activity taking place to keep you interested. The site is under the management of the local enterprise company Peterhead Projects Limited. The Martine Heritage Centre, a few minutes' walk from the site, has an excellent café. 2 acre site. 25 touring pitches. Caravan pitches. Motorhome pitches. Tent pitches. 14 statics.

Open: Mar-Oct **Last departure:** noon

Pitches: * 🚐 fr £18 🚎 fr £18 Å fr £10
Facilities: 🏕️ 🅿️ 🛁 🕐 🚻 ♻
Services: 🔌 🛒 🛍️
Within 3 miles: ⚙ 🏕️ 🍴 🎣 ⚓ 🛒 🛍️ ♻

Notes: No ball games, no nuisance noise after 22.00hrs. Dogs must be kept on leads.

PORTSOY — Map 23 NJ56

Places to visit

Banff Museum, BANFF, AB45 1AE, 01261 812941

Duff House, BANFF, AB45 3SX, 01261 818181 www.historic-scotland.gov.uk

Great for kids: Macduff Marine Aquarium, MACDUFF, AB44 1SL, 01261 833369
www.macduff-aquarium.org.uk

Portsoy Links Caravan Park
►►► 74%

tel: 01261 842695 **Links Rd, Portsoy AB45 2RQ**
email: contact@portsoylinks.co.uk
dir: *At Portsoy from A98 into Church St. 2nd right into Institute St (follow brown camping sign). At T-junct right, down slope to site.* grid ref: *NJ591660*

Taken into community ownership under the auspices of the Scottish Traditional Boats Festival, this is a lovely links-type site with stunning views across the bay.

LEISURE: 🏊 Indoor swimming pool 🏊 Outdoor swimming pool ⚑ Children's playground 🎯 Kid's club 🎾 Tennis court 🎱 Games room ▭ Separate TV room ⚙ golf course 🚤 Boats for hire 🎬 Cinema 🎵 Entertainment 🎣 Fishing ⛳ Mini golf 🏄 Watersports 💪 Gym 🏟️ Sports field Spa ♘ Stables
FACILITIES: 🛁 Bath 🚿 Shower ⚡ Electric shaver 🅿️ Hairdryer ❄️ Ice Pack Facility 🛂 Disabled facilities ☎ Public telephone 🛒 Shop on site or within 200yds 🏪 Mobile shop (calls at least 5 days a week) 🍖 BBQ area ⚞ Picnic area WiFi Wi-fi 🖥️ Internet access ♻ Recycling ❶ Tourist info 🐕 Dog exercise area

There is a large, safe fenced play area for smaller children and the toilet facilities are kept clean and well maintained. Portsoy is a typical small fishing port and has various eateries and shops; it is very convenient for visiting the other small fishing villages on the North East Scotland's Coastal Trail. 0.8 acre site. 51 touring pitches. 2 hardstandings. 6 seasonal pitches. Caravan pitches. Motorhome pitches. Tent pitches. 16 statics.

Open: 30 Mar-Oct **Last arrival:** 20.00hrs **Last departure:** noon

Pitches: 🚐 🚍 🛆

Leisure: ⚓

Facilities: 🌣 ᴕ 🞓 ⓦⓘⓕⓘ 𝟋

Services: 🔌 🔄 🛢

Within 3 miles: 🛝 🛒 🐾 🛶 🛒

Feughside Caravan Park
► ► ► ► 80%

tel: 01330 850669 **AB31 6NT**
email: info@feughsidecaravanpark.co.uk
dir: From Banchory take B974 to Strachan, 3m, take B976, 2m to Feughside Inn, follow site signs. **grid ref:** NO636913

A small, well maintained family-run site, set amongst mature trees and hedges and located five miles from Banchory. The site is ideally suited to those wishing for a peaceful location that is within easy reach of scenic Royal Deeside. 5.5 acre site. 27 touring pitches. 10 hardstandings. 12 seasonal pitches. Caravan pitches. Motorhome pitches. Tent pitches. 54 statics.

Open: Apr-Oct **Last arrival:** 22.00hrs **Last departure:** noon

Pitches: * 🚐 £18-£24 🚍 £18-£24 🛆 £10-£24

Leisure: ⚓

Facilities: 🌣 ⊙ ᴕ ❄ ᴕ ⓦⓘⓕⓘ 𝟋

Services: 🔌 🔄 🛢 ∅ 📍 🛝

Within 3 miles: 🛒 🐾 🛶 🔶 🔶 ♾

Notes: Quiet after 22.00hrs, no open fires. Dogs must be kept on leads & exercised off site.

AA Pubs & Restaurants nearby: Raemoir House Hotel, BANCHORY, AB31 4ED, 01330 824884

Turriff Caravan Park
► ► ► 75%

tel: 01888 562205 **Station Rd AB53 4ER**
email: turriffcaravanpark@btconnect.com
dir: On A947, S of Turriff. **grid ref:** NJ727492

Located on the outskirts of Turriff on the site of an old railway station, this site is owned by the local community. The pitches are level and the attractive landscaping is well maintained. The site also has a rally field. There is a large public park close to the site which has a boating pond and a large games park where the annual agricultural show is held. The town is only five minutes' walk through the park and has a good variety of shops to suit all tastes. This is an ideal base for touring rural Aberdeenshire and the nearby Moray coastline with its traditional fishing villages. 5 acre site. 70 touring pitches. 4 hardstandings. Caravan pitches. Motorhome pitches. Tent pitches. 14 statics.

Open: Apr-Oct **Last arrival:** 18.00hrs **Last departure:** noon

Pitches: 🚐 🚍 🛆

Leisure: ⚓ 🎱 **Facilities:** 🌣 ᴕ ᴕ ⓦⓘⓕⓘ ♻ 𝟋

Services: 🔌 🔄 🛢 🛝 **Within 3 miles:** 🛝 🐾 🔶 🔶

Notes: Dogs must be kept on leads.

AA Pubs & Restaurants nearby: The Redgarth, OLDMELDRUM, AB51 0DJ, 01651 872353

Riverview Caravan Park
► ► ► ► 82%

tel: 01382 535471 & 817979 **Marine Dr DD5 4NN**
email: info@riverview.co.uk
dir: From Dundee on A930 follow signs to Monifieth, past supermarket, right signed golf course, left under rail bridge. Site signed on left. **grid ref:** NO502322

A well-landscaped seaside site where the touring pitches are set in small areas; they are neatly divided by hedges and mature trees which are trimmed to allow light in; those on the beachfront enjoy excellent views. The site is a few minutes' walk from Monifieth and a pleasant stroll along the beachfront will take you to the nearby town of Broughty Ferry with its numerous boutique shops and other amenities. The site has good facilities, including a steam room and sauna and a gym. This is a good site for a traditional seaside holiday. 5.5 acre site. 49 touring pitches. 45 hardstandings. Caravan pitches. Motorhome pitches. 46 statics.

Open: Mar-Jan **Last arrival:** 22.00hrs **Last departure:** 12.30hrs

Pitches: 🚐 🚍

Leisure: 🎯 ⚓ 🎱 ♣ **Facilities:** 🌣 ⊙ ᴕ ᴕ 🕒 ᴕ ⓦⓘⓕⓘ 🖥 ♻ 𝟋

Services: 🔌 🔄 🛢 🔵 🛝 🛝 **Within 3 miles:** 🛝 🔶 🔶 🔶 ♾

Notes: Dogs must be kept on leads.

AA Pubs & Restaurants nearby: The Royal Arch Bar, BROUGHTY FERRY, DD5 2DS, 01382 779741

ARGYLL & BUTE

CARRADALE
Map 20 NR83

Carradale Bay Caravan Park
▶ ▶ ▶ 90%

tel: 01583 431665 **PA28 6QG**
email: info@carradalebay.com
dir: *A83 from Tarbert towards Campbeltown, left onto B842 (Carradale road), right onto B879. Site 0.5m.* **grid ref:** *NR815385*

A beautiful, natural site on the sea's edge with superb views over Kilbrannan Sound to the Isle of Arran. Pitches are landscaped into small bays broken up by shrubs and bushes, and backed by dunes close to the long sandy beach. The toilet facilities are appointed to a very high standard. An environmentally-aware site that requires the use of green toilet chemicals - available on the site. Lodges and static caravans for holiday hire. 8 acre site. 74 touring pitches. Caravan pitches. Motorhome pitches. Tent pitches. 15 statics.

Open: Apr-Sep **Last arrival:** 22.00hrs **Last departure:** noon

Pitches: 🚐 🚍 Å

Facilities: 🐾 ☉ 🎣 ✳ ⚫ ⚓ 🖼 🏪 🚻 🐕 📶 ♻ ❼

Services: 🔌 🗑

Within 3 miles: ⌊ ✦ 🎣 ⚓ 🏪 🗑 ∪

GLENDARUEL
Map 20 NR98

Places to visit
Benmore Botanic Garden, BENMORE, PA23 8QU, 01369 706261 www.rbge.org.uk

Glendaruel Caravan Park
▶ ▶ ▶ 79%

tel: 01369 820267 **PA22 3AB**
email: mail@glendaruelcaravanpark.com
dir: *A83 onto A815 to Strachur, 13m to site on A886. By ferry from Gourock to Dunoon take B836, then A886 for approx 4m N. (NB this route not recommended for towing vehicles - 1:5 uphill gradient on B836).* **grid ref:** *NR005865*

Glendaruel Gardens, with an arboretum, is the peaceful setting for this pleasant, well established wooded site in a valley surrounded by mountains. It is set back from the main road and screened by trees so that a peaceful stay is ensured. It has level grass and hardstanding pitches. A regular local bus service and a ferry at Portavadie (where there are retail outlets and eateries) make a day trip to the Mull of Kintyre a possibility. The Cowal Way, a long distance path, and a national cycle path pass the site. Static caravans and a camping lodge are available for hire. 6 acre site. 27 touring pitches. 15 hardstandings. 12 seasonal pitches. Caravan pitches. Motorhome pitches. Tent pitches. 32 statics. 1 wooden pod.

Open: Apr-Oct **Last arrival:** 22.00hrs **Last departure:** noon

Pitches: 🚐 🚍 Å 🏠

Leisure: ⚠ ⚙ **Facilities:** 🐾 ☉ 🎣 ✳ 🏪 🚻 🐕 📶 ♻ ❼

Services: 🔌 🗑 🛢 ⊘ T ⚱

Within 3 miles: 🎣 🏪 🗑

Notes: Dogs must be kept on leads. Sea trout & salmon fishing, woodland walks, 24-hour emergency phone.

OBAN
Map 20 NM82

Places to visit
Dunstaffnage Castle and Chapel, OBAN, PA37 1PZ, 01631 562465
www.historic-scotland.gov.uk

Bonawe Historic Iron Furnace, TAYNUILT, PA35 1JQ, 01866 822432
www.historic-scotland.gov.uk

Oban Caravan & Camping Park
▶ ▶ ▶ 80%

tel: 01631 562425 **Gallanachmore Farm, Gallanach Rd PA34 4QH**
email: info@obancaravanpark.com
dir: *From Oban centre follow signs for Mull Ferry. After terminal follow Gallanach signs. 2m to site.* **grid ref:** *NM831277*

Situated two miles from Oban this is a lovely site, with pleasant terraced areas that are separated by large swathes of well maintained grass and natural landscaping. Many pitches overlook the busy ferry route between Oban and the Isle of Colonsay. The site is convenient for the ferry terminal in Oban, and the train and bus stations provide easy access for public transport, making this an ideal site for both main holidays or for shorter stays. The owners have invested in new washroom facilities and have plans to install family rooms together with a new washroom block in the near future. Three well-equipped camping pods have been installed and located in an area that offers privacy. 15 acre site. 120 touring pitches. 35 hardstandings. 10 seasonal pitches. Caravan pitches. Motorhome pitches. Tent pitches. 17 statics. 3 wooden pods.

Open: Etr & Apr-Oct (rs Etr-end May & Sep-Oct shop closed) **Last arrival:** 23.00hrs
Last departure: noon

Pitches: * 🚐 £17-£20 🚍 £17-£20 Å £15-£17 🏠

Leisure: ⚠ ⚫ ▢

Facilities: 🐾 ☉ 🎣 ✳ ⚫ 🏪 🚻 🐕 📶 ❼

Services: 🔌 🗑 🛢 ⊘ T ⚱ ⬇

Within 3 miles: ⌊ ✦ 🎡 🎣 ⚓ 🏪 🗑 ∪

Notes: No commercial vehicles, no noise after 23.00hrs. Dogs must be kept on leads. Indoor kitchen for tent campers.

AA Pubs & Restaurants nearby: Coast, OBAN, PA34 5NT, 01631 569900

LEISURE: 🏊 Indoor swimming pool ⚲ Outdoor swimming pool ⚠ Children's playground 👟 Kid's club ⚾ Tennis court ◆ Games room ▢ Separate TV room ⌊ golf course ⚓ Boats for hire 🎬 Cinema 🎵 Entertainment 🎣 Fishing ◎ Mini golf ⚲ Watersports 🎡 Gym ⚙ Sports field Spa ∪ Stables

FACILITIES: 🛁 Bath 🐾 Shower ☉ Electric shaver 🎣 Hairdryer ✳ Ice Pack Facility ⚫ Disabled facilities ⚓ Public telephone 🏪 Shop on site or within 200yds 🛒 Mobile shop (calls at least 5 days a week) 🍴 BBQ area 🚻 Picnic area 📶 Wi-fi ▦ Internet access ♻ Recycling ❼ Tourist info 🐕 Dog exercise area

NORTH AYRSHIRE

SALTCOATS   Map 20 NS24

Places to visit

North Ayrshire Heritage Centre, SALTCOATS, KA21 5AA, 01294 464174
www.north-ayrshire.gov.uk/museums

Kelburn Castle and Country Centre, LARGS, KA29 0BE, 01475 568685
www.kelburnestate.com

Great for kids: Scottish Maritime Museum, IRVINE, KA12 8QE, 01294 278283
www.scottishmaritimemuseum.org

Sandylands
HOLIDAY CENTRE 80%

tel: 0871 664 9767 & 01294 469411 **James Miller Crescent, Auchenharvie
Park KA21 5JN**
email: sandylands@park-resorts.com
dir: *From Glasgow take M77 & A77 to Kilmarnock, A71 towards Irvine. Follow signs for
Ardrossan. Take A78 follow Stevenston signs. Through Stevenston, past Auchenharvie
Leisure Centre, 1st left follow signs to site on left.* **grid ref:** *NS258412*

A holiday centre with on-site recreational and entertainment facilities for all ages,
including an indoor swimming pool. With good transport links and easy access to
the ferry terminal in Ardrossan, day trips to the Isle of Arran are possible. The smart
amenity block provides touring customers with modern facilities. There is a links
golf course nearby. 55 acre site. 20 touring pitches. 20 hardstandings. Caravan
pitches. Motorhome pitches. Tent pitches. 438 statics.

Open: Apr-Oct **Last arrival:** mdnt **Last departure:** 10.00hrs

Pitches: ⌂ ⌂ ▲

Leisure: ▨ ⌂ ⌂ ⌂ ♫

Facilities: ⌂ ⌂ ⌂ ⌂ ⌂ ⌂ WiFi ⌂ ⌂ ⌂

Services: ⌂ ⌂ ⌂ ⌂ ⌂ ⌂

Within 3 miles: ⌂ ⌂ ⌂ ⌂ ⌂

Notes: Dogs must be kept on leads.

▶ **Find out about staying
at a Holiday Centre
in our feature on page 26**

SOUTH AYRSHIRE

AYR   Map 20 NS32

Places to visit

Robert Burns Birthplace Museum, ALLOWAY, KA7 4PQ, 0844 493 2601
www.burnsmuseum.org.uk

Great for kids: Heads of Ayr Farm Park, ALLOWAY, KA7 4LD, 01292 441210
www.headsofayrfarmpark.co.uk

Craig Tara Holiday Park
HOLIDAY CENTRE 82%

tel: 0871 231 0866 & 01292 265141 **KA7 4LB**
email: craigtara@haven.com **web:** www.haven.com/craigtara
dir: *A77 towards Stranraer, 2nd right after Bankfield rdbt. Follow signs for A719
& to park.* **grid ref:** *NS300184*

A large, well-maintained holiday centre with on-site entertainment and sporting
facilities to suit all ages. The touring area is set apart from the main complex at
the entrance to the park, and campers can use all the facilities, including a water
world, soft play areas, sports zone, show bars, and supermarket with in-house
bakery. There is direct access from the park to the beach and a bus service to Ayr.
213 acre site. 45 touring pitches. 45 hardstandings. Caravan pitches. Motorhome
pitches. 1100 statics.

Open: mid Mar-end Oct (rs mid Mar-May & Sep-Oct some facilities may be
limited) **Last arrival:** 20.00hrs **Last departure:** 10.00hrs

Pitches: ⌂ ⌂

AYR *continued*

Leisure: 🏊🏕️🎣🎯🎵🎶

Facilities: 🍴⊙🚿🚻🛁🔌🛒🏪📶♻️ℹ️

Services: 🔌🗑️🚽🚿💧🍽️🛒

Within 3 miles: ⛳🎡🎣◎🏪🛒⛴️

Notes: No commercial vehicles, no bookings by persons under 21yrs unless a family booking, max 2 dogs per booking, certain dog breeds banned. Dogs must be kept on leads.

AA Pubs & Restaurants nearby: Fairfield House Hotel, AYR, KA7 2AS, 01292 267461

The Kirkton Inn, DALRYMPLE, KA6 6DF, 01292 560241

See advert below

BARRHILL
Map 20 NX28

Barrhill Holiday Park
▶▶▶▶ 79%

tel: 01465 821355 **KA26 0PZ**
email: barrhillholidaypark@gmail.com
dir: On A714 Newton Stewart to Girvan road. 1m N of Barrhill. **grid ref:** NX216835

A small, friendly park in a tranquil rural location, screened from the A714 by trees. The park is terraced and well landscaped, and a high quality amenity block includes disabled facilities. The local bus to Girvan stops at the site entrance. 6 acre site. 30 touring pitches. 30 hardstandings. Caravan pitches. Motorhome pitches. Tent pitches. 42 statics.

Open: Mar-Jan **Last arrival:** 22.00hrs **Last departure:** 10.00hrs

Pitches: * 🚐 £15 🚐 £15 🏕️ £7-£15

Leisure: 🏕️ **Facilities:** 🍴⊙🏪🚿🛁🔌🛒♻️ℹ️

Services: 🔌🗑️💧🚽🛒

Within 3 miles: 🎣🛒

Notes: 🐕 No noise after 23.00hrs.

Places to visit

Robert Burns Birthplace Museum, ALLOWAY, KA7 4PQ, 0844 493 2601
www.burnsmuseum.org.uk

Sundrum Castle Holiday Park
HOLIDAY CENTRE 82%

GOLD

tel: 0844 335 3756 **KA6 5JH**
email: touringandcamping@parkdeanholidays.com
dir: From A77 (E of Ayr) take A70 signed Coylton. Approx 4m left at site sign.
grid ref: NS405208

A large family holiday park, in rolling countryside and just a 10-minute drive from the centre of Ayr, with plenty of on-site entertainment. Leisure facilities include an indoor swimming pool complex with flume, crazy golf, clubs for young children and teenagers. The touring pitch areas and amenity block have been appointed to a high standard. 30 acre site. 30 touring pitches. Caravan pitches. Motorhome pitches. Tent pitches. 247 statics.

Open: mid Mar-Oct **Last arrival:** 21.00hrs **Last departure:** 10.00hrs

Pitches: 🚐🚐🏕️

Leisure: 🏊🏕️🎣🎱🖥️🎵

Facilities: 🍴⊙🏪🔌🛒📶

Services: 🔌🗑️🚽💧🍽️🛒�

Within 3 miles: ⛳🎡🎣◎🏪🛒⛴️

Notes: No cars by tents. Dogs must be kept on leads. Nature trail.

AA Pubs & Restaurants nearby: Enterkine Country House, AYR, KA6 5AL, 01292 520580

LEISURE: 🏊 Indoor swimming pool 🏊 Outdoor swimming pool 🎠 Children's playground 👶 Kid's club 🎾 Tennis court 🎱 Games room 📺 Separate TV room 🏌️ golf course ⛵ Boats for hire 🎬 Cinema 🎵 Entertainment 🎣 Fishing ◎ Mini golf 🏄 Watersports 💪 Gym ⚽ Sports field Spa ⛴️ Stables
FACILITIES: 🛁 Bath 🚿 Shower ⊙ Electric shaver 🏪 Hairdryer ✳️ Ice Pack Facility 🔌 Disabled facilities 🕐 Public telephone 🛒 Shop on site or within 200yds 🏪 Mobile shop (calls at least 5 days a week) 🍖 BBQ area 🌲 Picnic area 📶 Wi-fi 🖥️ Internet access ♻️ Recycling ℹ️ Tourist info 🐕 Dog exercise area

Map 20 NX19

Turnberry Holiday Park
HOLIDAY HOME PARK 77%

BRONZE

tel: 01655 331288 **KA26 9JW**
email: enquiries@turnberryholidaypark.co.uk **web:** www.turnberryholidaypark.co.uk
dir: *Site signed from A77 between Turnberry & Girvan. 250mtrs to site adjacent to Dowhill Farm.* **grid ref:** *NS203033*

Situated in beautiful South Ayrshire with views of the Firth of Clyde and the iconic Ailsa Craig, this 26-acre park is between the busy seaside town of Ayr and the fishing town of Girvan. The many tourist attractions in the area include Turnberry Golf Course, The Burns Heritage Centre, Maidens and Culzean Castle and Country Park. The park is set in open farmland and continues to undergo major improvements. The Ailsa Bar provides family-centred entertainment as well as a café serving good food. There is a swimming pool, reception and sales office. There are 205 holiday homes, 9 statics, and a 3-bedroom chalet for hire.

Open: Mar- 4 Jan

Change over day: Mon, Fri & Sat

Arrival and departure times: Please contact the site

Statics: 15 Sleeps 8 Bedrms 2-3 Bathrms 1-2 (inc en suite) Toilets 1-2 Microwave Freezer TV Sky/FTV DVD Modem/Wi-fi Linen inc Elec inc Gas inc Grass area Low season £115-£398 High season £238-£573

Children: Cots Highchair **Dogs:** 2 on leads

Leisure: Cycle hire

Within 3 miles: Spa

See advert below

PITCHES: Caravans ⊑ Motorhomes ⚠ Tents ⌂ Glamping-style accommodation **SERVICES:** Electric hook up Launderette Licensed bar Calor Gas Camping Gaz T Toilet fluid Café/Restaurant Fast Food/Takeaway Battery charging Baby care Motorvan service point
ABBREVIATIONS: BH/bank hols – bank holidays Etr – Easter Spring BH – Spring Bank Holiday fr – from hrs – hours m – mile mdnt – midnight
rdbt – roundabout rs – restricted service wk – week wknd – weekend x-rds – cross roads No credit or debit cards No dogs Children of all ages accepted

DUMFRIES & GALLOWAY

ANNAN
Map 21 NY16

Places to visit

Ruthwell Cross, RUTHWELL, 0131 550 7612 www.historic-scotland.gov.uk

Great for kids: Caerlaverock Castle, CAERLAVEROCK, DG1 4RU, 01387 770244 www.historic-scotland.gov.uk

Galabank Caravan & Camping Group
▶▶ 74%

tel: 01461 203539 & 07999 344520 **North St DG12 5DQ**
email: margaret.ramage@hotmail.com
dir: *Enter site via North Street.* **grid ref:** *NY192676*

A tidy, well-maintained grassy little park with spotless facilities close to the centre of town but with pleasant rural views, and skirted by the River Annan. 1 acre site. 30 touring pitches. Caravan pitches. Motorhome pitches. Tent pitches.

Open: Mar-Oct **Last departure:** noon

Pitches: 🚐 🚗 ▲

Facilities: 🛆⊙🅿🛍🗚

Services: 🖿

Within 3 miles: 🛆🖽🗷🛍🔾

Notes: 🐾 Dogs must be kept on leads. Social club adjacent.

AA Pubs & Restaurants nearby: Del Amitri Restaurant, ANNAN, DG12 6DJ, 01461 201999

BRIGHOUSE BAY
Map 20 NX64

Places to visit

MacLellan's Castle, KIRKCUDBRIGHT, DG6 4JD, 01557 331856 www.historic-scotland.gov.uk

Broughton House & Garden, KIRKCUDBRIGHT, DG6 4JX, 0844 493 2246 www.nts.org.uk/Property/Broughton-House-and-Garden

Great for kids: Galloway Wildlife Conservation Park, KIRKCUDBRIGHT, DG6 4XX, 01557 331645 www.gallowaywildlife.co.uk

PREMIER PARK

Brighouse Bay Holiday Park
▶▶▶▶▶ 87%

GOLD

tel: 01557 870267 **DG6 4TS**
email: info@gillespie-leisure.co.uk
dir: *From Gatehouse of Fleet take A755 towards Kirkcudbright, onto B727 (signed Borgue). Or from Kirkcudbright take A755 onto B727. Site signed in 3m.* **grid ref:** *NX628453*

This top class park has a country club feel and enjoys a marvellous coastal setting adjacent to the beach and has superb views. Pitches have been imaginatively sculpted into the meadowland, where stone walls and hedges blend in with the site's mature trees. These features, together with the large range of leisure activities, make this an excellent park for families who enjoy an active holiday. Many of the facilities are at an extra charge. A range of self-catering units is available for hire. 120 acre site. 190 touring pitches. 100 hardstandings. 50 seasonal pitches. Caravan pitches. Motorhome pitches. Tent pitches. 275 statics.

Open: all year (rs Outside school hols leisure club closed Mon-Wed inclusive)
Last arrival: 20.00hrs **Last departure:** 11.30hrs

Pitches: 🚐 🚗 ▲

Leisure: 🏊🏌🏐🎣🎵🎿

Facilities: 🛆🛆⊙🅿✳🛆🕒🛍🗚🐾📶🖥♻🛈

Services: 🖿🛢🔌🛢🗷🗵🍴🛒🛍🛒🛆

Within 3 miles: 🛆🗷◎🛍🔾

Notes: Dogs must be kept on leads. Mini golf, 18-hole golf, PGA professional on site, horse riding, outdoor bowling green, jacuzzi, slipway, boating pond, coarse fishing, sea angling.

AA Pubs & Restaurants nearby: Selkirk Arms Hotel, KIRKCUDBRIGHT, DG6 4JG, 01557 330402

CREETOWN
Map 20 NX46

Places to visit

Cardoness Castle, CARDONESS CASTLE, DG7 2EH, 01557 814427 www.historic-scotland.gov.uk

Great for kids: Creetown Gem Rock Museum, CREETOWN, DG8 7HJ, 01671 820357 www.gemrock.net

PREMIER PARK

Castle Cary Holiday Park
▶▶▶▶▶ 79%

🏰

tel: 01671 820264 **DG8 7DQ**
email: enquiries@castlecarypark.f9.co.uk **web:** www.castlecary-caravans.com
dir: *Signed with direct access from A75, 0.5m S of village.* **grid ref:** *NX475576*

This attractive site in the grounds of Cassencarie House is sheltered by woodlands, and faces south towards Wigtown Bay. The park is in a secluded location with beautiful landscaping and excellent facilities. The bar/restaurant is housed in part of an old castle, and enjoys extensive views over the River Cree estuary. 12 acre site. 50 touring pitches. 50 hardstandings. Caravan pitches. Motorhome pitches. Tent pitches. 26 statics. 2 bell tents/yurts.

Open: all year (rs Oct-Mar reception/shop, no heated outdoor pool)
Last arrival: anytime **Last departure:** noon

Pitches: * 🚐 £21-£25 🚗 £21-£25 ▲ £16.15-£20.15 🏰

Leisure: 🏊🏊🏐🎣🛆

Facilities: 🛆🛆⊙🅿✳🛆🕒🛍🗚🐾📶🖥🛈

Services: 🖿🛢🔌🛢🗷🗵🍴🛒🛍🛒🛆

Within 3 miles: 🛆🖽🗷◎🛆🛍🔾

Notes: Dogs must be kept on leads. Crazy golf, coarse fishing, full size football pitch.

AA Pubs & Restaurants nearby: Creebridge House Hotel, NEWTON STEWART, DG8 6NP, 01671 402121

Cally Palace Hotel, GATEHOUSE OF FLEET, DG7 2DL, 01557 814341

Kirroughtree House, NEWTON STEWART, DG8 6AN, 01671 402141

LEISURE: 🏊 Indoor swimming pool 🏊 Outdoor swimming pool 🏐 Children's playground 🎣 Kid's club 🎾 Tennis court 🎣 Games room 🖵 Separate TV room 🏌 golf course 🚣 Boats for hire 🎬 Cinema 🎵 Entertainment 🎣 Fishing ◎ Mini golf 🎿 Watersports 🏋 Gym 🏐 Sports field Spa 🔾 Stables
FACILITIES: 🛆 Bath 🛆 Shower ⊙ Electric shaver 🅿 Hairdryer ✳ Ice Pack Facility 🛆 Disabled facilities 🕒 Public telephone 🛍 Shop on site or within 200yds 🛍 Mobile shop (calls at least 5 days a week) 🗚 BBQ area 🗚 Picnic area 📶 Wi-fi 🖥 Internet access ♻ Recycling 🛈 Tourist info 🐾 Dog exercise area

DALBEATTIE
Map 21 NX86

Places to visit

Threave Garden & Estate, CASTLE DOUGLAS, DG7 1RX, 0844 493 2245
www.nts.org.uk/Property/Threave-Estate

Orchardton Tower, PALNACKIE www.historic-scotland.gov.uk

Glenearly Caravan Park
►►►► 85%

tel: 01556 611393 **DG5 4NE**
email: glenearlycaravan@btconnect.com **web:** www.glenearlycaravanpark.co.uk
dir: From Dumfries take A711 towards Dalbeattie. Site entrance after Edingham Farm on right (200yds before boundary sign). **grid ref:** NX838628

An excellent small park set in open countryside with panoramic views of Long Fell, Maidenpap and Dalbeattie Forest. The park is located in 84 beautiful acres of farmland which visitors are invited to enjoy. The attention to detail here is of the highest standard, and this is most notable in the presentation of the amenity block. There is a regular bus service on the main road, making trips to the surrounding towns easy, and Dalbeattie is only a 10-minute walk away. The site is also convenient for visiting the Solway coast which provides good beaches and a variety of walks. Static holiday caravans are for hire. 10 acre site. 39 touring pitches. 33 hardstandings. Caravan pitches. Motorhome pitches. Tent pitches. 74 statics.

Open: all year **Last arrival:** 19.00hrs **Last departure:** noon
Pitches: * ⛺ £15.50-£17.50 ⛺ £15.50-£17.50 ▲ £15.50-£17.50
Leisure: 🅰 🔍
Facilities: 🏵⊙ℱ✳❄🕐🍴♻❶
Services: 🔌🗑 🔋➡🔧
Within 3 miles: ↕🚶ℱ◎⛷🗑🗑∪
Notes: No commercial vehicles. Dogs must be kept on leads.

ECCLEFECHAN
Map 21 NY17

Places to visit

Robert Burns House, DUMFRIES, DG1 2PS, 01387 255297 www.dumgal.gov.uk

Old Bridge House Museum, DUMFRIES, DG2 7BE, 01387 256904 www.dumgal.gov.uk

Great for kids: Dumfries Museum & Camera Obscura, DUMFRIES, DG2 7SW, 01387 253374 www.dumgal.gov.uk/museums

ECCLEFECHAN
Map 21 NY17

PREMIER PARK

Hoddom Castle Caravan Park
►►►►► 82%

tel: 01576 300251 **Hoddom DG11 1AS**
email: hoddomcastle@aol.com
dir: M74 junct 19, follow signs to site. From A75, W of Annan, take B723 for 5m, follow signs to site. **grid ref:** NY154729

A lovely, peaceful family park located close to Annan, with its large range of shops and eateries. The three amenity blocks, one being next to the reception, in part of the old castle buildings. The female showers have been updated to provide very good, modern amenities, and are indicative of the plans the owner has to modernise other facilities. There are extensive grounds, with many walks including the Annan Way which borders the River Annan. The park is neatly divided into statics, seasonal tourers and touring pitches with a large area for tents and 11 attractive wooden pods for hire. Fishing, a nine-hole golf course and a large children's play area are available; the small restaurant and café are open daily. 28 acre site. 200 touring pitches. 63 hardstandings. 94 seasonal pitches. Caravan pitches. Motorhome pitches. Tent pitches. 54 statics. 11 wooden pods.

Open: Etr or Apr-Oct **Last arrival:** 21.00hrs **Last departure:** 13.00hrs
Pitches: * ⛺ £16.50-£23.50 ⛺ £16.50-£23.50 ▲ £13.50-£23.50 🏠
Leisure: 🅰🔍♫♪
Facilities: 🏵🏵⊙ℱ✳❄🕐🗑🍴📶🖥♻❶
Services: 🔌🗑 🔋🔧⌇🔋T🍴🔋🔧
Within 3 miles: ↕ℱ◎🗑🗑
Notes: No electric scooters, no gazebos, no fires, no noise after mdnt. Dogs must be kept on leads.
AA Pubs & Restaurants nearby: Del Amitri Restaurant, ANNAN, DG12 6DJ, 01461 201999

GATEHOUSE OF FLEET
Map 20 NX55

Places to visit

MacLellan's Castle, KIRKCUDBRIGHT, DG6 4JD, 01557 331856 www.historic-scotland.gov.uk

Great for kids: Galloway Wildlife Conservation Park, KIRKCUDBRIGHT, DG6 4XX, 01557 331645 www.gallowaywildlife.co.uk

Auchenlarie Holiday Park
HOLIDAY CENTRE 89%

tel: 01556 506200 & 206201 **DG7 2EX**
email: enquiries@auchenlarie.co.uk
dir: Direct access from A75, 5m W of Gatehouse of Fleet. **grid ref:** NX536522

A well-organised family park set on cliffs overlooking Wigtown Bay, with its own sandy beach. The tenting area, in sloping grass surrounded by mature trees, has its own sanitary facilities, while the marked caravan pitches are in paddocks, with open views and the provision of high quality toilets. The leisure centre includes a swimming pool, gym, solarium and sports hall. There are six self-catering holiday
continued

PITCHES: ⛺ Caravans ⛺ Motorhomes ▲ Tents 🏠 Glamping-style accommodation **SERVICES:** 🔌 Electric hook up 🗑 Launderette 🍴 Licensed bar 🔋 Calor Gas ⌀ Camping Gaz T Toilet fluid 🍴 Café/Restaurant 🔧 Fast Food/Takeaway 🔋 Battery charging ➡ Baby care 🔧 Motorvan service point **ABBREVIATIONS:** BH/bank hols – bank holidays Etr – Easter Spring BH – Spring Bank Holiday fr – from hrs – hours m – mile mdnt – midnight rdbt – roundabout rs – restricted service wk – week wknd – weekend x-rds – cross roads ⊘ No credit or debit cards ⊗ No dogs 👪 Children of all ages accepted

GATEHOUSE OF FLEET *continued*

apartments for let. 32 acre site. 49 touring pitches. 52 hardstandings. Caravan pitches. Motorhome pitches. Tent pitches. 400 statics.

Open: Mar-Oct **Last arrival:** 20.00hrs **Last departure:** noon

Pitches: * 🚐 £20-£25 🚍 £20-£25 ⛺ £20-£25

Leisure: 🏊‍♀️ 🎣 🎮 💆 🎱 🎵

Facilities: 🏠 ⊙ ℙ ✳ ♿ 🕐 🛁 🚻 🪮 📶 🖥 ♻ ❶

Services: 🚐 🔋 📶 🛢 🍽 🛒 🗑 ⛲

Within 3 miles: ⌀ ℒ ◎ 🛒 ⚓ ∪

Notes: Dogs must be kept on leads. Crazy golf, teenagers' zone, baby changing facilities.

AA Pubs & Restaurants nearby: Cally Palace Hotel, GATEHOUSE OF FLEET, DG7 2DL, 01557 814341

Anwoth Caravan Site
►►►► 79%

tel: 01557 814333 & 01556 506200 **DG7 2JU**
email: enquiries@auchenlarie.co.uk
dir: *From A75 into Gatehouse of Fleet, site on right towards Stranraer. Signed from town centre.* **grid ref:** *NX595563*

A very high quality park in a peaceful sheltered setting within easy walking distance of the village, ideally placed for exploring the scenic hills, valleys and coastline. Grass, hardstanding and fully serviced pitches are available and guests may use the leisure facilities at the sister site, Auchenlarie Holiday Park. 2 acre site. 28 touring pitches. 13 hardstandings. Caravan pitches. Motorhome pitches. Tent pitches. 44 statics.

Open: Mar-Oct **Last arrival:** 20.00hrs **Last departure:** noon

Pitches: * 🚐 £12.50-£15 🚍 £12.50-£15 ⛺ £12.50-£15

Facilities: 🛁 🏠 ⊙ ℙ ✳ ♿ 🕐 🚻 📶 ♻ ❶

Services: 🚐 🔋 🛢 ⛲

Within 3 miles: ⌀ ℒ 🛒 🔋

Notes: Dogs must be kept on leads.

AA Pubs & Restaurants nearby: Cally Palace Hotel, GATEHOUSE OF FLEET, DG7 2DL, 01557 814341

GRETNA

Places to visit

Carlisle Cathedral, CARLISLE, CA3 8TZ, 01228 548071
www.carlislecathedral.org.uk

Tullie House Museum & Art Gallery Trust, CARLISLE, CA3 8TP, 01228 618718
www.tulliehouse.co.uk

Great for kids: Carlisle Castle, CARLISLE, CA3 8UR, 01228 591992
www.english-heritage.org.uk/daysout/properties/carlisle-castle

GRETNA   Map 21 NY36

Braids Caravan Park
►►►► 78%

tel: 01461 337409 **Annan Rd DG16 5DQ**
email: enquiries@thebraidscaravanpark.co.uk
dir: *On B721, 0.5m from village on right, towards Annan.* **grid ref:** *NY313674*

A very well-maintained park conveniently located on the outskirts of Gretna village. Within walking distance is Gretna Gateway Outlet Village, and Gretna Green with the World Famous Old Blacksmith's Shop is nearby. It proves a convenient stop-over for anyone travelling to and from both the north of Scotland, and Northern Ireland (via the ferry at Stranraer). The park has first-class toilet facilities and generously-sized all-weather pitches. Please note that tents are not accepted. A rally field and a meeting room are available. 5 acre site. 50 touring pitches. 42 hardstandings. Caravan pitches. Motorhome pitches.

Open: all year **Last arrival:** 21.00hrs **Last departure:** noon

Pitches: * 🚐 £16-£20 🚍 £16-£20

Facilities: 🏠 ⊙ ℙ ✳ ♿ ♻   **Services:** 🚐 🔋 ❚ 🍽 ⛲   **Within 3 miles:** 🔋

Notes: Latest arrival time 20.00hrs in winter. Dogs must be kept on leads.

AA Pubs & Restaurants nearby: Smiths at Gretna Green, GRETNA, DG16 5EA, 01461 337007

King Robert the Bruce's Cave Caravan & Camping Park
►►►► 76%

tel: 01461 800285 & 07779 138694 **Cove Estate, Kirkpatrick Fleming DG11 3AT**
email: enquiries@brucescave.co.uk **web:** www.brucescave.co.uk
dir: *Exit A74(M) junct 21 for Kirkpatrick Fleming, follow N through village, pass Station Inn, left at Bruce's Court. Over rail crossing to site.* **grid ref:** *NY266705*

The lovely wooded grounds of an old castle and mansion are the setting for this pleasant park. The mature woodland is a haven for wildlife, there is a riverside walk to Robert the Bruce's Cave and on-site coarse fishing is available. A toilet block with en suite facilities is especially useful to families. The site is convenient for the M74 and there is a good local bus service available nearby; the site is also on a National Cycle Route. 80 acre site. 75 touring pitches. 60 hardstandings. Caravan pitches. Motorhome pitches. Tent pitches. 35 statics.

Open: Apr-Nov (rs Nov shop closed, water restriction) **Last arrival:** 22.00hrs **Last departure:** 16.00hrs

Pitches: 🚐 £14-£20 🚍 £14-£20 ⛺ £10-£25

Leisure: ⚠ 🎣 ⚓ 📺   **Facilities:** 🛁 🏠 ⊙ ℙ ✳ ♿ 🕐 🛁 🚻 🪮 📶 🖥 ♻ ❶

LEISURE: 🏊‍♀️ Indoor swimming pool 🏊 Outdoor swimming pool ⚠ Children's playground 💆 Kid's club 🎾 Tennis court 🎱 Games room 📺 Separate TV room
⛳ golf course 🚣 Boats for hire 🎦 Cinema 🎵 Entertainment 🎣 Fishing ◎ Mini golf 🏄 Watersports 🏋 Gym ⚽ Sports field Spa ∪ Stables
FACILITIES: 🛁 Bath 🏠 Shower ⊙ Electric shaver ℙ Hairdryer ✳ Ice Pack Facility ♿ Disabled facilities 🕐 Public telephone 🛒 Shop on site or within 200yds
🚐 Mobile shop (calls at least 5 days a week) 🍽 BBQ area 🪮 Picnic area 📶 Wi-fi 🖥 Internet access ♻ Recycling ❶ Tourist info 🪮 Dog exercise area

Services: 🔌🔲🍺🚿T🚽🛒⬇ Within 3 miles: ⬆目🐾🚲🎣👣🛥∪

Notes: No noise after 23.00hrs. Dogs must be kept on leads. BMX bike hire, first aid available.

AA Pubs & Restaurants nearby: Smiths at Gretna Green, GRETNA, DG16 5EA, 01461 337007

KIPPFORD	Map 21 NX85

Places to visit

Orchardton Tower, PALNACKIE www.historic-scotland.gov.uk

Kippford Holiday Park
▶▶▶78%

Best of British — GOLD

tel: 01556 620636 **DG5 4LF**
email: info@kippfordholidaypark.co.uk **web:** www.kippfordholidaypark.co.uk
dir: *From Dumfries take A711 to Dalbeattie, left onto A710 (Solway coast road) for 3.5m. Park 200yds beyond Kippford turn on right.* **grid ref:** NX844564

An attractively landscaped park set in hilly countryside close to the Urr Water estuary and a sand and shingle beach, and with spectacular views. The level touring pitches are on grassed hardstands with private garden areas, and many are fully serviced; and there are attractive lodges for hire. The Doon Hill and woodland walks separate the park from the lovely village of Kippford. Red squirrels can be spotted in the woods, and opportunities to fish and to play golf are very close by. 18 acre site. 45 touring pitches. 35 hardstandings. 15 seasonal pitches. Caravan pitches. Motorhome pitches. Tent pitches. 119 statics.

Open: all year **Last arrival:** 21.30hrs **Last departure:** noon
Pitches: 🚐 £22-£29 🚍 £22-£29 ▲ £20-£27

Leisure: ⚑🎱
Facilities: 🔦⊙📶🍴✂&🛁🎣♿🐕📶🖥♻𝒊
Services: 🔌🔲🍺🚿T🚽⬇
Within 3 miles: ⬆🐾◎🎣👣🛥∪

Notes: No camp fires. Dogs must be kept on leads.

AA Pubs & Restaurants nearby: Balcary Bay Hotel, AUCHENCAIRN, DG7 1QZ, 01556 640217

KIRKCUDBRIGHT	Map 20 NX65

Places to visit

The Stewartry Museum, KIRKCUDBRIGHT, DG6 4AQ, 01557 331643 www.dumgal.gov.uk/museums

Tolbooth Art Centre, KIRKCUDBRIGHT, DG6 4JL, 01557 331556 www.dumgal.gov.uk/museums

Great for kids: Broughton House & Garden, KIRKCUDBRIGHT, DG6 4JX, 0844 493 2246 www.nts.org.uk/Property/Broughton-House-and-Garden

---

PREMIER PARK

Seaward Caravan Park
▶▶▶▶▶78%

tel: 01557 870267 & 331079 **Dhoon Bay DG6 4TJ**
email: info@gillespie-leisure.co.uk
dir: *2m SW of Kirkcudbright take A755 W then B727 signed Borgue.* **grid ref:** NX662492

An attractive park with outstanding views over Kirkcudbright Bay which forms part of the Dee Estuary. Access to a sandy cove with rock pools is just across the road. Facilities are well organised and neatly kept, and the park offers a very peaceful atmosphere. The leisure facilities at the other Gillespie Parks are available to visitors to Seaward Caravan Park. 23 acre site. 25 touring pitches. 3 seasonal pitches. Caravan pitches. Motorhome pitches. Tent pitches. 54 statics.

Open: Mar-Oct (rs Mar-until Spring BH & Sep-Oct swimming pool closed)
Last arrival: 20.00hrs **Last departure:** 11.30hrs

Pitches: 🚐🚍▲
Leisure: 🏊⚑🎱
Facilities: 🛁🔦⊙📶🍴✂&🎣♿🐕📶𝒊
Services: 🔌🔲🍺🚿T
Within 3 miles: ⬆🐾◎👣🛥∪

Notes: Dogs must be kept on leads. Mini golf, sea angling.

AA Pubs & Restaurants nearby: Selkirk Arms Hotel, KIRKCUDBRIGHT, DG6 4JG, 01557 330402

PITCHES: 🚐 Caravans 🚍 Motorhomes ▲ Tents 🏠 Glamping-style accommodation **SERVICES:** 🔌 Electric hook up 🔲 Launderette 🍺 Licensed bar 🍾 Calor Gas 🛢 Camping Gaz T Toilet fluid 🍴 Café/Restaurant 🍟 Fast Food/Takeaway 🚼 Battery charging 🚼 Baby care ⬇ Motorvan service point **ABBREVIATIONS:** BH/bank hols – bank holidays Etr – Easter Spring BH – Spring Bank Holiday fr – from hrs – hours m – mile mdnt – midnight rdbt – roundabout rs – restricted service wk – week wknd – weekend x-rds – cross roads 🚫 No credit or debit cards 🚫 No dogs 👫 Children of all ages accepted

LANGHOLM
Map 21 NY38

Places to visit

Hermitage Castle, HERMITAGE, TD9 0LU, 01387 376222
www.historic-scotland.gov.uk

Ewes Water Caravan & Camping Park
►►66%

tel: 013873 80386 **Milntown DG13 0BG**
dir: *Access directly from A7 approx 0.5m N of Langholm. Site in Langholm Rugby Club.*
grid ref: *NY365855*

On the banks of the River Esk, this attractive park lies in a sheltered wooded valley close to an unspoilt Borders' town. 2 acre site. 24 touring pitches. Caravan pitches. Motorhome pitches. Tent pitches.

Open: Apr-Sep **Last departure:** noon

Pitches: ⊕ ⊕ Å

Facilities: ⬈⊙✳⬟⬤⬟⬈⬈ **Services:** ⬤⬟⬟⬟

Within 3 miles: ⬟⬟⬟ **Notes:** ⬤ Large playing area.

LOCKERBIE

See Ecclefechan

NEWTON STEWART
Map 20 NX46

Places to visit

Kirroughtree Visitor Centre, NEWTON STEWART, DG8 7BE, 01671 402165
www.forestry.gov.uk/gallowayforestpark

Creebridge Caravan Park
►►►67%

tel: 01671 402324 & 402432 **Minnigaff DG8 6AJ**
email: john_sharples@btconnect.com
dir: *0.25m E of Newton Stewart at Minnigaff on bypass, signed off A75.*
grid ref: *NX415656*

A small family-owned site a short walk from the town's amenities. The site is surrounded by mature trees, and the toilet facilities are clean and functional. 5.5 acre site. 26 touring pitches. 9 hardstandings. Caravan pitches. Motorhome pitches. Tent pitches. 60 statics.

Open: all year (rs Mar only one toilet block open) **Last arrival:** 20.00hrs
Last departure: 10.30hrs

Pitches: * ⊕ £16 ⊕ £16 Å £14

Leisure: ⬟

Facilities: ⬈⊙⬟✳⬟⬟⬟⬟⬈⬟⬟

Services: ⬤⬟⬟⬟

Within 3 miles: ⬟⬟⬟⬟⬟⬟⬟

Notes: Dogs must be kept on leads. Security lighting.

AA Pubs & Restaurants nearby: Creebridge House Hotel, NEWTON STEWART, DG8 6NP, 01671 402121

Kirroughtree House, NEWTON STEWART, DG8 6AN, 01671 402141

PALNACKIE
Map 21 NX85

Places to visit

Orchardton Tower, PALNACKIE www.historic-scotland.gov.uk

Barlochan Caravan Park
►►►79%

tel: 01556 600256 & 01557 870267 **DG7 1PF**
email: info@gillespie-leisure.co.uk
dir: *On A711, Dalbeattie to Auchencaim rd. Signed before Palnackie.* **grid ref:** *NX819572*

A small terraced park with quiet landscaped pitches in a level area backed by rhododendron bushes. There are spectacular views over the River Urr estuary, and the park has its own coarse fishing loch nearby. The amenity block includes combined wash facilities. The leisure facilities at Brighouse Bay are available to visitors. 9 acre site. 20 touring pitches. 10 hardstandings. 6 seasonal pitches. Caravan pitches. Motorhome pitches. Tent pitches. 65 statics.

Open: Apr-Oct (rs Apr-until Spring BH & Sep-Oct swimming pool closed)
Last arrival: 20.00hrs **Last departure:** 11.30hrs

Pitches: ⊕ ⊕ Å

Leisure: ⬟⬟⬤⬟ **Facilities:** ⬈⬟⬟✳⬟⬟⬈⬈⬟⬟⬟⬟

Services: ⬤⬟⬟⬟⬟⬟ **Within 3 miles:** ⬟⬟⬤⬟⬟

Notes: Dogs must be kept on leads. Pitch & putt.

AA Pubs & Restaurants nearby: Balcary Bay Hotel, AUCHENCAIRN, DG7 1QZ, 01556 640217

PARTON
Map 20 NX67

Places to visit

Threave Garden & Estate, CASTLE DOUGLAS, DG7 1RX, 0844 493 2245
www.nts.org.uk/Property/Threave-Estate

Threave Castle, CASTLE DOUGLAS, DG7 1TJ, 07711 223101
www.historic-scotland.gov.uk

Loch Ken Holiday Park
►►►►84%

GOLD

tel: 01644 470282 **DG7 3NE**
email: office@lochkenholidaypark.co.uk
dir: *On A713, N of Parton. (NB do not follow Sat Nav directions. Site on main road).*
grid ref: *NX687702*

Run with energy, enthusiasm and commitment by the hands-on Bryson family, this busy and popular park, with a natural emphasis on water activities, is set on the eastern shores of Loch Ken. With superb views, it is in a peaceful and beautiful spot opposite the RSPB reserve, with direct access to the loch for fishing and boat launching. The park offers a variety of watersports (canoeing, sailing, water skiing) as well as farm visits and nature trails. Static caravans are available for hire. 15 acre site. 40 touring pitches. 20 hardstandings. 15 seasonal pitches. Caravan pitches. Motorhome pitches. Tent pitches. 35 statics.

Open: Feb-mid Nov (rs Feb-Mar (ex Etr) & Nov restricted shop hours)
Last departure: noon

Pitches: ⊕ ⊕ Å

Leisure: ⬟⬟⬤⬟ **Facilities:** ⬈⊙⬟✳⬟⬟⬈⬈⬟⬟⬟

LEISURE: ⬤ Indoor swimming pool ⬤ Outdoor swimming pool ⬟ Children's playground ⬟ Kid's club ⬟ Tennis court ⬤ Games room ⬟ Separate TV room ⬟ golf course ⬟ Boats for hire ⬟ Cinema ⬟ Entertainment ⬟ Fishing ⬤ Mini golf ⬟ Watersports ⬟ Gym ⬤ Sports field Spa ⬟ Stables
FACILITIES: ⬟ Bath ⬟ Shower ⊙ Electric shaver ⬟ Hairdryer ✳ Ice Pack Facility ⬟ Disabled facilities ⬟ Public telephone ⬟ Shop on site or within 200yds ⬟ Mobile shop (calls at least 5 days a week) ⬟ BBQ area ⬟ Picnic area ⬟ Wi-fi ⬟ Internet access ⬟ Recycling ⬟ Tourist info ⬟ Dog exercise area

Services: 🔌🔲🔋⌀T🛒 **Within 3 miles:** ⚓🎣🚲🏊🏦🛒

Notes: No noise after 22.00hrs. Dogs must be kept on leads. Bike, boat & canoe hire.

AA Pubs & Restaurants nearby: Cross Keys Hotel, NEW GALLOWAY, DG7 3RN, 01644 420494

PORT WILLIAM	Map 20 NX34

Places to visit

Glenluce Abbey, GLENLUCE, DG8 0AF, 01581 300541
www.historic-scotland.gov.uk

Whithorn Priory and Museum, WHITHORN, DG8 8PY, 01988 500508
www.historic-scotland.gov.uk

Kings Green Caravan Site
► ► ► 79%

tel: 01988 700489 **South St DG8 9SG**
dir: Direct access from A747 at junct with B7085 towards Whithorn. **grid ref:** NX340430

Located on the edge of Port William, with beautiful views across Luce Bay as far as the Isle of Man, this is a community run site which offers good facilities and large grass pitches with direct access to the pebble shore where otters have been seen. The road which runs along the coast is relatively traffic free so does not detract from the tranquillity of this small site. Two public boat launches are available. There are several good shops in the village and a local bus, with links to Whithorn, Garlieston and Newton Stewart, runs past the site. 3 acre site. 30 touring pitches. Caravan pitches. Motorhome pitches. Tent pitches.

Open: mid Mar-Oct **Last arrival:** 20.00hrs **Last departure:** noon

Pitches: 🚐 🚏 ⋏

Facilities: 🌳☉🅿&🕒🔲🛋♨🚻WiFi❶ **Services:** 🔌🔲

Within 3 miles: ⚓🎣🏊🛒

Notes: ⊗ No golf or fireworks permitted. Dogs must be kept on leads. Free book lending.

AA Pubs & Restaurants nearby: The Steam Packet Inn, ISLE OF WHITHORN, DG8 8LL, 01988 500334

SANDHEAD	Map 20 NX04

Places to visit

Glenwhan Gardens, STRANRAER, DG9 8PH, 01581 400222
www.glenwhangardens.co.uk

Ardwell House Gardens, ARDWELL, DG9 9LY, 01776 860227

Great for kids: Castle Kennedy Gardens, STRANRAER, DG9 8BX, 01776 702024
www.castlekennedygardens.co.uk

Sands of Luce Holiday Park
► ► ► ► 84%

tel: 01776 830456 & 830296 **Sands of Luce DG9 9JN**
email: info@sandsofluceholidaypark.co.uk
dir: From S & E: left from A75 onto B7084 signed Drummore. Site signed at junct with A716. From N: A77 through Stranraer towards Portpatrick, 2m, follow A716 signed Drummore, site signed in 5m. **grid ref:** NX103510

This is a large, well-managed holiday park overlooking Luce Bay. The site has a private boat launch and direct access to a wide sandy beach, which is proving popular with kite surfers. There is a small café, two games rooms and a nice play area for children; adults might like to visit the Lighthouse Bar at the site's entrance. A bus stops at the site entrance so this makes an ideal base for exploring the Mull of Galloway, and Port Logan Botanical Gardens is within easy driving distance. The site is tailored mainly for statics but touring customers are well catered for. 30 acre site. 100 touring pitches. 20 hardstandings. 50 seasonal pitches. Caravan pitches. Motorhome pitches. Tent pitches. 250 statics.

Open: Mar-Jan (rs Nov-Jan toilet block & shower closed) **Last arrival:** 20.00hrs **Last departure:** noon

Pitches: * 🚐 £20-£25 🚏 £20-£25 ⋏ £10-£22

Leisure: 🄰☺🎣🎵 **Facilities:** 🌳☉🅿❄&🕒🔲🛋♨🚻WiFi🖥♨❶

Services: 🔌🔲🍽🍴🛒🚮🚽 **Within 3 miles:** ⚓⚓🎣🏊🏦🛒U

Notes: No quad bikes, owners must clear up after their dogs. Dogs must be kept on leads. Boat launching & storage.

AA Pubs & Restaurants nearby: Tigh Na Mara Hotel, SANDHEAD, DG9 9JF, 01776 830210

Knockinaam Lodge, PORTPATRICK, DG9 9AD, 01776 810471

SANDYHILLS	Map 21 NX85

Places to visit

Threave Garden & Estate, CASTLE DOUGLAS, DG7 1RX, 0844 493 2245
www.nts.org.uk/Property/Threave-Estate

Orchardton Tower, PALNACKIE www.historic-scotland.gov.uk

Great for kids: Threave Castle, CASTLE DOUGLAS, DG7 1TJ, 07711 223101
www.historic-scotland.gov.uk

Sandyhills Bay Leisure Park
► ► ► ► 75%

tel: 01557 870267 & 01387 780257 **DG5 4NY**
email: info@gillespie-leisure.co.uk
dir: On A710, 7m from Dalbeattie, 6.5m from Kirkbean. **grid ref:** NX892552

A well-maintained park in a superb location beside a beach, and close to many attractive villages. The level, grassy site is sheltered by woodland, and the south-facing Sandyhills Bay and beach are a treasure trove for all the family, with their caves and rock pools. The leisure facilities at Brighouse Bay are available to visitors here. Two wigwams with TV, fridge, kettle and microwave are available for hire. 15 acre site. 24 touring pitches. Caravan pitches. Motorhome pitches. Tent pitches. 32 statics. 2 wooden pods.

Open: Apr-Oct **Last arrival:** 20.00hrs **Last departure:** 11.30hrs

Pitches: 🚐 🚏 ⋏ 🏕

Leisure: 🄰 **Facilities:** 🌳☉🅿❄🕒🔲🛋♨🚻WiFi❶

Services: 🔌🔲🔋⌀T🛒🚮🚽 **Within 3 miles:** ⚓🎣🏦🛒U

Notes: No motorised scooters, jet skis or own quad bikes. Dogs must be kept on leads.

PITCHES: 🚐 Caravans 🚏 Motorhomes ⋏ Tents 🏕 Glamping-style accommodation **SERVICES:** 🔌 Electric hook up 🔲 Launderette 🍽 Licensed bar 🔋 Calor Gas ⌀ Camping Gaz T Toilet fluid 🍴 Café/Restaurant 🚮 Fast Food/Takeaway 🛒 Battery charging 🚽 Baby care ⌄ Motorvan service point
ABBREVIATIONS: BH/bank hols – bank holidays Etr – Easter Spring BH – Spring Bank Holiday fr – from hrs – hours m – mile mdnt – midnight rdbt – roundabout rs – restricted service wk – week wknd – weekend x-rds – cross roads ⊗ No credit or debit cards ⊗ No dogs 👪 Children of all ages accepted

SOUTHERNESS | Map 21 NX95

Places to visit

Sweetheart Abbey, NEW ABBEY, DG2 8BU, 01387 850397
www.historic-scotland.gov.uk

New Abbey Corn Mill, NEW ABBEY, DG2 8BX, 01387 850260
www.historic-scotland.gov.uk

Southerness Holiday Village
HOLIDAY CENTRE 87%

tel: 0844 335 3756 **Off Sandy Ln DG2 8AZ**
email: touringandcamping@parkdeanholidays.com
dir: *From S: A75 from Gretna to Dumfries. From N: A74, exit at A701 to Dumfries. Take A710 (coast road), approx 16m, site easily visible.* **grid ref:** *NX976545*

There are stunning views across the Solway Firth from this holiday park at the foot of the Galloway Hills. A sandy beach on the Solway Firth is accessible directly from the park. The emphasis is on family entertainment, and facilities include an indoor pool, show bar, coast bar and kitchen. A very well organised park with excellent all-weather, fully serviced pitches and five 'Star Pitches' (grass or hardstanding) with electricity, water supply and direct drainage system for showers and sinks. 50 acre site. 99 touring pitches. 7 seasonal pitches. Caravan pitches. Motorhome pitches. Tent pitches. 611 statics.

Open: mid Mar-Oct **Last arrival:** 21.00hrs **Last departure:** noon

Pitches: ⛺ ⛺ ⛺

Leisure: 🏊 ⛹ 🛶 ⚽ 🎵

Facilities: 🚿 ⊙ ℗ ✳ ⅏ ⏰ 📵 WiFi 🖥 ❶

Services: 🚿 🗑 🛢 🍴 🚰 🚽 🍽 🛒 🛒

Within 3 miles: ⅃ ℓ ◎ 🛒 🛒

Notes: Dogs must be kept on leads. Amusements centre.

STRANRAER | Map 20 NX06

Places to visit

Glenwhan Gardens, STRANRAER, DG9 8PH, 01581 400222
www.glenwhangardens.co.uk

Great for kids: Castle Kennedy Gardens, STRANRAER, DG9 8BX, 01776 702024
www.castlekennedygardens.co.uk

Aird Donald Caravan Park
▶▶▶▶ 82%

tel: 01776 702025 **London Rd DG9 8RN**
email: enquiries@aird-donald.co.uk
dir: *From A75 left on entering Stranraer (signed). Opposite school, site 300yds.*
grid ref: *NX075605*

A spacious touring site set behind mature trees and within a five-minute walk of Stranraer town centre at the head of Loch Ryan. It is an ideal base to tour the

'Rinns of Galloway', to visit Port Logan Botanical Gardens or the lighthouse at the Mull of Galloway. It provides a very convenient stopover for the Cairnryan ferry to Ireland, but there's plenty to do in the area if staying longer. A 25 pitch rally field is available. 12 acre site. 50 touring pitches. 24 hardstandings. Caravan pitches. Motorhome pitches. Tent pitches.

Open: all year (rs Sep-Etr no tents) **Last departure:** 16.00hrs

Pitches: ⛺ ⛺ ⛺

Leisure: ⅏

Facilities: 🚿 ⊙ ℗ ⅏ 🚶 WiFi ❶

Services: 🚿 🗑 🛢 🖊 🛒 🛒

Within 3 miles: ⅃ 🛶 🗄 ℓ 🛒 🛒 ♨

Notes: 🐕 Dogs must be kept on leads.

AA Pubs & Restaurants nearby: Knockinaam Lodge, PORTPATRICK, DG9 9AD, 01776 810471

Corsewall Lighthouse Hotel, STRANRAER, DG9 0QG, 01776 853220

WIGTOWN | Map 20 NX45

Drumroamin Farm Camping & Touring Site
▶▶▶ 90%

tel: 01988 840613 & 07752 471456 **1 South Balfern DG8 9DB**
email: enquiry@drumroamin.co.uk
dir: *A75 towards Newton Stewart, onto A714 for Wigtown. Left on B7005 through Bladnoch, A746 through Kirkinner. Take B7004 signed Garlieston, 2nd left opposite Kilsture Forest, site 0.75m at end of lane.* **grid ref:** *NX444512*

An open, spacious site overlooking Wigtown Bay and the Galloway Hills. Located near Wigtown and Newton Stewart, this is an easily accessible site for those wishing to stay in a rural location. The toilet and other facilities are maintained in an exemplary manner. There is a large and separate tent field with a well-equipped day room, while the touring pitches can easily accommodate rally events. The RSPB's Crook of Baldoon Reserve is located a 10-minute walk away. There is a good bus service at the top of the road which goes to Newton Stewart, Wigtown and Whithorn. Two of the three statics on site are for hire. 5 acre site. 48 touring pitches. Caravan pitches. Motorhome pitches. Tent pitches. 3 statics.

Open: all year **Last arrival:** 21.00hrs **Last departure:** noon

Pitches: ⛺ £18 ⛺ £18 ⛺ £15-£18

Leisure: ⅏ ⚽

Facilities: 🚿 ⊙ ℗ ✳ ⅃ 🚶 ♻ ❶

Services: 🚿 🗑 🛒 🛒

Within 3 miles: ⅃ ℓ 🛒

Notes: No fires, no noise after 22.00hrs. Dogs must be kept on leads. Ball games area.

AA Pubs & Restaurants nearby: Creebridge House Hotel, NEWTON STEWART, DG8 6NP, 01671 402121

Kirroughtree House, NEWTON STEWART, DG8 6AN, 01671 402141

LEISURE: 🏊 Indoor swimming pool 🏊 Outdoor swimming pool ⅏ Children's playground 🛝 Kid's club ♨ Tennis court ⚽ Games room ▭ Separate TV room ⅃ golf course 🛶 Boats for hire 🎦 Cinema 🎵 Entertainment ℓ Fishing ◎ Mini golf 🏄 Watersports 🏋 Gym 🏟 Sports field ♨ Spa ♨ Stables
FACILITIES: 🛁 Bath 🚿 Shower ⊙ Electric shaver ℗ Hairdryer ✳ Ice Pack Facility ⅏ Disabled facilities 📞 Public telephone 🛒 Shop on site or within 200yds 🛒 Mobile shop (calls at least 5 days a week) 🍴 BBQ area 🌲 Picnic area WiFi Wi-fi 🖥 Internet access ♻ Recycling ❶ Tourist info 🚶 Dog exercise area

WEST DUNBARTONSHIRE

BALLOCH
Map 20 NS38

Places to visit

Loch Lomond Bird of Prey Centre, BALLOCH, G83 8NB, 07751 862416
www.llbopc.co.uk

The Tall Ship at Riverside, GLASGOW, G3 8RS, 0141 357 3699
www.thetallship.com

PREMIER PARK

Lomond Woods Holiday Park
► ► ► ► ► 80%

tel: 01389 755000 **Old Luss Rd G83 8QP**
email: lomondwoods@holiday-parks.co.uk
dir: From A82, 17m N of Glasgow, take A811 (Stirling to Balloch road). Left at 1st rdbt, follow holiday park signs, 150yds on left. **grid ref:** NS383816

This site is ideally placed on the southern end of Loch Lomond, the UK's largest inland water and a designated National Park. This site has something to suit all tastes from the most energetic visitor to those who just wish to relax. Fully serviced pitches are available and there are three family rooms. There are loch cruises and boats to hire, plus retail outlets, superstores and eateries within easy walking distance. A drive or cycle ride along Loch Lomond reveals breathtaking views. There are two large boat storage areas. Please note that this site does not accept tents. Holiday caravans and lodges and three camping pods are available to let. 13 acre site. 100 touring pitches. 100 hardstandings. Caravan pitches. Motorhome pitches. 35 statics. 3 wooden pods.

Open: all year **Last arrival:** 20.00hrs **Last departure:** noon

Pitches: * 🚐 £21-£27 🚍 £21-£27 🏠

Leisure: ⚼ 🎱 ▭

Facilities: 🚿 📞 ⊙ 🄿 ✳ ⚿ ⑤ ⌁ ➤ WiFi ♻ ❻

Services: 🔌 ⑤ 🔒 ⏻ 🅣 📇 ↯

Within 3 miles: ♨ ⚘ ⚯ ⚷ ⑤ ⑤ ∪

Notes: No jet skis. Dogs must be kept on leads.

AA Pubs & Restaurants nearby: The Cameron Grill, BALLOCH, G83 8QZ, 01389 722582

FIFE

ST ANDREWS

Places to visit

St Andrews Castle, ST ANDREWS, KY16 9AR, 01334 477196
www.historic-scotland.gov.uk

British Golf Museum, ST ANDREWS, KY16 9AB, 01334 460046
www.britishgolfmuseum.co.uk

Great for kids: St Andrews Aquarium, ST ANDREWS, KY16 9AS, 01334 474786
www.standrewsaquarium.co.uk

ST ANDREWS
Map 21 NO51

PREMIER PARK

Cairnsmill Holiday Park
► ► ► ► ► 94%

tel: 01334 473604 **Largo Rd KY16 8NN**
email: cairnsmill@aol.com **web:** www.cairnsmill.co.uk
dir: A915 from St Andrews towards Lathones. Approx 2m, site on right.
grid ref: NO502142

Hidden behind mature trees and hedging in open countryside on the outskirts of St Andrews, this top quality park is ideally placed for visiting St Andrews and exploring the Fife area. It is a family owned and run site providing high levels of customer care and excellent facilities, including a swimming pool, licensed bar and café, numerous play areas for children and a small fishing lochan, stocked annually with rainbow trout. Toilet facilities are first class, and the tent area has its own amenity block and outdoor kitchen area. The local bus to St Andrews stops at the site entrance. 27 acre site. 62 touring pitches. 33 hardstandings. 24 seasonal pitches. Caravan pitches. Motorhome pitches. Tent pitches. 194 statics.

Open: all year (rs Winter prior bookings only) **Last arrival:** flexible
Last departure: 11.00hrs

Pitches: * 🚐 £26.50-£28.50 🚍 £24.50-£26 ⚑ £10-£10.50

Leisure: ⚲ ⚼ 🎱 ▭ ♪ Spa **Facilities:** 📞 ⊙ 🄿 ✳ ⚿ ⓢ ⑤ ➤ WiFi 🖥 ♻ ❻

Services: 🔌 ⑤ 🕮 🔒 ⏻ 🅣 🍽 📇 ↯

Within 3 miles: ♨ ⚘ 🅓 ⚯ ◎ ⚷ ⑤ ⑤ ∪

Notes: No noise after mdnt, 1 car per pitch. Dogs must be kept on leads.

PITCHES: 🚐 Caravans 🚍 Motorhomes ⚑ Tents 🏠 Glamping-style accommodation **SERVICES:** 🔌 Electric hook up ⑤ Launderette 🕮 Licensed bar 🔒 Calor Gas ⏺ Camping Gaz 🅣 Toilet fluid 🍽 Café/Restaurant 🍴 Fast Food/Takeaway 📇 Battery charging 🔌 Baby care ↯ Motorvan service point **ABBREVIATIONS:** BH/bank hols – bank holidays Etr – Easter Spring BH – Spring Bank Holiday fr – from hrs – hours m – mile mdnt – midnight rdbt – roundabout rs – restricted service wk – week wknd – weekend x-rds – cross roads Ⓢ No credit or debit cards ⊗ No dogs 💒 Children of all ages accepted

ST ANDREWS *continued*

Craigtoun Meadows Holiday Park

►►►►► 92%

GOLD

tel: 01334 475959 **Mount Melville KY16 8PQ**
email: info@craigtounmeadows.co.uk **web:** www.craigtounmeadows.co.uk
dir: *M90 junct 8, A91 to St Andrews. Just after Guardbridge right for Strathkinness. At 2nd x-rds left for Craigtoun.* **grid ref:** NO482150

An attractive site set unobtrusively in mature woodlands, with large pitches in spacious hedged paddocks. All pitches are fully serviced, and there are also some patio pitches and a summerhouse containing picnic tables and chairs. The modern toilet block provides cubicled en suite facilities as well as spacious showers, baths, disabled facilities and baby changing areas. The licensed restaurant and coffee shop are popular, and there is a takeaway, indoor and outdoor games areas and a launderette. Located half a mile from St Andrews town centre which has sandy beaches, shops and restaurants, and being 'the home of golf', there are, of course, numerous golf courses including The Dukes, which borders the site. 32 acre site. 57 touring pitches. 57 hardstandings. 7 seasonal pitches. Caravan pitches. Motorhome pitches. Tent pitches. 199 statics.

Open: 15 Mar-Oct (rs Mar-Etr & Sep-Oct no shop & restaurant open shorter hours) **Last arrival:** 21.00hrs **Last departure:** 11.00hrs

Pitches: * ⚐ £21-£26.50 ⊟ £21-£26.50 ▲ £18-£21

Leisure: ⚙ ☺ ✎

Facilities: ➤ ⚑ ☉ ⌒ & ◔ ⌒ wifi 🖳 ♻ ❶

Services: ⚑ 🗐 ⏀ 🎒 🚽 ⚒

Within 3 miles: ↨ ⚘ ☗ ✎ ◎ ⚕ 🗐 🗐 ∪

Notes: ⊗ No groups of unaccompanied minors, no pets. Putting green, zip wire, all-weather football pitch.

AA Pubs & Restaurants nearby: Road Hole Restaurant, ST ANDREWS, KY16 9SP, 01334 474371

The Inn at Lathones, ST ANDREWS, KY9 1JE, 01334 840494

BALMACARA
Map 22 NG82

Places to visit

Balmacara Estate & Lochalsh Woodland Garden, BALMACARA, IV40 8DN, 0844 493 2233 www.nts.org.uk/property/balmacara-estate-woodland-walks

Eilean Donan Castle, DORNIE, IV40 8DX, 01599 555202 www.eileandonancastle.com

Reraig Caravan Site

►►► 79%

tel: 01599 566215 **IV40 8DH**
email: warden@reraig.com
dir: *On A87, 3.5m E of Kyle, 2m W of junct with A890.* **grid ref:** NG815272

A lovely site, on the saltwater Sound of Sleet, set back from the main road amongst mature trees in a garden-type environment. It is located near the Skye Bridge and very handy for exploring the surrounding area including Plockton. There is a regular bus that stops at the site entrance. 2 acre site. 40 touring pitches. 36 hardstandings. Caravan pitches. Motorhome pitches. Tent pitches.

Open: May-Sep **Last arrival:** 22.00hrs **Last departure:** noon

Pitches: * ⚐ £14.40-£14.90 ⊟ £14.40-£14.90 ▲ £13.50

Facilities: ⚑ ☉ ⌒ & ◔ wifi ♻ ❶

Services: ⚑ ⚒

Within 3 miles: 🗐

Notes: No awnings Jul & Aug, only small tents permitted. Dogs must be kept on leads. Charge for WiFi.

AA Pubs & Restaurants nearby: The Waterside Seafood Restaurant, KYLE OF LOCHALSH, IV40 8AE, 01599 534813

Plockton Inn & Seafood Restaurant, PLOCKTON, IV52 8TW, 01599 544222

The Plockton Hotel, PLOCKTON, IV52 8TN, 01599 544274

CORPACH
Map 22 NN07

Places to visit

West Highland Museum, FORT WILLIAM, PH33 6AJ, 01397 702169 www.westhighlandmuseum.org.uk

Great for kids: Inverlochy Castle, FORT WILLIAM, PH33 6SN, 01667 460232 www.historic-scotland.gov.uk

Linnhe Lochside Holidays

►►►►► 87%

GOLD

tel: 01397 772376 **PH33 7NL**
email: relax@linnhe-lochside-holidays.co.uk
dir: *On A830, 1m W of Corpach, 5m from Fort William.* **grid ref:** NN074771

Set on the shores of Loch Eil, on the outskirts of Corpac, this site has views over Ben Nevis and Sunart and is only a few miles from Fort William, the Scottish outdoor enthusiasts mecca. There is direct access from the site for kayaking and

LEISURE: 🏊 Indoor swimming pool 🏊 Outdoor swimming pool ⚙ Children's playground 🪁 Kid's club ⚘ Tennis court ✎ Games room 🖵 Separate TV room ↨ golf course ⚓ Boats for hire 🎬 Cinema ♫ Entertainment ✎ Fishing ◎ Mini golf ⚕ Watersports 🏋 Gym ☺ Sports field Spa ∪ Stables
FACILITIES: ➤ Bath ⚑ Shower ☉ Electric shaver ⌒ Hairdryer ✳ Ice Pack Facility & Disabled facilities ◔ Public telephone 🗐 Shop on site or within 200yds 🗐 Mobile shop (calls at least 5 days a week) 🍖 BBQ area ⌒ Picnic area wifi Wi-fi 🖳 Internet access ♻ Recycling ❶ Tourist info 🐾 Dog exercise area

sailing and the steam train to Mallaig passes under the site access bridge with the drivers always whistling to anyone on the bridge. The pitches are set in very well maintained landscaping with mature trees and shrubs and some have loch views. Tenters are well catered for in sheltered areas and there are also some pitches directly on the lochside. The owners have worked hard over the years to provide a site where nature and campers can be in unison. This is a great site for relaxation or if you wish to be more active the choices are limitless. 5.5 acre site. 85 touring pitches. 63 hardstandings. 20 seasonal pitches. Caravan pitches. Motorhome pitches. Tent pitches. 20 statics.

Open: Dec-Oct (rs Dec-Etr shop closed out of season) **Last arrival:** 21.00hrs **Last departure:** 11.00hrs

Pitches: 🚐 🚙 ⛺

Leisure: ⌂

Facilities: 🚽 🏾⊙🝫 🌣 🕹 ⏱ ⊡ 💺 🚿 ⌨ 🚮 ➌ ❶

Services: 🔌 🛢 🍴⊘ T 🚕 ⚖

Within 3 miles: ↕ ⚓ 🥾 ◎ 🎣 🛒🚲

Notes: No cars by tents. No large groups. Dogs must be kept on leads. Launching slipway, free fishing.

AA Pubs & Restaurants nearby: Inverlochy Castle Hotel, FORT WILLIAM, PH33 6SN, 01397 702177

Moorings Hotel, FORT WILLIAM, PH33 7LY, 01397 772797

DORNOCH
Map 23 NH78

Places to visit
Dunrobin Castle, GOLSPIE, KW10 6SF, 01408 633177 www.dunrobincastle.co.uk

---

Grannie's Heilan Hame Holiday Park
HOLIDAY CENTRE 83%

tel: 0844 335 3756 Embo IV25 3QD
email: touringandcamping@parkdeanholidays.com
dir: A949 to Dornoch, left in square. Follow Embo signs. **grid ref:** NH818924

A 60-acre holiday park situated in Embo that has direct access to the beach on the Dornoch Firth. Within a few miles of the historic town of Dornoch and with easy access to the A9 and regular bus services, this makes an excellent touring base. There is a swimming pool, spa, sauna, solarium, mini ten-pin bowling, a children's club, a bar and restaurant and a good shop. The main amenity block provides good facilities and is well maintained. 60 acre site. 125 touring pitches. Caravan pitches. Motorhome pitches. Tent pitches. 273 statics.

Open: Mar-Nov **Last arrival:** 21.00hrs **Last departure:** 10.00hrs

Pitches: 🚐 🚙 ⛺

Leisure: 🏊 ⌂ ⚽ 🎱 🎣 🎵

Facilities: 🏾⊙🝫 🌣 🕹 ⏱ 💺 🚮 📶 🖥 ➌ ❶

Services: 🔌 🛢 🍴 🛢⊘ T 🍴 🚕 🍺

Within 3 miles: ↕⚓ ◎ 🛒🚲

Notes: No noise after mdnt. Dogs must be kept on leads.

AA Pubs & Restaurants nearby: Dornoch Castle Hotel, DORNOCH, IV25 3SD, 01862 810216

DUNDONNELL
Map 22 NH08

Badrallach Cottage & Campsite
▶▶▶▶ 73%

tel: 01854 633281 & 07745 409130 Croft 9, Badrallach IV23 2QP
email: mail@badrallach.com
dir: From Inverness on A9 take A835 signed Ullapool, left onto A832 signed Gairloch. 10m, right onto single track signed Badrallach, 7m to site. **grid ref:** NH065917

Set near the shores of Little Loch Broom, this campsite has been carefully created by the owners on a croft that has stunning scenery and an abundance of wildlife. It is a place to relax and unwind whether you use the campsite, the bothy or the cottage. Kayaks, bikes and kites are available for hire, and walking in the nearby mountains directly from the campsite is a possibility. It's an easy drive from Inverness, although the last seven miles are along a narrow single track road. To avoid disappointment pre-booking is advised, and for caravans and motorhomes it is essential. Please note, there is no CDP on site and the nearest shops are 12 miles away. 2 acre site. 19 touring pitches. Caravan pitches. Motorhome pitches. Tent pitches.

Open: 9 Mar-23 Sep **Last arrival:** anytime **Last departure:** 11.00hrs

Pitches: 🚐 £15-£18 🚙 £15-£18 ⛺ £15-£18

Leisure: 🎣 **Facilities:** 🏾⊙🝫 🌣 🕹 ⏱ 🚮 ➌ ❶

Services: 🔌 **Within 3 miles:** 🥾 ⚓ 🎣

Notes: 🚫 Dogs must be kept on leads.

DUROR
Map 22 NM95

Places to visit
Glencoe & North Lorn Folk Museum, GLENCOE, PH49 4HS, 01855 811664 www.glencoemuseum.com

Glencoe & Dalness, GLENCOE, PH49 4LA, 0844 493 2222 www.nts.org.uk/Property/Glencoe-Dalness

---

Achindarroch Touring Park
▶▶▶ 78%

tel: 01631 740329 PA38 4BS
email: stay@achindarrochtp.co.uk
dir: A82 onto A828 at Ballachulish Bridge then towards Oban for 5.2m. In Duror site on left, signed. **grid ref:** NM997554

A long established, well-laid out park which continues to be maintained to a high standard by an enthusiastic and friendly family team. There is a well-appointed heated toilet block and spacious all-weather pitches and there are also 2- and 4-person camping pods for hire. The park is well placed for visits to Oban, Fort William and Glencoe. A wide variety of outdoor sports is available in the area. 5 acre site. 40 touring pitches. 21 hardstandings. 10 seasonal pitches. Caravan pitches. Motorhome pitches. Tent pitches. 2 wooden pods.

Open: 24 Jan-16 Jan **Last departure:** 11.00hrs

Pitches: 🚐 🚙 ⛺ ⋒

Facilities: 🏾⊙🝫 🌣 🕹 🚮 📶 ➌ ❶ **Services:** 🔌 🛢 🍴⊘ 🚕 ⚖

Within 3 miles: ⚓ ⛳

Notes: Groups by prior arrangement only. Dogs must be kept on leads. Campers' kitchen (freezer, toaster, kettle, microwave, boot dryer).

AA Pubs & Restaurants nearby: Loch Leven Hotel, NORTH BALLACHULISH, PH33 6SA, 01855 821236

FORT WILLIAM
Map 22 NN17

See also Corpach

Places to visit

West Highland Museum, FORT WILLIAM, PH33 6AJ, 01397 702169
www.westhighlandmuseum.org.uk

Great for kids: Inverlochy Castle, FORT WILLIAM, PH33 6SN, 01667 460232
www.historic-scotland.gov.uk

Glen Nevis Caravan & Camping Park
►►►►90%

tel: 01397 702191 **Glen Nevis PH33 6SX**
email: holidays@glen-nevis.co.uk
dir: *From A82 (N outskirts of Fort William) follow Glen Nevis signs at mini rdbt. Site 2.5m on right.* **grid ref:** *NN124722*

A tasteful site with well-screened enclosures, at the foot of Ben Nevis in the midst of some of the most spectacular Highland scenery; an ideal area for walking and touring. The park boasts a restaurant which offers a high standard of cooking and provides good value for money. 30 acre site. 380 touring pitches. 150 hardstandings. Caravan pitches. Motorhome pitches. Tent pitches. 30 statics.

Open: 15 Mar-Oct (rs Mar & Oct limited shop & restaurant facilities)
Last arrival: 22.00hrs **Last departure:** noon

Pitches: 🚐 🚛 Å

Leisure: 🎠

Facilities: 🌣⊙🅿✳️🔥🕓🖎🔥📶🖥♻️ℹ️

Services: 🔌🖸🍴🔋🧺🚰🕅🎪⛽

Within 3 miles: ⚓🎣🏪🖸

Notes: Quiet from 23.00hrs-08.00hrs.

GAIRLOCH
Map 22 NG87

Places to visit

Gairloch Heritage Museum, GAIRLOCH, IV21 2BP, 01445 712287
www.gairlochheritagemuseum.org

Inverewe Garden, POOLEWE, IV22 2LG, 0844 493 2225
www.nts.org.uk/Property/Inverewe-Garden-and-Estate

Gairloch Caravan Park
►►►79%

tel: 01445 712373 **Strath IV21 2BX**
email: info@gairlochcaravanpark.com
dir: *From A832 take B8021 signed Melvaig towards Strath. In 0.5m turn right, just after Millcroft Hotel. Immediately right again.* **grid ref:** *NG798773*

A clean, well-maintained site on flat coastal grassland close to Loch Gairloch. The owners and managers are hard working and well organised and continued investment in recent years has seen significant improvements around the park, including the hardstandings, good shrub and flower planting, and the building of a bunkhouse that provides accommodation for families. 6 acre site. 70 touring pitches. 13 hardstandings. 8 seasonal pitches. Caravan pitches. Motorhome pitches. Tent pitches.

Open: Apr-Oct **Last arrival:** 21.00hrs **Last departure:** noon

Pitches: 🚐 🚛 Å

Facilities: 🌣⊙🅿✳️🕓🖎📶♻️ℹ️

Services: 🔌🖸🔋🕅🚰⛽

Within 3 miles: ⚓🎣◉🏊🏪🖸⛴

Notes: No noise after 23.00hrs. Dogs must be kept on leads.

AA Pubs & Restaurants nearby: The Old Inn, GAIRLOCH, IV21 2BD, 01445 712006

GLENCOE
Map 22 NN15

Places to visit

Glencoe & Dalness, GLENCOE, PH49 4LA, 0844 493 2222
www.nts.org.uk/Property/Glencoe-Dalness

Great for kids: Glencoe & North Lorn Folk Museum, GLENCOE, PH49 4HS,
01855 811664 www.glencoemuseum.com

Invercoe Caravan & Camping Park
►►►►85%

tel: 01855 811210 **PH49 4HP**
email: holidays@invercoe.co.uk **web:** www.invercoe.co.uk
dir: *Exit A82 at Glencoe Hotel onto B863 for 0.25m.* **grid ref:** *NN098594*

A level grass site set on the shore of Loch Leven, with excellent mountain views. The area is ideal for both walking and climbing, and also offers a choice of several freshwater and saltwater lochs. Convenient for the good shopping in Fort William. 5 acre site. 60 touring pitches. Caravan pitches. Motorhome pitches. Tent pitches. 4 statics. 2 wooden pods.

Open: all year **Last departure:** noon

Pitches: 🚐 🚛 Å 🏠

Leisure: 🎠

Facilities: 🌣⊙🅿✳️🕓🖎📶🔥

Services: 🔌🖸🚰🕅🚰⛽

Within 3 miles: ⚓🏊🎣🏪🖸

Notes: No large group bookings.

AA Pubs & Restaurants nearby: Clachaig Inn, GLENCOE, PH49 4HX, 01855 811252

LEISURE: 🏊 Indoor swimming pool 🏊 Outdoor swimming pool 🎠 Children's playground 🪁 Kid's club 🎾 Tennis court 🎱 Games room 📺 Separate TV room ⚓ golf course 🚣 Boats for hire 🎦 Cinema 🎵 Entertainment 🎣 Fishing ◉ Mini golf 🏄 Watersports 🏋️ Gym ⚽ Sports field Spa ♨ Stables
FACILITIES: 🛁 Bath 🌣 Shower ⊙ Electric shaver 🅿 Hairdryer ✳️ Ice Pack Facility 🖎 Disabled facilities 🕓 Public telephone 🖸 Shop on site or within 200yds 🏪 Mobile shop (calls at least 5 days a week) 🍴 BBQ area 🔥 Picnic area 📶 Wi-fi 🖥 Internet access ♻️ Recycling ℹ️ Tourist info 🔥 Dog exercise area

JOHN O'GROATS
Map 23 ND37

Places to visit
The Castle & Gardens of Mey, THURSO, KW14 8XH, 01847 851473
www.castleofmey.org.uk

John O'Groats Caravan Site
►►►82%

tel: 01955 611329 & 07762 336359 **KW1 4YR**
email: info@johnogroatscampsite.co.uk
dir: At end of A99. **grid ref:** ND382733

An attractive site in an open position above the seashore and looking out towards the Orkney Islands. Nearby is the passenger ferry that makes day trips to the Orkneys, and there are grey seals to watch, and sea angling can be organised by the site owners. 4 acre site. 90 touring pitches. 30 hardstandings. Caravan pitches. Motorhome pitches. Tent pitches.

Open: Apr-Sep **Last arrival:** 22.00hrs **Last departure:** 11.00hrs
Pitches: * ⚏ fr £16.50 ⚐ fr £16.50 Å fr £13
Facilities: ⌂ ⊙ ℱ ✳ & ◯ ⇥ ⅏ 🗑 ❼
Services: ⚡ 🗇 ⊘ ⛟ ↯
Within 3 miles: ℐ 🏧 🗇
Notes: ⊛ No noise after 22.00hrs. Dogs must be kept on leads.

LAIDE
Map 22 NG89

Gruinard Bay Caravan Park
►►►71%

tel: 01445 731225 **IV22 2ND**
email: gruinard@ecosse.net
dir: From Inverness or Ullapool take A832 to Gairloch, follow signs to Laide. (NB on Inverness to Gairloch road - short stretch of single-track road with passing places just prior to Gairloch). **grid ref:** NG904919

With views across Gruinard Bay to the Summer Isles and the mountains, this is a lovely, small park in a particularly peaceful location. There is direct access to a small sandy beach and a small hotel nearby with a restaurant and free WiFi access; the small post office provides basic groceries, while larger shops can be found in Aultbuie, Poolewe, Gairloch and Ullapool, where there are ferries to the Outer Hebrides. Being beside a beach the site has no hardstandings but the grass pitches are on well-compacted shingle. 3.5 acre site. 35 touring pitches. 2 seasonal pitches. Caravan pitches. Motorhome pitches. Tent pitches. 20 statics.

Open: Apr-Oct **Last arrival:** 22.00hrs **Last departure:** noon
Pitches: * ⚏ £15-£17 ⚐ £15-£17 Å £14-£15
Facilities: ⌂ ⊙ ℱ ✳ 🆆 🗑 ❼
Services: ⚡ 🗇 ⅏ ⛟
Within 3 miles: ℐ 🏧 🗇
Notes: No noise after 22.00hrs. Dogs must be kept on leads.

LAIRG
Map 23 NC50

Dunroamin Caravan and Camping Park
►►►74%

tel: 01549 402447 **Main St IV27 4AR**
email: enquiries@lairgcaravanpark.co.uk
dir: 300mtrs from Lairg centre on S side of A839. **grid ref:** NC585062

An attractive little park with clean and functional facilities, adjacent to a licensed restaurant. The park is close to the lower end of Loch Shin. 4 acre site. 20 touring pitches. 8 hardstandings. Caravan pitches. Motorhome pitches. Tent pitches. 9 statics.

Open: Apr-Oct **Last arrival:** 21.00hrs **Last departure:** noon
Pitches: ⚏ ⚐ Å
Facilities: ⌂ ⊙ ℱ ✳ 🆆 🗑 ❼
Services: ⚡ 🗇 ⅏ ⊘ T 🍽 🍴 ⛟ ⅏ ↯
Within 3 miles: ⅍ ℐ 🚣 🏧 🗇
Notes: No vehicles to be driven on site between 21.00hrs-07.00hrs. Dogs must be kept on leads.

Woodend Caravan & Camping Site
►►►69%

tel: 01549 402248 **Achnairn IV27 4DN**
dir: 4m N of Lairg exit A836 onto A838, signed at Achnairn. **grid ref:** NC551127

A clean, simple site set in hilly moors and woodland with access to Loch Shin. The area is popular with fishing and boating enthusiasts, and there is a choice of golf courses within a 30 mile radius. A spacious campers' kitchen is a useful amenity. There's also a holiday cottage to hire. 4 acre site. 55 touring pitches. 5 hardstandings. Caravan pitches. Motorhome pitches. Tent pitches.

Open: Apr-Sep **Last arrival:** 23.00hrs
Pitches: ⚏ ⚐ Å
Leisure: /𝔸
Facilities: ⌂ ⊙ ℱ ✳
Services: ⚡ 🗇
Within 3 miles: ⅍ ℐ 🗇
Notes: ⊛

This symbol indicates that a site offers glamping-style accommodation

---

PITCHES: ⚏ Caravans ⚐ Motorhomes Å Tents 🏕 Glamping-style accommodation **SERVICES:** ⚡ Electric hook up 🗇 Launderette 🍺 Licensed bar ⬛ Calor Gas ⊘ Camping Gaz T Toilet fluid 🍽 Café/Restaurant ⅏ Fast Food/Takeaway ⛟ Battery charging ⇥ Baby care ↯ Motorvan service point **ABBREVIATIONS:** BH/bank hols – bank holidays Etr – Easter Spring BH – Spring Bank Holiday fr – from hrs – hours m – mile mdnt – midnight rdbt – roundabout rs – restricted service wk – week wknd – weekend x-rds – cross roads ⊛ No credit or debit cards ⊗ No dogs ⅋ Children of all ages accepted

NAIRN
Map 23 NH85

Places to visit

Sueno's Stone, FORRES, 01667 460232 www.historic-scotland.gov.uk

Dallas Dhu Distillery, FORRES, IV36 2RR, 01309 676548
www.historic-scotland.gov.uk

Great for kids: Brodie Castle, BRODIE CASTLE, IV36 2TE, 0844 493 2156
www.nts.org.uk/property/brodie-castle

Nairn Lochloy Holiday Park
HOLIDAY CENTRE 79%

GOLD

tel: 0844 335 3756 **East Beach IV12 5DE**
email: touringandcamping@parkdeanholidays.com
dir: *From A96 (Bridge St) in Nairn follow site signs onto unclassified road at Bridgemill Direct shop.* **grid ref:** *NH895574*

A small touring site situated within a popular holiday park with a wide range of leisure facilities including heated pool, sauna, spa bath, children's play area and clubs, toddlers' pool, crazy golf, amusements, bars, restaurant and mini supermarket. A small, well-maintained toilet block exclusively serves the touring area where all pitches have electricity. Handily placed in the centre of Nairn, only minutes from the beach and within striking distance of Inverness and the Highlands. 15 acre site. 13 touring pitches. Caravan pitches. Motorhome pitches. Tent pitches. 263 statics.

Open: Mar-Nov **Last arrival:** 21.00hrs **Last departure:** noon

Pitches: ⇞ ⇞ Å

Leisure: ⚓ ⌂ ♨ ♦ ♫

Facilities: ⚲ ⚲ ☉ ℘ ⚲ ⚲ ⚲ 🚾 ♻ ⓘ

Services: ⚲ ⚲ ⚲ ⚲ ⚲ ⚲

Within 3 miles: ⚲ ℘ ◎ ⚲ ⚲ ⚲

Notes: Dogs must be kept on leads.

AA Pubs & Restaurants nearby: Cawdor Tavern, CAWDOR, IV12 5XP, 01667 404777

Boath House, NAIRN, IV12 5TE, 01667 454896

Golf View Hotel & Spa, NAIRN, IV12 4HD, 01667 452301

ULLAPOOL
Map 22 NH19

Broomfield Holiday Park
►►► 78%

tel: 01854 612020 & 612664 **West Shore St IV26 2UT**
email: sross@broomfieldhp.com **web:** www.broomfieldhp.com
dir: *Into Ullapool on A893, 2nd right past harbour.* **grid ref:** *NH123939*

Set right on the water's edge of Loch Broom and the open sea, with lovely views of the Summer Isles. This clean, well maintained and managed park is close to the harbour and town centre with their restaurants, bars and shops. The Ullapool ferry allows easy access to the Hebridian islands for day trips or longer visits. 12 acre site. 140 touring pitches. Caravan pitches. Motorhome pitches. Tent pitches.

Open: Etr or Apr-Sep **Last departure:** noon

Pitches: * ⇞ fr £19 ⇞ fr £18 Å £15-£19

Leisure: ⌂

Facilities: ⚲ ☉ ☀ ⚲ ⚲ 🚾

Services: ⚲ ⚲ ⚲ ⚲

Within 3 miles: ⚲ ⊟ ℘ ⚲ ⚲

Notes: No noise at night. Dogs must be kept on leads.

LEISURE: ⚓ Indoor swimming pool ⚓ Outdoor swimming pool ⌂ Children's playground ♦ Kid's club ♨ Tennis court ♦ Games room ⊟ Separate TV room ⚲ golf course ⚲ Boats for hire ⊟ Cinema ♫ Entertainment ℘ Fishing ◎ Mini golf ⚓ Watersports ⚲ Gym ⚲ Sports field Spa ⚲ Stables
FACILITIES: ⚲ Bath ⚲ Shower ☉ Electric shaver ℘ Hairdryer ☀ Ice Pack Facility ⚲ Disabled facilities ⚲ Public telephone ⚲ Shop on site or within 200yds ⚲ Mobile shop (calls at least 5 days a week) ⚲ BBQ area ⚲ Picnic area 🚾 Wi-fi ⚲ Internet access ♻ Recycling ⓘ Tourist info ⚲ Dog exercise area

SOUTH LANARKSHIRE

ABINGTON Map 21 NS92

Places to visit

Hidden Treasures Museum of Lead Mining, WANLOCKHEAD, ML12 6UT, 01659 74387 www.leadminingmuseum.co.uk

---

Mount View Caravan Park
►►► 79%

tel: 01864 502808 **ML12 6RW**
email: info@mountviewcaravanpark.co.uk **web:** www.mountviewcaravanpark.co.uk
dir: M74 junct 13, A702 S into Abington. Left into Station Rd, over river & railway. Site on right. **grid ref:** NS935235

A delightfully maturing family park, surrounded by the Southern Uplands and handily located between Carlisle and Glasgow. It is an excellent stopover site for those travelling between Scotland and the south, and the West Coast Railway passes beside the park. 5.5 acre site. 42 touring pitches. 42 hardstandings. 18 seasonal pitches. Caravan pitches. Motorhome pitches. Tent pitches. 28 statics.

Open: Mar-Oct **Last arrival:** 20.45 **Last departure:** 11.30hrs

Pitches: * 🚐 £18-£25 🚐 £18-£25 ▲ £14-£30

Leisure: 🅰

Facilities: 🏪 ☺ 🅿 ⚅ 🚿 🅰 ❸

Services: 🔌 🗑 🍺

Within 3 miles: ✐ 🗑 🗑

Notes: 5mph speed limit, dogs must be exercised off site, credit cards not accepted (only debit cards). Dogs must be kept on leads. Emergency phone.

EAST LOTHIAN

ABERLADY Map 21 NT47

Places to visit

Dirleton Castle and Gardens, DIRLETON, EH39 5ER, 01620 850330 www.historic-scotland.gov.uk

Hailes Castle, EAST LINTON www.historic-scotland.gov.uk

Great for kids: Myreton Motor Museum, ABERLADY, EH32 0PZ, 01875 870288 www.myretonmotormuseum.co.uk

---

Aberlady Caravan Park
►►► 77%

tel: 01875 870666 **Haddington Rd EH32 0PZ**
email: aberladycaravanpark@hotmail.co.uk **web:** www.aberladycaravanpark.co.uk
dir: From Aberlady take A6137 towards Haddington. Right in 0.25m, site on right. **grid ref:** NT482797

A small family-run site that is peacefully located within the grounds of the old Aberlady railway station, and is pleasantly landscaped with an open outlook towards the nearby hills; it is within easy reach of many seaside towns, beaches, golf courses and attractions including the National Museum of Flight at East Fortune. The A1 is nearby, making Edinburgh easily accessible. 4.5 acre site. 22 touring pitches. 12 hardstandings. Caravan pitches. Motorhome pitches. Tent pitches. 3 wooden pods.

Open: all year (rs Nov-Feb a maximum of 5 caravans/motorhomes at any one time) **Last arrival:** 21.00hrs **Last departure:** noon

Pitches: * 🚐 £18-£20 🚐 £20-£25 ▲ £12.50-£30 🏠

Leisure: 🅰

Facilities: 🏪 ☺ 🅿 ☼ 🅰 🛏 🆆🅸🅵🅸 ♻ ❸

Services: 🔌 🗑 🍺 ⌀ Ⓣ 🔋 🛒

Within 3 miles: 🛤 ✐ ◎ 🏊 🗑 ∪

Notes: 🚫 No ball games, no loud music. Dogs must be kept on leads.
AA Pubs & Restaurants nearby: La Potinière, GULLANE, EH31 2AA, 01620 843214
Macdonald Marine Hotel & Spa, NORTH BERWICK, EH39 4LZ, 01620 897300

PITCHES: 🚐 Caravans 🚐 Motorhomes ▲ Tents 🏠 Glamping-style accommodation **SERVICES:** 🔌 Electric hook up 🗑 Launderette 🍺 Licensed bar 🍺 Calor Gas ⌀ Camping Gaz Ⓣ Toilet fluid 🍽 Café/Restaurant 🍔 Fast Food/Takeaway 🔋 Battery charging 🍼 Baby care 🛒 Motorvan service point **ABBREVIATIONS:** BH/bank hols – bank holidays Etr – Easter Spring BH – Spring Bank Holiday fr – from hrs – hours m – mile mdnt – midnight rdbt – roundabout rs – restricted service wk – week wknd – weekend x-rds – cross roads 🚫 No credit or debit cards 🚫 No dogs 👶 Children of all ages accepted

DUNBAR
Map 21 NT67

Places to visit

Preston Mill & Phantassie Doocot, EAST LINTON, EH40 3DS, 0844 493 2128
www.nts.org.uk/Property/Preston-Mill-Phantassie-Doocot

Great for kids: Tantallon Castle, NORTH BERWICK, EH39 5PN, 01620 892727
www.historic-scotland.gov.uk

PREMIER PARK

Thurston Manor Leisure Park

▶▶▶▶▶ 90%

tel: 01368 840643 **Innerwick EH42 1SA**
email: holidays@thurstonmanor.co.uk
dir: *4m S of Dunbar, signed from A1.* **grid ref:** *NT712745*

A pleasant park set in 250 acres of unspoilt countryside. The touring and static areas of this large park are in separate areas. The main touring area occupies an open, level position, and the toilet facilities are modern and exceptionally well maintained. The park boasts a well-stocked fishing loch, a heated indoor swimming pool, steam room, sauna, jacuzzi, mini-gym and fitness room plus seasonal entertainment. There is a superb family toilet block. 250 acre site. 120 touring pitches. 53 hardstandings. 52 seasonal pitches. Caravan pitches. Motorhome pitches. Tent pitches. 570 statics.

Open: 17 Feb-5 Jan **Last arrival:** 23.00hrs **Last departure:** 10.00hrs

Pitches: * ⚏ £12.75-£32.95 ⚍ £12.75-£32.95 ▲ £12.75-£32.95

Leisure: 🏊 ⛳ Ⓜ ⬇ ⚓ ▢ 🎵 Spa

Facilities: ⚏ ⊙ 🅿 ✳ ⛇ ⓢ ⓢ ⫙ 📅 WIFI 🖥 ♻ ❶

Services: ⚏ ⓢ 🛠 🍶 ⓣ 🍴 ⬛ ⬇ ⫚

Within 3 miles: 🎣 ⓢ ⓢ

Notes: Quiet after 23.00hrs. Dogs must be kept on leads.

AA Pubs & Restaurants nearby: Macdonald Marine Hotel & Spa, NORTH BERWICK, EH39 4LZ, 01620 897300

Belhaven Bay Caravan & Camping Park

▶▶▶ 75%

GOLD

tel: 01368 865956 **Belhaven Bay EH42 1TS**
email: belhaven@meadowhead.co.uk
dir: *A1 onto A1087 towards Dunbar. Site (1m) in John Muir Park.* **grid ref:** *NT661781*

Located on the outskirts of Dunbar, this is a sheltered park within walking distance of the beach. There is a regular bus service to Dunbar where there is an East Coast Main Line railway station. The site is convenient for the A1 and well placed to visit the area's many seaside towns and various visitor attractions. There is a large children's play area. 40 acre site. 52 touring pitches. 11 hardstandings. Caravan pitches. Motorhome pitches. Tent pitches. 64 statics.

Open: Mar-13 Oct **Last arrival:** 20.00hrs **Last departure:** noon

Pitches: ⚏ ⚍ ▲

Leisure: Ⓜ

Facilities: ⬅ ⚏ ⊙ 🅿 ✳ ⛇ ⓢ ⓢ ⫙ 📅 WIFI 🖥 ♻ ❶

Services: ⚏ ⓢ ⓣ ⫚

Within 3 miles: ⬇ 🎣 ◎ 🏊 ⓢ ⓢ ∪

Notes: No rollerblades or skateboards, no open fires, no noise 23.00hrs-07.00hrs. Dogs must be kept on leads.

AA Pubs & Restaurants nearby: Macdonald Marine Hotel & Spa, NORTH BERWICK, EH39 4LZ, 01620 897300

LONGNIDDRY
Map 21 NT47

Places to visit

Prestongrange Museum, PRESTONPANS, EH32 9RX, 0131 653 2904
www.prestongrange.org

Great for kids: Myreton Motor Museum, ABERLADY, EH32 0PZ, 01875 870288
www.myretonmotormuseum.co.uk

Seton Sands Holiday Village

HOLIDAY HOME PARK 87%

GOLD

tel: 0871 231 0867 **EH32 0QF**
email: setonsands@haven.com
dir: *A1 to A198 exit, take B6371 to Cockenzie. Right onto B1348. Site 1m on right.* **grid ref:** *NT420759*

A well-equipped holiday centre with plenty of organised entertainment, clubs and bars, plus restaurants, and sports and leisure facilities. A multi-sports court, heated swimming pool and various play areas ensure that there is plenty to do, and there is lots to see and do in and around Edinburgh which is nearby; there is a regular bus service from the site entrance, which makes Edinburgh easily accessible. The touring field is in a small area to the side of the entertainment complex and has all grass pitches. A 45-acre site with 600 statics; 110 are for hire.

Open: mid Mar-end Oct (rs mid Mar-May & Sep-Oct some facilities may be reduced)

Leisure: 🏊 ⬇ Ⓜ

Within 3 miles: ∪

MUSSELBURGH
Map 21 NT37

Places to visit

Prestongrange Museum, PRESTONPANS, EH32 9RX, 0131 653 2904
www.prestongrange.org

Inveresk Lodge Garden, INVERESK, EH21 7TE, 0844 493 2126
www.nts.org.uk/Property/Inveresk-Lodge-Garden

Great for kids: Edinburgh Butterfly & Insect World, DALKEITH, EH18 1AZ, 0131 663 4932 www.edinburgh-butterfly-world.co.uk

---

Drum Mohr Caravan Park

▶▶▶▶ 82%

tel: 0131 665 6867 **Levenhall EH21 8JS**
email: admin@drummohr.org
dir: *Exit A1 at A199 junct through Wallyford, at rdbt onto B1361 signed Prestonpans. 1st left, site 400yds.* **grid ref:** *NT373734*

This attractive park is carefully landscaped and sheltered by mature trees on all sides. It is divided into separate areas by mature hedging, trees and ornamental shrubs. The generously sized pitches include a number of fully serviced pitches, plus there are first-class amenities. The site is ideally located for exploring East Lothian area with its numerous seaside towns, and the National Museum of Flight

LEISURE: 🏊 Indoor swimming pool 🏊 Outdoor swimming pool Ⓜ Children's playground ⬇ Kid's club ⚟ Tennis court ⚓ Games room ▢ Separate TV room ⛳ golf course ⚓ Boats for hire ⊟ Cinema 🎵 Entertainment 🎣 Fishing ◎ Mini golf ⚟ Watersports ⛹ Gym ⊛ Sports field Spa ∪ Stables
FACILITIES: ⬅ Bath ⚏ Shower ⊙ Electric shaver 🅿 Hairdryer ✳ Ice Pack Facility ⛇ Disabled facilities ⓢ Public telephone ⓢ Shop on site or within 200yds ⓢ Mobile shop (calls at least 5 days a week) ⬛ BBQ area ⫙ Picnic area WIFI Wi-fi 🖥 Internet access ♻ Recycling ❶ Tourist info ⫚ Dog exercise area

at East Fortune just 15 miles away. It's an easy drive on the nearby A1 to Edinburgh or alternatively, there is a regular bus service which stops near the site. There are camping pods and luxury lodges with hot tubs for hire. 9 acre site. 120 touring pitches. 50 hardstandings. Caravan pitches. Motorhome pitches. Tent pitches. 12 statics. 17 wooden pods.

Open: all year (rs Winter arrivals by prior arrangement) **Last arrival:** 18.00hrs **Last departure:** noon

Pitches: * 🚐 £20-£30 🚏 £20-£30 ▲ £20-£27 🏠

Leisure: 🅰

Facilities: 🖈☉📁☼🕭🗑🚻🅗🏧 ♻ ⓘ

Services: 🔌🖸 🔋🖉🇹🚮♨

Within 3 miles: ⚓🖉🗑🖸

Notes: Max 2 dogs per pitch. Dogs must be kept on leads. Freshly baked bread & croissants, tea & coffee.

AA Pubs & Restaurants nearby: The Kitchin, EDINBURGH, EH6 6LX, 0131 555 1755

Plumed Horse, EDINBURGH, EH6 6DE, 0131 554 5556

WEST LOTHIAN

EAST CALDER   Map 21 NT06

Places to visit

Almond Valley Heritage Trust, LIVINGSTON, EH54 7AR, 01506 414957
www.almondvalley.co.uk

Malleny Garden, BALERNO, EH14 7AF, 0844 493 2123
www.nts.org.uk/property/malleny-garden

Linwater Caravan Park
►►►►82%

tel: 0131 333 3326 **West Clifton EH53 0HT**
email: queries@linwater.co.uk
dir: *M9 junct 1, B7030 (brown Linwater sign). Or from Wilkieston on A71.*
grid ref: *NT104696*

A farmland park in a peaceful rural area within easy reach of Edinburgh. The very good facilities are housed in a Scandinavian-style building, and are well maintained by resident owners; they are genuinely caring hosts and nothing is too much trouble. There are 'timber tents' for hire and nearby are plenty of pleasant woodland walks. 5 acre site. 60 touring pitches. 22 hardstandings. Caravan pitches. Motorhome pitches. Tent pitches. 4 wooden pods.

Open: mid Mar-late Oct **Last arrival:** 21.00hrs **Last departure:** noon

Pitches: * 🚐 £18-£24 🚏 £18-£24 ▲ £16-£20 🏠

Leisure: 🅰

Facilities: 🖈☉📁☼🕭🅗🚮📶 ♻ ⓘ

Services: 🔌🖸 🔋🖉🇹♨♨

Within 3 miles: ⚓🖉🗑🖸

Notes: No noise after 23.00hrs. Dogs must be kept on leads. Takeaway food can be ordered.

AA Pubs & Restaurants nearby: The Bridge Inn, RATHO, EH28 8RA, 0131 333 1320

LINLITHGOW   Map 21 NS97

Places to visit

Linlithgow Palace, LINLITHGOW, EH49 7AL, 01506 842896
www.historic-scotland.gov.uk

House of The Binns, LINLITHGOW, EH49 7NA, 0844 493 2127
www.nts.org.uk/Property/House-of-the-Binns

Great for kids: Blackness Castle, LINLITHGOW, EH49 7NH, 01506 834807
www.historic-scotland.gov.uk

Beecraigs Caravan & Camping Site
►►►►86%

tel: 01506 844516 & 848943 **Beecraigs Country Park, The Visitor Centre EH49 6PL**
email: mail@beecraigs.com **web:** www.beecraigs.com
dir: *M9 junct 3 or 4, A803 from Linlithgow or Bathgate. Follow B792, signs to country park. Reception within visitor centre.* **grid ref:** *NT006746*

A wildlife enthusiast's paradise where even the timber facility buildings are in keeping with the environment. Beecraigs is situated peacefully in the open countryside of the Bathgate Hills. Small bays with natural shading offer intimate pitches. The smart toilet block on the main park includes en suite facilities, and there is a luxury toilet block for tenters. 6 acre site. 36 touring pitches. 36 hardstandings. Caravan pitches. Motorhome pitches. Tent pitches.

Open: all year (rs 25-26 Dec & 1-2 Jan no new arrivals) **Last arrival:** 20.00hrs **Last departure:** noon

Pitches: * 🚐 £18.21-£22.50 🚏 £18.21-£22.50 ▲ £15-£22.50

Leisure: 🅰

Facilities: ♨🖈☉📁☼🕭🅗🚮🏧♻ⓘ

Services: 🔌🖸 🔋🇹♨

Within 3 miles: ⚓🖉♨🗑🖸⚲

Notes: No cars by tents. No ball games near caravans, no noise after 22.00hrs. Dogs must be kept on leads. Country park facilities including Ranger Service events, child bath available.

AA Pubs & Restaurants nearby: Champany Inn, LINLITHGOW, EH49 7LU, 01506 834532

MORAY

ABERLOUR
Map 23 NJ24

Places to visit

Balvenie Castle, DUFFTOWN, AB55 4DH, 01340 820121
www.historic-scotland.gov.uk

Glenfiddich Distillery, DUFFTOWN, AB55 4DH, 01340 820373
www.glenfiddich.com

Aberlour Gardens Caravan Park
►►►80%

Best of British
GOLD

tel: 01340 871586 **AB38 9LD**
email: info@aberlourgardens.co.uk
dir: *Midway between Aberlour & Craigellachie on A95 turn onto unclassified road. Site signed. NB vehicles over 10' 6" use A941 Dufftown to Craigellachie road. Park is signed.*
grid ref: *NJ282434*

This attractive parkland site is set in the five-acre walled garden of the Victorian Aberlour House, surrounded by the spectacular scenery of the Cairngorm National Park, through pine clad glens, to the famous Moray coastline; the park is also well placed for the world renowned Speyside Malt Whisky Trail. It offers a small, well-appointed toilet block, laundry and small licensed shop. 5 acre site. 34 touring pitches. 16 hardstandings. 10 seasonal pitches. Caravan pitches. Motorhome pitches. Tent pitches. 32 statics.

Open: Mar-27 Dec (rs Winter park opening dates weather dependant)
Last arrival: 19.00hrs **Last departure:** noon

Pitches: * ⊕ £19.65-£24.50 ⊕ £19.65-£24.50 Å £15.50-£24.50

Leisure: ∕⋒

Facilities: ⋒ ⊙ ⅌ ☀ ᴪ ⅙ ⓒ 🖪 ⅏ 🖩 ♺ ❻

Services: ⊕ 🖾 🛍 ∅ T ᘔ

Within 3 miles: ᝋ ⌱ 🖪 🖾

Notes: No ball games, max 5mph speed limit, no noise after 23.00hrs. Dogs must be kept on leads.

ALVES

Places to visit

Pluscarden Abbey, ELGIN, IV30 8UA, 01343 890257 www.pluscardenabbey.org

Elgin Museum, ELGIN, IV30 1EQ, 01343 543675 www.elginmuseum.org.uk

Great for kids: Duffus Castle, DUFFUS, IV30 5RH, 01667 460232
www.historic-scotland.gov.uk

ALVES
Map 23 NJ16

North Alves Caravan Park
►►►67%

tel: 01343 850223 **IV30 8XD**
dir: *From Elgin towards Forres on A96, follow signs for site (sign in Alves), turn right onto unclassified road. Approx 1m site on right.* **grid ref:** *NJ122633*

A quiet rural site in attractive rolling countryside within three miles of a good beach. The site is on a former farm, and the stone buildings are quite unspoilt. 10 acre site. 45 touring pitches. Caravan pitches. Motorhome pitches. Tent pitches. 45 statics.

Open: Apr-Oct **Last arrival:** 23.00hrs **Last departure:** noon

Pitches: ⊕ ⊕ Å

Leisure: ∕⋒ ⊕ ✎ ⌷ **Facilities:** ⋒ ⊙ ⅌ ☀ ᴪ

Services: ⊕ 🖾 ∅ T ᘔ **Within 3 miles:** ᝋ ⌱ 🖯 ⌱ 🖾 U

Notes: ⊛ Dogs must be kept on leads.

AA Pubs & Restaurants nearby: The Old Mill Inn, FORRES, IV36 2TD, 01309 641605

LOSSIEMOUTH
Map 23 NJ27

Places to visit

Elgin Cathedral, ELGIN, IV30 1HU, 01343 547171 www.historic-scotland.gov.uk

Duffus Castle, DUFFUS, IV30 5RH, 01667 460232 www.historic-scotland.gov.uk

PREMIER PARK

Silver Sands Leisure Park
►►►►82%

tel: 01343 813262 **Covesea, West Beach IV31 6SP**
email: info@richmondwight.com
dir: *Take B9040 from Lossiemouth, 2m to site.* **grid ref:** *NJ205710*

This is an ideal family park located on the Moray coast two miles from the busy seaside town of Lossiemouth. There is direct access to a sandy beach and the entertainment complex caters for both children and adults, with a pool, sauna, steam room and a large gym. There is a well-stocked shop, takeaway food and a small bistro-style café on site. With a golf course next to the park and several others within easy driving distance (including the world famous Nairn Golf Course), this site makes a perfect base for touring the area. The are 98 fully serviced hardstandings (68 newly created for the 2014 season) and 15 static caravans for hire. 60 acre site. 140 touring pitches. 105 hardstandings. 35 seasonal pitches. Caravan pitches. Motorhome pitches. Tent pitches. 200 statics.

Open: 15 Feb-15 Jan (rs 15 Feb-Jun & Oct-15 Jan shops & entertainment restricted) **Last arrival:** 22.00hrs **Last departure:** noon

Pitches: * ⊕ £17.60-£27.50 ⊕ £17.60-£27.50 Å £13.20-£23.10

Leisure: ∕⋒ ⅃ ⊛ ✎ ⌷ ♫

Facilities: ⅃ ⋒ ⊙ ⅌ ☀ ᴪ ⅙ ⓒ 🖪 ⌷ ᴪ 🖩 ⬛ ♺ ❻

Services: ⊕ 🖾 🛐 ∅ T ⓒ ᘔ ⬛ ⇄

Within 3 miles: ᝋ ⌱ ⌱ ⊚ ⌱ 🖯 🖾 U

Notes: Dogs must be kept on leads.

LEISURE: 🏊 Indoor swimming pool 🏊 Outdoor swimming pool ∕⋒ Children's playground ᴪ Kid's club ⅃ Tennis court ✎ Games room ⌷ Separate TV room ⌱ golf course ⅃ Boats for hire ⅃ Cinema ♫ Entertainment ⌱ Fishing ⊚ Mini golf ⅃ Watersports ᴪ Gym ⊛ Sports field Spa U Stables
FACILITIES: ⅃ Bath ⋒ Shower ⊙ Electric shaver ⅌ Hairdryer ☀ Ice Pack Facility ⅙ Disabled facilities ⓒ Public telephone 🖪 Shop on site or within 200yds 🖯 Mobile shop (calls at least 5 days a week) ᴪ BBQ area ⌷ Picnic area 🖩 Wi-fi ⬛ Internet access ♺ Recycling ❻ Tourist info ᴪ Dog exercise area

PERTH & KINROSS

BLAIR ATHOLL
Map 23 NN86

Places to visit

Blair Castle, BLAIR ATHOLL, PH18 5TL, 01796 481207 www.blair-castle.co.uk

Killiecrankie Visitor Centre, KILLIECRANKIE, PH16 5LG, 0844 493 2194 www.nts.org.uk/property/killiecrankie

PREMIER PARK

Blair Castle Caravan Park
► ► ► ► ► 90%

tel: 01796 481263 **PH18 5SR**
email: mail@blaircastlecaravanpark.co.uk
dir: From A9 onto B8079 at Aldclune, follow to Blair Atholl. Site on right after crossing bridge in village. **grid ref:** NN874656

An attractive site set in impressive seclusion within the Atholl Estate, surrounded by mature woodland and the River Tilt. Although a large park, the various groups of pitches are located throughout the extensive parkland, and each has its own sanitary block with all-cubicled facilities of a very high standard. There is a choice of grass pitches, hardstandings and fully serviced pitches. This park is particularly suitable for the larger type of motorhome. 32 acre site. 226 touring pitches. 155 hardstandings. 68 seasonal pitches. Caravan pitches. Motorhome pitches. Tent pitches. 97 statics.

Open: Mar-Nov **Last arrival:** 21.30hrs **Last departure:** noon

Pitches: * 🚐 £23-£26 🚍 £23-£26 ▲ £18-£21

Leisure: 🄰 ⊛ ✎

Facilities: ➟ 🏕 ⊙ 🕑 ✳ ⟳ ⊙ 🛋 🗚 🏕 WiFi 🖳 ♻ ❼

Services: 🔌 📇 🛢 ⊘ ⊤ 🍴 🚼 🔫

Within 3 miles: ↻ ✐ ⊚ 🛢 🛢 ∪

Notes: Family park, no noise after 23.00hrs. Dogs must be kept on leads.

AA Pubs & Restaurants nearby: Killiecrankie Hotel, KILLIECRANKIE, PH16 5LG, 01796 473220

PREMIER PARK

River Tilt Caravan Park
► ► ► ► ► 84%

tel: 01796 481467 **PH18 5TE**
email: stuart@rivertilt.co.uk
dir: 7m N of Pitlochry on A9, take B8079 to Blair Atholl & site at rear of Tilt Hotel.
grid ref: NN875653

An attractive park with magnificent views of the surrounding mountains, idyllically set in hilly woodland country on the banks of the River Tilt, adjacent to the golf course. There is also a leisure complex with heated indoor swimming pool, sun lounge area, spa pool and multi-gym, all available for an extra charge; outdoors there is a short tennis court. The toilet facilities are very good. 2 acre site. 30 touring pitches. Caravan pitches. Motorhome pitches. Tent pitches. 69 statics.

Open: 16 Mar-12 Nov **Last arrival:** 21.00hrs **Last departure:** noon

Pitches: 🚐 🚍 ▲

Leisure: ⊛ ⅋ Spa

Facilities: 🏕 ⊙ 🕑 ✳ 🛋 🗚 🏕 WiFi 🖳 ♻ ❼

Services: 🔌 📇 🛢 🛢 ⊘ 🍴 🔫

Within 3 miles: ↻ ≟ ✐ ⊚ 🛢 🛢 ∪

Notes: Dogs must be kept on leads. Sauna, solarium, steam room.

AA Pubs & Restaurants nearby: Killiecrankie Hotel, KILLIECRANKIE, PH16 5LG, 01796 473220

DUNKELD
Map 21 NO04

Places to visit

The Ell Shop & Little Houses, DUNKELD, PH8 0AN, 0844 493 2192 www.nts.org.uk/Property/Dunkeld

Loch of the Lowes Visitor Centre, DUNKELD, PH8 0HH, 01350 727337 www.swt.org.uk

Inver Mill Farm Caravan Park
► ► ► ► 80%

tel: 01350 727477 **Inver PH8 0JR**
email: invermill@talk21.com
dir: A9 onto A822 then immediately right to Inver. **grid ref:** NO015422

A peaceful park on level former farmland, located on the banks of the River Braan and surrounded by mature trees and hills. The active resident owners keep the park in very good condition. 5 acre site. 65 touring pitches. 3 hardstandings. Caravan pitches. Motorhome pitches. Tent pitches.

Open: end Mar-Oct **Last arrival:** 22.00hrs **Last departure:** noon

Pitches: * 🚐 £20-£22 🚍 £20-£22 ▲ £10-£22

Facilities: 🏕 ⊙ 🕑 ✳ ⟳ ⊙ WiFi ♻ ❼

Services: 🔌 📇 🛢 ⊘ 🚼

Within 3 miles: ↻ ✐ 🛢 📇

Notes: ⊛ Dogs must be kept on leads.

PITCHES: 🚐 Caravans 🚍 Motorhomes ▲ Tents 🏠 Glamping-style accommodation **SERVICES:** 🔌 Electric hook up 📇 Launderette 🍴 Licensed bar 🛢 Calor Gas ⊘ Camping Gaz ⊤ Toilet fluid 🍴 Café/Restaurant 🚼 Fast Food/Takeaway 🔋 Battery charging 🚼 Baby care 🔫 Motorvan service point
ABBREVIATIONS: BH/bank hols – bank holidays Etr – Easter Spring BH – Spring Bank Holiday fr – from hrs – hours m – mile mdnt – midnight rdbt – roundabout rs – restricted service wk – week wknd – weekend x-rds – cross roads ⊛ No credit or debit cards ⊗ No dogs 🕯 Children of all ages accepted

KINLOCH RANNOCH
Map 23 NN65

Kilvrecht Campsite
▶ 74%

tel: 01350 727284 **PH16 5QA**
email: tay.fd@forestry.gsi.gov.uk **web:** www.forestry.gov.uk
dir: *From north shore: B846 to Kinloch Rannoch. Follow South Loch Rannoch sign. Over river bridge, 1st right signed Kilvrecht. Approach via unclassified road along loch, with Forestry Commission signs.* **grid ref:** NN623567

Set within a large forest clearing, approximately half a mile from the road to Kinloch Rannoch which runs along the loch. This is a beautifully maintained site, with good clean facilities, for those who wish for a peaceful break. It also makes an ideal base for those who prefer the more active outdoor activities of hill walking (Schiehallion is within easy reach) or mountain biking; it is a great spot to observe the multitude of birds and wildlife in the area. Please note the site has no electricity. 17 acre site. 60 touring pitches. Caravan pitches. Motorhome pitches. Tent pitches.

Open: Apr-Oct **Last arrival:** 22.00hrs **Last departure:** 10.00hrs
Pitches: ⊞ ⌑ Å
Facilities: ᴄ ⌐ *ℹ* **Within 3 miles:** ⅓ ℘ ⑤
Notes: 🐾 No fires. Dogs must be kept on leads.

PITLOCHRY

Places to visit

Edradour Distillery, PITLOCHRY, PH16 5JP, 01796 472095 www.edradour.com

Great for kids: Scottish Hydro Electric Visitor Centre, Dam & Fish Pass, PITLOCHRY, PH16 5ND, 01796 473152 www.scottish-hydro-centre.co.uk

PITLOCHRY
Map 23 NN95

Milton of Fonab Caravan Park
▶▶▶▶ 88%

tel: 01796 472882 **Bridge Rd PH16 5NA**
email: info@fonab.co.uk
dir: *From S on A924, pass petrol station on left, next left opposite Bell's Distillery into Bridge Rd. Cross river, site on left. From N (& Pitlochry centre) on A924, under rail bridge, right opposite Bell's Distillery into Bridge Rd.* **grid ref:** NN945573

Set on the banks of River Tummel on the outskirts of the picturesque town of Pitlochry, this is a family-owned site with excellent toilet facilities and large spacious pitches. The town, with various tourist attractions – Bells Distillery and the Pitlochry Festival Theatre to name but two – has a wide variety of shops and eateries to suit all tastes. The site makes a great base for touring beautiful rural Perthshire. 15 acre site. 154 touring pitches. Caravan pitches. Motorhome pitches. Tent pitches. 34 statics.

Open: Apr-Oct **Last arrival:** 21.00hrs **Last departure:** 13.00hrs
Pitches: ⊞ ⌑ Å
Facilities: ⇤ ↾ ⊙ ℘ ✳ ᴄ ⑤ ⑤ ⌐ ₩₣ ♻ *ℹ*
Services: ⊞ ⑤ ▮ ⌀
Within 3 miles: ⅓ ⅓ ℘ ⊙ ⑤ ⑤
Notes: 🐾 Couples & families only, no motor cycles. Dogs must be kept on leads.
AA Pubs & Restaurants nearby: Moulin Hotel, PITLOCHRY, PH16 5EH, 01796 472196
Killiecrankie Hotel, KILLIECRANKIE, PH16 5LG, 01796 473220

Faskally Caravan Park
▶▶▶▶ 82%

tel: 01796 472007 **PH16 5LA**
email: info@faskally.co.uk
dir: *1.5m N of Pitlochry on B8019.* **grid ref:** NN916603

A large park near Pitlochry, which is divided into smaller areas by mature trees and set within well-tended grounds. This family-owned site has two large amenity blocks and an entertainment complex with a heated swimming pool, bar, restaurant and indoor games area. There are numerous walks from the site and it is ideal for either a longer stay to explore the area or as a convenient stopover. A regular bus service is available at the site entrance. 27 acre site. 300 touring pitches. 45 hardstandings. Caravan pitches. Motorhome pitches. Tent pitches. 130 statics.

Open: 15 Mar-Oct **Last arrival:** 23.00hrs **Last departure:** 11.00hrs
Pitches: * ⊞ £20.50-£22.50 ⌑ £20.50-£22.50 Å £20.50-£22.50
Leisure: ⌂ ⌸ ♦ ♫ Spa
Facilities: ↾ ⊙ ℘ ✳ ᴄ ⑤ ⑤ ₩₣ 💻 ♻ *ℹ*
Services: ⊞ ⑤ ▯ ▮ ⌀ ⊤ ⑩
Within 3 miles: ⅓ ⅓ ℘ ⑤ ⑤ ∪
Notes: Dogs must be kept on leads.
AA Pubs & Restaurants nearby: Moulin Hotel, PITLOCHRY, PH16 5EH, 01796 472196
Killiecrankie Hotel, KILLIECRANKIE, PH16 5LG, 01796 473220

LEISURE: ⌂ Indoor swimming pool ⌐ Outdoor swimming pool ⌸ Children's playground ♦ Kid's club ♨ Tennis court ♦ Games room ☐ Separate TV room ⅓ golf course ⅓ Boats for hire ⌸ Cinema ♫ Entertainment ℘ Fishing ⊙ Mini golf ≋ Watersports ♦ Gym ⊙ Sports field Spa ∪ Stables
FACILITIES: ⇤ Bath ↾ Shower ⊙ Electric shaver ℘ Hairdryer ✳ Ice Pack Facility ᴄ Disabled facilities ⊙ Public telephone ⑤ Shop on site or within 200yds ⑤ Mobile shop (calls at least 5 days a week) ⍾ BBQ area ⌐ Picnic area ₩₣ Wi-fi 💻 Internet access ♻ Recycling *ℹ* Tourist info ⌐ Dog exercise area

TUMMEL BRIDGE
Map 23 NN75

Places to visit
Queen's View Visitor Centre, QUEEN'S VIEW, PH16 5NR, 01350 727284
www.forestry.gov.uk

Tummel Valley Holiday Park
HOLIDAY CENTRE 82%

tel: 0844 335 3756 **PH16 5SA**
email: touringandcamping@parkdeanholidays.com
dir: *From Perth take A9 N to bypass Pitlochry. In 3m take B8019 signed Tummel Bridge. Site 11m on left.* **grid ref:** *NN764592*

A well-developed site amongst mature forest in an attractive valley, beside the famous bridge on the banks of the River Tummel. Play areas and the bar are sited alongside the river, and there is an indoor pool, children's clubs and live family entertainment. This is an ideal base in which to relax. Please note that this park does not accept tents or trailer tents. 55 acre site. 26 touring pitches. 28 hardstandings. Caravan pitches. Motorhome pitches. 169 statics.

Open: mid Mar-Oct **Last arrival:** 21.00hrs **Last departure:** 10.00hrs

Pitches: 🚐 🚍

Leisure: 🏊 ⚙ 🎱 ♦ 🎵

Facilities: ♿ 🛒 ⊙ ☕ ✳ ❄ ⚓ ① 🔥 📶

Services: 🔌 🗑 🍴 🍵 🚚 🍼 ♿

Within 3 miles: ⚽ ◎ 🍴

Notes: Dogs must be kept on leads. Sports courts, sauna, solarium, toddlers' pool, amusements, rod hire.

AA Pubs & Restaurants nearby: Killiecrankie Hotel, KILLIECRANKIE, PH16 5LG, 01796 473220

SCOTTISH BORDERS

EYEMOUTH

Places to visit
Berwick-upon-Tweed Barracks, BERWICK-UPON-TWEED, TD15 1DF, 01289 304493 www.english-heritage.org.uk/daysout/properties/berwick-upon-tweed-barracks-and-main-guard

Great for kids: Eyemouth Museum, EYEMOUTH, TD14 5JE, 018907 50678

EYEMOUTH
Map 21 NT96

Eyemouth
HOLIDAY CENTRE 74%

tel: 0871 664 9740 **Fort Rd TD14 5BE**
email: eyemouth@park-resorts.com
dir: *From A1, approx 6m N of Berwick-upon-Tweed take A1107 to Eyemouth. On entering town, site signed. Right after petrol station, left at bottom of hill into Fort Rd.*
grid ref: *NT941646*

A cliff-top holiday park on the outskirts of the small fishing village of Eyemouth, within easy reach of Edinburgh and Newcastle. The site is handily placed for exploring the beautiful Scottish Borders and the magnificent coastline and countryside of north Northumberland. 22 acre site. 17 touring pitches. 7 hardstandings. 17 seasonal pitches. Caravan pitches. Motorhome pitches. 276 statics.

Open: Apr-Oct **Last arrival:** mdnt **Last departure:** 10.00hrs

Pitches: 🚐 🚍

Leisure: 🏊 ⚙ 🎱 ♦ 🎵 **Facilities:** 🛒 ☕ ♿ ① 🔥 📶 🖥 ♻ ❼

Services: 🔌 🗑 🍴 🍵 🚚 **Within 3 miles:** ⚽ ◎ 🚴 🍴

Notes: Dogs must be kept on leads.

LAUDER
Map 21 NT54

Places to visit
Abbotsford, MELROSE, TD6 9BQ, 01896 752043 www.scottsabbotsford.co.uk

LAUDER
Map 21 NT54

Thirlestane Castle Caravan & Camping Site
▶▶▶ 76%

tel: 01578 718884 & 07976 231032 **Thirlestane Castle TD2 6RU**
email: thirlestanepark@btconnect.com
dir: *Signed from A68 & A697, just S of Lauder.* **grid ref:** *NT536473*

Located on the outskirts of Lauder, close to the A68 and within the grounds of Thirlestane Castle, this is an ideal site from which to explore the many attractions in the Scottish Borders. The amenity block is immaculately maintained and the pitches are behind the estate boundary wall to provide a secluded and peaceful location. There is a regular service bus near the site entrance. 5 acre site. 60 touring pitches. 22 hardstandings. 30 seasonal pitches. Caravan pitches. Motorhome pitches. Tent pitches. 27 statics.

Open: Apr-1 Oct **Last arrival:** 20.00hrs **Last departure:** noon

Pitches: 🚐 🚍 🏕

Facilities: 🛒 ⊙ ✳ ① 🖥 ♻ ❼ **Services:** 🔌 🗑 ♿

Within 3 miles: ⚽ ◎ 🍴 **Notes:** Dogs must be kept on leads.

continued

PITCHES: 🚐 Caravans 🚍 Motorhomes 🏕 Tents 🏠 Glamping-style accommodation **SERVICES:** 🔌 Electric hook up 🗑 Launderette 🍴 Licensed bar 🔋 Calor Gas ⊘ Camping Gaz T Toilet fluid 🍵 Café/Restaurant 🍔 Fast Food/Takeaway 🔌 Battery charging 🍼 Baby care ♿ Motorvan service point **ABBREVIATIONS:** BH/bank hols – bank holidays Etr – Easter Spring BH – Spring Bank Holiday fr – from hrs – hours m – mile mdnt – midnight rdbt – roundabout rs – restricted service wk – week wknd – weekend x-rds – cross roads ⊘ No credit or debit cards ⊗ No dogs 🚸 Children of all ages accepted

PEEBLES — Map 21 NT24

Places to visit

Kailzie Gardens, PEEBLES, EH45 9HT, 01721 720007 www.kailziegardens.com

Robert Smail's Printing Works, INNERLEITHEN, EH44 6HA, 0844 493 2259
www.nts.org.uk/property/robert-smails-printing-works

Crossburn Caravan Park
►►►►81%

tel: 01721 720501 **Edinburgh Rd EH45 8ED**
email: enquiries@crossburncaravans.co.uk **web:** www.crossburn-caravans.com
dir: *0.5m N of Peebles on A703.* **grid ref:** NT248417

A peaceful, family-run park, on the edge of Peebles and within easy driving distance for Edinburgh and the Scottish Borders. The park is divided by well-maintained landscaping and mature trees, and has good views over the countryside. There is a regular bus service at the site entrance and Peebles has a wide range of shops and attractions. The facilities are maintained to a high standard. There is also a main caravan dealership on site and a large stock of spares and accessories are available. 6 acre site. 45 touring pitches. 15 hardstandings. Caravan pitches. Motorhome pitches. Tent pitches. 85 statics. 2 wooden pods.

Open: Apr-Oct **Last arrival:** 21.00hrs **Last departure:** 14.00hrs

Pitches: * 🚐 £25-£27 🚐 £25-£27 ▲ £21-£25 🏠

Leisure: 🛝

Facilities: 🚿 🥾 ☺ 🕯 ⚕ 🛗 WiFi ♻ 🛈

Services: 🔌 🗑 🛢 🚰 T 🛒 ⛏

Within 3 miles: 🎣 ⛳ 🛍 ∪

Notes: Dogs must be kept on leads.

AA Pubs & Restaurants nearby: Cringletie House, PEEBLES, EH45 8PL, 01721 722510
Macdonald Cardrona Hotel, Golf & Spa, PEEBLES, EH45 8NE, 0844 879 9024

STIRLING

ABERFOYLE — Map 20 NN50

PREMIER PARK

Trossachs Holiday Park
►►►►►84%

GOLD

tel: 01877 382614 **FK8 3SA**
email: info@trossachsholidays.co.uk **web:** www.trossachsholidays.co.uk
dir: *Access on E side of A81, 1m S of junct A821 & 3m S of Aberfoyle.*
grid ref: NS544976

An attractively landscaped and peaceful park with outstanding views towards the hills, including the Munro, Ben Lomond. Set within the Loch Lomond National Park, boating, walking, cycling and beautiful drives over the Dukes Pass through the Trossachs are just some of the attractions within easy reach. Bikes can be hired from the reception and there is an internet café that sells home baked items. There are lodges for hire. 40 acre site. 66 touring pitches. 46 hardstandings. Caravan pitches. Motorhome pitches. Tent pitches. 84 statics.

Open: Mar-Oct **Last arrival:** 21.00hrs **Last departure:** noon

Pitches: 🚐 🚐 ▲

Leisure: 🛝 🎣 🖵 **Facilities:** 🥾 ☺ 🕯 ✳ 🕙 🛍 🛒 🛗 WiFi 🖥

Services: 🔌 🗑 🛢 T 🍴 🛒 **Within 3 miles:** 🎣 ≋ ⛳ 🛍 🗑 ∪

Notes: Groups by prior arrangement only.

AA Pubs & Restaurants nearby: The Clachan Inn, DRYMEN, G63 0BG, 01360 660824

See advert opposite

BLAIRLOGIE
Map 21 NS89

Places to visit

Alloa Tower, ALLOA, FK10 1PP, 0844 493 2129
www.nts.org.uk/property/alloa-tower

The National Wallace Monument, STIRLING, FK9 5LF, 01786 472140
www.nationalwallacemonument.com

AA CAMPSITE OF THE YEAR FOR SCOTLAND 2015

Witches Craig Caravan & Camping Park
►►►►90%

tel: 01786 474947 **FK9 5PX**
email: info@witchescraig.co.uk
dir: *3m NE of Stirling on A91 Hillfoots to St Andrews road.* **grid ref:** *NS821968*

In an attractive setting with direct access to the lower slopes of the dramatic Ochil Hills, this is a well-maintained family-run park. It is in the centre of 'Braveheart' country, with easy access to historical sites and many popular attractions. 5 acre site. 60 touring pitches. 60 hardstandings. 6 seasonal pitches. Caravan pitches. Motorhome pitches. Tent pitches.

Open: Apr-Oct **Last arrival:** 20.00hrs **Last departure:** noon

Pitches: * ♚ £21-£24 ♚ £21-£24 ▲ £17-£19.50

Leisure: ⚠ **Facilities:** ⋔⊙℘✻⚸⊞★⊞ ♻ ❶

Services: �R⊡⯊⊘⊤≐⯊ **Within 3 miles:** ⅃⊟℘⊚⑤⑤∪

Notes: Dogs must be kept on leads. Food preparation area, cooking shelters, baby bath & changing area.

CALLANDER
Map 20 NN60

Places to visit

Doune Castle, DOUNE, FK16 6EA, 01786 841742 www.historic-scotland.gov.uk

Gart Caravan Park
►►►►87%

tel: 01877 330002 **The Gart FK17 8LE**
email: enquiries@theholidaypark.co.uk
dir: *1m E of Callander on A84.* **grid ref:** *NN643070*

A very well appointed and spacious parkland site within easy walking distance of the tourist and outdoor activity-friendly town of Callander. The site is in an excellent location for touring the area; Loch Katrine (where there are trips on the *SS* Sir Walter Scott), The Trossachs and the Rob Roy Centre are only a few of the many nearby attractions. Free fishing is available on the River Teith which runs along the edge of the site. The statics vans are in a separate area. Please note that tents are not accepted. 26 acre site. 128 touring pitches. 45 hardstandings. Caravan pitches. Motorhome pitches. 66 statics.

Open: Etr or Apr-15 Oct **Last arrival:** 22.00hrs **Last departure:** 11.30hrs

Pitches: * ♚ £23.50-£27.50 ♚ £23.50-£27.50

Leisure: ⚠⚙ **Facilities:** ⋔⊙✻⚸⊙★⊞ ▣ ♻ ❶

Services: ⊟⊡⯊⯊ **Within 3 miles:** ⅃⊁℘⊚≐⑤⑤∪

Notes: No commercial vehicles. Dogs must be kept on leads.

AA Pubs & Restaurants nearby: Roman Camp Country House Hotel, CALLANDER, FK17 8BG, 01877 330003

The Lade Inn, CALLANDER, FK17 8HD, 01877 330152

PITCHES: ♚ Caravans ♚ Motorhomes ▲ Tents ⋒ Glamping-style accommodation **SERVICES:** ⊟ Electric hook up ⊡ Launderette ⬚ Licensed bar ⬚ Calor Gas ⬚ Camping Gaz ⊤ Toilet fluid ⬚ Café/Restaurant ⬚ Fast Food/Takeaway ≐ Battery charging ⬚ Baby care ⯊ Motorvan service point
ABBREVIATIONS: BH/bank hols – bank holidays Etr – Easter Spring BH – Spring Bank Holiday fr – from hrs – hours m – mile mdnt – midnight rdbt – roundabout rs – restricted service wk – week wknd – weekend x-rds – cross roads ⬚ No credit or debit cards ⊗ No dogs ⬚ Children of all ages accepted

LUIB
Map 20 NN42

Glendochart Holiday Park
►►►► 74%

tel: 01567 820637 **FK20 8QT**
email: info@glendochart-caravanpark.co.uk
dir: On A85 Oban to Stirling road, midway between Killin & Crianlarich.
grid ref: NN477278

A small site located on the A85 some eight miles from Killin, with boating and fishing available on Loch Tay. It is also convenient for Oban, Fort William and Loch Lomond. Hill walkers have direct access to numerous walks to suit all levels including the nearby Munro of Ben More. There is a regular bus service at the site entrance and nearby Crianlarich provides access to the West Highland Railway known as Britain's most scenic rail route, and also the West Highland Way. An ideal site as a stopover to the west coast or for a longer holiday. 15 acre site. 35 touring pitches. 28 hardstandings. Caravan pitches. Motorhome pitches. Tent pitches. 60 statics.

Open: Mar-Nov **Last arrival:** 21.00hrs **Last departure:** noon

Pitches: * ⛺ £18.50-£20 ⛺ £18.50-£20 ▲ £15-£17

Facilities: ⬀⊙🅟✳⭑🖀🛒🅯

Services: 🔌🗑🔌⊘🚽 **Within 3 miles:** 🎣

Notes: Dogs must be kept on leads.

AA Pubs & Restaurants nearby: The Lade Inn, CALLANDER, FK17 8HD, 01877 330152

STIRLING

See Blairlogie

STRATHYRE
Map 20 NN51

Immervoulin Caravan and Camping Park
►►► 77%

tel: 01877 384285 **FK18 8NJ**
dir: On A84, approx 1m S of Strathyre. **grid ref:** NN560164

A family-run park on open meadowland beside the River Balvaig, where fishing, canoeing and other water sports can be enjoyed. A riverside walk leads to Loch Lubnaig, and the small village of Strathyre has various pubs offering food. Located on the A84, the site is ideally located for exploring this lovely area. The park has a modern well-appointed amenity block. 5 acre site. 50 touring pitches. Caravan pitches. Motorhome pitches. Tent pitches.

Open: Mar-Oct **Last arrival:** 22.00hrs

Pitches: ⛺ ⛺ ▲

Facilities: ⬀⊙🅟✳⭑🕐🖀🛒🅯

Services: 🔌🗑🔌⊘🚽⊤🛒

Within 3 miles: 🎣🖀

Notes: No noise after 23.00hrs.

AA Pubs & Restaurants nearby: Creagan House, STRATHYRE, FK18 8ND, 01877 384638

SCOTTISH ISLANDS

ISLE OF ARRAN

KILDONAN
Map 20 NS02

Places to visit

Brodick Castle, Garden & Country Park, BRODICK, KA27 8HY, 0844 493 2152
www.nts.org.uk/Property/Brodick-Castle-Garden-and-Country-Park

Isle of Arran Heritage Museum, BRODICK, KA27 8DP, 01770 302636
www.arranmuseum.co.uk

Sealshore Camping and Touring Site
►►►► 82%

tel: 01770 820320 **KA27 8SE**
email: enquiries@campingarran.com
dir: From ferry terminal in Brodick turn left, 12m, through Lamlash & Whiting Bay. Left to Kildonan, site on left. **grid ref:** NS024210

On the south coast of Arran and only 12 miles from the ferry at Brodick, this is a peaceful, family-run site with direct access to a sandy beach. There are fabulous views across the water to Pladda Island and Ailsa Craig, and an abundance of wildlife. The site is suited for all types of touring vehicles but caters very well for non-motorised campers. The resident owner, also a registered fisherman, sells fresh lobster and crab, and on request will give fishing lessons on a small, privately owned lochan. There is an undercover BBQ, campers' kitchen and day room with TV. A bus, which stops on request, travels around the island. 3 acre site. 43 touring pitches. 8 hardstandings. Caravan pitches. Motorhome pitches. Tent pitches. 2 wooden pods.

Open: Mar-Oct **Last arrival:** 21.00hrs **Last departure:** noon

Pitches: ⛺ fr £20.50 ⛺ fr £20.50 ▲ fr £15 🏠

Leisure: 🎣▭ **Facilities:** ⬀⊙🅟✳⭑🖀🛒📶🖥♻🅯

Services: 🔌🗑🔌⊘⊤🍽🛒⬇

Within 3 miles: ⬇🎣◎🖀🗑

Notes: No cars by tents. No fires, no noise after 22.00hrs. Dogs must be kept on leads.

Interested in camping on an island? Take a look at page 20

ISLE OF MULL

CRAIGNURE · Map 20 NM73

Places to visit

Duart Castle, CRAIGNURE, PA64 6AP, 01680 812309 www.duartcastle.com

Shieling Holidays
▶▶▶▶ 84%

tel: 01680 812496 & 0131 556 0068 **PA65 6AY**
email: sales@shielingholidays.co.uk
dir: *From ferry left onto A849 to Iona. 400mtrs left at church, follow site signs towards sea.* **grid ref:** *NM724369*

A lovely site on the water's edge with spectacular views, and less than one mile from the ferry landing. Hardstandings and service points are provided for motorhomes, and there are astro-turf pitches for tents. The park also offers unique, en suite cottage tents for hire and bunkhouse accommodation for families. There is also a wildlife trail on site. 7 acre site. 90 touring pitches. 30 hardstandings. Caravan pitches. Motorhome pitches. Tent pitches. 15 statics.

Open: 6 Mar-2 Nov **Last arrival:** 22.00hrs **Last departure:** noon

Pitches: * � £17.50-£19.50 ☎ £17.50-£19.50 ▲ £16.50-£18

Leisure: ⚙◢▢ **Facilities:** ♿♠☺☞☀♿☺♨☐♨🛜♲❂

Services: ⚡☐ ♠⌀☐☷⇊

Within 3 miles: ⚓☞☖☐

Notes: Dogs must be kept on leads. Bikes available.

ISLE OF SKYE

EDINBANE · Map 22 NG35

Places to visit

Dunvegan Castle and Gardens, DUNVEGAN, IV55 8WF, 01470 521206
www.dunvegancastle.com

Skye Camping & Caravanning Club Site
▶▶▶▶ 90%

tel: 01470 582230 **Loch Greshornish, Borve, Arnisort IV51 9PS**
email: skye.site@thefriendlyclub.co.uk
dir: *Approx 12m from Portree on A850 (Dunvegan road). Site by loch shore.*
grid ref: *NG345527*

Situated on the beautiful Isle of Skye, this campsite stands out for its stunning waterside location and glorious views, the generous pitch density, the overall range of facilities, and the impressive ongoing improvements under enthusiastic franchisee owners. The layout maximises the beauty of the scenery and genuine customer care is very evident with an excellent tourist information room and campers' shelter being just two examples. The amenities block has smart, modern fittings, including excellent showers, a generously proportioned disabled room and a family bathroom. This is a green site that uses only green toilet fluids, which are available on site. There is an on-site shop, two camping pods to let, plus car hire is available on the site. Non-members are very welcome too. 7.5 acre site. 105 touring pitches. 36 hardstandings. Caravan pitches. Motorhome pitches. Tent pitches. 2 wooden pods.

Open: Apr-Oct **Last arrival:** 22.00hrs **Last departure:** noon

Pitches: � ☎ ▲ ⌂

Facilities: ♠☺☞☀♿☺♨☐♨🛜♲❂

Services: ⚡☐ ♠⌀☐☷⇊

Within 3 miles: ☞☖☐

Notes: Barrier locked 23.00hrs-07.00hrs. Dogs must be kept on leads. Fresh fish van visits weekly.

AA Pubs & Restaurants nearby: Stein Inn, STEIN, IV55 8GA, 01470 592362

Loch Bay Seafood Restaurant, STEIN, IV55 8GA, 01470 592235

The Three Chimneys, COLBOST, IV55 8ZT, 01470 511258

STAFFIN · Map 22 NG46

Staffin Camping & Caravanning
▶▶▶ 80%

tel: 01470 562213 **IV51 9JX**
email: staffincampsite@btinternet.com
dir: *On A855, 16m N of Portree. Turn right before 40mph signs.* **grid ref:** *NG492670*

A large sloping grassy site with level hardstandings for motorhomes and caravans, close to the village of Staffin. The toilet block is appointed to a very good standard and the park has a laundry. Mountain bikes are available for hire. 2.5 acre site. 50 touring pitches. 18 hardstandings. Caravan pitches. Motorhome pitches. Tent pitches.

Open: Apr-Oct **Last arrival:** 22.00hrs **Last departure:** 11.00hrs

Pitches: * � fr £16 ☎ fr £16 ▲ fr £14

Facilities: ♠☺☞☀♿☐♨🛜♲❂

Services: ⚡☐ ♠⌀☷

Within 3 miles: ⚓☞☖☐

Notes: ⊗ No music after 22.00hrs. Dogs must be kept on leads. Picnic tables, kitchen area, campers' bothy.

AA Pubs & Restaurants nearby: The Glenview, STAFFIN, IV51 9JH, 01470 562248

PITCHES: �CA Caravans ☎ Motorhomes ▲ Tents ⌂ Glamping-style accommodation **SERVICES:** ⚡ Electric hook up ☐ Launderette ☷ Licensed bar ♠ Calor Gas ⌀ Camping Gaz ☐ Toilet fluid ☺ Café/Restaurant ⿻ Fast Food/Takeaway ☷ Battery charging ☷ Baby care ⇊ Motorvan service point
ABBREVIATIONS: BH/bank hols – bank holidays Etr – Easter Spring BH – Spring Bank Holiday fr – from hrs – hours m – mile mdnt – midnight rdbt – roundabout rs – restricted service wk – week wknd – weekend x-rds – cross roads ⊗ No credit or debit cards ⊗ No dogs ♟ Children of all ages accepted

Wales

Wales – a place of myth and legend, a country loved passionately by actors and poets and male voice choirs, a land of rugged mountain grandeur and craggy, meandering coastline. Crossing the Severn Bridge, you sense at once you are entering a completely different country. The culture is different, so are the traditions and so are the physical characteristics. With its lush hills and dramatic headlands, it has echoes of other Celtic lands – most notably, Ireland and Scotland.

Wales's legacy of famous names from the world of the arts is truly impressive. Richard Burton hailed from the valleys in South Wales, Anthony Hopkins originates from Port Talbot and Dylan Thomas was born a century ago in a house on a hilltop street in Swansea. His birthplace in Cwmdonkin Drive can be hired for self-catering breaks and holidays and there is even the chance to sleep in the poet's tiny bedroom. Thomas described the house as 'a provincial villa…a small, not very well painted gateless house…very nice, very respective.'

Further west is the house where he lived in his final years. Thomas and his wife Caitlin moved to the Boat House at Laugharne, 40 miles from Swansea, in the spring of 1949. With its magnificent views across an expansive estuary, this was Dylan Thomas's perfect retreat and much of his creative writing was completed in the modest wooden shed on a bluff above the house. The Boat House is open to visitors and nearby Brown's Hotel, his favourite watering hole, offers the chance to relax and enjoy something to eat and drink.

On the Pembrokeshire coast, renowned for its beautiful beaches, is another, less familiar link with Dylan Thomas. The old fishing village of Lower Fishguard was home to a film unit of almost 100 people in the early months of 1971. Presided over by the film director Andrew Sinclair, filming of Thomas's classic play *Under Milk Wood* began, with Richard Burton and Peter O'Toole among the many film stars seen around the village. A young, virtually unknown David Jason, also appeared in the film. Sinclair and his team built false fronts on the dock cottages and created an undertaker's parlour – among other work. The National Eisteddfod in Llangollen is one of the most important events in the Welsh cultural calendar, celebrating the country's long heritage of storytelling, music and poetry.

Think of Wales and you often think of castles. The formidable Caernarfon Castle, the setting for the investure of the Prince of Wales in 1969, stands in the northwest corner of the country. Harlech Castle was built around 1283 by Edward I and from it are seen the peaks of Snowdonia. This glorious region of towering summits and crags, which has the highest range of mountains in England and Wales and is now a National Park, has long attracted walkers and climbers. Edmund Hillary and his team rehearsed here for the first successful assault on Everest in 1953. However, Snowdonia is not just about mountain peaks. There are plenty of gentler alternatives, including an extensive network of lowland routes, forest trails and waymarked walks. Below Snowdon lies the historic village of Llanberis, one of the region's most popular attractions and ideally placed for touring Snowdonia. Betws-y-Coed is another mountain resort with a range of delightful walks exploring picturesque river scenery and pretty, pastoral uplands.

For the buzz and vibrancy of the city, Swansea and Cardiff cannot be beaten, the latter boasting a lively café culture, docklands-style apartments, a science discovery centre that's fun for all the family, and the internationally renowned Wales Millennium Centre (Canolfan Mileniwm Cymru). However, in terms of Welsh scenery, there is so much waiting to be discovered and explored; the grand, immensely varied landscape of the Brecon Beacons, and the gentler, pastoral acres of the Welsh Borders – among a host of famed beauty spots throughout Wales.

◁ Snowdonia National Park

ISLE OF ANGLESEY

BEAUMARIS
Map 14 SH67

Places to visit

Beaumaris Castle, BEAUMARIS, LL58 8AP, 01248 810361
www.cadw.wales.gov.uk

Kingsbridge Caravan Park
▶▶▶▶ 82%

tel: 01248 490636 & 07774 842199 **Camp Rd, Llanfaes LL58 8LR**
email: info@kingsbridgecaravanpark.co.uk
dir: *From either Menai Bridge or Britannia Bridge follow signs for Beaumaris & A545. In Beaumaris (castle on left) take B5109 towards Llangoed, 2m to x-rds, turn left signed Kingsbridge.* **grid ref:** *SH605784*

Peacefully located two miles from historic Beaumaris, this long-established park has been transformed by its caring owners into a must-stay destination for lovers of walking and wildlife. The generously sized pitches are located in two separate touring areas — one for families and one for adults only — each has its own modern, well-equipped amenities block that are smartly presented with quality decor and fittings. Please note that a laundry is not provided but modern facilities are available in nearby Beaumaris. 14 acre site. 90 touring pitches. 21 hardstandings. 15 seasonal pitches. Caravan pitches. Motorhome pitches. Tent pitches. 29 statics.

Open: Mar-Oct **Last arrival:** 21.00hrs **Last departure:** noon

Pitches: * 🚐 £17-£23 🚌 £17-£23 ▲ £17-£30

Leisure: 🅰 🌀

Facilities: 📶 ⊙ 🅿 ✳ 🕒 🛢 ♻ 🔰

Services: 🚰 🛢 🝵 🅃 🔧 🔩

Within 3 miles: ↨ 🏌 ⛵ 🛒 🛢 ∪

Notes: No noise after 23.00hrs, no camp fires. Dogs must be kept on leads.

AA Pubs & Restaurants nearby: Ye Olde Bulls Head Inn, BEAUMARIS, LL58 8AP, 01248 810329

The Ship Inn, RED WHARF BAY, LL75 8RJ, 01248 852568

See which sites have been awarded Gold Pennants on page 36

DULAS
Map 14 SH48

Places to visit

Din Lligwy Hut Group, LLANALLGO, 01443 336000 www.cadw.wales.gov.uk

PREMIER PARK

Tyddyn Isaf Caravan Park
▶▶▶▶▶ 90%

tel: 01248 410203 & 410667 **Lligwy Bay LL70 9PQ**
email: mail@tyddynisaf.co.uk **web:** www.tyddynisaf.co.uk
dir: *Take A5025 through Benllech to Moelfre rdbt, left towards Amlwch to Brynrefail. Turn right to Lligwy at phone box. Site 0.5m down lane on right.* **grid ref:** *SH486873*

A beautifully situated, and very spacious family park on rising ground adjacent to a sandy beach, with magnificent views overlooking Lligwy Bay. A private footpath leads directly to the beach and there is an excellent nature trail around the park. The site has very good toilet facilities, including a block with underfloor heating and excellent unisex privacy cubicles, a well-stocked shop, and bar/restuarant serving meals, which are best enjoyed on the terrace with its magnificent coast and sea views. 16 acre site. 80 touring pitches. 60 hardstandings. 50 seasonal pitches. Caravan pitches. Motorhome pitches. Tent pitches. 56 statics.

Open: Mar-Oct (rs Mar-Jul & Sep-Oct bar & shop opening limited)
Last arrival: 21.30hrs **Last departure:** 11.00hrs

Pitches: 🚐 🚌 ▲

Leisure: 🅰 ▭

Facilities: 📶 ⊙ 🅿 ✳ ♿ 🕒 🛢 🎡 ㅐ 📶 🖥 ♻ 🔰

Services: 🚰 🔧 🝵 🛢 🅃 🍽 🛒 🔩

Within 3 miles: ↨ 🕊 🏌 🛢 ∪

Notes: 🐾 No groups, loud music or open fires, maximum 3 units together. Dogs must be kept on leads. Baby changing unit.

AA Pubs & Restaurants nearby: The Ship Inn, RED WHARF BAY, LL75 8RJ, 01248 852568

Ye Olde Bulls Head Inn, BEAUMARIS, LL58 8AP, 01248 810329

Bishopsgate House Hotel, BEAUMARIS, LL58 8BB, 01248 810302

LEISURE: 🏊 Indoor swimming pool 🏊 Outdoor swimming pool 🅰 Children's playground 🧒 Kid's club 🎾 Tennis court 🎯 Games room ▭ Separate TV room ⛳ golf course ⛵ Boats for hire 🎬 Cinema 🎵 Entertainment 🎣 Fishing ◉ Mini golf 🏄 Watersports 🏋 Gym 🌀 Sports field Spa ∪ Stables
FACILITIES: 🛁 Bath 📶 Shower ⊙ Electric shaver 🅿 Hairdryer ✳ Ice Pack Facility ♿ Disabled facilities 🕒 Public telephone 🛢 Shop on site or within 200yds 🚚 Mobile shop (calls at least 5 days a week) 🍖 BBQ area 🪑 Picnic area 📶 Wi-fi 🖥 Internet access ♻ Recycling 🔰 Tourist info 🐾 Dog exercise area

MARIAN-GLAS
Map 14 SH58

Places to visit
Din Lligwy Hut Group, LLANALLGO, 01443 336000 www.cadw.wales.gov.uk

PREMIER PARK

Home Farm Caravan Park
▶▶▶▶▶ 93%

Best of British

GOLD

tel: 01248 410614 **LL73 8PH**
email: enq@homefarm-anglesey.co.uk **web:** www.homefarm-anglesey.co.uk
dir: On A5025, 2m N of Benllech. Site 300mtrs beyond church. **grid ref:** SH498850

A first-class park run with passion and enthusiasm, set in an elevated and secluded position sheltered by trees, and with good planting and landscaping. The peaceful rural setting affords views of farmland, the sea and the mountains of Snowdonia. The modern toilet blocks are spotlessly clean and well maintained, and there are excellent play facilities for children both indoors and out. Facilities also include a visitors' parking area and a smart reception and shop. The area is blessed with sandy beaches, and the local pubs and shops cater for everyday needs. 12 acre site. 102 touring pitches. 65 hardstandings. Caravan pitches. Motorhome pitches. Tent pitches. 84 statics.

Open: Apr-Oct **Last arrival:** 21.00 **Last departure:** noon
Pitches: * ▭ £25.50-£35 ▭ £25.50-£35 ▲ £16.50-£29
Leisure: ⚲ ⛱ ☺ ✎ ▢
Facilities: ⬅ ♙ ☉ ℱ ☼ ⬤ ◔ ⑤ ✠ WiFi 🖳 ♻ ⊘
Services: ⬛ ⑤ ⊘ Ⓣ ≟ ⬇
Within 3 miles: ⇃ ℐ ⬚ ⚲ ⑤ ⬚ ∪
Notes: No roller blades, skateboards or scooters.
AA Pubs & Restaurants nearby: The Ship Inn, RED WHARF BAY, LL75 8RJ, 01248 852568
Ye Olde Bulls Head Inn, BEAUMARIS, LL58 8AP, 01248 810329
Bishopsgate House Hotel, BEAUMARIS, LL58 8BB, 01248 810302

PENTRAETH
Map 14 SH57

Places to visit
Bryn Celli Ddu Burial Chamber, BRYN CELLI DDU, 01443 336000 www.cadw.wales.gov.uk

Plas Newydd, PLAS NEWYDD, LL61 6DQ, 01248 714795 www.nationaltrust.org.uk/main/plasnewydd

St David's Park
▶▶▶▶ 87%

tel: 01248 852341 & 852702 **Red Wharf Bay LL75 8RJ**
email: info@stdavidspark.com
dir: A55 junct 8, A5025 towards Benllech. Approx 8m, right towards Red Wharf Bay, site 0.5m on left. **grid ref:** SH529811

In a stunning location with panoramic coastal and mountain views and direct access to sandy beaches, this long-established holiday village has been transformed in recent years to provide 105 pitches, 44 of which are allocated to seasonal customers. A haven for campers, the all-tent pitches have electric hook-up facilities and a stylish modern amenities block with hi-spec facilities. The Tavern Bistro and Bar offers a wide range of imaginative food and beverages. 47 acre site. 45 touring pitches. 44 seasonal pitches. Caravan pitches. Motorhome pitches. Tent pitches. 180 statics.

Open: 15 Mar-end Sep **Last arrival:** 21.00hrs **Last departure:** noon
Pitches: * ▭ £25-£36 ▭ £25-£36 ▲ £25-£36
Leisure: ⚲ ♻ **Facilities:** ⬅ ♙ ℱ ☼ ⬤ ⑤ WiFi ♻ ⊘
Services: ⬛ ⑤ ⬇ ▤ ⬤
Within 3 miles: ⇃ ≟ ℐ ⬚ ⑤ ⬚ ∪
Notes: ⊗ No group bookings, no jet skis, gazebos or disposable BBQs, no noise after 23.00hrs.

Rhos Caravan Park
▶▶▶ 78%

tel: 07788 772268 **Rhos Farm LL75 8DZ**
dir: On A5025, 1m N of Pentraeth. **grid ref:** SH517794

A warm welcome awaits families at this spacious park on level, grassy ground with easy access to the main road to Amlwch. A 200-acre working farm that has two play areas and farm animals to keep children amused, with good beaches, pubs, restaurants and shops nearby. The two toilet blocks are kept to a good standard by enthusiastic owners who are constantly improving the facilities. 15 acre site. 98 touring pitches. Caravan pitches. Motorhome pitches. Tent pitches. 66 statics.

Open: Mar-Oct **Last arrival:** 22.00hrs **Last departure:** 16.00hrs
Pitches: ▭ ▭ ▲
Leisure: ⚲ **Facilities:** ♙ ⬤ ☼ ✠ ⊘
Services: ⬛ ⑤ ⬇ ⊘ ≟
Within 3 miles: ⇃ ≟ ℐ ⬚ ⑤ ⬚ ∪
Notes: ⬤
AA Pubs & Restaurants nearby: The Ship Inn, RED WHARF BAY, LL75 8RJ, 01248 852568
Ye Olde Bulls Head Inn, BEAUMARIS, LL58 8AP, 01248 810329
Bishopsgate House Hotel, BEAUMARIS, LL58 8BB, 01248 810302

RHOS LLIGWY
Map 14 SH48

Places to visit
Din Lligwy Hut Group, LLANALLGO, 01443 336000 www.cadw.wales.gov.uk

Ty'n Rhos Caravan Park
►►►68%

tel: 01248 852417 **Lligwy Bay, Moelfre LL72 8NL**

email: robert@bodafonpark.co.uk

dir: *Take A5025 from Benllech to Moelfre rdbt, right to T-junct in Moelfre. Left, approx 2m, pass x-rds leading to beach, site 50mtrs on right.* **grid ref:** *SH495867*

A family park close to the beautiful beach at Lligwy Bay, and cliff walks along the Heritage Coast. Historic Din Lligwy, and the shops at picturesque Moelfre are nearby. All the touring pitches have water, electric hook-up and TV connection. Please note that guests should register at Bodafon Caravan Park in Benllech where detailed directions will be given and pitches allocated. 10 acre site. 30 touring pitches. 4 hardstandings. 48 seasonal pitches. Caravan pitches. Motorhome pitches. Tent pitches. 80 statics. 20 bell tents/yurts.

Open: Mar-Oct **Last arrival:** 20.00hrs **Last departure:** noon

Pitches: 🚐 🚏 Å ⛺

Leisure: 🏌

Facilities: 📷 ⊙ ✳ 🔥 🕙 🐕 📶 🖥 🎁

Services: 🔌 🔯 🔒

Within 3 miles: 🏌 ℘ 🏊 🛒 🎠

Notes: No campfires, no noise after 23.00hrs. Dogs must be kept on leads.

AA Pubs & Restaurants nearby: The Ship Inn, RED WHARF BAY, LL75 8RJ, 01248 852568

Ye Olde Bulls Head Inn, BEAUMARIS, LL58 8AP, 01248 810329

Bishopsgate House Hotel, BEAUMARIS, LL58 8BB, 01248 810302

RHOSNEIGR
Map 14 SH37

Ty Hen
►►►77%

tel: 01407 810331 **Station Rd LL64 5QZ**

email: info@tyhen.com

dir: *From A55 junct 5 follow signs to Rhosneigr, at clock turn right. Entrance (red gate post) 50mtrs before Rhosneigr railway station.* **grid ref:** *SH327738*

This site is in an attractive seaside location near a large fishing lake and riding stables. Surrounded by lovely countryside, this former working farm is close to RAF Valley, which is great for plane spotters, but expect some aircraft noise during the

day. The friendly owners are always on hand. 7.5 acre site. 38 touring pitches. 5 hardstandings. 33 seasonal pitches. Caravan pitches. Motorhome pitches. Tent pitches. 42 statics.

Open: mid Mar-Oct **Last arrival:** 21.00hrs **Last departure:** noon

Pitches: 🚐 🚏 Å

Leisure: 🏊 Å 🎣 🎵 **Facilities:** 📷 ⊙ 🔥 🐕 📶 ♻ 🎁

Services: 🔌 🔯 🔒 🛒 ⛏

Within 3 miles: 🏌 ℘ 🏊 🛒 🔯

Notes: 1 motor vehicle per pitch, children must not be out after 22.00hrs. Dogs must be kept on leads. Fishing, family room, walks.

BRIDGEND

PORTHCAWL
Map 9 SS87

Places to visit
Newcastle Castle, BRIDGEND, 01443 336000 www.cadw.wales.gov.uk

Coity Castle, COITY, CF35 6BG, 01443 336000 www.cadw.wales.gov.uk

Brodawel Camping & Caravan Park
►►►82%

tel: 01656 783231 **Moor Ln, Nottage CF36 3EJ**

email: info@brodawelcamping.co.uk

dir: *M4 junct 37, A4229 towards Porthcawl. Site on right off A4229 signed Brodawel.* **grid ref:** *SS816789*

A lovely family park close to sea and other attractions, with a lush grass touring field that provides generously sized pitches; most have electric hook-up. There is a smart amenities block appointed to a high standard, a well-stocked shop and WiFi. 4 acre site. 100 touring pitches. 4 hardstandings. 40 seasonal pitches. Caravan pitches. Motorhome pitches. Tent pitches.

Open: Apr-mid Oct **Last arrival:** 19.00hrs **Last departure:** 11.00hrs

Pitches: 🚐 £14-£20 🚏 £14-£20 Å £14-£20

Leisure: Å 🎣

Facilities: 🛁 📷 ⊙ 🔥 ✳ 🕙 🎁 🍴 📶 ♻ 🎁

Services: 🔌 🔯 🔒 🛒 🚽 T

Within 3 miles: 🏌 ⛴ ⊟ ℘ ◎ 🏊 🎁 🔯 🎠

Notes: Dogs must be kept on leads. Free electrical sockets, undercover picnic area, baby changing facility.

AA Pubs & Restaurants nearby: Prince of Wales Inn, KENFIG, CF33 4PR, 01656 740356

CARMARTHENSHIRE

LLANDOVERY
Map 9 SN73

Places to visit

Dolaucothi Gold Mines, PUMSAINT, SA19 8US, 01558 650177
www.nationaltrust.org.uk/main/w-dolaucothigoldmines

PREMIER PARK

Erwlon Caravan & Camping Park
▶▶▶▶▶85%

tel: 01550 721021 & 720332 **Brecon Rd SA20 0RD**
email: peter@erwlon.co.uk **web:** www.erwlon.co.uk
dir: 0.5m E of Llandovery on A40. **grid ref:** SN776343

A long-established, family-run site set beside a brook in the Brecon Beacons foothills. The town of Llandovery and the hills overlooking the Towy Valley are a short walk away. The superb, Scandinavian-style facilities block has cubicled washrooms, family and disabled rooms and is an impressive feature. 8 acre site. 75 touring pitches. 15 hardstandings. Caravan pitches. Motorhome pitches. Tent pitches.

Open: all year **Last arrival:** anytime **Last departure:** noon

Pitches: 🚐 🚏 🛆

Leisure: 🅰

Facilities: 🌊 ⊙ 🏪 ✳ & ⓢ 🚻 🚽 📶 ♻ ❼

Services: 🔌 🔳 🛢 🚿 🔋 ⛟

Within 3 miles: ↕ 🚣 🛒 🏦 ⛳ ♨

Notes: Quiet after 22.30hrs. Dogs must be kept on leads. Fishing, cycle storage & hire.

AA Pubs & Restaurants nearby: The Kings Head, LLANDOVERY, SA20 0AB, 01550 720393

Llandovery Caravan Park
▶▶▶77%

tel: 01550 721065 & 07970 650 606 **Church Bank SA20 0DT**
email: llandoverycaravanpark@gmail.com
dir: A40 from Carmarthen, over rail crossing, past junct with A483 (Builth Wells). Turn right for Llangadog, past church, 1st right signed Rugby Club & Camping.
grid ref: SN762342

Within easy walking distance of the town centre and adjacent to the notable Llandovery Dragons Rugby Club, this constantly improving park is an ideal base for touring the Brecon Beacons and many local attractions. Most pitches have both water and a hardstanding, and guests are welcome to use the popular on-site rugby club lounge bar. Please note a laundry is not provided but there is one in the town. 8 acre site. 100 touring pitches. 10 hardstandings. 40 seasonal pitches. Caravan pitches. Motorhome pitches. Tent pitches.

Open: all year **Last arrival:** 20.00hrs **Last departure:** 20.00hrs

Pitches: 🚐 £12-£15 🚏 £12-£15 🛆 £9-£15

Leisure: 🅰 ⊙ 🖵 **Facilities:** 🌊 ⊙ & 🚻 ♻ ❼

Services: 🔌 🍴 🛢

Within 3 miles: ↕ 🎏 🚣 🛒 🏦 ♨

Notes: 🐕 Dogs must be kept on leads.

AA Pubs & Restaurants nearby: The Kings Head, LLANDOVERY, SA20 0AB, 01550 720393

LLANGADOG
Map 9 SN72

Places to visit

Dinefwr Park and Castle, LLANDEILO, SA19 6RT, 01558 823902
www.nationaltrust.org.uk/dinefwrpark

Carreg Cennen Castle, CARREG CENNEN CASTLE, SA19 6UA, 01558 822291
www.cadw.wales.gov.uk

Abermarlais Caravan Park
▶▶▶78%

tel: 01550 777868 & 777797 **SA19 9NG**
dir: On A40 midway between Llandovery & Llandeilo, 1.5m NW of Llangadog.
grid ref: SN695298

An attractive, well-run site with a welcoming atmosphere. This part-level, part-sloping park is in a wooded valley on the edge of the Brecon Beacons National Park, beside the River Marlais. 17 acre site. 88 touring pitches. 2 hardstandings. Caravan pitches. Motorhome pitches. Tent pitches.

Open: 15 Mar-15 Nov (rs Mar & Nov 1 toilet block, water point no hot water) **Last arrival:** 23.00hrs **Last departure:** noon

Pitches: * 🚐 £12-£14 🚏 £12-£14 🛆 £12-£14

Leisure: 🅰 **Facilities:** 🌊 ⊙ ✳ & ⓢ 🏦 🚻 ❼

Services: 🔌 🛢 🚿 Ⓣ 🔋

Within 3 miles: 🚣 🏦 🛒 ♨

Notes: No open fires, quiet from 23.00hrs-08.00hrs. Dogs must be kept on leads. Volleyball, badminton court, softball tennis net.

AA Pubs & Restaurants nearby: The Angel Hotel, LLANDEILO, SA19 6EN, 01558 822765

The Kings Head, LLANDOVERY, SA20 0AB, 01550 720393

PITCHES: 🚐 Caravans 🚏 Motorhomes 🛆 Tents 🏠 Glamping-style accommodation **SERVICES:** 🔌 Electric hook up 🔳 Launderette 🍴 Licensed bar 🛢 Calor Gas 🚿 Camping Gaz Ⓣ Toilet fluid 🍽 Café/Restaurant 🍟 Fast Food/Takeaway 🔋 Battery charging 🚼 Baby care ⛟ Motorvan service point
ABBREVIATIONS: BH/bank hols – bank holidays Etr – Easter Spring BH – Spring Bank Holiday fr – from hrs – hours m – mile mdnt – midnight
rdbt – roundabout rs – restricted service wk – week wknd – weekend x-rds – cross roads 🚫 No credit or debit cards 🚫 No dogs 👫 Children of all ages accepted

LLANGENNECH
Map 8 SN50

Places to visit

WWT LLanelli Wetland Centre, LLANELLI, SA14 9SH, 01554 741087
www.wwt.org.uk/wetland-centres/llanelli/

NEW South Wales Caravan Park
►►► 90%

tel: 01554 820420 **Llwynifan Farm SA14 8AX**
email: info@southwalescaravanpark.com
dir: *M4 junct 48, A4138 signed Llanelli. In 11.5m right at rdbt. In 425yds left between bungalows into farm road.* **grid ref:** *SN554027*

This site is located in an elevated position close to Llanelli. The touring pitches, including 10 that are fully serviced, are on three terraced levels providing stunning countryside views. The grounds are immaculately maintained with a wide variety of trees, shrubs and pretty seasonal flowers, and a very well-equipped gym is also available. A same-day laundry service is provided too. Excellent customer care is assured; hands-on management from owners Cathrin and Hywel Davies means that visitors will have a memorable stay. 5 acre site. 30 touring pitches. Caravan pitches. Motorhome pitches.

Open: Feb-Nov **Last arrival:** 19.00hrs **Last departure:** noon
Pitches: * ⊞ £15-£20 ⊞ £15-£20
Notes: Adults only.

NEWCASTLE EMLYN
Map 8 SN34

Places to visit

Cilgerran Castle, CILGERRAN, SA43 2SF, 01239 621339 www.cadw.wales.gov.uk

Castell Henllys Iron Age Fort, CRYMYCH, SA41 3UT, 01239 891319 www.castellhenllys.com

Great for kids: Felinwynt Rainforest Centre, FELINWYNT, SA43 1RT, 01239 810882 www.butterflycentre.co.uk

---

NEWCASTLE EMLYN
Map 8 SN34

PREMIER PARK

Cenarth Falls Holiday Park
►►►►► 87%

Best of British

tel: 01239 710345 **Cenarth SA38 9JS**
email: enquiries@cenarth-holipark.co.uk **web:** www.cenarth-holipark.co.uk
dir: *From Newcastle Emlyn on A484 towards Cardigan. Through Cenarth, site on right.* **grid ref:** *SN265421*

Located close to the village of Cenarth where the River Teifi, famous for its salmon and trout fishing, cascades through the Cenarth Falls Gorge. With beautifully landscaped grounds and spotless amenities, the park also benefits from an indoor heated swimming pool, sauna, fitness suite and a restaurant with bar. 2 acre site. 30 touring pitches. 30 hardstandings. Caravan pitches. Motorhome pitches. Tent pitches. 89 statics.

Open: Mar-Nov (rs Off peak bar & meals restricted to wknds only) **Last arrival:** 20.00 **Last departure:** 11.00hrs
Pitches: * ⊞ £17-£28 ⊞ £17-£28 ▲ £17-£28
Leisure: ⊜ ⊜ ⍢ ⋀ ⬤ ♫
Facilities: ⍢ ⊙ ⍢ ✳ ⬤ ⬤ WiFi ⬤ ⊘
Services: ⬤ ⍢ ⍢ ⬤ ⬤ ⍢ ⍢ ⬤
Within 3 miles: ⍢ ⍢ ⍢ ⬤ ⬤
Notes: No skateboards. Dogs must be kept on leads. Pool table.
AA Pubs & Restaurants nearby: Nags Head Inn, ABERCYCH, SA37 0HJ, 01239 841200

Moelfryn Caravan & Camping Park
►►►► 85%

tel: 01559 371231 **Ty-Cefn, Pant-y-Bwlch SA38 9JE**
email: info@moelfryncaravanpark.co.uk
dir: *A484 from Carmarthen towards Cynwyl Elfed. Pass the shops on right, 200yds take left fork onto B4333 towards Hermon. In 7m follow brown sign on left. Turn left, site on right.* **grid ref:** *SN321370*

A small, beautifully maintained, family-run park in a glorious elevated location overlooking the valley of the River Teifi. Pitches are level and spacious, and well screened by hedging and mature trees. The centrally located amenities block was completely refurbished for the 2014 season; it has stylish decor, smart cladding, provision of good privacy options and excellent fixtures and fittings. 3 acre site. 25 touring pitches. 16 hardstandings. 12 seasonal pitches. Caravan pitches. Motorhome pitches. Tent pitches.

Open: Mar-10 Jan **Last arrival:** 22.00hrs **Last departure:** noon
Pitches: * ⊞ fr £13.50 ⊞ fr £13.50 ▲ fr £12
Leisure: ⋀
Facilities: ⍢ ⊙ ⍢ ✳ ⬤ WiFi ⬤ ⊘
Services: ⬤ ⍢ ⬤ ⬤ ⍢
Within 3 miles: ⍢ ⍢ ⍢ ⍢ ⬤ ⬤ ⬤ ⬤
Notes: Games to be played in designated area only. Dogs must be kept on leads. Caravan storage.
AA Pubs & Restaurants nearby: Nags Head Inn, ABERCYCH, SA37 0HJ, 01239 841200
Webley Waterfront Inn & Hotel, ST DOGMAELS, SA43 3LN, 01239 612085

LEISURE: ⊜ Indoor swimming pool ⊜ Outdoor swimming pool ⋀ Children's playground ⬤ Kid's club ⬤ Tennis court ⬤ Games room ⬤ Separate TV room ⬤ golf course ⬤ Boats for hire ⬤ Cinema ♫ Entertainment ⬤ Fishing ⬤ Mini golf ⬤ Watersports ⍢ Gym ⬤ Sports field Spa ⬤ Stables
FACILITIES: ⬤ Bath ⍢ Shower ⊙ Electric shaver ⬤ Hairdryer ✳ Ice Pack Facility ⬤ Disabled facilities ⬤ Public telephone ⬤ Shop on site or within 200yds ⬤ Mobile shop (calls at least 5 days a week) ⬤ BBQ area ⬤ Picnic area WiFi Wi-fi ⬤ Internet access ⬤ Recycling ⊘ Tourist info ⬤ Dog exercise area

Argoed Meadow Caravan and Camping Site
►►►►82%

tel: 01239 710690 **Argoed Farm SA38 9JL**
web: www.cenarthcampsite.co.uk
dir: *From Newcastle Emlyn on A484 towards Cenarth, take B4332. Site 300yds on right.*
grid ref: *SN268415*

A warm welcome is assured at this attractive and immaculately maintained site, situated on the banks of the River Teifi and close to Cenarth Falls Gorge. The spotlessly clean amenities block provides very good privacy options for the less able visitors. 3 acre site. 30 touring pitches. 5 hardstandings. Caravan pitches. Motorhome pitches. Tent pitches. 5 statics.

Open: all year **Last arrival:** anytime **Last departure:** noon

Pitches: 🚐 🚐 ▲

Facilities: 🎇 ⊙ 🧺 ✳ 🕁 🕔 🖻 🛒 🏕 ♻ ❷

Services: 🔌 🗑 🛢 ⊘ 🔋 🚼

Within 3 miles: 🎱 🎣 🛒 🗑 ∪

Notes: 🚫 No bikes or skateboards. Dogs must be kept on leads.

AA Pubs & Restaurants nearby: Nags Head Inn, ABERCYCH, SA37 0HJ, 01239 841200

Webley Waterfront Inn & Hotel, ST DOGMAELS, SA43 3LN, 01239 612085

Afon Teifi Caravan & Camping Park
►►►►80%

tel: 01559 370532 **Pentrecagal SA38 9HT**
email: afonteifi@btinternet.com **web:** www.afonteifi.co.uk
dir: *Signed from A484, 2m E of Newcastle Emlyn.* **grid ref:** *SN338405*

Set on the banks of the River Teifi, a famous salmon and sea trout river, this secluded, family-owned and run park has good views. It is only two miles from the market town of Newcastle Emlyn. The smart amenities block is appointed to a high standard. 6 acre site. 110 touring pitches. 22 hardstandings. 25 seasonal pitches. Caravan pitches. Motorhome pitches. Tent pitches. 15 statics.

Open: Apr-Oct **Last arrival:** 23.00hrs

Pitches: * 🚐 £18-£20 🚐 £18-£20 ▲ £10-£20

Leisure: 🎱 ⊕ 🔍

Facilities: 🎇 ⊙ 🧺 ✳ 🕁 🕔 🖻 🛒 🏕 ♻ ❷

Services: 🔌 🗑 🛢 ⊘ T 🚼

Within 3 miles: 🎱 🎣 🏊 🗑 ∪

Notes: 🚫 Dogs must be kept on leads.

AA Pubs & Restaurants nearby: Nags Head Inn, ABERCYCH, SA37 0HJ, 01239 841200

Webley Waterfront Inn & Hotel, ST DOGMAELS, SA43 3LN, 01239 612085

PITCHES: 🚐 Caravans 🚐 Motorhomes ▲ Tents 🏠 Glamping-style accommodation **SERVICES:** 🔌 Electric hook up 🗑 Launderette 🍷 Licensed bar 🛢 Calor Gas ⊘ Camping Gaz T Toilet fluid 🍽 Café/Restaurant 🍔 Fast Food/Takeaway 🔋 Battery charging 🚼 Baby care 🚐 Motorvan service point
ABBREVIATIONS: BH/bank hols – bank holidays Etr – Easter Spring BH – Spring Bank Holiday fr – from hrs – hours m – mile mdnt – midnight rdbt – roundabout rs – restricted service wk – week wknd – weekend x-rds – cross roads 🚫 No credit or debit cards 🚫 No dogs 👫 Children of all ages accepted

CEREDIGION

ABERAERON
Map 8 SN46

Places to visit
Llanerchaeron, ABERAERON, SA48 8DG, 01545 570200 www.nationaltrust.org.uk

Aeron Coast Caravan Park
▶▶▶ 90%

tel: 01545 570349 **North Rd SA46 0JF**
email: enquiries@aeroncoast.co.uk
dir: On A487 (coast road), N outskirts of Aberaeron, signed. Filling station at entrance.
grid ref: SN460631

A well-managed family holiday park on the edge of the attractive resort of Aberaeron, with direct access to the beach. The spacious pitches are all level. On-site facilities include an extensive outdoor pool complex, a multi-activity outdoor sports area, an indoor children's play area, a small lounge bar which serves food, a games room and an entertainment suite. 22 acre site. 100 touring pitches. 30 hardstandings. Caravan pitches. Motorhome pitches. Tent pitches. 200 statics.

Open: Mar-Oct **Last arrival:** 23.00hrs **Last departure:** 11.00hrs

Pitches: * ⊕ £17-£27 ⊕ £17-£27 ▲ £17-£27

Leisure: ⬡⬡⬡⬡⬡⬡⬡

Facilities: ⬡⬡⬡⬡⬡⬡⬡⬡⬡⬡

Services: ⬡⬡⬡⬡⬡⬡⬡⬡⬡⬡⬡⬡⬡

Within 3 miles: ⬡⬡⬡⬡⬡

Notes: Families only, no motorcycles. Dogs must be kept on leads.

AA Pubs & Restaurants nearby: The Harbourmaster, ABERAERON, SA46 0BT, 01545 570755

Ty Mawr Mansion, ABERAERON, SA48 8DB, 01570 470033

ABERYSTWYTH
Map 8 SN58

Places to visit
The National Library of Wales, ABERYSTWYTH, SY23 3BU, 01970 632565 www.llgc.org.uk

Vale of Rheidol Railway, ABERYSTWYTH, SY23 1PG, 01970 625819 www.rheidolrailway.co.uk

Ocean View Caravan Park
▶▶▶ 82%

tel: 01970 828425 & 623361 **North Beach, Clarach Bay SY23 3DT**
email: enquiries@oceanviewholidays.com
dir: Exit A487 in Bow Street. Straight on at next x-rds. Site 2nd on right.
grid ref: SN592842

This site is in a sheltered valley on gently sloping ground, with wonderful views of both the sea and the countryside. The beach of Clarach Bay is just 200 yards away, and this welcoming park is ideal for all the family. There is a children's football field and dog walking area. Campers may use the pool, gym, restaurant and bar at Clarach Bay which is within walking distance of the site. 9 acre site. 24 touring pitches. 15 hardstandings. 20 seasonal pitches. Caravan pitches. Motorhome pitches. Tent pitches. 56 statics.

Open: Mar-Oct **Last arrival:** 20.00hrs **Last departure:** noon

Pitches: ⊕ £14.50-£20 ⊕ £14.50-£20 ▲

Leisure: ⬡

Facilities: ⬡⬡⬡⬡⬡⬡⬡⬡⬡⬡⬡⬡⬡

Services: ⬡⬡⬡⬡

Within 3 miles: ⬡⬡⬡⬡⬡⬡⬡⬡

Notes: Dogs must be kept on leads.

BORTH
Map 14 SN69

Places to visit
The National Library of Wales, ABERYSTWYTH, SY23 3BU, 01970 632565 www.llgc.org.uk

Brynowen Holiday Park
HOLIDAY CENTRE 76%

tel: 01970 871366 **SY24 5LS**
email: brynowen@park-resorts.com
dir: Signed from B4353, S of Borth. **grid ref:** SN608893

Enjoying spectacular views across Cardigan Bay and the Cambrian Mountains, a small touring park in a large and well-equipped holiday centre. The well-run park offers a wide range of organised activities and entertainment for all the family from morning until late in the evening. A long sandy beach is a few minutes' drive away. 52 acre site. 16 touring pitches. 16 hardstandings. 4 seasonal pitches. Caravan pitches. Motorhome pitches. 480 statics.

Open: Apr-Oct **Last arrival:** mdnt **Last departure:** 10.00hrs

Pitches: ⊕ ⊕

Leisure: ⬡⬡⬡⬡⬡⬡⬡⬡

Facilities: ⬡⬡⬡⬡⬡⬡⬡⬡⬡⬡

Services: ⬡⬡⬡⬡⬡

Within 3 miles: ⬡⬡⬡

Notes: No cars by caravans. Dogs must be kept on leads. Mini ten-pin bowling.

NEW QUAY
Map 8 SN35

Places to visit
Llanerchaeron, ABERAERON, SA48 8DG, 01545 570200 www.nationaltrust.org.uk

Quay West Holiday Park
HOLIDAY HOME PARK 86%

tel: 01545 560477 **SA45 9SE**
email: quaywest@haven.com **web:** www.haven.com/quaywest
dir: From Cardigan on A487 left onto A486 into New Quay. Or from Aberystwyth on A487 right onto B4342 into New Quay. **grid ref:** SN397591

This holiday park enjoys a stunning clifftop position overlooking picturesque New Quay and Cardigan Bay. It's an easy walk to a glorious sandy beach, and the all-action on-site activities include heated swimming pools, SplashZone, football, archery and fencing (with professional tuition) and the Aqua Bar and terrace. There is a good range of holiday caravans.

LEISURE: 🏊 Indoor swimming pool 🏊 Outdoor swimming pool 🎠 Children's playground 👶 Kid's club 🎾 Tennis court 🎱 Games room 📺 Separate TV room ⛳ golf course 🚤 Boats for hire 🎬 Cinema 🎵 Entertainment 🎣 Fishing 🏌 Mini golf 🏄 Watersports 🏋 Gym 🏐 Sports field ♨ Spa ♘ Stables
FACILITIES: 🛁 Bath 🚿 Shower 🔌 Electric shaver 💈 Hairdryer ❄ Ice Pack Facility ♿ Disabled facilities 📞 Public telephone 🏪 Shop on site or within 200yds 🚐 Mobile shop (calls at least 5 days a week) 🍖 BBQ area 🏕 Picnic area 📶 Wi-fi 💻 Internet access ♻ Recycling ℹ Tourist info 🐕 Dog exercise area

Open: Mar-Oct

Change over day: Mon, Fri, Sat

Arrival and departure times: Please contact the site

Statics: 125 Sleeps 6-8 Bedrms 2-3 Bathrms 1-2 Toilets 1-2 Microwave Freezer TV Sky/FTV Elec inc Gas inc Grass area

Children: ♦♦ Cots Highchair **Dogs:** 2 on leads No dangerous dogs

Leisure: ♨ ⊜ ♒ Cycle hire ♨ /⋀

CONWY

BETWS-YN-RHOS
Map 14 SH97

Places to visit

Bodelwyddan Castle, BODELWYDDAN, LL18 5YA, 01745 584060
www.bodelwyddan-castle.co.uk

Bodnant Garden, TAL-Y-CAFN, LL28 5RE, 01492 650460
www.nationaltrust.org.uk/bodnant-garden

Hunters Hamlet Caravan Park
►►►► 85%

tel: 01745 832237 & 07721 552106 **Sirior Goch Farm LL22 8PL**
email: huntershamlet@aol.com
dir: From A55 W'bound, A547 junct 24 into Abergele. At 2nd lights turn left by George & Dragon pub, onto A548. 2.75m right at x-rds onto B5381. Site 0.5m on left. **grid ref:** SH928736

A warm welcome is assured at this long established, family-run working farm park next to the owners' Georgian farmhouse. Well-spaced pitches, including 15 with water, electricity and TV hook-up, are within two attractive hedge-screened grassy paddocks. The well-maintained amenities block, includes unisex bathrooms. Please note that this site does not accept tents. 2 acre site. 30 touring pitches. 30 hardstandings. Caravan pitches. Motorhome pitches.

Open: Mar-Oct **Last arrival:** 22.00hrs **Last departure:** noon

Pitches: ⊞ £18-£29 ⊞ £18-£29

Leisure: /⋀

Facilities: ⬥ ⋔⊙ℙ☼⅋⬤WiFi ♻ ❼

Services: ⊕⊙ ▮⊨

Within 3 miles: ↓✎⑤

Notes: No football, dogs must not be left unattended. Dogs must be kept on leads. Baby bath & changing facilities.

AA Pubs & Restaurants nearby: The Hawk & Buckle Inn, LLANNEFYDD, LL16 5ED, 01745 540249

The Kinmel Arms, ABERGELE, LL22 9BP, 01745 832207

Plas Farm Caravan Park
►►►► 83%

tel: 01492 680254 & 07831 482176 **LL22 8AU**
email: info@plasfarmcaravanpark.co.uk **web:** www.plasfarmcaravanpark.co.uk
dir: A55 junct 24, A547 through Abergele, straight on at 2 mini rdbts, follow Rhyd-Y-Foel signs, 3m. Left, follow signs. **grid ref:** SH897744

Ideally located for exploring the many attractions of north Wales and within easy travelling distance of historic Chester, this beautifully landscaped park, adjacent to a 16th-century farmhouse, is certainly a popular choice. Major investment within recent years has resulted in superb pitches, many fully serviced on terraced area; the camping area sited in woodland ensures tranquillity and relaxation, with only birdsong to disturb the peace. There are two modern amenities blocks, a good laundry and a well-equipped campers' kitchen. 10 acre site. 54 touring pitches. 54 hardstandings. Caravan pitches. Motorhome pitches. Tent pitches.

Open: Mar-Oct **Last arrival:** 19.00hrs **Last departure:** 11.00hrs

Pitches: ⊞ £17.50-£27.50 ⊞ £17.50-£27.50 ⋀ £10-£25

Leisure: /⋀

Facilities: ⋔⊙ℙ☼⅋⬤⊙⑤⊟⬤WiFi ♻ ❼

Services: ⊕⊙ ▮⊤⊨⬤⬥

Within 3 miles: ↓⊟✎⑤⑤

Notes: Quiet after 23.00hrs, no campfires, no large groups. Dogs must be kept on leads. Woodland walk.

AA Pubs & Restaurants nearby: The Kinmel Arms, ABERGELE, LL22 9BP, 01745 832207

Peniarth Bach Farm
►►► 87%

tel: 07545 572744 **Roadside LL22 8PL**
email: geoff-wilson@btinternet.com
dir: A55 junct 25, left into Abergele. Left at lights onto B5381 towards Llanfairth. Right after 3m signed Betws-yn-Rhos. Site signed on right. **grid ref:** SH926737

A campsite for only a few years and part of a working farm which also offers quality stone holiday cottages for hire. Most pitches are hardstanding, with electric hook-up and water supply, and the smart purpose-built amenities block provides modern and efficient facilities. 40 acre site. 38 touring pitches. 15 hardstandings. Caravan pitches. Motorhome pitches. Tent pitches.

Open: Mar-Oct **Last arrival:** flexible **Last departure:** 11.00hrs

Pitches: ⊞ ⊞ ⋀

Facilities: ⋔⊙ℙ☼⅋⬤⊟⬤WiFi ♻ ❼

continued

PITCHES: ⊞ Caravans ⊞ Motorhomes ⋀ Tents ⋒ Glamping-style accommodation **SERVICES:** ⊕ Electric hook up ⊙ Launderette ⊡ Licensed bar ▮ Calor Gas ⊘ Camping Gaz ⊤ Toilet fluid ⊙ Café/Restaurant ⬛ Fast Food/Takeaway ⊨ Battery charging ⬥ Baby care ⬥ Motorvan service point
ABBREVIATIONS: BH/bank hols – bank holidays Etr – Easter Spring BH – Spring Bank Holiday fr – from hrs – hours m – mile mdnt – midnight rdbt – roundabout rs – restricted service wk – week wknd – weekend x-rds – cross roads ⊘ No credit or debit cards ⊗ No dogs ♦♦ Children of all ages accepted

BETWS-YN-RHOS *continued*

Services: 🔧🔋 T 💼⚡

Within 3 miles: ↨⚓🎯🏌🎣◎⚓🏐🎱∪

Notes: 🔇 No noise after mdnt. Dogs must be kept on leads. Family room.

AA Pubs & Restaurants nearby: The Hawk & Buckle Inn, LLANNEFYDD, LL16 5ED, 01745 540249

The Kinmel Arms, ABERGELE, LL22 9BP, 01745 832207

LLANDDULAS
Map 14 SH97

Places to visit

Rhuddlan Castle, RHUDDLAN, LL18 5AD, 01745 590777 www.cadw.wales.gov.uk

Bodelwyddan Castle, BODELWYDDAN, LL18 5YA, 01745 584060 www.bodelwyddan-castle.co.uk

---

PREMIER PARK

Bron-Y-Wendon Caravan Park
►►►►► 85%

tel: 01492 512903 **Wern Rd LL22 8HG**
email: stay@northwales-holidays.co.uk
dir: *Take A55 W. Right at Llanddulas/A547 junct 23 sign, sharp right. 200yds, under A55 bridge. Park on left.* **grid ref:** *SH903785*

A top quality site in a stunning location, with panoramic sea views from every pitch and excellent purpose-built toilet facilities including heated shower blocks. Pitch density is excellent, offering a high degree of privacy, and the grounds are beautifully landscaped and immaculately maintained. Super pitches are available. Staff are helpful and friendly, and everything from landscaping to maintenance has a stamp of excellence. An ideal seaside base for touring Snowdonia and visiting Colwyn Bay, Llandudno and Conwy. 8 acre site. 130 touring pitches. 85 hardstandings. Caravan pitches. Motorhome pitches.

Open: all year **Last arrival:** anytime **Last departure:** 11.00hrs

Pitches: * 🚐 £21-£25 🚐 £21-£25

Leisure: 🎱

Facilities: 🌲⊙🎯☀☕🏧 WiFi 🖥 ♻ ❶

Services: 🔧🔋 🔋⚡

Within 3 miles: ↨⚓🎣⚓🏐🎱∪

Notes: Dogs must be kept on leads.

AA Pubs & Restaurants nearby: Pen-y-Bryn, COLWYN BAY, LL29 6DD, 01492 533360

LLANRWST
Map 14 SH86

Places to visit

Gwydir Uchaf Chapel, LLANRWST, 01443 336000 www.cadw.wales.gov.uk

Trefriw Woollen Mills, TREFRIW, LL27 0NQ, 01492 640462 www.t-w-m.co.uk

Great for kids: Conwy Valley Railway Museum, BETWS-Y-COED, LL24 0AL, 01690 710568 www.conwyrailwaymuseum.co.uk

---

AA CAMPSITE OF THE YEAR FOR WALES 2015

PREMIER PARK

Bron Derw Touring Caravan Park
►►►►► 85%

tel: 01492 640494 **LL26 0YT**
email: bronderw@aol.com **web:** www.bronderw-wales.co.uk
dir: *A55 onto A470 for Betws-y-Coed & Llanrwst. In Llanrwst left into Parry Rd signed Llanddoged. Left at T-junct, site signed at 1st farm entrance on right.*
grid ref: *SH798628*

Surrounded by hills and beautifully landscaped from what was once a dairy farm, Bron Derw has been built to a very high standard and is fully matured, with stunning flora and fauna displays. All pitches are fully serviced, and there is a heated, stone-built toilet block with excellent and immaculately maintained facilities. The Parc Derwen adults-only field has 28 fully serviced pitches and its own designated amenities block. CCTV security cameras cover the whole park. 4.5 acre site. 48 touring pitches. 48 hardstandings. 17 seasonal pitches. Caravan pitches. Motorhome pitches.

Open: Mar-Oct **Last arrival:** 22.00 **Last departure:** 11.00hrs

Pitches: 🚐 🚐

Facilities: 🌲⊙🎯☕🏧⚡🅿 WiFi ♻ ❶

Services: 🔧🔋 T ⚡

Within 3 miles: 🎣🏐🔋

Notes: Children must be supervised, no bikes, scooters or skateboards. Dogs must be kept on leads.

AA Pubs & Restaurants nearby: Ty Gwyn Inn, BETWS-Y-COED, LL24 0SG, 01690 710383

The Old Ship, TREFRIW, LL27 0JH, 01492 640013

Bodnant Caravan Park

►►►► 84%

tel: 01492 640248 **Nebo Rd LL26 0SD**
email: ermin@bodnant-caravan-park.co.uk
dir: *S in Llanrwst, at lights exit A470 opposite Birmingham garage onto B5427 signed Nebo. Site 300yds on right, opposite leisure centre.* **grid ref:** *SH805609*

This well maintained and stunningly attractive park is filled with flower beds, and the landscape includes shrubberies and trees. The statics are unobtrusively sited and the quality, spotlessly clean toilet blocks have fully serviced private cubicles. All caravan pitches are multi-service, and the tent pitches serviced. There is a separate playing field and rally field, and there are lots of farm animals on the park to keep children entertained, and Victorian farming implements are on display around the touring fields. 5 acre site. 54 touring pitches. 20 hardstandings. Caravan pitches. Motorhome pitches. Tent pitches. 2 statics.

Open: Mar-end Oct **Last arrival:** 21.00hrs **Last departure:** 11.00hrs

Pitches: ⊞ ⇆ ⋀

Facilities: ⋔☉⋔⅄⅃⦵⋔⊙�

Services: ⊞⋔⊘

Within 3 miles: ⅃⅄⋔⅊⊞⊙

Notes: No bikes, skateboards or camp fires, main gates locked 23.00hrs-08.00hrs, no noise after 23.00hrs. Dogs must be kept on leads.

AA Pubs & Restaurants nearby: Ty Gwyn Inn, BETWS-Y-COED, LL24 0SG, 01690 710383
The Old Ship, TREFRIW, LL27 0JH, 01492 640013

TAL-Y-BONT (NEAR CONWY)   Map 14 SH76

Places to visit

Bodnant Garden, TAL-Y-CAFN, LL28 5RE, 01492 650460
www.nationaltrust.org.uk/bodnant-garden

Great for kids: Smallest House, CONWY, LL32 8BB, 07925 049786
www.thesmallesthouseingreatbritain.co.uk

Tynterfyn Touring Caravan Park

► 89%

tel: 01492 660525 **LL32 8YX**
dir: *5m S of Conwy on B5106, signed Tal-y-Bont, 1st on left.* **grid ref:** *SH768695*

A quiet, secluded little park set in the beautiful Conwy Valley, and run by family owners. The grounds are tended with care, and the older-style toilet facilities sparkle. There is lots of room for children and dogs to run around. 2 acre site. 15 touring pitches. 4 hardstandings. Caravan pitches. Motorhome pitches. Tent pitches.

Open: Mar-Oct (rs 28 days in year tent pitches only) **Last arrival:** 22.00hrs
Last departure: noon

Pitches: * ⊞ fr £12.80 ⇆ fr £13.50 ⋀ fr £5

Leisure: ⌖ ⊙

Facilities: ⋔☉⋔⅄⅃⦵⋔⊙�

Services: ⊞⋔⊘⊟

Within 3 miles: ⅄⅊⅃⊞⊙

Notes: Dogs must be kept on leads.

AA Pubs & Restaurants nearby: The Old Ship, TREFRIW, LL27 0JH, 01492 640013

TOWYN (NEAR ABERGELE)   Map 14 SH97

Places to visit

Rhuddlan Castle, RHUDDLAN, LL18 5AD, 01745 590777 www.cadw.wales.gov.uk

Bodelwyddan Castle, BODELWYDDAN, LL18 5YA, 01745 584060
www.bodelwyddan-castle.co.uk

Great for kids: Welsh Mountain Zoo, COLWYN BAY, LL28 5UY, 01492 532938
www.welshmountainzoo.org

Ty Mawr Holiday Park

HOLIDAY CENTRE 76%

tel: 01745 832079 **Towyn Rd LL22 9HG**
email: admin.tymawr@parkresorts.com **web:** www.park-resorts.com
dir: *On A548, 0.25m W of Towyn.* **grid ref:** *SH965792*

Located between Chester and the Isle of Anglesey and close to many attractions including the lively resort of Rhyl. This is a very large coastal holiday park with extensive leisure facilities including sports and recreational amenities. The touring areas are on two level, grassy fields and all amenities blocks are centrally located. The entertainment facilities are ideal for both adults and families, and a choice of eating outlets is available, including a stylish new Boathouse Bar & Restaurant which opened in 2014. 18 acre site. 406 touring pitches. Caravan pitches. Motorhome pitches. Tent pitches. 464 statics.

Open: Apr-Oct (rs Apr (excl Etr)) **Last arrival:** mdnt **Last departure:** 10.00hrs

Pitches: ⊞ ⇆ ⋀

Leisure: ⌖ ⌖ ⋀ ⅃ ⊙ ● ♫

Facilities: ⋔☉⅄⅃⊞⋔⊙ WiFi ▤

Services: ⊞⊙⅊⅊⊡⋔

Within 3 miles: ⅃⊞⅊⊙⊡⊙∪

See advert on page 426

PITCHES: ⊞ Caravans ⇆ Motorhomes ⋀ Tents ⋔ Glamping-style accommodation **SERVICES:** ⊞ Electric hook up ⊙ Launderette ⋔ Licensed bar ⋔ Calor Gas ⊘ Camping Gaz ⊞ Toilet fluid ⍨ Café/Restaurant ⋔ Fast Food/Takeaway ⋔ Battery charging ⋔ Baby care ⋔ Motorvan service point
ABBREVIATIONS: BH/bank hols – bank holidays Etr – Easter Spring BH – Spring Bank Holiday fr – from hrs – hours m – mile mdnt – midnight rdbt – roundabout rs – restricted service wk – week wknd – weekend x-rds – cross roads ⊗ No credit or debit cards ⊗ No dogs ⋔ Children of all ages accepted

DENBIGHSHIRE

LLANDRILLO
Map 15 SJ03

Places to visit

Rug Chapel, CORWEN, LL21 9BT, 01490 412025 www.cadw.wales.gov.uk

Bala Lake Railway, LLANUWCHLLYN, LL23 7DD, 01678 540666 www.bala-lake-railway.co.uk

Hendwr Country Park
►►►80%

tel: 01490 440210 **LL21 0SN**
dir: *From Corwen (A5) take B4401 for 4m. Right at Hendwr sign. Site 0.5m on right down tree-lined drive. Or follow brown signs from A5 at Corwen.* **grid ref:** *SJ042386*

Surrounded by the Berwen Mountains, this well-established site has a stream meandering through it – the sound of running water and birdsong are the only distractions. A tree-lined drive welcomes visitors on to the immaculately maintained pitches. Fly fishing instruction can be arranged on the river which borders the park. Scandinavian-style lodges are available. 11 acre site. 40 touring pitches. 3 hardstandings. 30 seasonal pitches. Caravan pitches. Motorhome pitches. Tent pitches. 80 statics.

Open: Apr-Oct **Last arrival:** 22.00hrs **Last departure:** 16.00hrs

Pitches: 🚐 🚗 ▲

Facilities: 🌡️⊙❄️⑤🛒 📶 ♻️ ❂

Services: 🔌⑤🔒⊘🅣♨️⏚

Within 3 miles: ✏️⑤

Notes: No open fires. Dogs must be kept on leads. Wet weather camping facilities.

PRESTATYN
Map 15 SJ08

Presthaven Sands Holiday Park
HOLIDAY CENTRE 82%

tel: 0871 231 0888 **Gronant LL19 9TT**
email: presthavensands@haven.com **web:** www.haven.com/presthavensands
dir: *A548 from Prestatyn towards Gronant. Site signed. NB for Sat Nav use LL19 9ST.*
grid ref: *SJ091842*

Set beside two miles of superb sandy beaches and dunes (with donkeys on site at weekends) this constantly improving holiday park provides a wide range of both indoor and outdoor attractions. The site can boast happy returning visitors. The small touring field at the park entrance offers good electric pitches – the majority are hardstandings and include five super pitches. The centrally located entertainment area includes two indoor swimming pools, excellent children's activities and a choice of eating outlets. 21 acre site. 34 touring pitches. 33 hardstandings. Caravan pitches. Motorhome pitches. 1052 statics.

Open: mid Mar-end Oct (rs mid Mar-May & Sep-Oct facilities may be reduced)
Last arrival: 20.00hrs **Last departure:** 10.00hrs

Pitches: 🚐 🚗

Leisure: 🏊🏄♨️🖐️🎵🎶

Facilities: 🌡️⊙♿🕐⑤ 📶 ♻️ ❂

Services: 🔌⑤🍟🍴🍔⏚

Within 3 miles: ⛳🎣✏️◎⑤⑤U

Notes: No commercial vehicles, no bookings by persons under 21yrs unless a family booking, max 2 dogs per booking, certain dog breeds banned. Dogs must be kept on leads.

See advert on page 428

PITCHES: 🚐 Caravans 🚗 Motorhomes ▲ Tents 🏠 Glamping-style accommodation **SERVICES:** 🔌 Electric hook up ⑤ Launderette 🍺 Licensed bar
🔒 Calor Gas ⊘ Camping Gaz 🅣 Toilet fluid 🍴 Café/Restaurant 🍔 Fast Food/Takeaway ♨️ Battery charging 🚼 Baby care ⏚ Motorvan service point
ABBREVIATIONS: BH/bank hols – bank holidays Etr – Easter Spring BH – Spring Bank Holiday fr – from hrs – hours m – mile mdnt – midnight
rdbt – roundabout rs – restricted service wk – week wknd – weekend x-rds – cross roads ◎ No credit or debit cards ⊗ No dogs ♿ Children of all ages accepted

RHUALLT
Map 15 SJ07

Places to visit

Rhuddlan Castle, RHUDDLAN, LL18 5AD, 01745 590777 www.cadw.wales.gov.uk

Bodelwyddan Castle, BODELWYDDAN, LL18 5YA, 01745 584060 www.bodelwyddan-castle.co.uk

Great for kids: Denbigh Castle, DENBIGH, LL16 3NB, 01745 813385 www.cadw.wales.gov.uk

Penisar Mynydd Caravan Park
►►►► 90%

tel: 01745 582227 & 07831 408017 **Caerwys Rd LL17 0TY**
email: contact@penisarmynydd.co.uk
dir: *From A55 junct 29 follow Dyserth & brown caravan signs. Site 500yds on right.*
grid ref: *SJ093770*

A very tranquil, attractively laid-out park set in three grassy paddocks with superb facilities block including a disabled room and dishwashing area. The majority of pitches are super pitches. Immaculately maintained throughout, the park is within easy reach of historic Chester and the seaside resort of Rhyl. 6.6 acre site. 71 touring pitches. 71 hardstandings. Caravan pitches. Motorhome pitches. Tent pitches.

Open: Mar-15 Jan **Last arrival:** 21.00hrs **Last departure:** 21.00hrs

Pitches: ⊕ ⊕ Å

Leisure: ⊛

Facilities: ⬡ ⊙ ❉ ⬡ ⬡ ⬡ ⬡ ⬡ ⬡ ⬡ ⬡ ⬡ ⬡

Services: ⬡ ⬡ ⬡ ⬡ ⬡

Within 3 miles: ⬡ ⬡ ⬡ ⊚ ⬡ ⬡ ⬡ ∪

Notes: No cycling, no fires. Dogs must be kept on leads. Rally area.

AA Pubs & Restaurants nearby: The Plough Inn, ST ASAPH, LL17 0LU, 01745 585080

RUABON
Map 15 SJ34

Places to visit

Plas Newydd, LLANGOLLEN, LL20 8AW, 01978 861314 www.denbighshire.gov.uk

Valle Crucis Abbey, LLANGOLLEN, LL20 8DD, 01978 860326 www.cadw.wales.gov.uk

Great for kids: Horse Drawn Boats Centre, LLANGOLLEN, LL20 8TA, 01978 860702 www.horsedrawnboats.co.uk

James' Caravan Park
►►► 75%

tel: 01978 820148 **LL14 6DW**
email: ray@carastay.demon.co.uk
dir: *From Oswestry on A483 take slip road signed Llangollen & A539. At rdbt left onto A539 (Llangollen). Site 500yds on left. Or from Wrexham on A483 follow Llangollen & A539 signs. Right at rdbt onto A539, at next rdbt straight on, site on left.*
grid ref: *SJ300434*

A well-landscaped park on a former farm, with modern heated toilet facilities. Old farm buildings house a collection of restored original farm machinery, and the village shop, four pubs, takeaway and launderette are a 10-minute walk away. 6 acre site. 40 touring pitches. 4 hardstandings. Caravan pitches. Motorhome pitches.

Open: all year **Last arrival:** 21.00hrs **Last departure:** 11.00hrs

Pitches: ⊕ ⊕

Facilities: ⬡ ⊙ ⬡ ❉ ⬡ ⬡ ⬡

Services: ⬡ ⬡ ⬡ ⬡

Within 3 miles: ⬡ ⬡ ⬡

Notes: ⊘ No fires. Dogs must be kept on leads. Chest freezer available.

AA Pubs & Restaurants nearby: The Boat Inn, ERBISTOCK, LL13 0DL, 01978 780666

GWYNEDD

ABERSOCH
Map 14 SH32

Places to visit

Plas-yn-Rhiw, PLAS YN RHIW, LL53 8AB, 01758 780219
www.nationaltrust.org.uk

Penarth Fawr, PENARTH FAWR, 01443 336000 www.cadw.wales.gov.uk

Deucoch Touring & Camping Park
►►►►83%

tel: 01758 713293 & 07740 281770 **Sarn Bach LL53 7LD**
email: info@deucoch.com
dir: From Abersoch take Sarn Bach road, at x-rds turn right, site on right in 800yds.
grid ref: SH301269

A colourful, sheltered site with stunning views of Cardigan Bay and the mountains, and situated just a mile from Abersoch and a long sandy beach. The friendly, enthusiastic, hands-on proprietors make year-on-year improvements to enhance their visitors' experience. Facilities include outside hot showers, a superb dish washing facility, housed in an attractive log cabin, and caravan repairs. 5 acre site. 70 touring pitches. 10 hardstandings. Caravan pitches. Motorhome pitches. Tent pitches.

Open: Mar-Oct **Last arrival:** 20.00hrs **Last departure:** 11.00hrs

Pitches: ♔ ⌔ Å

Leisure: ⚙ ✦

Facilities: ⌁ ☉ ⌒ ✳ ⅙ WIFI ♻ ❶

Services: ♚ ⓢ ⅃

Within 3 miles: ⅃ ✝ ⌿ ⌁ ⓢ ⓢ ∪

Notes: ⊘ Families only. Dogs must be kept on leads.

AA Pubs & Restaurants nearby: Porth Tocyn Hotel, ABERSOCH, LL53 7BU, 01758 713303

Beach View Caravan Park
►►►►82%

tel: 01758 712956 **Bwlchtocyn LL53 7BT**
dir: Through Abersoch & Sarn Bach. Over x-rds, next left signed Porthtocyn Hotel. Pass chapel to another Porth Tocyn Hotel sign. Turn left, site on left. **grid ref:** SH316262

A compact family park run by a very enthusiastic owner who makes continual improvements. Just a six-minute walk from the beach, the site's immaculately maintained grounds, good hardstanding pitches (mostly seasonal) and excellent facilities are matched by great sea and country views. 4 acre site. 47 touring pitches. 47 hardstandings. 40 seasonal pitches. Caravan pitches. Motorhome pitches. Tent pitches.

Open: mid Mar-mid Oct **Last arrival:** 19.00hrs **Last departure:** 11.00hrs

Pitches: ♔ ⌔ Å

Facilities: ⌁ ☉ ⌒ ✳ ⌁ ❶

Services: ♚ ⓢ ⌷ ⌀ ⩲

Within 3 miles: ⅃ ✝ ⌿ ⌁ ⓢ ∪

Notes: ⊘ Dogs must be kept on leads.

AA Pubs & Restaurants nearby: Porth Tocyn Hotel, ABERSOCH, LL53 7BU, 01758 713303

Tyn-y-Mur Touring & Camping
►►►84%

tel: 01758 712328 **Lon Garmon LL53 7UL**
email: info@tyn-y-mur.co.uk **web:** www.tyn-y-mur.co.uk
dir: From Pwllheli into Abersoch on A499, sharp right at Land & Sea Garage. Site approx 0.5m on left. **grid ref:** SH304290

A family-only park in a glorious hill-top location overlooking a lush valley and with views extending across Abersoch to the mountains beyond Cardigan Bay. Good, clean, modern toilet facilities and spacious tent pitches in a level grassy field are on offer. There is a pathway from the site to private river fishing, and the beach at Abersoch is just a short walk away. The park offers boat storage facilities. 22 acre site. 90 touring pitches. 37 hardstandings. 37 seasonal pitches. Caravan pitches. Motorhome pitches. Tent pitches.

Open: Apr-Oct **Last arrival:** 22.00hrs **Last departure:** 11.00hrs

Pitches: ♔ ⌔ Å

Leisure: ⚙ ☺

Facilities: ⌁ ☉ ✳ ⅙ ⌁ ⌁ WIFI ♻ ❶

Services: ♚ ⓢ ⌷ ⌀ T ⩲ ⌸

Within 3 miles: ⅃ ✝ ⌿ ⌁ ⓢ ⓢ ∪

Notes: No open fires, no motorcycles, no noisy activity after 23.00hrs, 1 dog per unit. Dogs must be kept on leads.

AA Pubs & Restaurants nearby: Porth Tocyn Hotel, ABERSOCH, LL53 7BU, 01758 713303

PITCHES: ♔ Caravans ⌔ Motorhomes Å Tents ⌂ Glamping-style accommodation **SERVICES:** ♚ Electric hook up ⓢ Launderette ⌷ Licensed bar
⌀ Calor Gas ⌀ Camping Gaz T Toilet fluid ⌾ Café/Restaurant ⌸ Fast Food/Takeaway ⩲ Battery charging ⌁ Baby care ⅃ Motorvan service point
ABBREVIATIONS: BH/bank hols – bank holidays Etr – Easter Spring BH – Spring Bank Holiday fr – from hrs – hours m – mile mdnt – midnight
rdbt – roundabout rs – restricted service wk – week wknd – weekend x-rds – cross roads ⊘ No credit or debit cards ⊗ No dogs ⅋ Children of all ages accepted

ABERSOCH *continued*

Bryn Bach Caravan & Camping Site
►►►81%

tel: 01758 712285 & 07789 390808 **Tyddyn Talgoch Uchaf, Bwlchtocyn LL53 7BT**
email: brynbach@abersochcamping.co.uk
dir: *From Abersoch take Sarn Bach road for approx 1m, left at sign for Bwlchtocyn. Site approx 1m on left.* **grid ref:** *SH315258*

This well-run, elevated park overlooks Abersoch Bay, with lovely sea views towards the Snowdonia mountain range. Pitches are well laid out in sheltered paddocks, with well-placed modern facilities. Fishing, watersports and golf are all nearby. The site has a private shortcut to the beach. 4 acre site. 8 touring pitches. 1 hardstanding. 30 seasonal pitches. Caravan pitches. Motorhome pitches. Tent pitches. 2 statics.

Open: Mar-Oct **Last arrival:** 20.00hrs **Last departure:** 11.00hrs

Pitches: 🚐 🚌 Å

Leisure: /⚲ ⚽

Facilities: 🐾 ☉ ℱ ✳ ⚅ 🗛 🎦 📶 ♻ ❼

Services: 🔌 🗓 🛢 ⊘ 🗓 ⅏

Within 3 miles: ⚲ ⚵ 🎣 🐟 ⚓ 🛶 🖸 🗓 ⅋

Notes: Families & couples only. Dogs must be kept on leads. Boat storage.

AA Pubs & Restaurants nearby: Porth Tocyn Hotel, ABERSOCH, LL53 7BU, 01758 713303

Rhydolion
►►►70%

tel: 01758 712342 **Llangian LL53 7LR**
email: enquiries@rhydolion.co.uk
dir: *From A499 take unclassified road to Llangian for 1m, left, through Llangian. Site 1.5m after road forks towards Hell's Mouth/Porth Neigwl.* **grid ref:** *SH283276*

A peaceful small site with good views, on a working farm close to the long sandy surfers beach at Hell's Mouth. The simple toilet facilities are kept to a high standard by the friendly owners, and nearby Abersoch is a mecca for boat owners and water sports enthusiasts. 1.5 acre site. 28 touring pitches. Caravan pitches. Motorhome pitches. Tent pitches.

Open: Mar-Oct **Last arrival:** 22.00hrs **Last departure:** noon

Pitches: 🚐 🚌 Å

Leisure: /⚲ ⚽

Facilities: 🐾 ☉ ✳ ⚓ ♻ ❼

Services: 🔌 🗓 🛢

Within 3 miles: ⚲ ⚵ 🎣 🐟 ⚓ 🖸 🗓 ⅋

Notes: ⚲ Families & couples only, dogs only accepted by prior arrangement. Dogs must be kept on leads. 3 fridge freezers.

AA Pubs & Restaurants nearby: Porth Tocyn Hotel, ABERSOCH, LL53 7BU, 01758 713303

Places to visit
Bala Lake Railway, LLANUWCHLLYN, LL23 7DD, 01678 540666
www.bala-lake-railway.co.uk

Great for kids: Ewe-Phoria Sheepdog Centre, CORWEN, LL21 0PE, 01490 460369
www.ewe-phoria.co.uk

Pen-y-Bont Touring Park
►►►►83%

tel: 01678 520549 **Llangynog Rd LL23 7PH**
email: penybont-bala@btconnect.com
dir: *From A494 take B4391. Site 0.75m on right.* **grid ref:** *SH932350*

A family-run, attractively landscaped park in a woodland country setting. It is set close to Bala Lake and the River Dee with plenty of opportunities for water sports including kayaking and white-water rafting. The park offers good facilities including a motorhome service point, and many pitches have water and electricity. Around the park are superb, large wood carvings of birds and mythical creatures depicting local legends. Two reproduction Romany caravans are available for hire. 6 acre site. 95 touring pitches. 47 hardstandings. 20 seasonal pitches. Caravan pitches. Motorhome pitches. Tent pitches.

Open: Mar-Oct **Last arrival:** 21.00hrs **Last departure:** noon

Pitches: * 🚐 fr £16 🚌 fr £16 Å fr £16 🏠

Facilities: 🐾 ☉ ℱ ✳ ⚅ 🕓 🗓 🗛 🚿 📶 ♻ ❼

Services: 🔌 🗓 🛢 ⊘ 🗓 ⚎ ⅏

Within 3 miles: ⚲ ⚵ 🗓 🎣 🛶 🖸 🗓 ⅋

Notes: No camp fires, BBQs must be kept off ground, quiet after 22.30hrs. Dogs must be kept on leads.

Tyn Cornel Camping & Caravan Park
►►►►80%

tel: 01678 520759 **Frongoch LL23 7NU**
email: tyncornel@mail.com
dir: *From Bala take A4212 Porthmadog road for 4m. Site on left before National White Water Centre.* **grid ref:** *SH895400*

A delightful riverside park with mountain views that is popular with those seeking a base for river kayaking and canoeing — The National White Water Centre is adjacent, and there's a pleasant riverside walk to reach its café. The resident owners are always improving the already very well maintained and colourful grounds. 10 acre site. 67 touring pitches. 10 hardstandings. 14 seasonal pitches. Caravan pitches. Motorhome pitches. Tent pitches.

Open: Etr-Oct **Last arrival:** 20.00hrs **Last departure:** 11.00hrs

Pitches: * 🚐 £14-£23 🚌 £14-£27 Å £15-£34

Leisure: ⚽

Facilities: 🐾 ☉ ℱ ✳ ⚅ 🕓 🗛 🚿 📶 ♻ ❼

Services: 🔌 🗓 🛢 ⊘ ⚎ ⅏

Within 3 miles: ⚲ ⚵ 🗓 🎣 🛶 🖸 🗓 ⅋

Notes: Quiet after 23.00hrs, no cycling, no camp fires or wood burning. Dogs must be kept on leads. Fridge, freezer & tumble dryer available.

LEISURE: 🏊 Indoor swimming pool 🏊 Outdoor swimming pool /⚲ Children's playground 🏌 Kid's club 🎾 Tennis court 🎱 Games room 📺 Separate TV room
⛳ golf course 🚣 Boats for hire 🎬 Cinema 🎵 Entertainment 🎣 Fishing ◎ Mini golf 🛶 Watersports 🏋 Gym ⚽ Sports field Spa ⅋ Stables
FACILITIES: 🛁 Bath 🚿 Shower ☉ Electric shaver ℱ Hairdryer ✳ Ice Pack Facility ⚅ Disabled facilities 🕓 Public telephone 🗓 Shop on site or within 200yds
🏪 Mobile shop (calls at least 5 days a week) 🍖 BBQ area 🗛 Picnic area 📶 Wi-fi 💻 Internet access ♻ Recycling ❼ Tourist info 🐕 Dog exercise area

BANGOR

Map 14 SH57

Places to visit

Penrhyn Castle, BANGOR, LL57 4HN, 01248 353084
www.nationaltrust.org.uk/penrhyncastle

Gwynedd Museum, BANGOR, LL57 1DT, 01248 353368
www.gwynedd.gov.uk/museums

Great for kids: GreenWood Forest Park, Y FELINHELI, LL56 4QN, 01248 670076
www.greenwoodforestpark.co.uk

Treborth Hall Farm Caravan Park
▶▶▶72%

tel: 01248 364399 **The Old Barn, Treborth Hall Farm LL57 2RX**
email: enquiries@treborthleisure.co.uk
dir: A55 junct 9, 1st left at rdbt, straight over 2nd rdbt, site approx 800yds on left.
grid ref: SH554707

Set in eight acres of beautiful parkland with its own trout fishing lake and golf course, this park offers serviced pitches in a sheltered, walled orchard. Tents have a separate grass area, and there is a good clean toilet block. This is a useful base for families, with easy access for the Menai Straits, Anglesey beaches, Snowdon and the Lleyn peninsula. 8 acre site. 34 touring pitches. 34 hardstandings. Caravan pitches. Motorhome pitches. Tent pitches. 4 statics.

Open: Etr-end Oct **Last arrival:** 22.30 **Last departure:** 10.30hrs

Pitches: * 🚐 £19-£25 🚉 £19-£25 ▲ £12-£20

Leisure: ⚐ ♨

Facilities: 🌂 ⏚ 📶 ♻ ❻

Services: 🚐

Within 3 miles: ♨ ♪ ◉ 🎣 🔒 🔄

Notes: Dogs must be kept on leads.

BARMOUTH

Map 14 SH61

Places to visit

Harlech Castle, HARLECH, LL46 2YH, 01766 780552 www.cadw.wales.gov.uk

Cymer Abbey, CYMER ABBEY, LL40 2HE, 01443 336000 www.cadw.wales.gov.uk

---

PREMIER PARK

Trawsdir Touring Caravans & Camping Park
▶▶▶▶▶ 92%

tel: 01341 280999 **Llanaber LL42 1RR**
email: enquiries@barmouthholidays.co.uk
dir: 3m N of Barmouth on A496, just past Wayside pub on right. **grid ref:** SH596198

Well run by the owners, this quality park enjoys spectacular views to the sea and hills, and is very accessible to motor traffic. The facilities are appointed to a very high standard, and include spacious cubicles containing showers and washbasins, individual showers, smart toilets with sensor-operated flush and under-floor heating. Tents and caravans have their own designated areas divided by dry-stone walls (both have spacious fully serviced pitches), the site is very convenient for large recreational vehicles, and there are eight camping pods for hire. There is an excellent children's play area, plus glorious seasonal

floral displays and an illuminated dog walk that leads directly to the nearby pub! 15 acre site. 70 touring pitches. 70 hardstandings. 30 seasonal pitches. Caravan pitches. Motorhome pitches. Tent pitches. 8 wooden pods.

Open: Mar-Jan **Last arrival:** 17.00 **Last departure:** 11.00hrs

Pitches: * 🚐 £18-£34 🚉 £18-£34 ▲ £12-£24 🏠

Leisure: ⚐

Facilities: 🌂 ⊙ 🅿 ⚘ ⏚ 🖐 🚻 📶 ♻ ❻

Services: 🚐 🗂 🔒 🚰 Ⓣ 🥡 🔄

Within 3 miles: ♪ 🎣 🔒 🔄

Notes: Families & couples only. Dogs must be kept on leads. Milk, bread etc available from reception, takeaway food can be delivered from sister site.

AA Pubs & Restaurants nearby: Victoria Inn, LLANBEDR, LL45 2LD, 01341 241213

PREMIER PARK

Hendre Mynach Touring Caravan & Camping Park
▶▶▶▶▶ 85%

tel: 01341 280262 **Llanaber Rd LL42 1YR**
email: info@hendremynach.co.uk **web:** www.hendremynach.co.uk
dir: 0.75m N of Barmouth on A496. **grid ref:** SH605170

A constantly improving site where the enthusiastic owners invest year on year to enhance the customer experience. Although there is a steep decent to the arrivals' area, staff are always on hand to assist. The beautifully maintained touring areas benefit from attractive hedge screening around the large well-spaced pitches that are equipped with water and TV hook-ups. There is direct access to the seafront which leads to the town centre and its many attractions. 10 acre site. 240 touring pitches. 75 hardstandings. 23 seasonal pitches. Caravan pitches. Motorhome pitches. Tent pitches. 1 static.

Open: Mar-9 Jan (rs Winter months shop closed) **Last arrival:** 22.00
Last departure: 11.30hrs

Pitches: 🚐 🚉 ▲

Leisure: ⚐

Facilities: 🌂 ⊙ 🅿 ⚘ ⏚ ⏲ 🅢 📶 🖥 ♻ ❻

Services: 🚐 🗂 🔒 🚰 Ⓣ 🔄

Within 3 miles: ⛳ ♪ 🔒 🔄 ⛳

Notes: No open fires. Dogs must be kept on leads.

AA Pubs & Restaurants nearby: Victoria Inn, LLANBEDR, LL45 2LD, 01341 241213

PITCHES: 🚐 Caravans 🚉 Motorhomes ▲ Tents 🏠 Glamping-style accommodation **SERVICES:** 🚐 Electric hook up 🗂 Launderette 🍺 Licensed bar
🔒 Calor Gas ⚗ Camping Gaz Ⓣ Toilet fluid 🍴 Café/Restaurant 🍟 Fast Food/Takeaway 🔋 Battery charging 🥡 Baby care 🔄 Motorvan service point
ABBREVIATIONS: BH/bank hols – bank holidays Etr – Easter Spring BH – Spring Bank Holiday fr – from hrs – hours m – mile mdnt – midnight
rdbt – roundabout rs – restricted service wk – week wknd – weekend x-rds – cross roads 🚫 No credit or debit cards 🚫 No dogs 👫 Children of all ages accepted

BETWS GARMON
Map 14 SH55

Places to visit

Snowdon Mountain Railway, LLANBERIS, LL55 4TY, 01286 870223
www.snowdonrailway.co.uk

Great for kids: Dolbadarn Castle, LLANBERIS, LL55 4UD, 01443 336000
www.cadw.wales.gov.uk

Bryn Gloch Caravan & Camping Park
►►►► 82%

tel: 01286 650216 **LL54 7YY**
email: eurig@bryngloch.co.uk **web:** www.campwales.co.uk
dir: On A4085, 5m SE of Caernarfon. **grid ref:** SH534574

An excellent family-run site with immaculate modern facilities, and all level pitches in beautiful surroundings. The park offers the best of two worlds, with its bustling holiday atmosphere and the peaceful natural surroundings. The 28 acres of level fields are separated by mature hedges and trees, guaranteeing sufficient space for families wishing to spread themselves out. Excellent fully serviced camping pitches were introduced in the 2014 season. There are static holiday caravans for hire and plenty of walks in the area. 28 acre site. 160 touring pitches. 80 hardstandings. 80 seasonal pitches. Caravan pitches. Motorhome pitches. Tent pitches. 17 statics.

Open: all year **Last arrival:** 23.00hrs **Last departure:** 17.00hrs

Pitches: * ⊞ £18-£30 ⊞ £18-£30 ▲ £15-£30

Leisure: ⚠ ✎ ☐

Facilities: ➡ ❢ ⊙ �P ✳ ⅋ ◔ ᷉ ᛤ ᚼ ᗯᎥᖴᎥ ▦ ✿ ❼

Services: ⊞ ᛃ ⮂ ◪ ◲ ᝨ ⮂ ↯

Within 3 miles: ↕ ⚵ ᵖ ◎ ᎥᎥᎥ U

Notes: Dogs must be kept on leads. Heated family bathroom, mother & baby room.

CAERNARFON
Map 14 SH46

See also Dinas Dinlle & Llandwrog

Places to visit

Segontium Roman Museum, CAERNARFON, LL55 2LN, 01286 675625
www.segontium.org.uk

Welsh Highland Railway, CAERNARFON, LL55 2YD, 01766 516024
www.festrail.co.uk

Great for kids: Caernarfon Castle, CAERNARFON, LL55 2AY, 01286 677617
www.cadw.wales.gov.uk

Llys Derwen Caravan & Camping Site
►►►► 86%

tel: 01286 673322 **Ffordd Bryngwyn, Llanrug LL55 4RD**
email: llysderwen@aol.com
dir: A55 junct 11, take sliproad to Llanberis. Take 2nd exit off rdbt onto A4244, 5m. Take 1st exit at rdbt for Llanberis. Right at T-junct for Caernarfon onto A4086 through Llanrug, left at The Glyntwrog Pub, site 500mtrs on right. **grid ref:** SH539629

On the outskirts of the village of Llanrug, three miles from Caernarfon on the way to Llanberis and Snowdon. A beautifully maintained site with enthusiastic owners who are constantly investing to improve their customers' experience. The amenities block is appointed to a high standard and the immaculately maintained grounds are planted with an abundance of colourful shrubs and seasonal flowers. 5 acre site. 20 touring pitches. Caravan pitches. Motorhome pitches. Tent pitches. 2 statics.

Open: Mar-Oct **Last arrival:** 22.00hrs **Last departure:** noon

Pitches: * ⊞ £14-£16 ⊞ £14-£16 ▲ £14-£16

Facilities: ❢ ⊙ Ꮲ ✳ ⅋ ᚼ ✿ ❼

Services: ⊞ ◲ ⮂

Within 3 miles: ↕ ⚵ ᵖ ⚵ ᎥᎥᎥ U

Notes: ⊘ No open fires, no noise after 22.00hrs, no ball games. Dogs must be kept on leads.

AA Pubs & Restaurants nearby: Seiont Manor Hotel, CAERNARFON, LL55 2AQ, 01286 673366

LEISURE: 🏊 Indoor swimming pool 🏊 Outdoor swimming pool ⚠ Children's playground 🧒 Kid's club 🎾 Tennis court ✎ Games room ☐ Separate TV room
⚑ golf course ⚓ Boats for hire ☐ Cinema ♫ Entertainment ᵖ Fishing ◎ Mini golf ⚵ Watersports ✌ Gym ⚵ Sports field Spa U Stables
FACILITIES: ➡ Bath ❢ Shower ⊙ Electric shaver Ꮲ Hairdryer ✳ Ice Pack Facility ⅋ Disabled facilities ◔ Public telephone Ꭵ Shop on site or within 200yds
ᗯ Mobile shop (calls at least 5 days a week) ☐ BBQ area ᚼ Picnic area ᗯᎥᖴᎥ Wi-fi ▦ Internet access ✿ Recycling ❼ Tourist info ᚼ Dog exercise area

Riverside Camping
►►►► 85%

tel: 01286 678781 **Seiont Nurseries, Pont Rug LL55 2BB**
email: info@riversidecamping.co.uk
dir: 2m from Caernarfon on right of A4086 towards Llanberis, look for signs on entrance.
grid ref: SH505630

Set in the grounds of a former garden centre and enjoying a superb location along the River Seiont, this park is approached by an impressive tree-lined drive. Immaculately maintained by the owners, there are a mixture of riverside grassy pitches and fully serviced pitches for caravans and motorhomes. In addition to the smart amenities blocks, other facilities include an excellent café/restaurant, a volley ball court and boules pitch. River fishing permits are available. Hardstanding pitches have electric hook-up, water, drainage and TV connection (especially suitable for motorhomes). A haven of peace close to Caernarfon, Snowdonia and some great walking opportunities. 5 acre site. 73 touring pitches. 16 hardstandings. 10 seasonal pitches. Caravan pitches. Motorhome pitches. Tent pitches.

Open: 14 Mar-Oct **Last arrival:** anytime **Last departure:** noon

Pitches: * 🚐 £20-£23 🚐 £23-£26 ▲ £15-£23

Leisure: ⚑

Facilities: 🌢 ⊙ 🏴 ❊ ㋡ ⚓ 🎍 📶 🖥 ♻ ❸

Services: 🔌 🗑 🍴 🎦 🚚 🔧

Within 3 miles: ⤷ ⚲ 🏛 🖊 ◎ 🚣 🛒 🛍 ∪

Notes: No fires, no loud music, debit (not credit) cards accepted. Dogs must be kept on leads. Family shower room, baby-changing facilities.

AA Pubs & Restaurants nearby: Seiont Manor Hotel, CAERNARFON, LL55 2AQ, 01286 673366

Plas Gwyn Caravan & Camping Park
►►► 81%

tel: 01286 672619 **Llanrug LL55 2AQ**
email: info@plasgwyn.co.uk
dir: A4086, 3m E of Caernarfon, site on right. Between River Seiont & Llanrug.
grid ref: SH520633

A secluded park in an ideal location for visiting the glorious nearby beaches, historic Caernarfon, the attractions of Snowdonia and for walking opportunities. The site is set within the grounds of Plas Gwyn House, a Georgian property with colonial additions, and the friendly owners constantly improve facilities to enhance their visitors' experience. A 'breakfast butty' service with fresh tea or coffee is available for delivery to individual pitches. The all-electric pitches include hardstandings and five are fully serviced. Three timber camping tents and five statics are available for hire. 3 acre site. 42 touring pitches. 8 hardstandings. 8 seasonal pitches. Caravan pitches. Motorhome pitches. Tent pitches. 18 statics. 3 wooden pods.

Open: Mar-Oct **Last arrival:** 22.00hrs **Last departure:** 11.30hrs

Pitches: * 🚐 £17.50-£21 🚐 £17.50-£21 ▲ £10.50-£25 🏠

Facilities: 🌢 ⊙ 🏴 ❊ 🎍 📶 🖥 ♻ ❸

Services: 🔌 🗑 🛢 ⌀ 🎦 🚚 🔧 **Within 3 miles:** ⤷ ⚲ 🖊 🚣 🛒 🛍 ∪

Notes: Minimal noise between 22.00hrs-mdnt, complete quiet between mdnt-08.00hrs.

AA Pubs & Restaurants nearby: Seiont Manor Hotel, CAERNARFON, LL55 2AQ, 01286 673366

Cwm Cadnant Valley
►►► 80%

tel: 01286 673196 **Llanberis Rd LL55 2DF**
email: aa@cwmcadnant.co.uk **web:** www.cwmcadnant.co.uk
dir: On outskirts of Caernarfon on A4086 towards Llanberis, adjacent to fire station.
grid ref: SH487628

Set in an attractive wooded valley with a stream is this terraced site with secluded pitches, a good camping area for backpackers and clean, modernised toilet facilities. It is located on the outskirts of Caernarfon in a rural location, close to the main Caernarfon-Llanberis road and just a 10-minute walk from the castle and town centre. 4.5 acre site. 60 touring pitches. 9 hardstandings. 5 seasonal pitches. Caravan pitches. Motorhome pitches. Tent pitches.

Open: 14 Mar-3 Nov **Last arrival:** 22.00hrs **Last departure:** 11.00hrs

Pitches: * 🚐 £14-£22 🚐 £14-£22 ▲ £10-£22

Leisure: ⚑ **Facilities:** 🌢 ⊙ 🏴 ❊ ㋡ ⚓ 🖊 🎍 📶 ♻ ❸

Services: 🔌 🗑 🛢 ⌀ 🎦 🚚 **Within 3 miles:** ⤷ ⚲ 🖊 🚣 🛒 🛍 ∪

Notes: No noise after 23.00hrs, no wood fires. Dogs must be kept on leads. Family room with baby-changing facilities.

AA Pubs & Restaurants nearby: Seiont Manor Hotel, CAERNARFON, LL55 2AQ, 01286 673366

Ty'n yr Onnen Caravan Park
►►► 79%

tel: 01286 650281 & 07976 529428 **Waunfawr LL55 4AX**
email: tynronnen.farm@btconnect.com
dir: At Waunfawr on A4085, onto unclassified road opposite church. Site signed.
grid ref: SH533588

A gently sloping site on a 200-acre sheep farm set in magnificent surroundings close to Snowdon and enjoying stunning mountain views. This secluded park is well equipped and the amenity blocks were refurbished to a high standard ready for the 2014 season. Access is via a narrow, unclassified road. 3.5 acre site. 20 touring pitches. 25 seasonal pitches. Caravan pitches. Motorhome pitches. Tent pitches.

Open: Apr-Oct **Last arrival:** 22.00hrs **Last departure:** noon

Pitches: * 🚐 £16-£22 🚐 £16-£22 ▲ £14-£20

Leisure: ⚑ ◣ ▢ **Facilities:** 🌢 ⊙ ❊ ⚓ 🎍 📶 ♻

Services: 🔌 🗑 🚚 **Within 3 miles:** ⤷ ⚲ 🖊 ◎ 🚣 🛒 🛍 ∪

Notes: No music after 23.00hrs. Dogs must be kept on leads.

AA Pubs & Restaurants nearby: Snowdonia Parc Brewpub & Campsite, WAUNFAWR, LL55 4AQ, 01286 650409

PITCHES: 🚐 Caravans 🚐 Motorhomes ▲ Tents 🏠 Glamping-style accommodation **SERVICES:** 🔌 Electric hook up 🗑 Launderette 🍴 Licensed bar 🛢 Calor Gas ⌀ Camping Gaz 🎦 Toilet fluid 🍴 Café/Restaurant 🚚 Fast Food/Takeaway 🚚 Battery charging 🔧 Baby care 🔧 Motorvan service point
ABBREVIATIONS: BH/bank hols – bank holidays Etr – Easter Spring BH – Spring Bank Holiday fr – from hrs – hours m – mile mdnt – midnight rdbt – roundabout rs – restricted service wk – week wknd – weekend x-rds – cross roads ⊗ No credit or debit cards ⊗ No dogs ♦♦ Children of all ages accepted

CRICCIETH
Map 14 SH43

Places to visit

Criccieth Castle, CRICCIETH, LL52 0DP, 01766 522227 www.cadw.wales.gov.uk

Portmeirion, PORTMEIRION, LL48 6ER, 01766 772306
www.portmeirion-village.com

Great for kids: Ffestiniog Railway, PORTHMADOG, LL49 9NF, 01766 516024
www.festrail.co.uk

Eisteddfa
►►►► 83%

tel: 01766 522696 **Eisteddfa Lodge, Pentrefelin LL52 0PT**
email: info@eisteddfapark.co.uk
dir: *From Porthmadog take A497 towards Criccieth. Approx 3.5m, through Pentrefelin, site signed 1st right after Plas Gwyn Nursing Home.* **grid ref:** *SH518394*

A quiet, secluded park on elevated ground, sheltered by the Snowdonia Mountains and with lovely views of Cardigan Bay; Criccieth is nearby. The owners are carefully improving the park whilst preserving its unspoilt beauty, and are keen to welcome families, who will appreciate the cubicled facilities. There's a field and play area, woodland walks, a cocoon pod, two tipis, six superb slate-based hardstandings, three static holiday caravans for hire, and a three-acre coarse fishing lake adjacent to the park. 24 acre site. 100 touring pitches. 17 hardstandings. Caravan pitches. Motorhome pitches. Tent pitches. 3 statics. 2 tipis. 1 wooden pod.

Open: Mar-Oct **Last arrival:** 22.30 **Last departure:** 11.00hrs

Pitches: * 🚐 £15-£22 🚃 £15-£22 Å £13-£19 🏠

Leisure: 🅰 😊 🔍

Facilities: 🏹 ⊙ 🅿 ✳ 🅱 🎋 🛪 ♻ 🛈

Services: 🔋 🔲 🔋 🍴

Within 3 miles: ⌁ ⚘ 🎿 🕈 ℓ ◎ 🎿 🔋 🛍 U

Notes: No noise after 22.30hrs. Dogs must be kept on leads. Baby bath available.

AA Pubs & Restaurants nearby: Bron Eifion Country House Hotel, CRICCIETH, LL52 0SA, 01766 522385

Plas Bodegroes, PWLLHELI, LL53 5TH, 01758 612363

Llwyn-Bugeilydd Caravan & Camping Site
►► 82%

tel: 01766 522235 & 07714 196137 **LL52 0PN**
email: cazzyanne1@hotmail.com
dir: *From Porthmadog on A497, 1m N of Criccieth on B4411. Site 1st on right. From A55 take A487 through Caernarfon. After Bryncir right onto B4411, site on left in 3.5m.* **grid ref:** *SH498398*

A quiet rural site, convenient for touring Snowdonia and coastal areas. It is set amid stunning scenery and has well-tended grass pitches enhanced by shrubs and seasonal flowers. The smartly presented amenities block is kept spotlessly clean. 6 acre site. 45 touring pitches. 2 hardstandings. Caravan pitches. Motorhome pitches. Tent pitches.

Open: Mar-Oct **Last arrival:** anytime **Last departure:** 11.00hrs

Pitches: 🚐 🚃 Å

Leisure: 🅰 😊
Facilities: 🏹 ⊙ 🅿 ✳ 🛪 ♻ 🛈
Services: 🔋 🔲 🍴
Within 3 miles: ⌁ ⚘ 🎿 ℓ ◎ 🎿 🔋 🛍 U

Notes: 🚫 No skateboards. Dogs must be kept on leads.

AA Pubs & Restaurants nearby: Bron Eifion Country House Hotel, CRICCIETH, LL52 0SA, 01766 522385

Plas Bodegroes, PWLLHELI, LL53 5TH, 01758 612363

DINAS DINLLE
Map 14 SH45

Places to visit

Inigo Jones Slateworks, GROESLON, LL54 7UE, 01286 830242
www.inigojones.co.uk

Caernarfon Castle, CAERNARFON, LL55 2AY, 01286 677617
www.cadw.wales.gov.uk

Great for kids: Welsh Highland Railway, CAERNARFON, LL55 2YD, 01766 516024
www.festrail.co.uk

Dinlle Caravan Park
►►►► 87%

tel: 01286 830324 **LL54 5TW**
email: enq@thornleyleisure.co.uk
dir: *From A487 at rdbt onto A499 (signed Pwllheli). Right at sign for Caernarfon Airport (& brown camping sign).* **grid ref:** *SH438568*

A very accessible, well-kept, grassy site adjacent to a sandy beach and with good views towards Snowdonia. The park is situated in acres of flat grassland that provides plenty of space for large groups. The man-made dunes offer campers additional protection from sea breezes. The lounge bar and family room are comfortable places in which to relax, and children will enjoy the exciting adventure playground. Five camping pods with outside deck area were added in 2014. A golf club, a nature reserve and the Airworld Aviation Museum at Caernarfon Airport can all be accessed from the beach road. 20 acre site. 175 touring pitches. 20 hardstandings. Caravan pitches. Motorhome pitches. Tent pitches. 167 statics. 5 wooden pods.

Open: Mar-Nov **Last arrival:** 23.00hrs **Last departure:** noon

Pitches: 🚐 🚃 Å 🏠

Leisure: 🌊 🅰 🔍 🎵

Facilities: 🏹 ⊙ 🅿 ✳ 🅱 📶 🛈

Services: 🔋 🔲 🔋 🔋 ♻ ♿

Within 3 miles: ℓ 🛍 U

Notes: No skateboards. Dogs must be kept on leads.

DYFFRYN ARDUDWY
Map 14 SH52

Places to visit
Cymer Abbey, CYMER ABBEY, LL40 2HE, 01443 336000 www.cadw.wales.gov.uk

Great for kids: Harlech Castle, HARLECH, LL46 2YH, 01766 780552
www.cadw.wales.gov.uk

Murmur-yr-Afon Touring Park
►►►81%

tel: 01341 247353 **LL44 2BE**
email: murmuryrafon1@btinternet.com
dir: On A496 N of village. **grid ref:** SH586236

A pleasant family-run park alongside a wooded stream on the edge of the village, and handy for large sandy beaches. Expect good, clean facilities, and lovely views of rolling hills and mountains. 6 acre site. 78 touring pitches. 37 hardstandings. Caravan pitches. Motorhome pitches. Tent pitches.

Open: Mar-Oct **Last arrival:** 22.00hrs **Last departure:** 11.00hrs

Pitches: ⊡ ⊡ ▲

Leisure: ⋀

Facilities: ⊡⊙⊡⋇⊡⊙⊡⋔⊙

Services: ⊡⊡⋤

Within 3 miles: ⊡⋤⊡

Notes: Dogs must be kept on leads.

AA Pubs & Restaurants nearby: Victoria Inn, LLANBEDR, LL45 2LD, 01341 241213

LLANDWROG
Map 14 SH45

Places to visit
Welsh Highland Railway, CAERNARFON, LL55 2YD, 01766 516024
www.festrail.co.uk

Great for kids: Caernarfon Castle, CAERNARFON, LL55 2AY, 01286 677617
www.cadw.wales.gov.uk

White Tower Caravan Park
►►►►82%

tel: 01286 830649 & 07802 562785 **LL54 5UH**
email: whitetower@supanet.com
dir: From Caernarfon take A487 (Porthmadog road). 1st right into Pant Rd signed Llanfaglan & Saron. Site 3m on right. **grid ref:** SH453582

There are lovely views of Snowdonia from this park located just two miles from the nearest beach at Dinas Dinlle. A well-maintained toilet block has key access, and the hardstanding pitches have water and electricity. Popular amenities include an outdoor heated swimming pool, a lounge bar with family room, and a games and TV room. 6 acre site. 60 touring pitches. 60 hardstandings. 58 seasonal pitches. Caravan pitches. Motorhome pitches. Tent pitches. 71 statics.

Open: Mar-10 Jan (rs Mar-mid May & Sep-Nov bar open wknds only)
Last arrival: 23.00hrs **Last departure:** noon

Pitches: * ⊡ £20-£28 ⊡ £20-£28 ▲ £20-£28

Leisure: ⋥⋀⋐⊡⋔

Facilities: ⊡⊙⊡⋇⊙⊙⊡⊡⋤⊙⊙

Services: ⊡⊙⊡⋔⊙⋣⋤

Within 3 miles: ⊡⋤⊡⋤⊡⊙U

Notes: Dogs must be kept on leads.

AA Pubs & Restaurants nearby: Black Boy Inn, CAERNARFON, LL55 1RW, 01286 673604

PONT-RUG

See Caernarfon

PORTHMADOG
Map 14 SH53

Places to visit
Portmeirion, PORTMEIRION, LL48 6ER, 01766 772306
www.portmeirion-village.com

Great for kids: Ffestiniog Railway, PORTHMADOG, LL49 9NF, 01766 516024
www.festrail.co.uk

Greenacres Holiday Park
HOLIDAY CENTRE 83%

tel: 0871 231 0886 **Black Rock Sands, Morfa Bychan LL49 9YF**
email: greenacres@haven.com **web:** www.haven.com/greenacres
dir: From Porthmadog High Street follow Black Rock Sands signs between The Factory Shop & Post Office. Park 2m on left at end of Morfa Bychan. **grid ref:** SH539374

A quality holiday park on level ground just a short walk from Black Rock Sands, and set against a backdrop of Snowdonia National Park. All touring pitches are on hardstandings surrounded by closely-mown grass, and near the entertainment complex. A full programme of entertainment, organised clubs, indoor and outdoor sports and leisure, pubs, shows and cabarets all add to a holiday experience here. A bowling alley and a large shop/bakery are useful amenities. A competely new touring area with fully serviced Euro pitches and new amenities block is planned for

continued

PITCHES: ⊡ Caravans ⊡ Motorhomes ▲ Tents ⋔ Glamping-style accommodation **SERVICES:** ⊡ Electric hook up ⊡ Launderette ⊡ Licensed bar
⊡ Calor Gas ⊘ Camping Gaz ⊡ Toilet fluid ⊙ Café/Restaurant ⊞ Fast Food/Takeaway ⋤ Battery charging ⋣ Baby care ⋔ Motorvan service point
ABBREVIATIONS: BH/bank hols – bank holidays Etr – Easter Spring BH – Spring Bank Holiday fr – from hrs – hours m – mile mdnt – midnight
rdbt – roundabout rs – restricted service wk – week wknd – weekend x-rds – cross roads ⊗ No credit or debit cards ⊗ No dogs ⋔ Children of all ages accepted

PORTHMADOG *continued*

the 2015 season. 121 acre site. 46 touring pitches. 46 hardstandings. Caravan pitches. Motorhome pitches. 900 statics.

Greenacres Holiday Park

Open: mid Mar-end Oct (rs mid Mar-May & Sep-Oct some facilities may be reduced) **Last arrival:** anytime **Last departure:** 10.00hrs

Pitches: ⛺ ⛺

Leisure: 🏊 ⛲ 👋 ⚽ ♠ 🎵

Facilities: 🏪 ☺ 📷 ♿ 🕐 📷 🍴 WiFi ♻ 🛈

Services: 🔌 📷 🚰 🛢 🧴 🍴 🍴 🛒

Within 3 miles: ⬇ ☺ 🛒 🛒 ♨ 🐴

Notes: No commercial vehicles, no bookings by persons under 21yrs unless a family booking, max 2 dogs per booking, certain dog breeds banned. Dogs must be kept on leads.

AA Pubs & Restaurants nearby: Royal Sportsman Hotel, PORTHMADOG, LL49 9HB, 01766 512015

The Hotel Portmeirion, PORTMEIRION, LL48 6ET, 01766 770000

See advert below

PWLLHELI   Map 14 SH33

Places to visit

Penarth Fawr, PENARTH FAWR, 01443 336000 www.cadw.wales.gov.uk

Lloyd George Museum, LLANYSTUMDWY, LL52 0SH, 01766 522071 www.gwynedd.gov.uk/museums

Great for kids: Criccieth Castle, CRICCIETH, LL52 0DP, 01766 522227 www.cadw.wales.gov.uk

---

Hafan y Môr Holiday Park
HOLIDAY CENTRE 89%

GOLD

tel: 0871 231 0887 **LL53 6HJ**
email: hafanymor@haven.com **web:** www.haven.com/hafanymor
dir: *From Caernarfon take A499 to Pwllheli. A497 to Porthmadog. Park on right, approx 3m from Pwllheli. Or from Telford, A5, A494 to Bala. Right for Porthmadog. Left at rdbt in Porthmadog signed Criccieth & Pwllheli. Park on left 3m from Criccieth.*
grid ref: *SH431368*

Located between Pwllheli and Criccieth, and surrounded by mature trees that attract wildlife, this popular holiday centre provides a wide range of all-weather

---

LEISURE: 🏊 Indoor swimming pool   🏊 Outdoor swimming pool   🎠 Children's playground   👋 Kid's club   🎾 Tennis court   ♠ Games room   📺 Separate TV room   ⛳ golf course   🚤 Boats for hire   🎬 Cinema   🎵 Entertainment   🎣 Fishing   ⛳ Mini golf   🏄 Watersports   💪 Gym   ⚽ Sports field   Spa   🐴 Stables
FACILITIES: 🛁 Bath   🚿 Shower   ⚡ Electric shaver   💈 Hairdryer   ❄ Ice Pack Facility   ♿ Disabled facilities   📞 Public telephone   🛒 Shop on site or within 200yds   🏪 Mobile shop (calls at least 5 days a week)   🍖 BBQ area   🏕 Picnic area   WiFi Wi-fi   💻 Internet access   ♻ Recycling   🛈 Tourist info   🐕 Dog exercise area

attractions. Activities include a sports hall, an ornamental boating lake, a large indoor swimming pool and show bar, to name but a few, and a high ropes activity and Segways are now available. There are also great eating options - the Mash and Barrel bar and bistro, Traditional Fish and Chips, Burger King, Papa John's and a Starbucks café. The touring area includes 75 fully serviced all-weather pitches and a top notch, air-conditioned amenities block. 500 acre site. 75 touring pitches. 75 hardstandings. Caravan pitches. Motorhome pitches. 800 statics.

Open: mid Mar-end Oct (rs mid Mar-May & Sep-Oct reduced facilities)
Last arrival: 21.00hrs **Last departure:** 10.00hrs

Pitches: 🚐 🚍

Leisure: 🏊 ⚏ 🖐 🎵

Facilities: 🐾 ℗ ♿ 🕐 ⑤ 📶

Services: 🔌 🗄 🚽 🛢 🍽 ♨

Within 3 miles: ⚓ 🎣 ⛳ ◎ 🛶 🏪 ⑤ 🔵 ∪

Notes: No commercial vehicles, no bookings by persons under 21yrs unless a family booking, max 2 dogs per booking, certain dog breeds banned. Dogs must be kept on leads.

See advert below

Abererch Sands Holiday Centre
►►►71%

tel: 01758 612327 **LL53 6PJ**
email: enquiries@abererch-sands.co.uk **web:** www.abererch-sands.co.uk
dir: On A497 (Porthmadog to Pwllheli road), 1m from Pwllheli. **grid ref:** SH403359

Glorious views of Snowdonia and Cardigan Bay can be enjoyed from this very secure, family-run site adjacent to a railway station and a four-mile stretch of sandy beach. A large heated indoor swimming pool, snooker room, pool room, fitness centre and children's play area make this an ideal holiday venue. 85 acre site. 70 touring pitches. 70 hardstandings. Caravan pitches. Motorhome pitches. Tent pitches. 90 statics.

Open: Mar-Oct **Last arrival:** 21.00hrs **Last departure:** 21.00hrs

Pitches: 🚐 🚍 ⛺

Leisure: 🏊 ⚏ 🎱

Facilities: 🐾 ⊙ ❄ ♿ 🕐 ⑤ 🚿 📶 ♻

Services: 🔌 🗄 🛢 🧺 Ⓣ 🔋 ⟱

Within 3 miles: ⚓ 🎣 🏦 ⛳ 🛶 🏪 ⑤ 🔵 ∪

Notes: Dogs must be kept on leads.

AA Pubs & Restaurants nearby: Plas Bodegroes, PWLLHELI, LL53 5TH, 01758 612363

PITCHES: 🚐 Caravans 🚍 Motorhomes ⛺ Tents 🏕 Glamping-style accommodation **SERVICES:** 🔌 Electric hook up ⑤ Launderette 🍺 Licensed bar 🛢 Calor Gas ⊘ Camping Gaz Ⓣ Toilet fluid 🍽 Café/Restaurant ♨ Fast Food/Takeaway 🔋 Battery charging 🍼 Baby care ⟱ Motorvan service point **ABBREVIATIONS:** BH/bank hols – bank holidays Etr – Easter Spring BH – Spring Bank Holiday fr – from hrs – hours m – mile mdnt – midnight rdbt – roundabout rs – restricted service wk – week wknd – weekend x-rds – cross roads Ⓐ No credit or debit cards ⊗ No dogs ♦♦ Children of all ages accepted

TALSARNAU
Map 14 SH63

Places to visit
Portmeirion, PORTMEIRION, LL48 6ER, 01766 772306
www.portmeirion-village.com

Harlech Castle, HARLECH, LL46 2YH, 01766 780552 www.cadw.wales.gov.uk

Great for kids: Ffestiniog Railway, PORTHMADOG, LL49 9NF, 01766 516024
www.festrail.co.uk

Barcdy Touring Caravan & Camping Park
▶▶▶▶ 84%

tel: 01766 770736 **LL47 6YG**
email: anwen@barcdy.co.uk **web:** www.barcdy.co.uk
dir: From Maentwrog take A496 for Harlech. Site 4m on left. **grid ref:** SH620375

A quiet picturesque park on the edge of the Vale of Ffestiniog near the Dwryd estuary. Two touring areas serve the park, one near the park entrance, and the other with improved and more secluded terraced pitches beside a narrow valley. The tent area is secluded and peaceful, and the toilet facilities are clean and tidy. Footpaths through adjacent woodland lead to small lakes and an established nature trail. 12 acre site. 80 touring pitches. 40 hardstandings. 15 seasonal pitches. Caravan pitches. Motorhome pitches. Tent pitches. 30 statics.

Open: Apr-Oct (rs Selected dates 2nd facility building closed (excl high season & school hols)) **Last arrival:** 21.00hrs **Last departure:** noon

Pitches: * ⊞ £20-£27 ⊟ £20-£27 ▲ £15-£26

Facilities: ⬠☉🅟✳🎄📶♻🅘

Services: ⊟🖥🛢🧺

Within 3 miles: ↧🅟🅢∪

Notes: ⊗ No noisy parties, quiet families & couples only, no groups except Duke of Edinburgh Award participants.

AA Pubs & Restaurants nearby: The Hotel Portmeirion, PORTMEIRION, LL48 6ET, 01766 770000

TAL-Y-BONT

Places to visit
Cymer Abbey, CYMER ABBEY, LL40 2HE, 01443 336000 www.cadw.wales.gov.uk

Harlech Castle, HARLECH, LL46 2YH, 01766 780552 www.cadw.wales.gov.uk

TAL-Y-BONT
Map 14 SH52

PREMIER PARK

Islawrffordd Caravan Park
▶▶▶▶▶ 90%

tel: 01341 247269 **LL43 2AQ**
email: info@islawrffordd.co.uk **web:** www.islawrffordd.co.uk
dir: In village of Tal-y-Bont, take turn towards village railway halt, park signed.
grid ref: SH584215

Situated on the coast between Barmouth and Harlech, and within the Snowdonia National Park, with clear views of Cardigan Bay, the Lleyn Peninsula and the Snowdonia and Cader Idris mountain ranges, this excellent, family-run and family-friendly park has seen considerable investment over recent years. Fully matured, the touring area boasts fully serviced pitches, a superb toilet block with under-floor heating and top-quality fittings, and the park has private access to miles of sandy beach. 25 acre site. 105 touring pitches. 75 hardstandings. 50 seasonal pitches. Caravan pitches. Motorhome pitches. Tent pitches. 201 statics.

Open: Mar-1 Nov **Last arrival:** 20.00 **Last departure:** noon

Pitches: ⊞ ⊟ ▲

Leisure: ⬒⛰🎱☐ **Facilities:** ⬠☉🅟✳🅑🕐🅢📶♻🅘

Services: ⊟🖥🍴🛢🧺🅣🍽🎗🚿⚡ **Within 3 miles:** ↧🅟◎🎣🅢🅢∪

Notes: Strictly families & couples only. Dogs must be kept on leads.

AA Pubs & Restaurants nearby: Victoria Inn, LLANBEDR, LL45 2LD, 01341 241213

See advert on opposite page

ISLAWRFFORDD CARAVAN PARK

A family owned park Est. 1957

TALYBONT, NR BARMOUTH, GWYNEDD, LL43 2AQ, NORTH WALES

01341 247269

Email: info@islawrffordd.co.uk   www.islawrffordd.co.uk

"AA CAMPSITE OF THE YEAR 2012"

Family owned and run since being established in 1957, Islawrffordd Caravan Park offers the very best in quality which you are immediately aware of when entering the award winning reception building which now has similar architectural design to the laundry, bar and amusement/ take-away facilities.

Situated at the southern end of the magnificent Snowdonia National Park coastline in the village of Talybont, Islawrffordd offers 201 holiday home bases, 75 touring caravan/motorhome plots and 30 camping pitches all benefiting from the very best facilities, including a heated indoor swimming pool/sauna/ jacuzzi and tanning suite.

Nigel Mansell, O.B.E. & 1992 Formula 1 World Champion & Indy Car World Champion 1993 has a Holiday Home association with Islawrffordd that stretches back from the present day to his childhood and his opinion of the Snowdonia Coastline area and our park is still the same
"It's absolutely fantastic".

Choice of a Champion

TYWYN
Map 14 SH50

Places to visit

Talyllyn Railway, TYWYN, LL36 9EY, 01654 710472 www.talyllyn.co.uk

Castell-y-Bere, LLANFIHANGEL-Y-PENNANT, 01443 336000 www.cadw.wales.gov.uk

Great for kids: King Arthur's Labyrinth, MACHYNLLETH, SY20 9RF, 01654 761584 www.kingarthurslabyrinth.co.uk

Ynysymaengwyn Caravan Park
▶▶▶▶81%

tel: 01654 710684 **LL36 9RY**
email: rita@ynysy.co.uk
dir: On A493, 1m N of Tywyn, towards Dolgellau. **grid ref:** SH602021

A lovely park set in the wooded grounds of a former manor house, with designated nature trails through 13 acres of wildlife-rich woodland, scenic river walks, fishing and a sandy beach nearby. The attractive stone amenity block is clean and well kept, and this smart municipal park is ideal for families. 4 acre site. 80 touring pitches. Caravan pitches. Motorhome pitches. Tent pitches. 115 statics.

Open: Etr or Apr-Oct **Last arrival:** 23.00hrs **Last departure:** noon

Pitches: 🚐 🚐 Å

Leisure: ⚠

Facilities: 🌂 ⊙ 🖤 ⚒ 🕭 🕓 🖾 🎋 🚻

Services: 🕹 🗑 🛡 🧺 🛒

Within 3 miles: ↕🏇🐾 ◎ ⛾ 🖺 🖻 U

Notes: 🐕 Dogs must be kept on leads.

MONMOUTHSHIRE

ABERGAVENNY
Map 9 SO21

Places to visit

Big Pit National Coal Museum, BLAENAVON, NP4 9XP, 029 20573650 www.museumwales.ac.uk

Hen Gwrt, LLANTILIO CROSSENNY, 01443 336000 www.cadw.wales.gov.uk

Great for kids: Raglan Castle, RAGLAN, NP15 2BT, 01291 690228 www.cadw.wales.gov.uk

Wernddu Caravan Park
▶▶▶▶83%

tel: 01873 856223 **Old Ross Rd NP7 8NG**
email: info@wernddu-golf-club.co.uk
dir: From A465, N of Abergavenny, take B4521 signed Skenfrith. Site on right in 0.25m. **grid ref:** SO321153

Located north of the town centre, this former fruit farm, adjacent to a golf club and driving range, is managed by three generations of the same family, and has been transformed into an ideal base for those visiting the many nearby attractions. The well-spaced touring pitches have water, electricity and waste water disposal, and the smart modern amenities block provides very good privacy options. Site guests are welcome to use the golf club bar which also serves meals during the busy months; they are also eligible for half-price green fees. There is no shop on site but a daily newspaper service is provided, and a mini-market is less than a mile away. 6 acre site. 70 touring pitches. 20 hardstandings. 30 seasonal pitches. Caravan pitches. Motorhome pitches. Tent pitches.

Open: Mar-Oct **Last arrival:** 21.00hrs **Last departure:** noon

Pitches: * 🚐 £13.50-£17.50 🚐 £13.50-£17.50 Å £13.50-£17.50

Leisure: ⚓

Facilities: 🌂 ⚒ 🕭 🎋 🚻 WiFi ❼

Services: 🕹 🗑 🚽 🍴 🛒 ⛟

Within 3 miles: ↕🏇🐾 ◎ 🖺 🖻 U

Notes: Adults only. Dogs must be kept on leads. 9-hole pitch & putt, driving range, bar with sports TV.

AA Pubs & Restaurants nearby: Walnut Tree Inn, ABERGAVENNY, NP7 8AW, 01873 852797

Angel Hotel, ABERGAVENNY, NP7 5EN, 01873 857121

Pyscodlyn Farm Caravan & Camping Site
▶▶▶▶ 81%

tel: 01873 853271 & 07816 447942 **Llanwenarth Citra NP7 7ER**
email: pyscodlyn.farm@virgin.net
dir: *From Abergavenny take A40 (Brecon road), site 1.5m from entrance of Nevill Hall Hospital, on left 50yds past phone box.* **grid ref:** *SO266155*

With its outstanding views of the mountains, this quiet park in the Brecon Beacons National Park makes a pleasant holiday venue for country lovers. The Sugarloaf Mountain and the River Usk are within easy walking distance and, despite being a working farm, dogs are welcome. The separate ladies and gents amenities blocks have been refurbished to a high standard in recent years. Please note that credit cards are not taken at this site. 4.5 acre site. 60 touring pitches. Caravan pitches. Motorhome pitches. Tent pitches. 6 statics.

Open: Apr-Oct

Pitches: 🚐 £15-£16 🚍 £14-£16 ▲ £14-£16

Facilities: 📶⊙⚹⚿♿ ⚲ ❄ **Services:** 🔌🗑💧⚗🚾

Within 3 miles: 🎣🍴⚘◎🛒🍺⛳

Notes: 🚫 No noise after 23.00 hrs. Dogs must be kept on leads.

AA Pubs & Restaurants nearby: Angel Hotel, ABERGAVENNY, NP7 5EN, 01873 857121
Walnut Tree Inn, ABERGAVENNY, NP7 8AW, 01873 852797

| **DINGESTOW** | Map 9 SO41 |

Places to visit
Raglan Castle, RAGLAN, NP15 2BT, 01291 690228 www.cadw.wales.gov.uk

Tintern Abbey, TINTERN PARVA, NP16 6SE, 01291 689251 www.cadw.wales.gov.uk

Great for kids: The Nelson Museum & Local History Centre, MONMOUTH, NP25 3XA, 01600 710630

Bridge Caravan Park & Camping Site
▶▶▶ 84%

tel: 01600 740241 **Bridge Farm NP25 4DY**
email: info@bridgecaravanpark.co.uk
dir: *Phone for detailed directions.* **grid ref:** *SO459104*

The River Trothy runs along the edge of this quiet village park, which has been owned by the same family for many years. Touring pitches are both grass and hardstanding, and there is a backdrop of woodland. The quality facilities are enhanced by good laundry equipment. River fishing is available on site, and there is a dog walking area. The village shop is within 100 yards and a play field within 200 yards. 4 acre site. 94 touring pitches. 15 hardstandings. 50 seasonal pitches. Caravan pitches. Motorhome pitches. Tent pitches. 3 statics.

Open: Etr-Oct **Last arrival:** 22.00hrs **Last departure:** 16.00hrs

Pitches: 🚐 £15-£18 🚍 £15-£18 ▲ £15-£18

Facilities: 📶⊙📶⚹♿🛒 ❄ 🚲 **Services:** 🔌🗑💧⚗🚽🚾

Within 3 miles: 🎣🍴⚘◎🛒⛳

Notes: 🚫 Dogs must be kept on leads.

AA Pubs & Restaurants nearby: The Beaufort Arms Coaching Inn & Brasserie, RAGLAN, NP15 2DY, 01291 690412

| **USK** | Map 9 SO30 |

Places to visit
Caerleon Roman Fortress and Baths, CAERLEON, NP18 1AE, 01663 422518 www.cadw.wales.gov.uk

Big Pit National Coal Museum, BLAENAVON, NP4 9XP, 029 20573650 www.museumwales.ac.uk

Great for kids: Greenmeadow Community Farm, CWMBRAN, NP44 5AJ, 01633 647662 www.greenmeadowcommunityfarm.org.uk

| **PREMIER PARK** |

Pont Kemys Caravan & Camping Park
▶▶▶▶▶ 86%

tel: 01873 880688 **Chainbridge NP7 9DS**
email: info@pontkemys.com **web:** www.pontkemys.com
dir: *From Usk take B4598 towards Abergavenny. Approx 4m, over river bridge, bear right, 300yds to site. For other routes contact site for detailed directions.* **grid ref:** *SO348058*

A peaceful park next to the River Usk, offering an excellent standard of toilet facilities with family rooms. A section of the park has fully serviced pitches. The park is in a rural area with mature trees and country views, and attracts quiet visitors who enjoy the many attractions of this area. The local golf club is open during the day and serves breakfast and lunches. 8 acre site. 65 touring pitches. 29 hardstandings. 25 seasonal pitches. Caravan pitches. Motorhome pitches. Tent pitches.

Open: Mar-Oct **Last arrival:** 21.00 **Last departure:** noon

Pitches: * 🚐 £16-£20 🚍 £16-£20 ▲ £16-£20

Leisure: ⚽◻

Facilities: 📶⊙📶⚹♿🛒🚲❄ 🚲

Services: 🔌🗑💧⚗🚽🚾

Within 3 miles: 🎣⚘⚘🛒

Notes: No music. Dogs must be kept on leads. Mother & baby room, kitchen facilities for groups.

AA Pubs & Restaurants nearby: The Raglan Arms, USK, NP15 1DL, 01291 690800
The Nags Head Inn, USK, NP15 1BH, 01291 672820
The Three Salmons Hotel, USK, NP15 1RY, 01291 672133

PITCHES: 🚐 Caravans 🚍 Motorhomes ▲ Tents 🏠 Glamping-style accommodation **SERVICES:** 🔌 Electric hook up 🗑 Launderette 🍺 Licensed bar 💧 Calor Gas ⚗ Camping Gaz 🚽 Toilet fluid 🍴 Café/Restaurant 🍔 Fast Food/Takeaway 🔋 Battery charging 👶 Baby care 🚾 Motorvan service point
ABBREVIATIONS: BH/bank hols – bank holidays Etr – Easter Spring BH – Spring Bank Holiday fr – from hrs – hours m – mile mdnt – midnight rdbt – roundabout rs – restricted service wk – week wknd – weekend x-rds – cross roads 🚫 No credit or debit cards 🚫 No dogs 👶 Children of all ages accepted

PEMBROKESHIRE

BROAD HAVEN
Map 8 SM81

Places to visit
Llawhaden Castle, LLAWHADEN, 01443 336000 www.cadw.wales.gov.uk

Great for kids: Scolton Manor Museum & Country Park, SCOLTON, SA62 5QL, 01437 731328 (Museum) www.pembrokeshire.gov.uk

Creampots Touring Caravan & Camping Park
▶▶▶ 86%

tel: 01437 781776 **Broadway SA62 3TU**
email: creampots@btconnect.com
dir: *From Haverfordwest take B4341 to Broadway. Turn left, follow brown tourist signs to site.* **grid ref:** SM882131

Set just outside the Pembrokeshire National Park, this quiet site is just one and a half miles from a safe sandy beach at Broad Haven, and the coastal footpath. The park is well laid out and carefully maintained, and the toilet block offers a good standard of facilities. The owners welcome families. 8 acre site. 72 touring pitches. 32 hardstandings. Caravan pitches. Motorhome pitches. Tent pitches. 1 static.

Open: Mar-Nov **Last arrival:** 21.00hrs **Last departure:** 11.00hrs

Pitches: 🚐 🚙 🅰

Facilities: 🅿 ⊙ 🅿 ✳ ⅌ 🛋 📶 ♻ ❶

Services: 🔌 🔊 🎣 🧺 🛒

Within 3 miles: 🎣 🎡 ⌗ 🏊 🛒 🏌 ∪

Notes: Dogs must be kept on leads.

AA Pubs & Restaurants nearby: The Swan Inn, LITTLE HAVEN, SA62 3UL, 01437 781880

South Cockett Caravan & Camping Park
▶▶▶ 78%

tel: 01437 781296 & 781760 & 07774 782572 **South Cockett SA62 3TU**
email: esmejames@hotmail.co.uk
dir: *From Haverfordwest take B4341 to Broad Haven, at Broadway turn left, site 300yds.* grid ref: SM878136

A warm welcome is assured at this small site on a working farm. The touring areas are divided into neat paddocks by high, well-trimmed hedges, and there are good toilet facilities. The lovely beach at Broad Haven is only about two miles away. 6 acre site. 73 touring pitches. 25 seasonal pitches. Caravan pitches. Motorhome pitches. Tent pitches.

Open: Etr-Oct **Last arrival:** 22.30hrs

Pitches: 🚐 🚙 🅰

Leisure: ⊕

Facilities: 🅿 ⊙ ✳ ⌗ 🛒 ♻ ❶

Services: 🔌 🔊 🎣 🧺 🛒

Within 3 miles: 🎣 🏌 🏊 🛒 🏌 ∪

Notes: 🐕 Dogs must be kept on leads.

AA Pubs & Restaurants nearby: The Swan Inn, LITTLE HAVEN, SA62 3UL, 01437 781880

FISHGUARD
Map 8 SM93

Places to visit
Pentre Ifan Burial Chamber, NEWPORT, 01443 336000 www.cadw.wales.gov.uk

Great for kids: OceanLab, FISHGUARD, SA64 0DE, 01348 874737 www.ocean-lab.co.uk

Fishguard Bay Caravan & Camping Park
▶▶▶ 90%

tel: 01348 811415 **Garn Gelli SA65 9ET**
email: enquiries@fishguardbay.com **web:** www.fishguardbay.com
dir: *NB if approaching Fishguard from Cardigan on A487 ignore Sat Nav to turn right. Turn at camp site sign onto single track road.* **grid ref:** SM984383

Set high up on cliffs with outstanding views of Fishguard Bay, this site has the Pembrokeshire Coastal Path running right through its centre, so affording many opportunities for wonderful walks. The park is extremely well kept, with a good toilet block, a common room with TV, a lounge/library, decent laundry and a well-stocked shop. 5 acre site. 50 touring pitches. 6 hardstandings. Caravan pitches. Motorhome pitches. Tent pitches. 50 statics.

Open: Mar-9 Jan **Last arrival:** anytime **Last departure:** noon

Pitches: * 🚐 £19-£23 🚙 £19-£23 🅰 £18-£22

Leisure: 🅰 🎣 🖵

Facilities: 🅿 ⊙ 🅿 ✳ ⓒ 🛋 ⌗ 📶 ♻ ❶

Services: 🔌 🔊 🎣 🧺 🆃 🛒

Within 3 miles: 🎣 ⌗ 🏊 🛒 🏌 ∪

Notes: Dogs must be kept on leads.

AA Pubs & Restaurants nearby: The Sloop Inn, PORTHGAIN, SA62 5BN, 01348 831449

The Shed, PORTHGAIN, SA62 5BN, 01348 831518

Salutation Inn, NEWPORT, SA41 3UY, 01239 820564

Gwaun Vale Touring Park
►►►78%

tel: 01348 874698 **Llanychaer SA65 9TA**
email: margaret.harries@talk21.com
dir: B4313 from Fishguard. Site 1.5m on right. **grid ref:** SM977356

Located in the beautiful Gwaun Valley, this carefully landscaped park, with colourful, seasonal flowers, is set on the hillside with generously sized, tiered pitches on two levels that provide superb views of the surrounding countryside. 1.6 acre site. 29 touring pitches. 5 hardstandings. Caravan pitches. Motorhome pitches. Tent pitches. 1 static.

Open: Apr-Oct **Last arrival:** anytime **Last departure:** 11.00hrs

Pitches: * ⬛ £18-£21 ⬛ £18-£21 ▲ £16-£23

Leisure: ⚲

Facilities: 🌂⊙🍴☼☏🚻⚙❶

Services: 🔌🗑

Within 3 miles: 🎣🏇🚶🏪🛒♨

Notes: No skateboards. Dogs must be kept on leads. Guidebooks available.

AA Pubs & Restaurants nearby: The Sloop Inn, PORTHGAIN, SA62 5BN, 01348 831449

The Shed, PORTHGAIN, SA62 5BN, 01348 831518

Salutation Inn, NEWPORT, SA41 3UY, 01239 820564

Hasguard Cross Caravan Park
►►►83%

tel: 01437 781443 **SA62 3SL**
email: hasguard@aol.com
dir: From Haverfordwest take B4327 towards Dale. In 7m right at x-rds. Site 1st right. **grid ref:** SM850108

A very clean, efficient and well-run site in the Pembrokeshire National Park, just one and a half miles from the sea and beach at Little Haven, and with views of the surrounding hills. The toilet and shower facilities are immaculately clean, and there is a licensed bar (evenings only) serving a good choice of food. 4.5 acre site. 12 touring pitches. 3 hardstandings. Caravan pitches. Motorhome pitches. Tent pitches. 42 statics.

Open: all year (rs Aug tent field for 28 days) **Last arrival:** 21.00hrs
Last departure: 10.00hrs

Pitches: ⬛ ⬛ ▲

Leisure: ♨

Facilities: 🌂⊙🍴☼♿☏🚻⚙❶

Services: 🔌🗑🍺🔋🍴🏪🚐

Within 3 miles: 🚶🎣🏇♨🏪🛒♨

Notes: Dogs must be kept on leads.

AA Pubs & Restaurants nearby: The Swan Inn, LITTLE HAVEN, SA62 3UL, 01437 781880

Places to visit

Llawhaden Castle, LLAWHADEN, 01443 336000 www.cadw.wales.gov.uk

Great for kids: Oakwood Theme Park, NARBERTH, SA67 8DE, 01834 815170 www.oakwoodthemepark.co.uk

Nolton Cross Caravan Park
►►81%

tel: 01437 710701 **Nolton SA62 3NP**
email: info@noltoncross-holidays.co.uk
dir: 1m from A487 (Haverfordwest to St Davids road) at Simpson Cross, towards Nolton & Broadhaven. **grid ref:** SM879177

High grassy banks surround the touring area of this park next to the owners' working farm. It is located on open ground above the sea and St Bride's Bay (within one and a half miles), and there is a coarse fishing lake close by — equipment for hire and reduced permit rates for campers are available. 4 acre site. 15 touring pitches. Caravan pitches. Motorhome pitches. Tent pitches. 30 statics.

Open: Mar-Dec **Last arrival:** 22.00hrs **Last departure:** noon

Pitches: * ⬛ £8.70-£15.80 ⬛ £8.70-£15.80 ▲ £8.70-£15.80

Leisure: ⚲

Facilities: 🌂⊙☼☏🛒🚻📶⚙❶

Services: 🔌🗑🚿🔌🚐

Within 3 miles: 🏇♨🏪🛒♨

Notes: No youth groups. Dogs must be kept on leads.

AA Pubs & Restaurants nearby: The Swan Inn, LITTLE HAVEN, SA62 3UL, 01437 781880

See Hasguard Cross

PITCHES: ⬛ Caravans ⬛ Motorhomes ▲ Tents ⌂ Glamping-style accommodation **SERVICES:** 🔌 Electric hook up 🗑 Launderette 🍺 Licensed bar 🔋 Calor Gas ⊘ Camping Gaz 🔲 Toilet fluid 🍴 Café/Restaurant 🏪 Fast Food/Takeaway 🔋 Battery charging 🚼 Baby care 🚐 Motorvan service point **ABBREVIATIONS:** BH/bank hols — bank holidays Etr — Easter Spring BH — Spring Bank Holiday fr — from hrs — hours m — mile mdnt — midnight rdbt — roundabout rs — restricted service wk — week wknd — weekend x-rds — cross roads 🚫 No credit or debit cards 🚫 No dogs 👪 Children of all ages accepted

ST DAVIDS

Map 8 SM72

Places to visit

St Davids Bishop's Palace, ST DAVIDS, SA62 6PE, 01437 720517
www.cadw.wales.gov.uk

St Davids Cathedral, ST DAVID'S, SA62 6PE, 01437 720202
www.stdavidscathedral.org.uk

PREMIER PARK

Caerfai Bay Caravan & Tent Park

▶▶▶▶▶ 90%

tel: 01437 720274 **Caerfai Bay SA62 6QT**
email: info@caerfaibay.co.uk **web:** www.caerfaibay.co.uk
dir: From E on A487 towards St Davids left into Caerfai Rd (Ffordd Caerfai) signed
Caerfai & parking. Right at end of road. **grid ref:** SM759244

Magnificent coastal scenery and an outlook over St Bride's Bay can be enjoyed
from this delightful site, located just 300 yards from a bathing beach. The
excellent toilet facilities include four family rooms, which are a huge asset to the
park, and ongoing improvements include a second, solar-heated wet suit shower
room, upgraded roadways, and modernised water points. There is an excellent
farm shop just across the road. 10 acre site. 106 touring pitches. 26
hardstandings. Caravan pitches. Motorhome pitches. Tent pitches. 30 statics.

Open: Mar-mid Nov **Last arrival:** 21.00 **Last departure:** 11.00hrs
Pitches: * 🚐 £18-£23 🚍 £12.50-£17 ▲ £12.50-£17
Facilities: 🚿⊙☂✳&🕙🚽📶 🖥 ♻ ❼
Services: 🔌🔲 🔒⌀🛒↯
Within 3 miles: ⌄≭🦯≋💲🗐
Notes: No dogs in tent field mid Jul-Aug, no skateboards or rollerblades. Dogs must
be kept on leads.
AA Pubs & Restaurants nearby: Cwtch, ST DAVIDS, SA62 6SD, 01437 720491
The Sloop Inn, PORTHGAIN, SA62 5BN, 01348 831449
The Shed, PORTHGAIN, SA62 5BN, 01348 831518

Tretio Caravan & Camping Park

▶▶▶ 82%

tel: 01437 781600 **SA62 6DE**
email: info@tretio.com
dir: From St Davids take A487 towards Fishguard, left at Rugby Football Club, straight on
for 3m. Site signed, left to site. **grid ref:** SM787292

An attractive site in a very rural spot with distant country views, and close to
beautiful beaches; the tiny cathedral city of St Davids is only three miles away. A
mobile shop calls daily at peak periods, and orienteering advice and maps are
available for couples and families. 6.5 acre site. 40 touring pitches. 8 seasonal
pitches. Caravan pitches. Motorhome pitches. Tent pitches. 30 statics.

Open: Mar-Oct **Last arrival:** 20.00hrs **Last departure:** 10.00hrs
Pitches: * 🚐 £16.50-£30.50 🚍 £16.50-£30.50 ▲ £11.50-£30.50
Leisure: 🄰⊛♨ **Facilities:** 🚿⊙☂✳&🕙♻❼
Services: 🔌🔲⌀🝙🛒 **Within 3 miles:** ⌄≭🦯◎≋💲🗐
Notes: Dogs must be kept on leads. Pitch & putt, climbing wall, play area.
AA Pubs & Restaurants nearby: Cwtch, ST DAVIDS, SA62 6SD, 01437 720491
The Sloop Inn, PORTHGAIN, SA62 5BN, 01348 831449
The Shed, PORTHGAIN, SA62 5BN, 01348 831518

Hendre Eynon Camping & Caravan Site

▶▶▶ 81%

tel: 01437 720474 **SA62 6DB**
email: hendreeynoninfo@gmail.com **web:** www.hendreeynon.co.uk
dir: Take A487 (Fishguard road) from St Davids, left at rugby club signed Llanrhian. Site
2m on right NB do no take turn to Whitesands. **grid ref:** SM771284

A peaceful country site on a working farm, with a modern toilet block including
family rooms. Within easy reach of many lovely sandy beaches, and two miles from
the cathedral city of St Davids. 7 acre site. 50 touring pitches. 20 seasonal pitches.
Caravan pitches. Motorhome pitches. Tent pitches.

Open: Apr-Sep **Last arrival:** 21.00hrs **Last departure:** noon
Pitches: * 🚐 £14-£21 🚍 £14-£21 ▲ £14-£21
Facilities: 🚿⊙✳🕙🚽❼ **Services:** 🔌🔲 🔒⌀🛒
Within 3 miles: ⌄≭🦯≋💲🗐
Notes: 🚫 Maximum 2 dogs per unit. Dogs must be kept on leads.
AA Pubs & Restaurants nearby: Cwtch, ST DAVIDS, SA62 6SD, 01437 720491
The Sloop Inn, PORTHGAIN, SA62 5BN, 01348 831449
The Shed, PORTHGAIN, SA62 5BN, 01348 831518

LEISURE: 🏊 Indoor swimming pool 🏊 Outdoor swimming pool 🄰 Children's playground 👶 Kid's club 🎾 Tennis court 🎱 Games room 📺 Separate TV room
⛳ golf course ⛵ Boats for hire 🎬 Cinema 🎵 Entertainment 🎣 Fishing ◎ Mini golf 🏄 Watersports 💪 Gym 🏟 Sports field Spa ♨ Stables
FACILITIES: 🛁 Bath 🚿 Shower ⊙ Electric shaver ☂ Hairdryer ✳ Ice Pack Facility & Disabled facilities 🕙 Public telephone 🛒 Shop on site or within 200yds
🏪 Mobile shop (calls at least 5 days a week) 🍖 BBQ area 🏞 Picnic area 📶 Wi-fi 🖥 Internet access ♻ Recycling ❼ Tourist info 🐕 Dog exercise area

TENBY

Map 8 SN10

Places to visit

Tudor Merchant's House, TENBY, SA70 7BX, 01834 842279
www.nationaltrust.org.uk/tudormerchantshouse

Tenby Museum & Art Gallery, TENBY, SA70 7BP, 01834 842809
www.tenbymuseum.org.uk

Great for kids: Colby Woodland Garden, AMROTH, SA67 8PP, 01834 811885
www.nationaltrust.org.uk/main

Kiln Park Holiday Centre
HOLIDAY CENTRE 86%

tel: 0871 231 0889 **Marsh Rd SA70 7RB**
email: kilnpark@haven.com **web:** www.haven.com/kilnpark
dir: *Follow A477, A478 to Tenby for 6m. Then follow signs to Penally, site 0.5m on left.*
grid ref: *SN119002*

A large holiday complex complete with leisure and sports facilities and lots of entertainment for all the family. There are bars and cafés and plenty of security.

This touring, camping and static site is on the outskirts of town, and it's only a short walk through dunes to the sandy beach. The modern amenities block provides a stylish interior with under-floor heating and superb fixtures and fittings. 103 acre site. 130 touring pitches. 60 hardstandings. Caravan pitches. Motorhome pitches. Tent pitches. 703 statics.

Open: mid Mar-end Oct (rs mid Mar-May & Sep-Oct some facilities may be reduced) **Last arrival:** dusk **Last departure:** 10.00hrs

Pitches: 🚐 🚐 ⛺

Leisure: 🏊 ⛱ 🎾 🏆 👶 🎣 🎵 ♪

Facilities: 🍳 🐕 ♿ 🕐 💷 WiFi ♻

Services: 🔌 🔋 💷 🍽 🚿 ♨ 🍴 🛒

Within 3 miles: ↓ 🎣 🎿 🏇 🐎 ⛳ 🚴 🎢 🎱 U

Notes: No commercial vehicles, no bookings by persons under 21yrs unless a family booking, max 2 dogs per booking, certain dog breeds banned. Dogs must be kept on leads. Entertainment complex, bowling & putting green.

AA Pubs & Restaurants nearby: Hope and Anchor, TENBY, SA70 7AX, 01834 842131

See advert below

TENBY *continued*

Trefalun Park
►►►►87%

tel: 01646 651514 **Devonshire Dr, St Florence SA70 8RD**
email: trefalun@aol.com **web:** www.trefalunpark.co.uk
dir: *1.5m NW of St Florence & 0.5m N of B4318.* **grid ref:** *SN093027*

Open: Etr-Oct **Last arrival:** 19.00hrs **Last departure:** noon

Pitches: * 🚐 £15-£27 🚎 £15-£24 ⛺ £15-£24

Leisure: 🎪

Facilities: 🖙⊙𝄞⚒&⊙🚿WiFi♻𝒊

Services: 🔌🗑🛢🧺T🛒↯

Within 3 miles: ↨⚓🎣◎⛵🛍🛍

Notes: No motorised scooters, no gazebos. Dogs must be kept on leads.

AA Pubs & Restaurants nearby: Hope and Anchor, TENBY, SA70 7AX, 01834 842131

See advert below

Set within 12 acres of sheltered, well-kept grounds, this quiet country park offers well-maintained level grass pitches separated by bushes and trees, with plenty of space to relax in. Children can feed the park's friendly pets. Plenty of activities are available at the nearby Heatherton Country Sports Park, including go-karting, indoor bowls, golf and bumper boating. 12 acre site. 90 touring pitches. 54 hardstandings. 45 seasonal pitches. Caravan pitches. Motorhome pitches. Tent pitches. 10 statics.

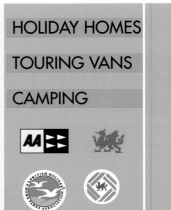
LEISURE: 🏊 Indoor swimming pool 🏊 Outdoor swimming pool 🎪 Children's playground 👶 Kid's club 🎾 Tennis court 🎱 Games room 📺 Separate TV room ⛳ golf course ⛵ Boats for hire 🎬 Cinema 🎵 Entertainment 🎣 Fishing ◎ Mini golf 🏄 Watersports 🏋 Gym 🏟 Sports field Spa ♘ Stables
FACILITIES: 🛁 Bath 🚿 Shower ⊙ Electric shaver 𝄞 Hairdryer ❄ Ice Pack Facility ♿ Disabled facilities 📞 Public telephone 🛍 Shop on site or within 200yds 🛒 Mobile shop (calls at least 5 days a week) 🍖 BBQ area 🏕 Picnic area WiFi Wi-fi 💻 Internet access ♻ Recycling 𝒊 Tourist info 🐕 Dog exercise area

Well Park Caravan & Camping Site
►►►►82%

tel: 01834 842179 **SA70 8TL**
email: enquiries@wellparkcaravans.co.uk
dir: A478 towards Tenby. At rdbt at Kilgetty follow Tenby/A478 signs. 3m to next rdbt, take 2nd exit, site 2nd right. **grid ref:** SN128028

An attractive, well-maintained park with good landscaping from trees, ornamental shrubs and flower borders. The amenities include a launderette and indoor dishwashing, games room with table tennis, and an enclosed play area. The park is ideally situated between Tenby and Saundersfoot; Tenby just a 15-minute walk away, or the town can be reached via a traffic-free cycle track. 10 acre site. 100 touring pitches. 16 hardstandings. Caravan pitches. Motorhome pitches. Tent pitches. 42 statics.

Open: Mar-Oct (rs Mar-mid Jun & mid Sep-Oct bar may be closed) **Last arrival:** 22.00hrs **Last departure:** 11.00hrs

Pitches: ⊞ ⊟ Å
Leisure: ⚠ ✎ ▢
Facilities: ⌐ ☉ ℱ ✳ ⅋ ⓢ ⊟ WiFi ♻ ❼
Services: ⊞ ⊡ ⊡ ⊟ ⊟ ⅄
Within 3 miles: ↥ ⅏ ⌀ ⊚ ⊱ ⊟ ⊟ ∪

Notes: Family groups only. Dogs must be kept on leads. TV hook-ups.
AA Pubs & Restaurants nearby: Hope and Anchor, TENBY, SA70 7AX, 01834 842131

Wood Park Caravans
►►►78%

tel: 01834 843414 & 0844 4141464 (winter) **New Hedges SA70 8TL**
email: info@woodpark.co.uk
dir: At rdbt 2m N of Tenby follow A478 towards Tenby, take 2nd right & right again. **grid ref:** SN128025

Situated in beautiful countryside between the popular seaside resorts of Tenby and Saundersfoot, and with Waterwynch Bay just a 15-minute walk away, this peaceful site provides a spacious and relaxing atmosphere for holidays. The slightly sloping touring area is divided by shrubs and hedge-screened paddocks and a licensed bar and games room are also available. 10 acre site. 60 touring pitches. 40 hardstandings. 10 seasonal pitches. Caravan pitches. Motorhome pitches. Tent pitches. 90 statics.

Open: Spring BH-Sep (rs Etr-Spring BH & Sep bar, laundrette & games room may not be open) **Last arrival:** 22.00hrs **Last departure:** 10.00hrs

Pitches: * ⊞ £14-£25 ⊟ £14-£25 Å £13-£23
Leisure: ⚠ ✎
Facilities: ⌐ ☉ ℱ ✳ WiFi ♻ ❼
Services: ⊞ ⊡ ⊡ ⊟ ⊘ ⊟
Within 3 miles: ↥ ⅏ ⌀ ⊚ ⊱ ⊟ ⊟

Notes: No groups, 1 car per unit, only small dogs accepted, no dogs Jul-Aug & BHs. Dogs must be kept on leads.
AA Pubs & Restaurants nearby: Hope and Anchor, TENBY, SA70 7AX, 01834 842131

POWYS

BRECON
Map 9 SO02

Places to visit
Regimental Museum of The Royal Welsh, BRECON, LD3 7EB, 01874 613310 www.royalwelsh.org.uk

Tretower Court & Castle, TRETOWER, NP8 1RD, 01874 730279 www.cadw.wales.gov.uk

PREMIER PARK

Pencelli Castle Caravan & Camping Park
►►►►►90%

tel: 01874 665451 **Pencelli LD3 7LX**
email: pencelli@tiscali.co.uk
dir: Exit A40 2m E of Brecon onto B4558, follow signs to Pencelli. **grid ref:** SO096248

Lying in the heart of the Brecon Beacons National Park, this charming park offers peace, beautiful scenery and high quality facilities. It is bordered by the Brecon and Monmouth Canal. The attention to detail is superb, and the well-equipped heated toilets with en suite cubicles are matched by a drying room for clothes and boots, full laundry, and a shop. Regular buses stop just outside the gate and go to Brecon, Abergavenny and Swansea. 10 acre site. 80 touring pitches. 40 hardstandings. Caravan pitches. Motorhome pitches. Tent pitches.

Open: Feb-27 Nov (rs 30 Oct-Etr shop closed) **Last arrival:** 22.00 **Last departure:** noon

Pitches: ⊞ ⊟ Å
Leisure: ⚠ ⊛
Facilities: ⌐ ☉ ℱ ✳ ⅋ ⓢ ⊟ ⊟ WiFi ♻ ❼
Services: ⊞ ⊡ ⊟ ⊘ T ⊟ ⅄
Within 3 miles: ⅏ ⊟ ⌀ ⊟ ⊟ ∪

Notes: No radios, music or camp fires, assistance dogs only. Cycle hire.
AA Pubs & Restaurants nearby: Star Inn, TALYBONT-ON-USK, LD3 7YX, 01874 676635
The Usk Inn, BRECON, LD3 7JE, 01874 676251

Follow us on Facebook
www.facebook.com/TheAAUK

PITCHES: ⊞ Caravans ⊟ Motorhomes Å Tents ⋒ Glamping-style accommodation **SERVICES:** ⊞ Electric hook up ⊡ Launderette ⊟ Licensed bar ⊟ Calor Gas ⊘ Camping Gaz T Toilet fluid ⊟ Café/Restaurant ⊟ Fast Food/Takeaway ⅄ Battery charging ⊟ Baby care ⅄ Motorvan service point **ABBREVIATIONS:** BH/bank hols – bank holidays Etr – Easter Spring BH – Spring Bank Holiday fr – from hrs – hours m – mile mdnt – midnight rdbt – roundabout rs – restricted service wk – week wknd – weekend x-rds – cross roads ⊗ No credit or debit cards ⊗ No dogs ⅋ Children of all ages accepted

BRONLLYS
Map 9 SO13

Places to visit
Regimental Museum of The Royal Welsh, BRECON, LD3 7EB, 01874 613310
www.royalwelsh.org.uk

Anchorage Caravan Park
►►►►82%

tel: 01874 711246 & 711230 **LD3 0LD**
web: www.anchoragecp.co.uk
dir: *8m NE of Brecon in village centre.* **grid ref:** *SO142351*

A well-maintained site with a choice of south-facing, sloping grass pitches and superb views of the Black Mountains, or a more sheltered lower area with a number of excellent super pitches. The site is a short distance from the water sports centre at Llangorse Lake. 8 acre site. 110 touring pitches. 8 hardstandings. 60 seasonal pitches. Caravan pitches. Motorhome pitches. Tent pitches. 101 statics.

Open: all year (rs Nov-Mar TV room closed) **Last arrival:** 23.00hrs
Last departure: 18.00hrs

Pitches: ⊞ fr £13 ⇞ fr £13 ▲ fr £13

Leisure: ⚙◻

Facilities: ⛏⊙℗✳⚒☺⑤ᙢᄼ㎿ ♻ ❼

Services: ⊟⑤🗑⊘⊤🎫

Within 3 miles: ℘⑤⑤∪

Notes: Dogs must be kept on leads. Post office, hairdresser.

AA Pubs & Restaurants nearby: The Harp Inn, GLASBURY, HR3 5NR, 01497 847373
The Old Black Lion, HAY-ON-WYE, HR3 5AD, 01497 820841

BUILTH WELLS
Map 9 SO05

Fforest Fields Caravan & Camping Park
►►►►►84%

tel: 01982 570406 **Hundred House LD1 5RT**
email: office@fforestfields.co.uk **web:** www.fforestfields.co.uk
dir: *From town centre follow New Radnor signs on A481. 4m to signed entrance on right, 0.5m before Hundred House village.* **grid ref:** *SO100535*

A constantly improving, sheltered park surrounded by magnificent scenery and an abundance of wildlife. The spacious pitches are well spaced to create optimum privacy, and the superb eco-friendly amenities block is fuelled by solar panels and a bio-mass boiler. The historic town of Builth Wells and The Royal Welsh Showground are just four miles away. 12 acre site. 80 touring pitches. 17 hardstandings. 12 seasonal pitches. Caravan pitches. Motorhome pitches. Tent pitches.

Open: all year (rs 4 Jan-end Mar no shop; caravan & motorhome hardstandings only) **Last arrival:** 21.00 **Last departure:** 18.00hrs

Pitches: * ⊞ £14-£20 ⇞ £14-£20 ▲ £14-£20

Leisure: ✪

Facilities: ⛏⊙℗✳⚒☺⑤ᙢ㎿ 🖥 ♻ ❼

Services: ⊟⑤🗑⊘⊤🎫

Within 3 miles: ↥⊟℘≋⑤⑤

Notes: No loud music or revelry.

AA Pubs & Restaurants nearby: The Laughing Dog, LLANDRINDOD WELLS, LD1 5PT, 01597 822406

LEISURE: 🏊 Indoor swimming pool 🏊 Outdoor swimming pool ⚠ Children's playground 🪁 Kid's club 🎾 Tennis court 🎱 Games room ▭ Separate TV room ⛳ golf course ⛵ Boats for hire 🎬 Cinema 🎵 Entertainment ℘ Fishing ◎ Mini golf 🌊 Watersports 🏋 Gym ✪ Sports field Spa ∪ Stables
FACILITIES: 🛁 Bath 🚿 Shower ⊙ Electric shaver ℗ Hairdryer ✳ Ice Pack Facility ⚒ Disabled facilities 🕾 Public telephone ⑤ Shop on site or within 200yds 🛒 Mobile shop (calls at least 5 days a week) 🍖 BBQ area ᙢ Picnic area ㎿ Wi-fi 🖥 Internet access ♻ Recycling ❼ Tourist info ᄼ Dog exercise area

CHURCHSTOKE
Map 15 SO29

Places to visit
Montgomery Castle, MONTGOMERY, 01443 336000 www.cadw.wales.gov.uk

PREMIER PARK

Daisy Bank Caravan Park

►►►►► 84%

tel: 01588 620471 & 07918 680713 **Snead SY15 6EB**
email: enquiries@daisy-bank.co.uk
dir: On A489, 2m E of Churchstoke. **grid ref:** SO309926

Peacefully located between Craven Arms and Churchstoke and surrounded by rolling hills, this idyllic, adults-only park offers generously sized, fully serviced pitches; all are situated in attractive hedged areas, surrounded by lush grass and pretty seasonal flowers. The immaculately maintained amenity blocks provide smart, modern fittings and excellent privacy options. Camping pods, a pitch and putt course and free WiFi are also available. 7 acre site. 80 touring pitches. 75 hardstandings. 30 seasonal pitches. Caravan pitches. Motorhome pitches. Tent pitches. 2 wooden pods.

Open: all year **Last arrival:** 20.00 **Last departure:** 13.00hrs

Pitches: 🚐 �car 🅰 🏕

Facilities: 🎣 📡 ☼ ⅙ ⊙ 🖵 ⚓ WIFI 🖥 ♻ ❼

Services: 🔌 🔄 🍴 ⌀ 🇹

Within 3 miles: ◎ 🏧 📷

Notes: Adults only. Dogs must be kept on leads. Caravan storage.

AA Pubs & Restaurants nearby: The Three Tuns Inn, BISHOP'S CASTLE, SY9 5BW, 01588 638797

CRICKHOWELL
Map 9 SO21

Places to visit
Tretower Court & Castle, TRETOWER, NP8 1RD, 01874 730279
www.cadw.wales.gov.uk

Big Pit National Coal Museum, BLAENAVON, NP4 9XP, 029 20573650
www.museumwales.ac.uk

Riverside Caravan & Camping Park
►►► 80%

tel: 01873 810397 **New Rd NP8 1AY**
dir: On A4077, well signed from A40. **grid ref:** SO215184

A very well tended adults-only park in delightful countryside on the edge of the small country town of Crickhowell. The adjacent riverside park is an excellent facility for all, including dog-walkers. Crickhowell has numerous specialist shops including a first-class delicatessen. Within a few minutes' walk of the park are several friendly pubs with good restaurants. 3.5 acre site. 35 touring pitches. Caravan pitches. Motorhome pitches. Tent pitches. 20 statics.

Open: Mar-Oct **Last arrival:** 21.00hrs

Pitches: * 🚐 fr £16 �car fr £16 🅰 fr £12

Facilities: 🎣 ⊙ 📡 ☼ ⅙ 🖼 ❼

Services: 🔌 🔋 🖃

Within 3 miles: ⅃ ♨ 🏧 ↻

Notes: Adults only. 🚫 No hang gliders or paragliders. Dogs must be kept on leads. Large canopied area for drying clothes & cooking etc.

AA Pubs & Restaurants nearby: The Bear, CRICKHOWELL, NP8 1BW, 01873 810408

LLANDRINDOD WELLS
Map 9 SO06

Disserth Caravan & Camping Park

►►►► 83%

tel: 01597 860277 **Disserth, Howey LD1 6NL**
email: disserthcaravan@btconnect.com
dir: 1m from A483, between Newbridge-on-Wye & Howey, by church. Follow brown signs from A483 or A470. **grid ref:** SO035583

A delightfully secluded and predominantly adult park, by a 13th-century church, that sits in a beautiful valley on the banks of the River Ithon, a tributary of the River Wye. It has a small bar which is open at weekends and during busy periods. The amenities block and laundry are appointed to a high standard and provide good privacy options. 4 acre site. 30 touring pitches. 6 hardstandings. Caravan pitches. Motorhome pitches. Tent pitches. 25 statics. 1 wooden pod.

Open: Mar-Oct **Last arrival:** sunset **Last departure:** noon

Pitches: * 🚐 £10-£25 🚗 £15-£25 🅰 £10-£30 🏕

Facilities: 🎣 ⊙ 📡 ☼ ⅙ WIFI ♻ ❼

Services: 🔌 🔄 🍴 🔋 ⌀ 🇹 🖃

Within 3 miles: ⅃ ♨ ♒ 🏧 📷 ↻

Notes: Dogs must be kept on leads. Private trout fishing.

AA Pubs & Restaurants nearby: The Laughing Dog, LLANDRINDOD WELLS, LD1 5PT, 01597 822406

Dalmore Camping & Caravanning Park
►► 82%

tel: 01597 822483 **Howey LD1 5RG**
dir: 3m S of Llandrindod Wells, off A483. 4m N of Builth Wells, at top of hill. **grid ref:** SO045575

An intimate and well laid out adults-only park. Pitches are attractively terraced to ensure that all enjoy the wonderful views from this splendidly landscaped little park. 3 acre site. 20 touring pitches. 12 hardstandings. 6 seasonal pitches. Caravan pitches. Motorhome pitches. Tent pitches. 20 statics.

Open: Mar-Oct **Last arrival:** 22.00hrs **Last departure:** noon

Pitches: * 🚐 £9-£12 🚗 £9-£12 🅰 £9-£12

Facilities: 🎣 ⊙ 📡 ☼ ⊙ ⚓ ❼

Services: 🔌 🔋 ⌀ 🖃 ↯

Within 3 miles: ⅃ ♨ ♒ ◎ 🏧 📷

Notes: Adults only. 🚫 Gates closed 23.00hrs-07.00hrs, no ball games. Dogs must be kept on leads. Separate male & female washing areas, no cubicles.

AA Pubs & Restaurants nearby: The Laughing Dog, LLANDRINDOD WELLS, LD1 5PT, 01597 822406

LLANGORS
Map 9 SO12

Places to visit

Regimental Museum of The Royal Welsh, BRECON, LD3 7EB, 01874 613310
www.royalwelsh.org.uk

Great for kids: Tretower Court & Castle, TRETOWER, NP8 1RD, 01874 730279
www.cadw.wales.gov.uk

Lakeside Caravan Park
►►►78%

tel: 01874 658226 **LD3 7TR**
email: holidays@llangorselake.co.uk
dir: *Exit A40 at Bwlch onto B4560 towards Talgarth. Site signed towards lake in Llangors centre.* **grid ref:** *SO128272*

Surrounded by spectacular mountains and set alongside Llangors Lake, with mooring and launching facilities, this is a must-do holiday destination for lovers of outdoor pursuits, from walking to watersports and even pike fishing for which the lake is renowned. The hedge- or tree-screened touring areas provide generously sized pitches. There's a well-stocked shop, bar and café, with takeaway, under the same ownership. 2 acre site. 40 touring pitches. 8 hardstandings. Caravan pitches. Motorhome pitches. Tent pitches. 72 statics.

Open: Etr or Apr-Oct (rs Mar-May & Oct clubhouse, restaurant, shop limited)
Last arrival: 21.30 **Last departure:** 10.00hrs

Pitches: 🚐 🚙 Å

Leisure: 🛝 🎱

Facilities: 🌡️ ☉ 🍽️ ✳️ 🛁 🛒 🚻 WiFi ♻️ 🛈

Services: 🔌 🛢️ 🍴 💧 ⊘ 🚰 T 🍴 🛗

Within 3 miles: 🎣 🌊 🏌️ 🛒 🛒 ∪

Notes: No open fires, no dogs in hire caravans. Dogs must be kept on leads. Boat hire (summer).

AA Pubs & Restaurants nearby: The Usk Inn, BRECON, LD3 7JE, 01874 676251

Star Inn, TALYBONT-ON-USK, LD3 7YX, 01874 676635

MIDDLETOWN

Places to visit

Powis Castle & Garden, WELSHPOOL, SY21 8RF, 01938 551929
www.nationaltrust.org.uk

MIDDLETOWN
Map 15 SJ31

Bank Farm Caravan Park
►►►80%

tel: 01938 570526 **SY21 8EJ**
email: bankfarmcaravans@yahoo.co.uk
dir: *13m W of Shrewsbury, 5m E of Welshpool on A458.* **grid ref:** *SJ293123*

An attractive park on a small farm, maintained to a high standard. There are two touring areas, one on either side of the A458, and each with its own amenity block, and immediate access to hills, mountains and woodland. A pub serving good food, and a large play area are nearby. 2 acre site. 40 touring pitches. Caravan pitches. Motorhome pitches. Tent pitches. 33 statics.

Open: Mar-Oct **Last arrival:** 20.00hrs

Pitches: * 🚐 fr £15 🚙 fr £15 Å fr £14

Leisure: 🛝 🎱

Facilities: 🌡️ ☉ ✳️ 🛁 🚻 🐾 WiFi ♻️ 🛈

Services: 🔌 🛢️ 💧 🛒

Within 3 miles: 🌊

Notes: 🐕 Dogs must be kept on leads. Coarse fishing, jacuzzi, snooker room.

AA Pubs & Restaurants nearby: The Old Hand and Diamond Inn, COEDWAY, SY5 9AR, 01743 884379

RHAYADER
Map 9 SN96

Places to visit

Great for kids: Gilfach Nature Discovery Centre and Reserve, RHAYADER, LD6 5LF, 01597 823298 www.rwtwales.org

Wyeside Caravan & Camping Park
►►►76%

tel: 01597 810183 **Llangurig Rd LD6 5LB**
email: wyesidecc@powys.gov.uk
dir: *400mtrs N of Rhayader town centre on A470.* **grid ref:** *SO967690*

With direct access from the A470, the park sits on the banks of the River Wye. Situated just 400 metres from the centre of the market town of Rhayader, and next to a recreation park with tennis courts, bowling green and children's playground. There are good riverside walks from here, though the river is fast flowing and unfenced, and care is especially needed when walking with children. 6 acre site. 120 touring pitches. 22 hardstandings. 21 seasonal pitches. Caravan pitches. Motorhome pitches. Tent pitches. 39 statics.

Open: Mar-Oct **Last arrival:** 20.00hrs **Last departure:** noon

Pitches: 🚐 🚙 Å

Facilities: 🌡️ ☉ 🍽️ ✳️ 🛁 🕐 ♻️ 🛈

Services: 🔌 🛢️ 💧 ⊘ T 🛒

Within 3 miles: 🌊 ◎ 🛒 🛒 ∪

Notes: No noise after 23.00hrs. Dogs must be kept on leads.

SWANSEA

PONTARDDULAIS
Map 8 SN50

Places to visit

The National Botanic Garden of Wales, LLANARTHNE, SA32 8HG, 01558 667149 www.gardenofwales.org.uk

Great for kids: Plantasia, SWANSEA, SA1 2AL, 01792 474555 www.plantasia.org

PREMIER PARK

River View Touring Park
▶▶▶▶▶85%

tel: 01269 844876 **The Dingle, Llanedi SA4 0FH**
email: info@riverviewtouringpark.com **web:** www.riverviewtouringpark.com
dir: M4 junct 49, A483 signed Llandeilo. 0.5m, 1st left after layby, follow lane to site.
grid ref: SN578086

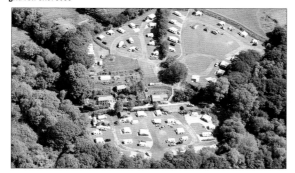

This peaceful park is set on one lower and two upper levels in a sheltered valley with an abundance of wild flowers and wildlife. The River Gwli flows around the bottom of the park where fishing for brown trout is possible. The excellent toilet facilities are an added bonus. This park is ideally situated for visiting the beaches of south Wales, The Black Mountains and the Brecon Beacons. 6 acre site. 60 touring pitches. 46 hardstandings. 20 seasonal pitches. Caravan pitches. Motorhome pitches. Tent pitches.

Open: Mar-mid Nov **Last arrival:** 20.00 **Last departure:** noon
Pitches: * ⊕ £14-£23 ⊕ £14-£23 Ⓐ £14-£23

Leisure: ⊛
Facilities: ⬤⊙⬤✳⬤⬤⬤ WiFi ⬤ ⬤
Services: ⬤⬤⬤⬤⬤Ⓣ⬤
Within 3 miles: ⬤⬤⬤⬤⬤⬤
Notes: Reduced noise after 22.00hrs. Dogs must be kept on leads.

PORT EYNON
Map 8 SS48

Places to visit

Weobley Castle, LLANRHIDIAN, SA3 1HB, 01792 390012 www.cadw.wales.gov.uk

Gower Heritage Centre, PARKMILL, SA3 2EH, 01792 371206 www.gowerheritagecentre.co.uk

Great for kids: Oxwich Castle, OXWICH, SA3 1ND, 01792 390359 www.cadw.wales.gov.uk

Carreglwyd Camping & Caravan Park
▶▶▶▶83%

tel: 01792 390795 **SA3 1NL**
dir: A4118 to Port Eynon, site adjacent to beach. **grid ref:** SS465863

Set in an unrivalled location alongside the safe sandy beach of Port Eynon on the Gower Peninsula, this popular park is an ideal family holiday spot; it is also close to an attractive village with pubs and shops. The sloping ground has been partly terraced and most pitches have sea views; excellent toilet facilities include three superb family bathrooms 12 acre site. 150 touring pitches. Caravan pitches. Motorhome pitches. Tent pitches.

Open: all year **Last arrival:** 22.00hrs **Last departure:** 15.00hrs
Pitches: ⊕ ⊕ Ⓐ
Facilities: ⬤⊙⬤⬤⬤ WiFi ⬤ ⬤
Services: ⬤⬤⬤⬤Ⓣ⬤
Within 3 miles: ⬤⬤⬤⬤
Notes: Dogs must be kept on leads.
AA Pubs & Restaurants nearby: Fairyhill, REYNOLDSTON, SA3 1BS, 01792 390139
King Arthur Hotel, REYNOLDSTON, SA3 1AD, 01792 390775

Find out about the AA's Pennant rating scheme on pages 10-11

PITCHES: ⊕ Caravans ⊕ Motorhomes Ⓐ Tents ⬤ Glamping-style accommodation **SERVICES:** ⬤ Electric hook up ⬤ Launderette ⬤ Licensed bar ⬤ Calor Gas ⬤ Camping Gaz Ⓣ Toilet fluid ⬤ Café/Restaurant ⬤ Fast Food/Takeaway ⬤ Battery charging ⬤ Baby care ⬤ Motorvan service point
ABBREVIATIONS: BH/bank hols – bank holidays Etr – Easter Spring BH – Spring Bank Holiday fr – from hrs – hours m – mile mdnt – midnight
rdbt – roundabout rs – restricted service wk – week wknd – weekend x-rds – cross roads ⬤ No credit or debit cards ⬤ No dogs ⬤ Children of all ages accepted

RHOSSILI
Map 8 SS48

Places to visit
Weobley Castle, LLANRHIDIAN, SA3 1HB, 01792 390012 www.cadw.wales.gov.uk

Gower Heritage Centre, PARKMILL, SA3 2EH, 01792 371206 www.gowerheritagecentre.co.uk

Great for kids: Oxwich Castle, OXWICH, SA3 1ND, 01792 390359 www.cadw.wales.gov.uk

Pitton Cross Caravan & Camping Park
▶▶▶90%

tel: 01792 390593 **SA3 1PT**
email: admin@pittoncross.co.uk **web:** www.pittoncross.co.uk
dir: 2m W of Scurlage on B4247. **grid ref:** SS434877

Surrounded by farmland close to sandy Mewslade Bay, which is within walking distance across the fields, this grassy park is divided by hedging into paddocks; hardstandings for motorhomes are available. Some areas are deliberately left uncultivated, resulting in colourful displays of wild flowers including roses and orchids. Rhossili Beach, which is popular with surfers, and the Wales Coastal Path are nearby. Both children's kites and power kites are sold on site, and instruction is available. Geocaching and paragliding are possible too. 6 acre site. 100 touring pitches. 25 hardstandings. Caravan pitches. Motorhome pitches. Tent pitches.

Open: all year (rs Nov-Mar no bread, milk or papers) **Last arrival:** 20.00hrs
Last departure: 11.00hrs

Pitches: * ▦ £20-£26 ▦ £20-£26 ▲ £10-£35

Leisure: ⚑

Facilities: ⌂⊙☗✳☗⚙⑤♨♺❢

Services: ⚡⑤🖤⊘Ⓣ

Within 3 miles: ⚓⚖⑤⑤

Notes: Quiet at all times, charcoal BBQs must be off ground, no fire pits or log burning. Dogs must be kept on leads. Baby bath available.

AA Pubs & Restaurants nearby: Fairyhill, REYNOLDSTON, SA3 1BS, 01792 390139

King Arthur Hotel, REYNOLDSTON, SA3 1AD, 01792 390775

Kings Head, LLANGENNITH, SA3 1HX, 01792 386212

SWANSEA
Map 9 SS69

Places to visit
Swansea Museum, SWANSEA, SA1 1SN, 01792 653763 www.swanseaheritage.co.uk

Great for kids: Plantasia, SWANSEA, SA1 2AL, 01792 474555 www.plantasia.org

Riverside Caravan Park
HOLIDAY CENTRE 77%

tel: 01792 775587 **Ynys Forgan Farm, Morriston SA6 6QL**
email: reception@riversideswansea.com
dir: Exit M4 junct 45 towards Swansea. Left into private road signed to site.
grid ref: SS679991

A large and busy park close to the M4 but in a quiet location beside the River Taw. This friendly, family orientated park has a licensed club and bar with a full high-season entertainment programme. There is a choice of eating outlets – the clubhouse restaurant, takeaway and chip shop. The park has a good indoor pool. 5 acre site. 90 touring pitches. Caravan pitches. Motorhome pitches. Tent pitches. 256 statics.

Open: all year (rs Winter months pool & club closed) **Last arrival:** mdnt
Last departure: noon

Pitches: ▦ ▦ ▲

Leisure: ⚓⚑♦▢

Facilities: ⌂⊙☗✳☗⚙⑤♨♺❢WiFi

Services: ⚡⑤🖤▮⊘Ⓣ🖤🏛

Within 3 miles: ⚓⚖☗⚖⑤⑤♆

Notes: Dogs by prior arrangement only (no aggressive dog breeds permitted). Fishing on site by arrangement.

AA Pubs & Restaurants nearby: Hanson at the Chelsea Restaurant, SWANSEA, SA1 3LH, 01792 464068

The Dragon Hotel, SWANSEA, SA1 5LS, 01792 657100

> **Find out about staying at a Holiday Centre** in our feature on page 26

VALE OF GLAMORGAN

LLANTWIT MAJOR   Map 9 SS96

Places to visit

Old Beaupre Castle, ST HILARY, 01443 336000 www.cadw.wales.gov.uk

Great for kids: Ogmore Castle, OGMORE, 01443 336000 www.cadw.wales.gov.uk

---

Acorn Camping & Caravan Site
▶▶▶84%

tel: 01446 794024 **Ham Lane South CF61 1RP**
email: info@acorncamping.co.uk
dir: *B4265 to Llantwit Major, follow camping signs. Approach site through Ham Manor residential park.* **grid ref:** *SS973678*

A peaceful country site in level meadowland, with some individual pitches divided by hedges and shrubs. It is about one mile from the beach, which can be reached via a cliff top walk, and the same distance from the historic town of Llantwit Major. An internet station and a full-size snooker table are useful amenities. 5.5 acre site. 90 touring pitches. 10 hardstandings. Caravan pitches. Motorhome pitches. Tent pitches. 25 statics.

Open: Feb-Nov **Last arrival:** 21.00hrs **Last departure:** 11.00hrs

Pitches: 🚐 🚃 ⛺

Leisure: ⚂ 🎣

Facilities: 🐾⊙🅿✳🛁🖾 WiFi ♻ ❶

Services: 🔌🖾 🔋🍳🚽🍴🎒🚮🛒⚒

Within 3 miles: ⬇🖾 🛁🖾Ü

Notes: No noise 23.00hrs-07.00hrs. Dogs must be kept on leads.

AA Pubs & Restaurants nearby: Blue Anchor Inn, EAST ABERTHAW, CF62 3DD, 01446 750329

WREXHAM

BRONINGTON   Map 15 SJ43

Places to visit

Erddig, WREXHAM, LL13 0YT, 01978 355314 www.nationaltrust.org.uk/erddig

---

NEW The Little Yurt Meadow
▶▶▶▶86%

tel: 01948 780136 & 07984 400134 **Bay Tree Barns, Mill Rd SY13 3HJ**
email: info@thelittleyurtmeadow.co.uk
dir: *Phone for detailed directions.* **grid ref:** *SJ483397*

An exciting new glamping retreat for 2014. A former meadow on the Shropshire/Welsh borders has been carefully and sympathetically transformed into a luxury glamping destination for those wishing to escape from the pressures of everyday life. Three spacious yurts with stylishly furnished interiors are equipped with sumptuous beds, two settees (one converts to a sofa bed), a wood-burning stove, mini-cooker and lots of quality extras. Each yurt has its own luxury shower room

and there are areas for communal outdoor and indoor relaxation. 3 acre site. 3 touring pitches. Tent pitches. 3 bell tents/yurts.

Open: all year **Last arrival:** 23.00hrs **Last departure:** 11.00hrs

Pitches: * ⛺ £140-£180 🏠

Leisure: ⚂

Facilities: 🐾🅿✳🛁🖾🚮♻❶

Services: 🔌🖾

Within 3 miles: ⬇🍴🖾◎🛁🖾🖾

Notes: 🚫 🐕 No cars by tents. No noise after 23.00hrs. No credit or debit cards, Paypal only. Self-catering kitchen area, wet rooms.

EYTON   Map 15 SJ34

Places to visit

Erddig, WREXHAM, LL13 0YT, 01978 355314 www.nationaltrust.org.uk/erddig

Chirk Castle, CHIRK, LL14 5AF, 01691 777701
www.nationaltrust.org.uk/main/w-chirkcastle

EYTON   Map 15 SJ34

PREMIER PARK

Plassey Holiday Park
▶▶▶▶▶93%

Best of British
GOLD

tel: 01978 780277 **The Plassey LL13 0SP**
email: enquiries@plassey.com **web:** www.plassey.com
dir: *From A483 at Bangor-on-Dee exit onto B5426 for 2.5m. Site entrance signed on left.* **grid ref:** *SJ353452*

A lovely park set in several hundred acres of quiet farm and meadowland in the Dee Valley. The superb toilet facilities include individual cubicles for total privacy and security, while the Edwardian farm buildings have been converted into a restaurant, coffee shop, beauty studio and various craft outlets. There is plenty here to entertain the whole family, from scenic walks and a swimming pool to free fishing, and use of the 9-hole golf course. 10 acre site. 90 touring pitches. 60 hardstandings. 60 seasonal pitches. Caravan pitches. Motorhome pitches. Tent pitches. 15 statics.

continued

PITCHES: 🚐 Caravans 🚃 Motorhomes ⛺ Tents 🏠 Glamping-style accommodation **SERVICES:** 🔌 Electric hook up 🖾 Launderette 🍺 Licensed bar 🔋 Calor Gas 🛢 Camping Gaz 🅣 Toilet fluid 🍴 Café/Restaurant 🍟 Fast Food/Takeaway 🔌 Battery charging 👶 Baby care ⚒ Motorvan service point
ABBREVIATIONS: BH/bank hols – bank holidays Etr – Easter Spring BH – Spring Bank Holiday fr – from hrs – hours m – mile mdnt – midnight rdbt – roundabout rs – restricted service wk – week wknd – weekend x-rds – cross roads 🚫 No credit or debit cards 🐕 No dogs 👫 Children of all ages accepted

EYTON continued

Plassey Holiday Park

Open: Feb-Nov **Last arrival:** 20.30hrs **Last departure:** noon

Pitches: * 🚐 £17.90-£28.60 🚃 £17.90-£28.60 ⛺ £17.90-£28.60

Leisure: 🐟 🎯 🎱 🎲 **Facilities:** 🚿 ☉ 📷 ✳ ♿ 🕐 🍴 🪑 🚻 📶 ♻ ❶

Services: 🔌 🗑 🚰 🛢 ⚡ 🇹 🍴 🛒 🏧 🚲 ♿

Within 3 miles: ♿ 🎱 🎣 ⊙ 🍴 🍴 ∪

Notes: No footballs or skateboards. Dogs must be kept on leads. Sauna, badminton & table tennis.

AA Pubs & Restaurants nearby: The Boat Inn, ERBISTOCK, LL13 0DL, 01978 780666

See advert below

The Trotting Mare Caravan Park

►►►► 83%

tel: 01978 711963 **LL13 0LE**

email: info@thetrottingmare.co.uk

dir: *From Oswestry towards Whitchurch take A495. In Ellesmere take A528 towards Overton. Site on left. Or from Wrexham take A525 signed Whitchurch. In Marchwiel turn right onto A528 towards Overton. Through Overton, site on right.* **grid ref:** *SJ374396*

Located between Overton-on-Dee and Ellesmere, this adults-only touring park is quietly located behind The Trotting Mare pub. The majority of pitches are fully serviced, and creative landscaping and a free coarse-fishing lake are additional benefits. Please note that there is no laundry on this site but facilities are available at either Ellesmere or Overton. 4.2 acre site. 53 touring pitches. 50 hardstandings. Caravan pitches. Motorhome pitches. Tent pitches. 11 statics. 3 tipis. 3 bell tents/yurts.

Open: all year **Last arrival:** 20.00hrs **Last departure:** noon

Pitches: * 🚐 £20-£30 🚃 £20-£30 ⛺ £20-£30 🏕

Facilities: 🚿 ☉ ✳ 🐕 📶 🖥 ♻

Services: 🔌 🚰 🇹 🍴 🛒 ♿

Within 3 miles: ♿ 🎣 ⊙ ∪

Notes: Adults only. Open fires prohibited, no gas bottles outside caravan/awning, no bikes, no commercial vehicles, no ball games, no noise after 23.00 hrs. Dogs must be kept on leads.

AA Pubs & Restaurants nearby: The Boat Inn, ERBISTOCK, LL13 0DL, 01978 780666

LEISURE: 🏊 Indoor swimming pool 🏊 Outdoor swimming pool 🛝 Children's playground 🧒 Kid's club 🎾 Tennis court 🎱 Games room 📺 Separate TV room ⛳ golf course 🚤 Boats for hire 🎬 Cinema 🎵 Entertainment 🎣 Fishing ◉ Mini golf 🏄 Watersports 🏋 Gym 🏟 Sports field Spa ∪ Stables

FACILITIES: 🛁 Bath 🚿 Shower ☉ Electric shaver 💇 Hairdryer ✳ Ice Pack Facility ♿ Disabled facilities 🕐 Public telephone 🛒 Shop on site or within 200yds 🏪 Mobile shop (calls at least 5 days a week) 🍴 BBQ area 🪑 Picnic area 📶 Wi-fi 🖥 Internet access ♻ Recycling ❶ Tourist info 🐕 Dog exercise area

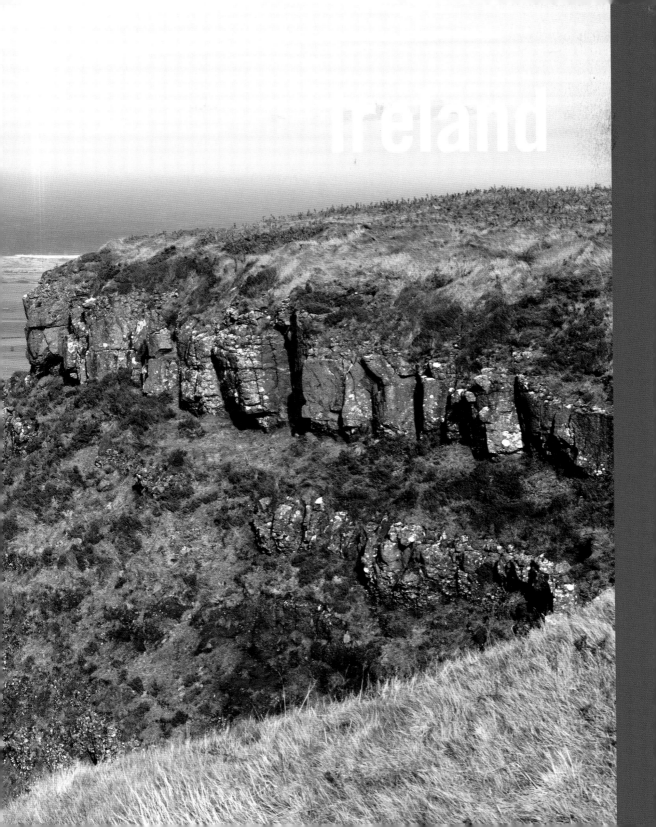

NORTHERN IRELAND

COUNTY ANTRIM

ANTRIM
Map 1 D5

Places to visit

Antrim Round Tower, ANTRIM, BT41 1BJ, 028 9023 5000
www.discovernorthernireland.com/Antrim-Round-Tower-Antrim-P2813

Great for kids: Belfast Zoological Gardens, BELFAST, BT36 7PN, 028 9077 6277
www.belfastzoo.co.uk

Six Mile Water Caravan Park
►►► 83%

tel: 028 9446 4963 & 9446 3113 **Lough Rd BT41 4DG**
email: sixmilewater@antrim.gov.uk
dir: *From A6 (Dublin road) into Lough Rd signed Antrim Forum & Loughshore Park. Site at end of road on right.* **grid ref:** *J137870*

A pretty tree-lined site in a large municipal park, within walking distance of Antrim and the Antrim Forum leisure complex yet very much in the countryside. The modern toilet block is well equipped, and other facilities include a laundry and electric hook-ups. All the pitches are precisely set on generous plots. 9.61 acre site. 45 touring pitches. 37 hardstandings. Caravan pitches. Motorhome pitches. Tent pitches.

Open: Mar-Oct (rs Feb & Nov wknds only) **Last arrival:** 21.00hrs **Last departure:** noon

Pitches: 🚐 🚏 👤

Leisure: 🔍 ▢

Facilities: 🅿 ⊙ ℱ 👤 🛒 ⬚ 📶 ♻ ⚙

Services: 🖥 🗄 🍴 🕎 ⬇

Within 3 miles: 🏌 🎇 ⌖ ◎ ⬆ 🏪 🗄

Notes: Max stay 7 nights, no noise between 22.00hrs-08.00hrs. Dogs must be kept on leads. Watersports, angling stands.

AA Pubs & Restaurants nearby: Galgorm Resort & Spa, BALLYMENA, BT42 1EA, 028 2588 1001

BALLYMONEY

Places to visit

Bonamargy Friary, BALLYCASTLE, 028 2076 2225
www.discovernorthernireland.com/Bonamargy-Friary-Ballycastle-P2818

Great for kids: Dunluce Castle, PORTBALLINTRAE, BT57 8UY, 028 2073 1938
www.discovernorthernireland.com/Dunluce-Castle-P15619

BALLYMONEY
Map 1 C6

PREMIER PARK

Drumaheglis Marina & Caravan Park
►►►►► 83%

tel: 028 2766 0280 & 2766 0227 **36 Glenstall Rd BT53 7QN**
email: drumaheglis@ballymoney.gov.uk **web:** www.ballymoney.gov.uk
dir: *Signed from A26, approx 1.5m from Ballymoney towards Coleraine. Also accessed from B66, S of Ballymoney.* **grid ref:** *C901254*

An exceptionally well-designed and laid out park beside the Lower Bann River that has seen serious investment and improvements over the past two years. It has 55 very spacious pitches (all fully serviced), two quality toilet blocks, a new, stylish reception building, which also houses a games room and IT suite, and five new camping pods. There's table tennis, picnic and BBQ areas, a grass volleyball court and a nature walk. This makes an ideal base for watersport enthusiasts and for those touring County Antrim. 16 acre site. 53 touring pitches. 53 hardstandings. 20 seasonal pitches. Caravan pitches. Motorhome pitches. Tent pitches. 5 wooden pods.

Open: 17 Mar-Oct **Last arrival:** 20.00hrs **Last departure:** 13.00hrs

Pitches: * 🚐 £24-£25 🚏 £24-£25 👤 £17 🏠

Leisure: 🛝

Facilities: 🅿 ⊙ ℱ ✳ 👤 ⊙ 🛒 ⬚ 📶 ♻ ⚙

Services: 🖥 🗄 🛒 ⬇

Within 3 miles: 🏌 ⌖ ⬆ 🏪 🗄

Notes: Dogs must be kept on leads. Marina berths, outdoor gym.

LEISURE: 🏊 Indoor swimming pool 🏊 Outdoor swimming pool 🛝 Children's playground Kid's club 🎾 Tennis court 🔍 Games room ▢ Separate TV room 🏌 golf course ⛵ Boats for hire 🎬 Cinema 🎵 Entertainment 🎣 Fishing ◎ Mini golf ⬆ Watersports 💪 Gym Sports field Spa ♨ Stables
FACILITIES: 🛁 Bath 🚿 Shower ⊙ Electric shaver ℱ Hairdryer ✳ Ice Pack Facility 👤 Disabled facilities ☏ Public telephone 🏪 Shop on site or within 200yds 🚚 Mobile shop (calls at least 5 days a week) 🍴 BBQ area ⬚ Picnic area 📶 Wi-fi Internet access ♻ Recycling ⚙ Tourist info 🐕 Dog exercise area

BUSHMILLS
Map 1 C6

Places to visit
Old Bushmills Distillery, BUSHMILLS, BT57 8XH, 028 2073 1521
www.bushmills.com

PREMIER PARK

Ballyness Caravan Park
►►►►► 91%

GOLD

tel: 028 2073 2393 **40 Castlecatt Rd BT57 8TN**
email: info@ballynesscaravanpark.com
dir: *0.5m S of Bushmills on B66, follow signs.* **grid ref:** *C944397*

A quality park with superb toilet and other facilities, on farmland beside St Columb's Rill, the stream that supplies the famous nearby Bushmills Distillery. The friendly owners created this park with the discerning camper in mind and they continue to improve it to ever higher standards. There is a pleasant walk around several ponds, and the park is peacefully located close to the beautiful north Antrim coast. There is a spacious play barn and a holiday cottage to let. 16 acre site. 48 touring pitches. 50 hardstandings. Caravan pitches. Motorhome pitches. 65 statics.

Open: 17 Mar-Oct **Last arrival:** 21.00hrs **Last departure:** noon

Pitches: * 🚐 £24 🚍 £24

Leisure: 🄰 😊 🐾 🔍 ▢

Facilities: 🚽 🖍 ☉ 🅿 ✳ ⚷ 🕚 🖺 🚮 📶 ♻ 🛈

Services: 🔌 🔋 🛢 ⌀ 🅃 🖚 ⚡

Within 3 miles: ⚲ ⚑ ⑤

Notes: No skateboards or rollerblades. Dogs must be kept on leads. Library.

AA Pubs & Restaurants nearby: Bushmills Inn Hotel, BUSHMILLS, BT57 8QG, 028 2073 3000

BELFAST

DUNDONALD
Map 1 D5

Places to visit
Mount Stewart House & Gardens, NEWTOWNARDS, BT22 2AD, 028 4278 8387
www.nationaltrust.org.uk/mount-stewart

Giant's Ring, BELFAST, 028 9023 5000
www.discovernorthernireland.com/Giants-Ring-Belfast-P2791

Great for kids: Belfast Zoological Gardens, BELFAST, BT36 7PN, 028 9077 6277
www.belfastzoo.co.uk

Dundonald Touring Caravan Park
►►► 77%

tel: 028 9080 9123 & 9080 9129 **111 Old Dundonald Rd BT16 1XT**
email: sales@castlereagh.gov.uk **web:** www.theicebowl.com
dir: *From Belfast city centre follow M3 & A20 to City Airport. Then A20 to Newtownards, follow signs to Dundonald & Ulster Hospital. At hospital right at sign for Dundonald Ice Bowl. Follow to end, turn right, Ice Bowl on left.* **grid ref:** *J410731*

A purpose-built park in a quiet corner of Dundonald Leisure Park on the outskirts of Belfast. This peaceful park is ideally located for touring County Down and exploring

continued

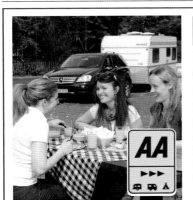
PITCHES: 🚐 Caravans 🚍 Motorhomes 🄰 Tents 🏕 Glamping-style accommodation **SERVICES:** 🔌 Electric hook up 🖻 Launderette 🍺 Licensed bar 🛢 Calor Gas ⌀ Camping Gaz 🅃 Toilet fluid 🍽 Café/Restaurant 🖚 Fast Food/Takeaway 🔋 Battery charging 👶 Baby care ⚡ Motorvan service point
ABBREVIATIONS: BH/bank hols – bank holidays Etr – Easter Spring BH – Spring Bank Holiday fr – from hrs – hours m – mile mdnt – midnight rdbt – roundabout rs – restricted service wk – week wknd – weekend x-rds – cross roads 🚫 No credit or debit cards 🚫 No dogs 👪 Children of all ages accepted

DUNDONALD *continued*

the capital. In the winter it offers an 'Aire de Service' for motorhomes. 1.5 acre site. 22 touring pitches. 22 hardstandings. Caravan pitches. Motorhome pitches. Tent pitches.

Dundonald Touring Caravan Park

Open: 14 Mar-Oct (rs Nov-Mar Aire de Service restricted to motorhomes/caravans with own bathroom facilities) **Last arrival:** 23.00hrs **Last departure:** noon

Pitches: * ➡ £8.50-£23.50 ➡ £8.50-£23.50 ▲ £15.50-£23.50

Facilities: ⬛⊙ℱ❊⭑⭒☉🎔⭐🚻WIFI ♻ ❼

Services: ⬛⭯ 🏧⭳

Within 3 miles: ⭑🏇⭏◎⭏⭏∪

Notes: No commercial vehicles. Dogs must be kept on leads. Bowling, indoor play area, Olympic-size ice rink (additional charges apply).

See advert on page 459

COUNTY FERMANAGH

BELCOO   Map 1 C5

Places to visit

Florence Court, ENNISKILLEN, BT92 1DB, 028 6634 8249 www.nationaltrust.org.uk

PREMIER PARK

Rushin House Caravan Park
►►►►►83%

tel: 028 6638 6519 **Holywell BT93 5DY**
email: enquiries@rushinhousecaravanpark.com
dir: *From Enniskillen take A4 W for 13m to Belcoo. Right onto B52 towards Garrison for 1m. Site signed.* **grid ref:** H835047

This park occupies a scenic location overlooking Lough MacNean, close to the picturesque village of Belcoo, and is the product of meticulous planning and execution. There are 24 very generous, fully serviced pitches standing on a terrace overlooking the lough, with additional tenting pitches below; all are accessed via well-kept, wide tarmac roads. Play facilities include a lovely well-equipped play area and a hard surface and fenced five-a-side football pitch. There is a slipway providing boat access to the lough and, of course, fishing. The excellent toilet facilities are purpose-built and include family rooms. 5 acre site.

38 touring pitches. 38 hardstandings. Caravan pitches. Motorhome pitches. Tent pitches.

Open: mid Mar-Oct (rs Nov-Mar Aire de Service facilities available)
Last arrival: 21.00hrs **Last departure:** 13.00hrs

Pitches: ➡ ➡ ▲

Leisure: �†⭯☉▭ **Facilities:** ⬛⊙ℱ❊⭑⭒☉🎔⭐🚻WIFI ♻ ❼

Services: ⬛⭯ 🏧⭯⭏⭳ **Within 3 miles:** ⭑⭏⭏⭏⭏

Notes: No cars by tents. Dogs must be kept on leads. Lakeside walk.

IRVINESTOWN   Map 1 C5

Places to visit

Castle Coole, ENNISKILLEN, BT74 6JY, 028 6632 2690 www.nationaltrust.org.uk

Great for kids: Castle Balfour, LISNASKEA, 028 9023 5000 www.discovernorthernireland.com/Castle-Balfour-Lisnaskea-Enniskillen-P2901

Castle Archdale Caravan Park & Camping Site
►►►►82%

tel: 028 6862 1333 **Lisnarick BT94 1PP**
email: info@castlearchdale.com **web:** www.castlearchdale.com
dir: *From Irvinestown take B534 signed Lisnarick. Left onto B82 signed Enniskillen. Approx 1m right by church (site signed).* **grid ref:** H176588

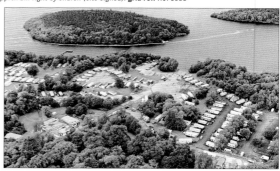

This park is located within the grounds of Castle Archdale Country Park on the shores of Lough Erne which boasts stunning scenery, forest walks and also war and wildlife museums. The site is ideal for watersport enthusiasts with its marina and launching facilities. Also on site are a shop, licenced restaurant, takeaway and play park. There are 56 fully serviced, hardstanding pitches. 11 acre site. 158 touring pitches. 120 hardstandings. Caravan pitches. Motorhome pitches. Tent pitches. 144 statics.

Open: Apr-Oct (rs Apr-Jun & Sep-Oct shop, restaurant & bar open wknds only)
Last departure: noon

Pitches: * ➡ £25-£30 ➡ £25-£30 ▲ £10-£40

Leisure: ⚠ **Facilities:** ⬛⊙❊⭑☉⭏🚻⭐WIFI ❼

Services: ⬛⭯ 🍴⭯⭏◰🍴⭏⭳⭳ **Within 3 miles:** ⭑⭏⭏⭏⭏⭏∪

Notes: No open fires. Dogs must be kept on leads.

AA Pubs & Restaurants nearby: Lough Erne Resort, ENNISKILLEN, BT93 7ED, 028 6632 3230

LISNASKEA
Map 1 C5

Places to visit

Castle Balfour, LISNASKEA, 028 9023 5000
www.discovernorthernireland.com/Castle-Balfour-Lisnaskea-Enniskillen-P2901

Florence Court, ENNISKILLEN, BT92 1DB, 028 6634 8249
www.nationaltrust.org.uk

Great for kids: Castle Coole, ENNISKILLEN, BT74 6JY, 028 6632 2690
www.nationaltrust.org.uk

Lisnaskea Caravan Park
►►► 81%

tel: 028 6772 1040 **BT92 0NZ**
dir: From Lisnaskea take B514 signed Carry Bridge, site signed. **grid ref:** H297373

A pretty riverside site set in peaceful countryside, with well-kept facilities and friendly owners. Fishing is available on the river, and this quiet area is an ideal location for touring the lakes of Fermanagh. 6 acre site. 43 touring pitches. 43 hardstandings. Caravan pitches. Motorhome pitches. Tent pitches. 8 statics.

Open: Mar-Sep **Last arrival:** 21.00hrs **Last departure:** 14.00hrs

Pitches: * ⊞ fr £20 ⊞ fr £20 ▲ fr £14

Leisure: ⚲ **Facilities:** ⬍⊙✲⬥⊞

Services: ⊟⊡⬛ **Within 3 miles:** ⬍⬍⊞⬍⬍⊞⊡∪

Notes: ⊗ Dogs must be kept on leads.

AA Pubs & Restaurants nearby: Lough Erne Resort, ENNISKILLEN, BT93 7ED, 028 6632 3230

COUNTY TYRONE

DUNGANNON
Map 1 C5

Places to visit

The Argory, MOY, BT71 6NA, 028 8778 4753 www.nationaltrust.org.uk

U S Grant Ancestral Homestead, BALLYGAWLEY, BT70 1TW, 028 8555 7133
www.dungannon.gov.uk

Great for kids: Mountjoy Castle, MOUNTJOY, 028 9023 5000
www.discoverloughneagh.com/wb/pages/topics/mountjoy-castle.php

Dungannon Park
►►► 81%

tel: 028 8772 8690 **Moy Rd BT71 6DY**
email: dpreception@dungannon.gov.uk
dir: M1 junct 15, A29 towards Dungannon, left at 2nd lights. **grid ref:** H805612

A modern caravan park in a quiet area of a stunning public park with fishing lake and excellent facilities, especially for disabled visitors. 4 acre site. 37 touring pitches. 24 hardstandings. Caravan pitches. Motorhome pitches. Tent pitches.

Open: Mar-Oct **Last arrival:** 20.30hrs **Last departure:** 14.00hrs

Pitches: ⊞ £19 ⊞ £19 ▲ £12-£19

Leisure: ⚲⬍⊙ **Facilities:** ⬍⊙⊓✲⬥⊙⊓⎁⊞ ♻ ⊘

Services: ⊟⊡⬛ **Within 3 miles:** ⬍⬍⊟⬍⊞⊡∪

Notes: Dogs must be kept on leads. Retail unit selling crafts, souvenirs etc.

REPUBLIC OF IRELAND

COUNTY CORK

BALLINSPITTLE
Map 1 B2

Garrettstown House Holiday Park
►►►► 80%

tel: 021 4778156 & 4775286
email: reception@garrettstownhouse.com
dir: 6m from Kinsale, through Ballinspittle, past school & football pitch on main road to beach. Beside stone estate entrance. **grid ref:** W588445

Elevated holiday park with tiered camping areas and superb panoramic views. Plenty of on-site amenities, and close to beach and forest park. 7 acre site. 60 touring pitches. 20 hardstandings. Caravan pitches. Motorhome pitches. Tent pitches. 80 statics.

Open: 4 May-9 Sep (rs Early season-1 Jun shop closed) **Last arrival:** 22.00hrs **Last departure:** noon

Pitches: ⊞ ⊞ ▲

Leisure: ⬍⚲⬍⬍⬍⊡⎁♫

Facilities: ⬍⊙⊓✲⬥⊙⊞⊓⊞ ♻ ⊘

Services: ⊟⊡⬛⊘⊓⬛⬛⬛

Within 3 miles: ⬍⬍⊞⊙⬍⊞⊡∪

Notes: ⊗ Dogs must be kept on leads. Crazy golf, video shows, snooker, adult reading lounge, tots' playroom.

BALLYLICKEY
Map 1 B2

Eagle Point Caravan and Camping Park
►►►► 85%

tel: 027 50630
email: eaglepointcamping@eircom.net
dir: From Cork: N71 to Bandon, R586 to Bantry, then N71, 4m to Glengarriff, opposite petrol station. From Killarney: N22 to Macroom, R584 to Ballickey Bridge, N71 to Glengarriff. **grid ref:** V995535

An immaculate park set in an idyllic position on a headland overlooking the rugged Bantry Bay and the mountains of West Cork. There are boat launching facilities, small and safe pebble beaches, a football field, tennis court, a small playground, and TV rooms for children and adults on the park. There is an internet café at reception and a shop and petrol station across from the park entrance. Nearby are two golf courses, riding stables, a sailing centre and cycle hire facilities. 20 acre site. 125 touring pitches. 20 hardstandings. 60 seasonal pitches. Caravan pitches. Motorhome pitches. Tent pitches.

Open: 17 Apr-21 Sep **Last arrival:** 21.00hrs **Last departure:** noon

Pitches: ⊞ €26-€29 ⊞ €26-€29 ▲ €26-€29

Leisure: ⚲⬍⊙⊡

Facilities: ⬍⊙✲⬥⊞⊞ ⬛ ♻ ⊘

Services: ⊟⊡⬍

Within 3 miles: ⬍⊟⬍⊞⊡

Notes: ⊗ No commercial vehicles, bikes, skates, scooters or jet skis.

AA Pubs & Restaurants nearby: Seaview House Hotel, BALLYLICKEY, 027 50073

PITCHES: ⊞ Caravans ⊞ Motorhomes ▲ Tents ⋒ Glamping-style accommodation **SERVICES:** ⊟ Electric hook up ⊡ Launderette ⊓ Licensed bar ⬛ Calor Gas ⊘ Camping Gaz ⊞ Toilet fluid ⊡ Café/Restaurant ⬛ Fast Food/Takeaway ⬛ Battery charging ⬍ Baby care ⬍ Motorvan service point **ABBREVIATIONS:** BH/bank hols – bank holidays Etr – Easter Spring BH – Spring Bank Holiday fr – from hrs – hours m – mile mdnt – midnight rdbt – roundabout rs – restricted service wk – week wknd – weekend x-rds – cross roads ⊗ No credit or debit cards ⊗ No dogs ⬍ Children of all ages accepted

COUNTY DONEGAL

PORTNOO
Map 1 B5

Places to visit

Glebe House & Gallery, LETTERKENNY, 074 9137071
www.heritageireland.ie/en/glebehouseandgallery/

Tower Museum, LONDONDERRY, BT48 6LU, 028 7137 2411
www.derrycity.gov.uk/museums

Boyle's Caravan Park
►►70%

tel: 074 9545131 & 086 8523131
email: pboylecaravans@gmail.com
dir: Exit N56 at Ardra onto R261, 6m. Follow signs for Santa Anna Drive.
grid ref: G702990

This open park sits among the sand dunes overlooking Narin Beach and close to a huge selection of water activities, including wind surfing, fishing, scuba diving and kayaking on a magnificent stretch of the Atlantic on the Donegal coast. There is an 18-hole golf links, and a café and shop at the entrance to the site. The park is very well maintained by the Boyle family. 1.5 acre site. 20 touring pitches. Caravan pitches. Motorhome pitches. Tent pitches. 80 statics.

Open: 18 Mar-Oct **Last arrival:** 23.00hrs **Last departure:** 11.00hrs

Pitches: 🚐 🚌 Å

Leisure: 🔲

Facilities: 🐾⊙✳🔥🕭🛒🗚🏧🚾 ♻ ❼

Services: 🔌🍴🛢🗑🎨🍴⛲

Within 3 miles: ↨‡🎣 🏊🛒🗒🛶

Notes: 🚫 No skateboards. 1.5m Blue Flag beach.

COUNTY DUBLIN

CLONDALKIN
Map 1 D4

Places to visit

Castletown, CELBRIDGE, 01 6288252 www.heritageireland.ie/en/castletown/

Irish Museum of Modern Art, DUBLIN, 01 6129900 www.imma.ie

Great for kids: Dublin Zoo, DUBLIN, 01 4748900 www.dublinzoo.ie

Camac Valley Tourist Caravan & Camping Park
►►►►81%

tel: 01 4640644 **Naas Rd, Clondalkin**
email: info@camacvalley.com
dir: M50 junct 9, N7 (South), exit 2, follow signs for Corkagh Park. **grid ref:** O056300

A pleasant, lightly wooded park with good facilities, security and layout, situated within an hour's drive, or a bus ride, from the city centre. 15 acre site. 163 touring pitches. 113 hardstandings. Caravan pitches. Motorhome pitches. Tent pitches.

Open: all year **Last arrival:** 22.00hrs **Last departure:** noon

Pitches: 🚐 🚌 Å

Leisure: 🅰️⊕🔲

Facilities: 🐾⊙🗚✳🕭🔥🏧🚾 ♻ ❼

Services: 🔌🗑🛢🗨🎨🇹🚮⛲

Within 3 miles: ↨🗒🏊 ⊚🗒🛶

Notes: Lights out 23.00hrs. Dogs must be kept on leads.

AA Pubs & Restaurants nearby: Finnstown Country House Hotel, LUCAN, 01 6010700

COUNTY MAYO

CASTLEBAR
Map 1 B4

Lough Lannagh Caravan Park
►►►►80%

tel: 094 9027111 **Old Westport Rd**
email: info@loughlannagh.ie **web:** www.loughlannagh.ie
dir: N5, N60, N84 to Castlebar. At ring road follow signs for Westport. Signs for Lough Lannagh Village on all approach roads to Westport rdbt. **grid ref:** M140890

This park is part of the Lough Lannagh Village which is situated in a wooded area a short walk from Castlebar. Leisure facilities include tennis courts, boules, children's play area and café. 2.5 acre site. 20 touring pitches. 20 hardstandings. Caravan pitches. Motorhome pitches. Tent pitches.

Open: 3 Apr-Aug **Last arrival:** 18.00hrs **Last departure:** 10.00hrs

Pitches: * 🚐 €21-€25 🚌 €21-€25 Å €21-€25

Leisure: 🎾⊕

Facilities: 🛁🐾⊙🗚✳🕭🔥🚾🖥 ♻ ❼

Services: 🔌🗑🎨🚐

Within 3 miles: ↨‡🗒🏊 ⊚🗒🛶

Notes: Pets accepted by prior arrangement only, no pets in Jul & Aug. Dogs must be kept on leads.

AA Pubs & Restaurants nearby: Knockranny House Hotel, WESTPORT, 098 28600

LEISURE: 🀢 Indoor swimming pool 🀣 Outdoor swimming pool 🅰 Children's playground 👐 Kid's club 🎾 Tennis court 🀫 Games room 🔲 Separate TV room ↨ golf course 🚣 Boats for hire 🎬 Cinema 🎵 Entertainment 🎣 Fishing ⊚ Mini golf 🏊 Watersports 🏋 Gym ⊕ Sports field Spa 🛶 Stables
FACILITIES: 🛁 Bath 🐾 Shower ⊙ Electric shaver 🗚 Hairdryer ✳ Ice Pack Facility 🕭 Disabled facilities 🕓 Public telephone 🗒 Shop on site or within 200yds 🗨 Mobile shop (calls at least 5 days a week) 🔥 BBQ area 🛒 Picnic area 🚾 Wi-fi 🖥 Internet access ♻ Recycling ❼ Tourist info 🏧 Dog exercise area

KNOCK
Map 1 B4

Knock Caravan and Camping Park
►►►► 76%

tel: 094 9388100 **Claremorris Rd**
email: caravanpark@knock-shrine.ie
dir: *From rdbt in Knock, through town. Site on left in 1km, opposite petrol station.*
grid ref: M408828

A pleasant, very well maintained camping park within the grounds of Knock Shrine, offering spacious terraced pitches and excellent facilities. 10 acre site. 88 touring pitches. 88 hardstandings. Caravan pitches. Motorhome pitches. Tent pitches. 12 statics.

Open: last Sun Mar-1st Sun Oct **Last arrival:** 22.00hrs **Last departure:** noon

Pitches: 🚐 🚏 🛆

Leisure: ⚲ 🎣 ▢

Facilities: 🖍 ⊙ 🏳 ✳ ♿ 🛝 🎋 🔨 WiFi ♻ ❶

Services: 🔌 🔄 🔋 ⊘ T 🍽 🔋 ⚓

Within 3 miles: ⚓ 🚴 🎣 ♨ 📷 ⟳

Notes: 🚫 Dogs must be kept on leads.

COUNTY ROSCOMMON

BOYLE
Map 1 B4

Places to visit
King House – Georgian Mansion & Military Barracks, BOYLE, 071 9663242
www.kinghouse.ie

Lough Key Caravan & Camping Park
►►► 74%

tel: 071 9662212 **Lough Key Forest Park**
email: info@loughkey.ie
dir: *3km E of Boyle on N4. Follow Lough Key Forest Park signs, site within grounds. Approx 0.5km from entrance.* **grid ref:** G846039

Peaceful and very secluded site within the extensive grounds of a beautiful forest park. Lough Key offers boat trips and waterside walks, and there is a viewing tower. 15 acre site. 72 touring pitches. 52 hardstandings. Caravan pitches. Motorhome pitches. Tent pitches.

Open: Apr-20 Sep **Last arrival:** 18.00hrs **Last departure:** noon

Pitches: 🚐 🚏 🛆

Leisure: ⚲

Facilities: ⬅ 🖍 ⊙ ♿ 🛝 🎋 🔨

Services: 🔌 🔄

Within 3 miles: ⚓ 🚴 🎣 ♨ 📷 📷

Notes: 🚫 No cars by tents.

COUNTY WATERFORD

DUNGARVAN
Map 1 C2

Casey's Caravan & Camping Park
►►►► 83%

tel: 058 41919 **Clonea**
dir: *From R675 (Dungarvan road), follow signs to Clonea Bay. Site at end of road.*
grid ref: X320937

A spacious, well-kept park with excellent toilet facilities, situated next to the beach. 4.5 acre site. 111 touring pitches. 34 hardstandings. Caravan pitches. Motorhome pitches. Tent pitches. 170 statics.

Open: 5 Apr-9 Sep **Last arrival:** 21.30hrs **Last departure:** noon

Pitches: 🚐 🚏 🛆

Leisure: ⚲ 🎣 ▢

Facilities: 🖍 ⊙ 🏳 ✳ ♿ 📷

Services: 🔌 🔋 ⊘ ⚓

Within 3 miles: ⚓ 🏊 🔒 🎣 📷

Notes: 🚫 Dogs must be kept on leads. Crazy golf, games room & tiny tots' play area.

PITCHES: 🚐 Caravans 🚏 Motorhomes 🛆 Tents 🏠 Glamping-style accommodation **SERVICES:** 🔌 Electric hook up 📷 Launderette 🍷 Licensed bar 🔋 Calor Gas ⊘ Camping Gaz T Toilet fluid 🍽 Café/Restaurant 🍟 Fast Food/Takeaway 🔋 Battery charging ⚓ Baby care ⚓ Motorvan service point **ABBREVIATIONS:** BH/bank hols – bank holidays Etr – Easter Spring BH – Spring Bank Holiday fr – from hrs – hours m – mile mdnt – midnight rdbt – roundabout rs – restricted service wk – week wknd – weekend x-rds – cross roads 🚫 No credit or debit cards 🚫 No dogs 👪 Children of all ages accepted

County maps

The county map shown here will help you identify the counties within each country. You can look up each county in the guide using the county names at the top of each page. To find towns featured in the guide use the atlas and the index.

England

1 Bedfordshire
2 Berkshire
3 Bristol
4 Buckinghamshire
5 Cambridgeshire
6 Greater Manchester
7 Herefordshire
8 Hertfordshire
9 Leicestershire
10 Northamptonshire
11 Nottinghamshire
12 Rutland
13 Staffordshire
14 Warwickshire
15 West Midlands
16 Worcestershire

Scotland

17 City of Glasgow
18 Clackmannanshire
19 East Ayrshire
20 East Dunbartonshire
21 East Renfrewshire
22 Perth & Kinross
23 Renfrewshire
24 South Lanarkshire
25 West Dunbartonshire

Wales

26 Blaenau Gwent
27 Bridgent
28 Caerphilly
29 Denbighshire
30 Flintshire
31 Merthyr Tydfil
32 Monmouthshire
33 Neath Port Talbot
34 Newport
35 Rhondda Cynon Taff
36 Torfaen
37 Vale of Glamorgan
38 Wrexham

Na h-Eileanan
an Iar

Highland

Moray

City of
Aberdeen

Aberdeenshire

SCOTLAND

Angus

Perth &
Kinross

Argyll
& Bute

Stirling

City of
Dundee

Fife

East
Lothian

North
Ayrshire

24

Scottish
Borders

South
Ayrshire

19

Dumfries &
Galloway

Northumberland

Tyne & Wear

Cumbria

Durham

Isle
of Man

North
Yorkshire

Lancashire

West Yorkshire

East Riding
of Yorkshire

Isle of
Anglesey

Merseyside

6

South
Yorkshire

Lincolnshire

Conwy

30

Cheshire

Derbyshire

11

29

38

Gwynedd

13

ENGLAND

Norfolk

Shropshire

9

12

WALES

15

Suffolk

Ceredigion

Powys

14

10

5

Pembrokeshire

16

1

Carmarthenshire

7

Swansea

Gloucestershire

4

8

Essex

3

Oxfordshire

Greater
London

Wiltshire

2

Kent

Somerset

Surrey

Hampshire

West
Sussex

East
Sussex

Devon

Dorset

Isle of
Wight

Cornwall

Isles of
Scilly

Guernsey

Jersey

Orkney Islands

Shetland Islands

Argyll
& Bute

Stirling

18

22

Fife

25

20

Falkirk

Inverclyde

23

17

North
Lanarkshire

West
Lothian

City of
Edinburgh

North
Ayrshire

21

Midlothian

19

South Lanarkshire

Scottish
Borders

31

26

32

33

35

28

36

27

34

37

Cardiff

| 0 | 20 | 40 | 60 | 80 | 100 miles |

| 0 | 20 40 60 | 80 100 120 | 140 160 kilometres |

KEY TO ATLAS

2

	Symbol	Description
	M6	Motorway/toll motorway
		Motorway junction full/ restricted. Service area
	A33	Primary route single/ dual carriageway
	A34	Other A road single/ dual carriageway
	B3400	B road
		Unclassified road
	V	Vehicle ferry
	C	Fast vehicle ferry or catamaran

● Ashbourne	Caravan and Camping
● Helmsley	AA Campsite Award Winner
○ Oundle	Town/Village name
	National boundary
ESSEX	English county name & boundary
CONWY	Welsh county name & boundary
MORAY	Scottish county name & boundary
	National Park

ISLES OF SCILLY

Bryher
New Grimsby · Tresco
St Martin's
Higher Town
Hugh Town · St Mary's
ISLES OF SCILLY ST MARY'S
Middle Town · Old Town
St Agnes

SV

SW

Lundy

Hartland Point
Hartland

Morwenstow

Kilkhampton

Bude
Bude · Str
Bay
Widemouth Bay · Bridg
Wee
St Ma
Crackington Haven
Jacobsto

Boscastle
Tintagel

Delabole
Camelford

Port Isaac · Pendoggett
Polzeath
St Minver
St Tudy · Bolventor
Harlyn · Rock · BODMIN MOOR
St Merryn · Padstow · Blisland
Porthcothan · A389
Wadebridge

Mawgan Porth · Rumford · St Ruthernbridge · C O R N W A L L · St Cle
Watergate Bay · Mawgan · Bodmin · Dobwalls
St Columb Major · Lanivet · Liskea
Newquay · White · A30 · Roche · St Keyne
West Pentire · Cross · Bugle · Luxulyan · Lostwithiel
Holywell Bay · Cubert · Indian Queens · Pelynt
Rejerrah · Summercourt · St Blazey Gate · St Blazey
Perranporth · Goonhavern · St Austell · Fowey
St Agnes · Ladock · St Stephen · Carlyon Bay · Polruan · Polper
St Allen · Pentewan
Porthtowan · Grampound · Mevagissey
Portreath · Blackwater · Gorran · Gorran Haven
Chacewater · Truro · Tregony
St Day · Carnon Downs · Portloe
St Ives Bay · Gwithian · Redruth
St Ives · Camborne
Zennor · A392 · St Just-in-Roseland
Lelant · Hayle · Portscatho
Leedstown · Penryn · St Mawes
St Just · Edgcumbe · Falmouth
Penzance · Marazion · St Hilary · Constantine · Mawnan Smith
Land's End · Rosudgeon · Ashton · Helston · Gweek
Newlyn · Praa · Porthleven · Manaccan
Sennen · Mousehole · Sands · St Keverne
Porthcurno · Treen · Mount's Bay
Mullion · Coverack
Kennack Sands
Cadgwith
Lizard
Lizard Point

For continuation pages refer to numbered arrows

Harwi

Ardleigh

COLCHESTER

Wix

Thorpe
le-Soken

Walton on the Naze

Elmstead
Market

Wivenhoe

Thorrington

Little
Clacton

Frinton-
on-Sea

Brightlingsea

Mersea
Island

St
Osyth

CLACTON-
ON-SEA

West Mersea

TM

Bradwell-on-Sea

River Bla

Steeple

St Lawrence

Latchingdon

Southminster

South Woodham
Ferrers

Burnham-on-Crouch

Hockley

Rayleigh · Rochford

Great Wakering

SOUTHEND-
ON-SEA

Canvey
Island

Grain

Sheerness

Minster

Eastchurch

Leysdown-
on-Sea

MARGATE

Reculver

Birchington

St Nicholas
at Wade

Broadstairs

Herne Bay

Isle of Sheppey

Iwade

CHESTER
GILLINGHAM
THAM

Sittingbourne

Whitstable

Sarre

Minster

Ramsgate

Bredhurst

Teynham

Faversham

Upstreet

Hersden

Sandwich

Ospringe

Blean

Sturry

Fordwich

Ash

Doddington

Boughton
Street

Canterbury

Wingham

Hollingbourne

Chilham

Chartham

Bridge

Eastry

Deal

Lenham

Challock

Aylesham

Kingsdown

Charing

KENT

Sutton
Valence

Wye

Elham

Densole

Alkham

St Margaret's
at Cliffe

Pluckley

Headcorn

Lyminge

Hawkinge

DOVER

Smarden

Ashford

Sellindge

Staplehurst

Bethersden

High
Halden

Kingsnorth

Sissinghurst

Lympne

FOLKESTONE

Biddenden

Woodchurch

Lymne

Hythe

Cranbrook

Benenden

Tenterden

Hamstreet

Rolvenden

Dymchurch

Wittersham

Appledore

Brenzett

St Mary's Bay

Northiam

Brookland

New
Romney

Peasmarsh

Rye

Lydd

Camber

Channel Tunnel (Rail)

STRAIT OF DOVER

Brede

Winchelsea

Dungeness

Westfield

Guestling
Green

Fairlight

HASTINGS

●	Caravan and Camping
●	AA Campsite Award Winner
○	Town/Village name

0   10 miles

0   10   20 kilometres

CARDIGAN BAY

SM

SR

SS

SN

PEMBROKESHIRE

CARMARTHENSHIRE

SWANSEA

St David's Head

Scrumble Head

Strumble Head

Aberdaron

Borth

Llandre

Aberystwyth

Llanfarian

Llanrhystud

Llansantffraid

Aberarth

C E R

New Quay

Aberaeron

Llangranog

Aberporth

Temple Bar

Tan-y-groes

Blaenporth

Talgarreg

Lampeter

St Dogmaels

Cardigan

Llechryd

Rhydowen

Llandysul

Llanybydder

Nevern

Newcastle Emlyn

Llandyssul

Llangeler

Newport

Eglwyswrw

Brechfa

Fishguard

PEMBROKESHIRE COAST NATIONAL PARK

MYNYDD PRESELI

Cynwyl Elfed

Tai

Letterston

Wolf's Castle

St Davids

Solva

Newgale

Roch

Llandissilio

Carmarthen

Nantgaredig

Llanarthne

A40

St Brides Bay

PEMBROKESHIRE COAST NATIONAL PARK

Robeston Wathen

Whitland

St Clears

Llanddarog

Cross Hands

Broad Haven

Haverfordwest

Narberth

Red Roses

Laugharne

Llansteffan

Pontyberem

Pontyates

Johnston

Kilgetty

Amroth

Pendine

Kidwelly

Marloes

Hasguard Cross

Milford Haven

Neyland

Carew

Saundersfoot

Hendy

Pontardulais

Broad Sound

Dale

Angle

Pembroke Dock

St Florence

Tenby

Carmarthen Bay

Pembrey

M4

Llangennech

Pembroke

Penally

Pwll

Burry Port

Llanelli

Gorseinon

Castlemartin

PEMBROKESHIRE COAST NATIONAL PARK

Manorbier

Gowerton

Bosherston

Llanrhidian

Dunvant

Llangennith

Reynoldston

SWANSEA

Bishopston

Rhossili

Worms Head

Oxwich

Port Einon

Lundy

Ilfracombe

Combe

Mortehoe

Lee

Berrynarbor

Caravan and Camping
AA Campsite Award Winner
Town/Village name

0   10 miles

0   10   20 kilometres

14

For continuation pages refer to numbered arrows

NA

NB

NA H–EILEANAN
AN IAR

NF

NG

NL

NM

20

Cape Wrath

Rudha Rhobhanais
(Butt of Lewis)
Port Nis
(Port of Ness)

Cellar
Head

Scourie

Great
Bernera

LEWIS

Tiumpan
Head

Inchnadar

Carlabhagh
(Carloway)

ISLE

OF

Steornabhagh
(Stornoway)

STORNOWAY

Lochinver

A858

A857

A857

A858

A859

A858

A859

A866

A835

A837

A894

A838

A837

Scarp

Taransay

Tairbeart
(Tarbert)

Scalpay

HARRIS

Gruinard
Bay

Laide

Ullapool

Dundonnell

Pabbay

Boreray

Berneray

Loch nam Madadh
(Lochmaddy)

NORTH UIST

Gairloch

Kinlochewe

A832

A832

A832

Achnasheen

A835

A890

A832

Benbecula

Ronay

Wiay

Uig

A87

Dunvegan

Edinbane

ISLE

Portree

Raasay

Inner Sound

A896

A890

A87

SOUTH
UIST

OF

A863

SKYE

Drynoch

Scalpay

Kyle of
Lochalsh

Balmacara

Cannich

Loch Baghasdail
(Lochboisdale)

Eriskay

Soay

Ardvasar

Sound of Sleat

Invergarry

A887

A87

A87

BARRA

A888

Bàgh a Chaisteil
(Castlebay)

Sandray

Canna

Rùm

Mallaig

Arisaig

A830

Corpach

Spean
Bridge

A82

Fort William

Mingulay

(Mar Ort)

Muck

Eigg

Point of
Ardnamurchan

Acharacle

A861

A861

A830

Kinlochleven

A82

(Mar Ort)

INNER HEBRIDES

Coll

Arinagour

Tobermory

NORTH WEST HIGHLANDS

Ballachulish

Glencoe

Duror

A828

Tiree

Scarinish

Ulva

ISLE

A848

A884

Lochaline

Lismore

A828

A85

Iona

Fionnphort

OF

A849

MULL

Kerrera

Craignure

Oban

A828

Dalmally

Crian

A849

A816

A85

Glamping sites

These campsites offer one or more types of glamping accommodation, i.e. wooden pods, tipis, yurts, bell tents, safari tents, shepherd's huts, Airstream caravans and vintage caravans.

ENGLAND

CORNWALL

BLISLAND
South Penquite Farm

BOSCASTLE
Lower Pennycrocker Farm

CARLYON BAY
East Crinnis Camping & Caravan Park

CRANTOCK (NEAR NEWQUAY)
Trevella Tourist Park

GOONHAVERN
Silverbow Park

HAYLE
St Ives Bay Holiday Park

HELSTON
Poldown Caravan Park

KILKHAMPTON
Upper Tamar Lake

LOOE
Tregoad Park

NEWQUAY
Hendra Holiday Park
Porth Beach Tourist Park

PERRANPORTH
Tollgate Farm Caravan & Camping Park

PORTREATH
Tehidy Holiday Park

RUTHERNBRIDGE
Ruthern Valley Holidays

ST AUSTELL
Meadow Lakes

ST MINVER
Gunvenna Holiday Park

WADEBRIDGE
St Mabyn Holiday Park

WIDEMOUTH BAY
Widemouth Bay Caravan Park

CUMBRIA

AMBLESIDE
Low Wray National Trust Campsite

APPLEBY-IN-WESTMORLAND
Wild Rose Park

BOOT
Eskdale Camping & Caravanning Club Site

GREAT LANGDALE
Great Langdale National Trust Campsite

KESWICK
Castlerigg Hall Caravan & Camping Park

KIRKBY LONSDALE
Woodclose Caravan Park

MILNTHORPE
Hall More Caravan Park

PATTERDALE
Sykeside Camping Park

PENRITH
Lowther Holiday Park

PENTON
Twin Willows

POOLEY BRIDGE
Waterfoot Caravan Park

SANTON BRIDGE
The Old Post Office Campsite

SILLOTH
Stanwix Park Holiday Centre

WASDALE HEAD
Wasdale Head National Trust Campsite

WATERMILLOCK
The Quiet Site
Ullswater Caravan, Camping & Marine Park

WINDERMERE
Park Cliffe Camping & Caravan Estate

DERBYSHIRE

ROSLISTON
Beehive Woodland Lakes

DEVON

BERRYNARBOR
Mill Park Touring Site

CLYST ST MARY
Crealy Meadows Caravan and Camping Park

DAWLISH
Lady's Mile Holiday Park

ILFRACOMBE
Hele Valley Holiday Park

KENTISBEARE
Forest Glade Holiday Park

PAIGNTON
Whitehill Country Park

TAVISTOCK
Harford Bridge Holiday Park
Langstone Manor Camping & Caravan Park
Woodovis Park

WOOLACOMBE
Europa Park

DORSET

ALDERHOLT
Hill Cottage Farm Camping and Caravan Park

BERE REGIS
Rowlands Wait Touring Park

BRIDPORT
Graston Copse Holiday Park

CHARMOUTH
Newlands Caravan & Camping Park

CHIDEOCK
Golden Cap Holiday Park

SHAFTESBURY
Blackmore Vale Caravan & Camping Park

SWANAGE
Herston Caravan & Camping Park

WAREHAM
Lookout Holiday Park

WIMBORNE MINSTER
Merley Court

HAMPSHIRE

BRANSGORE
Harrow Wood Farm Caravan Park

FORDINGBRIDGE
Sandy Balls Holiday Village

HEREFORDSHIRE

EARDISLAND
Arrow Bank Holiday Park

PEMBRIDGE
Townsend Touring Park

HERTFORDSHIRE

HODDESDON
Lee Valley Caravan Park Dobbs Weir

ISLE OF WIGHT

BRIGHSTONE
Grange Farm

WHITECLIFF BAY
Whitecliff Bay Holiday Park

KENT

WHITSTABLE
Homing Park

LANCASHIRE

BOLTON LE SANDS
Bay View Holiday Park

CROSTON
Royal Umpire Caravan Park

SILVERDALE
Silverdale Caravan Park

THORNTON
Kneps Farm Holiday Park

LINCOLNSHIRE

TATTERSHALL
Tattershall Lakes Country Park

WOODHALL SPA
Woodhall Country Park

LONDON

E4, CHINGFORD
Lee Valley Campsite

N9, EDMONTON
Lee Valley Camping & Caravan Park

NORFOLK

KING'S LYNN
King's Lynn Caravan and Camping Park

NORTHUMBERLAND

BAMBURGH
Waren Caravan & Camping Park

BELLINGHAM
Bellingham Camping & Caravanning Club Site

BERWICK-UPON-TWEED
Ord House Country Park

HALTWHISTLE
Herding Hill Farm

WOOLER
Riverside Leisure Park

NOTTINGHAMSHIRE

TEVERSAL
Teversal Camping & Caravanning Club Site

OXFORDSHIRE

CHARLBURY
Cotswold View Touring Park

SHROPSHIRE

WEM
Lower Lacon Caravan Park

SOMERSET

BREAN
Holiday Resort Unity

CHEDDAR
Cheddar Bridge Touring Park

DULVERTON
Wimbleball Lake

GLASTONBURY
Isle of Avalon Touring Caravan Park
The Old Oaks Touring Park

TAUNTON
Ashe Farm Camping & Caravan Site

WELLS
Wells Holiday Park

STAFFORDSHIRE

CHEADLE
Quarry Walk Park

SUSSEX, WEST

BARNS GREEN
Sumners Ponds Fishery & Campsite

WILTSHIRE

BERWICK ST JAMES
Stonehenge Campsite & Glamping Pods

YORKSHIRE, EAST RIDING OF

BRANDESBURTON
Dacre Lakeside Park

SPROATLEY
Burton Constable Holiday Park & Arboretum

Glamping sites *continued*

YORKSHIRE, NORTH

ALNE
Alders Caravan Park

FILEY
Flower of May Holiday Park

CHOP GATE
Lordstones Country Park

NORTHALLERTON
Otterington Park

RICHMOND
Brompton Caravan Park

ROBIN HOOD'S BAY
Grouse Hill Caravan Park
Middlewood Farm Holiday Park

ROSEDALE ABBEY
Rosedale Caravan & Camping Park

WHITBY
Ladycross Plantation Caravan Park

WYKEHAM
St Helens Caravan Park

CHANNEL ISLANDS

JERSEY

ST MARTIN
Beuvelande Camp Site

ST OUEN
Daisy Cottage Campsite

SCOTLAND

ARGYLL & BUTE

GLENDARUEL
Glendaruel Caravan Park

OBAN
Oban Caravan & Camping Park

DUMFRIES & GALLOWAY

CREETOWN
Castle Cary Holiday Park

ECCLEFECHAN
Hoddom Castle Caravan Park

SANDYHILLS
Sandyhills Bay Leisure Park

DUNBARTONSHIRE, WEST

BALLOCH
Lomond Woods Holiday Park

HIGHLAND

DUROR
Achindarroch Touring Park

GLENCOE
Invercoe Caravan & Camping Park

LOTHIAN, EAST

ABERLADY
Aberlady Caravan Park

MUSSELBURGH
Drum Mohr Caravan Park

LOTHIAN, WEST

EAST CALDER
Linwater Caravan Park

SCOTTISH BORDERS

PEEBLES
Crossburn Caravan Park

SCOTTISH ISLANDS

ISLE OF ARRAN

KILDONAN
Sealshore Camping and Touring Site

ISLE OF SKYE

EDINBANE
Skye Camping & Caravanning Club Site

WALES

ANGLESEY, ISLE OF

RHOS LLIGWY
Ty'n Rhos Caravan Park

GWYNEDD

BALA
Pen-y-Bont Touring Park

BARMOUTH
Trawsdir Touring Caravans & Camping Park

CAERNARFON
Plas Gwyn Caravan & Camping Park

CRICCIETH
Eisteddfa

DINAS DINLLE
Dinlle Caravan Park

POWYS

CHURCHSTOKE
Daisy Bank Caravan Park

LLANDRINDOD WELLS
Disserth Caravan & Camping Park

WREXHAM

BRONINGTON
The Little Yurt Meadow

OVERTON
The Trotting Mare Caravan Park

NORTHERN IRELAND

COUNTY ANTRIM

BALLYMONEY
Drumaheglis Marina & Caravan Park

Index

Entries are listed alphabetically by town name, then campsite name. The following abbreviations have been used: C&C – Caravan & Camping; HP – Holiday Park; CP – Caravan Park; C&C Club – Camping & Caravanning Club Site

Acknowledgments

AA Media would like to thank the following photographers, companies and picture libraries for their assistance in the preparation of this book.

Abbreviations for the picture credits are as follows – (t) top; (b) bottom; (c) centre; (l) left; (r) right; (b/g) background; (AA) AA World Travel Library.

Cover
Background Derek Croucher/Alamy.

Interior
3 AA/Adam Burton; 4 AA/James Tims; 6 Grouse Hill Caravan Park, Fylingdales; 14-15 b/g AA/Adam Burton; 14l AA/Adam Burton; 14r Oakdown Country Holiday Park, Sidmouth; 15l Witches Craig Caravan & Camping Park, Blairlogie; 15r Bron Derw Touring Caravan Park, Llanwrst; 16-17 b/g AA/Adam Burton; 16l Fauxquets Valley Campsite, Castel; 16r Orchards Holiday Caravan Park, Newbridge; 17l Longnor Wood Holiday Park, Longnor; 17r Manor Wood Country Caravan Park, Coddington; 18-19 b/g AA/Adam Burton; 18l Golden Square Caravan & Camping Park, Helmsley; 18r Park Foot Caravan & Camping Park, Pooley Bridge; 19l Wells Holiday Park, Wells; 19r Churchill Farm Campsite, Buckfastleigh; 20-21 Stuart Abraham/Alamy; 23 Colin Church; 24-25 DGB/Alamy; 26-27 Hafan y Môr Holiday Park, Pwllheli; 29 Hafan y Môr Holiday Park, Pwllheli; 31 AA/James Tims; 39 AA/Adam Burton; 42 AA/James Tims; 53 AA/Jeff Beazley; 54 AA/Adam Burton; 65 AA/John Wood; 74 AA/John Wood; 125 AA/Adam Burton; 127 AA/A Mockford & N Bonetti; 142 AA/A Mockford & N Bonetti; 149 AA/Andy Midgley; 150 AA/Guy Edwardes; 175 AA/Caroline Jones; 186 AA/Andrew Newey; 210 AA/Adam Burton; 222 AA/David Hall; 231 AA/James Tims; 233 AA/Andrew Newey; 262 AA/Tom Mackie; 291 AA/Caroline Jones; 292 AA/James Tims; 295 AA/James Tims; 312-313 AA/Caroline Jones; 314 AA/Tom Mackie; 323 AA/Tom Mackie; 325 AA/John Miller; 338-339 AA/Caroline Jones; 341 AA/James Tims; 379 AA/Steve Day; 414 AA/Stephen Lewis; 427 AA/Mark Bauer; 455 AA/Ian Burgum; 463 AA/Simon McBride; 491 AA/James Tims; 495 Stephen Dorey/Alamy.

Country openers
ENGLAND AA/Adam Burton; SCOTLAND AA/Steve Day; WALES AA/Stephen Lewis; IRELAND AA/Chris Hill.

Every effort has been made to trace the copyright holders, and we apologise in advance for any unintentional omissions or errors. We would be pleased to apply any corrections in a following edition of this publication.

Readers' Report Form

Please send this form to:–
The Editor, AA Caravan & Camping Guide,
AA Lifestyle Guides,
13th Floor,
Fanum House,
Basingstoke RG21 4EA

email: lifestyleguides@theAA.com

Please use this form to tell us about any site that you have visited, whether it is in the guide or not currently listed. Feedback from readers helps us to keep our guide accurate and up to date. However, if you have a complaint during your visit, we recommend that you discuss the matter with the management there and then, so that they have a chance to put things right before your visit is spoilt.

Please note that the AA does not undertake to arbitrate between you and the establishment, or to obtain compensation or engage in protracted correspondence.

Date

Your name (BLOCK CAPITALS)

Your address (BLOCK CAPITALS)

Post code

E-mail address

Name of site/park

Location

Comments

(please attach a separate sheet if necessary)

Please tick here ☐ if you DO NOT wish to receive details of AA offers or products   PTO

Readers' Report Form *continued*

Have you bought this guide before? ☐ YES ☐ NO

How often do you visit a caravan park or camp site? (tick one choice)
Once a year ☐   Twice a year ☐   Three times a year ☐
More than three times a year ☐

How long do you generally stay at a park or site? (tick one choice)
One night ☐   Up to a week ☐   1 week ☐
2 weeks ☐   Over 2 weeks ☐

Do you have a: (tick all that apply)
Tent ☐   Caravan ☐   Motorhome ☐

Please answer these questions to help us make improvements to the guide:
Which of these factors are the most important when choosing a site? (tick one choice)
Location ☐   Toilet/washing facilities ☐   Personal Recommendation ☐
Leisure facilities ☐
Other (please state)

Do you read the editorial features in the guide? ☐ YES ☐ NO

Do you use the location atlas? ☐ YES ☐ NO

What elements of the guide do you find most useful when choosing a site/park? (tick all that apply)
Description ☐   Photo ☐   Advertisement ☐

Is there any other information you would like to see added to this guide?

Readers' Report Form

Please send this form to:–
The Editor, AA Caravan & Camping Guide,
AA Lifestyle Guides,
13th Floor,
Fanum House,
Basingstoke RG21 4EA

email: lifestyleguides@theAA.com

Please use this form to tell us about any site that you have visited, whether it is in the guide or not currently listed. Feedback from readers helps us to keep our guide accurate and up to date. However, if you have a complaint during your visit, we recommend that you discuss the matter with the management there and then, so that they have a chance to put things right before your visit is spoilt.

Please note that the AA does not undertake to arbitrate between you and the establishment, or to obtain compensation or engage in protracted correspondence.

Date

Your name (BLOCK CAPITALS)

Your address (BLOCK CAPITALS)

Post code

E-mail address

Name of site/park

Location

Comments

(please attach a separate sheet if necessary)

Please tick here ☐ if you DO NOT wish to receive details of AA offers or products

PTO

Readers' Report Form *continued*

Have you bought this guide before? ☐ YES ☐ NO

How often do you visit a caravan park or camp site? (tick one choice)
Once a year ☐   Twice a year ☐   Three times a year ☐
More than three times a year ☐

How long do you generally stay at a park or site? (tick one choice)
One night ☐   Up to a week ☐   1 week ☐
2 weeks ☐   Over 2 weeks ☐

Do you have a: (tick all that apply)
Tent ☐   Caravan ☐   Motorhome ☐

Please answer these questions to help us make improvements to the guide:
Which of these factors are the most important when choosing a site? (tick one choice)
Location ☐   Toilet/washing facilities ☐   Personal Recommendation ☐
Leisure facilities ☐
Other (please state)

Do you read the editorial features in the guide? ☐ YES ☐ NO

Do you use the location atlas?   ☐ YES ☐ NO

What elements of the guide do you find most useful when choosing a site/park? (tick all that apply)
Description ☐   Photo ☐   Advertisement ☐

Is there any other information you would like to see added to this guide?